The Gallup Poll

Public Opinion 2016

Other Gallup Publications Available from SR Books:

The Gallup Poll Cumulative Index: Public Opinion, 1935–1997
ISBN 0-8420-2587-1 (1999)

The Gallup Poll: Public Opinion Annual Series
2010 (ISBN 978-1-4422-0991-6)
2009 (ISBN 978-1-4422-0519-2)
2008 (ISBN 978-1-4422-0105-7)
2007 (ISBN 0-7425-6239-5)
2006 (ISBN 0-7425-5876-2)
2005 (ISBN 0-7425-5258-6)
2004 (ISBN 0-7425-5138-5)
2003 (ISBN 0-8420-5003-5)
2002 (ISBN 0-8420-5002-7)
2001 (ISBN 0-8420-5001-9)
2000 (ISBN 0-8420-5000-0)
1999 (ISBN 0-8420-2699-1)
1998 (ISBN 0-8420-2698-3)
1997 (ISBN 0-8420-2697-9)
1996 (ISBN 0-8420-2696-0)
1995 (ISBN 0-8420-2695-2)
1994 (ISBN 0-8420-2560-X)
1993 (ISBN 0-8420-2483-2)
1992 (ISBN 0-8420-2463-8)
1991 (ISBN 0-8420-2397-6)
1990 (ISBN 0-8420-2368-2)
1989 (ISBN 0-8420-2344-5)
1988 (ISBN 0-8420-2330-5)
1987 (ISBN 0-8420-2292-9)
1986 (ISBN 0-8420-2275-0)
1985 (ISBN 0-8420-2249-X)
1984 (ISBN 0-8420-2234-1)
1983 (ISBN 0-8420-2220-1)
1982 (ISBN 0-8420-2214-7)
1981 (ISBN 0-8420-2200-7)
1980 (ISBN 0-8420-2181-7)
1979 (ISBN 0-8420-2170-1)
1978 (ISBN 0-8420-2159-0)
1972–77 (ISBN 0-8420-2129-9, 2 vols.)
1935–71 (ISBN 0-394-47270-5, 3 vols.)

International Polls

The International Gallup Polls: Public Opinion, 1979
ISBN 0-8420-2180-9 (1981)

The International Gallup Polls: Public Opinion, 1978
ISBN 0-8420-2162-0-9 (1980)

The Gallup International Opinion Polls: France, 1939, 1944–1975
2 volumes ISBN 0-394-40998-1 (1976)

The Gallup International Opinion Polls: Great Britain, 1937–1975
2 volumes ISBN 0-394-40992-2 (1976)

The Gallup Poll

Public Opinion 2016

EDITED BY
FRANK NEWPORT

ROWMAN & LITTLEFIELD
Lanham • Boulder • New York • Toronto • Plymouth, UK

ACKNOWLEDGMENTS

The Gallup Poll represents the efforts of a number of talented and dedicated individuals. I wish to express my gratitude to James Clifton, Chairman and CEO of Gallup, whose continuing vision and commitment to the value of social and economic analysis of the poll data undergirds all that is in this volume. I also acknowledge the central role of the poll staff, including Jeffrey Jones; Lydia Saad; Alyssa Brown, and Art Swift; and all of the authors whose names appear on the by-lines within this volume. Professor Fred Israel, City University of New York, George Gallup Jr. (1930–2011), and Alec Gallup (1928–2009) deserve special credit for their contributions to the first 38 volumes in this series.

Published in the United States of America by Rowman & Littlefield Publishers, Inc.
A wholly owned subsidiary of The Rowman & Littlefield Publishing Group, Inc.
4501 Forbes Boulevard, Suite 200, Lanham, Maryland 20706, www.rowman.com

Unit A, Whitacre Mews, 26-34 Stannary Street, London SE11 4AB

ISSN 0195-962X
Cloth ISBN-13: 978-1-5381-0009-7
eISBN: 978-1-5381-0010-3

∞™ The paper used in this publication meets the minimum requirements of American National Standard for Information Sciences—Permanence of Paper for Printed Library Materials, ANSI/NISO Z39.48-1992.

Printed in the United States of America

CONTENTS

INTRODUCTION

The Gallup Poll: Public Opinion 2016 contains the findings of the more than 500 Gallup Poll reports released to the American public during the year 2016. The latest volume reveals the attitudes and opinions of individuals and key groups within the American population concerning national and international issues and events of the year, and reports on Americans' views of the economy, their personal financial situation and well-being, and the political arena.

The 2016 volume is the most recent addition to the 43-volume Gallup collection, *Public Opinion, 1935–2016* the largest compilation of public opinion findings ever published. The Gallup collection documents the attitudes and opinions of Americans on national and international issues and events from Franklin D. Roosevelt's second term to the present.

Shown in detail are results of tens of thousands of questions that the Gallup Poll—the world's oldest and most respected public opinion poll—has asked of the public over the last eight decades. Results of the survey questions appear in the Gallup Poll reports reproduced in the 43 volumes. These reports, the first of which was released on October 20, 1935, have been provided on a continuous basis since that time, most recently as daily updates on Gallup's website, gallup.com.

The 43-volume collection documents public opinion from 1935 to the present in the following six separate and distinct areas:

1. *Measuring the Strength of Support for the President, Political Candidates, and Political Parties.* For over 70 years, Gallup has measured, on a continuous basis, the strength of support for the president, for the congressional opposition, and for various political candidates and parties in national elections.
2. *Monitoring the Economy.* An important Gallup Poll objective has been monitoring the U.S. economy in all of its permutations from the perspective of the American consumer. Gallup now measures unemployment and job creation and assesses Americans' views on economic conditions, the job market, and personal financial concerns on a daily basis—providing a continuous record of this vital component of the U.S. economy.
3. *Gauging and Charting the Public's Mood.* From its earliest days the Gallup Poll has sought to determine, on an ongoing basis, Americans' satisfaction or dissatisfaction with the direction in which the nation appeared to be headed and with the way they thought that their personal lives were progressing. This process also has involved regular assessments of the people's mood regarding the state of the nation's economy as well as the status of their personal finances, their jobs, and other aspects of their lives.
4. *Recording the Public's Response to Major News Events.* Gallup has recorded the public's attitudes and opinions in response to major news events of the last seven decades. Examples include Adolf Hitler's invasion of the Soviet Union, the bombing of Pearl Harbor, the dropping of the atomic bomb on Hiroshima, the assassination of President John F. Kennedy, the moon landing, the taking of U.S. hostages in Iran, the O. J. Simpson trial verdict, the impeachment of President Bill Clinton, the 9/11/2001 terrorist attacks, the Iraq War, Hurricane Katrina and its aftermath, and the election of the nation's first black president in 2008.
5. *Measuring Americans' Views on Key Policy Issues.* A primary ongoing Gallup polling activity has been to document the collective will of the American people in terms of major policy issues and initiatives under consideration by elected representatives. Gallup routinely measures Americans' priorities, including monthly assessments of the most important problem facing the nation, interest in and awareness of issues and pending legislation, and overall sentiments on pressing national issues.
6. *Tracking America's Well-Being and Health.* Since 2008, Gallup has tracked America's subjective well-being and personal health assessments on a daily basis as part of the Gallup-Healthways Well-Being Index.

Two of the most frequently asked questions concerning the Gallup Poll are: Who pays for or provides financial support to the Poll? And who determines which topics are covered by the Poll or, more specifically, who decides which questions are asked on Gallup surveys? Since its founding in 1935, the Gallup Poll has been underwritten by Gallup itself, in the public interest, and by the nation's media. The Gallup Poll also receives financial support from subscriptions to Gallup Analytics, this annual volume, and partners with innovative businesses who are vitally interested in understanding human attitudes and behavior.

Suggestions for poll questions come from a wide variety of sources, including print and broadcast media, from institutions as well as from individuals, and from broad editorial consideration of the key and pressing issues facing the nation. In addition, the public themselves are regularly questioned about the problems and issues facing the nation as they perceive them. Their answers establish priorities and provide an up-to-the-minute list of topic areas to explore through the Poll.

The Gallup Poll, as it is known today, began life on October 20, 1935, as a nationally syndicated newspaper feature titled *America Speaks—the National Weekly Column of Public Opinion*. For brevity's sake, the media quickly came to refer to the column as the Gallup Poll, after its founder and editor-in-chief, Dr. George H. Gallup. Although Dr. Gallup had experimented during the 1934 congressional and 1932 presidential election campaigns to develop more accurate techniques for measuring public opinion, including scientific sampling, the first Gallup survey results to appear in print were those reported in the initial October 20, 1935, column.

Although the new scientific opinion polls enjoyed almost immediate popular success, their initial efforts were met with skepticism from many quarters. Critics questioned, for example, how it was possible to determine the opinions of the entire American populace based on only 1,000 interviews or less, or how one knows whether people were telling the truth. The credibility of the polls as well as their commercial viability was enhanced significantly, however, when Gallup correctly predicted that Roosevelt would win the 1936 presidential election in a landslide, directly contradicting the forecast of the Literary Digest Poll, the poll of record at that time. The Digest Poll, which was not based on scientific sampling procedures, claimed that FDR's Republican challenger, Alfred M. Landon, would easily win the election.

Over the subsequent eight decades, scientifically based opinion polls have gained a level of acceptance to where they are used today to investigate virtually every aspect of human experience in most nations of the world.

In 2008, Gallup began an unprecedented program of daily tracking surveys, interviewing 1,000 national adults virtually each day of the year as part of the Gallup-Healthways Well-Being Index project. Daily interviewing allows Gallup to track important health, well-being, political and economic indicators on a continuous basis and also creates large databases used for detailed analysis of small demographic, political and regional subgroups. The benefits of this major initiative in survey research procedures will be apparent to the reader as he or she reviews the content of this volume.

Frank Newport

THE SAMPLE

Most Gallup Poll findings are based on telephone surveys. The majority of the findings reported in Gallup Poll surveys are based on samples consisting of a minimum of 1,000 interviews.

Design of the Sample for Telephone Surveys

The findings from the telephone surveys are based on Gallup's standard national residential and cell telephone samples, consisting of directory-assisted random-digit telephone samples utilizing a proportionate, stratified sampling design. The random-digit aspect of the residential telephone sample is used to avoid "listing" bias. Numerous studies have shown that households with unlisted telephone numbers are different from listed households. "Unlistedness" is due to household mobility or to customer requests to prevent publication of the telephone number. To avoid this source of bias, a random-digit procedure designed to provide representation of both listed and unlisted (including not-yet-listed) numbers is used.

Beginning in 2008, Gallup began including cellphone telephone numbers in its national samples to account for the growing proportion of Americans who are "cellphone only." Cellphone samples are also based on random-digit-dial procedures using lists of all cellphone exchanges in the United States.

Telephone numbers for the continental United States are stratified into four regions of the country. The sample of telephone numbers produced by the described method is representative of all telephone households within the continental United States.

Only working banks of telephone numbers are selected. Eliminating nonworking banks from the sample increases the likelihood that any sampled telephone number will be associated with a residence.

Within each household contacted on a residential landline, an interview is sought with the adult eighteen years of age or older living in the household who has had the most recent birthday (this is a method commonly employed to make a random selection within households without having to ask the respondent to provide a complete roster of adults living in the household). In the event that the sample becomes disproportionately female (due to higher cooperation rates typically observed for female respondents), the household selection criteria are adjusted to select only the male in the household who has had the most recent birthday (except in households where the adults are exclusively female). Calls made on cellphones do not use the same respondent selection procedure since cellphones are typically associated with a single individual rather than shared among several members of a household.

A minimum of three calls (and up to six calls) is attempted to each selected telephone number to complete an interview. Time of day and the day of the week for callbacks are varied to maximize the chances of reaching a respondent. All interviews are conducted on weekends or weekday evenings in order to contact potential respondents among the working population.

The final sample is weighted so that the distribution of the sample matches current estimates derived from the U.S. Census Bureau's Current Population Survey (CPS) for the adult population living in households with a landline or cellular telephone in the continental United States.

Weighting Procedures

After the survey data have been collected and processed, each respondent is assigned a weight so that the demographic characteristics of the total weighted sample of respondents match the latest estimates of the demographic characteristics of the adult population available from the U.S. Census Bureau. Gallup weights data to census estimates for gender, race, age, Hispanic ethnicity, educational attainment, region, population density, and phone status.

The procedures described above are designed to produce samples approximating the adult civilian population (18 and older) living in private households. Survey percentages may be applied to census estimates of the size of these populations to project percentages into numbers of people. The manner in which the sample is drawn also produces a sample that approximates the distribution of private households in the United States. Therefore, survey results also can be projected to numbers of households.

Sampling Tolerances

In interpreting survey results, it should be borne in mind that all sample surveys are subject to sampling error—that is, the extent to which the results may differ from what would be obtained if the whole population surveyed had been interviewed. The size of such sampling errors depends largely on the number of interviews. The design of the survey methodology, including weighting the sample to population estimates, should also be taken into account when figuring sample error.

DESCRIPTIONS OF GALLUP ECONOMIC MEASURES USED IN THIS VOLUME

Gallup's **Employment/Underemployment Index** provides continuous monitoring of U.S. employment and underemployment and serves as a key adjunct to the U.S. government's monthly tracking. This index—based on the combination of responses to a set of questions about employment status—is designed to measure U.S. employment accurately, in accordance with International Conference of Labour Statisticians standards. Based on an individual's responses to the question series (some of which are asked of only a subset of respondents), Gallup classifies respondents into one of six employment categories: employed full time for an employer; employed full time for self; employed part time, but do not want to work full time; employed part time, but want to work full time; unemployed; and out of the workforce. Using these categorizations, Gallup further divides the workforce into those who are employed and those who are underemployed. Employed respondents are those in the workforce who are either employed full time or working part time but do not want to work full time. Underemployed respondents are those in the workforce who are either unemployed or employed part time but want to work full time. Gallup interviews 1,000 Americans daily—or about 30,000 per month. Because of its daily tracking of other political, business, and well-being measures, Gallup provides insights not available from any other source on the health, well-being, optimism, financial situations, and politics of those who are working or seeking work.

Gallup's **Economic Confidence Index** is based on the combined responses to two questions asking Americans, first, to rate economic conditions in this country today and, second, whether they think economic conditions in the country as a whole are getting better or getting worse. Gallup's Economic Confidence Index is updated daily, based on interviews conducted the previous night, as well as weekly, providing a far more up-to-date assessment than the monthly reports from the other indices, which are often weeks old when issued.

Gallup's **Job Creation Index** is based on employed Americans' estimates of their companies' hiring and firing practices. Gallup asks its sample of employed Americans each day whether their companies are hiring new people and expanding the size of their workforces, not changing the size of their workforces, or letting people go and reducing the size of their workforces. The resulting index—computed on a daily and a weekly basis by subtracting the percentage of employers letting people go from the percentage hiring—is a real-time indicator of the nation's employment picture across all industry and business sectors. Gallup analysis indicates that the Job Creation Index is an excellent predictor of weekly jobless claims that the U.S. Labor Department reports each Thursday. In some ways, Gallup's Job Creation Index is more meaningful than the government's weekly new jobless claims measure, given that not everyone who is laid off files for unemployment. The index may also pick up hiring trends days or weeks before they are manifested in the official unemployment rate or other lagging indicators. Finally, the index measures job creation (hiring) and job loss (letting go) on a continuous basis. This provides additional real-time insight not available from broadly aggregated indicators and unemployment data.

Gallup's **Consumer Spending** measure is calculated from responses to a basic question asking Americans each day to estimate the amount of money they spent "yesterday," excluding the purchase of a home or an automobile or normal household bills. The result is a real-time indicator of discretionary retail spending, fluctuations in which are sensitive to shifts in the economic environment. Changes in Gallup's spending estimates are related to changes in both direction and magnitude of actual consumer spending as reported by the government. Further, Gallup's Consumer Spending measure provides estimates on a continuing basis, giving an early read on what the government eventually reports roughly two weeks after the close of each month. Gallup's continuous surveying allows for analysis of spending patterns on a daily and a weekly basis, which is particularly important to understanding seasonal variations in spending. The spending measure allows business and investment decisions to be based on essentially real-time information.

ABOUT THE GALLUP-HEALTHWAYS WELL-BEING INDEX®

The **Gallup-Healthways Well-Being Index** includes more than 2.2 million surveys and captures how people feel about and experience their daily lives. Levels of well-being correlate with healthcare (utilization and cost) and productivity measures (absenteeism, presenteeism, and job performance), all critical to organizational and economic competitiveness.

Well-Being Index data provide a comprehensive view of well-being across five elements:

Purpose: Liking what you do each day and being motivated to achieve your goals

Social: Having supportive relationships and love in your life

Financial: Managing your economic life to reduce stress and increase security

Community: Liking where you live, feeling safe and having pride in your community

Physical: Having good health and enough energy to get things done daily

STATE OF THE STATES POLLS

A number of stories included in this volume are based on Gallup's "State of the States" series, analyses that examine state-by-state differences on the political, economic, and well-being measures that Gallup tracks each day. State of the States stories are based on aggregated data for six-month or full-year time periods, providing large enough samples for meaningful analyses of responses in each of the 50 states and the District of Columbia.

January 07, 2016
U.S. UNINSURED RATE 11.9% IN FOURTH QUARTER OF 2015

by Stephanie Marken

Story Highlights

- *Uninsured rate essentially unchanged throughout 2015*
- *Rate down 5.2 points since just before key provision of health law took effect*
- *Uninsured rate has declined most among Hispanics*

WASHINGTON, D.C. – In the fourth quarter of 2015, 11.9% of U.S. adults were without health insurance, up slightly from 11.6% in the third quarter and back to where it was in the first quarter of 2015. Still, the uninsured rate declined 5.2 percentage points since the fourth quarter of 2013, right before the key provision of the health law requiring Americans to carry health insurance took effect in early 2014.

Percentage Uninsured in the U.S., by Quarter

Do you have health insurance coverage?

Among adults aged 18 and older

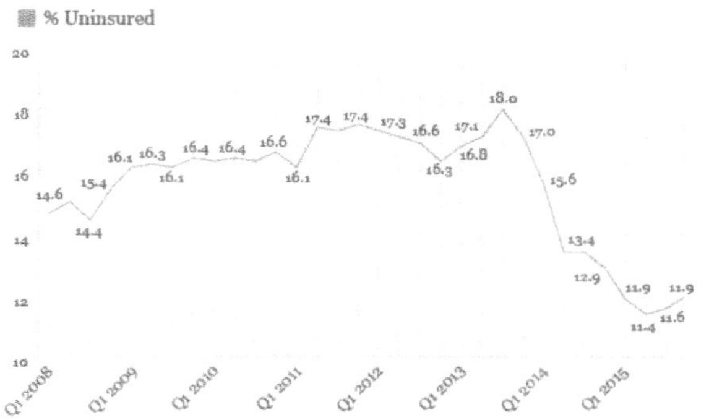

Quarter 1 2008-Quarter 4 2015
Gallup-Healthways Well-Being Index

GALLUP

Despite the uninsured rate not changing much over the course of 2015, it has been lower in each quarter compared with the same quarter in 2014.

Results for the fourth quarter are based on nearly 43,000 interviews with U.S. adults aged 18 and older from Oct. 1-Dec. 30, 2015, conducted as part of the Gallup-Healthways Well-Being Index. Gallup and Healthways ask 500 U.S. adults each day whether they have health insurance, which, on an aggregated basis, allows for precise and ongoing measurement of the percentage of Americans with and without health insurance.

Uninsured Rate Declines Most Among Hispanics

Across key subgroups, the largest dip in the uninsured rate since the fourth quarter of 2013 – right before the key provision of the Affordable Care Act took effect – has been among Hispanics. The uninsured rate among Hispanics was 30.9% in the fourth quarter of 2015, down 7.8 points from the fourth quarter of 2013. Similarly, the uninsured rate has declined 7.4 points among blacks over this same period. The sharper declines among these groups in part reflect that they had much higher uninsured rates to begin with. Even with the declines over the past two years, blacks and Hispanics still have relatively higher uninsured rates than the rest of the population.

Across income groups, the greatest decline in the uninsured rate has been among lower-income Americans. Among those with an annual household income of $36,000 or less, the uninsured rate declined 8.8 points since the fourth quarter of 2013. Those in lower income households remain far more likely than those in middle- and upper-income households to lack health insurance.

Percentage of Uninsured U.S. Adults, by Subgroup

Do you have health insurance coverage?

	Q4 2013	Q4 2015	Net change
	%	%	(pct. pts.)
National adults	17.1	11.9	-5.2
18 to 25	23.5	15.9	-7.6
26 to 34	28.2	20.9	-7.3
35 to 64	18.0	12.0	-6.0
65+	2.0	2.0	0.0
Whites	11.9	7.4	-4.5
Blacks	20.9	13.5	-7.4
Hispanics	38.7	30.9	-7.8
Less than $36,000	30.7	21.9	-8.8
$36,000 to $89,999	11.7	9.2	-2.5
$90,000+	5.8	3.2	-2.6

Gallup-Healthways Well-Being Index

GALLUP

The uninsured rates have declined significantly within age groups since late 2013, with the exception of seniors, most of whom were already covered by Medicare before the recent changes in health insurance.

Large Uptick in Those Paying for Own Health Plan

To assess changes in insurance type, Gallup and Healthways focus on adults aged 18 to 64, because nearly all Americans aged 65 and older have Medicare. The percentage of 18- to 64-year-olds who are covered by an insurance plan fully paid for by themselves or a family member was 21.6% in the fourth quarter, up from 17.6% in the fourth quarter of 2013. The percentages of Americans with Medicaid and Medicare insurance also have increased over this period.

Type of Health Insurance Coverage in the U.S., Among 18- to 64-Year-Olds

Is your health insurance coverage through a current or former employer, a union, Medicare, Medicaid, military or veteran's coverage or a plan fully paid for by you or a family member?

Primary and secondary insurance combined

	Q4 2013	Q4 2015	Net change
	%	%	(pct. pts.)
Current or former employer	44.2	43.2	-1.0
Plan fully paid for by self or family member	17.6	21.6	4.0
Medicaid	6.9	9.1	2.2
Medicare	6.1	7.5	1.4
Military/Veteran's	4.6	4.6	0.0
A union	2.5	2.7	0.2
(Something else)	3.5	3.8	0.3
No insurance	20.8	14.3	-6.5

Gallup-Healthways Well-Being Index

GALLUP

Gallup and Healthways began asking Americans about the source of their health insurance using the current question wording in August 2013, in anticipation of shifts in how people receive their health insurance as a result of the Affordable Care Act. Respondents are asked, "Is your primary health insurance coverage through a current or former employer, a union, Medicare, Medicaid, military or veteran's coverage or a plan fully paid for by you or a family member?" Respondents are also asked if they have secondary health insurance coverage and if so, what type of coverage it is. The results reported here are a combined estimate of primary and secondary insurance types.

Implications

The uninsured rate among U.S. adults dipped in the second and third quarters of 2015, before returning to where it was in the first quarter. Stability in the insurance rate was generally expected in the second, third and fourth quarters of 2015 because the open enrollment period for state and federal health insurance exchanges ended in the first quarter. The uninsured rate in the first quarter of 2016 – reflecting the start of insurance plans that new enrollees sign up for during the open enrollment period that began in November 2015 and ends on Jan. 31 – is more likely to show a decline.

The sharp drop in the uninsured rate seen in the first year after the insurance exchanges opened has leveled off in the second year, with smaller declines seen in 2015 compared with 2014. This validates concerns that similarly large reductions may not be possible in the future because the remaining uninsured are harder to reach or less inclined to become insured more generally. Future reductions will likely require significant outreach and expanded programs targeting those who have not yet taken advantage of the health insurance marketplace.

Survey Methods

Results are based on telephone interviews conducted Oct. 1-Dec. 31, 2015, as part of the Gallup-Healthways Well-Being Index survey, with a random sample of 42,998 adults, aged 18 and older, living in all 50 U.S. states and the District of Columbia. For results based on the total sample of national adults, the margin of sampling error is ±1 percentage point at the 95% confidence level. Each quarter dating to Quarter 1, 2014, has approximately 44,000 respondents. Each quarter from 2008 through 2013 has approximately 88,000 respondents.

January 08, 2016
TV HITS NEW LOW AS FAVORITE WAY IN U.S. TO SPEND EVENING

by Jim Norman

Story Highlights

- *Only 16% of Americans list TV as their favorite thing to do at night*
- *"Staying home" still America's favorite, 34% name this*
- *Relaxing (13%), reading (12%) are also popular choices*

WASHINGTON, D.C. – Television viewing was once so beloved by Americans that nearly half said it was their favorite thing to do at night, but it is now less popular than ever as an evening pastime. Fifty years ago, 48% of the public said it was their "favorite way of spending an evening"; this percentage has decreased steadily through the decades and now stands at a record-low 16%.

Staying Home With Family Eclipses Television Viewing as Americans' Favorite

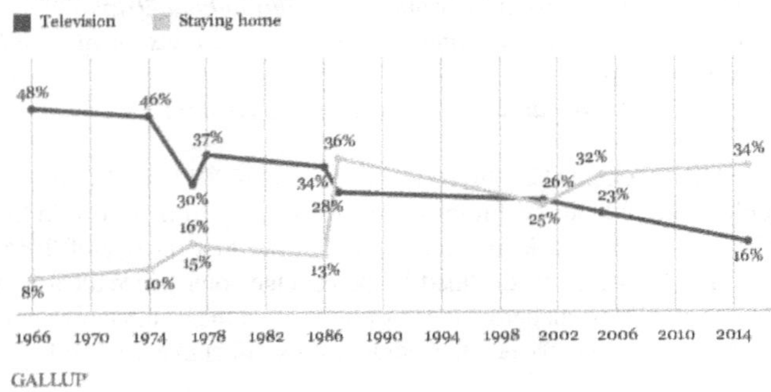

Meanwhile, the top choice for U.S. adults when asked how they like to spend an evening is "staying home" with 34% mentioning this activity in Gallup's December Lifestyle poll. Resting/Relaxing (13%) and reading (12%) are the third and fourth favorites, respectively. Both have been among the top choices all 11 times Gallup has asked the question since 1966.

The previous low for television viewing – which also includes mentions of watching DVDs or videocassettes – was 23% in 2005, the last time Gallup asked U.S. adults how they like to spend an evening. That was a slight drop from 26% in 2001.

As watching TV dropped in popularity through the years, "staying home" mentions soared – from 5% in 1966 to 16% in 1977 to 36% in 1987. After dropping back to 25% in 2001, it climbed to 32% in 2005 and 34% in the current poll.

Parents Most Likely to Favor Staying Home

In the current poll, those most likely to say staying home with the family is their favorite thing to do at night include those younger than 55, parents and workers. The only major demographic group as likely to say television is their favorite as staying home is the 55-and-older group: 25% say television, 23% list staying at home. Less than half that many choose television among those aged 35 to 54 (12%) and 18 to 34 (10%).

Percentage of Americans Who Say Stay at Home or Television Is Favorite Way to Spend an Evening

	Staying home	Television
18-34	39%	10%
35-54	39%	12%
55 and older	23%	25%
Employed	38%	14%
Not employed	27%	19%
Children younger than 18	49%	13%
No children younger than 18	27%	17%

Dec. 2-6, 2015

GALLUP

Decades Bring Major Changes in Evening Favorites

The percentage of U.S. adults who favor spending their nights reading, relaxing or visiting with friends has, for the most part, changed little over the past half-century, while the rise in the popularity of staying home and the fall of television watching have been generally steady during that time, with a few blips. However, going out for the night – whether to dine, see a movie, go dancing or go to bars – grew substantially in popularity between 1966 and 1986, only to take a steep dive in the new century.

What Is Your Favorite Way of Spending an Evening?

	A month ago (December 2015)	Eleven years ago (2005)	Thirty years ago (1986)	Fifty years ago (1966)
Staying at home	34%	32%	13%	8%
Television	16%	22%	34%	48%
Resting/Relaxing	13%	8%	14%	7%
Reading	12%	11%	14%	14%
Going out	6%	10%	21%	12%
Visiting with friends	6%	4%	8%	7%

GALLUP

Bottom Line

Gallup's question on Americans' favorite way to spend an evening serves as a barometer of changing lifestyles. It has captured the steady descent of television as the nation's favorite evening activity. Perhaps most tellingly, it has illustrated the changing mindset of Americans who have embraced staying at home over time.

Many factors could be behind the shift away from TV as a top choice. Television is now only one of many screens available to U.S. adults, and with Americans looking at smartphones and tablets on a near-constant basis throughout the day, the idea of sitting down to watch TV at night as a special thing to do may have lost its glow over the years.

Survey Methods

Results for this Gallup poll are based on telephone interviews conducted Dec. 2-6, 2015, on the Gallup U.S. Daily survey, with a random sample of 824 adults, aged 18 and older, living in all 50 U.S. states and the District of Columbia. For results based on the total sample of national adults, the margin of sampling error is ±4 percentage points at the 95% confidence level. All reported margins of sampling error include computed design effects for weighting.

January 19, 2016
BLACKS LEAST LIKELY AMONG U.S. RACIAL GROUPS TO SAY HOME IDEAL

by Rebecca Riffkin

Story Highlights

- *Blacks less likely than whites, Hispanics and Asians to say home ideal*
- *Blacks also least likely to say city or area is perfect place for them*

WASHINGTON, D.C. – Blacks are less likely than other major U.S. racial groups to be happy with their homes. Sixty-four percent of blacks agree that their house or apartment is ideal for them and their family, significantly lower than the 75% of whites, 71% of Asians and 70% of Hispanics who say the same.

Blacks Less Likely Than Other Racial and Ethnic Groups to See House as Ideal

On a 5-point scale, where 5 means strongly agree and 1 means strongly disagree, please rate your level of agreement with the following items: The house or apartment that you live in is ideal for you and your family.

	Whites	Blacks	Asians	Hispanics
% Agree (4+5)	75	64	71	70
% Neutral (3)	14	16	19	15
% Disagree (1+2)	11	20	11	15

Gallup Healthways Well-Being Index
Jan. 1-Nov. 30, 2015

GALLUP

Regardless of income, blacks are more likely than whites, Asians and Hispanics to disagree that their housing is ideal. This means that income variations alone cannot explain the differences in perceptions of housing among racial and ethnic groups.

These findings are based on interviews conducted from January-November 2015 as part of the Gallup Healthways Well-Being Index. Gallup asked U.S. adults to use a 5-point scale – where 5 means strongly agree and 1 means strongly disagree – to rate their level agreement with the following statement: "The house or apartment that you live in is ideal for you and your family." Nationally, 73% of adults agree with this statement, responding with a 4 or 5 on the scale, 13% disagree, responding with a 1 or 2 on the scale, and 15% are neutral, responding with a 3 on the scale.

Blacks Least Likely to See Their City as Perfect Place for Them

Results from a question asking Americans about the city or area where they live show a similar pattern. A majority of U.S. adults across racial and ethnic groups agree that the city or area where they live is a perfect place for them, but blacks (52%) are less likely than whites (64%), Hispanics (67%) and Asians (62%) to agree.

Blacks Less Likely Than Other Races to See City as Perfect Place for Them

On a 5-point scale, where 5 means strongly agree and 1 means strongly disagree, please rate your level of agreement with the following items: The city or area where you live is a perfect place for you.

	Whites	Blacks	Asians	Hispanics
% Agree (4+5)	64	52	62	67
% Neutral (3)	20	23	25	18
% Disagree (1+2)	15	25	14	15

Gallup Healthways Well-Being Index
Jan. 1-Nov. 30, 2015

GALLUP

Bottom Line

Housing needs and what qualifies as an "ideal house" can vary widely for each person. Factors such as cost, size, location and neighborhood safety can affect whether individuals feel their house meets their needs. And issues such as access to a safe place to exercise, proximity to quality schools, commute times, the availability of good jobs and access to fresh produce can affect whether an individual feels either their city or their home is right for them. Previous Gallup and Healthways research shows that those who see their home as ideal are more likely to have a stronger sense of purpose, a thriving social life, strong ties to their community, financial security and better physical health than those who don't think their home is perfect for them.

Various factors might help explain why blacks have a somewhat less positive view of their homes and communities than other racial groups do. According to the U.S. Census Bureau, blacks are the least likely racial or ethnic group to own their home. Gallup data aggregated from 2013-2015 also shows that 70% of U.S. whites report owning a home, compared with 41% of blacks and 43% of Hispanics. By renting, these groups have less autonomy to change aspects of their house or apartment to suit their needs.

Further, a study by Johns Hopkins University found that blacks who purchased their first home in the years shortly before the Great Recession have since had a significant loss in their net worth compared with an increase in the net worth of whites who purchased their first home during the same time period. In addition, lagging home prices in minority neighborhoods compared with steady or growing home prices in primarily white or mixed neighborhoods following the recession could be further negatively affecting blacks' views of their cities in general.

Additionally, an investigative report by ProPublica found that judgments on debt collection lawsuits happen almost twice as much in majority black neighborhoods than in mostly white communities, which could potentially influence how blacks from these neighborhoods view their cities or areas.

Despite these factors, a majority of blacks say they live in an ideal home and a perfect city. Increases in black home ownership and other key improvements in majority black communities could help close the racial and ethnic gap in perceptions of housing and communities.

Survey Methods

Results are based on telephone interviews conducted Jan. 1- Nov. 30, 2015, as part of the Gallup-Healthways Well-Being Index survey, with a random sample of 98,533 adults, aged 18 and older, living in all 50 U.S. states and the District of Columbia. For results based on the total sample of national adults, the margin of sampling error is ±0.3 percentage points at the 95% confidence level. For results based on the total sample of 9,061 blacks, the margin of sampling error is ±1 percentage point at the 95% confidence level. All reported margins of sampling error include computed design effects for weighting.

January 25, 2016

IN U.S., MODERATE DRINKERS HAVE EDGE IN EMOTIONAL HEALTH

by Nader Nekvasil and Diana Liu

Story Highlights

- *Moderate drinkers less likely to have had depression diagnosis*
- *Moderate drinkers more likely to experience positive emotions*

WASHINGTON, D.C. – U.S. adults who drink in moderation – one to 14 drinks per week – are slightly less likely than both nondrinkers and heavy drinkers to have been diagnosed with depression in their lifetime. Thirteen percent of moderate drinkers have been diagnosed with depression at some point in their lives, compared with 19% of nondrinkers and 17% of heavy drinkers. Moderate drinkers (7%) and heavy drinkers (8%) are also less likely than nondrinkers (11%) to report that they currently have or are being treated for depression.

U.S. Adults' Depression Diagnoses, by Number of Alcoholic Drinks Per Week

Results shown control for age, gender, race, ethnicity, education, income, marital status and children in household.

	0%	1 to 14%	15+ %
Depressed at some point in lifetime	19	13	17
Depressed currently	11	7	8

Jan. 2, 2014-Dec.15, 2015
Gallup-Healthways Well-Being Index

These findings, based on daily interviews conducted from Jan. 2, 2014-Dec. 15, 2015, are from the 2015 Gallup-Healthways Well-Being Index. Similar to the way the U.S. Centers for Disease Control and Prevention (CDC) define it, Gallup and Healthways define moderate drinking as having one to two drinks per day. Using the moderate drinking threshold of one to two drinks a day, this analysis termed moderate drinking as one to 14 drinks a week. While the CDC defines heavy drinking differently for men and for women, for this study, Gallup and Healthways defined heavy drinking for both genders as consuming 15 or more drinks per week. These results control for age, gender, race, ethnicity, education, income, marital status and children in household.

Overall, more than half of U.S. adults, 54.9%, say they have zero drinks per week, while 41.4% report drinking one to 14 drinks per week and 3.7% have 15 or more drinks.

Moderate Drinkers More Likely to Report Experiencing Positive Emotions

Positive Emotions, by Number of Alcoholic Drinks Per Week

Results shown control for age, gender, race, ethnicity, education, income, marital status and children in household.

	0%	1 to 14%	15+%
Happiness most of the day yesterday	89	92	89
Enjoyment most of the day yesterday	85	89	83
Smile or laugh a lot nearly every day	81	85	81

Jan. 2, 2014-Dec.15, 2015
Gallup-Healthways Well-Being Index

In addition to being less likely to have been diagnosed with depression at some point in their lives, moderate drinkers are also more likely than nondrinkers and heavy drinkers to report experiencing positive emotions on any given day, including happiness, enjoyment, and smiling or laughing. Nondrinkers and heavy drinkers do not differ significantly from each other in their reports of positive emotions.

Negative Emotions, by Number of Alcoholic Drinks Per Week

Results shown control for age, gender, race, ethnicity, education, income, marital status and children in household.

	0%	1 to 14%	15+%
Worry most of the day yesterday	31	29	35
Sadness most of the day yesterday	17	16	19
Little interest or pleasure in doing things nearly every day	16	13	18

Jan. 2, 2014-Dec.15, 2015
Gallup-Healthways Well-Being Index

Negative daily emotions, in turn, are less common among moderate drinkers. Moderate drinkers are slightly less likely than nondrinkers and heavy drinkers to report experiencing negative emotions, including worry or stress "yesterday" and having little interest or pleasure in doing things nearly every day. Moderate drinkers and nondrinkers report similar rates of sadness, but both groups are slightly less likely than heavy drinkers to experience sadness. Still, while heavy drinkers and nondrinkers report similar levels of positive emotions, heavy drinkers report experiencing more negative emotions than nondrinkers.

Bottom Line

Research into how alcohol consumption affects health has shown that moderate drinking is linked to lower rates of cardiovascular disease, diabetes and mortality, but could still increase one's risk of developing breast cancer. When it comes to the effect of alcohol consumption on mental and emotional health, a prominent medical study conducted in 1985 by clinical psychologist Cynthia Baum-Baicker showed that both heavy drinkers and nondrinkers have higher rates of clinical depression than moderate drinkers. The study also found that moderate alcohol consumption can increase overall happiness, euphoria, friendliness and pleasant feelings. A more recent study published in the *Oxford Journal* in 2006 found that for both men and women, moderate alcohol consumption led to improved cognition and fewer symptoms of depression.

The latest results from the Gallup-Healthways Well-Being Index are consistent with these findings and add to a body of research showing that for those who can safely drink alcohol, moderate consumption may yield mental and emotional health benefits. However, any study of the effect of drinking alcohol on health must take into account that drinking can be very harmful to those who abuse it and to those with certain medical conditions.

It is important to note that while this study controlled for the effect of a number of demographic variables, the relationship between alcohol use and depression is complex, and other variables may play a role in the relationship. It is also true that the directionality between the two is not established in these results. It is possible that people with poorer emotional health are more likely to choose abstaining from alcohol or heavy drinking than those with good emotional health. However, it could also be the case that moderate drinking is linked to emotional health benefits.

Previous Gallup research has shown that fewer than one in five, 17%, of Americans believe that moderate drinking is good for one's health, well below the 28% who say moderate drinking is bad for one's health and the 52% who say it makes no difference. However, with Gallup-Healthways data showing the link between moderate drinking and lower depression rates and more positive emotions, the recently reported decline in U.S. adults' belief that moderate drinking is good for one's health may be at least partially misplaced.

Survey Methods

Results are based on telephone interviews conducted Jan. 2, 2014-Dec. 15, 2015, as part of the Gallup-Healthways Well-Being Index survey, with a random sample of 347,915 adults, aged 18 and older, living in all 50 U.S. states and the District of Columbia. For results based on the total sample of national adults, the margin of sampling error is ±0.21 percentage points at the 95% confidence level.

For results based on the total sample of nondrinkers, the margin of sampling error is ±0.28 percentage points at the 95% confidence level.

For results based on the total sample of moderate drinkers, the margin of sampling error is ±0.31 percentage points at the 95% confidence level.

For results based on the total sample of heavy drinkers, the margin of sampling error is ±1.06 percentage points at the 95% confidence level.

All reported margins of sampling error include computed design effects for weighting.

January 27, 2016

HAWAII RECLAIMS TOP SPOT IN U.S. WELL-BEING

by Dan Witters

Story Highlights

- *Alaska, Montana, Colorado and Wyoming round out the top five*
- *West Virginia has lowest well-being for the seventh straight year*
- *Hawaii, Colorado and Montana are only states in the top 10 every year since 2012*

WASHINGTON, D.C. – Hawaii residents had the highest well-being of any state in the nation in 2015, reaching the top spot for the fifth time since Gallup and Healthways began tracking well-being in 2008. Alaska, which was the top state for well-being in 2014, slipped to second place. Residents of West Virginia and Kentucky have the lowest and second-lowest well-being, respectively, for the seventh consecutive year.

States With Highest and Lowest Well-Being in 2015

State	Well-Being Index Score	State	Well-Being Index Score
Hawaii	64.8	West Virginia	58.5
Alaska	64.1	Kentucky	60.3
Montana	63.8	Oklahoma	60.4
Colorado	63.6	Ohio	60.5
Wyoming	63.5	Indiana	60.5
South Dakota	63.5	Missouri	60.8
Minnesota	63.3	Arkansas	60.9
Utah	63.1	Mississippi	60.9
Arizona	63.0	Louisiana	61.1
California	62.7	Georgia	61.2
Texas	62.7	New York	61.2
Florida	62.4	Michigan	61.3
Wisconsin	62.4	Nevada	61.5
Iowa	62.4	Tennessee	61.5
North Dakota	62.3	Idaho	61.5

Gallup-Healthways Well-Being Index

GALLUP

Hawaii and Colorado are the only two states that have made the list of the 10 highest well-being states each year since 2008, while Alaska's well-being was among the top five in the nation for the fifth time. Montana was ranked in the top 10 each year except for 2010, and California had the 10th highest well-being in 2015, its best ranking since finishing ninth in 2008. North Dakota and Iowa, two states that have had multiple high well-being years but were outside of the top 15 in 2014, re-entered this list in 2015.

Most of the lowest well-being states in 2015 have frequented this list in the past.

These state-level data are based on more than 177,000 interviews with U.S. adults across all 50 states, conducted across 350 days from January-December 2015. The Well-Being Index is calculated on a scale of 0 to 100, where 0 represents the lowest possible well-being and 100 represents the highest possible well-being. The Gallup-Healthways Well-Being Index score for the nation and for each state comprises metrics affecting overall well-being and each of the five essential elements of well-being:

- **Purpose:** liking what you do each day and being motivated to achieve your goals
- **Social:** having supportive relationships and love in your life
- **Financial:** managing your economic life to reduce stress and increase security
- **Community:** liking where you live, feeling safe and having pride in your community
- **Physical:** having good health and enough energy to get things done daily

In most cases, a difference of 0.5 to 1.0 point in the Well-Being Index score between any two states represents a statistically significant gap and is characterized by meaningfully large differences in at least some of the individual metrics that make up the overall Gallup-Healthways Well-Being Index.

The Well-Being Index score for the U.S. in 2015 was 61.7, essentially unchanged from 61.6 in 2014. Gallup and Healthways have been tracking well-being since 2008 and updated the Well-Being Index survey instrument and scoring methodology in 2014 to provide a more comprehensive measure of well-being. The Well-Being Index scores for 2008-2013 are not directly comparable to the scores for 2014 and 2015 without appropriate adjustments because those prior scores are calculated using some different survey items and a different scoring method. State rankings across years, however, can be compared.

As in prior years, well-being in the U.S. shows regional patterns. The northern Plains and Mountain West are higher well-being areas, along with some western states and pockets of the Northeast and Atlantic. The lowest well-being states are in the south and through the industrial Midwest.

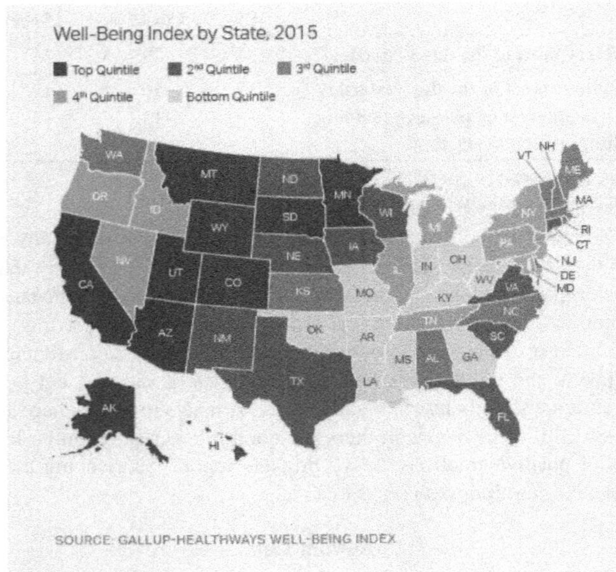

South Carolina Has Best Social Well-Being; Delaware Highest in Purpose

In addition to Hawaii residents having the highest overall well-being, they also had the highest physical well-being nationally. Alaska led all states in financial well-being, just edging out North Dakota. South Carolina residents had the best social well-being, and Delaware had the highest purpose well-being in 2015. Community well-being was highest in Montana.

West Virginians reported the lowest well-being in four of the five elements. The exception was financial well-being, which was lowest in Mississippi.

States With the Highest and Lowest Well-Being in Each Element

Purpose: Highest 5 States	Social: Highest 5 States	Financial: Highest 5 States	Community: Highest 5 States	Physical: Highest 5 States
Delaware	South Carolina	Alaska	Montana	Hawaii
Texas	Connecticut	North Dakota	Hawaii	Colorado
Wyoming	Utah	Hawaii	South Dakota	California
Hawaii	Florida	Minnesota	Wyoming	Montana
Alaska	Alaska	Iowa	Utah	Connecticut

Purpose: Lowest 5 States	Social: Lowest 5 States	Financial: Lowest 5 States	Community: Lowest 5 States	Physical: Lowest 5 States
West Virginia	West Virginia	Mississippi	West Virginia	West Virginia
Vermont	Arkansas	Georgia	New Jersey	Kentucky
New Hampshire	North Dakota	Idaho	Maryland	Oklahoma
Massachusetts	Oklahoma	West Virginia	New York	Arkansas
New York	Missouri	Louisiana	Ohio	Indiana

Gallup-Healthways Well-Being Index, 2015

GALLUP

Consistently High- and Low-Performing States in Well-Being

Over the past four years, Hawaii, Colorado, Montana, South Dakota and Minnesota have had the highest average well-being ranks nationally, followed closely by Utah, Nebraska and Iowa. Alaska and Vermont round out the top 10 states for high well-being ranks during this period. Only Hawaii, Colorado and Montana have been in the top 10 each year during this period.

After West Virginia and Kentucky, Ohio, Mississippi and Arkansas are the three states with the lowest well-being ranks in the past four years.

Well-Being 2012-2015: Highest and Lowest States Across Most Recent Years

Based on average Well-Being Index state rank from 2012 through 2015

Highest 10 states	Average rank	Lowest 10 states	Average rank
Hawaii	3	West Virginia	50
Colorado	5	Kentucky	49
Montana	5	Ohio	46
South Dakota	6	Mississippi	46
Minnesota	6	Arkansas	45
Utah	8	Indiana	44
Nebraska	9	Tennessee	43
Iowa	12	Oklahoma	43
Alaska	13	Missouri	42

Gallup-Healthways Well-Being Index

GALLUP

Implications

Overall, well-being across the U.S. has shown little improvement since 2008, although there are a number of individual metrics of the Well-Being Index that have improved. These include a decline in the uninsured rate, a decline in the smoking rate and an increase in reported exercise. Food insecurity, defined as not having enough money for food at least once in the last 12 months, has also dropped significantly since 2013 to a seven-year low.

Not all trends have pointed in the positive direction, however. Obesity in the U.S. has continued its relentless upward climb, reaching a new high mark last year. And the trend may continue as half of all overweight adults say they are not seriously trying to lose weight. And among workers, the rate of those working part-time jobs but seeking full-time work has been slow to improve, which is problematic for their well-being, as these "involuntarily part-time" workers exhibit financial well-being that is no better than the unemployed.

Actively seeking improvement in physical wellness is better than doing nothing at all, but research has shown that those who have high well-being across all five elements of well-being perform better than those who are physically fit alone. Those who seek to improve the well-being of their population, including large employers and state and local government leaders, should advocate for a holistic approach to well-being, with a long-term goal of their state being among the highest well-being states in the nation.

Read the State of American Well-Being report to see the complete state well-being rankings.

Survey Methods

Results are based on telephone interviews conducted Jan. 2-Dec. 30, 2015, as a part of the Gallup-Healthways Well-Being Index, with a random sample of 177,281 adults, aged 18 and older, living in all 50 U.S. states and the District of Columbia. For results based on the total sample of national adults, the margin of sampling error for the Well-Being Index score is ±0.1 point at the 95% confidence level. The margin of sampling error for most states is about ±0.6 points, although this increases to about ±1.6 points for the smallest population states such as North Dakota, Wyoming, Hawaii and Delaware. All reported margins of sampling error include computed design effects due to weighting.

February 01, 2016

DEMOCRATS, REPUBLICANS AGREE ON FOUR TOP ISSUES FOR CAMPAIGN

by Frank Newport

Story Highlights

- *All rate the economy, terrorism, jobs and healthcare as important*
- *Republicans put more priority on fixing government and the deficit*
- *Democrats rate climate change, inequality as more important*

PRINCETON, N.J. – Republicans and Democrats agree on the importance of the presidential candidates' positions on the economy, terrorism, jobs and healthcare. Beyond these, however, the two partisan groups differ significantly on the importance they assign to other campaign issues.

Importance of Campaign Issues, by Party

Now I am going to read a list of some of the issues that will probably be discussed in this year's presidential election campaign. As I read each one, please tell me how important the candidates' positions on that issue will be in influencing your vote for president -- extremely important, very important, somewhat important or not important.

% Extremely/Very important

	Republicans/ Republican leaners	Democrats/ Democratic leaners
ABOVE AVERAGE IN IMPORTANCE TO BOTH PARTIES		
Terrorism and national security	92	82
The economy	92	85
Employment and jobs	80	88
Healthcare and the Affordable Care Act	75	83
ABOVE AVERAGE IN IMPORTANCE TO REPUBLICANS ONLY		
The federal budget deficit	83	62
Foreign affairs	77	65
The size and efficiency of the federal government	77	49
Immigration	76	62
Taxes	74	66
ABOVE AVERAGE IN IMPORTANCE TO DEMOCRATS ONLY		
Education	67	90
The distribution of income and wealth in the United States	49	75
BELOW AVERAGE IN IMPORTANCE TO BOTH PARTIES		
Gun policy	61	70
Government regulation of Wall Street and banks	47	69
Social issues such as gay marriage and abortion	34	46
Climate change	21	69

Jan. 21-25, 2016

GALLUP'

These data, from Gallup's Jan. 21-25 Election Benchmark survey, are based on Americans' responses to a question asking them to rate the importance of the candidates' positions on 15 issues. Overall, Americans rate the economy, terrorism, jobs, healthcare and education as most important. The detailed results are at the end of this article.

The accompanying table groups each issue based on the issue's importance among Republicans and Republican-leaning independents and among Democrats and Democratic-leaning independents. Republicans' average importance rating across the 15 issues is 67%, while Democrats' is 71%.

The economy, terrorism, jobs and healthcare clearly are the four issues that share higher-than-average importance among both partisan groups.

Issues Important to Only One Party

Five issues are well above average in importance for Republicans, but are not as important to Democrats. These are:

- The federal budget deficit
- Foreign affairs
- The size and efficiency of the federal government
- Immigration
- Taxes

Of these five, the size and efficiency of the federal government receives particularly low ratings from Democrats. It is the second lowest of any issue tested for that partisan group. Democrats' importance ratings for the other four are below the Democratic average.

One issue has slightly above-average importance for Democrats but is well below average for Republicans: the distribution of income and wealth in the U.S. One other issue, education, is way above average for Democrats (it is their highest-rated issue), while just at the average importance rating among Republicans.

Issues Below Average in Importance to Both Parties

Four issues have below-average importance ratings for both partisan groups, although three of these are barely below the average for Democrats. These are:

- Gun policy
- Government regulation of Wall Street and banks
- Social issues such as gay marriage and abortion
- Climate change

Climate change is the lowest rated of the 15 issues tested among Republicans, while coming in just below average for Democrats. Social issues clearly have low importance across partisan lines; they are the lowest rated among Democrats and second lowest among Republicans.

Across the 15 issues, six show the largest discrepancy in rated importance between Republicans and Democrats, making these highly partisan concerns in the 2016 election environment:

- *Climate change.* Democrats' importance rating is 48 percentage points higher than Republicans', making this the single most discrepant issue of the 15 tested.
- *Size and efficiency of the federal government.* Republicans rate it more important than Democrats by 28 points.
- *The distribution of income and wealth in the U.S.* (Democrats: more important, by 26 points)
- *Education.* (Democrats, +23 points)
- *Government regulation of Wall Street and banks.* (Democrats, +22)
- *The federal budget deficit.* (Republicans, +21)

Top-of-Mind Priorities

A separate, open-ended question asked Americans to name the single issue or challenge they are most interested in having the next president address when he or she takes office next January. Americans' most frequently given responses involve the economy, followed by mentions of immigration, defense/national security, healthcare and terrorism – generally similar to the top-ranked issues in the list format.

The biggest differences between the two partisan groups on this question involve defense and national security, mentioned spontaneously by 19% of Republicans as the most important issue for the next president, but by only 5% of Democrats. Republicans are also more likely than Democrats to mention immigration and, to a lesser extent, the economy.

For their part, Democrats are more likely to mention education, as well as issues revolving around wages and Americans' ability to make a decent wage and, to a lesser extent, the environment.

The two partisan groups are about equally likely to mention healthcare and terrorism.

Regardless of who wins the election, what single issue or challenge are you most interested in having the next president address when he or she takes office next January? [OPEN-ENDED]

	Republicans/ Republican leaners	Democrats/ Democratic leaners
The economy	19	13
Immigration	19	11
Defense/National defense/Homeland security	19	5
Healthcare/Healthcare costs/Healthcare reform	11	12
Terrorism	7	7
Education	1	12
Jobs/Unemployment	5	6
The federal deficit/The budget	8	5
Foreign policy/affairs	6	4
Gun control	3	5
Wages/Earning a decent wage	*	7
The environment/Pollution	1	5
Poverty/The poor/Homelessness	2	4
Race relations/Equal rights	1	3
Taxes	3	1
Restoring respect to the office of president	3	1
Moral issues/Ethics/Religion	3	1
Social Security	1	2
Big government/Government invasion of privacy	2	1
Campaign finance reform	*	3
Abortion	2	1
Wars	2	1
Drugs	1	1
Medicare	1	1
Family/Youth issues	1	1
Crime	*	2
Care for the elderly	*	1
Trade/Foreign trade	1	*
Gay rights issues	1	--
Gas prices	--	1
Welfare/Welfare reform	*	1
Appointments to Supreme Court	--	1
Relations with China	--	*
Prescription drugs/High cost of prescription drugs	*	*
Farm/Agricultural issues	--	*
Other	3	3
Nothing	2	2
No opinion	3	4

* Less than 0.5%

Jan. 21-25, 2016

GALLUP

Bottom Line

Republicans and Democrats alike generally agree that the presidential candidates – and the next president, whoever that might be – should focus on the economy, on jobs, on terrorism and national security and on healthcare.

Beyond that agreement, the interests of the two partisan groups diverge, with Republicans giving more importance to certain specific issues and Democrats to others.

These differences across groups are meaningful at this point in the campaign, given that candidates are firmly focused on getting votes from their own partisans in the caucus and primary process that begins with Feb. 1 voting in Iowa. However, as the campaign pivots to the general election, the parties' nominees to some degree will need to pay more attention to issues of importance to those outside their party – in the effort to gain votes of weakly affiliated partisans and of independents. And, of course, the research reviewed here deals only with the importance that Americans put on each concern as a campaign issue. This leaves the candidates to deal with the challenge of presenting proposals for solving the issue that resonate with their own party's voters in the primary process, but also with a broader constituency in the general election.

These data on priorities help in evaluating how well-connected the candidates are with various constituents in the current election process. The Democratic candidates, for example, have focused on inequality and what they perceive to be the inordinate power of Wall Street – issues that are not among the most important for rank-and-file Democrats whose votes they need in the fight for their party's nomination, unless the candidates can tie them in to broader concerns about the economy and jobs.

Republican candidates who focus on gun rights and social issues such as abortion and gay marriage likewise find themselves addressing concerns that are not among the top issues for their party's constituents as a whole, although perhaps more so for smaller segments of the party such as evangelicals.

Overall, these data aid in the process of continuing to understand the attitudes and priorities of the American people as the election process unfolds, ultimately helping measure how well what the candidates are discussing and proposing fits with the views of the people they are vying to lead as chief executive.

The complete responses to both sets of questions are presented here:

Now I am going to read a list of some of the issues that will probably be discussed in this year's presidential election campaign. As I read each one, please tell me how important the candidates' positions on that issue will be in influencing your vote for president -- extremely important, very important, somewhat important or not important.

Sorted by % "Extremely important"

	Extremely important	Very important	Somewhat important	Not important
	%	%	%	%
Terrorism and national security	46	39	11	4
The economy	39	48	11	2
Healthcare and the Affordable Care Act	37	42	15	6
Education	36	43	17	3
Employment and jobs	35	49	14	1
Gun policy	31	35	22	12
The federal budget deficit	30	41	22	5
Immigration	28	38	28	5
Foreign affairs	28	40	26	5
The distribution of income and wealth in the United States	26	37	22	14
Taxes	25	44	26	4
The size and efficiency of the federal government	23	38	31	8
Government regulation of Wall Street and banks	21	37	32	9
Social issues such as gay marriage and abortion	18	22	29	31
Climate change	16	29	27	28

Jan. 21-25, 2016

GALLUP

Regardless of who wins the election, what single issue or challenge are you most interested in having the next president address when he or she takes office next January? [OPEN-ENDED]

	Jan 21-25, 2016
	%
The economy	17
Immigration	14
Defense/National defense/Homeland security	11
Healthcare/Healthcare costs/Healthcare reform	10
Terrorism	7
Education	6
Jobs/Unemployment	6
The federal deficit/The budget	6
Foreign policy/affairs	5
Gun control	4
Wages/Earning a decent wage	4
The environment/Pollution	3
Poverty/The poor/Homelessness	3
Race relations/Equal rights	3
Taxes	2
Restoring respect to the office of president	2
Moral issues/Ethics/Religion	2
Social Security	2
Big government/Government invasion of privacy	2
Campaign finance reform	1
Abortion	1
Wars	1
Drugs	1
Medicare	1
Family/Youth issues	1
Crime	1
Care for the elderly	1
Trade/Foreign trade	1
Gay rights issues	*
Gas prices	*
Welfare/Welfare reform	*
Appointments to Supreme Court	*
Relations with China	*
Prescription drugs/High cost of prescription drugs	*
Farm/Agricultural issues	*

* Less than 0.5%

GALLUP

These data are available in Gallup Analytics.

Survey Methods

Results for this Gallup poll are based on telephone interviews conducted Jan. 21-25, 2016, with a random sample of 1,022 adults, aged 18 and older, living in all 50 U.S. states and the District of Columbia. For results based on the total sample of national adults, the margin of sampling error is ±4 percentage points at the 95% confidence level. For results based on the total sample of 479 Republicans and Republican-leaning independents, the margin of sampling error is ±6 percentage points at the 95% confidence level. For results based on the total sample of 460 Democrats and Democratic-leaning independents, the margin of sampling error is ±6 percentage points at the 95% confidence level. All reported margins of sampling error include computed design effects for weighting.

February 03, 2016
RED STATES OUTNUMBER BLUE FOR FIRST TIME IN GALLUP TRACKING

by Jeffrey M. Jones

Story Highlights

- *20 states solidly or leaning Republican, 14 solidly or leaning Democratic*
- *Wyoming most Republican state; Vermont, Hawaii most Democratic*
- *Alabama and Idaho are most conservative states*

PRINCETON, N.J. – Gallup's analysis of political party affiliation at the state level in 2015 finds that 20 states are solidly Republican or leaning Republican, compared with 14 solidly Democratic or leaning Democratic states. The remaining 16 are competitive. This is the first time in Gallup's eight years of tracking partisanship by state that there have been more Republican than Democratic states. It also marks a dramatic shift from 2008, when Democratic strength nationally was its greatest in recent decades.

Political Composition of the 50 U.S. States

Based on annual state averages of party affiliation from Gallup Daily tracking

District of Columbia not included

	'08	'09	'10	'11	'12	'13	'14	'15
Solid Democratic	29	23	13	11	13	12	11	11
Lean Democratic	6	10	9	7	6	5	6	3
Competitive	10	12	18	15	19	19	18	16
Lean Republican	1	1	5	7	3	2	5	8
Solid Republican	4	4	5	10	9	12	10	12
Total Democratic	35	33	22	18	19	17	17	14
Total Republican	5	5	10	17	12	14	15	20
Net Democratic	+30	+28	+12	+1	+7	+3	+2	-6

Notes:

-- Solid states are defined as those in which one party has at least a 10-percentage-point advantage over the other in party affiliation (identification + leaning).

-- Leaning states are those in which one party has more than a 5-point but less than a 10-point advantage in party affiliation.

-- Competitive states are those in which the parties are within 5 points of each other in party affiliation.

GALLUP

Importantly, even though Republicans claim a greater number of states, Democrats continue to hold an edge nationally in partisanship. In 2015 Gallup Daily tracking data, 43% of all U.S. adults identified as Democrats or leaned Democratic, compared with 40% identifying as Republican or leaning Republican. That is largely because many of the most populous states, including California, New York and Illinois, are Democratically aligned.

Gallup asks Americans each day as part of its Daily tracking survey whether they identify politically as a Democrat, a Republican or an independent. Independents are then probed as to whether they lean toward the Democratic or Republican Party. Combining the percentage of party identifiers and leaners gives a sense of the relative strength of each party in a given state, particularly because the percentage of political independents varies widely from state to state and can be high in states in which one party dominates electoral outcomes. The estimates are based on Gallup Daily tracking interviewing throughout 2015 and include no fewer than 488 residents in any state, with most state samples greater than 1,000.

Gallup considers states to be solidly favoring one party when they have a greater-than 10-percentage-point advantage over the other in party affiliation among the state's adult population. "Leaning" states are those in which one party has an advantage of more than five points but less than 10 points. Competitive states show the parties within five points of each other.

In 2008, Democrats enjoyed a better-than 10-point advantage in party affiliation nationwide, as President George W. Bush suffered through low job approval ratings as a result of the recession and the ongoing war in Iraq. That year, Gallup classified a total of 35 states as solidly Democratic or Democratic leaning, compared with only five solidly or leaning Republican states.

In the last several years, excluding 2012 when President Barack Obama won re-election, there has been a roughly equal number of Democratic and Republican states. But that changed last year, when many more states' political leanings moved in a Republican rather than a Democratic direction, giving Republicans a lead in more states than Democrats.

In all, 13 states' political classifications changed between 2014 and 2015, with 11 of these shifting in a more Republican direction. The Democrats lost three states – Maine, Pennsylvania and Michigan – each of which moved from Democratic-leaning to competitive. Meanwhile, Republicans gained five states – New Hampshire, West Virginia, Missouri, South Carolina and Texas – all moving from competitive to leaning or solidly Republican. Additionally, Alaska and Oklahoma shifted from leaning Republican to being solidly Republican, and Delaware from being solidly Democratic to leaning Democratic.

Nebraska and New Mexico are the two states that moved in a more Democratic direction, though Nebraska remains in the Republican column, shifting from solidly Republican to leaning Republican. New Mexico moved from a leaning Democratic state to a solid one.

The following map displays the political classification of each state based on 2015 data. The full party results for each state appear at the end of the article.

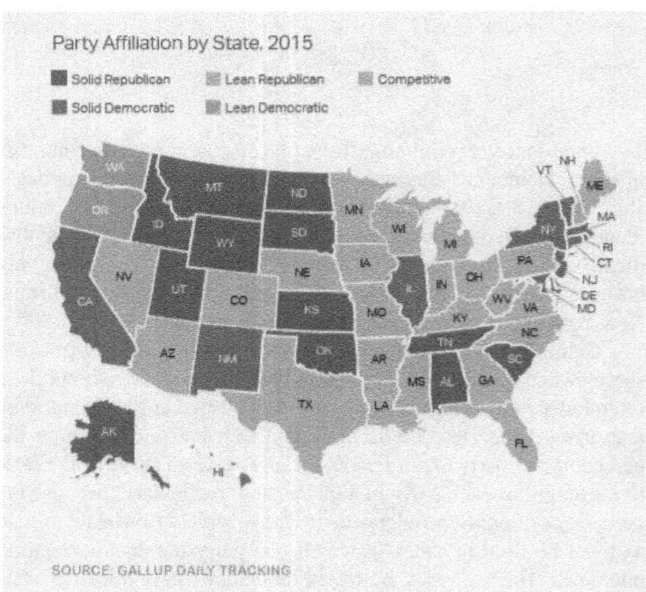

Wyoming Most Republican State; Vermont and Hawaii Most Democratic

The Republican Party had its biggest advantage in state party affiliation in Wyoming in 2015 – 60% of Wyoming adults identified as Republican or leaned Republican, while 28% identified as Democrats or leaned Democratic – a 32-point gap. The GOP advantage was nearly as large in Idaho and Utah, at roughly 30 points each. Vermont and Hawaii were the most Democratic states, with advantages in favor of the Democratic Party in excess of 20 points.

Most Republican and Most Democratic States, 2015

Republican states based on % Republican/Lean Republican minus % Democratic/Lean Democratic

Democratic states based on % Democratic/Lean Democratic minus % Republican/Lean Republican

Most Republican	Republican advantage	Most Democratic	Democratic advantage
Wyoming	31.8	Vermont	21.7
Idaho	30	Hawaii	20.8
Utah	29.9	Rhode Island	19.4
North Dakota	20.8	Massachusetts	18.6
Alabama	17.3	New York	18.4
Alaska	17.2	California	15.5
South Dakota	15.8	Maryland	15
Montana	14.4	New Mexico	11.6
Oklahoma	13.4	Illinois	10.8
Kansas	13.1	Connecticut	10.5

Gallup Daily tracking, January-December 2015

GALLUP

The most Republican and most Democratic states have been fairly consistent over time. Wyoming, Utah, Idaho and Kansas have been among the 10 most Republican states in each of the last eight years, and Montana, Alaska, Alabama, Nebraska and North Dakota have appeared in the top 10 in seven of the eight years. There is even greater consistency among Democratic states – all but two of the 10 most Democratic states in 2015 (New Mexico and Connecticut) have ranked in the top 10 in each of the last eight years, with Connecticut appearing seven times. New Mexico ranked among the top 10 states for the first time in 2015, with Delaware falling out of the top 10.

Ohio, North Carolina, Minnesota, Wisconsin and Florida are the most evenly balanced states politically, with less than one point separating Democratic and Republican Party preferences in those states. These states have been among the most highly contested "swing states" in recent presidential elections.

Alabama, Idaho Most Conservative States

In addition to assessing party leanings, Gallup asks Americans whether they identify politically as liberal, moderate or conservative. Nationally, many more Americans say they are conservative than liberal, and consequently, conservatives outnumber liberals in all but three states – Vermont, Massachusetts and Rhode Island. The full data on ideology by state appear at the end of the article.

Partisanship and ideology are highly correlated. As a result, there is usually much overlap between the most conservative and most Republican states and, alternatively, between the most liberal and most Democratic states. Seven of the 10 most Republican states also rank among the most conservative, although Alabama, the fifth-most Republican state, ties Idaho as the most conservative. Vermont ranks as the most liberal state by a wide margin over second-place Massachusetts.

Most and Least Conservative States, 2015

% Conservative minus % Liberal

Most conservative	Conservative advantage	Least conservative	Conservative advantage
Alabama	31.9	Vermont	-15.3
Idaho	31.8	Massachusetts	-5.8
Arkansas	30.0	Rhode Island	-0.9
North Dakota	27.8	New York	0.6
Utah	27.7	Hawaii	1.3
Mississippi	27.6	Connecticut	1.6
Wyoming	27.6	California	1.6
Louisiana	26.9	Oregon	2.7
Oklahoma	26.3	New Jersey	3.3
South Dakota	25.3	Washington	3.4

Gallup Daily tracking, January-December 2015

GALLUP

States that rank among the most conservative but not the most Republican include Arkansas, Mississippi and Louisiana, three Southern states that recently have voted Republican but were strongly Democratic states decades ago. Oregon, New Jersey and Washington rank among the least conservative states, but not among the most Democratic. However, those three states rank just outside the 10 most Democratic.

Implications

Monday's voting in the Iowa caucuses marked the beginning of voting in the 2016 presidential election campaign. The ultimate winner will be determined according to electoral votes won, based on each state's popular vote on Election Day this November. Presidential campaign strategists spend a lot of time developing their campaign plan and allocating resources based on which states' outcomes are uncertain to determine where campaigning can make the biggest difference.

The partisanship of the state population is a starting point in determining a state's likely vote, and there are more states in the Republican column heading into 2016 – a positive sign for the GOP. But because electoral votes are based on state population, the size of the state matters as much as the number of states each party holds. The 20 states that Gallup classifies as solidly Republican or leaning Republican account for 152 electoral votes, less than the 187 accounted for by the 14 solidly or leaning Democratic states plus the heavily Democratic District of Columbia.

But the election will not be merely a reflection of party preferences among adults in each state. If party preferences led directly to vote outcomes, Democrats would surely have won most presidential elections in the past, given their historical advantage in party preferences nationally.

Turnout is another key factor in determining the outcome, and it will especially be key in the 16 competitive states, which together account for 199 electoral votes. Republicans typically have an advantage in voter turnout in elections, and they will need to at least match Democratic turnout in competitive states in which they have a slight party advantage among all adults, such as Georgia, Virginia and Arizona. And the GOP will likely need to exceed Democratic turnout to win some of the larger, most politically balanced states like Florida, Ohio and North Carolina.

These data are available in Gallup Analytics.

Survey Methods

Results for this Gallup poll are based on telephone interviews conducted Jan. 1-Dec. 31, 2015, on the Gallup U.S. Daily survey, with a random sample of 177,991 adults, aged 18 and older, living in all 50 U.S. states and the District of Columbia. For results based on the total sample of national adults, the margin of sampling error is ±1 percentage point at the 95% confidence level.

Margins of error for individual states are no greater than ±6 percentage points and are ±3 percentage points in most states. All reported margins of sampling error include computed design effects for weighting.

Party Identification and Leaning, by State, 2015

	% Democratic/ Lean Democratic	% Republican/ Lean Republican	Democratic advantage	Gallup classification	N
Vermont	51.9	30.2	21.7	Solid Dem	571
Hawaii	51.6	30.8	20.8	Solid Dem	542
Rhode Island	48.3	28.9	19.4	Solid Dem	600
Massachusetts	50.8	32.2	18.6	Solid Dem	3,778
New York	49.9	31.5	18.4	Solid Dem	10,190
California	48.1	32.6	15.5	Solid Dem	17,507
Maryland	49.9	34.9	15.0	Solid Dem	3,039
New Mexico	48.1	36.5	11.6	Solid Dem	1,473
Illinois	46.8	36	10.8	Solid Dem	5,616
Connecticut	47.3	36.8	10.5	Solid Dem	1,939
New Jersey	46.5	36.3	10.2	Solid Dem	4,706
Washington	46.6	37.5	9.1	Lean Dem	4,366
Delaware	45.1	39.3	5.8	Lean Dem	504
Oregon	45.0	39.2	5.8	Lean Dem	2,972
Michigan	42.7	38.7	4.0	Competitive	5,024
Pennsylvania	44.6	41.6	3.0	Competitive	8,294
Florida	41.4	40.7	0.7	Competitive	10,580
Minnesota	42.9	42.4	0.5	Competitive	3,267
North Carolina	41.5	41.3	0.2	Competitive	5,716
Ohio	42.2	42	0.2	Competitive	6,418
Wisconsin	42.6	43.3	-0.7	Competitive	3,633
Arizona	40.0	41.4	-1.4	Competitive	4,273
Colorado	41.6	43.0	-1.4	Competitive	3,370
Louisiana	41.1	42.7	-1.6	Competitive	2,534
Virginia	40.9	42.5	-1.6	Competitive	5,151
Kentucky	42.2	45.0	-2.8	Competitive	2,697
Iowa	39.6	42.9	-3.3	Competitive	1,974
Maine	38.8	42.5	-3.7	Competitive	1,062
Georgia	39.8	43.7	-3.9	Competitive	5,215
Nevada	39.4	43.5	-4.1	Competitive	1,494
Mississippi	38.8	44.0	-5.2	Lean Rep	1,762
Texas	37.4	42.9	-5.5	Lean Rep	13,314
Indiana	38.2	44.2	-6	Lean Rep	3,934
West Virginia	39.6	45.7	-6.1	Lean Rep	1,253
Arkansas	38.5	45.4	-6.9	Lean Rep	1,964
Missouri	37.6	45.5	-7.9	Lean Rep	3,416
Nebraska	39.2	47.9	-8.7	Lean Rep	1,399
New Hampshire	37.6	46.4	-8.8	Lean Rep	819
Tennessee	36.1	46.4	-10.3	Solid Rep	4,379
South Carolina	35.4	47.9	-12.5	Solid Rep	2,839
Kansas	34.9	48.0	-13.1	Solid Rep	1,678
Oklahoma	35.9	49.3	-13.4	Solid Rep	2,623
Montana	33.2	47.6	-14.4	Solid Rep	1,044
South Dakota	36.1	51.9	-15.8	Solid Rep	542
Alaska	33.5	50.7	-17.2	Solid Rep	593
Alabama	34.1	51.4	-17.3	Solid Rep	3,099
North Dakota	30.8	51.6	-20.8	Solid Rep	488
Utah	26.1	56.0	-29.9	Solid Rep	2,165
Idaho	25.8	55.8	-30.0	Solid Rep	1,198
Wyoming	27.8	59.6	-31.8	Solid Rep	533

Gallup Daily tracking, January-December 2015

GALLUP

Self-Identified Ideology, by State, 2015

Sorted by Conservative advantage

	% Conservative	% Moderate	% Liberal	Conservative advantage (pct. pts.)	N
Alabama	47.5	31.5	15.6	31.9	3,099
Idaho	47.0	34.1	15.2	31.8	1,198
Arkansas	45.7	33.5	15.7	30.0	1,964
North Dakota	47.0	30.3	19.2	27.8	488
Utah	44.9	33.6	17.2	27.7	2,165
Mississippi	43.2	32.9	15.6	27.6	1,762
Wyoming	45.1	32.9	17.5	27.6	533
Louisiana	43.8	33.7	16.9	26.9	2,534
Oklahoma	43.0	35.2	16.7	26.3	2,623
South Dakota	44.0	34.2	18.7	25.3	542
South Carolina	42.7	34.5	17.6	25.1	2,839
Tennessee	41.7	35.2	17.3	24.4	4,379
Kentucky	43.1	33.8	18.8	24.3	2,697
West Virginia	42.0	34.4	18.7	23.3	1,253
Montana	42.0	34.8	18.8	23.2	1,044
Georgia	39.9	35.0	18.9	21.0	5,215
Indiana	40.3	34.8	19.6	20.7	3,934
Missouri	39.7	35.0	19.7	20.0	3,416
Texas	39.9	34.5	20.1	19.8	13,314
North Carolina	39.1	36.3	19.6	19.5	5,716
Alaska	38.3	40.6	19.0	19.3	593
Nebraska	37.9	39.4	19.3	18.6	1,399
Kansas	37.2	38.1	19.5	17.7	1,678
Iowa	37.3	37.7	20.0	17.3	1,974
Ohio	36.5	38.6	20.2	16.3	6,418
Wisconsin	37.0	36.6	22.1	14.9	3,633
Florida	35.9	36.0	21.9	14.0	10,580
Virginia	35.3	37.3	21.9	13.4	5,151
Arizona	35.0	37.4	22.2	12.8	4,273
Pennsylvania	35.1	37.5	22.8	12.3	8,294
New Hampshire	35.3	37.5	23.3	12.0	819
Michigan	34.4	36.8	22.8	11.6	5,024
Maine	35.4	36.5	24.2	11.2	1,062
Minnesota	34.5	37.4	23.6	10.9	3,267
Nevada	34.7	35.6	24.8	9.9	1,494
Delaware	32.5	37.8	23.2	9.3	504
Colorado	33.4	36.6	25.3	8.1	3,370
New Mexico	33.2	35.8	26.3	6.9	1,473
Illinois	31.0	37.2	25.9	5.1	5,616
Maryland	31.1	37.0	26.6	4.5	3,039
Washington	31.6	36.3	28.2	3.4	4,366
New Jersey	29.5	38.4	26.2	3.3	4,706
Oregon	32.3	34.0	29.6	2.7	2,972
California	30.2	35.5	28.6	1.6	17,507
Connecticut	29.3	37.6	27.7	1.6	1,939
Hawaii	28.2	39.0	26.9	1.3	542
New York	29.3	35.7	28.7	0.6	10,190
Rhode Island	27.5	38.6	28.4	-0.9	600
Massachusetts	26.7	36.6	32.5	-5.8	3,778
Vermont	24.4	31.2	39.7	-15.3	571

Gallup Daily tracking, January-December 2015

GALLUP

February 03, 2016

OBAMA RATED BEST IN HAWAII IN 2015, WORST IN WEST VIRGINIA

by Lydia Saad

Story Highlights

- *Hawaii's 58% approval rating was Obama's best in 2015*
- *Less than a quarter rated him positively in West Virginia*
- *Majorities approved of Obama in 10 states, up from five in 2014*

PRINCETON, N.J. – President Barack Obama's average job approval rating in 2015 was 46%, up four percentage points from 2014. Accordingly, the number of majority-approving states doubled from five to 10 in that period. Hawaii led these states, with 58% approving of Obama's overall job performance, slightly ahead of 56% in New York and California. All but one of the seven other states in his top 10 were in the East; Obama's most recent home state of Illinois was the exception.

Top 10 States for Obama Job Approval, 2015

% Approve

	%
Hawaii	58
New York	56
California	56
Massachusetts	55
Rhode Island	55
Maryland	55
New Jersey	52
Illinois	52
Vermont	51
Delaware	51

Gallup Daily tracking
January-December 2015

GALLUP

Obama's lowest average statewide approval rating in 2015 was in West Virginia (24%), but his ratings were nearly as low in Wyoming (25%) and Idaho (26%). The remainder of Obama's bottom 10 states gave him approval ratings ranging from 31% to 35%, more than 10 points below the national average.

Bottom 10 States for Obama Job Approval, 2015

% Approve

	%
West Virginia	24
Wyoming	25
Idaho	26
Oklahoma	31
North Dakota	31
Utah	32
Kentucky	34
Montana	34
Arkansas	35
Alabama	35
Alaska	35

Gallup Daily tracking
January-December 2015

GALLUP

These results are based on 177,990 Gallup Daily tracking interviews conducted nationally throughout 2015, including roughly 500 respondents in the least populous states and more than 1,000 in most other states. Gallup weighted each state's sample to match U.S. Census Bureau demographic parameters for that state's adult population. The full results by state appear at the end of this article.

The improvement in Obama's nationwide approval rating, and the related expansion in the number of states where majorities approve of his job performance, might seem to contradict the decline in the number of "blue" states nationally in 2015. However, the slight improvement in Obama's approval rating among all party groups in 2015 largely explains this.

Approval of Obama increased by four points among Democrats and Democratic leaners and by two points among Republicans and Republican leaners, as well as by eight points among the relatively small group of Americans who identify as independents with no partisan leanings. Thus, while the percentage of Republicans rose in many states, the increase in Republicans' and other party groups' approval of Obama produced a more favorable national picture for him.

President Barack Obama's Job Approval Rating Nationally

Annual averages by Party ID

	2014	2015	Change
	%	%	(pct. pts.)
Republican/Lean Republican	11	13	+2
Independent, no leaning	30	38	+8
Democrat/Lean Democratic	76	80	+4

Gallup Daily tracking

GALLUP

Coastal vs. Central Dichotomy in Obama Ratings Continues

The 50 states fall into five categories according to their average 2015 approval ratings:

- Well above average = approval rating of 55% or higher
- Above average = approval rating of 51% to 54%
- Average = approval rating within four percentage points of the 46% national average – in other words, 42% to 50%
- Below average = approval rating of 38% to 41%
- Well below average = approval rating below 38%

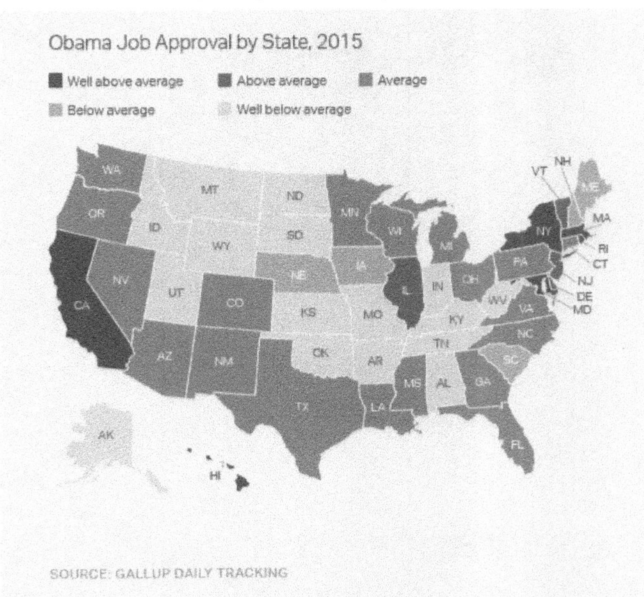

Obama's job approval rating increased at least slightly in nearly all 50 states in 2015, and as a result, the categorization of states with above- or below-average approval generally stayed the same as in 2014. Obama's strongest states remained clustered in the East, with the addition of California, Hawaii and Illinois, and his weakest states were located in the Rocky Mountain region, the Midwest and the South.

Bottom Line

A president's approval rating has considerable political significance in re-election years, as it indicates the incumbent's likelihood of re-election. In years when the president is not running for re-election, such as this one, the approval rating provides a broader indicator of his party's health, but generally needs to be reviewed in combination with other metrics, particularly party identification and party ratings.

This election year, knowledge of how well the president is perceived in each state may be useful in creating his campaign travel schedule, guiding him to those states – particularly swing states – where he is most popular and therefore may be most helpful to the Democratic nominee. The good news for that person, whomever he or she may be, is that at the start of 2016, Obama is bumping up against 50% approval, a significant improvement over his 2015 average. If this continues, it could mean there is less popular demand for change than when the presidential race started taking shape about a year ago.

Survey Methods

Results for this Gallup poll are based on telephone interviews conducted Jan. 2-Dec. 30, 2015, on the Gallup U.S. Daily tracking survey, with a random sample of 177,990 adults, aged 18 and older, living in all 50 U.S. states and the District of Columbia. For results based on the total sample of national adults, the margin of sampling error is ±1 percentage point at the 95% confidence level.

Margins of error for individual states are no greater than ±6 percentage points, and are ±3 percentage points in most states. All reported margins of sampling error include computed design effects for weighting.

February 04, 2016

ARKANSAS, KENTUCKY SET PACE IN REDUCING UNINSURED RATE

by Dan Witters

Story Highlights

- *Medicaid expansion, state exchanges linked to greater reductions*
- *45 states have had statistically significant declines since 2013*
- *No states have had statistically significant increases since 2013*

WASHINGTON, D.C. – Arkansas and Kentucky have had the sharpest net reductions in their uninsured rates since the healthcare law took effect at the beginning of 2014, followed closely by Oregon. West Virginia and California round out the top five states with the greatest declines in the percentage of adult residents without health insurance.

States With the Largest Reductions in the Percentage of Uninsured, 2013 vs. 2015

"Do you have health insurance?" (% no)

State	% of residents without health insurance, 2013	% of residents without health insurance, 2015	Percentage-point change in uninsured, 2013 to 2015	Medicaid expansion and/or state/partnership exchange by Sep 1, 2015?
Arkansas	22.5	9.6	-12.9	Both
Kentucky	20.4	7.5	-12.9	Both
Oregon	19.4	7.3	-12.1	Both
West Virginia	17.6	7.7	-9.9	Both
California	21.6	11.8	-9.8	Both
Washington	16.8	7.4	-9.4	Both
Alaska	18.9	10.3	-8.6	One
North Dakota	15.0	6.9	-8.1	One
Rhode Island	13.3	5.6	-7.7	Both
Mississippi	22.4	14.7	-7.7	One

Gallup-Healthways Well-Being Index

GALLUP

Seven of the 10 states with the largest reductions in uninsured rates have expanded Medicaid and established a state-based marketplace exchange or state-federal partnership, while the remaining three have implemented one or the other. The marketplace exchanges opened on Oct. 1, 2013, with new insurance plans purchased during the last quarter of that year typically starting on Jan. 1, 2014. Medicaid expansion among initially participating states also began at the beginning of 2014. As such, 2013 serves as a benchmark year for uninsured rates before the two major mechanisms of the healthcare law took effect: Medicaid expansion and marketplace exchanges.

Through the end of 2015, nine states had uninsured rates below 7.0%: Massachusetts, Hawaii, Vermont, Rhode Island, Minnesota, Wisconsin, Iowa, Connecticut and North Dakota. In the six-year span between 2008 and 2013, Massachusetts had been the only state to be at or below this rate in any year. No state has reported a statistically significant increase in its percentage of uninsured in 2015 compared with 2013.

Nationwide, the uninsured rate fell from 17.3% in 2013 to 11.7% in 2015.

States Not Embracing Health Law Less Likely to See Improvement

The only states that did not have statistically significant reductions in their respective uninsured rates since 2013 are Virginia, Wyoming, Kansas, Delaware and South Dakota. Four of these five states neither established a locally managed and promoted exchange nor expanded Medicaid – South Dakota is the exception, having implemented both.

Of the 10 states with the smallest declines since 2013, half have not implemented either of these major mechanisms of the Affordable Care Act (ACA). Four other states have implemented both – Massachusetts, Hawaii, Delaware and Iowa – and these were among the lowest six uninsured states nationwide in 2013, and thus they had less room for further reduction than most others.

States With Smallest Reductions in the Percentage of Uninsured, 2013 vs. 2015

"Do you have health insurance?" (% no)

State	% of residents without health insurance, 2013	% of residents without health insurance, 2015	Percentage-point change in uninsured, 2013 to 2015	Medicaid expansion and/or state/partnership exchange by Sep 1, 2015?
Virginia	13.3	12.6	-0.7	Neither
Massachusetts	4.9	3.5	-1.4	Both
Kansas	12.5	11.0	-1.5	Neither
Wyoming	16.6	14.0	-2.6	Neither
Hawaii	7.1	4.2	-2.9	Both
Delaware	10.5	7.4	-3.1	Both
Utah	15.6	12.4	-3.2	One
Iowa	9.7	6.3	-3.4	Both
South Dakota	14.0	10.6	-3.4	Neither
Missouri	15.2	11.6	-3.6	Neither

Gallup-Healthways Well-Being Index

GALLUP

These data, collected as part of the Gallup-Healthways Well-Being Index, are based on Americans' answers to the question, "Do you have health insurance coverage?" These state-level data are based on daily surveys conducted from January through December 2015 and include sample sizes that range from 494 randomly selected adult residents in Hawaii to more than 17,000 in California. The data for 2013 were collected over the same 12-month period and yielded sample sizes similar to those in 2015 for each state. A full list of the 2013 and 2015 uninsured rates for all 50 states appears at the end of the article.

For the eighth year in a row, Massachusetts had the lowest uninsured rate nationally, and Texas had the highest. In general, Southern, Southwestern and Mountain West states have the highest uninsured rates in the U.S.

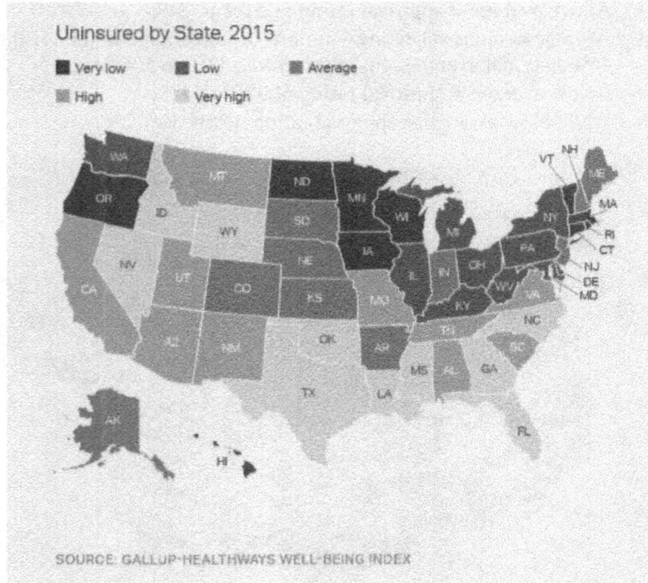

Implications

Americans' attitudes about the health law known as "Obamacare" have shown little change since 2013. More Americans continue to disapprove of the law than approve of it, even as uninsured rates for nearly all states have declined since that time. Political identity is closely related to approval or disapproval of the ACA, so entrenched attitudes toward the Obama presidency are likely driving the stability in Americans' views of the ACA.

The Gallup-Healthways Well-Being Index does not provide estimates for the number of American adults who have gained insurance or the number who have lost insurance during the ACA era. Rather, it measures the net change in the uninsured rate, which reflects both effects simultaneously. As such, the national decline from 17.3% without insurance in 2013 to 11.7% in 2015 represents a net increase of about 13.7 million adults with health insurance over this two-year period.

Medicaid expansion, one of the two major uninsured reduction mechanisms of the ACA, continues to slowly spread nationally. In addition to Alaska's implementation, effective Sept. 1, 2015, Montana cleared federal waiver approval and has officially expanded Medicaid effective Jan. 1, 2016; thus, the two have become the 29th and 30th states (plus the District of Columbia) to expand. Louisiana is in the process of expanding its coverage, and will become the 31st state to do so once the wider coverage is in effect.

With 19 states still eligible to expand Medicaid, this mechanism for reducing the uninsured rate continues to have the potential to be effective. But in most of the remaining states, there is substantial political opposition to taking that step. Still, some states such as Utah continue to debate expansion, and a few others such as South Dakota and Virginia have included aspects of expansion in their fiscal year 2017 budgets. Unless most of the remaining states choose to expand, however, the marketplace exchanges that enable people to select and purchase their own plan directly from insurers will likely be the primary means by which the national uninsured rate might continue to decline in the immediate future.

Survey Methods

Results are based on telephone interviews conducted Jan. 2-Dec. 30, 2013, and Jan. 2-Dec. 30, 2015, as part of the Gallup-Healthways Well-Being Index, with a random sample of 178,072 adults in 2013 and 177,281 adults in 2015, aged 18 and older, living in all 50 U.S. states and the District of Columbia. The margin of sampling error is ±1 to ±2 percentage points for most states, but climbs as high as ±4 percentage points for 2015 results for states with small populations such as North Dakota, Wyoming, Vermont and Alaska. All reported margins of sampling error include computed design effects for weighting.

For data collected before Sept. 1, 2015, each daily sample of national adults includes a minimum quota of 50% cellphone respondents and 50% landline respondents. For data collected between Sept. 1, 2015, and Dec. 30, 2015, each daily sample of national adults includes a minimum quota of 60% cellphone respondents and 40% landline respondents. Additional minimum quotas are by time zone within region.

Uninsured Rates for 2013 and 2015, by State

State	2015 sample sizes	% of residents without health insurance, 2013	% of residents without health insurance, 2015	Percentage-point change in uninsured, 2013 to 2015	Medicaid expansion and/or state/partnership exchange by Sep 1, 2015?
Alabama	3,063	17.7	13.0	-4.7	Neither
Alaska	520	18.9	10.3	-8.6	One
Arizona	4,324	20.4	13.7	-6.7	One
Arkansas	2,034	22.5	9.6	-12.9	Both
California	17,203	21.6	11.8	-9.8	Both
Colorado	3,456	17.0	10.3	-6.7	Both
Connecticut	1,971	12.3	6.4	-5.9	Both
Delaware	502	10.5	7.4	-3.1	Both
Florida	10,362	22.1	15.7	-6.4	Neither
Georgia	5,210	21.4	15.9	-5.5	Neither
Hawaii	494	7.1	4.2	-2.9	Both
Idaho	1,248	19.9	15.2	-4.7	One
Illinois	5,557	15.5	8.7	-6.8	Both
Indiana	3,967	15.3	10.8	-4.5	One
Iowa	1,988	9.7	6.3	-3.4	Both
Kansas	1,813	12.5	11.0	-1.5	Neither
Kentucky	2,743	20.4	7.5	-12.9	Both
Louisiana	2,589	21.7	15.7	-6.0	Neither
Maine	1,097	16.1	8.8	-7.3	Neither
Maryland	3,088	12.9	7.5	-5.4	Both
Massachusetts	3,687	4.9	3.5	-1.4	Both
Michigan	4,978	12.5	7.6	-4.9	Both
Minnesota	3,241	9.5	5.8	-3.7	Both
Mississippi	1,667	22.4	14.7	-7.7	One
Missouri	3,423	15.2	11.6	-3.6	Neither
Montana	1,031	20.7	13.3	-7.4	Neither
Nebraska	1,383	14.5	10.6	-3.9	Neither
Nevada	1,489	20.0	14.5	-5.5	Both
New Hampshire	849	13.8	8.8	-5.0	Both
New Jersey	4,638	14.9	9.7	-5.2	One
New Mexico	1,423	20.2	12.8	-7.4	Both
New York	10,258	12.6	8.6	-4.0	Both
North Carolina	5,880	20.4	14.4	-6.0	Neither
North Dakota	510	15.0	6.9	-8.1	One
Ohio	6,331	13.9	7.6	-6.3	One
Oklahoma	2,679	21.4	16.5	-4.9	Neither
Oregon	2,984	19.4	7.3	-12.1	Both
Pennsylvania	8,178	11.0	7.4	-3.6	Both
Rhode Island	560	13.3	5.6	-7.7	Both
South Carolina	2,840	18.7	12.3	-6.4	Neither
South Dakota	533	14.0	10.6	-3.4	Neither
Tennessee	4,250	16.8	13.0	-3.8	Neither
Texas	13,190	27.0	22.3	-4.7	Neither
Utah	2,067	15.6	12.4	-3.2	One
Vermont	601	8.9	4.7	-4.2	Both
Virginia	5,039	13.3	12.6	-0.7	Neither
Washington	4,504	16.8	7.4	-9.4	Both
West Virginia	1,224	17.6	7.7	-9.9	Both
Wisconsin	3,628	11.7	5.9	-5.8	Neither
Wyoming	591	16.6	14.0	-2.6	Neither

Gallup-Healthways Well-Being Index

GALLUP

February 04, 2016

NEW HAMPSHIRE NOW LEAST RELIGIOUS STATE IN U.S.

by Frank Newport

Story Highlights

- *20% in New Hampshire very religious, compared with 63% in Mississippi*
- *Most religious states continue to be in South, along with Utah*
- *Least religious states in Northeast and Northwest, plus Hawaii*

PRINCETON, N.J. – New Hampshire is the least religious state in the U.S., edging out Vermont in Gallup's 2015 state-by-state analysis. Mississippi has extended its eight-year streak as the most religious state, followed closely by neighboring Alabama.

Most Religious States, Based on % Very Religious

State	Very religious
Mississippi	63%
Alabama	57%
Utah	55%
Louisiana	54%
Tennessee	53%
Arkansas	52%
Georgia	51%
South Carolina	51%
North Carolina	49%
Kentucky	47%
Texas	47%

Gallup Daily tracking, January-December 2015

GALLUP

Least Religious States, Based on % Very Religious

State	Very religious
New Hampshire	20%
Vermont	22%
Maine	26%
Massachusetts	27%
Oregon	29%
Washington	29%
Hawaii	30%
Rhode Island	32%
New York	32%
Alaska	32%
Wyoming	32%

Gallup Daily tracking, January-December 2015

GALLUP

These state-by-state results are based on over 174,000 interviews conducted as part of Gallup Daily tracking in 2015, including more than 480 interviews in every state and more than 1,000 interviews in most states. Complete results and sample sizes are shown at the end of the article.

Gallup classifies Americans into three religious groups based on their responses to a question measuring religious service attendance and how important religion is in their daily life. Very religious Americans are those who say religion is important to them and who attend services every week or almost every week. Nonreligious Americans are those for whom religion is not important and who seldom or never attend religious services. Moderately religious Americans meet just one of the criteria, either saying religion is important or that they attend services almost every week or more.

Gallup began tracking several religious indicators on a daily basis in 2008. Some of these indicators have shown significant change over this time, most notably the percentage of Americans who report no formal religious identity when asked to name their religious preference. But the percentage classified as very religious on the basis of their attendance and view on the importance of religion has stayed remarkably stable. In 2008, 41% of Americans were very religious, 29% moderately religious and 30% nonreligious. In 2015, those same percentages are almost identical: 40%, 29% and 31%, respectively.

Religiosity by Year: 2008-2015

	Very Religious	Somewhat Religious	Nonreligious
	%	%	%
2015	40	29	31
2014	41	29	30
2013	41	29	29
2012	40	29	31
2011	41	28	31
2010	42	28	30
2009	42	28	30
2008	41	29	30

GALLUP

Over the past eight years, New Hampshire and Vermont have vied for the bottom position on Gallup's ranking of the most religious states. This year, New Hampshire comes in two percentage points lower than Vermont, and those two states are significantly lower in religiosity than the next two states, also in New England: Maine and Massachusetts.

New Hampshire is in the national spotlight this week as the presidential candidates focus on next Tuesday's primary in the Granite State. According to entrance polls of Iowa caucus voters, Ted Cruz's win in the GOP caucus on Feb. 1 in Iowa was driven by his strong appeal to highly religious or evangelical Republicans – who turned out in large numbers. Although Iowa as a state has only average religiosity, it is still significantly more religious than New Hampshire, suggesting that Cruz will have fewer evangelicals to bring out to vote in that state's primary.

However, the next contest in the GOP campaign, the Feb. 20 South Carolina primary, will take place in the nation's seventh most religious state. More broadly, as is usually the case, the overall most religious states are mainly in the South. In addition to Mississippi, Alabama and South Carolina, these include Louisiana, Tennessee, Arkansas, Georgia, North Carolina, Kentucky and Texas. Utah, with the majority of its population identifying as Mormons (the most religious group in the U.S.), is the only non-Southern state among the top states for religiosity.

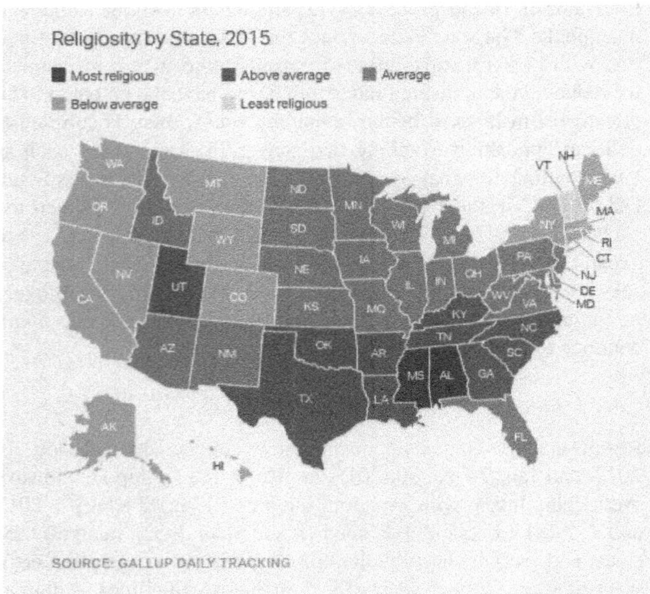

As has been the case since 2008, the least religious states generally are those in the two northern corners of the country. Rhode Island and New York join New Hampshire, Vermont, Massachusetts and Maine in the Northeast, while Oregon, Washington, Wyoming and Alaska are among the least religious states in the Northwest. The one additional state among the least religious is Hawaii.

Implications

The basic geographic structure of religion in America is stable, with only minor fluctuations in religiousness at the state level from year to year. The most religious states continue to be in the South, along with Utah, while the least religious Americans tend to live in the Northeast, in the Northwest, and in Alaska and Hawaii.

There are many explanations for the variations in religiosity by state, including the historical and cultural norms and patterns of each state, the types of people who choose to migrate to specific states and, to some degree, the demographic composition of the states.

Religion today is significantly linked to politics in the U.S., with Republicans, on average, significantly more religious than Democrats, so it could be expected that more religious states would be more Republican. This tends to be true in general, with many of the most religious states classified as solid or lean Republican in Gallup's recent analysis of 2015 party identification data.

However, there are exceptions to this pattern. Louisiana, Georgia, North Carolina and Kentucky are among the most religious states but are classified as politically competitive based on their party identification. Alaska, as another example, is one of the least religious states in the union, but is classified as solid Republican. And, as the most outstanding example of a disjuncture between religiousness and partisanship, New Hampshire is the least religious state in the union, yet is classified as a lean Republican state by Gallup and as a swing state by observers.

These data are available in Gallup Analytics.

Religiosity by State, 2015

	Very religious Americans	Moderately religious Americans	Nonreligious Americans	n
Mississippi	63%	26%	11%	1,713
Alabama	57%	29%	14%	3,033
Utah	55%	15%	31%	2,144
Louisiana	54%	29%	17%	2,492
Tennessee	53%	30%	18%	4,316
Arkansas	52%	30%	18%	1,921
South Carolina	51%	31%	18%	2,788
Georgia	51%	30%	19%	5,126
North Carolina	49%	29%	22%	5,617
Kentucky	47%	31%	23%	2,653
Texas	47%	31%	22%	13,042
Oklahoma	46%	31%	22%	2,568
South Dakota	45%	32%	23%	531
Kansas	45%	28%	27%	1,660
West Virginia	45%	30%	25%	1,226
Nebraska	45%	29%	27%	1,387
North Dakota	44%	32%	24%	481
Idaho	44%	25%	32%	1,178
Indiana	43%	29%	28%	3,862
New Mexico	42%	26%	32%	1,442
Missouri	42%	30%	28%	3,364
Virginia	41%	31%	28%	5,037
Ohio	40%	30%	30%	6,309
Iowa	39%	29%	32%	1,950
Maryland	38%	31%	31%	2,982
Michigan	38%	29%	33%	4,938
Minnesota	38%	30%	32%	3,215
Pennsylvania	38%	29%	34%	8,158
Wisconsin	38%	29%	33%	3,572
Illinois	37%	31%	32%	5,522
Florida	37%	31%	32%	10,362
Arizona	36%	30%	34%	4,199
Delaware	36%	30%	34%	495
New Jersey	35%	32%	33%	4,607
Montana	34%	29%	37%	1,033
Colorado	34%	27%	39%	3,315
California	33%	28%	38%	17,179
Connecticut	33%	28%	39%	1,919
Nevada	33%	28%	39%	1,472
Wyoming	32%	30%	38%	527
Alaska	32%	26%	42%	581
New York	32%	30%	38%	9,938
Rhode Island	32%	30%	38%	592
Hawaii	30%	26%	44%	530
Washington	29%	26%	45%	4,301
Oregon	29%	26%	45%	2,914
Massachusetts	27%	28%	46%	3,710
Maine	26%	24%	50%	1,041
Vermont	22%	23%	56%	558
New Hampshire	20%	24%	55%	809

Gallup Daily tracking, January-December 2015

GALLUP

Survey Methods

Results for this Gallup poll are based on telephone interviews conducted Jan. 1-Dec. 31, 2015, on the Gallup U.S. Daily survey, with a random sample of 174,745 adults, aged 18 and older, living in all 50 U.S. states and the District of Columbia. For results based on the total sample of national adults, the margin of sampling error is ±1 percentage point at the 95% confidence level.

Margins of error for individual states are no greater than ±6 percentage points and are ±3 percentage points in most states. All reported margins of sampling error include computed design effects for weighting.

February 05, 2016

IN 2016, ISSUES TRUMP ELECTABILITY IN CHOOSING A NOMINEE

by Justin McCarthy

Story Highlights

- *Six in 10 in U.S. prefer candidate who agrees with them on issues*
- *One in three prefer candidate with best chance of winning*
- *Democrats, Republicans share these preferences about equally*

WASHINGTON, D.C. – Americans are about twice as likely to prefer that their party nominate a candidate who agrees with them on almost all the issues they care about but does not have the best chance of winning, rather than one who has the best chance of winning but doesn't agree with them on the issues they care about. Republicans and Democrats have similar preferences.

Americans' Preferences for Their Party's Nomination, by Subgroup

Which type of candidate would you prefer to see your party nominate for president in 2016 -- a candidate who agrees with you on almost all of the issues you care about but does not have the best chance of winning or a candidate who has the best chance of winning, but who does not agree with you on almost all of the issues you care about?

	Agrees on issues	Best chance of winning
	%	%
National adults	60	33
Republicans/Republican leaners	58	37
Democrats/Democratic leaners	60	35

Jan. 21-25, 2016

GALLUP

The issue of the importance of a candidate's electability has been hotly discussed in the 2016 presidential election campaign, as establishment candidates who were widely perceived as the inevitable party nominees have been formidably challenged by political outsiders or politicians who operate mainly outside the party establishment. Democrats and Democratic-leaning independents, and Republicans and Republican-leaning independents, share the preference for a nominee who is more agreeable to them on the issues than for someone who is more likely to be elected.

Within the Democratic Party, many Hillary Clinton supporters argue that Sen. Bernie Sanders, perhaps because of his embrace of socialist ideals, could not win a general election contest. Gallup found in June – prior to Sanders' rise in support – that Americans were least likely to support a socialist among hypothetical presidential candidates with certain characteristics. It is unclear whether those views have changed in light of Sanders' success to date. Sanders' supporters, however, take issue with many of Clinton's previous votes and positions, such as her vote to authorize military action against Iraq in 2003.

Meanwhile, many GOP leaders are reeling from the surprising rise of Donald Trump as well as the Iowa victory of Sen. Ted Cruz, who has a troubled relationship with many in his party. Many question whether these candidates would be able to win a general election despite their relative popularity among Republican voters. Apparently, as these data would suggest, Republicans have been focused more on these candidates' positions on the issues than on their electability.

Adults Under 30 Far More Likely to Seek Issue-Agreeable Party Nominee

While Americans of all age groups prefer a candidate who largely agrees with them on the issues they care about, the percentage who have this preference is much higher among voters younger than 30. Between 46% and 59% of adults aged 30 or older are focused on issue agreement, compared with 82% of younger adults – those 18 to 29.

This disparity among age groups is revealing of the rift between Clinton and Sanders supporters in the debate over electability. While Clinton's base is generally older, and older Americans are more likely to say they prefer a candidate with greater ability to win, Sanders boasts a stronger rapport with younger adults, who are more likely to prefer a candidate who is most agreeable, issue-wise.

Americans' Preferences for Their Party's Nomination, by Subgroup

Which type of candidate would you prefer to see your party nominate for president in 2016 -- a candidate who agrees with you on almost all of the issues you care about but does not have the best chance of winning or a candidate who has the best chance of winning, but who does not agree with you on almost all of the issues you care about?

	Agrees on issues	Best chance of winning
	%	%
18 to 29	82	15
30 to 49	56	37
50 to 64	59	39
65+	46	41
Liberal Democrats	57	40
Conservative/Moderate Democrats	64	31
Liberal/Moderate Republicans	65	31
Conservative Republicans	55	40

Jan. 21-25, 2016

GALLUP

The poll also suggests that moderates within both political parties value issue agreement over electability compared with the more ideological wings of each party's base.

Preference for Issue-Agreeable Nominee Is Reminiscent of the 2012 Election

Americans' current preference for nominees who agree with them on the issues is not dissimilar to what it was in December 2011. As Republican presidential candidates entered the 2012 primary season to determine who would face President Barack Obama, two in three Americans said they preferred a party nominee who agreed with them on almost all issues – a slightly higher percentage than the current figure.

The figure hasn't changed much for Republicans, who also had a large field of candidates to choose from in 2012. For Democrats, the issues-versus-electability debate may have been a moot point that year because they enjoyed the advantage of having an incumbent president from their party.

Americans' Preference for a Candidate Who Agrees With Them on Almost All Issues, 2012 Election vs. 2016 Election

% Prefer a candidate who agrees but does not have the best chance of winning

	December 2011	January 2016
	%	%
National adults	67	60
Republicans/Republican leaners	62	58
Democrats/Democratic leaners	70	60

GALLUP

Bottom Line

As they did in the previous presidential election, Americans today value issue agreement over electability – and the way the 2016 primaries are playing out so far reflects this preference for issues rather than potential viability in the November general election.

The preference for a nominee with greater issue agreement can prove challenging for "establishment" candidates like Clinton, former Gov. Jeb Bush and Sen. Marco Rubio. Each walks a shaky political tightrope on myriad issues in an effort not to alienate key voting blocs – compared with some of their competitors who don't seem to shy away from divisive positions that could complicate their chances in a general election.

For Republicans, their party in 2016 has had one of its largest fields in modern political history, and with that, a wide spectrum of candidates and issue positions to select from. This complicates the GOP's ultimate goal of winning the general election, because Republicans and Republican-leaning independents may prefer candidates whom they find most agreeable now, but will in the end want a candidate who can win in November.

Democrats face a similar conundrum – one that consists of only two candidates, but is arguably just as divisive for their party. The recent Iowa caucuses highlighted a sharp divide among Democratic voters, and raised the question of what these voters truly value in a candidate – and whether they even believe that Clinton is more electable than Sanders.

These data are available in Gallup Analytics.

Survey Methods

Results for this Gallup poll are based on telephone interviews conducted Jan. 21-25, 2016, with a random sample of 1,022 adults, aged 18 and older, living in all 50 U.S. states and the District of Columbia. For results based on the total sample of national adults, the margin of sampling error is ±4 percentage points at the 95% confidence level. All reported margins of sampling error include computed design effects for weighting.

February 08, 2016

STATE GOVERNOR BEST EXPERIENCE FOR PRESIDENCY

by Jim Norman

Story Highlights

- *Public says government experience a plus for presidents*
- *Time in Congress or as secretary of state seen as good preparation*
- *GOP, Democrats split on value of time in Congress*

WASHINGTON, D.C. – Almost three in four U.S. adults – 72% – say that governing a state provides excellent or good preparation for someone to be an effective president. This number is slightly higher than the percentages who say the same about being in the U.S. Senate or House of Representatives (65%) or serving as secretary of state (63%). Smaller majorities believe that serving as a member of the president's Cabinet (56%) or being a business executive (51%) provides this level of preparation.

How Well Occupations Prepare Candidates for the Presidency

Do you consider each of the following occupations to be excellent, good, fair or poor for preparing someone to be an effective president? How about -- [RANDOM ORDER]?

	Excellent/Good	Excellent	Good	Fair	Poor
	%	%	%	%	%
Governor of a state	72	27	45	21	6
A member of U.S. Senate/ House of Representatives	65	25	40	24	10
U.S. secretary of state	63	28	35	21	14
A member of the president's Cabinet	56	23	33	25	17
A business executive	51	17	34	30	18

Jan. 21-25, 2016

GALLUP

Similar percentages of Republicans (76%) and Democrats (74%) say that being a governor helps prepare someone for the presidency, but there is a major split between the parties on the perceived effectiveness of serving in Congress. About the same percentage in each party thinks serving in Congress is good preparation (43% of Democrats and 45% of Republicans), but only 16% of Republicans believe it is excellent preparation, compared with 30% of Democrats.

Despite the public's belief that experience as a governor is a positive attribute in presidential candidates, being a governor has not paid off in the early stages of both parties' 2016 presidential nomination contests. Six of the nine Republican candidates who have been governor – Rick Perry, Scott Walker, Mike Huckabee, George Pataki, Bobby Jindal and Jim Gilmore – have already dropped out of the race. None of the other three – John Kasich, Jeb Bush and Chris Christie – finished among the top five vote-getters in last week's Iowa caucus. The only Democratic candidate with gubernatorial experience, Martin O'Malley, dropped out after finishing third in Iowa.

Both of the major candidates left in the Democratic contest – Hillary Clinton and Bernie Sanders – have been senators. On the Republican side, Sen. Ted Cruz won in Iowa, and Sen. Marco Rubio finished third.

Public Values Experience More Now Than in 2003

Though approval ratings for Congress have dropped from 41% in 2003 to 16% now, the percentage of U.S. adults who think being in Congress is excellent or good preparation for someone to be an effective president has held steady – 64% then vs. 65% now. Further, the percentage who say it is excellent preparation has grown from 14% in 2003 to 25% now.

The percentages who think being governors or business executives is excellent preparation for being president have also grown since 2003:

- 17% of U.S. adults in 2003 said being governor of a state was excellent for preparing to be an effective president. That number has grown to 27% now.
- Nine percent said in 2003 that being a business executive was excellent preparation; now 17% say it is.

Views on Preparing for the Presidency, 2003 and 2016

Do you consider each of the following occupations to be excellent, good, fair or poor for preparing someone to be an effective president? How about -- [RANDOM ORDER]?

	2003 Excellent	2016 Excellent	2003 Good	2016 Good	2003 Excellent/ Good	2016 Excellent/ Good
	%	%	%	%	%	%
Governor of a state	17	27	51	45	72	68
A member of U.S. Senate/ House of Representatives	14	25	50	40	64	65
A business executive	9	17	38	34	47	51

GALLUP

Bottom Line

A strong majority of Americans say that experience in major governmental offices – whether as a senator, governor or Cabinet member – is an asset for anyone seeking the presidency.

Every president since 1961 has come to office having served as either a governor, a U.S. senator or a member of the U.S. House. Over the past 40 years, voters have tended to favor candidates with gubernatorial experience over those who served in Congress. In the eight campaigns in which a candidate with gubernatorial experience ran against a candidate with congressional experience, governors and ex-governors won six times (1976, 1984, 1992, 1996, 2000 and 2004), compared with two wins for candidates with experience in Congress (1988 and 2012).

With President Barack Obama's success in the last two presidential elections, including his victory over former Massachusetts Gov. Mitt Romney in 2012, candidates with experience in Congress seemed to have gained the upper hand.

However, the 2016 presidential campaign has put candidates with either kind of experience – whether as governor or in Congress – on the defense against attacks that they are too tied to their party's establishment. Most successful in launching such attacks has been billionaire businessman Donald Trump, who has done well in early polling for the Republican nomination selling his qualifications as a nonpolitician. On the Democratic side, a sitting senator, Sanders, has shown strength running as an outsider whom Americans elected as an independent.

With majorities still saying they think experience as a governor or a member of Congress is an asset, one of the keys to this year's election will be how much value voters attach to such experience. If Trump can overcome those views and succeed in winning the election, he will be the first president who has been neither a governor nor a member of Congress since Dwight Eisenhower left office in January 1961.

Learn more about how Gallup Poll Social Series works.

Survey Methods

Results for this Gallup poll are based on telephone interviews conducted Jan. 21-25, 2016, with a random sample of 1,022 adults, aged 18 and older, living in all 50 U.S. states and the District of Columbia. For results based on the total sample of national adults, the margin of sampling error is ±4 percentage points at the 95% confidence level. All reported margins of sampling error include computed design effects for weighting.

February 10, 2016
IN U.S., A THIRD SEE GOVERNMENT PROBLEMS AS CRISES

by Andrew Dugan

Story Highlights

- *30% say failure of the government to solve major challenges is a crisis*
- *33% say special interests having too much power is a crisis*
- *More Republicans than Democrats name government failure as a crisis*

WASHINGTON, D.C. – Three in 10 Americans say that the failure of the government to solve major challenges facing the country is a "crisis." Similar percentages see two other issues – party leaders making decisions based on what is in the best interest of their party, and special interests having too much control over the government – as crises.

How Americans Rate Problems With the Way Things Work in Washington

Next, I'm going to read you a list of things that are considered by some to be problems with the way things work in Washington. For each, please tell me whether you, personally, consider it to be a crisis, a major problem, a minor problem or not a problem.

	Crisis	Major problem	Minor problem	Not a problem
	%	%	%	%
The failure of the government to solve the major challenges facing the country in the last few years	30	51	14	4
Democratic and Republican leaders making decisions based on what is best for their party even if it is not in the best interest of the country	30	55	11	3
Powerful special interests having too much control over what the government does	33	51	13	3

Jan. 21-25, 2016

GALLUP'

Additionally, a majority of Americans consider each item to be a major problem. In total, over eight in 10 see each issue as either a crisis or a major problem.

These results come from a Jan. 21-25 Gallup poll. Americans have expressed an ever-rising level of dissatisfaction with the federal government in recent years, including in 2014 and 2015, when pluralities of U.S. adults mentioned some aspect of government as the nation's top problem. Diagnosing the precise problems of the federal government, however, is no easy task. Gallup has tested three prominent theories as to why the government may work in ways that earn the country's disapproval, and has found that Americans rate the seriousness of all three similarly.

Americans' belief that these factors are corroding the nation's political system is nothing new. Similar percentages judged each of these issues to be as serious in 2008 as they do today.

These major concerns about the workings of Washington are undoubtedly fueling the rise of unconventional presidential candidates in the 2016 election, such as Donald Trump and Bernie Sanders – both of whom scored big wins in the New Hampshire primary Tuesday night.

Reps More Likely Than Dems to See Government Failure as Crisis

Republicans are twice as likely as Democrats to say that the government's failure to solve the country's major challenges represents a crisis, at 41% and 20%, respectively. Independents fall in between, with 32% saying this issue is a crisis.

How Americans Rate Problems With the Way Things Work in Washington -- by Party ID

Percentage saying each item is a "crisis"

	Republicans	Independents	Democrats
	%	%	%
The failure of the government to solve the major challenges facing the country in the last few years	41	32	20
Democratic and Republican leaders making decisions based on what is best for their party even if it is not in the best interest of the country	33	33	26
Powerful special interests having too much control over what the government does	34	37	32

Jan. 21-25, 2016

GALLUP'

The three political identities are in greater accord on the other two theories tested. Both 33% of Republicans and 33% of independents believe political leaders who put their party first constitutes a crisis, and about as many Democrats (26%) agree. On the third theory, the identities are almost perfectly aligned, with 34% of Republicans, 37% of independents and 32% of Democrats saying the level of governmental influence that special interests possess is a crisis.

Bottom Line

Americans' frustration with the federal government has been a rising force in politics, and may play a decisive role in how many Americans vote in this primary campaign and in the general election. These findings confirm that the vast majority of Americans consider the inability to fix problems, partisanship and the influence of special interests to be major problems or crises for the nation.

Such perceptions could produce unexpected outcomes in the various phases of the 2016 presidential election, such as a political outsider or "anti-establishment" candidate winning the presidency. In 2008, Barack Obama, a freshman senator, perhaps benefited from Americans' desire to elect a politician less steeped in the Washington political culture – and that desire seems to be burning just as bright in this election, if not brighter. But the lack of improvement in public opinion on these three dimensions since 2008 suggests the next president, like Obama, may struggle to change these pessimistic views.

These data are available in Gallup Analytics.

Survey Methods

Results for this Gallup poll are based on telephone interviews conducted Jan. 21-25, 2016, with a random sample of 1,022 adults, aged 18 and older, living in all 50 U.S. states and the District of Columbia. For results based on the total sample of national adults, the margin of sampling error is ±4 percentage points at the 95% confidence level. All reported margins of sampling error include computed design effects for weighting.

February 10, 2016
AMERICANS CITE CYBERTERRORISM AMONG TOP THREE THREATS TO U.S.

by Justin McCarthy

Story Highlights

- *International terrorism, nuclear weapons in Iran also top list*
- *Democrats far more likely to view global warming as "critical"*
- *Dems, GOP about equally likely to view cyberterrorism as "critical"*

WASHINGTON, D.C. – As President Barack Obama rolls out a proposal to increase U.S. cybersecurity funding, Americans view cyberterrorism as a leading threat to U.S. vital interests in the next 10 years. U.S. adults rank cyberterrorism (73%) along with international terrorism (79%) and development of nuclear weapons by Iran (75%) as the highest of a dozen potential threats.

Critical Threats to the United States

I am going to read you a list of possible threats to the vital interests of the United States in the next 10 years. For each one, please tell me if you see this as a critical threat, an important but not critical threat or not an important threat at all?

	% Critical threat	% Important but not critical threat
International terrorism	79	18
Development of nuclear weapons by Iran	75	18
Cyberterrorism, the use of computers to cause disruption or fear in society	73	22
The spread of infectious diseases throughout the world	63	33
The conflict in Syria	58	32
The military power of North Korea	58	29
Large numbers of refugees trying to come to Europe and North America	52	32
Global warming or climate change	50	28
The conflict between Israel and the Palestinians	45	41
The military power of China	41	46
The economic power of China	41	45
The military power of Russia	39	47

Feb. 3-7, 2016

GALLUP

In prior years, Americans have been most likely to identify international terrorism, which is down slightly from last year's 84%, and development of nuclear weapons by Iran as critical threats to the U.S. This is the first year Gallup has asked about cyberterrorism, defined in the poll as "the use of computers to cause disruption or fear in society."

In the Feb. 3-7 Gallup poll, 63% of U.S. adults consider the spread of infectious diseases throughout the world a critical threat. This comes as the first known case of Zika virus transmission in the U.S. was discovered in Texas, after many confirmed infections throughout the world. After this poll was conducted, Obama announced his intention to request additional emergency funding to combat Zika in the U.S.

The majority of Americans also see the military power of North Korea (58%) as a critical threat. On Sunday, the last day of the poll's field period, North Korea launched a rocket that illustrated the country's improvements in its missile technology.

Similarly, 58% of Americans name the conflict in Syria as a critical threat to the U.S., and a majority (52%) express concern over the potential of large numbers of refugees attempting to enter Europe and North America. Views of these threats as "critical" come as the conflict in Syria rages on, and the question of whether the U.S. would take in Syrian refugees has been hotly discussed in the 2016 presidential campaign.

Some of the issues perceived as less threatening are global warming or climate change (50% say it is a critical threat), the conflict between Israel and the Palestinians (45%), the military power and, separately, the economic power of China (both 41%), and the military power of Russia (39%). The percentage rating Russia's military power as a critical threat is down 10 points from last year as the Russia-Ukraine conflict has become less of a U.S. flashpoint.

Partisan Differences Small on Cyberterrorism, Infectious Diseases

Republicans and Democrats, including independents who lean toward each party, differ considerably in their assessments of what constitutes a critical threat to the vital interests of the U.S. Republicans and Republican-leaning independents are much more likely to categorize most issues as a "critical threat."

The largest gap exists on the issue of global warming or climate change, which three in four Democrats and Democratic-leaning independents describe as a "critical threat," while only one in four Republicans and GOP leaners agree. Conversely, Republicans and Republican-leaning independents (70%) are nearly twice as likely as Democrats and Democratic leaners (37%) to view the issue of refugees entering Europe and North America in large numbers as a "critical threat."

On a couple of issues, however, the differences between the two groups are negligible. When asked about cyberterrorism, about three-quarters of both Democrats and Republicans view the issue as a "critical threat." Similarly, seven percentage points separate the views of the two party groups on the issue of infectious diseases.

Critical Threats to the United States -- According to Democrats, Republicans

	Republicans+ Republican leaners	Democrats+ Democratic leaners	Difference (Republicans/leaners minus Democrats/leaners)
	% Critical threat	% Critical threat	(pct. pts.)
Global warming or climate change	25	75	-50
The spread of infectious diseases throughout the world	59	66	-7
Cyberterrorism, the use of computers to cause disruption or fear in society	77	72	5
The military power of Russia	44	34	10
The conflict in Syria	64	54	10
International terrorism	86	74	12
The economic power of China	48	34	14
The conflict between Israel and the Palestinians	53	38	15
The military power of North Korea	67	51	16
The military power of China	49	33	16
Development of nuclear weapons by Iran	87	66	21
Large numbers of refugees trying to come to Europe and North America	70	37	33

Feb. 3-7, 2016

GALLUP

Bottom Line

Given the spate of news on the fronts of international terrorism, cyberterrorism and nuclear weapons negotiations with Iran, it's perhaps unsurprising that these issues are at the forefront of Americans' concerns about potential threats to the U.S. over the next 10 years. And the president's high-profile efforts – for example, his *Wall Street Journal* op-ed on cyberterrorism Tuesday – align with the importance Americans place on such issues.

But an issue's prominence might be less of a factor in Americans' assessments than the seriousness of its consequences if it should happen. In the past year alone, Americans have seen the ramifications of the Paris terrorist attacks and of Chinese hackers' infiltration of U.S. federal government data.

Of course, Republicans and Democrats often don't agree about what constitutes a "critical" threat to the vital interests of the U.S. Still, for lawmakers, Americans' widespread agreement on issues such as cyberterrorism and infectious diseases may provide a welcome opening for bipartisan agreement and progress on issues whose importance has broad public consensus.

Historical data are available in Gallup Analytics.

Survey Methods

Results for this Gallup poll are based on telephone interviews conducted Feb. 3-7, 2016, with a random sample of 1,021 adults, aged 18 and older, living in all 50 U.S. states and the District of Columbia. For results based on the total sample of national adults, the margin of sampling error is ±4 percentage points at the 95% confidence level. All reported margins of sampling error include computed design effects for weighting.

February 11, 2016
ECONOMY TOPS AMERICANS' MINDS AS MOST IMPORTANT PROBLEM

by Rebecca Riffkin

Story Highlights

- *17% of Americans mention the economy as top problem*
- *A net of 39% name an economic issue as most important*
- *Democrats, independents more likely than GOP to name jobs*

WASHINGTON, D.C. – Americans in February are slightly more likely to name the economy generally as the "most important problem facing the country" than they have been in the last two months. Seventeen percent of Americans name this issue as the top problem, up from 13% last month and 9% in December. In those months, the government and terrorism were more prominent in Americans' minds, edging out the economy as the No. 1 problem.

Recent Trends in Most Important U.S. Problems

What do you think is the most important problem facing this country today? [OPEN-ENDED]

	Nov 2015	Dec 2015	Jan 2016	Feb 2016
	%	%	%	%
Economy	17	9	13	17
Government	15	13	16	13
Immigration	9	5	8	10
Unemployment/Jobs	7	6	5	10
National security	3	5	3	7
Terrorism	3	16	9	7
Federal budget deficit/Federal debt	5	2	5	6
Poor healthcare/High cost of healthcare	6	3	4	6

Shown are problems listed by at least 6% of Americans in February 2016

GALLUP

In addition to the economy, at least 10% of U.S. adults mention dysfunctional government, immigration and unemployment/jobs as the top problem facing the nation.

The 7% of U.S. adults who name national security as the most important problem is higher than at any point since 2004. Seven percent of Americans also mentioned terrorism in February, but that is down from 9% in January and 16% in December as Americans responded to the Paris and San Bernardino, California, terrorist attacks. Mentions of guns and gun control as the top problem also fell in February to 2%, after 7% named this issue in January and December.

Altogether, 39% of Americans named some economic issue – including the economy in general, unemployment/jobs, the federal budget, wages and others – as the most important problem in February. That is up from less than 30% in December and January.

Republicans, Democrats Differ on What Is Most Important

While the economy in general ranked as a top issue among Republicans, independents and Democrats, partisans differ in what else they perceive to be most important. Republicans are more likely than Democrats and independents to name the federal budget deficit, immigration and national security. Democrats and independents are more likely than Republicans to name unemployment or jobs as most important. Democrats are also slightly more likely than independents and Republicans to name race relations, education and healthcare.

Most Commonly Named Problems Facing the U.S., by Party ID

What do you think is the most important problem facing this country today? [OPEN-ENDED] February 2016

	Republicans	Independents	Democrats
	%	%	%
Economy	16	19	14
Government	17	13	10
Immigration	15	7	8
Unemployment/Jobs	7	10	12
National security	13	6	3
Terrorism	8	7	6
Federal budget deficit	10	6	3
Healthcare	5	5	8
Race relations/Racism	2	6	8
Education	3	4	8

Note: Issues mentioned by less than 8% of either group not shown

GALLUP

Bottom Line

The economy and unemployment are again prominent in Americans' minds as important problems, while noneconomic issues such as terrorism have faded. This could be important to Washington lawmakers as they attempt to agree on the next budget. President Barack Obama presented Congress with a budget outline, but Republican congressional leaders immediately rejected it.

As far as average Americans are concerned, the most pressing priority for the nation is keeping the economy vibrant and growing, fixing the way government itself operates, dealing with immigration and keeping the nation safe, especially from terrorism.

Exactly how well any final budget will address Americans' priorities for the nation remains to be seen. Obama's proposed budget continues to have a deficit, and 6% of Americans consider the federal budget deficit to be the most important problem facing the U.S. However, the president's proposed budget also has significant spending to help young Americans get their first job and plans to reform unemployment insurance, both of which could respond to the 10% of Americans who say unemployment is the most important problem.

On the campaign front, several Republican candidates continue to talk about national security and stopping terrorism. These issues speak to fellow Republicans, for whom national security and terrorism are among the most important problems facing the country, but not to independents and Democrats, who are less likely to name these issues.

Historical data are available in Gallup Analytics.

Survey Methods

Results for this Gallup poll are based on telephone interviews conducted Feb. 3-7, 2016, on the Gallup U.S. Daily survey, with a random sample of 1,021 adults, aged 18 and older, living in all 50 U.S. states and the District of Columbia. For results based on the total sample of national adults, the margin of sampling error is ±4 percentage points at the 95% confidence level. All reported margins of sampling error include computed design effects for weighting.

February 12, 2016

U.S. OBESITY RATE CLIMBS TO RECORD HIGH IN 2015

by Dan Witters

Story Highlights

- *In U.S., 28.0% of adults are obese*
- *Diabetes rate was 11.4% in 2015, matching all-time high*
- *Whites show sharpest uptick in obesity and diabetes rates*

WASHINGTON, D.C. – The obesity rate among U.S. adults in 2015 climbed to a new high of 28.0%, up 2.5 percentage points since 2008. This represents an increase of about 6.1 million U.S. adults who are obese.

U.S. Adult Obesity Rate, 2008-2015

Obesity rate (BMI of 30+) among U.S. adults, based on self-reported height and weight

Gallup-Healthways Well-Being Index

GALLUP'

These results are based on more than 175,000 interviews conducted each year from 2013 to 2015 and more than 350,000 interviews conducted each year from 2008 to 2012 as part of the Gallup-Healthways Well-Being Index. Unlike some government estimates of obesity, the Well-Being Index uses respondents' self-reported height and weight to calculate body mass index (BMI). It does not involve in-home clinical measurements that typically result in higher obesity estimates.

In addition to the 28.0% who are obese, another 35.6% of adults are classified as overweight, with 34.6% normal weight and 1.8% underweight, as reported in 2015.

As with obesity, diabetes generally has trended upward since 2008. The rates of both conditions declined slightly in 2011, only to see annual upticks in the years since. The obesity and diabetes trends typically parallel each other given the close relationship between the two health conditions, but are not always in lockstep. In 2015, 11.4% of Americans reported having been diagnosed with diabetes, unchanged from 2014. This equates to about 27.9 million adults living with diabetes.

U.S. Adult Diabetes Rate, 2008-2015

Has a doctor or nurse ever told you that you have diabetes? (% Yes)

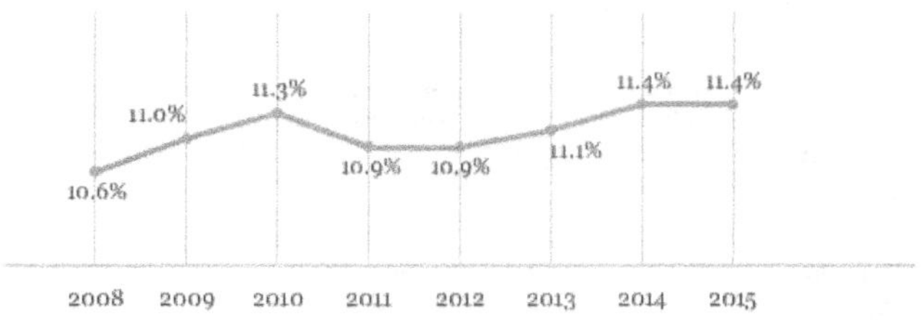

Gallup-Healthways Well-Being Index

GALLUP'

The Well-Being Index does not measure new onset of diabetes, but rather the percentage of adults who report ever having been diagnosed with it in their lifetime. The Well-Being Index does not discern between Type 1 and Type 2 diabetes.

Whites See Sharpest Uptick in Obesity, Diabetes Rates

Across racial and ethnic groups, increases in obesity and diabetes rates since 2008 have been uneven. Both rates have increased much more among whites than among blacks, Asians and Hispanics.

Blacks have the highest obesity rate by far of the major racial and ethnic groups, followed by Hispanics, but these two groups have had comparatively modest increases in obesity since 2008, and have shown little to no change in diabetes diagnoses during this time.

Obesity and Diabetes Rates, 2008-2015, by Race and Ethnicity

	2008	2015	Change
OBESE	%	%	(pct. pts.)
Whites	24.2	27.0	+2.8
Hispanics	27.4	28.6	+1.2
Asians	8.6	9.8	+1.2
Blacks	35.1	35.6	+0.5
DIABETIC	%	%	(pct. pts.)
Whites	10.1	11.0	+0.9
Blacks	14.3	14.5	+0.2
Hispanics	10.7	10.7	0.0
Asians	5.8	5.2	-0.6

Gallup-Healthways Well-Being Index

GALLUP

There is a discernible link between obesity and diabetes among both individuals and large populations. The increased probability of a diabetes diagnosis among those who are obese compared with those of normal weight is similar across all major race and ethnic groups, and is thus an equally important health issue regardless of racial or ethnic identity. Overall, adults who are currently obese are about 4.7 times more likely to be diabetic compared with those who are normal weight, a probability that doesn't vary significantly for individual racial or ethnic groups. Diabetes diagnoses can and do occur among normal-weight individuals, though it is much less likely.

U.S. Diabetes Rate When Normal Weight vs. Obese, by Race and Ethnicity

Has a doctor or nurse ever told you that you have diabetes? (% Yes)

	Normal weight	Obese	Difference (pct. pts.)	Increased probability of diabetes diagnosis when obese
U.S. adults	4.6%	21.7%	17.1	4.7x
Whites	4.4%	21.9%	17.5	5.0x
Blacks	5.9%	23.4%	17.5	4.0x
Hispanics	5.0%	18.7%	13.7	3.7x
Asians	3.1%	15.3%	12.2	4.9x

Gallup-Healthways Well-Being Index

GALLUP

Implications

The obesity rate has continued to rise in the U.S. after leveling off from 2011 to 2013, and has done so despite rising public concern. Past research has demonstrated that obesity and its associated chronic conditions including diabetes cost the U.S. economy $153 billion per year in unplanned absenteeism due to poor health, a figure that has increased since the time of that study. And while blacks suffer disproportionately from chronic conditions associated with obesity, the sharp increase in obesity measured among whites since 2008 signifies that this is not a problem isolated to one racial or ethnic group.

Obesity affects all elements of well-being, not just physical wellness. It is associated, for example, with lower financial and social well-being. While obesity can diminish overall well-being, the relationship can also work in reverse; high well-being can reduce the chances of being obese. Those who have high or improving well-being across all five elements – purpose, social, financial, community and physical – are less likely to be obese or to become obese in the future than those who do not.

States, communities and workplaces alike can develop interventions targeting the behaviors linked to obesity. While exercise, produce consumption and healthy eating are all important factors, less obvious aspects of poor well-being are also key predictors of its occurrence, including smoking, depression, food insecurity, not having a safe place to exercise, not having a personal doctor and exhibiting poor dental habits. Having an accountability partner who encourages healthy choices and learning new and interesting things daily are also demonstrated deterrents to obesity. It is also important to recognize those occupations that are most at risk for obesity, including transportation, manufacturing/production and installation/repair workers. By addressing obesity on all relevant fronts, it is possible to reverse the upward trend and, in turn, decrease diabetes rates as well.

Survey Methods

Results are based on telephone interviews conducted Jan. 2-Dec. 30 in each year from 2008 through 2015, as part of the Gallup-Healthways Well-Being Index, with a random sample of over 350,000 adults in 2008-2012 and over 175,000 adults in 2013-2015, aged 18 and older, living in all 50 U.S. states and the District of Columbia. For results based on the total sample of national adults, the margin of sampling error is ±0.2 points at the 95% confidence level. The margin of sampling error for the four major race and ethnic groups ranges from ±0.3 points for whites to less than ±2.0 points for Asians. All reported margins of sampling error include computed design effects due to weighting.

February 12, 2016

ANTI-INCUMBENT MOOD TOWARD CONGRESS STILL GOING STRONG

by Lydia Saad

Story Highlights

- *Half of voters say their own representative deserves re-election*
- *Barely a quarter say most members deserve another term*
- *Both figures are near their two-decade low*

PRINCETON, N.J. – Barely half of U.S. voters think their own member of Congress deserves re-election, and just 27% say most members deserve another turn. These findings are on par with voters' attitudes in October 2014 and slightly improved from the historically weak levels seen in early 2014 but otherwise are among the weakest for incumbents since 1992.

Percentage Saying Each Type of Office-Holder Deserves to Be Re-Elected

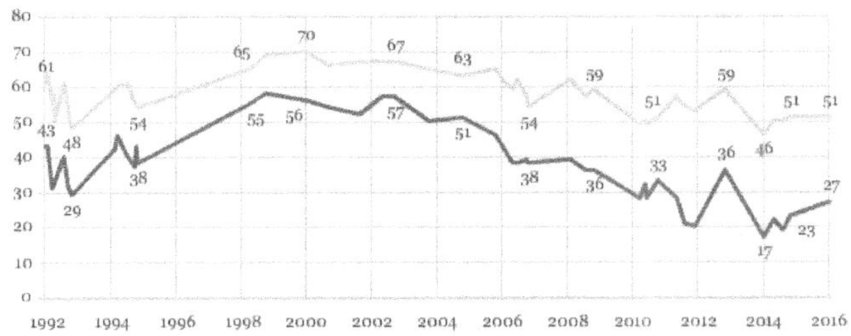

Voters' support for congressional incumbents' re-election has been relatively low since 2006. Since then, voters' belief that most members deserve re-election continued to decline through 2014 while their support for their own members' re-election has steadied between 51% and 59%.

Support for members of Congress on both measures exceeded 50% from 1998 through 2004 – a period of relative prosperity and solid support for governmental leaders in the years following the 9/11 attacks. This environment was good for congressional Republicans, who were able to maintain their majorities over this period with ease. However, in years just before – 1992 and 1994 – Gallup recorded another low point in public support for incumbents with 38% of U.S. adults saying most members of Congress deserved re-election in November 1994, likely contributing to the GOP takeover in that year's midterm elections.

The 2016 figures are based on a Jan. 21-25 Gallup poll. Despite the current Republican majority in Congress – and mirroring the recent political parity seen in approval of Congress – rank-and-file Republicans and Democrats have similar views about whether their own member, as well as most members, should be re-elected.

Percentage Saying Each Type of Office-Holder Deserves to Be Re-Elected, by Party ID

	Most members of Congress	Own representative
	%	%
Republicans	26	55
Independents	25	45
Democrats	31	54

Based on registered voters
Jan. 21-25, 2016

GALLUP

Bottom Line

The historically low levels of Americans saying that their own and most members deserve re-election reflect Congress' dismal job rating, mostly registering at or below 20% in Gallup's monthly polling for the past five years. If the anti-incumbent mood continues into the fall, Congress could see relatively high turnover, similar to 1992 and 2010 when fewer than 93% of incumbents were re-elected. On the other hand, incumbents did quite well in 2014 – with a 95% re-election rate in the House – in spite of historically low "deserves to be re-elected" numbers. The turnover that did occur was all in the Republicans' favor.

When anti-incumbency fervor coincides with a presidential year, the other possibility is that the losing party in the presidential race takes the brunt of the seat losses, which happened to Republicans in 2008. And while that's not a guarantee, the heft of the Republicans' current majority means the GOP has the most to lose from the public's desire for change in Congress.

Survey Methods

Results for this Gallup poll are based on telephone interviews conducted Jan. 21-25, 2016, with a random sample of 1,022 adults, aged 18 and older, living in all 50 U.S. states and the District of Columbia. For results based on the total sample of 903 registered voters, the margin of sampling error is ±4 percentage points at the 95% confidence level. All reported margins of sampling error include computed design effects for weighting.

February 15, 2016

MAJORITY OF AMERICANS VIEW CUBA FAVORABLY FOR FIRST TIME

by Jim Norman

Story Highlights

- *Favorability jumps from 38% in 2014 to 54% now*
- *Improvement matches timeline of Obama's overtures to Cuba*
- *Partisan gap on issue has doubled in last two years*

WASHINGTON, D.C. – A majority of the American public, which for decades has viewed Cuba in a decidedly negative light, sees the country favorably for the first time in Gallup polling history. Fifty-four percent now view Cuba positively – an increase of eight percentage points from last year, 16 points from two years ago and 33 points since 2006.

Cuba's Long March to Favorable Status

What is your overall opinion of Cuba?

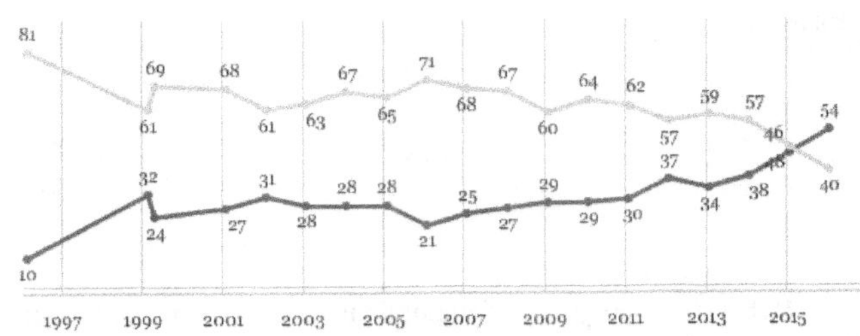

Americans' attitudes about Cuba have changed dramatically since 1996 when Gallup first asked the current version of the question. Only 10% that year said they had a favorable opinion. An earlier version of the question that measured favorability with a numerical scale not directly comparable to the current format found strong majorities of the U.S. public in 1976, 1979 and 1980 viewing Cuba unfavorably.

Public's Views of Cuba Tied to U.S. Government's Actions

The public's increasingly positive view of Cuba comes against the backdrop of President Barack Obama's vigorous campaign over the past two years to rebuild relations between the two countries. The biggest change took place last summer when formal diplomatic relations, severed in 1961 after the U.S. objected to the revolutionary regime led by Fidel Castro, were restored, and both countries reopened their embassies.

Over the past two decades, the views of the American public have tended to move in tandem with the ups and downs of relations between the two governments.

- Gallup measured the highest unfavorable rating, 81%, in 1996 – the year the U.S. Congress passed the Helms-Burton Act tightening an embargo on Cuba.
- About two-thirds of Americans viewed Cuba negatively in most years from 2001 through 2008, as President George W. Bush maintained a hard-line approach to relations between the two nations.
- In 2009, Obama was sworn into office, and unfavorable attitudes about Cuba dropped to 60%, with 29% favorable. During Obama's presidency, with its emphasis on finding ways to decrease hostilities between the two nations, Cuba's favorable ratings have climbed 25 points.

Perceptions of Cuba Divide Along Partisan Lines

Most of the shift in attitudes over the past two years has occurred among Democrats and independents. The percentage of Republicans with a favorable view grew by just six points from 2014 (28%) to now (34%) and still represents only a third of those in the GOP. Meanwhile, there has been a 15-point increase among independents from 2014 to 2015 (38% to 53%, respectively), and a 28-point change among Democrats – from less than a majority (45%) holding a favorable view in 2014 to almost three-fourths (73%) today.

Partisan Gap Grows Wider

Percent with overall favorable view of Cuba

	2014	2015	2016
	%	%	%
All national adults	38	46	54
Democrats	45	59	73
Independents	38	45	53
Republicans	28	30	34

GALLUP'

With a strong majority of Republicans seeing Cuba in a negative light and an even larger majority of Democrats viewing it positively, candidates for the parties' presidential nominations this year have mostly echoed those views. Both candidates on the Republican side with Cuban backgrounds – Ted Cruz and Marco Rubio – blasted Obama's reopening of the U.S. embassy in Havana. Two of the other top vote-getters in last week's New Hampshire primary, John Kasich and Jeb Bush, have also been critical of the move. On the Democratic side, Hillary Clinton and Bernie Sanders have strongly supported Obama's attempts to normalize relations.

Republican front-runner Donald Trump has taken a different tack, saying he agrees with reopening relations with Cuba – with the caveat that "we should have made a stronger deal."

Bottom Line

Americans' views of Cuba have become dramatically more positive in recent years, mostly because Democrats now overwhelmingly view Cuba favorably. During the past few years, Americans' opinions about Cuba have become sharply polarized by political party, with the Democrat-Republican gap in favorability more than doubling in the last two years – from 17 points in 2014 to 39 points today.

The momentum of public opinion seems to favor Democratic presidential candidates; the public backed their stances on reopening diplomatic relations with Cuba even before Obama's moves in the past two years. The wild card in this, as in so many other aspects of the upcoming election, is Trump, who seems to lean closer to a Democratic point of view than a Republican one.

Survey Methods

Results for this Gallup poll are based on telephone interviews conducted Feb. 3-7, 2016, on the Gallup U.S. Daily survey, with a random sample of 1,021 adults, aged 18 and older, living in all 50 U.S. states and the District of Columbia. For results based on the total sample of national adults, the margin of sampling error is ±4 percentage points at the 95% confidence level. All reported margins of sampling error include computed design effects for weighting.

February 15, 2016

AMERICANS LESS LIKELY TO SEE U.S. AS NO. 1 MILITARILY

by Frank Newport

Story Highlights

- *49% say U.S. is No. 1 military power in world, down from last year*
- *Views that U.S. is spending too little on defense are edging up*
- *Republicans much more likely to say military spending is too little*

PRINCETON, N.J. – Americans are evenly split when asked if the U.S. is No. 1 in the world militarily, with 49% saying "yes" and 49% saying "no." The current percentage who view the U.S. as No. 1 is, by a small margin, the lowest Gallup has recorded in its 23-year trend. It also marks a significant downturn from last February, when 59% said the U.S. was the world's top military power.

Americans' Views on How U.S. Military Ranks

Do you think the United States is No. 1 in the world militarily, or that it is only one of several leading military powers?

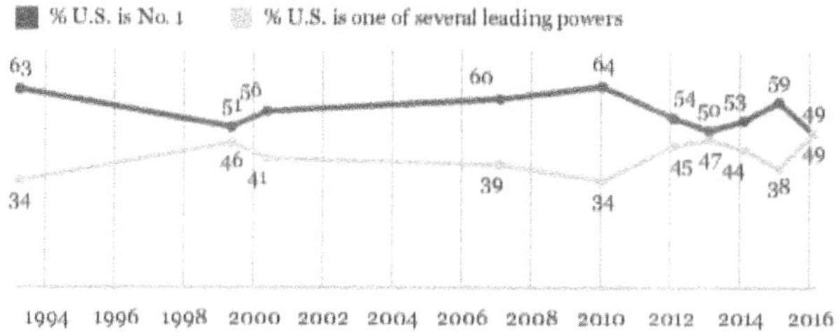

GALLUP

A separate question included in Gallup's Feb. 3-7 World Affairs poll asked Americans about the *importance* of the nation being No. 1 militarily. Two-thirds of Americans say it *is* important, in line with sentiments measured since Gallup first asked this question in 1993.

Importance of the U.S. Being No. 1 in the World Militarily

Do you feel that it's important for the United States to be No. 1 in the world militarily, or that being No. 1 is not that important, as long as the U.S. is among the leading military powers?

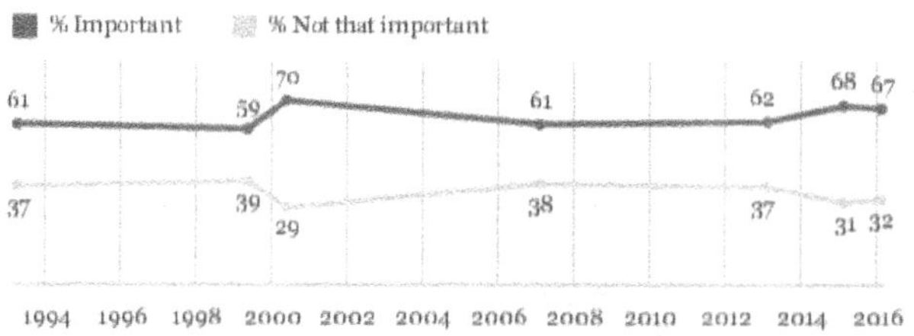

GALLUP

Views That U.S. Spends Too Little on Military Up, but Still in Minority

As might be expected given the less positive views of U.S. military power, more Americans than in recent years say the country is spending too little on its military. In the February survey, 37% say the government in Washington is spending too little on "national defense and military purposes," up slightly from last year and the highest since before the 9/11 terrorist attacks. Even with this shift, however, the "spending too little" sentiment remains relatively low. Nearly as many, 32%, say the U.S. is spending "too much," and the remainder, 27%, say defense spending is "about right."

Spending on National Defense and Military Purposes

There is much discussion as to the amount of money the government in Washington should spend for national defense and military purposes. How do you feel about this? Do you think we are spending too little, about the right amount or too much?

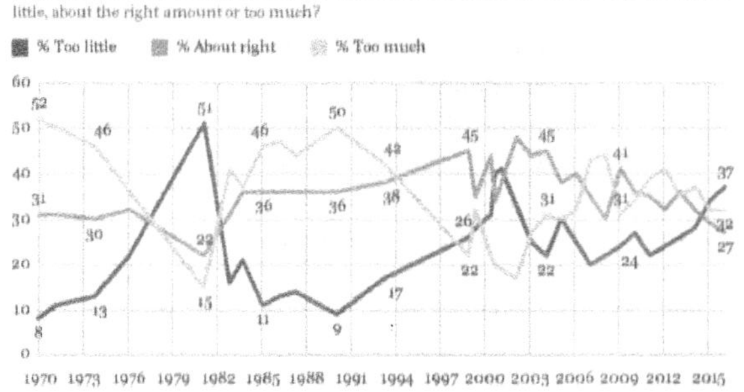

GALLUP

Gallup has asked this defense spending question since 1969, with responses fluctuating a good deal over the years. The broad patterns show that Americans' belief that military spending is too low rise after the real-world level of such spending goes down. This is evident in the sharp spike in views that the nation was spending too little on defense in January 1981, as newly elected President Ronald Reagan took office – winning in part on a platform emphasizing the need to bolster the military to counter the growing Soviet threat. The "spending too little" measure also rose in February 2001 as newly elected President George W. Bush took office after a two-term Bill Clinton presidency in which military spending fell.

U.S. military spending rose sharply after 9/11, peaking in 2010, and Americans' views that the government was spending too little on the military dropped concomitantly. Now that military spending has been dropping in the last several years because of sequestration and a reduced involvement in Iraq and Afghanistan, Americans' views that the U.S. is spending too little on defense have begun to increase.

Republicans More Than Three Times as Likely as Democrats to Say Spending Is Too Little

Defense and military spending have been a significant talking point for Republican presidential candidates this year, with most calling for a sharply increased military budget. Sen. Ted Cruz, for example, says, "In order to restore America's safety and security, we must rebuild our military. If you think defending the country is expensive, try not defending it." Donald Trump says he would "build up the military so nobody messes with us," and Marco Rubio says he would "work to ... begin to undo the damage caused by $1 trillion in indiscriminate defense cuts." On the other hand, Democratic candidate Bernie Sanders says he has "very serious concerns about our nation's bloated military budget and ... misplaced national priorities."

Rank-and-file Republicans across the country generally share the hawkish views of their party's presidential candidates, with about two-thirds agreeing that there is too little spending on the military. In sharp contrast, 20% of Democrats say the U.S. spends too little while 45% say the government spends too much. Independents are largely divided, but the greatest percentage of that group says the U.S. spends too much.

Views on U.S. Military Spending, by Partisanship

	Republicans	Independents	Democrats
	%	%	%
Spending too little	66	27	20
Spending about right	23	26	32
Spending too much	9	39	45

Feb. 3-7, 2016

GALLUP

Implications

The 10-point drop in the percentage of Americans who believe the U.S. is the No. 1 military power in the world may reflect worries about international terrorism, which the public views as the most critical international threat the nation faces. It may also reflect the discussion of the military and defense in the current presidential election campaign. The uptick in Americans' view that the nation is spending too little on its military may partly reflect these two dynamics, but also follows the classic ebb and flow of attitudes about military spending in response to ups and downs in the nation's actual spending.

Although more Americans now than in the years after 9/11 say there is too little spending on defense, that percentage is nowhere near as high as it was immediately after the Jimmy Carter years when Reagan took office and began years of massively increased military spending. Nor is it as high as in the years just before 9/11. And even with the recent shifts in attitudes, the majority of Americans remain convinced that the nation's military budget is about right or is too high.

Republicans' and Democrats' very different views on the current level of military spending suggest this could become a contentious issue in the general election this fall.

As commander in chief, the president is a critical determinant of the nation's defense posture. This means the direction of military spending in the years ahead will be quite different, depending on whether a Republican or a Democrat is elected in November, and the public's attitudes about the strength of the U.S. military will most likely follow in turn.

Historical data are available in Gallup Analytics.

Survey Methods

Results for this Gallup poll are based on telephone interviews conducted Feb. 3-7, 2016, with a random sample of 1,021 adults, aged 18 and older, living in all 50 U.S. states and the District of Columbia. For results based on the total sample of national adults, the margin of sampling error is ±4 percentage points at the 95% confidence level. All reported margins of sampling error include computed design effects for weighting.

February 17, 2016

ILLINOIS RESIDENTS LEAST CONFIDENT IN THEIR STATE GOVERNMENT

by Jeffrey M. Jones

Story Highlights

- *25% of Illinois residents confident in state government*
- *North Dakota residents most confident, at 81%*
- *Residents in larger states have less confidence, on average*

PRINCETON, N.J. – One in four Illinois residents are confident in their state government, the lowest among the 50 states by a significant margin. Rhode Island (33%) and Connecticut (39%) join Illinois as states with less than 40% government confidence. North Dakota residents are the most trusting; 81% say they are confident in their state government.

States With Least and Most Confidence in Their State Government

In [state name], do you have confidence in each of the following or not? How about the [state name] government in general?

	% Confident	% Not confident
LEAST CONFIDENCE		
Illinois	25	74
Rhode Island	33	66
Connecticut	39	60
New Jersey	41	59
Louisiana	44	55
Kansas	45	53
Pennsylvania	46	53
New York	46	53
MOST CONFIDENCE		
North Dakota	81	18
Wyoming	76	23
Nebraska	74	25
Montana	72	27
South Dakota	71	28
Utah	70	29
Minnesota	69	31

2015 Gallup 50-State Poll

GALLUP

These results are based on Gallup's 50-state poll, conducted March through December 2015. Gallup asked respondents whether they do or do not have confidence in their state's "government in general." The full data for each state appear at the end of this article.

Illinoisans' lack of confidence likely stems from the state's long history of political corruption, with several recent governors having been found guilty of crimes. The state is also in the midst of an eight-month-long impasse over the 2016 state budget between Republican Gov. Bruce Rauner and the Democratic legislature.

Corruption and challenging economic times likely contribute to other states ranking among the least confident in their government. Louisiana, like Illinois, is renowned for corruption in politics, and many of the other lower-confidence states have had high-ranking elected officials convicted of crimes in recent years.

There is a strong positive relationship between residents' ratings of their state's economy and their confidence in state government. In addition to Illinois, Rhode Island, Connecticut, New Jersey and Kansas all rank among the states in which residents are the least positive about their state's economy. North Dakota, Utah, Minnesota and Nebraska are four states in which residents rate their state's economy positively and express high confidence in their state government.

Gallup also conducted a 50-state poll in 2013, which included a question asking respondents how much "trust and confidence" they have in the government of their state to handle "state problems." Despite the differences in question wording between the 2013 and 2015 polls, there is much overlap between the top-ranking states and bottom-ranking states in the two studies. Illinois residents also had the least trust in their state government in 2013, with Rhode Island, Pennsylvania and Louisiana among the lowest as well. North

Dakota, Wyoming, Utah and Nebraska ranked among the states with the highest levels of trust in their government in 2013, just as they do in the current study.

In [state name], do you have confidence in each of the following or not? How about the [state name] government in general?

	% Confident	% Not confident	% No opinion
North Dakota	81	18	1
Wyoming	76	23	1
Nebraska	74	25	0
Montana	72	27	1
South Dakota	71	28	1
Utah	70	29	1
Minnesota	69	31	1
New Hampshire	68	30	1
Iowa	68	31	1
Colorado	66	32	2
Massachusetts	66	32	2
Delaware	65	34	1
Texas	64	33	3
Alaska	64	34	3
Arkansas	63	35	1
Idaho	63	36	1
Tennessee	63	36	1
Nevada	61	37	2
Vermont	60	39	1
Oklahoma	60	40	1
Georgia	59	40	1
South Carolina	59	40	0
Ohio	59	39	2
Virginia	58	41	1
Florida	57	42	1
Maryland	56	41	3
Hawaii	55	44	1
Mississippi	55	43	2
Washington, D.C.	55	43	2
Indiana	55	44	1
Oregon	55	44	1
North Carolina	55	43	2
California	54	43	3
Kentucky	54	45	1
Washington	54	45	1
West Virginia	51	47	1
Missouri	50	48	2
Wisconsin	49	50	1
Arizona	49	49	3
New Mexico	48	50	2
Michigan	48	51	1
Alabama	48	51	2
Maine	48	52	1
New York	46	53	1
Pennsylvania	46	53	1
Kansas	45	53	2
Louisiana	44	55	1
New Jersey	41	59	0
Connecticut	39	60	1
Rhode Island	33	66	1
Illinois	25	74	1

2015 Gallup 50-State Poll

GALLUP

State Size a Factor in Government Confidence

Gallup's 2013 analysis of state trust in government found a negative relationship between state population size and trust in government, meaning residents in less populous states tended to have greater confidence in their state government than those living in states that are more populous. That relationship is also apparent in the current data. An average of 64% of residents in the smallest 10 states have confidence in their state government, compared with an average of 51% confidence among residents in the 10 largest states.

Confidence in State Government, by State Characteristics

	% Confident
POPULATION SIZE	
Largest 10 states	51
Second-largest 10 states	54
10 middle states	56
Second-smallest 10 states	59
Smallest 10 states	64
REGION OF COUNTRY	
West	61
Midwest	58
South	57
East	50

2015 Gallup 50-State Poll

Note: States are grouped by population size according to 2014 U.S. Census Bureau's Current Population Survey.

GALLUP

More populous states contain a mix of urban and rural areas and a more diverse population financially, including areas with high concentrations of poverty. Thus, these states likely have greater challenges in delivering needed services to residents than do smaller states, which tend to have more homogeneous populations.

On a regional basis, residents in Western states tend to express the highest confidence in their state governments, largely because no Western states rank among the lowest states while Wyoming, Utah and Montana are among the states with the most confidence in government. The Midwest's average score is held down by Illinois' low level of trust, but the Midwest still ranks second among regions at 58%. The East has the lowest average confidence score, as it is home to five of the states where residents have the lowest confidence in their state government.

Politics Not Strongly Related to Trust

The Illinois budget impasse is an example of the political gridlock that can ensue when states have a governor and legislature of opposing political parties that fail to find common ground on pressing state issues. In general, however, divided party government or unified party government has little relation to confidence in state government. On average, 58% of residents in states in which the same political party controls the governorship and both houses of the state legislature have confidence in their state government, compared with 55% of those in states in which party control of the government is divided.

Confidence in State Government, by State Political Characteristics

	% Confident
DIVIDED VS. UNIFIED GOVERNMENT	
Unified government (governor and legislature from same party)	58
Divided government (governor and one or more houses from different parties)	55
GOVERNOR POLITICAL PARTY	
Republican	58
Democrat	55

2015 Gallup 50-State Poll

GALLUP

Similarly, there is little difference in confidence in government depending on whether the governor of the state is a Republican or a Democrat. Average confidence is 58% in states led by a Republican chief executive and 55% in states led by a Democrat.

Confidence is higher, on average, in the 22 states that have a Republican governor and GOP majority in both houses of the legislature (60%) than in the seven states that have a Democratic governor and Democratic majority in both houses (52%). The Democratic state average is held down by Rhode Island and Connecticut. Delaware (65%) and Vermont (60%) are two Democratic-controlled states with higher confidence. Many of the Republican-controlled states are less populous states such as Wyoming, Utah, North Dakota and South Dakota.

Implications

In all representative forms of government, residents of a city, state or nation elect officials to conduct business and pass policies on their behalf, for the betterment of all residents. Trust in elected officials is essential to making the system work, but it is severely lacking in many U.S. states.

Given the strong relationship between residents' perceptions of their state's economic health and their confidence in state government, some of the states with less confidence could see that turn around if economic conditions in the state improve. And by the same token, states that have higher trust in their government could see that erode if the state's economy worsens, something that bears watching in energy-producing states like Wyoming and North Dakota, where residents are less optimistic about the direction their economy is headed.

In other states, particularly those with a long history of corruption such as Illinois and Louisiana, there may be cultural or institutional hurdles to overcome, and it may take more than an improving economy to engender confidence in those states' elected officials.

These data are available in Gallup Analytics.

Survey Methods

Results for this Gallup poll are based on telephone interviews conducted March 30-Dec. 22, 2015, with random samples of approximately 500 adults, aged 18 and older, living in each of the 50 U.S. states. Data are weighted to account for unequal selection probability, nonresponse and double coverage of landline and cellphone users in the two sampling frames. Data are also weighted to state estimates of gender, age, race, Hispanic ethnicity, education and phone status (cellphone only, landline only, both, and cellphone mostly).

For results based on the total sample of adults in each state, the margin of sampling error is ±6 percentage points at the 95% confidence level. All reported margins of sampling error include computed design effects for weighting.

February 17, 2016
AFTER NUCLEAR DEAL, U.S. VIEWS OF IRAN REMAIN DISMAL

by Andrew Dugan

Story Highlights

- *14% of Americans have a favorable view of Iran*
- *30% of Americans approve; 57% disapprove of the Iran nuclear deal*
- *9% of Republicans approve of deal versus 51% of Democrats*

WASHINGTON, D.C. – Iran's long-standing negative image in the U.S. remains unchanged, even as the deal designed to limit Iran's nuclear program has come into effect. Fourteen percent of Americans say they have a favorable view of Iran, essentially unchanged from a 2015 poll conducted before the nuclear deal was finalized but just a hair above the 11% average favorable rating the country has received over Gallup's 27-year trend.

Americans' Favorability Ratings of Iran

Next, I'd like your overall opinion of some foreign countries. What is your overall opinion of Iran? Is it very favorable, mostly favorable, mostly unfavorable or very unfavorable?

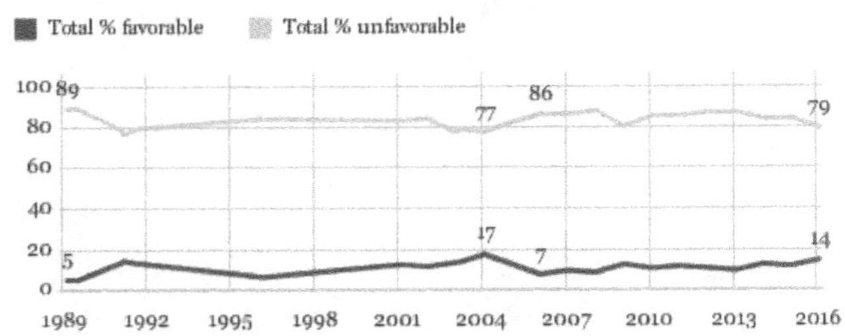

GALLUP

Iran was once a close U.S. ally, when the former was ruled by the autocratic Shah, but the 1979 Iranian Revolution birthed a "new" Iran, one ruled by a theocratic government and guided by staunchly anti-American convictions. The protracted U.S. hostage crisis that stemmed from the revolution undoubtedly sullied Iran's image in many Americans' minds. When Gallup began polling about Iran's favorable ratings in 1989, 5% said they saw the country favorably, a rating that would only modestly improve in the ensuing years. Iran's highest favorable rating of 17% was recorded in 2004, when the U.S. occupied Iraq, the two countries' common enemy.

These results are based on a Gallup poll conducted Feb. 3-7.

Iran also retains its position as one of the least popular countries and territories of the 21 that Gallup measures on an annual basis. Only Syria and North Korea have lower favorable ratings this year, at 12% and 8%, respectively.

Republicans Most Negative Toward Iran

Republicans, Democrats and independents all view Iran unfavorably, but Republicans' views are the most negative. Currently, 4% of Republicans rate Iran very or mostly favorably, compared with 18% of Democrats and 19% of independents. Independents' views of Iran are more positive than last year, but Republicans' and Democrats' opinions are basically unchanged.

Iran's Image Among Americans, by Party Affiliation

% Who have "very" or "mostly" favorable view of Iran

	February 2015 %	February 2016 %	Change (pct. pts.)
Republicans	6	4	-2
Independents	10	19	+9
Democrats	15	18	+3

GALLUP

Three in 10 Americans Approve of Iran Nuclear Agreement

One clear reason that the Iran nuclear deal has done nothing to bolster Iran's image in the U.S. is that most Americans don't approve of the agreement. Nearly twice as many Americans disapprove of the deal as approve, 57% versus 30%. Fourteen percent have no opinion.

Americans' Views on the Iran Nuclear Deal

Do you approve or disapprove of the Iran nuclear agreement?

	Approve %	Disapprove %	Net approval (pct. pts.)
National adults	30	57	-27
Republicans	9	80	-71
Independents	30	53	-23
Democrats	51	38	13

Feb. 3-7, 2016

GALLUP

Approval of the Iran nuclear deal varies significantly by party. Just 9% of Republicans approve of the deal negotiated by the Obama administration, compared with 30% of independents and 51% of Democrats.

In stark contrast to Americans' views of the nuclear deal, Gallup has found that a clear majority of Iranian adults are optimistic about it. More than two-thirds of Iranians believe their national leaders negotiated a good deal for their country. And 51% of Iranians believe the deal will improve Iranian-U.S. relations – a hope that seems bleak, given Americans' still-dismal views of Iran.

Americans nonetheless implicitly agree with the Obama administration's overarching aim in negotiating this deal, namely, stopping Iran from producing nuclear weapons. But the reaching of and the implementation of the agreement appear to have done little to assuage Americans' concerns about Iranian nuclear weapons. Three-quarters of U.S. adults say the potential development of nuclear weapons by Iran represents a critical threat to the vital interests of the U.S. in the next 10 years. This is nearly equivalent to the 77% who answered similarly last year, prior to the finalization of the deal in July 2015. Only when it comes to international terrorism do more Americans see this as a critical threat than Iran's possible production of nuclear weapons, across 12 existing or emerging threats Gallup tested.

Threats to the Vital Interests of the United States in Next 10 Years: Development of Nuclear Weapons by Iran

Next, I am going to read you a list of possible threats to the vital interests of the United States in the next 10 years. For each one, please tell me if you see this as a critical threat, an important but not critical threat, or not an important threat at all.

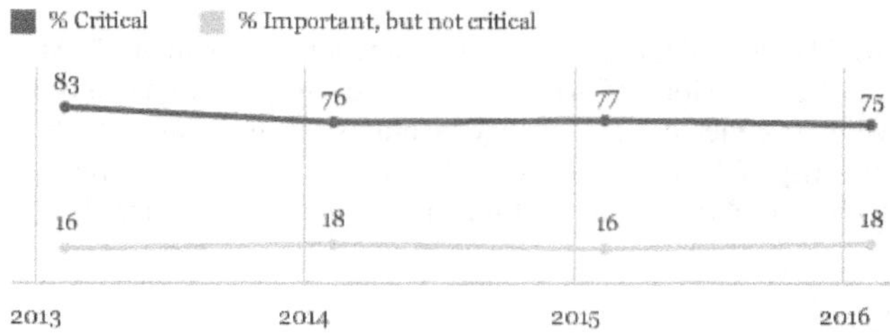

GALLUP

Of Americans who consider the development of Iranian nuclear weapons a "critical" threat, 23% approve of the Iran deal. For those who say the development of such weapons is an important but not critical threat or not important at all, 53% approve of the nuclear deal.

Bottom Line

Last month was a historic one for Iran – the International Atomic Energy Agency officially verified that Iran has taken significant steps to curtail its nuclear program. With this verdict, Iran is freed from the devastating effects of international economic sanctions. Iran is already re-engaging the global economy; the country shipped its first oil to Europe in the post-sanctions era several days ago. Additionally, the U.S. waived some sanctions against Iran, allowing the latter to rejoin the international financial system.

But these milestones notwithstanding, Gallup's data suggest that American perceptions' of Iran have not changed. Iran retains its spot as one of the least popular countries in the eyes of U.S. adults. Congressional Republicans' fierce opposition to the nuclear deal, as well as Israeli Prime Minister Benjamin Netanyahu's disapproval, may have helped shape the sour national mood on this issue. But whatever the cause of Americans' skepticism, it may take years of demonstrated Iranian compliance with the terms of the deal before most U.S. adults come around to the agreement, if they ever do.

Historical data are available in Gallup Analytics.

Survey Methods

Results for this Gallup poll are based on telephone interviews conducted Feb. 3-7, 2016, with a random sample of 1,021 adults, aged 18 and older, living in all 50 U.S. states and the District of Columbia. For results based on the total sample of national adults, the margin of sampling error is ±4 percentage points at the 95% confidence level. All reported margins of sampling error include computed design effects for weighting.

February 18, 2016

AMERICANS SEE RUSSIA LESS NEGATIVELY, AS LESS OF A THREAT

by Art Swift

Story Highlights

- *30% have a favorable impression of Russia, 65% unfavorable*
- *Younger Americans give highest ratings*
- *39% say Russia's military power is a critical threat to the U.S.*

WASHINGTON, D.C. – After reaching a new low in 2015, Americans' impressions of Russia have recovered somewhat this year, with 30% viewing the country favorably versus 24% in 2015. The majority of Americans continue to view the nation unfavorably, and their favorability rating is still half as high as it was a decade ago.

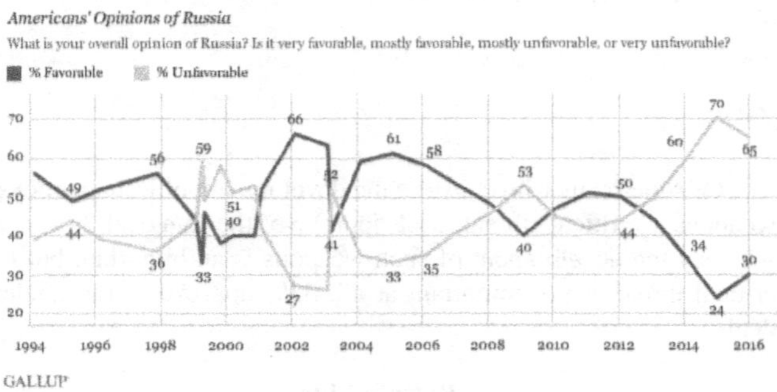

Russia and the U.S. have a tempestuous history. As part of the Soviet Union, the Russian government engendered fear and resentment among Americans for decades after World War II during the Cold War. Hostilities began to ease during the era of *glasnost* in the mid-1980s. Through much of the 1990s and 2000s, Americans' favorable opinions of Russia climbed, swelling to 66% in 2002. This sentiment began to crash when Vladimir Putin returned to the presidency in 2012. Some of his policies and actions, including discriminatory policies against gays and Russia's involvement in Ukraine, contributed to favorability dropping to a low point of 24% last year.

But in Gallup's annual World Affairs update survey conducted Feb. 3-7, Americans' favorability toward Russia has edged back up. The reason for this may be that Russia simply isn't dominating news headlines as it did in 2013 and 2014. Putin's interventions in the Middle East and Ukraine have arguably been most in the news in the past year, while Russia has also been prominent for its economic free fall as oil prices collapsed worldwide. The economic free fall, however, may not inspire a negative or positive response in Americans.

Younger Americans Have Highest Favorable Opinion Toward Russia

Americans between the ages of 18 and 34 gave Russia the highest favorable rating across all age groups at 43%. This is significantly higher than those aged 35 to 54, and more than double the percentage of Americans aged 55 and older. In the past four years, young Americans have maintained a relatively positive opinion of Russia, with the exception of last year. This may be attributable to most of this age group not living through the Cold War and not viewing Russia as the enemy to the U.S. that other generations experienced.

Americans' Opinions of Russia, by Age and Party ID

% Favorable

	2013	2014	2015	2016
18-29	53	42	28	43
35-54	45	35	34	30
55 and older	35	27	13	21
Republican	39	31	20	30
Independent	44	37	25	32
Democrat	48	33	26	29

Feb. 3-7, 2016

GALLUP

In the political spectrum, favorability of Russia is similarly low across party lines, with Republicans, Democrats and political independents all giving Russia a favorable rating between 29% and 32%.

Perceptions of Russia's Military Power as a Critical Threat Decline

As Americans' opinions of Russia improve, a smaller percentage believes Russia's military power is a critical threat to the U.S. Thirty-nine percent of Americans say Russia's military power is a critical threat, down 10 percentage points from last year, but still above where it was from 2004 through 2014.

Nearly two years since Crimea became part of Russia, stirring up a hornet's nest of geopolitical tension in Eastern Europe, many of the concerns voiced by NATO countries have not materialized. Russia has not invaded other former Soviet republics or made any pronouncements of aggression toward the U.S. Americans' perception of the military power of Russia as a critical threat comes in far below the threats that Americans are most concerned about, including international terrorism and cyberterrorism.

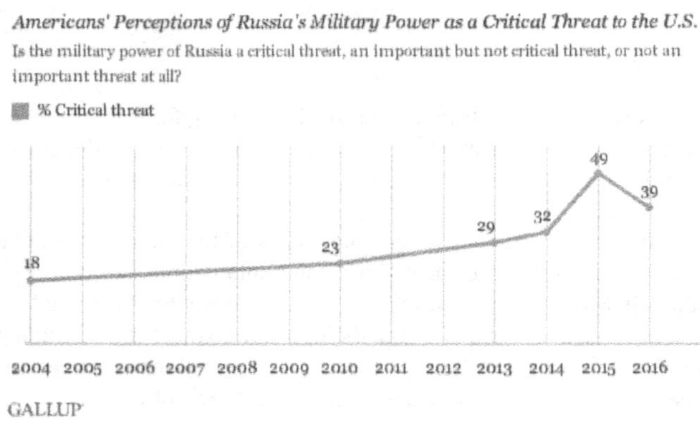

Bottom Line

Russia's image has become slightly less negative this year among U.S. adults, although it remains near the lowest level Gallup has recorded. After a period of several years that Putin has expressed criticism of the U.S., harbored alleged cyberterrorist Edward Snowden, restricted gay rights in his country and annexed Crimea, Americans do not have the same positive feelings toward Russia than in the halcyon period following the end of the Cold War. It will be interesting to see if the next president reaches out to Putin, potentially boosting the favorable ratings of Russia in the U.S.

Historical data are available in Gallup Analytics.

Survey Methods

Results for this Gallup poll are based on telephone interviews conducted Feb. 3-7, 2016, on the Gallup U.S. Daily survey, with a random sample of 1,021 adults, aged 18 and older, living in all 50 U.S. states and the District of Columbia. For results based on the total sample of national adults, the margin of sampling error is ±4 percentage points at the 95% confidence level. All reported margins of sampling error include computed design effects for weighting.

February 19, 2016

FOUR IN FIVE AMERICANS VIEW SYRIA UNFAVORABLY

by Justin McCarthy

Story Highlights

- *Highest unfavorable rating for Syria in Gallup's trend*
- *Americans divided on best course for U.S. military in Syria*
- *Republicans most likely to say more involvement needed*

WASHINGTON, D.C. – Syria's negative image in the U.S. increased over the past year to the point that four in five Americans now say they have an unfavorable view of the country, up from 74% a year ago. Syria now has the second-worst image of 21 countries rated in a new Gallup poll, with only North Korea rated worse.

Americans' Favorability Ratings of Syria

Next, I'd like your overall opinion of some foreign countries. What is your overall opinion of Syria? Is it very favorable, mostly favorable, mostly unfavorable or very unfavorable?

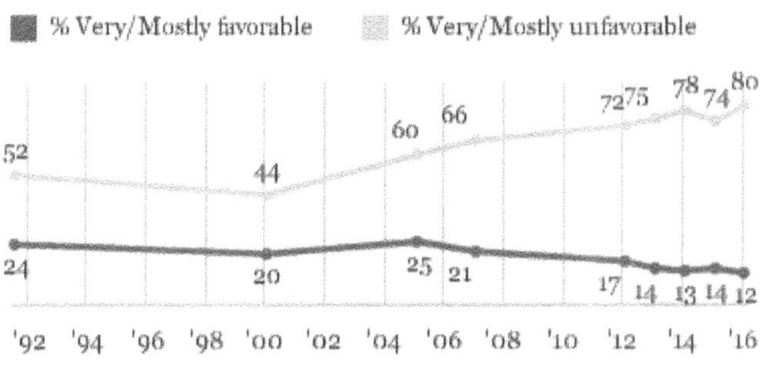

GALLUP

Over the 25 years Gallup has asked Americans about Syria, the country's image has never been very positive. No more than 25% have ever viewed the nation favorably, and that has now dwindled to 12%. The percentage viewing it unfavorably has almost doubled since 2000 – first jumping to 60% in 2005 as U.S.-Syrian tensions were escalating over Syria's role in supporting regional terrorism. Its negative rating crossed the 70% threshold in 2012 as a popular uprising in Syria was mounting, and it has since remained high through the five-year civil war. Meanwhile, the percentage with no opinion of Syria has declined from 36% in 2000 to 8% today.

The current data, from Gallup's Feb. 3-7 World Affairs poll, comes as a ceasefire in the Syrian civil war appears less and less likely to occur. Although several world powers convened last week to agree on a "cessation of hostilities" and the delivery of aid to Syria, the country's president has expressed doubt such a truce is feasible.

As they watch the unfolding news from Damascus, Americans of all political stripes view Syria negatively, but Republicans have the worst views. Nine in 10 Republicans have an unfavorable view of the country, compared with about three in four independents and Democrats, respectively.

Americans' Favorability Ratings of Syria

Next, I'd like your overall opinion of some foreign countries. What is your overall opinion of Syria? Is it very favorable, mostly favorable, mostly unfavorable or very unfavorable?

	Favorable	Unfavorable
	%	%
National adults	12	80
Republicans	7	90
Independents	14	77
Democrats	16	76

Feb. 3-7, 2016

GALLUP

Gallup has also found that a majority (58%) of Americans view the conflict in Syria as a critical threat to the vital interests of the U.S.

Americans Divided on U.S. Military's Approach in Syria

A separate question asked Americans about U.S. military involvement in the country. The results show that Americans are about as likely to say the U.S. military should get more involved in Syria (34%) as they are to say the current involvement is about right (29%) or that it should be less involved (30%).

Independents and Democrats are fairly split over whether the U.S. military should maintain, step up or scale back its involvement. But Republicans lean heavily toward increasing it (49%).

Americans' Views on U.S. Military Action in Syria

Based on what you know or have read, do you think the U.S. military should be -- more involved in Syria than it is now, is its involvement about right or should the U.S. military be less involved in Syria than it is now?

	More involved	Involvement is about right	Less involved
	%	%	%
National adults	34	29	30
Republicans	49	22	23
Independents	30	29	33
Democrats	26	36	34

Feb. 3-7, 2016

GALLUP

Bottom Line

Syrian President Bashar al-Assad has used chemical weapons against his own people, maintains close ties with Russian President Vladimir Putin and keeps his grip on a country that has rebelled against him for several years. Now with conflict creating an international refugee crisis, it's not surprising that Americans' views of the country are at a low ebb.

At the same time, the American public – perhaps reflecting the lack of consensus seen among the 2016 presidential candidates on the issue – is divided over how deeply the U.S. military should be involved. Republican candidates have repeatedly focused on the need for more extensive U.S. efforts in the region. Rank-and-file Republicans across the country are much more likely to favor more involvement than independents or Democrats, but there is hardly any agreement on the matter. Half of Republicans say that current involvement is about right or that the U.S. should be less involved.

Historical data are available in Gallup Analytics.

Survey Methods

Results for this Gallup poll are based on telephone interviews conducted Feb. 3-7, 2016, on the Gallup U.S. Daily survey, with a random sample of 1,021 adults, aged 18 and older, living in all 50 U.S. states and the District of Columbia. For results based on the total sample of national adults, the margin of sampling error is ±4 percentage points at the 95% confidence level. All reported margins of sampling error include computed design effects for weighting.

February 22, 2016
NAPLES-IMMOKALEE-MARCO ISLAND, FLORIDA, NO. 1 IN WELL-BEING

by Dan Witters

Story Highlights

- *Naples-Immokalee-Marco Island, Florida, up from No. 7 in 2012-2013*
- *Charleston, West Virginia, had the lowest well-being in 2014-2015*
- *San Jose-Sunnyvale-Santa Clara, California, topped all large metro areas*

WASHINGTON, D.C. – Residents of Naples-Immokalee-Marco Island, Florida, had the highest well-being across 190 communities Gallup and Healthways surveyed in 2014-2015, edging out Salinas, California. The remaining communities rounding out the top five were North Port-Bradenton-Sarasota, Florida; Fort Collins, Colorado; and the Town of Barnstable, Massachusetts.

Top 15 Communities in Overall Well-Being, 2014-2015

Among 190 Metropolitan Statistical Areas nationwide

	Well-Being Index score
Naples-Immokalee-Marco Island, Florida	65.0
Salinas, California	65.0
North Port-Bradenton-Sarasota, Florida	64.7
Fort Collins, Colorado	64.6
Town of Barnstable, Massachusetts	64.6
Santa Cruz-Watsonville, California	64.6
Boulder, Colorado	64.5
Charlottesville, Virginia	64.5
Anchorage, Alaska	64.4
San Luis Obispo-Paso Robles-Arroyo Grande, California	64.3
McAllen-Edinburg-Mission, Texas	64.3
Santa Maria-Santa Barbara, California	64.3
Urban Honolulu, Hawaii	64.2
Provo-Orem, Utah	63.8
San Jose-Sunnyvale-Santa Clara, California	63.7

Gallup-Healthways Well-Being Index

"Metropolitan Statistical Areas" as defined by the U.S. Office of Management and Budget

GALLUP

Naples-Immokalee-Marco Island's top ranking is an improvement from its No. 7 position in 2012-2013, and its Well-Being Index score in 2014-2015 slightly exceeded Salinas' score when extended to two decimal points. Other communities that typically have ranked in the top 15 for well-being since 2008 include Boulder, Colorado; Honolulu, Hawaii; and Provo-Orem, Utah.

Charleston, West Virginia, earned the lowest well-being score in 2014-2015, with a number of Rust Belt communities accounting for most of the remaining lowest-ranked states. Many of the lowest well-being communities in 2014-2015 have consistently been among the lowest since 2008, including Charleston; Fort Smith, Arkansas-Oklahoma; Hickory-Lenoir-Morganton, North Carolina; Huntington-Ashland, West Virginia-Kentucky-Ohio; and Youngstown-Warren-Boardman, Ohio-Pennsylvania.

Baton Rouge, Louisiana, and Indianapolis-Carmel-Anderson, Indiana, had much higher rankings in prior years and appeared on the list of lowest well-being communities for the first time in 2014-2015.

Bottom 15 Communities in Overall Well-Being, 2014-2015

Among 190 Metropolitan Statistical Areas nationwide

	Well-Being Index score
Charleston, West Virginia	57.1
Fort Smith, Arkansas-Oklahoma	58.2
Hickory-Lenoir-Morganton, North Carolina	58.3
Huntington-Ashland, West Virginia-Kentucky-Ohio	58.3
Chico, California	58.6
Youngstown-Warren-Boardman, Ohio-Pennsylvania	58.7
Toledo, Ohio	59.3
Worcester, Massachusetts-Connecticut	59.3
Dayton, Ohio	59.3
Rockford, Illinois	59.4
Scranton--Wilkes-Barre--Hazleton, Pennsylvania	59.7
Baton Rouge, Louisiana	59.9
Flint, Michigan	59.9
Utica-Rome, New York	59.9
Indianapolis-Carmel-Anderson, Indiana	59.9

Gallup-Healthways Well-Being Index

"Metropolitan Statistical Areas" as defined by the U.S. Office of Management and Budget

GALLUP

These community-level data are based on more than 353,000 interviews with U.S. adults across all 50 states, conducted Jan. 2, 2014, through Dec. 30, 2015. The Gallup-Healthways Well-Being Index is calculated on a scale of 0 to 100, where 0 represents the lowest possible well-being and 100 represents the highest possible well-being. The Well-Being Index scores for the nation and for each community are composed of metrics within each of the five essential elements of well-being:

- **Purpose:** liking what you do each day and being motivated to achieve your goals
- **Social:** having supportive relationships and love in your life
- **Financial:** managing your economic life to reduce stress and increase security
- **Community:** liking where you live, feeling safe and having pride in your community
- **Physical:** having good health and enough energy to get things done daily

In most cases, a difference of 1.0 to 2.0 points in the Well-Being Index score of any two communities represents a statistically significant gap, and is characterized by meaningfully large differences in at least some of the individual metrics that make up the Gallup-Healthways Well-Being Index. The Well-Being Index for the U.S. in 2015 was 61.7, essentially unchanged from 61.6 in 2014.

Corpus Christi, Texas, Leads Communities in Purpose and Social Well-Being

Naples-Immokalee-Marco Island residents had the highest community well-being nationally, contributing to the community's top well-being ranking overall. Corpus Christi, Texas, led the nation in both purpose and social well-being, but did not perform as well in the other three elements, resulting in an overall rank of 35th. North Port-Bradenton-Sarasota had the best financial well-being, while Boulder topped all communities in physical well-being.

Communities With the Highest Well-Being in Each Element, 2014-2015

Among 190 Metropolitan Statistical Areas nationwide; first listed is highest

Purpose: Highest 5	Social: Highest 5	Financial: Highest 5	Community: Highest 5	Physical: Highest 5
Corpus Christi, Texas	Corpus Christi, Texas	North Port-Bradenton-Sarasota, Florida	Naples-Immokalee-Marco Island, Florida	Boulder, Colorado
McAllen-Edinburg-Mission, Texas	North Port-Bradenton-Sarasota, Florida	Urban Honolulu, Hawaii	Fort Collins, Colorado	Salinas, California
Salinas, California	Port St. Lucie, Florida	Anchorage, Alaska	San Luis Obispo-Paso Robles-Arroyo Grande, California	Town of Barnstable, Massachusetts
Naples-Immokalee-Marco Island, Florida	Town of Barnstable, Massachusetts	San Jose-Sunnyvale-Santa Clara, California	Asheville, North Carolina	Bridgeport-Stamford-Norwalk, Connecticut
El Paso, Texas	Daphne-Fairhope-Foley, Alabama	Boulder, Colorado	Daphne-Fairhope-Foley, Alabama	San Jose-Sunnyvale-Santa Clara, California

Gallup-Healthways Well-Being Index

"Metropolitan Statistical Areas" as defined by the U.S. Office of Management and Budget

GALLUP

Residents of Charleston had the lowest or second lowest well-being in three of the five elements: purpose, financial and physical. Similarly, Fort Smith was among the lowest three communities for social, financial and physical well-being. Flint, Michigan, which has suffered from a water purity crisis in recent months, was in the bottom three for community well-being, trailing only Fayetteville, North Carolina, and Rockford, Illinois. Flint has historically been among the lowest communities for overall well-being.

Communities With the Lowest Well-Being in Each Element, 2014-2015

Among 190 Metropolitan Statistical Areas nationwide; first listed is lowest

Purpose: Lowest 5	Social: Lowest 5	Financial: Lowest 5	Community: Lowest 5	Physical: Lowest 5
Worcester, Massachusetts-Connecticut	Fort Wayne, Indiana	Hickory-Lenoir-Morganton, North Carolina	Fayetteville, North Carolina	Charleston, West Virginia
Charleston, West Virginia	Fort Smith, Arkansas-Oklahoma	Charleston, West Virginia	Rockford, Illinois	Fort Smith, Arkansas-Oklahoma
Chico, California	Huntington-Ashland, West Virginia-Kentucky-Ohio	Fort Smith, Arkansas-Oklahoma	Flint, Michigan	Hickory-Lenoir-Morganton, North Carolina
Utica-Rome, New York	Charleston, West Virginia	Jackson, Mississippi	Binghamton, New York	Huntington-Ashland, West Virginia-Kentucky-Ohio
Burlington-South Burlington, Vermont	Lexington-Fayette, Kentucky	Savannah, Georgia	Toledo, Ohio	Chico, California

Gallup-Healthways Well-Being Index

"Metropolitan Statistical Areas" as defined by the U.S. Office of Management and Budget

GALLUP

San Jose-Sunnyvale-Santa Clara Tops All Large Metros in Well-Being

San Jose-Sunnyvale-Santa Clara residents had the highest well-being among the nation's 53 largest communities, those with at least 1 million residents. Austin-Round Rock, Texas, placed second among large communities. Both have commonly been among the top large metropolitan areas for overall well-being since measurement began in 2008.

Washington-Arlington-Alexandria, D.C.-Virginia-Maryland-West Virginia, historically one of the highest well-being cities in the U.S., had a lower score in 2014-2015 than in previous years, dropping to eighth among large communities and 38th overall nationally.

Detroit-Warren-Dearborn, Michigan, and Cleveland-Elyria, Ohio, join Indianapolis-Carmel-Anderson among the lowest three large communities.

Highest and Lowest Large Communities in Overall Well-Being, 2014-2015

Among 53 Metropolitan Statistical Areas with at least 1 million residents

Highest five	Well-Being Index score	Lowest five	Well-Being Index score
San Jose-Sunnyvale-Santa Clara, California	63.7	Indianapolis-Carmel-Anderson, Indiana	59.9
Austin-Round Rock, Texas	63.5	Detroit-Warren-Dearborn, Michigan	60.0
San Antonio-New Braunfels, Texas	63.3	Cleveland-Elyria, Ohio	60.2
San Diego-Carlsbad, California	63.3	Memphis, Tennessee-Mississippi-Arkansas	60.3
Minneapolis-St. Paul-Bloomington, Minnesota-Wisconsin	63.0	Cincinnati, Ohio-Kentucky-Indiana	60.4

Gallup-Healthways Well-Being Index

"Metropolitan Statistical Areas" as defined by the U.S. Office of Management and Budget

GALLUP

Implications

U.S. communities are at the front lines of American well-being. City leaders are often able to create and sustain a culture of well-being in ways that leaders of more geographically diverse states cannot. This is critical, as well-being can have a very real effect on a wide variety of outcomes for a community. For example, communities with low well-being, as a whole, have residents with significantly higher obesity rates and double the heart attack incidence, thus incurring substantially higher healthcare costs. Conversely, communities with high well-being tend to have residents who learn and do interesting things daily, have safe places to exercise, have high energy levels and believe that their water is safe to drink.

One area that is critical to creating and maintaining high well-being in communities is jobs. Globally, individuals who report that now is a "good time" to find a job have substantially higher well-being than those who do not, and those who are employed full time for an employer evaluate their lives much better than others in the workforce do. In addition, being unemployed or involuntarily employed part time has been linked to depression, a common characteristic of individuals and communities with low well-being. The economic vibrancy of communities, in turn, reflects these broader relationships. San Jose-Sunnyvale-Santa Clara, for example, leads the nation in economic confidence, and seven of the top 10 large metros nationally in economic confidence are among the highest 12 large metro areas in well-being.

As community leaders think about strategies to improve residents' lives, they should simultaneously consider the relationship between good jobs and well-being. Good jobs in a community boost the well-being of its residents, and residents with higher well-being attract potential employers seeking a workforce that has better job performance, less absenteeism and lower healthcare utilization.

Read the State of Community Well-Being report to see the full rankings.

Survey Methods

Results are based on a subset of 353,983 telephone interviews with U.S. adults across all 50 states and the District of Columbia, conducted Jan. 2, 2014, through Dec. 30, 2015. In 2014, 176,702 interviews were conducted nationally; in 2015, 177,281 interviews were conducted. Gallup conducts 500 telephone interviews daily, resulting in a sample that projects to an estimated 95% of all U.S. adults. Metropolitan Statistical Areas (MSAs) are based on U.S. Office of Management and Budget definitions. Only MSAs with at least 300 completed interviews are reported, and results for each MSA are uniquely weighted according to Nielsen Claritas demographic targets.

The margin of sampling error for the reported communities ranges from ±1.7 points for the least populated to ±0.3 points for the most heavily populated. All reported margins of sampling error include computed design effects due to weighting.

February 22, 2016
FOUR NATIONS TOP U.S.'S GREATEST ENEMY LIST

by Jim Norman

Story Highlights

- *Americans most likely to name North Korea, Russia, China or Iran*
- *All four seen as important military or nuclear threats to U.S.*
- *Wider spread among nations named as enemies than in earlier years*

WASHINGTON, D.C. – Americans are less likely than ever to agree on which country is the greatest enemy of the U.S., but the four countries that crowd the top of the list this year are the same as in Gallup polls in 2014 and 2015: North Korea (16%), Russia (15%), Iran (14%) and China (12%).

N. Korea, Russia, Iran, China Rotate Top Spots on "Greatest Enemy" List

What one country anywhere in the world do you consider to be the United States' greatest enemy today? (open-ended)

	2014	2015	2016
	%	%	%
North Korea	16	15	16
Russia	9	18	15
Iran	16	9	14
China	20	12	12
Countries in which ISIS operates	0	4	5
Iraq	7	8	5
Afghanistan	5	3	4
Syria	3	4	4
Other	13	15	11
None	2	1	4
No opinion	9	12	11

GALLUP

Americans are continuing last year's trend of identifying a wide array of entities – including, for the second year in a row, the Islamic State group – as the United States' greatest enemy.

- At least 5% of the public named one of six different entities – five nations and the Islamic State group – as the top threat.
- The 16% total for North Korea is the lowest percentage for any country listed as the top threat since Gallup began asking the question. Russia's 18% last year had been the lowest, and China's 20% two years ago was the lowest before that. (The country named by the highest percentage of Americans since 2001 is Iraq, which accounted for 38% of the responses in 2001.)

Though the responses are more dispersed, there is continuity at the top. North Korea, Iran and China have consistently ranked high on the list of enemies, dating back to 2005. Americans have not as consistently regarded Russia as the greatest U.S. enemy, but that nation led the list last year.

Majorities Dislike All Four, but Make Clear Distinctions

Gallup's February World Affairs survey features two other updates on Americans' views of foreign countries: favorability ratings and the perceived economic and military threat that a country poses. A majority of Americans view each of the four countries at the top of the "greatest enemy" list unfavorably. Majorities also see each of the four as threatening the U.S. through military power, economic power or the development of nuclear weapons.

But the basic ratings of the countries are not monolithic. Americans are more than five times as likely to have a favorable opinion of China (44%) as to have one of North Korea (8%).

Favorability Trends for the Four Countries Americans Rate as "Greatest U.S. Enemies" in 2016

Percentage of Americans with a favorable view of each country

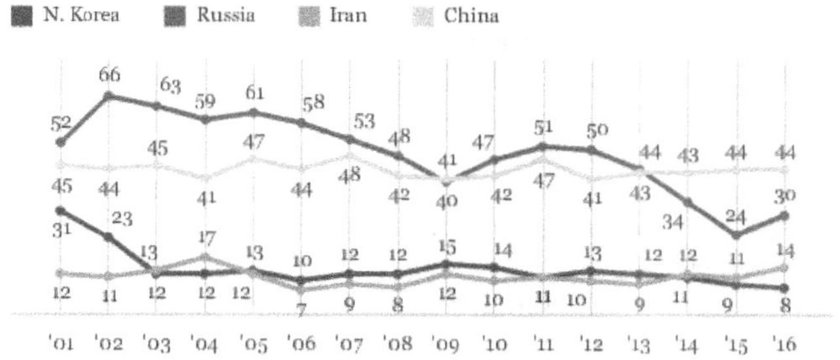

GALLUP

Likewise, they are almost twice as likely to consider the development of nuclear weapons by Iran (75%) as a "critical" threat as they are to see Russia's military power (39%) that way.

Here's a closer look at the four:

North Korea: The nation named most often as the greatest U.S. enemy this year also has the most unfavorable rating of the 21 countries and territories rated – and has had the lowest rating for three straight years. A majority of U.S. adults (58%) regard its military power as a "critical" threat.

Russia: Only four years ago, half of the American public viewed Russia favorably, and only 2% viewed it as the United States' greatest enemy. But a series of events pitting the U.S. and Russia against each other has soured the relationship. Only 30% now have a favorable view of Russia, and 86% regard Russia's military power as either an important (47%) or a critical threat (39%).

Iran: Iran topped the "greatest enemy" list five straight times from 2006 to 2012. China moved ahead of it on the 2014 list, as the percentage naming Iran fell from 32% in 2012 to 16% in 2014. It shrank again to 9% in 2015 before the slight increase to 14% this year. Meanwhile, Americans are only slightly more likely to view Iran favorably now (14%) than they were in 2012 (10%), and 75% think the development of nuclear weapons by Iran constitutes a critical threat to the U.S.

China: A slim majority of Americans (52%) view China unfavorably, but 87% view its military power as an important or critical threat to the U.S.; 86% feel the same about China's economic power.

Bottom Line

Though no one country dominates Americans' thinking when they are asked to name the United States' greatest enemy, they most frequently mention North Korea, Russia, Iran and China, and all have ranked highly in recent years.

For the past two years, strong majorities of Americans have seen each of the four as threatening to the vital interests of the U.S. in some way – the military power of Russia and North Korea, the military and the economic power of China and the threat of nuclear weapons for Iran.

With almost three-fourths (73%) of the public thinking all four nations are, at the least, an important threat to the U.S., the reason no single nation is thought of as the greatest enemy may not be because Americans see so few threats, but because they see so many.

Survey Methods

Results for this Gallup poll are based on telephone interviews conducted Feb. 3-7, 2016, on the Gallup U.S. Daily survey, with a random sample of 1,021 adults, aged 18 and older, living in all 50 U.S. states and the District of Columbia. For results based on the total sample of national adults, the margin of sampling error is ±4 percentage points at the 95% confidence level. All reported margins of sampling error include computed design effects for weighting.

February 23, 2016

"DISHONEST" AND "SOCIALIST" LEAD U.S. REACTIONS TO DEMS

by Frank Newport and Lydia Saad

Story Highlights

- *Top overall impression of Clinton is "dishonest"*
- *Her highest positive is for being capable, qualified*
- *Sanders most commonly identified as "socialist"*

PRINCETON, N.J. – Hillary Clinton and Bernie Sanders have multifaceted images among the American public. But the most common responses Americans give when asked to say what comes to mind when they think of each are "dishonest" and "dislike her" for Clinton, and "socialist" and "old" for Sanders. On the positive side, a fair number of Americans view Clinton as capable and experienced, and Sanders as a fresh face and honest.

Top Unaided Reactions to "Hillary Clinton"

	U.S. adults
	%
Dishonest/Liar/Don't trust her/Poor character	21
Dislike her	9
Like her	8
Capable of being president/Qualified	7
Criminal/Crooked/Thief/Belongs in jail	7
Experienced	5
Good politician	3
Strong	3
Wouldn't be good for the country	3

Results mentioned by fewer than 3% are not shown

Feb. 13-14, 2016

GALLUP

Top Unaided Reactions to "Bernie Sanders"

	U.S. adults
	%
Socialist	12
Older/Aged	6
Favorable	5
Fresh face/New ideas/Change for the better	5
Honest/Trustworthy	4
Crazy/Delusional/Idiot/Unrealistic	4
Unfavorable	4
Cares about the people/For the middle class/Fair	3
I like him	3
Liberal/Progressive	3
Strong/Opinionated	3
Communist	3
Giving money away/Free stuff/Expensive ideas/Idealist	3

Results mentioned by fewer than 3% are not shown
Feb. 13-14, 2016

GALLUP

These findings are from a Feb. 13-14 survey. Separately, Gallup Daily tracking of the presidential candidates' favorable ratings shows that only 10% of Americans do not know enough about Clinton to say whether they have a favorable or unfavorable opinion of her, and 20% have no opinion of Sanders. In line with that, 12% of Americans could not articulate a top-of-mind impression of Clinton in the latest poll, while nearly one in five could not think of anything to say about Sanders.

Negative Comments Outnumber Positives for Clinton

These top-of-mind impressions clearly show that negative perceptions about Clinton's character and trustworthiness continue to dog her.

In addition to the 21% of responses in the "dishonest/don't trust her" category, another 7% of Americans use even stronger words in a similar negative vein, including "criminal," "crooked" and "thief." Nine percent say they dislike her. Smaller percentages (shown at the end of this article) associate her with Bill Clinton, with the controversy surrounding her use of a private email server while secretary of state and with the Benghazi terrorist attack.

The perceptions of Hillary Clinton as dishonest are not new. When Gallup asked the same question in 2008, "dishonest" was Americans' most frequent response. And, in a Gallup poll conducted in September 2015, Americans overwhelmingly referred to the email scandal when asked to mention what they had read or heard about Clinton.

On the positive side, 8% of Americans say they like her, 7% describe her as capable and qualified, 5% as experienced, 3% as strong and 3% as a good politician. Smaller percentages consider her honest or smart.

Overall, 29% of Americans offer a positive observation about Clinton while 51% express something negative. The rest have either a neutral comment or no opinion. This loosely fits with her overall image among national adults as measured on Gallup tracking, which is 42% favorable and 51% unfavorable.

Sanders' National Image Is More Mixed; Many Cite His Ideology

Sanders is a self-avowed democratic socialist and, accordingly, 12% of Americans think first of the word "socialist" when they hear his name; another 3% say "communist." Six percent of top-of-mind reactions to Sanders center on his age (he is 74 and would be 75 when inaugurated).

Clear-cut negative impressions of Sanders include people saying they view him unfavorably; describing him as "crazy" or "delusional"; and claiming that he would provide government freebies or simply give money away.

On the positive side, in addition to views that Sanders is a fresh face and honest, Americans mention that he cares about people and the middle class, that he is personable and that he is intelligent.

The public's comments about Sanders can be summarized as 26% positive and 20% negative, with the rest categorized as neutral, other or no opinion. The neutral grouping includes a significant number of references to "socialist," "liberal," "higher taxes" and his being older – which, as noted, can be construed as either positive or negative, depending on the respondents' perspectives. Most of the references to Sanders' being a "socialist" come from Republicans, and Americans rated "a socialist" as the least appealing type of presidential candidate in a recent Gallup poll. But because some Democrats also call him a socialist, the response was categorized as neutral.

Democrats' Impressions Are More Positive, but Touch on Same Themes

In this primary and caucus stage of the presidential campaign, the constituency that matters for these two candidates is Democrats. Clinton has a broadly favorable image among Democrats and Democratic leaners in Gallup tracking, and Democrats' most frequently mentioned responses when asked what comes to mind when they think of her are positive, as would be expected. These include the broad positives ("I like her"), that she is capable of being president and that she is experienced. These are followed by views of her as dishonest, with positive responses below those.

Overall, Democrats' top-of-mind comments about Clinton split 52% positive and 27% negative.

Just 4% of Democrats mention "socialist" when they talk about Sanders, significantly less than is the case among the national adult population. Democrats are most likely, perhaps paradoxically, to talk about Sanders' age and to say he would bring fresh, new ideas to the presidency. Other comments Democrats make about Sanders are general positives: that he cares about middle-class people, that he is honest and that he is strong in his views.

Altogether, 38% of Democrats' comments about Sanders can be described as clearly positive and 12% as clearly negative, with 28% classified as neutral.

Republicans, including Republican-leaning independents, offer mostly negative reactions. Overall, 77% of Republicans' top-of-mind impressions of Clinton are negative, with their most frequent responses focusing on views of her as dishonest and crooked. By contrast, 29% of Republicans' views of Sanders are negative, with many of the rest either neutral or in the "no opinion" category.

Implications

Although many Americans cannot articulate much that is of substance when asked about Sanders, the most frequent comments about him revolve around his unique ideological branding as a democratic socialist and his advanced age. By contrast, the comments about Clinton are more personal in nature, including a large number of mentions of her lack of honesty and character, along with positive associations as a competent and well-qualified public servant.

Unfortunately for Clinton, the negative associations currently outnumber the positive ones by a sizable margin, and even among Democrats, the negatives are fairly high. Throughout her more-than two-decades-long career in the public eye as first lady, U.S. senator, secretary of state, two-time presidential candidate and bestselling author, she has acquired a fairly well-developed image among Americans – for better and for worse.

Survey Methods

Results for this Gallup poll are based on telephone interviews conducted Feb. 13-14, 2016, on the Gallup U.S. Daily survey, with a random sample of 1,014 adults, aged 18 and older, living in all 50 U.S. states and the District of Columbia. For results based on the total sample of national adults, the margin of sampling error is ±4 percentage points at the 95% confidence level. For results based on the sample of 424 Democrats and Democratic-leaning independents, the margin of error for responses near 50% is ±6 percentage points at the 95% confidence level. For responses near 10%, the margin of error is ±4 percentage points. For responses below 5%, the margin of error is no more than ±2 percentage points. For results based on the sample of 472 Republicans and Republican-leaning independents, the margin of error for responses near 50% is ±6 percentage points at the 95% confidence level. For responses near 10%, the margin of error is ±4 percentage points. For responses below 5%, the margin of error is no more than ±2 percentage points. All reported margins of sampling error include computed design effects for weighting.

Americans' Top-of-Mind Reactions to Hillary Clinton

What comes to your mind when you think about Hillary Clinton? (Open-ended)

	U.S. adults	Democrats/ Democratic leaners	Republicans/ Republican leaners
	%	%	%
POSITIVE (Net 29%)			
Like her	8	13	2
Capable of being president/Qualified	7	13	2
Experienced	5	9	2
Good politician	3	5	0
Strong	3	5	0
Honest/Trustworthy/Good morals	2	3	0
Intelligent/Smart	2	3	0
Like her views	1	2	0
NEUTRAL (Net 6%)			
Would be first woman president	2	4	2
Democrat	1	1	1
Not electable/People aren't ready for a female president	1	2	1
Outspoken/Loud and opinionated	1	1	1
NEGATIVE (Net 51%)			
Dishonest/Liar/Don't trust her/Poor character	21	8	35
Dislike her	9	4	15
Criminal/Crooked/Thief/Belongs in jail	7	3	13
Wouldn't be good for the country	3	2	5
Emails/Email scandal	2	1	2
Riding Bill's shirttails	2	1	3
Unqualified/Incompetent	2	3	1
Benghazi	1	0	2
Dislike her views	1	2	1
Power hungry/Pushy	1	2	1
Too liberal	1	1	2
Wishy-washy/Doesn't take a clear stand on issues	1	1	1
All the baggage with Bill and the past history	0	0	1
Other	5	7	4
Nothing/No opinion	12	10	8
	104%	106%	105%

Adds to more than 100% because of multiple mentions

Feb. 13-14, 2016

GALLUP

February 24, 2016
AMERICANS' PERCEPTIONS OF OBAMA'S WORLD STANDING IMPROVE

by Justin McCarthy

Story Highlights

- *45% of Americans say Barack Obama is respected internationally*
- *GOP no more likely than last year to say Obama is respected*
- *Obama's approval on handling foreign affairs up slightly*

WASHINGTON, D.C. – Forty-five percent of Americans believe world leaders respect President Barack Obama, up from 37% a year ago. Still, the percentage who say international leaders respect Obama falls short of the 51% to 67% who held this view from 2009 to 2013.

Americans' Perceptions of President Barack Obama's World Standing

Do you think leaders of other countries around the world have respect for Barack Obama, or do you think they don't have much respect for him?

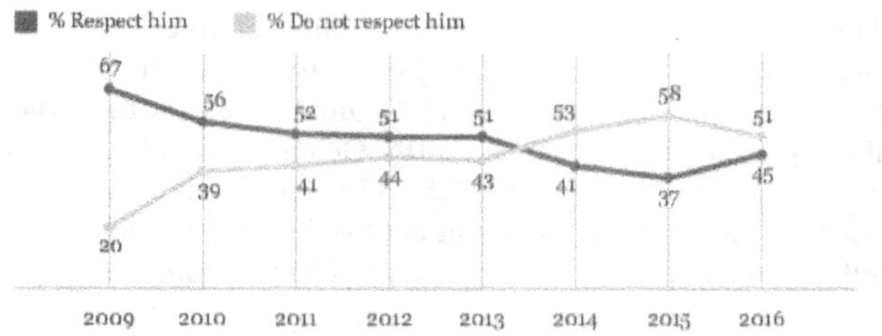

GALLUP

The latest world-respect figure, from Gallup's Feb. 3-7 World Affairs poll, represents the first time in Gallup's eight-year trend that Americans' perceptions of Obama's world standing have improved. When Obama first took office in 2009, 67% of Americans believed he was respected by leaders of other countries. Within two years, the percentage holding this view dropped to 52%, and by 2014 it fell to 41%.

Perceptions that Obama is respected on the world stage bottomed out last year after the Islamic State group emerged as a serious threat to the U.S., and as Russia-U.S. relations became increasingly tense over Russia's involvement in Ukraine. Obama was also grappling with the fallout of Edward Snowden's leaks of classified information.

In the past year, U.S.-Russia tensions over Ukraine eased after a ceasefire helped slow hostilities in the region. Additionally, Obama succeeded in reaching a major international agreement with Iran to limit that country's ability to develop nuclear weapons, although that agreement remains controversial.

Americans' views of Obama's international standing are divided across party lines. While about four in five Democrats say foreign leaders respect the president, only about one in seven Republicans agree. And a majority of independents say leaders of other countries do *not* respect Obama.

The rise in Americans' belief that Obama is respected on the world stage stems from increased percentages of Democrats and independents holding this view today compared with a year ago. Republicans are essentially unchanged.

Perceptions of Barack Obama's World Standing, by Party ID

Do you think leaders of other countries around the world have respect for Barack Obama, or do you think they don't have much respect for him? (% Respect him)

	2015	2016	Change
	%	%	(pct. pts.)
National adults	37	45	+8
Republicans	16	14	-2
Independents	32	43	+11
Democrats	61	79	+18

Feb. 3-7, 2016

GALLUP

Obama's Approval Rating on Handling Foreign Affairs Up Slightly

Americans' approval of Obama's handling of foreign affairs has also edged up compared with last February's measure. Thirty-nine percent of Americans approve of Obama's work on the issue, up slightly from 36% in February 2015. Obama's overall job approval rating was 50% in this year's Feb. 3-7 survey, compared with 46% last February – so the uptick in approval on foreign affairs partly reflects a more positive view of the president overall.

Approval of President Barack Obama's Handling of Foreign Affairs

Do you approve or disapprove of the way Barack Obama is handling foreign affairs?

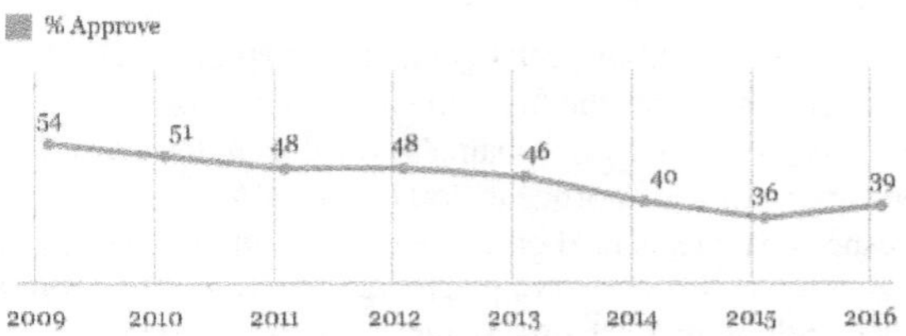

All figures shown are from February polls.

GALLUP

In addition to the annual February updates, Gallup has measured Obama's approval rating on foreign affairs numerous other times during the years since he first took office. Overall, his foreign affairs approval rating has generally waned over the course of his presidency but has spiked a few times. His approval rating on handling foreign affairs was highest in his first year in office, at 61% in March 2009. It fell below 50% for most of 2010 and 2011, but rose to 51% after the killing of Osama bin Laden in May 2011.

Bottom Line

Obama's securing of an Iran nuclear deal may have increased Democrats' faith that the president is respected by international leaders, which boosted Americans' views overall. But while perceptions of the respect Obama receives from foreign leaders has improved, a majority of Americans still feel he is *not* respected, and Republicans' views have not improved. Americans' political views, which are especially polarized in an election year, likely affect their opinions of Obama's standing among world leaders.

Obama's approval rating on handling foreign affairs is not the lowest recorded for him, but it is substantially lower than earlier in his presidency. Over the course of his time in office, Obama's shift in focus moved from killing bin Laden and exiting Iraq to arguably more complicated matters such as the rise of the Islamic State group, tensions with Russia and civil war in Syria. While the Iran nuclear deal may have boosted Americans' perception of Obama as a president who can negotiate with other leaders, the unpopularity of the deal itself among Americans may have been a factor in why his approval rating on foreign affairs didn't receive a similarly sized increase.

Historical data are available in Gallup Analytics.

Survey Methods

Results for this Gallup poll are based on telephone interviews conducted Feb. 3-7, 2016, with a random sample of 1,021 adults, aged 18 and older, living in all 50 U.S. states and the District of Columbia. For results based on the total sample of national adults, the margin of sampling error is ±4 percentage points at the 95% confidence level. All reported margins of sampling error include computed design effects for weighting.

Each sample of national adults includes a minimum quota of 60% cellphone respondents and

February 25, 2016

FRANCE'S FAVORABLE RATING IN U.S. ZOOMS TO 87%, A NEW HIGH

by Lydia Saad

Story Highlights

- *France's favorable rating rises five points in past year to 87%*
- *Increase in recent years driven by improved ratings from Republicans*
- *France now Americans' third-highest-rated country*

PRINCETON, N.J. – France's favorable rating in the U.S. is now 87%, up five percentage points from a year ago and marking a record high for France in Gallup's 25-year trend. This continues the gradual improvement in France's image in the U.S. after that nation's favorability plummeted at the start of the Iraq War in 2003.

Americans' Overall Opinion of France, 1991-2016

What is your overall opinion of [France]? Is it very favorable, mostly favorable, mostly unfavorable or very unfavorable?

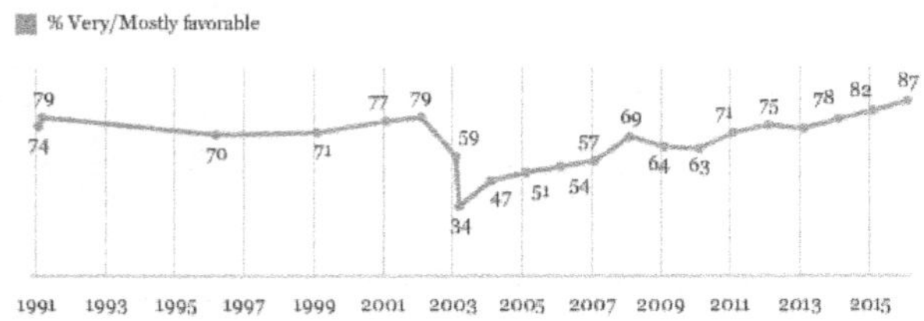

GALLUP

This year's reading comes three months after terrorists associated with the Islamic State group conducted a series of deadly attacks in and around Paris, killing 130. The 82% of Americans viewing France favorably a year ago was recorded a month after terrorists killed 12 people in a mass shooting at the *Charlie Hebdo* magazine office building in Paris.

The latest results are from Gallup's Feb. 3-7 World Affairs poll.

France now ranks third in overall favorability with Americans among major countries the U.S. interacts with on the world stage. Only Great Britain and Canada earned higher total favorable scores this year. However, France still falls well short of those countries in the percentage of Americans viewing each very favorably. Its 29% "very favorable" score this year is similar to the 30% for Germany, which places fourth in overall favorability, but still trails Great Britain's 43% and Canada's 56%.

Top Five Countries in Americans' Favorability Ratings in 2016

	Very favorable	Mostly favorable	Mostly unfavorable	Very unfavorable	TOTAL favorable	TOTAL unfavorable
	%	%	%	%	%	%
Canada	56	37	3	2	93	5
Great Britain	43	47	3	1	90	4
France	29	58	6	2	87	8
Germany	30	55	8	2	85	10
Japan	29	53	8	4	82	12

Feb. 3-7, 2016

GALLUP

Republicans' Rating Rises Most Since 2013

France's image fell much more steeply among Republicans than Democrats at the start of the Iraq War in 2003, stemming from that nation's opposition to Republican President George W. Bush's effort to win U.N. support for use of force against Iraq. Between February 2002 and March 2003, Republicans' favorability toward France dropped more than 60 points, from 81% to 20%, versus a 34-point decline among Democrats, from 79% to 45%.

A sizable partisan gap in France's ratings persisted throughout the first decade of its image recovery, but during the past three years, the gap has nearly closed. That reflects Republicans' finally closing in on Democrats' high level of favorability toward France. This may be the result of France's support for the U.S.-led coalition against the Islamic State in Syria in 2013, as well as sympathy for France stemming from the recent terrorist attacks.

Americans' Overall View of France, by Party ID -- % Very/Mostly Favorable

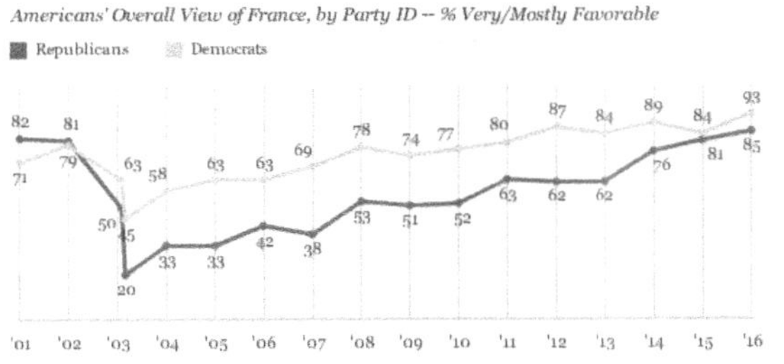

Note: Independents not shown

GALLUP

Bottom Line

After diplomatic differences in 2003 soured relations between the two countries, France and the U.S. have found a common interest in combating international terrorism, and the mission has become personal for both countries. This has helped bring about a major turnaround in how Americans view what Secretary of State John Kerry has called the United States' "oldest ally." France's image was already on the mend, but the significant increase in the percentage of Republicans viewing France favorably over the past three years has pushed its image to new heights.

Survey Methods

Results for this Gallup poll are based on telephone interviews conducted Feb. 3-7, 2016, with a random sample of 1,021 adults, aged 18 and older, living in all 50 U.S. states and the District of Columbia. For results based on the total sample of national adults, the margin of sampling error is ±4 percentage points at the 95% confidence level. All reported margins of sampling error include computed design effects for weighting.

February 25, 2016
MAJORITY OF AMERICANS SAY THE WORLD VIEWS THE U.S. FAVORABLY

by Rebecca Riffkin

Story Highlights

- *54% think the rest of the world views the U.S. favorably*
- *Views have been consistent since end of Iraq War in 2011*
- *Majority dissatisfied with the United States' global position*

WASHINGTON, D.C. – Slightly more than half of Americans, 54%, believe the rest of the world views the U.S. favorably, while 45% believe the world views the U.S. unfavorably. This is consistent with how Americans have perceived the nation's global image for the past several years. But it is a change from the last years of George W. Bush's presidency and the first year of Barack Obama's administration, when the majority thought the world viewed the U.S. unfavorably.

Americans' Perceptions of How U.S. Rates in the Eyes of the World

In general, how do you think the United States rates in the eyes of the world -- very favorably, somewhat favorably, somewhat unfavorably or very unfavorably?

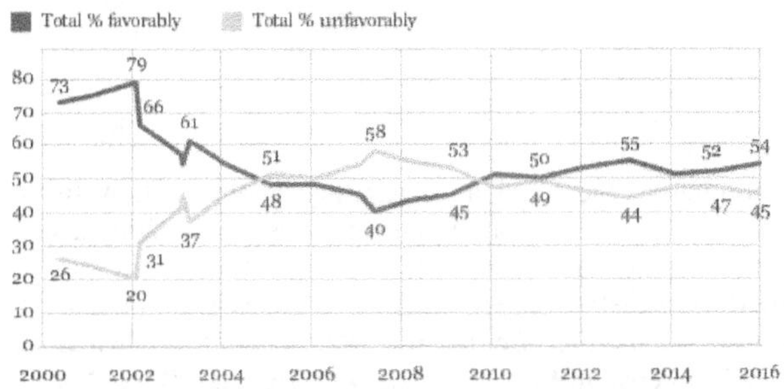

GALLUP

From 2000 until 2004, strong majorities of Americans said the world viewed the U.S. favorably. This sentiment peaked in early 2002, five months after the 9/11 attacks, when 79% said the world had a favorable view of the U.S. and 20% an unfavorable view. But Americans' perceptions of the country's image slowly worsened as the U.S. entered the Iraq War with opposition from some in the international community.

By 2005, slightly more Americans said the world viewed the U.S. unfavorably than favorably, the first time attitudes had tilted negative. Attitudes continued to sour and in June 2007, 40% said they thought the rest of the world viewed the U.S. favorably, the lowest such reading in the 16-year trend. This coincided with a sharp increase of U.S. ground troops in Iraq and followed earlier revelations of the U.S. military's poor treatment of Iraqi prisoners at Abu Ghraib and the absence of weapons of mass destruction. Furthermore, in 2007 and 2008, Americans' views that the U.S. was rated unfavorably may have stemmed from a general weariness with President Bush and the war in Iraq.

In 2010 and especially 2011, Americans were torn over whether the world viewed the U.S. favorably or unfavorably. But since the official end of the Iraq War in 2011, a clear majority of Americans have generally expressed the opinion that the world views the

U.S. favorably. Part of the recent increase in perceived favorability may be related to Obama's foreign policy decisions – which have largely favored opening relations with other nations, notably Cuba and Iran – as well as a major new trade deal. Additionally, Obama's perceived popularity abroad improved this year and is generally up from Bush's popularity abroad during his second term.

In the latest poll, more Democrats (68%) than Republicans (39%) believe the rest of the world views the U.S. favorably – not surprising with a Democrat in the White House.

A Majority of Americans Are Dissatisfied With U.S.'s Global Position

At the same time that Americans believe the international community views the U.S. favorably, they are largely dissatisfied with the United States' position in the world. Currently, 36% are satisfied and 63% are dissatisfied. A majority of Americans have been dissatisfied since 2004, but the percentage who are dissatisfied is down slightly from its 2008 peak of 68%.

Americans' Satisfaction With United States' Position in the World

On the whole, would you say that you are satisfied or dissatisfied with the position of the United States in the world today?

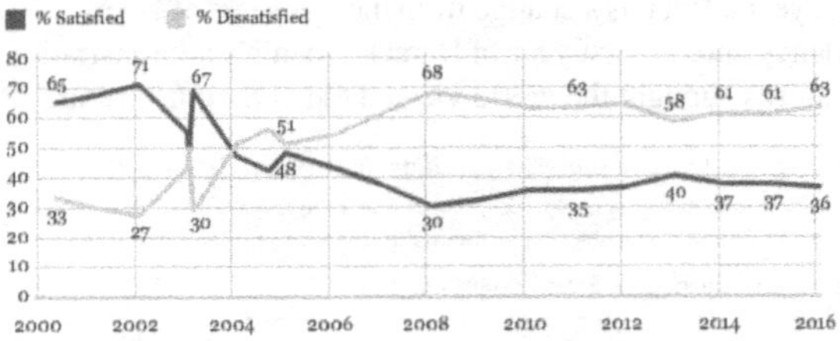

Trend since 2000

GALLUP

Similar to the trend in Americans' views on how the world rates the U.S., satisfaction with the country's international standing was high in the early years of the 2000s and fell in the mid-2000s. Americans' satisfaction with the United States' position in the world spiked in the months after the Iraq War began, from 48% in February 2003 to 69% in March. It remained high at 67% in April 2003, though by February 2004, satisfaction was back down to 47%.

Democrats (52%) are currently more likely than Republicans (19%) to be satisfied with the U.S.'s position in the world. Still, only a slim majority of Democrats are satisfied, suggesting some level of concern about the U.S.'s position even among members of the president's own party.

Bottom Line

Although Americans' perceptions of the United States' global image have been at least partially repaired since the height of the Iraq War, the public remains dissatisfied with the country's position in the world. The latter likely reflects public uncertainty stemming from a mounting number of complex international issues: terrorism, the Syrian refugee crisis, North Korea's rocket launches, and Russian and Chinese expansionism. Americans themselves have become less likely than they were a few years ago to say the U.S. is the No. 1 military power in the world. Furthermore, approval of U.S. leadership is down in both Africa and Asia, and U.S. leadership on average has never received majority approval from those polled globally.

While a majority of Americans believe the world views the U.S. favorably, Americans have been consistently dissatisfied with the U.S.'s position in the world. This aligns with the views of most Republican presidential candidates this year – who say the U.S., especially the military, is weak, while Obama strongly disagrees. The two Democratic candidates often spar over their respective votes about going to war in Iraq, but do not express much disagreement with Obama's foreign policy decisions.

Historical data are available in Gallup Analytics.

Survey Methods

Results for this Gallup poll are based on telephone interviews conducted Feb. 3-7, 2016, with a random sample of 1,021 adults, aged 18 and older, living in all 50 U.S. states and the District of Columbia. For results based on the total sample of national adults, the margin of sampling error is ±4 percentage points at the 95% confidence level. All reported margins of sampling error include computed design effects for weighting.

February 26, 2016

RHODE ISLAND, MICHIGAN RESIDENTS LEAST SATISFIED WITH ROADS

by Jeffrey M. Jones

Story Highlights

- *31% of Rhode Island and 35% of Michigan residents are satisfied*
- *Satisfaction with local roads highest in North Dakota, at 81%*
- *State spending on roads is positively related to satisfaction levels*

PRINCETON, N.J. – Rhode Island (31%) and Michigan (35%) residents are less likely to be satisfied with the roads and highways where they live than are residents in any other state. North Dakota has the highest satisfaction at 81%, followed closely by Wyoming, Utah and Kansas.

Satisfaction With Local Roads and Highways -- Top and Bottom States

In the city or area where you live, are you satisfied or dissatisfied with the roads and highways?

	% Satisfied	% Dissatisfied
BOTTOM STATES		
Rhode Island	31	68
Michigan	35	65
Hawaii	38	61
West Virginia	39	61
Louisiana	40	60
Oklahoma	42	58
South Carolina	47	53
Pennsylvania	49	51
New York	54	45
Mississippi	54	46
TOP STATES		
North Dakota	81	19
Wyoming	78	21
Utah	77	22
Kansas	77	23
South Dakota	74	25
Idaho	74	26
Nevada	74	26
Montana	74	26
Minnesota	73	26
Arizona	72	28

2015 Gallup 50-State poll

GALLUP

The results are based on Gallup's 2015 50-State poll, which consists of interviews with at least 500 residents in each state. The data for each state appear at the end of the article.

States vary widely in how much they spend on road construction and maintenance, and how they raise that revenue. There is a modest positive correlation between state spending on roads per capita and residents' satisfaction with roads – states that spend more tend to have higher satisfaction.

The 10 states spending the most per capita on roads average 67% satisfaction, compared with 61% satisfaction among the 10 states spending the least per capita on roads. The middle 30 states average 60% satisfaction.

North Dakota, Wyoming and Utah rank among the top-spending states on roads and, along with Kansas, are the states where residents are most satisfied. Michigan spent the least per capita on roads, according to the most recent data from the U.S. Census Bureau, with Rhode Island ranking in the bottom third of states.

Rhode Island and Michigan have consistently ranked among the states with the worst-quality roads, based on studies of road conditions from government agencies and independent research organizations. Michigan voters named roads as the most important problem facing the state in a 2014 poll. State political leaders there have struggled to find a way to increase spending on roads. The governor and state lawmakers agreed on a deal in late 2014 that asked voters to approve an increase in state sales and gasoline taxes to help pay for road improvements, among other things, but voters overwhelmingly rejected that ballot proposal. Last fall, the governor and legislature finally agreed on legislation to raise the gas tax and increase vehicle registration fees to raise revenues to fix the roads.

In Rhode Island, the governor signed legislation this month to impose driver tolls on trucks as a way to raise money to fix the state's ailing roads and bridges.

Hawaii Only Western State With Below-Average Satisfaction

Many of the states with above-average resident satisfaction with local roads and highways are in the Upper Midwest and Upper West regions of the country. In the West, all the states have above-average or average satisfaction except Hawaii. The remaining states with below-average satisfaction are in the South and East, along with Michigan in the Midwest.

Many of the states whose residents are most likely to be satisfied with local roads and highways are less densely populated. An analysis of the data confirms there is a negative correlation between state population density and satisfaction with roads – more densely

In the city or area where you live, are you satisfied or dissatisfied with the roads and highways?

	% Satisfied	% Dissatisfied	State Spending on Roads Per Capita
North Dakota	81	19	$754
Wyoming	78	21	$968
Utah	77	22	$541
Kansas	77	23	$355
South Dakota	74	25	$604
Idaho	74	26	$441
Nevada	74	26	$226
Montana	74	26	$724
Minnesota	73	26	$275
Arizona	72	28	$226
Wisconsin	71	29	$302
Florida	71	29	$264
New Hampshire	70	29	$394
Delaware	70	30	$571
Missouri	70	30	$336
North Carolina	69	31	$297
Alaska	68	31	$2,032
Oregon	67	32	$348
Georgia	67	33	$211
Illinois	66	34	$412
Kentucky	66	34	$411
Nebraska	65	34	$357
Tennessee	65	35	$236
Alabama	65	35	$273
California	64	36	$231
Vermont	64	36	$540
New Mexico	64	36	$407
Maryland	62	37	$355
Iowa	62	38	$445
Texas	61	38	$220
Washington	61	39	$349
Virginia	60	40	$295
Indiana	60	40	$289
Colorado	60	40	$423
Maine	60	40	$201
Ohio	60	40	$214
Massachusetts	59	41	$267
Arkansas	58	41	$265
New Jersey	57	43	$306
Connecticut	55	44	$301
Mississippi	54	46	$357
New York	54	45	$239
Pennsylvania	49	51	$530
South Carolina	47	53	$252
Oklahoma	42	58	$415
Louisiana	40	60	$440
West Virginia	39	61	$618
Hawaii	38	61	$345
Michigan	35	65	$154
Rhode Island	31	68	$279

Satisfaction data from 2015 Gallup 50-State poll; state spending on roads from 2010 U.S. census

GALLUP

populated states' residents tend to be less satisfied with road and highway conditions.

Implications

Solid infrastructure, including well-designed and well-maintained roads and bridges, are key to the functioning of a local economy. But supporting a state's infrastructure requires a significant investment from the government, and states differ in terms of how much revenue they are willing to raise from citizens and on what projects they are willing to spend it. While there isn't a strong relationship between state spending on roads and state residents' satisfaction with local roads and highways, states that spend more tend to have modestly higher satisfaction than states that spend less.

In two states in which residents are least satisfied with the condition of roads and highways – Rhode Island and Michigan – state lawmakers have recently agreed on plans to greatly increase the amount of money the state devotes toward upkeep of its roads and bridges. Other states with low satisfaction, including West Virginia and South Carolina, are also considering measures to increase funding for roads, but passage of these measures is far from assured.

These data are available in Gallup Analytics.

Survey Methods

Results for this Gallup poll are based on telephone interviews conducted March 30-Dec. 22, 2015, with random samples of approximately 500 adults, aged 18 and older, living in each of the 50 U.S. states. Data are weighted to account for unequal selection probability, nonresponse and double coverage of landline and cellphone users in the two sampling frames. Data are also weighted to state estimates of gender, age, race, Hispanic ethnicity, education and phone status (cellphone only, landline only, both, and cellphone mostly).

For results based on the total sample of adults in each state, the margin of sampling error is ±6 percentage points at the 95% confidence level. All reported margins of sampling error include computed design effects for weighting.

February 29, 2016
IMAGES OF CRUZ AND TRUMP FALL AS GOP CAMPAIGN HEATS UP

by Frank Newport

Story Highlights

- *Cruz's image among GOP has fallen more than any GOP candidate*
- *Rubio remains far more popular than Trump, Cruz*
- *Trump's popularity among Republicans is near his campaign low*

PRINCETON, N.J. – Ted Cruz's and Donald Trump's images among Republicans have dropped to all-time lows in recent days as exchanges between the Republican presidential candidates have turned highly negative and personal. Cruz's net favorable rating among Republicans is now +14, his lowest to date and essentially the same as Trump's +15. Marco Rubio's image is less positive than it has been at previous points in the campaign, but at +34, it is the same as in early January. Rubio's net favorable score is now twice as high as the scores of either of his major two competitors.

Cruz, Rubio and Trump Net Favorable Ratings Among Republicans/Leaners

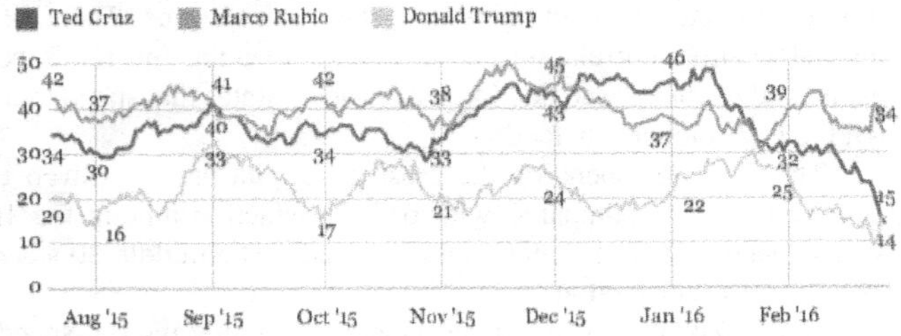

Based on two-week rolling averages through Feb. 23; one-week averages since Feb. 24

GALLUP

The net favorable ratings Republicans and Republican-leaning independents give to Cruz, Trump and Rubio are all at or near their lowest since tracking began, underscoring the clear toll the campaign has apparently taken on how Republicans view these contenders. The latest update comes from Gallup polling conducted Feb. 21-27. During this time, the leading Republican candidates intensified their rhetoric against one another, including at the 10th Republican debate on Feb. 25 and at a Trump campaign event on Friday during which New Jersey Gov. Chris Christie endorsed Trump.

Ted Cruz

- Cruz registered his campaign's highest net favorable score (+48) among Republicans and Republican leaners in late December, but his image has soured since. His current score of +14 is the lowest since Gallup began tracking images in July. Cruz, who has come under attack by not only Trump and Rubio, but also by GOP candidate Ben Carson for his perceived use of underhanded campaign tactics, has seen his popularity drop farther than any other GOP candidate in 2016.
- Cruz's image has worsened across most groups of Republicans when compared with his standings in the first two weeks of this year. Only among "very conservative" and highly religious Republicans is Cruz's level of popularity roughly where it was in the first two weeks of January.
- Cruz continues to have a more positive image among men than among women, among core Republican identifiers than among independents who lean Republican, and among conservative Republicans. (He has a net negative score among moderate/liberal Republicans.)
- Cruz is more popular among those with at least some college education, and those who are highly religious (with a negative net favorable score among those who are not religious).

Donald Trump

- Trump has long been relatively unpopular among national Republicans, and his average net favorable score of +22 in the nine months Gallup has been tracking images is well below Rubio's or Cruz's average over the same period.
- Trump's net favorable rating with Republicans reached +9 for the seven days ending Feb. 24, its lowest point since tracking began, before edging back to his current +15.

- Trump's highest net favorable rating during the campaign was +33, registered in late August and early September.
- Among Republicans, Trump is viewed most positively by men, those aged 55 and older and those with some college education but no degree. He is viewed more negatively than positively by women, 18- to 34-year-olds and those with a postgraduate education.

Marco Rubio

- Though yet to finish first in any primary contest, Rubio is the most popular of the three major candidates among national Republicans. His current net favorable score of +34 is more than twice that of either Cruz or Trump. Rubio began the year with a +34 net favorable, identical to his current rating.
- Rubio's average net favorable score of +40 since tracking began is higher than the average of either of the other top two candidates.
- Rubio's most positive net favorable score was +50, reached in mid-November. This marked the second-highest net favorable score earned by any of the 17 candidates Gallup has measured – behind only the scores in the 50-point and 60-point range registered by Carson in the late summer and early fall.
- Rubio's image skews highest among Republican identifiers, conservative Republicans, those with a college education and those who are highly religious. His biggest improvement this year has been with Republican women, who now give him a net favorable score about nine points higher than he received earlier this year.

Implications

While there has been no shortage of unflattering remarks throughout much of the GOP campaign, the increased amount of personal attacks and insults over the past week likely have negatively affected both Cruz's and Trump's images, although the latter's image has recovered slightly in recent days. Cruz is less well-liked by Republicans and Republican-leaning independents than at any point since Gallup tracking began nine months ago. Rubio maintains a considerably more positive image than either Trump or Cruz, but his net favorable rating is lower than it has been at previous points in the campaign.

Republicans' much more favorable image of Rubio than of Trump or Cruz has not translated into first-place finishes in primary contests so far for the Florida senator. This may partly reflect that Trump's appeal is not based on his being likable or personable, but rather on his rough, critical and reaction-generating persona. As was on display this past Friday, Rubio has made the decision to emulate that more negative, baiting style associated with Trump. Undoubtedly, this is a risk for Rubio. He could hurt his own image more than Trump's by engaging in this type of dialogue. But given Trump's impressive performance thus far in the primaries, Rubio and his advisers may think this is his best gamble to wrestle the lead from the current front-runner.

Historical data are available in Gallup Analytics.

Survey Methods

Results for this Gallup poll are based on telephone interviews conducted on a continuous basis on the Gallup U.S. Daily survey. The latest update used in this report is based on interviewing conducted Feb. 21-27, 2016, with random samples of between 754 and 810 Republicans and Republican-leaning independents, aged 18 and older, living in all 50 U.S. states and the District of Columbia, rating each of the three candidates. For results based on the total sample of Republicans, the margin of sampling error is ±4 percentage points at the 95% confidence level. All reported margins of sampling error include computed design effects for weighting.

February 29, 2016

AMERICANS' VIEWS TOWARD ISRAEL REMAIN FIRMLY POSITIVE

by Lydia Saad

Story Highlights

- *Six in 10 continue to sympathize more with Israelis than Palestinians*
- *Republicans remain especially likely to favor the Israelis*
- *More in U.S. still favor than oppose establishment of Palestinian state*

PRINCETON, N.J. – Americans' views about the Israeli-Palestinian conflict remained steady over the past year, with 62% of Americans saying their sympathies lie more with the Israelis and 15% favoring the Palestinians. About one in four continue to be neutral, including 9% who sympathize with neither side, 3% who sympathize with both, and 11% expressing no opinion.

Americans' Sympathies in Mideast Conflict -- Trend Since 2001

In the Middle East situation, are your sympathies more with the Israelis or more with the Palestinians?

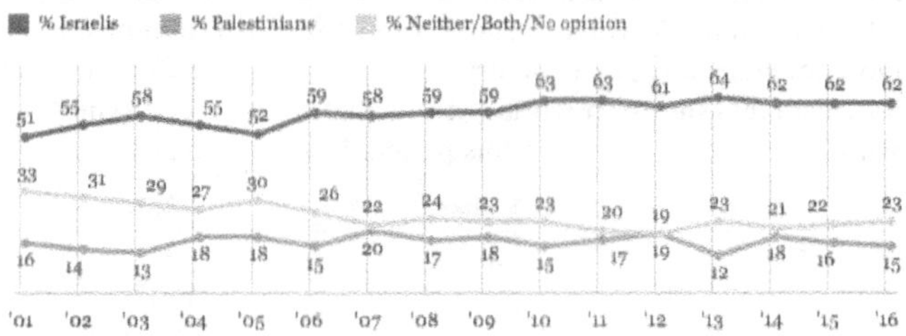

Trends shown are from annual February World Affairs survey

GALLUP'

Americans have consistently shown more support for Israel than for the Palestinians over the past 15 years. However, sympathy for Israel increased in 2006 to 59%, from 52% the year before, in a Gallup poll conducted shortly after the January 2006 Palestinian elections in which Hamas – which the U.S. government has classified as a terrorist group – won the majority of parliamentary seats. Support for Israel has since remained at 58% or higher.

All major demographic and political subgroups of Americans lean toward Israel over the Palestinians on this question. However, several characteristics are related to the extent of public support for Israel.

Chief among these are religious preference and party identification. Gallup finds a 31-percentage-point difference in sympathy for Israel between Protestants (72%) and nonreligious Americans

(41%), and a 26-point difference between Republicans (79%) and Democrats (53%). That contrasts with a 19-point difference between highly religious and nonreligious Americans, and an 18-point difference between older and younger Americans.

All of these differences from Gallup's Feb. 3-7, 2016, World Affairs poll are similar to the recent patterns in Americans' Mideast sympathies.

Americans' Sympathies in the Israeli-Palestinian Conflict, by Key Subgroups

Feb. 3-7, 2016

	Israelis	Palestinians	Both (vol.)	Neither (vol.)/ No opinion
	%	%	%	
U.S. adults	62	15	3	20
Men	64	15	3	18
Women	60	15	4	22
18 to 29 years	54	23	3	21
30 to 49 years	54	18	4	25
50 and older	72	10	3	14
Republicans	79	7	2	12
Independents	56	15	5	24
Democrats	53	23	3	21
Attend worship service weekly	75	9	2	13
Attend nearly weekly	65	13	1	20
Never/seldom attend	56	19	5	20
Catholics	58	11	6	25
Protestants/Other Christians	72	10	3	15
No religion	41	29	4	26

(vol.) = Volunteered response

GALLUP

As Gallup has reported in the past, the partisan gap in Americans' support for Israel has widened over the past decade and a half as Republicans warmed toward Israel during George W. Bush's administration. This likely stems from the Bush administration's close relationship to that country as well as post-9/11 attitudes about terrorism and the Arab world. Meanwhile, Democrats' sympathies with Israel also grew during this period, just not as much.

Percentage Sympathizing More With the Israelis Than the Palestinians in Mideast Situation

by Party ID

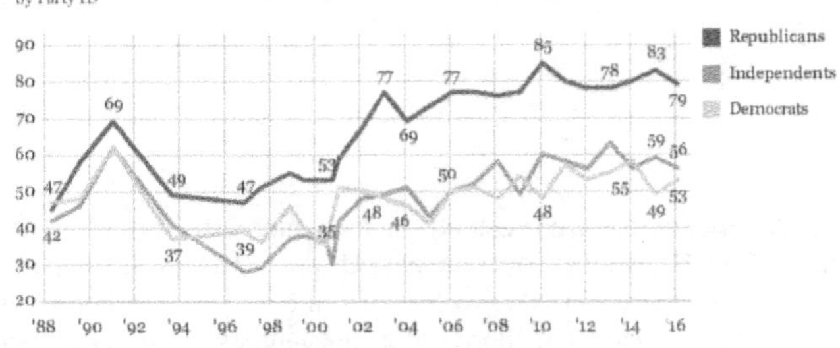

Trend since 2001 includes only results from annual February World Affairs survey

GALLUP

Separately, Gallup measures Americans' favorability toward Israel and the Palestinian Authority individually. The results are similar to the "sympathies" split, with 71% of Americans holding a very or mostly favorable view of Israel, versus 19% viewing the Palestinian Authority favorably.

These attitudes were also steady over the past year, though they show increased favorability toward Israel compared with 2000. At the same time, the trend shows no long-term change in favorability toward the Palestinian Authority. Apart from the occasional dip and spike, this has tended to be near 20%.

Americans' Overall Views of Israel and the Palestinian Authority

Percentage viewing each very favorably or mostly favorably

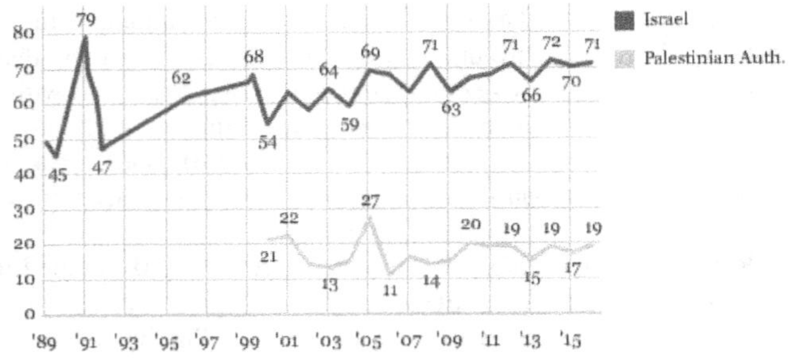

GALLUP

More Still Favor Than Oppose an Independent Palestinian State

One other trend question asked in the survey shows somewhat more U.S. understanding for the Palestinians. By a slight margin, 44% to 37%, more Americans favor than oppose the establishment of an independent Palestinian state on the West Bank and Gaza Strip. Those results are in line with what Gallup has measured since 2013; however, there were larger margins in favor of a Palestinian state in most prior years.

Americans' Support for an Independent Palestinian State

Do you favor or oppose the establishment of an independent Palestinian state on the West Bank and the Gaza Strip?

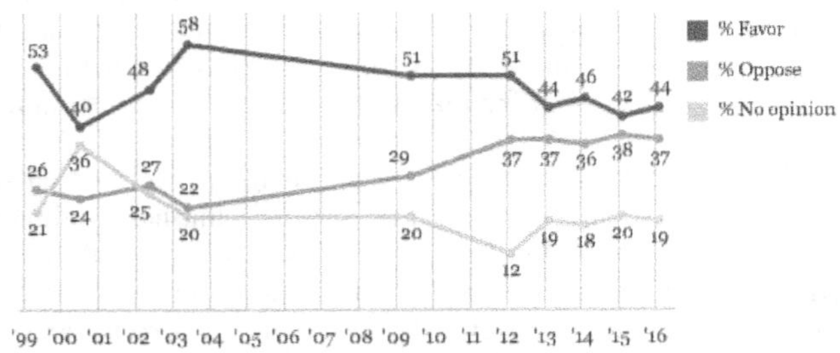

GALLUP

On this question, the two political parties have substantively different views, with 58% of Democrats supporting the establishment of a Palestinian state, compared with 26% of Republicans.

Bottom Line

Americans have become more sympathetic toward Israel over the past 15 years, and that more pro-Israel view held steady in the past year. While Republicans show extraordinarily high support for Israel – an affinity evident at the Republican presidential debate in Houston last week, where every candidate professed his strong support for the Jewish state – the majority of Democrats and independents are also on the same page.

Given this, it is intriguing that more Americans continue to favor than oppose the creation of a Palestinian state. The finding suggests that despite the lack of U.S. diplomatic activity on this issue in recent years, it is still something Americans would generally welcome should the next president be willing to work toward it.

Historical data are available in Gallup Analytics.

Survey Methods

Results for this Gallup poll are based on telephone interviews conducted Feb. 3-7, 2016, with a random sample of 1,021 adults, aged 18 and older, living in all 50 U.S. states and the District of Columbia. For results based on the total sample of national adults, the margin of sampling error is ±4 percentage points at the 95% confidence level. All reported margins of sampling error include computed design effects for weighting.

March 01, 2016
UN JOB RATING AMONG AMERICANS HIGHER, BUT STILL LOW

by Jim Norman

Story Highlights

- *38% of Americans say U.N. is doing a good job*
- *Job rating is highest since start of Iraq War in 2003*
- *Independents much more likely to give good rating than in 2015*

WASHINGTON, D.C. – Americans are slightly more likely than they were a year ago to think the United Nations is doing a good job of trying to solve the problems it faces. The small gain – from 35% in 2015 to 38% now – pushes the U.N.'s job rating to its highest level since before it balked at supporting the Iraq War in 2003.

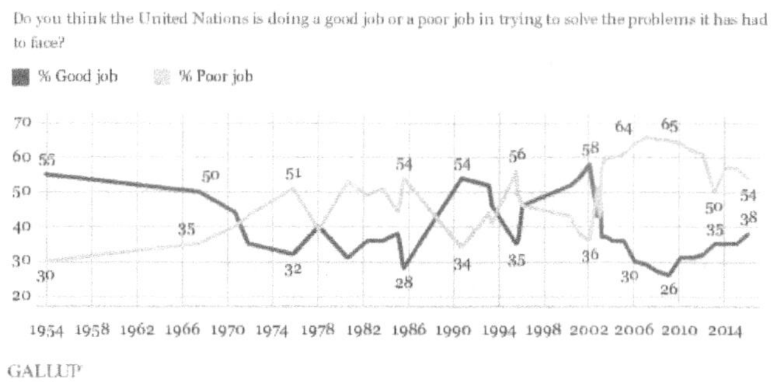

The percentage of Americans judging the U.N.'s work favorably has now risen 12 percentage points since 2009. At that time, 26% of Americans said the U.N. was doing a good job – the lowest point in the 38 times Gallup has polled on the subject, going back to 1953. This year's slight climb comes after the percentage saying the U.N. was doing a good job stalled at 35% for three consecutive years.

Fourteen years have passed since a majority of U.S. adults have said the U.N. is doing a good job, following a familiar pattern that goes back decades. Fifty-five percent of Americans supported the U.N.'s efforts when the question was first asked in 1953, and 50% did so in 1967. However, the percentage dropped to 44% in 1970, and since then, attitudes about the U.N.'s work have been marked by lengthy stretches of negative ratings. The two exceptions since then were brief periods of majority support around the times of the first Gulf War in 1991 and the 9/11 terrorist attacks.

2015 a Tumultuous Year for the UN

In judging the U.N.'s performance this year, U.S. adults had several major events on which to base their opinions:

- In July, the U.N. Security Council unanimously approved an agreement designed to limit Iran's nuclear program – a deal that has not been popular in the United States.
- In November, the Security Council unanimously approved a resolution calling for action against the Islamic State group. The action came a week after attacks by Islamic extremists killed 130 people in Paris.
- In December, the United Nations Climate Change Conference produced the Paris Agreement, a global deal on the reduction of climate change reached after 20 years of negotiations on the subject.
- On Feb. 3, the U.N. suspended peace talks focused on ending Syria's civil war just a few days after they began.

The United Nations' support of the Iran nuclear deal touched on an issue that a majority of Americans opposed, but its action on global warming dealt with a subject that has strong support overall in the U.S. The U.N.'s quick reaction against the Islamic State group after the Paris attacks also mirrored the attitudes of most Americans.

UN Job Rating Improves Most Among Independents

Over the past year, the United Nations' support of the global warming treaty and the Iran nuclear deal drew criticism from Republicans in Congress. Not surprisingly, the percentage of Republicans saying the U.N. is doing a good job fell from 25% in 2015 to 17% now. Nevertheless, the overall U.N. job rating rose because the percentage of independents saying it is doing a good job spiked from 29% to 43%. In doing so, independents – for the second time in a decade – moved closer to the Democratic view than to the Republican view. Democrats' opinions of the U.N. showed no significant change in 2016 after improving by 11 percentage points last year.

Meanwhile, the partisan gap between the two parties, after widening from 15 points in 2014 to 27 points last year, now stands at 37 points – the largest divide since Gallup began asking the question annually in the February World Affairs poll in 2004.

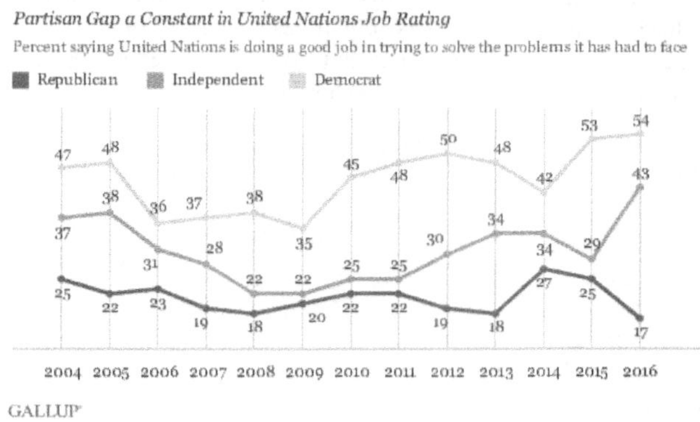

Bottom Line

Although the United Nations has made incremental advances in the eyes of the American public over the past seven years, only slightly more than a third of Americans think it is doing a good job. Furthermore, the U.N. lost ground among Republicans in the past year, possibly as a result of its support for the Iran nuclear deal and the global warming treaty.

But despite Americans' consistent disapproval of the United Nations since 2003, the American public has indicated again and again that the U.N. has a vital role to play. More than 60% said in 2014 that the U.N. should play a leading or major role in world affairs. In 2013, 58% said that working with the U.N. should be a very important foreign policy goal for the U.S., and 66% said that the U.N. "plays a necessary role in the world today." While the majority of Americans generally have not been happy with the way the United Nations deals with the world's problems, few have wanted to see it fade into oblivion, as did its post-World War I predecessor, the ill-fated League of Nations.

Survey Methods

Results for this Gallup poll are based on telephone interviews conducted Feb. 3-7, 2016, with a random sample of 1,021 adults, aged 18 and older, living in all 50 U.S. states and the District of Columbia. For results based on the total sample of national adults, the margin of sampling error is ±4 percentage points at the 95% confidence level. All reported margins of sampling error include computed design effects for weighting.

March 02, 2016

AMERICANS SAY E-CIGS SHOULD BE REGULATED LIKE TOBACCO CIGS

by Alyssa Davis and Diana Liu

Story Highlights

- *60% say e-cigarettes should be regulated like tobacco cigarettes*
- *Half say e-cigarettes are a threat to public health*
- *48% want e-cigarettes totally banned in restaurants*

WASHINGTON, D.C. – Most U.S. adults favor some type of regulation for e-cigarettes. A majority, 60%, say e-cigarettes should be regulated as much as tobacco cigarettes. An additional 19% say e-cigarettes should be regulated, but not as much as regular cigarettes. Seventeen percent say they should not be regulated at all.

Americans' Views on Regulating E-Cigarettes

In your opinion, which of the following best describes how e-cigarettes should be regulated?

	U.S. adults	Current tobacco cigarette smokers	Have tried e-cigarettes
	%	%	%
Regulated as much as cigarettes	60	50	50
Regulated less than cigarettes	19	23	31
Not regulated at all	17	26	18
Don't know/Refused	4	2	1

Dec. 1-30, 2015

Gallup-Healthways Well-Being Index

GALLUP

The 17% of U.S. adults who currently smoke regular tobacco cigarettes and the 19% who have tried e-cigarettes are somewhat less likely than U.S. adults overall to say e-cigarettes should be regulated as much as tobacco cigarettes. But regardless of Americans' personal experience with tobacco or e-cigarettes, the prevailing opinion is that both products should be regulated similarly.

The Food and Drug Administration proposed regulations in April 2014 that would extend its tobacco authority to cover e-cigarettes. These regulations, which include banning sales to minors and requiring warning labels, have not yet been implemented.

In the absence of federal regulations, some state and local governments have passed laws and policies regulating e-cigarettes. Forty-eight states prohibit sales of electronic cigarettes to minors, as of December 2015. Seven states include e-cigarettes in their definitions of "tobacco products" in state statutes, as of May 2015. Fifteen states have at least one restriction on where e-cigarettes can be used.

Many Americans Believe E-Cigs Are Not as Harmful as Tobacco Cigs

Advocates of e-cigarettes, or vaping, say they are an effective smoking-cessation product, although the FDA has not approved e-cigarettes for this purpose. Its proponents see e-cigarettes as less harmful than regular cigarettes and, in turn, believe they should be regulated less strictly. Opponents argue that e-cigarettes are a gateway to regular cigarettes, particularly for young adults, and should be regulated the same way as tobacco products.

Americans tend to say e-cigarettes are less harmful than tobacco cigarettes to personal health. While one in three say e-cigarettes are just as bad as tobacco cigarettes for someone's health, the majority either say e-cigarettes are less harmful to one's health than tobacco cigarettes (48%) or are not harmful to personal health at all (11%). Current tobacco cigarette smokers and those who have tried e-cigarettes are, not surprisingly, less likely than U.S. adults overall to say e-cigarettes are just as harmful as tobacco cigarettes.

Americans' Views on How E-Cigarettes Affect Personal Health

Which of the following best describes your opinion regarding e-cigarettes and a person's health?

	U.S. adults	Currently smoke tobacco cigarettes	Have tried e-cigarettes
	%	%	%
Just as bad as tobacco cigarettes	33	23	17
Not as bad as tobacco cigarettes, but still harmful	48	52	58
Not harmful	11	20	23
Don't know/Refused	8	5	2

Dec. 1-30, 2015

Gallup-Healthways Well-Being Index

GALLUP

Despite the potential for e-cigarettes to help some smokers quit using tobacco, when asked about the effect of e-cigarettes on public health, half of U.S. adults say they are harmful, 14% say they are helpful and 28% say they have no effect. Cigarette smokers and those who have tried e-cigarettes are significantly less likely than U.S. adults overall to say e-cigarettes are harmful to public health. These groups tilt toward saying e-cigarettes have no effect on public health.

Americans' Views on E-Cigarettes' Effect on Public Health and Environment

Based on what you have seen or heard, are e-cigarettes helpful, harmful or do they have no impact on the following?

	Harmful	No impact	Helpful
	%	%	%
PUBLIC HEALTH			
U.S. adults	50	28	14
Current tobacco cigarette smokers	29	41	26
Have tried e-cigarettes	29	41	27
THE ENVIRONMENT			
U.S. adults	40	40	11
Current tobacco smokers	19	57	18
Have tried e-cigarettes	17	58	22

Dec. 1-30, 2015
Gallup-Healthways Well-Being Index

GALLUP

Little is known about how the manufacturing, use and disposal of e-cigarettes affect the environment, according to an FDA/Center for Tobacco Products literature review. Americans are slightly less likely to say e-cigarettes harm the environment as they are to say the same about public health, with equal percentages saying e-cigarettes are either harmful to the environment or have no impact (40%). Eleven percent believe they help the environment. Majorities of current tobacco smokers and those who have tried e-cigarettes say they have no impact on the environment.

No Consensus on Whether to Ban E-Cigarette Use in Public Places

Americans are not in favor of completely banning e-cigarettes in restaurants, workplaces, hotels, bars and public parks. Of these venues, Americans are most likely to say e-cigarettes should be totally banned from restaurants (48%) and least likely to say they should be banned from public parks (29%). In contrast, a majority of U.S. adults believe cigarette smoking should be illegal in all public places.

Americans' Views on Banning E-Cigarettes

Should they set aside certain areas, should they totally ban e-cigarettes or should there be no restrictions on using e-cigarettes in the following venues?

	Totally ban	Set aside certain areas	No restrictions
	%	%	%
Restaurants	48	34	16
Workplaces	41	41	16
Hotels and motels	34	41	23
Bars	31	36	31
Public parks	29	30	39

Dec. 1-30, 2015
Gallup-Healthways Well-Being Index

GALLUP

Not surprisingly, regular and e-cigarette smokers are much less supportive of total bans.

Bottom Line

Research into how e-cigarettes affect people's health and the public in general provides mixed results, with some researchers hailing it as a next-generation method of tobacco cessation, while others see it as a gateway to tobacco use. It is also unclear whether e-cigarettes have their own harmful health effects. With the growth of e-cigarette use being a relatively recent phenomenon, it may take some time before researchers reach a consensus on the effect e-cigarettes have on personal, public and environmental health.

Gallup and Healthways will publish additional research this month on e-cigarette usage.

Survey Methods

Results are based on telephone interviews conducted Dec. 1-Dec. 30, 2015, as part of the Gallup-Healthways Well-Being Index survey, with a random sample of 13,648 adults, aged 18 and older, living in all 50 U.S. states and the District of Columbia. For results based on the total sample of national adults, the margin of sampling error is ±1.0 percentage points at the 95% confidence level. For results based on the total sample of adults who currently smoke tobacco cigarettes, the margin of sampling error is ±2.6 percentage points at the 95% confidence level. For results based on the total sample of adults who have tried e-cigarettes, the margin of sampling error is ±6.8 percentage points at the 95% confidence level. All reported margins of sampling error include computed design effects for weighting.

March 03, 2016

ECONOMIC ISSUES ARE TRUMP'S STRONG SUIT AMONG REPUBLICANS

by Frank Newport and Lydia Saad

Story Highlights

- *Most Republicans pick Trump over rivals as best on economic issues*
- *Trump also seen as strong on immigration, but weaker on abortion*
- *Few think Trump has best temperament*

PRINCETON, N.J. – More than six in 10 Republicans and independents who lean Republican say Donald Trump would be best at dealing with the economy/jobs and the federal budget deficit as president, compared with less than 20% who pick either Ted Cruz or Marco Rubio.

Republicans' Preference for GOP Candidates on the Issues

Now I'm going to read several issues facing the country. Regardless of who you might vote for, please say if [Ted Cruz, Marco Rubio (or) Donald Trump] would be best at dealing with that issue as president.

	Donald Trump	Marco Rubio	Ted Cruz	Other (vol.)	None/No opinion
	%	%	%	%	%
The economy and jobs	64	17	13	1	5
The federal budget deficit	61	16	16	1	6
Immigration	52	25	18	1	5
National defense and security against terrorism	46	24	22	1	7
Healthcare and the Affordable Care Act	44	23	22	2	9
Abortion	29	24	29	2	16

Based on Republicans/Republican leaners
Feb. 26-28, 2016

GALLUP

Most likely reflecting his front-runner status, Trump also holds convincing leads in Republicans' perceptions of which candidate would best handle immigration, national defense and healthcare. The only issue of the six Gallup tested in the Feb. 26-28 poll on which Trump doesn't have a big advantage is abortion. He ties with Cruz on this issue at 29%, while Rubio is close behind at 24%.

Trump's strength on economic issues, compared with his major competitors, most likely reflects the billionaire's business resume and the emphasis he places on his business experience on the campaign trail. Neither Cruz nor Rubio has a business background, and the percentages favoring these two on the economy are only 13% and 17%, respectively.

Trump Also the "Can Do" Candidate

Republicans see Trump – more so than Rubio or Cruz – as the candidate who would accomplish what he sets out to do as president and as the candidate who would improve the United States' standing in the world. At the same time, he does not have nearly the same perceived strengths on other leadership dimensions.

Republicans are, in fact, significantly more likely to say Cruz, as opposed to either Trump or Rubio, would govern as a true conservative, and Trump holds only a slim lead over Cruz as the candidate most likely to protect Americans' constitutional rights. Republicans see Rubio, whose campaign rhetoric has arguably generated less controversy than that of Trump or Cruz, as having the right temperament to be president, a dimension on which Trump is the least likely to be chosen. Rubio effectively ties Trump as being able to best deal effectively with Congress. Though both Rubio and Cruz are U.S. senators, Cruz is better known for opposing legislation than for advancing it, including legislation supported by his own party.

Republicans' View of GOP Candidates' Leadership Qualities

Now please say if each of the following descriptions applies best to [Ted Cruz, Marco Rubio (or) Donald Trump]?

	Donald Trump	Marco Rubio	Ted Cruz	Other (vol.)	None/No opinion
	%	%	%	%	%
Would accomplish what he sets out to do	56	21	16	1	6
Would improve the United States' standing in the world	45	27	20	2	7
Would protect citizens' constitutional rights	38	24	31	1	6
Would deal effectively with Congress	35	32	23	3	8
Would govern as a true conservative	25	24	42	2	8
Has the right temperament to be president	25	36	29	3	7

Based on Republicans/Republican leaners
Feb. 26-28, 2016

GALLUP

Trump Supporters See Strengths and Flaws in Their Candidate

Trump's own supporters – Republicans and Republican leaners who say they would like to see him win the nomination – favor him by overwhelming margins as being the best candidate to deal with the economy, the deficit, immigration, improving the U.S. world standing and accomplishing what he sets out to do. Between 89% and 97% of Trump supporters say he is the best candidate for each of these, underscoring the centrality of these issues and characteristics to his success.

Trump's supporters are somewhat less likely to see him as the best candidate to handle national security, healthcare, protecting citizens' rights and dealing effectively with Congress, although large majorities still name him as best on these. Trump's relative weaknesses among his supporters are in the areas of abortion, presidential temperament and governing as a true conservative, all things his opponents have criticized him for during the campaign. Barely half of those who want to see Trump become the nominee consider him to be the best candidate on these three dimensions. In essence, his supporters are aware that these are not his strengths, even while favoring him for the nomination.

Percentage of Republican Trump Supporters Choosing Trump as Best GOP Candidate on These Issues and Qualities

Based on Republicans/Republican leaners who favor Donald Trump for GOP nomination

	Feb. 26-28, 2016
	%
Dealing with the economy	97
Dealing with the federal budget deficit	97
Accomplishing what he sets out to do	94
Dealing with immigration	92
Improving the United States' standing in the world	89
Dealing with national security and defense	83
Dealing with healthcare and the Affordable Care Act	79
Protecting citizens' constitutional rights	76
Dealing effectively with Congress	70
Dealing with abortion	56
Having the right temperament to be president	56
Governing as a true conservative	52

GALLUP

Bottom Line

Republicans choose Donald Trump, who promises to "make America great again" – as the best GOP candidate for handling the economy and federal budget deficit as president. These strengths appear to be at the core of his support, tying in with the persistent economic anxiety Republicans express on a host of Gallup measures, such as confidence in the economy and their own economic progress.

Republicans also give Trump considerable credit for being able to handle immigration, the issue that launched his candidacy and has generated much controversy during the campaign – and for accomplishing what he sets out to do and improving the standing of the U.S. in the world.

At the same time, Republicans – including many who favor his nomination – seem to be well aware that Trump has weaknesses. They implicitly acknowledge Trump's unusual brashness, giving Rubio the most credit for having the right temperament to be president. Republicans also acknowledge that Trump is not the most conservative candidate, giving Cruz credit for the conservatism that has become his signature message. Given that Republicans in this poll favor Trump to win their party's nomination, they appear to be willing to overlook the front-runner's deficiencies.

Survey Methods

Results for this Gallup poll are based on telephone interviews conducted Feb. 26-28, 2016, on the Gallup U.S. Daily survey, with a random sample of 681 Republicans and independents who lean Republican, aged 18 and older, living in all 50 U.S. states and the District of Columbia. For results based on the total sample of national adults, the margin of sampling error is ±5 percentage points at the 95% confidence level. All reported margins of sampling error include computed design effects for weighting.

March 04, 2016

TRUMP SUPPORT BUILT ON OUTSIDER STATUS, BUSINESS EXPERIENCE

by Frank Newport and Lydia Saad

Story Highlights

- *Top reason Trump supporters back him is he's not a politician*
- *Trump's business background ranks second*
- *Rubio and Cruz voters are less specific in their reasons for support*

PRINCETON, N.J. – Republicans who want to see Donald Trump win their party's nomination are most likely to say it is Trump's status as a nonpolitician and an outsider that drives their support, followed by his experience as a businessman. A number of Trump supporters also prefer him because he is outspoken.

Most Important Reasons for Supporting Donald Trump for Republican Nomination

What are one or two of the most important reasons why you prefer Donald Trump for the Republican nomination? (open-ended)

Republicans/Republican leaners

	%
He's not a career politician/Outsider	22
Good businessman	16
Speaks his mind/Outspoken	14
Immigration	8
Would accomplish what he sets out to do/Strong	7
Self-funded/Not taking lobbyist money	7
Honest/Trust him	6
Would improve the United States' standing in the world	6
Like his decisions/views/outlook	4
Would protect citizens' constitutional rights/Stands up for citizens	4
Best candidate to pick/Don't care for the others	4
Need a change/Fresh ideas	4
National defense and security against terrorism/Border protection	4
Good financial plan/Get budget under control	3
The economy and jobs	2

Feb. 26-28, 2016

GALLUP

These findings are based on Gallup's Feb. 26-28 poll in which Republicans and Republican-leaning independents were asked whether they would prefer to see Trump, Ted Cruz or Marco Rubio win their party's nomination, and then to indicate in their own words what lies behind their preference. Responses to the latter question were coded into major categories as displayed in the accompanying table.

According to Trump supporters, his unconventional résumé and style have helped attract their support for his candidacy, more so than his positions on issues or specific policies. In fact, other than his signature issue of immigration, mentioned by 8% of his supporters, no other issue is named by more than half that many – with between 2% and 4% mentioning his ability to deal with terrorists, his financial planning and budget expertise, and his handling of the economy and employment.

This is not to say Trump supporters don't think he has strengths on specific issues. In the same poll, Trump gets substantially more credit than his major competitors for being able to handle the economy and the deficit, as well as immigration. But it is his nonpolitician background that comes to mind first, not his positions on issues, when supporters are asked to explain why they want him as their party's nominee.

In addition to the perception that Trump is an outsider and a businessman, Republicans who support Trump also frequently mention that he would accomplish what he sets out to do, that his campaign has so far been self-funded, that he is honest and that his election as president would improve the stature of the U.S. around the world.

Cruz's Conservatism Is an Attraction, While Rubio Is Liked, Seen as Honest

Fewer Republicans in this survey say they would prefer Rubio as their party's nominee. Those who do generally offer less specific – and certainly less unique – reasons for supporting him than is seen for Trump. Their most-frequently mentioned reasons include generic justifications that he is the best candidate or at least better than the others, that he is honest, and that they like him and his decisions.

Cruz has the fewest supporters of the three Republican candidates in this survey, but those who do want him to be the GOP nominee provide only somewhat more specific reasons than is true for Rubio. In addition to the generic "I like him" justification, Cruz's supporters mention that he would stand up for constitutional rights, one of the Texas senator's central campaign themes, and that he would govern as a true conservative.

Most Important Reasons for Supporting Marco Rubio and Ted Cruz for Republican Nomination

Republicans/Republican leaners

What are one or two of the most important reasons why you prefer Marco Rubio for the Republican nomination?	What are one or two of the most important reasons why you prefer Ted Cruz for the Republican nomination?
Best candidate to pick/Don't care for the others	Like his decisions/views/outlook
Honest/Trust him	Would protect citizens' constitutional rights
Like his decisions/views/outlook	Best candidate to pick/Don't care for the others
Experienced	Would govern as true conservative
Smart/Intelligent	Experienced

Feb. 26-28, 2016

GALLUP

Implications

If Trump wins the Republican nomination, his opponent in the general election – who right now is most probably Hillary Clinton – will likely seek to attack him for his idiosyncratic temperament and bombastic ways. Previewing this possible line of attack, a member of his own party, 2012 Republican presidential nominee Mitt Romney, heavily criticized Trump on Thursday in a speech in Utah, using words like "bullying … showing off … absurd third-grade theatrics … ridiculous."

The insight from the new poll – conducted before Trump engaged in additional nonconventional references and personal attacks in the March 3 GOP debate – is that rank-and-file Republicans may be willing to look beyond these qualities and, by extension, that general-election swing voters could do the same. Republicans who support Trump's candidacy like him for being an anti-politician, and Trump's willingness to say things that flout conventional norms governing political speech may only strengthen his authenticity as an outsider.

More generally, the responses given by Republicans who want to see Trump prevail show that Trump's outsider message is clearly reaching its target through the free media on which he relies.

His supporters' discussion of his outsider status, his business background, that he says what he thinks, his position on immigration, that he would get things done, and his being self-funded are all centerpieces of Trump's debate and numerous off-the-cuff comments.

Survey Methods

Results for this Gallup poll are based on telephone interviews conducted Feb. 26-28, 2016, on the Gallup U.S. Daily survey, with a random sample of 681 Republicans and independents who lean Republican, including 277 who prefer Trump as the Republican nominee, 174 who prefer Rubio and 124 who prefer Cruz, aged 18 and older, living in all 50 U.S. states and the District of Columbia. For results based on each candidate's supporters, and based on results near 20%, the margin of sampling error is no more than ±7 percentage points at the 95% confidence level. All reported margins of sampling error include computed design effects for weighting.

March 04, 2016

NEVADANS MOST LIKELY TO SAY STATE GOOD PLACE FOR IMMIGRANTS

by Justin McCarthy

Story Highlights

- *W. Virginians least likely to say their area good for immigrants*
- *East Coast residents view their states as being most hospitable*
- *Southern, Midwestern states least likely to say area a "good place"*

WASHINGTON, D.C. – Ninety percent of Nevada residents indicate their area is hospitable to immigrants, the highest among the 50 U.S. states and the District of Columbia. Nevada is followed closely by four states – Massachusetts, Hawaii, Delaware and California, plus Washington, D.C. – all at 89%.

States Whose Residents Are Most Likely/Least Likely to Say Their Area Is a Good Place for Immigrants to Live

Is the city or area where you live a good place or not a good place to live for immigrants from other countries?

Most likely states	2015	Least likely states	2015
	% Good place		% Good place
Nevada	90	West Virginia	67
Massachusetts	89	Tennessee	72
Washington, D.C.	89	Arkansas	73
Hawaii	89	Oklahoma	75
Delaware	89	Kentucky	75
California	89	Mississippi	75
Florida	88	North Dakota	76
New York	88	Alabama	76
New Jersey	88		
Virginia	88		

Gallup Poll, March-December 2015

GALLUP

West Virginia has the lowest proportion of residents, 67%, who say their state is a good place for immigrants to live, though this is still a solid majority.

Residents of several East Coast states are among the most likely to say the city or area where they live is a good place for immigrants from other countries. In addition to Massachusetts and Delaware, in Florida, New York, New Jersey and Virginia, along with the District, at least 88% of residents express this sentiment. This is also true for residents of Nevada, Hawaii and California.

Meanwhile, residents of several Southern states are among the least likely to say their city or area is hospitable to immigrants. Between 72% and 77% of adults in Tennessee, Arkansas, Mississippi, Kentucky, Oklahoma and Alabama say this. North Dakotans are also among the least likely to say this about their area. The complete list of states can be found at the end of this article.

An average of 82% nationwide say their local area is a good place for immigrants to live in Gallup's 2015 comprehensive poll of 50 states and Washington, D.C. The poll consisted of 500 interviews or more in each state and the District. Interviewing was conducted from March-December 2015, at a time when immigration was a major issue in the presidential campaign. The immigration debate focused largely on building a wall on the U.S.-Mexico border, how to address the status of immigrants currently in the country illegally and whether the U.S. should take in Syrian refugees who fled the civil war there.

Good Place for Immigrants to Live by State, 2015

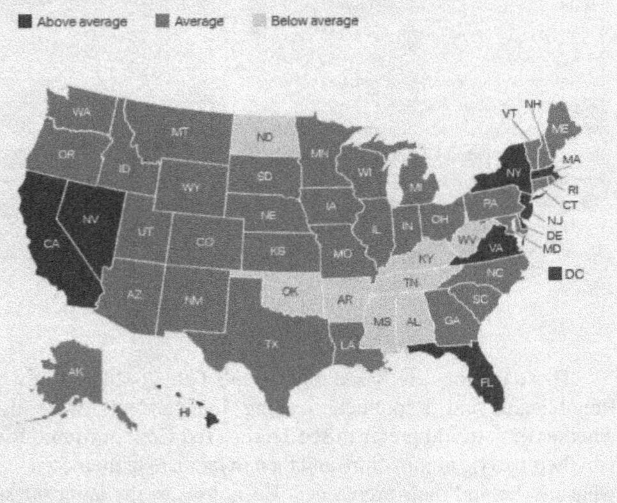

SOURCE: GALLUP POLL, MARCH-DECEMBER 2015

In Arizona, where residents still live under the controversial SB 1070 – a state law considered one of the strictest anti-illegal-immigration measures in the country when it passed in 2010 – 81% say their area is a good place for immigrants to live. Although a strong majority, the figure is slightly below average, and falls at least five percentage points below the scores of neighboring states – California, Nevada, Utah, Colorado and New Mexico.

While Alabama residents, who also live under a controversial anti-illegal immigration law, are among the least likely to indicate that their city or area is hospitable to immigrants (76%), residents just across the border in Florida (88%) are much more likely to say this.

Bottom Line

In each of the 50 states and the District of Columbia, a solid majority of residents feel their city or area is a good place for immigrants to live. But responses to this question vary somewhat by state.

The status and future of immigrants who are in the U.S. illegally – about half of whom are Mexicans – have produced a bevy of hot-button political issues this election year. While about two in three Americans support a path to citizenship for such immigrants, many have flocked to support GOP presidential front-runner Donald Trump. Trump has insisted that Mexico is "not sending [its] best" to the U.S., suggesting that immigrants from that country are bringing problems such as drugs and rape, and that a wall must be built on the countries' common border and paid for by Mexico.

Although many have rejected Trump's comments and positions, he recently received the endorsements of former Arizona Gov. Jan Brewer, who signed the state's anti-illegal immigration bill, and another anti-illegal-immigration icon, Alabama Sen. Jeff Sessions.

Americans' views of their area as a good place for immigrants to live might not necessarily be related to their views on how to address illegal immigration, but the latter could be a factor in how the states vary. Regardless of residents' views on illegal immigration, they may not be inclined to say anything that would make it appear that their local area is unwelcoming to outsiders, which could play a role in why the percentages are fairly high in all of the states. It seems that, despite variations across the country, a strong majority of Americans everywhere believe their towns would welcome "huddled masses yearning to breathe free."

These data are available in Gallup Analytics.

Survey Methods

Results for this Gallup poll are based on telephone interviews conducted March 30-Dec. 22, 2015, with random samples of approximately 500 adults, aged 18 and older, living in each of the 50 U.S. states. Data are weighted to account for unequal selection probability, nonresponse and double coverage of landline and cellphone users in the two sampling frames. Data are also weighted to state estimates of gender, age, race, Hispanic ethnicity, education and phone status (cellphone only, landline only, both, and cellphone mostly).

For results based on the total sample of adults in each state, the margin of sampling error is ±6 percentage points at the 95% confidence level. All reported margins of sampling error include computed design effects for weighting.

March 07, 2016
ALMOST ALL HAWAII RESIDENTS SAY AREA GOOD FOR MINORITIES

by Frank Newport

Story Highlights

- *94% of Hawaii residents say their area is good for minorities*
- *At the low end of the list, 74% of West Virginians are positive*
- *These attitudes are related to actual minority population in states*

PRINCETON, N.J. – Ninety-four percent of Hawaii residents say their city or area is a good place to live for racial and ethnic minorities, the highest of the 50 U.S. states and the District of Columbia. Other states in which at least nine in 10 residents have a positive view of how hospitable their state is for minorities are Alaska, Texas, Nevada, Virginia, New Mexico and Arizona.

States Whose Residents Are Most Likely to Say Their Area Is a Good Place for Racial and Ethnic Minorities to Live

Is the city or area where you live a good place or not a good place to live for racial and ethnic minorities?

	2015
	% Good place
Hawaii	94
Alaska	93
Texas	92
Nevada	91
Virginia	91
New Mexico	90
Arizona	90

Gallup 50-State poll, March-December 2015

GALLUP

These results come from a Gallup 50-State poll conducted from March-December 2015, with at least 500 residents in each state. The full results for each state are shown at the end of this story.

Statistical analysis shows that attitudes about minorities are clearly related to the actual demographic makeup of the states. In particular, the seven states whose residents are most positive about the environment for minorities all have above-average minority populations. Hawaii – the most prominent example – has the lowest percentage of non-Hispanic whites (23%) of any state in the union according to census data, meaning over three-quarters of that state's residents identify their race as something other than white, or identify their ethnicity as Hispanic. Less than half of the residents of two other states – New Mexico and Texas – are non-Hispanic white, and both of these states are above average in residents' positive attitudes about minorities.

Residents of West Virginia are least likely to believe (74%) that their place of residence is good for minorities. Other states with a below-average percentage positive about the climate for minorities include Missouri, Wisconsin and Arkansas. West Virginia's population includes relatively few minorities; the census classifies 93% of the residents of the Mountain State as non-Hispanic white, the third highest of all states. Missouri, Wisconsin and Arkansas all have above-average white populations as well.

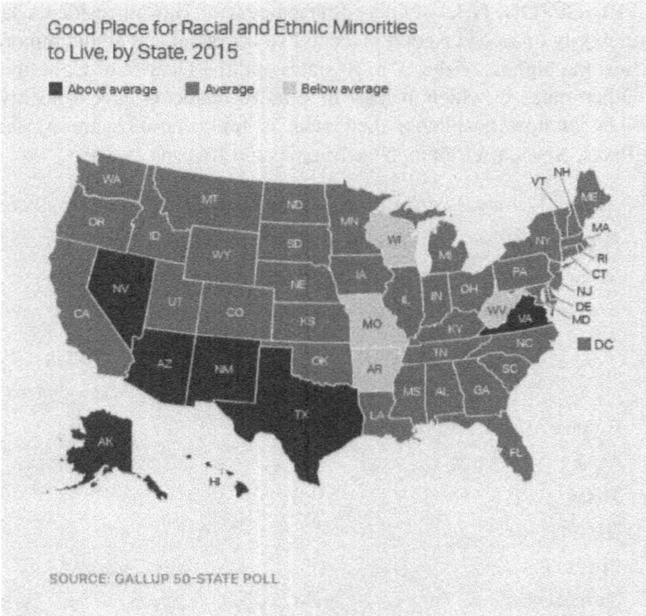

Despite state-level differences in these attitudes, residents of all 50 states are generally positive that their place of residence is a good place for minorities – as was the case in Gallup's initial 50-State poll in 2013.

State-by-state differences in Americans' attitudes about the climate for racial and ethnic minorities have been quite stable over the past three years. The top three states on this year's list – Hawaii, Alaska and Texas – were also the top three states in 2013. And three of the four states that are lowest on the 2016 list – West Virginia, Missouri and Arkansas – were at the bottom of the list three years ago.

Implications

Americans generally remain positive about their local city or area as a place for racial and ethnic minorities to live, as was the case two years ago, and residents in states with the most minorities tend to be the most positive. In states like Hawaii and Texas, non-Hispanic whites are themselves a minority group, with well over half of state residents identifying their race and ethnicity as something other than non-Hispanic white. This makes it perhaps not surprising that these states' residents would say their state is a good place for racial and ethnic minorities. But even in states whose residents are mostly non-Hispanic white, clear majorities say they believe their state is a good place for minorities.

Additionally, it takes only a few individuals to create a hostile situation for minorities, even if most residents of a state perceive themselves as welcoming and positive. Seventy-six percent of Missouri residents, for example, say their state is a good place for minorities. That leaves plenty of Missouri residents who perceive their local area as having a poor environment for minorities – some of whom may live in and around the St. Louis suburb of Ferguson, or are responding in terms of the racial unrest in that city.

Many Americans may feel it appropriate to indicate that they view their area positively on this measure, and other research shows that non-minorities are typically more positive about race relations than minorities themselves. In addition, although the measure reviewed here is quite positive in general, a long line of social science research shows that self-reported attitudes about race do not always predict actual behaviors.

These data are available in Gallup Analytics.

Survey Methods

Results for this Gallup poll are based on telephone interviews conducted March 30-Dec. 22, 2015, with random samples of approximately 500 adults, aged 18 and older, living in each of the 50 U.S. states. Data are weighted to account for unequal selection probability, nonresponse and double coverage of landline and cellphone users in the two sampling frames. Data are also weighted to state estimates of gender, age, race, Hispanic ethnicity, education and phone status (cellphone only, landline only, both, and cellphone mostly).

For results based on the total sample of adults in each state, the margin of sampling error is ±6 percentage points at the 95% confidence level. All reported margins of sampling error include computed design effects for weighting.

March 10, 2016
AMERICANS NAME ECONOMY, GOVERNMENT AS TOP PROBLEMS

by Jeffrey M. Jones

Story Highlights

- *17% mention economy, 15% dissatisfaction with government*
- *Mentions of unemployment remain elevated*
- *27% are satisfied with the way things are going in the U.S.*

PRINCETON, N.J. – The economy and dissatisfaction with the government, two issues regularly at the top of Gallup's monthly most important problem list, rank as Americans' top issues in March. Mentions of unemployment are in the double digits for a second consecutive month after hitting a seven-year low in January.

Recent Trend, Most Important Problem

What do you think is the most important problem facing this country today? [OPEN-ENDED]

	Jan 2016	Feb 2016	March 2016
	%	%	%
Economy in general	13	17	17
Dissatisfaction with government	16	13	15
Unemployment/Jobs	5	10	11
Immigration	8	10	8
Healthcare	4	6	8
Race relations/Racism	6	5	6
Terrorism	9	7	6
Election/Election reform	2	*	5
Federal budget deficit	5	6	5
Moral/Ethical decline	4	2	4
Education	3	5	4

Issues mentioned by 4% or more of respondents in March 2016 shown.

GALLUP

The results are based on Gallup's March 2-6 poll. Beyond the top three problems, at least 5% of Americans mention several other issues. These include immigration, healthcare, race relations, terrorism, the election and the federal budget deficit.

Mentions of the election, at 5%, are not high in an absolute sense, but they are the highest since Gallup began tracking the category in 2001. The prior high was 2% on several occasions, usually shortly after an election took place. Many of the responses in the current survey specifically mention Donald Trump and his role in the election. Those citing the election as the most important problem are primarily independents and Democrats.

The greatest party differences in perceptions of the most important problem facing the nation are on the economy, given a sharp increase in Republican mentions of it this month. Currently, 28% of Republicans say the economy is the most important problem, up from 16% in February and 8% in December. By contrast, the percentages of independents and Democrats naming the issue are currently 16% and 12%, respectively, mostly consistent with the past six months. Republicans' heightened concern about the economy could reflect their agreement with Republican presidential candidates' rhetoric about the economic problems the country is facing.

Percent Mentioning Economy in General as Most Important Problem, by Political Party

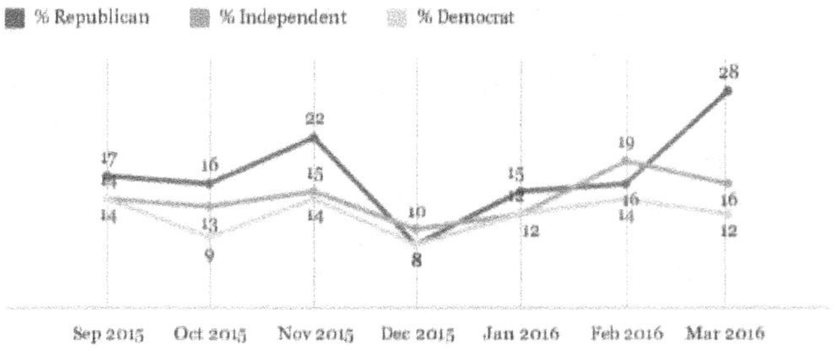

GALLUP

Other notable party differences in perceptions about the country's top problem are Republicans' greater likelihood than Democrats to mention immigration, terrorism and national security. And Democrats are more likely than Republicans to name race relations and the government.

Roughly One in Four Satisfied With State of Nation

The poll also finds 27% of Americans saying they are satisfied with the way things are going in the country, including 44% of Democrats and 25% of independents, but only 10% of Republicans.

The current satisfaction level among all Americans is in line with what Gallup has measured the last four years, but significantly below the historical average of 37%.

Below-average satisfaction at the time of an election is often a sign of trouble for the incumbent presidential party's ability to win, as in 1980 (19%), 1992 (22%) and 2008 (13%). However, President Barack Obama won re-election in 2012 when satisfaction was only slightly better (33%) than it is now.

The president's party typically has won elections when satisfaction was above the historical average, which was the case in 1984 (48%), 1988 (56%), 1996 (39%) and 2004 (44%). The exception was in 2000 when the Democrats lost the election by virtue of the Electoral College vote even though satisfaction was 62%.

Implications

Americans remain much more dissatisfied than satisfied with the state of the nation, and the economy and the way the government is operating are two of the major issues of concern. The economy and the government have consistently been named as the most important problems facing the country over the past five years.

Satisfaction levels usually do not improve greatly over the course of a presidential election year, but they did improve in 1988, 1996 and 2012. With current levels of satisfaction just below what they were in November 2012, even a slight increase may be enough to improve Democrats' chances of retaining the White House.

Historical data are available in Gallup Analytics.

Survey Methods

Results for this Gallup poll are based on telephone interviews conducted March 2-6, 2016, with a random sample of 1,019 adults, aged 18 and older, living in all 50 U.S. states and the District of Columbia. For results based on the total sample of national adults, the margin of sampling error is ±4 percentage points at the 95% confidence level. All reported margins of sampling error include computed design effects for weighting.

March 10, 2016
OBAMA'S JOB APPROVAL AT HIGHEST LEVEL SINCE MAY 2013

by Andrew Dugan and Frank Newport

Story Highlights

- *50% approve of Obama's job performance in latest weekly reading*
- *Nearly nine in 10 Democrats approve, up from 81% in early 2016*
- *Americans view Obama's final year similarly to Reagan's thus far*

WASHINGTON, D.C. – President Barack Obama earned a 50% job approval rating for the week ending March 6, his highest weekly average since May 2013.

Barack Obama's Job Approval Ratings -- Weekly Averages

Latest weekly average: Feb. 29-March 6, 2016

Gallup U.S. Daily tracking

GALLUP

Obama's current 50% weekly average exceeds the 46% he averaged in his seventh year in office, which ended on Jan. 19 of this year. This latest rating also exceeds his 47% average since taking office in 2009, spanning nearly two full terms.

Throughout his seven years in office, Obama's ratings have been among the most politically polarized of any modern president. His current higher overall rating continues to reflect an extreme degree of party polarization, with 87% of Democrats approving of the job Obama is doing as president versus 11% of Republicans.

Obama's current standing with Democrats is four percentage points higher than his average approval rating among Democrats since taking office in 2009. At the same time, his job approval ratings from Republicans and independents are close to his term averages for these groups. Obama's current 87% reading among Democrats is also up from 81% at the beginning of this year, while his ratings among independents and Republicans have been more stable over the past two months.

Barack Obama's Weekly Job Approval Ratings, by Party

% Approve

	U.S. adults	Democrats	Independents	Republicans
	%	%	%	%
Feb 29-Mar 6, 2016	50	87	45	11
Dec 28, 2015-Jan 3, 2016	45	81	42	10
Average weekly rating to date	47	83	43	13

Gallup U.S. Daily tracking

GALLUP

While it's hard to pinpoint precisely why Obama's approval rating has risen among Democrats recently, there are a number of plausible explanations. The unusual status of the Republican primary race – exemplified in particular by front-runner Donald Trump's campaign style and rhetoric – may serve to make Obama look statesmanlike in comparison. The campaign season also may activate latent partisan loyalty among those broadly in the Democratic camp.

Obama's Approval Ahead of Bush's, Below Clinton's and on Par With Reagan's

Although up, Obama's overall job approval rating is still lower than that of his most recent Democratic predecessor, Bill Clinton, at a comparable point in his two-term presidency. In early March 2000, Clinton's approval rating was 63%. At that point, Clinton fared about as well as Obama among Democrats – 89% approved of Clinton then, compared with the 87% who approve of Obama now. But unlike Obama, a majority of independents (65%) and close to a third of Republicans (31%) rated Clinton well, reflecting a much less polarized environment 16 years ago.

Obama is doing significantly better than his most recent predecessor, George W. Bush, who had a 32% job approval rating in March 2008. Bush was rated equally poorly by the opposing party as Obama is today. However, unlike Obama, he did not enjoy the same high level of support from his own party, with fewer than three in four Republicans (72%) approving of his job performance at that time.

In March 1988, 51% of U.S. adults approved of Ronald Reagan's job performance, almost identical to Obama's current rating. Reagan's profile across party lines was not as polarized as Obama's, however, with 81% approval among Republicans and 28% among Democrats.

Approval of Recent Two-Term U.S. Presidents in March of Final Year in Office

% Approve

	U.S. adults	Democrats	Independents	Republicans
	%	%	%	%
Barack Obama	50	87	45	11
George W. Bush	32	9	23	72
Bill Clinton	63	89	65	31
Ronald Reagan	51	28	51	81

Gallup U.S. Daily tracking

GALLUP

Implications

After averaging 48% in the first two months of the year, Obama's weekly job approval rating has edged up to 50%. This increase has been driven partly by Democrats' approval of Obama rising to a nearly three-year high. Obama's popularity among Democrats has been improving steadily over the past year – perhaps one reason why presidential candidate Hillary Clinton is tacking herself tightly to the Obama legacy.

In comparison, the two most recent candidates running to succeed a two-term president of the same party – John McCain running to follow the unpopular Bush, and Al Gore trying to succeed the popular but scandal-prone Bill Clinton – went to greater pains to ensure they were not associated with the outgoing president. Prior to that, George H.W. Bush in 1988 presented himself as a natural heir to the Reagan legacy and was able to win his own term.

These data are available in Gallup Analytics.

Survey Methods

Results for this Gallup poll are based on telephone interviews conducted Feb. 29-March 6, 2016, on the Gallup U.S. Daily survey, with a random sample of 3,563 adults, aged 18 and older, living in all 50 U.S. states and the District of Columbia. For results based on the total sample of national adults, the margin of sampling error is ±2 percentage points at the 95% confidence level. All reported margins of sampling error include computed design effects for weighting.

March 10, 2016

NORTH DAKOTA RESIDENTS MOST POSITIVE ABOUT SCHOOLS

by Stephanie Marken and Vanessa Maturo

Story Highlights

- *89% of North Dakota residents rate schools as excellent or good*
- *Nevada and New Mexico residents least positive about their schools*
- *Residents see link between quality K-12 education and workplace success*

WASHINGTON, D.C. – North Dakota residents (89%) are more likely than those living in any other U.S. state to rate the K-12 education provided in their state as excellent or good, followed closely by those living in Minnesota and Nebraska. In stark contrast, about half as many Nevada and New Mexico residents, 42% in each, rate their public education systems positively.

States With Most and Least Positive Ratings of the Quality of Education

Overall, how would you rate the quality of public education provided in grades K through 12 in the state -- as excellent, good, only fair or poor?

Most Positive States	% Excellent/good	Least Positive States	% Excellent/good
North Dakota	89	Nevada	42
Minnesota	82	New Mexico	42
Nebraska	82	Hawaii	47
Iowa	80	Louisiana	49
Massachusetts	80	Arizona	50
New Hampshire	80	Alabama	52
Wyoming	79	California	52
South Dakota	78	Mississippi	53
Vermont	75	Oregon	54
Virginia	75	Rhode Island	54

Gallup Poll, March-December 2015

GALLUP

North Dakota also ranked at the top when Gallup first measured state residents' perceptions of public education quality in 2013, while Nevada and New Mexico were at the bottom.

These results are based on a Gallup poll conducted March 30-Dec. 22, 2015, with approximately 500 interviews in every state. Full results for each state appear at the end of the article.

North Dakota Residents Report School System Prepares Students for Workplace Success

Residents in states where a large share of residents rate the quality of education as excellent or good are also more likely to believe their public school system prepares students for success in the workplace. About nine in 10 North Dakota residents report their public school system prepares students for success in the workplace. Nebraska and South Dakota residents follow closely behind at 81%. On the other end of the spectrum, less than half of Nevada, New Mexico and Hawaii residents feel that their state education system prepares students for workplace success.

There is a moderate relationship between unemployment rates and residents' perceptions that their public education system prepares students for workplace success. In December 2015, North Dakota, Nebraska and South Dakota – states with positive perceptions of public education – had the three lowest unemployment rates among all states and the District of Columbia, according to the Bureau of Labor Statistics. Nevada and New Mexico – the two states with the least positive perceptions of schools – had significantly higher unemployment rates and ranked 46th and 48th in December 2015 among all 50 states and the District of Columbia.

States With Most and Least Positive Views That Their Public School System Prepares Students for Success in the Workplace

Do you believe your state public school system prepares students for success in the workplace?

Most Positive States	% Yes	Least Positive States	% Yes
North Dakota	89	Nevada	47
Nebraska	81	New Mexico	48
South Dakota	81	Hawaii	49
Wyoming	78	Rhode Island	51
Minnesota	76	California	53
Iowa	75	Oregon	55
Kansas	75	Florida	56
Virginia	75	Arizona	57
New Hampshire	74	Louisiana	57
Massachusetts	73	Illinois	58
		New York	58

Gallup Poll, March-December 2015

GALLUP

Implications

Gallup data reveal a strong relationship between states' economic conditions and residents' perceptions that their public education systems are providing high-quality education that will prepare students for workplace success. Public education systems require strong financial support at the state and local level, and challenging economic conditions can make it more difficult to provide the funding required for schools to deliver a high-quality education. Additionally, students living in states with higher unemployment rates may face different challenges in finding a good job.

Nationally, leaders continuously suggest programmatic changes to improve the quality of education in the U.S. Gallup data suggest that Americans believe a key component of a high-quality education is providing students with skills that can easily transfer to the workplace.

Survey Methods

Results for this Gallup poll are based on telephone interviews conducted March 30-Dec. 22, 2015, with random samples of approximately 500 adults, aged 18 and older, living in each of the 50 U.S. states. Data are weighted to account for unequal selection probability, nonresponse and double coverage of landline and cellphone users in the two sampling frames. Data are also weighted to state estimates of gender, age, race, Hispanic ethnicity, education and phone status (cellphone only, landline only, both and cellphone mostly).

For results based on the total sample of adults in each state, the margin of sampling error is ±6 percentage points at the 95% confidence level. All reported margins of sampling error include computed design effects for weighting.

Percentage of State Residents Who Rate the Quality of Public Education in Grades K Through 12 in Their State as Excellent or Good

Overall, how would you rate the quality of public education provided in grades K through 12 in the state -- as excellent, good, only fair or poor?

	% Excellent/good
North Dakota	89
Minnesota	82
Nebraska	82
Iowa	80
Massachusetts	80
New Hampshire	80
Wyoming	79
South Dakota	78
Vermont	75
Virginia	75
Montana	73
Connecticut	71
Kansas	71
Texas	71
Utah	71
Wisconsin	71
Alaska	70
Maine	70
Ohio	68
Colorado	67
Indiana	67
Arkansas	65
Washington	65
Missouri	64
New Jersey	64
Kentucky	62
Maryland	61
New York	61
Georgia	60
Michigan	60
South Carolina	60
Tennessee	60
Pennsylvania	59
West Virginia	59
Delaware	58
North Carolina	58
Idaho	56
Oklahoma	56
Florida	55
Illinois	55
Oregon	54
Rhode Island	54
Mississippi	53
Alabama	52
California	52
Arizona	50
Louisiana	49
Hawaii	47
Nevada	42
New Mexico	42

Gallup Poll, March-December 2015

GALLUP

Percentage of State Residents Who Agree Their State Public School System Prepares Students for Success in the Workplace

Do you believe your state public school system prepares students for success in the workplace?

	% Yes
North Dakota	89
Nebraska	81
South Dakota	81
Wyoming	78
Minnesota	76
Iowa	75
Kansas	75
Virginia	75
New Hampshire	74
Massachusetts	73
Alaska	72
Wisconsin	72
Montana	71
Utah	70
Vermont	70
Texas	69
Arkansas	68
Connecticut	68
Indiana	68
Ohio	67
Maine	66
Alabama	65
Washington	65
Colorado	64
Delaware	64
Michigan	64
Mississippi	64
Missouri	64
New Jersey	63
South Carolina	63
Oklahoma	62
Kentucky	61
Maryland	61
Pennsylvania	61
Tennessee	61
West Virginia	61
North Carolina	60
Georgia	59
Idaho	59
Illinois	58
New York	58
Arizona	57
Louisiana	57
Florida	56
Oregon	55
California	53
Rhode Island	51
Hawaii	49
New Mexico	48
Nevada	47

Gallup Poll, March-December 2015

GALLUP

March 11, 2016

TRUMP HAS A MAJOR IMAGE PROBLEM WITH HISPANICS

by Frank Newport

Story Highlights

- *Trump has 12% favorable, 77% unfavorable image among Hispanics*
- *Trump has become better known, but more disliked since summer*
- *Rubio, Kasich and Cruz have much more positive images among Hispanics*

PRINCETON, N.J. – Presidential candidate Donald Trump has a major image problem among U.S. Hispanics, with 77% saying they view him unfavorably and just 12% viewing him favorably. This gives Trump by far the most negative image among Hispanics of any of the four Republican candidates. He also has a much more negative image among Hispanics than the two Democratic candidates.

Favorable and Unfavorable Opinions of Presidential Candidates, Among Hispanics
Ranked by net favorable

	Favorable	Unfavorable	No opinion	Familiarity	Net favorable
	%	%	%	%	(pct. pts.)
Hillary Clinton	59	26	15	85	+33
Bernie Sanders	35	16	49	51	+19
Marco Rubio	32	26	42	58	+6
John Kasich	15	14	71	29	+1
Ted Cruz	26	30	44	56	-4
Donald Trump	12	77	11	89	-65

Jan. 2-March 8, 2016

GALLUP

This latest update is based on Gallup Daily tracking data collected Jan. 2-March 8. When Gallup started tracking the candidates in July and August of 2015, Trump was not quite as well-known as he is now. However, his image was already very negative, with 66% of Hispanics viewing him unfavorably and 14% favorably. As he has become better known among Hispanics, his image has worsened.

The major factor most likely contributing to Trump's image deficit among Hispanics is one of the first highly publicized controversies of his presidential campaign in June, when he called for building a giant wall along the Mexican border. He also characterized Mexicans coming into the U.S. as drug traffickers and rapists. Since then, Trump's strong and controversial stances against other immigrant groups may have reinforced the ill will among Hispanics, the majority of whom immigrated to this country within the last several generations.

Trump is well-known among Hispanics. At this point, 89% are familiar enough with the billionaire businessman to have an opinion about him, substantially higher than Hispanics' familiarity with Marco Rubio and Ted Cruz (58% and 56% familiarity, respectively) and much higher than Hispanics' low familiarity with John Kasich (29%). In fact, Hispanics are now slightly more familiar with Trump than with Hillary Clinton.

Trump's Negative Image Among Hispanics Goes Beyond Party Leanings

Hispanics tilt Democratic, with 50% identifying as Democratic or leaning Democratic in the Jan. 2-March 8 period, contrasted with 23% who identify as Republican or who lean Republican. Trump's negative image, however, is not merely a result of Hispanics' Democratic political orientation – evident in the substantially more positive images that Hispanics have of the other three Republican candidates. Two of these – Rubio and Kasich – actually have slightly more positive than negative ratings, while Cruz's image tilts just slightly negative.

Trump also has significant image issues among the relatively small group of Hispanic Republicans interviewed in this period. He is the only one of the four GOP candidates with a negative image among Hispanic Republicans, with a net favorable rating of -29. By contrast, Rubio, Cruz and Kasich all have net positive images among Hispanic Republicans, with Rubio's +34 the best of the group. Trump is significantly less popular with Hispanic Republicans than the two *Democratic* candidates in the race, Clinton and Bernie Sanders.

Favorable and Unfavorable Opinions of Presidential Candidates, Among Hispanic Republicans
Ranked by net favorable

	Favorable	Unfavorable	No opinion	Familiarity	Net favorable
	%	%	%	%	(pct. pts.)
Marco Rubio	53	19	28	72	+34
Ted Cruz	43	22	35	65	+21
John Kasich	24	19	57	43	+5
Bernie Sanders	29	37	34	66	-8
Hillary Clinton	39	50	11	89	-11
Donald Trump	31	60	9	91	-29

Jan. 2-March 8, 2016

GALLUP

Bottom Line

Hispanics' views of Trump can be an important factor not only in forthcoming primary contests in states such as Florida and Arizona with high Hispanic populations, but also in the general election – should he win the GOP nomination. Just this week a news report indicated that billionaire George Soros and other liberal donors are bankrolling a multimillion-dollar campaign to motivate Hispanic voters to get out and vote in key swing states such as Colorado, Florida and Nevada. A *New York Times* article this week cited anecdotal evidence that disliking Trump has led to a situation in which Hispanics living in the U.S. are increasingly attempting to become U.S. citizens between now and November specifically to vote against him.

Exit polls show that Mitt Romney received 27% of the Hispanic vote in his 2012 run against Barack Obama, and Gallup polling in the fall of that year showed that Romney's image among Hispanics, while net negative, was still much more positive than Trump's is today.

This suggests that if Trump ends up being the GOP nominee, his unusually negative image among Hispanics could make it difficult for him to equal Romney's 2012 share of the Hispanic vote. In particular, this could present a challenge for Trump in key swing states where Hispanics are a sizable percentage of the electorate.

Historical data are available in Gallup Analytics.

Survey Methods

Results for this Gallup poll are based on telephone interviews conducted on a continuous basis on the Gallup U.S. Daily survey. The latest update used in this report is based on interviewing conducted Jan. 2 - March 8, 2016, with random samples of between 1,173 and 1,236 Hispanic adults who rated each candidate, aged 18 and older, living in all 50 U.S. states and the District of Columbia, rating each of the three candidates. For results based on the total sample, the margin of sampling error is ±4 percentage points at the 95% confidence level. Reports of Hispanic Republicans are based on random samples of between 294 and 331 Hispanics who identify as Republicans or lean Republican, with a margin of sampling error of ±7. All reported margins of sampling error include computed design effects for weighting.

March 14, 2016
MORE AMERICANS VIEW OBAMA POSITIVELY ON KEY ISSUES

by Jim Norman

Story Highlights

- *45% now say Obama doing good job of making America prosperous*
- *48% say he is doing good job on energy, up from 39% in 2015*
- *54% say good job on environment, slight boost from 2015*

WASHINGTON, D.C. – More Americans say President Barack Obama is doing a good job of improving the nation's energy policy (48%) and making America prosperous (45%) than at most points in his presidency. On another key measure of his presidency, 54% say Obama is doing a good job of protecting the nation's environment, a slight boost from last year but mostly in line with his recent readings.

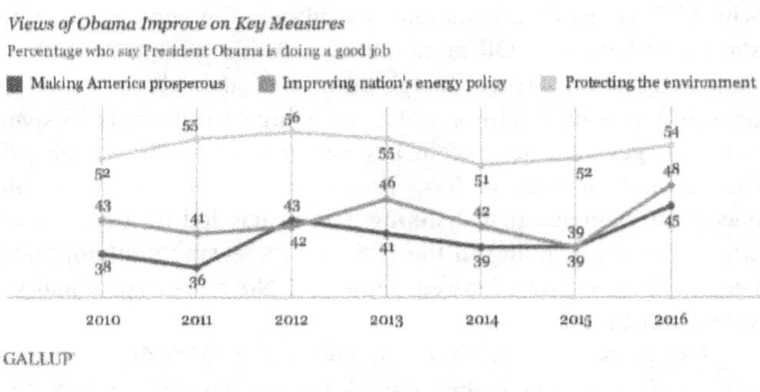

In Obama's final year in office, U.S. adults are still more likely to say he is doing a poor job (49%) rather than a good job (45%) of making America prosperous, but the margin has shrunk to four points from 14 points last year. The percentages saying Obama is doing a good job on the environment, energy and the economy are clustered more closely than they have been in any previous year of his presidency. The improvement on all three from last year mirrors the improvement in Obama's overall job approval rating, now the best it has been since 2013.

In a Gallup poll conducted March 5-8, 2009, during the first weeks of Obama's presidency, 79% of Americans said they thought he would do a good job on the environment, 72% said he would do a good job with energy policy and 61% said he would do a good job of making America prosperous.

Environment, Energy, Economy All Made Headlines in 2015

The issues of prosperity, energy and the environment all made major news in the past year, and the White House claims major accomplishments in all three areas.

Making America Prosperous: That Obama's rating on making America prosperous is higher than it was last year but still not a majority reflects the mix of good and bad news on the nation's economic front. On the positive side, unemployment dropped from 5.5% in February 2015 to 4.9% last month. On the negative side, the Dow Jones industrial average was down to 16,899 on March 2 from 18,289 a year earlier. A drop of more than 25% in gasoline prices over the past 12 months has been good news for most consumers but very bad news for some investors and workers.

Obama's effort to tout low unemployment and his trade deal with 12 Pacific Rim nations as economic successes have clearly resonated with some of the public. But this year's presidential campaign is presenting significant obstacles to Obama's assertions, with major candidates from both parties attacking the trade deal and claiming the economy is failing most Americans.

Improving U.S. Energy Policy: The drop in gas prices was accompanied by a plethora of stories on the "oil glut" that caused the lower prices. Americans are now less concerned about the possibility of a critical energy shortage and more likely than in recent years to think protection of the environment should take precedence over developing energy supplies. In January, Obama pushed strongly during his final State of the Union address for cutbacks in "dirty energy" such as oil and coal; instead, he promoted major investments in "clean energy." Obama has made strides in public opinion over the past year on energy policy, with the percentage saying he is doing a good job increasing from 39% to 48% and thereby gaining approval from the bulk of Americans.

Protecting the Environment: Throughout his time as president, Obama has sounded warnings about the need to combat climate change, and his administration has consistently pushed programs to invest in "clean energy." A White House list of his top 10 accomplishments in 2015 includes the Paris Agreement on climate change that 195 nations adopted in December. Americans' views of Obama's record on protecting the environment have varied little over the past seven years, with the percentage saying he is doing a good job reaching a high of 56% in 2012 and a low of 51% in 2014.

Democrats' Support More Solid Than Republicans' Opposition

Almost identical percentages of Democrats give Obama credit for doing a good job on the environment (81%), prosperity (81%) and energy (80%). Only small minorities of Republicans say he is doing a good job on the three, with more variation than among Democrats: 27% of Republicans say he is doing a good job on the environment, 18% on energy, 10% on prosperity.

Americans Who Say President Obama Is Doing a "Good Job" on Three Key Issues, by Party

Do you think Barack Obama is doing a good job or a poor job in handling each of the following issues as president?

	Democrats%	Independents%	Republicans%
Protecting the nation's environment	81	48	27
Improving the nation's energy policy	80	42	18
Making America prosperous	81	38	10

Gallup, March 2-6, 2016

Combining results across the three items reveals that 70% of Democrats say Obama is doing a good job in all three areas. In contrast, 57% of Republicans say he is doing a poor job on all three.

On two of the measures – protecting the environment and making America prosperous – Democrats' ratings improved while Republicans' were stagnant over the past year. Democrats' ratings increased by six points on the environment and eight points on making America prosperous. Ratings on improving energy policy increased for both Republicans (five points) and Democrats (12 points).

Bottom Line

Obama has made some headway in gaining Americans' approval on his handling of the economy and energy policy over the past year, mostly because Democrats are viewing his presidency more favorably as Americans prepare to choose his successor. However, he is still locked into an enduring partisan split that seems to leave little room for significant changes in views of his presidency. His overall approval rating has rarely dipped below 40% or risen above 55%, and the percentage of the public saying he has done a good job on energy, prosperity or the environment has never been lower than 36% (prosperity) or higher than 56% (environment). By comparison, Obama's predecessor, George W. Bush, saw greater extremes: 63% said Bush was doing a good job on prosperity five months after the Sept. 11 terrorist attacks, and only 23% in 2008 said he was doing a good job on energy.

Methodology

Results for this Gallup poll are based on telephone interviews conducted March 2-6, 2016, with a random sample of 1,019 adults, aged 18 and older, living in all 50 U.S. states and the District of Columbia. For results based on the total sample of national adults, the margin of sampling error is ±4 percentage points at the 95% confidence level. All reported margins of sampling error include computed design effects for weighting.

March 14, 2016
AMERICANS ATTRIBUTE WARM WINTER WEATHER TO CLIMATE CHANGE

by Rebecca Riffkin

Story Highlights

- *63% say winter was warmer than usual; 10% say it was colder*
- *Most who say it was warmer attribute this to climate change*
- *In previous two years, majorities said winter was colder than usual*

WASHINGTON, D.C. – A majority of Americans, 63%, say the weather in their local area this winter was warmer than usual. When asked what they think caused these abnormal temperatures, more Americans say the shift was the result of human-caused climate change rather than normal variations. Just 10% of Americans say it was a colder winter than usual, and 26% say the weather was about the same.

Americans' Experience of Extremes in Local Weather and the Perceived Cause

Have temperatures in your local area been – [ROTATED: colder than usual this winter, about the same, (or) warmer than usual this winter]? (Asked of those who say the weather has been colder/warmer than usual:) Do you think temperatures are colder/warmer mainly due to – [ROTATED: human-caused climate change (or to) normal year-to-year variation in temperatures]?

	2015%	2016%
Winter temperatures in your local area		
Colder than usual	51	10
(Due to normal variation in temperatures)	31	6
(Due to human-caused climate change)	19	4
About the same	29	26
Warmer than usual	18	63
(Due to normal variation in temperatures)	8	26
(Due to human-caused climate change)	9	34

Gallup, March 2-6, 2016

Most recently, Americans who have said they've experienced abnormal winter temperatures have been more likely to attribute those changes to normal variations than to climate change. The shift this year is likely because a larger, more regionally and politically diverse group of Americans is reporting warmer temperatures this year.

Majorities of Americans of all political identities say this winter was warmer than usual. However, more Democrats (76%) than Republicans (51%) say this, and Democrats who say it was warmer are more than twice as likely as Republicans to attribute the rise in temperatures to climate change, as Gallup has found in the past.

Gallup's annual March Environment poll has asked Americans since 2012 to report on weather conditions in their local areas. Americans appear to be reasonably accurate in their temperature assessments. This year and in 2012, majorities have said it was warmer than usual. This year's poll was conducted just before warm, spring-like temperatures came early for much of the U.S. East Coast but a few weeks after summer-like temperatures in California and much of the Southwestern region. El Nino is probably one cause of this abnormal weather.

In 2014 and 2015, Americans were most likely to say the weather was colder than usual, an assessment generally in line with official statistics.

Local Winter Temperatures Compared With Prior Winters

Next, I'd like you to think about the weather in your local area this winter season compared to past winters. Have temperatures in your local area been -- [ROTATED: colder than usual this winter, about the same (or) warmer than usual this winter]?

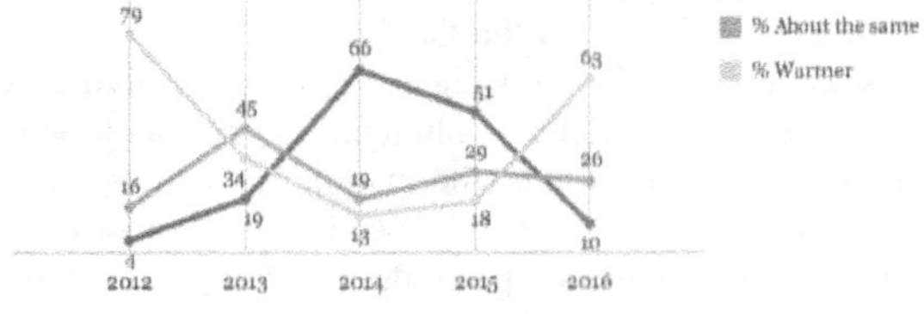

GALLUP

The highest proportions of adults saying it was warmer than usual this winter – more than seven in 10 – were in the East and Midwest, the regions most likely to experience cold winters. But even a majority of Southerners reported warmer-than-normal temperatures. Americans in the West were the least likely of all four regions to say the winter was warmer than usual; still, 49% said this.

Winter Temperatures Compared With Prior Winters, by Region

Next, I'd like you to think about the weather in your local area this winter season compared to past winters. Have temperatures in your local area been – [ROTATED: colder than usual this winter, about the same (or) warmer than usual this winter]?

	East%	Midwest%	South%	West%
Colder	5	6	11	19
About the same	17	21	31	31
Warmer	78	72	57	49

Gallup, March 2-6, 2016

Last year, Americans' views of their winter weather varied more by region. Westerners were more likely to say it was warmer rather than colder, and their responses were the most similar to this year's. In the other regions, especially the East, residents were more likely to say it was colder than usual last year. This again largely matched the varying weather patterns found in different parts of the country last winter.

Bottom Line

Scientists say 2015 was the warmest year on record across the globe, and temperatures increased by one of the largest amounts found since record keeping began in 1880. U.S. temperatures were also high, and that trend appears to have continued this winter, as El Nino has affected the weather. And, while scientists say climate change is driving global temperatures up, they say the more recent changes also reflect a spike in the usual patterns. Still, Americans were more likely this year to attribute the extreme weather to climate change rather than normal variations, including El Nino.

Cold weather was partially to blame for low U.S. gross domestic product figures in the first quarter of last year, because snow and cold temperatures discourage shopping and traveling and encourage people to bundle up at home, not spending money. But in the late 1990s, an El Nino event boosted GDP by at least a small amount, something that could happen again this year. So the warm weather Americans have reported this winter could be a good sign for the GDP in the first quarter, even if it means fewer people buying snow shovels and salt for sidewalks and driveways over the past few months.

Historical data are available in Gallup Analytics.

Survey Methods

Results for this Gallup poll are based on telephone interviews conducted March 2-6, 2016, on the Gallup U.S. Daily survey, with a random sample of 1,019 adults, aged 18 and older, living in all 50 U.S. states and the District of Columbia. For results based on the total sample of national adults, the margin of sampling error is ±4 percentage points at the 95% confidence level. All reported margins of sampling error include computed design effects for weighting.

March 15, 2016

IN U.S., PERCENTAGE PREDICTING ENERGY SHORTAGE AT NEW LOW

by Jeffrey M. Jones

Story Highlights

- *31% believe U.S. will face critical energy shortage during next five years*
- *This is down from 50% in 2012*
- *28% describe energy situation in U.S. as very serious*

PRINCETON, N.J. – As Americans continue to pay relatively low prices for gas, they are now less likely than at any point in Gallup's trend to predict a critical energy shortage in the country in the next five years. Currently, 31% of Americans believe this will happen, down sharply from 50% when the question was last asked in 2012, and 14 percentage points below the previous low.

Do you think that the United States is or is not likely to face a critical energy shortage during the next five years?

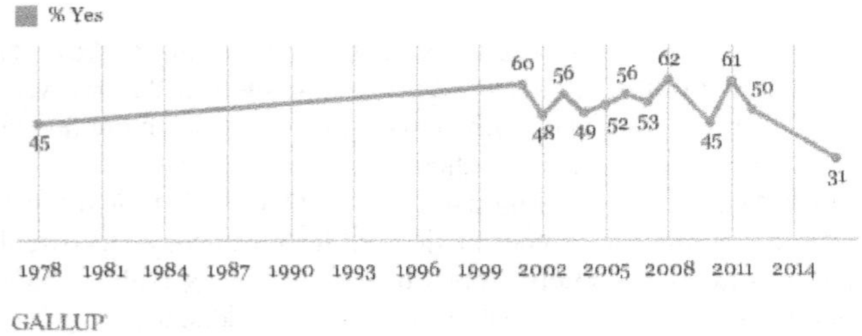

The results are from Gallup's annual Environment poll, conducted March 2-6.

The prior low point in Gallup's trend, first asked in 1978 and updated most years since 2001, was 45%. That occurred on two occasions: in November 1978 after President Jimmy Carter signed the National Energy Act, but before the 1979 oil crisis, and again in 2010.

Americans have been most likely to believe energy shortages were imminent when gas prices were high, as was the case in 2001, 2008 and 2011. The 2001 reading also came at a time when the state of California experienced a widely publicized energy crisis. Between 60% and 62% of Americans said the U.S. was likely to face an energy shortage in those three years.

Compared with when Gallup last asked the question in 2012, expectations of an impending U.S. energy shortage have significantly declined across all key subgroups. Among the groups least likely to believe the U.S. will face shortages are those with a postgraduate education (18%), upper-income Americans (22% of those whose annual household income is $75,000 or more), and men (22%).

By contrast, at least four in 10 lower-income Americans (those whose annual income is less than $30,000), young adults (18 to 29 years old), and nonwhites believe there will be an energy shortage, the highest among key subgroups.

Percentage Describing Energy Situation as Very Serious Near Historical Low

The decline in predictions of an energy shortage are consistent with the decreasing percentage of Americans who describe the U.S.

energy situation as "very serious." Currently, 28% say it is very serious, similar to the last two years but down 14 points since 2012.

How serious would you say the energy situation is in the United States -- very serious, fairly serious or not at all serious?

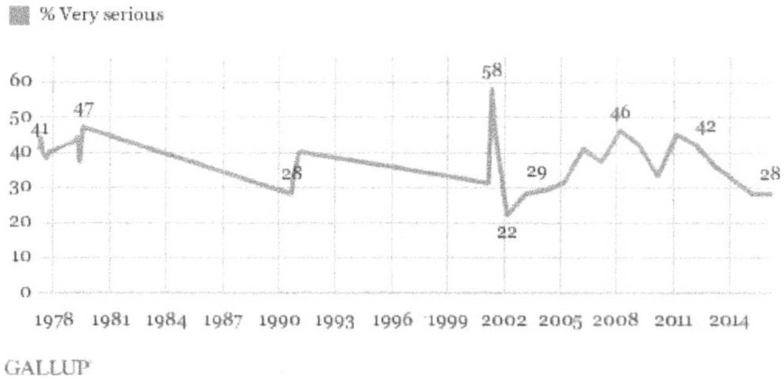

The high point in perceptions that the energy situation was very serious came in a May 2001 poll, when California had instituted "rolling blackouts" to address electricity shortages in that state and gas prices were rising nationwide.

Less than a year later, in March 2002, only 22% described the situation as very serious, the low point in the trend. That lower reading partly reflected not only the easing of the California energy crisis, but also Americans' changing priorities after the 9/11 terror attacks.

The 2002 poll was conducted just months after the 9/11 terror attacks, when terrorism was a dominant concern in Americans' minds. Even though the energy situation may have been worse in 2002 than it is today – indeed, many more (48%) predicted a future energy shortage then compared with today (31%) – Americans viewed the energy situation as less serious, arguably because other issues seemed far less serious compared with the threat of terrorism.

Worry About Energy at 15-Year Low

A separate question in the new survey finds 27% of Americans saying they worry "a great deal" about the "availability and affordability of energy." This ties a March 2003 reading as the lowest in Gallup's trend dating back to 2001. The level of worry was much higher in 2001 and in most years between 2006 and 2012.

Percent Worried About the Availability of Affordable Energy

Next, I'm going to read a list of problems facing the country. For each one, please tell me if you personally worry about this problem a great deal, a fair amount, only a little or not at all? First, how much do you personally worry about -- the availability and affordability of energy?

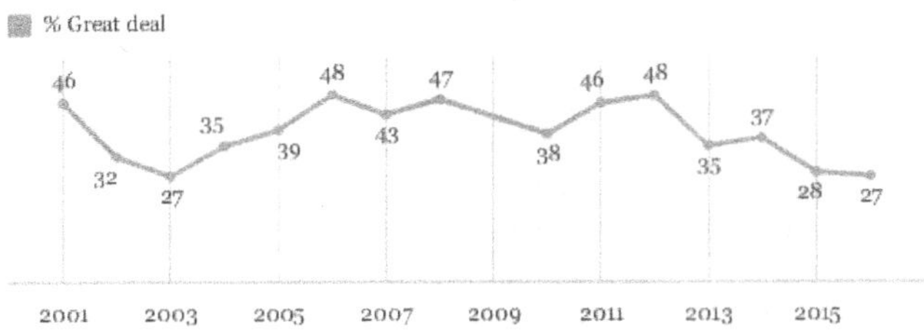

In addition to the 27% who worry a great deal about the availability and affordability of energy, another 34% say they worry "a fair amount." The total 61% who worry at least a fair amount is the lowest in Gallup's trend.

Implications

Americans' current assessments of the energy situation, taken as a whole, are the least negative Gallup has recorded in the past 15 years, if not dating back even further. A record-low 31% believe the U.S. is likely to face a critical energy shortage in the next few years, and slightly more than one in four describe the U.S. energy situation as very serious or say they worry a great deal about the availability and affordability of energy.

Low gas prices are likely the reason for the positive assessment, as the price at the pump is an obvious and frequent reminder to Americans about the U.S. energy supply. Regions of the U.S. and the world that produce energy are well aware of the oil glut, which has contributed to declining prices for consumers. In the past, Americans' concerns about the U.S. energy situation have been highest when gas prices were historically high or rising significantly.

Also, a warmer winter combined with lower heating costs only adds to Americans' contentment with the energy issue. Energy was a major issue discussed during the 2008 and 2012 presidential campaigns, but it may not receive much attention this year since Americans are less concerned about energy shortfalls or high energy prices.

Historical data are available in Gallup Analytics.

Survey Methods

Results for this Gallup poll are based on telephone interviews conducted March 2-6, 2016, with a random sample of 1,019 adults, aged 18 and older, living in all 50 U.S. states and the District of Columbia. For results based on the total sample of national adults, the margin of sampling error is ±4 percentage points at the 95% confidence level. All reported margins of sampling error include computed design effects for weighting.

March 15, 2016

IN U.S., PERCENTAGE PREDICTING ENERGY SHORTAGE AT NEW LOW

by Jeffrey M. Jones

Story Highlights

- *31% believe U.S. will face critical energy shortage during next five years*
- *This is down from 50% in 2012*
- *28% describe energy situation in U.S. as very serious*

PRINCETON, N.J. – As Americans continue to pay relatively low prices for gas, they are now less likely than at any point in Gallup's trend to predict a critical energy shortage in the country in the next five years. Currently, 31% of Americans believe this will happen, down sharply from 50% when the question was last asked in 2012, and 14 percentage points below the previous low.

Do you think that the United States is or is not likely to face a critical energy shortage during the next five years?

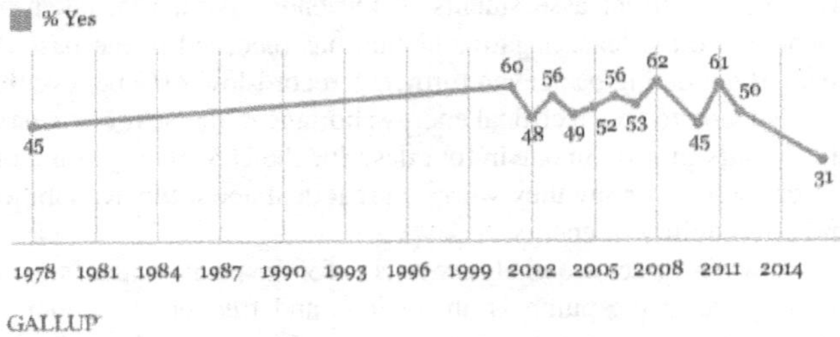

The results are from Gallup's annual Environment poll, conducted March 2-6.

The prior low point in Gallup's trend, first asked in 1978 and updated most years since 2001, was 45%. That occurred on two occasions: in November 1978 after President Jimmy Carter signed the National Energy Act, but before the 1979 oil crisis, and again in 2010.

Americans have been most likely to believe energy shortages were imminent when gas prices were high, as was the case in 2001, 2008 and 2011. The 2001 reading also came at a time when the state of California experienced a widely publicized energy crisis. Between 60% and 62% of Americans said the U.S. was likely to face an energy shortage in those three years.

Compared with when Gallup last asked the question in 2012, expectations of an impending U.S. energy shortage have significantly declined across all key subgroups. Among the groups least likely to believe the U.S. will face shortages are those with a postgraduate education (18%), upper-income Americans (22% of those whose annual household income is $75,000 or more), and men (22%).

By contrast, at least four in 10 lower-income Americans (those whose annual income is less than $30,000), young adults (18 to 29 years old), and nonwhites believe there will be an energy shortage, the highest among key subgroups.

Percentage Describing Energy Situation as Very Serious Near Historical Low

The decline in predictions of an energy shortage are consistent with the decreasing percentage of Americans who describe the U.S. energy situation as "very serious." Currently, 28% say it is very serious, similar to the last two years but down 14 points since 2012.

How serious would you say the energy situation is in the United States -- very serious, fairly serious or not at all serious?

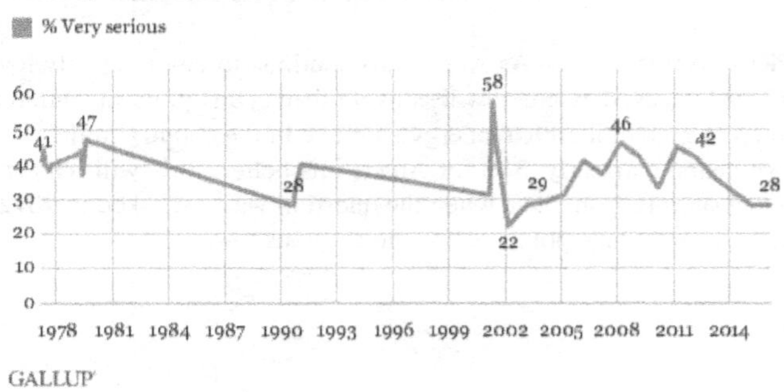

The high point in perceptions that the energy situation was very serious came in a May 2001 poll, when California had instituted "rolling blackouts" to address electricity shortages in that state and gas prices were rising nationwide.

Less than a year later, in March 2002, only 22% described the situation as very serious, the low point in the trend. That lower reading partly reflected not only the easing of the California energy crisis, but also Americans' changing priorities after the 9/11 terror attacks.

The 2002 poll was conducted just months after the 9/11 terror attacks, when terrorism was a dominant concern in Americans' minds. Even though the energy situation may have been worse in 2002 than it is today – indeed, many more (48%) predicted a future energy shortage then compared with today (31%) – Americans viewed the energy situation as less serious, arguably because other issues seemed far less serious compared with the threat of terrorism.

Worry About Energy at 15-Year Low

A separate question in the new survey finds 27% of Americans saying they worry "a great deal" about the "availability and affordability of energy." This ties a March 2003 reading as the lowest in Gallup's trend dating back to 2001. The level of worry was much higher in 2001 and in most years between 2006 and 2012.

Percent Worried About the Availability of Affordable Energy

Next, I'm going to read a list of problems facing the country. For each one, please tell me if you personally worry about this problem a great deal, a fair amount, only a little or not at all? First, how much do you personally worry about -- the availability and affordability of energy?

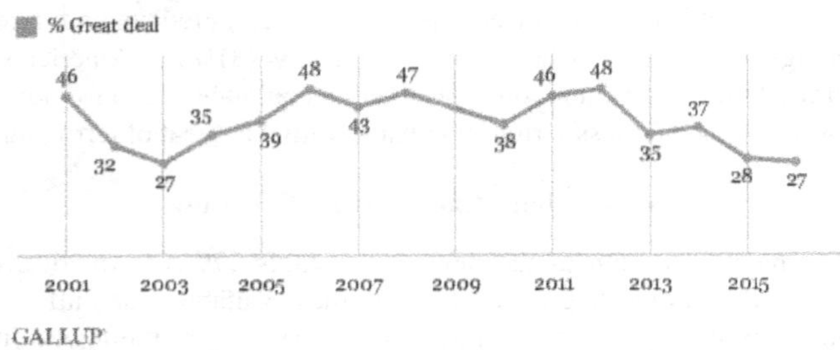

In addition to the 27% who worry a great deal about the availability and affordability of energy, another 34% say they worry "a fair amount." The total 61% who worry at least a fair amount is the lowest in Gallup's trend.

Implications

Americans' current assessments of the energy situation, taken as a whole, are the least negative Gallup has recorded in the past 15 years, if not dating back even further. A record-low 31% believe the U.S. is likely to face a critical energy shortage in the next few years, and slightly more than one in four describe the U.S. energy situation as very serious or say they worry a great deal about the availability and affordability of energy.

Low gas prices are likely the reason for the positive assessment, as the price at the pump is an obvious and frequent reminder to Americans about the U.S. energy supply. Regions of the U.S. and the world that produce energy are well aware of the oil glut, which has contributed to declining prices for consumers. In the past, Americans' concerns about the U.S. energy situation have been highest when gas prices were historically high or rising significantly.

Also, a warmer winter combined with lower heating costs only adds to Americans' contentment with the energy issue. Energy was a major issue discussed during the 2008 and 2012 presidential campaigns, but it may not receive much attention this year since Americans are less concerned about energy shortfalls or high energy prices.

Historical data are available in Gallup Analytics.

Survey Methods

Results for this Gallup poll are based on telephone interviews conducted March 2-6, 2016, with a random sample of 1,019 adults, aged 18 and older, living in all 50 U.S. states and the District of Columbia. For results based on the total sample of national adults, the margin of sampling error is ±4 percentage points at the 95% confidence level. All reported margins of sampling error include computed design effects for weighting.

March 16, 2016
U.S. CONCERN ABOUT GLOBAL WARMING AT EIGHT-YEAR HIGH

by Lydia Saad and Jeffrey M. Jones

PRINCETON, N.J. – Americans are taking global warming more seriously than at any time in the past eight years, according to several measures in Gallup's annual environment poll. Most emblematic is the rise in their stated concern about the issue. Sixty-four percent of U.S. adults say they are worried a "great deal" or "fair amount" about global warming, up from 55% at this time last year and the highest reading since 2008.

How Much Americans Worry About Global Warming

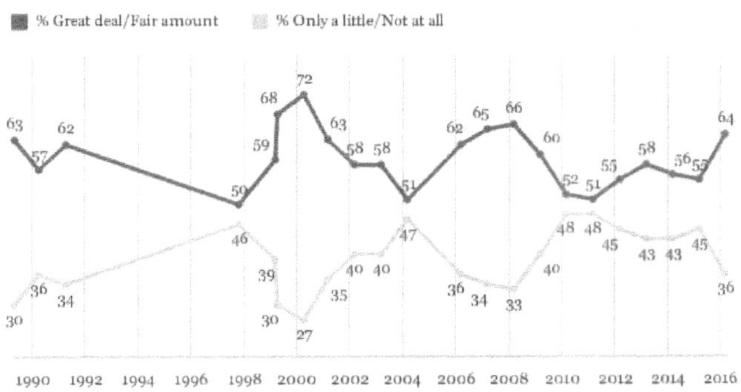

GALLUP

Mirroring this, the March 2-6 survey – conducted at the close of what has reportedly been the warmest winter on record in the U.S. – documents a slight increase in the percentage of Americans who believe the effects of global warming have already begun. Nearly six in 10 (59%) today say the effects have already begun, up from 55% in March 2015. Another 31%, up from 28% in 2015, believe the effects are not currently manifest but will be at some point in the future. That leaves only 10% saying the effects will never happen, down from 16% last year and the lowest since 2007.

U.S. Views About When Effects of Global Warming Will Occur

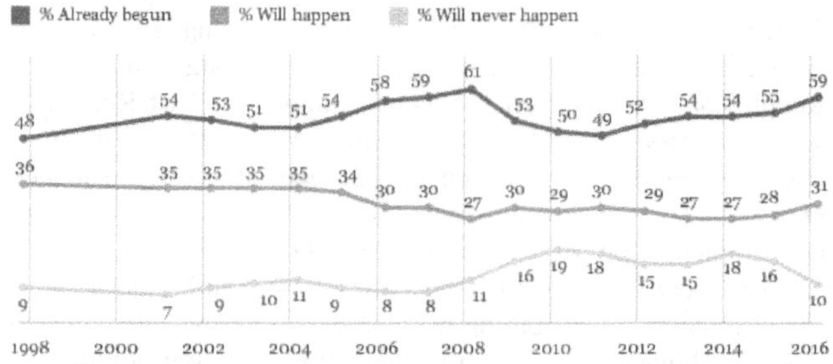

% "Will happen" includes those who think effects will happen in their lifetime, or not in their lifetime but in the future

GALLUP

A third key indicator of public concern about global warming is the percentage of U.S. adults who believe the phenomenon will eventually pose a serious threat to them or their way of life. Forty-one percent now say it will, up from 37% in 2015 and, by one point, the highest in Gallup's trend dating back to 1997.

Americans' Perception of Global Warming as a Serious Threat

Do you think that global warming will pose a serious threat to you or your way of life in your lifetime?

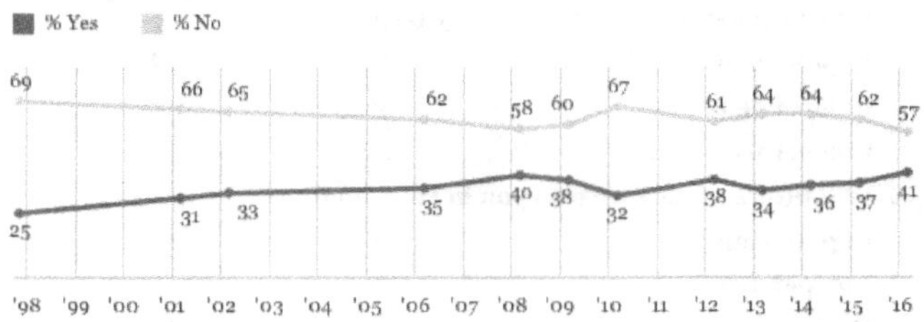

GALLUP

Americans' clear shift toward belief in global warming follows a winter that most described in the same poll as being unusually warm. Sixty-three percent say they experienced an unusually warm winter, and the majority of this group ascribes the warm weather pattern to human-caused climate change.

Record 65% Blame Human Activity for Rising Temperatures

That finding relates to another record broken in the new poll – the 65% of Americans now saying increases in the Earth's temperature over the last century are primarily attributable to human activities rather than natural causes. This represents a striking 10-percentage-point increase in the past year and is four points above the previous high of 61% in 2007.

Perceived Cause of Global Warming

And from what you have heard or read, do you believe increases in the Earth's temperature over the last century are due more to – [the effects of pollution from human activities (or) natural changes in the environment that are not due to human activities]?

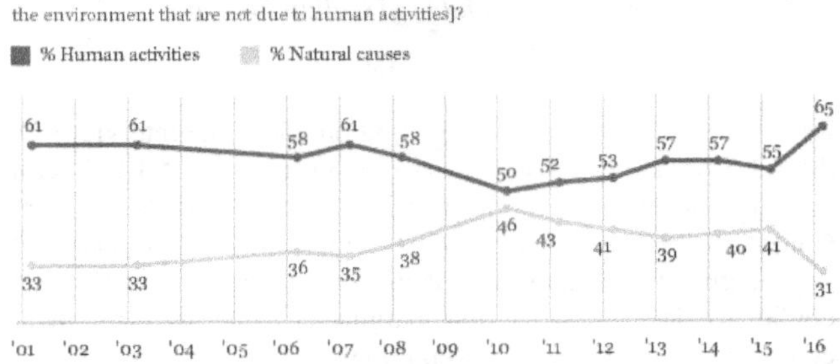

GALLUP

All Party Groups Show Increased Concern

Concern about global warming has increased among all party groups since 2015, although it remains much higher among Democrats than Republicans and independents. For example, 40% of Republicans say they worry a great deal or fair amount about global warming, up from 31% last year. The percentage of independents expressing concern has also increased nine points, from 55% to 64%. Democrats' concern is up slightly less, from 78% to 84%.

Democrats and independents also show double-digit increases in the percentages attributing warmer temperatures to human activities. Republicans show a more modest uptick of four points on this question.

Changes in Attitudes About Global Warming, 2015-2016, by Political Party Identification

	2015%	2016%	Change(pct. pts.)
Worried a great deal/fair amount about global warming			
Republicans	31	40	+9
Independents	55	64	+9
Democrats	78	84	+6
Effects of global warming already begun			
Republicans	36	40	+4
Independents	55	55	0
Democrats	72	77	+5
Will pose serious threat to you in your lifetime			
Republicans	18	20	+2
Independents	37	43	+6
Democrats	53	58	+5
Increased temperatures due to human activities			
Republicans	34	38	+4
Independents	56	68	+12
Democrats	74	85	+11

Gallup Environment Poll

Bottom Line

A confluence of factors – the economic downturn, the Climategate controversy and some well-publicized pushback against global warming science – may have dampened public concern about global warming from about 2009 to 2015. However, Americans are now expressing record- or near-record-high belief that global warming is happening, as well as concern about the issue. Several years of unseasonably warm weather – including the 2011-2012, 2012-2013 and 2015-2016 winters – has potentially contributed to this shift in attitudes. If that's true, continuation of such weather patterns would likely do more than anything politicians and even climate-change scientists can to further raise public concern.

Historical data are available in Gallup Analytics.

Survey Methods

Results for this Gallup poll are based on telephone interviews conducted March 2-6, 2016, with a random sample of 1,019 adults, aged 18 and older, living in all 50 U.S. states and the District of Columbia. For results based on the total sample of national adults, the margin of sampling error is ±4 percentage points at the 95% confidence level. All reported margins of sampling error include computed design effects for weighting.

Learn more about how the Gallup Poll Social Series works.

March 17, 2016

AMERICANS REACT TO PRESIDENTIAL CANDIDATES' TAX PROPOSALS

by Frank Newport

Story Highlights

- *Most support for closing loopholes for the rich and cutting the estate tax*
- *Least support for cutting everyone's taxes and a 10% flat tax*
- *Many Americans uncertain about these tax reform proposals*

PRINCETON, N.J. – Tax reform is a central issue in this year's GOP presidential nomination race, with Republican candidates proposing a number of ways to simplify and reduce taxes. When asked to react to six of these tax-related proposals, Americans generally are more positive than negative about all, although by widely varying margins. Americans are most in favor of eliminating tax deductions and loopholes available to the very rich, followed by eliminating the estate tax – the only two proposals to get majority support. They are less likely to favor sweeping proposals to cut income taxes for everyone or to install a 10% flat tax plan. A significant segment of Americans say they don't know enough about these tax proposals to have an opinion.

Views on Six Proposals to Reform Tax System in U.S.

Next, I'm going to read several proposals recently made by candidates running for president. For each proposal, please tell me if you agree or disagree with the proposal, or if you don't know enough about it to have an opinion.

	Proposed by	Agree%	Disagree%	Don't know enough to have an opinion%	Net agree (pct. pts.)
Eliminate most federal income tax deductions and loopholes available to the very rich	Trump	63	17	19	46
Eliminate the estate tax that is paid when a person dies	Trump, Cruz	54	19	26	35
Simplify the federal tax code into four tax brackets instead of the current seven	Trump	47	12	41	35
Replace the current federal income tax system with a 10% flat tax	Cruz	45	28	26	17
Lower the federal corporate tax rate to 15%	Trump	43	30	27	13
Cut federal income taxes for all income levels	Trump	47	34	19	13

March 9-13, 2016
Gallup Daily tracking

Views on Six Proposals to Reform Tax System in U.S.

Americans were asked about their views on these tax proposals as part of Gallup's ongoing effort to test public support for specific policy recommendations made by candidates from both parties in this year's election cycle.

Americans' support for tax reform ideas generally lands in the middle of the group of all proposals tested to date. They generate less support than the top-rated proposals – such as providing easier access to healthcare for veterans – but are viewed much more positively than widely rejected proposals such as eliminating entire cabinet-level departments of government such as the Departments of Education and Energy.

Five of the six tax proposals tested here are part of Donald Trump's detailed tax reform plan. Ted Cruz has championed the idea of a 10% flat tax, and Cruz joins Trump in advocating for eliminating the estate or "death" tax.

Almost two-thirds of Americans agree with the idea of closing loopholes and removing deductions "available to the very rich." This finding is consistent with previous Gallup research showing that a majority of Americans favor heavier taxes on the wealthy. Just 1% of Americans consider themselves to be upper class and most likely don't think they would be affected by tax changes aimed at the very rich. In addition to Trump, Democratic candidates Bernie Sanders and Hillary Clinton have also put forth broadly similar proposals aimed at higher-income tax payers.

Overall, broad plans to cut taxes for all income levels (part of Trump's plan) and to reduce the current complex system to a simple 10% flat tax (Cruz's proposal) are by no means big winners – even though they seemingly could benefit everyone. Less than half of Americans agree with these proposals, and about three in 10 disagree with them. Sizable percentages say they don't know enough to have an opinion. Americans give about the same level of support for Trump's idea of lowering the federal corporate income tax rate to 15% for all businesses.

Trump's idea of simplifying the tax code into four brackets, rather than the current seven, receives about four times as much support as opposition – 47% vs. 12% – but 41% of Americans, the highest for any proposal tested, say they don't know enough about it to have an opinion.

Over half of Americans agree with the idea of eliminating the estate tax "paid when a person dies," with a relatively low level of disagreement.

Implications

Tax reform is not a high priority for the average American. Few mention taxes when asked to name the most important problem facing the nation today, and taxes also rank below average when Americans rate the importance of various issues that will help determine their vote for president.

Despite the public's apparent lack of urgency about reforming taxes, the leading GOP presidential candidates have offered detailed proposals to change the tax system, most likely because they believe that taxes represent the most obvious way in which the federal government factors into citizens' lives. (Democratic candidates' proposals on economic-related issues will be reviewed in future releases.)

The tax proposals tested in this analysis generate more agreement than disagreement among Americans, but only two – closing loopholes/eliminating deductions available to the rich and eliminating the estate tax – have majority support. Americans do not appear to be highly enthusiastic about broad plans to cut everyone's taxes or move to a flat tax system, but they aren't entirely unenthusiastic either.

Many Americans say they don't know enough about these proposals to have an opinion, so it is likely support could change, in either direction, as Americans become familiar with them in the remaining months of the election season.

These data are available in Gallup Analytics.

Survey Methods

Results for this Gallup poll are based on telephone interviews conducted March 9-13, 2016, on the Gallup U.S. Daily survey, with each proposal rated by between 516 and 559 national adults living in all 50 U.S. states and the District of Columbia. Results for each proposal have a margin of error of ±6 percentage points at the 95% confidence level. All reported margins of sampling error include computed design effects for weighting.

March 17, 2016

AMERICANS' CONCERNS ABOUT WATER POLLUTION EDGE UP

by Justin McCarthy

Story Highlights

- *Levels of worry tick up on six environmental issues*
- *Worry about polluted drinking water highest, at 61%*
- *Concerns about pollution of rivers, lakes up nine percentage points*

WASHINGTON, D.C. – After declining last year, Americans' worries about several environmental issues ticked upward in 2016, and are now mostly back to 2014 levels. A majority express "a great deal" of concern about polluted drinking water (61%) and the pollution of rivers, lakes and reservoirs (56%). These increases come as details surrounding the water crisis in Flint, Michigan, continue to emerge.

Americans' Concerns About Environmental Problems

I'm going to read you a list of environmental problems. As I read each one, please tell me if you personally worry about this problem a great deal, a fair amount, only a little or not at all.

	A great deal, 2014%	A great deal, 2015%	A great deal, 2016%
Pollution of drinking water	60	55	61
Pollution of rivers, lakes and reservoirs	53	47	56
Air pollution	46	38	43
Extinction of plant and animal species	41	36	42
The loss of tropical rain forests	41	33	39
Global warming or climate change	34	32	37

Gallup Poll Social Series: Environment

Gallup's annual Environment survey, conducted March 2-6 this year, also documents the percentages of Americans who say they personally worry "a great deal" about air pollution (43%), the extinction of plant and animal species (42%), the loss of tropical rain forests (39%) and global warming or climate change (37%). The percentage saying they worry a great deal about each issue increased by five or more percentage points from last year, after each showed a decline from 2014 to 2015. Concerns about air pollution, climate change and the pollution of rivers, lakes and reservoirs are similar to where they were in 2014, as are levels of concern regarding the other three issues.

Polluted drinking water and the pollution of rivers, lakes and reservoirs have consistently topped Americans' concerns throughout Gallup's 27-year trend measuring these environmental issues. Climate change worries have regularly appeared at the bottom of the list.

From a longer-term perspective, the current percentages of Americans worrying a great deal about polluted drinking water and the pollution of rivers, lakes and reservoirs are on the high end of figures recorded over the past 16 years, but remain below where they were in the 1980s and 1990s.

Americans' Concerns About Water Pollution

% Worried "a great deal"

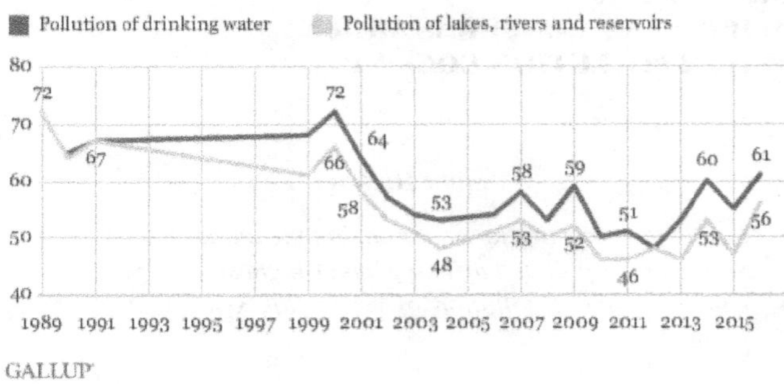

Democrats Worry More About Environmental Issues

In general, Americans' concerns about most environmental issues have receded from higher levels seen in the 1980s and 1990s, when a renewed sentiment of environmentalism prevailed.

Republicans, however, have consistently expressed less worry than Democrats about each of the environmental issues. This year, Democrats' levels of concern range from 71% worried about polluted drinking water to 47% worried about the loss of tropical rain forests. Among Republicans, levels of concern range from 48% worried about polluted drinking water to 18% worried about climate change.

While levels of concern among the two major parties stayed the same or declined from 2014 to 2015, they reverted this year to 2014 levels. Democrats' concerns about polluted drinking water and the pollution of rivers, lakes and reservoirs are higher now than two years ago.

Americans' Concerns About Environmental Problems, by Political Party

% Worried a great deal

	2014%	2015%	2016%
Democrats/Democratic leaners			
Pollution of drinking water	67	64	71
Pollution of rivers, lakes and reservoirs	62	55	67
Air pollution	57	53	55
The loss of tropical rain forests	51	39	47
Extinction of plant and animal species	50	46	49
Global warming or climate change	53	52	53
Republicans/Republican leaners			
Pollution of drinking water	50	43	48
Pollution of rivers, lakes and reservoirs	41	36	40
Air pollution	30	22	27
The loss of tropical rain forests	27	24	26
Extinction of plant and animal species	28	24	30
Global warming or climate change	16	13	18

Gallup Poll Social Series: Environment

Bottom Line

As details about the Flint water crisis emerge following a congressional hearing on the matter, Americans' concerns about water pollution are slightly higher than last year, but generally mirror trend averages. The Flint crisis may have simply underlined a recurring concern, given that worries about water pollution have appeared atop the public's environmental concern list in all previous years.

The 2016 presidential election shines a spotlight on these ecological issues – and others such as climate change, carbon emissions and hydraulic fracturing – by forcing candidates to address key policy decisions they would have to make as commander in chief. The viewpoints of their respective party's rank and file differ drastically, however, which complicates the next president's ability to alleviate the concerns of all Americans.

Historical data are available in Gallup Analytics.

Editor's Note: An earlier version of this story contained data from a different question on climate change. This story has since been revised to reflect the climate change question in the environmental trend.

Survey Methods

Results for this Gallup poll are based on telephone interviews conducted March 2-6, 2016, on the Gallup U.S. Daily survey, with a random sample of 1,019 adults, aged 18 and older, living in all 50 U.S. states and the District of Columbia. For results based on the total sample of national adults, the margin of sampling error is ±4 percentage points at the 95% confidence level. All reported margins of sampling error include computed design effects for weighting.

March 18, 2016
FOR FIRST TIME, MAJORITY IN U.S. OPPOSE NUCLEAR ENERGY

by Rebecca Riffkin

Story Highlights

- *54% of Americans oppose nuclear energy, 44% in favor*
- *First time in Gallup's trend that majority oppose nuclear energy*
- *Both major parties less likely to favor nuclear energy than in 2015*

WASHINGTON, D.C. – For the first time since Gallup first asked the question in 1994, a majority of Americans say they oppose nuclear energy. The 54% opposing it is up significantly from 43% a year ago, while the 44% who favor using nuclear energy is down from 51%.

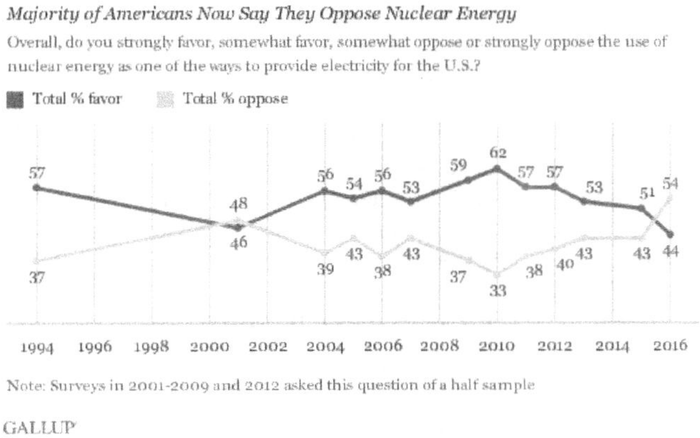

Gallup asks Americans as part of its annual Environment poll if they favor or oppose the use of nuclear energy as one way to provide electricity. Each year from 2004 to 2015, a majority of Americans said they favored the use of nuclear energy, including a high of 62% in 2010.

In 2011, Gallup conducted its annual Environment poll a few days before the Fukushima nuclear plant disaster in Japan, and at that time, 57% of Americans were in favor of nuclear energy. The next time the question was asked in 2012, a similar majority still favored the use of nuclear energy.

And although there have not been any major nuclear incidents since Fukushima in 2011, a majority of U.S. adults now oppose nuclear energy. This suggests that energy prices and the perceived abundance of energy sources are the most relevant factors in attitudes toward nuclear power, rather than safety concerns prompted by nuclear incidents.

Lower gasoline prices over the past year are likely driving greater opposition toward the use of nuclear power. As Americans have paid less at the pump, their level of worry about the nation's energy situation has dropped to 15-year-low levels. This appears to have resulted in more Americans prioritizing environmental protection and fewer backing nuclear power as an alternative energy source.

Democrats and Republicans Less Likely to Favor Nuclear Energy

Republicans continue to be more likely than Democrats and independents to be in favor of nuclear energy. Still, support for the use of nuclear energy among Republicans and Democrats has declined in comparison to 2015. A slight majority of Republicans, 53%, are in favor of nuclear energy, down significantly from 68% last year. One in three Democrats, 34%, favor it, down from 42% in 2015. Independents' support is essentially unchanged from last year, but is down from the high Gallup found in 2010.

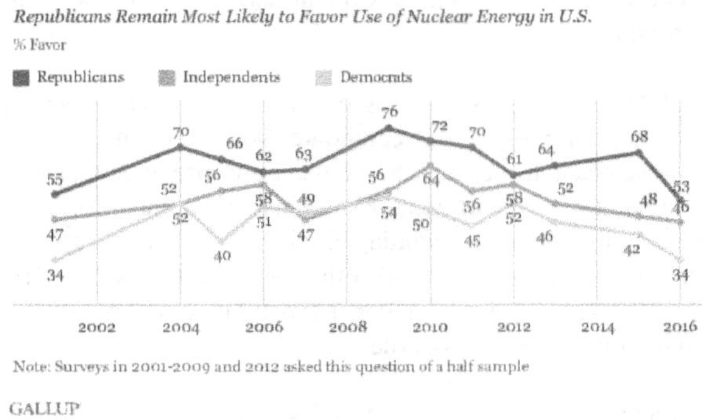

In previous years, as many as three in four Republicans were in favor of nuclear energy, peaking at 76% in 2009. The percentage of Democrats favoring nuclear energy also reached its high the same year, at 54%. Independents have typically been less likely than Republicans to favor nuclear energy but have usually been more likely than Democrats to favor it, particularly in recent years.

Bottom Line

Gas prices have been relatively low over the past year, likely because of the sharp decline in oil and natural gas prices and the apparent glut of oil around the world. This seems to have lessened Americans' perceptions that energy sources such as nuclear power are needed. The increased opposition to nuclear power does not seem to result from a fear of it, as there have been no major nuclear disasters anywhere in the world since 2011.

Nuclear power plants are expensive to build, often costing billions upfront, although they require relatively low maintenance costs once they are running. And nuclear energy has lower greenhouse gas emissions than other power sources, especially coal, so it is considered a clean provider of electricity. Still, nuclear energy is a bet that the cost over time of coal or natural gas to power an electric plant will be higher than the upfront cost of building a nuclear reactor. And at a time when oil prices are low, it seems Americans are not in favor of making that bet.

Historical data are available in Gallup Analytics.

Survey Methods

Results for this Gallup poll are based on telephone interviews conducted March 2-6, 2016, with a random sample of 1,019 adults, aged 18 and older, living in all 50 U.S. states and the District of Columbia. For results based on the total sample of national adults, the margin of sampling error is ±4 percentage points at the 95% confidence level. All reported margins of sampling error include computed design effects for weighting.

March 21, 2016

AMERICANS SAY "YES" TO SPENDING MORE ON VA, INFRASTRUCTURE

by Frank Newport

Story Highlights

- Proposal allowing vets to receive care at civilian facilities gets strong support
- Americans strongly agree with spending more to modernize the VA
- Spending more federal money on infrastructure wins widespread approval

PRINCETON, N.J. – Americans overwhelmingly agree with proposals made by presidential candidate Donald Trump and others to allow veterans to get healthcare from any provider that accepts Medicare, not just Department of Veterans Affairs medical facilities. Americans also support spending more federal money on the VA in general, and widely agree with the idea championed by Trump, Hillary Clinton and Bernie Sanders to spend more federal money on improving the nation's infrastructure.

Views on Proposals to Reform VA and Spend More on Infrastructure

I'm going to read several proposals recently made by candidates running for president. For each proposal, please tell me if you agree or disagree with the proposal, or if you don't know enough about it to have an opinion.

	Agree%	Disagree%	Don't know%	Net agree (pct. pts.)
Allow veterans to get healthcare at any healthcare provider that accepts Medicare, not just Veterans Administration medical facilities (proposed by Trump, Cruz)	91	2	6	89
Spend federal money to modernize the Veterans Administration (proposed by Trump)	74	7	19	67
Spend more federal money to improve infrastructure, including roads, buildings and waterways (proposed by Clinton, Sanders, Trump)	75	11	13	64

March 9-13, 2016
Gallup Daily tracking

Gallup asked Americans about these proposals in a March 9-13 poll as part of an ongoing effort to test public support for specific policy recommendations made by presidential candidates of both parties in this year's election cycle. All three of these proposals are extremely popular with Americans, with high levels of agreement and little disagreement, putting them at the top of the list of all presidential proposals tested to date.

Support for Veterans

While most presidential candidates have addressed veterans' issues, the two proposals tested have been a key part of Trump's campaign platform. Trump says that under his administration, "all veterans eligible for VA healthcare can bring their veteran's ID card to any doctor or care facility that accepts Medicare to get the care they need immediately," in part reacting to the 2014 controversy over the quality of healthcare veterans receive. Ted Cruz has also called for more flexibility in veterans' ability to get healthcare outside of VA medical facilities.

In addition, Trump proposes to increase funding for a variety of VA projects, including "accelerating and expanding investments in state-of-the-art technology" and spending more for job training, placement services, educational support and business loans.

Americans have more confidence in the military than in any other U.S. institution, and this high regard extends to military veterans as well. The idea of allowing veterans to get their healthcare from any provider that accepts Medicare receives almost no pushback from Americans. Only 2% disagree with the idea, while 91% agree. Support for increased federal spending for VA-related projects is not quite as high, with 74% agreement and 7% disagreement. The lesser support, however, is largely a result of a higher percentage of Americans saying they don't know enough to have an opinion.

Federal Spending on Infrastructure

Both Trump and the two Democratic presidential candidates have proposed increased government spending on the nation's infrastructure. Trump said in December, "We've spent $4 trillion trying to topple various people. If we could've spent that $4 trillion in the United States to fix our roads, our bridges and all of the other problems – our airports and all of the other problems we've had – we would've been a lot better off." Clinton promises to "boost federal investment [in infrastructure] by $275 billion over the next five years," and Sanders has proposed the "Rebuild America Act, to invest $1 trillion over five years to modernize our infrastructure."

The general idea of spending more federal money on infrastructure, like the suggestions to improve the situation for veterans, meets with strong public approval; 75% of Americans say they agree, while 11% disagree.

Implications

All of the presidential candidate proposals reviewed here require additional federal spending – in the case of Sanders' infrastructure proposal, as much as $1 trillion. As is the case when candidates reference these types of proposals in speeches or debates, the wording used in this research did not specify where the funding for increased spending on veterans or infrastructure would come from. But the results clearly show that these proposals strike a responsive chord with Americans when they hear them in capsule form, which means that they play well on the campaign trail.

If a candidate who promises these types of initiatives is elected, the challenge will be for him or her to figure out exactly how to pay for them: with increased taxes or cost savings, or by shifting funding from other programs. That process has the potential to dilute the public's current high levels of support.

Historical data are available in Gallup Analytics.

Survey Methods

Results for this Gallup poll are based on telephone interviews conducted March 9-13, 2016, on the Gallup U.S. Daily survey, with each proposal rated by between 494 and 559 national adults living in all 50 U.S. states and the District of Columbia. Results for each proposal have a margin of error of ±6 percentage points at the 95% confidence level. All reported margins of sampling error include computed design effects for weighting.

March 21, 2016
U.S. SUPPORT FOR GARLAND AVERAGE FOR SUPREME COURT NOMINEES

by Jeffrey M. Jones

Story Highlights

- *52% favor, 29% oppose Senate confirmation of Garland*
- *Opponents believe next president should make nomination*
- *Republican opposition to Garland no greater than for prior Obama nominees*

PRINCETON, N.J. – Americans are more likely to favor (52%) than oppose (29%) Senate confirmation of Merrick Garland to the Supreme Court, according to Gallup's first reading on public support for his nomination. That level of support essentially matches the average 51% in initial readings for the eight nominees Gallup has tested since 1991.

Support for Confirmation of Merrick Garland and Other Recent Supreme Court Nominees

As you may know, Merrick Garland is a federal judge who has been nominated to serve on the Supreme Court. Would you like to see the Senate vote in favor of Garland serving on the Supreme Court, or not?

	Poll dates	Vote in favor%	Not vote in favor%	No opin.%
Merrick Garland	Mar 18-19, 2016	52	29	19
Elena Kagan	May 24-25, 2010	46	32	22
Sonia Sotomayor	May 29-31, 2009	54	28	19
Samuel Alito	Nov 7-10, 2005	50	25	25
Harriet Miers	Oct 13-16, 2005	44	36	20
John Roberts	Jul 22-24, 2005	59	22	19
Ruth Bader Ginsburg	Jun 18-21, 1993	53	14	33
Clarence Thomas	Jul 11-14, 1991	52	17	31

Note: Data are based on first Gallup survey conducted after nomination was made.
Gallup

As with all recent nominees, a significant proportion of Americans, 19%, do not have an opinion on Garland's confirmation.

The results are based on a Gallup poll conducted March 18-19, days after President Barack Obama nominated Garland to fill the Supreme Court vacancy after the death of Justice Antonin Scalia. Scalia's passing during a presidential election year ignited a political battle over whether a president in his last year in office should fill the vacancy or if the process should be delayed until after a new president is in office.

Amid the political storm, initial public support for Garland's confirmation is similar to what it has been for other Supreme Court nominees. It exceeds that for 2010 Obama nominee Elena Kagan (46%) and 2005 George W. Bush nominee Harriet Miers (44%). Miers requested that Bush withdraw her nomination as opposition to her confirmation grew among elected officials from both parties and the general public. Just before her withdrawal, 42% Americans favored and 43% opposed Senate confirmation of her.

Only John Roberts, at 59%, had significantly higher initial support than Garland among recent high court nominees.

Gallup also measured support for Ronald Reagan's 1987 appointee Robert Bork. That initial reading found 31% in favor of Senate confirmation, 25% opposed and a higher 44% not having an opinion. If Bork's data are included, the average level of support for prior nominees drops to 49%. Further Gallup polling on the Bork nomination in September 1987 found a significant increase in Americans' opposition to Bork's confirmation, with Americans ending up about evenly divided as to whether the Senate should (38%) or should not (35%) confirm him. The Senate eventually voted against confirming Bork.

Gallup did not measure support for 1994 Bill Clinton nominee Stephen Breyer, 1990 George H. W. Bush nominee David Souter, or 1987 Reagan nominees Douglas Ginsburg and Anthony Kennedy.

Garland Opponents Believe Next President Should Choose Nominee

Given a choice, Americans who believe the Senate should not confirm Garland largely say their opposition stems from their belief that the next president should fill the vacancy (67%), rather than specific concerns they have about Garland himself (20%).

That finding is not surprising because Americans have limited familiarity with Garland at this point, with a majority saying they have heard or read "very little" (31%) or "nothing at all" (28%) about the judge's qualifications and record. Only 7% say they have heard "a great deal," with another 34% saying they have heard "a fair amount."

Slim Majority of Republicans Oppose Garland Confirmation

Since little is known specifically about Garland, support or opposition to his nomination at this point may mostly reflect Americans' partisanship and, by extension, their views of Obama. Consistent with this, 76% of Democrats say they favor Senate confirmation of Garland to the Supreme Court. Republicans are more likely to oppose (51%) than support (33%) Garland's confirmation, but Republican opposition is not nearly as widespread as Democratic support. Independents tilt in favor of Senate confirmation.

Support for Confirmation of Merrick Garland to Supreme Court, by Political Party

	Vote in favor%	Not vote in favor%	No opinion%
Democrats	76	11	14
Independents	44	31	25
Republicans	33	51	16

Gallup, March 18-19, 2016

Despite the controversy over the election-year nomination, the 51% of Republicans initially opposing Garland's confirmation is no higher than initial Republican opposition to Obama's prior Supreme Court nominees – Kagan (51%) and Sonia Sotomayor (57%). And more Republicans say they want the Senate to vote to confirm Garland (33%) than said this about either Kagan (26%) or Sotomayor (24%).

Initial Support for Confirmation of President Barack Obama's Nominees to Supreme Court, by Political Party

	Vote in favor %	Not vote in favor %	No opinion %
Republicans			
Garland	33	51	16
Kagan	26	51	22
Sotomayor	24	57	20
Democrats			
Garland	76	11	14
Kagan	68	12	20
Sotomayor	76	6	17
Independents			
Garland	44	31	25
Kagan	43	33	25
Sotomayor	54	27	19

Note: Data are based on first Gallup survey conducted after nomination was made.
Gallup

Democratic support for Garland is higher than it was for Kagan and similar to what it was for Sotomayor. Independents were much more positive about the Sotomayor nomination than the Kagan and Garland nominations.

Implications

The passing of Scalia has made the ideological makeup of the Supreme Court more salient in an already intense political year. It is understandable that Republicans do not want Obama to appoint Scalia's successor, given that this could tilt the balance of the Supreme Court if he appointed a liberal, or even a moderate, justice to replace the conservative Scalia. However, Obama and the Democrats are arguing that the president and Senate should put politics aside and fulfill their respective constitutional obligations to fill the Supreme Court vacancy.

Although the political context surrounding Garland's nomination is different from the context for any other recent Supreme Court nominee, the public's reaction is similar to what it has been for past nominees. A slight majority favors confirmation, and nearly twice as many support as oppose it when factoring out those without an opinion.

Obama chose a nominee that many regard as a moderate judge, and one several current Senate Republicans voted to confirm to his current federal judgeship. Obama may hope that the public can persuade reluctant Republicans to relent and vote to confirm his choice, and some GOP senators facing tough re-election battles may feel pressure to do so. Public opinion on Garland's confirmation is largely divided along partisan lines, but not any more so than it has been for other Obama nominees.

Importantly, with the exceptions of Bork and Miers, there has been little change in Americans' fundamental support for the confirmation of past high court nominees between Gallup's initial readings and subsequent measurements leading up to their confirmation hearings. As such, unless forthcoming reviews of Garland's qualifications and past judicial rulings raise serious concerns, the public is likely to continue to back his confirmation.

Historical data are available in Gallup Analytics.

Survey Methods

Results for this Gallup poll are based on telephone interviews conducted March 18-19, 2016, on the Gallup U.S. Daily survey, with a random sample of 1,019 adults, aged 18 and older, living in all 50 U.S. states and the District of Columbia. For results based on the total sample of national adults, the margin of sampling error is ±4 percentage points at the 95% confidence level. All reported margins of sampling error include computed design effects for weighting.

March 22, 2016
TRUMP'S IMAGE AMONG REPUBLICANS CONTINUES TO TILT POSITIVE

by Frank Newport

Story Highlights

- Between 54% and 61% of Republicans have viewed Trump favorably since July
- Trump's image more negative than other GOP front-runners in previous years
- Republicans who view Trump positively are older, more likely to be men

PRINCETON, N.J. – Republicans nationwide remain more positive than negative in their views of Donald Trump, with 55% viewing him favorably and 41% unfavorably so far in March. Despite Trump's extraordinary journey since last summer as the central – and controversial – focus of the 2016 election, Republicans' views of the billionaire businessman have generally held steady. His image today is roughly where it was last July.

Republicans' Views of Donald Trump

Monthly averages, among Republicans and Republican-leaning independents

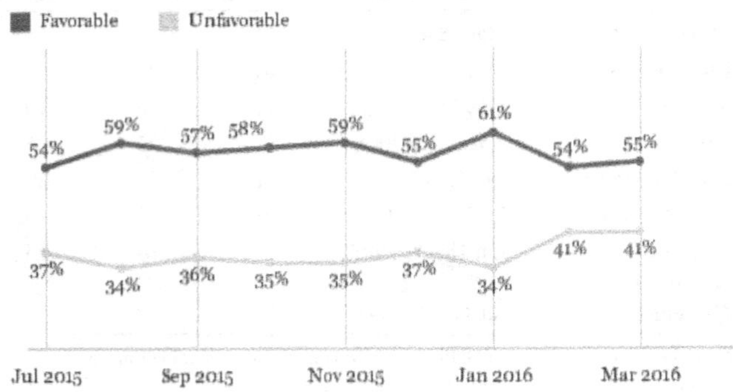

Gallup Daily tracking

GALLUP

These trend data are based on Gallup Daily tracking of more than 1,600 Republicans who have rated Trump each month since July.

Overall, Trump has averaged a 57% favorable rating and a 37% unfavorable rating among Republicans over that period. Since Trump's favorable rating peaked at 61% in January, it has been lower each of the past two months. But from a broad perspective, the month-to-month changes have been relatively minor.

The relative stability in Trump's favorable percentage – ranging between 54% and 61% – shows that his supporters are fairly locked into their support and are not dramatically affected by what Trump says or does, or by what the media and rival candidates say about him. This, in turn, may reflect that Trump was well-known early on, and that many Republicans formed a fairly firm opinion of him in the early stages of the campaign.

On a comparative basis, Trump's popularity among Republicans is roughly similar to where Mitt Romney was in February 2012 (59% favorable, 31% unfavorable), although fewer Republicans had an opinion of Romney four years ago, giving him a higher net favorable than Trump's today. In March of election years prior to that, the eventual Republican nominee had much higher favorable ratings among his own partisans, with John McCain in 2008, George W. Bush in 2000 and Bob Dole in 1996 all earning favorable ratings among Republicans in the 80% to 90% range.

Few Young, Female Republicans Are Pro-Trump

Opinions of Trump essentially divide the GOP into two segments – the pro-Trump majority and the anti-Trump minority. This division is based on opinions of Trump and does not necessarily correlate with actual voting. But the opinion data can be used to examine the types of Republicans who like Trump and those who don't.

The age difference between the two groups is significant; 59% of pro-Trump Republicans are aged 50 and older, compared with 43% of the anti-Trump group.

Another key difference between the two groups is how older men and younger women in the GOP base react to Trump. A third of pro-Trump Republicans are men aged 50 and older, compared with 21% of anti-Trump Republicans. Likewise, 14% of pro-Trump Republicans are women aged 18 to 49, contrasted with 31% of anti-Trump Republicans.

Age and Gender Composition of Pro- and Anti-Trump Republicans

	Gender/Age distribution of pro-Trump Republicans %	Gender/Age distribution of anti-Trump Republicans %	Gap between pro- and anti-Trump Republicans %
Men aged 18 to 49	27	26	1
Men aged 50+	33	21	12
Women aged 18 to 49	14	31	-17
Women aged 50+	26	22	4

March 1-20, 2016
Gallup Daily tracking

Pro-Trump Group Less Educated, Less Religious

Older Americans are less likely to be college graduates than those who are younger, and this relationship helps explain the finding that pro-Trump supporters – who skew older – are less well-educated. Twenty-seven percent of pro-Trump Republicans are college graduates, compared with 39% of anti-Trump Republicans. But education has at least some effect in each age group, and pro-Trump Republicans are proportionately more likely to be 35- to 54-year-old non-college graduates, in particular.

Additionally, pro-Trump Republicans are significantly less likely to be highly religious than their anti-Trump counterparts: 44% of Trump's Republican fans are highly religious versus 60% of his detractors.

The pro- and anti-Trump segments of the GOP differ modestly in terms of race and ethnicity. Within the constraints of the Republican Party's highly white skew, 91% of pro-Trump Republicans are non-Hispanic whites, compared with 81% of anti-Trump Republicans.

Implications

It is possible that Donald Trump will not secure enough delegates before July's Republican National Convention in Cleveland to have the nomination in hand when he arrives, leading to a contested convention. While some within the Republican Party are already plotting against Trump's nomination, a majority of the rank-and-file members of the party – typically in the 55% to 60% range – have a favorable view of the businessman, and this has been a persistent finding over the last nine months. Thus, there is by no means a majority negative reaction to Trump among Republicans nationwide, even though his image may be less robust at this point than other front-runners in past elections, and less robust than Hillary Clinton's is now among Democrats. Past Gallup research also indicates that Trump's image may improve if he were to become the presumptive nominee.

The pro-Trump segment of the GOP does have some distinctive demographic characteristics. Pro-Trump Republicans are older, more likely to be male, less well-educated, more likely to be non-Hispanic white and less religious than the anti-Trump group. But these differences are not huge, suggesting that Trump's appeal to Republicans goes beyond traditional demographic categories. Trump's consistently favorable rating among over half of Republicans most likely reflects a combination of psychological and emotional factors leading to differences in the way those in his party perceive his style, personality, nonpolitical background, business credentials and policy promises.

These data are available in Gallup Analytics.

Survey Methods

Results for this Gallup poll are based on telephone interviews conducted on a monthly basis from July 2015 to March 2016 on the Gallup U.S. Daily survey, with random monthly samples of between 1,640 and 2,587 Republicans and Republican-leaning independents, aged 18 and older, living in all 50 U.S. states and the District of Columbia. For results based on each month's total sample of Republicans, the margin of sampling error is ±3 percentage points at the 95% confidence level. All reported margins of sampling error include computed design effects for weighting.

March 23, 2016
WORRY ABOUT TERROR ATTACKS IN U.S. HIGH, BUT NOT TOP CONCERN

by Justin McCarthy

Story Highlights

- *Before Brussels, 48% worried "a great deal" about future attacks*
- *Percent worried "a great deal" similar to 2015, up from 2004-2014*
- *Americans more concerned about healthcare, the economy and crime*

WASHINGTON, D.C. – Before the terrorist attacks Tuesday that killed at least 30 in Brussels, 48% of Americans worried "a great deal" about the possibility of future terrorist attacks in the U.S. While this percentage is higher than in most years since 2004, a possible terrorist attack was not Americans' top concern. More Americans expressed "a great deal" or "a fair amount" of worry about domestic problems such as healthcare, the economy and crime than about terrorism among a list of 13 different issues.

Americans' Concerns for Problems Facing the U.S.

Next, I'm going to read a list of problems facing the country. For each one, please tell me if you personally worry about this problem a great deal, a fair amount, only a little or not at all? First, how much do you personally worry about – ?

	Great deal%	Fair amount%	Only a little/ Not at all%
The availability and affordability of healthcare	55	27	17
The economy	55	28	18
Crime and violence	53	26	22
The possibility of future terrorist attacks in the U.S.	48	23	29
Hunger and homelessness	47	29	24
The Social Security system	46	25	28
Drug use	44	23	33
The quality of the environment	42	31	26
Unemployment	39	29	31
Illegal immigration	37	23	39
Race relations	35	27	37
Climate change	33	27	40
The availability and affordability of energy	27	34	38

March 2-6, 2016
Gallup Poll Social Series: Environment

Worries about terrorism generally take a back seat to at least a few domestic problems, but concerns about the issue increased in 2002 and 2003 after 9/11.

The latest attacks, which took place at an airport and metro station in Brussels, could affect Americans' level of concern about terrorism. In the wake of the terrorist attacks in Paris and San Bernardino, California, terrorism climbed to the top of Americans' list of the most important problems facing the U.S. in December. But by early March, mentions of terrorism declined significantly.

Before the attacks in Brussels, Americans already reported a heightened state of worry because of the increasing worldwide threat of terrorism, in particular from the Islamic State group, which has already claimed responsibility for Tuesday's attacks. Both last year and in Gallup's latest poll, conducted March 2-6, about half of Americans say they have "a great deal" of worry about another terrorist attack on U.S. soil, up from percentages mostly around or less than 40% in the previous 11 years.

Americans' Concerns About the Possibility of Future Terrorist Attacks in the U.S.

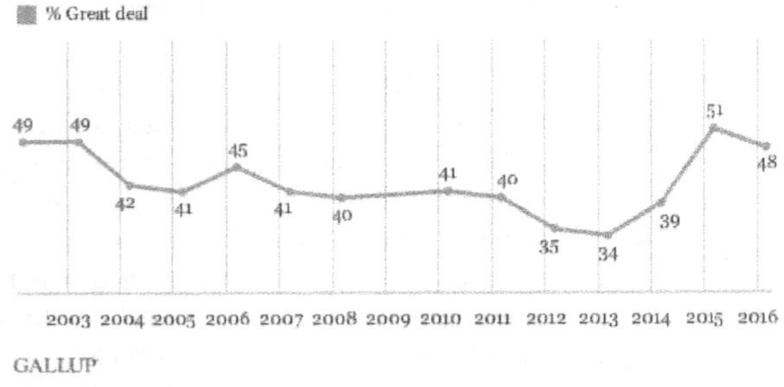

Gallup's longer-term trend on terrorism concerns, first asked in 1995 and last updated in December, also found about half of Americans saying they are "very" or "somewhat" worried about personally becoming a victim of terrorism. And a January poll also found a decrease in Americans' satisfaction with the nation's security from terrorism.

Worries About Future Terrorist Attacks Higher Among Seniors, Republicans

Older Americans appear to worry more than younger Americans about potential terrorist attacks in the U.S. Less than half of Americans under the age of 50 say they worry "a great deal" about the issue. Meanwhile, about half of those between the ages of 50 and 64 (49%) and the majority of seniors aged 65 and older (58%) report worrying "a great deal."

Concern about possible terrorist attacks also differs by party. Republicans (64%) are much more likely than Democrats (36%) to say they worry "a great deal" about the possibility of future terrorist attacks in the U.S. About half of independents (48%) share this degree of worry on the issue.

Americans' Concerns About the Possibility of Future Terrorist Attacks in the U.S., by Party ID and Age

Next, I'm going to read a list of problems facing the country. For each one, please tell me if you personally worry about this problem a great deal, a fair amount, only a little or not at all? How much do you personally worry about the possibility of future terrorist attacks in the U.S.?

	Great deal%
Republicans	64
Independents	48
Democrats	36
18 to 29	42
30 to 49	46
50 to 64	49
65+	58

March 2-6, 2016
Gallup Poll Social Series: Environment

Bottom Line

Because Gallup has found an increase in Americans' worries about terrorism in the aftermath of past high-profile attacks, worry might increase after the attacks in Brussels, at least in the short term. Even before the latest attacks occurred, the level of concern was relatively high by post-9/11 standards. However, Americans are overall more likely to voice concern about pressing domestic matters such as the economy and healthcare.

Historical data are available in Gallup Analytics.

Survey Methods

Results for this Gallup poll are based on telephone interviews conducted March 2-6, 2016, with a random sample of 1,019 adults, aged 18 and older, living in all 50 U.S. states and the District of Columbia. For results based on the total sample of national adults, the margin of sampling error is ±4 percentage points at the 95% confidence level. All reported margins of sampling error include computed design effects for weighting.

March 24, 2016

IN U.S., 73% NOW PRIORITIZE ALTERNATIVE ENERGY OVER OIL, GAS

by Zac Auter

Story Highlights

- *73% want U.S. to emphasize alternative energy rather than oil and gas*
- *Support increased among both Democrats and Republicans since 2013*
- *Higher support for alternative energy coincides with falling gas prices*

WASHINGTON, D.C. – Seventy-three percent of Americans say they prefer emphasizing alternative energy, rather than gas and oil production, as the solution to the nation's energy problems. This marks the highest percentage of Americans prioritizing alternative energy since Gallup first asked the question in 2011.

Americans' Preferred Solution to Energy Problems

Which of the following approaches to solving the nation's energy problems do you think the U.S. should follow right now?

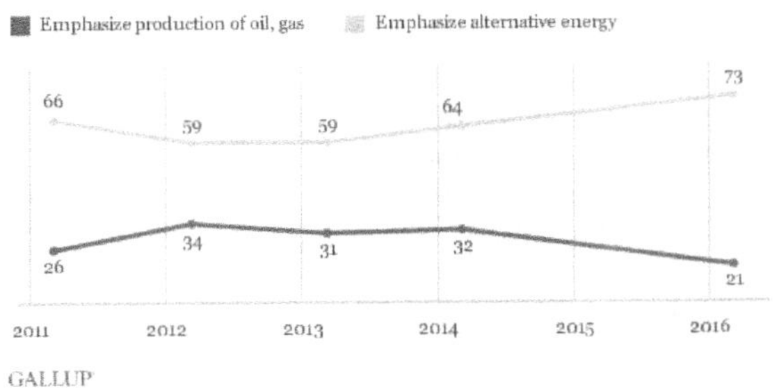

While a majority of Americans have preferred alternative energy solutions since 2011, support has increased substantially since 2013 (59%) and 2014 (64%).

These results are from Gallup's annual Environment poll, conducted March 2-6. From 2012 to 2014, the gap separating traditional and alternative energy advocates was stable, with differences between the two groups ranging from 25 to 32 percentage points. But this year, the gap has widened to 52 points.

Majority of Republicans Now Support Alternative Energy

While a majority of Democrats and Democratic-leaning independents have favored emphasizing alternative energy over traditional fossil fuel sources since 2011, this year marks the first time a majority of Republicans and Republican-leaning independents prefer an alternative energy strategy. The 51% of Republicans who now favor alternative energy is up from the previous high of 46% in 2011.

Both Democrats' and Republicans' support for an alternative energy strategy has grown steadily since 2013. Republicans' support grew eight points from 2014 to 2016, while Democrats' support increased five points over that same time period.

Desire to Emphasize Alternative Energy, by Party Identification

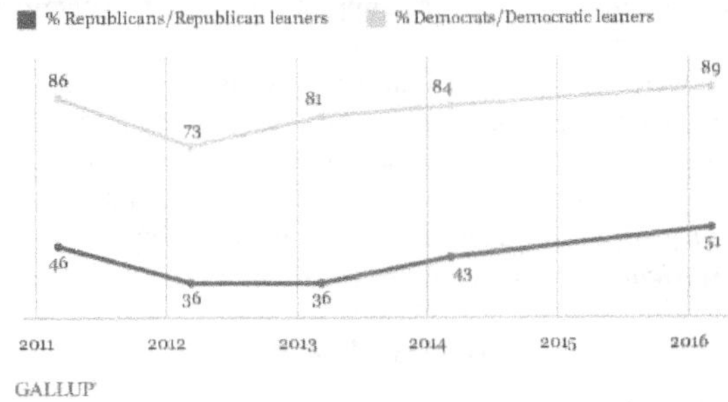

Support for Alternative Energy Coincides With Falling Fuel Prices

The increase in the share of Americans – both Republican and Democrat – preferring an alternative energy strategy in 2016 coincides with an oil supply surplus that has caused fuel prices to plummet. High fuel costs may prime American consumers to prefer increased production of oil and gas as a means to alleviate burdensome prices at the pump. Low fuel costs, however, might be paving the way for a greater willingness to support alternative energy solutions.

In the two years with the highest average gas price for the month preceding Gallup's survey ($3.64 in 2012 and $3.74 in 2013), alternative energy had its fewest advocates (59%). However, the spike in alternative energy proponents in 2016 corresponds with the lowest average fuel cost ($1.87) since Gallup first asked about energy solutions in 2011. If Americans view the price of gas as an indication that traditional fuel is in good supply, they may be more willing to sanction an emphasis on alternative sources because there is little risk of exhausting fossil fuel even with the shift in emphasis.

Link Between Gas Prices and Emphasizing Alternative Energy

	Average Gas Price$	Emphasize Alternative Energy%
March 2-6, 2016	1.87	73
March 6-9, 2014	3.43	64
March 7-10, 2013	3.74	59
March 8-11, 2012	3.64	59
March 3-6, 2011	3.26	66

Gas price data from U.S. Energy Information Administration. Average gas prices taken from month before poll.
Gallup Poll, March 2-6, 2016

Implications

In a time of notable partisan polarization, growing support for alternative energy among Republicans and Democrats represents a rare instance where a bipartisan coalition could form in support of an alternative energy strategy. Even though a substantial gap remains between Republicans and Democrats in emphasizing alternative sources, a majority of Republicans now support the idea. In fact, recent Gallup polls show Americans' concern about global warming is at an eight-year high, with both Democrats and Republicans stating a sharply higher concern for the issue in 2016.

Meanwhile, the perception that fuel is not in short supply – as indicated by low gas prices – may also contribute to more Americans now favoring alternative energy solutions. Absent an urgent desire to offset high fuel costs with increased fuel production, Americans may believe that greater investment in alternative energy strategies is a low-risk endeavor. As a result, if Americans perceive that the fuel supply is abundant, support for alternative energy could increase.

Last week, the Obama administration announced its plan to halt offshore oil and gas drilling set to take place in several southern U.S. states. Taken together, lower fuel prices and Americans' growing concern about global climate change could provide the groundwork for a policy shift toward alternative energy solutions.

Historical data are available in Gallup Analytics.

Survey Methods

Results for this Gallup poll are based on telephone interviews conducted March 2-6, 2016, with a random sample of 504 adults, aged 18 and older, living in all 50 U.S. states and the District of Columbia. For results based on the total sample of national adults, the margin of sampling error is ±6 percentage points at the 95% confidence level. All reported margins of sampling error include computed design effects for weighting.

March 25, 2016

THOUGHT ABOUT ELECTION UP, BUT ENTHUSIASM EDGES DOWN

by Frank Newport

Story Highlights

- *Those giving quite a lot of thought up to 71% from 63% in January*
- *At the same time, enthusiasm about voting down five points to 43%*
- *Republicans have lost the enthusiasm edge they held in January*

PRINCETON, N.J. – The bruising presidential primary season appears to be taking a toll on Americans' enthusiasm about the election this year. While Americans are giving more thought to the presidential election now than in January, their enthusiasm about voting for president has slipped.

Thoughts About Election and Enthusiasm About Voting

January and March 2016

	January 2016%	March 2016%
Quite a lot of thought given to election	63	71
Extremely or very enthusiastic about voting this year	48	43

Gallup Poll

The latest update on these two key indicators is based on Gallup interviewing conducted March 21-23. Gallup has not asked the enthusiasm question on a systematic basis in past elections, but did measure enthusiasm in January and March of 2012. Those results also showed a downtick in enthusiasm in the early months of the election year, with Americans' enthusiasm (extremely/very enthusiastic) falling from 47% in January 2012 to 38% in March. This suggests the primary and caucus season, a time when Americans are paying more attention to the campaign and when there is greater scrutiny of the candidates' records, can dampen voter enthusiasm. Enthusiasm stayed low in 2012 until fall, when it began to edge up during the intense part of the general election campaign.

Gallup's only measure of enthusiasm from 2008 was in January, when 58% of voters were extremely or very enthusiastic about voting, significantly higher than has been the case in either January or March of this year, or in 2012.

How enthusiastic are you about voting for president in this year's election?

	Extremely/Very enthusiastic%
National adults	
Mar 21-23, 2016	43
Jan 21-25, 2016	48
Mar 25-26, 2012	38
Jan 27-28, 2012	47
Jan 10-13, 2008	58

Gallup Poll

Republicans' enthusiasm about voting since January has slipped more than Democrats', leaving an equal 46% of both partisan groups extremely or very enthusiastic at this point. The overall average of 43% is pulled down by the very low enthusiasm among independents who do not identify with or lean toward either party. In contrast to the parity in enthusiasm today, Republicans had a five-percentage-point edge in enthusiasm in January.

The two partisan groups were also equal in enthusiasm in March of 2012. By contrast, Democrats had a marked edge in January 2008, most likely reflecting the excitement generated by the strong candidacies of Barack Obama and Hillary Clinton on the Democratic side of the political equation.

Both Republicans and Democrats Are Giving More Thought to Election

Even as they are becoming less enthusiastic about voting, Americans are giving more thought to the election compared with January. The current thought level is higher than was the case in March of the 2004 and 2000 election years. All of these measures are eclipsed, however, by the higher level of thought measured in March 2008. The historical record suggests that thought given to the election will increase further in the months ahead – as the nominees are determined, the conventions are held, the debates take place and the November election draws nigh.

How much thought have you given to the upcoming election for president – quite a lot, or only a little?

	Quite a lot%	Some (vol.)%	Only a little%	None%
Mar 21-23, 2016	71	1	25	3
Jan 21-25, 2016	63	4	32	2
Mar 14-16, 2008	75	3	19	1
Mar 26-28, 2004	64	2	31	3
Mar 5-7, 2004	62	3	32	3
Mar 30-Apr 2, 2000	42	7	46	5
Mar 10-12, 2000	50	7	38	5

Gallup Poll

Republicans' and Democrats' levels of thought given to the election rose by identical margins from January to March, preserving the Republican advantage seen in January. In comparison, Democrats gave a bit more thought to the election in March 2008, while Republicans had a very slight edge in March 2004. None of these differences between party groups, then or now, are large.

Thought Given to 2016 Presidential Election, by Subgroup

How much thought have you given to the upcoming election for president – quite a lot, or only a little? % Quite a lot

	Jan 21-25, 2016%	Mar 21-23, 2016%	Change (pct. pts.)
U.S. adults	63	71	8
Republican/Lean Republican	70	77	7
Democrat/Lean Democratic	63	70	7

Gallup Poll

Bottom Line

Americans have become somewhat less enthusiastic about voting as the election process has moved through the first two-and-a-half months of the year, even though they are giving more thought to the election. Most of this appears to be caused by the drop in enthusiasm among Republicans, who were more enthusiastic than Democrats in January, but not any longer.

Other research has shown that Republicans have also become less likely to say the election process is working as it should. These findings underscore the conclusion that the GOP campaign so far this year, particularly the controversy generated by front-runner Donald Trump and reactions to it, is having a negative effect on how rank-and-file Republicans are looking at the whole process.

Americans are clearly paying attention to the election, and given that thought is a good predictor of turnout in November, this year could see a rebound from the 2012 turnout levels. In that election, turnout was lower than the two elections that preceded it. The key issue relating to increased turnout from the candidates' perspectives is exactly who it is that is more likely to vote. While Republicans are continuing to give more thought to the election than Democrats – a key predictor of turnout – Republicans are losing the edge on enthusiasm they appeared to have in January.

Historical data are available in Gallup Analytics.

Survey Methods

Results for this Gallup poll are based on telephone interviews conducted March 21-23, 2016, on the Gallup U.S. Daily survey, with a random sample of 1,518 adults, aged 18 and older, living in all 50 U.S. states and the District of Columbia. For results based on the total sample of national adults, the margin of sampling error is ±3 percentage points at the 95% confidence level. For results based on the total sample of 683 Republicans and Republican-leaning independents, the margin of error is ±5 percentage points at the 95% confidence level. For results based on the total sample of 677 Democrats and Democratic-leaning independents, the margin of error is ±5 percentage points at the 95% confidence level. All reported margins of sampling error include computed design effects for weighting.

March 25, 2016

REPUBLICANS SOUR ON WAY ELECTION PROCESS IS WORKING

by Frank Newport

Story Highlights

- *30% in U.S. say election process is working, down from 37% in January*
- *Republicans' views have soured most – down from 46% to 30%*
- *Most Americans still say there is at least one good candidate running*

PRINCETON, N.J. – Thirty percent of Americans say the presidential election process is working as it should, down from 37% in January. The decline is driven mainly by Republicans' increasingly cynical views as the campaign season has progressed. The percentage of Republicans and Republican-leaning independents who say the election process is working has fallen from 46% to 30% since January. Democrats' and Democratic leaners' views haven't changed.

Does the way the presidential campaign is being conducted make you feel as though the election process is working as it should, or not?

% Yes, as it should

	January 2016%	February 2016%	March 2016%
National adults	37	33	30
Republicans/Leaners	46	41	30
Democrats/Leaners	32	29	32

Gallup Poll

The latest update, based on interviewing conducted March 16-17, shows that Republicans and Democrats now have similarly low levels of belief that the election process is working properly, based on their views of the way the presidential campaign is being conducted. This situation differs from what Gallup found in January, when Republicans were much more positive. Since then, the GOP field has narrowed substantially from a large number of candidates to the three still in the race – Donald Trump, Ted Cruz and John Kasich. And the lion's share of attention is going to the controversial Trump, the clear front-runner at this point. By contrast, Hillary Clinton and Bernie Sanders have remained the two main Democratic candidates all year.

It is unclear from the data if partisans are reacting to the developments in their own party's nomination race, the other party's nomination race or both. Republicans' increasingly dour sentiments may be related to Trump – either the increasing inevitability that he will gain his party's nomination, or the way controversial aspects of his campaign have dominated the news. Trump is the least popular Republican nominee among members of his own party in recent elections going back to 1996, and he is much less well-liked than Hillary Clinton is among Democrats. Democrats' more stable but still cynical views may be based on their views of what is happening on the GOP side, or they may not be pleased with something about their own party's campaign.

Another factor could be the increasingly contentious campaigns, particularly on the Republican side, where personal attacks have been an almost daily occurrence and violence between supporters and protestors has broken out at some Trump rallies.

Gallup asked the election-process question on a limited basis during the 2000, 2008 and 2012 election cycles. The high point in positive reactions came in January 2008, when 67% answered affirmatively. That was an open-seat election year, with a particularly well-liked Barack Obama battling Hillary Clinton for the Democratic nomination, and John McCain and Rudy Giuliani among a large field running for the Republican nod.

A majority of Americans were also positive about the process in January and March 2000, another open-seat election year, when the two parties' nominees – Al Gore for the Democrats and George W. Bush for the Republicans – were already the clear front-runners. The most cynical response before this year was measured in December 2011, when Barack Obama was running for re-election and the fight for the GOP nomination was underway.

Does the way the presidential campaign is being conducted make you feel as though the election process is working as it should, or not?

	Yes, as it should%	No, not%	No opinion%
Mar 16-17, 2016	30	66	4
Feb 15-16, 2016	33	64	3
Jan 15-16, 2016	37	60	4
Dec 15-18, 2011	39	58	3
Jan 10-13, 2008	67	30	3
Mar 10-12, 2000	53	43	4
Jan 7-10, 2000	57	37	6

Gallup poll

Most Americans Say at Least One Candidate Running Would Be Good President

Americans' negativity toward the election process does not seem to be based on the view that there is a dearth of good candidates. More than two-thirds, 68%, say there is a candidate running who they think would make a good president. Even 63% of those who say the process is not working the way it should still say there is a candidate running who would make a good president.

And although the percentage of Americans who say the election process is working has dropped, views that there is at least one good candidate running are stable and generally in line with what Gallup has found in previous election years.

Republicans' views about there being a candidate running who would make a good president have stayed relatively constant since January, while Democrats have become modestly more positive. Democrats are now more likely than Republicans to say a good candidate is running, 78% vs. 69%, respectively.

Is there any candidate running who you think would make a good president, or not?

% Yes

	January 2016%	February 2016%	March 2016%
National adults	66	67	68
Republicans/Leaners	71	70	69
Democrats/Leaners	69	71	78

Gallup poll

Implications

A recent March 17-20 *New York Times*/CBS News survey found that 60% of Republican registered voters say the Republican presidential campaign has made them feel mostly embarrassed by the Republican Party rather than mostly proud. In the same poll, only 13% of Democratic registered voters said they were mostly embarrassed about their party's campaign. These findings support the hypothesis that Republicans' views that the campaign is not working properly are being driven by their negative views of the candidates' campaigns, most likely related to Trump. Republican establishment leaders' attempt to prevent Trump from getting the GOP nomination may be adding to rank-and-file Republicans' views that the process is not working, either because they support or because they oppose these efforts. House Speaker Paul Ryan said earlier this week,

"Looking around at what's taking place in politics today, it is easy to get disheartened," and apparently many Republicans may agree.

These data are available in Gallup Analytics.

Survey Methods

Results for this Gallup poll are based on telephone interviews conducted March 16-17, 2016, on the Gallup U.S. Daily survey, with a random sample of 1,012 adults, aged 18 and older, living in all 50 U.S. states and the District of Columbia. For results based on the total sample of national adults, the margin of sampling error is ±4 percentage points at the 95% confidence level. All reported margins of sampling error include computed design effects for weighting.

March 28, 2016
TRUMP AND CLINTON SUPPORTERS LEAD IN ENTHUSIASM

by Lydia Saad

Story Highlights

- *Two-thirds of Republicans backing Trump are highly enthusiastic*
- *Less than 40% of other GOP candidates' supporters are enthusiastic*
- *Clinton's supporters lead Sanders' 54% to 44% in enthusiasm*

PRINCETON, N.J. – As the 2016 primaries continue, with neither party's nominee yet decided, Gallup finds sharp differences in the enthusiasm expressed by supporters of the various candidates. Among Republicans and Republican leaners, voters who support Donald Trump are the most enthusiastic by far, with a combined 65% describing themselves as extremely or very enthusiastic. This is nearly twice the level of fervor expressed by Republicans backing Gov. John Kasich (33%), and well eclipses the enthusiasm from those backing Sen. Ted Cruz (39%).

Enthusiasm for Voting in 2016 Among Republican Candidate Supporters

Based on Republicans/Republican leaners who are registered to vote

	Trump supporters %	Cruz supporters %	Kasich supporters %
Extremely enthusiastic	37	22	16
Very enthusiastic	28	17	17
Somewhat enthusiastic	23	25	15
Not too enthusiastic	5	19	20
Not at all enthusiastic	5	16	31
No opinion	2	0	1
Extremely/Very enthusiastic	65	39	33

Gallup, March 21-23, 2016

On the Democratic side, Hillary Clinton's supporters are more enthusiastic than Sen. Bernie Sanders' supporters, 54% vs. 44%.

Enthusiasm for Voting in 2016 Among Democratic Candidate Supporters

Based on Democrats/Democratic leaners who are registered to vote

	Clinton supporters %	Sanders supporters %
Extremely enthusiastic	25	23
Very enthusiastic	29	21
Somewhat enthusiastic	23	27
Not too enthusiastic	12	19
Not at all enthusiastic	10	9
No opinion	1	0
Extremely/Very enthusiastic	54	44

Gallup, March 21-23, 2016

In both parties, people's enthusiasm for voting in the election could reflect a combination of factors – including excitement about their preferred candidate's presence in the race as well as confidence that the candidate will succeed in winning either the nomination or the general election. The latter could be particularly relevant on the Democratic side, where Clinton is widely seen as the likely nominee and is poised to be the first female major-party nominee. That contrasts with the Republican nomination, which remains unclear given the real likelihood that no candidate will garner the necessary number of delegates to secure the nomination before the convention.

These findings are from Gallup Daily tracking interviews conducted March 21-23 with 1,358 registered voters, including 635 Republicans and independents who lean Republican, and 610 Democrats and Democratic leaners. The poll coincided with the March 22 Democratic primaries that resulted in two wins for Sanders and one for Clinton, but preceded Saturday's voting in Alaska, Hawaii and Washington state – which Sanders swept.

Overall, 47% of registered voters nationwide say they are extremely or very enthusiastic about voting this year. That is down from 54% in January, but is slightly higher than the 42% level of enthusiasm recorded in March 2012.

Separately, Gallup asked voters how much thought they have given to the election – an important past indicator of voter turnout. Here Gallup finds that the various candidates' supporters are paying fairly similar attention to the election. Three-quarters of Clinton and Sanders supporters say they have given quite a lot of or some thought to the election, along with 79% of Cruz supporters and slightly higher percentages of Trump (83%) and Kasich (85%) supporters.

How much thought have you given to the upcoming election for president – quite a lot, or only a little?

Based on registered voters

	Cruz^ supporters %	Trump^ supporters %	Kasich^ supporters %	Clinton^^ supporters %	Sanders^^ supporters %
Quite a lot/ Some (vol.)	79	83	85	76	75
Only a little/ None (vol.)	20	17	16	24	25
No opinion	1	0	0	0	0

^ Cruz, Trump and Kasich supporters based on Republicans/Republican leaners; ^^ Clinton and Sanders supporters based on Democrats/Democratic leaners

Gallup, March 21-23, 2016; (vol.) = Volunteered response

Bottom Line

Voter enthusiasm is not necessarily a good indicator of voter turnout, but it could play a role come convention time when the parties need to bring the losing candidates' supporters on board with the party's choice for nominee. Should these findings persist, the extraordinarily high enthusiasm seen among Trump's supporters could be an impediment to Republican Party unity if he is not chosen. On the Democratic side, enthusiasm for Sanders – most evident in the overflow rallies he has enjoyed throughout the campaign – could portend party dissension should Clinton become the nominee. However, contrary to what the optics of the campaign might project, it is Clinton's supporters right now who are more enthusiastic.

Historical data are available in Gallup Analytics.

Survey Methods

Results for this Gallup poll are based on telephone interviews conducted March 21-23, 2016, on the Gallup U.S. Daily survey, with a random sample of 1,358 registered voters, aged 18 and older, living in all 50 U.S. states and the District of Columbia. For results based on the total sample of national adults, the margin of sampling error is ±3 percentage points at the 95% confidence level. For results based on the total sample of 635 Republicans and Republican-leaning independents, the margin of error is ±5 percentage points at the 95% confidence level. For results based on the total sample of 610 Democrats and Democratic-leaning independents, the margin of error is ±5 percentage points at the 95% confidence level. All reported margins of sampling error include computed design effects for weighting.

March 28, 2016

AMERICANS BELIEVE 2015 WAS RECORD-WARM, BUT SPLIT ON WHY

by Riley E. Dunlap

Gallup Scholar for the Environment

Story Highlights

- *69% of Americans believe reports of record-high temperatures*
- *Republicans are least likely to believe the reports*
- *49% think reason for record warmth is human-caused climate change*

PRINCETON, N.J. – U.S. government scientists recently reported that 2015 was the Earth's warmest year since reliable record keeping began. Majorities of U.S. adults surveyed in Gallup's annual Environment poll are aware of this finding and believe it is accurate, but they are almost evenly divided on whether the record-high temperatures are attributable mainly to human-caused climate change (49%) or natural variability (46%).

U.S. Views on Record-Warm 2015

	Yes%	No%	No opinion%
Heard reports that 2015 was Earth's warmest year on record	63	37	*
Believe reports are accurate	69	27	4

* Less than 0.5%
Gallup, March 2-6, 2016

U.S. Views on Main Cause of Record 2015 Temperatures

	Main cause%
Human-caused climate change	49
Natural changes in the Earth's temperatures	46
Other/No opinion	5

Gallup, March 2-6, 2016

Majority of Americans Aware of Reports of Record Temperatures for 2015

When asked if they had heard that scientists recently reported that 2015 was the Earth's warmest year on record, 63% of U.S. adults said they had. This awareness varies somewhat among key demographic sectors – particularly education, age and race.

College graduates are substantially more likely than those with no college to have heard of the reports, 76% vs. 53%. A large gap is also evident by age: 70% of those aged 55 and older are familiar with the reports, compared with 53% of 18- to 34-year-olds. Whites (68%) are more likely than nonwhites (52%) to have heard. Partisan differences are insignificant, with 66% of Democrats and 64% of Republicans hearing about the reports of record temperatures in 2015.

U.S. Public's Awareness of 2015 Record Warmth

As you may know, scientists recently reported that 2015 was the Earth's warmest year on record. Had you heard about these reports before now, or not?

	Yes, had heard%	No, had not heard%
U.S. adults	63	37
18 to 34	53	47
35 to 54	63	37
55+	70	29
White	68	32
Nonwhite	52	47
College graduate	76	24
Some college	62	38
No college	53	46
Republican	64	36
Independent	62	37
Democrat	66	34

Gallup, March 2-6, 2016

Majority Also Believe the Reports Are Accurate

All adults were next asked whether they believe the reports are accurate. A somewhat larger majority than had heard of the reports say they are accurate, 69%, while 27% say they are not. Compared with the question about awareness of the reports, the patterns by subgroup change substantially on the question of their accuracy.

While Republicans and Democrats are similarly aware of the reports about 2015's record warmth, there are striking partisan differences in terms of belief in the reports' accuracy: 84% of Democrats believe them, compared with 52% of Republicans.

Young adults (aged 18 to 34) are more likely to believe the reports than their older (55 and older) counterparts, 78% vs. 65%. There is a modest difference between whites (67%) and nonwhites (74%) in the perceived accuracy of the reports. College graduates are also modestly more likely to believe the reports than those with no college, 75% vs. 67%.

U.S. Public's Views on Accuracy of 2015 Climate Report

Just your best guess, do you generally believe these reports are accurate or not accurate?

	Accurate %	Not accurate%	No opinion %
U.S. adults	69	27	4
18 to 34	78	20	2
35 to 54	68	29	4
55+	65	31	4
White	67	29	3
Nonwhite	74	23	3
College graduate	75	22	2
Some college	66	29	5
No college	67	29	3
Republican	52	45	3
Independent	70	26	4
Democrat	84	12	3
Heard of 2015 climate reports	76	26	1
Had not heard of reports	58	35	7

Gallup, March 2-6, 2016

Americans Split on Primary Cause of Record Warmth

A third question in the March 2-6 poll asked adults if, assuming the reports are true, they think the record 2015 global temperatures are mainly attributable to human-caused climate change or to natural changes in the Earth's temperatures. Here, the U.S. public is sharply divided. Forty-nine percent attribute the record temperatures to human-caused climate change, while 46% attribute them to natural changes.

Not surprisingly, given the degree to which climate change has become a highly polarized political issue, there is a chasm between Republicans and Democrats on the source of 2015's record-high global temperatures. While 72% of Democrats attribute the record temperatures to human-caused climate change, only 27% of Republicans do so. This mirrors the continued large partisan gap in views of global warming documented in other items in this year's Environment poll.

Younger adults (those 18 to 34) are also much more likely than older Americans (55 and older) to attribute the record warmth to human-caused climate change, 61% vs. 39%. There are also noticeable differences by education and race: College graduates are more likely than those with no college to choose human causation (56% vs. 42%), and nonwhites are more likely than whites to do so (58% vs. 46%).

Attribute Record 2015 Warmth to Human-Caused Climate Change or Natural Changes?

Assuming these reports are accurate, do you think the record temperatures in 2015 were mainly due to – [human-caused climate change (or to) natural changes in the Earth's temperatures]?

	Climate change %	Natural changes %	Reports are not accurate (vol.)%	No opinion%
U.S. adults	49	46	2	3
18 to 34	61	38	1	*
35 to 54	52	45	2	1
55+	39	54	2	5
White	46	51	2	2
Nonwhite	58	37	2	4
College graduate	56	40	1	3
Some college	52	44	2	2
No college	42	53	2	3
Republican	27	72	1	1
Independent	47	48	3	2
Democrat	72	24	1	2
Heard of 2015 climate reports	53	43	2	2
Had not heard of reports	43	52	2	4
Reports are accurate	62	35	1	2
Reports are not accurate	20	74	3	3

(vol.) = Volunteered response; * Less than 0.5%
Gallup, March 2-6, 2016

As Gallup reported previously, the same poll found 63% of Americans saying that temperatures where they live have been warmer than usual this winter and 10% saying they were colder than usual. About half of each group – or 38% of all Americans – attribute the unusual winter weather to climate change caused by human activity. That is somewhat less than the percentage attributing last year's record warmth at the global level to human-caused climate change.

Bottom Line

A strong majority of Americans, including 52% of Republicans, accept that 2015 was a record-setting warm year. However, they are sharply divided, especially on the basis of political affiliation, on the sources of the record temperatures. This is yet another indication of the extreme degree of partisan polarization surrounding climate change that has evolved in the U.S. over the past decade.

Riley E. Dunlap is Gallup Scholar for the Environment and Regents Professor of Sociology at Oklahoma State University.

Survey Methods

Results for this Gallup poll are based on telephone interviews conducted March 2-6, 2016, with a random sample of 1,019 adults, aged 18 and older, living in all 50 U.S. states and the District of Columbia. For results based on the total sample of national adults, the margin of sampling error is ±4 percentage points at the 95% confidence level. All reported margins of sampling error include computed design effects for weighting.

March 30, 2016
AMERICANS' VIEWS OF TRUMP, CRUZ AT NEW LOWS IN MARCH

by Frank Newport

PRINCETON, N.J. – The primary and caucus season is taking its toll on the images of three of the major presidential candidates. Republicans Donald Trump and Ted Cruz, in particular, have suffered significant drops in their images over the past two months. Trump continues to have the most negative image of any of the five active presidential candidates. Cruz's image has suffered as much as Trump's, although he remains the better liked of the two GOP contenders.

Clinton, Trump, Cruz, Sanders and Kasich Net Favorable Ratings

Monthly averages, among U.S. adults

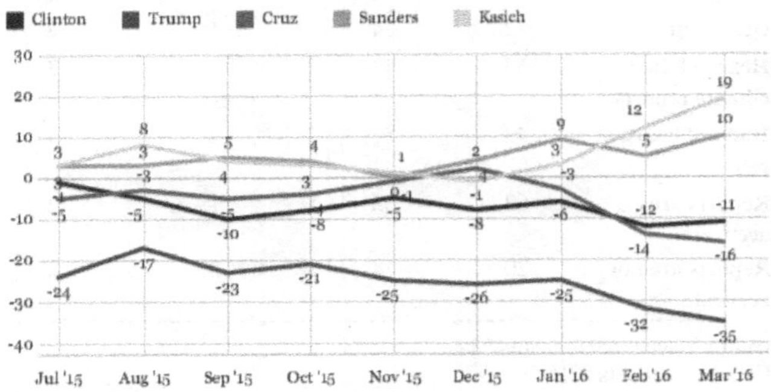

Gallup Daily tracking

GALLUP'

Hillary Clinton's image has slipped marginally in the past two months, while Bernie Sanders' and John Kasich's ratings have improved. Kasich now has the most positive net favorable rating of any of these five candidates.

These month-by-month image averages are based on Gallup Daily tracking conducted since July, with more than 3,600 U.S. adults rating each candidate each month. The net favorable ratings are based on the difference between those with a favorable opinion and those with an unfavorable opinion of each candidate.

Americans' views of these candidates have fluctuated, but in the past several months, the intense focus of the primary and caucus season has clearly affected the images of all five – some for the better, and some for the worse.

Trump has always had the worst image of any of these five candidates, and his image has slipped further among Americans since January. His current -35 net favorable rating (30% favorable and 65% unfavorable) is the worst for him in any month since tracking began.

Cruz, like Trump, has seen his image deteriorate in recent months, and Cruz's net favorable score of -16 (based on 32% favorable and 48% unfavorable) is now the second lowest of the five candidates. Cruz used to be significantly more popular; at one point in November, he was basically tied with Kasich and Sanders as having the highest net favorable rating of any of these five candidates.

Clinton's image has been somewhat more stable than both Trump's and Cruz's over the past six months. Her net favorable rating dropped modestly in February and has stayed at that level so far in March. Her current net favorable score of -11 (42% favorable and 53% unfavorable) puts her in the middle of these five.

Kasich and Sanders – most likely as a result of their not being perceived as front-runners and thus being out of the main focus of campaign brickbats and intense media coverage – have both seen significant improvement in their images as they have become better known. Both still lag their respective party's front-runner in the percentage of Americans who are familiar with them. They are the only candidates with net favorable images in positive territory. Each now has his most positive rating since tracking began, with Sanders at +10 and Kasich at +19.

Sanders Has Gained Most in Familiarity Since July

Sanders, Kasich and Cruz have all seen their name recognition increase by double digits since July. Kasich remains the least known of any of the candidates, with a familiarity score of 62%, but that is up by 34 percentage points since July. About eight in 10 Americans know of Sanders and Cruz. Sanders' jump from 44% familiarity in July to 82% today is the largest gain among any of these candidates.

Trump and Clinton were already well-known when Gallup tracking began last July. Their familiarity scores have edged up in the months since, and are now at the point where they have nearly universal recognition levels of 94% to 95%.

Clinton, Trump, Sanders, Cruz and Kasich Familiarity, Among U.S. Adults

	Familiar with candidate in July 2015* %	Familiar with candidate in March 2016** %	Gain in familiarity from 2015 to 2016(pct. pts.)
Hillary Clinton	90	95	+5
Donald Trump	88	94	+6
Bernie Sanders	44	82	+38
Ted Cruz	57	81	+24
John Kasich	28	62	+34

* July 8-31, 2015; ** March 1-28, 2016

Gallup Daily tracking

Bottom Line

The intense campaign season has clearly affected the images of the remaining presidential candidates, especially Trump and Cruz. Americans now view both in a worse light than in any month since Gallup tracking began last July. Clinton's favorable image is down, but not by nearly as much. At this point in the campaign, notably, front-runners Trump and Clinton both have net negative images among the American public.

Even as they have become better known, Sanders and Kasich have seen their images improve in recent months, although Kasich remains less well-known than any of the other candidates.

Historical data are available in Gallup Analytics.

Survey Methods

Results for this Gallup poll are based on telephone interviews conducted on a monthly basis from July 8, 2015, to March 28, 2016, on the Gallup U.S. Daily survey, with each candidate rated each month by a random sample of between 3,648 and 7,302 national adults, aged 18 and older, living in all 50 U.S. states and the District of Columbia. For results based on each month's total sample of national adults rating each candidate, the margin of sampling error is ±2 percentage points at the 95% confidence level. All reported margins of sampling error include computed design effects for weighting.

March 30, 2016
OPPOSITION TO FRACKING MOUNTS IN THE U.S.

by Art Swift

Story Highlights

- *Opposition to fracking rises to 51% from 40% in 2015*
- *Drop in fracking mirrors Americans' turn away from nuclear energy*
- *Republicans fuel drop in support for fracking*

WASHINGTON, D.C. – Opposition to the practice of hydraulic fracturing or "fracking" has increased significantly in the past year as environmental concerns, such as earthquakes, have grown, even though the procedure has helped keep oil prices low.

Fracking in the United States

Do you favor or oppose hydraulic fracturing or "fracking" as a means of increasing the production of natural gas and oil in the U.S.?

	Favor%	Oppose%	No opinion%
Mar 2-6, 2016	36	51	13
Mar 5-8, 2015	40	40	19

Gallup

In the past year, the price of oil has fluctuated between roughly $25 and $60 per barrel, a staggering drop from its peak of around $120 in mid-2014. One major reason the price of this commodity has remained so low is fracking, which now accounts for half of the oil production in the U.S. As recently as 2000, fracking made up only 2% of the nation's oil output.

In Gallup's 2016 Environment survey, conducted March 2-6, Americans have a clearer position on fracking than they did a year ago. Last year, 40% said they favored fracking and 40% were opposed, with a substantial 19% not knowing about or having no opinion on fracking. In 2016, support for fracking has slipped to 36%, while opposition has climbed to 51%. The percentage of Americans with no opinion has dropped to 13%, perhaps as the term becomes more commonplace in the culture, or as the media has more extensively covered the arguments for and against fracking.

Americans' turn against fracking comes as the percentage predicting there will be a critical energy shortage in the next five years has fallen to a new low, likely because of lower gas prices. With oil and gas relatively cheap, many Americans may not see the need to fracture the earth through fracking. Lower oil and gas prices may also be the reason a majority of Americans are opposed to nuclear energy for the first time. Additionally, more people would like to prioritize alternative energy over traditional energy sources. Fracking, while a relatively new way to extract oil, is still a means of harnessing fossil-fuel energy, helping explain why Americans may be growing averse to it.

Republicans Not as Supportive of Fracking in 2016

Republicans had the biggest drop in support for fracking, falling from 66% support in 2015 to 55% this year. Still, Republicans' support for fracking far exceeds support among independents (34%) and Democrats (25%). Views among the last two groups are essentially unchanged from last year.

Fracking in the United States

Americans in favor, by political party

	2015%	2016%
Republican	66	55
Independent	35	34
Democrat	26	25

Gallup, March 2-6, 2016

Bottom Line

Fracking has become a contentious topic in American life. In recent years, it has been seen as a source of great prosperity for the nation's crude oil producers, yet it has also become part of a global tug of war with Saudi Arabia. The Middle Eastern oil behemoth has been engaged in a pricing battle with American oil companies, with its goal being lower prices to make the cost of fracking too expensive for U.S. companies to pursue.

Fracking is potentially a cause of earthquakes across sections of the U.S. that are not used to these types of natural disasters. The U.S. Geological Survey said this week that 7 million Americans are at risk of experiencing earthquakes caused by fracking in the states of Oklahoma, Kansas, Texas, Colorado, New Mexico and Arkansas. With more than 1,000 earthquakes in the central U.S. alone last year, these events could be linked to the rising percentage of Americans who oppose fracking.

For the foreseeable future, fracking appears to be a way to extract oil from shale. Oil producers nationwide have said that if oil prices remain above $40 per barrel, it is prudent to use fracking to drill for crude oil. Previously, producers had said that price needed to be $70. With the U.S. effectively swimming in shale oil, the deliberation over fracking will likely continue for years to come.

Historical data are available in Gallup Analytics.

Survey Methods

Results for this Gallup poll are based on telephone interviews conducted March 2-6, 2016, with a random sample of 1,019 adults, aged 18 and older, living in all 50 U.S. states and the District of Columbia. For results based on the total sample of national adults, the margin of sampling error is ±4 percentage points at the 95% confidence level. All reported margins of sampling error include computed design effects for weighting.

March 31, 2016

CLINTON PREFERRED FOR EXPERIENCE; SANDERS, FOR CARE

by Justin McCarthy

Story Highlights

- *Her platform and a desire for a female president also among top reasons*
- *His backers most likely to support him for his care for people*

WASHINGTON, D.C. – Democrats and Democratic-leaning independents who would like to see Hillary Clinton win the Democratic presidential nomination most frequently cite her qualifications, White House experience and care for the needs of the people as the reasons they favor her over Sen. Bernie Sanders.

Most Important Reasons for Supporting Hillary Clinton for the Democratic Nomination

What are one or two of the most important reasons why you prefer Hillary Clinton for the Democratic nomination? (open-ended) Among Democrats/Democratic leaners

	Mar 21-23, 2016%
Capable of being president/Qualified/ Experienced	29
Hillary Clinton's political background/White House experience/Bill Clinton	19
Care for and about the people/Connected to their needs	10
Hillary Clinton's a woman/Need a woman/ Equal for women	9
Like/Agree with views/Good platform	8
Intelligent/Smart/Knowledgeable	8
Strong/Good leadership abilities	4
Well-versed in foreign policy/International dealings	4
Will win the election	3
Need a change/Different	3
Consistent/Stable stand by their decision	3
None/No opinion	9

Note: Responses mentioned by at least 3% are listed
Gallup

Other reasons Clinton supporters give to explain why they back her include the desire or need for a female president, her platform and overall views and her intelligence. Nine percent did not offer an opinion as to why they support the former first lady, U.S. senator and secretary of state.

These data, based on a March 21-23 Gallup poll, come as Clinton and Sanders gear up for important primary contests in Wisconsin and New York.

Gallup asked Democrats and Democratic-leaning independents who said they would support Clinton or Sanders to indicate in their own words what lies behind their preference. Responses to this question were coded into major categories as displayed in the accompanying tables.

As the results show, Clinton supporters tend to cite aspects of her background and character as reasons for her supporting her. Beyond the 8% saying they like her platform, the only specific mention of issues or policy is her being well-versed in foreign policy (4%). This, however, is likely tied in to her experience as secretary of state.

More Sanders supporters reference aspects of his policy stances, such as his focus on education and college tuition (10%) and healthcare problems (4%). These are in addition to the 19% who more generally say they agree with his views.

The single most common mention about the Vermont senator, however, is that he cares about and connects with the people and their needs (22%).

Most Important Reasons for Supporting Bernie Sanders for the Democratic Nomination

What are one or two of the most important reasons why you prefer Bernie Sanders for the Democratic nomination? (open-ended) Among Democrats and Democratic leaners

	Mar 21-23, 2016%
Care for and about the people/Connected to their needs	22
Like/Agree with views/Good platform	19
Honest/Trustworthy	16
Like his/her focus on education/College tuition views	10
Dislike or don't care for other candidate	8
He's a man/Don't want women in office	6
Capable of being president/Qualified/ Experienced	5
Don't trust her/him	5
Is not controlled by corporate money/big business	5
Cares about the healthcare problems	4
Need a change/Different	3
Has more socialistic views/ways	3
Other (vol.)	3
None/No opinion	4

Note: Responses mentioned by at least 3% are listed; (vol.) = Volunteered response
Gallup

About one in six Sanders supporters say they prefer him because he is honest and trustworthy, something few Clinton supporters (1%) mention as a reason they support her. Perceptions of dishonesty were the most common responses about Clinton in a previous Gallup open-ended question among all Americans. At the same time, few Sanders supporters cite the experience (5%) that is most often mentioned by Clinton supporters (29%).

Bottom Line

Clinton supporters and Sanders supporters offer fairly different reasons why they prefer their candidate to be the Democratic nominee, mostly focusing on the candidates' relative strengths.

Clinton's supporters commonly prefer her for what she has accomplished, in terms of her résumé and job experience. Sanders' supporters more commonly mention his care for Americans' needs and his platform positions. It is unclear whether these responses reflect Democrats' principal reasons for their support of Clinton or Sanders, or if the responses largely reflect what Democrats think of first when they are asked to explain their choice in an open-ended question format.

Once the nomination is settled, supporters of the losing candidate most likely will join with supporters of the victor as he or she prepares to face the Republican nominee in the general election. And as the campaign shifts from the nomination to the general election phase, those who supported the losing candidate for the Democratic nomination will likely find reasons to embrace the Democratic nominee over the Republican.

Survey Methods

Results for this Gallup poll are based on telephone interviews conducted March 21-23, 2016, on the Gallup U.S. Daily survey, with a random sample of 677 Democrats and independents who lean Democratic, including 384 who prefer Clinton as the Democratic nominee and 254 who prefer Sanders, aged 18 and older, living in all 50 U.S. states and the District of Columbia. For results based on Clinton's supporters, and based on results near 20%, the margin of sampling error is ±5 percentage points at the 95% confidence level. For results based on Sanders' supporters, and based on results near 20%, the margin of sampling error is ±6 percentage points at the 95% confidence level. All reported margins of sampling error include computed design effects for weighting.

April 01, 2016
DEMOCRATS INCREASING THEIR EDGE IN U.S. PARTY AFFILIATION

by Jeffrey M. Jones

Story Highlights

- *Democrats hold six-percentage-point edge in party affiliation*
- *One of largest advantages in Obama's second term*
- *Parties were even last fall*

PRINCETON, N.J. – Forty-six percent of Americans now identify politically as Democrats or say they lean Democratic, while 40% identify as Republican or lean Republican. As recently as October, the parties had equal levels of support.

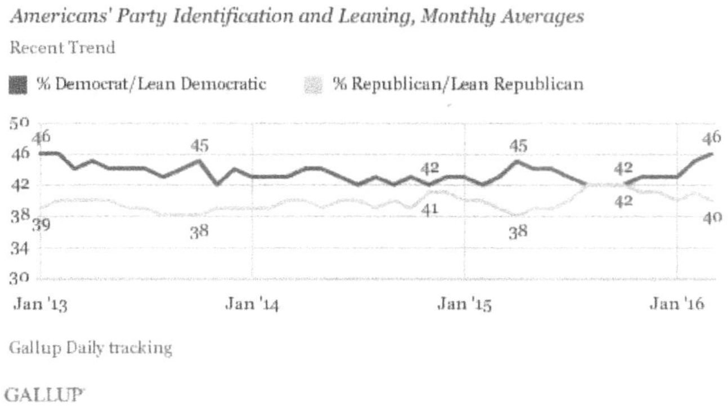

The six-percentage-point Democratic advantage in party loyalties in Gallup Daily tracking throughout March is one of the larger leads for the party during Barack Obama's second presidential term. Democrats have held a seven-point lead over Republicans on three occasions during this time, including January 2013, the month of Obama's second inauguration; October 2013, during the partial federal government shutdown; and April 2015, as the 2016 presidential field was beginning to take shape and Hillary Clinton was the best-known, and best-liked, candidate.

These results are based on monthly averages of Gallup Daily tracking data, including more than 13,000 interviews each month. Each night, Gallup asks Americans whether they identify politically as Democrats, Republicans or independents. Independents are subsequently asked if they lean more toward the Republican or Democratic Party. Party "leaners" usually share similar attitudes and behaviors to those who identify outright with the party. Consequently, the combined percentage of party identifiers and leaners gives a sense of the relative strength of each party within the U.S.

The recent shifts toward, and away from, the GOP may reflect the twists and turns in the presidential campaign. As Clinton became embroiled in a controversy over storing classified government communications on a private server last spring, her image suffered. Meanwhile, Donald Trump's presence in the campaign, a GOP contest with a large field of 17 candidates, and widely viewed television debates offered a great deal of publicity for the party. But the large field also created greater uncertainty about the likely outcome than the Democratic contest in which Clinton was regarded as the clear front-runner, notwithstanding Bernie Sanders' spirited challenge.

In August, September and October, the parties were tied in party affiliation, at 42%.

Since then, particularly in the past two months as Trump and his GOP challengers have frequently resorted to personal attacks in debates, at campaign rallies and on social media, Americans' party loyalties have shifted, giving the Democratic Party a clear advantage. Republicans are also facing the real possibility that no candidate will emerge from the contentious nomination campaign with the majority of delegates needed to ensure his nomination, thus leaving the ultimate choice of the nominee to convention delegates.

Amid the presidential campaign, a time when latent party loyalties are activated given the intense focus on political matters, Obama's job approval rating has improved. Last week, an average of 53% of Americans approved of the job Obama was doing, his highest weekly average since late January/early February 2013. Obama's rising popularity could also be a factor in Americans' greater likelihood of aligning with the Democratic Party.

Implications

Democrats' current six-point edge in party affiliation gives them strong positioning heading toward this fall's election. Given that Republicans tend to vote at higher rates than Democrats, a bigger advantage in basic party loyalties gives Democrats more of a cushion if their turnout fails to match or approach that of Republicans.

The Democratic lead in party affiliation was smaller than it is now in the months preceding the 2012 election, ranging from two to four percentage points. But it pales in comparison to the double-digit advantages it held in 2008, which grew even larger after Obama won the election.

If the GOP nomination is settled in a way that doesn't ignite further controversy, Republicans may gain back some of the support the party has lost, particularly considering the numerous shifts in party affiliation over the past 12 months. But at this point, with neither party nomination settled and Election Day still seven months away, Democrats hold the upper hand.

These data are available in Gallup Analytics.

Survey Methods

Results for this Gallup poll are based on telephone interviews conducted March 1-31, 2016, on the Gallup U.S. Daily survey, with a random sample of 15,253 adults, aged 18 and older, living in all 50 U.S. states and the District of Columbia. For results based on the total sample of national adults, the margin of sampling error is ±1 percentage point at the 95% confidence level. All reported margins of sampling error include computed design effects for weighting.

April 01, 2016
SEVEN IN 10 WOMEN HAVE UNFAVORABLE OPINION OF TRUMP

by Frank Newport and Lydia Saad

Story Highlights

- *Trump has a 70% unfavorable and 23% favorable image among women*

- *Men also give Trump net negative rating, but it is significantly better*
- *Trump's gender gap is larger than any other major candidate's*

PRINCETON, N.J. – Donald Trump's image among U.S. women tilts strongly negative, with 70% of women holding an unfavorable opinion and 23% a favorable opinion of the Republican front-runner in March. Trump's unfavorable rating among women has been high since Gallup began tracking it last July, but after rising slightly last fall, it has increased even further since January.

Donald Trump's Image Among Women

Monthly averages

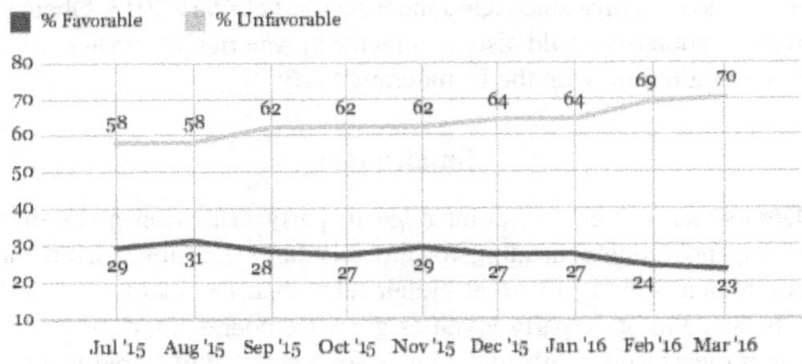

Gallup Daily tracking

GALLUP

These monthly averages are based on interviews with more than 3,600 U.S. adults rating Trump as well as the other major candidates in the race each month as part of Gallup Daily tracking.

Trump's image is also more negative than positive among men. As a result, his overall image is the most negative of any of the five remaining major candidates from both parties who are running for president. Still, men are not nearly as negative toward Trump as women are. The gap between his favorable and unfavorable rating among men averaged 22 percentage points in March 1-28 interviewing, compared with a 47-point gap among women.

Donald Trump's Image Among Men

Monthly averages

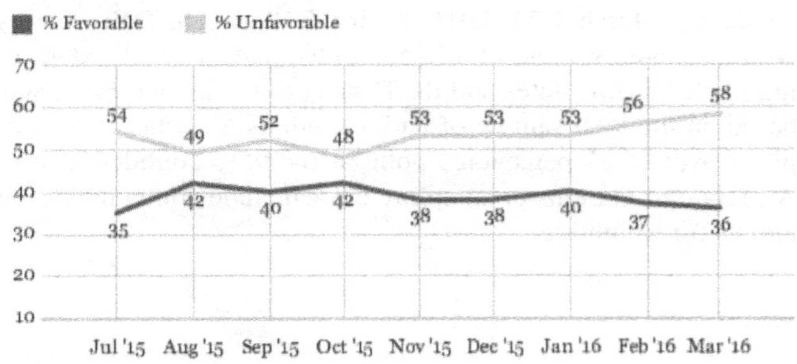

Gallup Daily tracking

GALLUP

Since last year, Trump's net favorable rating (% favorable minus % unfavorable) among all adults nationally has worsened, to -35 in March from -17 in August. But despite a nearly constant string of controversies that raise questions about Trump's attitudes toward and treatment of women, the decline in his image among men has been similar to that among women.

One possible explanation for Trump's better image among men is that men overall are more likely to identify as Republicans, while women are more likely to identify as Democrats.

But attitudes toward Republican candidates Ted Cruz and John Kasich belie this partisan explanation, given that men and women nationally have similar views of each of these two candidates. Cruz's image tilts about equally negative among both genders, while the two genders view Kasich equally positively. Cruz's image has become much more negative among both men and women over the past two months, but generally in lock step. The one-point difference in his net favorable rating between men (-15) and women (-16) in March is on par with the average four-point difference seen since July.

Hillary Clinton, like Trump and Cruz, is viewed more negatively than positively by both men and women, though of these two, women are far less negative. This likely reflects the basic female gender skew among Democrats and that Clinton is the only female candidate in the race. Clinton's stronger performance among women than among men has been a constant over the past nine months. Her average net favorable rating has been 21 points higher among women than among men, close to her current 17-point gap in March.

Vermont Sen. Bernie Sanders has a better image among women than among men, although with a smaller gap than is the case for Clinton.

Trump, Kasich, Cruz, Sanders and Clinton Images, by Gender

	Net favorable rating, women (pct. pts.)	Net favorable rating, men (pct. pts.)	Image gender gap, women minus men (pct. pts.)
Donald Trump	-47	-22	-25
John Kasich	+18	+20	-2
Ted Cruz	-16	-15	-1
Bernie Sanders	+15	+6	+9
Hillary Clinton	-3	-20	+17

Gallup Daily tracking, March 1-28, 2016

Trump's Gender Gap Mostly Among Republicans

Most of the gender gap in views of Trump is a result of Republicans' views, with ratings of Trump much more positive among Republican men (61% favorable, 36% unfavorable) than among Republican women (49% favorable, 46% unfavorable). Among Democrats, men and women are more united in their dislike of the candidate, with high unfavorable ratings of Trump among both groups.

Donald Trump's Image, by Gender and Party

	Favorable%	Unfavorable%
REPUBLICANS/LEANERS		
Male	61	36
Female	49	46
DEMOCRATS/LEANERS		
Male	12	84
Female	7	89

Gallup Daily tracking, March 1-28, 2016

Bottom Line

There was a sizable gender gap in Americans' views of Trump as early as last July. But even as his overall image has worsened among both genders in recent months, the size of the gender gap has been fairly steady. Trump's "woman problem" has come into sharper focus this week with his latest high-visibility comments about women and abortion. It is too early to measure what effect those comments may be having on his image. But even before these remarks, fewer than one in four women viewed him favorably, suggesting he may already be down to a core of rock-hard supporters whose opinions aren't likely to change.

These data are available in Gallup Analytics.

Survey Methods

Results for this Gallup poll are based on telephone interviews conducted on a monthly basis from July 8, 2015, to March 28, 2016, on the Gallup U.S. Daily survey, with each candidate rated each month by a random sample of between 3,648 and 7,302 national adults, aged 18 and older, living in all 50 U.S. states and the District of Columbia. For results based on each month's total sample of national adults rating each candidate, the margin of sampling error is ±2 percentage points at the 95% confidence level. For results based on subsamples of between 1,717 and 3,863 men and women who rated each candidate each month, the margin of sampling error is ±3 percentage points at the 95% confidence level. All reported margins of sampling error include computed design effects for weighting.

April 04, 2016

MORE COLLEGE STUDENTS THAN U.S. ADULTS SAY FREE SPEECH IS SECURE

by Lydia Saad and Jeffrey M. Jones

Story Highlights

- *73% of students, 56% of adults say free speech is secure in U.S. today*
- *Students more positive than adults about all five First Amendment freedoms*
- *Students believe free speech rights stronger than in past; adults disagree*

PRINCETON, N.J. – Social media, student activism and school policies are testing the limits of First Amendment rights on campuses around the country. But a new study, sponsored by the John S. and James L. Knight Foundation in partnership with the Newseum Institute and Gallup, finds U.S. college students feeling more confident than the public as a whole about the security of these rights in the country today. Most notably, three-quarters of college students (73%) believe free speech rights are secure, compared with 56% of U.S. adults overall.

Do you think each of the following rights is very secure, secure, threatened or very threatened in the country today?

% Very secure/Secure

	College students %	U.S. adults%	Difference (pct. pts.)
Freedom to petition the government	76	58	18
Freedom of the press	81	64	17
Freedom of speech	73	56	17
Freedom of religion	68	60	8
Freedom to assemble peacefully	66	60	6

February-March 2016
Knight Foundation "Free Expression on Campus" study

The Free Expression on Campus study finds a similar gap in college students' and U.S. adults' views that freedom to petition the government is secure in the U.S. today (76% vs. 58%, respectively). Additionally, 81% of students versus 64% of all U.S. adults say freedom of the press is secure.

The two groups share similar views about freedom of assembly and freedom of religion, although college students are slightly more confident about the security of those rights as well.

These findings come from two nationally representative surveys – a March 5-8 telephone survey of 2,031 U.S. adults and a separate Feb. 29-March 15 telephone survey of 3,072 U.S. college students currently enrolled in four-year higher education institutions. Additionally, the study includes a nationally representative telephone survey of 250 U.S. Muslims, interviewed March 4-10.

Racial Gulf in College Students' Perceptions of Freedom of Assembly

Non-Hispanic black college students are less confident than non-Hispanic white college students about the security of all five First Amendment freedoms, but they are especially doubtful about freedom of assembly. Just 39% of black students, compared with seven in 10 white students, say this freedom is secure. In addition to recent student protests over campus race relations – most notably, at the University of Missouri – nationwide protests in the past year over police treatment of young black males may be influencing how black students perceive this right.

U.S. College Students' Perceptions of First Amendment Rights – by Race

% Very secure/Secure

	Whites %	Blacks %	Difference (pct. pts.)
Freedom to assemble peacefully	70	39	31
Freedom of speech	74	61	13
Freedom of religion	69	57	12
Freedom of the press	82	73	9
Freedom to petition the government	78	69	9

February-March 2016
Knight Foundation "Free Expression on Campus" study

A similar pattern is seen among U.S. adults overall, with 62% of whites versus 45% of blacks saying freedom of assembly is secure. Blacks are also less confident than whites about press freedom (58% vs. 66%, respectively). However, blacks' views regarding the security of freedom of religion, freedom to petition the government and freedom of speech are similar to those of whites.

U.S. Adults' Perceptions of First Amendment Rights – by Race and Party ID

% Very secure/Secure

	Whites %	Blacks %	Dems %	Independents %	Reps %
Freedom of the press	66	58	76	61	59
Freedom to assemble peacefully	62	45	67	60	55
Freedom to petition the government	59	58	73	56	49
Freedom of religion	58	63	75	63	43
Freedom of speech	57	53	73	53	45

February-March 2016

Knight Foundation "Free Expression on Campus" study

The study finds sharp differences in perceptions of the status of First Amendment rights by party identification among U.S. adults, with Republicans far less confident than Democrats about the security of all five rights. This is, perhaps, a result of ideological differences in the way the two groups view these rights, but it likely also reflects greater Democratic confidence and Republican cynicism about First Amendment protections under a Democratic president.

The largest difference by party involves freedom of religion: 75% of Democrats versus 43% of Republicans consider this right secure, a 32-percentage-point difference. Large partisan gaps are also seen for freedom of speech and freedom to petition the government. Smaller gaps are seen for freedom of the press and freedom of assembly – the only two freedoms that the majority of Republicans think are secure today.

In contrast to the pattern among U.S. adults, college students show little partisan differences in their perceptions that First Amendment rights are secure. The one exception, that Republican students (76%) are more likely than Democratic students (60%) to say freedom of assembly is secure, likely reflects the substantial racial gap on this item.

U.S. Muslims' views about the security of First Amendment rights are mostly similar to those of college students; however, Muslims are a bit less confident than students about freedom of the press and freedom of religion. The 60% of Muslims believing freedom of religion is secure is on par with U.S. adults.

U.S. Adults See Greater Deterioration of Free Speech

The study also measured U.S. adults' and college students' perceptions of how free speech rights have changed in the past 20 years. Students are more positive than adults overall regarding the trend in freedom of speech: 40% of U.S. adults, compared with 22% of college students, believe Americans' ability to exercise these rights is weaker today. Conversely, half of college students versus a third of U.S. adults believe it is stronger.

From what you have heard or read, do you think Americans' ability to exercise their free speech rights is stronger, about the same or weaker than it was 20 years ago?

	College students %	U.S. adults %
Stronger	50	31
About the same	27	27
Weaker	22	40
No opinion	1	2

February-March 2016
Knight Foundation "Free Expression on Campus" study

These results are mirrored in generational differences among the U.S. adult population. The percentage saying free speech is weaker today is only 29% among all 18- to 29-year-olds, but rises to 39% among those aged 30 to 49 and to 46% among those aged 50 and older.

Bottom Line

U.S. colleges have long been places where open expression and debate are encouraged to further their goals of educating students and teaching them skills to help them be productive and responsible citizens. As such, colleges have a history of being places for activism – for raising awareness of issues affecting not only students but also the country and world more generally. At the same time, increasing diversity on campuses and in the U.S. can sometimes put free expression rights to the test when that expression is insensitive or hurtful toward members of certain subgroups.

Despite their exposure to these issues at college, most students believe the five rights guaranteed to Americans by the First Amendment are secure in this country today. Further, students are more likely than U.S. adults overall to believe in the security of these rights.

Digging deeper, the study finds that U.S. adults' views are far more influenced by political considerations than are college students', perhaps reflecting Republican adults' greater sensitivity to having a Democratic president in office. But politics alone is not a complete explanation of the difference between college students and adults. In many instances, college students are just as optimistic as Democratic adults, if not more so, about the security of rights such as freedom of the press and freedom of speech. Whatever the reason, college students hold a more optimistic and idealistic view of First Amendment freedoms than U.S. adults do.

Survey Methods

Results for U.S. adults are based on telephone interviews conducted March 5-8, 2016, on the Gallup U.S. Daily tracking survey, with a random sample of 2,031 adults, aged 18 and older, living in all 50 U.S. states and the District of Columbia. For results based on the total sample of U.S. adults, the margin of sampling error is ±3 percentage points at the 95% confidence level.

Results for college students are based on telephone interviews conducted Feb. 29-March 15, 2016, with a random sample of 3,072 U.S. college students, aged 18 to 24, who are currently enrolled full time at four-year institutions. The college sample consists of a random subset of full-time students at 32 randomly selected U.S. four-year colleges that were stratified based on region, enrollment size and private versus public control. For results based on the total sample of college students, the margin of sampling error is ±3 percentage points at the 95% confidence level.

Results for Muslims are based on telephone interviews conducted March 4-10, 2016, with a sample of 250 U.S. adults who were previously interviewed for the Gallup U.S. Daily tracking survey, who identified their religion as Muslim and who agreed to be re-contacted by Gallup for future interviews. For results based on the total sample of Muslims, the margin of sampling error is ±8 percentage points at the 95% confidence level.

April 05, 2016
COLLEGE STUDENTS OPPOSE RESTRICTIONS ON POLITICAL SPEECH

by Jeffrey M. Jones

Story Highlights

- *72% oppose restrictions on expression of offensive political views*
- *Students favor restrictions on slurs, stereotypical costumes*
- *Most say students should not be able to block press access to protests*

PRINCETON, N.J. – U.S. college students mostly reject the idea that colleges should be able to establish policies restricting the expression of political views that upset or offend certain groups. At the same time, students support restricting language or expression that intentionally hurts or offends others, such as using racial or ethnic slurs or wearing costumes that stereotype certain groups.

College Students' Views of Acceptable Restrictions on Speech

Do you think colleges should or should not be able to establish policies that restrict each of the following types of speech or expression on campus?

	Should be able to restrict%	Should not be able to restrict%
Using slurs and other language on campus that is intentionally offensive to certain groups	69	31
Wearing costumes that stereotype certain racial or ethnic groups	63	37
Expressing political views that are upsetting or offensive to certain groups	27	72

February-March 2016
Knight Foundation "Free Expression on Campus" Study

First Amendment freedoms on college campuses have been a major flashpoint this academic year, following a wave of protests about racial matters that swept across the country. In March, students at Emory University in Atlanta gathered to protest chalk messages supporting Donald Trump's presidential candidacy. Last week, anti-Muslim "#StopIslam" markings accompanied similar pro-Trump writings that appeared across the University of Michigan campus. And Yale University's attempts to discourage the wearing of stereotypical Halloween costumes last fall led to a rebuttal by a faculty member that sparked considerable controversy.

On Monday, Knight Foundation and the Newseum Institute released the Free Expression on Campus study. Gallup surveyed a nationally representative sample of more than 3,000 U.S. college students for the study.

College students' views on First Amendment freedoms on campus are complex, reflecting the sometimes-competing tensions in allowing a wide range of viewpoints to be heard while still respecting student diversity and the desire to make students feel safe on campus.

Nearly eight in 10 college students (78%) believe colleges should strive to create open learning environments that expose students to all types of viewpoints, even if it means allowing speech that is offensive toward certain groups of people. On the other hand, 22% believe colleges should create positive learning environments for all students by prohibiting speech or the expression of views that are offensive to certain groups.

But students' preference for an open campus environment has limits, with roughly two-thirds saying colleges should be allowed to establish policies restricting the use of slurs and other language that is intentionally offensive to certain groups, as well as the wearing of costumes that stereotype racial or ethnic groups.

At the same time, 72% of students regard the expression of offensive political views as beyond what college officials should regulate, while 27% think colleges should be able to prohibit the expression of such views.

Majorities of all key student subgroups oppose college policies restricting offensive political speech – but majorities also believe colleges should be able to restrict slurs and stereotypical costumes.

Students Say Press Has Right to Cover Campus Protests

Perhaps the greatest test of First Amendment freedoms on campus occurred last fall, when some protesters exercising their rights of free speech and free assembly attempted to deny members of the press their right to report on those events. This occurred at the University of Missouri and at Smith College in Massachusetts during protests about matters of racial inclusion.

College students generally do not support denying reporters access to campus protests: 70% believe student protesters should not be able to prevent the press from covering protests, while 28% believe they should.

However, as with free speech, college students' commitment to a free press appears stronger in the abstract than it does when they are asked to evaluate reasons protesters might give for denying the press access. Roughly half of students say it would be acceptable to resist reporters if protesters believe the press will be unfair in its reporting (49%) or if the protesters assert a right to be left alone (48%). Slightly less, 44%, believe protesters can bar reporters from their event if the protesters want to tell their own story on the Internet or on social media.

College Students' Views of Reasons to Deny Press Access to Protests

Do you believe each of the following is – or is not – a legitimate reason for people attending a protest or other public gathering to deny the press access to an event?

	A legitimate reason %	Not a legitimate reason %
The people at the protest believe the press will be unfair to them in its reporting.	49	50
The people at the protest or public gathering say they have a right to be left alone.	48	51
The people at the protest or public gathering want to tell their own story on the Internet and social media.	44	56

February-March 2016
Knight Foundation "Free Expression on Campus" Study

Majorities of female college students and black college students believe all three reasons are legitimate for denying the press access to campus protests.

Implications

College students' complex views of First Amendment freedoms and the recent actions of some students raise questions as to how committed students are to those rights. Students themselves, much more so than U.S. adults more generally, largely believe these rights are secure in the U.S. today. And college students believe free speech rights are stronger today than in the past.

Recent events touching on free expression issues on campus suggest new controversies will continue to emerge, even though college students largely show consensus on what types of expression they think are and are not permissible. As in the case of the recent "Trump 2016" and "#StopIslam" messages, the controversies may arise out of the ambiguity of whether such messages are permissible expressions of controversial political viewpoints or impermissible expressions designed to hurt or threaten members of certain groups.

Survey Methods

Results are based on telephone interviews conducted Feb. 29-March 15, 2016, with a random sample of 3,072 U.S. college students, aged 18 to 24, who are currently enrolled full time at four-year institutions. The college sample consists of a random subset of full-time students at 32 randomly selected U.S. four-year colleges that were stratified based on region, enrollment size and private versus public control. For results based on the total sample of college students, the margin of sampling error is ±3 percentage points at the 95% confidence level.

April 05, 2016
U.S. ECONOMIC CONFIDENCE INDEX EDGES UP TO -10 IN MARCH

by Rebecca Riffkin

Story Highlights

- *Economic Confidence Index up slightly from February*
- *Scores similar to those recorded since July*
- *Democrats remain more confident than Republicans in the economy*

WASHINGTON, D.C. – Americans were slightly more confident in the economy in March than they were in February; however, their confidence has not drastically changed in the past nine months. Gallup's U.S. Economic Confidence Index averaged -10 in March, up slightly from -13 in February and on the high end of the -10 to -14 range found since July.

Gallup's U.S. Economic Confidence Index -- Monthly Averages
January 2008-March 2016

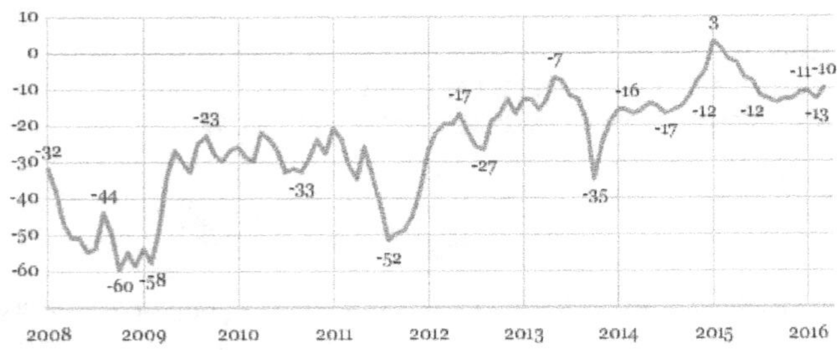

Gallup Daily tracking

GALLUP

Overall, Americans' economic confidence is much higher than it was during the recession and immediate post-recession years, but it remains down from recent high points measured in early 2015.

Gallup's Economic Confidence Index for the week ending April 3, 2016, was also -10, recovering from a slightly lower -13 reading the week of the Brussels terrorist attacks.

Gallup's index is the average of two components: how Americans rate current economic conditions and whether they feel the economy is getting better or getting worse. Both of these components increased slightly in March from February.

In March, the current conditions score was -3, up from -5 the previous month. This was the result of 26% of Americans rating current economic conditions in the U.S. as "excellent" or "good," and 29% rating them as "poor." Americans continue to view current economic conditions more favorably than their outlook of the economy, as they have since March 2015. In the most recent polling, 39% of Americans said the economy was "getting better," while 56% said it was "getting worse." This resulted in an economic outlook score of -17, up from -20 in February.

Gallup's U.S. Economic Confidence Index Components -- Monthly Averages
March 2015-March 2016

* % (Excellent + Good) minus % Poor
** % Getting better minus % Getting worse

Gallup Daily tracking

GALLUP

Democrats, Higher-Income Americans Most Confident in Economy

In March, the U.S. Economic Confidence Index among Democrats was +14, much higher than the -35 average among Republicans and the -13 average among independents. Economic confidence among Americans with different political identities is influenced by what party is in the White House. Democrats have been more confident in the economy than Republicans since 2009, when President Barack Obama took office.

Gallup's U.S. Economic Confidence Index – Monthly Averages, by Political Party and Annual Household Income

	March 2016 index average
Democrats	+14
Independents	-13
Republicans	-35
Household income of less than $24,000 a year	-16
Household income of $24,000 to $59,999	-17
Household income of $60,000 to $89,999	-10
Household income of $90,000 a year or more	0

Gallup Daily tracking

Gallup has also found that Americans' financial standing generally affects their confidence in the U.S. economy. Economic confidence is consistently higher among upper-income Americans than it is among lower-income Americans. March was no exception, with an index average of 0 among the highest-income Americans and an index average of -16 among the lowest-income Americans.

Bottom Line

Americans' slightly negative evaluation of the U.S. economy mirrors other mixed economic indicators. The Bureau of Labor Statistics reported that the economy gained a larger number of jobs than expected in March, but the unemployment rate also slightly increased. This reflects a small rise in the labor force participation rate, meaning that more Americans began actively looking for work after previously exiting the job market. However, wage growth in March was minimal, which is a disappointing sign. The federal government will release the U.S. gross domestic product figures in late April, which will provide indicators of whether the economy is growing.

These data are available in Gallup Analytics.

Survey Methods

Results for this Gallup poll are based on telephone interviews conducted March 1-31, 2016, on the Gallup U.S. Daily survey, with a random sample of 15,216 adults, aged 18 and older, living in all 50 U.S. states and the District of Columbia. For results based on the total sample of national adults, the margin of sampling error is ±1 percentage points at the 95% confidence level. All reported margins of sampling error include computed design effects for weighting.

April 06, 2016
IN U.S., CONCERN ABOUT CRIME CLIMBS TO 15-YEAR HIGH

by Alyssa Davis

Story Highlights

- *53% worry "a great deal" about crime, compared with 39% in 2014*
- *44% are concerned about drug use, also up significantly since 2014*

WASHINGTON, D.C. – Americans' level of concern about crime and violence is at its highest point in 15 years. Fifty-three percent of U.S. adults say they personally worry "a great deal" about crime and violence, an increase of 14 percentage points since 2014. This figure is the highest Gallup has measured since March 2001.

Americans' Level of Concern About Crime and Violence

I'm going to read a list of problems facing the country. For each one, please tell me if you personally worry about this problem a great deal, a fair amount, only a little or not at all. How much do you personally worry about crime and violence?

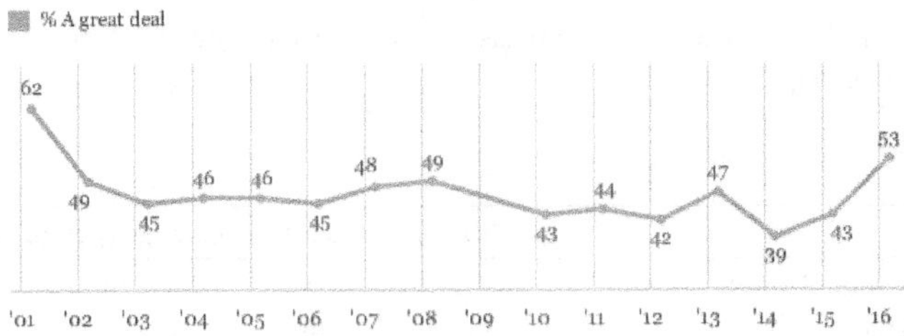

Note: Asked of a half sample in 2014

GALLUP'

Twenty-six percent of U.S. adults currently worry "a fair amount" about crime and violence, while 22% worry "only a little" or "not at all."

When Gallup first asked Americans about their level of concern regarding crime and violence in March 2001, 62% said they worried a great deal. That figure remains the highest level of worry in Gallup's 15-year trend on this question. In the months leading up to 9/11, Americans consistently mentioned crime and violence as one of the most important problems facing the country in response to a separate Gallup question. But after 9/11, crime and violence no longer appeared among the list of problems Americans identified as most important, with terrorism rising to the top.

In turn, the percentage saying they personally worry about crime and violence plunged to 49% by March 2002. Crime worry remained at a lower level over the next decade, as Americans named other issues such as the situation in Iraq, terrorism, the economy, dissatisfaction with government and healthcare as the most important problems facing the country. After falling to a record-low 39% in 2014, worry about crime and violence increased in 2015 and 2016.

The rise in Americans' level of concern about crime could reflect actual, albeit modest, increases in crime, as well as increasing media coverage of it. The number of violent crimes reported to police across the country in the first half of 2015 was up by 1.7% compared with the same period in 2014, according to the FBI's 2015 *Uniform Crime Report*. Many large U.S. cities reported spikes in their homicide rates in 2015, including Milwaukee, St. Louis,

Baltimore and Washington, D.C. From a long-term perspective, though, violent crime is down significantly since the 1990s.

Gallup's annual Environment survey asks Americans how much they personally worry about a number of specific problems facing the country. In addition to crime and violence, only two other issues have Americans just as concerned: the economy and the availability and affordability of healthcare. Concern about crime and violence slightly exceeds concern about the possibility of terrorist attacks.

Worry About Crime Rises Across All Major Subgroups

Americans across all major subgroups show heightened worry about crime compared with 2014. Worry has increased the most among those without a college degree and those living in households earning $30,000 to less than $75,000 annually.

More broadly, those with no college education are roughly twice as likely as those with a college degree to worry about crime, and those living in households earning less than $30,000 per year are much more likely than those earning at least $75,000 to worry about crime and violence. Nonwhites' concern about crime is much higher than whites' worry about the issue.

Americans' Level of Concern About Crime and Violence, by Subgroup

% A great deal

	2014%	2016%	Change (pct. pts.)
National adults	39	53	14
Men	32	49	17
Women	46	56	10
Whites	32	46	14
Nonwhites	59	68	9
18 to 34	34	52	18
35 to 54	40	48	8
55+	43	58	15
High school or less	50	70	20
Some college	32	52	20
Graduated college	31	32	1
Less than $30,000	59	66	7
$30,000 to $74,999	37	57	20
$75,000+	28	36	8
Republicans	38	53	15
Democrats	44	52	8
Independents	36	53	17

Gallup poll

Women and older Americans are more worried than their male and younger counterparts about crime and violence. Worry about crime and violence is similar across party groups, though Republicans' and independents' levels of worry have increased more than Democrats' since 2014.

Americans' Worry About Drug Use Also Up Sharply

Americans' worry about drug use has followed the same basic pattern over the last 15 years as worry about crime and violence. Forty-four percent of U.S. adults say they worry a great deal about drug use, up 10 points from the low found in 2014. This level of concern is on the higher end of what Gallup has found since first asking the question in 2001, but is comfortably below the peak of 58% measured that year.

This rise in worry about drug use preceded President Barack Obama's announcement on March 29 about his plan to reduce drug abuse and overdose deaths.

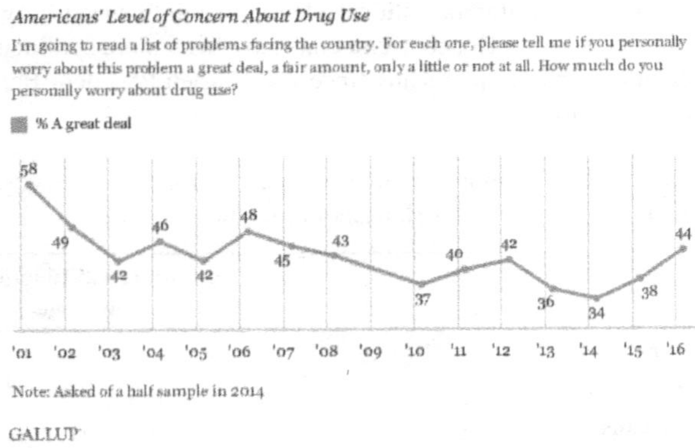

The uptick in worry about drug use since 2014 spans most subgroups. In general, concern about drug use is higher among those with less education, those with lower incomes, older Americans, women, nonwhites and Republicans. Drug use worry is comparatively low among college graduates and those in households earning at least $75,000 annually.

Americans' Level of Concern About Drug Use, by Subgroup

% A great deal

	2014%	2016%	Change (pct. pts.)
National adults	34	44	10
Men	30	40	10
Women	38	47	9
Whites	27	41	14
Nonwhites	52	49	-3
18 to 34	22	37	15
35 to 54	35	41	6
55+	43	51	8
High school or less	46	62	16
Some college	27	41	14
Graduated college	25	22	-3
Less than $30,000	52	55	3
$30,000 to $74,999	34	47	13
$75,000+	21	28	7
Republicans	37	48	11
Democrats	39	42	3
Independents	28	41	13

Gallup poll

Implications

Gallup reported in October 2015 that Americans perceived more crime in the U.S. than the year before. However, perceptions of local crime held steady. Together, these findings suggest that even if many Americans are not aware of increased crime where they live, they may be exposed to media coverage of rising crime and violence throughout the U.S.

On the drug front, the rise in overdose deaths and media coverage of the nation's opioid abuse and heroin epidemic may be playing into Americans' rising level of worry. The number of drug overdose deaths reached a record high in 2014 and increased 6.5% from 2013, according to the Centers for Disease Control and Prevention. New Hampshire's heroin epidemic has been a hot topic in the 2016 presidential election, elevating the issue of drug use to the national stage.

Obama's initiatives to address the nation's opioid abuse epidemic, with the goal of treating this type of drug addiction as a public health problem rather than a criminal issue, could assuage Americans' worry about drug use. But those initiatives could also draw more attention to the issue, resulting in increased public concern.

Historical data are available in Gallup Analytics.

Survey Methods

Results for this Gallup poll are based on telephone interviews conducted March 2-6, 2016, with a random sample of 1,019 adults, aged 18 and older, living in all 50 U.S. states and the District of Columbia. For results based on the total sample of national adults, the margin of sampling error is ±4 percentage points at the 95% confidence level.

April 06, 2016
U.S. JOB CREATION INDEX SHOWS FIRST GAIN IN 10 MONTHS

by Jim Norman

Story Highlights

- *Index gains three points, matching its previous high of +32*
- *Increase is first for the index since May 2015*
- *Hiring picture improves for government workers*

WASHINGTON, D.C. – Gallup's monthly U.S. Job Creation Index climbed to +32 in March, matching the highest level of its eight-year history. The increase from February's +29 reading is the first upward movement since May of last year, when the index first reached the +32 level.

U.S. Job Creation Index, Monthly Averages, January 2008-March 2016

Percentage of U.S. workers who say their employers are hiring new people minus percentage who say their employers are letting people go

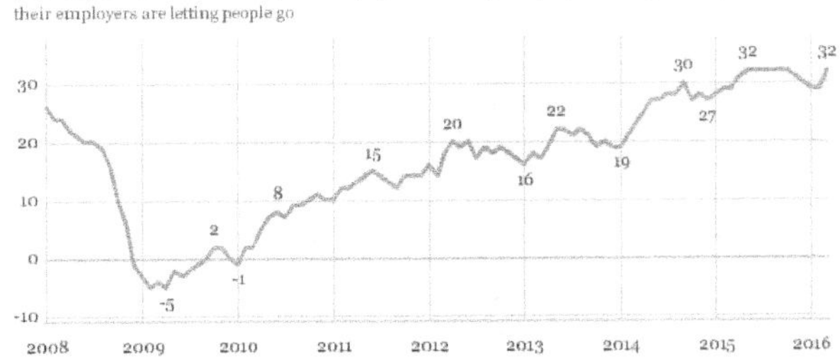

GALLUP

The latest results are based on interviews conducted March 1-31 with 17,997 full- and part-time U.S. workers. As part of Gallup's Daily tracking survey, interviewers ask a random sample of employed workers nationwide each day whether their employers are increasing, reducing or maintaining the size of their workforce. In March, 43% of workers reported an increase and 11% a decrease, resulting in the Job Creation Index score of +32.

Gallup's initial measurement of hiring activity in January 2008 recorded a +26 score, but the index dropped steadily for the next 13 months in the midst of the nation's economic crash. After bottoming out in February 2009 at -5 – a month when 28% of workers reported workforce reductions, while only 23% reported increases – the index has taken a slow, bumpy path upward, with major gains in 2010 and 2014.

Government Job Creation Increases, Still Behind Nongovernment

The March Job Creation Index for government workers was +27 – an increase of two points from February's +25, seven points from +20 a year ago and 29 points from -2 in March 2013. The nongovernment workers' index for March increased three points to +33.

Nongovernment workers have been more likely to report greater job growth than government workers in all but five of the 92 months since Gallup included the government/nongovernment breakdown in the index in late 2008. However, the gap between the two – as large as 34 points in June 2011 – has closed considerably over the past three years, from 22 points in March 2013 to six points now.

U.S. Job Creation Index for Government and Nongovernment Workers, August 2008-March 2016

Percentage who say their employers are expanding the workforce minus percentage who say their employers are reducing the workforce

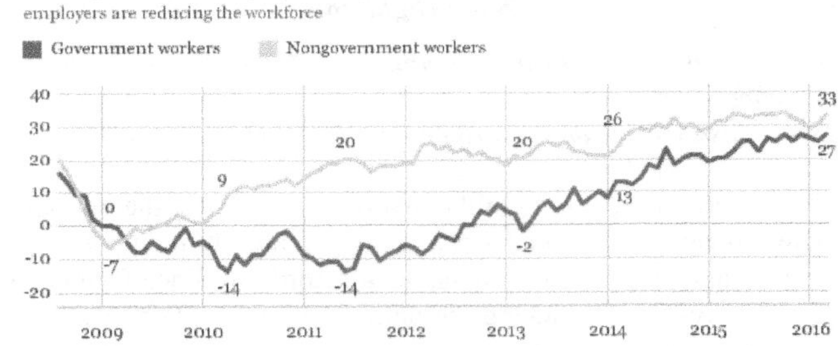

GALLUP

East, Weakest Region in Job Creation, Gains Four Points in March

Job Creation Indexes for all four major regions – East, Midwest, South and West – showed gains in March. The East, which has trailed the other three regions for most of the past three years, climbed closer to them with a four-point gain, from +26 in February to +30 in March. The other three regions each gained two points: the South, from +29 to +31; the Midwest, from +30 to +32; and the West, from +32 to +34.

Bottom Line

A three-point or greater increase in the monthly Job Creation Index may not seem impressive at first glance, but it has been achieved only six times in the eight-plus years since the index was created – and had not occurred since May 2013.

Further, March's +32 rating provides additional proof that, despite global economic concerns and months of volatility in the

U.S. stock market, American employers by and large are still in a hiring mood. It's a finding backed up by the Bureau of Labor Statistics report on April 1 that the U.S. economy added 215,000 jobs in March.

The increase in available jobs across the U.S. helps explain the growth of the U.S. labor force by nearly 400,000 people in March, and the continuing rise in the share of adults who are either working or actively looking for work.

Survey Methods

Results for this Gallup poll are based on telephone interviews conducted March 1-31, 2016, on the Gallup U.S. Daily survey, with a random sample of 17,997 employed adults, aged 18 and older, living in all 50 U.S. states and the District of Columbia. For results based on the total sample of employed adults, the margin of sampling error is ±1 percentage point at the 95% confidence level. All reported margins of sampling error include computed design effects for weighting.

April 07, 2016

U.S. UNINSURED RATE AT 11.0%, LOWEST IN EIGHT-YEAR TREND

by Stephanie Marken

Story Highlights

- *Uninsured rate down 6.1 points since individual mandate took effect*
- *Uninsured rate down most among Hispanics and blacks*

WASHINGTON, D.C. – In the first quarter of 2016, the uninsured rate among all U.S. adults was 11.0%, down from 11.9% in the fourth quarter of 2015. This marks a record low since Gallup and Healthways began tracking the uninsured rate in 2008. The uninsured rate has declined 6.1 percentage points since the fourth quarter of 2013, which was right before the individual mandate provision of the Affordable Care Act took effect in early 2014 that required Americans to carry health insurance.

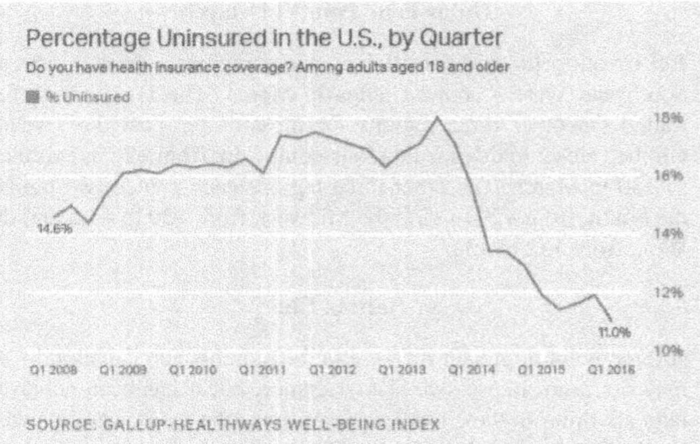

Results for the first quarter are based on nearly 45,000 interviews with U.S. adults aged 18 and older, from Jan. 2 to March 31, 2016, conducted as part of the Gallup-Healthways Well-Being Index. Gallup and Healthways ask 500 U.S. adults each day whether they have health insurance, which, on an aggregated basis, allows for precise and ongoing measurement of the percentage of U.S. adults with and without health insurance and the net change in the uninsured rate over time.

The uninsured rate for the first quarter accounts for interviews conducted both before and after the Jan. 31 deadline to purchase a 2016 health plan from government insurance exchanges. The percentage without health insurance in the second quarter of 2016 may decline slightly, as it will be the first quarterly measurement this year to reflect interviews that were all conducted after the exchanges closed.

Uninsured Rate Declines Most Sharply Among Hispanics and Blacks

Across key subgroups, blacks and Hispanics have experienced the largest declines in their uninsured rates since the fourth quarter of 2013. The rate among Hispanics was 28.3% in the first quarter of 2016, still significantly higher than for all U.S. adults, but down 10.4 points from the fourth quarter of 2013. Similarly, the uninsured rate has declined 9.5 points among blacks over this same period to its current 11.4%. These larger declines for blacks and Hispanics partly reflect higher uninsured rates among those demographic groups relative to whites before the implementation of the new healthcare law.

Percentage of Uninsured U.S. Adults, by Subgroup

Do you have health insurance coverage?

	Q4 2013%	Q1 2016%	Net change (pct. pts.)
National adults	17.1	11.0	6.1
18 to 25	23.5	14.8	8.7
26 to 34	28.2	18.5	9.7
35 to 64	18.0	10.7	7.3
65+	2.0	1.6	0.4
Whites	11.9	6.4	5.5
Blacks	20.9	11.4	9.5
Hispanics	38.7	28.3	10.4
Less than $36,000	30.7	20.0	10.7
$36,000 to $89,999	11.7	8.2	3.5
$90,000+	5.8	2.9	2.9

Gallup-Healthways Well-Being Index

The uninsured rate has declined significantly for all age groups below age 65 since late 2013. Seniors, most of whom were already covered by Medicare before the recent changes in health insurance took place, continue to almost universally report being insured.

More Americans Have Self-Paid and Medicaid Insurance Plans

Gallup and Healthways focus on adults aged 18 to 64 because nearly all Americans 65 and older have Medicare. Compared with the fourth quarter of 2013, the largest increase in insurance type has occurred among those paying for a plan themselves. In the first quarter of 2016, 21.8% of U.S. adults aged 18 to 64 had a plan fully paid for by themselves or a family member, up 4.2 percentage points from the fourth quarter of 2013. The percentage of U.S. adults with Medicaid has also increased to 9.4% in the first quarter of 2016, up 2.5 points from the fourth quarter of 2013.

Type of Health Insurance Coverage in the U.S., Among Adults Aged 18 to 64

Is your health insurance coverage through a current or former employer, a union, Medicare, Medicaid, military or veteran's coverage or a plan fully paid for by you or a family member? Primary and secondary insurance combined

	Q4 2013%	Q1 2016%	Net change (pct. pts.)
Current or former employer	44.2	43.4	-0.8
Plan fully paid for by self or family member	17.6	21.8	4.2
Medicaid	6.9	9.4	2.5
Medicare	6.1	7.6	1.5
Military/Veteran's	4.6	5.2	0.6
A union	2.5	2.6	0.1
(Something else)	3.5	4.4	0.9
No insurance	20.8	12.9	-7.9

Gallup-Healthways Well-Being Index

Implications

The uninsured rate has dropped considerably since the fourth quarter of 2013 when the key provision of the new healthcare law requiring U.S. adults to obtain health insurance took effect. After declining significantly in earlier quarters, the rate of uninsured U.S. adults leveled off in 2015. Most healthcare policy watchers had anticipated this, as those who remain uninsured are among the most difficult to insure. The drop in the first quarter of 2016 suggests that the rate may continue to decline in future years, although less markedly and maybe only in the first quarter of each year as U.S. adults continue to make use of the exchanges to obtain health insurance.

The open enrollment period concluded on Jan. 31, 2016, meaning slight changes are expected in the second quarter of 2016 when the totality of interviews are conducted after the exchanges have closed, but further significant changes to the uninsured rate are unlikely until the first quarter of 2017.

Survey Methods

Results are based on telephone interviews conducted Jan. 2-March 31, 2016, as part of the Gallup-Healthways Well-Being Index survey, with a random sample of 44,557 adults, aged 18 and older, living in all 50 U.S. states and the District of Columbia. For results based on the total sample of national adults, the margin of sampling error is ±1 percentage point at the 95% confidence level. Each quarter dating to the first quarter of 2014 has approximately 44,000 respondents. Each quarter from 2008 through 2013 has approximately 88,000 respondents.

April 07, 2016

COLLEGE PRESIDENTS STILL REPORT POSITIVE RACE RELATIONS ON CAMPUS

by Jeffrey M. Jones

Story Highlights

- *84% rate their campus race relations positively, unchanged from 2015*
- *Sharply fewer rate race relations on U.S. campuses positively*
- *College students also say the racial climate on their campus is good*

PRINCETON, N.J. – During a year marked by numerous college protests over race and diversity issues, presidents of U.S. colleges and universities describe race relations on their own campus positively, and no worse than they did in 2015. However, their broader perceptions of race relations on campuses nationwide are significantly worse than a year ago. Currently, just 24% of presidents rate race relations on U.S. campuses as either excellent or good, down sharply from 43% in 2015.

Change in College Presidents' Assessments of Race Relations

Generally speaking, would you say the state of race relations [on your campus/on college and university campuses in this country] is excellent, good, fair or poor?

	2015%	2016%	Change%
Own Campus			
Excellent	18	20	+2
Good	63	64	+1
Fair	18	16	-2
Poor	1	1	0
U.S. College Campuses			
Excellent	1	0	-1
Good	42	24	-18
Fair	51	65	+14
Poor	5	10	+5

Inside Higher Ed Survey of College and University Presidents

These results are based on the *Inside Higher Ed* annual survey of U.S. college presidents, conducted by Gallup.

Protests about the treatment of racial and ethnic minority students erupted last fall on a number of college campuses, including the University of Missouri, Yale University, Princeton University and Ithaca College. Student concerns ultimately led to the resignation of the president of the Missouri state university system and the chancellor of the main campus in Columbia. The president of Ithaca College also resigned under student and faculty pressure for his handling of race matters on that campus.

These protests received widespread media attention and likely contribute to presidents' more negative assessment this year – fewer than one in four presidents now say race relations are "excellent" or "good" on campuses across the country. The majority of presidents, 65%, describe race relations on U.S. campuses as "fair," and 10% say they are "poor." The latter figure is up from 5% a year ago.

But in a year of high-profile student activism on race relations issues on U.S. campuses, college presidents continue to be just as positive about race relations on their own campus as they were in early 2015. The survey finds 84% of presidents saying race relations on their campus are "excellent" or "good," similar to the 81% of presidents who rated their campus race relations positively a year ago. Just 1% of presidents say race relations on their campus are poor, the same as in 2015.

These findings could indicate that a few highly publicized incidents of racial tensions on campuses have had a dramatic influence on the way presidents perceive the state of race relations at most U.S. colleges and that racial strife is not the norm at colleges. College presidents' more positive assessments of race relations on their own campus, compared with campuses nationally, may also reflect individuals' tendency to rate their own situation more positively than the situation in the country as a whole.

College Students Report Positive Racial Climate on Campus

It is not just college presidents who perceive race relations positively on their campus. A new Knight Foundation/Newseum Institute survey of U.S. college students, conducted by Gallup, finds college students are generally positive about the racial climate on their campus. Nearly three-quarters of college students describe interactions between students of different races and their treatment of one another on campus as either excellent (26%) or good (48%). Only 6% say the racial climate on their campus is poor.

Majorities of all major racial and ethnic groups are positive about the racial climate on their campus. At least seven in 10 whites (76%), Hispanics (74%) and Asians (70%) describe the racial climate as either excellent or good. Blacks are slightly less positive, with 62% evaluating their campus' racial climate positively.

Blacks are more than twice as likely as whites to say the racial climate on their campus is poor (13% vs. 5%, respectively).

College Students' Ratings of Racial Climate on Their Campus

Thinking about how students of different races interact and treat one another, how would you rate the overall racial climate on your college's campus – as excellent, good, only fair or poor?

	All%	White%	Black%	Hispanic %	Asian%
Excellent	26	27	21	15	27
Good	48	49	41	59	43
Fair	20	20	26	16	25
Poor	6	5	13	10	5

Knight Foundation/Newseum Institute/Gallup Survey of College Students

Students' views of the quality of race relations on campus are related to their perceptions of how racially and ethnically diverse they perceive the student body to be. While 87% of those who believe their campus is "highly diverse" rate the racial climate positively, 34% of those who say their campus is "not diverse at all" do.

College students were not asked to rate the racial climate on colleges nationwide.

Implications

Both presidents and students at U.S. colleges and universities assess the racial climate on their campuses positively. And presidents see the situation as no worse than a year ago, even though a wave of college protests on racial matters is likely contributing to their considerably more negative assessment of race relations on campuses nationwide.

While the poll results paint a generally positive picture of race relations on campus, they do show that there is still progress to be made, given that about one in six presidents and about one in four students rate the racial climate at their college as fair or poor.

Survey Methods

Results for college presidents are based on Web interviews conducted Jan. 7-Feb. 2, 2016, with 727 presidents of U.S. colleges and universities with student enrollment greater than 500 students. The sampling frame for the study was the universe of 3,046 presidents of colleges with greater than 500 students, with weighting adjustments made to correct for nonresponse using institutional characteristics (region of the country, private versus public control, two-year or four-year degree-granting, and student enrollment size. The weighted sample results can be viewed as representative of the views of presidents at colleges nationwide.

Results for college students are based on telephone interviews conducted Feb. 29-March 15, 2016, with a random sample of 3,072 U.S. college students, aged 18 to 24, who are currently enrolled full time at four-year institutions. The college sample consists of a random subset of full-time students at 32 randomly selected U.S. four-year colleges that were stratified based on region, enrollment size and private versus public control. For results based on the total sample of college students, the margin of sampling error is ±3 percentage points at the 95% confidence level. All reported margins of sampling error include computed design effects for weighting.

April 08, 2016

SANDERS, THE OLDEST CANDIDATE, LOOKS BEST TO YOUNG AMERICANS

by Frank Newport

Story Highlights

- *Sanders has a +39 net favorable rating among 18- to 24-year-olds*
- *Clinton does much worse among those 18 to 24, with a -23 net favorable*
- *Sanders-Clinton age gap among young Americans also seen among young Dems*

PRINCETON, N.J. – Although he is the oldest candidate in the presidential race, Bernie Sanders receives his highest rating, +39, from the youngest U.S. adults. The image of his Democratic competitor, Hillary Clinton, among this group is her worst, at -23. This disparity in ratings is the largest found for the two candidates among all age groups.

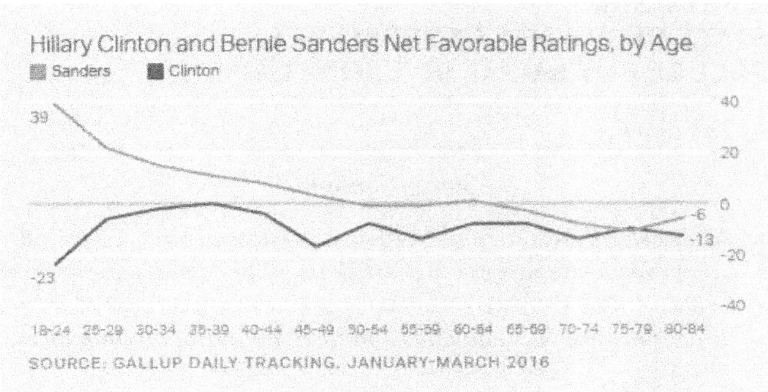

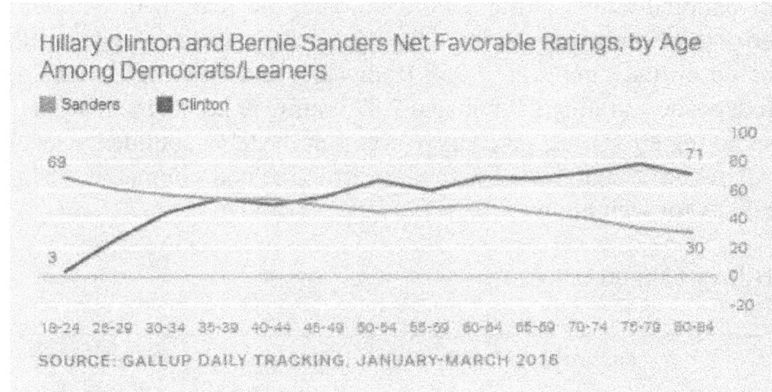

These results are based on ratings of the two Democratic candidates in Gallup Daily tracking from January through March, based on a large sample of more than 18,000 national adults, allowing for a detailed analysis of the candidates' images across the age spectrum. Over this period, an average 43% of all U.S. adults viewed Sanders favorably and 35% unfavorably, while Clinton's ratings tilted negative: 42% favorable, 52% unfavorable.

Sanders' positive image among younger Americans partly reflects the general tendency of younger people to identify as Democrats, although, as noted, even among those aged 18 to 24 he is viewed much more favorably than Clinton.

The positive sentiments of those younger than age 50 are the main drivers of Sanders' overall net positive image among all U.S. adults. Those aged 50 to 64 roughly break even, favorable versus unfavorable, in their views of Sanders. Despite his own relatively advanced age (74), Americans aged 65 to 84 see him more negatively than positively.

Clinton's image varies less than Sanders' across age groups, with her weakest standing among the youngest U.S. adults and her most positive among those aged 30 to 44.

The most striking difference in the images of the two candidates is among those aged 18 to 24, 59% of whom hold a positive opinion of the Vermont senator, compared with 20% who view him negatively. Clinton's image is almost the reverse among this group, with 34% favorable and 57% unfavorable.

The image gap between the two Democratic candidates narrows among those aged 25 to 29, and then generally gets smaller among older age groups. Clinton is viewed (slightly) more positively than Sanders only among the 75 to 79 age group. Complete ratings for each candidate by age group are at the end of this article.

Democrats See Both Candidates More Positively, With Same Patterns by Age

Among Democrats and Democratic-leaning independents, young people also view Sanders much more favorably than they do Clinton. Sanders' net favorable rating among 18- to 24-year-old Democrats is +69, compared with +3 for Clinton. That gap shrinks among the next-oldest age groups. The two candidates are seen roughly equally among Democrats aged 35 to 44, with Clinton gaining the image advantage among Democrats aged 45 and older.

In general, Clinton's net favorable rating rises almost linearly across Democratic age groups until the 80 to 84 group. Sanders' image shows the opposite pattern, tending to get worse with each successively older group of Democrats.

Implications

Sanders would be – by a wide margin – the oldest president to take office in U.S. history. Ronald Reagan was 69 when he became president in 1981 and was 77 when he left office. If elected, Sanders would within three years be the oldest person ever to hold the office, and would be well into his 80s if he were to serve two terms. Clinton, if elected, would be the same age as Reagan when he first took office.

Sanders' extraordinary appeal to the youngest group of potential voters is clearly not based on their belief that he shares their life experiences and contemporary outlook. It presumably is based on the appeal of his ideas, approaches to policy or his personality. Ten percent of those who support Sanders say it is because of his focus on education, including his proposal to make all public universities free to any qualified student, and that policy may appeal to the youngest Americans, many of whom are in college.

Sanders is clearly a liberal in his social policies, and young people are not particularly liberals based on self-definitions, instead tending to label themselves as moderates. But many of Sanders' left-leaning policies apparently appeal strongly to the young.

Clinton too is generally on the left of the political spectrum, and seemingly might have a special appeal to young people for the same reasons – but that isn't the case. Clinton has a long and often controversial public history, and something about that background, her policy proposals or her personality has apparently turned many young people against her.

The real-world value of Sanders' appeal to the young – in terms of helping him procure the nomination and win in November if he is the nominee – is debatable, given young adults' lower election turnout rates. Two early indicators suggest this won't change this election: Young people are paying the lowest levels of attention to the election in general, and have the lowest enthusiasm about voting.

Young people did serve as a key component of the winning Barack Obama coalition in 2008 and in 2012. Even if young adults continue to have below-average turnout levels, Clinton undoubtedly would like to re-create that winning combination this year. But if she wins the nomination, it is unclear how likely young people would be to transfer their excitement about Sanders over to her campaign.

Historical data are available in Gallup Analytics.

Survey Methods

Results for this Gallup poll are based on telephone interviews conducted Jan. 2-March 31, 2016, on the Gallup U.S. Daily survey, with random samples of 18,298 adults aged 18 and older, living in all 50 U.S. states and the District of Columbia, rating Hillary Clinton and 18,392 rating Bernie Sanders. For results based on the total sample of national adults rating each candidate, the margin of sampling error is ±1 percentage point at the 95% confidence level. For results based on the sample of 7,955 Democrats and Democratic-leaning independents rating Clinton and 7,877 rating Sanders, the margin of sampling error is ±2 percentage points at the 95% confidence level. All reported margins of sampling error include computed design effects for weighting.

Hillary Clinton Image

	Favorable %	Unfavorable %	Heard of, no opinion (vol.) %	Never heard of (vol.) %
18 to 24	34	57	6	2
25 to 29	41	48	7	3
30 to 34	44	46	7	3
35 to 39	46	46	6	1
40 to 44	45	49	3	2
45 to 49	39	56	3	1
50 to 54	44	52	3	1
55 to 59	41	55	2	1
60 to 64	44	52	3	0
65 to 69	44	52	3	1
70 to 74	42	56	2	1
75 to 79	43	53	2	1
80 to 84	41	54	3	1

Jan. 2-March 31, 2016
Gallup Daily tracking; (vol.) = Volunteered response

Bernie Sanders Image

	Favorable %	Unfavorable %	Heard of, no opinion (vol.) %	Never heard of (vol.) %
18 to 24	59	20	6	15
25 to 29	46	24	8	21
30 to 34	44	29	10	17
35 to 39	41	31	9	18
40 to 44	41	33	10	14
45 to 49	41	38	10	11
50 to 54	40	40	9	10
55 to 59	41	42	9	8
60 to 64	43	42	8	7
65 to 69	42	44	7	7
70 to 74	38	47	7	7
75 to 79	36	48	7	8
80 to 84	38	44	8	8

Jan. 2-March 31, 2016
Gallup Daily tracking; (vol.) = Volunteered response

April 08, 2016

STATE RESIDENTS GENERALLY FEEL SECURE BUT RACIAL DIVISIONS EXIST

by Zac Auter

Story Highlights

- *Midwestern, Western and Northeastern states score well on index*
- *Idaho residents express highest sense of personal security from crime*
- *Blacks express less confidence in local police than non-blacks*

WASHINGTON, D.C. – Residents of Idaho express the highest sense of personal security according to Gallup's Law and Order Index of U.S. states in 2015 with a score of 88 out of 100, just ahead of New Hampshire and Utah. Residents in most states generally feel secure, as the lowest two states on the scale, South Carolina and New Mexico, still had relatively high scores of 72.

Top and Bottom States on Gallup's Law and Order Index

	Index
Top states	
Idaho	88
New Hampshire	87
Utah	87
Wisconsin	86
Montana	86
Nebraska	86
South Dakota	86
North Dakota	86
Wyoming	86
Minnesota	86
Bottom states	
New Mexico	72
South Carolina	72
Louisiana	73
Mississippi	74
West Virginia	75
Delaware	76
Tennessee	76
California	77

March 30-Dec. 22, 2015
Gallup Poll

Overall, Midwestern, Western and Northeastern states placed highly on the index, while several Southern states found themselves near the bottom. Looking at the distribution of states on the index, those with larger minority populations occupy the lower half of the scale, while more racially homogenous states tend to score higher. This suggests that, rather than regional differences, state index scores may reflect Americans' divergent attitudes about personal security as it relates to their own race.

Gallup constructs a global Law and Order Index using Gallup World Poll data on people's confidence in their local police, feelings of personal safety and self-reported incidence of theft. The index ranges from 0 to 100 by averaging "positive" responses to these three questions. Higher scores correspond to a higher percentage of the population reporting feeling secure.

The results reported here apply that same index to the U.S. using data collected in Gallup's 2015 50-state poll. The survey was conducted March 30-Dec. 22, 2015, with approximately 500 respondents in every state.

Law and Order Index and State Crime Rates Uncorrelated

The state rankings of the Law and Order Index provide a comparative picture of how the people in each state feel about their personal security and reflect the confidence they have in their local law enforcement. These perceptions, however, do not necessarily relate to official crime statistics in each state.

For example, a state's crime rate does not correlate with people's confidence in local police – one of the three components of the index. If the states are ranked according to their crime rates using FBI data, confidence in local police remains strong whether a person lives in a state in the top or bottom 20% of the nation. In the bottom quintile of states ranked by crime rate, 82% of Americans report having confidence in local law enforcement, on par with the 79% of residents in the top quintile.

A small relationship exists between respondents' perceptions of their safety – another component of the index – and state crime rates. While 81% of those in states with the lowest 20% of crime rates report feeling safe walking alone at night, Americans' perceptions of their safety in states within the highest 20% of national crime rates drop nine percentage points to 72%.

State Crime Rates and Perceptions of Personal Security

	Bottom 20% crime rate	Second quintile	Third quintile	Fourth quintile	Top 20% crime rate
% Confident in local police	82	80	80	80	79
% Not confident in local police	18	20	20	20	21
% Yes, feel safe walking alone at night	81	78	78	76	72
% No, do not feel safe walking alone at night	19	22	22	24	28

March 30-Dec. 22, 2015
Gallup Poll

Racial Divisions Drive Index Components

Previous Gallup research finds nonwhites, and black adults in particular, to be less likely to say they have confidence in the police. This most recent survey confirms these trends, with 66% of blacks living in all 50 states reporting confidence in local police, compared with 82% of non-blacks. Likewise, though 79% of non-blacks feel safe walking alone at night, only 62% of blacks concur.

These national racial divides – where black Americans are more likely to express less confidence in police and to feel less safe – explain, in part, why several Southern states with higher black populations rank near the bottom of the index. Of the eight lowest-scoring states on the index, seven of them rank among the top 11 states with the highest black populations in the U.S. (Washington, D.C., No. 1; Mississippi, No. 2; Louisiana, No. 3; South Carolina, No. 6; Delaware, No. 9; Tennessee, No. 11).

Race and Perceptions of Personal Security

	Black	Non-black
% Confident in local police	66	82
% Not confident in local police	34	18
% Yes, feel safe walking alone at night	62	79
% No, do not feel safe walking alone at night	38	21

March 30-Dec. 22, 2015
Gallup Poll

Implications

While Americans' concern about crime – among both whites and nonwhites – has reached a 15-year peak, their confidence in local law enforcement and perceptions of their safety differ starkly along racial lines. Blacks report substantially lower confidence in their local law enforcement and express a greater uneasiness about walking alone at night. In this sense, the U.S. Law and Order Index taps into a nuanced assessment of personal security, rather than a general conception about fear of crime. It assesses multiple facets of individual perceptions of safety, including the institution charged with preventing crime and enforcing laws.

On the heels of several high-profile incidents involving police and black Americans over the past year, the racial divisions reflected in the components of the Law and Order Index have played a central role in discussions of criminal law reform. As analysis of two of the index's components shows here, a racial schism in perceptions of police and personal security, rather than the actual crime rate itself, may be the principal driver of ongoing unrest between minorities and the justice system.

Data on the components of the Law and Order Index are available in Gallup Analytics.

Survey Methods

Results are based on telephone interviews conducted March 30-Dec. 22, 2015, with random samples of approximately 500 adults, aged 18 and older, living in each of the 50 U.S. states and the District of Columbia. For results based on the total state samples, the margin of sampling error is ±5 percentage points at the 95% confidence level.

Data are weighted to account for unequal selection probability, nonresponse and double coverage of landline and cellphone users in the two sampling frames. Data are also weighted to state estimates of gender, age, race, Hispanic ethnicity, education and phone status (cellphone only, landline only, both, and cellphone mostly).

April 11, 2016

U.S. WORRIES ABOUT RACE RELATIONS REACH A NEW HIGH

by Jim Norman

Story Highlights

- *35% of Americans are worried a great deal about race relations*
- *Number has more than doubled in past two years*
- *Race relations still ranks low among issues causing worry*

WASHINGTON, D.C. – More than a third (35%) of Americans now say they are worried "a great deal" about race relations in the U.S. – which is higher than at any time since Gallup first asked the question in 2001. The percentage who are worried a great deal rose seven percentage points in the past year and has more than doubled in the past two years.

Race Relations Worries Are Growing in U.S.

Percentage of Americans who worry "a great deal" about the problem of race relations

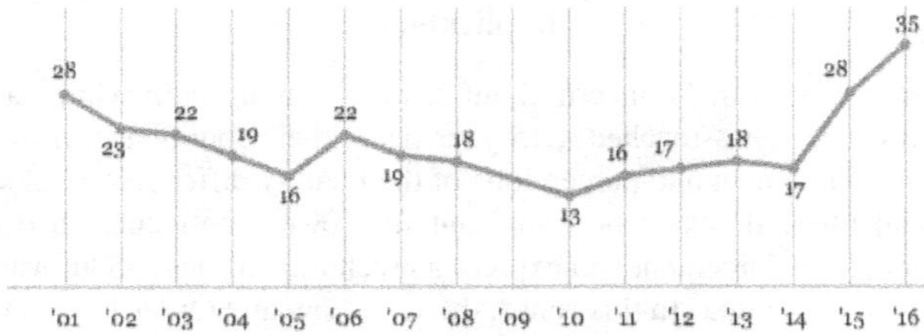

GALLUP

Concern about race relations in the U.S. has risen during an 18-month period marked by a series of deaths of unarmed blacks at the hands of police officers. These deaths sparked major, sometimes violent, protests and fueled the nationwide rise of the "Black Lives Matter" movement.

Democrats, Liberals More Worried Than Republicans, Conservatives

Concern about race relations over the past two years has increased among Republicans and Democrats, conservatives and liberals, and blacks and whites. But the gap between the groups who were already most worried before 2015 – Democrats, liberals and blacks – and those less worried has not shrunk, and in some cases has widened. Of particular note is the 53% to 27% "worried" gap between blacks and whites, up from the 31% to 14% gap between blacks and whites in the 2012-2014 combined polls.

Percentage Who Say They Worry "a Great Deal" About Race Relations in the U.S.

	2001-2011%	2012-2014%	2015-2016%
Democrats + leaners	25	22	37
Republicans + leaners	14	14	26
Liberals	25	24	42
Moderates	19	14	27
Conservatives	17	16	28
Blacks	45	31	53
Whites	15	14	27

Combined Gallup polls: 2001-2011, 2012-2014, 2015-2016

Race Relations Low on the List of Major Concerns

Prior to 2015, race relations was much less of a concern to Americans, relative to other national issues. In almost every one of 13 polls from 2001 to 2014, Americans were significantly less likely to be worried about race relations than about any of the other dozen or so issues tested. Even this year, though the percentage concerned is up, race relations still ranks near the bottom of the list of concerns, along with energy, climate change and illegal immigration. None of the four elicited a great deal of concern from more than 37% (illegal immigration) of the public, compared with more than 50% for healthcare, the economy, and crime and violence.

Bottom Line

Race relations may not worry as many Americans as do issues such as the economy, affordable healthcare or crime, but Gallup's polling clearly shows that racial tensions over the past few years have significantly affected public opinion.

Not only are far more Americans – no matter their race or political beliefs – worried about race relations, Americans have also become less satisfied with the way blacks are treated and more likely to list race relations as the most important problem the nation faces.

The rising concern about race relations as the nation's first black president completes his last year in office is a retreat from the optimism that swept the country in the immediate aftermath of President Barack Obama's first election win in 2008. A Gallup poll one night after Obama won found that seven in 10 Americans believed race relations would improve because of his victory.

In fact, a mid-2015 Gallup poll indicated that treatment of blacks had not worsened during Obama's time in office, even while concerns about race relations and treatment of blacks were rising. However, the poll also did not show any significant lessening of perceived racial discrimination among blacks.

In the current presidential election cycle, both conservatives and liberals have attacked Republican front-runner Donald Trump for his campaign's racist overtones, and conservative pundits are already claiming that history will conclude the Obama presidency worsened race relations. These factors, along with the ever-growing number of racial protests on college campuses and elsewhere, make it unlikely that Americans' concerns about race relations will diminish in 2016.

Survey Methods

Results for this Gallup poll are based on telephone interviews conducted March 2-6, 2016, with a random sample of 1,019 adults, aged 18 and older, living in all 50 U.S. states and the District of Columbia. For results based on the total sample of national adults, the margin of sampling error is ±4 percentage points at the 95% confidence level. All reported margins of sampling error include computed design effects for weighting.

April 11, 2016
AMERICANS STILL SAY POSTSECONDARY EDUCATION VERY IMPORTANT

by Jeffrey M. Jones

Story Highlights

- *70% of Americans say postsecondary education "very important"*
- *Blacks and Hispanics attach greater importance than whites*
- *Individuals seen as most responsible for increasing percent attaining degree*

PRINCETON, N.J. – Americans strongly endorse the value of postsecondary education, with 70% saying it is "very important" for adults to have a degree or professional certificate beyond high school. The percentage of Americans who view having a degree or certificate as very important has held steady near 70% since 2012, even amid declining college enrollment and growing discussions in this country about the value of higher education.

Americans' Rating of the Importance of Postsecondary Education

How important is it for adults in this country to have a degree or professional certificate beyond high school -- very important, somewhat important, not very important or not at all important?

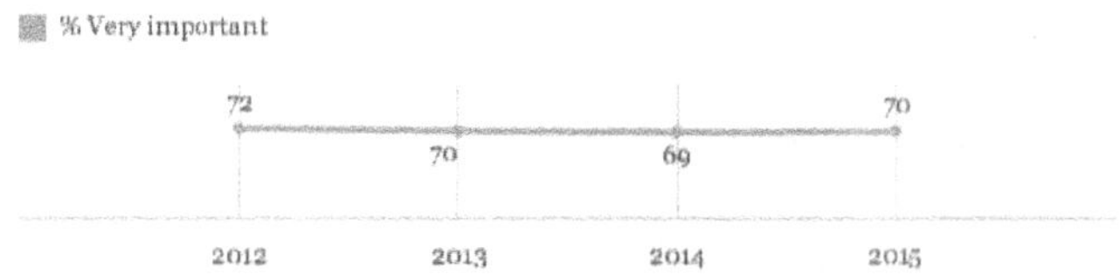

2015 Gallup-Lumina Foundation

GALLUP

Blacks and Hispanics, who have lower levels of college degree attainment than whites according to the National Center for Education Statistics, place a greater value on postsecondary education than whites do. Seventy-nine percent of blacks and 78% of Hispanics say education beyond high school is very important, compared with 67% of whites.

These results are based on the fifth annual Gallup-Lumina Foundation poll on Americans' opinions about higher education. The latest study was conducted Oct. 1-Nov. 5, 2015, with 1,616 U.S. adults, including 300 blacks and 302 Hispanics.

The poll also finds Americans place a value on postsecondary education in its own right – 66% strongly agree or agree that taking some college classes is a good idea even if it does not lead to a degree.

However, perhaps echoing research on lifetime earnings by educational attainment, Americans also see a strong connection between completing a postsecondary education program and finding a good job. Seven in 10 Americans strongly agree (39%) or agree (31%) that having a professional certificate or degree beyond high school is essential for getting a good job. Although solid majorities of whites, blacks and Hispanics agree that a postsecondary education is essential for getting a good job, Hispanics (58%) and blacks (50%) are much more likely than whites (33%) to *strongly* agree.

Americans' Views of a Degree or Certificate as Being Essential for Getting a Good Job

On a 5-point scale, where 1 means strongly disagree and 5 means strongly agree, please rate your level of agreement with the following item: Having a professional certificate or degree beyond high school is essential for getting a good job.

	5 - Strongly agree%	4 - Agree %	Total agree%
U.S. adults	39	31	70
Non-Hispanic whites	33	35	68
Non-Hispanic blacks	50	23	73
Hispanics	58	21	79

2015 Gallup-Lumina Foundation Survey on Higher Education

And despite frequent news stories of recent college graduates being unable to get a job in their chosen field after investing tens of thousands of dollars in college tuition, 70% of Americans say having a postsecondary degree or professional certificate will be "more important" in the future to getting a good job; only 7% predict it will be less important.

Consistent with these views, 58% of Americans say it is very important to increase the proportion of people in the U.S. who have a degree or professional certificate beyond high school. That view is held by 71% of Hispanics, 70% of blacks and 54% of whites.

Americans Say Individuals Most Responsible for Increasing Postsecondary Education

A public consensus on the value of postsecondary education is just the first step in increasing education levels in the U.S. population. The survey asked Americans which institutions or actors are most responsible for increasing the proportion of Americans with a college degree or professional certificate.

Americans overwhelmingly believe that individuals themselves are responsible for ensuring that more people in the U.S. earn degrees or certificates beyond high school, with 72% saying individuals are "very responsible." But most Americans also see a variety of U.S. institutions as "very" or "somewhat responsible" for increasing educational attainment, including colleges and universities, government institutions, local communities and businesses.

Americans' Views on How Responsible Various Actors Are for Increasing Postsecondary Degree and Certificate Attainment

How responsible are each of the following to ensuring that more Americans have a degree or certificate beyond high school – very responsible, somewhat responsible, not too responsible or not responsible at all?

	Very responsible%	Somewhat responsible%
Individuals themselves	72	24
Colleges and universities	53	40
State governments	38	42
The federal government	36	37
The president of the United States	35	31

	Very responsible %	Somewhat responsible %
Local communities	31	49
Businesses	27	49

2015 Gallup-Lumina Foundation Survey on Higher Education

Among Those Without Degree, 15% Enrolled in a Degree Program

In addition to assessing how much they value higher education, the survey asked Americans about their intentions for completing a college degree program. The 59% of respondents who have not received an associate degree or higher were asked about their current or prospective enrollment in a college degree program. Fifteen percent report they are currently enrolled in a degree program, while another 24% say they plan to enroll in the next five years. The remaining 61% have no plans to enroll in a degree program in the next five years.

Enrollment intentions are particularly high among younger adults; 35% of those between the ages of 18 and 34 say they are currently enrolled and 39% in this age group plan to enroll in the next five years. Also, more than one-third of Americans between the ages of 35 and 49 are enrolled (8%) or plan to enroll (30%) in some education program.

If all those who are enrolled in a degree program or who plan to enroll completed the program, the percentage of U.S. adults with an associate degree or higher would increase from 41% to 64%.

Implications

Although the value of postsecondary education is a matter of increasing debate, Americans are largely convinced that such education is important, is essential to getting a good job and will be more important in the future. That strong commitment to education suggests younger as well as older adults will continue to find ways to attain a degree or professional certificate. And despite the financial obstacles to higher education, 59% of Americans believe postsecondary education is available to anyone in this country who needs it.

In a changing U.S. job market that sees fewer manufacturing positions and more jobs in the information, technology and service fields, the importance of learning advanced skills taught in college or in professional settings is clear. Americans view individuals themselves as most responsible for helping to increase the proportion of those in this country with degrees or certificates, but Americans also see many government and nongovernment institutions as bearing at least some responsibility.

Hispanics and blacks place an especially high value on postsecondary education, even though, on average, those groups are less likely to complete college degree programs than whites or Asians. To some degree, these facts indicate considerable barriers to postsecondary educational attainment still exist. Cost may be the most obvious barrier, and Americans largely share this view, with 76% saying education beyond high school is not affordable to anyone who needs it.

Survey Methods

Results for this Gallup poll are based on telephone interviews conducted Oct. 1-Nov. 5, 2015, with a random sample of 1,616 adults, aged 18 and older, living in all 50 U.S. states and the District of Columbia. The sample included oversamples of 300 non-Hispanic blacks and 302 Hispanics. For results based on the total sample of national adults, the margin of sampling error is ±3 percentage points at the 95% confidence level.

For results based on the total sample of 930 non-Hispanic whites, the margin of sampling error is ±4 percentage points at the 95% confidence level.

For results based on the total sample of 300 non-Hispanic blacks, the margin of sampling error is ±7 percentage points at the 95% confidence level.

For results based on the total sample of 302 Hispanics, the margin of sampling error is ±7 percentage points at the 95% confidence level.

All reported margins of sampling error include computed design effects for weighting.

April 12, 2016
MOST U.S. INVESTORS HAPPY WITH THEIR 401(K)

by Lydia Saad

Story Highlights

- *Nine in 10 employed investors view their 401(k) plan positively*
- *Majority seek allocation advice from personal financial adviser*
- *Younger plan holders also rely on Internet, family advice*

PRINCETON, N.J. – The vast majority of employed U.S. investors who participate in a 401(k) savings plan, the primary means of retirement savings for many working Americans, view it positively. Nine in 10 investors say they are satisfied with their own 401(k) plan as a tool for saving for their retirement, including 44% who are "very" satisfied and 47% who are "somewhat" satisfied. Just 9% are somewhat or very dissatisfied.

Overall, how satisfied are you with your 401(k) plan as a tool for saving for your retirement?

Based on employed 401(k) participants

	Total participants %	Investments of \$100,000+ %	Investments of less than \$100,000 %
Very satisfied	44	46	43
Somewhat satisfied	47	47	47
Somewhat dissatisfied	7	6	7
Very dissatisfied	2	1	3

Jan. 29-Feb. 7, 2016
Wells Fargo/Gallup Investor and Retirement Optimism Index

Satisfaction is just as high among those with less than $100,000 invested (90%) as it is among higher-asset investors (93%), indicating the 401(k)'s egalitarian appeal.

These findings are from the latest Wells Fargo/Gallup Investor and Retirement Optimism Index survey, conducted Jan. 29-Feb. 7, 2016, among 1,012 U.S. investors. Approximately 40% of U.S. adults meet the survey's criteria as investors; these criteria involve having $10,000 or more invested in stocks, bonds or mutual funds, either in an investment or retirement account. Seven in 10 employed investors say their current employer offers a 401(k) – and of these, 88% say they participate.

Although 401(k) plans offer tremendous opportunity for investors to achieve financial freedom in retirement, the onus for managing them falls on individuals. Along with saving enough, making the right investment decisions at each stage of a worker's career – which involves maximizing growth while managing risk – is key to building wealth.

Internet, Personal Adviser Tie as Preferred Source of Advice

Among six tools or resources that investors use to help them allocate their 401(k) investments, Internet research and personal financial advisers tie for the most commonly used – with 58% of investors naming each. These are followed by online investment calculators, at 46%, and advice from family and friends, at 40%. One in five investors (21%) use target-date funds, which automate allocation based on the date investors plan to start taking withdrawals.

Although 78% of investors who are currently enrolled in a 401(k) say they have access to a financial call center through their plan, only 15% say they rely on it for allocation advice.

Majorities of investors younger than age 50 and those closer to retirement age say they rely on a personal financial adviser. However, it is the top resource used by those aged 50 and older while it ranks second to Internet research among those aged 18 to 49.

Which of the following tools or resources do you use to help you decide how to allocate your 401(k) investments?

Based on employed 401(k) participants

	Total%	18 to 49%	50+%
A personal financial adviser	58	52	63
Internet research	58	66	49
Online investment calculators and other financial tools	46	58	35
Advice from family or friends	40	50	30
Target-date funds	21	23	18
Advice through a financial call center	15	10	21

Jan. 29-Feb. 7, 2016
Wells Fargo/Gallup Investor and Retirement Optimism Index

Other age-related differences in preference for receiving allocation advice underscore generational gaps in the use of digital versus traditional resources:

- A majority of investors younger than 50 (58%) versus a third of those aged 50 and older (35%) use online investment calculators.
- Older investors are twice as likely as those aged 18 to 49 to consult a financial call center (21% vs. 10%, respectively).
- Younger investors (50%) are also much more likely than older investors (30%) to turn to family or friends for allocation advice.

Bottom Line

According to a 2015 Wells Fargo/Gallup Investor and Retirement Optimism Index survey, roughly two-thirds of employed investors who have a 401(k)-type plan said they can manage it on their own while 35% said they need advice. And when asked which of five areas of investing they need the most help with, the largest percentages mentioned knowing what to invest in (32%) and knowing when to reallocate funds (29%). The latest research clarifies how investors go about answering these important questions.

The majority turn to a personal financial adviser, but many – particularly younger investors – also identify Internet research and online investment tools as helpful. Although financial call centers are commonly available, relatively few investors take advantage of them for allocation advice, and those who do tend to be older.

Survey Methods

Results for the Wells Fargo/Gallup Investor and Retirement Optimism Index survey are based on questions asked Jan. 29-Feb. 7, 2016, on the Gallup Daily tracking survey, of a random sample of 1,012 U.S. adults having investable assets of $10,000 or more.

For results based on the total sample of investors, the margin of sampling error is ±4 percentage points at the 95% confidence level. All reported margins of sampling error include computed design effects for weighting.

April 13, 2016

U.S. CONGRESS APPROVAL REMAINS LOW

by Justin McCarthy

Story Highlights

- *17% of Americans approve, up slightly from 13% in March*
- *Although GOP controls both houses, Democrats are more approving*

WASHINGTON, D.C. – The substantial majority of Americans still disapprove of the job Congress is doing, while just 17% approve. This is up slightly from the 13% approval rating Congress received in March. Congress' approval rating has not exceeded 20% since October 2012.

Congressional Job Approval Ratings: 2001-2016

Do you approve or disapprove of the way Congress is handling its job?

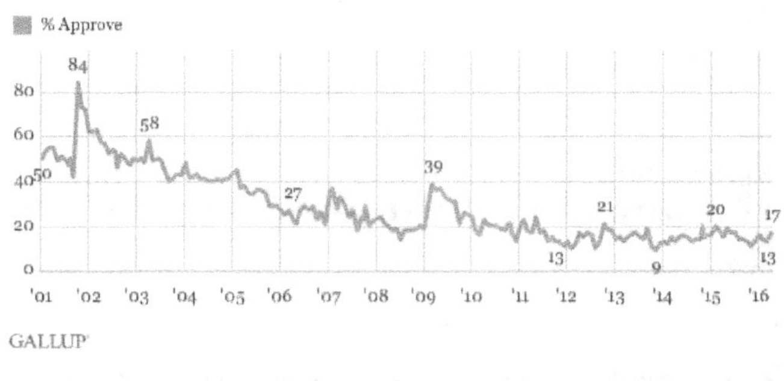

These data, collected April 6-10, come three months into Paul Ryan's tenure as House speaker, and as 34 Senate seats and all 435 House of Representatives seats are up for grabs in November's elections. In addition to the question of which party will control each chamber next year, two sitting U.S. senators – Sens. Bernie Sanders and Ted Cruz – are running for president.

Amid the backdrop of the presidential and congressional elections, Congress is grappling with a variety of issues, ranging from a Supreme Court nomination in the Senate to debt management in Puerto Rico. Congressional action has seemingly been more muted and less controversial in 2016, given the deal struck late last year by outgoing Speaker John Boehner that passed a budget and debt ceiling package, allowing incoming Speaker Ryan to avoid a high-stakes partisan battle. Congress may also be hesitant to vote on controversial measures during an election year. Regardless, its approval rating has not moved appreciably since the deal was struck.

Although Republicans control both the House and Senate, Democrats nationwide (20%) remain more approving than Republicans (12%) of the job Congress is doing. Congressional Republicans are still dealing with the fallout of a showdown between newer, more conservative Republicans who eschew compromise, versus more moderate, establishment party members who are willing to make deals with Democrats to pass legislation. This divide may still be dampening rank-and-file Republicans' approval of Congress.

Meanwhile, 17% of independents approve of the job Congress is doing.

Bottom Line

Congress has long been the least popular of the three federal government branches, but the consistency of its low ratings over the past 6 ½ years has been remarkable. The current rating is not much higher than the institution's all-time low approval rating of 9% and is far below the all-time high rating of 84%, measured shortly after the 9/11 terrorist attacks.

With approval ratings as low as they have been for several years, it is unlikely that they will change markedly in the coming months, as congressional gridlock complicates any efforts to enact major legislation – especially during an election year.

Historical data are available in Gallup Analytics.

Survey Methods

Results for this Gallup poll are based on telephone interviews conducted April 6-10, 2016, with a random sample of 1,015 adults, aged 18 and older, living in all 50 U.S. states and the District of Columbia. For results based on the total sample of national adults, the margin of sampling error is ±4 percentage points at the 95% confidence level. All reported margins of sampling error include computed design effects for weighting.

April 14, 2016
ECONOMY, GOVERNMENT TOP U.S. PROBLEM LIST

by Zac Auter

Story Highlights

- *Economy tops Americans' concern as most important issue*
- *Overall, 71% of Americans dissatisfied with country's direction*
- *GOP dissatisfaction with country's course outpaces Democrats'*

WASHINGTON, D.C. – Americans in April continue to cite the economy as the single most important problem for the U.S, with mentions holding steady at 17% over the past several months. Dissatisfaction with the government also retains the second-place spot, with 13% of Americans naming it as the leading U.S. concern.

Recent Trend, Most Important Problem

What do you think is the most important problem facing this country today? [OPEN-ENDED]

	Feb '16%	Mar '16%	Apr '16%
Economy in general	17	17	17
Dissatisfaction with government	13	15	13
Unemployment/Jobs	10	11	9
Immigration	10	8	8
Race relations/Racism	5	6	7
Terrorism	7	6	6
Federal budget deficit	6	5	5
National security	7	3	5
Healthcare	6	8	5
Election/Election reform	*	5	4

April 6-10, 2016
Gallup Poll

The results are based on Gallup's April 6-10 update of Americans' views of the most important problem facing the U.S. While concerns about the economy and government are the only problems named by at least one in 10 Americans, several other issues register a notable level of concern, including unemployment (9%) and immigration (8%).

Seven percent of Americans name racial issues – including racism and race relations – as America's top problem. This continues a trend of recent elevated concern about the issue, with between 5% and 7% mentioning it each of the past four months. Americans' mentions of racism and race relations as the most important problem facing the country spiked in December 2014 to 13% amid protests over high-profile incidents of police brutality toward blacks. For more than a decade prior to December 2014, no more than 5% of Americans had named racism or race relations as the top problem facing the U.S., with the figure often measuring 0%.

This month's result ties for the highest percentage of Americans naming race relations as America's leading issue since July 2015. That month, 9% of Americans cited race relations as the country's top concern, weeks after white South Carolina resident Dylann Roof killed nine black parishioners at the historic Emanuel African Methodist Episcopal Church in Charleston.

Overall, 40% of Americans mention at least one problem that is economic in nature, similar to the past two months. These economic concerns include generic mentions of the economy and unemployment, as well as the federal budget deficit, inequality and wage issues.

However, as has been the case for some time, an even larger proportion of Americans – 69% – mention a noneconomic problem, with the chief ones being government, immigration issues, race issues and terrorism.

GOP More Concerned About Economy and Country's Direction

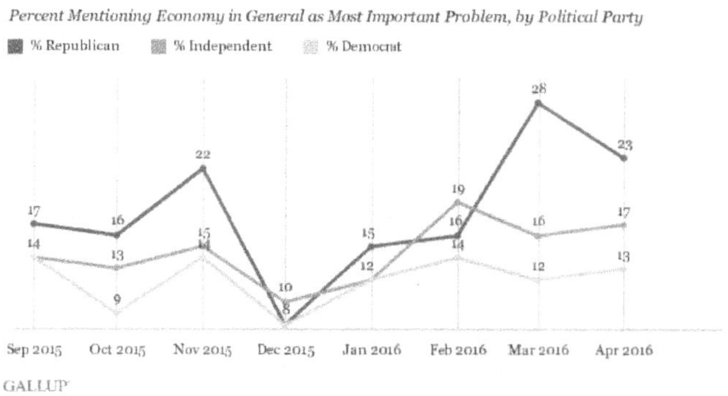

In last month's poll, concerns about the economy revealed a stark partisan gap, with 28% of Republicans citing the economy as the country's top issue, compared with 12% of Democrats – a net difference of 16 percentage points. Though Republicans continue to be more likely than Democrats and independents to cite the economy as the leading U.S. concern, the partisan gap contracted somewhat in April. Now, 10 percentage points separate the parties, with 23% of Republicans mentioning the economy as the county's top concern and Democrats holding steady at 13%.

Americans' Dissatisfaction With the Way Things Are Going in the U.S.

	Satisfied	Dissatisfied
Republicans	14%	85%
Independents	22%	75%
Democrats	42%	54%
Total	26%	71%

April 6-10, 2016
Gallup Poll

The partisan gap in concern about the economy echoes broader assessments about the country's direction. While a large majority of Americans are dissatisfied with the country's course (71%), there is a wide partisan gap. Though majorities of both Republicans and Democrats say they are dissatisfied with the country's direction, Republican dissatisfaction (85%) far outpaces that of Democrats (54%).

Implications

No single issue appears to be weighing on Americans as a dominant national concern, with no more than 17% naming one issue. However, recently elevated mentions of economic problems in the past three months, tied with broad dissatisfaction with the direction of the country, help to explain the negative flavor of the 2016 election cycle. The candidates are talking less about maintaining the progress that's been made since the recession or about building on successes in domestic policy, and more about correcting significant problems in the labor market, such as wages, immigration, national security and other important areas.

Historical data are available in Gallup Analytics.

Survey Methods

Results for this Gallup poll are based on telephone interviews conducted April 6-10, 2016, on the Gallup U.S. Daily survey, with a random sample of 1,015 adults, aged 18 and older, living in all 50 U.S. states and the District of Columbia. For results based on the total sample of national adults, the margin of sampling error is ±4 percentage points at the 95% confidence level.

April 14, 2016
MOST AMERICANS IN 15 YEARS SAY THEIR TAX BILL IS TOO HIGH

by Jim Norman

Story Highlights

- *57% say they pay too much in federal income taxes*
- *Highest percentage since the 2001 tax cut*
- *47% say their taxes are unfair, highest since 1999*

WASHINGTON, D.C. – As the deadline looms for filing federal income taxes, 57% of Americans say they are paying too much in taxes – a six-percentage-point increase from last year and the highest percentage in 15 years.

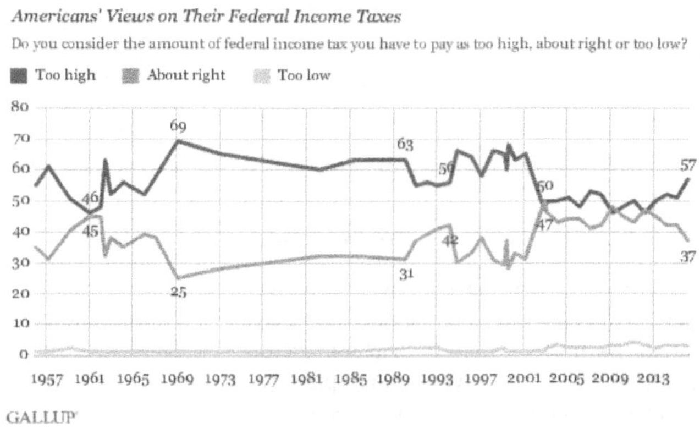

The results, from an April 6-10 Gallup poll, mark the first time since a major tax cut was enacted during the Bush administration in 2001 that more than 53% of Americans have said their taxes are too high. In three years during that time (2003, 2009 and 2012), Americans were more likely to say they were paying the right amount than to say they were paying too much. This is something that had not occurred in the 28 times Gallup asked the question from 1956 to 2001.

Partisan Gap Widens as More Republicans Say They Pay Too Much

The partisan gap in views of the fairness of taxes widened this year, as the percentage of Republicans saying they pay too much increased 10 points, to 73%, while the percentage of Democrats increased only three points, to 44%.

The changes among age groups went against the grain of typical views on political issues. Though those under 30 typically move in tandem with Democrats and those 65 and older with Republicans, the opposite is happening with views on taxes. In 2015, a minority of those under 30 (38%) thought that they were paying too much – the lowest of all age groups – but now a majority in this age group (55%) feel that way. Meanwhile, those 65 and older went from 46% saying they were paying too much last year to 39% saying the same now.

This year also saw a closing of the gender gap on the issue. Forty-seven percent of women last year said they paid too much, nine points less than men (56%) who said the same. But while men stayed about the same this year (55%), the percentage of women who think they pay too much jumped 11 points to 58%.

Fewer Feel Their Tax Bill Is Fair

A separate question included in the April survey asks Americans to say if the amount they are paying in taxes is fair or unfair. This year, the 47% who say their tax bill is unfair is the highest Gallup has measured since 1999, when 49% felt that way. This year's figure is a seven-point increase from last year's 40% and a 13-point increase from 10 years ago.

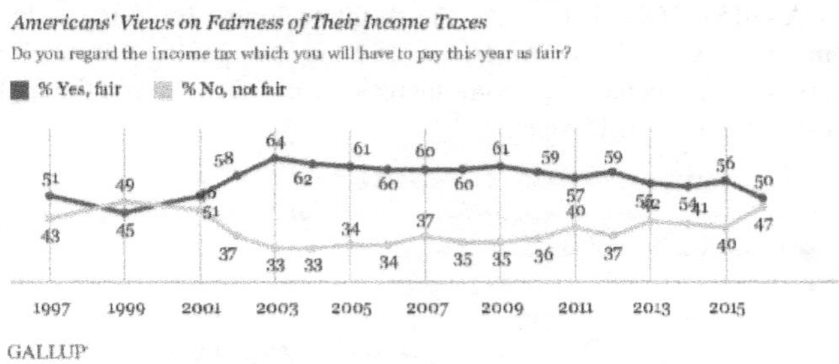

Bottom Line

Americans clearly have grown unhappier about their taxes in the past year, and the presidential candidates' various proclamations about tax fairness may be a major factor. The candidate who has made the most news with his tax plans is Bernie Sanders, an independent running as a Democrat. Sanders has charged that the current system gives huge breaks to the rich at the expense of everyone else. His Democratic opponent, Hillary Clinton, agrees that the rich pay too little in taxes, though her proposed solutions are not as far-reaching. On the Republican side, both Ted Cruz and Donald Trump have complained about the unfairness of the current system and have called for tax cuts.

In looking at this year's increase in the number of people who think they pay the federal government too much in income taxes, it's important to remember that it comes after a period of historically low unhappiness with tax payments. The 57% who this year say they pay too much is only one point higher than the 56% average for the 43 times Gallup has asked the question.

The change in views on tax payments, and the fact that they align so closely with the historic average, raises the question of whether this year's results are simply an adjustment back toward attitudes of the past. The political season ahead should provide some answers as, almost certainly, the Republican nominee will push for tax cuts while the Democratic nominee will emphasize the unfairness of the current tax laws and call for tax hikes for the rich.

Survey Methods

Results for this Gallup poll are based on telephone interviews conducted April 6-10, 2016, with a random sample of 1,015 adults, aged 18 and older, living in all 50 U.S. states and the District of Columbia. For results based on the total sample of national adults, the margin of sampling error is ±4 percentage points at the 95% confidence level.

April 15, 2016
SLIM MAJORITY IN U.S. SEE GOOD LOCAL JOB MARKET CONDITIONS

by Nawal Abouelala and Steve Ander

Story Highlights

- *51% say now is a good time to find a job in their area*
- *Those employed full time for an employer are more positive*
- *White Americans less likely to rate local job market positively*

WASHINGTON, D.C. – Americans are slightly more likely to say now is a good time (51%) rather than a bad time (46%) to find a good job in their local area. Their views of conditions locally are more positive than their views of the U.S. job market more broadly. A separate April 6-10 Gallup poll finds 40% of Americans saying now is a good time to find a "quality job" in the U.S.

Perceptions of Local Job Market, by Employment Status

Thinking about the job situation in the city or area where you live today, would you say that it is now a good time or bad time to find a good job?

	Good time%	Bad time%
National adults	51	46
Consistently employed 30+ hours per week for an employer	60	38
Employed full time for self/Employed part time^	47	51

March 31-April 2, 2016; ^Includes those who don't want a full-time job and those who do
Gallup Daily tracking

Gallup's question about local job market conditions augments its ongoing assessments of how the public views national economic conditions. In general, as is usually the case when they are asked to rate local conditions, Americans are more positive about the job situation at home than the situation nationally.

About six in 10 Americans who are employed full time for an employer – what Gallup considers a "good job" – rate the local job market positively. This percentage is higher than the national average of 51%, and higher than the percentage among those who have other types of employment (47%). This underscores the degree to which Americans' personal situations act as a filter through which they view the world; as such, those with a "good job" tend to think the climate is better for finding a good job than do those who are not in that position.

Nonwhites More Positive Than Whites About Local Job Market

An identical gap in perceptions of local jobs exists between white U.S. adults and nonwhites, with 60% and 47%, respectively, saying now is a good time to find a good job in their local area. Political party affiliation could be influencing these differences, as nonwhites are generally more likely than whites to be Democrats. The poll finds 63% of Democrats, compared with 40% of Republicans, saying now is a good time to find a good job.

Perceptions of Local Job Market, by Employment Status

Thinking about the job situation in the city or area where you live today, would you say that it is now a good time or bad time to find a good job?

	Good time%	Bad time%
Whites	47	50
Nonwhites	60	39

March 31-April 2, 2016
Gallup Daily tracking

Bottom Line

The U.S. labor market, like the U.S. economy more broadly, has made incremental gains since the recession. The U.S. unemployment rate is now half of what it was in 2010. Given this, it may be surprising that barely half of U.S. adults currently believe the local economic climate is good for job seekers. However, 2016 is the first time Gallup has asked Americans about local job market conditions on the U.S. Daily survey, and it is likely that today's modest optimism represents a marked improvement over the recession and immediate post-recession years. This would likely parallel the improvement in perceptions of job opportunity nationally, where positive perceptions have increased from 8% in 2011 to 40% or better in recent months.

Survey Methods

Results for this Gallup poll are based on telephone interviews conducted March 31-April 2, 2016, with a random sample of 1,526 adults, aged 18 and older, living in all 50 U.S. states and the District of Columbia. For results based on the total sample of national adults, the margin of sampling error is ±4 percentage points at the 95% confidence level. For perceptions of local market, the margin of sampling error is ±7 percentage points at the 95% confidence level. For whites, the margin of sampling error is ±4 percentage points at the 95% confidence level and for nonwhites, the margin of sampling error is ±6 percentage points at the 95% confidence level. All reported margins of sampling error include computed design effects for weighting.

April 15, 2016
AMERICANS STILL SAY UPPER-INCOME PAY TOO LITTLE IN TAXES

by Frank Newport

Story Highlights

- *Americans say money and wealth should be more evenly distributed*
- *Belief that upper-income pay too little in taxes has been evident for 25 years*
- *Slight majority favoring heavy taxes on rich is unchanged over last three years*

PRINCETON, N.J. – Six in 10 Americans continue to believe that upper-income Americans pay too little in taxes. This attitude has been steady over the past five years, but is lower than in the early 1990s, when as many as 77% said those with higher incomes paid too little in taxes.

Americans' Views on Tax Burden of Upper-Income Americans

As I read off some different groups, please tell me if you think they are paying their FAIR share in federal taxes, paying too MUCH or paying too LITTLE? First, how about upper-income people?

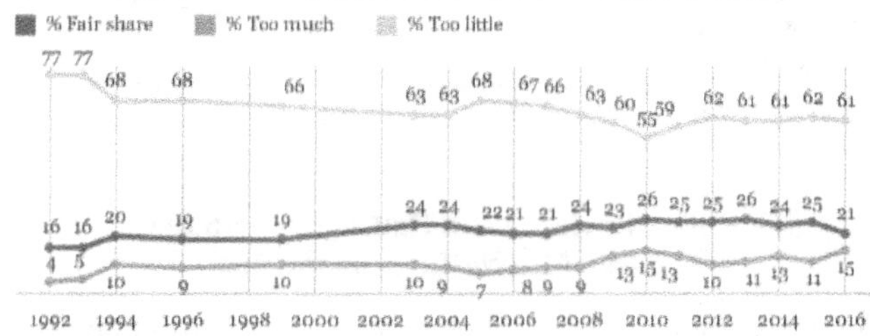

Latest results from April 6-10, 2016

GALLUP

The latest update comes from Gallup's April 6-10 Economy and Personal Finance survey – conducted during a presidential election year in which taxes have been a major area of focus for the candidates. In particular, Democratic presidential candidate Bernie Sanders has made the reduction of inequality the central motif of his campaign, saying, "The issue of wealth and income inequality is the great moral issue of our time, it is the great economic issue of our time, and it is the great political issue of our time." He has called for "higher income tax rates for the richest Americans." His Democratic opponent, Hillary Clinton, also has called for the need to "reform our tax code so the wealthiest pay their fair share."

Republicans, in contrast, have called for simplified tax plans, which will end up reducing the income taxes all Americans pay. Ted Cruz says that under his tax plan, "All income groups will see a double-digit increase in after-tax income." Donald Trump's plan would simplify the tax code into fewer tax brackets. Although it would reduce or eliminate "most deductions and loopholes available to the very rich," the rich likely would pay less in taxes because upper-income taxpayers under Trump's plan would have a lower tax rate.

The Democratic presidential candidates are the most in sync with overall public opinion on the issue of taxing the rich, given the significant majority who say upper-income Americans pay too little in taxes.

Americans' attitudes on whether upper-income Americans pay too little in taxes are split along political lines. Three-quarters of

Democrats say the rich pay too little, compared with less than half of Republicans. Independents mirror the national average. Those with an annual income of at least $75,000 per year, Gallup's highest income category for this analysis, have views that are broadly similar to those earning lower incomes.

Americans' Views on Tax Burden of Upper-Income Americans

As I read off some different groups, please tell me if you think they are paying their FAIR share in federal taxes, paying too MUCH or paying too LITTLE? First, how about upper-income people?

	Fair share%	Too much%	Too little%
National adults	21	15	61
Democrats	14	9	75
Independents	18	16	62
Republicans	32	20	45
Conservatives	30	20	46
Moderates	20	11	67
Liberals	10	12	76
Under $30,000	15	19	63
$30,000 to $74,999	21	11	64
$75,000+	26	16	57

April 6-10, 2016
Gallup

Slightly More Than Half Agree With the Idea of Heavy Taxes on the Rich

A separate Gallup trend question addressing the issue of taxes paid by the well-to-do finds that a slight majority of Americans agree with the proposition that the government should redistribute wealth by "heavy taxes on the rich." *Fortune* Magazine first asked this question in the late 1930s, during the Depression, and at that point only about a third agreed. When Gallup updated the question in 1998, 45% agreed. Although the exact figures have fluctuated since, public opinion has been about evenly divided. Most recently, in 2013, 2015 and this year, 52% say the government should redistribute wealth by taxing the rich.

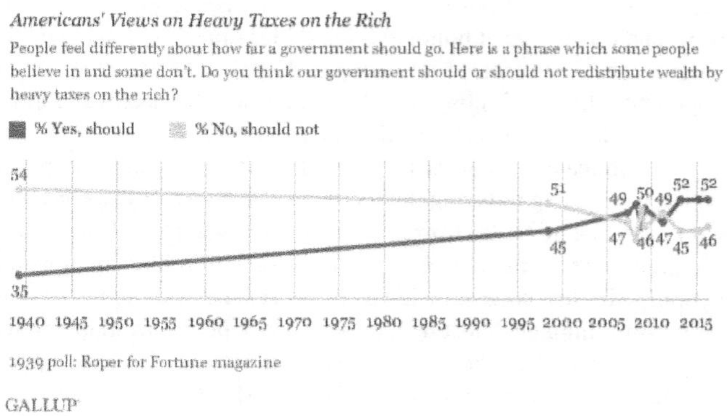

Views on heavily taxing the rich to redistribute wealth are strongly related to political orientation, with a huge gap between Republicans (22% of whom agree with the idea) and Democrats (80%), and a similar gap between conservatives and liberals. As household income rises, support for this idea drops, with those making at least $75,000 per year rejecting the idea of heavy taxes on the rich by a 59% to 40% margin. Young people, who tend to skew more Democratic in orientation, are most likely of the age groups o favor the idea.

Views on Government Redistribution of U.S. Wealth

People feel differently about how far a government should go. Here is a phrase which some people believe in and some don't. Do you think our government should or should not redistribute wealth by heavy taxes on the rich?

	Yes, redistribute by heavy taxes on rich%	No, should not redistribute wealth%	Don't know/ Refused%
National adults	52	46	2
Democrats	80	19	2
Independents	50	47	3
Republicans	22	76	1
Conservatives	26	71	3
Moderates	57	42	1
Liberals	77	21	2
Under $30,000	61	35	3
$30,000 to $74,999	57	41	2
$75,000+	40	59	1

April 6-10, 2016
Gallup

Americans Generally Favor More Equal Distribution

A clear majority of Americans agree that money and wealth in the U.S. should be more evenly distributed among a larger percentage of people, as has been true since Gallup first asked this question in 1984. The percentage agreeing was generally in the 60% range from 1984 through April 2008 and then dropped slightly in the fall of 2008 just before Barack Obama won the presidential election. The current 59% agreement is right at the average of what Gallup has found since 2009.

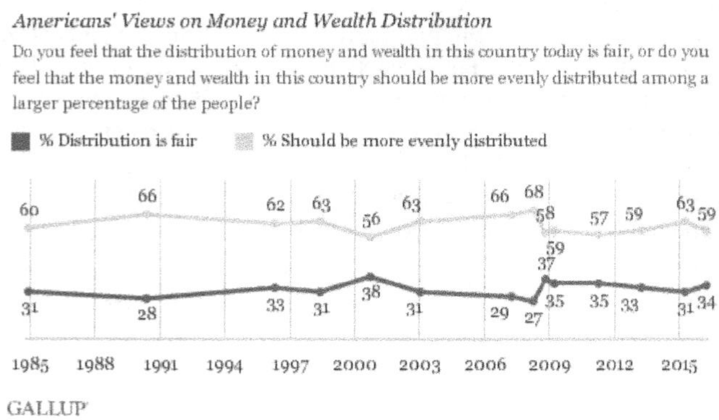

Implications

Americans are generally on board – as they consistently have been in recent decades – with the concept that wealth and income should be distributed more equally in the U.S. Americans also tend to agree that upper-income Americans pay too little in taxes and that the rich should be more heavily taxed in order to achieve a more even distribution of wealth.

These attitudes are divided along partisan lines, with wide gaps in opinion between Republicans and Democrats, reflecting the starkly different positions of the two parties' presidential candidates on this issue.

Sanders has been most focused on the issue of income inequality in his campaign, and his position clearly strikes a highly responsive chord with his own partisans, although Democrats interviewed in this survey who support Clinton for their party's nomination are little different on these measures from those who support Sanders. Cruz and Trump may find a similarly responsive chord among their partisans for their "lower all taxes" positions, with again little difference between Republicans who support one or the other for their party's nomination.

Overall, the Democrats continue to have a more resonant position than Republicans with the general public on the use of taxes to help redistribute income and wealth. Other Gallup research shows, however, that Americans have become less likely to say the amount they *personally* pay in taxes is fair, and the Republican candidates' calls for lowering taxes in general may be more in sync with the public's views.

Inequality does not show up as an extremely high priority when Americans are asked about campaign issues, and relatively few Americans mention inequality or taxes more generally as the most important problem facing the nation today.

Historical data are available in Gallup Analytics.

Survey Methods

Results for this Gallup poll are based on telephone interviews conducted April 6-10, 2016, with a random sample of 1,015 adults, aged 18 and older, living in all 50 U.S. states and the District of Columbia. For results based on the total sample of national adults, the margin of sampling error is ±4 percentage points at the 95% confidence level. All reported margins of sampling error include computed design effects for weighting.

April 18, 2016
AMERICANS MOST CONFIDENT IN SANDERS, KASICH ON ECONOMY

by Justin McCarthy

Story Highlights

- *Nearly half express confidence in Sanders (47%), Kasich (46%)*
- *Clinton not far behind, at 43%*
- *Trump (30%), Cruz (35%) evoke least confidence on economy*

WASHINGTON, D.C. – Nearly half of Americans express a "great deal" or "fair amount" of confidence in Sen. Bernie Sanders (47%) and Gov. John Kasich (46%) to recommend the right thing for the U.S. economy – the highest ratings among the five remaining presidential candidates. Americans have the least confidence in Donald Trump (30%).

Americans' Confidence in Presidential Candidates to Handle the Economy

As I read some names and groups, please tell me how much confidence you have in each to do or to recommend the right thing for the economy – a great deal, a fair amount, only a little or almost none.

	Great deal/Fair amount%	Only a little/Almost none%
Vermont Sen. Bernie Sanders	47	49
Ohio Gov. John Kasich	46	43
Hillary Clinton	43	56
Texas Sen. Ted Cruz	35	60
Donald Trump	30	68

April 6-10, 2016
Gallup Poll Social Series

These data, from an April 6-10 Gallup poll, come just three months before both parties' nominating conventions and as the candidates clamor for the remaining delegates for their respective nomination contests.

Hillary Clinton ranks within striking distance of her Democratic competitor, Sanders, with 43% of Americans saying they have a great deal or fair amount of confidence in the former secretary of state. However, a majority of Americans (56%) say they have "only a little" or "almost [no]" confidence in her to recommend the right thing for the economy. Americans' economic confidence in Clinton is lower now than during her 2008 campaign, when 51% were confident in her economic leadership.

Republican candidates Trump (30%) and Sen. Ted Cruz (35%) fall short of their GOP competitor, Kasich, in terms of the confidence Americans have in their handling of the economy. Majorities report having only a little or almost no confidence in Trump (68%) and Cruz (60%).

All five candidates currently inspire less economic confidence than President Barack Obama does.

Sanders' sentiments for greater economic equality may resonate with his supporters, with a platform that includes a nationwide $15 minimum wage, a detail-limited call to break up large banks, and free college tuition at public colleges and universities. Among all five candidates, Kasich is the only candidate with executive experience in managing a state economy, as governor of Ohio. Kasich also served as chairman of the House Budget Committee during the late 1990s, a time when the economy was strong and President Bill Clinton and the Republican Congress produced consecutive balanced budgets.

It is important to note that ratings of the candidates on this economic confidence measure track closely with their overall favorable ratings among national adults. Sanders (46% favorable, 39% unfavorable) and Kasich (38% favorable, 24% unfavorable) are the only two candidates who have positive net favorable ratings among U.S. adults. Americans view Clinton (39% favorable, 55% unfavorable), Cruz (31% favorable, 51% unfavorable) and Trump (31% favorable, 64% unfavorable) more negatively than positively.

These ratings of the candidates' ability to recommend or do the right thing for the economy may merely reflect their overall image in the eyes of Americans, and may have less to do with their specific experience or proposals on economic matters.

Clinton Most Trusted Among Dems; Cruz and Trump Among GOP

Kasich and Sanders may receive the most positive ratings overall on this measure because of the higher levels of confidence they evoke in independents (43% and 46%, respectively). But among their particular party's rank-and-file, Kasich and Sanders fall short of their competitors.

Americans' Confidence in Candidates to Handle the Economy, by Party ID

% Great deal/Fair amount

	Cruz %	Trump %	Kasich %	Sanders %	Clinton %
Republicans	59	58	54	17	12
Independents	32	30	43	46	35
Democrats	22	9	46	74	79

April 6-10, 2016
Gallup Poll Social Series

Republicans are a bit more likely to express confidence in Cruz and Trump, with about six in 10 saying they have a great deal or fair amount of confidence in each candidate when it comes to recommendations on the economy. Kasich is not far behind, however, with a majority of 54%. Republicans report having very little confidence in Democrats Sanders (17%) and Clinton (12%).

Democrats express much higher levels of confidence in their party's candidates compared with the GOP. About four in five Democrats report having confidence in Clinton (79%) – five percentage points higher than Sanders (74%). Though their confidence is low for Republicans Cruz (22%) and Trump (9%), about half of Democrats report having confidence in Kasich (46%).

Bottom Line

Within each contender's respective party, no candidate garners a decisively higher level of confidence among the Democratic Party and Republican Party faithful. In each party, candidates rate within five points of their competitors on economic confidence.

Among all Americans, however, Kasich and Sanders – both of whom appear unlikely to secure their party's nomination at this point – lead the other candidates in their perceived ability to handle the economy. Kasich is the only candidate whose economic confidence rating approaches 50% among the opposing party.

The Ohio governor's relevant experience in handling economic matters in his home state and in Congress may give him a boost in how Americans rate his ability to do the right thing economically, since his economic confidence rating is significantly higher than his overall favorable rating. Meanwhile, Trump's business background seems to buy him little from the public in terms of perceptions that he can handle the economy, as his 30% confidence rating matches his 31% overall favorable rating. Clinton, Sanders and Cruz have less experience that speaks to their ability to manage the economy, and as such, their ratings for handling the economy may simply reflect whether people view them positively or negatively overall.

These data are available in Gallup Analytics.

Survey Methods

Results for this Gallup poll are based on telephone interviews conducted April 6-10, 2016, with a random sample of 1,015 adults, aged 18 and older, living in all 50 U.S. states and the District of Columbia. For results based on the total sample of national adults, the margin of sampling error is ±4 percentage points at the 95% confidence level. All reported margins of sampling error include computed design effects for weighting.

April 18, 2016
HALF IN U.S. REMAIN CONFIDENT IN OBAMA'S ECONOMIC LEADERSHIP

by Jeffrey M. Jones

PRINCETON, N.J. – Half of Americans say they have "a great deal" or "a fair amount" of confidence in President Barack Obama to do or to recommend the right thing for the U.S. economy, generally similar to the readings through most of his presidency. Americans expressed more confidence in the president in 2009 (71%) and 2013 (57%), the first years of his first and second terms, and less confidence in him in 2014 (42%).

Confidence in Barack Obama's Economic Leadership

As I read some names and groups, please tell me how much confidence you have in each to do or to recommend the right thing for the economy -- a great deal, a fair amount, only a little or almost none. How about -- President Barack Obama?

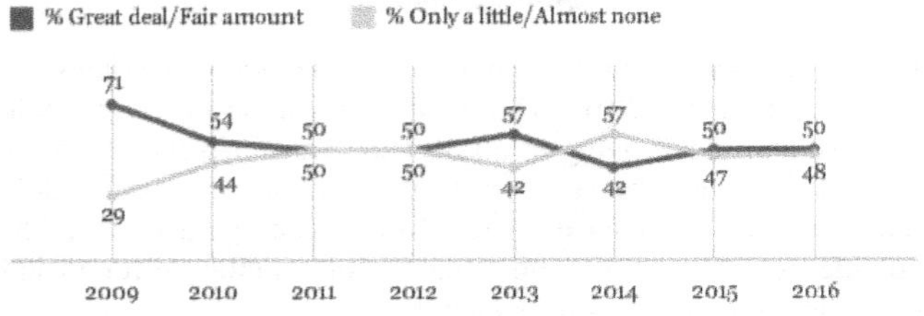

GALLUP

The results are based on Gallup's April 6-10 Economy and Personal Finance poll. Gallup has asked the same question each April throughout Obama's eight years as president. An average of 53% of Americans over that period have expressed confidence in Obama's ability to manage the economy.

That is similar to the 54% average from 2001 to 2008 for George W. Bush, the only other president about whom Gallup has asked this question. Bush's ratings varied more over the course of his presidency. Two-thirds or more of Americans were confident in him during the first three years of his presidency – a time when Bush had high job approval ratings after the 9/11 terrorist attacks – and just 34% were confident in his final year as the nation was in an economic recession.

Confidence in Obama is strongly related to one's party identification, as 86% of Democrats but only 14% of Republicans trust the president to do the right thing for the economy. Forty-six percent of independents are confident in Obama's economic leadership.

Americans Split as to Whether They Trust Yellen

Arguably the second-most important economic leader in the U.S. after the president is the chair of the Federal Reserve Board. Janet Yellen has held that post since February 2014, but one in four Americans still do not know her well enough to say whether they are confident in her ability to do the right thing for the economy. Currently, 38% have a great deal or fair amount of confidence in her, 35% say they have "only a little" or almost no confidence and 26% do not have an opinion.

Confidence in Yellen has been roughly 40% during her tenure, while the percentage expressing no confidence has varied between a high of 43% in 2014 and a low of 31% last year.

Confidence in Janet Yellen's Economic Leadership

As I read some names and groups, please tell me how much confidence you have in each to do or to recommend the right thing for the economy -- a great deal, a fair amount, only a little or almost none. How about -- Federal Reserve Chair Janet Yellen?

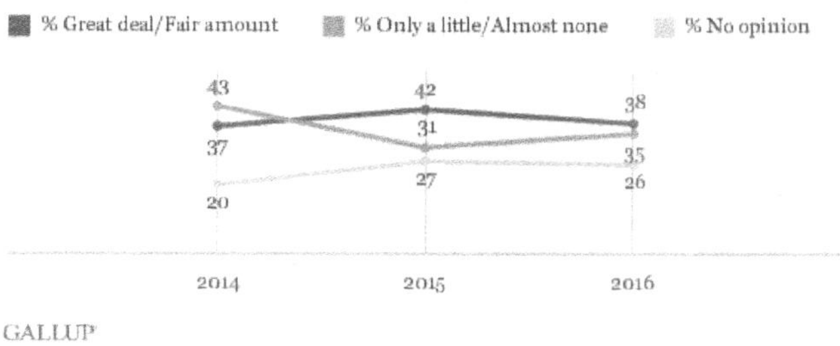

Yellen's 38% average rating thus far is slightly lower than former Fed Chair Ben Bernanke's 44% average from 2006 through 2013, partly because Bernanke was better known than Yellen is. Bernanke's predecessor, Alan Greenspan, averaged a 65% confidence rating over the last five years of his chairmanship. Greenspan was much better known than either of his successors and presided over the Fed during a time when the economy was generally strong.

Despite their lack of familiarity with her, Republicans are much more likely to say they are confident in Yellen (37%) than in Obama (14%). Fifty-two percent of Democrats express confidence in the Fed chair.

Majority Do Not Trust Democratic Leaders in Congress

Forty-two percent of Americans have confidence in Democratic congressional leaders on the economy, while 57% are not confident. The current level of confidence in Democratic leaders is in the lower range of what Gallup has measured since 2001, but above the low of 35% in 2014.

There have been several times when a majority of Americans were confident in Democratic leaders, including 2001 through 2003 when ratings of government leaders tended to be higher because of the strong economy and post-9/11 rally effect; in 2007 after Democrats became the majority party in Congress; and in 2009 after Obama's election as president.

Confidence in Democratic Congressional Leaders' Economic Leadership

As I read some names and groups, please tell me how much confidence you have in each to do or to recommend the right thing for the economy -- a great deal, a fair amount, only a little or almost none. How about -- the Democratic leaders in Congress?

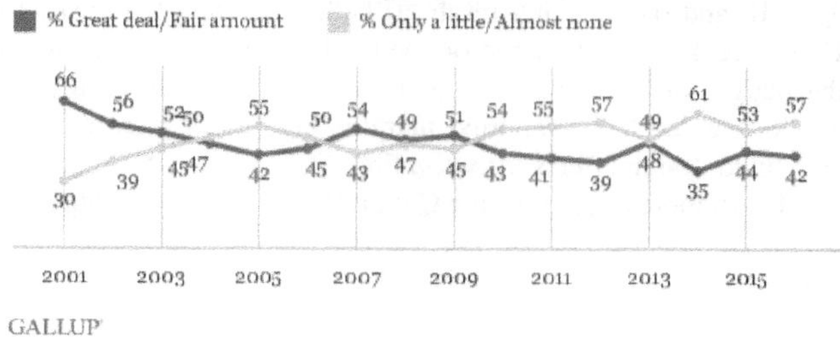

Americans Least Trusting in Republican Leaders in Congress

Americans are significantly less confident in the economic stewardship of Republican leaders in Congress than in Democratic leaders, with 33% saying they are confident in GOP congressional leaders. That represents a slight decline from 38% last year but is above the 2014 low point of 24%. A majority of Americans were confident in Republicans from 2001 through 2003, but since then, the percentage has held below 50%, including only two readings above 40% since 2008.

Confidence in Republican Congressional Leaders' Economic Leadership

As I read some names and groups, please tell me how much confidence you have in each to do or to recommend the right thing for the economy -- a great deal, a fair amount, only a little or almost none. How about -- the Republican leaders in Congress?

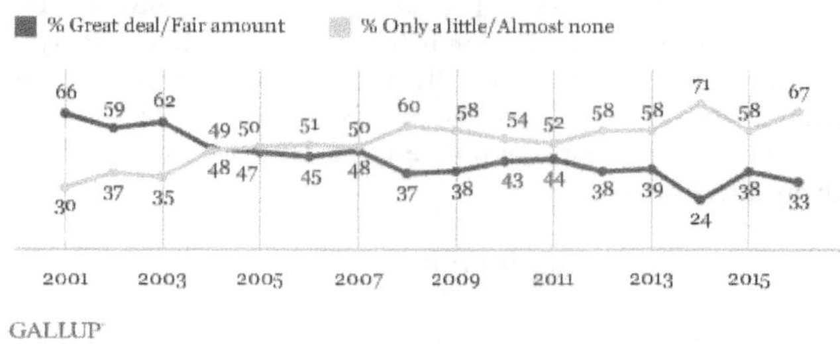

Bottom Line

Of the four major federal leaders or groups of leaders responsible for economic policy, Americans are most likely to say they are confident in Obama. His higher confidence rating is partly related to Americans' lack of familiarity with Yellen and their generally negative views of Congress as an institution.

Apart from the strong 71% rating Americans gave Obama during the honeymoon phase of his presidency, their confidence in him to manage the economy has not varied a great deal during his presidency. This is the case even though Americans' assessments of the U.S. economy have improved over the past seven years. Given the large partisan gap in Obama's confidence ratings, these may be rooted more in fundamental agreement or disagreement with the president's approach to economic policy than on how the economy is doing on his watch.

Historical data are available in Gallup Analytics.

Survey Methods

Results for this Gallup poll are based on telephone interviews conducted April 6-10, 2016, with a random sample of 1,015 adults, aged 18 and older, living in all 50 U.S. states and the District of Columbia. For results based on the total sample of national adults, the margin of sampling error is ±4 percentage points at the 95% confidence level. All reported margins of sampling error include computed design effects for weighting.

Learn more about how the Gallup Poll Social Series works.

April 19, 2016
REPUBLICANS SAY CAMPAIGN TAKING TOLL ON PARTY IMAGE

by Lydia Saad and Frank Newport

Story Highlights

- *More than six in 10 Republicans fear nomination process is hurting the GOP*
- *Just 24% of Democrats say the same about their party's campaign*
- *Democrats slightly more content with their primary field*

PRINCETON, N.J. – With the 2016 presidential primary season more than half over, 63% of Republicans say the continuing campaign for the GOP nomination is hurting the Republican Party. By contrast, Democrats are markedly more comfortable with the effect the primaries are having on their party's image. Only 24% of Democrats believe the campaign for the Democratic nomination is negatively affecting their party.

Is the Campaign Hurting the Party?

Do you think the continuing campaign for the [Republican/Democratic] nomination is hurting the party or not hurting the party?

	Hurting %	Not hurting %	No opinion %
Republican/Lean Republican	63	34	3
Democrat/Lean Democratic	24	71	5

April 15-17, 2016
Gallup

Republicans are more likely now to say the campaign is hurting their party than they were in February 2012, earlier in that year's campaign, when responses to this same question showed 40% saying it was hurting the party and 57% saying it was not.

These findings are based on interviewing conducted April 15-17 as part of Gallup Daily tracking. The large difference between Republicans' and Democrats' perceived effect of the campaign is notable because neither party has settled on a nominee, and both are witnessing rancorous battles between the candidates who are still standing.

Republicans' higher level of concern about the effect of the campaign on their party may reflect the harsh personal nature of some of the Republican candidates' attacks and counterattacks, and the looming potential battles over delegates and convention procedures in Cleveland in July. While Donald Trump's GOP detractors may not like what the businessman's front-runner status means for their party, just over half of Republicans view him favorably, and many of these supporters may be troubled by speculation that party insiders are conspiring to deny Trump the nomination.

Democrats also have some disputes over "superdelegates" and other details of the nominating process, but neither of the Democratic candidates has been vociferously critical of their party's structure, as has been the case on the Republican side.

About six in 10 Trump and Ted Cruz supporters say the campaign is hurting the party. The smaller number of Republicans who support John Kasich are somewhat more likely than the others to say the process is hurting the party.

Democrats More Likely Than Republicans to Be Pleased With Selection of Candidates

A slight majority of Democrats and Democratic-leaning independents – 55% – say they are pleased with the selection of candidates in the 2016 presidential race, while 42% say they wish someone else were running. Republicans are less likely to be content; 44% of them are pleased with the Republican candidates and 55% wish for an alternative.

Pleased With Selection of Candidates?

Are you generally pleased with the selection of the candidates running for the [Republican/Democratic] nomination, or do you wish someone else was running for president?

	Generally pleased %	Wish someone else was running %	No opinion %
Democrat/Lean Democratic	55	42	3
Republican/Lean Republican	44	55	2

April 15-17, 2016
Gallup

Republican dissatisfaction with the selection of candidates may reflect disappointment with the winnowed-down field of three GOP candidates still in the running, after at least 15 candidates started the process of running last year. Additionally, none of the three remaining GOP candidates have high favorability scores among Republicans, with Trump at 55% favorable, Cruz at 52% and Kasich at 50%.

Still, although Republicans' satisfaction with their nomination choices trails that of Democrats, it is similar to past elections. The 44% satisfied with their choice is identical to what Gallup found in February 2012, when Mitt Romney was battling Rick Santorum, Newt Gingrich and Ron Paul for that year's Republican nomination. It is also similar to the 46% who were generally pleased with the GOP field in February 1996, when Bob Dole was the runaway leader.

By contrast, majorities of Republicans were pleased in February and March 1992, when Republican President George H.W. Bush was running for re-election. And even larger percentages – 61% and 70% – were pleased in the spring and fall of 2007 with the emerging 2008 GOP field, although the question used in those surveys was slightly different.

Democrats' current satisfaction with their field exceeds the 42% satisfied in 1992 and the 48% in 2002. Gallup did not ask a comparable question of Democrats in the 1996 or 2012 elections, when a Democratic president was running for re-election, but in 2007, 73% to 80% were pleased with the field as it was shaping up – led by Hillary Clinton and Barack Obama. At this point, both Clinton and Bernie Sanders have a favorable rating from about two-thirds or more of Democrats.

On both sides, partisans who support their party's front-runners are the most likely to say they are pleased with the selection of candidates running for the nomination. Trump supporters (60%) are more likely to be pleased with the selection of candidates than are Cruz (44%) or in particular Kasich (12%) supporters. And among Democrats, Clinton supporters (62%) are somewhat more likely to be pleased than Sanders supporters (47%). Presumably, some supporters of candidates who are not in the lead interpret the question to be measuring pleasure with the leading candidates at this juncture.

Bottom Line

The contest for the Republican nomination has been a long and arduous battle among a large field of candidates, with Trump playing a starring role. A long string of nationally televised candidate debates has drawn huge audiences. But more recently, the big GOP newsmaker has been engaged in increasing levels of back-and-forth criticism with the remaining candidates, coupled with reports that some prominent Republicans are trying to foil Trump's bid.

Whatever the precise reason, most Republicans now believe the primary process is hurting the party, and this could imply that Republicans fear this in turn will cause the party to suffer in the fall general election. Still, while the majority of Republicans would like to see someone else in the race, the 44% who are satisfied with the current slate of candidates is not historically low.

Meanwhile, the Democratic race has also been heating up, with Clinton and Sanders showing more willingness to launch unfettered attacks on the other's policies and fitness for the presidency. Yet the majority of Democrats are satisfied with the field, and most doubt the lingering battle is doing their party much harm.

These data are available in Gallup Analytics.

Survey Methods

Results for this Gallup poll are based on telephone interviews conducted April 15-17, 2016, on the Gallup U.S. Daily survey, with a random sample of 1,537 adults, aged 18 and older, living in all 50 U.S. states and the District of Columbia. For results based on the total sample of national adults, the margin of sampling error is ±3 percentage points at the 95% confidence level.

For results based on the sample of 719 Republicans and Republican-leaning independents, the margin of error is ±5 percentage points at the 95% confidence level. For results based on the sample of 672 Democrats and Democratic-leaning independents, the margin of error is ±5 percentage points at the 95% confidence level. All reported margins of sampling error include computed design effects for weighting.

April 20, 2016
JUST OVER HALF OF AMERICANS OWN STOCKS, MATCHING RECORD LOW

by Justin McCarthy

Story Highlights

- *About half of Americans (52%) say they invest in stocks*
- *Current figure down slightly from 2014 and 2015*
- *Middle-class adults, those younger than 35 less likely to invest*

WASHINGTON, D.C. – With the Dow Jones industrial average near its record high, slightly more than half of Americans (52%) say they currently have money in the stock market, matching the lowest ownership rate in Gallup's 19-year trend.

Percentage of U.S. Adults Invested in the Stock Market

Do you, personally, or jointly with a spouse, have any money invested in the stock market right now -- either in an individual stock, a stock mutual fund or in a self-directed 401(k) or IRA?

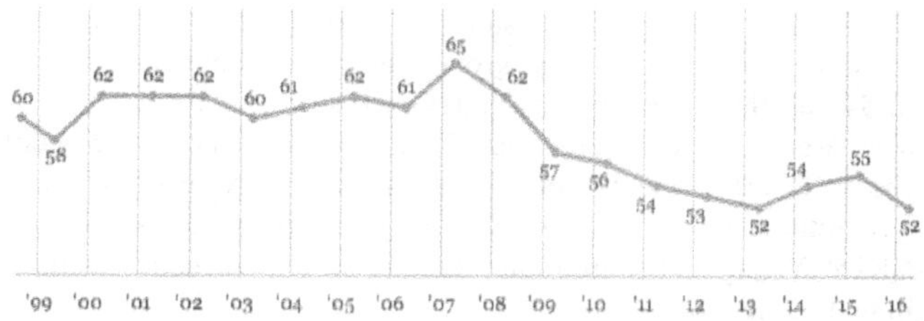

Selected trends closest to April for each year, from Gallup's annual Economy and Personal Finance survey

GALLUP

In 2007, nearly two in three American adults (65%) reported investing in the stock market, the high in Gallup's selected trend on this question for April of each year. But this percentage shrank each year from 2008 to 2013 as the effects of the Great Recession and big market losses took their toll on Americans' sense of job security, confidence in the economy and financial means to invest – as well as their general confidence in stocks as a place to invest their money.

Though the Dow Jones industrial average has made great gains since bottoming out in 2009, Americans' stock ownership has yet to recover to the level reported prior to the recession.

There were modest gains in the percentage of Americans with stock investments in 2014 and 2015, but reported ownership fell back this year, possibly because of the Dow's tumultuous performance over the past year. Americans' views of stocks as the best long-term investment also dipped this year.

Middle-Class Americans Most Likely to Leave Market

Although Americans in all income groups are less likely to have stock investments now than before the Great Recession, middle-class Americans have been the most likely to flee the market. Nearly three in four middle-class Americans, with annual household incomes ranging from $30,000 to $74,999, said they invested money in the stock market in 2007. Today, only half report having stock investments. This 22-percentage-point drop is more than double the changes seen in stock investing among higher and lower income groups.

Americans Invested in the Stock Market – Selected Trend

By age and income

	April 2007 %	April 2016 %	Change (pct. pts.)
National adults	65	52	-13
Less than $30,000	28	23	-5
$30,000 to $74,999	72	50	-22
$75,000 or more	90	79	-11
18 to 34	52	38	-14
35 to 54	73	62	-11
55+	65	56	-9

Gallup Poll Social Series

Adults younger than 35 are also less likely to invest since the recession. Slightly more than half (52%) said they invested money in the stock market in 2007. But nearly a decade later, fewer than four in 10 report investing in stocks. The 14-point dip for this group is the largest among all age groups; however, Americans aged 35 to 54 and those aged 55 and older each saw roughly double-digit decreases. Although many financial advisers say that young people should invest as much money as possible to maximize their long-term returns, the majority of 18- to 34-year-olds are not heeding that advice. Young adults are more likely to save their money or invest in real estate.

Bottom Line

While a slight majority of Americans report investing their money in the stock market, it's a far cry from pre-recession levels that spanned 58% to 65%. Confidence in the stock market and levels of financial literacy have clearly suffered in recent years, and investment rates lag significantly behind the overall rebound the market has made.

While Americans are likely still recovering from the fallout of the financial crisis, the market's behavior over the past year hasn't helped regain their confidence. The Dow's major drops in August and September of last year and again in January and February 2016 are now behind investors, but the unpredictability of its trajectory may have hampered the plans of potential investors to join them in the market. Fewer Americans – particularly those in middle-income families – are benefiting from the recent gains in stock values than would have been the case a decade ago.

Historical data are available in Gallup Analytics.

Survey Methods

Results for this Gallup poll are based on telephone interviews conducted April 6-10, 2016, on the Gallup U.S. Daily tracking survey, with a random sample of 1,015 adults, aged 18 and older, living in all 50 U.S. states and the District of Columbia. For results based on the total sample of national adults, the margin of sampling error is ±4 percentage points at the 95% confidence level. All reported margins of sampling error include computed design effects for weighting.

April 20, 2016
MORE AMERICANS SAY REAL ESTATE IS BEST LONG-TERM INVESTMENT

by Jim Norman

Story Highlights

- *35% of Americans now say real estate is best long-term investment*
- *Stocks (22%) and gold (17%) fall further behind as top choice*
- *Age, income, education, gender all related to views of best investment*

WASHINGTON, D.C. – Real estate, already Americans' top pick as the "best long-term investment" for the last two years, has increased its lead over four other investment choices. Thirty-five percent of Americans now choose real estate, compared with 22% for stocks and mutual funds, 17% for gold, 15% for savings accounts/CDs and 7% for bonds.

Americans' Choice of Best Long-Term Investment

Percentage who choose real estate, stocks/mutual funds, gold, savings/CDs or bonds as the best long-term investment

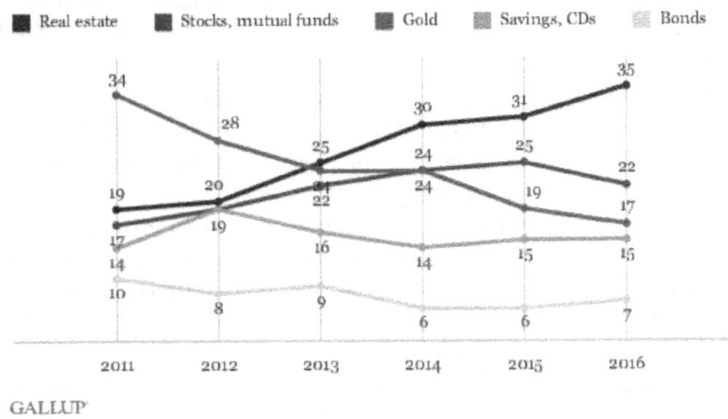

Real estate and gold have switched positions over the last five years as gold prices tumbled and home sales recovered from the 2007-2009 housing market collapse. In August 2011, 34% of Americans named gold as the best investment for the long term, compared with 19% for real estate.

Stocks and mutual funds, in spite of making major gains in the past five years after the historic 2008 stock market crash, have struggled to gain favor in the public's eyes. In August 2011, with the Dow Jones Industrial Average still below pre-crash levels, 17% of Americans chose stocks and mutual funds as the top long-term investment. The Dow in April 2016 is above its pre-crash high of 14,164 by almost 4,000 points, but the percentage choosing stocks or mutual funds as the best long-term strategy has grown only to 22%. That figure did reach 25% last April, but dipped slightly this year after the Dow's roller-coaster ride in recent months.

Meanwhile, as the average sale price of new homes in the U.S. increased from $259,300 in August 2011 to $348,900 in February of this year, the percentage of Americans picking real estate as the best long-term investment almost doubled. During approximately the same time span – from August 2011 to April of this year – gold prices plunged from $1,910 to $1,254 per ounce, and the percentage thinking gold would be the best investment was cut in half.

Age, Income, Education, Gender All Relate to Investment Views

Combined results from the 2015 and 2016 Gallup polls that asked about long-term investment preferences reveal some clear differences among key subgroups.

- Men are more likely than women to think gold is the best investment. Women are more likely than men to favor savings accounts.
- College graduates are more than twice as likely as nongrads to favor stocks – 37% to 17%. Those without a degree are more likely than grads to favor gold (21% to 12%) and savings (19% to 8%).
- Americans younger than 30 are the least likely (26%) age group to think real estate is the best investing choice and are the most likely (26%) to favor savings.
- Americans with higher incomes are more likely than those with lower incomes to favor stocks and less likely to choose savings.
- Stock owners are much more likely (33%) to pick stocks as the best investment than those who do not own stocks (12%).
- Renters are about as likely (32%) as homeowners (34%) to list real estate as the best choice.

Which of the following do you think is the best long-term investment?

	Real estate %	Stocks, mutual funds %	Gold %	Savings, CDs %	Bonds %
Men	32	25	22	12	5
Women	33	21	14	18	8
College degree	35	37	12	8	5
No college degree	32	17	21	19	7
18 to 29	26	20	18	26	8
30 to 49	37	27	15	12	6
50 to 64	34	22	21	13	6
65 and older	33	22	19	13	6
Less than $30,000	28	14	19	25	8
$30,000-$74,999	34	22	22	13	7
$75,000	37	34	13	9	4
Stock investors	34	33	15	10	6
Noninvestors	32	12	22	22	8
Homeowner	34	26	19	11	6
Renter	32	19	18	20	8

Combined results from April 9-12, 2015, and April 6-10, 2016, Gallup polls

Bottom Line

Both the housing market and the stock market have recovered from catastrophic losses suffered in the last decade, with average house prices and the Dow well above their pre-crash high marks. But Americans have been much more likely to regain confidence in real estate than in stocks as "the best" long-term place to invest their money. The split between the two investment options grew again in the last year as the stock market's volatility increased investors' concerns. With housing prices showing a steadier path upward in recent months, even stock investors are about as likely in the April 2016 poll to choose real estate (37%) as stocks (32%) as the best long-term investment.

The growing gap between stocks and real estate, and the continued rise of the latter as the preferred choice for long-term investments, may simply be a return to the norm. In a 2002 Gallup poll that did not include gold as a choice, 50% named real estate as the best long-term investment, compared with only 18% for stocks, 16% for savings accounts and 13% for bonds.

Survey Methods

Results for this Gallup poll are based on telephone interviews conducted April 6-10, 2016, with a random sample of 1,015 adults, aged 18 and older, living in all 50 U.S. states and the District of Columbia. For results based on the total sample of national adults, the margin of sampling error is ±4 percentage points at the 95% confidence level.

April 21, 2016
OBAMA JOB APPROVAL UP TO AVERAGE 49.5% IN 29TH QUARTER

by Jeffrey M. Jones

Story Highlights

- *Approval ratings averaged nearly three points higher than 28th quarter*
- *Democrats, independents more likely to approve of Obama*
- *Obama's 29th quarter average similar to Reagan's 29th*

PRINCETON, N.J. – President Barack Obama averaged 49.5% job approval in Gallup Daily tracking from Jan. 20 through April 19, his 29th quarter in office. That is nearly three percentage points higher than his 28th quarter average of 46.6%, and one of the higher quarterly averages in his presidency to date.

President Barack Obama's Quarterly Job Approval Averages

GALLUP

The nearly three-point increase from the previous quarter is one of the larger quarter-to-quarter gains for Obama during his presidency; the best to date was a four-point improvement between his

15th and 16th quarters, the period surrounding his re-election as president in the fall of 2012.

Obama's 29th quarter approval average ranks as the second-best quarter in his second term as president, behind a 49.7% average from Jan. 20-April 19, 2013, after Obama's second inauguration. He has had only six higher quarterly averages in his seven-plus years as president.

Obama's job approval rating averaged 50% or higher for six consecutive weeks from Feb. 29 through April 10, including an average 53% approval rating the week of March 21-27, his best since Jan. 28-Feb. 3, 2013. Most of the president's more recent three-day approval ratings have been just below 50%, but the latest Gallup Daily tracking estimate, for April 17-19, is 51%.

Democrats and independents led the improvement in the president's job approval ratings during his 29th quarter. Democrats' approval ratings of the president increased from 84% to 86%, while independents' went up from 43% to 47%. Republicans' ratings remained low and were essentially unchanged.

Change in President Barack Obama's Job Approval Ratings, 28th to 29th Quarter, by Political Party

	Quarter 28 %	Quarter 29 %	Change pct. pts.
Democrats	83.6	86.1	+2.5
Independents	43.3	47.2	+3.9
Republicans	9.6	10.2	+0.6

Gallup Daily tracking

The increase came as both parties are in the process of choosing their party's nominee to be Obama's successor. In this time of heightened political attention, there is more focus on the state of the nation and Obama's record as president, which some Democrats and independents may now be viewing more positively.

Obama, Reagan Near 50% Approval in 29th Quarter

Obama is the sixth president since World War II to serve 29 quarters in office, joining Harry Truman, Dwight Eisenhower, Ronald Reagan, Bill Clinton and George W. Bush. Clinton and Eisenhower were the two most popular at this stage of their presidencies, as both had job approval ratings above 60%. Reagan, like Obama, was right around the 50% mark. Truman and Bush were highly unpopular, with approval ratings near 30%, as the nation dealt with economic problems and prolonged and increasingly unpopular U.S. wars in Korea and Iraq.

Average Presidential Job Approval Ratings During 29th Quarter in Office, Gallup Polls

President	Dates of 29th quarter	Average approval rating	Number of polls
Truman	Apr 20-Jul 19, 1952	29.8	4
Eisenhower	Jan 20-Apr 19, 1960	64.3	3
Reagan	Jan 20-Apr 19, 1988	50.0	4
Clinton	Jan 20-Apr 19, 2000	61.0	7
G.W. Bush	Jan 20-Apr 19, 2008	31.3	8
Obama	Jan 20-Apr 19, 2016	49.5	89

Gallup

Obama might not expect his job approval rating to improve further in his 30th quarter if history is a guide. To date, Truman is the only president thus far who saw improvement in his ratings during his 30th quarter, although Truman's 30th quarter ratings were still historically low at 32%. Eisenhower, Clinton and Bush all had declines of between two and five percentage points in their 30th quarters, while Reagan's job approval ratings were stable.

Implications

Obama's job approval ratings have been some of the most politically polarized of any post-World War II president, and that polarization has held his ratings down. He has averaged 47% job approval to date over his seven-plus years in office. Aside from higher approval during his "honeymoon period" in early 2009, Obama's ratings have held above the 50% level for only brief periods, including the time just before and after his re-election and the recent stretch in March and early April.

As Americans look to choose Obama's successor and decide whether they generally want to continue with the policy course he has set or change the nation's direction, the public will naturally reflect on how he has done as president. Obama and the Democrats hope his approval ratings will increase between now and the election, to help the Democratic Party's efforts to accomplish the rare modern feat of winning three consecutive presidential elections.

These data are available in Gallup Analytics.

Survey Methods

Results for this Gallup poll are based on telephone interviews conducted Jan. 20-April 19, 2016, on the Gallup U.S. Daily survey, with a random sample of 45,221 adults, aged 18 and older, living in all 50 U.S. states and the District of Columbia. For results based on the total sample of national adults, the margin of sampling error is ±1 percentage point at the 95% confidence level. All reported margins of sampling error include computed design effects for weighting.

April 22, 2016
WOMEN PAYING LESS ATTENTION THAN MEN TO 2016 ELECTION

by Frank Newport

Story Highlights

- *44% of men following election very closely, compared with 31% of women*
- *Gender gap larger in April than in previous months*
- *Gap exists among both Republicans and Democrats*

PRINCETON, N.J. – Men over the last two months have been paying significantly more attention to news about the 2016 presidential election than are women. In April, 44% of men say they are following election news very closely, compared with 31% of women. This 13-percentage-point gap has expanded from previous months, particularly February, when the gap was a narrow two points.

How closely are you following the news about the 2016 presidential election campaign -- very closely, somewhat closely, not too closely or not at all?

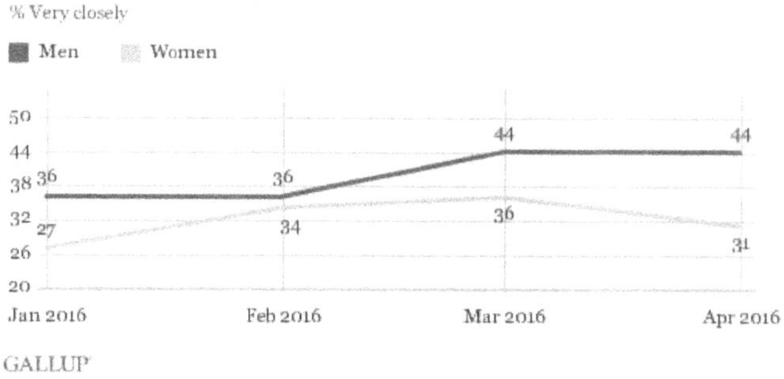

This measure of attention paid to the campaign is based on Gallup Daily tracking interviews conducted since January, in the middle of each month, with the latest update from April 15-17. Men's attention to the election increased in March and remains unchanged in April, while women's stayed about the same in February and March, but dropped five points in April. Complete results are at the end of this article.

As is usually the case, Republicans (48%) are following news of the election significantly more closely than are Democrats (34%). Men are more likely than women to identify as Republicans, suggesting that one possible explanation for the gender gap could be underlying gender differences in partisan composition.

But the gender gap persists within both parties. An aggregated analysis of March and April responses shows that Republican men are eight points more likely than Republican women to be following the election very closely, while Democratic men are 11 points more likely than Democratic women. "Pure" independents – those who do not lean to either party – are following the news less closely than those in either party, regardless of gender, as would be expected. But even with overall lower levels of interest, independent men are significantly more likely than independent women to say they are following the news very closely.

How Closely Following News About Election, by Gender and Party

% Very closely

	Men %	Women %	Difference (pct. pts.)
REPUBLICANS/LEANERS	52	44	+8
INDEPENDENTS/NO LEAN	24	6	+18
DEMOCRATS/LEANERS	41	30	+11

March 16-17 and April 15-17, 2016
Gallup Daily tracking

Age, too, does not appear to be a direct factor in this relationship. The gender gap in the percentages who very closely follow election news persists across all three major age groups: nine points among those 18 to 34 years old, 14 points among 35- to 54-year-olds and 13 points among those 55 and older.

How Closely Following News About Election, by Gender and Age

% Very closely

	Men %	Women %	Difference (pct. pts.)
18-34	26	17	+9
35-54	46	32	+14
55+	57	44	+13

March 16-17 and April 15-17, 2016
Gallup Daily Tracking

The gender gap in paying attention to the election also persists regardless of education level. Attention to the news is generally higher as education level increases, but men with a college degree are more likely than degree-holding women to be paying close attention to election news (a 16-point gap), and the trend is consistent with men and women without college degrees (a 10-point gap).

How Closely Following News About Election, by Gender and Education

% Very closely

	Men %	Women %	Difference (pct. pts.)
COLLEGE GRADUATE	59	43	+16
NOT COLLEGE GRADUATE	38	28	+10

March 16-17 and April 15-17, 2016
Gallup Daily Tracking

Implications

Men are more likely than women to be Republicans, and not only is overall Republican interest higher in this election so far, but turnout in Republican primaries has also been higher. But even within ranks of both parties, men are paying more attention than women – indicating there is more causing the gap in attention to the election than just the underlying fact that Republicans are more interested than Democrats so far this year.

Much of the news coverage in this year's presidential campaign has been focused on Donald Trump, and data from the April survey indicate that his supporters are more likely than those who support any of the other major candidates to say they are following the news very closely. Since Trump's supporters skew male, it could be that the Trump factor is helping fuel the higher male interest within the ranks of Republicans. But that doesn't help explain the gender gap among Democrats.

Data show that there has been a gender gap in attention paid to historical elections as well. One possible, although difficult-to-document hypothesis, is that the general absence of women as candidates for the major parties' nominations over time could be a factor in women's overall lower attention to the race. Even this year, despite the presence of Hillary Clinton as the Democratic front-runner, only one other individual out of the more than 20 candidates who began the presidential race is a woman – Carly Fiorina.

The implications of the gender gap in election interest are unclear at this point. Women may well vote at their usual levels – women constituted 53% of the presidential vote in 2012 based on exit polling – even if their interest levels stay relatively low. It's also entirely possible that women's relative interest may pick up once the two parties hold their conventions in July and the nominees are solidified.

How Closely Following News About Election, by Gender and Month

	Very closely %	Somewhat closely %	Not too closely %	Not at all closely %
JANUARY				
Men	36	36	20	8
Women	27	40	23	8
FEBRUARY				
Men	36	36	18	10
Women	34	37	19	9
MARCH				
Men	44	34	15	6
Women	36	35	24	5
APRIL				
Men	44	34	15	6
Women	31	43	19	7

Gallup Daily Tracking

These data are available in Gallup Analytics.

Survey Methods

Results for this Gallup poll are based on telephone interviews conducted April 15-17, 2016, on the Gallup U.S. Daily survey, with a random sample of 1,537 adults, aged 18 and older, living in all 50 U.S. states and the District of Columbia. For results based on the total sample of national adults, the margin of sampling error is ±3 percentage points at the 95% confidence level.

For results based on the sample of 719 Republicans and Republican-leaning independents, the margin of error is ±5 percentage points at the 95% confidence level. For results based on the sample of 672 Democrats and Democratic-leaning independents, the margin of error is ±5 percentage points at the 95% confidence level. All reported margins of sampling error include computed design effects for weighting.

April 22, 2016
AMERICANS' IDENTIFICATION AS "ENVIRONMENTALISTS" DOWN TO 42%

by Jeffrey M. Jones

Story Highlights

- *Percentage identifying as environmentalists is down from 78% in 1991*
- *Party gap has emerged in last 25 years*
- *Concern about environmental problems also down*

PRINCETON, N.J. – As Americans observe Earth Day, Gallup finds 42% of Americans identifying themselves as environmentalists, down from an average of 76% in the late 1980s and early 1990s.

Americans' Self-Identification as "an Environmentalist"

Do you consider yourself an environmentalist or not?

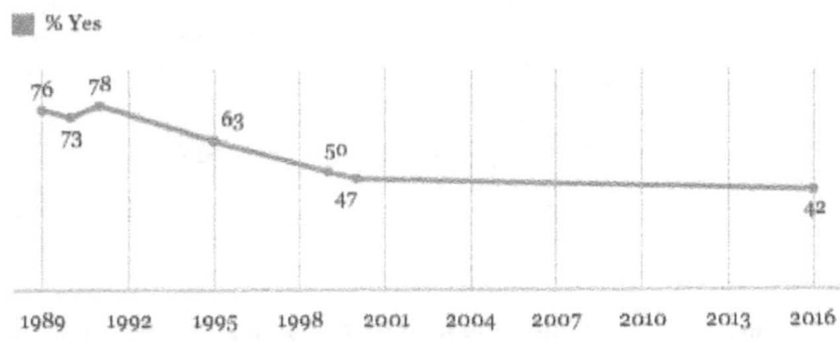

GALLUP

The results are based on Gallup's annual Environment poll, conducted March 2-6. When last asked, in 2000, 47% of Americans identified as environmentalists, which in turn was down from 63% in 1995. In 1991 – one year after Earth Day became a global event celebrated each April 22 – a high of 78% of Americans described themselves that way.

One reason for the decline is that the environment has become politicized as an issue, especially in terms of the debate over climate change and how to address it. In 1991, the same high percentage of Republicans and Democrats – 78% – considered themselves environmentalists. Today, 27% of Republicans think of themselves that way, compared with 56% of Democrats, a partisan gap of 29 percentage points.

Americans' Self-Identification as "an Environmentalist," by Political Party

Do you consider yourself an environmentalist or not?

Figures indicate % Yes

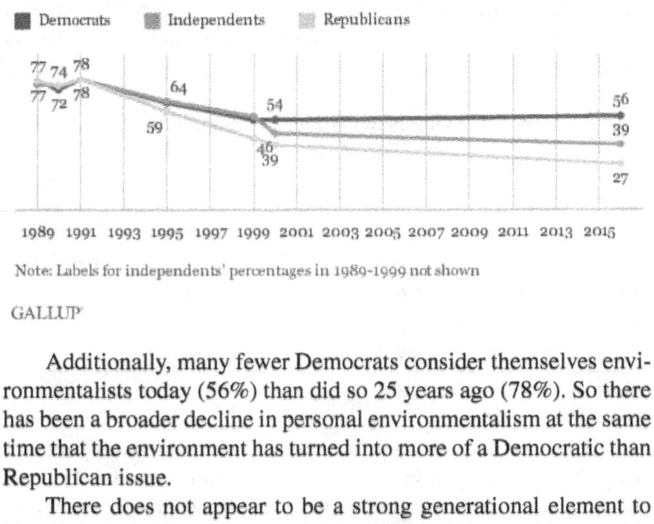

Note: Labels for independents' percentages in 1989-1999 not shown

GALLUP

Additionally, many fewer Democrats consider themselves environmentalists today (56%) than did so 25 years ago (78%). So there has been a broader decline in personal environmentalism at the same time that the environment has turned into more of a Democratic than Republican issue.

There does not appear to be a strong generational element to identifying as an environmentalist – 46% of 18- to 29-year-olds describe themselves that way, compared with between 39% and 43% of older age groups. There were only modest age differences in 1991 as well.

Another possibility for the decline is that the "environmentalist" term may just be less commonly used than it was 25 years ago and may not resonate with Americans as much as it did in the past.

To some degree, too, the term "environmentalism" may be associated with protestors who have taken more radical actions to protect the environment against perceived threats. The Gallup survey does not attempt to define the word "environmentalist" for respondents, so their likelihood of identifying themselves that way, now or in the past, depends on their own understanding of the label.

Also, many environmentally sensitive actions are now commonplace. As a result, it may take more significant action than recycling or conserving energy for one to consider oneself an environmentalist today, but that may not have been the case in the past.

Americans Less Concerned About Some Environmental Matters

Consistent with their drop in identification as environmentalists, Americans express less concern about certain environmental problems now than in the late 1980s and early 1990s, but that varies by the problem. Americans are much less concerned now than they were a generation ago about air pollution and pollution of rivers, lakes and reservoirs. Their concern about polluted drinking water is down slightly, while they are slightly more concerned about global warming or climate change than in the late 1980s and early 1990s. However, on a relative basis, global warming is still of less concern than most of the other problems.

Changes in Americans' Concern About Environmental Problems

Percentage worried "a great deal" about each problem

	1989-1990 %	2016 %	Change pct. pts.
Pollution of rivers, lakes and reservoirs	68	56	-12
Pollution of drinking water	65	61	-4
Air pollution	61	43	-18
The loss of tropical rain forests	41	39	-2
Global warming/Climate change	33	37	+4

Data are an average of 1989 and 1990 polls for all items except for pollution of drinking water, which was asked only in 1990
Gallup

Also, when considering trade-offs between protecting the environment and promoting economic growth, Americans are less inclined to prioritize the environment today (56% to 37%) than they were in 1991 (71% to 20%).

Implications

The decline in Americans' willingness to identify themselves as environmentalists is likely a result of many factors, including the politicization of environmental issues and the routine nature of recycling and other simple, environmentally friendly actions people might have once associated with environmentalism. Also, it is possibly because the term is less commonly used or may have taken on a different meaning than in the past.

Gallup's data indicate that much of the drop in identification as an environmentalist occurred from the mid-1990s through 2000, with smaller declines since then. The Democratic-Republican gap in identification as an environmentalist did not become large until the late 1990s, suggesting politicization may account for more of the recent change but other factors drove the initial declines in the mid-1990s.

The key trend, however, is whether Americans' concern for and commitment to the environment has declined compared with a generation ago, when three-quarters of Americans described themselves as environmentalists. There is some evidence to suggest that it has, with fewer Americans today than in the late 1980s and early 1990s giving "pro-environment" responses to a variety of Gallup questions. But the declines are not evident on all items asked in the two time periods, and on those for which concern has declined, the changes are much less dramatic than for the drop in identification as environmentalists.

Thus, while dwindling identification of the public as environmentalists may not be a welcome development for supporters of the environmental movement, it may not reflect a substantial weakening of the movement and its ability to achieve its objectives.

Historical data are available in Gallup Analytics.

Survey Methods

Results for this Gallup poll are based on telephone interviews conducted March 2-6, 2016, with a random sample of 1,019 adults, aged 18 and older, living in all 50 U.S. states and the District of Columbia. For results based on the total sample of national adults, the margin of sampling error is ±4 percentage points at the 95% confidence level. All reported margins of sampling error include computed design effects for weighting.

Learn more about how the Gallup Poll Social Series works.

April 25, 2016

OBAMA RETAINS STRONG EDGE OVER CONGRESS IN JOB APPROVAL

by Lydia Saad

Story Highlights

- *Obama holds 34-percentage-point edge over Congress thus far in 2016*
- *Only George H.W. Bush enjoyed similar edge over Congress*
- *Obama approval remarkably high relative to U.S. satisfaction*

PRINCETON, N.J. – With President Barack Obama's job approval rating up nearly three percentage points in the first quarter, he continues to maintain a wide lead in approval over the popularity-challenged U.S. Congress. In fact, if maintained, the 34-percentage-point gap between Obama's 49% average job approval rating thus far in 2016 and the 15% average approval rating for Congress would be the widest of Obama's presidency, and one of the largest Gallup has measured since 1981.

*Presidential Job Approval vs. Congress Approval -- Annual Averages^*

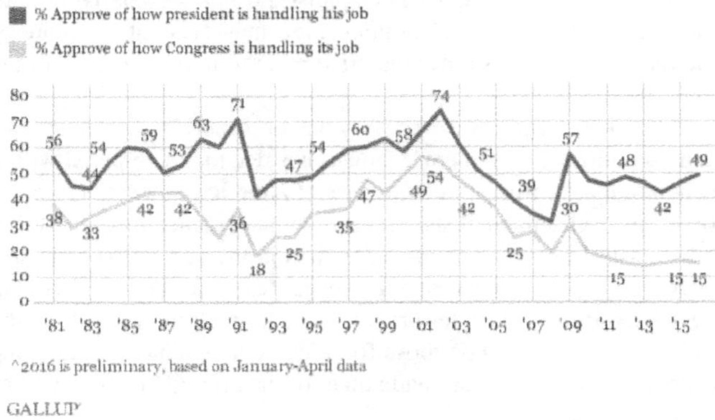

*Presidential Job Approval vs. U.S. Satisfaction -- Annual Averages^*

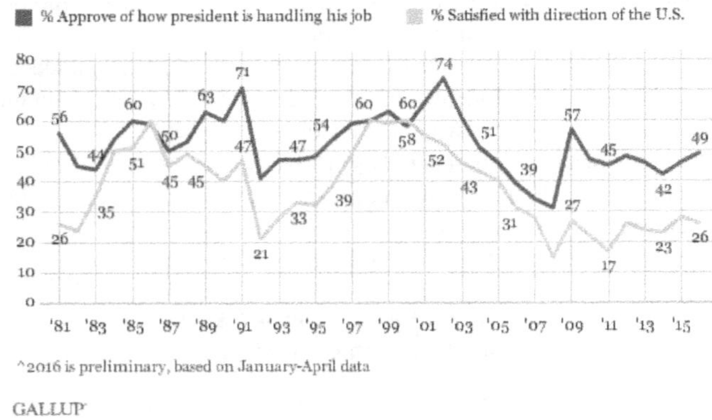

Congress approval was on the historically low side when Obama took office in 2009, related mainly to the troubled economy at the time. However, since then, his yearly job approval averages have managed to stay in the 40s while Congress' ratings have sunk to record-low levels. As a result, the gap between the two has averaged 30 points over the course of Obama's presidency and has not fallen below 27 points in any calendar year.

Obama's popularity edge over Congress is far from typical for recent presidents. George W. Bush's approval rating averaged 12 points higher than congressional approval across his two terms in office, from 2001 to 2008. Bill Clinton held an 18-point advantage over Congress in job approval from 1993 to 2000, while Ronald Reagan held a 13-point lead between 1981 and 1988 (with no congressional ratings in 1984 and 1985).

Only George H.W. Bush matches Obama in outperforming Congress in public approval, according to Gallup polling between 1990 and 1992. However, that is partly a reflection of Bush's extraordinarily high ratings stemming from the first Iraq War in the second and third years of his term, as well as image problems for Congress stemming from the "Keating Five" and the House banking scandal.

Obama Also Soars Above U.S. Satisfaction

Since the start of his presidency, Obama's average job approval rating has also been running substantially higher than Americans' average level of satisfaction with the nation, ranging from 18 to 30 points higher each year. Thus far in 2016, the gap between Obama's approval rating (49%) and public satisfaction with the direction of the country (26%) is a healthy 23 points. That compares with an average 12-point premium for George W. Bush and 10-point approval leads for Clinton and Reagan.

The only other president who consistently logged much higher job approval ratings than the prevailing level of U.S. satisfaction was George H.W. Bush. However, even his average 21-point job approval premium falls short of Obama's.

Bottom Line

Obama entered office with a significant advantage in popularity over Congress. But that gap has persisted long past his honeymoon period and could well emerge as one of the defining features of his presidency. However, it's not just Congress' low ratings that account for Obama's relatively high approval. He also receives higher approval than one would expect given Americans' low satisfaction with the direction of the country.

Obama's ability to outperform both congressional job approval and public satisfaction with the U.S. may be related to his personal popularity. Most recently, Gallup found 53% of Americans viewing him favorably. However, Obama's favorable rating is not unusually high relative to his job approval, at least compared with past presidents. The more important factor could be the extraordinarily high job approval he receives from Democrats, reflecting the strong political polarization in the country. This gives Obama a solid "floor" that keeps his job approval from falling too low, even while just 10% of Republicans approve. And that contrasts sharply with congressional ratings, which are poor among both parties, ensuring that the overall ratings for Congress remain low.

Historical data are available in Gallup Analytics.

Survey Methods

Obama's job approval ratings reviewed in this article are based on annual aggregates of data from the Gallup U.S. Daily tracking survey. The aggregates include roughly 150,000 interviews each year with a random sample of adults, aged 18 and older, living in all 50 U.S. states and the District of Columbia, interviewed by landline and cellular telephone. For annual results based on the total sample of national adults, the margin of sampling error is ±1 percentage point at the 95% confidence level. All reported margins of sampling error include computed design effects for weighting.

Congressional approval and U.S. satisfaction results are based on combined data from Gallup's monthly Gallup Poll Social Series surveys. These aggregates generally include at least 12,000 interviews each year with a random sample of adults, aged 18 and older, living in all 50 U.S. states and the District of Columbia, interviewed by landline and cellular telephone. For annual results based on the total sample of national adults, the margin of sampling error is ±1 percentage point at the 95% confidence level. All reported margins of sampling error include computed design effects for weighting.

April 25, 2016

NEARLY TWO-THIRDS OF AMERICANS PREFER SAVING TO SPENDING

by Jim Norman

Story Highlights

- *Preference for saving versus spending continues to climb*
- *Pre-financial crisis age differences have disappeared*
- *More say they are spending less than say they are spending more*

WASHINGTON, D.C. – Nearly two in three Americans now say they enjoy saving money more than spending it, further establishing the pro-savings trend that developed in the wake of the 2008 financial crisis. With 33% now saying they prefer spending, the gap between those who prefer saving and those who prefer spending is at its widest since Gallup first asked the question in 2001.

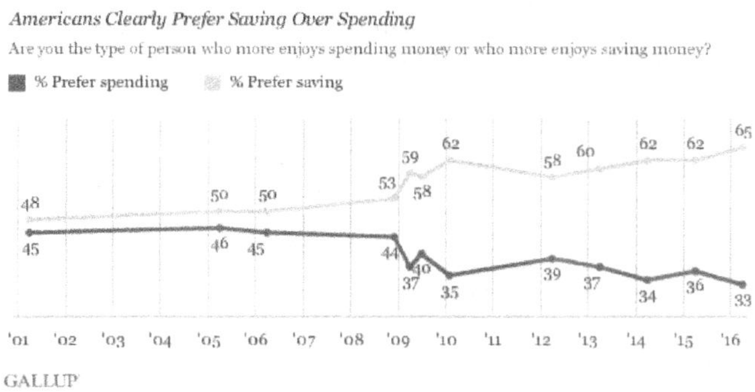

In three Gallup polls before the 2008 crisis, an average of 49% of U.S. adults said they preferred saving. The average has jumped to 60% in nine polls since then. The highest percentage yet measured (65%) is the most recent – from the April 6-10 Gallup Economy and Personal Finance poll.

The question does not measure actual spending and saving. Instead, it gives insight into what Americans would prefer to do – save or spend. In fact, those with the lowest incomes are generally more likely than those with the highest incomes to say they get greater enjoyment from saving.

Age Differences Disappear in Recent Years

A look at combined results for the three pre-crisis polls and the three most recent polls reveals the extent to which people in different age groups have changed their attitudes about saving and spending. Before the crisis, a slight majority of those younger than 30 favored spending; those aged 30 to 49 were split; those aged 50 to 64 slightly favored saving; and those aged 65 and older were clearly the most likely to prefer saving.

As the percentage preferring saving increased significantly in recent years, most of the movement in this direction occurred among the three younger age groups. The net result is that once-obvious differences among age groups before the crisis have now almost disappeared.

Major Differences Pre-Crisis, Few Differences Post-Crisis, by Age

Are you the type of person who more enjoys spending money or who more enjoys saving money?

	2001-2006%	2014-2016%
18 to 29		
Prefer spending	54	33
Prefer saving	43	66
30 to 49		
Prefer spending	50	38
Prefer saving	47	61
50 to 64		
Prefer spending	43	34
Prefer saving	51	64
65 and older		
Prefer spending	33	34
Prefer saving	58	62

Combined Gallup polls, 2001/2005/2006 and 2014/2015/2016

As Personal Finances Improve, So Does Appeal of Saving

The appeal of saving over spending shows some signs of being the new normal rather than a temporary reaction to the hard times after 2008. In April 2006, 51% of Americans thought their financial situation was good or excellent, but by April 2010, the percentage had dropped to 41%. During roughly the same period, with unemployment reaching as high as 10% and wages stagnant, the appeal of saving over spending grew from 50% to 62%.

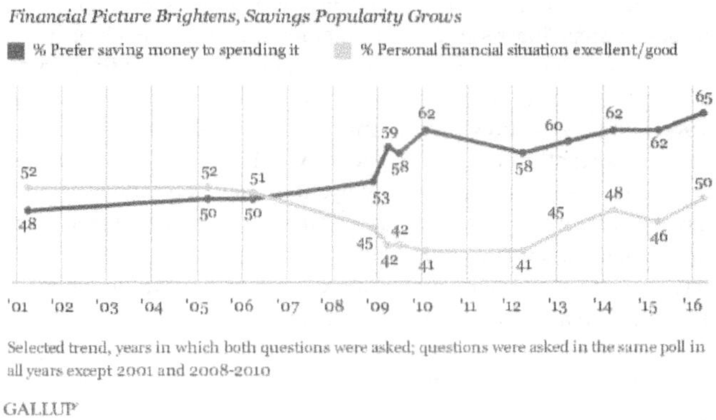

But even as the percentage of Americans considering their financial situation excellent or good has rebounded in the past few years, Americans have not moved back toward enjoying spending more. In Gallup's current poll, the 50% who say their financial situation is good or excellent is the highest since 2007, and the 33% who prefer spending is an all-time low.

Once Again, Americans More Likely to Say They Are Spending Less

The April Economy and Personal Finance survey also asks Americans directly if they have been spending more or spending less "in recent months." Each of the nine times since 2009 that Gallup has polled on the subject, Americans have been more likely to say they have been spending less in recent months than to say they have been spending more. The current poll is no exception – 38% say they are spending less and 28% spending more, with the rest saying their spending has not changed.

The gap between "spending less" and "spending more" has narrowed considerably since the question was asked in 2009 and 2010, when the U.S. struggled to emerge from the recession and half or more of Americans reported spending less. Today's 38% who report spending less in recent months is similar to the previous two years.

The poll also shows those who are spending more tend to think this is temporary, while those who are spending less are more likely to think it will be permanent – further supporting the conclusion that Americans are settling into a mode in which they are mentally focused on being thrifty. That has been the case in every poll since the questions were first asked in 2009. In the current poll:

- Seventeen percent of Americans say they are spending more and that the change is temporary; 11% say they are spending more and that it will become a new, normal pattern.
- Twenty-nine percent say they are spending less, and that the change will become a new, normal pattern; 9% say they are temporarily spending less.

Bottom Line

Some economists are expressing concern that Americans aren't spending enough to keep the U.S. economy growing at a healthy pace, even as savings rates remain well below historical levels.

The new reality, however, is that Americans are considerably more likely than they were in the easy-credit years preceding 2008 to perceive saving money as more enjoyable than spending it. And their actions have, at least to some extent, mirrored their attitudes. Saving rates that had dropped from the double-digit levels of the 1960s and 1970s down to an abysmal 1.9% rate in July 2005 are now consistently close to or above 5%. Even as Americans have seen their own finances improving, they have continued to value saving over spending. The question now becomes whether the apparent changes in attitude will affect savings rates more than they have to date – and what effect this will, in turn, have on the vitally important retail sector of the U.S. economy.

Survey Methods

Results for this Gallup poll are based on telephone interviews conducted April 6-10, 2016, with a random sample of 1,015 adults, aged 18 and older, living in all 50 U.S. states and the District of Columbia. For results based on the total sample of national adults, the margin of sampling error is ±4 percentage points at the 95% confidence level.

April 27, 2016

HEALTHCARE COSTS TOP U.S. FAMILIES' FINANCIAL CONCERNS

by Zac Auter

Story Highlights

- *15% of Americans say healthcare costs are family's top financial concern*
- *Those without money to live comfortably concerned with immediate living costs*
- *About one in 10 Americans say their family faces no financial problems*

WASHINGTON, D.C. – Fifteen percent of Americans cite healthcare costs as the most important financial problem facing their family. In addition to healthcare costs, Americans also point to low wages, debt, college expenses and housing costs as pressing financial concerns for their family. About one in 10 Americans say their family faces no financial problems.

Most Important Financial Problems Facing American Families

	U.S. adults %	Have enough money to live comfortably %	Do not have enough money to live comfortably %
Healthcare costs	15	15	11
Lack of money/ Low wages	13	6	17
Not enough money to pay debts	9	7	11
College expenses	9	9	6
Costs of owning/ renting a home	8	6	10
High cost of living/ Inflation	7	8	5
Unemployment/ Loss of job	6	5	8
Taxes	5	6	3
Retirement savings	5	7	1
Lack of savings	3	3	2
Social Security	2	2	2
State of the economy	1	1	2
Controlling spending	1	1	1
Energy costs/Oil and gas prices	1	1	1
Interest rates	1	1	0
Stock market/ Investments	1	1	0
None	11	13	4
Other	4	4	3

April 6-10, 2016
Gallup Poll

These results are from Gallup's annual Economy and Personal Finance poll, conducted April 6-10 this year.

While healthcare costs top the list of family financial concerns among Americans overall, the problems that Americans cite as most important differ between those with and without enough money to live comfortably. Thirteen percent of those with enough money to live comfortably say they have no important financial problems, compared with 4% among those who do not have enough to live comfortably.

Long-Term Saving Concerns Top List for Those Living Comfortably

Americans who say they have enough money to live comfortably are more likely to cite long-term saving concerns such as retirement savings and college expenses as their most pressing financial problem. Meanwhile, those without enough money to live comfortably express greater concern about more immediate financial problems, including low wages, debt payments and housing costs.

Among those living comfortably on their current income, for example, 7% mention retirement savings and 9% cite college expenses as their family's most pressing financial problem. These Americans tend to be older, more educated and wealthier: 74% of those aged 65 and older, 80% of college graduates and 88% of those living in households earning $75,000 or more per year report having enough money to live comfortably.

Financial Means to Live Comfortably – by Income, Education and Age

	Have enough money to live comfortably %	Do not have enough money to live comfortably %
Income		
Less than $30,000	36	64
$30,000 to less than $75,000	67	33
$75,000 or more	88	12
Education		
Graduated college	80	19
Did not graduate college	61	39
Age		
18 to 29	65	34
30 to 49	63	37
50 to 64	65	35
65+	74	25

April 6-10, 2016
Gallup Poll

Alternatively, those not living comfortably on their current income are more likely to point to immediate financial concerns about low wages (17%), debt payments (11%) and housing costs (10%). Compared with those who have the financial means to live comfortably, these Americans have less income and less education. Sixty-four percent of Americans earning less than $30,000 in annual household income and 39% of those without a college degree say they do not have enough money to live comfortably.

Bottom Line

These financial problems facing U.S. families parallel Americans' unease about the economy more broadly. In the past three months, Americans have consistently cited the economy as the most important issue facing the country. However, the contrasting nature of these concerns points to a much different reality for those without the financial means to live comfortably. Americans living in financial comfort emphasize concerns about meeting long-term financial goals, while those without enough money to live comfortably must instead sacrifice future financial goals to meet the immediate costs of living.

Historical data are available in Gallup Analytics.

Survey Methods

Results for this Gallup poll are based on telephone interviews conducted April 6-10, 2016, on the Gallup U.S. Daily survey, with a random sample of 1,015 adults, aged 18 and older, living in all 50 U.S. states and the District of Columbia. For results based on the total sample of national adults, the margin of sampling error is ±4 percentage points at the 95% confidence level. All reported margins of sampling error include computed design effects for weighting.

April 27, 2016

U.S. RENTERS WORRY MORE THAN HOMEOWNERS ABOUT HOUSING COSTS

by Jeffrey M. Jones

Story Highlights

- *49% of renters and 25% of homeowners worry about paying for housing*
- *More renters than homeowners worry at all income levels*
- *Gap in owner-renter worry growing for the middle- and upper-income*

PRINCETON, N.J. – Americans who rent their home are nearly twice as likely as those who own their home to say they worry about not being able to pay their housing costs. While upper-income Americans are more likely to own and lower-income Americans are more likely to rent, renters worry more than homeowners at all income levels.

Worry About Not Being Able to Pay Rent, Mortgage or Other Housing Costs, Homeowners vs. Renters

% "Very" or "moderately worried"

	Renters %	Homeowners %	Difference (pct. pts.)
National adults	49	25	24
Annual household income			
Less than $30,000	63	47	16
$30,000 to $74,999	42	27	15
$75,000 or more	29	15	14

2013-2016 Gallup Economy and Personal Finance Surveys

These results are based on more than 5,000 combined interviews from Gallup's 2013-2016 Economy and Personal Finance surveys, including 3,606 homeowners and 1,294 renters.

Overall, during this time, 33% of Americans said they were very (15%) or moderately (18%) worried about not being able to pay their "rent, mortgage or other housing costs."

As would be expected, lower-income Americans are more likely than upper-income Americans to worry about meeting their housing costs, and income is a stronger predictor of worry than homeownership status. For example, lower-income homeowners (47%) are more likely to worry about not being able to pay their housing obligations than are middle- or upper-income renters (42% and 29%, respectively). But at every income level, there is a roughly 15-percentage-point gap in worry between homeowners and renters.

Homeowners, regardless of income, may worry less than renters because they likely have more stable housing payments. Their principal and interest payments on a mortgage would be fixed in most cases, with only minor year-to-year increases in property taxes and insurance. Renters, on the other hand, probably could expect more significant year-to-year rent increases.

Also, rental payments for a given renter would mostly reflect current real estate market conditions, whereas mortgage payments for a given homeowner would mostly reflect home values at the time the home was purchased, which could be well below current home values in the area.

Finally, other financial considerations beyond household income may lead people to rent rather than own a home and to be more worried about their finances in general. These could include concerns about job security, high levels of personal debt or insufficient savings to come up with a down payment on a house.

Worry Gap for Middle- and Upper-Income Americans Widens

Gallup has consistently found that renters are more worried than homeowners about making housing payments, both overall and by household income level, in the 16 years it has conducted the Economy and Personal Finance survey. But the gap in homeowner-renter worry has increased among both middle- and upper-income owners compared with the past.

Homeowners and renters at all income levels became increasingly worried about paying housing costs from 2008 through 2012, during the recession and immediate post-recession years, compared with the 2001 through 2007 housing boom. In recent years, middle- and upper-income homeowners' worry has eased. But middle-income renters are only slightly less worried, and upper-income renters have become more likely to worry.

Trend in Worry About Not Being Able to Pay Rent, Mortgage or Other Housing Costs, Homeowners vs. Renters, by Annual Household Income

% "Very" or "moderately worried"

	Renters %	Homeowners %	Difference (pct. pts.)
Less than $30,000			
2001-2007	47	32	15
2008-2012	66	48	18
2013-2016	63	47	16
$30,000 to $74,999			
2001-2007	32	23	9
2008-2012	45	33	12
2013-2016	42	27	15
$75,000 or more			
2001-2007	16	11	5
2008-2012	25	20	5
2013-2016	29	15	14

Gallup

Those trends likely follow rent costs, which have consistently increased in recent years, particularly in higher-priced markets. There are some indications these gains may be leveling off as rental supply is now catching up to, or exceeding, rental demand.

Implications

The bursting of the housing bubble helped push the economy into recession and drove Americans' homeownership rate down to 62% from 73% in 2005-2007, according to Gallup's data. That decline is a result of multiple factors, including many former homeowners losing their homes to foreclosure and tighter lending requirements for getting new mortgages. Also, potential home buyers may not be as confident that homes will hold their value after seeing prices plummet in recent years. Finally, many within the growing retiree population may be choosing to sell their homes and rent, while young adults living on their own for the first time may look to live in cities or other areas where renting is more feasible than owning.

The declining percentage of homeowners and the increasing percentage of renters in the U.S. adult population help explain why Americans today are significantly more worried about being able to pay their housing costs than they were in the past. From 2001 through 2007, before the housing market crashed, an average 24% of Americans worried about paying their housing costs. Since then, an average of 35% have. Although Americans' worry about a variety of financial matters is up since 2007, worries about making housing payments are up the most.

In an era when most Americans are seeing slow wage growth, more are renting than in the past and rental costs have been rising significantly, it is understandable that an increasing percentage of Americans are worried about meeting one of their most basic financial obligations.

Historical data are available in Gallup Analytics.

Survey Methods

Results for this Gallup poll are based on combined telephone interviews conducted from Gallup's April 2013 to 2016 Economy and Personal Finance surveys, with a random sample of 5,073 adults, aged 18 and older, living in all 50 U.S. states and the District of Columbia. For results based on the total sample of national adults, the margin of sampling error is ±2 percentage points at the 95% confidence level.

For results based on the total sample of 3,606 homeowners, the margin of sampling error is ±2 percentage points at the 95% confidence level.

For results based on the total sample of 1,294 renters, the margin of sampling error is ±3 percentage points at the 95% confidence level.

All reported margins of sampling error include computed design effects for weighting.

April 28, 2016
AMERICANS SPLIT ON IDEA OF WITHDRAWING FROM TRADE TREATIES

by Frank Newport

Story Highlights

- *28% of Americans favor U.S. withdrawal from free trade treaties*
- *The same percentage are opposed, with 43% having no opinion*
- *Half favor stricter import duties on Chinese goods*

PRINCETON, N.J. – More than four in 10 Americans say they don't know enough to say whether the U.S. should end its participation in free trade deals such as the North American Free Trade Agreement (NAFTA) and the Trans-Pacific Partnership (TPP). Among Americans who do have an opinion, 28% favor withdrawing from trade treaties, and the same percentage oppose it.

"Next, I'm going to read several proposals recently made by candidates running for president. For each proposal, please tell me if you agree or disagree with the proposal, or if you don't know enough about it to have an opinion. … End U.S. participation in free trade deals, such as NAFTA and the Trans-Pacific Trade Agreement"

	Agree %	Disagree%	Don't know enough to say%
Apr 21-24, 2016	28	28	43

Gallup U.S. Daily

Gallup measured this proposal as part of a series of tests of how Americans react to ideas that presidential candidates have enunciated this year. Several candidates – particularly Donald Trump and Bernie Sanders – have campaigned on ending these trade agreements. The 28% agreement ranks this issue near the bottom of the list of more than 50 proposals tested, partly reflecting the higher percentage who don't have an opinion, but also a result of the split opinion.

Trump believes that trade agreements have been poorly negotiated, saying the TPP is "one of the worst trade deals" and "I would rather not have it," and calling NAFTA a "total disaster." Sanders has railed against NAFTA and the TPP, arguing that these have a severely negative effect on the U.S. job market. Sanders says the TPP "must be defeated" and that NAFTA "has led to the loss of nearly 700,000 jobs."

Last fall, Gallup measured reaction to the proposed idea in a different form, asking Americans how effective withdrawing from the free trade treaties would be in improving the U.S. economy. Sixteen percent of Americans in the Sept. 23-27 survey said that removing the U.S. from "the 12-country free trade agreement known as the Trans-Pacific Partnership" would be very effective in improving the economy. Eighteen percent said the same about ending U.S. participation in free trade deals "such as the North American Free Trade Agreement, or NAFTA, or the Central America Free Trade Agreement, or CAFTA." The scores placed these proposals near the bottom of the list of a large number of economic proposals tested, rank-ordered based on perceived effectiveness.

These questions on the trade pacts provide information on how Americans react to the basic idea of the U.S. getting out of the trade treaties, based on how the candidates might phrase the proposal on the campaign trail or in interviews.

A long-standing Gallup trend question provides broader context to Americans' opinions on trade. The question contrasts the idea that free trade agreements provide more of an economic opportunity because of exports, with the idea that free trade constitutes an economic threat because of imports.

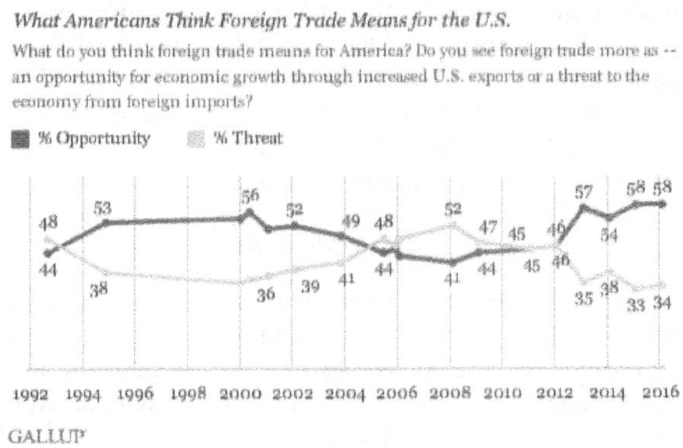

Americans' responses have varied since the question was first asked in the early 1990s. But over the past four years, a majority of Americans have consistently viewed trade as an economic opportunity rather than a threat – including 58% to 34% in February of this year. Thus, while many Americans don't have an opinion on the issue of withdrawing from specific trade agreements (and those with an opinion are split), they are positive on the overall concept of free trade as an economic plus rather than as a negative.

That more than four in 10 Americans say they don't know enough about the free trade pacts to have an opinion suggests that the public's opinions are rather weakly held, and that Americans may not be highly conversant with the details of specific trade deals. As a result, poll questions that mention that allowing more imports might cost jobs produce higher levels of support.

A separate policy proposal that Gallup tested in March asked Americans about the idea of imposing "higher import taxes on Chinese products coming into the U.S." Fifty percent of Americans agreed, 22% disagreed, and 27% said they didn't know enough to have an opinion. This question didn't remind respondents that products might cost more if they are subject to increased import duties, or that there might have to be a quid pro quo increase in tariffs on exported goods if this were to take place. But the results highlight that public support for specific trade-related policies can be greater than agreement with the broad idea of trade as a threat, or support for withdrawing completely from free trade treaties.

Implications

Trade policies, like most issues, may be highly important to highly specific segments of the population. As such, candidates' positions on trade could affect the presidential election outcome in certain states or areas within states. Recent academic research, for example, has shown that Americans living in areas disproportionately affected by trade competition are more likely than others to either vote more strongly left or more strongly right, suggesting that trade policies can, in fact, affect political behavior. Candidates also may find it useful to bring up trade as a campaign issue because it gives them a specific "enemy" to blame for economic woes and provides an easy explanation for the loss of manufacturing jobs.

But, trade is not top-of-mind to Americans when they are asked to name the most important problem facing the country or the most important priorities for the next president. Less than 1% mention trade in response to either of these open-ended questions, although trade may be a factor driving the concerns that *are* verbalized – the economy and jobs in particular.

More generally, Americans continue to say that trade is more of an economic opportunity than a threat to the nation. And, while many don't have a position on the proposal to withdraw U.S. participation from free trade treaties, those who do are split, and there is little indication that the public believes such actions would be highly effective in improving the U.S. economy.

Historical data are available in Gallup Analytics.

Survey Methods

Results for this Gallup poll are based on telephone interviews conducted April 21-24, 2016, on the Gallup U.S. Daily survey, with a random sample of 551 adults, aged 18 and older, living in all 50 U.S. states and the District of Columbia. For results based on the total sample of national adults, the margin of sampling error is ±5 percentage points at the 95% confidence level. All reported margins of sampling error include computed design effects for weighting.

April 28, 2016
AMERICANS' FINANCIAL WORRIES EDGE UP IN 2016

by Justin McCarthy

Story Highlights

- *Worries slightly higher in all seven financial issues measured*
- *Not having enough money for retirement still top concern (64%)*
- *Six in 10 worry about unexpected medical costs*

WASHINGTON, D.C. – Americans express slightly greater worries than they did last year about seven financial issues, with significant increases in concern about being able to pay medical costs in the event of a serious illness or accident and being able to maintain their standard of living. Americans continue to be most worried about not having enough money for retirement, with 64% saying they are "very worried" or "moderately worried" about this.

Americans' Specific Financial Worries, 2015 vs. 2016

Please tell me how concerned you are right now about each of the following financial matters, based on your current financial situation – are you very worried, moderately worried, not too worried or not worried at all?

	2015%	2016%	Change (pct. pts.)
Not being able to pay medical costs of a serious illness/ accident	55	60	+5
Not being able to maintain the standard of living you enjoy	46	51	+5
Not having enough to pay your normal monthly bills	36	41	+5
Not having enough money for retirement	60	64	+4
Not being able to pay medical costs for normal healthcare	42	45	+3
Not being able to pay your rent, mortgage or other housing costs	32	34	+2
Not being able to make the minimum payments on your credit cards	20	21	+1

April 6-10, 2016

Gallup has asked Americans how concerned they are about all seven financial issues each April since 2001 as part of the annual economically focused survey. These data come from Gallup's April 6-10 Economy and Personal Finance survey.

Worries about not having enough money for retirement increased four percentage points and edge out not being able to pay for serious medical costs as the No. 1 worry. Now a majority, 51%, also worry about maintaining their standard of living.

Nearly half of Americans report being concerned about not being able to pay medical costs for their normal healthcare (45%), while about one in three worry about not being able to pay their rent, mortgage or other housing costs (34%). Americans are least concerned about not being able to make minimum payments on their credit cards (21%), though like all of the issues measured, this is up from the prior year.

Additionally, 37% of Americans report being worried about not having enough money to pay for their children's college, which is consistent with the range of 34% to 43% who have reported such worries since Gallup first asked this question in 2007.

Retirement, Unexpected Medical Costs Have Consistently Been Greatest Concerns

Since Gallup began polling Americans in 2001 about their financial concerns, a majority have continually been worried about not being able to afford retirement – the top overall concern in each of those 16 years. Americans were less likely to worry about retirement in the early 2000s, with percentages ranging from 52% to 54%, but 60% or more have worried about retirement since 2005, including a peak of 67% in 2012.

Serious medical costs, meanwhile, have consistently ranked as the second-most-expressed concern since 2001, with majorities in all but one poll in the past decade who said they were worried about the costs. The level of worry about serious medical costs peaked in 2012, at 62%. Prior to 2005, a smaller 45% to 50% of Americans expressed such concern.

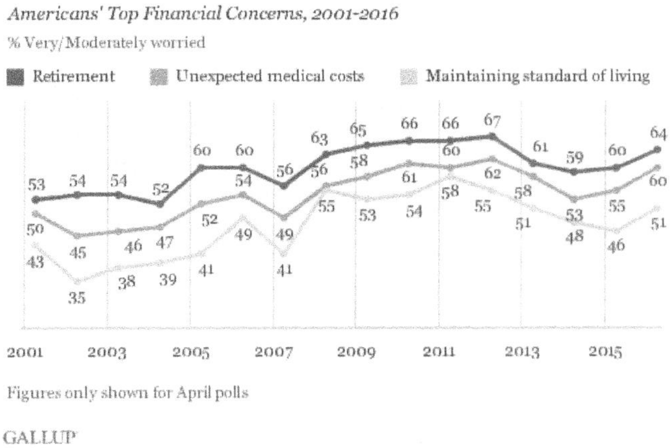

While less than half of Americans indicated concern about their ability to maintain their standard of living from 2001 to 2007, this became a majority concern by 2008 – peaking at 58% in 2011. Concern about maintaining one's current standard of living subsided gradually each year after 2011, settling at 46% in 2015 before climbing yet again this year to 51%.

Bottom Line

Americans' elevated concerns about various future or potential costs are in sync with their lower confidence in the U.S. economy now than a year ago and the fact that their spending has not changed over the prior year.

Americans' retirement funding remains atop their lists of concerns, with majorities also skeptical of their ability to pay for treatment of serious medical issues and worried their standard of living will deteriorate in the future. Despite some signs of gains for the economy, average Americans aren't feeling them – and are a bit more concerned than they have been in recent years.

Historical data are available in Gallup Analytics.

Survey Methods

Results for this Gallup poll are based on telephone interviews conducted April 6-10, 2016, on the Gallup U.S. Daily survey, with a random sample of 1,015 adults, aged 18 and older, living in all 50 U.S. states and the District of Columbia. For results based on the total sample of national adults, the margin of sampling error is ±4 percentage points at the 95% confidence level. All reported margins of sampling error include computed design effects for weighting.

April 29, 2016

MOST U.S. RETIREES LIVING WELL, BUT NONRETIREES UNCONVINCED

by Jim Norman

Story Highlights

- *48% expect to live comfortably in retirement*
- *74% of U.S. retirees say they are living comfortably*
- *Many affluent Americans expect to take a retirement hit*

WASHINGTON, D.C. – Almost half of Americans (47%) who are not retired think that when they do retire, they won't have enough money to live comfortably. And about the same number (48%) expect they will have enough. Those who have already made the move to retirement, however, tell a different story: 74% say they have enough money to live comfortably.

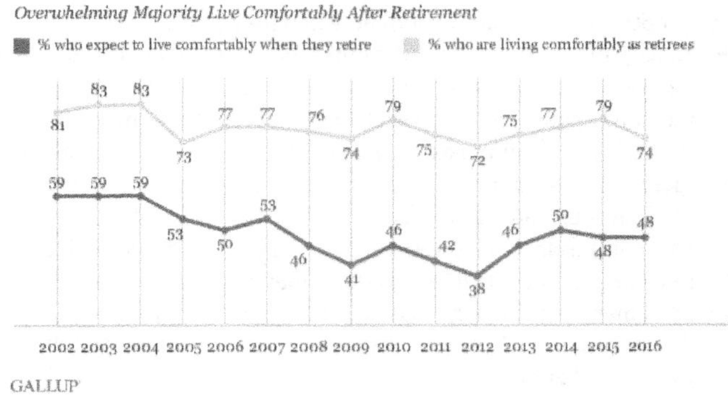

The gap between the percentage of U.S. nonretirees who think they will live comfortably once they retire and the percentage of retirees who actually are living comfortably is not a new phenomenon; it has existed since Gallup first asked both questions in 2002. The gap was widest in the economically tumultuous years from 2008 to 2012 – a period when plummeting property and stock values caused many still in the workforce to grow pessimistic about their long-term financial prospects.

The combination of falling house prices and the financial crisis affected some of the key income sources many Americans count on for retirement. In an April 2007 Gallup poll, 24% listed stocks as an expected major source when they retired; 30% listed equity in their homes; and 52% named 401(k), individual retirement account (IRA), Keogh or other retirement savings accounts. As each of these potential sources shrank in value for many Americans, optimism about living comfortably in retirement fell from 53% in 2007 to 41% in 2009 and bottomed out in 2012 at 38%.

Among those closest to retirement during the 2008-2012 period, those aged 50 to 64, only 35% said they expected to retire to a comfortable lifestyle. The percentage has not risen much among those aged 50 to 64 in the past four years, averaging 41%.

However, in combined polls from 2014 to 2016, three in four (75%) younger retirees – those aged 61 to 70 and therefore most likely to have retired since 2008 – say they are living comfortably. The percentage is only a few points lower than the 79% of older retirees who say they are living comfortably. These findings suggest that fears of being short of money among those looking retirement directly in the face are generally not borne out once they actually retire.

Largest Gap Occurs Among Most Affluent, Those Closest to Retirement

Combining the data from the three 2014-2016 Gallup Economy and Personal Finance polls allows a look at how income and age potentially affect optimism about living comfortably in retirement.

- Among younger adults, attitudes about current living situations come close to matching what they expect when they retire in the distant future. But at all other age levels, there is a pronounced gap. Sixty-three percent of those younger than age 30 say they are living comfortably now, and 58% expect to live comfortably when retired. The percentage expecting a comfortable retirement drops significantly among nonretirees aged 30 and older, while the percentage currently living comfortably stays at about the same level or increases. Among those between the ages of 60 and 69 who have not yet retired, 68% say they are living comfortably, but 50% expect that to continue when they retire.

- Nearly one in three (32%) nonretirees with annual household incomes below $30,000 say they are living comfortably now, and the same percentage expect to live comfortably in retirement. A clear divide emerges between the two measures as income increases, and among those earning $75,000 or more, 90% say they are currently living comfortably, but only 64% expect to live comfortably once retired. Those in the $75,000-and-above bracket are twice as likely to think they will live comfortably in retirement as those who earn less than $30,000, but they are also far more likely to expect that they will lose their comfortable lifestyle when they retire.

Retirement Optimism Gap Grows With Age, Affluence

	Living comfortably now%	Expect to live comfortably in retirement%	Differencepct. pts.
Age			
18-29	63	58	5
30-39	65	46	19
40-49	70	46	24
50-59	60	42	18
60-69	68	50	18
Annual Income			
Less than $30,000	32	32	0
$30,000-$49,999	59	43	16
$50,000-$74,999	70	47	23
$75,000 and above	90	64	26

2014, 2015 and 2016 Gallup polls of 1,034 nonretirees

Bottom Line

Americans have had concerns about the affordability of retirement for decades. A 1989 Gallup poll found that 74% of workers aged 30 or older worried they would not have enough money to live comfortably when they retired. More recently, workers have been given plenty of reasons to worry. The housing market collapse of 2007-2012 eroded the value of homes, and the financial crisis in 2008 made major inroads on savings heavily invested in the market. Politicians and pundits have sounded warnings about the solvency of Social Security, and articles describing long-term financial dangers facing retirees have proliferated.

This atmosphere has created retirement worries that reach far beyond those Americans facing serious financial difficulties. In Gallup's three most recent polls, 25% of nonretirees earning $100,000 or more annually do not expect to live comfortably when they retire. In those same three polls, more than half (58%) of nonretirees who are living comfortably now worry about having enough money for retirement. Even among those who are retired and living comfortably, 31% worry that it won't last.

The experience of recent retirees, most of whom report that they are living comfortably, provides some evidence that fears of retirement woes have been overblown. But complicating factors – including people living longer, the drying up of pension funds and the low levels of savings among Americans in recent years – seem to guarantee that no clear answers will be known for years to come.

Survey Methods

Results for this Gallup poll are based on telephone interviews conducted April 6-10, 2016, with a random sample of 1,015 adults, aged 18 and older, living in all 50 U.S. states and the District of Columbia. For results based on the total sample of national adults, the margin of sampling error is ±4 percentage points at the 95% confidence level.

May 02, 2016

AMERICANS BUY FREE PRE-K; SPLIT ON TUITION-FREE COLLEGE

by Lydia Saad

Story Highlights

- *Six in 10 Americans agree with making child care, pre-K free for all*
- *Americans divided on proposal to eliminate public college tuition*
- *Tuition proposal sparks different reactions by age, political party*

PRINCETON, N.J. – By more than 2-to-1 (59% vs. 26%), U.S. adults agree with the idea of providing free child care and pre-kindergarten programs for all Americans. They are divided, however, about eliminating tuition at public colleges and universities.

Americans' Support for Democrats' Education Policy Proposals

	Agree %	Disagree %	No opinion %
Enact free universal child care and pre-kindergarten programs for all children	59	26	16
Make tuition free at all public colleges and universities throughout America	47	45	9

April 21-24, 2016
Gallup

Vermont Sen. Bernie Sanders has strongly advanced these education proposals in his struggling bid for the Democratic presidential nomination, while Hillary Clinton says she would increase federal funding for free daycare and tuition assistance programs. Both candidates argue that government investments in early and higher education will pay the country big dividends in creating a better-educated, more economically secure workforce.

Americans' initial reaction to providing free early childhood education is positive, with the majority agreeing with this proposal. And while support is highest among women (65%), young adults (70%) and those living in lower-income households (69%), the demographic counterparts to these groups are also more likely to agree than disagree with the proposal.

The poll does find sharp differences on the basis of party identification: Just 36% of Republicans and independents who lean Republican favor it, compared with 81% of Democrats and independents who lean Democratic. However, even among Republicans and Republican leaners, less than half disagree outright with the proposal.

Support for Proposal to Enact Free Universal Child Care, Pre-K Programs

	Agree %	Disagree %	No opinion %
U.S. adults	59	26	16
Men	52	30	17
Women	65	21	14
18 to 34 years	70	12	18
35 to 54 years	62	24	14
55 years and older	49	36	15
Less than $36,000	69	13	18
$36,000 to $89,999	54	31	15
$90,000 or more	53	34	13
Republican/Lean Republican	36	46	18
Democratic/Lean Democratic	81	7	11

April 21-24, 2016
Gallup

Of course, government programs aren't free – everything has to be paid for through taxes or government debt that will eventually come due. And it is not clear whether Americans who favor these programs do so because they aren't thinking about the costs, because they assume "someone else" will pay them or because they believe the price in higher taxes is worth it.

A slightly different question Gallup tested on this topic nearly two years ago – using federal money to make sure quality pre-K is available to everyone who needs it – found 70% support. However, that slightly more positive response may reflect that the question did not offer the explicit "don't know enough to have an opinion" option that the current question does. Those without a well-formed opinion on the issue appear inclined to favor it.

Republicans and Associated Demographics Oppose Free Tuition

Free college tuition is the more controversial of the two proposals. While public opinion is evenly divided, Americans in different educational, age and party groups have opposing views. Majorities of 18- to 34-year-olds, those in lower-income households, those without a college degree and Democrats agree with the proposal. By contrast, majorities of those aged 55 and older, those earning $90,000 or more in annual household income, college graduates and Republicans oppose it.

The high level of young adults' support for free public college education – one of Sanders' signature themes – could partly explain their strong backing of the 74-year-old senator during the primaries.

Support for Proposal to Make College Tuition Free

	Agree %	Disagree %	No opinion %
U.S. adults	47	45	9
Men	48	45	6
Women	46	44	10
18 to 34 years	63	31	6
35 to 54 years	48	43	9
55 years and older	37	55	8
Less than $36,000	61	28	11
$36,000 to $89,999	48	46	6
$90,000 or more	42	54	4
Graduated from college	39	54	7
Did not graduate from college	52	39	9
Republican/Lean Republican	23	70	7
Democratic/Lean Democratic	67	28	5

April 21-24, 2016
Gallup

Gallup asked the early childhood and college tuition questions as part of an ongoing effort this election cycle to test Americans' reactions to specific policy proposals put forward by the various presidential candidates. As such, there is no attempt to explain the reasons for these programs or to balance the question with counter-arguments. The purpose is simply to measure the public's reaction to actual positions they might hear candidates promoting on the campaign trail.

Bottom Line

Both of the remaining Democratic candidates have proposed changes that would likely open up education to more Americans. Clinton's education proposals are intended to improve lower- and middle-income Americans' financial access to preschool and college. Sanders' would go further and make public education free for Americans, all the way from pre-K through college – essentially a major expansion of the K-12 public school system.

Clinton has amassed more delegates during this year's primaries and is widely expected to win the nomination. However, if Sanders follows through on his recent promise to take the battle to the convention and compete for superdelegates, Clinton may need to take bolder stances on some of Sanders' signature issues to help thwart that effort.

In terms of taking those positions into the general election, support for free child care and preschool would be an easier sell than free college tuition.

Survey Methods

Results for this Gallup poll are based on telephone interviews conducted April 21-24, 2016, on the Gallup U.S. Daily survey, with a random sample of 2,024 adults, aged 18 and older, living in all 50 U.S. states and the District of Columbia. Each respondent rated a randomly selected subset of five of the 18 proposals included in the survey. Each proposal was rated by between 533 and 590 national adults. Results for each proposal have a margin of error of ±5 percentage points at the 95% confidence level. All reported margins of sampling error include computed design effects for weighting.

May 03, 2016
ECONOMIC TURMOIL STIRS RETIREMENT PLANS OF YOUNG, OLD

by Jim Norman

Story Highlights

- *Younger nonretirees leaning more toward savings accounts for retirement*
- *Those aged 40 to 59 counting less on pensions, home equity*
- *Social Security, pensions still top money sources for retirees*

WASHINGTON, D.C. – Economic turmoil over the past eight years has reshaped the views of both older and younger American nonretirees on how they will pay for retirement – but in decidedly different ways. Those younger than 40 are more likely now than before 2008 to view savings and part-time work as major sources of retirement income, while nonretirees in their 40s and 50s are now less likely to say they will rely heavily on pensions and home equity.

Economic Turmoil Affects Retirement Plans

Percentage who say each of the following will be a major source of retirement income

	2002-2007 %	2013-2016 %	Change (pct. pts.)
Aged 18 to 39			
401(k), IRA, other retirement savings accounts	57	51	-6
Savings accounts, CDs	26	37	11
Pension plans	26	22	-4
Stocks, mutual funds	24	19	-5
Home equity	23	19	-4
Social Security	18	23	5
Part-time work	17	24	7
Aged 40 to 59			
401(k), IRA, other retirement savings accounts	48	46	-2
Savings accounts, CDs	12	15	3
Pension plans	34	26	-8
Stocks, mutual funds	19	19	0
Home equity	29	22	-7
Social Security	33	34	1
Part-time work	15	19	4

Combined results from Gallup surveys in 2002-2007 and 2013-2016

In the years leading up to the recession, a majority of U.S. nonretirees the furthest from retirement – those aged 18 to 39 – expected individual retirement accounts, or IRAs, and other 401(k)-type retirement savings accounts to be a major source of retirement funds. An average 57% in Gallup's annual Economy and Personal Finance polls from 2002 through 2007 predicted these accounts would be a primary foundation for them. At the same time, 26% said they expected savings accounts to be a major source of retirement money, 26% named pension plans, 24% mentioned stocks or mutual funds, and 23% listed home equity.

Then came a series of economic shocks, led by the bursting of the housing bubble in 2006 and 2007. Over the next few years, home values dropped by almost 30%, the Dow Jones industrial average lost more than 40% of its value, and the national unemployment rate doubled.

Since 2013, home values and stock prices have mostly recovered, and unemployment is back down to the 5% range. But many younger nonretirees who witnessed the turmoil may have decided that a savings account is the safest way to protect their earnings for retirement. In four Gallup polls from April 2013 through April 2016, an average 37% of those aged 18 to 39 list savings accounts as a major source of retirement money, up 11 percentage points from the 26% who named it in the 2002-2007 polls. Retirement savings accounts such as IRAs and 401(k)s are still the source mentioned most often, but the percentage naming retirement accounts has dropped from 57% to 51%. Savings accounts are now a clear second among this group, and between 19% and 24% of nonretirees mention the five remaining sources tested.

For those closer to retirement, who may have a better sense of what their options for major sources of retirement income will be, there has been less change overall, and the biggest changes have been decreases. Thirty-four percent of nonretirees in their 40s and

50s polled prior to 2008 expected pensions to be a major source of retirement income, but that has dropped to 26% in the polls after 2012. Home equity was listed as an expected source of retirement income by 29% of nonretirees in 2002-2007 – the period when the housing bubble pushed average home values up by more than 30%. But despite recent improvements in the housing market, only 22% in polling since 2012 have said they expect home equity to be a major money source during retirement.

Self-directed retirement savings plans such as 401(k)s and IRAs remain the top expected source for those between the ages of 40 and 59. Social Security has overtaken pension plans as the second most common expected source for this age group. Overall, despite negative media coverage of the long-term viability of Social Security, both age groups of nonretirees have maintained or increased their expectations for relying on it.

Social Security, Pensions Most Common Sources of Retirement Income

A separate measure on the April poll asks retirees how much they currently rely on most of the same sources of income. (Part-time workers are not included in Gallup's definition of retirees.) Combined Gallup polling on this measure from the last four years shows Social Security to be, by far, the most common source of retirement income for today's retirees, with an average 59% calling it a major source. Though many U.S. companies have phased out pensions in favor of 401(k) accounts, 37% of retirees currently name pensions as a major income source, while 23% say the same for retirement savings accounts such as 401(k)s and IRAs.

As in the past, there are significant differences between retirees' reliance on various income sources and nonretirees' expected reliance on the same sources. For example, 31% of nonretirees expect Social Security to be a major source of income when they retire, but 59% of current retirees say it is a major source for them. And while 23% of current retirees list retirement savings accounts as a major source, 47% of nonretirees expect them to be. Smaller gaps between retirees' experience and nonretirees' expectations are apparent concerning pensions, home equity, savings accounts and individual stock investments.

Nonretirees' Expectations vs. Retirees' Experience

Percentage of nonretirees who say each of the following will be a major source of retirement income; percentage of retirees who say each of the following is a major source of retirement income

	Will be a major source of retirement income (Nonretirees)%	Is a major source of income (Retirees)%
401(k), IRA, other retirement savings accounts	47	23
Social Security	31	59
Savings accounts, CDs	24	11
Pension plans	24	37
Home equity	20	18
Stocks, mutual funds	19	13

Combined results from Gallup surveys in 2002-2007 and 2013-2016

Reinforcing Americans' attachment to 401(k)-type savings plans to fund their retirement, the latest Wells Fargo/Gallup Investor and Retirement Optimism Index survey found that the vast majority of employed U.S. investors who participate in a 401(k) savings plan view it positively. More than four in 10 (44%) are "very" satisfied with their plan, and 47% are "somewhat" satisfied.

Bottom Line

The economic twists and turns of the past decade did not fundamentally change Americans' plans for how they will fund their days as retirees, but it did create some shifts in emphasis on different approaches. Older nonretirees are less likely than before the recession to think they can count on their home's equity or on pensions. Their younger counterparts – who have been less affected than older generations by inflation worries – are now more likely to want to salt their money away in a savings account. They also are more likely to think that part-time work might be a major element of their retirement security.

These changing expectations have not yet come into play in any major way. Younger retirees – those aged 61 to 70 in the 2013-2016 polls – do not differ greatly from older retirees when it comes to major sources of income. And Social Security, despite the dire warnings, still provides a major source of income for more than half of retired Americans. Nonretirees are no less likely to say they will rely on it than they were prior to the recession.

Survey Methods

Results for this Gallup poll are based on the combined results of two sets of Gallup Economy and Personal Finance surveys. Aggregated results from six surveys conducted in 2002, 2003, 2004, 2005, 2006 and 2007 are based on telephone interviews with a random sample of 1,764 retirees and 5,319 nonretirees. Aggregated results from four surveys conducted in 2013, 2014, 2015 and 2016 are based on telephone interviews with a random sample of 1,669 retirees and 3,404 nonretirees. All respondents were aged 18 and older, living in all 50 U.S. states and the District of Columbia. For results based on retirees, the margin of sampling error is ±3 percentage points at the 95% confidence level. For results based on nonretirees, the margin of sampling error is ±2 percentage points.

May 03, 2016
U.S. ECONOMIC CONFIDENCE DOWN IN APRIL

by Jeffrey M. Jones

Story Highlights

- *Economic Confidence Index averages -14, down from -10*
- *Americans' economic outlook is lowest since November 2013*
- *All party groups are slightly more negative about economy*

PRINCETON, N.J. – Americans' confidence in the economy retreated in April, with Gallup's Economic Confidence Index averaging -14 for the month, down from -10 in March. The April average ties with September 2015 as numerically the worst since confidence started climbing toward positive territory in late 2014 and early 2015 after gas prices began to decline.

Gallup's U.S. Economic Confidence Index -- Monthly Averages
January 2008-April 2016

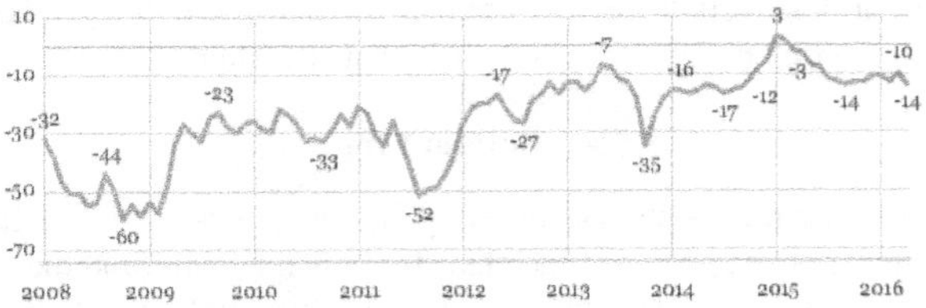

Gallup Daily tracking

GALLUP

The high point in confidence in Gallup's eight-year tracking trend occurred in January 2015, when the monthly index averaged +3, while the low point was -60 in October 2008. Gallup's U.S. Economic Confidence Index has a theoretical range of -100 to +100, with positive scores indicating Americans are more positive than negative about the economy. Scores have been primarily negative since 2008, although confidence has been much less negative in recent years than it was during the Great Recession.

Although the U.S. labor market remains strong and U.S. stock values are high, there are still questions about how strong the economy is. The government's recently released gross domestic product estimates indicate the economy barely grew in the first quarter of 2016, with retail spending especially weak. First quarter growth was also weak in 2014 and 2015, but those disappointing figures came amid particularly bad winter weather in many parts of the country; however, this year's winter brought milder temperatures.

Economic confidence varied significantly throughout April, with Gallup's three-day rolling averages falling as low as -20 on two separate occasions and as high as -8. The most recent weekly average, based on April 25-May 1 interviewing, shows the confidence index at -15, right around the monthly average.

Americans Less Negative About Current State of the Economy Than Its Outlook

Gallup's U.S. Economic Confidence Index is based on Americans' ratings of current conditions and their outlook on whether the economy is getting better or worse. Since March 2015, Americans have been more upbeat about the current state of the economy than about the direction in which it is headed. In late 2014 and early 2015, as gas prices dropped, the two ratings were generally similar.

In April, 24% of Americans rated current economic conditions as "excellent" or "good," while 30% said they were "poor," resulting in a current conditions score of -6. At the same time, 37% said the economy was "getting better" and 58% said it was "getting worse," for an economic outlook score of -21. The gap between the two ratings ties as the largest in the past year.

Gallup's U.S. Economic Confidence Index Components -- Monthly Averages
September 2014-April 2016

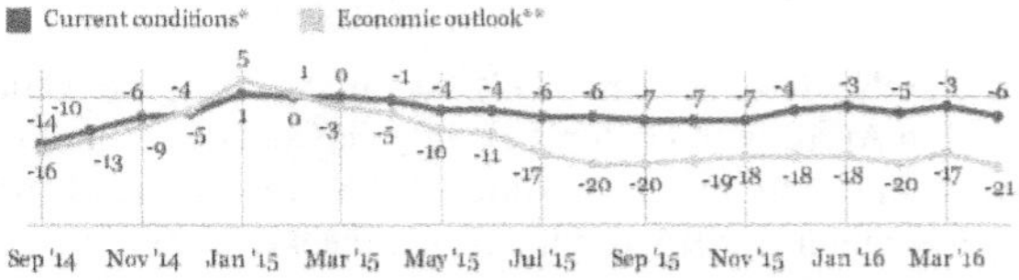

* % (Excellent + Good) minus % Poor
** % Getting better minus % Getting worse

Gallup Daily tracking

GALLUP

Gallup has not found a lower economic outlook score than the current one since November 2013, when 34% of Americans thought the economy was getting better and 61% thought it was getting worse.

All Party Groups More Negative About the Economy

Americans' confidence in the economy is influenced to a significant degree by political considerations, namely the match between an individual's party identification and the party of the U.S. president. As such, Democrats have consistently had greater confidence than independents and especially Republicans during Barack Obama's presidency.

Despite these consistent differences, confidence has mostly risen and fallen by similar amounts among each party group over the past few years, including in April. All three party groups showed slight drops of between two and four index points in April compared with March. The April U.S. Economic Confidence Index score was +10 among Democrats, -15 among independents and -38 among Republicans.

Gallup's U.S. Economic Confidence Index, by Political Party
September 2014-April 2016

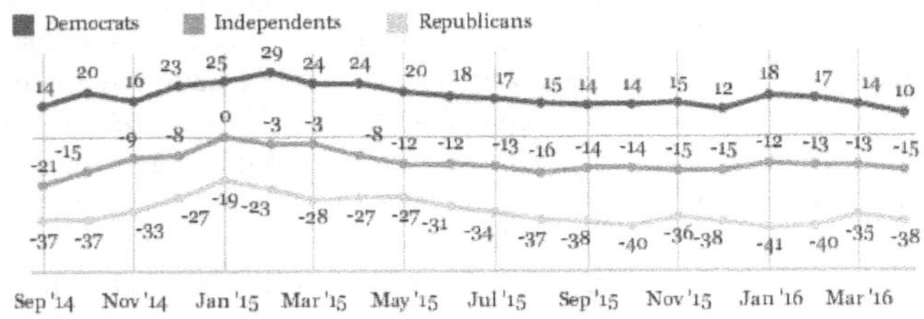

Gallup Daily tracking

GALLUP

Democrats' index score has mostly been in positive territory since February 2012, roughly when Obama's re-election campaign kicked off. The only exception occurred in October 2013; during the partial federal government shutdown, confidence plunged and Democrats' monthly index score dropped to -9.

Implications

Although U.S. employment numbers are strong and stock values are high, there are other indications – most notably GDP and retail spending – that raise doubts about whether the economy is currently healthy. This is reflected in Americans' slightly more negative assessment of the U.S. economy and presidential candidates' acknowledgement that certain aspects of the economy need to be addressed. It is also made clear by the Federal Reserve's caution to date in raising interest rates.

In 2014 and 2015, weak first quarter economic growth was followed by stronger growth and increased consumer spending in the second quarter, with many economists attributing the slower first quarters to poor weather. But the sluggish first quarter this year is not a result of poor winter weather holding down consumer activity; thus, it is less predictable whether GDP will bounce back in the second quarter.

One positive sign is that Gallup's measure of consumer spending – based on respondent self-reports of their actual spending – showed a strong increase in April, suggesting that second quarter consumer activity could be off to a relatively strong start.

These data are available in Gallup Analytics.

Survey Methods

Results for this Gallup poll are based on telephone interviews conducted April 1-30, 2016, on the Gallup U.S. Daily survey, with a random sample of 15,198 adults, aged 18 and older, living in all 50 U.S. states and the District of Columbia. For results based on the total sample of national adults, the margin of sampling error is ±1 percentage points at the 95% confidence level. All reported margins of sampling error include computed design effects for weighting.

May 04, 2016

AMERICANS' OPTIMISM ABOUT HOMEBUYING CLIMATE DIPS

by Alyssa Davis

Story Highlights

- *66% say it's a good time to buy, down slightly from recent years*
- *55% say house prices will increase in local area over next year*
- *Majority of nonhomeowners think they will buy home*

WASHINGTON, D.C. – Americans' optimism about the climate for buying a home has waned somewhat from recent years. By a slim margin, optimism sits at its lowest level since 2008. Sixty-six percent of Americans say now is a good time to buy a home, down slightly from an average of 71% between 2009 and 2015. Still, these views are much more positive than what Gallup measured from 2006 to 2008 amid the housing bubble crisis, when an average of 54% of U.S. adults said it was a good time to buy a home.

For people in general, do you think that now is a GOOD time or a BAD time to buy a house?

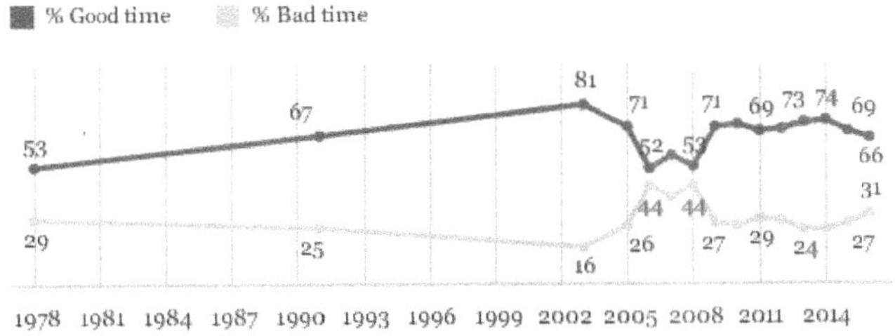

GALLUP

The latest results are based on Gallup's annual Economy and Personal Finance survey, conducted April 6-10. Americans' less optimistic views about the homebuying climate may be related to rising housing prices in many parts of the country, partly caused by a low supply of new and existing homes. Americans may also be factoring in their views of the investment returns on buying a house, although in the same poll, they chose real estate as a better long-term investment than stocks or other investments.

That the percentage saying it is a good time to buy a home has never dropped below 50%, even after the housing bubble burst, indicates that people's perceptions reflect not only prevailing housing market conditions, but also their views about the value of homeownership in general.

Regionally, Americans living in the Midwest and South are the most optimistic that now is a good time to buy a home, while those in the West are the least positive. Those aged 50 to 64 are more positive than other age groups. Upper- and middle-income Americans' views are more optimistic than those of lower-income Americans, who likely have more difficulty affording houses.

Views of Whether Now Is a Good Time to Buy a House, by Subgroup

	Good time%
Region	
East	61
West	55
Midwest	74
South	71
Age	
18-29	60
30-49	66
50-64	71
65+	63
Annual household income	
Less than $30,000	47
$30,000-74,999	71
$75,000 or more	74

Gallup

Current homeowners are significantly more upbeat than renters about it being a good time to buy a house, a change from 2005, when views were similar among both groups.

Now Is a Good Time to Buy a House, by Homeownership Status

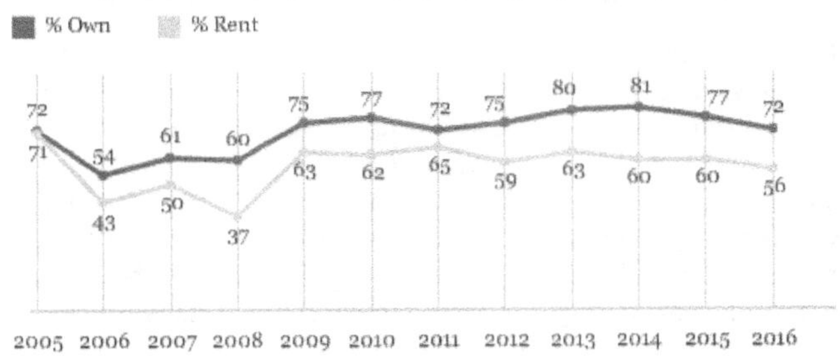

GALLUP

To a large degree, this wider gap in homeowners' and renters' views may reflect their own attitudes about owning a home in general, regardless of market conditions. Some renters may prefer renting and be less likely to endorse buying a home, given their own situation. With home values peaking during the housing bubble, renters may have seen the great potential in owning a home. But after the bubble burst, and home values dropped precipitously, it was probably harder for renters to see the financial virtues of owning a home.

Gallup's trends show a significant drop in homeownership compared with the mid-2000s, from 73% in 2007 to 62% today.

Majority Predict Local Housing Prices Will Increase

Likely reflecting recent increases in home values, a majority of U.S. adults predict housing prices in their local area will increase over the next year. Currently, 55% say housing prices will increase; 31% say they will stay the same; and 12% say they will decrease. These predictions are slightly less optimistic than last year, but similar to views found two years ago.

From 2008 to 2011, Americans were generally more likely to say local housing prices would decrease or stay the same than to say they would increase. As housing prices began to rise in 2012, Americans' predictions for local housing prices grew more optimistic. By 2013, Americans' views of increased housing values in their local area had jumped. They have stayed relatively high since. But the percentage saying housing prices will increase has not yet recovered to the levels seen in 2005 and early 2006, before the housing bubble burst.

Over the next year, do you think that the average price of houses in your area will increase, stay the same or decrease?

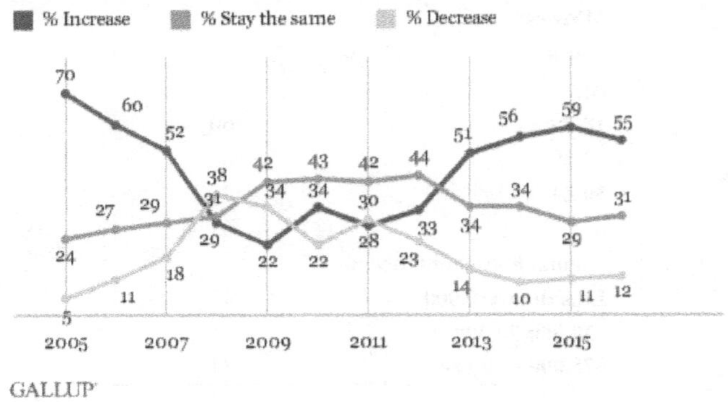

Americans living in the West (64%) and South (61%) are significantly more likely than those in the East (48%) and Midwest (45%) to say they expect local housing prices to increase.

Fewer Americans Think They Will Buy a Home

Regardless of views of the housing market, the majority of nonhomeowners continue to say they intend to buy a home in the foreseeable future. Currently, 59% of nonhomeowners think they will buy a home at some point within the next 10 years. This is down slightly from 67% in 2013, but similar to the 58% recorded in 2015. Of course, it is unlikely that all those who say they plan to buy a home will actually do so, but these figures indicate the extent to which homeownership is still a desirable goal for many Americans.

U.S. Nonhomeowners' Expectations for Buying Home

Based on what you know right now, do you think you will buy a home in the next year, in the next five years, in the next 10 years, or are you unlikely to buy a home in the forseeable future?

	2013%	2015%	2016%
Next year	8	7	9
Next five years	37	36	32
Next 10 years	22	15	18
Not for the foreseeable future	31	41	38

Gallup

Implications

Although economic confidence is higher now than at most points in recent years and mortgage rates remain low, Americans are a bit less positive about the homebuying climate than they have been since 2009. Americans' belief that home prices in their area are on the rise, coupled with reports indicating there is a lack of inventory of available homes in many areas, may leave many with the sense that market conditions currently favor sellers over buyers.

Still, the majority of nonhomeowners say they think they will buy a home in the future, and Americans continue to say real estate is the best long-term investment. But rising home prices, growing student debt burden, delayed marriage and childbearing, and worries about the state of the economy could result in more nonhomeowners delaying or forgoing a house. Young adults – the least likely across age groups to say real estate is the best long-term investment – may be reluctant to make a house their single most valuable asset after witnessing the housing market collapse. But rising rents, which make owning less expensive than renting in many areas, might nudge Americans toward homeownership.

Historical data are available in Gallup Analytics.

Survey Methods

Results for this Gallup poll are based on telephone interviews conducted April 6-10, 2016, with a random sample of 1,015 adults, aged 18 and older, living in all 50 U.S. states and the District of Columbia. For results based on the total sample of national adults, the margin of sampling error is ±4 percentage points at the 95% confidence level. For results based on the total sample of 687 homeowners, the margin of sampling error is ±5 percentage points at the 95% confidence level. All reported margins of sampling error include computed design effects for weighting.

Learn more about how the Gallup Poll Social Series works.

May 04, 2016
SMALL-BUSINESS OWNERS SAY CANDIDATES FAIL TO ADDRESS ISSUES

by Frank Newport and Coleen McMurray

Story Highlights

- *50% of small-business owners say election outcome is of major impact*
- *Most owners paying close attention to election*
- *Over two-thirds of owners say candidates not discussing their issues*

PRINCETON, N.J. – The latest Wells Fargo/Gallup Small Business Index survey finds that half of small-business owners say the outcome of the presidential election will have a major impact on their small business. At the same time, fewer than three in 10 (28%) say the presidential candidates are discussing the issues most important to them as small-business owners.

Small-Business Owners and the Presidential Election

Would you say that the outcome of this year's presidential election – that is, who wins in November – will have a major impact, a minor impact or not much impact at all on your small business?

	%
Major impact	50
Minor impact	23
Not much impact at all	23

April 4-8, 2016
Wells Fargo/Gallup Small Business Index

Small-Business Owners and the Presidential Election

As far as you are concerned, are the presidential candidates discussing the issues most important to you as a small-business owner, or not?

	%
Yes	28
No	69

April 4-8, 2016
Wells Fargo/Gallup Small Business Index

These results are based on interviews conducted April 4-8 as part of the Wells Fargo/Gallup Small Business Index, with a special focus on the ways in which small-business owners view the presidential election, the candidates and the issues.

In addition to the 50% who say the election will have a major impact on their small business, another 23% say it will have a minor impact, leaving 23% who say it will have not much impact at all. The 28% who say that the candidates are discussing the issues most important to them as a small-business owner is much lower than the 58% of national adults in a Gallup Poll who were asked a similar question in mid-April about the issues most important to them.

Business owners are paying especially close attention to the election. A total of 87% of owners say they are following the election either "very closely" (56%) or "somewhat closely" (31%), higher than what Gallup typically finds among national adults.

In addition to the widely held belief that the candidates are not focusing enough on the issues important to them, small-business owners are also split on how well they comprehend the candidates' positions. Overall, 79% of small-business owners say they understand the candidates' positions on issues that would affect small businesses "extremely," "very" or "somewhat" well – although only 47% put their level of understanding in the first two of these categories.

These findings suggest that small-business owners are keenly interested in the election, and a significant number believe that the election outcome will have a direct bearing on their business. However, the prevailing sentiment is that candidates are not adequately focused on the issues small-business owners think are most important.

The Most Important Campaign Issues for Small-Business Owners

Given the conviction of many small-business owners that the candidates are not talking about the issues that are most important to them, the question becomes one of ascertaining exactly what those specific issues are. To that end, the survey included an open-ended question asking owners to name the issues they would like candidates to focus on in the campaign. The results, displayed in the accompanying table, show that owners would most like the candidates to address how they would handle taxes that affect small businesses. Owners' next-most frequently mentioned issues are the economy, healthcare and jobs, followed by the impact of government regulations, and the desire for a general focus on small-business owners.

As a small-business owner, what is the most important issue that you would like the presidential candidates to focus on during this campaign?

	Mentioning%
Taxes	22
Economy	12
Healthcare	9
Jobs/employment	7
Small-business focus	7
Government regulations	7
National debt/spending	4
National security/terrorism	3
Immigration	3
Truth/honesty/good leadership	3
Government unity	3
Trade (import and export)	2
Financial stability/sustainability	2
Minimum wage	2
Welfare/socialism	1
Education	1
Other	5
None/nothing	1
Don't know/refused	6

April 4-8, 2016
Wells Fargo/Gallup Small Business Index

Owners were also asked in a separate sequence of questions to rate the importance of 15 specific issues to their small business when the new president – whoever he or she should be – takes office.

The percentage of those rating the issues as "extremely" or "very" important ranged from 83% for issues relating to the small-business implications of the tax code, tax regulations and tax rates, to 40% for the president's actions relating to environmental regulations and climate change.

Issues rated as extremely or very important by two-thirds or more of small-business owners, in addition to taxes, include economic policies relating to small businesses, healthcare, actions that would increase consumer confidence and terrorism/national security. In addition to climate change, other issues at the low end of the ranking included presidential actions relating to the Small Business Administration, the minimum wage and education.

Thinking ahead to when a new president takes office early next year, how important will each of the following be to your small business? Will __________ be extremely important, very important, somewhat important, not very important, or not at all important?

Rank ordered by extremely important + very important

	Extremely important %	Very important %	Somewhat important %	Not very important %	Not at all important %
Actions relating to changes in the tax code, tax regulations and tax rates for small businesses	34	49	14	2	1
Actions relating to economic policies that affect small-business owners	30	47	18	3	1
Actions relating to healthcare and the current healthcare law	33	40	17	6	3
Actions relating to the confidence consumers have in the economy	26	43	24	4	2
Actions relating to terrorism and national security	29	38	20	8	5
Actions relating to trade laws and regulations that could affect small businesses	22	42	22	10	3
Actions relating to job creation	22	41	22	9	6
Actions that could impact oil prices or energy costs	21	40	27	7	4
Actions relating to government regulations of banks	19	36	28	10	6
Actions relating to federal spending on infrastructure such as roads and bridges	18	36	29	11	6
Actions relating to immigration	20	33	22	14	10
Actions relating to education	16	35	29	13	7
Actions on increasing the minimum wage	20	30	23	15	11
Actions relating to the SBA or Small Business Administration	16	32	33	11	7
Actions relating to environmental regulations/climate change	15	25	30	17	12

April 4-8, 2016
Wells Fargo/Gallup Small Business Index

Survey Methods

Results are based on telephone interviews with 600 U.S. small-business owners in all 50 states, conducted April 4-8, 2016. The margin of sampling error is ±4 percentage points at the 95% confidence level.

May 05, 2016

HALF OF AMERICANS RATE THEIR FINANCIAL SITUATION POSITIVELY

by Justin McCarthy

Story Highlights

- *Positive financial situation ratings at highest since 2007*
- *Nearly half (47%) say their financial situation is improving*

WASHINGTON, D.C. – Fifty percent of Americans rate their personal financial situation as either "excellent" or "good," slightly higher than the 46% recorded last year and the highest level recorded since before the Great Recession.

How would you rate your financial situation today -- as excellent, good, only fair or poor?

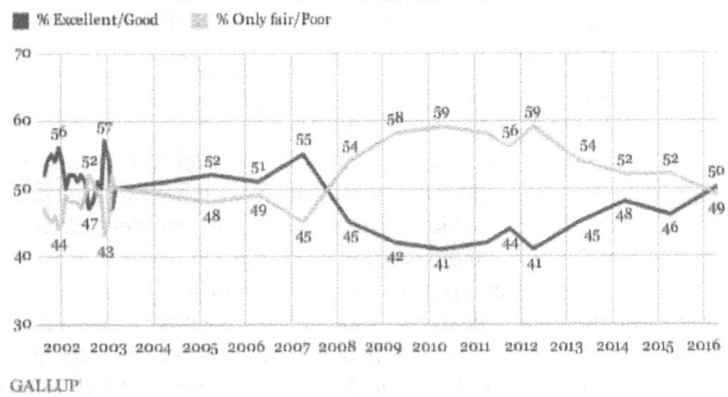

These data come from Gallup's annual Economy and Personal Finance survey, conducted April 6-10. When Gallup began asking this question in 2001, Americans were a bit more likely to rate their financial situation positively, with slight majorities saying their situation was excellent or good in most polls from 2001 to 2007.

These ratings dropped during the recession, however, and remained low in the years that followed. In 2008, less than half described their situation positively, and a record-low 41% of Americans gave excellent or good ratings in 2010 and 2012. Americans' ratings began to improve in 2013. These data are similar to Gallup's findings in January that Americans are more likely to report being "better off" financially than they were in the year prior – another measure in which Americans' assessments have recovered from the immediate post-recession years.

Americans More Likely Than in Post-Recession Years to Report Situation as Improving

Comparable to their views of their current financial situation, Americans' projections for the future of their finances have recovered from their fairly pessimistic lows during the recession and immediate post-recession years.

Currently, Americans are more likely to say their financial situation as a whole is "getting better" (47%) than to say it is "getting worse" (38%), the fifth consecutive year they have reported a net positive outlook. Positive outlook ratings for their finances are down, however, by five percentage points from last year's 52%, which was the first time since before the recession that this sentiment reached a majority level.

Right now, do you think that your financial situation as a whole is getting better or getting worse?

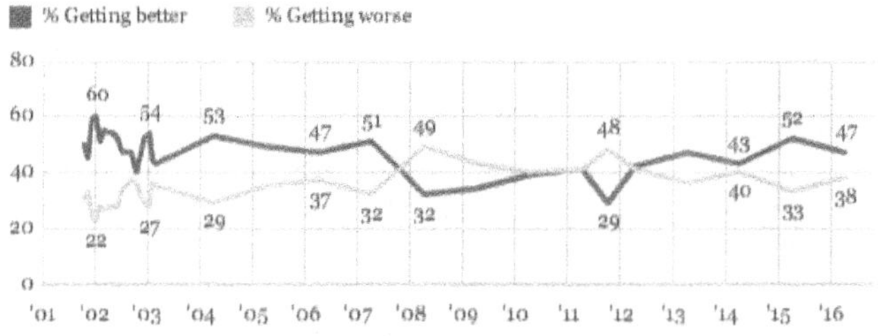

Americans were the most positive about their future finances in 2002, when 60% said their financial situation was improving. They were the least optimistic about future conditions in October 2011 (29%), following sharp declines in stock prices after the S&P downgraded the U.S. federal government's credit rating.

Bottom Line

Americans' assessments of their current financial situation and their expectations for the future have recovered quite a bit from the recession and immediate post-recession years. But these ratings aren't as positive as they were at most points prior to the recession.

Meanwhile, just as many Americans rate their financial situation negatively as they do positively, and they are a bit less likely to view their finances as improving. This aligns with their muted confidence in the U.S. economy, which was a bit rosier in 2015 than it has been so far this year.

Historical data are available in Gallup Analytics.

Survey Methods

Results for this Gallup poll are based on telephone interviews conducted April 6-10, 2016, on the Gallup U.S. Daily survey, with a random sample of 1,015 adults, aged 18 and older, living in all 50 U.S. states and the District of Columbia. For results based on the total sample of national adults, the margin of sampling error is ±4 percentage points at the 95% confidence level. All reported margins of sampling error include computed design effects for weighting.

May 06, 2016

AMERICANS' VIEWS OF SOCIALISM, CAPITALISM ARE LITTLE CHANGED

by Frank Newport

Story Highlights

- *Americans' negative image of socialism is little changed since 2010*
- *Small business has an almost universally positive image*
- *60% are positive about capitalism; 85% about free enterprise*

PRINCETON, N.J. – Even though Bernie Sanders, a self-described "Democratic socialist," has generated strong support for his presidential campaign, Americans' image of socialism is no better now than it was six years ago. Thirty-five percent of Americans have a positive view of the term socialism, similar to what was found in 2012 and 2010. The 60% who have a positive view of capitalism is also unchanged from six years ago.

Just off the top of your head, would you say you have a positive or negative image of each of the following?

% Positive

	May 2-4, 2016 %	Nov. 18-19, 2012 %	Jan. 26-27, 2010%
Small business	96	95	95
Entrepreneurs	87	86	84
Free enterprise	85	89	86
Capitalism	60	61	61
Big business	53	58	49
The federal government	44	51	46
Socialism	35	39	36

Gallup Daily tracking

Americans retain very positive images of small business, entrepreneurs and free enterprise. A little more than half have a positive view of big business, and less than half have a positive view of the federal government.

These seven terms were measured May 2-4 using Gallup Daily tracking, updating previous measurements taken in November 2012, just after that year's presidential election, and in January 2010.

The rank order of positive reactions has been the same at each of the three time periods, with only minor fluctuations in the percentage of Americans holding a positive image of each concept. Positive views of big business, for example, are down a little from 2012 but remain higher than in 2010. Views of the federal government are also slightly less positive than three-and-a-half years ago but are now about where they were in 2010.

Democratic presidential candidate Sanders focused his campaign on criticism of big business and promoted the value of a bigger role for the federal government in economic and social life, including his proposals for a "Medicare for all" federally funded healthcare system. At the same time, the presumptive Republican nominee, Donald Trump, is himself a businessman who has, along with many of the other Republican challengers, focused on criticizing the government while saying that he would run it more like a business. However, none of this has apparently made a major difference in the ways in which Americans think about these economic terms.

As would be expected, Republicans and Republican-leaning independents are somewhat more positive about big business, free enterprise and capitalism than are Democrats and Democratic-leaning independents.

Democrats, on the other hand, are much more positive than Republicans about the federal government and socialism. Notably, Democrats have a more positive image of socialism than they do of big business, and their images of socialism and capitalism are essentially the same. These broad patterns are similar to what was found in 2012.

Just off the top of your head, would you say you have a positive or negative image of each of the following?

% Positive, by party ID (including leaners)

	Republicans/ Republican leaners %	Democrats/ Democratic leaners %
Small business	97	96
Entrepreneurs	91	86
Free enterprise	92	83
Capitalism	68	56
Big business	57	48
The federal government	30	59
Socialism	13	58

May 2-4, 2016
Gallup Daily tracking

Younger Adults More Positive Than Older Adults About Socialism

Young Americans, aged 18-29, have more positive views of both the federal government and socialism than older Americans do. Young adults' ratings of the federal government, capitalism, big business and socialism are similar – between 55% and 58% positive for each.

Older Americans' views of capitalism are more positive than those of Americans under 50 years of age, and older Americans' views of socialism are more negative than those who are younger. Overall, Americans across most age groups see capitalism more positively than socialism. The exception is among those aged 18-29, who are equally positive about both.

Just off the top of your head, would you say you have a positive or negative image of each of the following?

% Positive, by age

	18-29 years %	30-49 years %	50-64 years %	65+ years %
Small business	98	94	96	93
Entrepreneurs	90	87	87	83
Free enterprise	78	84	89	91
Capitalism	57	54	69	63
Big business	57	49	52	53
The federal government	58	43	38	40
Socialism	55	37	27	24

May 2-4, 2016
Gallup Daily tracking

Implications

These results show the presidential campaign has not changed Americans' images of a number of commonly used political and economic terms. Americans react almost universally positively to the term small business and also have very positive reactions to free enterprise and entrepreneurs. Overall reactions to capitalism are also positive and significantly more so than views of socialism, which is the least-liked term of any tested.

Americans are mixed in their reactions to big business and the federal government, with slightly more positive views of the former than the latter. Notably, Americans are less positive about capitalism and big business than they are about free enterprise and small business, highlighting the different ways in which these terms resonate with the public.

The results show that several of these terms are politically charged. Republicans and Democrats diverge in their reactions to capitalism, big business, socialism and the federal government, with the biggest differences seen on the latter two terms. Sanders' strong challenge to Hillary Clinton for the Democratic nomination is a testament to the fact that his self-labeling as a "Democratic socialist" is not a strong negative among Democrats. His and Clinton's more positive views of the federal government and its role in society as espoused on the campaign trail also seem to fit with those of rank-and-file Democrats, the majority of whom are positive about the government.

It is notable that young Americans constitute the only age group that does not view the term socialism more negatively than capitalism. Older Americans' much more negative reactions to socialism could be based on different historical or conceptual references than is the case for young people. Americans being much more positive about the term free enterprise than capitalism also suggests that labels used to describe an economic system carry different connotations.

Historical data are available in Gallup Analytics.

Survey Methods

Results for this Gallup poll are based on telephone interviews conducted May 2-4, 2016, on the Gallup U.S. Daily survey, with a random sample of 1,544 adults, aged 18 and older, living in all 50 U.S. states and the District of Columbia. For results based on the total sample of national adults, the margin of sampling error is ±4 percentage points at the 95% confidence level. All reported margins of sampling error include computed design effects for weighting.

May 09, 2016

U.S. SMALL-BUSINESS OWNERS' OPTIMISM LEVELS OFF

by Frank Newport and Coleen McMurray

Story Highlights

- *Wells Fargo/Gallup Small Business Index at +64; was +67 in first quarter*
- *Despite fluctuations, owners' optimism returns to where it was a year ago*
- *Challenges are getting customers, government regulations, the economy*

PRINCETON, N.J. – Small-business owners' level of optimism about their business situation is essentially unchanged from the first quarter of this year and matches the level of optimism found one year ago. The Wells Fargo/Gallup Small Business Index is now at

+64, similar to the +67 recorded in the first quarter but up from +54 in the fourth quarter of 2015. Optimism remains well below the high points registered in the years before the recession.

Wells Fargo/Gallup Small Business Index

The Small Business Index consists of owners' ratings of their business' current situation and their expectations for the next 12 months, measured in terms of their overall financial situation, revenue, cash flow, capital spending, number of jobs and ease of obtaining credit.

Index conducted since August 2003 and quarterly from December 2003 to May 2016

GALLUP'

The quarterly survey, which measures small-business owners' ratings of their business' current situation and their expectations for the next 12 months, jumped in the first quarter of the year after posting three consecutive quarters of declines. The index score has returned to the level found one year ago, indicating that after some fluctuation, small-business owners' feelings about the state of their current and future financial situations have shown no net improvement year to year.

Small-business owners' estimates of their cash flow, which improved in the first quarter, have now settled back to the levels found in the second half of 2015. The other measures that make up the overall index score – which include small-business owners' financial situation, company revenue, capital spending, hiring and ease of obtaining credit – show little change compared with the first-quarter results.

Attracting Customers Continues to Be Top Challenge

When small-business owners are asked to identify the most important challenge facing their business, 16% cite attracting customers and finding new business. Other top concerns include the economy (10%), government regulations (10%), and hiring and retaining qualified staff (9%). Small-business owners have consistently reported these issues as top concerns since early 2013, although the order of concerns shifts slightly from quarter to quarter.

What do you think is the most important challenge facing you as a small-business owner today?

	Total %
Attracting customers/Targeting business opportunities/ Finding new business	16
Government regulations	10
The economy	10
Hiring qualified/good staff and retaining them	9
Taxes	9
Financial stability/Cash flow	6
Government (general)	6
Competition/Larger corporations/Internet	5
Costs of running the business/Having enough money for capital investment	5
Marketing/Advertising/Reaching out/Getting noticed	5
Credit availability	3
Healthcare/Costs of healthcare	2
Not enough time	2
Employee benefits	2
Challenge of being own boss/working for self	1
Product improvements/Updated products/Availability of products	1
Healthcare/Obamacare	1
No jobs/Lost job/Laid off	-
Accounting/Bill paying	-
No choice/Forced into it	-
Everything	-
Other	3

April 4-8, 2016
Wells Fargo/Gallup Small Business Index

Bottom Line

After steadily improving from the lows found during and after the Great Recession, small-business owners' optimism has leveled off over the last year and a half. The current index reading of +64 is more than 90 points higher than at points in 2010, but still well below readings for the years prior to 2008. The question remains as to whether small-business owners' optimism will eventually return to the more positive levels seen before the recession or whether that trauma ushered in a new normal of sorts, such that owners' optimism may never fully recover.

Survey Methods

Results are based on telephone interviews with 600 U.S. small-business owners in all 50 states, conducted April 4-8, 2016. The margin of sampling error is ±4 percentage points at the 95% confidence level.

May 09, 2016

U.S. WORKERS REGAIN FAITH IN FINDING GOOD JOB IF LAID OFF

by Jeffrey M. Jones

Story Highlights

- *63% say they likely would find a new job just as good*
- *Back to pre-recession levels after tumbling to 42% in 2010*
- *15% say they are likely to lose their job in next year*

PRINCETON, N.J. – After plummeting in 2010, Americans' confidence that they would find a job as good as their current one if they happened to be laid off has been restored. Currently, 63% believe it is very or somewhat likely that they would find a job as good as the one they have, up from 42% six years ago. The current figure is similar to what Gallup measured in early 2007, before the recession.

If you were to lose your job, how likely is it that you would find a job just as good as the one you have now -- very likely, somewhat likely, not very likely or not at all likely?

Based on those who are employed full or part time

% Very/Somewhat likely

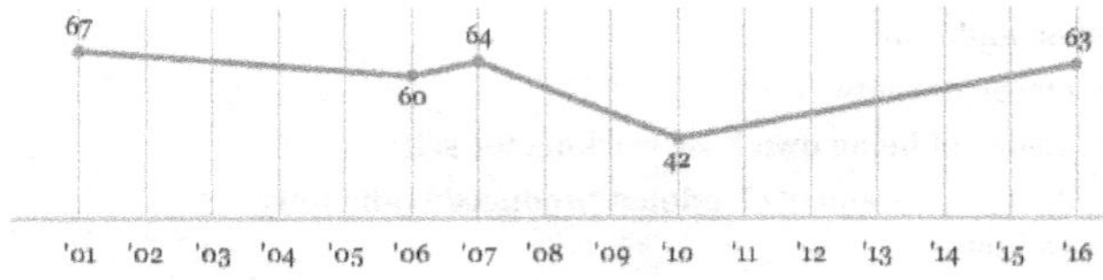

Figures represent annual averages in years in which the question was asked multiple times

GALLUP

When Gallup last asked this question, in April 2010, the Bureau of Labor Statistics unemployment rate was 9.9%. This April, it is 5.0%.

Those positive employment trends are likely one factor in Americans' greater confidence in finding comparable work if they were to lose their job. Whether their confidence is warranted is unclear, though, partly because the job growth in recent years has come disproportionately among lower-paying and part-time jobs.

The unemployment rates were similar to the current level – slightly below 5% – when Gallup asked the question in 2001, 2006 and 2007. In the 16-year history of the trend, the 2010 measurement is the only one in which the employment situation was dramatically different from the other years.

Upper-Income Workers' Assessments of Prospects Have Brightened Considerably

Six years ago, workers residing in upper-income households and those residing in middle- and lower-income households evaluated their job opportunities similarly, with 41% of each group saying it was likely that they would find a job similar to their current one. Now, upper-income workers (70%) are significantly more likely than middle- and lower-income workers (58%) to believe they could find a job just as good as their current one if they were laid off. This could indicate that the jobs recovery has not been equal among income groups, particularly for middle-income workers.

Workers of differing education levels, ages and genders show similar gains since 2010.

Changes in Perceived Likelihood of Being Able to Find a Job Just as Good as the Current One if Laid Off, by Subgroup

Based on adults employed full or part time

	2010%	2016%	Changepct. pts.
Age			
18 to 34 years	52	73	+21
35 to 54 years	40	60	+20
55+ years	30	51	+21
Education			
College graduate	48	69	+21
College nongraduate	38	59	+21
Annual Household Income			
Less than $75,000	41	58	+17
$75,000 or more	41	70	+29
Gender			
Male	42	63	+21
Female	41	62	+21

Gallup

Younger workers are much more likely than older workers to believe they would find a job just as good as the one they have if they were forced to find one. Currently, 73% of 18- to 34-year-old workers are optimistic about finding such a job, compared with 51% of workers aged 55 and older. Those age differences are typical of what Gallup has found previously and may reflect that younger workers have a wider range of opportunities, given that they are less likely to be established in a particular career or industry than older workers. Partly because of that, employers may prefer younger workers because they would tend to make less money than older workers.

College graduates (69%) are more optimistic than those without a college degree (59%) about finding a suitable new job if needed, as is typically the case.

Working men and working women are equally likely to believe they could find a job just as good as their current one.

Workers See Little Chance of Losing Their Job

Since 1975, Gallup has routinely asked U.S. workers to assess the likelihood that they will lose their job. The vast majority of workers have always viewed being laid off as a remote possibility. Today, just 15% say it is very or somewhat likely that they will be laid off in the next 12 months. That remains down from the high point of 21% in 2010, and essentially matches the historical average of 14%.

Thinking about the next 12 months, how likely do you think it is that you will lose your job or be laid off -- is it very likely, fairly likely, not too likely or not at all likely?

Based on those who are employed full or part time

% Very/Fairly likely

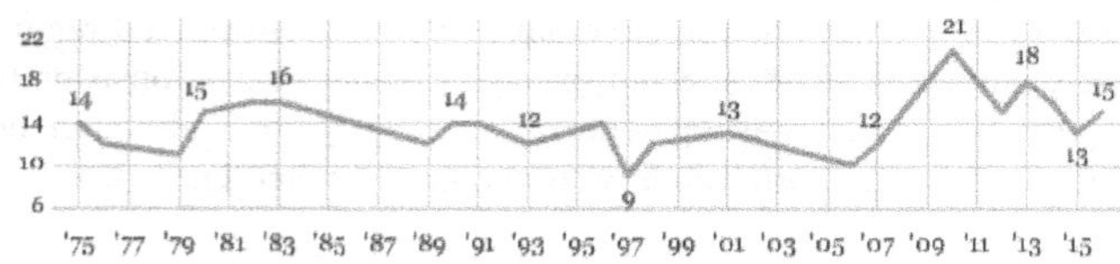

Figures represent annual averages in years in which the question was asked multiple times

GALLUP

Typically, workers' concerns about being laid off are similar by gender and age, but differ by socioeconomic status. Since 2001, an average of 17% of workers without a college degree have said it was likely that they would be laid off in the next 12 months, compared with 10% of workers with a degree. And 18% of workers in lower- and middle-income households worry about being laid off, compared with 9% of upper-income workers.

Implications

The Great Recession and its aftermath produced a period of heightened financial anxiety for many Americans. Amid unemployment rates near double digits, a record-high percentage of U.S. workers worried about being laid off, and workers' confidence in being able to find another decent job if that happened tumbled by 22 percentage points.

By June 2014, the Bureau of Labor Statistics estimated that the U.S. had recovered all the jobs lost in the recession. Americans are just as optimistic now as before the recession that they would find similar employment if they lost their job. At the same time, the jobs recovery has been uneven – stronger in some industries than others, and showing much more limited growth in middle-income jobs than in lower-paying jobs.

Americans' increasing optimism about their job prospects has been reflected in the growing number of employees quitting their job voluntarily, in most cases presumably because they have found another job. Whether that trend continues – especially in light of the BLS report showing that April job growth did not meet expectations – may depend on whether the U.S. economy can grow at a stronger pace than it did in the first quarter of 2016.

Historical data are available in Gallup Analytics.

Survey Methods

Results for this Gallup poll are based on telephone interviews conducted April 6-10, 2016, with a random sample of 525 adults, aged 18 and older, employed full or part time and living in all 50 U.S. states and the District of Columbia. For results based on the total sample of employed adults, the margin of sampling error is ±5 percentage points at the 95% confidence level. All reported margins of sampling error include computed design effects for weighting.

May 11, 2016

OBESITY RATE LOWEST IN HAWAII, HIGHEST IN WEST VIRGINIA

by Alyssa Davis and Diana Liu

Story Highlights

- *Hawaii and Colorado are the only two states with obesity rate below 20%*
- *Obesity rate exceeds 30.0% in 18 states*
- *Fourteen states have seen significant increases in obesity since 2008*

WASHINGTON, D.C. – At 18.5%, Hawaii has the lowest adult obesity rate in the U.S., closely followed by Colorado at 19.8%. They are the only two states in which the obesity rate is below 20%. West Virginia has the highest adult obesity rate, at 37.0%. In addition to West Virginia, at least one in three adults are obese in Mississippi, Delaware, Arkansas and Oklahoma.

Percentage of Obese Adults, by State

	Obese%
States with lowest obesity percentage	
Hawaii	18.5
Colorado	19.8
Massachusetts	23.6
New Mexico	23.7
Nevada	23.9
California	23.9
Montana	24.1
New Hampshire	24.3
Utah	24.5
New Jersey	24.7
States with highest obesity percentage	
West Virginia	37.0
Mississippi	35.5
Delaware	33.8
Arkansas	33.5
Oklahoma	33.5
Ohio	31.6
Maine	31.5
Michigan	31.5
Kentucky	31.4
South Carolina	31.4

Gallup-Healthways Well-Being Index, 2015

These data, from daily interviews conducted January through December 2015 as part of the Gallup-Healthways Well-Being Index, are based on U.S. adults' self-reports of their height and weight, which are then used to calculate Body Mass Index (BMI) scores. Americans who have a BMI of 30 or higher are classified as obese.

The national obesity rate reached a new high of 28.0% in 2015, up significantly from 25.5% in 2008, when Gallup and Healthways began tracking obesity. Fourteen states had statistically significant increases in their obesity rates from 2008 to 2015, while no state registered a statistically significant decline. Maine, West Virginia, Idaho and Oklahoma experienced the sharpest upticks in obesity.

States With Statistically Significant Increases in Obesity, 2008 to 2015

	2008%	2015%	Increasepct. pts.
Maine	24.9	31.5	6.6
West Virginia	30.5	37.0	6.5
Idaho	24.0	29.7	5.7
Oklahoma	28.0	33.5	5.5
Iowa	26.4	31.3	4.9
Michigan	26.7	31.5	4.8
Ohio	27.6	31.6	4.0
South Carolina	27.6	31.4	3.8
North Carolina	26.7	30.4	3.7
Texas	27.1	30.7	3.6
Georgia	26.0	28.8	2.8
Washington	24.5	27.1	2.6
Florida	24.2	26.5	2.3
Pennsylvania	27.2	29.2	2.0

Gallup-Healthways Well-Being Index

Obesity Remains Highest in the South, Lowest in the West

Of the 18 states with obesity rates of at least 30.0%, all but one are located in the South or Midwest. Meanwhile, all 11 states with obesity rates below 25.0% are located in the Northeast or West.

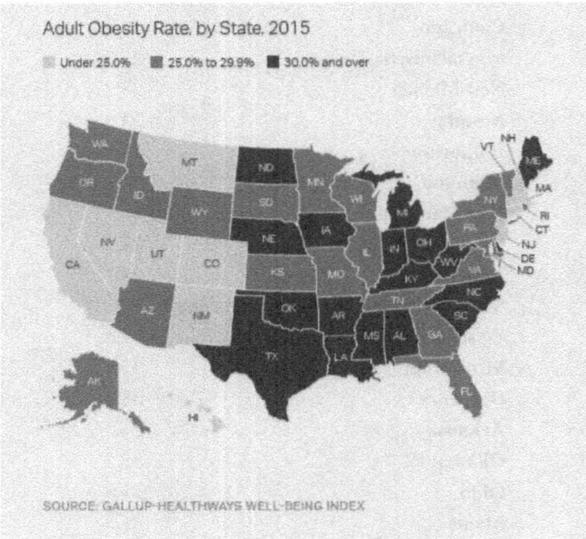

Since 2008, the obesity rate for the Midwest has increased by 3.2 percentage points, more than any other region. The South followed closely behind, with a 2.9-point increase. The Northeast and West have seen smaller, but still statistically significant, increases of 2.0 and 1.8 points, respectively.

Regional Changes in Adult Obesity Rates, 2008 to 2015

% Obese

	2008%	2015%	Increasepct. pts.
Midwest	26.8	30.0	+3.2
South	27.0	29.9	+2.9
Northeast	24.2	26.2	+2.0
West	22.8	24.6	+1.8

Gallup-Healthways Well-Being Index

As Obesity Rates Rise, So Do Healthcare Costs

Given that obesity is associated with illnesses such as heart disease, diabetes, stroke, osteoarthritis and some forms of cancer, the medical costs for an obese person amounted to $1,429 more per year than for a person of a normal weight, according to research conducted in 2008 by RTI International and the Centers for Disease Control and Prevention. After adjusting for inflation, the annual medical costs for 2015 are $1,573 more for a person who is obese than for a person of a normal weight.

Gallup calculated the incremental cost of healthcare per year for each state by multiplying the estimated number of obese people in the state's population by the annual incremental $1,573 cost of obesity per person.

In the five most obese states, the annual incremental cost of obesity per 100,000 residents averages $54 million. By contrast, the average cost is $34 million in the five least obese states. In other words, per capita medical costs attributable to obesity are about 1.6 times higher in the five states with the highest obesity rates than in the states with the five lowest rates. Additional annual medical costs attributable to obesity for each state appear at the end of the article.

States' Annual Incremental 2015 Healthcare Costs Attributable to Obesity

	Population (estimate)	Obese %	Annual healthcare cost per 100k adults	Annual healthcare costall adults
States with highest percentage of obese adults				
West Virginia	1,452,598	37.0	$58,273,467	$846,479,005
Mississippi	2,163,049	35.5	$55,914,797	$1,209,464,207
Delaware	697,965	33.8	$53,223,481	$371,481,197
Arkansas	2,215,461	33.5	$52,743,928	$1,168,521,191
Oklahoma	2,767,117	33.5	$52,647,884	$1,456,828,340
States with lowest percentage of obese adults				
Hawaii	1,049,465	18.5	$29,067,060	$305,048,588
Colorado	4,019,462	19.8	$31,109,252	$1,250,424,550
Massachusetts	5,144,065	23.6	$37,087,771	$1,907,818,922
New Mexico	1,596,641	23.7	$37,245,304	$594,673,741
Nevada	2,095,527	23.9	$37,539,385	$786,648,014

Gallup-Healthways Well-Being Index, 2015

Implications

As the adult obesity rate continues to rise both nationally and within many states, preventable healthcare costs will also rise. If states can lower their obesity rates, even modestly, they can achieve significant cost savings and improve their residents' well-being.

"There's no better time than now to comprehensively look at what drives people to make sustained changes in their lives, as the costs of obesity are staggering, both financially and personally," says Sean Slovenski, president, Population Health Services at Healthways. "We know from both science and experience that to be effective, the weight-loss journey needs to be personalized, easy to implement and supported."

But reducing obesity rates is no easy task. Gallup previously found that Americans are twice as likely to want to lose weight as to say they are seriously trying to do so. Most of the burden for reducing obesity falls on individuals and how motivated they are to consistently make healthier choices. This motivation is often difficult to find and maintain, but there are proven population health interventions that are effective in supporting sustained weight loss.

"We can reverse our nation's growing obesity epidemic," says Dan Buettner, National Geographic Fellow and founder of Blue Zones Project, a community well-being improvement initiative of Healthways and its community partners. "The key is creating an environment that makes the healthy choice not only easy but at times unavoidable – so that people will eat less, eat better, move more and connect socially. Communities that have the courage to implement simple, evidence-based designs and policies that support lasting change, such as Los Angeles Beach cities, are seeing a measurable reduction in obesity and healthcare costs, and an increase in well-being."

In the long run, interventions designed to prevent and reduce obesity at both the individual and community levels can potentially lead to substantial cost savings for families, employers and states.

Survey Methods

Results are based on telephone interviews conducted Jan. 2-Dec. 30, 2015, as a part of the Gallup-Healthways Well-Being Index, with a random sample of 177,281 adults, aged 18 and older, living in all 50 U.S. states and the District of Columbia. For results based on the total sample of national adults, the margin of sampling error for the Well-Being Index score is ±0.1 point at the 95% confidence level. The margin of sampling error for most states is about ±0.6 points, although this increases to about ±1.6 points for the smallest population states such as North Dakota, Wyoming, Hawaii and Delaware. All reported margins of sampling error include computed design effects for weighting.

May 11, 2016

MILLENNIALS LIKE SANDERS, DISLIKE ELECTION PROCESS

by Jim Norman

Story Highlights

- *Americans aged 20 to 36 favor Sanders over Trump, Clinton*
- *Millennials more positive than older generations about Sanders*
- *32% think 2016 election process is working as it should*

WASHINGTON, D.C. – Bernie Sanders is now considered a long shot for the Democratic presidential nomination, but his quest has accomplished one of his main goals – scoring major points in the contest for the hearts and minds of America's youngest voters. Millennials, the generation of Americans aged 20 to 36, are far more likely to have a favorable opinion of Sanders (55%) than presumptive Democratic nominee Hillary Clinton (38%) or her Republican counterpart, Donald Trump (22%).

Sanders Favored by Wide Variety of Millennials

Percentages with favorable opinions of Sanders, Clinton and Trump

	Sanders %	Clinton %	Trump %
All millennials	55	38	22
Men	53	32	28
Women	57	45	16
Whites	52	28	29
Blacks	67	60	14
Hispanics	52	50	14
Conservatives	29	26	36
Moderates	57	37	22
Liberals	78	51	9
No college	47	38	26
Some college	57	32	23
Graduated college	62	39	21
Postgraduate work	65	53	11

April 1-30, 2016

Gallup poll

Gallup Daily tracking polls conducted in April show Sanders bests Trump and Clinton among most millennial subgroups – specifically, with both men and women, with whites and blacks, with all education and most income levels, with moderates and liberals, and with Democrats and independents. Trump does better than Sanders or Clinton among Republicans and conservatives.

Millennials are significantly more likely than older Americans to view Sanders favorably, and are significantly less likely to have a favorable opinion of Trump. There is little difference between the two age groups concerning favorable views of Clinton. Millennials differ greatly from older Americans among several subgroups:

- Eighty-two percent of millennial Democrats view Sanders favorably, compared with 64% of older Democrats. Those figures are almost exactly reversed for Clinton: 64% of millennial Democrats view her favorably, compared with 81% of older Democrats.
- About half (51%) of conservatives aged 37 and older view Trump favorably, while 36% of millennial conservatives do.
- Eighty-two percent of blacks older than 36 view Clinton favorably. That figure drops to 60% among black millennials.

Sanders' popularity among younger Americans is not surprising. As the most liberal of the three candidates, he benefits from the fact that millennials have consistently been the most liberal of the generations that currently make up the U.S. electorate. Twenty-eight percent of millennials describe themselves as liberal, compared with 21% in Generation X (aged 37 to 51), 21% of baby boomers (aged 52 to 70) and 18% of traditionalists (aged 71 and older).

Millennials Most Likely to Lean Left

Percentages describing their political views as conservative, moderate or liberal

	Millennials %	Generation X %	Baby boomers %	Traditionalists %
Conservative	27	37	42	46
Moderate	39	37	34	30
Liberal	28	21	21	18

April 1-30, 2016

Gallup poll

Millennials: Good Candidates, but Bad Process

In Gallup polls conducted each month in 2016, majorities of millennials have consistently reacted positively to certain aspects of this year's presidential election, but have expressed dissatisfaction with the overall campaign process.

Combined results from Gallup's January-April polls show 60% of millennials say the presidential candidates are talking about issues they really care about. And when asked whether there is "any candidate running who you think would make a good president," a majority say that there is. But fewer millennials have much confidence in the campaign process so far: Just 32% say the way the presidential campaigns are being conducted makes them feel the election process is working.

Older Americans are more likely than millennials (70% vs. 59%, respectively) to think there is a good candidate running this year. On the other two questions, millennials' views align closely with those of older Americans.

Gallup also tracks how closely Americans follow election news. Millennials (21%) are less likely than the other three major generational voting groups to say they follow the news "very closely." Thirty-five percent of those in Generation X, 48% of baby boomers and 48% of traditionalists say they closely follow election news. This follows the pattern seen in previous elections in which younger adults were less likely to be deeply immersed in election news.

Bottom Line

The leading edge of the millennial generation had just turned 21 when terrorists attacked the U.S. on Sept. 11, 2001. Since then, millennials have also contended with wars in Iraq and Afghanistan, the collapse of the housing bubble, the Great Recession, and the nation's subsequent struggle to regain lost economic ground.

Faced with these challenges, millennials have responded positively to Sanders, whose platform calls for the most liberal and some of the most drastic changes to the U.S. economic and political landscape. Not only do millennials have favorable views of him personally, but there are also indications they are more likely than older generations to back his policies. Sanders is expected to lose his fight for the Democratic nomination, but he seems to be succeeding at building a foundation for his progressive movement among the voters who will have the greatest say about the nation's direction in the long run.

Download How Millennials Want to Work and Live for an in-depth look at how the millennial generation is reshaping politics, the economy, the workplace and the marketplace.

Survey Methods

Results for favorable attitudes toward the candidates are based on telephone interviews with 1,754 millennials and 7,101 adults aged 37 and older, conducted April 1-30, 2016. Results for views on how campaigns are being conducted are based on nightly polls conducted April 15-17 that included a random sample of 866 millennials and 3,606 older Americans. All respondents were aged 18 and older, living in all 50 U.S. states and the District of Columbia. For results based on the sample of 1,754 millennials, the margin of sampling error is ±3 percentage points at the 95% confidence level. For results based on the sample of 866 millennials, the margin of sampling error is ±4 percentage points at the 95% confidence level.

May 13, 2016
AMERICANS SLOWLY EMBRACING AFFORDABLE CARE ACT MORE

by Art Swift

Story Highlights

- *49% in U.S. disapprove of ACA; 47% approve*
- *22% say the law has helped their families; 26% say it has hurt*
- *Americans roughly divided about long-term effects on nation*

WASHINGTON, D.C. – Six years after its passage, Americans are almost evenly divided about the Affordable Care Act (ACA). Forty-nine percent say they disapprove of the act, while 47% approve of President Barack Obama's signature achievement. Approval is tied at its highest level since 2012.

Do you generally approve or disapprove of the 2010 Affordable Care Act, signed into law by President Obama that restructured the U.S. healthcare system?

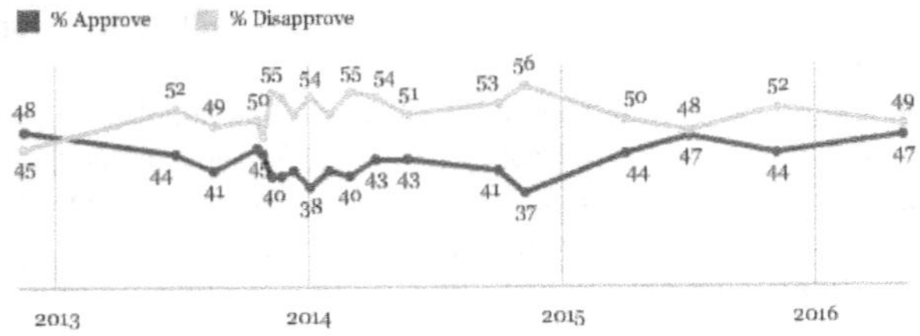

GALLUP

Americans' opinions of the ACA have fluctuated over the past four years. Just after Obama's reelection in November 2012, slightly more Americans (48%) said they approved of the law than disapproved (45%). Since then, more Americans have expressed disapproval in subsequent Gallup surveys. However, in several of these, including the latest May 6-8 survey, the gap between approval and disapproval is within the margin of error. The highest level of Americans' disapproval with the ACA (56%) was in November 2014, right after the election in which the Democrats lost the Senate.

More Americans Saying the ACA Helping Their Families

Slowly but steadily, the percentage of Americans who say Obamacare has helped them and their families has risen and, at 22%, is now at its highest since 2012. The percentage who say the law has hurt them is up 10 percentage points, now at 26%. The bulk of Americans continue to say the law has "had no effect," and that percentage is down significantly, from 70% in 2012 to 50% today. As the law is almost completely implemented nationwide, the financial effects of the ACA, along with the emotional effects it has either provided or not provided, are likely sinking in. The number of uninsured Americans has declined under Obamacare, though the law continues to be a hot point of contention in American life.

The Affordable Care Act's Effect on Families

As you may know, a number^ of the provisions of the healthcare law have already gone into effect. So far, has the law – [ROTATED: helped you and your family, not had an effect, (or has it) hurt you and your family]?

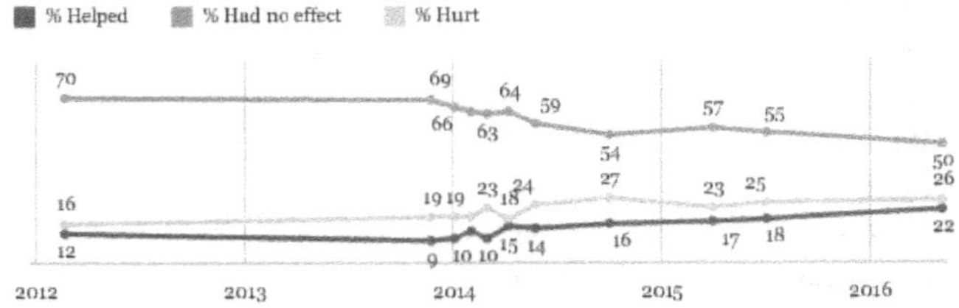

^ Wording from 2012 to April 2014: "a few"

GALLUP

The percentage of those who say the law has "had no effect" may be attributable to Obamacare not directly affecting them, including those on Medicare or those who have employer insurance.

Long Term, Americans Mixed on Effects

Americans continue to have mixed views on the ACA's long-term effects on themselves and their families. Overall, Americans are roughly divided among the beliefs that the ACA, in the long run, will make their healthcare situation better (26%), make it worse (33%) or not make much difference (39%). This three-way split is similar to what it was when Gallup first asked this question four years ago. The percentage who say ACA will improve their healthcare over time is up slightly from recent years and, by one point, is the highest measured. The percentage who say their healthcare situation will be worse is down from 38% in 2012.

Americans' Views of the ACA's Ability to Improve Families' Healthcare Situations

In the long run, how do you think the healthcare law will affect your family's healthcare situation? Will it -- [ROTATED: make things better, not make much difference, (or will it) make things worse]?

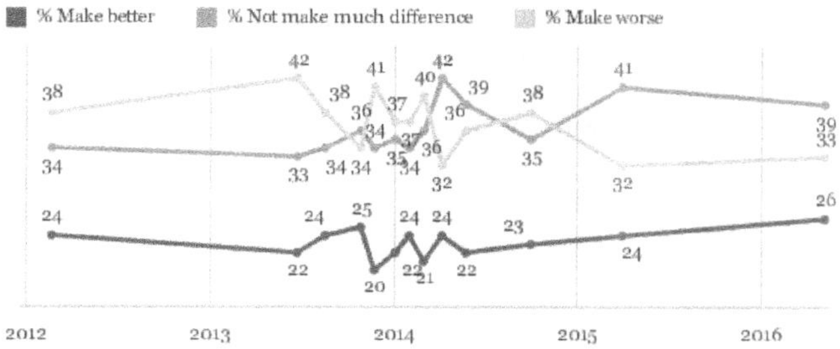

GALLUP

Americans are also divided on their views of the long-term effect of the law on the U.S. healthcare system. U.S. adults have consistently been more likely to say the law would make things worse rather than better over the past three years, but the gap has narrowed significantly.

In June 2013, 34% said the law would make healthcare nationwide better, and 47% said it would make things worse. Now, 40% say the nation's healthcare situation will be better in the long run, and 41% say it will be worse. Contrary to the sizable percentage of those who say the law hasn't personally affected them, a much smaller percentage (16%) say the ACA will not make much difference on healthcare in the U.S.

Americans' Views of the Long-Term National Impact of the Healthcare Law

In the long run, how do you think the healthcare law will affect the healthcare situation in the U.S.? Will it -- [ROTATED: make things better, not make much difference, (or will it) make things worse]?

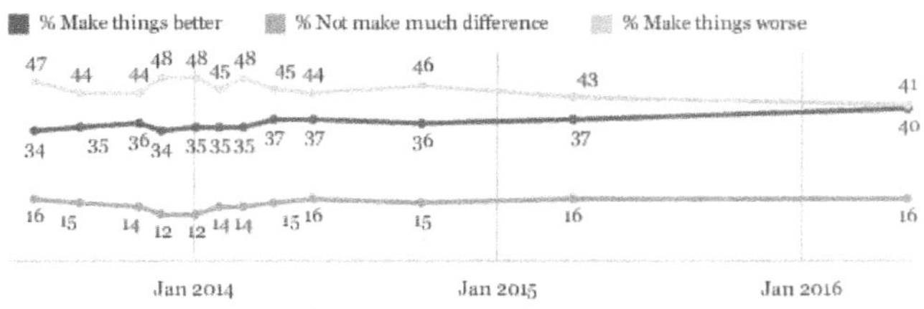

June 2013 asked on Gallup Poll News Service (non-tracking) poll

GALLUP

In this survey, Gallup asked Americans for the first time about the effect of the law so far in the U.S. Again, there is a split. Forty percent say the law has hurt the healthcare situation in the U.S., and 39% say it has helped. A much smaller percentage (14%) say it has had no effect.

Bottom Line

Americans are divided about whether they approve or disapprove of the Affordable Care Act, but support for the law has edged up from its lows in 2014. After the disastrous rollout of the U.S. government's website, along with the mass cancellation of healthcare policies in late 2013, Americans are slowly warming up to the law, its effects on themselves and their families, and the effect it will have long term for healthcare in the U.S. Support is nearly back to what it was in late 2012, a time, like now, when the president enjoyed majority job approval.

As they have been since the law's inception, views of the ACA are divided along party lines, with Democrats strongly positive and Republicans strongly negative. These attitudes on the part of rank-and-file partisans are carried over by the party's presumed nominees. While Donald Trump has vowed to repeal Obamacare immediately after taking office, it is clear that a significant portion of the public would denounce such a move. If Hillary Clinton becomes the Democratic nominee and eventually president, the Affordable Care Act will remain intact, at least for the short term. That may allow trends of greater acceptance of the healthcare law to continue into a Clinton presidency. On the other hand, if Republicans continue to be negative about the Affordable Care Act, divided approval and disapproval may continue as the norm, even if it remains the law.

Historical data are available in Gallup Analytics.

Survey Methods

Results for this Gallup poll are based on telephone interviews conducted May 6-8, 2016, on the Gallup U.S. Daily survey, with a random sample of 1,549 adults, aged 18 and older, living in all 50 U.S. states and the District of Columbia. For results based on the total sample of national adults, the margin of sampling error is ±3 percentage points at the 95% confidence level. All reported margins of sampling error include computed design effects for weighting.

May 13, 2016

THREE IN 10 U.S. WORKERS FORESEE WORKING PAST RETIREMENT AGE

by Lydia Saad

Story Highlights

- *Thirty-one percent of nonretirees plan to keep working past age 67*
- *A quarter of seniors are still working or retired after 67*
- *Four in 10 seniors retired early, before they turned 62*

PRINCETON, N.J. – Thirty-one percent of nonretired U.S. adults predict they will retire after age 67, the current minimum age for receiving full Social Security retirement benefits. Another 38% expect to retire between the ages of 62 and 67, spanning the existing Social Security age thresholds for benefits eligibility, while 23% expect to stop working before they turn 62 – that is, before becoming eligible for any Social Security retirement benefits.

U.S. Nonretirees' Expected Retirement Age

At what age do you expect to retire?

	U.S. nonretirees %
Will retire before age 62	23
Will retire between ages 62 and 67	38
Will retire at age 68 or older	31
Unsure	8

Gallup, April 6-10, 2016

These findings are from Gallup's 2016 Economy and Personal Finance Poll, conducted April 6-10. The average age at which U.S. workers predict they will retire is 66, consistent with the 65 to 67 age range found since the 2007-2009 recession ended. The expected retirement age is up slightly from about 64 years of age spanning 2004 to 2008, and is up from 60 in 1995.

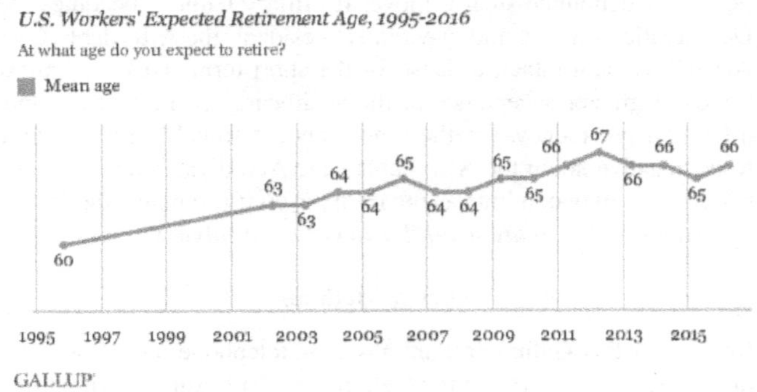

Lower-income workers plan to retire a bit later, on average, than those earning $75,000 or more annually. Young adults, those aged 18 to 29, plan to retire earlier than middle-aged and older adults, likely reflecting youthful optimism about their future income and savings.

U.S. Nonretirees' Expected Retirement Age

At what age do you expect to retire?

	U.S. nonretireesaverage age
Income	
Less than $30,000	70
$30,000 to less than $75,000	69
$75,000 or more	67
Age	
18 to 29	64
30 to 49	70
50 to 64	69
65+	*

* Sample size for 65+ nonretirees is insufficient for reporting

Gallup, April 6-10, 2016

Four in 10 Current Retirees Retired Before 62

In contrast with current workers' expectations about retirement, retired Americans report they stopped working at an average 61 years of age, significantly lower than the average 66 years at which today's nonretired Americans intend to stop working. More specifically, 42% of retirees say they stopped working before age 62, while just 13% continued working until they were 67 or older. Of course, current retirees span an age range of more than 40 years, meaning that some retired decades ago, while others may have retired the day before they were interviewed, and their age at retirement no doubt reflects societal and economic patterns in force at that time.

This doesn't tell the entire generational story, as approximately one in seven seniors (defined for this analysis as those aged 67 and older) are still in the workforce – working full time, working part time or unemployed. When these are factored into the equation, 26% of adults 67 and older are either still in the workforce (14%) or worked until they were 67 or older before retiring (12%). That is a bit less than the 31% of today's nonretirees who intend to work past 67. However, the greater discrepancy is in the percentage retiring before age 62: 36% of today's seniors say they did this, while just 23% of current workers intend to.

U.S. Retirees' Retirement Age

At what age did you retire?

	Retirees %
Retired before age 62	36
Retired at age 62 to 66	36
Retired at age 67 or older	12
Not yet retired (working or unemployed)	14
No opinion	3

Gallup, April 6-10, 2016

Bottom Line

Myriad factors go into determining the best time to retire, not all of which are within workers' control. Financial troubles, poor health, family needs or being let go at work can all disrupt the best-laid plans. At the same time, for those who depend on it, the Social Security system forces people to gamble on their life expectancy in deciding whether to retire early with partial benefits or later with full benefits.

Although many of these factors are constant, some have changed in recent decades. As a result, the age at which today's workers expect to retire is significantly older, on average, than the age current retirees say they already did retire: 66 vs. 61, respectively. Some of that difference undoubtedly reflects the gradual increase, which Congress mandated in 1983, in the Social Security system's age threshold for receiving full benefits – from 65 to 67. However, that does not explain the higher percentage of nonretirees who plan to work beyond age 67 compared with current retirees who report having worked this long – 31% vs. 26%, respectively.

One factor causing today's workers to think about delaying retirement could be their recognition that working may be healthier than staying home. A recent Wells Fargo/Gallup Investor and Retirement Optimism Index survey found 67% of nonretired investors – those with $10,000 or more in investments – agreeing that they want to work as long as possible, given the benefits to their physical and mental health. At the same time, unexpected health problems could explain why some current retirees retired early.

In reality, however, many working Americans simply can't afford to retire. Fewer workers today than in the past say a pension will be a major income source in retirement, and many have been unable to save sufficiently during the economic slowdown of the past decade. Seven in 10 employed adults told Gallup in April that they are worried about not having enough savings for retirement. As a result, they now need to work as long as possible to build up their retirement nest eggs.

At the moment, most workers are forgoing any thought of retiring before 62, the minimum age to receive partial Social Security retirement benefits, while nearly a third are planning to hold off until after age 67. These figures already represent a departure from how today's seniors have handled retirement, and could easily change further if the economy or the Social Security Administration throws workers any more curve balls.

Historical data are available in Gallup Analytics.

Survey Methods

Results for this Gallup poll are based on telephone interviews conducted April 6-10, 2016, with a random sample of 1,015 adults, aged 18 and older, living in all 50 U.S. states and the District of Columbia. For results based on the total sample of national adults, the margin of sampling error is ±4 percentage points at the 95% confidence level. For results based on the sample of 678 nonretirees, the margin of sampling error is ±5 percentage points. For results based on the sample of 525 adults employed full or part time, the margin of sampling error is ±5 percentage points. For results based on the sample of 337 retirees, the margin of sampling error is ±7 percentage points. All reported margins of sampling error include computed design effects for weighting.

May 16, 2016

ECONOMY CONTINUES TO RANK AS TOP U.S. PROBLEM

by Justin McCarthy

Story Highlights

- *Americans also mention dissatisfaction with government, unemployment*
- *Republicans' concerns about the economy edge higher*

WASHINGTON, D.C. – Eighteen percent of U.S. adults in May name the economy in general as the most important problem facing the U.S. This figure is similar to the 17% who mentioned the economy as the chief problem the prior three months. Mentions of the economy have increased slightly this year compared with last year.

Most Important Problem – Recent Trend

What do you think is the most important problem facing this country today? (Open-ended)

	March 2016 %	April 2016 %	May 2016 %
Economy in general	17	17	18
Dissatisfaction with government	15	13	13
Unemployment/Jobs	11	9	9
Immigration	8	8	7
Race relations/Racism	6	7	5
Federal budget deficit	5	5	5
Elections/Election reform	5	4	5
Terrorism	6	6	4
Healthcare	8	5	4
National security	3	5	4
Education	4	4	4
Poverty/Hunger/Homelessness	3	4	4
Gap between rich and poor	3	3	4

Issues mentioned by 4% or more of respondents in May 2016
Gallup Daily tracking

Americans in May continue to cite a wide variety of issues when asked to name the most important problem facing the U.S., including dissatisfaction with government (13%) and unemployment (9%). Americans also list immigration (7%), race relations (5%), the federal budget deficit (5%), and elections and election reform (5%).

Although the percentage of Americans mentioning each of these problems has varied slightly from month to month, the basic pattern of concerns has remained similar since February.

Many issues atop the list have ebbed slightly in prominence by one or two percentage points over the past month or so, and mentions of healthcare (4%) have fallen four points since March. But the economy in general has remained the problem mentioned most often for four consecutive months.

Republicans' Concerns About the Economy Edge Higher

The percentages of independents (16%) and Democrats (11%) naming the economy in general as the country's top problem have not changed much in recent months, while the percentage of Republicans mentioning the issue has increased sharply.

Since March, an average of 27% of Republicans have said the economy is the top problem facing the country, up from an average of 13% from December to February. Republicans' greater concern about this issue could reflect GOP presidential candidates' views on economic problems in the current presidential election.

Percentages Mentioning Economy as Most Important Problem, by Political Party

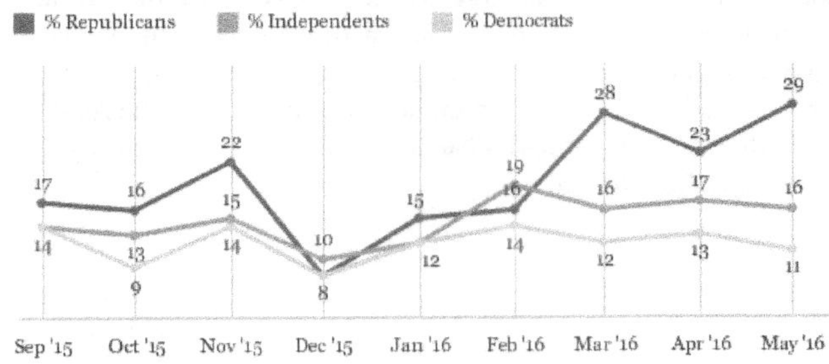

Gallup Daily tracking

GALLUP'

Bottom Line

With the presidential election campaign roaring on, the economy remains the single leading issue in Americans' minds as the biggest problem facing the country. Economic concerns more generally make up about 40% of all "most important problem" mentions. This comes as Americans' confidence in the economy has recently sagged a bit and as Americans prepare to elect their next leader to steer the country.

Gallup has found that the economy is one of the top campaign issues for both Democrats and Republicans. But while members of both parties agree the issue is a pressing one, Republicans are nearly three times as likely as Democrats to say the issue is the *top* problem facing the U.S. This is consistent with their confidence in the national economy – Democrats have much more positive views – and reflects the nature of how Americans view the economy through their party's lens.

Historical data are available in Gallup Analytics.

Survey Methods

Results for this Gallup poll are based on telephone interviews conducted May 4-8, 2016, on the Gallup Daily tracking survey, with a random sample of 1,025 adults, aged 18 and older, living in all 50 U.S. states and the District of Columbia. For results based on the total sample of national adults, the margin of sampling error is ±4 percentage points at the 95% confidence level. All reported margins of sampling error include computed design effects for weighting.

May 16, 2016

MAJORITY IN U.S. SUPPORT IDEA OF FED-FUNDED HEALTHCARE SYSTEM

by Frank Newport

Story Highlights

- *58% favor replacing the ACA with federally funded healthcare system*
- *About half would also be OK with keeping the ACA as is*
- *Separate question shows that just over half would favor repealing the ACA*

PRINCETON, N.J. – Presented with three separate scenarios for the future of the Affordable Care Act (ACA), 58% of U.S. adults favor the idea of replacing the law with a federally funded healthcare system that provides insurance for all Americans. At the same time, Americans are split on the idea of maintaining the ACA as it is, with 48% in favor and 49% opposed. The slight majority, 51%, favor repealing the act.

Favor or Oppose Three Proposals Relating to the Affordable Care Act

Please tell me whether you strongly favor, favor, oppose or strongly oppose each of the following.

	Favor %	Oppose %	No opinion %
Replacing the ACA with a federally funded healthcare program providing insurance for all Americans	58	37	5
Repealing the Affordable Care Act	51	45	3
Keeping the Affordable Care Act in place	48	49	2

Gallup, May 6-8, 2016

Gallup included these three questions in its interviewing on May 6-8 to provide insight into how Americans might react to the three remaining presidential candidates' proposals for dealing with the ACA. Bernie Sanders calls for replacing the ACA with a single-payer, federally administered system that he calls "Medicare for All." Donald Trump has said he would repeal the ACA, and Hillary Clinton generally says she would keep the ACA in place. Americans were asked in the survey to react to each of these proposals separately, and there was no mention of the candidates in the question wording.

The results show that many Americans are OK with several ways of handling the ACA rather than favoring only one possibility. In particular, 35% of all Americans say they would favor keeping the ACA in place and separately say they favor the idea of replacing it with a federally funded universal health insurance system. Among Democrats and Democratic leaners, 59% favor both of these approaches. In short, many Americans would apparently go along with Clinton's idea of keeping the ACA in place as it is now, or with Sanders' bolder proposal to replace it with a Medicare-for-All system.

Gallup also asked those who favor either keeping the ACA in place or replacing it with a federally funded system to choose between these two options. The federally funded system wins among this group by a 2-to-1 ratio, 64% to 32%, meaning this system garners the most support among the initial favor/oppose questions and wins when those who like both approaches are forced to choose.

Additionally, 27% of Americans say they favor repealing the ACA and say they favor replacing it with a federally funded system. This means the group of Americans in this survey who favor the law's repeal, a core policy proposal of many Republican presidential candidates during this campaign season, includes some who apparently want the ACA repealed to replace it with an even more liberal system. Only 22% of Americans say they want the ACA repealed and do not favor replacing it with a federally funded system.

Democrats Favor Keeping the ACA *and* Replacing It With Single-Payer System

The breakdown of reactions to these proposals by partisanship shows the expected patterns: Democrats and Democratic-leaning independents are highly likely to favor the two options put forth by the Democratic candidates, while Republicans and Republican leaners are highly likely to favor Trump's position, repeal of the ACA.

Proposals to Deal With Affordable Care Act, by Partisanship

	Democrats/Leaners %	Republicans/Leaners %
Replacing the ACA with a federally funded healthcare program providing insurance for all Americans		
Favor	73	41
Oppose	22	55
Repealing the Affordable Care Act		
Favor	25	80
Oppose	72	17
Keeping the Affordable Care Act in place		
Favor	79	16
Oppose	19	82

Gallup, May 6-8, 2016

One notable exception to the strong partisan skew in reactions to these proposals comes from Republicans when they are asked about replacing the ACA with a federally funded system. Forty-one percent of Republicans favor the proposal – much higher than the 16% who favor keeping the ACA in place. This may reflect either that Republicans genuinely think a single-payer system would be good for the country, or that they view any proposal to replace the ACA ("Obamacare") as better than keeping it in place.

Approval of the ACA and What Should Be Done About It

Responses to other questions included in the May 6-8 survey show that Americans remain split in their overall views of the ACA, with about as many approving as disapproving of the law. Almost nine in 10 of those who approve of the ACA in general subsequently say they would favor keeping it in place, which is logical. But 72% of those who approve of the ACA also would favor replacing it with a single-payer federally funded health system. This reinforces the idea that ACA supporters can agree simultaneously with several different ways of dealing with this law.

Bottom Line

Americans express considerable support for the idea of replacing the ACA with a federally run national healthcare system, which is similar to the proposal championed by presidential candidate Sanders. To be sure, many Americans, primarily Democrats, also favor the idea of just keeping the ACA in place. But given a choice, those who favor both proposals come down on the side of the Sanders-type proposal. Four in 10 Republicans also favor the idea of a federally funded system.

Additionally, Americans have been more positive than negative in two previous Gallup measures of the idea of a single-payer federally funded system, although when given a chance to say so, a sizable percentage of Americans say they don't know enough about it to have an opinion.

The current survey used shorthand descriptions to describe the alternatives for dealing with the ACA, and it's possible that not everyone understands the implications of each approach. Instituting a universal healthcare system, in particular, would be one of the most significant overhauls of a major part of American life in modern U.S. history, and would create huge consequences and challenges. Additionally, other research shows that when given a choice, Americans are philosophically more inclined to favor a private healthcare system than one run by the government. Americans are generally satisfied with their personal healthcare, something that also could slow down the process of adopting a major overhaul of the healthcare system. Still, the general idea of a single payer system seems to play well with the majority of Americans, something both the presumed Democratic nominee Clinton and the Republican nominee Trump will need to keep in mind as they debate healthcare in the months to come.

Historical data are available in Gallup Analytics.

Survey Methods

Results for this Gallup poll are based on telephone interviews conducted May 6-8, 2016, on the Gallup U.S. Daily survey, with a random sample of 1,549 adults, aged 18 and older, living in all 50 U.S. states and the District of Columbia. For results based on the total sample of national adults, the margin of sampling error is ±3 percentage points at the 95% confidence level. All reported margins of sampling error include computed design effects for weighting.

May 17, 2016
MOST "PRO-LIFE" AMERICANS UNSURE ABOUT TRUMP'S ABORTION VIEWS

by Lydia Saad

Story Highlights

- *Six in 10 "pro-life" adults unfamiliar with Trump's abortion views*
- *19% of pro-life Americans say they agree with Trump's views*
- *One in five Americans say abortion is a key voting issue for them*

PRINCETON, N.J. – Donald Trump, the presumptive Republican nominee who describes himself as "pro-life," still has significant work to do to convince the anti-abortion voting bloc that he is on their side. Sixty-three percent of Americans who describe themselves as "pro-life" are unable to say whether they agree or disagree with Trump on the abortion issue. The rest are about equally divided between agreeing (19%) and disagreeing (18%) with him.

Americans' Level of Agreement With Donald Trump on Abortion Issue

Based on what you know or have read, would you say you generally agree or generally disagree with Donald Trump on the abortion issue, or don't you know enough to say?

	U.S. adults %	"Pro-choice" %	"Pro-life" %
Agree	13	7	19
Disagree	31	46	18
No opinion	56	47	63

May 4-8, 2016
Gallup poll

Meanwhile, "pro-choice" Americans are much more likely to disagree than agree with Trump on abortion – 46% vs. 7%, respectively – while about half are unsure. Overall, a slight majority of Americans (56%) are uncertain about their level of agreement with Trump's abortion views; 13% agree with his views, and 31% disagree.

Hillary Clinton is unambiguously pro-abortion rights and has talked about her strong support for women's reproductive rights for decades. Nevertheless, the public is only a bit less vague about her stance on the issue compared with Trump's. Overall, 22% of Americans say they agree with her views and 32% disagree, while 46% are unsure.

Pro-choice Americans – who align with Clinton and the Democratic Party on the issue – are significantly more likely to agree than disagree with her views: 38% vs. 15%, respectively. Similar to pro-choice Americans' disagreement with Trump, about half of pro-life Americans (51%) disagree with Clinton.

Americans' Level of Agreement With Hillary Clinton on Abortion Issue

Based on what you know or have read, would you say you generally agree or generally disagree with Hillary Clinton on the abortion issue, or don't you know enough to say?

	U.S. adults %	"Pro-choice" %	"Pro-life" %
Agree	22	38	6
Disagree	32	15	51
No opinion	46	47	43

May 4-8, 2016
Gallup poll

These findings are from Gallup's 2016 Values and Beliefs poll, conducted May 4-8. The survey finds that 46% of Americans describe themselves as pro-life and 47% as pro-choice. That is a more even division than a year ago, when Americans leaned more toward the pro-choice side (50% vs. 44%) but is similar to attitudes in 2013 and 2014.

Abortion Not a Key Voting Issue for Most

Americans' general lack of familiarity with the leading Republican and Democratic presidential candidates' positions on abortion could reflect the relatively low profile the abortion issue has had in the campaign this cycle. Although discussion of the issue has flared at times, the economy, healthcare, immigration and national security tend to consume more air time.

Another reason, perhaps, that many Americans seem unclear as to where Clinton and Trump stand on abortion is that only 20% – similar to the level in 2012 – say the issue affects how they vote for major offices. One in five say they will only vote for a candidate who shares their views on abortion. Another 49% say it is one of many important factors they consider when voting, while 28% say it is not a major issue for them.

As in the past, slightly more in the pro-life than in the pro-choice camp – 23% vs. 17%, respectively – say that a candidate must share their views on abortion to win their support.

Effect Abortion Issue Has on Americans' Voting for Major Offices

Thinking about how the abortion issue might affect your vote for major offices, would you ... ?

	U.S. adults %	"Pro-choice" %	"Pro-life" %
Only vote for a candidate who shares your views on abortion	20	17	23
Consider a candidate's position on abortion as just one of many important factors when voting	49	48	51
Not see abortion as a major issue	28	32	22
No opinion	4	2	4

May 4-8, 2016
Gallup poll

Bottom Line

Abortion has not been a highly important voting issue for the public in the 2016 presidential election, at least not yet. And given the consistently low percentage of Americans who identify it as a key voting issue for them, that is not likely to change between now and November. Still, in a close election, even small constituency groups can have a pivotal effect on the outcome. Pro-choice Americans' clear leaning toward agreeing with Clinton's views could be advantageous for her. By contrast, Trump has failed to establish much of any image on abortion among self-described pro-lifers. How this develops between now and November could decide whether the 20% of pro-lifers who care deeply about the issue will come out and vote for him.

Survey Methods

Results for this Gallup poll are based on telephone interviews conducted May 4-8, 2016, with a random sample of 1,025 adults, aged 18 and older, living in all 50 U.S. states and the District of Columbia. For results based on the total sample of national adults, the margin of sampling error is ±4 percentage points at the 95% confidence level. For results based on the total sample of 480 adults who identify as "pro-choice" and 472 adults who identify as "pro-life," the margin of sampling error is ±5 percentage points at the 95% confidence level. All reported margins of sampling error include computed design effects for weighting.

May 18, 2016
MAJORITY IN U.S. DO NOT HAVE A WILL

by Jeffrey M. Jones

Story Highlights

- *44% report having a will*
- *Percentage was 51% in 2005, 48% in 1990*
- *Older Americans are more likely to have a will*

PRINCETON, N.J. – Forty-four percent of Americans say they have a will that describes how they would like their money and estate handled after their death. That is lower than in two prior Gallup polls: 51% in 2005 and 48% in 1990.

Do you have a will that describes how you would like your money and estate to be handled after your death?

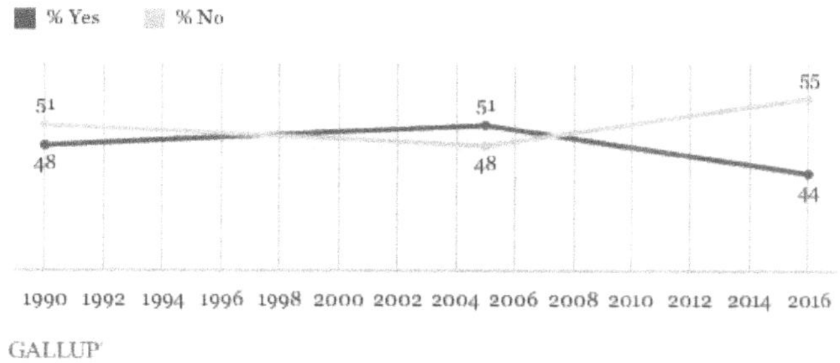

The issue of wills has been a topic in the news after the untimely death of the musician Prince. His sister filed court papers asserting he did not have a will, and so far, nobody has produced one. While most Americans are not as wealthy as Prince, his not having a will appears to be common in the U.S.

Lawyers and financial advisors recommend people write wills to ensure their wishes for transferring their property and assets are followed and to avoid protracted legal proceedings over the distribution of those assets.

The results are based on a May 4-8 Gallup poll, conducted two weeks after Prince's death. While it is unknown whether major news events that touch on the wishes of the dead or dying can influence Americans' self-reports of having a will, the higher 2005 estimate came in a poll conducted shortly after the Terri Schiavo saga.

Americans' likelihood of having a will depends largely on their age and socioeconomic status. Sixty-eight percent of those aged 65 and older have a will, compared with just 14% of those younger than age 30. Of Americans whose annual household income is $75,000 or greater, 55% have a will, compared with 31% of those with incomes of less than $30,000. And while 61% of those with a postgraduate education have a will, only 32% with a high school education or less do.

Likely reflecting those age and socioeconomic differences, nonwhite adults (28%) are about half as likely as white adults (51%) to have a will.

Given the relationships between age and income and having a will, the percentage who say they have a will rises to 75% among upper-income Americans aged 55 and older.

Since 2005, the percentage of those in most key subgroups who have a will has declined. The major exception is among those with a postgraduate education, for which there has been essentially no change. Declines have been above-average since 2005 in the subgroups that are least likely to have a will – younger, lower-income, less-educated and nonwhite Americans.

Percentage Having a Will, by Age, Income, Education and Race

	2005 %	2016 %	Changepct. pts.
National adults	51	44	-7
Age			
65+	78	68	-10
50-64	63	56	-7
30-49	43	35	-8
18-29	24	14	-10
Annual Household Income			
$75,000 or more	62	55	-7
$30,000-$74,999	48	38	-10
Less than $30,000	45	31	-14
Education			
Postgraduate	60	61	1
College graduate only	54	50	-4
Some college	54	47	-7
High school or less	45	32	-13
Race			
White	55	51	-4
Nonwhite	39	28	-11

Gallup

Implications

Prince's main legacy will undoubtedly be his music, but his unexpected death might leave him with another: an example of what can happen when someone dies without a will. Prince was certainly not alone in not writing a will, as the majority of Americans report they do not have one. Even a substantial minority of older and upper-income Americans – roughly three in 10 of those aged 65 years and older, and nearly four in 10 of those with household incomes of $100,000 or more – say they do not have a will.

The legal battles over the distribution of Prince's estate are just beginning, but as those play out in the coming months, it might persuade more Americans to formally and legally spell out their wishes for how to handle their estates after their death.

Historical data are available in Gallup Analytics.

Survey Methods

Results for this Gallup poll are based on telephone interviews conducted May 4-8, 2016, with a random sample of 1,025 adults, aged 18 and older, living in all 50 U.S. states and the District of Columbia. For results based on the total sample of national adults, the margin of sampling error is ±4 percentage points at the 95% confidence level. All reported margins of sampling error include computed design effects for weighting.

May 19, 2016

GALLUP ANALYSIS: MILLENNIALS, MARRIAGE AND FAMILY

by John Fleming

Story Highlights

- *59% of millennials are single and have never been married*
- *60% of millennials do not have any children under 18 in their household*

PRINCETON, N.J. – There are roughly 73 million millennials in the U.S. – those born between 1980 and 1996 – and to marketers, these consumers represent a huge economic opportunity. To some, millennials are hyperconnected and technology-savvy social media mavens. To others, millennials are the new generation of highly indebted narcissists forever credited with coining the term "selfie."

Marketers and business leaders have a keen interest in understanding how members of the millennial generation – now the largest generation after eclipsing the baby boomers – differ from members of other generations. Understanding millennials' attitudes, preferences and behaviors is critical because they have significant implications for many aspects of U.S. social and economic life.

The Gallup Daily tracking survey reveals that members of the millennials do in fact differ from other generations in some important ways – ways that millennials' relative youth alone does not explain. We would expect young people to differ from those who are older, as they always have, just as we would expect seniors to differ from those who are younger. These differences that the data reveal represent a departure from the patterns of older generations at the same points in their lives. Large sample sizes – approximately 175,000 per year – allow Gallup to examine extensive demographic breaks and crosstabulations of the daily measures. The 2014 Gallup Daily tracking data are one of the only sources to capture views of the entire span of the millennial generation, because the last of the millennials turned 18 in 2014.

Marital Status, by Generation

	Millennials %	Gen Xers %	Baby boomers %	Traditionalists %	TOTAL %
Single/Never married	59	16	10	4	25
Married	27	62	65	55	52
Separated	2	4	3	1	2
Divorced	3	11	14	9	9
Widowed	*	1	6	29	6
Domestic partnership/ Living with partner	9	6	3	1	5

* Less than 0.5%
Gallup U.S. Daily tracking, Jan. 2-Dec. 30, 2014

Millennials Are in No Rush to Marry

Contrary to what we would expect, given normal demographic patterns of adolescents' movement into early adulthood and family formation, the data show that significantly more millennials are currently single/never married than was true for those in older generations, and considerably more are in domestic partnerships. Specifically, more than half of all millennials (59%) have never married, and 9% are in domestic partnerships. Gallup has noted a trend toward fewer young adults being married in recent years.

In the 2014 Gallup Daily tracking data, just 27% of millennials were married. According to historical U.S. Census Bureau data, 36% of Generation Xers, 48% of baby boomers and 65% of traditionalists were married when they were the age that millennials are now. For millennials currently aged 18 to 30, just 20% are married, compared with nearly 60% of 18- to 30-year-olds in 1962, according to the U.S. Census. When Gen Xers were the same age, 32% were married; for baby boomers, it was more than 40%.

Millennials are clearly delaying marriage longer than any generation before them, in spite of evidence suggesting that many millennials intend to marry at some point. For example, a 2013 Gallup poll found that 86% of single/never married Americans aged 18 to 34 (roughly equivalent to the millennial generation) wanted to get married someday.

The percentage of single-adult households for millennials (18%) is no different from that of Gen Xers (16%) or baby boomers (19%), while the percentage of single-adult traditionalist households (31%) is larger for obvious mortality reasons. The percentage of current two-adult millennial households (46%) is significantly lower than that of Gen Xers (57%), baby boomers (52%) or traditionalists (55%). Significantly more millennials are currently in multi-adult households of three or more (36%) than is true for any other generation, suggesting that these reflect some form of communal living arrangement (77% of millennials in multi-adult households of three or more are single/never married, while 12% are married).

Adults Aged 18 or Older in Household, by Generation

	Millennials %	Gen Xers %	Baby boomers %	Traditionalists %	TOTAL %
One	18	16	19	31	20
Two	46	57	52	55	52
Three or more	36	27	29	14	28

Gallup U.S. Daily tracking, Jan. 2-Dec. 30, 2014

Millennials Are Intent on Having Children

The key point, however, is this: There doesn't appear to be any evidence that millennials – both married and single/never married – are putting off having children. Even among the small percentage (2%) of married 18-year-old millennials, less than half (44%) have no children, and the percentage decreases with age to just 17% at age 34. And while few single 18-year-old millennials have children (4%), that percentage rises to almost half by age 34. In other words, almost half of the oldest millennials who have never married nonetheless have children. In 2000, the comparable number for Gen Xers aged 30 to 34 was just 30%.

In fact, public perceptions of the moral acceptability of having children out of wedlock have increased dramatically over the past decade and a half. Gallup poll data show that the percentage who say this is morally acceptable currently stands at an all-time high (62% overall and 68% among millennials). As recently as 2002, just 45% overall said it was morally acceptable to have a child out of wedlock, while 50% said it was morally wrong.

In a 2013 Gallup poll, 87% of adults between 18 and 40 who did not yet have children said they wanted them someday. The current data suggest that for millennials, "having children someday" does not necessarily depend on being married. But when combined with the observation that the substantial majority of single/never married 18- to 34-year-olds would like to get married someday, it is possible that more single/never married millennials with children will ultimately get married in the months and years ahead. It is also possible that more millennials – married or not – will have children in the near future.

Children Under 18 in Household, by Generation

	Millennials %	Gen Xers %	Baby boomers %	Traditionalists %	TOTAL %
None	60	32	86	98	66
One	15	23	9	1	13
Two	13	26	4	1	12
Three or more	11	19	2	1	9

Gallup U.S. Daily tracking, Jan. 2-Dec. 30, 2014

Implications

Most millennials have not yet married, and they are waiting longer to marry. For 34-year-olds, just over half (56%) are married, and of these, 83% have children. But a substantial number (46%) of those who have never been married and are well into their 30s have children. This may represent a seismic shift in the connection between marriage and child rearing because as recently as 2000, the comparable percentage of single/never married 30- to 34-year-olds with children was just 30%.

More millennials currently live in multi-adult households than is true for other generations, and the data suggest that unlike those older generations, these multi-adult households consist primarily of single millennials living collectively. Domestic partnerships – not common in general – are much more common among millennials, and millennials are more than twice as likely as older Americans to identify as LGBT. No doubt this is a reflection of changing social standards within the larger American community. These last observations about marriage, family and sexuality tend to point to a generation that is beginning to rethink and reconstruct social norms to better fit its wants and needs, throwing off convention when it no longer serves a compelling purpose.

The face of the American family has profoundly changed during the past two generations, with millennials picking up where Gen Xers left off. Along with these changes, or perhaps as a result of them, social norms within American society have shifted – and with them, nearly every aspect of our daily lives. It would be wise for marketers and business leaders to stay abreast of the kinds of changes millennials bring to American society, because understanding how this large group of consumers approaches the world – and the marketplace – could be lucrative. Getting it wrong, however, could hamstring and hobble a company for decades.

Download Gallup's latest report, How Millennials Want to Work and Live, *to get further insight into what millennials really want from a job, manager and company, and what organizations can do to become this generation's employer of choice.*

These data are available in Gallup Analytics.

May 19, 2016

REPUBLICANS MORE POSITIVE ABOUT TRUMP, BUT MANY NOT PLEASED

by Frank Newport

Story Highlights

- *Trump's favorable rating among Republicans up to its highest point*
- *Trump's image still lags previous GOP nominees at this point*
- *Half of Republicans wish there was another nominee, not Trump*

PRINCETON, N.J. – As a number of Republican Party leaders express dissatisfaction with Donald Trump being their party's presumptive nominee, rank-and-file Republicans have become more positive about the billionaire businessman. Over the last seven days, Trump's favorable rating among Republicans and Republican-leaning independents has reached 66%, the highest since Gallup began tracking him nine months ago. His unfavorable rating is at 30%.

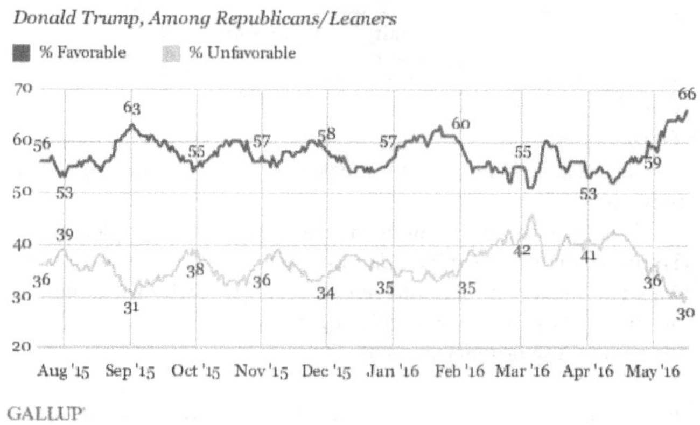

Trump has always been perceived more favorably than unfavorably by Republicans. His ratings were most negative in late February/early March, but in recent weeks, as his nomination has become all but certain, Trump's net favorable image among Republicans has improved steadily.

Trump's image among Republicans, however, is still significantly more negative than that of the last three Republican nominees at about this point in their presidential campaigns. Mitt Romney, John McCain and George W. Bush had coalesced their party's support into a more universally positive image by May or early June of 2012, 2008 and 2000, respectively, with favorable ratings in the 80% range and low unfavorable ratings.

Republican Candidates' Image Among Republicans/Leaners

Candidate	Date	Favorable %	Unfavorable %
Donald Trump	May 11-17, 2016	66	30
Mitt Romney	May 10-13, 2012	82	13
John McCain	May 30-June 1, 2008	84	11
George W. Bush	June 6-7, 2000	87	9

Gallup

The fact that Trump has a significantly more negative image than has been the norm for his party's nominees at this point in recent campaigns could partially reflect the time frame of the nomination process. Trump's battle against his competitors, for example, has gone on much longer than Bush's in 2000, who was never seriously challenged that year as his party's presumptive nominee. Similarly, McCain essentially became the presumptive GOP nominee by February 2008. Romney, like Trump, didn't sew up the GOP nomination until late April, but he held an 82% favorable rating among Republicans by mid-May, a contrast to Trump's current 66%.

Another Gallup measure reinforces the conclusion that Trump faces a more difficult than usual challenge in his effort to unite Republicans behind his candidacy. Republicans in May 13-15 interviewing were split down the middle when asked if they are pleased with Trump as their party's nominee, or if they wish it was someone else – 48% pleased and 50% wishing there was someone else.

Are you generally pleased with the selection of Donald Trump as the Republican nominee, or do you wish someone else was the Republican nominee?

Based on Republicans/leaning Republicans

	Generally pleased %	Wish someone else was running %	No opinion %
May 13-15, 2016	48	50	2

Gallup

There is no history of this measure providing a comparison with previous GOP nominees.

The groups of Republicans most likely to be pleased with Trump as the nominee include those who are older, men, conservatives and those without college degrees – generally adhering to the profile of those who have held the most favorable view of Trump throughout the primary process.

Are you generally pleased with the selection of Donald Trump as the Republican nominee, or do you wish someone else was the Republican nominee?

Based on Republicans/leaning Republicans

	Generally pleased %	Wish someone else was running %
AGE		
18-34	36	62
35-54	39	59
55+	59	39
GENDER		
Male	50	47
Female	44	55
PARTY ID AND IDEOLOGY		
Conservative Republican	53	46
Liberal/Moderate Republican	40	57
EDUCATION		
College grad	41	56
Not college grad	50	48

May 13-15, 2016
Gallup

Bottom Line

Trump's image among his fellow Republicans is improving and is now more positive than it has been at any point since the campaign process heated up last summer. But Trump's image is substantially more negative than the images of his predecessors at this point in their campaigns, and half of Republicans say they wish someone else was their party's nominee.

The relative lack of enthusiasm for Trump among his own party may not be his biggest challenge to winning the presidency – twice as many Americans overall have an unfavorable (60%) as a favorable (34%) opinion of him, reflecting strongly negative views among independents and Democrats. His likely competitor, Hillary Clinton, however, also has a negative image among all Americans, at 39% favorable and 55% unfavorable.

Both Trump and Clinton's next major opportunities to improve voters' perceptions will be their selection of a vice presidential running mate, and then the conventions in July.

These data are available in Gallup Analytics.

Survey Methods

Results for this Gallup poll are based on telephone interviews conducted May 11-17, 2016, on the Gallup U.S. Daily survey, with a random sample of 1,555 Republicans and Republican-leaning independents, aged 18 and older, living in all 50 U.S. states and the District of Columbia, and interviews conducted May 13-15, 2016, with a random sample of 677 Republicans and Republican-leaning independents. For results based on the first sample of Republicans, the margin of sampling error is ±4 percentage points at the 95% confidence level, and for the second sample, the margin of sampling error is ±5 percentage points at the 95% confidence level. All reported margins of sampling error include computed design effects for weighting.

May 19, 2016

AMERICANS' SUPPORT FOR GAY MARRIAGE REMAINS HIGH, AT 61%

by Justin McCarthy

Story Highlights

- *Support is up among each political party and age group*
- *About one in four say candidates must share their views on issue*
- *Gay marriage issue loses importance among GOP voters*

WASHINGTON, D.C. – Sixty-one percent of Americans say that marriages between same-sex couples should be recognized by the law as valid, consistent with the 58% and 60% recorded in 2015. Last year's Supreme Court decision made same-sex marriage legal nationwide – but the issue remains contentious at state and local levels, among religious groups and within the Republican Party.

Do you think marriages between same-sex couples should or should not be recognized by the law as valid, with the same rights as traditional marriages?

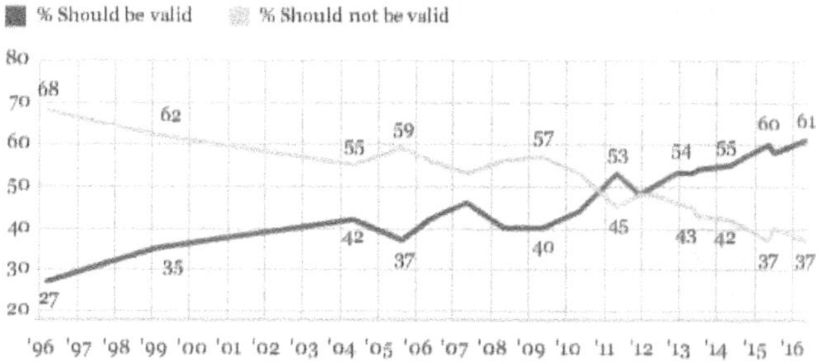

Note: Trend shown for polls in which same-sex marriage question followed questions on gay/lesbian rights and relations
1996-2005 wording: "Do you think marriages between homosexuals ..."

GALLUP

Public support for same-sex marriage has more than doubled over the past two decades. When Gallup first polled on the issue in 1996, about a quarter of Americans (27%) said such marriages should be recognized by law. Majority support was recorded for the first time in 2011, and the percentage has since grown.

The latest 61%, from the annual Values and Beliefs poll conducted May 4-8, is the highest in Gallup's trend so far by one percentage point.

With six months left until Election Day, the issue of gay marriage has been less prominent this year than in the past few presidential elections. The Supreme Court's ruling in 2015 makes the issue somewhat moot, and both Democratic candidates support it. Meanwhile, Republican front-runner Donald Trump has been fairly muted on the issue compared with some his GOP opponents, particularly those who backed a constitutional amendment defining marriage as a union between a man and a woman. While Trump says he opposes same-sex marriage, the issue does not appear on his campaign website, and he has been referred to as "the most gay-friendly Republican nominee for president ever" by the president of the Log Cabin Republicans, an organization for gay Republicans.

Trump's relatively subdued stance on the issue may be related to softened opposition from national Republicans. Four in 10 rank-and-file Republicans say same-sex marriage should be legally recognized. This is the highest support on record and is more than twice as high as the 16% found in 1996. The GOP remains the least supportive of gay marriage among the three main party groups, as strong majorities of independents (65%) and Democrats (79%) say such marriages should be recognized as valid under the law.

Support for Same-Sex Marriage, by Party

Do you think marriages between same-sex couples should or should not be recognized by the law as valid, with the same rights as traditional marriages?
% Should be valid

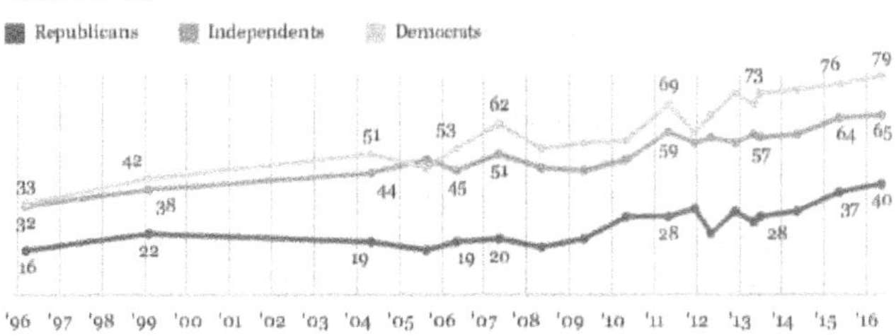

Note: Trend shown for polls in which same-sex marriage question followed questions on gay/lesbian rights and relations
1996-2005 wording: "Do you think marriages between homosexuals ..."

GALLUP

Majority of Oldest Americans Now Support Same-Sex Marriage

Support for gay marriage has consistently been highest among adults younger than 30 years, but support declines with each step up the age scale. At the same time, Americans in all four age groups have become more supportive since 1996.

This year marks the first time in Gallup's trend that the majority of adults aged 65 and older said gay marriage should be legal. Fifty-three percent of Americans aged 65 and older now support same-sex marriage. That is still well below the 83% support among 18- to 29-year-olds, the highest support among the age groups.

Support for Legal Same-Sex Marriage by Age, 1996-2016

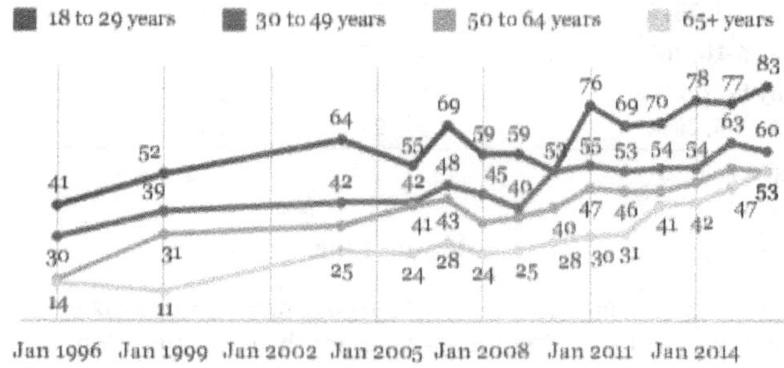

GALLUP

A Quarter of Adults Say Issue Could Affect Their Vote for a Candidate

Twenty-three percent of Americans say they would only vote for a candidate who shares their views on gay marriage, while 44% say it is one of many important factors. Three in 10 say it is not a major issue in terms of how they will vote. The percentage who say a candidate must agree with them on this issue to earn their vote is higher now than it was in 2004 and 2008.

Importance of Candidates' Stance on Gay Marriage in How Americans Vote

Thinking about how the gay marriage issue might affect your vote for major offices, would you – [ROTATED: only vote for a candidate who shares your views on gay marriage, consider a candidate's position on gay marriage as just one of many important factors when voting or would you not see gay marriage as a major issue]?

	Candidate must share views %	One of many important factors %	Not a major issue %
May 4-8, 2016	23	44	30
May 6-10, 2015	26	43	26
May 8-11, 2008	16	49	33
May 2-4, 2004	16	46	35

Gallup Poll

Americans who are opposed to gay marriage (29%) are much more likely than those in favor of it (19%) to say they would only vote for a candidate who shares their views. At the other end of the scale, 22% of gay marriage opponents compared with 32% of gay marriage supporters say it is not a major factor for their vote.

The percentage of Republicans saying gay marriage is a pivotal voting issue for them has fallen to 18% – down from 27% as recently as last year. Among Democrats, the issue has become more important, climbing to 32% after registering 26% a year ago and just 10% in 2008.

Americans Who Say Candidate Must Share Their Views on Gay Marriage

% Candidate must share views

	Pro-gay marriage %	Anti-gay marriage %	Republicans %	Democrats %
May 4-8, 2016	19	29	18	32
May 6-10, 2015	21	37	27	26
May 8-11, 2008	5	31	26	10
May 2-4, 2004	7	27	24	11

Gallup Poll

Bottom Line

Americans' heightened approval of gay marriage this year makes the issue a fairly straightforward one for the remaining Democratic presidential candidates. Not only do the vast majority of fellow Democrats agree with their stance, but they also have little to fear on the issue from the general electorate.

Trump might have found an ideal climate to run as a Republican with a somewhat murky record on gay marriage, given his party's tapering opposition to it and the reduced prominence of the issue to Republicans' votes. Though his opposition to gay marriage remains, he notably congratulated singer Elton John on his same-sex nuptial and even attended a gay wedding himself a year after his home state of New York legalized it. This is a marked departure from his former primary rival, Ted Cruz, who said he'd never attend a gay wedding if invited.

Attitudes on gay marriage, as well as on other LGBT issues, have been shifting since Gallup started measuring them. This has taken place across all political party and age groups, with each demographic subgroup demonstrating greater acceptance this year. With the Supreme Court's decision last year likely settling the matter of its legality, and especially since attempts by some local and state officials to defy the ruling were unsuccessful, the re-emergence of gay marriage as a divisive political issue is less likely.

Historical data are available in Gallup Analytics.

Survey Methods

Results for this Gallup poll are based on telephone interviews conducted May 4-8, 2016, with a random sample of 1,025 adults, aged 18 and older, living in all 50 U.S. states and the District of Columbia. For results based on the total sample of national adults, the margin of sampling error is ±4 percentage points at the 95% confidence level. All reported margins of sampling error include computed design effects for weighting.

May 20, 2016
DEMOCRATS MORE LIBERAL ON SOCIAL ISSUES THAN ECONOMIC ONES

by Jeffrey M. Jones

Story Highlights

- *57% of Democrats are liberal on social issues; 41% on economic*
- *Republicans more likely to be conservative on economic than social issues*
- *Similar percentages in U.S. are liberal or conservative socially*

PRINCETON, N.J. – A majority of Democrats, 57%, describe their views on social issues as liberal. At the same time, Democrats are about as likely to say they are moderate (37%) as liberal (41%) on economic issues. Most Republicans say they are conservative in both areas, but more say this about economic matters (73%) than social ones (62%).

Self-Described Economic and Social Ideology, by Political Party Identification

	U.S. adults %	Democrats %	Independents %	Republicans %
Social issues				
Liberal	32	57	31	10
Moderate	31	28	36	27
Conservative	34	13	28	62
Economic issues				
Liberal	20	41	18	4
Moderate	35	37	43	23
Conservative	41	21	34	73

Gallup, May 4-8, 2016

Political independents are most likely to describe their views on economic and social issues as moderate. Many more independents say they are conservative rather than liberal on economic issues, while roughly equal proportions are conservative or liberal on social issues.

These results are based on Gallup's May 4-8 Values and Beliefs poll. Each year, Gallup asks Americans to describe their views on social issues and, separately, economic issues using a five-point "very liberal" to "very conservative" scale.

Overall, Americans are evenly divided in their self-described ideology on social issues – 34% identify as conservative, 31% as moderate and 32% as liberal. On economic issues, Americans are more likely to say they are conservative (41%) than moderate (35%) or liberal (20%).

Americans' general tendency to be more conservative/less liberal on economic matters results from Republicans being much more likely to identify as conservative on those issues than Democrats are to identify as liberal, as well as independents' greater tilt toward economic conservatism. The roughly equal division in Americans' social ideology is because of Republicans' and Democrats' roughly equal likelihood of identifying as conservative and liberal, respectively, as well as independents' even split between social conservatism and social liberalism.

Social Liberalism More Common in U.S.

Americans have in recent years been more likely to identify as socially liberal, reducing what had been a consistent double-digit conservative advantage to a virtual tie. Those trends in self-identification are consistent with trends toward Americans' holding increasingly left-leaning positions on same-sex marriage, marijuana and a variety of moral issues.

The movement toward greater liberalism on social issues is Democrat-driven. The 57% of Democrats who currently say they are socially liberal is up from 35% in 2001. The trends in liberal social identification are mostly flat among independents and Republicans.

Trend in Liberal Self-Identification on Social Issues, by Political Party

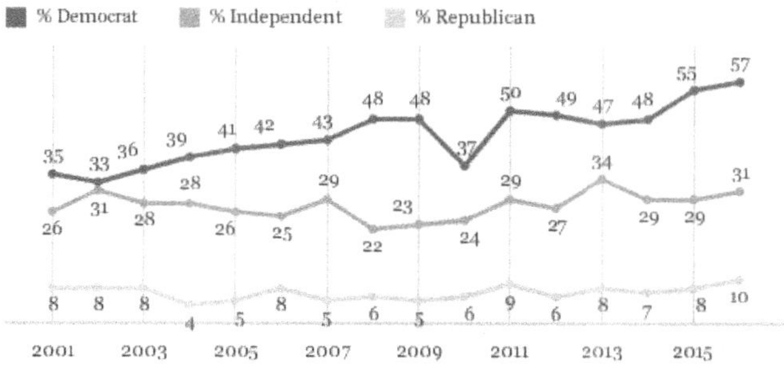

GALLUP

Since 2001, the conservative-liberal gap on economic self-identification has been no less than 20 percentage points. Democrats have become much more likely to identify as liberal on this dimension since 2001 (from 22% then to 41% today). Republicans have become more conservative (from 64% to 73%), with little change among independents. This has resulted in a slight narrowing of the conservative-liberal gap among all Americans over time.

Implications

Over the past decade, Americans have become more likely to identify as liberal on social issues, to the point at which there are roughly as many social liberals as social conservatives in the U.S. That makes likely Democratic presidential nominee Hillary Clinton's more socially liberal issue positions, including her shift toward favoring same-sex marriage over the past decade, less of a liability today than they might have been for prior Democratic candidates.

Americans' tendency to identify as conservative on economic issues may be an advantage for likely Republican nominee Donald Trump, although his positions on free trade and other economic issues have caused many to view him as more of a populist.

An analysis of the poll data by Americans' expressed likelihood of voting for Clinton and Trump reveals that the ideological makeup of probable supporters of the two presumptive nominees largely reflects the views of the party bases they will represent in the November election. Americans who do not exhibit a clear preference for either candidate at this point are similar in their views to the broader U.S. adult population, so their ideological preferences do not clearly indicate how they might vote in November.

Ideological fit between voters and the presidential candidates is just one of many factors that will help determine the outcome of the fall election, along with Americans' assessments of the state of the nation, their evaluations of the two major-party candidates, and voter turnout among supporters of each party and presidential candidate.

Survey Methods

Results for this Gallup poll are based on telephone interviews conducted May 4-8, 2016, with a random sample of 1,025 adults, aged 18 and older, living in all 50 U.S. states and the District of Columbia. For results based on the total sample of national adults, the margin of sampling error is ±4 percentage points at the 95% confidence level.

For results based on the samples of 342 Republicans, 304 Democrats and 361 independents, the margin of sampling error is ±7 percentage points at the 95% confidence level.

All reported margins of sampling error include computed design effects for weighting.

May 20, 2016
MOST DEMOCRATS SAY CONTINUED CAMPAIGN NOT HURTING THE PARTY

by Justin McCarthy

Story Highlights

- *70% say campaign is not damaging party*
- *Sanders, Clinton supporters about as likely to hold this view*
- *There is agreement across age groups*

WASHINGTON, D.C. – Although Bernie Sanders has scored a series of victories in recent primaries to slow down Hillary Clinton's likely presidential nomination, the vast majority of Democrats (70%) do not think the continuing campaign for the Democratic nomination is hurting the party. Sanders and Clinton supporters share this sentiment, and Democrats' views are unchanged from last month (71%).

Perceptions of the Campaign for the Democratic Nomination's Impact on the Party

Do you think the continuing campaign for the Democratic nomination is hurting the party or not hurting the party?

	Hurting the party %	Not hurting the party %
Democrats/Democratic-leaning independents	25	70
Clinton supporters	23	74
Sanders supporters	27	69

Gallup, May 13-15, 2016

Meanwhile, one in four Democrats do believe the process has damaged the party. This perception of party damage is much lower than what Gallup measured among Republicans last month. In April, before Ted Cruz and John Kasich suspended their campaigns, a majority (63%) of Republicans and Republican-leaning independents said they thought their party's continuing campaign for the nomination was hurting the party. That may have reflected the antipathy between Donald Trump and his Republican opponents in the race, as well as widespread speculation at the time that the party was headed for a brokered convention.

The latest data, collected May 13-15, come as a dispute at the state Democratic convention in Nevada has angered Sanders' supporters. They alleged corruption in the vote for the state-level delegates, as some of them booed and later sent threatening messages to the party official tasked with leading the convention.

Accusations that the party establishment has snubbed Sanders in favor of Clinton are not new, and date back to early in the nomination process. Last year, Sanders accused the party of scheduling debates during times of low viewership as a way to protect Clinton's candidacy. But the fallout from the events surrounding the Nevada Democratic convention underscores how difficult unifying the party after the nomination process could be.

Across Age Groups, Democrats Agree That Continuing Campaign Not Hurting Party

As of this recent poll, concluded Sunday, rank-and-file Democrats do not perceive the continuing campaign as having harmed their party. The process is coming to a close, as Clinton is fewer than 100 delegates away from clinching the nomination, with fewer than a dozen primaries left.

Age-wise, Democrats are on the same page about the nomination process' impact on the party. About one in four younger Democrats, who skew toward Sanders, and older Democrats, who lean toward Clinton, say the process is damaging the party, while majorities of each age group say the campaign isn't harming it.

Perceptions of the Campaign for the Democratic Nomination's Impact on the Party, by Age Group

Do you think the continuing campaign for the Democratic nomination is hurting the party or not hurting the party?

	Hurting the party %	Not hurting the party %
18 to 29	25	71
30 to 49	25	70
50 to 64	25	68
65+	23	73

Gallup, May 13-15, 2016

Bottom Line

Though tensions have boiled over recently, the dramatic events are not representative of the feelings of rank-and-file Democrats, who don't share with Republicans the view that a continuing campaign for their party's nomination is damaging the party itself. Republicans' more pessimistic views could stem from a long process that has involved a large group of candidates, name-calling and many heated, televised exchanges. While the Democratic candidates have had impassioned exchanges of their own, the temperament of the contest pales in comparison to that of the GOP.

Regardless, the process is almost over, as Clinton nears the required delegate threshold for the Democratic nomination and few contests remain – though Clinton's total delegate count includes many superdelegates, who can theoretically redirect their support to Sanders. But the larger challenge for the eventual nominee may not be how damaging the process has been, but whether he or she can unify the party in time to defeat presumed Republican nominee Trump. Democrats' current view that the process has been harmless could bode well for the party if, after the convention, supporters of the losing candidate continue to feel this way.

Survey Methods

Results for this Gallup poll are based on telephone interviews conducted May 13-15, 2016, on the Gallup U.S. Daily survey, with a random sample of 699 Democrats and Democratic-leaning independents, aged 18 and older, living in all 50 U.S. states and the District of Columbia. For results based on the total sample of national adults, the margin of sampling error is ±5 percentage points at the 95% confidence level. All reported margins of sampling error include computed design effects for weighting.

May 23, 2016
SANDERS' BACKERS MOST LIKELY TO SAY ELECTION PROCESS FAULTY

by Lydia Saad

Story Highlights

- *More than eight in 10 Sanders supporters say election process not working*
- *Fewer Clinton backers (60%) feel the same way*
- *Overall, almost three in 10 in U.S. say election working as it should*

PRINCETON, N.J. – Neither political party's supporters think the election process is working as it should, but Democrats who back Bernie Sanders (17%) are less than half as likely as those who prefer Hillary Clinton for the nomination (39%) to feel positively about the process. On the flip side, more than eight in 10 of the Vermont senator's supporters (81%) say the process is *not* working, exceeding the 60% of Democratic Clinton supporters who feel the same way.

Americans' Views of Election Process

Next, please try to answer each of the following questions based on what you may have heard or read so far about the presidential campaign and candidates from the Democratic and Republican parties. Does the way the presidential campaign is being conducted make you feel as though the election process is working as it should, or not?

	Yes, as it should	No, not as it should	No opinion
	%	%	%
Democrats/Democratic leaners			
Prefer Hillary Clinton as nominee	39	60	1
Prefer Bernie Sanders as nominee	17	81	1

	Yes, as it should	No, not as it should	No opinion
	%	%	%
Republicans/Republican leaners			
Pleased with selection of Trump	35	64	1
Wish someone else were nominee	23	75	2

Gallup, May 13-15, 2016

The views of Sanders and Clinton supporters about the process have not changed much over the past month.

Although the Republican nomination is essentially settled now that Donald Trump's main competitors have dropped out or suspended their campaigns, 35% of Republicans and Republican-leaning independents who are pleased with the selection of Trump – or about half of Republicans – say the election process is working. In April, when Ted Cruz was still waging a spirited campaign against Trump, just 25% of Republicans who backed Trump for the nomination thought the process was working well, compared with 32% of Cruz supporters.

Overall, 28% of all U.S. adults this month say the election process is working, similar to the 27% in April but down from 33% in February and 37% in January. Over these five months, Democrats' satisfaction with the process has been fairly steady near 30%, while Republicans' fell from 46% at the start of the year to 30% by March and has since remained near that level.

Monthly Trend in Public Perceptions That 2016 Election Process Is Working as It Should

Does the way the presidential campaign is being conducted make you feel as though the election process is working as it should, or not?

% Yes, as it should

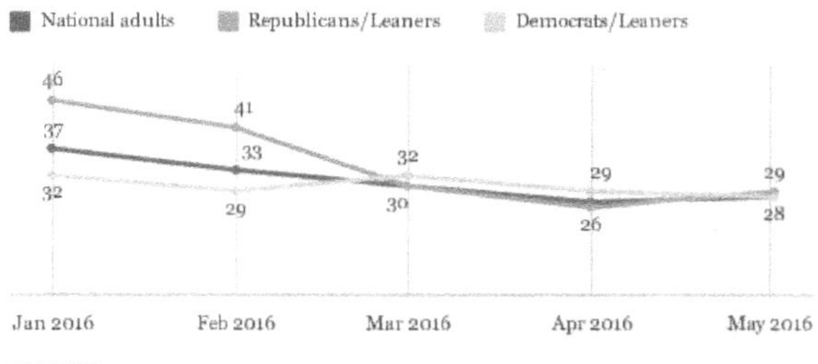

Current public skepticism about the election process contrasts with early 2000 and 2008, when about half or even two-thirds of Americans – including majorities of Republicans and Democrats – thought the process was working as it should.

Americans' View of Election Process, Trend by Party ID

Percentage saying the way the campaign is being conducted makes them feel the election process is working as it should

	National adults	Republicans/ Leaners	Democrats/ Leaners
	%	%	%
May 13-15, 2016	28	29	28
Apr 15-17, 2016	27	26	29
Mar 16-17, 2016	30	30	32
Feb 15-16, 2016	33	41	29
Jan 15-16, 2016	37	46	32
Dec 15-18, 2011	39	49	31
Jan 10-13, 2008	67	66	71
Dec 14-16, 2007	47	46	52
Mar 10-12, 2000	53	54	54

Gallup

Although Gallup's trend on this question is limited, only in December 2011 were attitudes nearly as dour as they are today. At that point, only 39% of Americans thought the election process was working well. And the results by party were remarkably similar to what Gallup found in January of this year: roughly half of Republicans (49%) versus nearly a third of Democrats (31%) thought the process was working well.

One similarity between the 2011-2012 and 2015-2016 election cycles is concern about overexposure of the Republican candidates because of the number of debates, the number of candidates or both. In January 2015, Reince Priebus, chairman of the Republican National Committee, said he thought the number of Republican debates and forums during the 2011-2012 cycle – 27 total – damaged the party's image by giving too much airtime to Republicans' attacks on each other. As a result, Priebus limited the number of debates this cycle; since last October, there have been 12. But the unprecedented number of candidates running this time, with Trump launching sharp attacks on his opponents, has produced as much if not more of a spectacle.

Bottom Line

Sanders' supporters have their reasons to be frustrated with an election process that seems destined to deliver the Democratic nomination to his opponent. Even if Sanders manages to win a similar number of delegates to Clinton's in the state primaries and caucuses, her commanding lead among Democratic "superdelegates" has tilted the nomination process strongly in Clinton's favor. That could explain the higher percentage of Sanders than Clinton supporters who today say the election process is not working as it should. However, Democrats have been critical of the process as far back as January, most likely reflecting their views of the Republicans' highly fractured and divisive race as much as the Democratic one.

And, echoing the sentiment from late 2011, the year began with Republicans feeling better than Democrats about the election process. But as GOP candidates started dropping out, and personal attacks among the remaining ones became the campaign's prominent feature, Republicans' satisfaction fell in March to match Democrats' and has since remained low.

Both parties have an opportunity to put a more positive spin on the process at their nominating conventions this summer, as well as during the presidential debates this fall. However, if those events fail to convince Americans that democracy is on course, voters' low satisfaction with the process could contribute to lower turnout in the election this fall.

Survey Methods

Results for this Gallup poll are based on telephone interviews conducted May 13-15, 2016, on the Gallup U.S. Daily survey, with a random sample of 1,537 adults, aged 18 and older, living in all 50 U.S. states and the District of Columbia. For results based on the total sample of national adults, the margin of sampling error is ±3 percentage points at the 95% confidence level.

For results based on the sample of 699 Democrats and Democratic-leaning independents, the margin of error is ±5 percentage points at the 95% confidence level. For results based on the sample of 677 Republicans and Republican-leaning independents, the margin of error is ±5 percentage points at the 95% confidence level. All reported margins of sampling error include computed design effects for weighting.

May 23, 2016
REPUBLICANS PAYING MORE ATTENTION TO ELECTION THAN DEMOCRATS

by Frank Newport

Story Highlights

- *47% of Republicans, 39% of Democrats following election news very closely*
- *General GOP advantage on this measure evident each month since January*
- *Overall, Americans paying slightly more attention now than in January*

PRINCETON, N.J. – Republicans continue to follow the news of the presidential election more closely than Democrats. In mid-May, 47% of Republicans and Republican-leaning independents say they are following election news "very closely," compared with 39% of Democrats and Democratic leaners. This eight-percentage-point gap is slightly smaller than in previous months, but the general pattern of Republicans paying closer attention than Democrats has been evident all year.

How closely are you following the news about the 2016 presidential election campaign -- very closely, somewhat closely, not too closely or not at all?

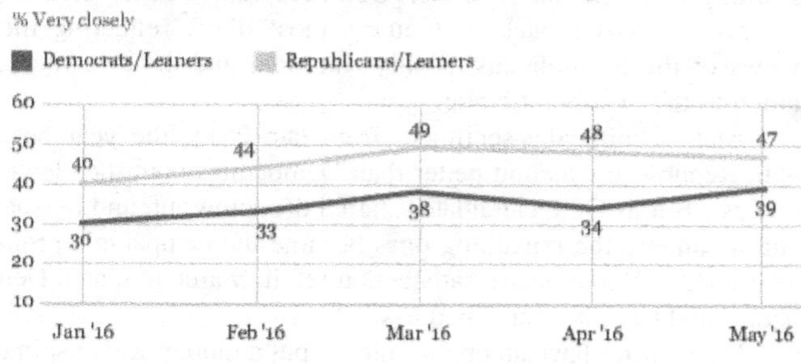

This measure of attention paid to the campaign is based on Gallup Daily tracking interviews conducted in the middle of each month since January, with the latest update from May 13-15.

That Republicans pay closer attention to elections is not a new phenomenon; the basic pattern was evident in the 2012 presidential election. Additionally, some real-world evidence – namely, higher television ratings for the Republican than for the Democratic presidential debates last fall and earlier this year – underscores the sense that the GOP primary process has been more engaging than the Democratic process for Americans. This may reflect the unusually large field of 17 GOP candidates, the presence of the iconoclastic Donald Trump, and greater uncertainty about who would ultimately prevail in the Republican race.

The groups paying the closest attention to the election generally are those most likely to identify as Republicans. These include men, those aged 50 and older, and whites.

How closely are you following the news about the 2016 presidential election campaign – very closely, somewhat closely, not too closely or not at all?

	Very closely %
NATIONAL ADULTS	40
GENDER	
Male	43
Female	37
AGE	
18 to 29	26
30 to 49	32
50 to 64	51
65+	51
EDUCATION	
H.S. or less	31
Some college	41
College grad only	48
Postgraduate	55
RACE	
Whites	45
Nonwhites	27
IDEOLOGY	
Conservative	45
Moderate	35
Liberal	40

Gallup, May 13-15, 2016

A Gallup analysis last month noted that the gender gap in paying attention to the election had been growing since February, with men 13 points more likely than women to be paying very close attention. This month, however, that gap has narrowed, although men continue to be paying closer attention than women.

Americans' Interest in the Election Rises Gradually Since January

American adults overall are paying slightly more attention to the presidential election as the primary season has gone on this year, although there has been little meaningful change in the percentage following "very closely" over the past three months. Forty percent are following election news very closely in May, up from 31% in January. More broadly, 79% report following news about the election very or somewhat closely now, compared with 69% in January. This leaves 21% who are following election news not too closely or not at all.

How closely are you following the news about the 2016 presidential election campaign?

	January %	February %	March %	April %	May %
Following closely (net)	69	71	75	75	79
Very closely	31	34	40	37	40
Somewhat closely	38	37	35	38	39
Following not too closely or not at all	30	29	25	24	21

Gallup

Implications

Although Republicans have been consistently more likely than Democrats to say they are following election news closely this year, more activity is left in the race for the Democratic nomination than for the GOP nomination, which appears to be settled. How this might affect the attention gap remains to be seen.

More broadly, attention to the election will most likely rise for all Americans in July, as the two parties hold their conventions, and then again in September and October, as the campaign comes down to its final two months. The latter period will include four planned debates, the first of which is scheduled for Sept. 26 at Wright State University in Dayton, Ohio. Whether the Democrats can generate more interest from their constituency and hence increase the probability of higher voter turnout is one of their central challenges moving toward November.

Historical data are available in Gallup Analytics.

Survey Methods

Results for this Gallup poll are based on telephone interviews conducted May 13-15, 2016, on the Gallup U.S. Daily survey, with a random sample of 1,537 adults, aged 18 and older, living in all 50 U.S. states and the District of Columbia. For results based on the total sample of national adults, the margin of sampling error is ±3 percentage points at the 95% confidence level. For results based on the total samples of 699 Democrats and Democratic-leaning independents and 677 Republicans and Republican-leaning independents, the margin of sampling error is ±5 percentage points at the 95% confidence level. All reported margins of sampling error include computed design effects for weighting.

May 24, 2016
HILLARY CLINTON MAINTAINS IMAGE ADVANTAGE OVER DONALD TRUMP

by Frank Newport

Story Highlights

- *Clinton has a 40% favorable rating, compared with 33% for Trump*
- *Trump's net favorable has climbed in May*
- *Trump's gains due to increased favorable rating among Republicans*

PRINCETON, N.J. – Democratic front-runner Hillary Clinton continues to have an image advantage over presumptive Republican nominee Donald Trump among the general American population. So far this month, 40% of Americans hold a favorable view of Clinton, while 54% have an unfavorable opinion, resulting in a net favorable rating of -14. For Trump, Americans' views are 33% favorable and 60% unfavorable for a net favorable rating of -27.

Views of Hillary Clinton and Donald Trump, May 1-22

	Favorable %	Unfavorable %	Net Favorable (pct. pts.)
Clinton	40	54	-14
Trump	33	60	-27

Gallup, May 1-22, 2016

Overall, Clinton's image has gradually worsened over the course of the campaign since Gallup began tracking the candidates' images 10 months ago, dropping from a -2 net favorable rating last July to -14 this month. Trump's image has also worsened, reaching a low point of -35 net favorable in March, but it improved this month to -27. His most recent seven-day average is also -27.

These data are from Gallup's Daily tracking, aggregated at the monthly level (except for May, which is based on interviewing conducted May 1-22).

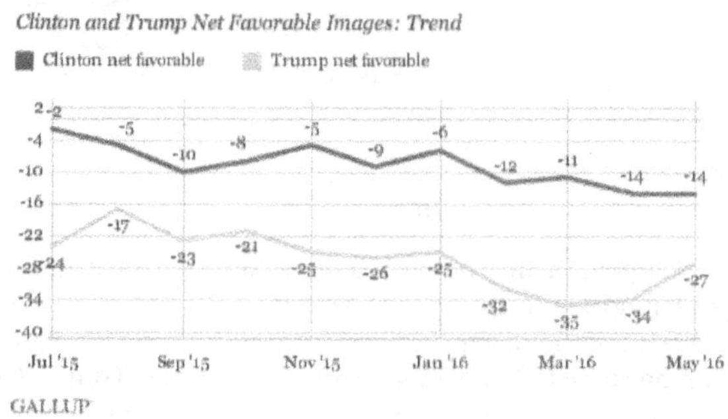

Trump More Popular Now Among Republicans

The uptick in Trump's overall image in recent weeks results from the presumptive nominee's popularity increasing among Republicans. With Trump essentially securing the nomination, many who supported other candidates are "coming home to roost," in essence, and now support the probable nominee. Trump lost a little ground among Republicans in February and March, but his current net favorable rating among Republicans (+33) is his highest monthly average yet within his own party. His decidedly negative net favorable rating among Democrats has remained essentially the same over the last three months, near -77, which is worse than it was among that group in 2015 and early 2016.

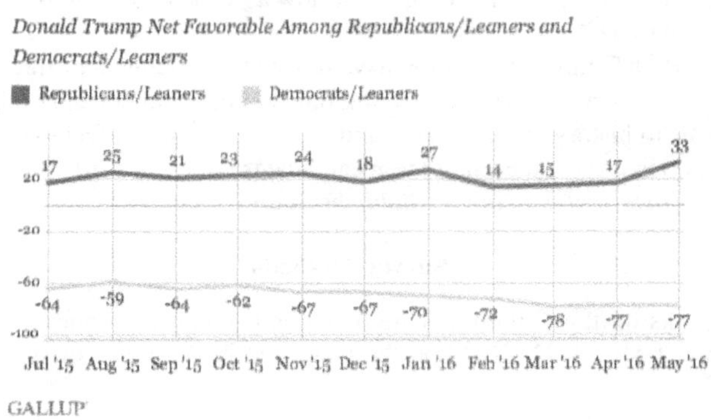

Clinton's image among Democrats remains more positive than Trump's is among Republicans, but her image – unlike his – has not yet recovered from a slow slide downward. Her image among Democrats will likely improve when Bernie Sanders officially drops out of the race or when he acknowledges her as the presumptive nominee – although that may not occur until late July at the Democratic National Convention in Philadelphia.

Clinton's very negative ratings among Republicans are identical to Trump's ratings among Democrats. This reinforces the conclusion that the difference in the overall way the two candidates are viewed is driven by the opinions of their respective partisan groups.

Hillary Clinton Net Favorable Among Republicans/Leaners and Democrats/Leaners

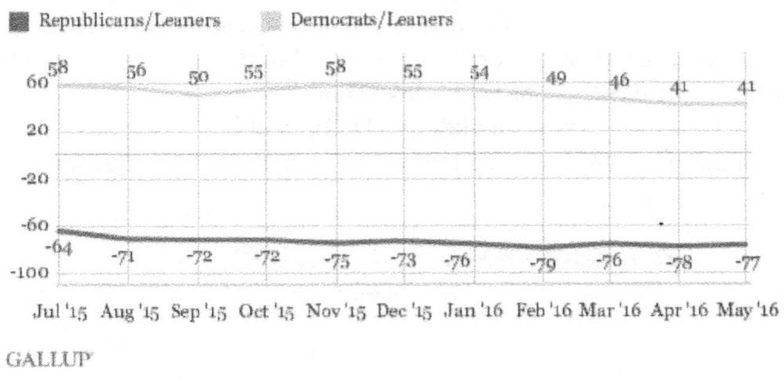

Implications

Hillary Clinton, at this point, retains a more positive image than Donald Trump among the general American population, but Trump's image among Republicans has improved, narrowing the image gap with his presumed Democratic challenger. Unlike Trump, Clinton continues to have an active challenger for the nomination, which may be depressing her image among some Democrats. Even still, she continues to retain a more positive image among her partisans than Trump does among his.

All major presidential candidates in recent elections have ended their campaigns with favorable ratings at 46% or higher, with many well into majority territory. A key element of this 2016 election to watch will be the degree to which Clinton and Trump manage to raise their favorable ratings, or if their images remain as negative as they are now going into the fall.

Both candidates will be highly visible at their conventions in July. Those occasions, coupled with their vice presidential selections, will provide the opportunity for a potential shift in their image ratings. The most relevant recent example of this effect is the case of Bill Clinton in 1992. Prior to the Democratic National Convention that year, his favorable rating was as low as 41%; immediately after, it rose to 62%.

Both Trump and Clinton have moved into a campaign stage in which they are actively criticizing one another, with specific references to history and character, and these tactics may affect the way Americans look at each of these candidates going forward.

Historical data are available in Gallup Analytics.

Survey Methods

Results for this Gallup poll are based on telephone interviews conducted May 1-22, 2016, on the Gallup U.S. Daily survey, with a random sample of 10,598 adults, aged 18 and older, living in all 50 U.S. states and the District of Columbia, rating Hillary Clinton, and 10,648 adults rating Donald Trump. For results based on each of these total samples of national adults, the margin of sampling error is ±1 percentage points at the 95% confidence level. All reported margins of sampling error include computed design effects for weighting.

May 25, 2016

AMERICANS REMAIN PESSIMISTIC ABOUT STATE OF MORAL VALUES

by Justin McCarthy

Story Highlights

- *Majority continues to say state of morals getting worse*
- *Americans most likely to describe morals in U.S. as "poor"*
- *Republicans, GOP leaners most negative on state of morals*

WASHINGTON, D.C. – Americans remain far more likely to say the state of moral values in the U.S. is getting worse (73%) than to say it is getting better (20%). Over a 15-year trend, solid majorities have consistently viewed the direction of the country's values negatively, ranging from 67% in 2002 and 2003 to 82% in 2007.

Americans' Outlook on State of Moral Values in the U.S.

Right now, do you think the state of moral values in the country as a whole is getting better or getting worse?

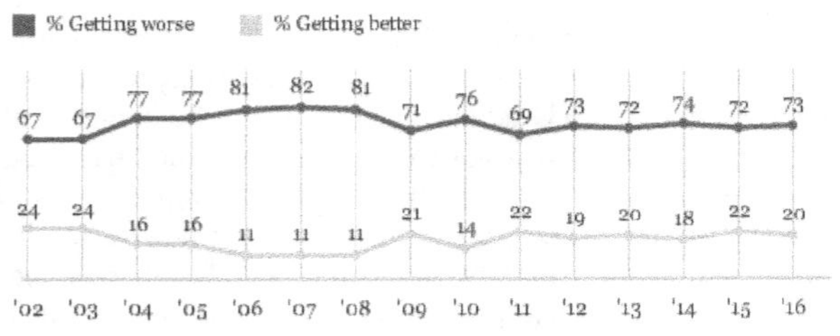

Trend based on Gallup's Values and Beliefs poll, conducted each May

GALLUP

As has been the case since 2007, Republicans and independents who lean Republican (84%) continue to be more likely than Democrats and independents who lean Democratic (61%) to say the state of moral values in the U.S. is getting worse. Prior to that, both groups were about equally likely to view the direction of the country's morals negatively.

From 2003 to 2007, Republicans became increasingly likely to say the state of morals in the U.S. was deteriorating; in 2007, that figure reached 88%. It has generally remained close to that level since, with most ratings in the mid-80s each year. Democrats, on the other hand, have become less likely to view the state of moral values as declining since the end of the George W. Bush administration. During Bush's two terms in office, between 69% and 79% of Democrats said moral values in the U.S. were getting worse, compared with 56% to 67% during Barack Obama's administration.

The latest figures were collected as part of Gallup's May 4-8 Values and Beliefs poll.

Outlook on State of Moral Values in the U.S., by Party Identification

Right now, do you think the state of moral values in the country as a whole is getting better or getting worse? (% Getting worse)

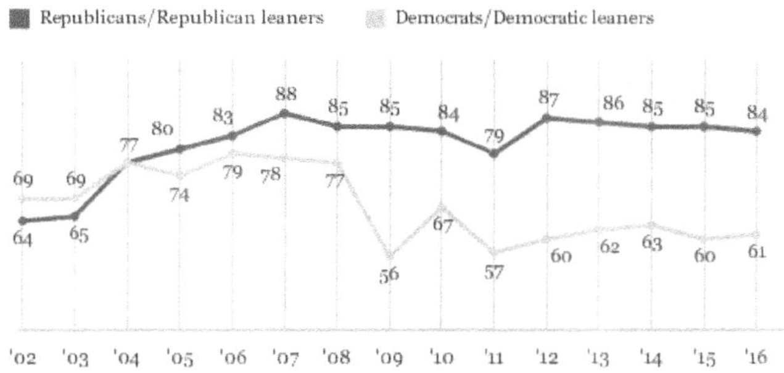

Trend based on Gallup's Values and Beliefs poll, conducted each May

GALLUP

Views on Current State of Moral Values in the U.S., by Party Identification

How would you rate the overall state of moral values in this country today -- as excellent, good, only fair or poor? (% Poor)

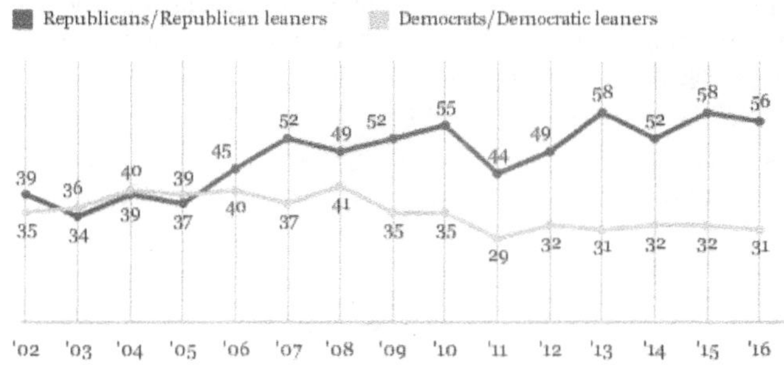

Trend based on Gallup's Values and Beliefs poll, conducted each May

GALLUP

Americans Most Likely to Describe State of Moral Values as "Poor"

In line with their pessimism about the direction of moral values in the country, U.S. adults are much more likely to describe the current state of moral values as "poor" (43%) or "only fair" (36%) than to say it is "excellent" or "good" (18%).

This has been the case for most of Gallup's trend, though in some years the percentages saying moral values were poor or only fair have been about even. The highest percentage ever saying that the state of moral values was excellent/good was 23% in 2011. Among the positive responses, however, few Americans rate the state of moral values as excellent – only between 1% and 3% have given this rating since 2002.

Americans' Views on Current State of Moral Values in the U.S.

How would you rate the overall state of moral values in this country today -- as excellent, good, only fair or poor?

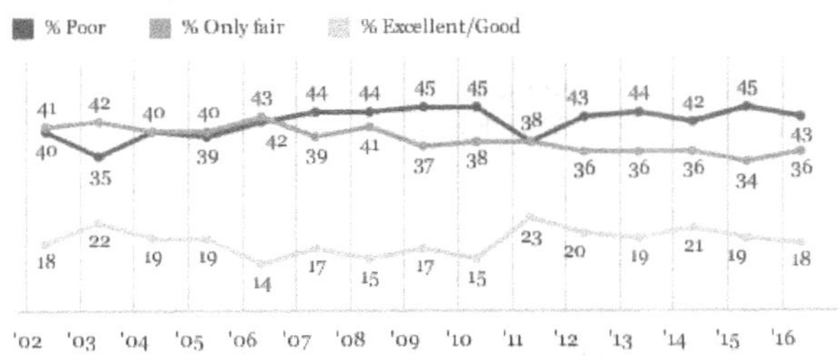

Trend based on Gallup's Values and Beliefs poll, conducted each May

GALLUP

Republicans and Republican-leaning independents' assessments of the current state of moral values in the U.S. are more negative than those of Democrats and Democratic-leaning independents. Republicans (56%) are nearly twice as likely as Democrats (31%) to describe the state of moral values as poor.

From 2002 to 2006, these groups were similarly likely to say the nation's moral fabric was poor, with differences between them not exceeding five percentage points. The disparities between the two have grown, however, with 25 points separating the groups in the latest poll.

Bottom Line

Negative views of the state of moral values in the U.S. are the norm for Americans – they are most likely to describe it as poor, and a strong majority say it is only getting worse.

Platform issues on moral values are frequently espoused by Republican candidates for office at all levels of U.S. government, so it may come as little surprise that those who identify as or lean Republican have a heightened sensitivity to the state of the nation's moral fabric. But a majority of Democrats and Democratic-leaning independents, too, say the state of moral values is declining.

While Americans point to many ways in which they see the country's morals getting worse, they are most likely to say they see a decline in U.S. standards and a lack of respect for one another, as well as poor values instilled by parents and reflected among government officials. Given Gallup's long-standing trend, it is likely that a majority of Americans will continue to view the direction of the nation's morals negatively.

Historical data are available in Gallup Analytics.

Survey Methods

Results for this Gallup poll are based on telephone interviews conducted May 4-8, 2016, on the Gallup U.S. Daily survey, with a random sample of 1,025 adults, aged 18 and older, living in all 50 U.S. states and the District of Columbia. For results based on the total sample of national adults, the margin of sampling error is ±4 percentage points at the 95% confidence level. All reported margins of sampling error include computed design effects for weighting.

May 25, 2016

IN U.S., PERCENTAGE STRUGGLING TO AFFORD FOOD AT NEW LOW

by Nader Nekvasil

Story Highlights

- *15.0% of U.S. adults struggled to afford food in past 12 months*
- *Blacks, Hispanics continue to struggle most to afford food*
- *Mississippi residents most likely to report struggling*

WASHINGTON, D.C. – Fifteen percent of U.S. adults reported in the first quarter of 2016 that there have been times in the past 12 months when they did not have enough money to buy food that they or their family needed. This is the lowest percentage of Americans experiencing food hardship in any quarter since Gallup and Healthways began tracking this measure in 2008.

Percentage of Americans Who Struggled to Afford Food in the Past Year

Have there been times in the past 12 months when you did not have enough money to buy food that you or your family needed?

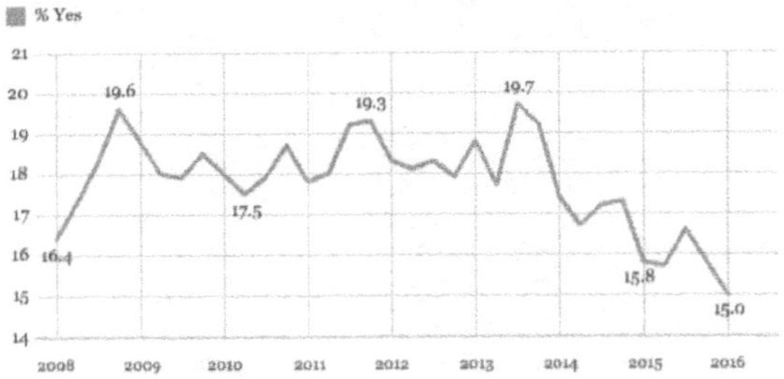

Data reflect Q1 2008-Q1 2016

Gallup-Healthways Well-Being Index

GALLUP

These findings are based on daily interviews conducted from January 2008 through March 2016 as part of the Gallup-Healthways Well-Being Index.

As fewer Americans report that they struggled to afford food, the April unemployment and underemployment rates as measured by Gallup reached their lowest levels since Gallup began tracking them in 2010. Previous Gallup and Healthways research has shown that those who are unemployed or are working part time but wanting full-time work are nearly three times as likely to lack enough money to afford food as those who are employed full time.

Along with the decline in the jobless rate, Americans' optimism about their personal financial situation is the highest it has been since 2007, and the percentage thriving in their financial well-being is up from the first quarter of 2014, when Gallup and Healthways began tracking it.

Despite these improvements, food hardship could still increase in the coming months. The Center on Budget and Policy Priorities predicts that between 500,000 and 1 million Americans will lose Supplemental Nutrition Assistance Program (SNAP) benefits, formerly known as food stamps, as 22 states re-establish three-month time limits and work requirements.

Blacks, Hispanics Continue to Struggle Most to Afford Food

Across key demographic groups, the percentage struggling to afford food declined somewhat over the past two years. Young adults aged 18-29 saw the most improvement across age groups, while blacks saw the most improvement across racial and ethnic groups. Still, blacks remain the most likely racial group to not have enough money to buy food. Blacks and Hispanics are roughly twice as likely as whites and more than three times as likely as Asians to say they have struggled to afford food at least once in the past year.

Percentage of Americans Who Did Not Have Enough Money to Buy Food in Past 12 Months, by Age and Race/Ethnicity

	Q1 2014 %	Q1 2016 %	Difference pct. pts.
Age			
18 to 29	20.3	17.0	-3.3
30 to 44	20.6	17.8	-2.8
45 to 64	18.6	15.9	-2.7
65+	8.3	7.9	-0.4
Race/Ethnicity			
Black	30.5	24.9	-5.6
Hispanic	25.2	22.4	-2.6
White	13.3	11.4	-1.9
Asian	9.5	7.2	-2.3

Gallup-Healthways Well-Being Index

Mississippi Residents Struggle Most, While North Dakota Residents Struggle Least

Along with these national findings from the first quarter of 2016, an aggregate of 2015 Gallup-Healthways data found Mississippi residents were most likely to struggle to afford food for the third consecutive year, followed by those living in Louisiana, Alabama, Oklahoma and West Virginia. Four of the five states with residents who were most likely to not have enough money to afford food were also among the states with the lowest overall well-being scores in 2015.

On the opposite end of the spectrum, North Dakota residents were least likely to struggle to afford food, which has been the case in all but one year since Gallup and Healthways began tracking this measure in 2008. All five states with residents who were least likely to struggle to afford food were also among the 2015 best-performing states in overall well-being.

States Most and Least Likely to Have Residents Who Did Not Have Enough Money to Buy Food in Past 12 Months

Has there been a time in the past 12 months when you did not have enough money to buy food that you or your family needed?

	Yes %
Most Likely	
Mississippi	22.9
Louisiana	21.4
Alabama	20.0
Oklahoma	19.5
West Virginia	19.3
Least Likely	
North Dakota	8.4
Hawaii	10.2
Minnesota	10.7
Alaska	10.8
Iowa	11.0

January-December 2015

Gallup-Healthways Well-Being Index

Similar to previous years, residents of Southern states are most likely to lack enough money to buy food, while residents of Midwest and Northern states are least likely.

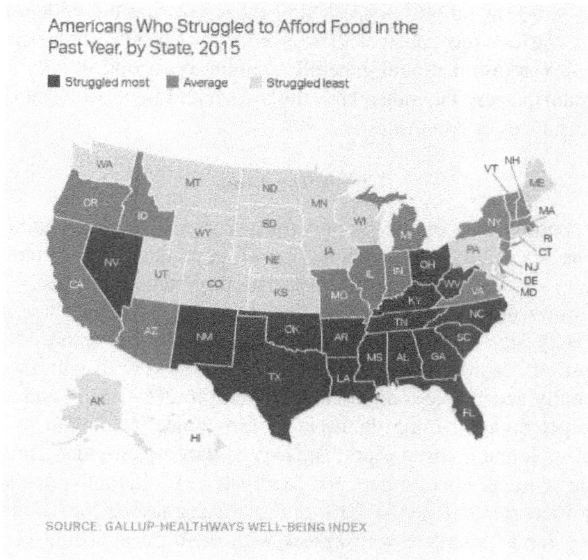

Bottom Line

Even though fewer Americans overall report not having enough money for food, wide disparities exist across regions and among racial and ethnic groups. Nearly all Southern states are above the national average in their percentage of residents who struggle to afford food. Additionally, blacks and Hispanics remain about twice as likely as whites to struggle to afford food.

Although there is strong evidence that the SNAP program helps alleviate food hardship, the significant drop in the percentage struggling to afford food cannot be attributed to increased dependency on SNAP. SNAP participation in February 2016 reached its lowest level in five years, according to the Food Research and Action Center.

Survey Methods

Results are based on telephone interviews conducted Jan. 1-March 31, 2016, as part of the Gallup-Healthways Well-Being Index survey, with a random sample of 44,558 adults, aged 18 and older, living in all 50 U.S. states and the District of Columbia. For results based on the total sample of national adults, the margin of sampling error is ±0.6 percentage points at the 95% confidence level.

For age and race, all reported margins of sampling error are at the 95% confidence interval.

Margin of Error, by Subgroup

Age	
18-29	+/- 1.38
30-44	+/- 1.24
45-64	+/- 0.93
65+	+/- 1.01
Race	
White	+/- 0.65
Black	+/- 1.8
Asian	+/- 3.56
Hispanic	+/- 1.68

Gallup-Healthways Well-Being Index

All reported margins of sampling error include computed design effects for weighting.

State results are based on telephone interviews conducted Jan. 2-Dec. 30, 2015, as a part of the Gallup-Healthways Well-Being Index, with a random sample of 177,281 adults, aged 18 and older, living in all 50 U.S. states and the District of Columbia. For results based on the total sample of national adults, the margin of sampling error for the Well-Being Index score is ±0.1 point at the 95% confidence level. The margin of sampling error for most states is about ±0.6 points, although this increases to about ±1.6 points for the smallest population states such as North Dakota, Wyoming, Hawaii and Delaware. All reported margins of sampling error include computed design effects for weighting.

May 25, 2016

AMERICANS' ATTITUDES TOWARD ABORTION UNCHANGED

by Lydia Saad

Story Highlights

- *U.S. adults split over whether abortion is morally acceptable*
- *Also divided in self-description as "pro-choice" or "pro-life"*
- *Largest segment – 50% – want abortion legal, but with limits*

PRINCETON, N.J. – U.S. public opinion on abortion was largely steady over the past year, as Americans remained split on the morality of abortion as well as in their preferences for the "pro-choice" vs. "pro-life" labels. The vast majority of adults continue to believe abortion should be legal to some extent, with 29% saying it should be legal in all circumstances and 50% favoring legality under certain circumstances.

Recent Trend in U.S. Abortion Views

	May 6-10, 2015 %	May 4-8, 2016 %
Morality of abortion		
Morally acceptable	45	43
Morally wrong	45	47
Abortion position		
"Pro-choice"	50	47
"Pro-life"	44	46
Legality of abortion		
Legal under any circumstances	29	29
Legal only under certain circumstances	51	50
Illegal in all circumstances	19	19

Gallup

Moral Acceptability Has Increased, Longer Term

The public's attitudes on the morality of abortion reflect a recent split, and contrast with a slightly more conservative stance seen in most years from 2002 through 2014. During that period, 50%

of Americans, on average, called abortion morally wrong, while only 39% called it morally acceptable. Analysis of the trend by age indicates the shift is mainly because older adults, those aged 55 and older, have grown more likely to consider abortion morally acceptable.

U.S. Adults' Views on Morality of Abortion

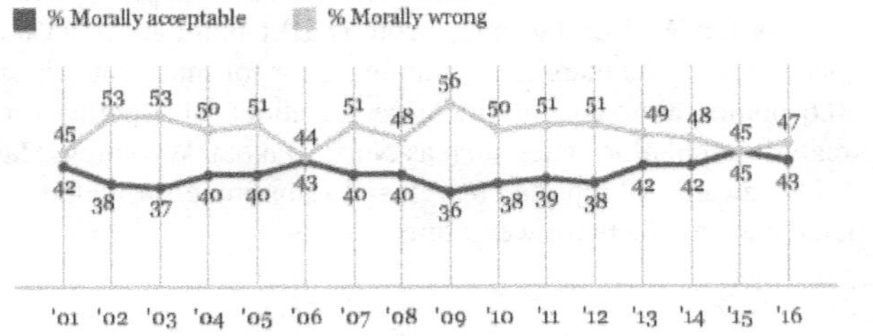

Surveys conducted in May of each year

GALLUP

Over the same period, Americans' perceptions of themselves as either "pro-choice" or "pro-life" in their abortion views have bounced around somewhat, but have generally broken fairly evenly since 2010. This contrasts with the period from 2004 through 2008, when the "pro-choice" position held a consistent edge.

With respect to the abortion issue, would you consider yourself to be pro-choice or pro-life?

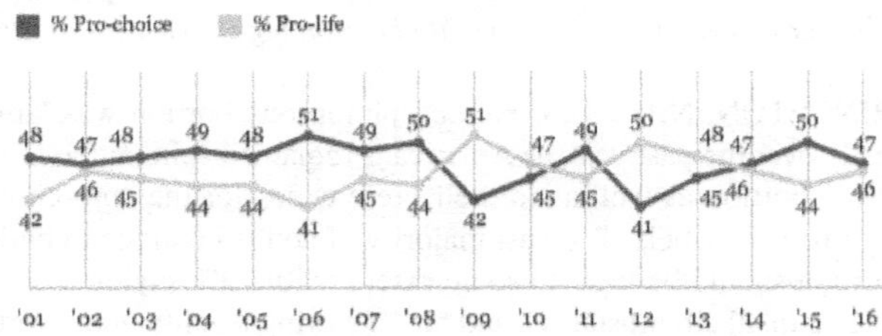

Surveys conducted in May of each year

GALLUP

Meanwhile, Americans' fundamental view about the legality of abortion has been broadly steady, with the largest segment consistently favoring the middle position of three that Gallup supplies, saying abortion should be legal only under certain circumstances. Of the remainder, more Americans lean to the left than to the right on the issue, with 29% saying abortion should be legal in all circumstances vs. 19% saying it should be *illegal* in all circumstances.

Do you think abortions should be legal under any circumstances, legal only under certain circumstances or illegal in all circumstances?

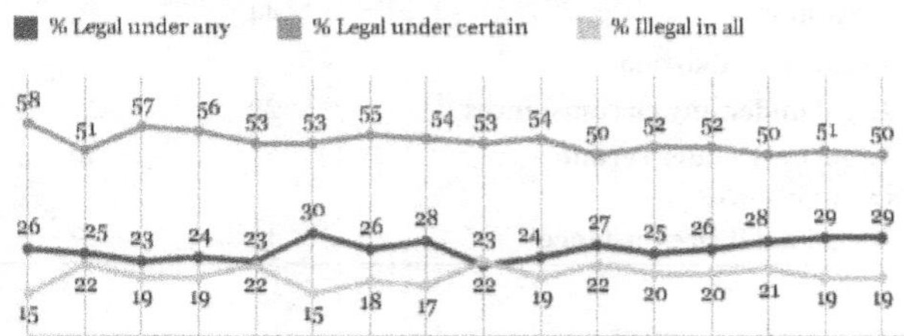

Surveys conducted in May of each year

GALLUP

A follow-up question asked of those favoring the middle position clarifies that most of these – constituting 37% of Americans – think abortion should generally be rare, occurring in only a few circumstances. The other 13% think it should be legal in most circumstances or are unsure.

Bottom Line

In contrast with public support for gay rights – more specifically, same-sex marriage – which has grown in recent years, Americans' views on abortion have been remarkably steady. Not only have attitudes changed little in the past year, but they also have been broadly steady over the past decade, spanning three presidential elections. While Americans are a bit more likely to call abortion morally acceptable today than they were in 2004, 2008 and 2012, the percentage calling themselves "pro-choice" is similar to what Gallup found in those years. The overall stability provides a predictable political environment for candidates. Additionally, as Gallup reported previously, the 20% of Americans saying they will vote only for a candidate who agrees with them on abortion has also remained steady, with pro-life voters slightly more likely than pro-choice voters to say the issue is critical to their vote.

Historical data are available in Gallup Analytics.

Survey Methods

Results for this Gallup poll are based on telephone interviews conducted May 4-8, 2016, with a random sample of 1,025 adults, aged 18 and older, living in all 50 U.S. states and the District of Columbia. For results based on the total sample of national adults, the margin of sampling error is ±4 percentage points at the 95% confidence level. All reported margins of sampling error include computed design effects for weighting.

May 26, 2016

U.S. RELIGIOUS GROUPS DISAGREE ON FIVE KEY MORAL ISSUES

by Jeffrey M. Jones

Story Highlights

- *Jews, nonreligious tend to be most liberal on morality*
- *Catholics say out-of-wedlock births, gay-lesbian relations moral*
- *Only Mormons view premarital sex, gambling as immoral*

PRINCETON, N.J. – Americans' religious faith greatly shapes their views of whether moral issues or practices are acceptable or not. In general, Jews and those with no religious preference are more liberal than Protestants, Catholics and Mormons in their views on various moral issues. These differences are most apparent on abortion and, to a lesser extent, doctor-assisted suicide and animal cloning. Catholics join with Jews and nonreligious Americans in saying gay-lesbian relations and out-of-wedlock births are morally OK.

Moral Issues on Which Major U.S. Religious Group Disagree

Percentage saying each is "morally acceptable"

	No religion %	Jewish %	Catholic %	Protestant %	Mormon %
Abortion	73	76	38	33	18
Doctor-assisted suicide	77	73	47	43	30
Cloning animals	50	50	33	28	33
Gay-lesbian relations	83	85	62	41	28
Having a baby outside of marriage	80	68	59	47	25

Note: Gay-lesbian relations based on 2005-2016 data
2001-2016 Gallup Values and Beliefs polls

Jews and those with no religious preferences have virtually identical views on the morality of abortion, doctor-assisted suicide, gay-lesbian relations and cloning animals. Jews are somewhat less likely than nonreligious Americans to believe having a baby outside of marriage is moral, 68% to 80%.

Mormons, Protestants and Catholics believe that abortion, doctor-assisted suicide and cloning animals are not morally acceptable practices. Mormons are more conservative than Protestants and Catholics on abortion, gay-lesbian relations, doctor-assisted suicide and out-of-wedlock births, but not on cloning animals.

These are five of 16 moral issues tested each year in Gallup's annual Values and Beliefs poll, conducted each May since 2001. As part of that survey, Gallup asks Americans to say whether a list of items dealing with sexuality, marriage, end-of-life issues, among others, are "morally acceptable" or "morally wrong."

The combined 2001 to 2016 samples yield enough data – more than 16,000 total interviews – to provide reliable estimates on the views of Jews and Mormons, each representing 2% of the U.S. adult population, as well as the larger groups of Protestants, Catholics and those with no religion.

The 16 issues that Gallup has included in the poll consistently since 2001 can be categorized into three groups: those on which there is disagreement among multiple religious groups, those on which the major U.S. religious groups broadly agree and those on which Mormons diverge from all other groups.

The estimates reported here represent an average of opinion since 2001. On most of these moral issues, Americans' views have shifted in a more liberal direction over the last 15 years, with the greatest change in views of the morality of gay-lesbian relations, premarital sex and having a baby outside of marriage. As a result, the 2001-2016 estimates show a slightly lower percentage believing certain issues are morally acceptable than is the case today. There has been no meaningful change in the views of all Americans on these issues between last year and this year.

Broad Agreement on Whether Many Moral Practices Are Acceptable or Wrong

Although it is the case that Jews and nonreligious Americans are more liberal on most moral issues, they do fall on the same side of the morally acceptable/morally wrong debate as Protestants, Catholics and Mormons on eight of the 16 issues included in the analysis. A majority in each of the five major U.S. religious groups agree that the death penalty, divorce, medical testing on animals and wearing clothing made of animal fur are morally acceptable. And a majority in all groups agree that extramarital affairs, polygamy, suicide and cloning humans are morally wrong.

Moral Issues on Which Major U.S. Religious Groups Generally Agree

Percentage saying each is "morally acceptable"

	No religion %	Jewish %	Catholic %	Protestant %	Mormon %
Divorce	86	86	69	61	55
Death penalty	62	54	61	66	79
Wearing clothing made of animal fur	57	63	57	61	67
Medical testing on animals	54	63	61	60	63
Suicide	36	38	12	11	8
Cloning humans	22	15	10	7	6
Polygamy	26	18	7	6	8
Extramarital affair	14	17	6	5	6

2001-2016 Gallup Values and Beliefs polls

There is broad agreement among the religious groups that divorce is morally acceptable, but Mormons are the least likely to say this, at 55%. Just shy of nine in 10 Jewish and nonreligious Americans believe divorce is OK. Jews, on the other hand, are least likely to say the death penalty is morally acceptable (54%), while Mormons (79%) are most likely to believe it is. The five groups show little variation in their views of the morality of medical testing on animals and wearing clothes made from animal fur.

Jews and those with no religion are also more likely than the other religious groups to see suicide, cloning humans, polygamy and extramarital sex as morally acceptable.

Mormons Distinct on Morality of Premarital Sex, Gambling

On three other moral issues – premarital sex, gambling and stem cell research – Mormons are alone in saying the practices are not morally acceptable. The percentage of Mormons believing stem cell research is moral falls just under the majority threshold at 46%. Mormons are far less likely to condone gambling (37%) and premarital sex (29%).

Moral Issues on Which Mormons Disagree With Other Major U.S. Religious Groups

Percentage saying each is "morally acceptable"

	No religion %	Jewish %	Catholic %	Protestant %	Mormon %
Gambling	81	81	74	56	37
Premarital sex	88	83	68	50	29
Stem cell research	78	85	60	54	46

2001-2016 Gallup Values and Beliefs polls

Jews and nonreligious Americans are more liberal than Protestants and Catholics on these three issues. A solid majority of

Catholics believe each is morally acceptable, while at or slightly more than half of Protestants agree.

Implications

The United States is one of the more religious western nations, and Americans' religious identity influences the way they view matters of morality. The Mormon religion and many Protestant faiths promote strict moral codes that frown on abortion and out-of-wedlock births, with those values mostly endorsed by adherents of those religions. Catholic Church doctrine also instructs Catholics how to think about moral issues, but American Catholics' views on many moral issues, including premarital sex, the death penalty and gay-lesbian relations, do not reflect the church's positions. Nevertheless, Catholics tend to be more conservative on morality than those with no religion and Jewish Americans.

Trends in U.S. religious identification – particularly the increasing percentage of Americans without a religious preference – have occurred at the same time as the movement toward more liberal attitudes on moral issues over the last 15 years. The explanations for both of these trends is most likely complex, having to do with genuine cultural shifts, differences in what survey respondents are willing to tell interviewers, demographic changes and other factors. Whatever the reasons behind these trends, it is probably more likely that they will continue in the same direction, with fewer Americans being religious and more espousing liberal views on morality, than that these trends will reverse course in the future.

Historical data are available in Gallup Analytics.

Survey Methods

Results for this Gallup poll are based on combined telephone interviews in Gallup's 2001 through 2016 annual Values and Beliefs poll, conducted each May with random samples of U.S. adults, aged 18 and older, living in all 50 U.S. states and the District of Columbia.

For results based on the total sample of 16,754 national adults, the margin of sampling error is ±1 percentage point at the 95% confidence level.

For results based on the total sample of 9,161 Protestants, the margin of sampling error is ±1 percentage point at the 95% confidence level.

For results based on the total sample of 3,893 Catholics, the margin of sampling error is ±2 percentage points at the 95% confidence level.

For results based on the total sample of 438 Jews, the margin of sampling error is ±6 percentage points at the 95% confidence level.

For results based on the total sample of 295 Mormons, the margin of sampling error is ±7 percentage points at the 95% confidence level.

For results based on the total sample of 1,915 adults with no religious preference, the margin of sampling error is ±3 percentage points at the 95% confidence level.

All reported margins of sampling error include computed design effects for weighting.

May 27, 2016
MOST ARE POSITIVE ABOUT AT LEAST ONE PRESIDENTIAL CANDIDATE

by Frank Newport

Story Highlights

- *58% of Democrats say Clinton would be great/good president*
- *Similar percentage of Republicans say Trump would be great/good president*
- *Most Americans are positive about the presidency of at least one candidate*

PRINCETON, N.J. – Twenty-two percent of Democrats and independents who lean Democratic say Hillary Clinton would be a great president if elected, similar to the 19% of Republicans and Republican leaners who say the same about Donald Trump. Most of the rest of each partisan group say their party's candidate would be either a good or an average president. Positive sentiments are by no means universal within either party, however; 21% of Republicans say Trump would be a poor or terrible president, while 13% of Democrats say that about Clinton.

In your view, what kind of president would each of the following be if he or she were elected in November [2016/2012/2008] – great, good, average, poor, terrible or don't you know enough to say?

	Great %	Good %	Average %	Poor %	Terrible %	Don't know %
Hillary Clinton						
Democrats/Democratic leaners						
May 18-22, 2016	22	36	26	8	5	3
Dec 14-16, 2007	33	43	17	4	3	1
Donald Trump						
Republicans/Republican leaners						
May 18-22, 2016	19	37	20	11	10	3
Apr 20-23, 2011	10	24	24	20	13	9

Gallup

These data are from a Gallup poll conducted May 18-22. Gallup asked similar questions about these two candidates at different times in previous election cycles – Clinton in December 2007 as she was making her first bid for the presidency and Trump in April 2011.

The percentage of Republicans who think Trump would be a great or good president is considerably higher now (56%) than was true in 2011 (34%). Trump's campaigning and status as the presumptive Republican nominee have apparently convinced Republicans of his potential virtues as president compared with what they might have thought when he was flirting with the idea of running before the 2012 election.

The opposite pattern has occurred relating to Democrats' views of Clinton. In December 2007, before her battle with Barack Obama for the Democratic nomination began in earnest, 76% of Democrats thought she would be a great or good president, higher than the 58% who feel that way today.

Fourteen Percent Say Both Trump and Clinton Would Be Poor or Terrible President

Because Gallup asked each American in this survey to rate potential Trump and Clinton presidencies, the responses can be combined to show how the two candidates are rated together. As the accompanying table shows (and as one would expect), Americans are most likely to rate one candidate positively and at the same time rate the other negatively. This includes the 26% who say Clinton would be great or good and at the same time think Trump would be poor or terrible, and the 23% who hold the opposite views – that Trump would be great or good and that Clinton would be poor or terrible.

In your view, what kind of president would each of the following be if he or she were elected in November 2016 – great, good, average, poor, terrible or don't you know enough to say?

Numbers represent percentages of total sample

	Trump: Great/Good %	Trump: Average %	Trump: Poor/ Terrible %
Clinton: Great/ Good	2	2	26
Clinton: Average	3	3	12
Clinton: Poor/ Terrible	23	9	14

Gallup, May 18-22, 2016

Of particular interest is the 14% of Americans who say *both* candidates would be poor or terrible presidents.

Roughly two-thirds of this group of 14% who are negative about potential Trump *and* Clinton presidencies identify initially as political independents (before they are asked which way they lean). Another 24% of this group are Republicans, while 12% are Democrats. Because Republicans and Democrats are about equally represented in the survey, the larger proportion of Republicans believing that both candidates would be bad presidents underscores that Republicans are more concerned than Democrats about their own party's nominee.

Views of Potential Clinton and Trump Presidencies, by Party Identification

	Republicans %	Independents %	Democrats %
Party identification among those who say both Trump and Clinton would be poor/terrible president	24	64	12
Party identification among those with all other views	28	42	30

Gallup, May 18-22, 2016

Americans younger than 30 are significantly overrepresented in the group of those who think both Clinton and Trump would be poor or terrible presidents. This is to some degree related to young people's support for Bernie Sanders for president. The views of Sanders' supporters could change when he eventually withdraws from the race.

Views of Potential Clinton and Trump Presidencies, by Age Distribution

	18 to 29 %	30 to 49 %	50 to 64 %	65+ %
Age distribution among those who say both Trump and Clinton would be poor/terrible president	36	34	21	10
Age distribution among those with all other views	19	32	27	22

Gallup, May 18-22, 2016

Implications

Some speculation in this presidential race has centered on the perception that Americans are dissatisfied with the prospect of either Clinton or Trump as the next president. This is partly based on Americans' low favorable ratings of each, as well as other measures indicating Americans' frustrations with how the nomination contests have played out. But these data reveal that only 14% of Americans think that both candidates would be poor or terrible presidents. Most Americans think that at least one of the two would be at least an average president if he or she were to take office next January.

Additionally, the substantial majority of Democrats and of Republicans believe that Clinton and Trump, respectively, would be at least an average president, with majorities saying they would be great or good. This positivity is muted, however, with about one-fifth of each partisan group willing to say their candidate would be a great president.

These perceptions may change as the campaign progresses, just as views of the type of president Clinton and Trump would be have changed since 2007 and 2011. For one thing, Sanders remains an active competitor to Clinton, and Sanders' supporters may be reluctant to say positive things about her until he exits the race. Trump is new on the political scene, and as his campaign continues, the public may become more convinced or less convinced of his ability to handle the job of being president.

These data are available in Gallup Analytics.

Survey Methods

Results for this Gallup poll are based on telephone interviews conducted May 18-22, 2016, with a random sample of 1,530 adults, aged 18 and older, living in all 50 U.S. states and the District of Columbia. For results based on the total sample of national adults, the margin of sampling error is ±3 percentage points at the 95% confidence level. For results based on the sample of 744 Republicans and Republican-leaning independents, the margin of sampling error is ±4 percentage points at the 95% confidence level. For results based on the sample of 697 Democrats and Democratic-leaning independents, the margin of sampling error is ±5 percentage points at the 95% confidence level. All reported margins of sampling error include computed design effects for weighting.

May 31, 2016
PARTY IMAGES STABLE AMID HEATED NOMINATION CONTESTS

by Justin McCarthy

Story Highlights

- *Forty-four percent of Americans view Democratic Party favorably*
- *Thirty-six percent have favorable view of Republican Party*
- *Democrats maintain favorability edge with independents*

WASHINGTON, D.C. – Amid a contentious primary season, Americans' favorable ratings of both the Democratic (44%) and Republican (36%) parties haven't changed much from March of last year, before any of the presidential candidates announced their intentions to run.

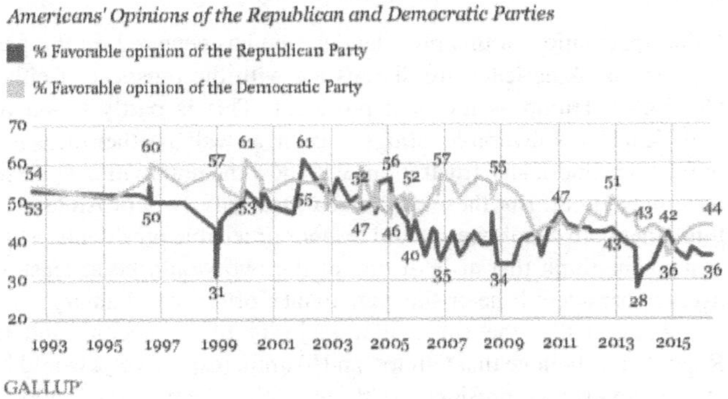

The latest findings from a May 18-22 Gallup survey indicate that the images of the two major parties have not suffered because of the belligerent primary process this year. Last month, most Republicans expressed concerns that the campaign was taking a toll on the party. Democrats were much less concerned when asked earlier this month.

On the Republican side, repeated onslaughts from outsider candidate Donald Trump toward his competitors and other party members have tempted some Republicans to seek a third-party candidate, with some admitting that they may vote for the Democratic nominee in November.

The Democratic contest hasn't been without its own infighting. Despite being mere delegates away from securing the nomination, Hillary Clinton remains in a drawn-out battle with Sen. Bernie Sanders, who is taking shots at the party establishment, including the party chairwoman. Many of his supporters vow not to vote for Clinton, who they feel has benefited from a "rigged" system.

But despite the political acrimony, Americans' views of the two parties haven't moved much since January. The lack of change could reflect that Americans' images of the parties were very poor to begin with, as both are near the low points in Gallup's historic trend dating back to 1992.

About Three in Four Republicans Have Favorable View of Their Party

Republicans' ratings of their own party remain near the 75% level seen since late 2013, while 28% of independents view the party favorably. Very few Democrats (7%) have a favorable view of the GOP.

While the Republican Party has enjoyed favorability of its own members since late 2013 with ratings ranging from 72% to 79%, Republicans used to think more highly of the GOP, with a 91% favorable rating near Election Day 2012. The party's ratings suffered amid the government shutdown, which was led by its own members.

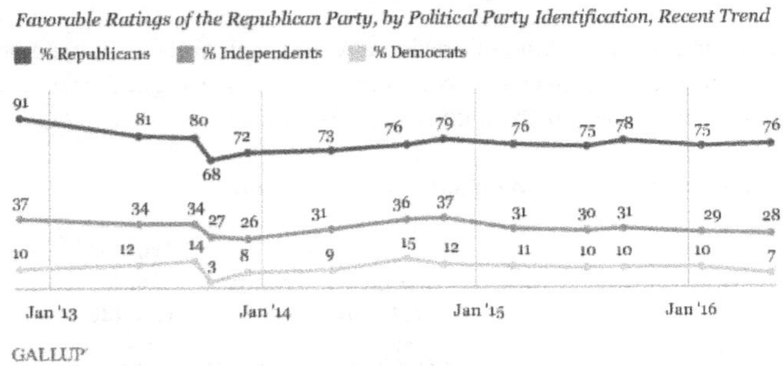

Democratic Party Enjoys Certain Advantages in Favorable Ratings

In addition to maintaining its edge in party affiliation, the Democratic Party enjoys other advantages over the Republican Party, including higher favorable ratings among its own party members. Democrats rate their own party more positively than Republicans do – 89%, compared with the GOP's 76% among Republicans. The Democratic Party also has higher favorability among independents (38%), whose ratings of the Republican Party are 10 percentage points lower.

Only 9% of Republicans say they have a favorable view of the Democratic Party, similar to the percentage of Democrats who hold a favorable view of the GOP.

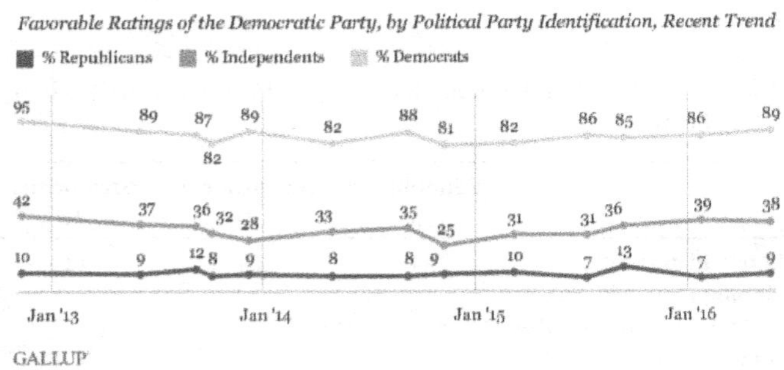

Bottom Line

Americans' views of the two major political parties have remained fixed over the past five months, even as both parties have been through tumultuous presidential nomination campaigns.

However, both parties' images have indeed taken hits from a long-term perspective. While majorities of Americans regularly viewed each party favorably in the 1990s and early 2000s, their ratings have dropped below 50% and have remained there for years. This is especially true for the Republican Party, which suffered in favorability in the second half of the George W. Bush administration and has yet to return to pre-2005 levels.

Majorities of Americans continue to express the need for a third party to emerge in order to adequately represent them, but systemic challenges – such as efforts to get on the ballot in all 50 states – make the chances of a viable third-party candidate low.

Historical data are available in Gallup Analytics.

Survey Methods

Results for this Gallup poll are based on telephone interviews conducted May 18-22, 2016, on the Gallup U.S. Daily survey, with a random sample of 1,530 adults, aged 18 and older, living in all 50 U.S. states and the District of Columbia. For results based on the total sample of national adults, the margin of sampling error is ±3 percentage points at the 95% confidence level. All reported margins of sampling error include computed design effects for weighting.

June 01, 2016
ECONOMY REMAINS TOP PRIORITY FOR NEXT PRESIDENT

by Frank Newport

Story Highlights

- *Economy tops list of Americans' priorities for next president*
- *Immigration second-most-frequently mentioned*
- *Other priorities include defense, healthcare, education*

PRINCETON, N.J. – Americans mention the economy more than any other concern when asked what single issue the next president should focus on when he or she takes office next January. They also frequently mention immigration, healthcare, defense and national security, and education as top priorities.

Regardless of who wins the election, what single issue or challenge are you most interested in having the next president address when he or she takes office next January? [OPEN-ENDED]

	May 18-22, 2016 %
The economy	19
Immigration	14
Healthcare/Healthcare costs/Healthcare reform	10
Defense/National Defense/Homeland security	9
Education	8
The federal deficit/The budget	7
Wages/Earning a decent wage/Decline of middle class	6
Jobs/Unemployment	6
Terrorism	5
Foreign policy/affairs	4
Big government/Government invasion of privacy	4
Race relations/Equal rights	3
Restoring respect to the office of president	3
Taxes	2
Poverty/The poor/Homelessness	2
The environment/Pollution	2
Gun control	2
Uniting Americans	2
Moral issues/Ethics/Religion	2
Nothing	3
No opinion	4

Note: Responses with at least 2% mentions are shown.
Gallup

These latest data are from Gallup's May 18-22 election benchmark survey. Americans' responses to this open-ended question are similar to those measured in January, showing that the issues on which the public wants the next president to focus haven't changed after five additional months of intense campaigning and issue discussion in the string of debates held during that time.

The next president, if intent on following the will of the people, will clearly need to keep a sustained focus on economic issues. Not only do Americans spontaneously mention the economy more often than any other issue, but they also name several other economically related priorities, including the federal deficit, wages and the decline of the middle class, jobs/unemployment, taxes and poverty.

The next president will at the same time face the challenge of responding to other public concerns, including the perennial challenge of keeping the nation safe and secure, immigration, healthcare and education.

Economy Also Ranks as Issue Most Important to Vote

A separate question included in the May poll asked Americans to rate the importance of each of 17 specific issues in determining their vote for president, on a scale from extremely important to not important. The economy tops this list too, with more than nine in 10 Americans ranking it as extremely or very important, followed by employment and jobs, terrorism and national security, education and healthcare.

Now I am going to read a list of some of the issues that will probably be discussed in this year's presidential election campaign. As I read each one, please tell me how important the candidates' positions on that issue will be in influencing your vote for president – extremely important, very important, somewhat important or not important.

	Extremely/Very important %
The economy	92
Employment and jobs	89
Terrorism and national security	87
Education	86
Healthcare and the Affordable Care Act	83
The federal budget deficit	78
Foreign affairs	74
Taxes	71
Immigration	69
The treatment of minority groups in this country	66
The distribution of income and wealth in the United States	65
The size and efficiency of the federal government	64
Gun policy	63
Trade with other nations	61
Government regulation of Wall Street and banks	59
Social issues such as gay marriage and abortion	48
Climate change	47

Gallup, May 18-22, 2016

The general rank-order of issues on this list is broadly similar to the responses to the open-ended question.

One exception is immigration, which is lower on the list when Americans evaluate its importance to their vote than it is when they offer top-of-mind responses about the issue they most want the next president to address. This could suggest that immigration is of high importance to a segment of the population, for whom it comes to mind immediately, but that it is of relatively low importance to the public at large.

Implications

The presidential candidates and, in turn, the next president of the United States, would be well-advised to keep a strong focus on the economy, which – although not the dominant issue it has been in previous elections – is clearly a common concern.

Americans also want their next president to focus on several fundamental issues: immigration, defense and national security, healthcare and education.

Although education is not solely or even the primary responsibility of the federal government, massive government initiatives such as No Child Left Behind and its recent successor law Every Student Succeeds have made it a clear target for federal intervention. Additionally, candidates in this election cycle have been called on to discuss their positions on the Common Core curriculum, and several have advocated major federal involvement in helping ensure that every child has pre-K education. Additionally, Sanders and Clinton have put forth proposals that in various ways call for lowered or free tuition at public colleges and community colleges.

Healthcare has become an even more important federal government focus in recent years with the 2010 passage of the Affordable Care Act, one of the most significant interventions of the federal government into the healthcare arena since Medicare. All candidates have taken positions on what should happen to the ACA, with Sanders proposing to replace it with a single-payer "Medicare for all" system, Trump proposing to repeal it, and Clinton advocating keeping it in place, albeit it with tweaks.

Notably, Americans appear to have low priorities for other issues that have been discussed on the campaign trail and in the debates, including gay marriage, abortion, climate change, foreign trade and Supreme Court nominations. The low priority for foreign trade as a presidential issue could obscure "hidden" concerns about trade in Americans' mentions of the economy and jobs.

Historical data are available in Gallup Analytics.

Survey Methods

Results for this Gallup poll are based on telephone interviews conducted May 18-22, 2016, with a random sample of 1,530 adults, aged 18 and older, living in all 50 U.S. states and the District of Columbia. For results based on the total sample of national adults, the margin of sampling error is ±3 percentage points at the 95% confidence level. All reported margins of sampling error include computed design effects for weighting.

June 02, 2016

TRUMP LEADS CLINTON ON TOP-RANKING ECONOMIC ISSUES

by Lydia Saad

Story Highlights

- *Trump leads Clinton as better able to handle the economy, jobs*
- *Education is highest-ranking issue on which Clinton leads*
- *Candidates each favored on eight of 17 issues; tied on trade*

PRINCETON, N.J. – If the race for president comes down to Donald Trump and Hillary Clinton, Trump could benefit from an edge in public confidence on the issues Americans are prioritizing most this election. A slight majority of Americans choose Trump as better able to handle the economy (53%) and jobs (52%), and 50% choose him – versus 46% who choose Clinton – on terrorism and national security.

Americans' Preference for Donald Trump vs. Hillary Clinton to Handle Each of Top Five Election Issues

Regardless of which presidential candidate you support, please tell me if you think Hillary Clinton or Donald Trump would better handle each of the following issues.

	High importance to vote^ %	Prefer Trump on issue %	Prefer Clinton on issue %	Advantage
The economy	92	53	43	Trump +10
Employment and jobs	89	52	45	Trump +7
Terrorism and national security	87	50	46	Trump +4
Education	86	35	61	Clinton +26
Healthcare and the Affordable Care Act	83	40	56	Clinton +16

^ Percentage saying the candidates' positions on the issue will be extremely/very important issue to influencing their vote for president

Gallup, May 18-22, 2016

At the same time, the Democratic front-runner boasts commanding leads over the presumptive Republican nominee in public perceptions of who can best handle education and healthcare, with 61% and 56%, respectively, choosing Clinton over Trump on these issues. Both issues rank among the top five Americans say will influence their vote for president.

These findings come from a May 18-22 Gallup poll in which U.S. adults were first asked to rate how important each of 17 prominent national issues will be to their vote for president this year, and then to say whether Clinton or Trump would best handle each issue. As Gallup reported previously, most of the issues Americans rate as highly important are economic and national defense-related. By contrast, most of the bottom eight involve social policy, trade and the environment. (See the full list in the table at the end of the story.)

Overall, Trump leads Clinton in public perceptions of who would better handle eight of the 17 issues. Beyond his modest leads on the economy (+10) and jobs (+7), and slight edge on terrorism (+4), he leads on several lower-ranked concerns: the federal budget deficit (+18), the size and efficiency of the federal government (+14), regulation of banks and Wall Street (+11), taxes (+8) and gun policy (+5).

Donald Trump Issue Advantages

Based on U.S. adults

	High importance to vote^ %	Prefer Trump on issue %	Prefer Clinton on issue %	Advantage
The economy	92	53	43	Trump +10
Employment and jobs	89	52	45	Trump +7
Terrorism and national security	87	50	46	Trump +4
The federal budget deficit	78	57	39	Trump +18
Taxes	71	52	44	Trump +8
The size and efficiency of the federal government	64	55	41	Trump +14
Gun policy	63	50	45	Trump +5
Government regulation of Wall Street and banks	59	53	42	Trump +11

^ Percentage saying the candidates' positions on the issue will be extremely/very important issue to influencing their vote for president
Gallup, May 18-22, 2016

Meanwhile, Clinton has advantages on eight other issues. However, aside from education (+26) and healthcare (+16) these tend to be lower-ranking concerns: climate change (+38), the treatment of minority groups in the U.S. (+38), social issues such as gay marriage and abortion (+33), foreign affairs (+21), income and wealth distribution (+8), and immigration (+8).

Hillary Clinton Issue Advantages

Based on U.S. adults

	High importance to vote^ %	Prefer Clinton on issue %	Prefer Trump on issue %	Advantage
Education	86	61	35	Clinton +26
Healthcare and the Affordable Care Act	83	56	40	Clinton +16
Foreign affairs	74	59	38	Clinton +21
Immigration	69	52	44	Clinton +8
The treatment of minority groups in this country	66	67	29	Clinton +38
The distribution of income and wealth in the U.S.	65	51	43	Clinton +8
Social issues such as gay marriage and abortion	48	64	31	Clinton +33
Climate change	47	66	28	Clinton +38

^ Percentage saying the candidates' positions on the issue will be extremely/very important issue to influencing their vote for president
Gallup, May 18-22, 2016

Trade, a relatively low-ranked election issue, is the one area where the candidates are tied. Neither Clinton's foreign policy credentials nor Trump's business credentials and emphasis on trade policies in his campaign have given either candidate an advantage on the issue. Both Trump and Clinton are on record opposing the Trans-Pacific Partnership now being debated in Congress.

Trump Leads on Higher-Profile Issues, but by Slimmer Margins

On average, 75% of Americans rate the eight issues Trump leads on as extremely or very important to their vote, slightly higher than the 67% who rate the eight issues Clinton leads on this highly.

At the same time, Clinton tends to have much larger advantages on the issues on which she is favored than Trump has on the issues on which he is favored. Clinton leads on her eight issues by an average of 24 points, while Trump leads by a 10-point average on his eight. Clinton's ratings on the issues may also be somewhat suppressed to the extent supporters of Bernie Sanders are reluctant to say positive things about her while he is still actively contesting the nomination.

Bottom Line

More Americans prefer Trump than Clinton to handle the issues of utmost importance to voters this fall – the economy in general as well as employment and jobs, specifically. More broadly, Trump's center of gravity on the issues is a little higher on the priority scale than Clinton's. On the other hand, the candidates are tied in the sheer number of issues on which each is preferred. And while Clinton tends to lead Trump by wide margins in the issues for which she is favored, Trump's leads are a bit tenuous and could more easily dwindle or disappear. Still, as of today, the issue advantage seems to go to Trump.

Survey Methods

Results for this Gallup poll are based on telephone interviews conducted May 18-22, 2016, with a random sample of 1,530 adults, aged 18 and older, living in all 50 U.S. states and the District of Columbia. For results based on the total sample of national adults, the margin of sampling error is ±3 percentage points at the 95% confidence level. All reported margins of sampling error include computed design effects for weighting.

2016 Election Issues and Americans' Preference for Donald Trump vs. Hillary Clinton to Handle Each

Based on U.S. adults

	Extremely/ Very important to vote %	Prefer Trump on issue %	Prefer Clinton on issue %	Candidate advantage pct. pts.
The economy	92	53	43	Trump +10
Employment and jobs	89	52	45	Trump +7
Terrorism and national security	87	50	46	Trump +4
Education	86	35	61	Clinton +26
Healthcare and the Affordable Care Act	83	40	56	Clinton +16

	Extremely/ Very important to vote %	Prefer Trump on issue %	Prefer Clinton on issue %	Candidate advantage pct. pts.
The federal budget deficit	78	57	39	Trump +18
Foreign affairs	74	38	59	Clinton +21
Taxes	71	52	44	Trump +8
Immigration	69	44	52	Clinton +8
The treatment of minority groups in this country	66	29	67	Clinton +38
The distribution of income and wealth in the U.S.	65	43	51	Clinton +8
The size and efficiency of the federal government	64	55	41	Trump +14
Gun policy	63	50	45	Trump +5
Trade with other nations	61	49	48	Trump +1
Government regulation of Wall Street and banks	59	53	42	Trump +11
Social issues such as gay marriage and abortion	48	31	64	Clinton +33
Climate change	47	28	66	Clinton +38

Issues ranked by % extremely/very important to vote
Gallup, May 18-22, 2016

June 03, 2016
AMERICANS FAVOR IDEA OF INCREASED OVERTIME ELIGIBILITY

by Frank Newport

Story Highlights

- *67% agree with concept of increasing worker overtime eligibility*
- *Majorities also favor requirements for paid sick leave, vacation and family leave*
- *On balance, Americans are negative about increased power for unions*

PRINCETON, N.J. – Americans agree with the idea of expanding the number of workers eligible for overtime pay, a change recently announced by the U.S. Department of Labor and one favored by presidential candidates Hillary Clinton and Bernie Sanders.

Expand Number of Workers Eligible for Overtime

	Agree %	Disagree %	Don't know enough to have an opinion %
Expand the number of workers eligible for overtime pay	67	14	18

Gallup, May 24-27, 2016

The change in overtime rules to be put in place by the Department of Labor raises the maximum annual salary at which employers are required to pay workers for overtime from $23,660 to $47,476. The expansion of overtime eligibility has been championed by both remaining Democratic candidates, Hillary Clinton and Bernie Sanders. At this point, the American public's initial reaction to the idea is quite positive.

Americans also agree with the idea of raising the minimum wage, as they generally have in the more than 70 years Gallup has tested it using different formats and different dollar amounts. The specific proposal tested in the current research is to raise the minimum wage to $20 per hour by the year 2020, agreed to by 56% of Americans. Both Sanders and Clinton have supported the idea of raising the minimum wage, with Sanders endorsing the specific proposal tested here. Donald Trump's position on the minimum wage has been characterized as shifting, although he has recently implied that the minimum wage does need to be increased.

Increase Minimum Wage

	Agree %	Disagree %	Don't know enough to have an opinion %
Increase the federal minimum wage from $7.25 to $15 an hour by 2020	56	36	7

Gallup, April 21-24, 2016

These measures of the American public's reaction to proposed changes affecting workers were tested in Gallup research conducted April 21-24 and May 24-27 of this year, and are part of Gallup's ongoing assessment of the ways in which Americans react to proposals made by presidential candidates. The research measures initial reactions to shorthand versions of proposals made by presidential candidates in speeches or in debates. Most policy changes are, in reality, complex, and the public's reactions could change if proposals became a matter of continuing public debate.

Americans Supportive of Mandatory Paid Vacation, Family Leave

A majority of Americans also favor workplace proposals that would require employers to provide seven days of paid sick leave, two weeks of paid vacation and at least 12 weeks of paid family and medical leave. Both Clinton and Sanders support these types of proposals, aimed at improving life for the nation's workers. Trump has not addressed the proposals.

Sick Leave, Vacation, and Family and Medical Leave

	Agree %	Disagree %	Don't know enough to have an opinion %
Require employers to provide all workers at least seven days of paid sick leave	75	16	9
Require employers to provide all workers at least two weeks of paid vacation	75	19	5
Require employers to provide at least 12 weeks of paid family and medical leave	62	27	10

Gallup, April 21-24, 2016

Both Clinton and Sanders have also argued for a strengthened role for labor unions as a mechanism designed to improve the situation for workers in this country. Unlike the reactions to the other aforementioned proposals, more of the public disagrees with this idea than agrees.

Increase Power of Labor Unions

	Agree %	Disagree %	Don't know enough to say %
Enact laws increasing the power of labor unions	32	41	27

Gallup, May 24-27, 2016

The net negative response to the idea of increasing the power of labor unions matches Gallup's ongoing union trends. Americans are positive about unions in general – 58% approve of them – though that level of support is much lower than what Gallup measured in the 1930s through the 1990s. But fewer than four in 10 Americans in Gallup's latest measure say the influence of labor unions in this country should increase. The majority of Americans say that unions' influence should either decrease or stay the same.

Bottom Line

Americans' reactions to presidential candidates' proposals concerning new laws or regulations aimed at improving the situation of the country's workers are generally positive. A majority of the public agrees with the idea of increasing eligibility for overtime, raising the minimum wage and requiring companies to offer specified amounts of paid sick leave, vacation, and family and medical leave. Americans do not, however, support the idea of increasing the power of labor unions.

Historical data are available in Gallup Analytics.

Survey Methods

Results reported in this article are based on telephone interviews with random samples of 2,024 national adults, aged 18+, living in all 50 states and the District of Columbia, conducted April 21-24, 2016, and 2,044 national adults conducted May 24-27, 2016.

Each respondent interviewed April 21-24 rated a randomly selected subset of five of 18 policy proposals included in the survey. Each proposal was rated by between 533 and 590 national adults. Results for each proposal have a margin of error of ±5 percentage points at the 95% confidence level.

Each respondent interviewed May 24-27 rated a randomly selected subset of six of 20 policy proposals included in the survey. Each proposal was rated by between 588 and 634 national adults. Results for each proposal have a margin of error of ±5 percentage points at the 95% confidence level.

All reported margins of sampling error include computed design effects for weighting.

June 03, 2016

CLINTON'S BEST ASSET, TRUMP'S BIGGEST LIABILITY: EXPERIENCE

by Justin McCarthy

Story Highlights

- *Americans twice as likely to say Clinton has experience it takes*
- *Honesty, trustworthiness a weak point for both candidates*
- *Majorities say both Clinton and Trump can get things done*

WASHINGTON, D.C. – Hillary Clinton holds double-digit advantages over Donald Trump in Americans' views of the two candidates' experience to be president, ability to work with both parties in Washington and likability. Trump's greatest relative strengths include being a strong and decisive leader and the ability to stand up to special interests.

Americans' Views of the Qualities and Characteristics of Hillary Clinton and Donald Trump

Thinking about the following characteristics and qualities, please say whether you think each applies or doesn't apply to Hillary Clinton/Donald Trump. How about – [RANDOM ORDER]?

	Applies to Clinton %	Applies to Trump %	Difference (Clinton minus Trump) %
Has the experience it takes to be president	62	31	31
Would work well with both parties to get things done in Washington	51	39	12
Is likable	46	36	10
Would display good judgment in a crisis	48	39	9
Can manage the government effectively	49	42	7
Cares about the needs of people like you	44	37	7
Has strong moral character	39	36	3
Is honest and trustworthy	32	33	-1
Can get things done	56	58	-2
Can bring about the changes this country needs	37	42	-5
Stands up to special interest groups	44	52	-8
Is a strong and decisive leader	51	60	-9

Gallup, May 18-22, 2016

These data, collected May 18-22, also find that Clinton has a slight edge in views of the candidates' ability to manage the government effectively and whether they care about the needs of people "like you." Americans are about equally likely to say Clinton and Trump have strong moral character and to say they are honest and trustworthy, though fewer than four in 10 say these apply to either candidate. On the other hand, nearly equivalent majorities of Americans view each candidate as being able to get things done.

More than six in 10 Americans say Clinton has the experience it takes to be president (62%) – twice as many as say this about Trump (31%). In fact, experience is Clinton's greatest overall strength from among those tested in the poll, and it is Trump's single weakest attribute.

Most adults also believe Clinton can get things done (56%), while about half say she would work well with both parties in Washington (51%) and that she is a strong and decisive leader (51%).

As is true of Clinton, most Americans believe Trump can get things done (58%), and they are more likely to view him than Clinton as a strong and decisive leader (60%) – the latter being the characteristic Trump scores highest on. And most say Trump is capable of standing up to special interests (52%) – more so than for Clinton (44%).

The candidates are both viewed as lacking in honesty – 32% say Clinton displays honesty and trustworthiness, her lowest score on any issue, but no worse than Trump's 33% on this dimension. The two candidates also both score relatively poorly on having strong moral character, being able to bring about the changes needed in the U.S. and caring about people's needs.

Both candidates receive majority positive ratings on getting things done and being strong leaders. Clinton gains a majority rating on experience and working well with both parties, and Trump also gets a majority positive rating on standing up to special interests. Otherwise, less than half of Americans say that any of the other dimensions apply to either candidate.

One in Three Trump Supporters Say Clinton Has Experience It Takes

As would be expected, solid majorities of self-identified Clinton supporters say the dozen characteristics apply to her, but there is a good deal of variation. The strongest majorities say she has the experience necessary to be president (92%) and can get things done (89%). At the other end of the spectrum, a much smaller 61% of those who say they would vote for her over Trump say honesty and trustworthiness apply to her, and 69% give her credit for standing up to special interests.

Few Trump supporters see these characteristics in Clinton – their lowest ratings for her are her honesty and trustworthiness and her ability to bring about the changes the country needs, at just 6% each.

However, sizable minorities of Trump's supporters are willing to grant that Clinton possesses certain positive qualities, including the necessary experience to be president (34%) and the ability to get things done (25%).

Views of Clinton's Qualities and Characteristics, by Supporters of Each Candidate

Thinking about the following characteristics and qualities, please say whether you think each applies or doesn't apply to Hillary Clinton. How about – [RANDOM ORDER]?

	Applies to Clinton (Clinton supporters) %	Applies to Clinton (Trump supporters) %
Has the experience it takes to be president	92	34
Can get things done	89	25
Would display good judgment in a crisis	85	15
Can manage the government effectively	85	16
Is a strong and decisive leader	85	19
Would work well with both parties to get things done in Washington	84	20
Cares about the needs of people like you	81	11
Is likable	75	18
Can bring about the changes this country needs	70	6
Has strong moral character	70	11
Stands up to special interest groups	69	22
Is honest and trustworthy	61	6

Gallup, May 18-22, 2016

One in Three Clinton Supporters Say Trump Is a Strong, Decisive Leader

Trump's supporters rate him relatively highly on all characteristics, but most widely on being a strong and decisive leader (94%) and the ability to get things done (94%). Trump's supporters are least likely to say he has the experience to be president (61%) or has strong moral character (64%).

Among Clinton's supporters, fewer view Trump as having these characteristics than is true for Trump's supporters regarding Clinton. On half of the characteristics, less than 10% of Clinton's supporters view them as applying to Trump. However, a few qualities strike a sizable minority of her supporters as applying to her GOP opponent.

One in three Clinton supporters say Trump is a strong and decisive leader (33%), while about three in 10 say he has the ability to stand up to special interests (30%) and can get things done (28%).

Views of Each Candidate's Supporters of Trump's Qualities and Characteristics

Thinking about the following characteristics and qualities, please say whether you think each applies or doesn't apply to Donald Trump. How about – [RANDOM ORDER]?

	Applies to Trump (Trump supporters) %	Applies to Trump (Clinton supporters) %
Can get things done	94	28
Is a strong and decisive leader	94	33
Can bring about the changes this country needs	84	9
Can manage the government effectively	82	8
Stands up to special interest groups	80	30
Cares about the needs of people like you	77	5
Would display good judgment in a crisis	76	9
Would work well with both parties to get things done in Washington	72	12

	Applies to Trump (Trump supporters) %	Applies to Trump (Clinton supporters) %
Is honest and trustworthy	69	5
Is likable	68	11
Has strong moral character	64	15
Has the experience it takes to be president	61	6

Gallup, May 18-22, 2016

Bottom Line

The candidates' respective supporters are drawn to Clinton's and Trump's unique résumés and personal qualities, but when it comes to the experience necessary for the presidency, Americans are more likely to say Clinton has that experience. But Trump has advantages of his own in Americans' eyes, such as his leadership and ability to confront special interests, although neither compares with Clinton's 2-to-1 advantage on experience. Americans are just as likely to say Trump can get things done as to say this about Clinton.

Almost as important for Clinton as her edge in experience is Trump's low score on honesty. Only one in three Americans view Clinton as honest, her single biggest liability. But Trump scores no better on this dimension, missing out on an area in which the Republican could have painted a strong contrast with Clinton in the general election contest.

Most broadly, Americans tend to see the two candidates as strong leaders, but ones lacking in honesty and morality.

Survey Methods

Results for this Gallup poll are based on telephone interviews conducted May 18-22, 2016, on the Gallup U.S. Daily survey, with a random sample of 1,530 adults, aged 18 and older, living in all 50 U.S. states and the District of Columbia. For results based on the total sample of national adults, the margin of sampling error is ±3 percentage points at the 95% confidence level. All reported margins of sampling error include computed design effects for weighting.

June 06, 2016
PARTY GROUPS AGREE ON IMPORTANCE OF BIG ELECTION ISSUES

by Lydia Saad

Story Highlights

- *Americans from both parties rate economy, jobs as important voting issues*
- *Republicans, Democrats also agree on education, healthcare, national security*
- *Climate change, minorities, government size spark differences*

PRINCETON, N.J. – Mirroring the top issue priorities of Americans as a whole, Republicans, independents and Democrats largely agree on the top issues that will affect their vote for president this fall. Education, the economy, jobs, healthcare and terrorism/national defense rank among the six most important voting issues for all three groups, with close to 80% or more rating each as extremely or very important.

Five Areas of Issue-Priority Agreement Among U.S. Party Groups

% Rating each extremely or very important to their vote for president

	Democrats %	Independents %	Republicans %
Education	92	85	80
The economy	91	90	95
Employment and jobs	91	87	91
Healthcare and the Affordable Care Act	88	79	81
Terrorism and national security	85	84	95

Gallup, May 18-22, 2016

At the same time, Democrats and Republicans have vastly different perspectives on three of 17 campaign issues rated in a recent Gallup survey. Democrats are much more likely than Republicans to say climate change and the treatment of minority groups will be key voting issues for them this fall. Republicans put much more emphasis than Democrats on the size and efficiency of government.

Sharpest Issue-Priority Disagreements Among U.S. Party Groups

% Rating each extremely or very important to their vote for president

	Democrats %	Independents %	Republicans %	Difference, Democrats vs. Republicans pct. pts.
Climate change	72	44	25	+47
The treatment of minority groups in this country	86	64	48	+38
The size and efficiency of the federal government	47	64	79	-32

Gallup, May 18-22, 2016

The importance gap between Democrats and Republicans is particularly wide for climate change, with 72% of Democrats vs. 25% of Republicans rating it an extremely or very important issue to their vote this year – a 47-percentage-point difference. There is a 38-point gap for the treatment of minority groups in the country, with 86% of Democrats vs. 48% of Republicans rating it highly important. And the gap is nearly as wide – 32 points, but in the other direction – for the size and efficiency of government, with 79% of Republicans vs. 47% of Democrats rating it as highly important.

Independents fall almost squarely between the two party groups on all three issues. These differences in the ways in which partisan groups look at priorities for the presidential candidates to discuss are generally similar to what they were in January, when Gallup last measured them.

The latest findings come from a May 18-22 Gallup survey in which U.S. adults were first asked to rate how important the candidates' positions on each of 17 prominent national issues will be to their vote for president this year. As Gallup reported previously, most of the issues at the top of the importance list are related to the economy and national defense. By contrast, the bottom eight touch heavily on social policy, as well as on trade and the environment.

Beyond the three issues that divide Americans most, Democrats place significantly more emphasis than Republicans do on four other areas: the distribution of income and wealth, government regulation of Wall Street and banks, education, and social issues such as gay marriage and abortion. Republicans put more emphasis on the federal budget deficit, immigration, taxes and national defense.

Party Groups' Ratings of Each Issue as Extremely/Very Important to Their Vote for President

Ranked by Democratic vs. Republican difference

	Democrats %	Independents %	Republicans %	Difference, Democrats vs. Republicans pct. pts.
Climate change	72	44	25	+47
The treatment of minority groups in this country	86	64	48	+38
The distribution of income and wealth in the United States	76	64	51	+25
Government regulation of Wall Street and banks	66	60	51	+15
Education	92	85	80	+12
Social issues such as gay marriage and abortion	56	45	44	+12
Healthcare and the Affordable Care Act	88	79	81	+7
Employment and jobs	91	87	91	0
Gun policy	67	57	67	0
The economy	91	90	95	-4
Foreign affairs	72	72	78	-6
Trade with other nations	59	59	66	-7
Terrorism and national security	85	84	95	-10
Taxes	66	71	76	-10
Immigration	66	65	77	-11
The federal budget deficit	70	78	88	-18
The size and efficiency of the federal government	47	64	79	-32

Gallup, May 18-22, 2016

Bottom Line

Republicans and Democrats place differing emphases on the importance of the candidates' positions on climate change, the treatment of minority groups and the size and scope of government. Additionally, Democrats put more emphasis on a variety of other social and income equality issues, while Republicans put greater emphasis on certain national security and fiscal issues.

Despite these differences, Republicans and Democrats are united on their top priorities: the economy, jobs, healthcare, national defense and education. These issues represent a common denominator for the electorate that should make it easy for the candidates to know where to focus their attention this year. The candidates' ability to convince Americans that they have a plan or the skill to solve these problems could go a long way toward enhancing their appeal to a broad base of voters.

Survey Methods

Results for this Gallup poll are based on telephone interviews conducted May 18-22, 2016, with a random sample of 1,530 adults, aged 18 and older, living in all 50 U.S. states and the District of Columbia. For results based on the total sample of national adults, the margin of sampling error is ±3 percentage points at the 95% confidence level. All reported margins of sampling error include computed design effects for weighting.

June 07, 2016
U.S. ECONOMIC CONFIDENCE INDEX FLAT IN MAY, AT -14

by Justin McCarthy

Story Highlights

- *Index remained the same as in April*
- *Democrats, Republicans at lowest levels of confidence since 2014*

WASHINGTON, D.C. – Americans' confidence in the U.S. economy was flat in May. Gallup's U.S. Economic Confidence Index averaged -14 – the same as in April, which was a seven-month low.

Gallup's U.S. Economic Confidence Index -- Monthly Averages

January 2008-May 2016

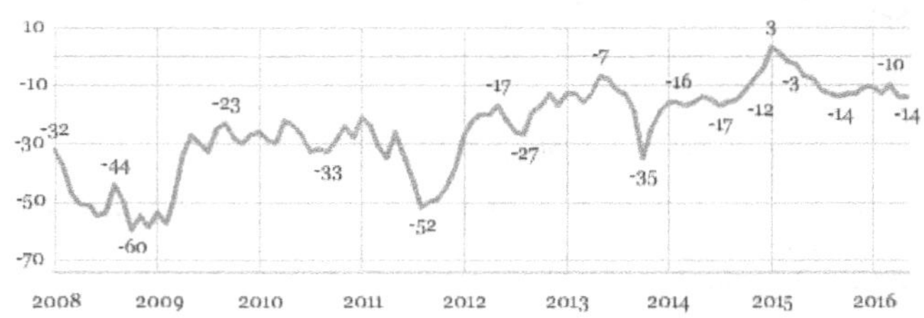

Gallup Daily tracking

GALLUP

The latest index score was quite a bit lower than the -7 registered one year earlier, in May 2015. This year's monthly scores have consistently been lower than the comparable months in 2015, and Americans' views of the national economy have consistently skewed negative since March 2015. Still, monthly index scores from the past couple of years have been well above most of the readings in Gallup's eight-year trend, particularly the dismally low ones recorded in the years after the Great Recession.

Examining the index on a weekly basis, however, reveals that confidence has recently improved somewhat. The past two weeks have both registered at -12, a minor improvement from the -14 to -16 weekly readings from mid-April to mid-May.

Gallup's U.S. Economic Confidence Index is the average of two components: how Americans rate current economic conditions and whether they feel the economy is improving or getting worse. The index has a theoretical maximum of +100 if all Americans say the economy is doing well and improving, and a theoretical minimum of -100 if all Americans say the economy is doing poorly and getting worse.

In May, the current conditions score registered -5, one point higher than in April. This was the result of 25% of U.S. adults rating the current economy as "excellent" or "good," and 30% rating it as "poor." Meanwhile, the economic outlook score went down one point to -22. This was the result of 37% of U.S. adults saying the economy was "getting better" and 59% saying it was "getting worse."

Gallup's U.S. Economic Confidence Index Components -- Monthly Averages

May 2015-May 2016

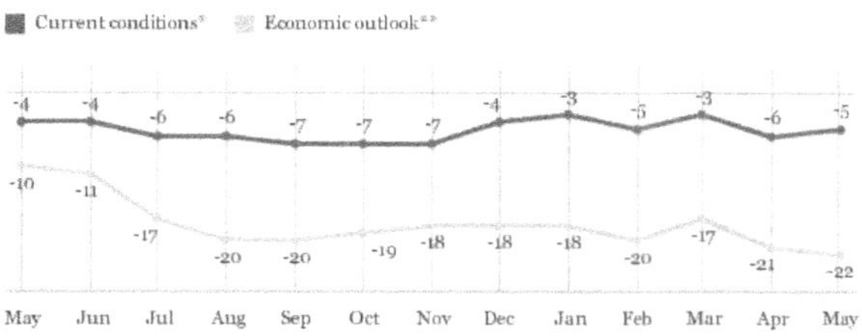

* % (Excellent + Good) minus % Poor

** % Getting better minus % Getting worse

Gallup Daily tracking

GALLUP'

Democrats, Republicans at Lowest Confidence Levels Since 2014

Each party group's index score in May was about 20 points down from where their scores were in early 2015. The latest monthly scores were Democrats' and Republicans' lowest levels of confidence since their respective lows in 2014.

Democrats' May index score (+9) represented another successive monthly decrease in confidence. While Democrats are still the only party group to have net positive views of the economy, the latest score was their lowest since July 2014.

Republicans' score of -42 was technically their lowest since March 2014 but was not markedly different from the -35 to -41 range they remained in from January to April.

Gallup's U.S. Economic Confidence Index, by Political Party

January 2014-May 2016

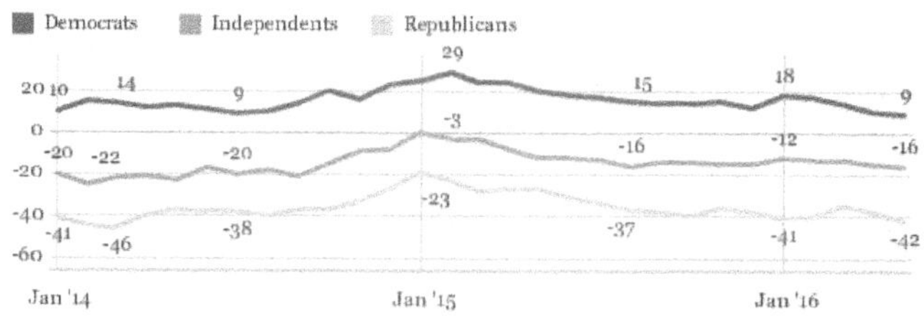

Gallup Daily tracking

GALLUP'

Bottom Line

Americans' confidence in the U.S. economy remains negative, although recent weekly readings of the index could mark a turning point. The consistent level of confidence reflects the balance of good and bad news from the Bureau of Labor Statistics' latest report – job growth slowed in May, but the unemployment rate dipped to its lowest rate since 2007.

The Dow Jones industrial average is on the upswing, but so are gas prices. The latter, however, could merely be seasonal increases Americans are accustomed to seeing each spring and summer. Overall, Americans are nearly neutral in their assessments of how the national economy is currently doing. Their outlook for its future, however, remains negative.

These data are available in Gallup Analytics.

Survey Methods

Results for this Gallup poll are based on telephone interviews conducted May 1-31, 2016, on the Gallup U.S. Daily survey, with a random sample of 15,700 adults, aged 18 and older, living in all 50 U.S. states and the District of Columbia. For results based on the total sample of national adults, the margin of sampling error is ±1 percentage point at the 95% confidence level. All reported margins of sampling error include computed design effects for weighting.

June 08, 2016

BIRTH CONTROL, DIVORCE TOP LIST OF MORALLY ACCEPTABLE ISSUES

by Art Swift

Story Highlights

- *89% say birth control morally acceptable; divorce, 72%*
- *10% believe extramarital affairs are acceptable; cloning humans, 13%*
- *Republicans and Democrats split on several issues*

WASHINGTON, D.C. – Birth control, divorce, sex between unmarried men and women, and gambling top a list of morally acceptable issues, while Americans deem polygamy, cloning humans and extramarital affairs as the least acceptable.

Moral Acceptability

Regardless of whether you think it should be legal, for each one, please tell me whether you personally believe that it is morally acceptable or morally wrong.

	2016 %
Highly acceptable	
Birth control	89
Largely acceptable	
Divorce	72
Sex between an unmarried man and woman	67
Gambling	67
Having a baby outside of marriage	62
Medical research using stem cells obtained from human embryos	60
Gay or lesbian relations	60
The death penalty	59
Buying and wearing clothing made of animal fur	59
Contentious	
Medical testing on animals	53
Doctor-assisted suicide	53
Abortion	43
Largely unacceptable	
Sex between teenagers	37
Pornography	34
Cloning animals	34
Highly unacceptable	
Suicide	18
Polygamy	14
Cloning humans	13
Married men and women having an affair	10

Gallup, May 4-8, 2016

For the past 15 years, Gallup has asked Americans to rate the moral acceptability of different issues. Of the 19 issues included in this year's survey, a majority of Americans view 11 as morally acceptable. Americans' willingness to describe many issues as morally acceptable has grown since 2001, namely for gay or lesbian relations, having a baby outside of marriage and sex between unmarried people. On other issues, including abortion, cloning animals and wearing clothing made of animal fur, there has been little to no change in the past 15 years. On a year-to-year basis, Americans' views of the moral acceptability of any of these issues have not changed much since 2015.

Birth control is the issue that the largest percentage of Americans approve of, with 89% deeming it morally acceptable. Eight others – ranging from divorce to medical research using stem cells obtained from human embryos – fall into the "largely acceptable" category, with solid majorities rating them as morally OK. Americans are split on three issues in the "contentious" category: medical testing on animals, doctor-assisted suicide and abortion.

At least half of Americans consider seven issues on the list "morally wrong." In the "largely unacceptable" category, sex between teenagers, pornography and cloning animals are deemed wrong by at least 56%, with roughly a third calling these acceptable. In the "highly unacceptable" category are suicide (18% morally acceptable vs. 73% morally unacceptable), polygamy (14% vs. 82%) and cloning humans (13% vs. 81%). Extramarital affairs rank as the least morally acceptable activity on this list, with 10% saying they are acceptable versus 88% saying they are not.

Republicans, Democrats Split on Moral Acceptability

There are some key differences in how partisans view these moral issues. Democrats are more likely than Republicans to deem sex between an unmarried man and woman as acceptable, along with having a baby outside of marriage and abortion. Republicans, on the other hand, are more likely than Democrats to believe the death penalty is acceptable, as well as to support buying and wearing clothing made of animal fur and medical testing on animals.

Moral Acceptability, by Party Identification

	Republicans	Independents	Democrats
Birth control	87	87	94
Divorce	67	68	83
Sex between an unmarried man and woman	54	70	78
Gambling	63	66	74
Having a baby outside of marriage	49	64	73
Medical research using stem cells obtained from human embryos	44	63	73
Gay or lesbian relations	44	62	75
The death penalty	74	56	47
Buying and wearing clothing made of animal fur	71	59	45
Doctor-assisted suicide	44	53	64
Medical testing on animals	64	52	43
Abortion	24	44	62
Sex between teenagers	25	36	52
Pornography	22	36	46
Cloning animals	31	33	39
Suicide	9	20	25
Polygamy	10	16	18
Cloning humans	10	13	17
Married men and women having an affair	8	12	9

Gallup, May 4-8, 2016

Bottom Line

Americans broadly agree on the moral acceptability of several prominent social issues. Most consider birth control and divorce as OK, while the vast majority disapprove of polygamy, cloning humans and extramarital affairs. Although polygamy and cloning humans have seen increases in acceptability in recent years, more than 80% of the public still oppose them.

Gay or lesbian relations, having a baby out of wedlock and sex between unmarried men and women have seen substantial increases in public acceptance since Gallup began asking about them, but issues such as the death penalty and medical testing on animals have seen declining acceptance. In general, in the 21st century, Americans believe more key issues are morally acceptable than they used to, consistent with other trends toward greater social liberalism.

Historical data are available in Gallup Analytics.

Survey Methods

Results for this Gallup poll are based on telephone interviews conducted May 4-8, 2016, on the Gallup U.S. Daily survey, with a random sample of 1,025 adults, aged 18 and older, living in all 50 U.S. states and the District of Columbia. For results based on the total sample of national adults, the margin of sampling error is ±4 percentage points at the 95% confidence level. All reported margins of sampling error include computed design effects for weighting.

June 08, 2016

THOUGHT GIVEN TO PRESIDENTIAL ELECTION MATCHES 2008 LEVELS

by Jim Norman

Story Highlights

- *75% of Americans have given "quite a lot" of thought to the election*
- *Republicans, as is typical, are more likely to have given it a lot of thought*
- *48% are less enthusiastic than usual about voting, 46% more enthusiastic*

WASHINGTON, D.C. – Three in four Americans are giving "quite a lot" of thought to the upcoming presidential election, a possible sign of high voter turnout this November. In the 2008 presidential campaign that produced the highest voter-turnout percentage in 40 years, a late-May poll showed a level of interest similar to this year's. In the lower-turnout 2000 and 2004 elections, smaller percentages said in May that they had given quite a bit of thought to the election.

Thought Given in May, Votes Cast in November

	Quite a lot	Only a little	Turnout percentage, Election Day
	%	%	%
2016	75	21	N/A
2008	73	20	58.2
2004	64	29	56.7
2000	42	43	51.2

Question on thought given to the election was not asked in May-June 2012
May Gallup polls in 2000, 2004, 2008 and 2016; The American Presidency Project, Voter Turnout in Presidential Elections

Fewer than half of Americans in May 2000 were paying a lot of attention to that year's presidential election, and the turnout reflected the lack of interest. About half of eligible voters (51.2%) cast a ballot, the third-lowest turnout rate (ahead of 1996 and 1988) since 1924.

Gallup did not measure thought about the election in the May-June period of the 2012 election, which produced a 54.9% turnout rate. In a July poll that year, 64% said they were thinking about the election quite a lot – fewer than in July 2008, about the same as in July 2004 and more than in July 2000.

Democrats and Republicans Giving More Thought to Election Than in January

The current level of thought Americans are giving to the election is significantly higher than before the first presidential primaries in February. Seventy-nine percent of Republicans, including independents who lean Republican, now say they have given quite a lot of thought to the election, up from 70% in January. Democrats and Democratic leaners are also more likely to say they are thinking about the election: 72% say "quite a lot" now, up from 63% in January.

Republicans are more likely than Democrats to say they are following the race closely, continuing a pattern seen in previous campaigns. Even in the final days of the Democratic victories in the 2008 and 2012 presidential elections, Republicans were more likely than Democrats to say they were thinking about the election quite a lot. Republicans also are following election news more closely, according to a May 13-15 Gallup poll.

Americans Split on Whether Their Enthusiasm Is Higher or Lower Than in Past

Though Americans are giving a lot of thought to the election, they are split on whether they are more enthusiastic (46%) or less enthusiastic (48%) about voting this year compared with prior election years. The only time Gallup asked this question in May or June of a presidential campaign year was during the high-turnout 2008 election. In a June 15-19 poll that year, about the same percentage (48%) said they were more enthusiastic as said so this year, but significantly fewer (37%) said they were less enthusiastic.

Republicans today are far more enthusiastic than in June 2008, when incumbent Republican President George W. Bush's approval rating was below 30%. Then, only 35% of Republicans and leaners said they were more enthusiastic than usual, and 51% were less enthusiastic. Now, 51% of Republicans are more enthusiastic and 43% less enthusiastic.

For Democrats and leaners, the situation is reversed. In June 2008, with Barack Obama on the way to being their party's nominee, 61% were more enthusiastic and 25% less enthusiastic. Now, 43% are more enthusiastic and 50% less.

Party Enthusiasm Has Flipped Since 2008

Compared to previous elections, are you more enthusiastic than usual about voting, or less enthusiastic?

	All adults	Democrats and leaners	Republicans and leaners
	%	%	%
May 18-22, 2016			
More enthusiastic	46	43	51
Less enthusiastic	48	50	43
Jun 15-19, 2008			
More enthusiastic	48	61	35
Less enthusiastic	37	25	51

Gallup

There have been three other notable shifts in enthusiasm from 2008 to now:

- In 2008, Gallup measured Americans' enthusiasm to vote just after Hillary Clinton gave up her bid for the Democratic nomination; this year's poll was conducted as she stood on the threshold of becoming the first female presidential nominee of a major party. Nevertheless, among Democratic and Democratic-leaning women, 59% in 2008 were more enthusiastic than usual about voting and 31% were less enthusiastic. But this year, 40% are more enthusiastic and 53% are less enthusiastic.
- Among ideological moderates from either party, 48% were more enthusiastic than usual in 2008 and 39% less enthusiastic. Now 38% are more enthusiastic and 56% less enthusiastic.
- Conservatives' enthusiasm has grown, while liberals' has faded. Fifty-two percent of conservatives are more enthusiastic this year, compared with 40% in 2008; at the same time, 48% of liberals are more enthusiastic now, compared with 63% in 2008.

Enthusiasm could grow in both parties. With the interparty battles of the primary season ending, the parties can switch their emphasis to healing internal wounds and attacking the other party's nominee. The fall campaign may also help energize voters in both parties – in the last three presidential election years, enthusiasm within the parties tended to peak in the month before the election.

Bottom Line

It is no surprise that a campaign with two heated battles for party nominations, each dominated by a candidate who has been among the nation's best-known public figures for decades, has drawn the attention of most Americans. It also is no surprise, with both Clinton and Donald Trump holding unusually high unfavorable ratings, that nearly half of Americans say they are less enthusiastic than usual about voting. Both nominees face the dual challenges of winning back support within their own party from campaign opponents and those opponents' supporters as well as improving their images with the general public.

The 2016 election has Americans pondering their choices with a focus similar to that of the high-turnout 2008 campaign, but there is a fundamental difference. Fewer than four in 10 Americans have a favorable view of either Clinton or Trump. At the beginning of June 2008, 58% viewed eventual Democratic nominee Barack Obama favorably, and 56% held that view of presumptive Republican nominee John McCain.

With the public engaged by the campaign but not favorably disposed toward the two major-party candidates, it is unclear whether high interest in the election will result in high turnout, or whether the current low regard for the candidates will lead to low turnout in November. Turnout may depend on the extent to which the candidates can change the public's views of them and can turn animosity toward their opponent into turnout at the polls for themselves.

Survey Methods

Results for this Gallup poll are based on telephone interviews conducted May 18-22, 2016, with a random sample of 1,530 adults, aged 18 and older, living in all 50 U.S. states and the District of Columbia. For results based on the total sample of national adults, the margin of sampling error is ±3 percentage points at the 95% confidence level. For results based on the total samples of 697 Democrats and Democratic-leaning independents and 744 Republicans and Republican-leaning independents, the margin of sampling error is ±5 percentage points at the 95% confidence level. All reported margins of sampling error include computed design effects for weighting.

June 10, 2016
REPUBLICANS CONTINUE TO RATE GOP-LED CONGRESS POORLY

by Jeffrey M. Jones

Story Highlights

- *12% of Republicans approve, below the 16% national average*
- *Republicans have registered lower approval since last summer*
- *Prior GOP-led Congresses rated much more positively by Republicans*

PRINCETON, N.J. – Just 12% of Republicans approve of the job Congress is doing, a lower rating than the historically subpar rating all Americans (16%) give the GOP-led institution. Immediately after the Republican Party took control of both houses of Congress in early 2015, Republican identifiers were more positive than the general public about Congress, but by the summer of that year Republicans' approval dropped below the national average.

Approval Ratings of Congress, Recent Trend, All Americans vs. Republicans

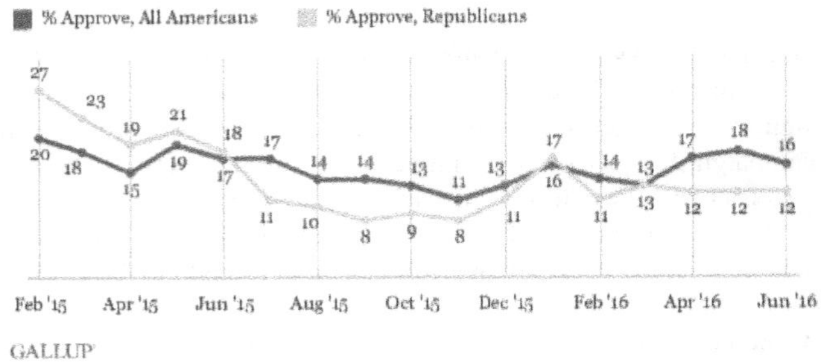

Since last July, Republican approval has averaged 11%, compared with 15% for independents and 17% for Democrats. The recent trends for all three major party groups are shown in a graph at the end of this article.

Republicans have failed to make progress in getting their preferred legislation passed since they gained control of the Senate in early 2015. John Boehner resigned as speaker last fall as a result of unhappiness with his leadership among many Republican House members, not to mention Republican Party supporters more generally. After a prolonged search to find a replacement, the GOP tapped Paul Ryan as its new House leader. However, that has done little to improve Republicans' evaluations of the way Congress is handling its job.

In the past, supporters of the majority party may have been happy just to have their party in power. Over the past two decades, the majority party's supporters have given Congress significantly higher job approval ratings than supporters of the opposition party when one party had control of both houses of Congress. These data go back to 1993, when Gallup began compiling approval of Congress by party.

Job Approval of Congress, by Party Identification and Party Control of Congress

Years	Majority party in House and Senate	Average approval, Republicans %	Average approval, Democrats %	Gap in favor of majority party pct. pts.
1993-1994	Democratic	21	31	+10
1995-2000	Republican	52	36	+16
2003-2006	Republican	55	25	+30
2007-2010	Democratic	18	33	+15
2015-2016	Republican	14	17	-3

Note: 2001-2002 and 2011-2014 not included because control of Congress was shared, with one party controlling the House and the other the Senate.
Gallup

To illustrate, when the GOP was the majority party in 1995 through 2000, Republican approval of Congress was 16 percentage points higher on average than that of Democrats, 52% to 36%. The gap was even larger – 30 points – from 2003 through 2006, perhaps because Republican George W. Bush was president at the time.

Democrats were also much more positive toward Congress in the two recent periods in which they were the majority party. From 1993 through 1994, Democrats' average approval rating of Congress was 10 points higher than that of Republicans. And from 2007 to 2010, Democrats' ratings were 15 points higher on average.

In the current period, which includes the initial months of 2015 when Republicans were more positive toward Congress, Republicans' approval ratings have averaged three points *lower* than Democrats', 14% to 17%.

Implications

Rank-and-file Republicans are not alone in having a negative opinion of Congress, as independents' and Democrats' approval ratings are also currently low from a historical perspective. But Republicans are unusual in giving Congress lower approval at a time when their party has control of both houses. In the past, supporters of the majority party typically had approval ratings at least 10 points higher than supporters of the opposition party.

Republicans' negativity toward the GOP-led Congress is not merely a function of there being divided government. Republicans were more positive than Democrats toward the GOP-led Congress when Democrat Bill Clinton was president in the 1990s. Likewise, Democrats were more positive than Republicans toward the Democratically controlled Congress in 2007 and 2008 when Bush was president.

Nor are Republicans' lower ratings of Congress attributable to unawareness of or confusion as to which party controls Congress – 64% of Americans and 69% of Republicans correctly identify the Republican Party as the majority party in the House. Those were easily the highest scores on five questions testing Americans' knowledge of Congress included in the June 1-5 poll.

Republicans' frustration with their own party leadership, in both the House and Senate, likely contributed to their negative evaluations of Congress. Some Republicans are probably upset with the leadership for not doing more to pass legislation to address the nation's problems, even if that meant compromising with Democrats. Other Republicans may have been unhappy with the leadership for failing to take a more aggressive approach against President Barack Obama and the Democrats, wanting Republicans to pass GOP-favored legislation even in the face of a certain presidential veto and to take active steps to thwart the president's ability to pass legislation he favored. Regardless, the change in the House leadership last fall seems to have done little to make Republicans feel better about Congress.

Republican approval of Congress would almost surely improve if Donald Trump were elected president in 2016 and the party maintained control of both houses of Congress, mainly because Republicans would see more of their preferred legislation passed than has been the case with Obama in the White House. However, if Hillary Clinton is elected along with a Republican Congress, it is unlikely that much would change to make Republicans feel better about the way Congress is doing its job.

Historical data are available in Gallup Analytics.

Survey Methods

Results for this Gallup poll are based on telephone interviews conducted June 1-5, 2016, with a random sample of 1,027 adults, aged 18 and older, living in all 50 U.S. states and the District of Columbia. For results based on the total sample of national adults, the margin of sampling error is ±3 percentage points at the 95% confidence level.

For results based on the total samples of 308 Republicans and 313 Democrats, the margins of sampling error are ±7 percentage points at the 95% confidence level.

For results based on the total sample of 386 independents, the margin of sampling error is ±6 percentage points at the 95% confidence level.

All reported margins of sampling error include computed design effects for weighting.

Approval Ratings of Congress, Recent Trend, by Political Party

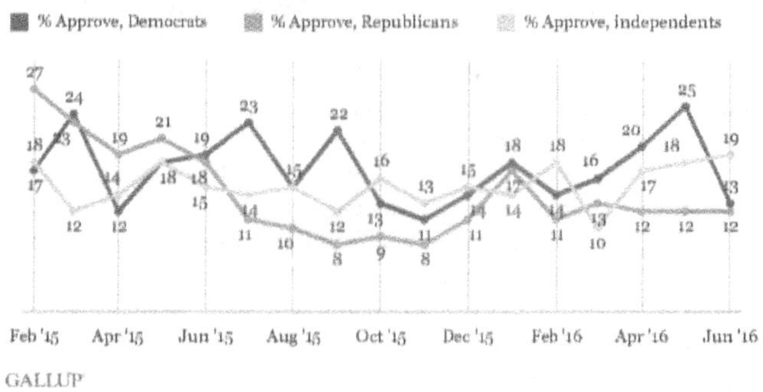

June 10, 2016
U.S. EMPLOYEE ENGAGEMENT SLIPS BELOW 33% IN MAY

by Amy Adkins

Story Highlights

- *32.7% of U.S. workers engaged in their jobs*
- *Monthly averages holding better than in 2015*

WASHINGTON, D.C. – The percentage of U.S. workers whom Gallup considers "engaged" in their jobs averaged 32.7% in May. While still among the better monthly averages on record, May follows two consecutive months in which employee engagement averages remained at or above 33.0% – a rare occurrence in Gallup's history of tracking the metric.

Employee engagement has generally been trending upward for the past three years. In 2015, the metric was largely stable, registering between 31.5% and 32.1% for much of the year. However, the monthly average for December rose to 32.8%, setting the stage for a stronger start to 2016. Aside from February's average, monthly employee engagement figures this year have tracked higher than monthly averages in 2015. Monthly averages in 2016 have not fallen below 32.5% at any point.

In May, an additional 50.9% of employees were "not engaged" and 16.4% were "actively disengaged."

The May 2016 employee engagement average is based on Gallup Daily tracking interviews conducted with 7,327 U.S. adults working for an employer. Gallup categorizes workers as "engaged" based on their level of agreement with key workplace elements – such as having an opportunity to do what they do best each day, having someone at work who encourages their development and believing their opinions count at work – that predict important organizational performance outcomes.

Engaged employees are involved in, enthusiastic about and committed to their work. Gallup's extensive research shows that employee engagement is strongly connected to business outcomes essential to an organization's financial success, such as productivity, profitability and customer engagement. Engaged employees drive the innovation, growth and revenue that their companies need.

Bottom Line

Despite dropping below 33.0%, the May employee engagement average remains higher than it was in 2015 and is in line with the generally stronger monthly averages Gallup has recorded over the past six months. Organizations appear to be making incremental – but important – progress in employee engagement, pushing engagement closer to the rare 33.0% mark. Certain economic factors may also be encouraging some improvement in engagement levels. For example, the Gallup Good Jobs rate and the Gallup Job Creation Index are at high points in their trends.

While employee engagement has not been found to be seasonal, monthly averages in June 2014 and 2015 were higher than averages for May in those same years. If the pattern repeats this year, engagement may return to or surpass 33.0%. However, employee engagement averages struggled to reach even 32.0% in the first week of June, perhaps signaling a return to pre-2016 levels.

Survey Methods

Results for this Gallup poll are based on telephone interviews conducted May 1-31, 2016, on the Gallup U.S. Daily survey, with a random sample of 7,327 U.S. adults employed full or part time for an employer, aged 18 and older, living in all 50 U.S. states and the District of Columbia. For results based on the total sample of employed adults, the margin of sampling error is ±2 percentage points at the 95% confidence level. All reported margins of sampling error include computed design effects for weighting.

June 13, 2016
AMERICANS' CONFIDENCE IN NEWSPAPERS AT NEW LOW

by Lydia Saad

Story Highlights

- *More in U.S. have low (36%) than high (20%) confidence in newspapers*
- *Democrats, young adults no longer confident in newspapers*
- *Decline for newspapers mirrors pattern for 14 major institutions*

PRINCETON, N.J. – The 20% of Americans who are confident in newspapers as a U.S. institution hit an all-time low this year, marking the 10th consecutive year that more Americans express little or no, rather than high, confidence in the institution. The percentage of Americans expressing "a great deal" or "quite a lot" of confidence in newspapers has been dwindling since 2000, and the percentage expressing "very little" or "none" finally eclipsed it in 2007. The percentage with low confidence has only expanded since, tying a previous high of 36%.

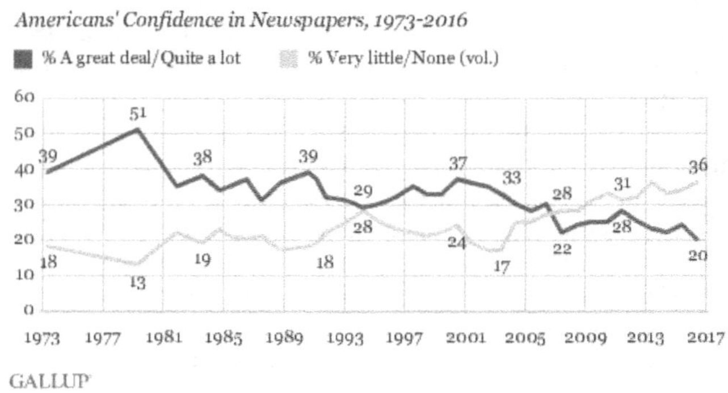

One in five U.S. adults now say they have a great deal or quite a lot of confidence in newspapers – the all-time low for newspapers in Gallup's trend dating to 1973. An additional 42% of U.S. adults say they have "some" confidence, meaning that the institution still sparks at least a measure of confidence in a majority of Americans.

However, the days when more than twice as many Americans expressed high rather than low confidence in newspapers are long gone. While this was common from the inception of Gallup's confidence in institutions trend through 1990, it has only been achieved once since – in 2002, during the aftermath of the 9/11 attacks when Americans rallied around most major U.S. institutions.

Newspapers Lose Vote of Confidence From Democrats

Historically, Gallup has found that Democrats, including independents who lean Democratic, are more likely than Republicans and Republican leaners to have a significantly better view of newspapers. That has held true even as confidence in newspapers among both groups has fallen over the past 16 years. This is the first year, however, that Democrats' confidence is no longer net positive: 27% have little or no confidence in newspapers, slightly exceeding the 25% saying they have a great deal or quite a lot of confidence. By contrast, Republicans' views toward the institution have tilted negative since 2004.

Net Confidence in Newspapers, by Party ID

Percentage "A great deal/Quite a lot" minus "Very little/None"^

	Republican/Lean Republican	Democratic/Lean Democratic
2016	-33	-2
2015	-25	7
2014	-25	5
2013	-29	2
2012	-23	12
2011	-19	17
2010	-26	10
2009	-25	13
2008	-20	9
2007	-25	12
2006	-14	18
2005	-10	15
2004	-11	23
2003	12	24
2002	10	24
2001	5	26

^ % None a volunteered response
Gallup

Young adults aged 18 to 34 have consistently been the most positive of all age groups about newspapers as an institution. However, the broader decline in confidence has finally reached the point that young adults are more likely to say they have very little or no confidence in newspapers than to say they have high confidence. This year marks the second straight year that newspapers are running a significant confidence deficit among young adults.

Net Confidence in Newspapers, by Age

Percentage "A great deal/Quite a lot" minus "Very little/None"^

	18 to 34	35 to 54	55+
2016	-5	-23	-18
2015	-7	-17	-8
2014	6	-12	-23
2013	4	-19	-20
2012	13	-8	-21
2011	15	-12	-7
2010	24	-26	-11
2009	-1	-2	-15
2008	18	-7	-14
2007	9	-6	-15
2006	10	-5	5
2005	10	-5	6
2004	12	2	2
2003	32	14	5
2002	30	15	9
2001	26	13	10

^ % None a volunteered response
Gallup

The decline in public confidence in newspapers since 2000 is part of a larger pattern of decline in Americans' confidence in U.S. institutions. However, since 2000, confidence in newspapers has fallen more steeply than the average of 14 institutions Gallup has tracked annually since 1993. While average confidence across all 14 institutions fell from 40% in 2000 to 32% the last two years, confidence in newspapers fell from 37% to 20% over the same period.

Confidence in newspapers was at a peak in 2000, after climbing between 1993 and that year. However, even compared with 1993, confidence in newspapers has fallen more than the 14-institution average.

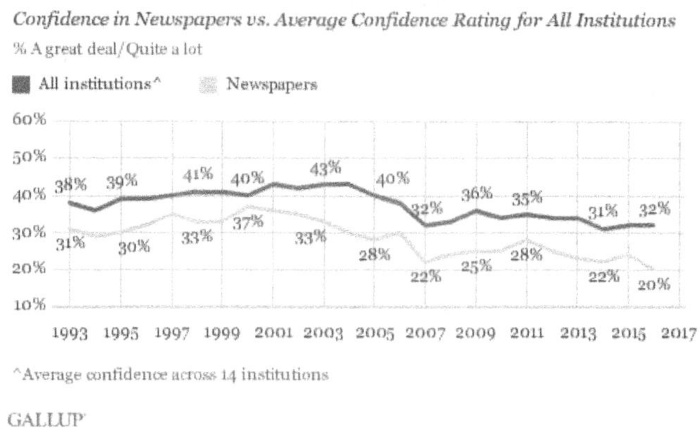

Bottom Line

Over half of Americans maintain at least some confidence in newspapers as a U.S. institution, but the percentage expressing high confidence – the kind that counts – has dwindled to 20%. The percentage with low confidence is now close to twice that rate. This reflects a downturn in confidence among all age and party groups to the point that young adults and Democrats, who once expressed solidly positive confidence in newspapers, are now neutral or net negative.

The public's mood over the past 16 years has been something of a whirlpool, pulling most major U.S. institutions underwater, but newspapers appear to be faring a bit worse than average. The rise of digital media could be a factor in the trust Americans place in a traditionally print medium such as newspapers, but perhaps more importantly, newspapers are suffering from the broader decline Gallup sees in Americans' trust in the mass media in general.

Survey Methods

Results for this Gallup poll are based on telephone interviews conducted June 1-5, 2016, on the Gallup U.S. Daily survey, with a random sample of 1,027 adults, aged 18 and older, living in all 50 U.S. states and the District of Columbia. For results based on the total sample of national adults, the margin of sampling error is ±4 percentage points at the 95% confidence level. All reported margins of sampling error include computed design effects for weighting.

June 13, 2016

AMERICANS' CONFIDENCE IN INSTITUTIONS STAYS LOW

by Jim Norman

Story Highlights

- *Confidence in institutions stays near historical lows*
- *Confidence in newspapers, organized religion now at record lows*
- *Confidence in institutions has slumped for a decade*

WASHINGTON, D.C. – Americans' confidence in the nation's major institutions continues to lag below historical averages, with two institutions – newspapers and organized religion – dropping to record lows this year. The overall average of Americans expressing "a great deal" or "quite a lot" of confidence in 14 institutions is below 33% for the third straight year.

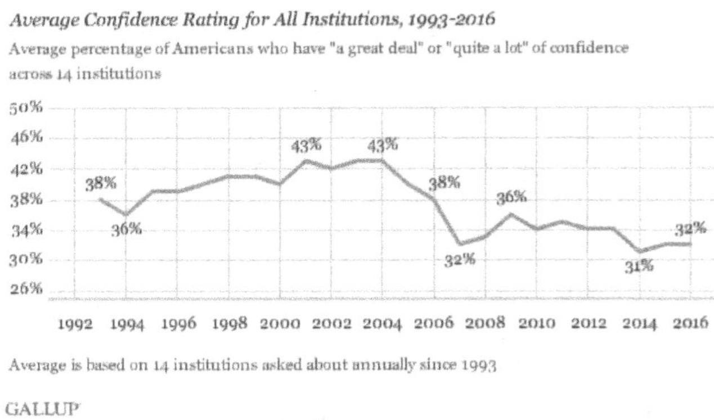

Americans' confidence in key U.S. institutions has remained relatively low since 2007. That year, the average for the 14 institutions Gallup has asked about annually since 1993 dropped to 32% from 38% in 2006. (Gallup began asking about a 15th institution, small business, in 2007.) From 1993 to 2006, the average had been below 38% only once – in 1994, when it dipped to 36%.

Banks, Organized Religion, News Media, Congress Fell Most Over Past Decade

Since 2006, Americans have lost confidence in 10 of those 14 institutions, with six suffering substantial losses. The remaining four institutions saw no change or a gain of no more than a few percentage points.

Many Institutions Lost Ground in Last Decade

Percentage with "a great deal" or "quite a lot" of confidence in the institution

	June 2006 %	June 2016 %	Difference, 2006 to 2016 pct. pts.
Military	73	73	0
Police	58	56	-2
Church or organized religion	52	41	-11
Medical system	38	39	+1
Presidency	33	36	+3
U.S. Supreme Court	40	36	-4
Public schools	37	30	-7
Banks	49	27	-22
Organized labor	24	23	-1
Criminal justice system	25	23	-2
Television news	31	21	-10
Newspapers	30	20	-10
Big business	18	18	0
Congress	19	9	-10

Gallup polls, June 1-4, 2006, and June 1-5, 2016

Confidence in banks – which took a hit amid the bursting housing bubble in 2007 and 2008, and dropped further after the ensuing financial crisis – fell the most, plunging from 49% in 2006 to 27% now. Confidence in organized religion, which has felt the effects of the scandals enveloping the Catholic Church, dropped from 52% to 41%, one point below last year's previous low of 42%. Television news, newspapers and Congress all dropped 10 points – pushing newspapers to a 20% confidence level, two points below their previous low of 22% in 2007 and 2014.

Despite the declining percentages of Americans having high confidence in these institutions, the majority have at least "some" confidence in all but one of them. Congress has the ignominious distinction of being the only institution sparking little or no confidence in a majority of Americans.

As has been the case in previous years, Americans have the most confidence in the military, and the least in Congress. The police and small business are the only other institutions garnering majority confidence. Joining Congress at the bottom of the list are big business, newspapers, television news, the criminal justice system and organized labor.

As Other Measures Climb, Confidence in Institutions Lags Behind

While the overall average confidence in institutions is still six points below where it was in 2006, the trends in two other key measures of the public's mood have – by contrast – recovered from major drops during the past decade.

- When Gallup asked about confidence in institutions in June 2006, the public's satisfaction with the way things were going in the nation was in the midst of a long fall, having dropped from 55% in January 2004 to 30%. The decline continued through the financial crisis of 2008 – bottoming out at 7% in October of that year. A long, bumpy climb has brought the percentage satisfied back up to 29% in June 2016, about where it was in June 2006.
- A Gallup measure of job market optimism asking whether "now is a good time or a bad time to find a quality job" fell from 41% in June 2006 to as low as 8% in November 2009 and 2011, but is now up to 43%.

U.S. Satisfaction and Job Market Optimism Recover Between 2006 and 2016; Confidence in U.S. Institutions Does Not

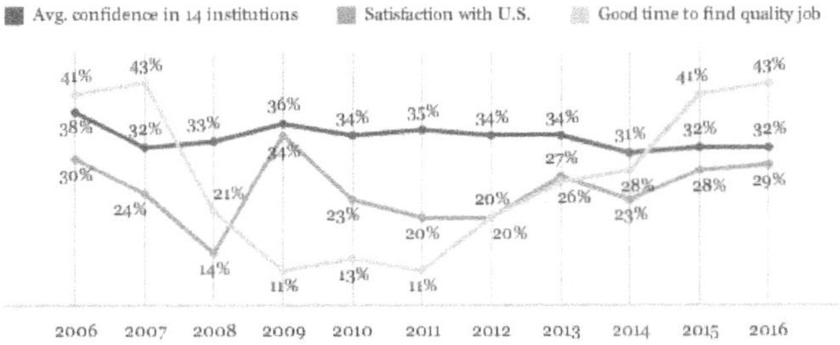

Based on June polling in each year

GALLUP

Bottom Line

Americans clearly lack confidence in the institutions that affect their daily lives: the schools responsible for educating the nation's children; the houses of worship that are expected to provide spiritual guidance; the banks that are supposed to protect Americans' earnings; the U.S. Congress elected to represent the nation's interests; and the news media that claims it exists to keep them informed.

Even as Americans regain confidence in the economy and are no longer in the depths of dissatisfaction with the way things are going in the nation, they remain reluctant to put much faith in these institutions at the core of American society.

Each institution has its own specific probable causes for this situation. But the loss of faith in so many at one time, while Americans are becoming more positive in other ways, suggests there are reasons that reach beyond any individual institution. The task of identifying and dealing with those reasons in a way that rebuilds confidence is one of the more important challenges facing the nation's leaders in the years ahead.

Survey Methods

Results for this Gallup poll are based on telephone interviews conducted June 1-5, 2016, with a random sample of 1,027 adults, aged 18 and older, living in all 50 U.S. states and the District of Columbia. For results based on this sample of national adults, the margin of sampling error is ±4 percentage points at the 95% confidence level. All reported margins of sampling error include computed design effects for weighting.

June 14, 2016
U.S. CONFIDENCE IN POLICE RECOVERS FROM LAST YEAR'S LOW

by Frank Newport

Story Highlights

- *56% of Americans have confidence in the police, up from 52% in 2015*
- *Confidence in police is third highest of 15 institutions measured*
- *Whites have a substantially higher confidence level than nonwhites*

PRINCETON, N.J. – Americans' confidence in the police has edged back up this year after dropping last year to its lowest point in 22 years. Currently, 56% of Americans have "a great deal" or "quite a lot" of confidence in the police, four percentage points higher than in 2015. Confidence is essentially back to where it was before a series of highly publicized incidents involving white police officers and young black men in several communities across the country.

Americans' Confidence in the Police

% A great deal/Quite a lot

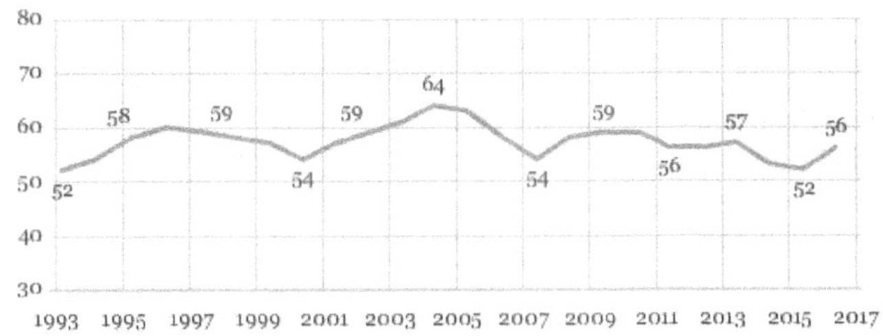

GALLUP

The latest update on Gallup's annual measure of confidence in U.S. institutions, conducted June 1-5, finds Americans' overall confidence in most institutions below the historical average, a pattern that encompasses the police, despite the small rise in confidence this year. Still, confidence in the police is high on a relative basis, lagging behind only the military and small business on a list of 15 institutions.

Americans' confidence in the police was at 52% when Gallup first measured it in 1993. This rating reflected the impact of the trial of four Los Angeles police officers for beating Rodney King and violating his civil rights two years earlier. Confidence in the police rose thereafter, reaching 60% by the mid-1990s and a record high of 64% in 2004. In the ensuing years, confidence in police slipped, as it did for most institutions. Last year, confidence tied the record low of 52%, reflecting police actions in Ferguson, Missouri, and other cities, before rebounding modestly this year as these events faded from the news.

At this point, 25% of Americans say they have a great deal of confidence in the police, 31% quite a lot, 29% "some," 13% "very little" and 1% "none." The combined 14% who have very little or no confidence in the police is down from 18% last year, which was the highest negative confidence reading in Gallup's history of rating the police.

As has been true historically, whites have a significantly higher level of confidence in the police than nonwhites, and the gap between the two racial groups widened this year as whites' confidence rose to 62%, while nonwhites stayed at 39% both years. Republicans and independents who lean Republican have more confidence in the police than Democrats and Democratic leaners, although Democrats' confidence rose to 48% from 41% last year, while Republicans stayed the same both years at 68%.

Implications

A slim majority of Americans have confidence in the police as an institution, and that confidence level has risen modestly since last year's low point, which most likely reflected the visibility of police incidents involving black citizens. The continuing gulf between whites and nonwhites in confidence in the police, however, has increased – reflecting the tension that exists between the police and some communities, a problem that will almost certainly take years to address in meaningful ways.

Historical data are available in Gallup Analytics.

Survey Methods

Results for this Gallup poll are based on telephone interviews conducted June 1-5, 2016, with a random sample of 1,027 adults, aged 18 and older, living in all 50 U.S. states and the District of Columbia. For results based on the total sample of national adults, the margin of sampling error is ±4 percentage points at the 95% confidence level. All reported margins of sampling error include computed design effects for weighting.

June 15, 2016

DEMOCRATS NOW MORE CONVINCED CANDIDATES HAVE GOOD IDEAS

by Frank Newport

Story Highlights

- *58% of Democrats say candidates have good ideas; 46% of Republicans agree*
- *Before March, Republicans much more positive about candidate ideas*
- *Independents are the most cynical; just 38% agree*

PRINCETON, N.J. – As the two major political parties have settled on their presumptive presidential nominees, Democrats (58%) have become significantly more likely than Republicans (46%) and independents (38%) to say any presidential candidate has come up with good ideas for solving the most important problem facing the U.S. From November to February, Republicans were the most positive on candidates' ideas for solving the nation's No. 1 problem. The two partisan groups were tied from March through May.

Any Candidate Come Up With Good Ideas for Solving Most Important Problem

% Yes, have come up with good ideas

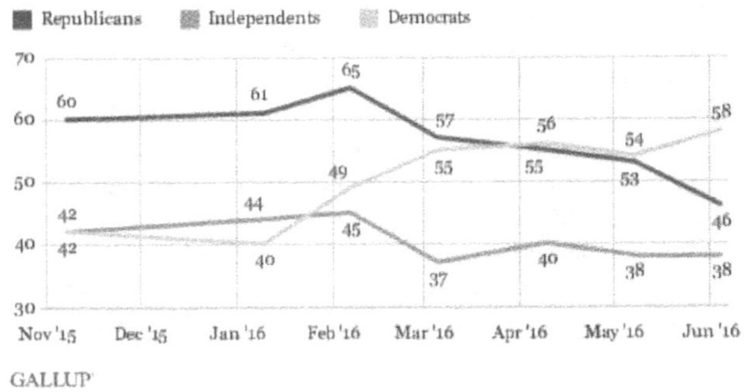

Gallup first asked this question last November and has updated it monthly since January. The most recent measurement was June 1-5, prior to the Orlando mass shooting. Gallup uses this question as a follow-up to a question asking Americans, in an open-ended fashion, to name the top problem facing the U.S.

As of the most recent June asking, the Republican nomination had been decided. Bernie Sanders was still battling Hillary Clinton for the Democratic nomination, although Clinton's nomination was all but assured at that point.

The trend in Republicans' responses to some degree parallels the narrowing of their party's field of candidates. Last November and in the first two months of this year, the Republican field was crowded. A significant drop in Republicans' positive views in March took place after the field narrowed with the withdrawal of Jeb Bush, Chris Christie, Rand Paul, Carly Fiorina and Mike Huckabee. At the time of the March survey, however, Ted Cruz, Marco Rubio and John Kasich were still campaigning against Donald Trump. It is possible that the negative turn in the tone of the GOP debates in March affected Republicans' perceptions of their candidates and their ideas.

Trump's two remaining challengers – Cruz and Kasich – both dropped out in early May just before that month's May 4-8 survey, but Republicans' views changed little in that poll. Another significant downturn in Republicans' positive views of candidate ideas took place in June, with Trump entrenched as the nominee.

On the Democratic side, no specific event coincided with the uptick in Democrats' positivity in the March survey. Clinton's main competition, Sanders, has continued campaigning up through this week's final primary in Washington, D.C., and Democrats have become even more positive still this month. Both Democrats and Republicans began paying more attention to the race in March.

Since February, independents have been less likely than Republicans or Democrats to say that any candidate has come up with good ideas for solving problems. This reflects independents' lack of strong allegiance to either party or a specific candidate.

Despite these significant shifts in how each party's constituents feel about candidates having come up with good ideas, the overall trend in this measure has stayed fairly stable. The exception to this pattern came in February, when – reflecting the uptick in both Republicans' and Democrats' positive responses – the "good ideas" percentage rose to 52%, the highest figure recorded for any month. By March, however, the overall trend had settled down, and although it is a little more negative in June, has not varied substantially. This reflects the fact that as one group of partisans became more positive, the other group became more negative. The overall trend shows that half of Americans at this juncture do not think any candidate has come up with good ideas for solving the nation's top problem.

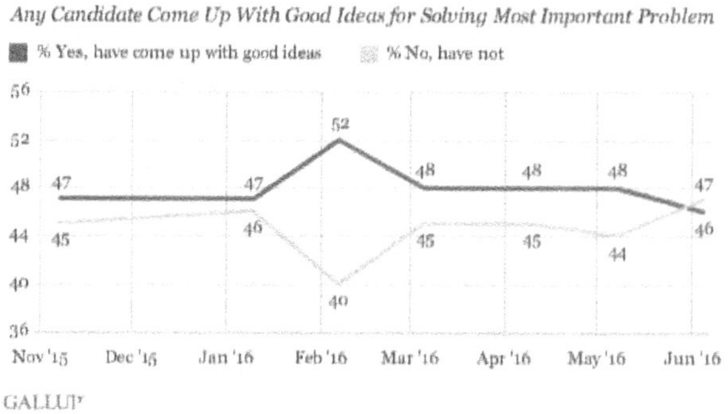

Implications

Republicans' and Democrats' perceptions of whether presidential candidates have come up with good ideas for solving the most important problem facing the U.S. have shifted notably over the course of the past eight months. The percentage of Republicans saying candidates have come up with solid plans to address the nation's most pressing issue dropped about 20 percentage points from February to June, while the percentage of Democrats holding that view rose by about the same amount from January to June.

It's not entirely clear what has driven these shifts. Clearly, the fact that the number of Republican candidates has gone from many to one could be a factor. About three in 10 Republicans now view Trump unfavorably, and given that there are no other GOP candidates in the field, these individuals could be the ones who now say that no candidates have good ideas for solving the nation's top problem. More broadly, the June data could simply reflect the fact that Democrats are more satisfied with the ideas generated by Clinton (and perhaps Sanders) than Republicans are about ideas generated by Trump.

Clinton has been the expected Democratic nominee for months now, although with dogged competition from Sanders. Her victories in the June 7 primaries that essentially sealed her status as the Democratic nominee occurred after Gallup's June update, thus this does not help explain why Democrats are more positive this month.

Whatever the reasons, the current data are an apparent plus for Democrats – if they can translate their partisans' positive feelings about candidates' (presumably their candidate's) ideas for solving the big problems into enthusiasm and turnout on Election Day.

Historical data are available in Gallup Analytics.

Survey Methods

Results for this Gallup poll are based on telephone interviews conducted June 1-5, 2016, with a random sample of 1,027 adults, aged 18 and older, living in all 50 U.S. states and the District of Columbia. For results based on the total sample of national adults, the margin of sampling error is ±4 percentage points at the 95% confidence level. For results based on the total sample of 308 Republicans, the margin of sampling error is ±6 percentage points at the 95% confidence level. For results based on the total sample of 386 independents, the margin of sampling error is ±6 percentage points at the 95% confidence level. For results based on the total sample of 313 Democrats, the margin of sampling error is ±6 percentage points at the 95% confidence level. All reported margins of sampling error include computed design effects for weighting.

June 15, 2016

HOW HIGH WILL TERRORISM CONCERNS RISE, HOW LONG WILL THEY LAST?

by Jim Norman

Story Highlights

- *Terrorism topped most important problem list in December, but not since*
- *Orlando massacre may push terrorism back to the top of the list*
- *Push for gun control could cause spike in concern about guns*

WASHINGTON, D.C. – Terrorism rose to the top of the list of Americans' concerns about their nation last December after deadly attacks in Paris and San Bernardino, and it could happen again in the wake of Sunday's horrific massacre in Orlando. But if the same pattern occurs this time, terrorism would likely not remain the most important problem for long.

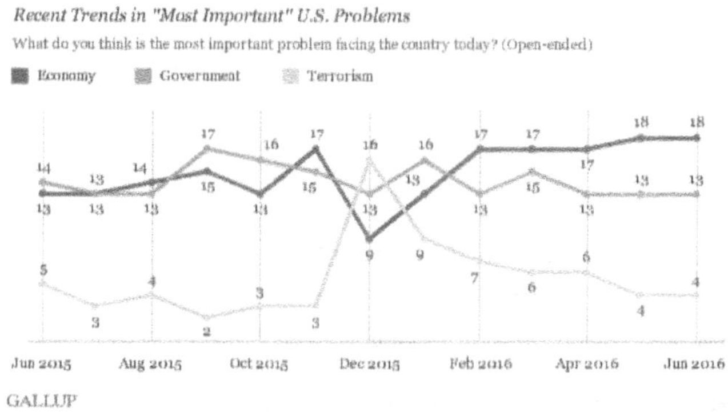

Three percent of Americans named terrorism as the most important problem in the U.S. last November. But after the attacks in San Bernardino and Paris, 16% in December listed terrorism as the top problem, moving it ahead of the economy (9%) and the government (13%). It was the first time in 19 months that the public had named an issue other than the government or the economy as the nation's most important problem.

In January, however, both the government (16%) and the economy (13%) moved back ahead of terrorism (9%) as the most important problem, and they have been the issues most often mentioned in every poll so far this year. In a poll earlier this month, before the Orlando shooting, 18% of U.S. adults said the economy was the nation's most important problem, 13% named the government and only 4% named terrorism.

The Orlando tragedy has been variously described as terrorism, a mass shooting and a hate crime. The likelihood that concern about terrorism will spike again in response to the incident is made more likely by the emphasis political leaders have placed on its role in the tragedy. President Barack Obama called it "an act of terror," as did both Republican presumptive presidential nominee Donald Trump and Democratic presumptive presidential nominee Hillary Clinton.

Since 9/11 Fears Faded, Terrorism Seldom Seen as Most Important Problem

In Gallup polls from 1939 to the beginning of September 2001, terrorism was never mentioned as the most important problem in the U.S. by enough respondents to be reported as a separate category. But a month after the 9/11 attacks in New York City and Washington,

D.C., 46% of Americans listed terrorism as the most important problem facing the nation.

The number slowly dwindled through the next two years, falling below 10% for the first time in April 2003 as Americans' concerns gravitated toward economic problems and the Iraq War. Since then, a few events have triggered a spike in mentions of terrorism as the nation's most important problem, but each time, concerns faded within a few months. For four years, from February 2010 through January 2015, no more than 4% in any month considered terrorism the top problem facing the country.

Percent of Americans Naming Terrorism as the Most Important U.S. Problem Since October 2001

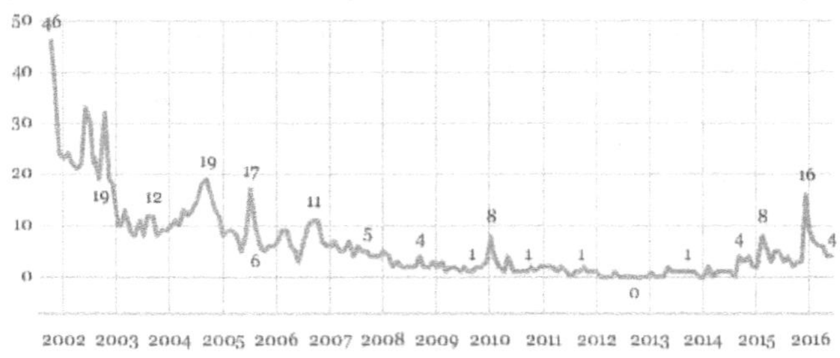

GALLUP

Rise in Mentions of Guns as Most Important Problem Also Possible

The widespread calls for more gun control after Sunday's Orlando shooting could result in a higher percentage of Americans naming guns as the nation's most important problem, as has happened after some past mass shootings:

- The highest percentage of Americans listing guns and gun control as the most important problem was 10% in May 1999, a month after two teenagers killed 12 students and a teacher at Columbine High School in Colorado. By January 2000, only 1% listed it as the nation's top problem. From then until late 2012, it was seldom mentioned as the most important problem.
- In the months after the December 2012 shooting deaths of 20 children and seven adults at an elementary school in Newtown, Connecticut, the percentage naming guns as the most important problem rose as high as 7%, but within a year, it fell below 1%.
- After a white supremacist killed nine people at a church in Charleston, South Carolina, in June 2015, polls in October showed 7% considered guns the most important problem.
- In the same December 2015 poll in which terrorism topped the list of most important problems, 7% named guns.

Percent of Americans Naming Guns as the Most Important U.S. Problem, November 2012 to June 2016

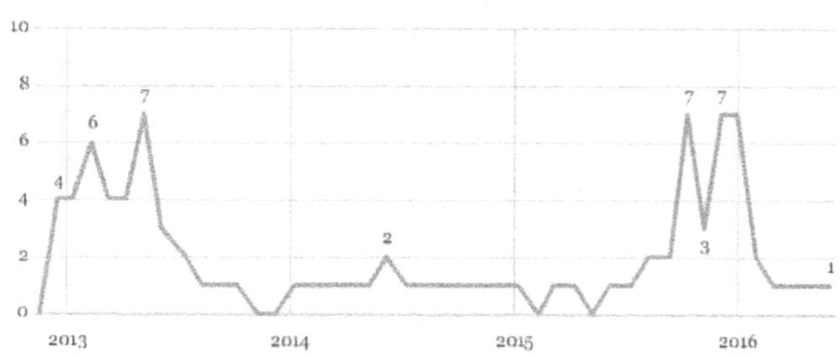

GALLUP

Bottom Line

Previous mass shootings and terrorist attacks – with the exception of 9/11 – have only temporarily increased the likelihood of Americans naming guns or terrorism as the nation's most important problem. That might be the case again this time, but there are some reasons why it might not.

The fact that 49 people were killed in Orlando makes it the worst mass shooting in the nation's modern history and the deadliest terrorist attack in the U.S. since 9/11. It happened in the middle of a bitter presidential contest already marked by harsh exchanges between the candidates on the issues of terrorism and gun control. The combination of these factors almost guarantees that terrorism and gun control will be major, persistent themes in the candidates' campaigns over the next five months.

Survey Methods

Results for this Gallup poll are based on telephone interviews conducted June 1-5, 2016, with a random sample of 1,027 adults, aged 18 and older, living in all 50 U.S. states and the District of Columbia. For results based on this sample of national adults, the margin of sampling error is ±4 percentage points at the 95% confidence level. All reported margins of sampling error include computed design effects for weighting.

June 16, 2016

MAJORITY IN U.S. SAY CONGRESS DOING A "POOR" OR "BAD" JOB

by Lydia Saad

Story Highlights

- *Republicans offer no better review of Congress than do Democrats*
- *Democrats give net positive review of Democrats in Congress*
- *Republicans are more negative than positive toward GOP caucus*

PRINCETON, N.J. – Americans' assessments of whether Congress is doing an excellent, good, fair, poor or bad job are decidedly negative, similar to a year ago. The majority of U.S. adults (53%) say Congress is doing a poor or bad job, while just 13% call its performance good or excellent. This results in a -40 net positive rating for Congress, similar to the -34 in June 2015.

Americans' Ratings of How the U.S. Congress Is Handling Its Job

	Excellent/Good %	Fair %	Poor/Bad %	Net positive pct. pts.
Jun 1-5, 2016^	13	32	53	-40
Jun 15-16, 2015	15	34	49	-34

^ Based on combined results from split sample in which half rated "The U.S. Congress in Washington" and half "The U.S. Congress"
Gallup

In contrast to Congress' negative job evaluation, state and local governments earn net positive ratings of +11 and +24, respectively. Americans' ratings of their respective state governments even improved slightly this year, with 37% rating them excellent or good, up from 31% in June 2015, resulting in an increase in the net positive score to +11 from +4.

Americans' Ratings of the Job Their State and Local Governments Are Doing

	Excellent/ Good %	Fair %	Poor/Bad %	Net positive pct. pts.
Your state government				
Jun 1-5, 2016	37	37	26	+11
Jun 15-16, 2015	31	40	27	+4
Your local government				
Jun 1-5, 2016	44	36	20	+24
Jun 15-16, 2015	39	40	19	+20

Gallup

These findings are from a June 1-5 Gallup survey conducted before this week's debate over the role congressional inaction on gun control played in the Orlando terrorist attack. The results are consistent with the broad public disapproval of Congress Gallup has found on a monthly basis for a decade. One reason this negativity has continued is that Americans who identify as Republican have remained persistently critical of Congress even as control of the institution has shifted from Democratic majorities in both chambers to split control, and, more recently, to full Republican control. One would expect Congress' overall approval rating to be lifted because supporters of the majority party typically give it higher ratings, but that has not occurred with Republicans in recent years.

Echoing this pattern, Republicans are no more likely than Democrats to say Congress is doing an excellent or good job, nor are they much less likely to say it is doing a poor or bad job.

Job the U.S. Congress Is Doing – by Party ID

	Excellent/ Good %	Fair %	Poor/ Bad %	Net positive pct. pts.
Republicans	12	36	51	-39
Independents	13	30	55	-42
Democrats	13	31	54	-41

Gallup, June 1-5, 2016

In the same June 1-5 poll, Gallup asked Americans for their separate assessments of the Republicans and the Democrats in Congress. Americans' ratings of the Republicans in Congress match those of Congress as a whole, while their ratings of Democrats in Congress are somewhat less negative.

- Thirteen percent of U.S. adults say the Republicans in Congress are doing an excellent or good job, while 54% call it poor or bad, giving the GOP a -41 net positive score. That is noticeably worse than the -32 Gallup recorded a year ago.
- The Democrats in Congress – currently the minority party in both the House and Senate – aren't rated quite so poorly, with 21% of Americans giving them high marks vs. 40% low, for a net positive rating of -19. This is essentially unchanged from last year.

Job the Republicans and Democrats in Congress Are Doing

	Excellent/ Good %	Fair %	Poor/Bad %	Net positive pct. pts.
Republicans in Congress				
Jun 1-5, 2016	13	30	54	-41
Jun 15-16, 2015	16	34	48	-32
Democrats in Congress				
Jun 1-5, 2016	21	36	40	-19
Jun 15-16, 2015	19	38	41	-22

Net positive = % excellent/good minus % poor/bad
Gallup

More Republicans Negative Than Positive About GOP Caucus

Rank-and-file Republicans are negative about Congress even when rating its GOP members specifically. Slightly more Republicans say the Republicans in Congress are doing a poor or bad job (30%) than say they are doing an excellent or good job (22%). By contrast, rank-and-file Democrats have a relatively positive view of the Democrats in Congress, with 41% rating them excellent or good and only 13% poor or bad. In short, Republicans are much more critical about their representation in Congress than Democrats are about theirs.

Job the Republicans and Democrats in Congress Are Doing – by Party ID

	Excellent/Good %	Fair %	Poor/Bad %	Net positive pct. pts.
Republicans in Congress				
Republicans	22	46	30	-8
Independents	10	31	55	-45
Democrats	10	14	75	-65
Democrats in Congress				
Republicans	6	28	64	-58
Independents	15	35	45	-30
Democrats	41	45	13	+28

Gallup, June 1-5, 2016

Bottom Line

Despite solid Republican majorities in Congress, neither rank-and-file Republicans nor Democrats think Congress is performing well. And while the explanation for this theoretically could be that Republicans evaluate Congress more on the basis of how the Democrats in Congress are behaving than on how the Republicans are performing, Republican identifiers are negative toward Congress even when rating the Republican caucus specifically. By contrast, Democrats rate the Democratic caucus more positively than negatively.

Somewhat more positively, fewer Americans say Congress is doing a poor or bad job (53%) than say they disapprove of the job Congress is doing (80%) in Gallup's standard approve/disapprove format. The 80% disapproving of Congress therefore includes some whose disapproval is not extremely negative. In the current survey, of those disapproving of Congress on the approve/disapprove question, just 23% rated the job Congress is doing in the worst possible terms, calling it "bad." Another 41% called it "poor," while 31% described it as "fair." In other words, Americans have a broadly negative view of how Congress is performing, but it could be worse.

This is the first in a series of Gallup reports investigating Congress' negative image. Future articles in this series will review Americans' specific criticisms of Congress as well as the factors that drive Americans' negative views of Congress.

Frank Newport and Mike Traugott contributed to this article.

Survey Methods

Results for this Gallup poll are based on telephone interviews conducted June 1-5, 2016, with a random sample of 1,027 adults, aged 18 and older, living in all 50 U.S. states and the District of Columbia. For results based on the total sample of national adults, the margin of sampling error is ±4 percentage points at the 95% confidence level. For results based on the total sample of 308 Republicans or 313 Democrats, the margin of sampling error is ±7 percentage points at the 95% confidence level. All reported margins of sampling error include computed design effects for weighting.

June 16, 2016

AMERICANS' CONFIDENCE IN BANKS STILL LANGUISHING BELOW 30%

by Justin McCarthy

Story Highlights

- *More than one in four have a great deal, quite a lot of confidence*
- *Level of confidence unchanged since 2013*
- *Liberals, conservatives share similarly low level of confidence*

WASHINGTON, D.C. – Americans' confidence in banks is unchanged from a year ago and remains below 30% for the eighth straight year after tumbling during the 2007-2009 recession. The 27% of U.S. adults who now say they have "a great deal" or "quite a lot" of confidence in the institution is slightly higher than the lows during the Great Recession and its aftermath. However, confidence in banks has been essentially at this level the past several years.

Americans' Confidence in Banks, 1979-2016 Trend

Now I am going to read you a list of institutions in American society. Please tell me how much confidence you, yourself, have in each one -- a great deal, quite a lot, some or very little.

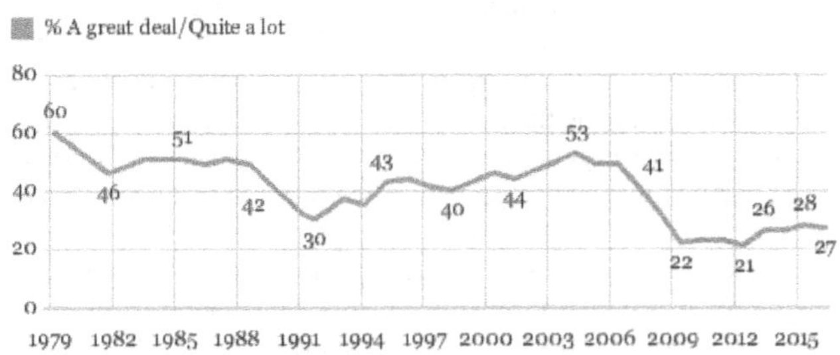

The current percentage of adults who say they have confidence in banks is just half of what it was in 2004 when 53% expressed confidence in the institution. The record high was 60% in 1979. In addition to those expressing high confidence in banks, nearly half of Americans say they have "some" confidence in them, while about a quarter (26%) have "very little" or no confidence.

About half of Americans expressed confidence in banks in most polls in the 1980s, but confidence suffered in the early 1990s after the Savings and Loan crisis, with confidence ranging from 30% to 37%. But by the late '90s, confidence improved, ranging from 40% to 44%. Confidence in banks gained in the early 2000s, reaching a majority level by 2004.

Like most institutions, confidence in banks began to fall in 2005 and 2006 as Americans' satisfaction with the way things were going suffered. By 2007, with housing prices starting to fall after peaking in 2006, banking confidence dipped to 41%. It then fell further to 32% in June 2008, after the recession began but before the October 2008 financial crisis. By June 2009, just 22% of Americans had confidence in banks, slightly worse than today.

Conservatives, Independents, Liberals Share Similarly Low Level of Confidence

Although railing against big banks has been the rallying cry of liberal Democrats such as Massachusetts Sen. Elizabeth Warren and presidential candidate Sen. Bernie Sanders, among the general population, conservatives and Republicans are no more likely than liberals and Democrats to have high confidence in banks.

About a quarter of Americans in each of the main political party and ideology groups say they have a great deal or quite a lot of confidence in banks. They differ in the percentages expressing low confidence, which is slightly higher for Democrats and liberals than for their Republican and conservative counterparts.

Confidence in banks differs a bit more among income groups. Adults whose households earn less than $30,000 annually (33%) are slightly more likely than those in the middle (24%) and higher (22%) income brackets to express high confidence in banks.

Americans' Confidence in Banks, by Self-Identified Party Affiliation

Please tell me how much confidence you, yourself, have in banks – a great deal, quite a lot, some or very little.

	A great deal/ Quite a lot %	Some %	Very little/None (vol.) %
Republicans	26	55	17
Independents	24	44	32
Democrats	27	48	24
Conservatives	27	50	23
Moderates	25	50	24
Liberals	25	44	30
$75K+	22	56	21
$30K-$74.9K	24	52	24
Less than $30K	33	36	29

(vol.) = Volunteered response
Gallup, June 1-5, 2016

Bottom Line

The fallout from the 2008 financial crisis continues to affect Americans' views of the banking industry. Despite some signs of economic recovery, views of the economy's overall health remain negative, and Americans are not much more willing to express confidence in banks.

Low confidence in banks is not unprecedented, and Americans' views of the institution have recovered in the past from severe dips. However, past events such as the Savings and Loan Crisis paled in comparison to the wide-ranging effects of the 2008 financial crisis that led the economy to depths unseen since the Great Depression. Regaining Americans' trust in recent years, then, appears to be a heavier lift for the banking industry. And it is unclear when – or if – Americans' confidence in banks will be restored to what it was a decade ago.

Historical data are available in Gallup Analytics.

Survey Methods

Results for this Gallup poll are based on telephone interviews conducted June 1-5, 2016, on the Gallup U.S. Daily survey, with a random sample of 1,027 adults, aged 18 and older, living in all 50 U.S. states and the District of Columbia. For results based on the total sample of national adults, the margin of sampling error is ±4 percentage points at the 95% confidence level. All reported margins of sampling error include computed design effects for weighting.

June 17, 2016
AMERICANS CONTINUE TO EXPRESS HIGHEST CONFIDENCE IN MILITARY

by Frank Newport

Story Highlights

- *73% of Americans are confident in the military, higher than any other institution*
- *Confidence in the military has remained high over the past decade and a half*
- *By contrast, Americans have become less confident in many other institutions*

PRINCETON, N.J. – While Americans' faith in many U.S. institutions has fallen from the levels of previous decades, the public's confidence in the military has remained consistently high. The average confidence level across all 14 institutions tested in 2004 was 43%, compared with 32% this year. In contrast, the 73% confidence rating that Americans give the military today is essentially unchanged from the 75% rating they gave it 12 years ago.

Confidence in Institutions: The Military, and 14-Institution Average

Figures are percentage with "a great deal"/"quite a lot" of confidence

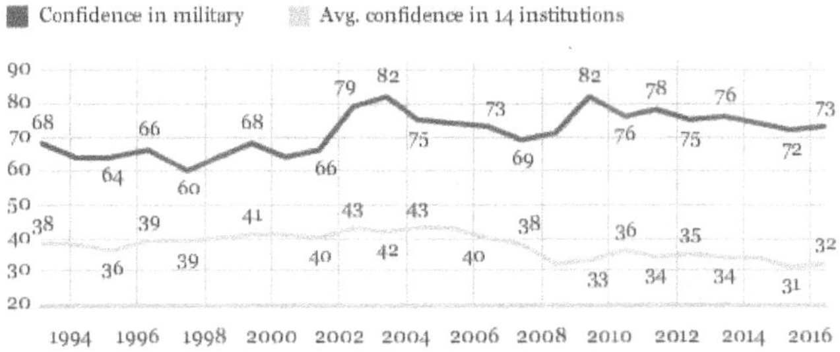

GALLUP

The military reached its highest level of confidence – 85% – in March 1991, just after the first Persian Gulf War. This rating remains the highest Gallup has yet recorded for any institution. There was another sharp uptick in Americans' confidence in the military after the 9/11 attacks. Confidence has fluctuated some in the years since 2001, but has generally remained high, dropping below 70% only once. From 1975 through early 2001, confidence in the military averaged 63%. Since 9/11, it has averaged 75%.

The last time when Americans' confidence in the military was *not* No. 1 on Gallup's confidence in institutions list was in 1997, when "small business" eclipsed it. Since 1998, however, the military has been No. 1 each year. Confidence in the military is currently five points higher than the second-ranking institution, small business (68%), and 17 points higher than the police (56%). Small business and the police are the only other two institutions with majority confidence in this year's survey.

Americans' Confidence in the Military

Figures are percentage with "a great deal"/"quite a lot" of confidence

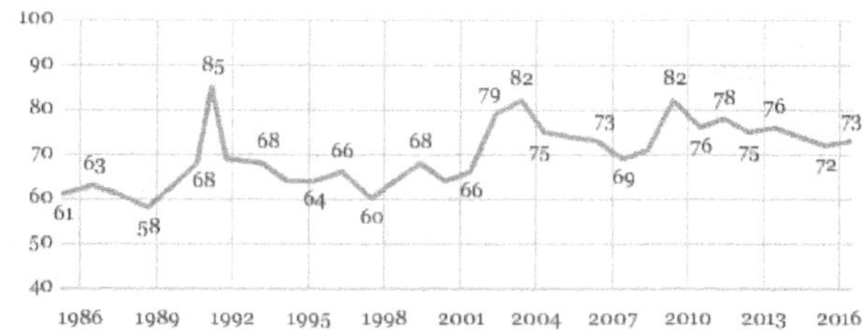

GALLUP

Confidence in Military Somewhat Lower Among Liberals, Young People

The high confidence ratings in the military reflect generally strong ratings across all segments of the population, although Republicans' 82% confidence level is significantly higher than Democrats' 65%. Seventy-eight percent of conservatives and moderates have confidence in the military, contrasted with 59% among liberals. The 60% confidence rating among young Americans (aged 18 to 29) is lower than that of those aged 50 to 64 (82%) and those 65 and older (79%).

Confidence in the Military, by Groups

	Great deal/Quite a lot of confidence %
National Adults	73
Men	74
Women	71
18-29	60
30-49	71
50-64	82
65+	79
Republicans/leaners	82
Democrats/leaners	65
Conservatives	78
Moderates	78
Liberals	59

Gallup, June 1-5, 2016

Implications

Americans continue to place more faith in their military than in any other societal institution, and despite some fluctuations over time, this high level of confidence has not abated. The military maintains this high level of respect even as the public's confidence in many other of society's institutions has declined compared with levels measured a decade ago and further back.

Americans' robust confidence in the military, which clearly rose after 9/11, has stayed high even as a majority of Americans came to believe that the most significant U.S. military action of the past two decades – the invasion of Iraq – was a mistake. Although Gallup did not ask about confidence in the military at the time of the Vietnam War, which likewise a majority of the public came to see as a mistake, a reading in 1981 showed confidence in the military had dropped to 50%. This was a time when Vietnam and its associated controversies were perhaps still relatively fresh on Americans' minds, and also a year after the aborted attempt to use the military to rescue American hostages in Iran. The 1980 presidential campaign in which Ronald Reagan consistently called for an increase in military spending would also have been fresh on Americans' minds in 1981.

Today is clearly a different era, and unlike the Vietnam era, members of the military are often applauded, given privileges and perks, and commonly greeted by the encomium, "Thank you for your service." It may be in particular that 9/11 and the specter of terrorism have been major factors in sustaining Americans' continuing high levels of faith in the men and women who don uniforms to protect and defend their country.

Historical data are available in Gallup Analytics.

Survey Methods

Results for this Gallup poll are based on telephone interviews conducted June 1-5, 2016, with a random sample of 1,027 adults, aged 18 and older, living in all 50 U.S. states and the District of Columbia. For results based on the total sample of national adults, the margin of sampling error is ±4 percentage points at the 95% confidence level. All reported margins of sampling error include computed design effects for weighting.

June 17, 2016
REPUBLICANS, DEMOCRATS INTERPRET ORLANDO INCIDENT DIFFERENTLY

by Jeffrey M. Jones

Story Highlights

- *79% of Republicans describe it as an act of Islamic terrorism*
- *60% of Democrats interpret it as domestic gun violence*
- *Blocking gun sales to terrorism suspects seen as best prevention*

PRINCETON, N.J. – Republicans and Democrats have starkly different interpretations of what the recent mass shooting at an Orlando nightclub represents. While 79% of Republicans view it primarily as an act of Islamic terrorism, the majority of Democrats, 60%, see it as an act of domestic gun violence. Given Republicans' more lopsided views, Americans as a whole tilt toward describing it as a terrorist act.

Perceptions of Orlando Mass Shooting Incident

From what you know or have heard, do you view the incident in Orlando over the weekend as more – [ROTATED: An act of Islamic terrorism (or more) an act of domestic gun violence]?

	U.S. adults %	Republicans %	Independents %	Democrats %
Islamic terrorism	48	79	44	29
Domestic gun violence	41	16	42	60
Both equally (vol.)	6	1	9	7

(vol.) = volunteered response
Gallup Daily, June 14-15, 2016

The results are based on a June 14-15 Gallup poll, conducted days after a Muslim U.S. citizen, Omar Mateen, perpetrated the deadliest mass shooting in U.S. history at an Orlando nightclub. Mateen had been listed on the federal government's terrorism watch list in 2013 and 2014, but was later removed. While both President Barack Obama and presumptive Democratic presidential nominee Hillary Clinton described the incident as an act of terror, presumptive Republican presidential nominee Donald Trump went further, tying the act to radical Islam.

Democrats' interpretation of the Orlando shooting may be influenced by Democratic leaders' calls for stricter gun laws in recent days. This was exemplified by a Democratic-led filibuster on the Senate floor Wednesday and Thursday, which ended after Republican leaders agreed to take up proposals on background checks and steps to prevent terrorists from obtaining guns.

Trump's statements on the event may be contributing to Republicans' views of the Orlando incident as an act of Islamic terrorism, but Republicans' tendency to define it as terrorism may also stem from their greater concern about terrorism in general.

Independents are evenly divided as to whether the Orlando shooting was an act of Islamic terrorism (44%) or domestic gun violence (42%).

Whether the Orlando incident was inspired by Islamic terrorism or the actions of a killer able to obtain guns is a debate that cannot be easily settled and, regardless, does nothing to diminish the tragedy of the event. But it is clear that Americans' political views influence how they interpret the tragedy and, by extension, shape their views of the policies leaders should pursue to prevent similar incidents.

Republicans, Democrats Agree on Denying Guns to Suspected Terrorists

Americans are most likely to believe banning gun sales to suspected terrorists would be most effective of seven steps the government could take to prevent future incidents like the Orlando shooting. Eighty percent of Americans believe such a move would be very or somewhat effective, including 84% of Democrats and 75% of Republicans.

At least six in 10 Americans also believe increasing U.S. airstrikes against the Islamic State or ISIS, changing state gun laws to allow more people to carry concealed weapons, and passing new laws to make it harder to buy assault weapons would be effective in preventing a repeat of the Orlando attack. The last two proposals garner almost identical public support, although one involves tightening gun restrictions and the other loosening them.

Many fewer think banning Muslims from entering the U.S., a move that Trump has specifically promoted, or requiring Muslims living in the U.S. to carry special IDs would be effective.

Americans' Perceived Effectiveness of Potential Actions to Prevent Incidents Like Orlando Mass Shooting

How effective do you think each of the following will be in preventing incidents such as the one that happened in Orlando this past weekend – very effective, somewhat effective, not too effective or not at all effective?

	Very/Somewhat effective %	Not too/Not at all effective %
Banning gun sales to people on the federal no-fly terrorism watch list	80	17
Increasing U.S. airstrikes against the Islamic State or ISIS to take out their leaders, heavy weapons and infrastructure	67	29
Changing state gun laws to allow more people to carry concealed weapons if they pass a background check and complete a training program	64	34
Pass new laws making it harder to buy assault weapons	63	36
Limit the sale of ammunition magazines to those with 10 rounds or less	52	46
A new law that would prevent any Muslim from entering the U.S.	32	63
Requiring Muslims, including those who are U.S. citizens, to carry a special ID	25	71

Gallup Daily, June 14-15, 2016

A wide partisan divide exists on all proposals except banning gun sales to suspected terrorists. More than eight in 10 Republicans believe increased airstrikes against the Islamic State and changing state gun laws to allow more Americans to carry concealed weapons would be effective in preventing similar incidents. Meanwhile, most Democrats think passing new laws regarding assault weapons and limiting the sale of ammunition magazines would be effective.

Perceptions of Potential Actions to Prevent Incidents Like Orlando Mass Shooting as "Very/Somewhat Effective," by Political Party

How effective do you think each of the following will be in preventing incidents such as the one that happened in Orlando this past weekend – very effective, somewhat effective, not too effective or not at all effective?

	Republicans %	Independents %	Democrats %
Banning gun sales to people on the federal no-fly terrorism watch list	75	80	84
Increasing U.S. airstrikes against the Islamic State or ISIS to take out their leaders, heavy weapons and infrastructure	85	62	57
Changing state gun laws to allow more people to carry concealed weapons if they pass a background check and complete a training program	83	65	45
Pass new laws making it harder to buy assault weapons	43	59	84
Limit the sale of ammunition magazines to those with 10 rounds or less	32	50	70
A new law that would prevent any Muslim from entering the U.S.	54	31	14
Requiring Muslims, including those who are U.S. citizens, to carry a special ID	35	26	16

Gallup Daily, June 14-15, 2016

A majority of Republicans, 54%, think the Trump-favored ban on Muslims would be effective at preventing similar incidents like the one in Orlando, but only 14% of Democrats agree. Because Mateen was born in the U.S. and lived there throughout his life, such a policy would not have prevented the Orlando incident.

Implications

The Orlando tragedy will long be remembered for the scope of the attack, ranking as the largest mass shooting in U.S. history. Given that it was orchestrated by a person of the Islamic faith who claimed allegiance to terrorist groups and who targeted gays and lesbians, the crime has elements of a mass shooting, terrorism and a hate crime.

In its aftermath, Americans' political leaders are trying to sort out what measures the government can take to prevent a reoccurrence. How Americans interpret the event undoubtedly influences what steps they favor, but it may also be that their policy preferences and partisanship influence their interpretations of the event.

Although the proposals members of both parties have put forth are surely well-intentioned, Democrats are focusing their efforts on advancing gun control legislation they long have favored, while Republicans are renewing their calls for tougher anti-terrorism efforts.

Where those two agendas intersect – namely in taking steps to prevent terrorists from obtaining guns – may be the place where lawmakers are most likely to find enough common ground to pass new laws. It is also the policy Americans are most likely to view as effective in preventing a repeat of the Orlando tragedy.

These data are available in Gallup Analytics.

Survey Methods

Results for this Gallup poll are based on telephone interviews conducted June 14-15, 2016, on the Gallup U.S. Daily survey, with a random sample of 1,021adults, aged 18 and older, living in all 50 U.S. states and the District of Columbia. For results based on the total sample of national adults, the margin of sampling error is ±4 percentage points at the 95% confidence level.

For results based on the total samples of 319 Democrats, 311 Republicans and 349 independents, the margin of sampling error is ±7 percentage points at the 95% confidence level.

All reported margins of sampling error include computed design effects for weighting.

June 20, 2016

IN U.S., HEALTHCARE INSECURITY AT RECORD LOW

by Jeffrey M. Jones and Nader Nekvasil

Story Highlights

- *15.5% of adults unable to afford necessary healthcare and/or medicine*
- *Decline coincides with drop in percentage of uninsured Americans*
- *Fewer insured and uninsured say they have struggled to afford healthcare*

WASHINGTON, D.C. – Fewer Americans reported not having enough money in the past 12 months to pay for necessary healthcare and/or medicines for themselves or their families than at any point since Gallup and Healthways began tracking this metric in 2008. From 2008 through 2013, the percentage of Americans who experienced difficulty in the past 12 months affording healthcare and medicine was fairly steady, hovering near the average of 18.7%. Since then, the average has been 16.4%, including the new quarterly low of 15.5% in the most recent quarter.

Have there been times in the past 12 months when you did not have enough money to pay for healthcare and/or medicines that you or your family needed?

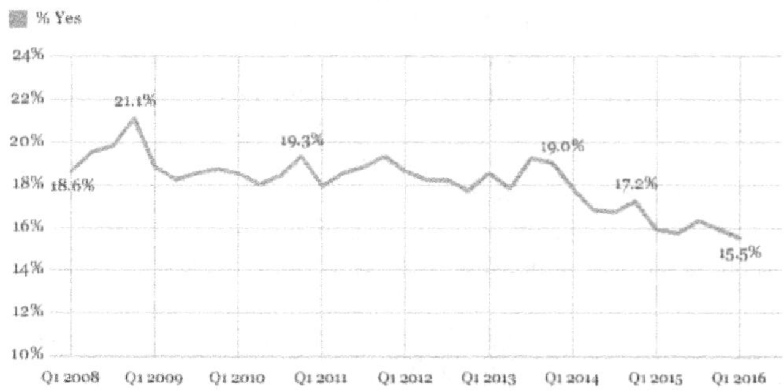

Data reflect Q1 2008-Q1 2016
Gallup-Healthways Well-Being Index

GALLUP

These findings are based on interviews conducted daily from January 2008 through March 2016 as part of the Gallup-Healthways Well-Being Index. Gallup and Healthways classify Americans as healthcare insecure if they report being unable to pay for healthcare and/or medicines they or their family needed at some point in the past 12 months.

Overall, the percentage of U.S. adults with healthcare insecurity has dropped 3.5 percentage points since the fourth quarter of 2013. This drop in healthcare insecurity coincides with the decline in the percentage of uninsured Americans, which has fallen from 17.1% in the fourth quarter of 2013 – just before the Affordable Care Act's requirement that Americans have health insurance went into effect – to 11.0% in the first quarter of this year.

The increase in the percentage of Americans having health insurance is likely a key reason why fewer Americans are struggling to pay for healthcare. Generally, those without health insurance are at least three times more likely to report not having enough money for healthcare/medicine than their counterparts with health insurance. In the most recent quarter, 41.8% of the uninsured said they had struggled to pay for healthcare costs, compared with 12.3% of those with insurance.

Still, the drop in the uninsured rate does not account for the entire reduction in the percentage of Americans experiencing healthcare insecurity.

Since late 2013, the percentages of both uninsured and insured Americans who report struggling to afford healthcare has declined. The decline has been larger among the uninsured population (from 45.0% to 41.8%), but the smaller decline among the much larger group of Americans with health insurance (from 13.6% to 12.3%) also contributes to the overall drop in healthcare insecurity.

Have there been times in the past 12 months when you did not have enough money to pay for healthcare and/or medicines that you or your family needed?

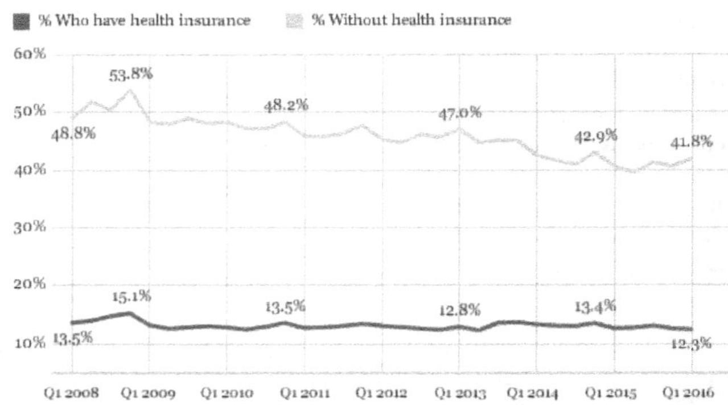

Data reflect Q1 2008-Q1 2016
Gallup-Healthways Well-Being Index

GALLUP

Both insured and uninsured Americans' greater ability to afford healthcare and medicine could also reflect an improving economy – most notably unemployment and underemployment rates that have returned to pre-recession levels.

But it could be that Americans are less burdened in other areas, such as energy costs from the decline in gas prices, which leaves more money for healthcare and other expenses. Also, the percentage of Americans struggling to afford food for themselves or their families is at a record low.

More generally, half of all Americans recently reported that their personal financial situation was either "excellent" or "good," the highest figure Gallup has recorded since 2008.

Bottom Line

Although roughly one in six Americans report having times in the past year when they were unable to afford the healthcare or medicine they needed, this is down significantly from just three years ago. The expansion of health insurance coverage to millions more Americans under the Affordable Care Act is likely a major factor in the decline of healthcare insecurity, demonstrating a concrete benefit of the law.

At the same time, there are growing concerns that health insurance costs are set to rise in many parts of the country, as insurers and states adjust to the new healthcare market. These increases would mostly affect Americans who do not qualify for a health insurance subsidy under the Affordable Care Act.

Also, the fate of the law itself remains uncertain. It has survived two Supreme Court challenges to date, but the presumptive Republican presidential nominee Donald Trump has vowed to make repeal of the law a priority if he is elected. If the Affordable Care Act is repealed under a new administration, 24 million Americans could become newly uninsured by 2021, according to a recent Urban Institute report.

Repealing the Affordable Care Act could easily halt or reverse the positive trends in healthcare access, which would certainly affect Americans' ability to pay for healthcare in the future.

Diana Liu contributed to this article

These data are available in Gallup Analytics.

Survey Methods

Results are based on telephone interviews conducted Jan. 1-March 31, 2016, as part of the Gallup-Healthways Well-Being Index survey, with a random sample of 44,558 adults, aged 18 and older, living in all 50 U.S. states and the District of Columbia. For results based on the total sample of national adults, the margin of sampling error is ±0.6 percentage points at the 95% confidence level.

June 20, 2016
DEMOCRATS MORE UPBEAT THAN REPUBLICANS ABOUT 2016 SLATE

by Lydia Saad

Story Highlights

- *Seven in 10 Democrats say someone who is running will make a good president*
- *Six in 10 Republicans feel the same way*
- *Trump admirers are most satisfied with candidates' attention to issues*

PRINCETON, N.J. – By 71% to 59%, more Democrats than Republicans in the U.S. are satisfied that someone is running this year who will make a good president. While this is similar to what Gallup found in May, the latest reading is the first since Hillary Clinton effectively clinched the Democratic nomination. Donald Trump became the inevitable GOP nominee a month earlier.

Is there any candidate running who you think would make a good president, or not?

% Yes

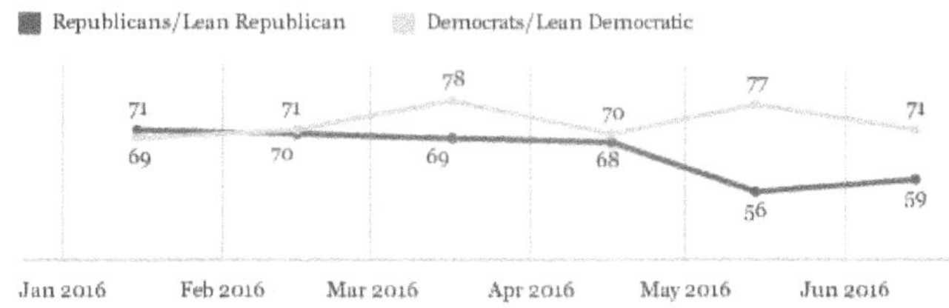

Gallup Daily tracking

GALLUP

Clinton secured her position as the presumptive Democratic nominee as a result of her victories in the June 7 primaries, while Ted Cruz's departure from the race on May 3 erased any reasonable doubt that Trump would be the Republican nominee. However, the narrowing of each party's field seems to have done more harm to Republicans' views of the field than to Democrats'.

Between mid-April and mid-May, spanning the time Cruz suspended his campaign and Trump became the inevitable nominee, the percentage of Republicans and Republican-leaning independents who believe there is a candidate who would make a good president fell from 68% to 56% and has since held near that level. Between mid-May and mid-June, spanning Clinton's clinching of the nomination, the percentage of Democrats and Democratic leaners who believe a good potential president is still running dropped less precipitously, from 77% to 71%.

Trump and Clinton Detractors Less Confident a Qualified Candidate Remains

Shifts on this question over the past few months mainly reflect the views of Republicans and Democrats who have watched with disappointment as their party's field of candidates has narrowed to an individual they don't like.

As recently as April, a majority of Republicans who viewed Trump *unfavorably* – 53% – said there was someone running who would make a good president; however, that was when several other GOP candidates were still in the race. The figure plummeted to 27% in May after Cruz and John Kasich dropped out. Meanwhile, a consistently high percentage of Republican Trump admirers have said there is a good president in the field.

Similarly, with Bernie Sanders' path to the Democratic nomination seeming to hit a dead end on June 7, Democrats who have an unfavorable view of Clinton became significantly less likely to say a candidate was running who would make a good president, dropping from 61% in May to 44% this month. The views of those who like Clinton remained solid, with over 80% confident that a good candidate is running.

Believe a Candidate Is Running Who Will Make a Good President

Based on views of Donald Trump among Republicans/Hillary Clinton among Democrats

	Apr 15-17, 2016 %	May 13-15, 2016 %	Jun 14-15, 2016 %
Republicans: favorable toward Trump	83	72	75
Republicans: unfavorable toward Trump	53	27	31
Democrats: favorable toward Clinton	75	84	83
Democrats: unfavorable toward Clinton	65	61	44

Gallup Daily Tracking

Republicans Slightly More Likely to Be Satisfied With Candidates' Issue Focus

Despite Democrats' advantage in perceptions that a good potential president is still in the race for president, the percentage of Republicans who say the candidates are talking about issues they care about reached a record high for the year in June, at 71%. The 61% figure for the Democrats on this question is about where it's been since March.

Percentage Who Say Presidential Candidates Are Talking About Issues They Really Care About

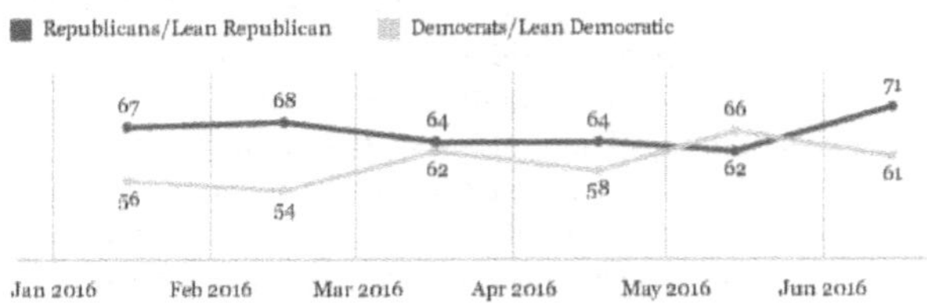

Gallup Daily tracking

GALLUP'

The uptick in Republicans' satisfaction with discussion of the issues this month is almost entirely attributable to an 11-percentage-point increase among those who view Trump favorably, now at 83%. By contrast, 63% of Democrats who view Clinton favorably feel satisfied about the discussion of the issues in June, essentially unchanged from May.

Notably, Clinton's Democratic detractors are far more likely to feel satisfied with the issues being addressed than are Trump's Republican detractors, 60% vs. 46%.

Percentage Who Say Presidential Candidates Are Talking About Issues They Really Care About

Based on views of Donald Trump among Republicans/Hillary Clinton among Democrats

	Apr 15-17, 2016 %	May 13-15, 2016 %	Jun 14-15, 2016 %
Republicans: favorable toward Trump	75	72	83
Republicans: unfavorable toward Trump	54	45	46
Democrats: favorable toward Clinton	65	67	63
Democrats: unfavorable toward Clinton	46	65	60

Gallup Daily Tracking

Bottom Line

In the aftermath of Clinton's securing of the delegates needed to become the 2016 Democratic presidential nominee at her party's national convention this summer, slightly fewer Democrats than last month – 71% now vs. 77% in May – are satisfied that someone is running who would make a good president. However, the drop in Democrats' satisfaction was somewhat less than the drop seen among Republicans in May after Trump became the presumptive GOP nominee. As a result, after being at parity with Republicans on this measure at the start of the year, Democrats now have an advantage in believing there is a candidate in the race who will make a good president.

While Republicans as a whole are more likely than Democrats to be satisfied with the discussion of issues they care about, there is a major breach between pro- and anti-Trump Republicans on this question. Much higher proportions of Trump's Republican admirers than Republican detractors are satisfied with the issues the candidates are talking about. By contrast, there is almost no difference between Democratic admirers and detractors of Clinton on this question. A uniformly modest level of contentment exists that the issues that matter to them are being addressed.

Survey Methods

Results for this Gallup poll are based on telephone interviews conducted June 14-15, 2016, on the Gallup U.S. Daily survey, with a random sample of 1,021 adults, aged 18 and older, living in all 50 U.S. states and the District of Columbia. For results based on the total sample of national adults, the margin of sampling error is ±4 percentage points at the 95% confidence level. For results based on the total sample of 447 Republicans and independents who lean Republican, the margin of sampling error is ±7 percentage points at the 95% confidence level. For results based on the total sample of 441 Democrats and independents who lean Democratic, the margin of sampling error is ±7 percentage points at the 95% confidence level. All reported margins of sampling error include computed design effects for weighting.

June 21, 2016
TRUMP'S IMAGE SLIPS; CLINTON'S HOLDS STEADY

by Frank Newport

Story Highlights

- *Trump's image is at -33 net favorable, compared with -28 in early May*
- *Clinton's image, at -13 net favorable, is little changed in last month and a half*
- *Americans see both candidates less positively now than 11 months ago*

PRINCETON, N.J. – Americans' views of Donald Trump have drifted slightly more negative over the past month and a half, with his net favorable rating slipping to -33 for June 13-19 from -28 in the first week of May. Americans' views of Hillary Clinton have remained significantly less negative than their views of Trump – and have been more stable, with her current -13 net favorable rating almost identical to her -14 from early May.

Hillary Clinton, Donald Trump Net Favorable Ratings

Net favorable represents the percentage with favorable views minus the percentage with unfavorable views

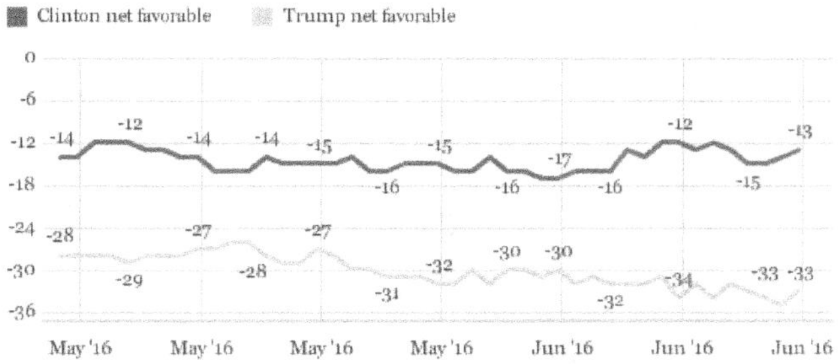

Note: Seven-day rolling averages

GALLUP

These results are from Gallup Daily tracking of the two candidates, with each estimate based on a seven-day rolling average of about 3,500 interviews.

The last month and a half has been an eventful period for both candidates. Trump secured the 1,237 delegates he needed to win the nomination the week of May 23. Shortly after, he attracted a great deal of attention by questioning the impartiality of the federal judge hearing a case related to Trump University because of the judge's Mexican heritage. Clinton basically secured the Democratic nomination on June 7 with her wins in California and other states. Both candidates also made highly publicized comments following the tragic shootings on June 12 in Orlando that left 49 dead, offering glimpses into how each would handle such an event as commander in chief.

Americans' views of Clinton improved modestly after she secured her party's nomination, but that basically represented a return to where her image had been in early May. The broad picture throughout the last month and a half for Clinton has been one of stability. On the other hand, Americans' views of Trump began to worsen in the final weeks of May and have continued to slip since. Importantly, the trend reflects a slow slide, rather than an abrupt change in response to any specific event of the past month and a half. Graphs showing the full trends in favorable and unfavorable ratings for both candidates appear at the end of this article.

Both Candidates' Images More Negative Now Than Last Summer

Gallup has been tracking the public's views of Clinton and Trump since mid-July 2015. Since then, both candidates' images have become more negative. Americans' views of Clinton have consistently been more positive than those of Trump, with the exception of a brief period in late August.

Americans held equally positive and negative views of Clinton in July 2015, but their views of the eventual Democratic nominee soured shortly thereafter, and her negative ratings have outweighed her positive ratings from last August to the present – although with significant ups and downs over that period. Americans' views of Clinton have been generally steady since mid-April.

Trump's image peaked in late August, although it remained more negative than positive, and then generally drifted downward through April, reaching a low of -39 net favorable. His image improved through mid-May and then began yet another downward slide to where it is today.

Hillary Clinton, Donald Trump Net Favorable Ratings

Net favorable represents the percentage with favorable views minus the percentage with unfavorable views

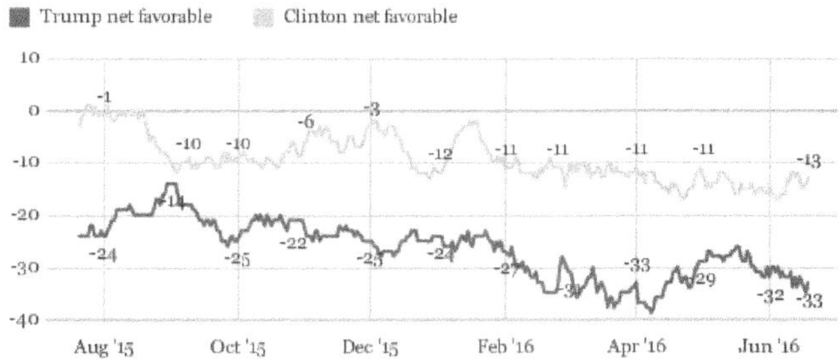

Note: Seven-day rolling averages

GALLUP

Despite the changes that have taken place over the past 11 months, the gap in the net favorable ratings of the two candidates is essentially the same now (20 points) as it was in July 2015 (21 points), when Gallup began tracking the candidates.

Implications

As the campaign has gone through its debate and primary-voting stages – with all that accompanies these political events – Americans have ended up with less positive views of both candidates compared with last July.

By this point in an election cycle, when each party's nomination has been clinched, candidates typically have more positive images than is the case for Clinton and Trump. Since 1992, Gallup has tracked few presidential candidates with negative net favorable ratings in June and July of an election year. The exceptions include Mitt Romney's -9 net favorable score in July 2012, as well as Bill Clinton's -6 and George H.W. Bush's -7 net favorable scores in June 1992. None of these candidates had net favorables in the summer as negative as Clinton's or Trump's today, however, and Clinton's and Romney's images became more positive closer to the election.

Americans can certainly change their minds about the candidates going forward, particularly during the party conventions that begin in mid-July. The public's views of Clinton have undergone significant shifts over the 25 years in which she has been in the national public eye as she has moved into and out of various political and nonpolitical roles, suggesting the possibility that views of her could shift once more. Trump is newer to the national political scene, and how much Americans will change their minds about him remains to be seen.

Donald Trump Favorability Ratings

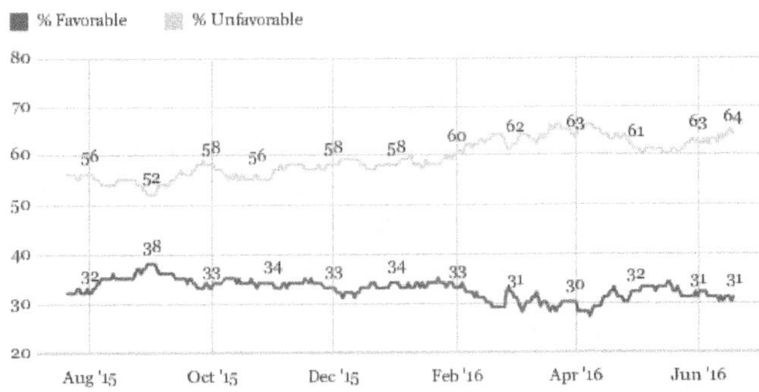

Note: Seven-day rolling averages

GALLUP

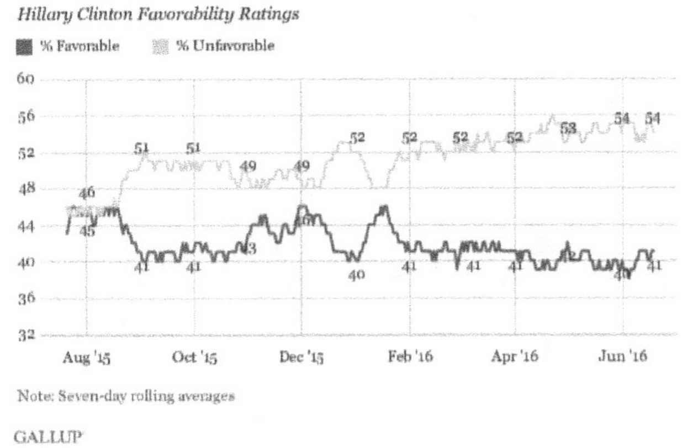

These data are available in Gallup Analytics.

Survey Methods

Results for the latest Gallup poll estimates are based on telephone interviews conducted June 13-19, 2016, on the Gallup U.S. Daily survey, with a random sample of 3,560 adults, aged 18 and older, living in all 50 U.S. states and the District of Columbia. For results based on the total sample of national adults, the margin of sampling error is ±2 percentage points at the 95% confidence level. All reported margins of sampling error include computed design effects for weighting.

June 22, 2016
SAME-SEX MARRIAGES UP ONE YEAR AFTER SUPREME COURT VERDICT

by Jeffrey M. Jones

Story Highlights

- *Nearly half of cohabiting same-sex couples now married*
- *Up from 38% before same-sex marriage legalized in all states*
- *9.6% of LGBT Americans married to same-sex spouse, up from 7.9%*

PRINCETON, N.J. – The proportion of same-sex cohabiting couples who are married has increased from 38% to 49% in the year since the U.S. Supreme Court legalized same-sex marriage nationwide.

Change in Percentage of Married Versus Unmarried Same-Sex Cohabiting Couples After Supreme Court Ruling on Same-Sex Marriage

Based on LGBT Americans

	Pre-Obergefell v. Hodges decision %	Post-Obergefell v. Hodges decision %
Married	38	49
Living together but not married	62	51

Note: Since Jan. 28, 2015, Gallup has measured sex of spouse/partner for LGBT respondents reporting they are married or living with a partner.
Gallup Daily tracking

On June 26, 2015, the Supreme Court in *Obergefell v. Hodges* struck down prohibitions on same-sex marriage in the 13 states that still had them. Since then, the same-sex marriage rate has grown significantly in those 13 states, but it has also grown in the states where it was already legal. The increase has been slightly greater (13 percentage points versus 10 points) in the states that had prohibited same-sex marriage before last June.

Change in Percentage of Married Versus Unmarried Same-Sex Couples Living Together After Supreme Court Ruling on Same-Sex Marriage, by Prior State Law

Based on LGBT Americans

Marital status	Pre-Obergefell v. Hodges decision %	Post-Obergefell v. Hodges decision %
Same-sex marriage NOT legal in state before June 26, 2015		
Married	26	39
Living together but not married	74	61
Same-sex marriage legal in state before June 26, 2015		
Married	42	52
Living together but not married	58	48

Note: Since Jan. 28, 2015, Gallup has measured sex of spouse/partner for LGBT respondents reporting they are married or living with a partner.
Gallup Daily tracking

The proportion of married same-sex couples remains higher in states in which the practice had been legal before the Supreme Court's ruling – 52% to 39%, with only a slight closing of the gap in the past year.

The results are based on Gallup Daily tracking interviews conducted throughout 2015 and 2016. Gallup asks U.S. adults if they identify as lesbian, gay, bisexual or transgender, and to indicate their marital status. Those who say they are LGBT and are either married or living in a domestic partnership are asked whether their spouse or partner is of the same sex or the opposite sex.

Gallup currently estimates 3.9% of U.S. adults are lesbian, gay, bisexual or transgender, and 0.4% of U.S. adults are married to a same-sex spouse. These figures can be used to estimate there are approximately 981,000 U.S. adults in a same-sex marriage and, thus, 491,000 same-sex marriages in the U.S. That latter estimate is up from roughly 368,000 a year ago.

One in 10 LGBT Adults Now Report Being Married to Same-Sex Spouse

Currently, 9.6% of LGBT adults report being married to a same-sex spouse, up from 7.9% before the landmark court decision. Meanwhile, the percentage of LGBT Americans who are living with a same-sex domestic partner has declined, from 12.8% to 10.1% – a larger decline compared with the increase in same-sex marriages. This indicates that while many unmarried same-sex couples who were living together got married in the past year, many others stopped living together or no longer consider themselves to be domestic partners. The largest percentage of LGBT Americans – 49.9% – continue to identify as single or never married, up from 47.4% a year ago.

Marital Status of LGBT Americans, Before and After Supreme Court Ruling Legalizing Same-Sex Marriage Nationwide

	Pre-Obergefell v. Hodges decision %	Post-Obergefell v. Hodges decision %	Change pct. pts.
Married to same-sex spouse	7.9	9.6	+1.7
Living with same-sex partner	12.8	10.1	-2.7
Single/Never married	47.4	49.9	+2.5
Living with opposite-sex partner	4.8	5	+0.2
Married to opposite-sex spouse	14.2	13.6	-0.6
Divorced	7.1	6.4	-0.7
Separated	2.5	2.2	-0.3
Widowed	2.8	2.9	+0.1

Gallup Daily tracking

At the time of Gallup's initial update on same-sex marriages after the Supreme Court ruling, 9.6% of LGBT Americans said they were married to a same-sex spouse. Since that November update, the percentage is essentially unchanged, at 9.5%. This suggests there was a burst of same-sex marriages in the first few months after the Supreme Court ruling but little additional increase since then.

Males who identify as LGBT are more likely than females who identify as LGBT to report being married to a same-sex spouse (10.5% vs. 8.8%, respectively). Gallup tracking documents similar increases since last June in the percentage of both groups who are in a same-sex marriage. A year ago, 8.7% of LGBT men and 7.2% of LGBT women said they were married to a same-sex spouse.

Implications

Gallup's data indicate a clear increase in same-sex marriages in the U.S. since the Supreme Court granted those unions legal status nationwide. Now, roughly half of all cohabiting same-sex couples are married, up from 38% a year ago. Gallup estimates that approximately 123,000 same-sex marriages have taken place since the *Obergefell v. Hodges* decision, with increases apparent among those living in states where same-sex marriage was already legal as well as those where it was not.

More recent data collected since Gallup's initial update on same-sex marriages in November show the growth in same-sex marriages may be leveling off. The *Obergefell v. Hodges* ruling appears to have provided the impetus for an initial surge in same-sex marriages, but that surge only lasted a short while. Going forward, as the nation moves further away in time from that June 2015 decision, increases in the same-sex marriage rate may be more evident in the long term rather than in the short term.

This is especially likely given that the U.S. LGBT population is decidedly young, and many who one day want to marry a same-sex spouse are not currently at a point in their lives when they are likely to seriously consider marriage.

These data are available in Gallup Analytics.

Survey Methods

Results for this Gallup poll are based on telephone interviews with a random sample of U.S. adults, aged 18 and older, living in all 50 U.S. states and the District of Columbia, on the Gallup U.S. Daily survey. Sample sizes and margins of error are shown in the accompanying table:

Margin of Error

Sample	Sample size	Margin of error %
Pre-Obergefell v. Hodges decision (Jan. 28-June 26, 2015)		
National adults	148,457	+/-1
LGBT	4,752	+/-2
Non-LGBT	135,643	+/-1
Post-Obergefell v. Hodges decision (June 27, 2015-June 19, 2016)		
National adults	351,880	+/-1
LGBT	11,588	+/-1
Non-LGBT	322,321	+/-1

Gallup Daily tracking

All reported margins of sampling error include computed design effects for weighting.

June 23, 2016
CONGRESS' HARSHEST CRITICS IDENTIFY A CRISIS OF INFLUENCE

by Frank Newport and Lydia Saad

Story Highlights

- *56% of critics strongly agree Congress too beholden to financial contributors*
- *Also agree strongly that Congress pays too much attention to lobbyists*
- *Most frequent general complaint about Congress: partisan gridlock*

PRINCETON, N.J. – Congress' harshest critics – the 53% of Americans who rate the job Congress is doing as poor or bad – feel more strongly about the undue influence that donors and lobbyists have on Congress than they do about any other major criticism of the institution. More than half of this group strongly agrees that members of Congress pay too much attention to what their contributors want them to do (56%) and what special interests and lobbyists want them to do (55%). Nearly half (46%) strongly agree that members of Congress should be willing to compromise more.

Americans' Specific Complaints About U.S. Congress

By rating of how Congress is doing its job

	Rate Congress' Job Poor or Bad (53%) %	Rate Congress' Job Excellent, Good or Fair (45%) %
Pay too much attention to financial contributors	56	23
Pay too much attention to special interests and lobbyists	55	23
Should be willing to compromise more	46	31
Spend too much time campaigning and raising money	43	19
Pay too much attention to party leaders	32	18
Congress not getting lots of important work accomplished	39	7
Congress has not worked hard to address issues you care most deeply about	37	8
Mainly out to gain personal glory and success	30	15
Mainly out to get rich	25	14
Are not honest	27	8
Congress has passed legislation you strongly object to	25	11
Do not care a lot about what their constituents want them to do	21	5
American public would be better off if Congress did less	14	8
Are not smart enough for their job	14	3

Based on agreement with negative statements or disagreement with positive statements about Congress
Gallup

By contrast, 4% of those most critical of Congress say its members care a lot about what their own constituents want them to do; 21% strongly disagree with this statement.

These results are part of a special Gallup analysis of the reasons behind Americans' extraordinarily low regard for Congress. Just 13% of Americans rate the job Congress is doing as excellent or good, and Congress' job approval is at 16%.

In a June 1-5 survey, Gallup asked Americans to react to a series of 14 positive and negative statements about Congress that encompass the major concerns that previous Gallup research shows most bothers Americans about the institution. The responses among Americans who are most critical of Congress, as well as those whose views of Congress are either positive or neutral, are shown in the accompanying table. As would be expected, those who rate the job Congress is doing as poor or bad are much more likely than others to judge Congress negatively across the 14 dimensions.

The views of the majority of Americans who say Congress is doing a poor or bad job may be particularly helpful in revealing the institution's core image problem. Additionally, those who are most critical of Congress are also the most knowledgeable about Congress, according to their answers to several factual questions about how Congress operates, underscoring the value of understanding what this group thinks.

The only two statements that a majority of those most critical of Congress strongly agree with are that Congress pays too much attention to financial contributors and too much attention to lobbyists and special interests. The related concern that members of Congress spend too much time raising money also ranks highly, with 43% strongly agreeing.

Notably, despite the 46% strongly agreeing that Congress should be willing to compromise more, only 32% of those most critical of Congress strongly agree that members pay too much attention to what their party leaders want them to do. Americans most critical of Congress thus apparently see partisanship, at least as it plays out in party leaders telling members what to do, taking a backseat to the influence of special interests in creating gridlock in Washington.

Americans who view Congress as doing an excellent, good or fair job are not nearly as likely to strongly agree with critical statements about Congress, but a substantial percentage still agree, even if not strongly. Among this group, lack of congressional compromise ranks first on the "strongly agree" list, with others falling behind. The complete results for this and other groups are reported at the end of this article.

Congressional Inaction Leads Top-of-Mind Concerns

A somewhat different perspective on Congress' image problem emerges from Americans' answers to an open-ended question about why they rate Congress the way they do. Almost half of Americans who say Congress is doing a poor or bad job cite congressional inaction or gridlock as the top reason for their view. This is consistent with the reasons Americans have traditionally given when asked open-ended questions about their views of Congress.

Relatively few in this group of critics spontaneously think of outside influences on Congress, such as lobbyists or financial contributors, even though these concerns spark relatively high levels of agreement when they are asked about specifically.

Thus, lack of compromise emerges as a leading concern about Congress in both the agree/disagree measure of what's wrong with Congress and the open-ended format. What is different about the results of the two approaches is that few Americans who are critical of Congress mention special interests or lobbyists in response to the open-ended question. This seeming disparity may indicate that Americans distinguish between what they believe Congress is doing wrong and the factors behind that failure. The open-ended questions reveal that Congress' lack of action on the nation's problems is the ultimate problem. At the same time, Americans' responses to the agree/disagree statements apparently tap into an underlying belief that special interests and big donors are thwarting the nation's business more generally.

Reason Given for Rating of Congress

What are some of the reasons you think the U.S. Congress is doing a/an [excellent/good/fair/poor/bad] job?

	Rate Congress Poor/Bad %	Rate Congress Excellent/Good %	Total %
Party gridlock/ obstruction	27	10	20
Needs to accomplish what they promised/ address the issues/take action	22	18	20
Represent party more than the people	9	5	7
Too much personal interest	9	2	6
Republicans opposing President Obama	7	5	6
Not doing a good job (nonspecific)	4	2	3
Corruption	3	0	2
Spending too much money/increasing the deficit	3	1	2
Lobbyists/special interests have too much influence on what Congress does	2	1	2
Are bipartisan/are compromising	2	3	2
Need term limits	2	1	1
Should pay better attention/be more focused	2	0	1
Should be more accountable	2	0	1
Lying	1	0	1
Doing a good job (nonspecific)	0	18	9
Some action being taken, need to take more	0	8	4
Other	2	2	2
No opinion	3	24	12

Gallup

Bottom Line

The explanations for Americans' low ratings of Congress as a whole appear to coalesce into two broad categories. First is Americans' belief that Congress is not accomplishing enough and suffers from gridlock. Second, and related to the first, is their belief that Congress is under the control of outside influences, including those with money and lobbyists, and is less interested in the interests of their constituents. These are also the primary factors explaining the particularly negative view of Congress' harshest critics.

Congress' failure to act on immigration reform in 2007 or pass a federal budget within the required time frame in 2013 are two of the more spectacular historical examples of legislative intransigence undermining public confidence in the institution. The inability of Congress to take action on gun control this week, despite much evidence that the public supports increases in background checks and restrictions on the sale of assault weapons, is a recent illustration of the public's chief complaints.

Gallup Senior Scientist Michael W. Traugott, Ph.D., contributed to this article.

Survey Methods

Results for this Gallup poll are based on telephone interviews conducted June 1-5, 2016, with a random sample of 1,027 adults, aged 18 and older, living in all 50 U.S. states and the District of Columbia. For results based on the total sample of national adults, the margin of sampling error is ±4 percentage points at the 95% confidence level. All reported margins of sampling error include computed design effects for weighting.

Americans' Reaction to Positive and Negative Assessments of Congress

Based on those who say Congress doing a poor or bad job

	Strongly agree %	Agree %	Neither %	Disagree %	Strongly disagree %
Pay too much attention to financial contributors	56	38	2	3	1
Pay too much attention to special interests and lobbyists	55	37	2	4	2
Should be willing to compromise more	46	41	3	7	2
Spend too much time campaigning and raising money	43	42	7	7	0
Congress getting lots of important work accomplished	1	3	4	51	39
Congress has worked hard to address issues you care most about	1	6	4	52	36
Pay too much attention to party leaders	32	52	6	8	2
Mainly out to gain personal glory and success	30	46	10	13	1
Are honest	1	7	13	51	27
Mainly out to get rich	25	40	13	19	1
Congress has passed legislation you strongly object to	25	41	13	14	4
Care a lot about what their constituents want them to do	4	23	10	41	21
American public would be better off if Congress did less	14	28	10	35	13
Smart enough for their job	3	35	14	32	14

June 1-5, 2016

Americans' Reaction to Positive and Negative Assessments of Congress

Based on those who say Congress doing an excellent/good/fair job

	Strongly agree %	Agree %	Neither %	Disagree %	Strongly disagree %
Should be willing to compromise more	31	56	5	6	2
Pay too much attention to special interests and lobbyists	23	52	9	13	2
Pay too much attention to financial contributors	23	55	8	11	2
Spend too much time campaigning and raising money	19	44	11	23	1
Pay too much attention to party leaders	18	56	11	12	2
Mainly out to gain personal glory and success	15	42	16	26	1
Mainly out to get rich	14	34	18	32	2
Congress has passed legislation you strongly object to	11	40	17	26	4
American public would be better off if Congress did less	8	31	15	36	8
Smart enough for their job	8	49	20	19	3
Care a lot about what their constituents want them to do	10	42	15	27	5
Congress getting lots of important work accomplished	4	28	18	42	7
Are honest	4	27	22	37	8
Congress has worked hard to address issues you care most about	4	28	17	43	8

June 1-5, 2016

June 24, 2016
IN U.S., SLIM MAJORITY CONFIDENT ABOUT FINANCIAL FUTURE

by Alyssa Davis

Story Highlights

- *53% "very" or "somewhat" confident about financial future*
- *Lower-income Americans most insecure*
- *Financial outlook linked to views of national economy*

WASHINGTON, D.C. – A small majority of Americans, 53%, say they feel at least somewhat confident about their financial future, including 15% who feel "very" confident. Meanwhile, nearly half (46%) report feeling at least somewhat insecure about their financial future, including 17% who feel "very" insecure.

Americans' Assessments of their Financial Future

Thinking about your income and expenses – do you feel very confident, somewhat confident, somewhat insecure or very insecure about your financial future?

	U.S. adults %
Very confident	15
Somewhat confident	38
Somewhat insecure	29
Very insecure	17

Gallup Poll, May 18-22, 2016

Americans' slight tilt toward feeling confident about their financial future in the May 18-22 Gallup poll comes as consumer spending remains healthy, gas prices are significantly lower than in recent years, and U.S. workers' reports of hiring activity are at a new high. There are also possible signs of wage growth, and fewer Americans report struggling to afford food and healthcare than at any point since 2008.

Gallup asked this question once before in January 2016, and the results were similar then.

Lower-Income, Those Nearing Retirement Age Most Insecure

Lower-income earners, the least financially confident of all groups, are more than four times as likely as upper-income earners and more than twice as likely as middle-income earners to feel very insecure. Those aged 50 to 64 are more likely than all other age groups to say they are very insecure about their financial future, possibly reflecting their concerns about saving enough for retirement.

Financial confidence is similar across party identification groups.

Americans' Confidence in Financial Future, by Subgroup

	Very confident %	Somewhat confident %	Somewhat insecure %	Very insecure %
Age				
18-29 years	14	36	32	18
30-49 years	16	42	26	15
50-64 years	13	36	31	21
65+ years	19	35	31	15
Annual household income				
Less than $30,000	5	28	28	37
$30,000 to less than $75,000	13	37	35	14
$75,000+	24	44	24	8
Party identification				
Republican	13	40	31	15
Independent	16	35	29	19
Democrat	16	39	27	17

Gallup Poll, May 18-22, 2016

Confidence in Financial Future Tied to Views of U.S. Economy

Americans' evaluations of their own financial future are closely related to how they view the broader U.S. economy. In the same May 18-22 survey, Gallup asked whether they think the U.S. economy is growing, staying the same or shrinking. Americans who say the U.S. economy is growing are more than twice as likely to say they are confident in their financial future as to say they are insecure. And the reverse is also true: Those who say the economy is shrinking are much more likely to be insecure than to be confident about their future financial situation.

Americans' Confidence in Financial Future, by Views of U.S. Economy

	Growing %	Staying the same %	Shrinking %
Very confident	23	12	11
Somewhat confident	45	45	29
Somewhat insecure	22	33	34
Very insecure	10	11	25

Gallup Poll, May 18-22, 2016

The relationship between financial confidence and views of the economy holds across all income groups. Those who are more positive about the U.S. economy are more confident in their financial future.

While there is a strong relationship between financial confidence and views of the economy, the direction is unclear. Americans' personal financial situations may color their views of the national economy, or their views of the national economy may be shaping their assessment of their financial future.

Implications

A slight majority of Americans are optimistic about their financial future, but there is significant room for improvement – even among those who are confident. More than twice as many Americans are only "somewhat" confident as opposed to "very" confident in their financial future, and confidence is uneven across key segments of the population.

Economists expect the gross domestic product to accelerate in the second quarter, driven by strong consumer spending. Given the relationship between financial optimism and views of the U.S. economy, news of improved economic growth could potentially boost Americans' financial confidence – at least temporarily. But the public likely would need to see evidence of sustained job creation and economic growth before their assessments of their financial future brighten.

Historical data are available in Gallup Analytics.

Survey Methods

Results for this Gallup poll are based on telephone interviews conducted May 18-22, 2016, with a random sample of 1,530 adults, aged 18 and older, living in all 50 U.S. states and the District of Columbia. For results based on the total sample of national adults, the margin of sampling error is ±3 percentage points at the 95% confidence level.

June 24, 2016

EUTHANASIA STILL ACCEPTABLE TO SOLID MAJORITY IN U.S.

by Art Swift

Story Highlights

- *69% say doctors should be allowed to end a patient's life by painless means*
- *51% say they would consider ending their lives if faced with terminal illness*
- *About half of Americans say doctor-assisted suicide is morally acceptable*

WASHINGTON, D.C. – A large majority of Americans continue to say euthanasia should be legal, a reversal from the 1940s and 1950s when most thought the practice should be illegal. Sixty-nine percent say that a doctor should be allowed to end a patient's life by painless means if the patient requests it, up from 36% in 1950. Americans' continued support for making euthanasia legal comes as California recently passed its own right-to-die law.

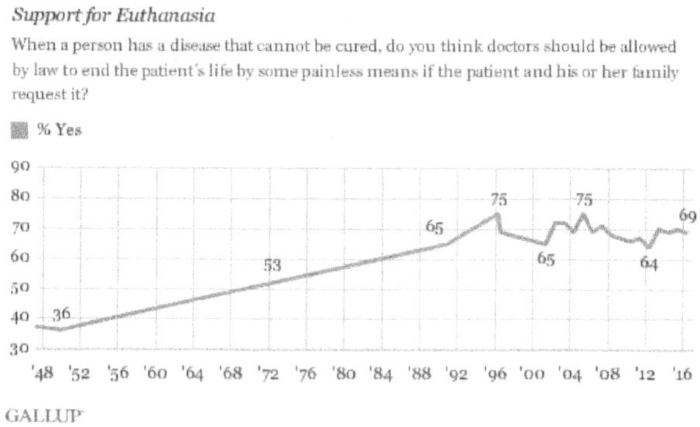

The new law in the nation's most populous state, passed last fall, will allow terminally ill patients who meet certain criteria to ask their doctor for life-ending medication. The legislation came as a result of the case of Brittany Maynard, who was diagnosed with terminal brain cancer in California, where physicians previously were barred from prescribing medication to allow terminally ill people to end their lives. Maynard ended her life in Oregon, where the practice was legal.

In 1973, Gallup for the first time found a majority in favor of doctors being legally permitted to end a patient's life if requested. That percentage grew to 65% in 1990. In the last 25 years, Americans have solidly been in favor of doctors having the ability to end patients' lives, with between 64% and 75% favoring the practice.

Americans More Reluctant to End Own Lives by Painless Means

While 69% in the U.S. say physicians should be allowed to end patients' lives by painless means, fewer Americans (51%) say they would consider ending their own lives if they personally had a disease that could not be cured and they were living in severe pain.

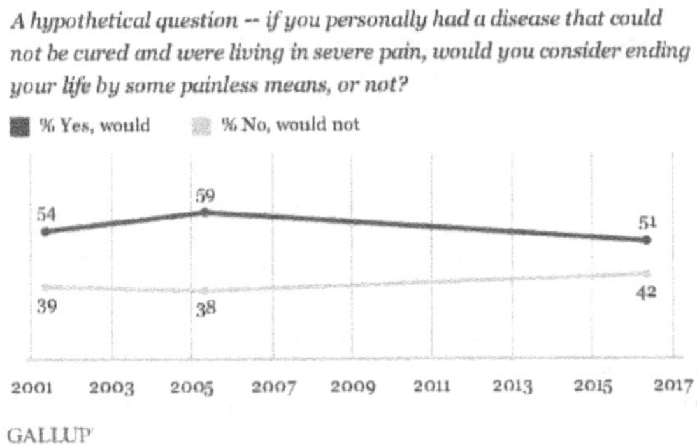

This is down from the last time Gallup asked this question in 2005 (59%), around the time of the Terri Schiavo controversy. Schiavo's husband advocated that Schiavo would not have wanted prolonged artificial life support without the ability to recover, and he chose to have hospice staff remove her feeding tube. The first time Gallup asked this question in 2001, 54% said they would consider ending their own lives if they had a terminal disease.

Americans Say Doctor-Assisted Suicide Morally Acceptable

In the same Values and Beliefs poll in May, Gallup asked Americans if they believe doctor-assisted suicide is morally acceptable or morally wrong. A slight majority (53%) say the practice is morally acceptable.

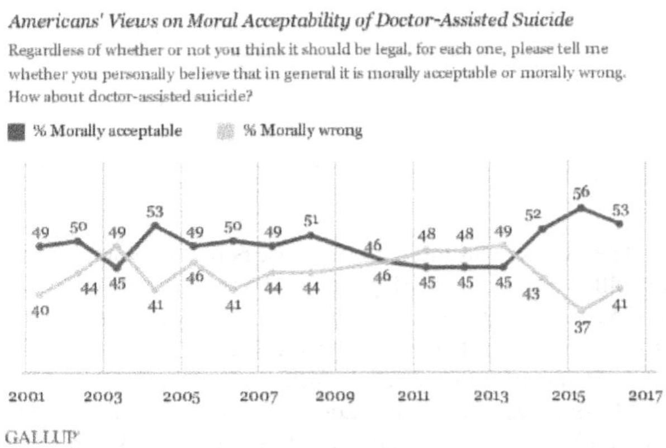

Over the past 15 years, the highest percentage of Americans saying doctor-assisted suicide is morally acceptable occurred in 2015, at 56%. This trend has fluctuated between 45% and 56% since 2001.

This question uses the word "suicide," which may affect Americans' responses. It is possible that some may not understand the distinction between patients dying with a self-administered medication and a doctor taking action to end a patient's life.

Bottom Line

California recently joined Oregon, Washington, Vermont, Montana and New Mexico as the only states to allow physician-assisted suicide. California, often a bellwether for change throughout the U.S., may persuade other states to consider passing legislation permitting physicians to allow terminally ill people to end their lives. While Americans appear to be solidly comfortable with the practice, the nation is more divided on the moral acceptability of doctor-assisted suicide.

Historical data are available in Gallup Analytics.

Survey Methods

Results for this Gallup poll are based on telephone interviews conducted May 4-8, 2016, with a random sample of 1,025 adults, aged 18 and older, living in all 50 U.S. states and the District of Columbia. For results based on the total sample of national adults, the margin of sampling error is ±4 percentage points at the 95% confidence level. For results based on the half-sample of 521 national adults, the margin of sampling error is ±5 percentage points. All reported margins of sampling error include computed design effects for weighting.

June 27, 2016

CLINTON, TRUMP GAINING FAVORABILITY WITHIN PARTIES

by Lydia Saad

Story Highlights

- *Clinton's favorability among Democrats up three points since June 5*
- *Trump's favorability among Republicans holds at improved level in June*
- *Trump has made gains among GOP each of the past two weeks*

PRINCETON, N.J. – Since clinching the Democratic nomination in early June, Hillary Clinton's favorable rating among Democrats and Democratic-leaning independents is up slightly to 71%, compared with 68% in April and May. Her image is now partly restored to what it was at the start of the year when 74% of Democrats viewed her favorably.

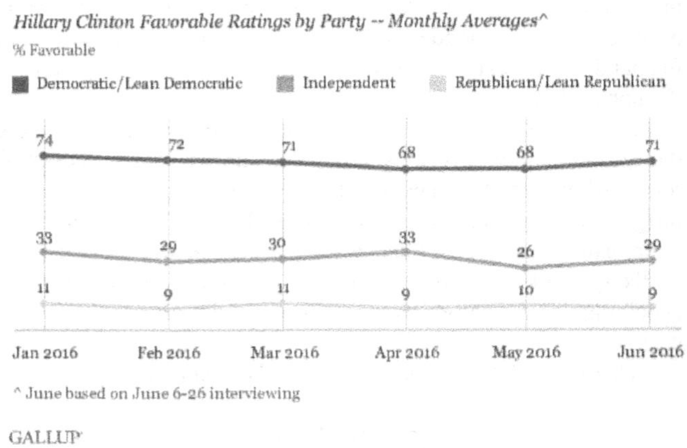

Meanwhile, Donald Trump has maintained higher favorable ratings among Republicans and Republican leaners since he emerged as the sole Republican candidate in May compared with earlier in the year. His favorable rating among Republicans averages 64% so far in June, the same as in May but higher than the 54% to 56% in the three prior months. His current favorable rating also exceeds the average 61% he earned from this partisan group in January.

Donald Trump Favorable Ratings by Party -- Monthly Averages

% Favorable

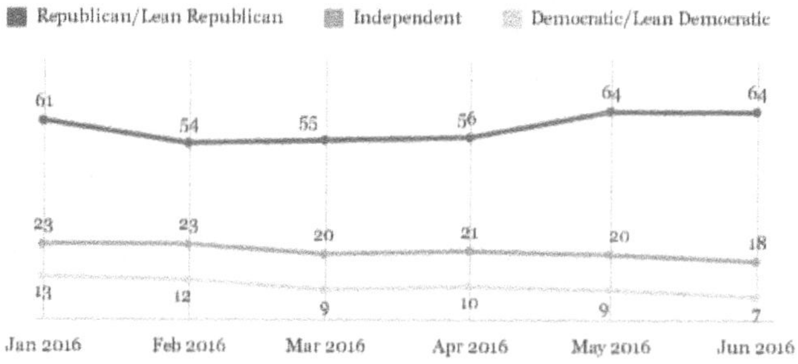

GALLUP

At the same time, Clinton and Trump have each lost ground over the course of 2016 among independents who lean toward neither party. Because of this, the candidates' national favorable ratings have stayed still or declined slightly, despite recent improved ratings from their own partisans. Clinton's overall favorable rating since clinching the nomination has averaged 41%, nearly matching her 40% in May but down slightly from 44% in January. Trump's average 31% thus far in June compares with 32% in May and 34% in January. However, the electoral importance of pure independents will likely be muted, as Gallup polling traditionally shows this group to be less engaged in politics and less likely to vote than those who identify with or lean toward one of the two major parties.

Additionally, the percentage of Democrats viewing Trump favorably has dwindled from 13% in January to 10% in April and 7% in June, also contributing to the decline in his overall favorable rating nationally. The percentage of Republicans viewing Clinton favorably has been steady, near 10%.

2016 Nominees Less Liked by Own Parties Than Their Predecessors

Although Clinton leads Trump in overall favorability thus far in June, she remains well behind the last several Democratic nominees, two of whom garnered 87% favorability among Democrats in June of their election years. Only Al Gore in June 2000 fell below that range, at 77%. Clinton's 9% average favorable rating from Republicans in June is also far lower than what most prior Democratic nominees have earned, although not too much lower than President Barack Obama's in 2012.

Democratic Nominees: % Favorable by Party in June of Each Election Year

	Democratic/ Lean Democratic %	Republican/ Lean Republican %
2016: Hillary Clinton	71	9
2012: Barack Obama	88	15
2008: Barack Obama	87	37
2004: John Kerry	87	28
2000: Al Gore	77	25

Note: 2012 results for Barack Obama based on May 10-13 survey
Gallup

Clinton's favorability problems are not necessarily a liability for her given that Trump fares even worse than her and relative to his Republican predecessors. The 64% of Republicans viewing Trump favorably in June is nearly 20 percentage points lower than any of the prior recent Republican nominees. And his 7% rating among Democrats and Democratic leaners in June is markedly lower than the crossover favorability that prior Republican nominees have earned.

Republican Nominees: % Favorable by Party in June of Each Election Year

	Republican/Lean Republican %	Democratic/Lean Democratic %
2016: Donald Trump	64	7
2012: Mitt Romney	82	20
2008: John McCain	88	37
2004: George W. Bush	94	21
2000: George W. Bush	88	36

Note: 2012 results for Mitt Romney based on May 10-13 survey
Gallup

One bright spot for Trump is that his average favorable rating from Republicans in June reflects improving scores on a weekly basis, rising from 60% for June 6-12 to 64% for June 13-19 and 67% for June 20-26. Over the same period, Clinton's weekly scores among Democrats were flat, registering 72%, 70% and 71%.

Bottom Line

Despite steady or even sagging ratings nationally, Trump and Clinton have begun the process of repairing their images within their own parties as they prepare to receive their nominations in July. Eliminating their challengers for the nomination may have been the first step in having their own party members view them more favorably. Shifting gears to a general election mode will be the next step, and the national party conventions next month should maximize whatever support the candidates will receive from their own parties' supporters nationally.

While Clinton may have earned a bump from clinching the Democratic nomination in early June, she has not built on that in the following weeks, perhaps because of Bernie Sanders' reluctance to withdraw from the race and endorse her. Trump, on the other hand, has picked up some additional steam among Republicans in June. However, advancing on a weekly basis is one thing – maintaining those gains on a monthly basis is another. It will be important to see if Trump can hold or build on his improved status among Republicans into July.

Historical data are available in Gallup Analytics.

Survey Methods

Results for this Gallup analysis are based on telephone interviews conducted Jan. 2-June 26, 2016, on the Gallup U.S. Daily survey with random samples of U.S. adults, aged 18 and older, living in all 50 U.S. states and the District of Columbia. Each candidate's monthly ratings are based on at least 4,000 U.S. adults, including at least 1,700 adults aligned with or leaning toward the Republican and Democratic Parties and at least 400 pure independents.

For monthly results based on the total sample of national adults, the margin of sampling error is no more than ±2 percentage points at the 95% confidence level. For monthly results based on Democrats and independents who lean Democratic as well as Republicans and independents who lean Republican, the margin of sampling error is no more than ±3 percentage points at the 95% confidence level. All reported margins of sampling error include computed design effects for weighting.

June 27, 2016

TRUMP NOT YET GENERATING EVANGELICAL REPUBLICAN ZEAL

by Frank Newport

Story Highlights

- *Trump's appeal to white Republicans is similar regardless of religiosity*
- *In contrast, Ted Cruz's appeal was highest among the highly religious*
- *Trump made special appeal to this group last week*

PRINCETON, N.J. – Highly religious white Protestant Republicans, a core group whose support presumptive Republican presidential nominee Donald Trump sought last week, are slightly more positive about Trump now than they were from February to May. However, this group remains no more likely to view Trump favorably than are white Protestant Republicans who are moderately or not religious. In contrast, while he was still in the race, former candidate Ted Cruz's appeal was significantly higher among highly religious members of this group than among those who were less religious.

Non-Hispanic White Protestant Republicans' Views of Donald Trump and Ted Cruz, by Religiosity

	Highly religious %	Moderately religious %	Not religious %
Ted Cruz (Feb. 1-May 3, 2016)	63	48	43
Donald Trump (Feb. 1-May 31, 2016)	57	70	64
Donald Trump (June 1-22, 2016)	66	73	65

Gallup U.S. Daily

These differences in attitudes toward the candidates are based on Gallup Daily tracking interviews conducted from February through May and June 1-22. Gallup classifies Americans as highly religious, moderately religious or not religious based on their self-reports of whether religion is important to them and how frequently they attend religious services.

Trump clearly considers evangelicals to be an important target for his presidential campaign. Last week, he met with nearly 1,000 Christian evangelical leaders in New York, with the presumed objective of shoring up his support and, ultimately, turnout among that group. He released a photo of himself and Christian conservative leader Jerry Falwell, Jr.; took a swipe at Hillary Clinton's religiousness, saying, "We don't know anything about Hillary in terms of religion"; and appointed a 21-person evangelical advisory board.

There is no universally agreed-upon definition of exactly who is and who is not an "evangelical," but the label typically refers to individuals who are highly religious and identify with a non-Catholic Christian (Protestant) faith. White Protestants who are highly religious are particularly important in a political context, because black Americans' views of the candidates appear to be more related to their race than their religiosity. For example, about two-thirds or more of blacks have positive opinions of Clinton regardless of their religiosity, and only 10% in any of the three religious categories view Trump favorably.

Highly religious white Americans skew Republican, but some of this group are Democrats, and thus are unlikely to vote for Trump. Therefore, the data on highly religious white Protestant Republicans serve as a good representation of evangelicals as they are usually considered. And, as seen, while white Republican Protestants overall have positive opinions of Trump, their opinions are broadly similar, regardless of religiosity.

In short, among Protestants – once partisanship and race are taken into account – religiosity doesn't appear to make much of a difference in views of Trump. This stands in contrast to this group's views of Cruz earlier this year, when he was still an active candidate for the GOP nomination. At that point, white Protestant Republicans who were highly religious were significantly more positive about Cruz than were those who were either moderately or not religious.

Implications

Based on personality, history and other factors, it's not clear whether Trump will ever generate the type of differentially strong appeal among evangelicals as was the case for Cruz. But, in terms of sheer numbers alone – 54% of white Protestant Republicans are highly religious – if there is a way for Trump to increase his image and support among this group, it would appear to have significant upside potential for his campaign.

Historical data are available in Gallup Analytics.

Survey Methods

Results for this Gallup poll are based on telephone interviews conducted June 1-22, 2016, on the Gallup U.S. Daily survey, with a random sample of 11,170 adults, aged 18 and older, living in all 50 U.S. states and the District of Columbia. For results based on the total sample of national adults, the margin of sampling error is ±2 percentage points at the 95% confidence level. For results based on the total sample of 2,630 white Protestant Republicans, the margin of sampling error is ±2 percentage points at the 95% confidence level. All reported margins of sampling error include computed design effects for weighting.

June 28, 2016
NO IMMEDIATE BREXIT EFFECT ON U.S. ECONOMIC CONFIDENCE

by Justin McCarthy

Story Highlights

- *Pre- and post-Brexit index scores match at -16*
- *Weekly index down slightly, at -17*
- *Economic outlook dips to lowest since November 2013*

WASHINGTON, D.C. – The United Kingdom's decision Thursday to exit the European Union did not immediately affect Americans' confidence in the U.S. economy. Gallup's U.S. Economic Confidence Index was -16 in three-day rolling averages recorded before *and* after the referendum. This might suggest that Americans are taking a wait-and-see approach before assessing the vote's effect on the U.S. economy, or that Americans are simply unconcerned with matters across the Atlantic.

Americans' Confidence in the U.S. Economy, Pre- and Post-Brexit

	Pre-Brexit (June 21-23)	Post-Brexit (June 24-26)
U.S. Economic Confidence Index	-16	-16

Gallup Daily tracking

There is a great deal of uncertainty surrounding how the Brexit decision will affect the global economy in the future. Many investors reacted negatively, including in the U.S., where the Dow Jones industrial average fell 610 points the day after the vote. Economists' opinions differ on what long-term influence the decision will have in the U.S.

In the short term, Americans appear unfazed by the decision – at least concerning their views of the U.S economy – and they are about as confident in the U.S. economy as they were in the week before the referendum. Gallup's U.S. Economic Confidence Index was -17 for the entire week ending June 26, including interviewing done partly before and after the Brexit results became known on Friday. Although this reading matches the low from the past year, the latest index reading is not markedly different from the -15 recorded in the previous week.

Confidence has been consistently negative for well over a year – similar to how it has been for most of Gallup's tracking of the index since 2008. While the weekly averages in 2016 have fallen short of the positive ones recorded in late 2014 and early 2015, they are still well above many of the dismally low figures registered in the aftermath of the Great Recession.

U.S. Economic Confidence Index -- Weekly Averages Since December 2014

Latest results for week ending June 26, 2016

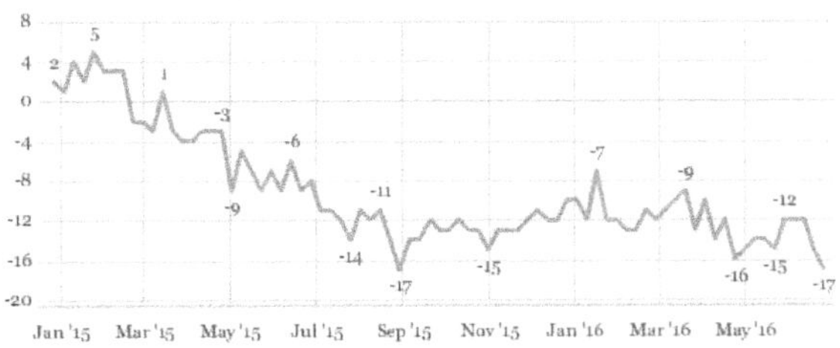

Gallup U.S. Daily tracking

GALLUP

Gallup's U.S. Economic Confidence Index is the average of two components: how Americans rate current economic conditions and whether they feel the economy is improving or getting worse. The index has a theoretical maximum of +100 if all Americans say the economy is doing well and improving, and a theoretical minimum of -100 if all Americans say the economy is doing poorly and getting worse.

For the week ending June 26, the current conditions score registered -6, consistent with the readings on this component over the past year. This latest score was the result of 24% of U.S. adults rating the current economy as "excellent" or "good," and 30% rating it as "poor."

Americans continue to be more pessimistic about the future of the economy. The latest economic outlook score of -27 was the lowest for this component since November 2013, based on 34% of U.S. adults saying the economy is "getting better" and 61% saying it is "getting worse." This figure has declined slightly each of the past two weeks, accounting for the drop in the overall weekly index from -12 the week of June 6-12 to the most recent -17.

U.S. Economic Confidence Index Components -- Weekly Averages Since June 2015

Latest results for week ending June 26, 2016

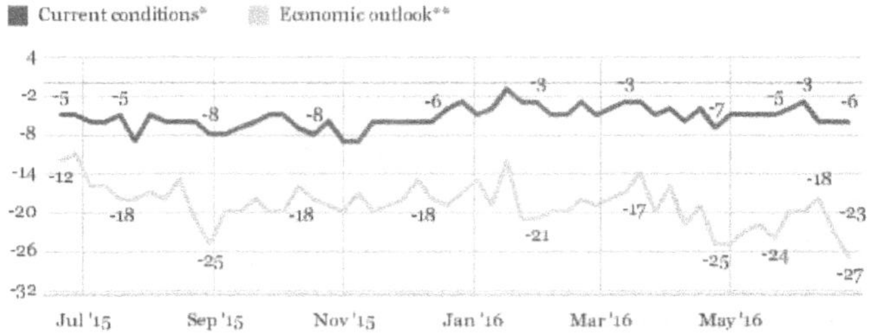

*% (Excellent + Good) minus % Poor

**% Getting better minus % Getting worse

Gallup U.S. Daily tracking

GALLUP

Bottom Line

Americans' confidence in the economy might be unmoved for the time being, but that's not to say it won't change in the weeks to come. The public's confidence has faltered after major political and economic events in the past, and the fallout from the Brexit might not have settled yet – particularly if it continues to affect U.S. stock values in the short run or hurts other aspects of the U.S. economy in the coming years. The referendum decision is literally foreign to Americans, and many might struggle to understand what it means.

Americans might be more likely to feel its effects on the behavior of their own stock market, which suffered in the immediate aftermath of the Brexit vote. But some argue that these are temporary setbacks and that the U.S. economy is resilient enough to weather any potential fallout from the U.K. – and could even stand to gain from it via lower costs for imports and gas.

These data are available in Gallup Analytics.

Survey Methods

Results for this Gallup poll are based on telephone interviews conducted June 20-26, 2016, on the Gallup U.S. Daily survey, with a random sample of 3,544 adults, aged 18 and older, living in all 50 U.S. states and the District of Columbia. For results based on the total sample of national adults, the margin of sampling error is ±2 percentage points at the 95% confidence level. All reported margins of sampling error include computed design effects for weighting.

June 29, 2016
MOST AMERICANS STILL BELIEVE IN GOD

by Frank Newport

Story Highlights

- *89% of Americans say they believe in God*
- *In a separate poll, 79% say "believe in God" and 10% "not sure"*
- *All measures of belief in God show declines from previous decades*

PRINCETON, N.J. – About nine in 10 Americans say they believe in God, and one in 10 say they do not. However, when presented with more than a "yes or no" option, about eight in 10 say they believe and one in 10 say they aren't sure. Belief in God, regardless of how the question is phrased to Americans, is down from levels in past decades.

Americans' Belief in God Using Different Question Wording

	Yes	No	No opinion
	%	%	%
Do you believe in God?	89	10	1
Do you believe in God or a universal spirit?	89	9	2

Gallup, June 14-23, 2016

For each of the following items I am going to read you, please tell me whether it is something you believe in, something you're not sure about or something you don't believe in: God.

	%
Believe in	79
Not sure about	10
Don't believe in	11

Gallup, May 4-8, 2016

These results are based on several different questions that Gallup has used over the years to ask Americans about their belief in God. The latest results come from surveys conducted May 4-8 and June 14-23.

When Gallup first asked Americans, "Do you, personally, believe in a God?" in 1944, 96% said they did. Between 94% and 98% of Americans said they believed in God in other surveys conducted through 1967. In 1976, Gallup modified the wording and asked Americans about their belief in "God or a universal spirit," with 94% to 96% responding in the affirmative through 1994.

Since 2011, Gallup has asked both questions of random half-samples of Americans. The results on both questions have been similar, indicating that adding "universal spirit" into the mix doesn't significantly affect how Americans respond to the question. Since 2013, the percentage believing in God or a universal spirit has been consistently in the upper 80% range. In the most recent June survey, both versions of the question netted 89% affirmative responses.

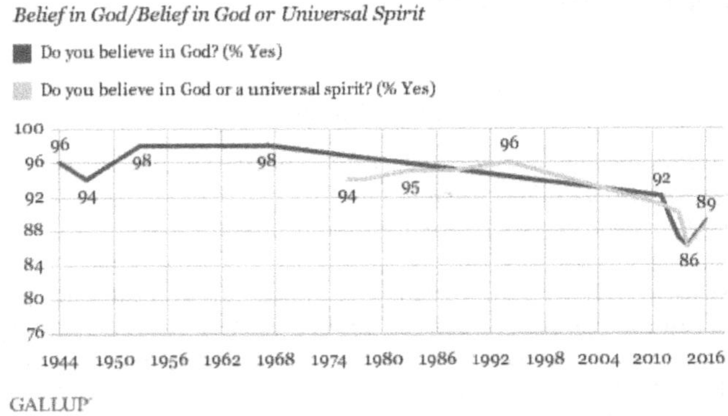

In 2001, 2004, 2007 and 2016, Gallup asked a separate question that gives Americans three options to characterize their beliefs: "believe in," "not sure about" and "don't believe in."

In 2001 and 2004, 90% of U.S. adults said they believed in God, with 7% and 5%, respectively, saying they were unsure. By 2007, the percentage choosing "believe in God" had dropped slightly to 86%, with another 8% expressing uncertainty. This year, "believe in God" dropped further to 79%, with 10% unsure. Still, the 89% who say they believe in God or are unsure (as opposed to saying they don't believe in God) is the same as the 89% who respond affirmatively when asked the simpler "yes or no" question, "Do you believe in God?"

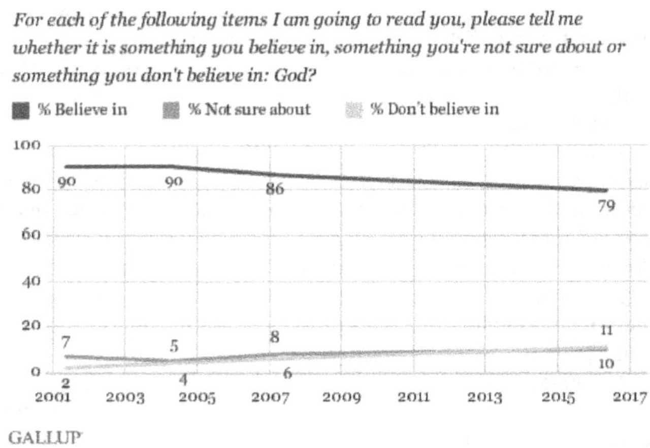

Gallup asked the question that includes the "not sure about" option in random rotation with questions about belief in four other religious concepts: angels, heaven, hell and the devil. Americans' belief in all of these is lower than their belief in God, ranging from 72% who say they believe in angels to 61% who say they believe in the devil, with 12% unsure on both. Belief in these four concepts is down at least marginally from when last measured in 2007, following the same pattern as the trend in belief in God using this question format.

For each of the following items I am going to read you, please tell me whether it is something you believe in, something you're not sure about or something you don't believe in.

	Believe in %	Not sure about %	Don't believe in %
God	79	10	11
Angels	72	12	16
Heaven	71	14	15
Hell	64	13	22
The devil	61	12	27

Gallup, May 4-8, 2016

Implications

About nine in 10 Americans believe in God – or when given the option, say they either believe in God or are unsure about it. Either way, that leaves roughly 10% who say they do not believe in God.

All of Gallup's questions about belief in God show declines from previous decades. The question that gives people the chance to say they're "not sure" shows a decline from as recently as nine years ago. This follows the general trend in drops in other religious indicators over the decades. Most notable among these is that close to 20% of Americans now say they do not identify with a specific religious group or denomination, compared with smaller percentages who had no religious identity in decades past.

The exact meaning of these shifts is unclear. Although the results can be taken at face value in showing that fewer Americans believe in God than did so in the past, it is also possible that basic beliefs have not changed – but rather Americans' willingness to express nonreligious sentiments to an interviewer has. Whatever the explanation for these changes over time, the most recent findings show that the substantial majority of Americans continue to give a positive response when asked about their belief in God.

Historical data are available in Gallup Analytics.

Survey Methods

Results for this Gallup poll are based on telephone interviews conducted June 14-23, 2016, with a random sample of 1,025 adults, aged 18 and older, living in all 50 U.S. states and the District of Columbia. For results based on the total sample of national adults, the margin of sampling error is ±4 percentage points at the 95% confidence level. For results based on the total sample of 1,025 adults interviewed May 4-8, 2016, the margin of sampling error is ±4 percentage points at the 95% confidence level. All reported margins of sampling error include computed design effects for weighting.

June 29, 2016
VIEWS OF OPPORTUNITY IN U.S. IMPROVE, BUT LAG THE PAST

by Jeffrey M. Jones

Story Highlights

- *54% believe it is likely today's youth can live better than their parents*
- *Up from 44% in 2011, but still below 66% from early 2008*
- *70% say there is plenty of opportunity in U.S. to get ahead*

PRINCETON, N.J. – Fifty-four percent of Americans believe it is likely that today's young people will have a better life than their parents. While still down from 66% in early 2008, the current figure shows continued improvement from the low point of 44% in April 2011.

Perceived Likelihood Today's Youth Can Live Better Than Their Parents

In America, each generation has tried to have a better life than their parents, with a better living standard, better homes, a better education and so on. How likely do you think it is that today's youth will have a better life than their parents -- very likely, somewhat likely, somewhat unlikely or very unlikely?

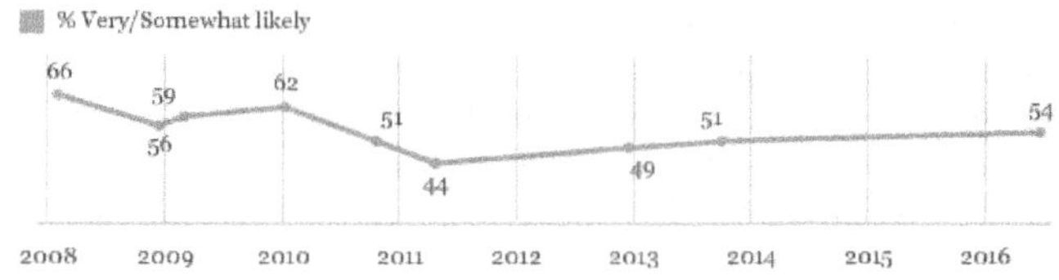

GALLUP

The latest results are based on a June 14-23 Gallup poll. Americans' optimism about young people being able to live better than their parents dampened only slightly during the Great Recession in 2008 and 2009. More substantial declines occurred in late 2010 and early 2011, after the unemployment rate had been 9.0% or higher for over a year.

By December 2012, with the unemployment rate back below 8.0%, Americans started to show renewed optimism about future generations' economic opportunities.

The question was asked before 2008 by other polling organizations. During the economic boom of the late 1990s and early 2000s, a high of 71% of Americans believed it was likely young people would live better than their parents, according to a July 1999 *New York Times* poll. That figure was matched in a December 2001 CBS News/*New York Times* poll conducted a few months after the 9/11 terrorist attacks.

The question was first asked by the Roper Organization in January 1983, another time of high unemployment. At that time, 54% said it was likely young people could live better than their parents, the same level as today.

Seven in 10 Say There Is "Plenty of Opportunity" in the U.S.

Americans are also more optimistic now than in recent years about how much opportunity there is in the U.S. Seven in 10 Americans say there is "plenty of opportunity" in the U.S. today for anyone who wants to work hard and get ahead, up from just over half in 2011 and 2013. However, while those attitudes have improved significantly, fewer today say there is plenty of opportunity than did so in 1998 (81%).

Perceptions of Opportunity in the U.S.

Some people say there's not much opportunity in America today -- that the average person doesn't have much chance to really get ahead. Others say there's plenty of opportunity and anyone who works hard can go as far as they want. Which one comes closer to the way you feel about this?

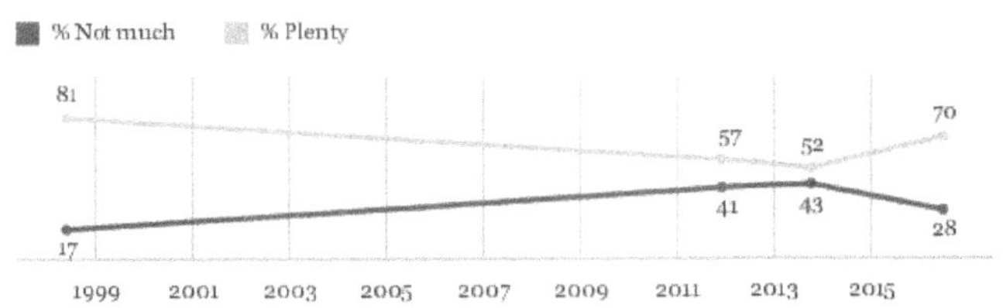

GALLUP

Republicans Less Optimistic About Youth Living Better Than Parents

Predictions of whether young people will be able to live better than their parents are similar across key U.S. subgroups, including by age, education level, employment status and household income. Views differ significantly across partisan groups, however, with 68% of Democrats and Democratic-leaning independents, but only 41% of Republicans and Republican leaners, saying it is likely today's youth will have a better life than their parents.

Both party groups were less optimistic in 2011 than they are today, and both have shown similar improvements since that time. In the January 2008 poll, when Republican George W. Bush was still president, Republicans were slightly more optimistic than Democrats. These party trends, to some degree, reflect the way Republicans' and Democrats' assessments of conditions in the country are influenced by the party of the president.

Perceived Likelihood Today's Youth Will Live a Better Life Than Their Parents, by Party Affiliation

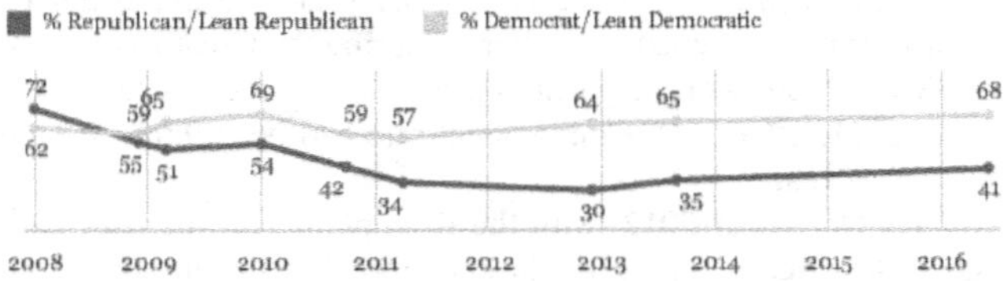

Figures are percentage saying it is very or somewhat likely today's youth will have a better life than their parents did.

GALLUP

In contrast, Republicans (70%) and Democrats (71%) are about equally likely to believe there is plenty of opportunity in the U.S. for those who want to get ahead. There were only modest differences between the party groups in 2013, when Americans were less positive about the ability of people to get ahead. At that time, 58% of Democrats and 48% of Republicans thought there was plenty of opportunity in the U.S.

Implications

A common theme in each party's presidential campaigns this year has been that Americans, particularly those in the middle class, are losing ground and do not have as bright a future as they used to. While Americans are less optimistic about economic opportunity today than they have been at times in the past, that optimism has been increasing rather than decreasing in recent years. The majority of Americans once again believe it is likely today's young people will have a better life than their parents did, and nearly seven in 10 believe ample opportunity to advance exists for those in the U.S. who want to work hard. For Americans' faith in economic opportunity to be fully restored to previous heights, it may necessitate a stronger economic recovery than has occurred to date, and renewed faith in major U.S. institutions.

Historical data are available in Gallup Analytics.

Survey Methods

Results for this Gallup poll are based on telephone interviews conducted June 14-23, 2016, with a random sample of 1,025 adults, aged 18 and older, living in all 50 U.S. states and the District of Columbia. The two questions reported here were asked of randomly determined half-samples of approximately 500 respondents each. For results based on these samples of national adults, the margin of sampling error is ±5 percentage points at the 95% confidence level. All reported margins of sampling error include computed design effects for weighting.

July 01, 2016

NEW LOW OF 52% "EXTREMELY PROUD" TO BE AMERICANS

by Jeffrey M. Jones

Story Highlights

- *Percentage extremely proud down from 57% in '13 and 70% in '03*
- *Young adults show largest decline in patriotism over time*
- *Republicans still prouder than before 9/11*

PRINCETON, N.J. – As the nation prepares to celebrate Independence Day, 52% of U.S. adults say they are "extremely proud" to be Americans, a new low in Gallup's 16-year trend. Americans' patriotism spiked after 9/11, peaking at 70% in 2003, but has declined since, including an eight-percentage-point drop in early 2005 and a five-point drop since 2013.

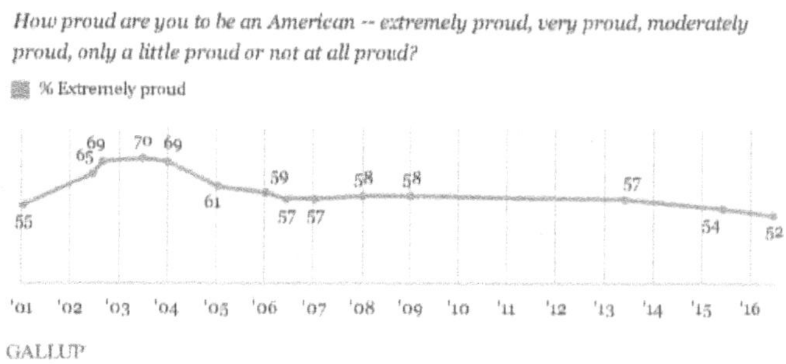

Americans' declining patriotism is likely related to broader dissatisfaction with the way things are going in the U.S. In January 2004, when 69% were extremely proud to be an American, 55% of Americans were satisfied with the way things were going in the U.S. That was the last time satisfaction has been at the majority level, and the percentage satisfied has mostly held below 30% since 2007, including the 29% in Gallup's most recent update.

Americans' patriotism stayed relatively flat from 2006 through 2013, a period that spanned the Great Recession and Barack Obama's election and first term as president. But over the last three years, Americans' willingness to say they are extremely proud to be an American has declined further.

In addition to the 52% who say they are extremely proud in the June 14-23 poll, another 29% say they are very proud and 13% moderately proud, meaning the vast majority of U.S. adults express at least a considerable amount of pride in being Americans. Five percent say they are "only a little proud" and 1% "not at all proud."

Young Adults Lead Decline in Patriotism

Since the 2003 peak, all major subgroups have shown significant declines in the percentage saying they are extremely proud to be Americans. The largest decline has come among young adults, from 60% to 34%. In 2003 as well as today, young adults rank among the subgroups least willing to say they are extremely proud to be Americans.

Changes in Percentage "Extremely Proud" to Be Americans, by Subgroup

	2001 %	2003 %	2016 %	Change, 2003 to 2016 (pct. pts.)
All	55	70	52	-18
Men	54	67	53	-14
Women	56	73	50	-23
18 to 29	51	60	34	-26
30 to 49	56	74	51	-23
50 to 64	57	73	64	-9
65+	57	68	55	-13
Whites	58	73	54	-19
Nonwhites	39	59	45	-14
College grads	58	63	47	-16
College nongrads	54	73	54	-19
Republicans	64	86	68	-18
Independents	46	62	44	-18
Democrats	53	65	45	-20
Conservatives	62	80	61	-19
Moderates	53	68	53	-15
Liberals	49	56	36	-20

Gallup

Young adults today are also one of the few subgroups that are significantly less likely to be patriotic than in January 2001, before the 9/11 rally effect. At that time, 51% of 18- to 29-year-olds were extremely proud to be Americans. Because no one who is 18 to 29 today was in that same age group in 2001 or 2003, the trends in patriotism among young adults could be evidence that those in the millennial generation are less patriotic than young adults in generations that preceded them. And that generational change may help explain why there has been further decline in patriotism among all U.S. adults over the last three years.

Political liberals (36%) join young adults as the least patriotic major subgroup today. Independents, Democrats, nonwhites and college graduates also show below-average patriotism.

Republicans (68%), conservatives (61%) and those aged 50 to 64 (64%) are the major subgroups most likely to say they are extremely proud to be Americans. Republicans, 50- to 64-year-olds and nonwhites are the only groups that are at least somewhat more patriotic today than before 9/11. As a result of Republicans' still-elevated percentage, the 23-point Republican-Democratic gap in patriotism is now roughly double what it was in January 2001.

Implications

The vast majority of U.S. adults indicate they are at least moderately proud to be Americans, but as they celebrate the Fourth of July this year, fewer say they are extremely proud than at any point in the last 16 years. Americans' continued frustration with national conditions – likely tied to their concern about the economy and lack of faith in public institutions – is probably one reason patriotism is at a recent low point.

It is unclear to what extent, if any, the presidential campaign that now pits two controversial and widely unpopular nominees against each other could be a factor in Americans' expressed pride. A year ago – long before the presidential field was set – there were signs that patriotism was declining further.

Millennials' greater reluctance than young adults before them to say they are extremely proud to be an American may also be a factor in the new low and, if so, could signal further declines in patriotism in the years and decades ahead.

Historical data are available in Gallup Analytics.

Survey Methods

Results for this Gallup poll are based on telephone interviews conducted June 14-23, 2016, with a random sample of 1,025 adults, aged 18 and older, living in all 50 U.S. states and the District of Columbia. For results based on the total sample of national adults, the margin of sampling error is ±4 percentage points at the 95% confidence level. All reported margins of sampling error include computed design effects for weighting.

Learn more about how the Gallup Poll Social Series work

July 01, 2016
AMERICANS' REACTIONS TO TRUMP, CLINTON EXPLAIN POOR IMAGES

by Justin McCarthy

Story Highlights

- *Half of Americans have negative reactions to Clinton*
- *Two in three react negatively to Trump*

WASHINGTON, D.C. – Americans' initial reactions to Hillary Clinton and Donald Trump are largely negative, which helps explain their negative images. When Americans are asked what comes to mind when they think of Clinton, many say they don't trust her (27%), don't like her (13%) and that she is a criminal or corrupt (8%). Trump elicits a variety of complaints about his personality, with 16% saying they dislike him, and others describing him as an "idiot" or a "joke" (12%), a "racist" or a "bigot" (10%), "reckless" or "dangerous" (8%), or someone who speaks without thinking (7%).

Top Unaided Reactions to "Hillary Clinton" and "Donald Trump"

What comes to your mind when you think about -- ? [OPEN-ENDED]

Hillary Clinton	%	Donald Trump	%
Don't trust her/Dishonest/Unethical	27	Dislike him/Negative view	16
Dislike/Don't care for her	13	Idiot/Joke/Embarrassing/Crazy	12
Capable of being president/ Qualified/Experienced	12	Racist/Bigot/Anti-women/Hater	10
Crook/Criminal/Corrupt/Should be in jail	8	Reckless/Unpredictable/Dangerous/ Scary	8
Strong/Ambitous/Confident/Good leadership abilities	6	Speaks without thinking/Big mouth/Boisterous	7
She's a woman/Need a woman/Equality for women	5	Strong/Businessman/Leader	7
Bill is her husband/History/Familiar with the whole presidential process	5	Will turn things around/New/Different ideas	7
Benghazi	3	Arrogant/Narcissist/Egotistical/Spoiled/ Selfish	6
Insider/Career politician/ Establishment/Same as Obama	3	Big bully/Dictator/Demagogue	5
Like her/Good person/Good qualities	3	Con artist/Liar/Don't trust	5
		Inexperienced/Unqualified	5
		Best/Good choice/Like him/Only choice	5
		Honest/Truthful/Says it like it is	4

Gallup, June 14-23, 2016

Note: Results mentioned by fewer than 3% are not shown

GALLUP

For Clinton, the latest responses – collected in a June 14-23 survey – reflect that many Americans continue to see her as dishonest and untrustworthy and dislike her in general. These perceptions also dogged her in Gallup's February survey when she was still competing against her Democratic rival, Sen. Bernie Sanders, and they were evident when the same question was asked during her fight for the Democratic nomination in 2008. As she pivots to the general election, she does not appear to have shaken these perceptions because they remain atop the list.

Additionally, 8% say Clinton is a "crook," corrupt or a criminal, while 3% mention Benghazi – a reference to the 2012 attack on the American diplomatic compound in Libya that resulted in the death of the U.S. ambassador to that country while Clinton was secretary of state.

Despite the leading negative responses, many Americans also have positive reactions to Clinton, saying she is capable and qualified to be president (12%), that she displays good leadership (6%) and that her husband's time in the White House gives her a familiarity with presidential responsibilities (5%). Another 5% express the need or desire for a female president.

Trump, too, struggles with Americans' negative perceptions of him – and to an even greater degree than Clinton does. The top four responses Americans offer about the presumptive GOP nominee are disparaging. Large segments simply don't like him generally (16%) or see him as a "joke" or "crazy" (12%). Ten percent describe him as racist or antagonistic or to various segments of the population, including blacks, Hispanics, women and Muslims. Another category of responses mentioned by 8% of Americans is that he is "scary" and that his presidency would pose a danger to the country.

At the same time, many Americans offer positive comments about Trump, focusing on his business acumen or his leadership (7%) and his ability to turn things around with new ideas (7%), and saying they like him (5%) and that he is honest (4%).

The weaknesses outlined here align closely with the language the two candidates are using to attack each other on the campaign trail, with Trump calling Clinton "Crooked Hillary" and Clinton recently warning that Trump is untrustworthy with nuclear codes because he is "thin-skinned and quick to anger."

Half Have Negative Reaction to Clinton; Two-Thirds React Negatively to Trump

One way to summarize the various responses about the candidates is to categorize each comment as positive or negative. Some comments do not have a clear direction and Gallup does not code them as positive or negative.

For both candidates, Americans are more likely to mention something negative than to mention something positive.

While about four in 10 Americans characterize Clinton in positive terms, about half characterize her negatively. Trump has an even greater deficit, with two in three Americans responding with what can be defined as negative impressions and about a quarter responding positively.

Unaided Positive vs. Negative Reactions to "Hillary Clinton" and "Donald Trump"

	Positive reactions	Negative reactions	Difference
	%	%	(pct. pts.)
Clinton	39	51	-12
Trump	27	67	-40

June 14-23, 2016

GALLUP

Bottom Line

With the primaries and caucuses ended, Americans' initial thoughts about the presumptive major-party nominees for president underscore the persistently negative tilt to their favorability ratings and raise serious questions about whether either can unify the country after the election. Because Trump and Clinton have been high-profile figures for many years, it will be challenging for either one to change this in the remaining four months of the campaign. Both, however, will have opportunities to improve the way Americans perceive them – at their party conventions later this month, during the presidential debates and in responding to the various issues that come up between now and Election Day.

Historical data are available in Gallup Analytics.

Survey Methods

Results for this Gallup poll are based on telephone interviews conducted June 14-23, 2016, with a random sample of 1,025 adults, aged 18 and older, living in all 50 U.S. states and the District of Columbia. For results based on the total sample of national adults, the margin of sampling error is ±4 percentage points at the 95% confidence level. All reported margins of sampling error include computed design effects for weighting.

July 01, 2016
TRUMP LEADS CLINTON IN HISTORICALLY BAD IMAGE RATINGS

by Lydia Saad

Story Highlights

- *Trump's poor favorability scores rival Barry Goldwater's*
- *Trump's high unfavorable score sets new record among candidates*
- *Clinton's image also low historically, just above Goldwater's*

PRINCETON, N.J. – Trump and Clinton are currently among the worst-rated presidential candidates of the last seven decades according to Gallup's long-term "scalometer" trend. In the race to the bottom, however, Trump's 42% highly unfavorable score easily outpaces Clinton's 33%. Prior to now, 1964 Republican nominee Barry Goldwater had the highest negative score, with 26% rating him highly unfavorably in October 1964.

Highly Favorable and Highly Unfavorable Ratings of Major Party Presidential Nominees, 1956-2016

Based on U.S. adults; Ranked by % highly favorable

	Nominee	Highly favorable % (+4 to +5)	Highly unfavorable % (-4 to -5)
1956 Oct 18-23	D. Eisenhower	57	4
1964 Oct 8-13	L. Johnson	49	5
1960 Oct 18-23	J. Kennedy	43	5
1984 Sep 21-24	R. Reagan	43	18
1976 Sep 24-27	J. Carter	42	5
1972 Oct 13-16	R. Nixon	41	11
1968 Oct 17-22	R. Nixon	39	8
1960 Oct 18-23	R. Nixon	37	8
2008 Oct 23-26	B. Obama	37	22
2012 Oct 27-28	B. Obama	36	24
2004 Oct 22-24	G.W. Bush	34	23
1956 Oct 18-23	A. Stevenson	34	16
1980 Oct 10-13	J. Carter	31	17
2012 Oct 27-28	M. Romney	30	22
1976 Sep 24-27	G. Ford	29	9
1968 Oct 17-22	H. Humphrey	29	11
1984 Sep 21-24	W. Mondale	28	15
2008 Oct 23-26	J. McCain	28	20
1992 Oct 23-25	B. Clinton	27	15
1980 Oct 10-13	R. Reagan	26	16
1992 Oct 23-25	G.H.W. Bush	25	18
2004 Oct 22-24	J. Kerry	22	22
2016 June 14-23	H. Clinton	22	33
1972 Oct 13-16	G. McGovern	21	20
1964 Oct 8-13	B. Goldwater	17	26
2016 June 14-23	D. Trump	16	42

2016 nominees are presumptive; Dates for all years except 2016 are final pre-election; No data for 1988, 1996 and 2000
Gallup

Gallup's 10-point scalometer favorability scale asks respondents to name a number between +1 and +5 to express a favorable view of a candidate, with +5 indicating a very favorable view. They are asked to name a number from -1 to -5 to indicate an unfavorable view, with -5 being very unfavorable. The survey was conducted by telephone June 14-23 with a nationwide sample of U.S. adults.

Since 1992, Gallup has primarily measured candidate favorability using a binary favorable/unfavorable choice. But Gallup does use the 10-point scale once or twice each campaign to allow for longer-term historical comparisons. The scalometer typically produces positive ratings about 10 points higher than the binary favorable scores.

Trump's Total Favorability Worse Than Goldwater's

In addition to his record-setting highly unfavorable rating, Trump's overall image on the scalometer tilts more negatively than Goldwater's did at his lowest point in 1964. Trump's combined ratings are 42% favorable and 59% unfavorable whereas Goldwater's broke about even at 43% favorable and 47% unfavorable.

Clinton's overall image on the scalometer – 51% favorable vs. 50% unfavorable – is also better than Trump's and slightly more positive than Goldwater's in October 1964. However, her ratings are no match for the Democratic incumbent in that year's election. President Lyndon Johnson had extraordinarily high positive ratings on the scale, reflecting his strong popularity less than a year after he assumed the presidency following John F. Kennedy's assassination. Johnson's total favorable score at the end of the 1964 race was a stellar 81%, with just 13% viewing him unfavorably, and he went on to win re-election by a historically high 61% to 38% in the popular vote.

Both Johnson and Goldwater were viewed a bit better at earlier points in the 1964 race than they were in October of that year. In particular, majorities viewed Goldwater favorably in Gallup's May and August polls. However, even Goldwater's 54% and 52% total favorable scores from these polls stand as some of the lowest in Gallup's records for a presidential nominee.

1964 Trend in Scalometer-Based Favorability Ratings for Barry Goldwater and Lyndon Johnson

Based on U.S. adults

	May 22-27, 1964 %	Aug 6-11, 1964 %	Oct 8-13, 1964 %
Total favorable (+1 to +5)			
L. Johnson	87	87	81
B. Goldwater	54	52	43
Highly favorable (+4 to +5)			
L. Johnson	59	54	49
B. Goldwater	15	21	17

Gallup

The following table displays the final scores for the major candidates in each election since 1956, with no ratings available for 1988, 1996 or 2000. In some cases, the final reading was higher than ratings earlier in the election year, and in other cases, the final reading was lower, making it unclear which way Clinton's and Trump's might go between now and November.

Total Favorable and Unfavorable Ratings of Major Party Presidential Nominees, 1956-2016

Based on U.S. adults; Ranked by % total favorable

	Nominee	Total favorable % (+1 to +5)	Total unfavorable % (-1 to -5)
1956 Oct 18-23	D. Eisenhower	84	12
1964 Oct 8-13	L. Johnson	81	13
1976 Sep 24-27	J. Carter	81	16
1960 Oct 18-23	J. Kennedy	80	14
1968 Oct 17-22	R. Nixon	79	22
1960 Oct 18-23	R. Nixon	79	20
1976 Sep 24-27	G. Ford	78	20
1972 Oct 13-16	R. Nixon	76	22
1968 Oct 17-22	H. Humphrey	72	28
1984 Sep 21-24	R. Reagan	71	30
1980 Oct 10-13	J. Carter	68	32
1984 Sep 21-24	W. Mondale	66	34
1992 Oct 23-25	B. Clinton	65	32
2008 Oct 23-26	J. McCain	64	35
1980 Oct 10-13	R. Reagan	64	37
2008 Oct 23-26	B. Obama	62	35
2012 Oct 27-28	B. Obama	62	37
1956 Oct 18-23	A. Stevenson	61	31
2004 Oct 22-24	G.W. Bush	61	39
1992 Oct 23-25	G.H.W. Bush	60	40
2004 Oct 22-24	J. Kerry	57	40
1972 Oct 13-16	G. McGovern	55	41
2012 Oct 27-28	M. Romney	55	43
2016 June 14-23	H. Clinton	51	50
1964 Oct 8-13	B. Goldwater	43	47
2016 June 14-23	D. Trump	42	59

2016 nominees are presumptive; Dates for all years except 2016 are final pre-election; No data for 1988, 1996 and 2000

Gallup

It is clear from this table that high favorability ratings on the 10-point scale are relegated to the past. No presidential candidate since Ronald Reagan in 1984 has ended his campaign with a total favorable scalometer score above 70%. The highest final pre-election favorable score for more recent candidates was 64%, earned by John McCain in 2008, just a week before he lost to Barack Obama, who was rated favorably by 62%.

It is also worth noting that the lowest final pre-election scalometer favorable rating of any winning candidate since 1956 was 61%, received by George W. Bush in 2004. His opponent that year, John Kerry, had a 57% total favorable score.

Candidates' Relative "Enthusiasm Quotient" May Matter Most

While the overall favorability of the Republican and Democratic candidates was similar in several years, important differences emerge when focusing on the percentage rating the candidate a "+5" or "+4," what Gallup has referred to in the past as the "enthusiasm quotient" (or "EQ") for each candidate.

For instance, although Obama and McCain had nearly identical total favorable scores in 2008, Obama's highly favorable rating was significantly better: 37% for Obama vs. 28% for McCain. A similar phenomenon occurred in 1960, 1976 and 2004, when the winning candidate had an insignificant lead in overall favorability but a sizeable lead in high favorability. And in fact, in all elections but 1980, the candidate with the higher final "EQ" score won the election. That 1980 reading, from mid-October, may not have reflected Americans' impressions of the candidates at the end of the campaign, particularly after the late October debate between Reagan and Jimmy Carter.

In 2016, Clinton leads Trump by six points in high favorability – 22% vs. 16% – even as she leads him by nine points in total favorability. The wild card in this year's ratings is that more Americans view Clinton and Trump highly unfavorably than highly favorably, and to an unprecedented degree. Only two other candidates received such ratings since 1956 – Goldwater in 1964 and independent candidate John Anderson in 1980 – and in both cases, the negative tilt was far less than is seen with Clinton and Trump.

Total Favorable and Unfavorable Ratings of Major Party Presidential Nominees, 1956-2016

Based on U.S. adults; Ranked by % total favorable

	Nominees	Highly favorable % (+4 to +5)	Highly unfavorable % (-4 to -5)
2016 Jun 14-23	Hillary Clinton (D)	22	33
	Donald Trump (R)	16	42
2012 Oct 27-28	Barack Obama (D)	36	24
	Mitt Romney (R)	30	22
2008 Oct 23-26	Barack Obama (D)	37	22
	John McCain (R)	28	20
2004 Oct 22-24	George W. Bush (R)	34	23
	John Kerry (D)	22	22
1992 Oct 23-25	Bill Clinton (D)	27	15
	George Bush (R)	25	18
	Ross Perot (I)	24	11
1984 Sep 21-24	Ronald Reagan (R)	43	18
	Walter Mondale (D)	28	10
1980 Oct 10-13	Jimmy Carter (D)	31	17
	Ronald Reagan (R)	26	16
	John Anderson (I)	11	15
1976 Sep 24-27	Jimmy Carter (D)	42	5
	Gerald Ford (R)	29	9
1972 Oct 13-16	Richard Nixon (R)	41	11
	George McGovern (D)	21	20
1968 Oct 17-22	Richard Nixon (R)	39	8
	Hubert Humphrey (D)	29	11
1964 Oct 8-13	Lyndon Johnson (D)	49	5
	Barry Goldwater (R)	17	26
1960 Oct 18-23	John F. Kennedy (D)	43	5
	Richard Nixon (R)	38	8
1956 Oct 18-23	Dwight Eisenhower (R)	57	4
	Adlai Stevenson (D)	34	16

2016 nominees are presumptive; Dates for all years except 2016 are final pre-election; No data for 1988, 1996 and 2000
Gallup

Bottom Line

Trump's image in 2016 is worse than Goldwater's was in 1964, giving Trump – at least for the moment – the distinction of having the highest negative scores on Gallup's scalometer of any presidential candidate rated since 1956. But that is only half the equation. Clinton's ratings are not much better than Trump's and are nowhere near as high as those of Goldwater's opponent in 1964, Lyndon Johnson – meaning the fundamentals are not in place for a re-run of the 1964 Democratic landslide.

Still, at present, Clinton beats Trump in total favorability as well as in high favorability from the American public. While favorable scores can and do change over the course of campaigns, she is currently positioned as the stronger candidate. However, her positioning would be improved by widening her lead over Trump in high favorability, not just total favorability.

Historical data are available in Gallup Analytics.

Survey Methods

Results for this Gallup poll are based on telephone interviews conducted June 14-23, 2016, with a random sample of 1,025 adults, aged 18 and older, living in all 50 U.S. states and the District of Columbia. For results based on the total sample of national adults, the margin of sampling error is ±4 percentage points at the 95% confidence level. All reported margins of sampling error include computed design effects for weighting.

Research Note

The 10-point scalometer was Gallup's standard method of measuring the likeability or favorability of public figures in the days of in-person interviewing. With its adoption of telephone polls in the 1980s, Gallup switched to a simpler "mostly favorable" to "mostly unfavorable" verbal scale before adopting the present day "favorable" or "unfavorable" question. Thus, the scalometer provides the only basis for systematically comparing the popularity of modern-day presidential candidates to those of 1984 or earlier. Additionally, Gallup has asked the question in October of each election year since 2004 to allow for historical comparison of the candidates in those election years.

Gallup research indicates that candidates score higher favorability on the scalometer than with today's favorable/unfavorable question. This is likely because some respondents who feel ambivalent about a candidate and would choose "unfavorable" on today's question offer a mild positive score when given the opportunity on the 10-point scalometer. This holds for the 2016 candidates as Clinton and Trump both receive 10 points higher favorable ratings with the scalometer than with the straight favorable question in Gallup Daily tracking over the same time period. Clinton and Trump's Daily tracking favorable scores are available in the Presidential Election 2016: Key Indicators center on Gallup.com.

July 05, 2016
AMERICANS' SELF-REPORTS OF SPENDING DOWN SLIGHTLY IN JUNE

by Jeffrey M. Jones

Story Highlights

- *Daily self-reports of spending averaged $88 in June*
- *Down from $93 in May and $95 in April*
- *June spending typically the same as or lower than May's*

PRINCETON, N.J. – Americans' daily self-reports of spending averaged $88 in June, a retreat from the higher levels recorded in April ($95) and May ($93).

Amount of Money Americans Report Spending "Yesterday," Monthly Averages

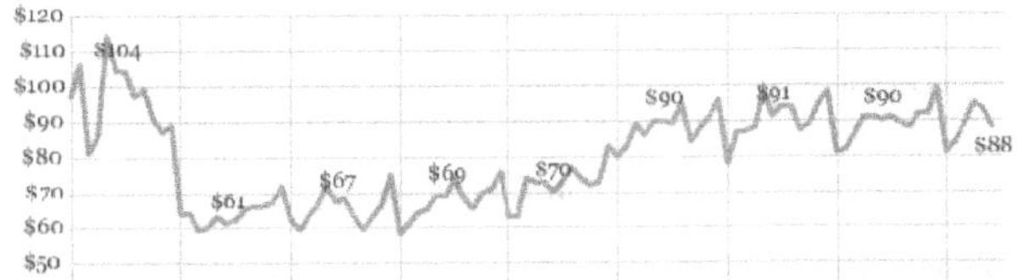

Figures shown are for June of each year.
Gallup Daily tracking

GALLUP

These results are based on Gallup Daily tracking interviews conducted throughout June. Gallup asks Americans each night to report how much they spent "yesterday," excluding normal household bills and major purchases such as a home or car. The measure gives an indication of discretionary spending.

Americans' spending in June started out strong, with U.S. adults' estimates of their spending averaging $95 from June 1 through June 15 – essentially in line with spending in April and May. But consumers appeared to pull back significantly in the second half of the month, with daily reports of spending averaging a much lower $82. Gallup did not observe meaningful differences in first-half versus second-half spending estimates in May or in any prior June.

Although the precise relationship between consumers' evaluations of the economy and their personal spending is unclear, Gallup's Economic Confidence Index also fell slightly in the second half of June compared with where it was in the first half. That decline was apparent prior to Britons' voting to leave the European Union, a move that sent financial markets around the world tumbling. U.S. stocks have since recovered most of the losses.

One possible explanation for the later June spending swoon is that consumers were curtailing their expenditures in anticipation of the July Fourth holiday. The average spending estimate for the first three days of July – data not reported in the figures for June – was $112. That is substantially higher than any prior July 1-3 estimate, which range from a low of $68 in 2009 to a high of $97 in 2008. Last year, the average for July 1-3 was $89.

June Spending Typically Similar to or Lower Than May's

There is nothing unusual about June's average spending level failing to match May's. In the nine years Gallup has asked its daily spending measure, the June average has yet to exceed the May average. This year's May-to-June drop, in fact, is similar to the average decline of $4 since 2008.

Monthly Averages of Amount Spent "Yesterday"

May through June, 2008-2016

	May $	June $	Change $
2016	93	88	-5
2015	91	90	-1
2014	98	91	-7
2013	90	90	0
2012	73	70	-3
2011	69	69	0
2010	72	67	-5
2009	63	61	-2
2008	114	104	-10

Gallup Daily tracking

Implications

Gallup's healthy April and May spending estimates were consistent with subsequent Department of Commerce reports of strong retail spending. And June was off to a solid start before consumers appeared to pull back significantly in the second half of the month. The reasons for that pullback are not entirely clear, but the late-month drop is not typical of normal spending patterns.

What is typical, however, is that Gallup's June spending reports usually fail to match those for May. From that perspective, the most recent June numbers are not necessarily disappointing, but the second-half drop does indicate June could have been a much stronger month than it ended up being.

Looking ahead, Gallup's July spending estimates are usually similar to those from June. In most cases, the July figure is slightly higher than June's – but not to a meaningful degree, with an average increase of $2 since 2008.

That said, this month is off to an auspicious start, with consumer reports of spending this past holiday weekend the best Gallup has measured for the first three days of July in any of the past nine years, and indicates that the late June pullback in spending was likely temporary.

These data are available in Gallup Analytics.

Survey Methods

Results for this Gallup poll are based on telephone interviews conducted June 1-30, 2016, on the Gallup U.S. Daily survey, with a random sample of 15,233 adults, aged 18 and older, living in all 50 U.S. states and the District of Columbia. For results based on the total sample of national adults, the margin of error for the spending mean is ±$4 at the 95% confidence level. All reported margins of sampling error include computed design effects for weighting.

July 05, 2016
U.S. ECONOMIC CONFIDENCE INDEX STEADY IN JUNE AT -14

by Justin McCarthy

Story Highlights

- *June's index average matched that of April and May*
- *Confidence higher in the first half of the month, fell in second half*
- *Economic outlook component remains lowest since November 2013*

WASHINGTON, D.C. – Gallup's U.S. Economic Confidence Index averaged -14 in June, the same reading as in April and May. Confidence ticked slightly higher earlier in the month – with the index averaging -12 each of the first two weeks – but retreated near the end, with subsequent weekly readings of -15 and -17.

Gallup's U.S. Economic Confidence Index -- Monthly Averages

January 2008-June 2016

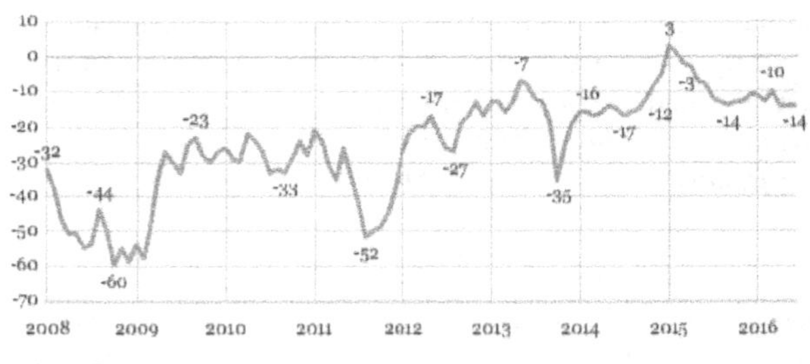

Gallup Daily tracking

GALLUP

As economists ponder the long-term effect of the United Kingdom's decision on June 23 to exit the European Union, Gallup's June data show no immediate effect on Americans' confidence in the U.S. economy. The referendum did cause instantaneous turmoil in U.S. markets, which have since recovered, but the long-term effect of Brexit on the U.S. economy – and by extension, Americans' confidence in it – is unclear.

Americans' economic confidence began to slide in the first week of June before the Brexit vote and remained lower the following week, perhaps related to the anxiety leading up to the British referendum. Although the latest weekly figure is on the low end of what Gallup recorded in 2015 and thus far in 2016, it is much higher than all monthly readings from 2008 to 2011.

Gallup's U.S. Economic Confidence Index is the average of two components: how Americans rate current economic conditions and whether they feel the economy is improving or getting worse. The index has a theoretical maximum of +100 if all Americans were to say the economy is doing well and improving, and a theoretical minimum of -100 if all Americans were to say the economy is doing poorly and getting worse.

In June, the current conditions score registered -6, the result of 25% of U.S. adults rating the current economy as "excellent" or "good" and 31% rating it as "poor." June's result is consistent with the -1 to -7 range for this component since April of last year. Meanwhile, the economic outlook score in June remained at -22, the same as in May and the lowest this component has been since November 2013. The outlook score is based on 37% of U.S. adults saying the economy is "getting better" and 59% saying it is "getting worse."

Gallup's U.S. Economic Confidence Index Components -- Monthly Averages

November 2013–June 2016

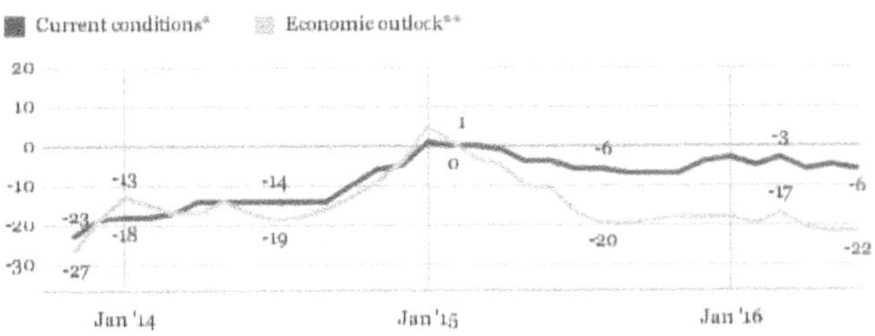

* % (Excellent + Good) minus % Poor

** % Getting better minus % Getting worse

Gallup Daily tracking

GALLUP

Bottom Line

Though economic confidence overall in June was flat compared with previous months, there was movement within the month, with more positive ratings earlier in the month yielding to more negative readings near the end.

There are reasons to be optimistic for July, however. The Dow Jones industrial average regained its footing after an immediate post-Brexit drop, and some members of the Federal Reserve Board predict the British referendum decision will have little to no effect on the U.S. economy.

These data are available in Gallup Analytics.

Survey Methods

Results for this Gallup poll are based on telephone interviews conducted June 1-30, 2016, on the Gallup U.S. Daily survey, with a random sample of 15,162 adults, aged 18 and older, living in all 50 U.S. states and the District of Columbia. For results based on the total sample of national adults, the margin of sampling error is ±1 percentage point at the 95% confidence level. All reported margins of sampling error include computed design effects for weighting.

July 06, 2016

AMERICANS: MAJOR DONORS SWAY CONGRESS MORE THAN CONSTITUENTS

by Michael W. Traugott

Story Highlights

- *64% say major donors have a lot of influence on congressional votes*
- *By contrast, only 14% say people in districts have a lot of influence*
- *These views are universal regardless of party identification*

PRINCETON, N.J. – Large majorities of Americans believe that major donors and lobbyists have a significant amount of influence on how members of Congress vote on legislation, while far fewer think members' constituents have this much influence.

How much influence do you think each of the following has on how members of Congress vote on legislation?

	A lot %	A fair amount %	Only a little %	None %	No opinion %
Major donors	64	21	10	3	2
Lobbyists	55	24	14	4	2
Party leaders in Congress	45	33	17	2	1
People in the district they represent	14	29	49	6	2

Gallup, June 1-5, 2016

These results, based on Gallup poll data collected June 1-5, help illustrate the nature of the contentious relationship between Americans and the elected officials who represent them in Congress. Of the four groups asked about, Americans perceive that major donors have the most influence – 64% say they have "a lot" of influence – followed by lobbyists (55%). Slightly less than half of U.S. adults (45%) say that party leaders in Congress have a lot of influence on voting decisions, while one in seven (14%) believe that constituents have the same level of influence.

Americans' responses to this direct question present a different view of the public's concerns about Congress compared with their answers to an open-ended question about why they rate Congress' performance as "poor" or "bad." The results of that question revealed a top-of-mind focus on Congress' inability to compromise and get things done, while these results help show possible reasons for Americans' perceptions of congressional inaction.

In the current study, perceptions of the extent to which each of the four groups has a lot of influence are unrelated to party identification. Similar percentages of Republicans, independents and Democrats say that each of the four groups has a major influence on congressional voting.

How much influence do you think each of the following has on how members of Congress vote on legislation? (by party ID)

% A lot

	Republicans %	Independents %	Democrats %	Total %
Major donors	67	63	62	64
Lobbyists	59	55	53	55
Party leaders in Congress	46	46	45	45
People in the district they represent	14	14	14	14

Gallup, June 1-5, 2016

The extent of a person's political knowledge and how much attention he or she pays to the news media do make a difference in these evaluations. Gallup constructed an index of political knowledge using five questions, with the score ranging from zero to 5 based on a person's number of correct answers. The questions cover five basic facts about Congress, its leadership and its operations.

Those who are the most knowledgeable (i.e., have the highest scores on the index) are more likely than less knowledgeable Americans to say major donors, lobbyists and party leaders in Congress have a lot of influence on voting decisions. By contrast, only 8% of the most knowledgeable – versus 18% of the least knowledgeable – believe that the people in members' districts have this same level of influence. These data confirm the same basic patterns found in previous research showing that the most knowledgeable Americans are the most negative about Congress.

How much influence do you think each of the following has on how members of Congress vote on legislation? (by political knowledge score)

% A lot

	Very knowledgeable (4-5) %	Somewhat knowledgeable (2-3) %	Not very knowledgeable (0-1) %	Total %
Major donors	78	75	49	64
Lobbyists	78	62	40	55
Party leaders in Congress	59	49	36	45
People in the district they represent	8	13	18	14

Gallup, June 1-5, 2016

Bottom Line

Previous research shows Americans are highly likely to agree with statements asserting that financial contributors, lobbyists and special interests have too much influence over members of Congress. The current findings reinforce this basic understanding of the way in which Americans view their elected representatives, and provide context for the low levels of confidence that Americans have in their members of Congress. U.S. adults are more than four times as likely to say major donors have a lot of influence on congressional voting as to say the same about congressional constituents, and those views are more pronounced among Americans who know the most about how Congress works.

Historical data are available in Gallup Analytics.

Michael W. Traugott, Ph.D., is a Gallup Senior Scientist.

Survey Methods

Results for this Gallup poll are based on telephone interviews conducted June 1-5, 2016, with a random sample of 1,027 adults, aged 18 and older, living in all 50 U.S. states and the District of Columbia. For results based on the total sample of national adults, the margin of sampling error is ±4 percentage points at the 95% confidence level. All reported margins of sampling error include computed design effects for weighting.

July 06, 2016

U.S. JOB CREATION HOLDS AT EIGHT-YEAR HIGH IN JUNE

by Justin McCarthy

Story Highlights

- *Index at high of +33, same as in May*
- *Perceptions of hiring in the Midwest reach new high for any region*

WASHINGTON, D.C. – U.S. workers' reports of hiring activity at their place of employment in June held at the record high first achieved in May. The +33 Job Creation Index score for June represents 44% of employees saying their employer is hiring workers and expanding the size of its workforce minus the 11% saying their employer is letting workers go.

Gallup Job Creation Index -- Monthly Averages, Full Trend

The index is computed as the percentage of workers who say their employer is hiring workers/expanding the size of its workforce minus the percentage who say their employer is letting workers go/reducing the size of its workforce.

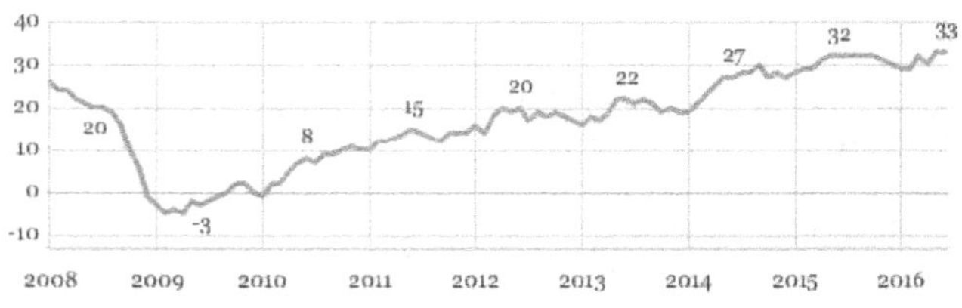

Note: Numbers shown are June readings for each year

Gallup U.S. Daily tracking

GALLUP

Gallup has asked workers to report on hiring activity at their places of employment since 2008. The index was negative between December 2008 and August 2009 amid the Great Recession – meaning more U.S. workers reported a loss of jobs rather than hiring at their places of employment – but steadily improved since then. For much of 2015, the Job Creation Index stayed at a then-record +32 before falling back in the late fall and winter months to scores of +29 and +30. But workers' reports brightened in the spring, with the index reaching a new high +33 in May.

The latest Job Creation Index is based on interviews with 17,930 U.S. adults who are employed full or part time, conducted throughout the month of June. In addition to the 44% of workers reporting a net hiring increase and the 11% reporting a net hiring decrease, 39% of employees say the size of their workforce is unchanged.

Hiring and Firing Nationwide, Monthly Averages, January 2008-June 2016

Note: Numbers shown are June readings for each year

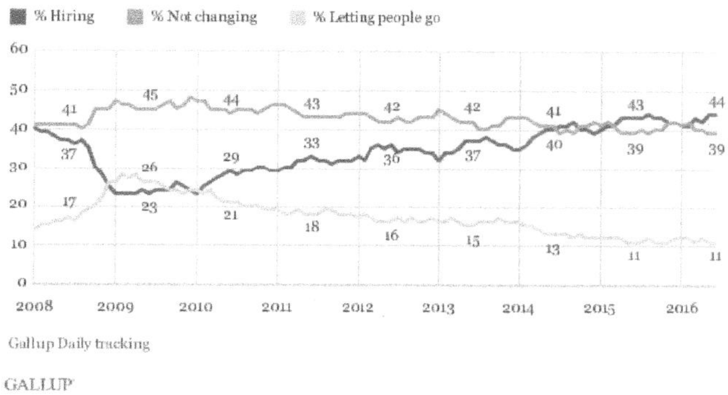

Perceptions of Hiring in the Midwest Best for Any Region Since '08

Of the four major U.S. regions, the Midwest has the highest job creation index (+37), followed by the West (+34), with the East and South (both +31) slightly further behind. The Midwest had led the other regions most of last summer before falling behind the West in the winter months. As the weather warms again, the Midwest has re-emerged as the strongest region for hiring.

The Midwest's +37 index score is notable as the highest Gallup has measured for any region in its eight-year trend, but it is not significantly better than the region's scores of +36 on two occasions last summer.

Gallup Job Creation Index -- Monthly Averages by Region, Recent Trend

The index is computed as the percentage of workers who say their employer is hiring workers/expanding the size of its workforce minus the percentage who say their employer is letting workers go/reducing the size of its workforce.

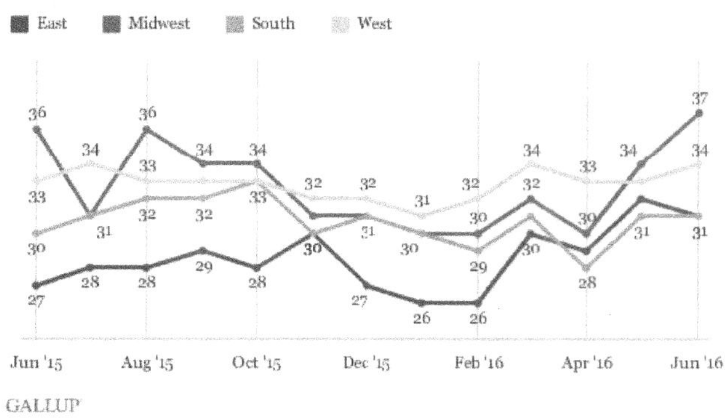

Bottom Line

Workers' perceptions of employers' hiring remain stronger than at any point in the last eight years. These perceptions of job creation can produce different results from other indicators of job growth the government measures in part because Gallup's measure gets at workers' general views of hiring and firing at the company level but does not quantify the extent of that activity or the types of jobs involved. However, the fact that only 11% of workers say that their employer is letting workers go, while four times that many say their company is hiring, suggests a relatively positive jobs situation at this juncture.

These data are available in Gallup Analytics.

Survey Methods

Results for this Gallup poll are based on telephone interviews conducted June 1-30, 2016, on the Gallup U.S. Daily survey, with a random sample of 17,930 adults, aged 18 and older, living in all 50 U.S. states and the District of Columbia who are employed full- or part-time. For results based on the total sample of working adults, the margin of sampling error is ±1 percentage points at the 95% confidence level. All reported margins of sampling error include computed design effects for weighting.

July 07, 2016

BUSH STILL LEADS OBAMA IN BLAME FOR U.S. ECONOMIC TROUBLES

by Lydia Saad

Story Highlights

- *More than six in 10 think Bush merits blame for economy's ills*
- *Half of Americans point finger at Obama*
- *Little change in these perceptions since 2011*

PRINCETON, N.J. – As Barack Obama's two-term presidency enters its final months, more Americans still blame George W. Bush than Obama for the nation's economic ills. When asked how much they blame each president for current economic problems, 64% of Americans say Bush deserves a "great deal" or "moderate amount" of blame, compared with 50% for Obama.

Amount Americans Blame Each President for Current Economic Problems

Thinking about the economic problems currently facing the United States, how much do you blame [George W. Bush/Barack Obama] for these -- a great deal, a moderate amount, not much or not at all?

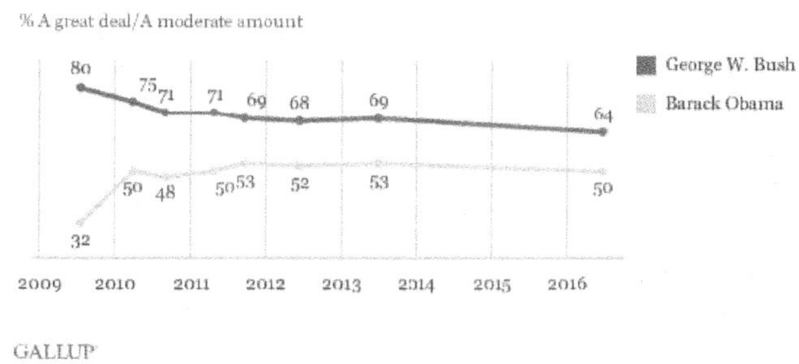

Both presidents receive slightly less blame in the June 14-23 Gallup poll than they did the last time Gallup asked this question in 2013, but the gap has held steady over the past three years, with Bush blamed more than Obama.

The overall percentage of Americans blaming Bush a great deal or moderate amount has consistently exceeded the percentage blaming Obama throughout Obama's presidency. However, it was much more lopsided in the first few years after Bush left office – namely in Obama's honeymoon year (2009), and to a lesser extent in 2010. That, of course, was in the aftermath of the 2008 Wall Street financial crisis that occurred on Bush's watch, an event that 60% of Americans described at the time as the biggest economic crisis the U.S. had faced in their lifetime.

Currently, a quarter of Americans blame each president "a great deal" for current economic problems. But more blame Bush than Obama "a moderate amount," leading to the finding that more Americans overall assign significant responsibility to the former president. Just 35% blame Bush "not much" or "not at all," compared with 50% assigning little or no blame to Obama.

Amount Americans Blame Each President for Current Economic Problems

	George W. Bush %	Barack Obama %
A great deal	27	25
A moderate amount	37	25
Not much	24	29
Not at all	11	21
No opinion	1	1

Gallup, June 14-23, 2016

Republicans More Likely to Blame Bush Than Democrats to Blame Obama

Americans' perspectives on each president's culpability for the current economy are largely rooted in their partisan orientation. More than four in five Democrats blame Bush a moderate amount or great deal, and a similar proportion of Republicans blame Obama to the same degree.

At the same time, Republicans are far more likely to blame Bush than Democrats are to blame Obama (44% vs. 19%, respectively). Political independents are more balanced in their finger-pointing but are still more likely to blame Bush (61%) than Obama (50%).

Amount Americans Blame Each President for Current Economic Problems, by Party ID

% A great deal/A moderate amount

	Republicans %	Independents %	Democrats %
George W. Bush	44	61	83
Barack Obama	83	50	19

Gallup, June 14-23, 2016

As president, Obama has not received stellar approval ratings on the economy. Since the end of his honeymoon period in 2009, more Americans have disapproved than approved of the job he is doing on the issue. However, the fact that Americans have consistently blamed Obama's predecessor more than they blame him for the country's economic problems may explain why his overall job approval rating has consistently exceeded his economic approval rating as well as Americans' general satisfaction with the country.

The following graph aligns the three ratings – Obama's overall job approval rating, his approval rating on the economy and the percentage of Americans satisfied with the direction of the country – from February 2009 through the most recent measure of Obama's economic approval rating in February 2016. It shows that his overall approval rating has consistently exceeded his economic rating and that both ratings have far exceeded Americans' broader satisfaction with the direction of the country.

President Barack Obama's Job Ratings and U.S. Satisfaction

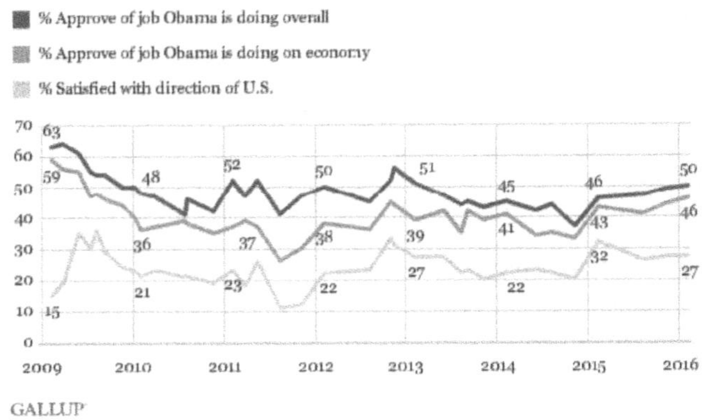

Bottom Line

Neither the passage of time nor Republicans' attempts to pin the nation's sluggish economic recovery on Obama's policies have erased many Americans' belief that the economic problems facing the country are rooted in George W. Bush's presidency. Although half of Americans think Obama is at least moderately to blame for current economic problems, they blame Bush more.

The broader finding – that more than seven years after Bush left office, nearly two-thirds of Americans still think he deserves significant blame for economic issues – speaks to the magnitude of the problems Obama inherited when he took office. Americans recognized them at the time and evidently haven't forgotten who was in charge when they occurred. This awareness has likely colored the entirety of Obama's presidency – keeping his job approval ratings at arm's length from Americans' persistently negative economic confidence and resulting low satisfaction with the direction of the country. In turn, it will likely be a major factor in how his presidency is defined in the coming years.

Historical data are available in Gallup Analytics.

Survey Methods

Results for this Gallup poll are based on telephone interviews conducted June 14-23, 2016, with a random sample of 1,025 adults, aged 18 and older, living in all 50 U.S. states and the District of Columbia. For results based on the total sample of national adults, the margin of sampling error is ±4 percentage points at the 95% confidence level. All reported margins of sampling error include computed design effects for weighting.

July 07, 2016
MOST IN U.S. OPPOSE COLLEGES CONSIDERING RACE IN ADMISSIONS

by Frank Newport

Story Highlights

- *Seven in 10 Americans say merit should be only basis for college admissions*
- *65% disagree with Supreme Court decision allowing race to be a factor*
- *By 50% to 44%, blacks favor merit, not race*

PRINCETON, N.J. – Americans continue to believe colleges should admit applicants based solely on merit (70%), rather than taking into account applicants' race and ethnicity in order to promote diversity (26%). These findings suggest Americans would disagree with the Supreme Court's recent decision in Fisher v. University of Texas, in which the court essentially ruled that colleges can continue to consider race as a factor in their admissions decisions to increase diversity on their campuses.

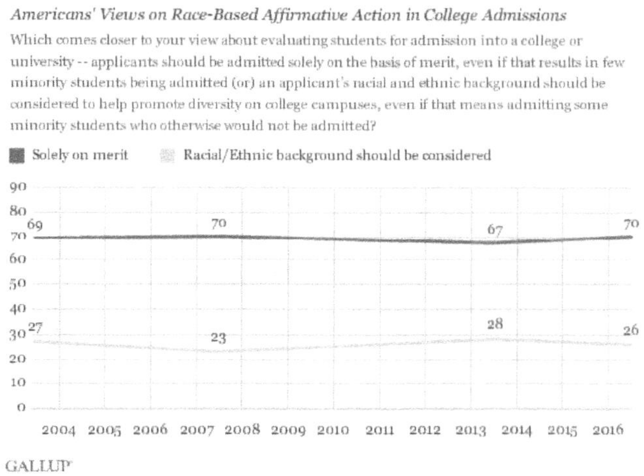

Gallup previously asked this question as part of its Minority Rights and Relations poll in 2003, 2007 and 2013, and Americans' views since 2003 have held steady.

Gallup, in collaboration with *Inside Higher Ed*, also asked a slightly different question focusing directly on the Fisher v. University of Texas decision in a separate June 29-July 2 poll. The question described it as "a case that confirms that colleges can consider the race or ethnicity of students when making decisions on who to admit to the college." The results were similar to the more generic Gallup trend question, with 65% disapproving and 31% approving of the Supreme Court decision.

The Supreme Court recently ruled on a case that confirms that colleges can consider the race or ethnicity of students when making decisions on who to admit to the college. Overall, do you approve or disapprove of the Supreme Court's decision?

	Approve %	Disapprove %	No opinion %
Jun 29-Jul 2, 2016	31	65	4

Gallup

Americans were asked in the latter poll to react to a list of nine factors that colleges and universities could consider when making admissions decisions. Using a question format that differed from the way the first two questions were asked, the results still showed that Americans tend to reject taking race into account in such decisions, with 63% saying race or ethnicity should not be a factor at all in admissions and 9% saying that they should be a "major factor."

Americans' low support for taking race/ethnicity into account stands in sharp contrast to their widespread agreement that high school grades should be a major factor in admissions. A majority of Americans also say that scores on standardized tests and the types of courses a student takes in high school should weigh heavily.

Next I'm going to read some different factors colleges and universities may consider when making admissions decisions. For each one, please say if you think it should be a major factor, a minor factor or not a factor at all in college admissions.

Sorted by "major factor"

	Major factor %	Minor factor %	Not a factor %	No opinion %
High school grades	73	20	6	1
Scores on standardized tests like the SAT or ACT	55	33	10	2
The types of courses the student took in high school	50	31	19	1
The family's economic circumstances	31	30	39	1
Whether the student would be the first person in the family to attend college	31	27	41	1
Athletic ability	15	40	44	1
Parent is an alumni of the school	11	35	52	2
Race or ethnicity	9	27	63	1
Gender	8	25	66	2

Gallup, June 29-July 2, 2016

Differences by Race

There are differences between whites, blacks and Hispanics in response to the question asking if race or ethnicity should be taken into account in college admissions decisions in order to promote diversity, with 44% of blacks agreeing, compared with 22% of whites and 29% of Hispanics. Still, half of blacks are more likely to agree with the merit approach.

At the same time, these groups' views of the Supreme Court decision are similar, with all three much more likely to disapprove of it than approve.

When asked about the list of nine possible factors colleges can consider in admissions, whites are less likely than blacks or Hispanics to say race should be a major factor in colleges' decisions. But the differences are only a matter of degree: 4% of whites, 17% of blacks and 26% of Hispanics say race and ethnicity should be a major factor.

Americans' Views on Consideration of Race in College Admissions

	Non-Hispanic whites %	Non-Hispanic blacks %	Hispanics %
Evaluating students for college admissions			
Admit applicants solely on merit	76	50	61
Take race/ethnicity into account	22	44	29
Approve or disapprove of Supreme Court's decision?			
Approve	30	35	25
Disapprove	66	63	65
How should race or ethnicity factor into admissions decisions?			
Should be a major factor	4	17	26
Should be a minor factor	29	26	20
Should not be a factor at all	67	57	47

Gallup, June 7-July 1, 2016 (Evaluating question); June 29-July 1, 2016 (Supreme Court and Factor questions)

Implications

The Fisher v. University of Texas Supreme Court decision does not require colleges to take race and ethnicity into account, but makes it constitutionally legal to do so if it promotes diversity in certain situations. Many colleges and universities who are selective in their admissions process already use racial and ethnic background as a factor in making admissions decisions, and college presidents have come out in support of the Supreme Court decision, which allows them to continue that practice. However, the process seems to run counter to Americans' belief that race should not be a factor in making college admissions decisions.

It is possible that when Americans think about taking race into account, they think mostly about race being used to discriminate against minorities and to prevent them from having equal opportunities – rather than the reverse issue at the heart of the Supreme Court decision, which involves taking race into account in ways that help minorities.

Americans also might not understand the reasons colleges feel committed to increasing racial and ethnic diversity. But Gallup finds that Americans who say they are most familiar with the college admissions process in the June 29-July 2 survey do not differ substantially from others in their views of the Supreme Court decision, or on whether race and ethnicity should be a factor in the college admissions process. Therefore, lack of knowledge about college admissions does not appear to be driving Americans' rejection of race-sensitive admissions.

Read Inside Higher Ed's analysis of the data.

These data are available in Gallup Analytics.

Survey Methods

Results for this Gallup poll are based on telephone interviews conducted June 7-July 1, 2016, with a sample of 3,270 adults, aged 18 and older, living in all 50 U.S. states and the District of Columbia, who had previously been interviewed in the Gallup Daily tracking poll and agreed to be re-interviewed for a later study. The sample is weighted to be representative of U.S. adults.

For results based on the total sample of national adults, the margin of sampling error is ±3 percentage points at the 95% confidence level. For results based on the sample of 1,320 non-Hispanic whites, the margin of sampling error is ±4 percentage points at the 95% confidence level. For results based on the sample of 912 non-Hispanic blacks, the margin of sampling error is ±5 percentage points at the 95% confidence level. For results based on the sample of 906 Hispanics, the margin of sampling error is ±6 percentage points at the 95% confidence level. (271 out of the 906 interviews with Hispanics were conducted in Spanish.)

All reported margins of sampling error include computed design effects for weighting.

Results for questions asked June 29-July 1, 2016, as part of Gallup Daily interviewing, are based on the total sample of 2,036 adults, aged 18 and older. For results based on the total sample of national adults, the margin of sampling error is ±3% at the 95% confidence level. For results based on the total sample of 1,526 non-Hispanic whites, the margin of sampling error is ±4 percentage points at the 95% confidence level. For results based on the total sample of 182 non-Hispanic blacks, the margin of sampling error is ±7 percentage points at the 95% confidence level. For results based on the total sample of 195 Hispanics, the margin of sampling error is ±7 percentage points at the 95% confidence level. All reported margins of sampling error include computed design effects for weighting.

Learn more about how the Gallup Poll Social Series works.

July 07, 2016

U.S. GALLUP GOOD JOBS RATE EDGES TO NEW HIGH IN JUNE

by Ben Ryan

Story Highlights

- *Highest Gallup Good Jobs rate in six years of measurement*
- *Unemployment down to 5.3%, lowest in any June since 2010*
- *Workforce participation at 67.5%*

WASHINGTON, D.C. – The Gallup Good Jobs (GGJ) rate in the U.S. was 46.0% in June. This is up nominally from May (45.5%) and stands as the highest monthly rate Gallup has recorded since measurement began in 2010. The current rate is also half a percentage point higher than in June 2015, suggesting an underlying increase in full-time work beyond seasonal changes in employment.

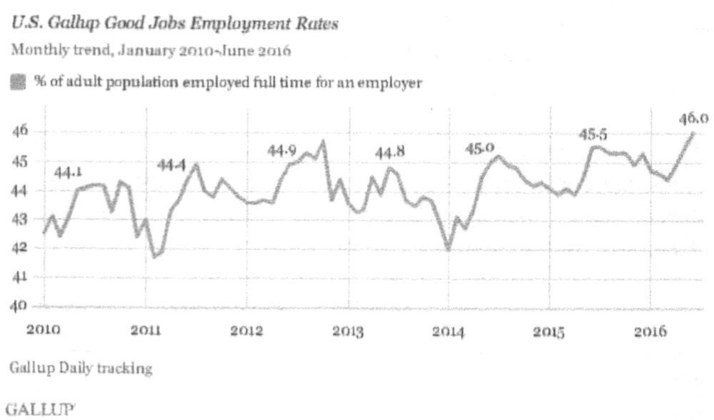

The GGJ metric tracks the percentage of U.S. adults, aged 18 and older, who work for an employer full time – at least 30 hours per week. Gallup does not count adults who are self-employed, work fewer than 30 hours per week, are unemployed or are out of the workforce as payroll-employed in the GGJ metric.

The latest results are based on Gallup Daily tracking interviews with 30,395 U.S. adults, conducted June 1-30 by landline telephone and cellphone. GGJ is not seasonally adjusted.

Workforce Participation at 67.5% in June

The percentage of U.S. adults in June who participated in the workforce – by working full time, part time or not working but actively seeking and being available for work – was 67.5%. This is up nominally from May's 67.3% and above the 66.9% average workforce participation rate since June 2013. Current workforce participation is slightly lower than the period from May 2010 to June 2013 when it averaged 67.7%.

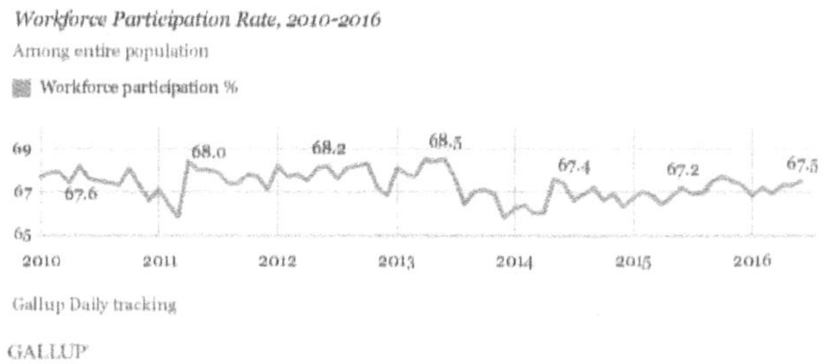

Unemployment at 5.3%

Gallup's unadjusted U.S. unemployment rate was 5.3% in June, down nominally from May's 5.5%. June's unemployment estimate is the second lowest for any month since Gallup began tracking the measure in 2010, after reaching 5.2% in April of this year. Gallup's U.S. unemployment rate represents the percentage of adults in the workforce who did not have any paid work in the past seven days, either for an employer or for themselves, and who were actively looking for and available to work.

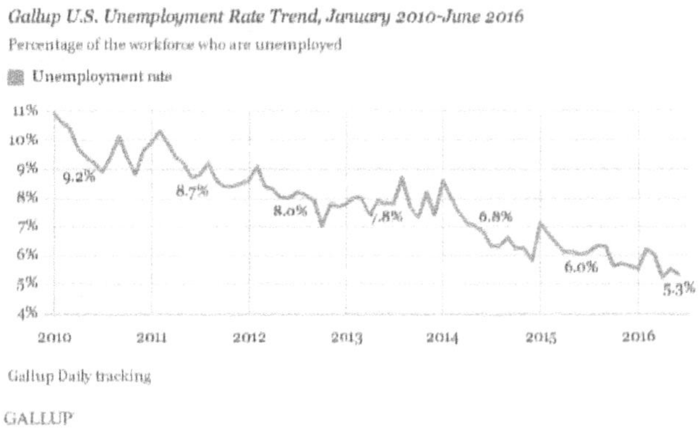

Unlike the Gallup Good Jobs rate, which is a percentage of the total population, the unemployment rates that Gallup and the U.S. Bureau of Labor Statistics (BLS) report are percentages of the labor force. While both Gallup and BLS data are based on surveys with large sample sizes, the two have important methodological differences – outlined at the end of this article. Additionally, the most-discussed unemployment rate released by the BLS each month is seasonally adjusted, while Gallup reports unadjusted numbers. Although Gallup's unemployment numbers strongly correlate with BLS rates, the BLS and Gallup estimates of unemployment do not always track precisely on a monthly basis.

Underemployment Down Slightly at 13.6%

Gallup's measure of *underemployment* in June was 13.6%, almost the same as May's (13.7%) yet also the lowest Gallup has recorded since 2010. June's rate also marks the fourth straight month of declining underemployment from February's rate of 14.7%. Gallup's U.S. underemployment rate combines the percentage of adults in the workforce who are unemployed (5.3%) with those who are working part time but desire full-time work (8.3%).

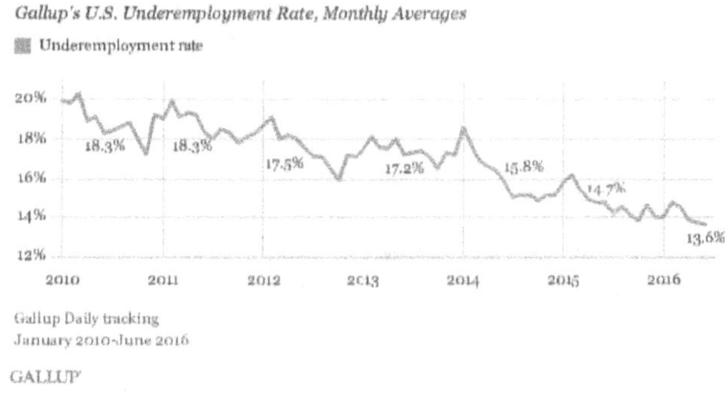

Bottom Line

Based on the seasonal patterns observed over the past six years, full-time employment generally peaks in midsummer at the same time that unemployment falls. In that sense, this past month's findings are in line with previously observed seasonal patterns. However, June 2016 stands out as having the highest GGJ rate of any June – or any month at all – dating back to 2010, as well as one of the lowest unemployment rates that Gallup has yet recorded. This is indicative of a broader, continuing improvement in the U.S. labor market beneath the seasonal ups and downs.

The data in this article are available in Gallup Analytics.

Gallup's U.S. Unemployment Measures, June 2016

	Most recent month (June 2016) %	Previous month (May 2016) %	Month a year ago (June 2015) %
Employed full time for employer (GGJ)*	46.0	45.5	45.5
Employed full time for self*	5.7	5.7	5.3
Workforce participation rate*	67.5	67.3	67.2
Unemployment rate**	5.3	5.5	6.0
Employed part time wanting full time**	8.3	8.2	8.7
Underemployment rate**	13.6	13.7	14.7

**Metrics represent percentages of the U.S. workforce.

*Metrics represent percentages of the U.S. population aged 18 or older who have a job or are actively seeking work.

Daily: Employment, Economic Confidence and Job Creation, Consumer Spending

Weekly: Employment, Economic Confidence, Job Creation, Consumer Spending

Read more about Gallup's economic measures.

View our economic release schedule.

Survey Methods

Results for this Gallup poll are based on telephone interviews conducted June 1-30, 2016, on the Gallup U.S. Daily survey, with a random sample of 30,395 adults, aged 18 and older, living in all 50 U.S. states and the District of Columbia. For results based on the total sample of national adults, the margin of sampling error is ±1 percentage point at the 95% confidence level. All reported margins of sampling error include computed design effects for weighting.

July 08, 2016

AMERICANS INCREASINGLY TURN TO SPECIFIC SOURCES FOR NEWS

by Jim Norman

Story Highlights

- *Those mentioning a type of media have fallen from 58% to 48% since 2013*
- *Specific mentions of media organizations have risen from 30% to 42%*
- *Those younger than 35 turning to social media sites for news*

WASHINGTON, D.C. – As the ways people consume news grow more complex, Americans are becoming less likely to view their news sources in terms of how they get news – radio, television, print or internet – and more in terms of who specifically provides it. Forty-eight percent of U.S. adults still identify a type of media as their main news source, but that is down from 58% just three years ago. Meanwhile, the percentage naming a specific media organization is up from 30% to 42%.

Thinking about various sources of news available today, what would you say is your main source of news about current events in the U.S. and around the world? (open-ended)

	2013 %	2016 %
Type of media (combined)	58%	48%
Television news	26	22
Internet/Computer/Online	18	16
Newspaper	6	5
Local television news	4	2
Radio	4	2
Media organization (combined)	30%	42%
Fox News	8	9
CNN	7	8
Facebook/Twitter/Social media	2	6
Specific internet site	1	4
NPR	1	2
MSNBC	1	2

Responses include all answers totaling at least 2% in 2016 poll

Gallup polls, June 20-24, 2013, and June 14-23, 2016

"Television news" and "internet/computer/online" are still the most popular answers when Americans are asked to name their "main source of news about current events in the U.S. and around the world." But they are slightly less likely to name each one than they were in 2013. Meanwhile, numerous individual media organizations such as Fox News, NPR and various internet sites saw small gains that were not statistically significant on an individual basis but showed a major increase when combined into total mentions of specific media organizations.

The poll was not designed to give a comprehensive listing of the most popular news organizations or the most popular means of receiving news. Instead, it provides insight into how Americans think about news sources in general.

The shift in thinking on the subject is partly powered by Americans' increasing ability to gather news from a single organization on multiple platforms. Every major television and print news organization has a presence on the internet, and internet sites produce videos that, through streaming devices, can be viewed on a television screen.

Women, who three years ago were significantly more likely to mention a method of receiving the news (type of media) than a specific media organization, are now about as likely as men to list a media organization. Democrats and those who lean Democratic have moved closer to Republicans and their leaners. The shift by age is even more striking.

Percentage of Americans Naming a Media Organization as Their Main News Source

	Media organizations, 2013 %	Media organizations, 2016 %
18 to 34 years old	32	53
35 to 54 years old	28	39
55 and older	31	37
Men	33	41
Women	26	43
Republicans + leaners	33	44
Democrats + leaners	27	45

Gallup polls, June 20-24, 2013, and June 14-23, 2016

Percentage of Americans Naming a Type of Media as Their Main News Source

	Type of media, 2013 %	Type of media, 2016 %
18 to 34 years old	54	38
35 to 54 years old	59	49
55 and older	60	55
Men	54	46
Women	63	49
Republicans + leaners	56	45
Democrats + leaners	62	47

Gallup polls, June 20-24, 2013, and June 14-23, 2016

Those Younger Than 35 Lead the Move to Social Media Sites

Social media sites such as Facebook and Twitter have had a major influence as primary news sources within the past three years. The overall percentage of mentions has grown only from 2% to 6% during that time, but this disguises the explosion in growth among younger Americans. This year, 15% of those aged 18 to 34 list a social media site as their main news source – up from 3% in 2013. Four percent of those aged 35 to 54 now list it as their main source, up from 1% in 2013. Among those aged 55 and older, 1% listed it as their main source three years ago, and 1% list it as their main source today.

Those younger than 35 are also more likely to list specific internet sites that are not part of social media, with 7% naming one as their main news source, compared with 3% of those 35 to 54 and 1% of those 55 or older.

Bottom Line

Americans' orientation to news is changing, with a growing emphasis on identifying more closely with a favorite media organization. Because America's youngest adults are moving most strongly in this direction, the change is likely to accelerate.

Clearly the change will affect individual media organizations as the battle for brand loyalty, especially among teens and young adults, ratchets up. But the implications could reach beyond individual companies to significantly affect U.S. politics and society. Will Americans become less willing to view the news through multiple lenses and viewpoints as they identify more with a specific media provider? Will they become more reliant on social media sites where news events are intermixed with less weighty topics? Answers to these and related questions could, among other things, change the definition of what qualifies as news.

Survey Methods

Results for this Gallup poll are based on telephone interviews conducted June 14-23, 2016, with a random sample of 1,025 adults, aged 18 and older, living in all 50 U.S. states and the District of Columbia. For results based on the total sample of national adults, the margin of sampling error is ±4 percentage points at the 95% confidence level. All reported margins of sampling error include computed design effects for weighting.

July 19, 2016
PAUL RYAN MAINTAINS POSITIVE IMAGE AMONG REPUBLICANS

by Justin McCarthy

Story Highlights

- *Ryan has higher favorable rating than Trump, Christie and Cruz*
- *71% of Republicans, 44% of U.S. adults view Ryan favorably*
- *Cruz's image has improved among Republicans*

WASHINGTON, D.C. – House Speaker Paul Ryan enjoys modestly higher favorable ratings among both Republicans (71%) and national adults (44%) than Ted Cruz and Chris Christie, who will speak this week at the Republican National Convention. Americans also view Ryan more favorably than they do presidential nominee Donald Trump. Of six key Republican leaders asked about, only former President George W. Bush has a higher favorable rating than Ryan does.

Favorability of Republican Party Figures

Next, we'd like to get your overall opinion of some people in the news. As I read each name, please say if you have a favorable or unfavorable opinion of that person – or if you have never heard of them.

	U.S. adults % Favorable	U.S. adults % Unfavorable	Republicans % Favorable	Republicans % Unfavorable
Attending convention				
Paul Ryan	44	35	71	16
Ted Cruz	36	49	59	31
Donald Trump	33	63	65	32
Chris Christie	31	46	52	26
Not attending convention				
George W. Bush	52	43	75	22
Mitt Romney	35	51	44	46

Gallup, July 13-17, 2016

These results come from a July 13-17 Gallup poll conducted just before the convention. Ryan, who has endorsed Trump but kept him at arm's length, skipped key party convention votes on Monday but will address the convention Tuesday. His speech is expected to be one rooted in his party's favored policies – including ones at odds with Trump's.

Both Cruz and Christie, Trump's rivals in the 2016 Republican primaries, will speak at the convention. Cruz's image has recovered quickly among the party base in recent months. At the time he suspended his campaign in early May, Republicans viewed him as negatively as they did positively. Today, they are almost twice as likely to view him favorably as unfavorably. Christie's favorable rating hasn't moved among Republicans since he ended his campaign in February. About half of Republicans had a favorable view of him then, similar to the rating he has now after spending months campaigning for Trump.

One notable Republican leader who is not attending the convention is 2012 GOP presidential nominee Mitt Romney, a vocal critic of Trump throughout the nomination process. The former Massachusetts governor's attempts to influence the outcome have not endeared him to the party, as Republicans now view him about as negatively (46%) as they do positively (44%). That is a far cry from September 2012, when about nine in 10 Republicans had a favorable view of Romney.

Like Romney, former President George W. Bush is a notable no-show at the convention. Republicans still view him favorably overall, and his 52% favorable rating among national adults is further evidence that his image is recovering from the 34% he finished his presidency with. Still, Americans continue to assign Bush more responsibility for current economic problems than they do President Barack Obama. Americans generally view former presidents more charitably than current presidents, even those like Bush who left office with low public support.

Ryan's Favorable Rating Among Republicans Back Above 70%

Since Romney selected Ryan as a vice presidential candidate in 2012, consistent majorities of Republicans have held favorable views of the House speaker. His current 71% favorable rating among Republicans is nearly back to where it was in late 2012 and early 2013. Ryan's favorable rating among Republicans dipped to 57% in 2014, when he was out of the spotlight and fewer held opinions of him. Now that he again has a prominent role within the party, his favorable rating is up – but so is his unfavorable rating, at 16%. This higher unfavorable rating likely reflects ongoing frustrations within the party over Republican congressional leadership.

Favorable and Unfavorable Ratings of Paul Ryan, Among Republicans

Recent trend

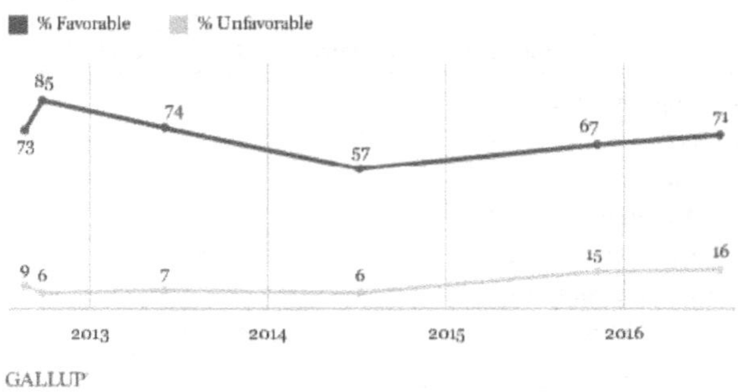

Still, Ryan retains high positive ratings among party loyalists after roughly nine months in the speakership. That stands in stark contrast to former Speaker John Boehner's ratings after he announced his resignation last fall, as well as ratings of current Senate Majority Leader Mitch McConnell in Gallup's last measurement of him in October.

Bottom Line

Many in his party have long respected Speaker Ryan as a unifying figure who can overcome steep political challenges. Rank-and-file Republicans hold him in high esteem. The 2016 presidential election is yet another challenge for Ryan, as he seeks to keep his party together after a divisive campaign season that rocked his party's establishment. Though he doesn't always refrain from criticizing Trump, Ryan has endorsed him.

With many key GOP figures skipping the convention this year, Ryan could play a critical role in uniting his party – not only for the general election, but also for the Republican majorities in Congress he seeks to maintain.

Historical data are available in Gallup Analytics.

Survey Methods

Results for this Gallup poll are based on telephone interviews conducted July 13-17, 2016, with a random sample of 1,023 adults, aged 18 and older, living in all 50 U.S. states and the District of Columbia. For results based on the total sample of national adults, the margin of sampling error is ±4 percentage points at the 95% confidence level. All reported margins of sampling error include computed design effects for weighting.

July 11, 2016
U.S. UNINSURED RATE REMAINS AT HISTORICAL LOW OF 11.0%

by Stephanie Marken

Story Highlights

- *Uninsured rate remains at trend low*
- *Rate down 6.1 points since key provision of health law took effect*
- *Uninsured rate has declined most among Hispanics, low-income*

WASHINGTON, D.C. – In the second quarter of 2016, the uninsured rate among all U.S. adults remains at the trend low of 11.0% reached in the first quarter of this year. This is down from 11.9% in the fourth quarter of 2015, which was prior to when health plans purchased through government exchanges during the most recent open enrollment period took effect in early 2016.

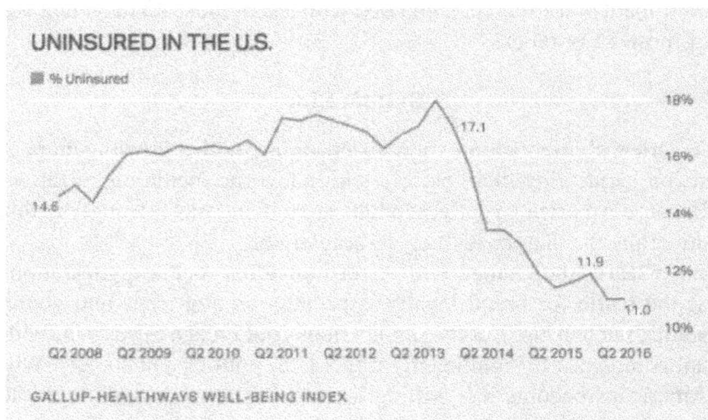

The rate has declined 6.1 percentage points since the fourth quarter of 2013, right before the key provision of the Affordable Care Act took effect, requiring Americans to carry health insurance in early 2014.

Results for the second quarter are based on approximately 46,000 interviews with U.S. adults aged 18 and older from April 1 to June 30, 2016, conducted as part of the Gallup-Healthways Well-Being Index. Gallup and Healthways ask 500 U.S. adults each day whether they have health insurance, which, on an aggregated basis, allows for precise and ongoing measurement of the percentage of Americans with and without health insurance.

Greatest Decline in Uninsured Rate Among Low-Income Households, Minorities

Across income groups, the uninsured rate has declined the most among those living in households making less than $36,000 annually. In the fourth quarter of 2013, 30.7% of these individuals were uninsured, compared with 20.4% of in the second quarter of 2016. This 10.3-percentage-point decline among low-income households contrasts with less than three-point declines among higher-income households.

The uninsured rate has also declined precipitously among Hispanics and blacks since the fourth quarter of 2013. In the fourth quarter of 2013, 38.7% of Hispanics were uninsured, compared with 27.8% in the second quarter of 2016, a 10.9-percentage-point decline. The uninsured rate among blacks has declined by 8.6 points since the fourth quarter of 2013, from 20.9% in the fourth quarter of 2013 to 12.3% in the second quarter of 2016.

Percentage of Uninsured U.S. Adults, by Subgroup

	Q4 2013 %	Q2 2016 %	Net change (pct. pts.)
National adults	17.1	11.0	-6.1
18 to 25	23.5	14.9	-8.6
26 to 34	28.2	19.4	-8.8
35 to 64	18.0	11.0	-7.0
65+	2.0	2.1	0.1
Whites	11.9	6.8	-5.1
Blacks	20.9	12.3	-8.6
Hispanics	38.7	27.8	-10.9
Less than $36,000	30.7	20.4	-10.3
$36,000 to $89,999	11.7	8.9	-2.8
$90,000+	5.8	3.2	-2.6

Gallup-Healthways Well-Being Index

Among Those 18 to 64, Self-Paid Plans Have Seen Greatest Change Since 2013

To assess changes in the type of insurance coverage people have, Gallup and Healthways focus on adults aged 18 to 64, because nearly all Americans aged 65 and older have Medicare. Since the fourth quarter of 2013, the percentage reporting they have a plan fully paid for by themselves or a family member has changed the most. In the final quarter of 2013, 17.6% of all U.S. adults were insured through these individually purchased health insurance plans, compared with 21.8% in the second quarter of 2016, a 4.2-point increase.

Type of Health Insurance Coverage in the U.S., Among 18-to 64-Year-Olds

Is your health insurance coverage through a current or former employer, a union, Medicare, Medicaid, military or veteran's coverage, or a plan fully paid for by you or a family member? Primary and secondary insurance combined

	Q4 2013 %	Q2 2016 %	Change (pct. pts.)
Current or former employer	44.2	43.5	-0.7
Plan fully paid for by self or family member	17.6	21.8	4.2
Medicaid	6.9	9.6	2.7
Medicare	6.1	7.4	1.3
Military/Veteran's	4.6	4.9	0.3
A union	2.5	2.5	0
(Something else)	3.5	4.3	0.8
No insurance	20.8	13.3	-7.5

Gallup-Healthways Well-Being Index

Gallup and Healthways began asking Americans about the source of their health insurance using the current question wording in August 2013, in anticipation of shifts in how people would receive their health insurance after the Affordable Care Act. Respondents are asked, "Is your primary health insurance coverage through a current or former employer, a union, Medicare, Medicaid, military or veteran's coverage, or a plan fully paid for by you or a family member?" Respondents are also asked if they have secondary health insurance coverage and, if so, what type of coverage it is. The results reported here are a combined estimate of primary and secondary insurance types.

Implications

The uninsured rate has been dropping fairly consistently on a quarterly basis since the ACA provision requiring U.S. adults to obtain health insurance took effect in 2013. The greatest change occurred early on in that period. While the rate was steady in the second quarter of 2016, it held at the trend low first reached in the first quarter. The stabilization of the rate is to be expected, given that the latest open enrollment period concluded on Jan. 31, 2016, and for the same reason, Gallup and Healthways anticipate little change in the uninsured rate for the remainder of 2016.

Survey Methods

Results are based on telephone interviews conducted April 1-June 30, 2016, as part of the Gallup-Healthways Well-Being Index survey, with a random sample of 46,060 adults, aged 18 and older, living in all 50 U.S. states and the District of Columbia. For results based on the total sample of national adults, the margin of sampling error is ±1 percentage point at the 95% confidence level. Each quarter dating to Quarter 1, 2014, has approximately 44,000 respondents. Each quarter from 2008 through 2013 has approximately 88,000 respondents.

July 11, 2016

MAJORITY IN U.S. PREFER STATE OVER FEDERAL GOVERNMENT POWER

by Justin McCarthy

Story Highlights

- *Fifty-five percent favor concentration of power at state level*
- *Thirty-seven percent favor power at federal government level*
- *Republicans more than four times as likely to favor state power*

WASHINGTON, D.C. – A majority of Americans (55%) favor the theory of government that concentrates power in state governments, outnumbering the 37% who favor power concentrated in the federal government. The latest update of this question – asked only twice before, in 1936 and 1981 – is from a June 14-23 Gallup poll. It comes as nearly half of the states sue the federal government over its directive to grant transgender students the right to use bathrooms and locker rooms that correspond with their gender identity. Schools that don't comply could risk losing federal funding.

Americans' Preferences for Concentration of Government Power, State vs. Federal

Which theory of government do you favor: concentration of power in the state government or concentration of power in the federal government?

	State government %	Federal government %	No opinion %
Jun 14-23, 2016	55	37	8
Sep 18-21, 1981	56	28	16
Jan 20-25, 1936	44	56	–

Gallup

Americans' preference for state power was similar in 1981 – the first year of the presidency of Ronald Reagan, who declared his support for states' rights on the prior year's campaign trail. In contrast, Americans slightly preferred federal power in the mid-1930s, after President Franklin D. Roosevelt unveiled a sweeping series of programs that increased the role of the federal government in Americans' lives.

The current lawsuit over transgender bathrooms, which is being brought predominantly by GOP-controlled states, is one of many battles states have fought against President Barack Obama's administration. Obama was unsuccessful this year in defending his executive order on allowing undocumented immigrants to stay in the U.S. but won the fight to uphold the Affordable Care Act he signed into law in his first term.

Views on this question are far from politically homogeneous. The majority of Democrats (62%) support concentrating power at the federal level, while majorities of independents (56%) and Republicans (78%) favor concentrating power at the state level.

Democrats' preference for federal power reflects their party's underlying ideology and is likely related to having a Democrat in the White House. Meanwhile, about two in three state governors in the U.S. are from the GOP, and Republicans are more than four times as likely to prefer concentration of power at the state versus the federal level.

Reflecting these partisan differences, a majority of Americans who approve of the job Obama is doing say they favor concentration of power in the federal government (53%), while 38% favor the states having it. By contrast, those who disapprove of Obama's job performance are more than three times as likely to favor concentration of power in the states (74%) as in the federal government (20%).

Americans' Preferences for Concentration of Government Power, by Demographic Group

Which theory of government do you favor: concentration of power in the state government or concentration of power in the federal government?

	State government %	Federal government %
Democrats	32	62
Independents	56	33
Republicans	78	17
Approve of Obama's job performance	38	53
Disapprove of Obama's job performance	74	20

June 14-23, 2016

Bottom Line

Americans' preferences for how power is distributed in the U.S. have differed over the past century, and could change again as the politics of the country continue to shift. A reading on these attitudes at the start of a Republican's presidency some 35 years ago found the public leaning toward states' rights, but a reading 80 years ago during a Democratic presidency revealed a slight preference for federal power.

If presumptive Democratic nominee Hillary Clinton loses this year's presidential election, Democrats could find themselves more amenable to concentration of power in state governments. Likewise, Republicans could become more open to federal power if a Republican again occupies the White House. Still, states' rights have long been a rallying cry of the GOP, and that seems unlikely to change as a result of the coming presidential election.

Regardless of public opinion, the U.S. Constitution outlines strong federal powers, while giving all unenumerated powers to the states. The Supreme Court may choose to review any disputes between the two.

Historical data are available in Gallup Analytics.

Survey Methods

Results for this Gallup poll are based on telephone interviews conducted June 14-23, 2016, on the Gallup U.S. Daily survey, with a random sample of 1,025 adults, aged 18 and older, living in all 50 U.S. states and the District of Columbia. For results based on the total sample of national adults, the margin of sampling error is ±4 percentage points at the 95% confidence level. All reported margins of sampling error include computed design effects for weighting.

July 12, 2016
AMERICANS USING CASH LESS COMPARED WITH FIVE YEARS AGO

by Art Swift and Steve Ander

Story Highlights

- *Percentage using cash for "all" transactions shrinks*
- *But few indicate they have given up cash altogether*
- *Young Americans report sharpest drop in cash usage from five years ago*

WASHINGTON, D.C. – Fewer Americans say they are making "all" or "most" of their purchases with cash, compared to what they say they did five years ago – a sign of a shift toward electronic payment methods as well as mobile payment apps. While few indicate they have given up cash altogether, more Americans say they are making merely "some" of their purchases with cash.

Americans Using Cash Now Versus Five Years Ago

Think about the purchases you make on a regular basis and the way you pay for them – including cash, check, credit card, debit card and other forms of electronic payment. Do you make ...

	Now %	Five Years Ago* %
All of your purchases with cash	10	19
Most of your purchases with cash	14	17
About half of your purchases with cash and half with other forms of payment	22	20
Some of your purchases with cash	41	33
None of your purchases with cash	12	10

*Self-reports of cash habits five years ago
Gallup

Gallup asked Americans in a survey June 22-23 about the extent to which they use cash for retail purchases – and how much they used cash five years ago. While 24% report currently making all or most of their purchases with cash, 36% say they were doing this five years ago. Conversely, the majority (53%) say they currently make only some or none of their purchases with cash, versus 43% saying this about their spending of five years ago.

As mobile technology and e-commerce have proliferated, Americans can use their cellphones and computers to make purchases. And, with the onset of PayPal, Google Wallet, Apple Pay and numerous other mobile payment options, Americans may find that paying for items electronically is more convenient than having to carry cash for in-person purchases. Additionally, "showrooming" – when shoppers inspect goods in-person but actually buy them online – may contribute to lower consumer demand for cash.

Younger Americans Say They Use Less Cash Than Five Years Ago

Twenty-one percent of young Americans – aged 23-34 – say they make all or most of their purchases with cash, down 18 percentage points from the 39% who say they used cash to that extent five years ago. While the economy has absorbed noncash payments for goods and services, among all age groups younger Americans have shown the most striking drop in using cash. In contrast, those aged 35-54 saw a two-point drop, while those 55 and older saw a six-point drop.

Americans Using Cash Now Versus Five Years Ago, By Age

All/Most purchases with cash

	Now %	Five Years Ago* %
23-34	21	39
35-54	21	23
55+	18	24

*Self-reports of cash habits five years ago
Gallup

These differences by age may be attributed to younger Americans generally embracing mobile technology and payments more systematically than older Americans do. Younger Americans may not see a particular cachet in using physical currency, especially when they are the most trusting of institutions like banks and credit card companies to safeguard their information.

Bottom Line

As technology and consumer preferences evolve, companies will constantly seek ways to make retail payments more efficient to gain an advantage with customers. The economy has become more internet-oriented, and it is already becoming easier to make purchases using mobile technology. People are more familiar and comfortable with cashless transactions and are now primed to use those services in live retail environments.

For an improved customer experience, it is going to become increasingly necessary for businesses to accept other forms of payment beyond cash. Americans say they are using less cash than they were five years ago, and with enhanced technology, this trend is likely to continue. The next generation of consumers might conduct even fewer cash transactions than the youngest Americans today. This shift is not unknown to mobile payment platform companies, banks and credit card companies as they increasingly compete for the future consumer. However, with a rising number of data breaches and bad actors disrupting cybersecurity, it is possible that some Americans may never turn away from using cash.

These data are available in Gallup Analytics.

Survey Methods

Results for this Gallup poll are based on telephone interviews conducted June 22-23, 2016, with a random sample of 1,024 adults, aged 18 and older, living in all 50 U.S. states and the District of Columbia. For results based on the total sample of national adults, the margin of sampling error is ±4 percentage points at the 95% confidence level.

July 13, 2016

IN U.S., HISPANICS LEAST WORRIED ABOUT ELECTION OUTCOME

by Jim Norman

Story Highlights

- *38% of Hispanics strongly agree they are afraid of election outcome*
- *64% of blacks, 53% of whites strongly agree they fear the outcome*
- *Fewer Hispanics than whites, blacks strongly agree stakes are higher*

WASHINGTON, D.C. – Despite Donald Trump's harsh anti-immigration rhetoric throughout this year's presidential campaign, Hispanics are less likely than either whites or blacks to "strongly agree" that they are afraid of what will happen if their candidate loses. Hispanics also are less likely to agree that the stakes in this year's presidential election are higher than usual.

Presidential Election Stakes and Fears by Race

	Strongly agree %	Somewhat agree %	Somewhat disagree %	Strongly disagree %
The stakes in this presidential election are higher than in previous years.				
All	61	24	9	5
Blacks	66	20	6	5
Hispanics	50	30	11	6
Non-Hispanic whites	63	24	8	5
I am afraid of what will happen if my candidate for president does not win.				
All	51	21	13	10
Blacks	64	13	9	11
Hispanics	38	31	14	12
Non-Hispanic whites	53	20	13	10

Gallup, June 7-July 1

Large majorities of all three major U.S. racial and ethnic groups agree the election stakes are higher this year than in prior years, with 66% of blacks, 63% of whites and 50% of Hispanics *strongly* agreeing. And while roughly seven in 10 or more of each group agree they are afraid of what will happen if their candidate does not win, 64% of blacks, compared with 53% of whites and only 38% of Hispanics, *strongly* agree.

U.S.-Born Hispanics More Concerned Than Hispanic Immigrants About Election

Hispanic immigrants account for most of the differences between the views of Hispanics and those of blacks and non-Hispanic whites. Sixty-nine percent of native-born Hispanics strongly agree that this year's election stakes are higher than usual, compared with 31% of Hispanic immigrants. Forty-five percent of Hispanics born in the U.S. strongly agree they are afraid of what will happen if their candidate for president does not win, compared with 30% of Hispanic immigrants.

Hispanics have been less likely than other racial or ethnic groups to vote in recent elections. The Democratic Party, which typically garners strong support from Hispanics who do vote, has mounted a major drive this year to build interest and increase the number of Hispanics registered to vote.

Among U.S.-born Hispanics, 87% say they are registered to vote, slightly less than the 93% of non-Hispanic whites who are registered to vote. Among Hispanic immigrants, 28% say they are registered, and another 27% plan to register before the election.

Younger Blacks, Black Women Most Afraid of Election Outcome

Almost three in four black women (72%) strongly agree that they are afraid of what will happen if their candidate loses, compared with 55% of black men. The gender gap is smaller among whites and virtually non-existent among Hispanics.

I am afraid of what will happen if my candidate for president does not win.

	Strongly agree %	Somewhat agree %	Somewhat disagree %	Strongly disagree %
Black men	55	12	15	16
Black women	72	14	4	7
Hispanic men	36	26	18	14
Hispanic women	39	35	10	11
Non-Hispanic white men	49	22	13	11
Non-Hispanic white women	56	18	12	9

Gallup, June 7-July 1

Although younger blacks (71%) are more likely than those who are older (54%) to strongly agree they are afraid of the election outcome, the reverse is true among Hispanics and whites – older Hispanics and whites express the most fear.

I am afraid of what will happen if my candidate for president does not win.

	Strongly agree %	Somewhat agree %	Somewhat disagree %	Strongly disagree %
Blacks ages 18-49	71	12	8	9
Black ages 50 and older	54	15	11	15
Hispanics ages 18-49	33	36	13	12
Hispanics ages 50 and older	48	20	14	13
Whites (non-Hispanic) ages 18-49	49	23	14	10
Whites (non-Hispanic) ages 50 and older	56	18	11	10

Gallup, June 7-July 1

Combining all races and ethnicities, Democrats (63%) are more likely than Republicans (53%) to strongly agree that they are afraid of what will happen if their candidate loses the election.

Bottom Line

Strong majorities of whites, blacks and Hispanics agree the stakes are high in the 2016 presidential election, and that they have reason be worried if their candidate loses. The two groups that mostly vote Democratic – blacks and Hispanics – seem, on the surface, to have widely differing views, but the differences almost dissolve when considering only native-born Hispanics. Non-Hispanic whites, who are more likely to be Republican, show similar levels of concern about the outcome of the election.

In less than a month, both Republicans and Democrats will have held their party's national convention and nominated their candidates. The tone at each of those events will give a preview of how much the fall campaigns will aim to capitalize on the fears most Americans have about the consequences if their candidate loses.

Survey Methods

Results for this Gallup poll are based on telephone interviews conducted June 7-July 1, 2016, with a sample of 3,270 adults, aged 18 and older, living in all 50 U.S. states and the District of Columbia, who had previously been interviewed in the Gallup Daily tracking poll and agreed to be re-interviewed for a later study. The sample is weighted to be representative of U.S. adults.

For results based on the total sample of national adults, the margin of sampling error is ±3 percentage points at the 95% confidence level. For results based on the sample of 1,320 non-Hispanic whites, the margin of sampling error is ±4 percentage points at the 95% confidence level. For results based on the sample of 912 non-Hispanic blacks, the margin of sampling error is ±5 percentage points at the 95% confidence level. For results based on the sample of 906 Hispanics, the margin of sampling error is ±6 percentage points at the 95% confidence level. (271 out of the 906 interviews with Hispanics were conducted in Spanish.)

All reported margins of sampling error include computed design effects for weighting.

July 13, 2016
BEFORE JULY SHOOTINGS, BLACKS DIVIDED ON POLICE BEHAVIOR

by Lydia Saad

Story Highlights

- *Nearly half of blacks say their local police treat blacks unfairly*
- *More whites say blacks treated unfairly in dealings with police*
- *Blacks who report personal mistreatment by police steady at 16%*

PRINCETON, N.J. – Just before the July 5 and July 6 fatal shootings of black men during routine law enforcement encounters in Louisiana and Minnesota, blacks in the U.S. were evenly divided over the treatment of blacks by their local police. Half of blacks responded in a June 7-July 1 Gallup poll that police in their local area treat blacks and other racial minorities *fairly,* while 48% said they treat blacks *unfairly.*

Blacks' Perceptions of Local Police Treatment of Blacks/Racial Minorities

How would you say local police in your area treat racial minorities including blacks – [very fairly, fairly, unfairly (or) very unfairly]?

	Jun 15-Jul 10, 2015 %	Jun 7-Jul 1, 2016 %
Very fairly	8	9
Fairly	44	41
Unfairly	33	29
Very unfairly	15	19
Total fairly	52	50
Total unfairly	48	48

Gallup

Nineteen percent of blacks thought local police treated blacks *very* unfairly, similar to what Gallup found in 2015.

These results are based on Gallup's Minority Rights and Relations survey. The 2016 poll was conducted by telephone with 3,270 national adults, including large oversamples of blacks and Hispanics.

Although young black men have been the focal point of recent news stories about police shootings, black women – along with younger blacks – are more likely to express criticism of the police than are black men and older blacks. Fifty-three percent of black women versus 43% of black men say local police treat blacks and other minorities unfairly. Similarly, 52% of blacks aged 18 to 49 versus 43% of blacks 50 and older think police treatment of minorities is unfair.

Perceptions of Police Treatment of Blacks in Local Area

	Very fairly/Fairly %	Very unfairly/Unfairly %
Black men	56	43
Black women	45	53
Blacks 18 to 49	47	52
Blacks 50+	55	43

Gallup, June 7-July 1, 2016

The views of male and female blacks, as well as younger and older blacks, are similar to what Gallup found when first asking this question last year.

Black Americans' perceptions of how racial minorities are treated by local police are markedly different from the views of Hispanics and non-Hispanic whites. While almost half of blacks believe racial minorities are treated unfairly, only 34% of Hispanics and 20% of whites agree.

Perceptions of Police Treatment of Blacks in Local Area

	Very fairly/Fairly %	Very unfairly/Unfairly %
Jun 7-Jul 1, 2016		
U.S. adults	71	26
Blacks	50	48
Hispanics	65	34
Non-Hispanic whites	77	20
Jun 15-Jul 10, 2015		
U.S. adults	73	25
Blacks	52	48
Hispanics	71	29
Non-Hispanic whites	78	19

Gallup

Whites Express Record-High Belief That Blacks Are Treated Worse by Police

A longer-term Gallup trend asking Americans how blacks in their community are treated compared with whites in "dealing with the police, such as traffic incidents" finds even broader dissatisfaction among blacks. Two-thirds of blacks say blacks are treated less fairly than whites in such encounters. While down slightly from last year's 73%, it is still higher than the 55% and 60% readings in the late 1990s.

Hispanics (45%) and non-Hispanic whites (40%) are far less likely than blacks to perceive a disparity in police treatment by race. However, the percentage of whites expressing this sentiment is up from 34% in 2015.

As a result, the overall percentage of Americans believing blacks receive worse treatment than whites from the police remains at a record high – 45%, statistically similar to the 43% recorded in 2015.

Percentage Believing Blacks Are Treated Less Fairly Than Whites in Dealing With the Police, Such as Traffic Incidents, 1997-2016

Just your impression, are blacks in your community treated less fairly than whites in the following situations?

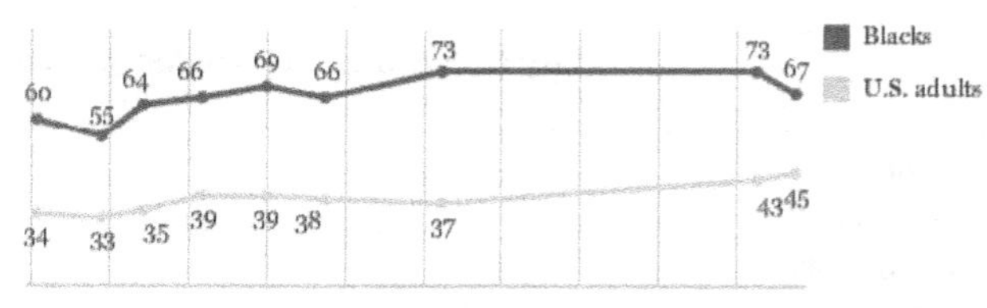

Meanwhile, the percentage of blacks reporting that they personally have experienced unfair treatment from police – now 16% – is similar to the level Gallup has recorded since 2013. From 1999 through 2007, the percentage was slightly higher than it is now, ranging between 20% and 25%.

Percentage of Blacks Who Feel They Were Treated Unfairly in Past 30 Days in Dealings With the Police, Such as Traffic Incidents, 1997-2016

Can you think of any occasion in the last 30 days when you felt you were treated unfairly in the following places because you were black?

Bottom Line

A video of several police officers beating Rodney King after a high-speed chase in Los Angeles in 1991 gave the public a rare, pre-smartphone glimpse of police brutality that proved explosive. The proliferation of camera phones and social media has made similar images commonplace in recent years, possibly contributing to heightened public concern about such events. Most notably, even before the recent shootings, four in 10 whites, up from 34% last year, thought the police in their community treat blacks less fairly than whites. Also, the percentage of blacks believing the police treat blacks and other racial minorities less fairly than whites was on the high side of Gallup's two-decade trend, even as the percentage who personally felt mistreated within the previous month remained on the low side.

More broadly, negative views of local police are by no means universal among black Americans. In fact, before the latest incidents, as many blacks said their local police are fair in their dealings with blacks as said they are unfair. But a huge racial gap remains, with the majority of Hispanics and non-Hispanic whites believing blacks are treated fairly.

Historical data are available in Gallup Analytics.

Survey Methods

Results for this Gallup poll are based on telephone interviews conducted June 7-July 1, 2016, with a sample of 3,270 adults, aged 18 and older, living in all 50 U.S. states and the District of Columbia, who had previously been interviewed in the Gallup Daily tracking poll and agreed to be re-interviewed for a later study. The sample is weighted to be representative of U.S. adults.

For results based on the total sample of national adults, the margin of sampling error is ±3 percentage points at the 95% confidence level. For results based on the sample of 1,320 non-Hispanic whites, the margin of sampling error is ±4 percentage points at the 95% confidence level. For results based on the sample of 912 non-Hispanic blacks, the margin of sampling error is ±5 percentage points at the 95% confidence level. For results based on the sample of 906 Hispanics, the margin of sampling error is ±6 percentage points at the 95% confidence level. (271 out of the 906 interviews with Hispanics were conducted in Spanish.)

All reported margins of sampling error include computed design effects for weighting.

July 14, 2016
MAJORITY IN U.S. STILL HOPEFUL FOR SOLUTION TO RACE PROBLEMS

by Frank Newport

Story Highlights

- *Before recent events, 57% said race issues will be worked out*
- *Whites more positive than blacks, by 57% to 48%*
- *53% rated current black-white relations as "good"*

PRINCETON, N.J. – Speaking at the services of five slain Dallas police officers on Tuesday, President Barack Obama said the recent violence makes Americans wonder "if the divides of race in America can ever be bridged," but he urged them to "reject such despair." The majority of Americans, at least from a long-term perspective, share the president's optimism. Fifty-seven percent of Americans in June said that a solution to relations between whites and blacks "will eventually be worked out," while 40% said that black-white relations "will always be a problem."

Do you think that relations between blacks and whites will always be a problem for the United States, or that a solution will eventually be worked out?
Based on national adults

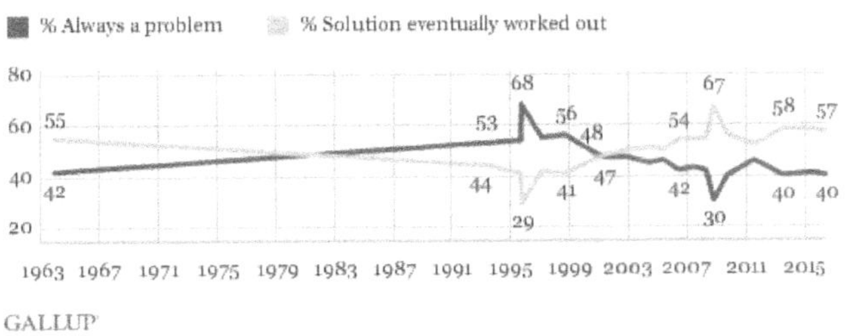

The latest results are from Gallup's June 7-July 1 Minority Rights and Relations poll, conducted before the events of the past two weeks in Louisiana, Minnesota and Texas – the latter the occasion for Obama's speech in Dallas.

Americans' optimism about black-white relations in the long term has held steady over the past three years, even with a number of incidents involving black men being killed in encounters with white police officers that sparked nationwide protests and, ultimately, the Black Lives Matter movement.

In 1963, the independent research organization NORC at the University of Chicago asked Americans about the long-term prospects for race relations in the U.S., and 55% said that a solution would eventually be worked out. Gallup started updating the trend on this question in the 1990s and found Americans' optimism by that point had dropped significantly. They were most negative after the verdict in the O.J. Simpson murder trial in October 1995, when an all-time low of 29% said a solution would eventually be worked out. The public grew more positive in the 2000s, and, across 13 different surveys conducted since 2002, at least half of Americans have said a solution to black-white relations will eventually be worked out. Americans were most optimistic in November 2008, just after Obama's election as the nation's first black president.

In 1963, blacks were significantly more optimistic than whites about an eventual solution to race relations issues. Since 1997, however, whites have consistently been more positive than blacks, with the size of the gap in attitudes between the two remaining fairly constant. This year's nine-percentage-point gap – 57% of whites saying that a solution will be worked out, compared with 48% of blacks – is about average for recent years.

Belief That a Solution to Black-White Relations Will Eventually Be Worked Out, by Race
Trend including polls with sufficient sample sizes of blacks

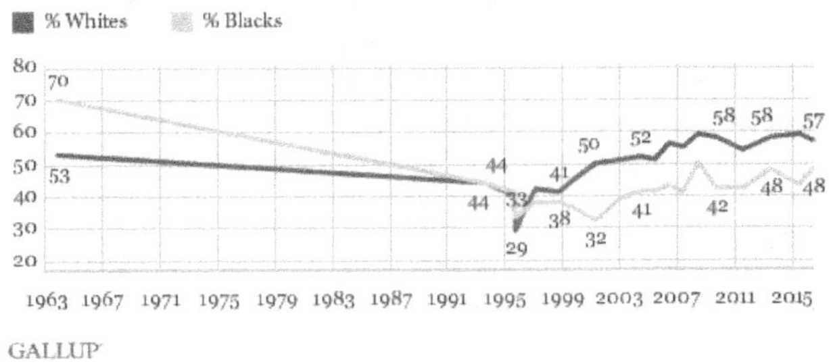

Majority of 53% Rates Current State of Race Relations as "Good"

Last year, Gallup reported a precipitous drop in Americans' positive views of the current state of relations between whites and blacks, from 70% in 2013 to 47% in 2015 – likely a response to the highly publicized deaths of several black men in dealings with police. In this year's survey, 53% of Americans rate relations between whites and blacks as "very" or "somewhat good," up marginally from year to year.

Even with this slight increase in positive attitudes about black-white relations, Americans' views remain – along with last year's – the most negative of any measured since this trend began in 2001. The high point was 72% "good" in 2004.

The uptick this year in positive views of race relations is driven mostly by a more optimistic view among whites, whose "good" rating rose from 45% to 55%. Blacks' views, in contrast, have stayed essentially the same, at 51% "good" last year and 49% "good" this year.

Ratings of Black-White Relations as Very/Somewhat Good

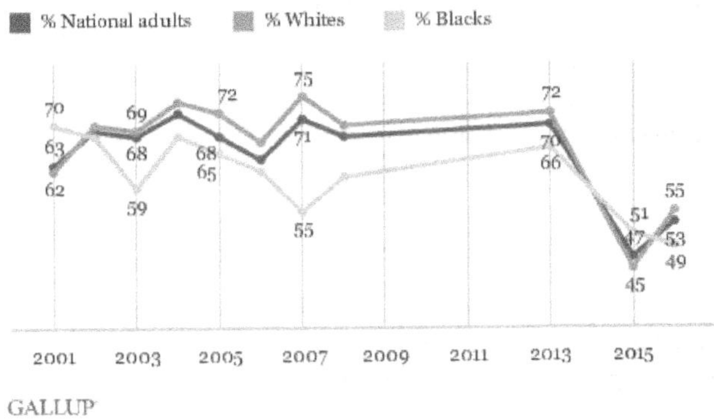

Bottom Line

A majority of Americans interviewed in June continue to say a solution to the problems associated with black-white relations will eventually be worked out. These attitudes about the long-term prospects for black-white relations have not changed materially over the past half-decade, even as race relations have been tested. The continued optimism about an eventual solution gives some hope that Obama's and others' calls for peace – and for the races to work together instead of enacting violence – may reach a receptive audience.

Despite this long-term optimism, however, Americans' assessment of the *current* state of black-white relations in the country is much worse than it was before 2015.

The racial breakdown in these results reinforces the general finding that whites and blacks tend to look at the world through different lenses. Similar to what is seen in terms of white and black attitudes toward the police, white Americans are more positive than black Americans about both the current state of race relations and about the prospect of a race relations solution eventually being worked out.

After race riots and massive civil rights demonstrations in the 1960s, the presidentially appointed Kerner Commission warned that "our nation is moving toward two societies, one black, one white – separate and unequal." These measures of current public opinion, along with a number of others showing that blacks and whites still see two different societies, continue to indicate the depth of the challenge in addressing what Swedish economist Gunnar Myrdal more than 70 years ago called the "American Dilemma."

Historical data are available in Gallup Analytics.

Survey Methods

Results for this Gallup poll are based on telephone interviews conducted June 7-July 1, 2016, with a sample of 3,270 adults, aged 18 and older, living in all 50 U.S. states and the District of Columbia, who had previously been interviewed in the Gallup Daily tracking poll and agreed to be re-interviewed for a later study. The sample is weighted to be representative of U.S. adults.

For results based on the total sample of national adults, the margin of sampling error is ±3 percentage points at the 95% confidence level. For results based on the sample of 1,320 non-Hispanic whites, the margin of sampling error is ±4 percentage points at the 95% confidence level. For results based on the sample of 912 non-Hispanic blacks, the margin of sampling error is ±5 percentage points at the 95% confidence level. For results based on the sample of 906 Hispanics, the margin of sampling error is ±6 percentage points at the 95% confidence level. (271 out of the 906 interviews with Hispanics were conducted in Spanish.)

All reported margins of sampling error include computed design effects for weighting.

July 15, 2016
AMERICANS' OPTIMISM ABOUT BLACKS' OPPORTUNITIES WANES

by Jeffrey M. Jones

Story Highlights

- *64% say blacks have same chance as whites to get a job*
- *New low of 71% say blacks have same chance to get good education*
- *70% say blacks have same chance to get housing, lowest since '89*

PRINCETON, N.J. – Sixty-four percent of Americans believe blacks have the same chance as whites in their local community to get a job for which they are qualified, but the percentage holding that view has declined in recent years and is the lowest since 1995.

Americans' Perceptions of Whether Blacks Have as Good a Chance as Whites in Their Community to Get a Job for Which They Are Qualified

The only time Americans were less optimistic about blacks' ability to secure jobs was in the 1960s civil rights era, when roughly four in 10 thought blacks and whites had equal job opportunities.

Americans' beliefs that blacks enjoy equality of opportunity relative to housing and education have also declined. Currently, 70% say blacks have the same chance as whites to get any housing they can afford, the lowest since 1989 and down from a peak of 83% in 1997.

Americans' Perceptions of Whether Blacks Have as Good a Chance as Whites in Their Community to Get Any Housing They Can Afford

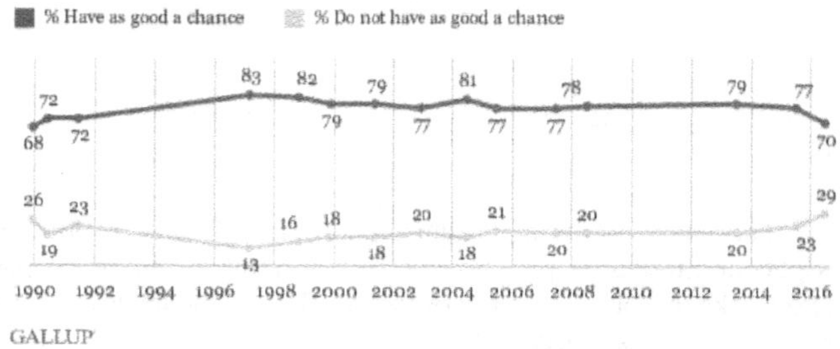

The 71% of Americans who believe black children have the same chance as whites of obtaining a good education is the lowest in Gallup's trend, including in 1962, less than a decade after the Supreme Court ruling desegregating public schools.

Americans' Perceptions of Whether Black Children Have as Good a Chance as White Children in Their Community to Get a Good Education

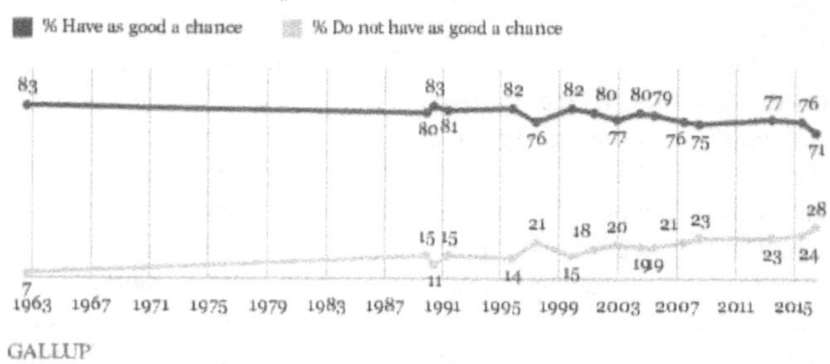

The results are based on the June 7-July 1 Gallup Minority Rights and Relations poll, conducted just before recent racial incidents in Minneapolis, Baton Rouge and Dallas.

Most Americans believe blacks have the same opportunities as whites in all three areas of life assessed in the new poll – jobs, housing and education – but fewer hold that view than at any point in at least the last two decades. One reason for the declines could be the attention given to racial and economic inequality by the candidates in this year's presidential campaign. Racial incidents involving police in recent years, and the resulting Black Lives Matter movement, could also be a factor, though declines in perceptions of black housing and educational opportunities were mostly evident this year.

Blacks Less Confident Than Whites About Equal Opportunity

Whites and blacks have different perceptions of equality of opportunity for members of racial groups. Whereas roughly seven in 10 whites believe that blacks and whites have the same opportunities to get a job, a good education and any housing they can afford, far fewer blacks agree. Slightly less than half of blacks believe that blacks and whites have the same chance to get a good education (49%) and to get any housing they can afford (46%). Even fewer blacks, 32%, say blacks and whites have equal job opportunities.

Compared with 1999 – the first year Gallup asked all three questions in a poll with a large oversample of blacks – both blacks and whites are now less optimistic about black opportunities in all three areas and by similar margins. Thus, while blacks and whites continue to hold widely differing views on black opportunities in the U.S., both groups are less positive than in the past about the situation for blacks.

Perceptions of Black vs. White Opportunities for Jobs, Housing and Education

Figures reflect percentages who believe blacks and whites have the same chance

	1999 %	2016 %	Change pct. pts.
Jobs			
National adults	74	64	-10
Whites	79	69	-10
Blacks	40	32	-8
Housing			
National adults	82	71	-11
Whites	86	75	-11
Blacks	56	49	-7
Education			
National adults	79	70	-9
Whites	83	74	-9
Blacks	53	46	-7

Gallup

Implications

Americans as a whole largely believe blacks and whites have equal opportunities in the workforce, in school and in finding a home, as opposed to believing blacks are disadvantaged in those areas. But fewer Americans – including both blacks and whites – believe equality of opportunity exists in these realms today than have done so in the previous 20 years or more. And more than 50 years after the civil rights movement began, blacks themselves are divided as to whether they have equal opportunities.

Racially charged incidents involving police, the resulting Black Lives Matter movement, and the Flint, Michigan, water crisis have all contributed to a robust national discussion about the challenges blacks face in society. And these concerns are likely magnified in the midst of a presidential campaign as the candidates react to the events and attempt to offer solutions to address the issues they raise. Barack Obama's election as the nation's first black president was a landmark achievement for blacks, but seven years into his presidency, the issues of race remain complex and are beyond what political leadership alone can change.

Historical data are available in Gallup Analytics.

Survey Methods

Results for this Gallup poll are based on telephone interviews conducted June 7-July 1, 2016, with a sample of 3,270 adults, aged 18 and older, living in all 50 U.S. states and the District of Columbia, who had previously been interviewed in the Gallup Daily tracking poll and agreed to be re-interviewed for a later study. The sample is weighted to be representative of U.S. adults.

For results based on the total sample of national adults, the margin of sampling error is ±3 percentage points at the 95% confidence level. For results based on the sample of 1,320 non-Hispanic whites, the margin of sampling error is ±4 percentage points at the 95% confidence level. For results based on the sample of 912 non-Hispanic blacks, the margin of sampling error is ±5 percentage points at the 95% confidence level. For results based on the sample of 906 Hispanics, the margin of sampling error is ±6 percentage points at the 95% confidence level. (271 out of the 906 interviews with Hispanics were conducted in Spanish.)

All reported margins of sampling error include computed design effects for weighting.

July 15, 2016
U.S. SATISFACTION HIGHER AMONG BLACKS, HISPANICS THAN WHITES

by Justin McCarthy

Story Highlights

- *About half of blacks, Hispanics satisfied with U.S. direction*
- *Twenty-eight percent of whites satisfied*
- *Large majority of each group satisfied with personal lives*

WASHINGTON, D.C. – Nearly half of American blacks (49%) and Hispanics (47%) are satisfied with the way things are going in the U.S., compared with 28% of whites. Satisfaction levels among these three groups have generally been steady in Minority Rights and Relations polls conducted since 2013.

In general, are you satisfied or dissatisfied with the way things are going in the United States at this time?

	Satisfied %
Total	34
Non-Hispanic whites	28
Blacks	49
Hispanics	47

Gallup, Jun 7-Jul 1, 2016

The latest reading, from Gallup's June 7-July 1 Minority Rights and Relations survey, was collected just before recent police shootings of black men in Minnesota and Louisiana that once again brought race relations to the forefront of public discussion. These data were also collected before the shooting deaths of five Dallas police officers during a protest march.

Polling conducted as part of Gallup Daily tracking earlier in the Obama administration, between 2009 and 2013, shows racial gaps in satisfaction similar to those seen today. By contrast, throughout the Bush administration from 2001 through 2008, whites were more satisfied with the direction of the country and blacks less satisfied, consistent with each racial groups' political leanings.

Blacks and Hispanics lean heavily Democratic, while whites lean Republican – which appears to influence their views of the way things in the U.S. are going under presidents of their own party versus those of the opposing party.

More Than Four in Five Americans Satisfied With Personal Lives

While two-thirds of Americans are dissatisfied with the way things are going in the country as a whole, Americans are generally upbeat about the direction of their own lives. No less than 85% of those in any of the three major racial and ethnic groups say they are very or somewhat satisfied with their lives. This follows the general truism that Americans tend to be more positive about their personal lives and where they live than they are about the country as a whole. Additionally, personal satisfaction across all racial and ethnic groups is much more consistent than is U.S. satisfaction.

Unlike the racial gaps seen with U.S. satisfaction, there are small differences among whites, blacks and Hispanics in personal satisfaction. Whites and blacks have virtually identical satisfaction levels, at 89% and 88%, respectively, with Hispanics just slightly lower, at 85%.

Overall, how satisfied are you with your life – are you very satisfied, somewhat satisfied, somewhat dissatisfied or very dissatisfied?

	Very/Somewhat satisfied %
Total	88
Non-Hispanic whites	89
Blacks	88
Hispanics	85

Gallup, Jun 7-Jul 1, 2016

Bottom Line

Even with the increased spotlight on police treatment of blacks and more focus on U.S. race relations, blacks' and Hispanics' satisfaction with the direction of the country remains about where it has been in recent years. These higher levels of satisfaction appear to reflect blacks' and Hispanics' Democratic orientation and their positive reaction to a Democratic president. Blacks are clearly more negative than whites about specific aspects of race relations, but their general outlook on the way things are going in the country is more positive.

Whites continue to be least satisfied with where the country is heading, most likely linked to their Republican orientation. It may also help explain why enough Republican voters gravitated toward Donald Trump's campaign promises about making America great again – and his continued criticism of the way things are going in the U.S. under President Barack Obama – to make Trump their party's nominee.

Regardless of race or ethnicity, most Americans have been satisfied with their own lives over the past 16 years, suggesting that even in times of widespread dissatisfaction with their country, Americans separate their personal circumstances from those going on in the country around them.

Historical data are available in Gallup Analytics.

Survey Methods

Results for this Gallup poll are based on telephone interviews conducted June 7-July 1, 2016, with a sample of 3,270 adults, aged 18 and older, living in all 50 U.S. states and the District of Columbia, who had previously been interviewed in the Gallup Daily tracking poll and agreed to be re-interviewed for a later study. The sample is weighted to be representative of U.S. adults.

For results based on the total sample of national adults, the margin of sampling error is ±3 percentage points at the 95% confidence level. For results based on the sample of 1,320 non-Hispanic whites, the margin of sampling error is ±4 percentage points at the 95% confidence level. For results based on the sample of 912 non-Hispanic blacks, the margin of sampling error is ±5 percentage points at the 95% confidence level. For results based on the sample of 906 Hispanics, the margin of sampling error is ±6 percentage points at the 95% confidence level (271 out of the 906 interviews with Hispanics were conducted in Spanish). All reported margins of sampling error include computed design effects for weighting.

July 15, 2016
MOST AMERICANS FORESEE DEATH OF CASH IN THEIR LIFETIME

by Art Swift and Steve Ander

Story Highlights

- *62% think society is likely to become cashless*
- *Older Americans prefer to always have cash on hand*
- *People in their peak earning years like to carry the most cash*

WASHINGTON, D.C. – Most Americans (62%) expect the U.S. to become a cashless society in their lifetime, with all purchases being made with credit cards, debit cards and other forms of electronic payment. They express these views as more Americans make payments from an expanding menu of electronic options, and fewer make cash transactions, and as younger populations are becoming more comfortable without cash in their pockets.

Cash and the Future Economy

How likely do you think it is that in your lifetime the United States will be a cashless society, in which all purchases are made with credit cards, debit cards and other forms of electronic payment?

	Jun 22-23, 2016 %
Very likely	30
Likely	32
Unlikely	25
Very unlikely	11

Gallup

Gallup asked Americans in a June 22-23 survey about their opinions of cash and its future role in the economy. Solid majorities in all age groups say they can foresee a U.S. society without cash, including 58% of those 65 and older and 63% of 18- to 29-year-olds.

Younger Americans Least Likely to Have Cash on Hand

As Americans move away from using tangible currency for their transactions, the majority (54%) still say they like to have cash on them at all times. Forty-two percent say they are comfortable not having cash on them. Younger Americans between the ages of 18 and 29 are the most likely to be comfortable not having cash. Americans aged 30 and older – including more than six in 10 among the oldest Americans – say they would prefer having cash on them at all times, as opposed to not having cash.

Americans' Tendencies to Have Cash, by Age

Are you someone who likes to have cash on you at all times when you are out of your home, or are you comfortable not having cash on you?

	Have cash on you at all times %	Comfortable not having cash %
National adults	54	42
18 to 29	42	56
30 to 49	54	42
50 to 64	55	39
65+	62	32

Gallup, June 22-23, 2016

Young adults' greater comfort in being cashless aligns with their self-reported behavior. They are using cash in a significantly smaller proportion of transactions than they were even five years ago, so they are clearly adapting to spending without cash.

Those in Peak Earning Years Carry the Most Cash

While older adults generally like to have cash always on hand, this does not mean they like to carry the most cash. Instead, those aged 30 to 49 like to have the most on hand, averaging $61.73. That is more than double the average amount of cash 18- to 29-year-olds like to carry.

Cash on Hand, by Age

About how much cash do you typically like to have on you when you are out of the house?

	Mean $	Median $
National adults	49	20
18 to 29	27.25	0
30 to 49	61.73	20
50 to 64	48.04	20
65+	52.30	25

Gallup, June 22-23, 2016

The ages of 30 to 49 are largely considered the peak earning years and the prime child-rearing years. Therefore, for those in this group, their relatively high amount of desired walking-around money may derive from both supply and demand – they have access to more money, and they likely have more reasons to spend it.

Bottom Line

The first article in this two-part series reported on Americans' decreasing use of cash in daily transactions. Accordingly, most Americans can already foresee a time when cash will be obsolete.

Cash is becoming less a part of Americans' purchasing behavior as they gravitate toward other payment options and shift toward online purchases, rather than transactions in a brick-and-mortar store. Younger American customers' lower likelihood to use cash and greater comfort with not having it on hand suggest that the economy will have to adapt. This has significant implications for the credit card, banking and e-commerce industries as well as the local stores and businesses in every U.S. town and city. In the short term, this shift will place greater pressure on these businesses to adapt and accept electronic payments. In the long term, Americans largely predict that cash will become a relic.

Historical data are available in Gallup Analytics.

Survey Methods

Results for this Gallup poll are based on telephone interviews conducted June 22-23, 2016, with a random sample of 1,024 adults, aged 18 and older, living in all 50 U.S. states and the District of Columbia. For results based on the total sample of national adults, the margin of sampling error is ±4 percentage points at the 95% confidence level.

July 18, 2016
TRUMP'S IMAGE OVER LAST YEAR STABLE – AND NEGATIVE

by Frank Newport

Story Highlights

- *Americans' favorable views of Trump at 34% now; 31% a year ago*
- *Trump's unfavorable also very similar now and in July 2015*
- *66% of Republicans view Trump favorably*

PRINCETON, N.J. – As Republicans gather in Cleveland and prepare to make Donald Trump their party's presidential nominee, a retrospective analysis shows that Americans' views of Trump have been generally stable and continually negative over the past year. Despite some ups and downs as the campaign progressed, Trump's current 34% favorable and 61% unfavorable ratings are within a few percentage points of where they were in July 2015 when the campaign was just starting.

Donald Trump Favorable and Unfavorable Image

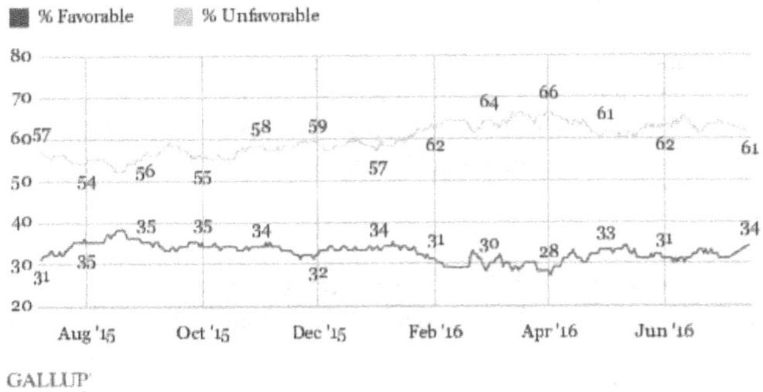

When Gallup began tracking Trump's favorability in July 2015, 31% of Americans viewed him favorably and 57% viewed him unfavorably, leaving 12% who had no opinion. The general trajectory of his image from that point through April this year has been negative, with his unfavorable rating rising to its high point of 66% several times in March and April. As it became increasingly evident that Trump would win his party's nomination, Trump's negative rating began to edge down slightly, ending at 61% for the last seven days ending July 16.

Trump's favorable rating was at its highest point of 38% in August 2015. His current 34% rating is higher than the lowest point of 27% in April 2016. Trump's overall favorable rating over the past 12 months has been 33%, while his average unfavorable rating has been 59%, meaning that his current image is just about average for the entire year.

Trump's current 61% unfavorable rating is among the most negative of any presidential candidate for whom Gallup has historical records on this question. Businessman Ross Perot, who ran as an independent candidate in 1992, had an unfavorable rating of 66% among registered voters in October of that year. Incumbent president and candidate George H.W. Bush's unfavorable rating reached as high as 57% during that same month. Candidates since 1992 have all had significantly lower unfavorable ratings.

Republicans Now a Bit More Positive About Trump

A little less than two-thirds of Republicans viewed their presidential nominee favorably in Gallup's June average, and that percentage is up slightly for the week ending July 16. Republicans' positive views were generally below the 60% mark until Trump essentially secured the nomination, and their ratings have edged higher since. Democrats' already low favorable opinions of Trump have drifted even lower as the campaign progressed, with a monthly high point of 17% in August 2015 and the low point of 7% in June 2016.

Donald Trump Favorability, by Party

% Favorable, monthly averages

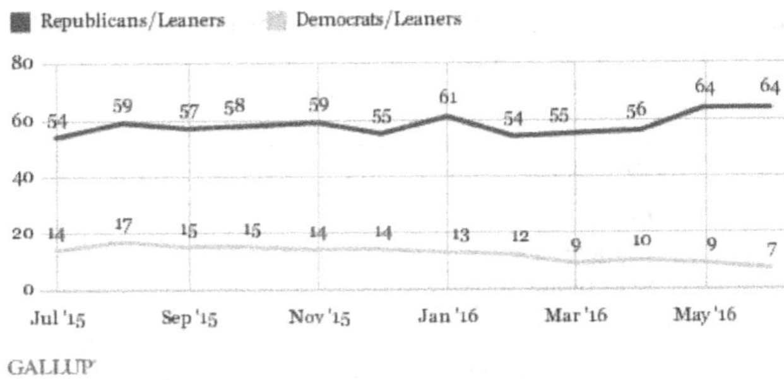

Trump's Favorable Image Among Blacks and Hispanics Between 10% and 12%

Trump's image is highly differentiated across the nation's racial and ethnic groups. Although still relatively low, his favorable rating among non-Hispanic whites over the past 12 months have been generally more than twice as high as his favorable rating among either blacks or Hispanics. The month-to-month favorable ratings among whites have ranged between a high of 44% last August to a low of 38% in March and April 2016. Blacks' favorable views of Trump have slid from 21% last August to 10% over the past two months. Hispanics' favorable views dropped to 12%.

Donald Trump Favorability, by Race

% Favorable, monthly averages

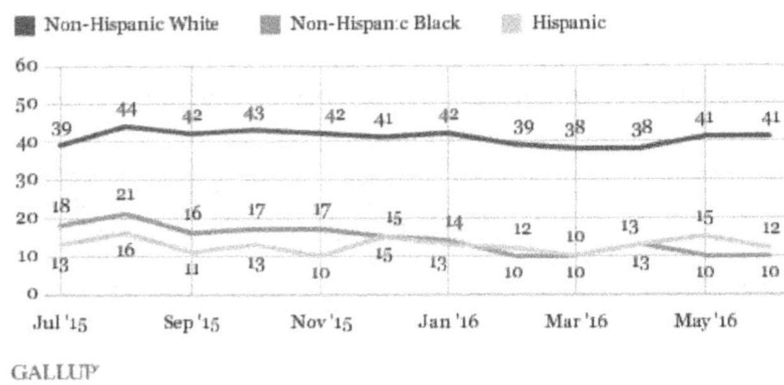

Men Consistently More Positive Than Women About Trump

Most Republican candidates are better liked by men than by women, and Trump is no exception. The gender gap has averaged 12 percentage points over the past 12 months and was at exactly that average in June – 38% of men held a favorable opinion, compared with 26% of women. The gender gap is slightly smaller over the seven days of interviewing ending July 16, however, at nine points. Trump's most recent seven-day average of 29% favorable rating among women is exactly the same as where he started last summer.

Donald Trump Favorability, by Gender

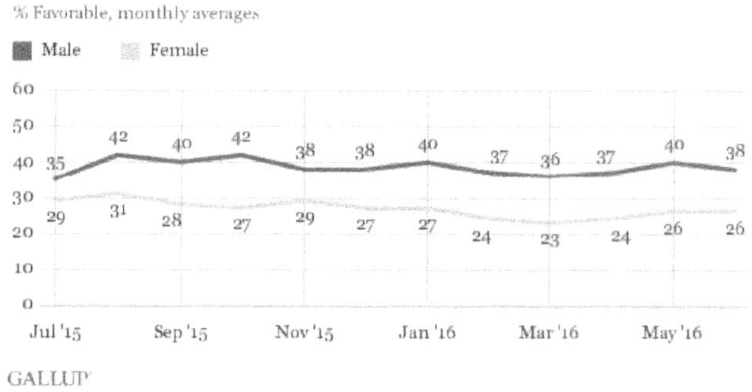

Bottom Line

The process by which non-politician Trump captured his party's presidential nomination will likely stand as one of most remarkable in contemporary U.S. political history. The billionaire businessman defied much of the conventional political logic about how to win a nomination, freewheelingly said things and criticized groups who previously had been off limits to major party candidates, used social media and avoided traditional paid television commercials. He won the nomination even as many professional politicians, media commentators and pundits said he had no chance.

Throughout the process, the audience to which Trump is ultimately playing – the American people – has ended up rating him just about how they did a year ago. When Gallup began tracking his image last July, it was just a shade less than a negative 2-to-1 ratio, and 12 months later, it is about the same. This stability raises the question of whether it is possible for Trump to change the way the people view him in the less than four months remaining in the campaign. If not, how possible will it be to convince Americans who don't like him in general to, nevertheless, end up voting for him?

The Republican National Convention now underway offers one of the best opportunities for a candidate like Trump to alter his image, as most candidates come out of their convention with a more positive standing than when it began.

Trump's candidacy thus far is credited with having created records for Republican primary voting turnout and primary debate ratings. This certainly suggests that the at-home audience for the GOP convention in Cleveland this week may be large, thus giving Trump one of the most important stages of his nascent political career so far.

Historical data are available in Gallup Analytics.

Survey Methods

Results for this Gallup poll are based on telephone interviews conducted July 9-16, 2016, on the Gallup U.S. Daily survey, with a random sample of 3,538 adults, aged 18 and older, living in all 50 U.S. states and the District of Columbia. For results based on the total sample of national adults, the margin of sampling error is ±3 percentage points at the 95% confidence level. All reported margins of sampling error include computed design effects for weighting.

July 18, 2016
VOTERS HAVE MUTED REACTION TO PENCE, HARDLY KNOW HIM

by Lydia Saad

Story Highlights

- *37% rate Pence positively as VP choice*
- *Slightly more, 45%, call Pence "only fair" or "poor" choice*
- *62% offer no opinion of Pence on favorability question*

PRINCETON, N.J. – Thirty-seven percent of U.S. voters rate Indiana Gov. Mike Pence an "excellent" or "pretty good" choice as Donald Trump's vice presidential running mate. Slightly more, 45%, rate him "only fair" or "poor." This is a replay of voters' reactions to Mitt Romney's choice of Wisconsin Rep. Paul Ryan as his running mate four years ago. Thirty-nine percent of registered voters rated Ryan positively and 45% rated him as only fair or poor.

U.S. Registered Voters' Reaction to Donald Trump's Choice of Mike Pence for Vice President

How would you rate Donald Trump's choice of Mike Pence for vice president? Would you rate this choice as – excellent, pretty good, only fair or poor?

	Excellent/ Pretty good %	Only fair/ Poor %	No opinion %
2016: Mike Pence	37	45	18
For comparison:			
2012: Paul Ryan	39	45	16
2008: Sarah Palin	46	37	17
2008: Joe Biden	47	33	20
2004: John Edwards	64	28	8
2000: Joe Lieberman	53	28	19
2000: Dick Cheney	55	34	11

Gallup

Since 2000, when Gallup began measuring voters' immediate reaction to vice presidential choices, only Ryan and Pence have elicited more negative than positive reactions upon being named as running mates.

Two other vice presidential picks, Sarah Palin and Joe Biden – both tapped in 2008 – were rated slightly more positively than negatively. Solid majorities rated three picks – John Edwards in 2004, Joe Lieberman in 2000 and Dick Cheney in 2000 – as excellent or pretty good. The less-positive reaction to vice presidential candidates in recent years could reflect the increasingly polarized political environment in the U.S.

Barely One in Four Republican Voters Appear Enthused About Pence

Overall, two-thirds of Republicans who are registered to vote consider Pence an excellent or pretty good choice for vice president; only 5% call him poor. But one of the jobs of a running mate is to help the nominee fire up his or her political base, and it appears Pence has yet to achieve that. Just 27% of Republican voters call him an excellent choice for vice president.

U.S. Voters' Reactions to Mike Pence as Trump's VP Choice, by Party ID

	Excellent %	Pretty good %	Only fair %	Poor %	No opinion %
U.S. registered voters	13	24	23	22	18
Republicans	27	40	17	5	13
Independents	9	21	28	21	22
Democrats	4	10	26	42	18

Gallup, July 15-16, 2016

Pence's "excellent" rating falls well short of the 39% of Republicans rating Ryan this highly in 2012, as well as 34% for Palin in 2008. Cheney sparked less enthusiasm in 2000, earning a mere 18% excellent rating from Republicans.

Pence Largely Unknown

More broadly, Pence is not a well-known figure nationally. Just 39% of registered voters have an opinion of him. More than six in 10 either have no opinion (18%) or have never heard of him (44%). Thus, while nearly as many voters currently view Pence unfavorably (18%) as favorably (21%), there is a great deal of opportunity for that to change as he becomes a household name.

Only Palin, newly named as John McCain's running mate in 2008, was more unfamiliar to voters than Pence is today, while slight majorities were unacquainted with Ryan, Biden and Lieberman at the time they were selected.

U.S. Registered Voters' Impressions of Mike Pence

Do you have a favorable or unfavorable opinion of Mike Pence, or have you never heard of him?

	Favorable %	Unfavorable %	Never heard of %	No opinion %
2016: Mike Pence	21	18	44	18
For comparison:				
2012: Paul Ryan	27	21	32	21
2008: Sarah Palin	22	7	51	20
2008: Joe Biden	34	15	23	28
2004: John Edwards	54	16	12	18
2000: Joe Lieberman	37	10	24	29
2000: Dick Cheney	51	11	7	31
1996: Jack Kemp	56	14	10	20
1992: Al Gore	59	13	–	28

Gallup, July 15-16, 2016

Pence Not Rocking the Vote

Roughly three in four registered voters claim that having Pence on the ticket will not influence their likelihood of voting for Trump for president, and that is typical – Gallup finds the majority saying this about the vice presidential selections in every election.

At the same time, by 14% to 10%, slightly more voters say Pence makes them more likely to support Trump in November rather than less likely. This is also typical; however, this minimal positive tilt is one of the weaker ones of the past eight elections. It is on par with Ryan's influence on the ticket in 2012 as well as Cheney's in 2000. Dan Quayle in 1988 is the only candidate who brought no net positive effect to the ticket.

Effect of Mike Pence on Likelihood of Voting for Donald Trump in November

Does having Mike Pence as his running mate make you more likely to vote for Donald Trump in November, less likely or will it not have much effect on your vote?

	More likely %	Less likely %	No effect %	Net more likely pct. pts.
2016: Mike Pence	14	10	74	4
For comparison:				
2012: Paul Ryan	17	13	68	4
2008: Sarah Palin	18	11	67	7
2008: Joe Biden	14	7	72	7
2004: John Edwards	24	7	66	17
2000: Joe Lieberman	16	4	76	12
2000: Dick Cheney	14	10	72	4
1996: Jack Kemp	26	8	63	18
1992: Al Gore	33	8	57	25
1988: Lloyd Bentsen §	26	9	60	17
1988: Dan Quayle ^	10	10	73	0

§ Time poll; ^ USA Today poll; NOTE: all vice presidential nominees shown are non-incumbents

Gallup

Less Than Half Say Pence Qualified to Be President if Necessary

Pence has yet to accomplish another important job – helping to patch one of the presumptive GOP nominee's image weaknesses. In Trump's case, that includes a perceived lack of experience needed to be president.

By 46% to 33%, more voters say Pence – a lawyer, current governor of Indiana and former six-term congressman from the state – is qualified to serve as president should it become necessary. While similar to 2012 voter perceptions of Ryan, whom 50% thought was qualified, the 46% saying Pence is qualified is on the low end of the percentages saying this about other vice presidential choices since 1992. Palin, another relatively unknown governor nationally, was rated worse.

These views may reflect some awareness that Pence is a governor and has at least earned Trump's confidence. However, with 22% of voters expressing no opinion on Pence's qualifications, there is room for change on this front as the campaign continues.

U.S. Voters' Perceptions of Mike Pence as Qualified to Serve as President

Based on what you know about Mike Pence, do you think he is qualified to serve as president if it becomes necessary, or not?

	Yes, qualified %	No, not %	No opinion %
2016: Mike Pence	46	33	22
For comparison:			
2012: Paul Ryan	50	31	19
2008: Sarah Palin	39	33	29
2008: Joe Biden	57	18	26
2004: John Edwards	57	29	14
2000: Joe Lieberman	52	13	35
2000: Dick Cheney	57	18	25
1996: Al Gore	60	34	6
1996: Jack Kemp	61	16	23
1992: Al Gore	64	19	17

Gallup, July 15-16, 2016

Bottom Line

In selecting Pence as his running mate, Trump has neither scored a home run nor struck out. Voters have reacted with modest approval – not convinced he is an excellent or even good choice, but more likely to believe he is qualified than not qualified, and slightly more likely to say he inspires them to vote for the GOP ticket. Still, Pence is largely unfamiliar to most voters, with 62% having no opinion of him, and therefore these attitudes can be viewed as only preliminary. For now, voters are most likely basing their views about Pence's selection or his qualifications on partisanship, their feelings about Trump or a general awareness of Pence's government credentials.

Research indicates that the name on the vice presidential line of the ballot has little influence on presidential elections – and may not even improve the ticket's chance of winning that person's home state. Voters corroborate this, telling pollsters that the vice presidential choice won't influence their vote. Proving the point, two superstars of vice presidential announcements, based on their favorability and excellent/pretty good ratings – Edwards and Lieberman – were on the losing side of the election despite the strongly positive reactions their announcements generated among voters.

Likewise, unpopular running mates don't necessarily doom a ticket. A Louis Harris and Associates poll conducted in 1988 – immediately after the Republican national convention at which George H.W. Bush announced Quayle as his running mate – found a majority of likely voters viewing Quayle as an only fair or poor choice. Although this was after several days of negative press about Quayle and thus doesn't represent as immediate a reaction as Pence's today, it does provide a guidepost for the degree to which a vice presidential candidate can be viewed negatively and yet not prevent a ticket from winning the election. And at this point, Pence is nowhere near that level.

Historical data are available in Gallup Analytics.

Survey Methods

Results for this Gallup poll are based on telephone interviews conducted July 15-16, 2016, on the Gallup U.S. Daily survey, with a random sample of 901 registered voters, aged 18 and older, living in all 50 U.S. states and the District of Columbia. For results based on the total sample of registered voters, the margin of sampling error is ±4 percentage points at the 95% confidence level. All reported margins of sampling error include computed design effects for weighting.

MORE REPUBLICANS FAVOR PATH TO CITIZENSHIP THAN WALL

by Jeffrey M. Jones

Story Highlights

- *76% of Republicans favor path to citizenship; 62% building a wall*
- *Two-thirds in U.S. oppose deporting illegal immigrants, building a wall*
- *84% in U.S. favor of path to citizenship for illegal immigrants*

PRINCETON, N.J. – Two-thirds of Americans oppose immigration plans advocated by Republican presidential nominee Donald Trump – building a wall along the U.S.-Mexico border and deporting immigrants living in the U.S. illegally. In contrast, 84% favor a path to citizenship for illegal immigrants living in the U.S., a plan backed by Democratic nominee Hillary Clinton. Notably, significantly more Republicans favor a path to citizenship than support building a border wall or deporting illegal immigrants.

Opinions of Immigration Proposals

	U.S. adults %	Democrats %	Independents %	Republicans %
Allowing immigrants living in the U.S. illegally the chance to become U.S. citizens if they meet certain requirements over a period of time				
Favor	84	91	85	76
Oppose	15	8	14	24
Building a wall along the entire U.S.-Mexico border				
Favor	33	12	33	62
Oppose	66	88	66	38
Deporting all immigrants who are living in the U.S. illegally back to their home country				
Favor	32	16	33	50
Oppose	66	83	65	48

June 7-July 1 Gallup poll

Republicans are divided on deporting all immigrants living in the U.S. illegally back to their home country, a proposal advanced by Trump during the primary season. Since then, he appears to have softened that stance.

Republicans are more likely to favor the border wall, but their 62% support for it stands in sharp contrast to Democrats' 88% opposition to the same proposal.

At least three in four Republicans (76%), independents (85%) and Democrats (91%) favor a path to citizenship for immigrants living in the U.S. illegally who meet certain requirements over a period of time.

The results are based on Gallup's June 7-July 1 Minority Rights and Relations poll, a survey of more than 3,000 U.S. adults including large oversamples of blacks and Hispanics. The sample is weighted to be representative of U.S. adults nationally.

Non-Hispanic Whites Show Greater Support for Deportation, Wall

Given white Americans' GOP leanings, it is not surprising that non-Hispanic whites are more likely than blacks or Hispanics to support deporting illegal immigrants and building a border wall. Still, most whites oppose these proposals – 59% oppose the U.S.-Mexico border wall, and 62% oppose deporting all illegal immigrants.

Fewer than one in five blacks and Hispanics favor the construction of a wall between the U.S. and Mexico, and fewer than one in four favor deporting illegal immigrants.

Blacks (84%) and whites (82%) show similar strong support for a path to citizenship, with Hispanics even higher, at 92%.

Opinions of Immigration Proposals, by Race and Ethnicity

	U.S. adults	Non-Hispanic whites	Non-Hispanic blacks	Hispanics
	%	%	%	%
Allowing immigrants living in the U.S. illegally the chance to become U.S. citizens if they meet certain requirements over a period of time				
Favor	84	82	84	92
Oppose	15	17	14	8
Building a wall along the entire U.S.-Mexico border				
Favor	33	41	18	16
Oppose	66	59	82	82
Deporting all immigrants who are living in the U.S. illegally back to their home country				
Favor	32	36	23	21
Oppose	66	62	76	78

June 7-July 1 Gallup poll

Hillary Clinton Given Edge on Immigration Issue

Perhaps not surprisingly, given the greater support for a path to citizenship than deportation or building a wall on the U.S.-Mexico border, Americans are more likely to say Hillary Clinton's immigration policies and proposals, rather than Trump's, come closer to their own. But the margin in favor of Clinton's ideas on immigration, 53% to 37%, is not as large as one might expect given the differences in support for her key immigration proposals versus Trump's.

That may reflect the realities of partisanship. Republicans widely say Trump's proposals on immigration are closer to their own, by 76% to 15%. Republicans may have a hard time saying they view Clinton as better than their own party's nominee on any issue, given their strong likelihood of voting for Trump in the election. Republicans may also be more comfortable with Trump's broad approach to immigration, even if sizable minorities in the party disagree with some of his specific plans. Still, the 76% of Republicans who say Trump is closer to them on immigration is smaller than the 90% of Democrats who say the same about Clinton.

Candidate Whose Views on Immigration Come Closer to Your Own, by Political Party

	U.S. adults	Democrats	Independents	Republicans
	%	%	%	%
Clinton	53	90	48	15
Trump	37	6	35	76

June 7-July 1 Gallup poll

Independents are more likely to say Clinton's views on immigration are closer to their own by 48% to 35%.

Non-Hispanic whites are about evenly divided about which candidate comes closer to their own views on immigration, with 47% saying Trump and 43%, Clinton. Trump, whose anti-Mexican rhetoric has raised questions about his ability to attract Hispanic support in the general election, is favored by 17% of Hispanics on immigration, compared with 73% who choose Clinton. That is actually a lower level of support for Clinton than among blacks, who favor her over Trump on the immigration issue by 83% to 9%, likely because of blacks' overwhelming support for the Democratic Party.

Candidate Whose Views on Immigration Come Closer to Your Own, by Race and Ethnicity

	U.S. adults	Non-Hispanic whites	Non-Hispanic blacks	Hispanics
	%	%	%	%
Clinton	53	43	83	73
Trump	37	47	9	17

June 7-July 1 Gallup poll

Implications

Immigration has been a major focus of the 2016 campaign, arguably because of the attention Trump has devoted to the issue and the controversy generated by his comments on the matter. Americans as a whole oppose his oft-repeated proposal of building a large wall along the U.S.-Mexico border to deter potential illegal immigrants from entering the country. And though a majority of Republicans favor this proposal, the 62% who do so is much smaller than the 76% who favor a path to citizenship for immigrants living here illegally, a key aspect of Clinton's immigration policy.

Should Trump be elected president, some may conclude his immigration proposals played a key part in that win. However, if Trump does prevail, it appears his victory would come in spite of his stance on immigration, not because of it.

Survey Methods

Results for this Gallup poll are based on telephone interviews conducted June 7-July 1, 2016, with a sample of 3,270 adults, aged 18 and older, living in all 50 U.S. states and the District of Columbia, who had previously been interviewed in the Gallup Daily tracking poll and agreed to be re-interviewed for a later study. The sample is weighted to be representative of U.S. adults.

For results based on the total sample of national adults, the margin of sampling error is ±3 percentage points at the 95% confidence level. For results based on the sample of 1,320 non-Hispanic whites, the margin of sampling error is ±4 percentage points at the 95% confidence level. For results based on the sample of 912 non-Hispanic blacks, the margin of sampling error is ±5 percentage points at the 95% confidence level. For results based on the sample of 906 Hispanics, the margin of sampling error is ±6 percentage points at the 95% confidence level (271 out of the 906 interviews with Hispanics were conducted in Spanish).

All reported margins of sampling error include computed design effects for weighting.

July 21, 2016
OBAMA AVERAGES 50.9% JOB APPROVAL IN 30TH QUARTER

by Jeffrey M. Jones

Story Highlights

- *Improves from 49.5% in 29th quarter*
- *Best quarter in his second term, fifth best overall*
- *Clinton, Eisenhower had higher averages, Reagan a similar one*

PRINCETON, N.J. – President Barack Obama averaged 50.9% job approval during his 30th quarter in office, which began on April 20 and ended on July 19. This is up from a 49.5% average in his 29th quarter and 46.6% during his 28th quarter.

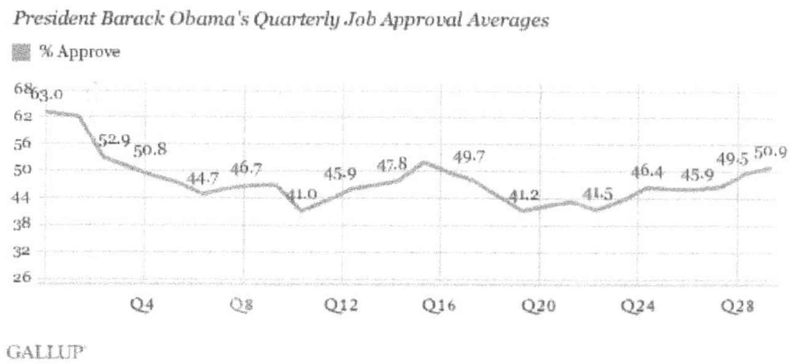

Obama's 30th quarter marks just the sixth time during his presidency that his quarterly average approval has been above the majority level. This includes his first four quarters in office, during the traditional honeymoon phase for presidents, as well as the last quarter during his first term, which coincided with his re-election and a subsequent boost in popularity.

By comparison, other recent two-term presidents had many more quarterly averages above 50% through their 30th quarter in office, including George W. Bush with 16, Bill Clinton with 21 and Ronald Reagan with 18.

Obama's approval ratings held above 50% for much of the latest quarter, including averaging 53% in mid-June. But over the last two weeks, his ratings have suffered as the nation has dealt with more fatal shootings of black men by police officers and two incidents of sniper attacks on police officers. In Gallup's most recent weekly average of presidential approval, based on July 11-17 polling, 49% of Americans approved of Obama's overall job performance.

Notwithstanding the recent slippage, Obama's approval rating has improved among all party groups since last fall, including one- to two-percentage-point increases among Democrats, independents and Republicans in the most recent quarter. Democrats' approval is now at 87.7%, up from 82.8% last fall. Independents' ratings are up by a similar amount, to 48.4%. Republicans' ratings of Obama remain low, but now exceed 10%.

Change in President Obama's Job Approval Ratings, by Political Party, Recent Quarters

Gallup Daily tracking

	Quarter 27 %	Quarter 28 %	Quarter 29 %	Quarter 30 %	Change since 27th quarter pct. pts.
Democrats	82.8	83.6	85.1	87.7	+4.9
Independents	43.7	43.3	47.2	48.4	+4.7
Republicans	9.6	9.6	10.2	12.2	+2.6

Gallup

Recent Obama Climb Reminiscent of Reagan

The improvement in Obama's job ratings since last fall is similar to the pattern seen in Ronald Reagan's ratings in 1987 and 1988. In the late summer and early fall of 1987, an average of 47.0% of Americans approved of the job Reagan was doing as president. As the calendar turned to 1988, that improved to 50.0% and generally stayed there into the summer. But during the late summer and early fall months, a time that included the 1988 party conventions and election campaign, Reagan's approval rating averaged 53.5%.

Improvement over the course of a president's final year in office has not been the norm historically for two-term presidents.

- Harry Truman, who was highly unpopular in 1951 and 1952, did show steady improvement during the 1952 election year, with his ratings going from an all-time low of 23.0% during his 27th quarter to 32.0% in his 30th.
- Dwight Eisenhower was well-regarded by Americans in 1959 and 1960, but his approval rating fell from 65.3% to 58.8% between his 27th and 30th quarters
- Bill Clinton was also popular as his presidency neared its end, but his approval ratings were relatively flat from the fall of 1999 (59.7%) to the spring and summer of 2000 (58.0%).
- George W. Bush's unpopularity rivaled Truman's, with his approval ratings falling from 33.2% in his 27th quarter to 29.0% in his 30th.

Overall, then, Obama is less popular than Clinton and Eisenhower were at this point in their presidencies, but like Reagan, Obama's ratings are improving at a time that could prove beneficial to his party in the looming presidential election.

Implications

Americans are now seeing Obama in a much better light than they did roughly a year ago. Democrats hope they can pull off the rare feat of a party winning three consecutive presidential elections. The improvement in Obama's job approval ratings harkens back to what occurred for Reagan in 1988, the last time a party won a third consecutive presidential election, with Reagan's vice president, George H.W. Bush, defeating Democrat Michael Dukakis.

While that historical pattern may offer hope for Democrats, recent events may serve to halt the improvement in Obama's ratings. The president's most recent approval ratings have primarily been below 50% as the nation struggles with high-profile violence between police and black citizens. Growing concern over race relations and violence is the likely reason Americans' satisfaction with the way things are going in the U.S. fell sharply in July.

Like the GOP in 1988, Democrats have a significant opportunity at their party convention next week to convince Americans that the president has done a good job and that their party should continue to hold the White House beyond his term. Whether Americans ultimately buy that argument may depend on whether their views of the state of the nation improve between now and Election Day.

These data are available in Gallup Analytics.

Survey Methods

Results for this Gallup poll are based on telephone interviews conducted April 20-July 19, 2016, on the Gallup U.S. Daily survey, with a random sample of 45,229 adults, aged 18 and older, living in all 50 U.S. states and the District of Columbia. For results based on the total sample of national adults, the margin of sampling error is ±1 percentage point at the 95% confidence level. All reported margins of sampling error include computed design effects for weighting.

July 21, 2016

AMERICANS' SATISFACTION WITH U.S. DROPS SHARPLY

by Art Swift

Story Highlights

- *Satisfaction now at 17%, down from 29% in June*
- *Lowest measure of satisfaction since October 2013*
- *Race relations surges to top of "most important problem" list*

WASHINGTON, D.C. – Americans' satisfaction with the way things are going in the U.S. dropped 12 percentage points in the past month, amid high-profile police killings of black men and mass shootings of police. Currently, 17% of Americans are satisfied with the state of affairs in the U.S.

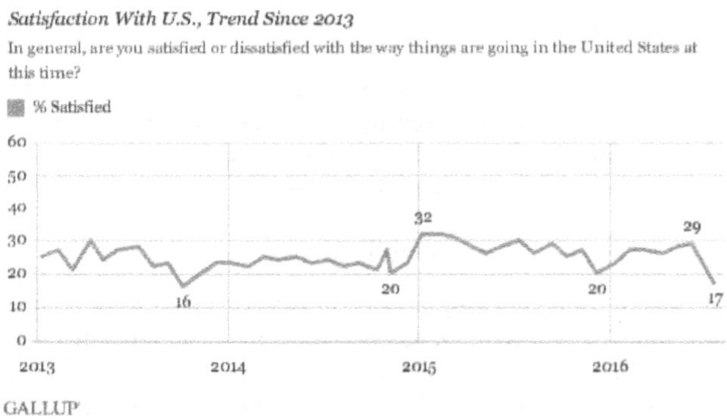

Satisfaction is the lowest it has been nationwide since October 2013, when Republican members in Congress led a federal government shutdown. For the past two years, satisfaction has been in the 20s and 30s, with low points of 20% in December 2015 and November 2014.

This 12-point drop in one month is tied for the largest decrease in satisfaction since Gallup started asking satisfaction monthly in 2001. The previous largest decrease during this period was also 12 points in October 2008, as the financial crisis was taking hold.

These data are from Gallup's latest monthly reading of Americans' satisfaction, taken July 13-17. Between the June reading and now, the U.S. has been rocked by deadly shootings of black men by police in Louisiana and Minnesota, and the targeted killing of police at a protest in Dallas. Also since the last survey, a gunman killed 49 people in a gay nightclub in Orlando. World news has not offered much solace, with a terrorist attack across the Atlantic in Nice, France, involving a truck ramming into a crowd on Bastille Day in mid-July, killing 84.

Race Relations Named as Most Important Problem in U.S.

The same July poll finds a surge in concern about race relations and racism, after the several recent incidents of violence between police and black men. In the July 13-17 update, 18% of Americans say race relations or racism is the most important problem facing the nation, a jump of 13 points in the past month.

Since 2000, mentions of race have only once previously been in double digits – in December 2014, when 13% mentioned race as the top problem facing the nation. Race was infrequently mentioned as the top problem facing the nation from 1970 through 2000, with the exception of May 1992, a week after the Rodney King verdicts in Los Angeles, when 15% mentioned race as the top problem.

There was little change in Americans' mention of terrorism this month, despite the Orlando shootings.

Recent Trend, Most Important Problem

What do you think is the most important problem facing this country today?

	April 2016 %	May 2016 %	June 2016 %	July 2016 %
Race relations/ Racism	7	5	5	18
Dissatisfaction with government	13	13	13	16
Economy in general	17	18	18	12
Unemployment/Jobs	9	9	8	7
Crime/Violence	2	2	3	6
Ethics/Moral decline	5	3	5	6
Immigration/Illegal aliens	8	7	7	6
National security	5	4	5	6
Terrorism	6	4	4	5
Guns/Gun control	1	1	1	5
Elections/Election reform	4	5	6	5

Gallup

Dissatisfaction with government ranks second among the most important problems this month, and at 16% generally remains in the range it has been in during recent months. Mentions of the "economy in general," No. 1 last month, fell to third at 12%. Americans this month are more likely to mention crime/violence (6%) and guns/gun control (5%) than they have been in previous months, most likely a reaction to the occurrence of violence and shootings in Louisiana, Minnesota, Texas and Florida.

Democrats' Satisfaction Drops Precipitously

The decline in Americans' satisfaction this month includes a particularly sharp drop among Democrats, whose satisfaction levels

– after registering 51% last month – dropped 22 points to 29% in July. This was a marked change from the 11-point jump in satisfaction Democrats expressed from May to June.

Satisfaction With U.S. by Party ID, Trend Since 2007

In general, are you satisfied or dissatisfied with the way things are going in the United States at this time?

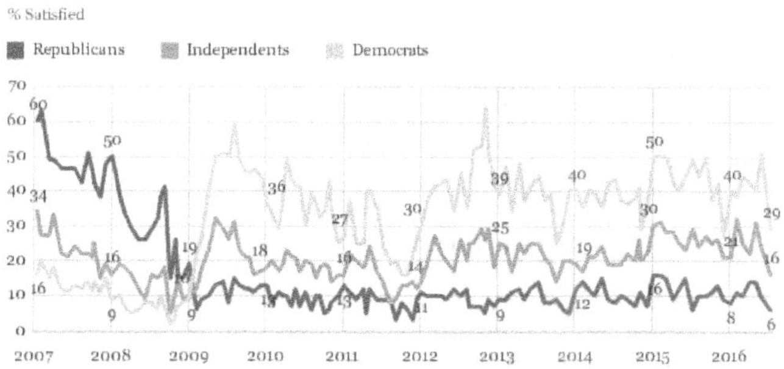

GALLUP

Republicans, on the other hand, have professed extremely low satisfaction with life in the U.S. throughout the Obama administration, ranging from 3% to 19% during Barack Obama's term in office. Independents' satisfaction dropped in the last month from 24% to 16%.

Bottom Line

Racial strife, epitomized in the recent police shootings and shootings of police, and highlighted in ongoing protests, appears to have ignited new concerns about the state of the U.S. The American public now says race relations/racism is the nation's single most important problem, and overall satisfaction with the way things are going in the country has dropped significantly.

Americans' satisfaction with the way things are going in the U.S. has generally been low in the past decade, even before the July downturn. In an era increasingly defined by wars in the Middle East, a Great Recession, ongoing economic uncertainty and heightened and polarized political rhetoric, it is not surprising that more than half of Americans have said they are not satisfied with the way things are going in the country for more than a decade.

As the summer continues, with political conventions and the possibility of ongoing racial unrest, satisfaction with the U.S. may remain low as uncertainty persists at least until the presidential election in November.

Historical data are available in Gallup Analytics.

Survey Methods

Results for this Gallup poll are based on telephone interviews conducted July 13-17, 2016, on the Gallup U.S. Daily survey, with a random sample of 1,023 adults, aged 18 and older, living in all 50 U.S. states and the District of Columbia. For results based on the total sample of national adults, the margin of sampling error is ±4 percentage points at the 95% confidence level. All reported margins of sampling error include computed design effects for weighting.

July 22, 2016
ABOUT HALF OF AMERICANS PLAY STATE LOTTERIES

by Zac Auter

Story Highlights

- *Nearly half of all U.S. adults say they have played the state lottery*
- *40% of lower-income Americans have bought a lottery ticket*
- *11% of the lower-income say they sometimes gamble more than they should*

WASHINGTON, D.C. – Roughly half of Americans say they have bought a state lottery ticket within the last year, similar to the figures recorded in 2003 and 2007, but down considerably from the 57% who said they played the state lottery in 1996 and 1999. This trend has occurred even as the number of states with lotteries grew over this period from 37 states and the District of Columbia to 44.

Trend in the Share of Americans Who Say They Bought a State Lottery Ticket in Past 12 Months

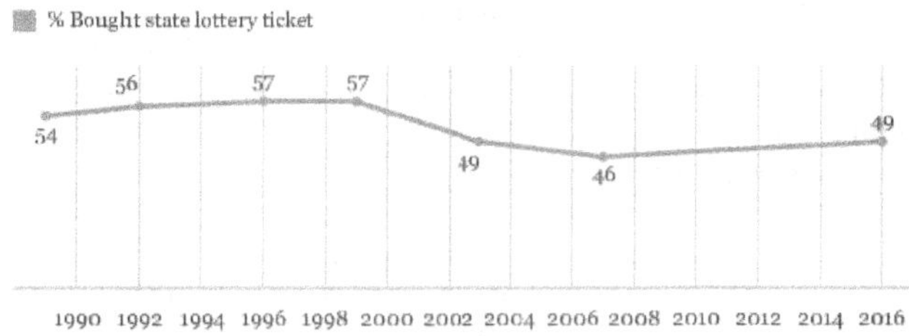

GALLUP

These latest data are from a Gallup survey conducted June 14-23. The exact reason for the decline in Americans' reports of playing the lottery during the last 13 years is not clear, although gamblers now also have a wider range of gambling avenues from which to choose, including the proliferation of online poker and online fantasy sports leagues.

Poorer, Less Educated Less Likely to Say They Bought State Lottery Ticket

Critics of state-sponsored lotteries argue that they disproportionately prey on the hopes of disadvantaged groups such as the poor and less educated, who can least afford to be spending on non-essentials. According to some lottery critics, lottery winnings can have an outsized appeal to economically vulnerable Americans who have less disposable income.

The latest Gallup update, however, shows that Americans whose annual household income is less than $36,000 per year were substantially less likely than higher-income Americans to say they have purchased a state lottery ticket within the past year. Four in 10 lower-income Americans say they bought a lottery ticket during that time, while more than half of middle- (56%) and upper-income Americans (53%) say the same.

U.S. Gambling Behavior by Annual Income

	Less than $36,000 %	$36,000 to $89,999 %	$90,000+ %
Bought state lottery ticket in past 12 months	40	56	53

Gallup, June 14-23, 2016

U.S. Gambling Behavior by Education

	High school or less %	Technical degree or some college %	College degree %	Postgraduate education %
Bought state lottery ticket in past 12 months	47	53	53	45

Gallup, June 14-23, 2016

There are also modest differences by education. Less than half of Americans (47%) with a high-school diploma or less say they have purchased a state lottery ticket – on par with those with postgraduate education (45%). However, more than half of Americans with some college, as well as those whose highest education is a college degree, say they have bought a state lottery ticket (53% each).

While these findings may defy common conceptions of gamblers as lower-income and less-educated Americans, they echo previous Gallup studies from 1999, 2004 and 2007. In each of those three years, higher-income Americans were *more* likely than lower-income Americans to say they gambled. In two of the three, Gallup found that more highly educated Americans were more likely than less-educated Americans to say they gambled.

Nearly Two-Thirds of Americans Gamble in Some Fashion

Playing a state lottery is the most popular of 11 common gambling activities measured in Gallup's latest update on gambling behavior, with barely a quarter of Americans reporting engaging in the second-most-popular mode of gambling – visiting a casino (26%). Other than participating in a sports-related office pool (15%), no more than one in 10 Americans say they participated in each of the other types of gambling tested within the past year, including wagering on professional sports events (10%) or playing video poker (9%).

Gambling Behavior Among U.S. Adults

	Yes, have done this in past 12 months %
Bought state lottery ticket	49
Visited casino	26
Participated in office pool on the World Series, Super Bowl or other game	15
Bet on professional sports event	10
Other type of gambling	9
Played video poker machine	9
Bet on horse race	6
Played bingo for money	6
Bet on college sports event	5
Bet on boxing match	3
Gambled for money on the internet	3
Overall, have gambled in past 12 months	
Yes	64%

Gallup, June 14-23, 2016

Few Americans Concerned About Their Gambling Behavior

Gambling does not appear to represent a major problem for Americans. Fewer than one in 10 (7%) say they sometimes gamble more than they should, and an identical 7% say gambling has at some point been a source of problems in their family. There has been little change in responses to these two questions over the years.

Lower-income Americans are slightly more likely than those making more money to say they sometimes gamble more than they should, but the differences are not large (11% vs. 6% or 7%). Similarly, one in 10 lower-income Americans report that gambling has been a source of problems in their family, compared with 6% of middle-income and 3% of upper-income Americans.

Implications

In a year marked by a record lottery jackpot in excess of $1 billion, many states are seeing increased revenues from lottery ticket sales. In fact, Massachusetts' state treasurer announced this week that the state saw record highs for both lottery sales and profits in the last fiscal year, selling $5.23 billion in lottery tickets. These trends are occurring despite little evidence of an increase in the percentage of the adult population who play the lottery in recent years.

Many states' lottery revenue supports dedicated policy funds, such as education (for example, Florida), environmental protection (Colorado) or assistance to the elderly (Pennsylvania). By tying revenues to support of public goods, states position their lotteries as a means to supplement popular policies. The role of the lottery remains controversial in some quarters, however. The nonprofit North Carolina Center for Public Policy Research has found that rather than supplementing the budgets of programs for which lottery revenues are dedicated, some states use lottery revenues to fund those programs at normal levels, and then move government funds to other budget items.

Whatever the big-picture consequences of state lotteries, about half of Americans find playing the lottery rewarding enough on a personal basis that they buy a ticket – at least occasionally.

These data are available in Gallup Analytics.

Survey Methods

Results for this Gallup poll are based on telephone interviews conducted June 14-23, 2016, with a random sample of 1,025 adults, aged 18 and older, living in all 50 U.S. states and the District of Columbia. For results based on the total sample of national adults, the margin of sampling error is ±4 percentage points at the 95% confidence level. All reported margins of sampling error include computed design effects for weighting.

July 25, 2016
CLINTON'S IMAGE AT LOWEST POINT IN TWO DECADES

by Frank Newport

Story Highlights

- *38% view Hillary Clinton favorably, 57% unfavorably*
- *Her favorable percentage was 55% as recently as two years ago*

PRINCETON, N.J. – As the Democratic National Convention gets underway in Philadelphia, Hillary Clinton's image is at its lowest point in the 24 years of her national career, with 38% of Americans viewing her favorably and 57% unfavorably. Americans' most positive view of Clinton, 67% favorable, came in December 1998. Before last year, her lowest favorable ratings since she became well-known had been 43% in January 1996 and 44% in March 2001.

Hillary Clinton's Favorable and Unfavorable Ratings

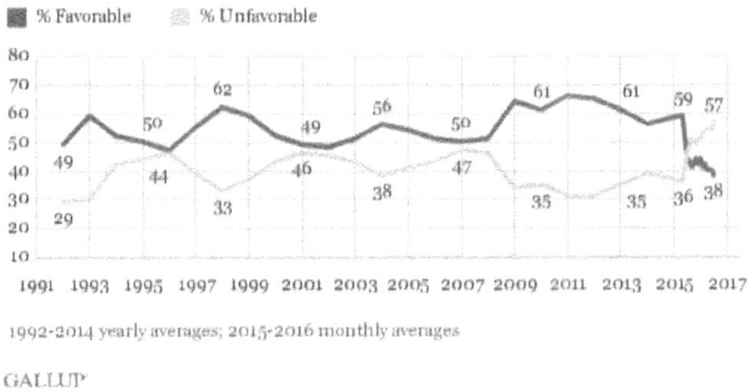

Clinton was at 41% favorable in mid-June but drifted down to 37% by mid-July. Her favorable ratings have since held near that level, including through last week's Republican National Convention. Republican nominee Donald Trump's image for the past seven days was 36% favorable and 59% unfavorable, only slightly less positive than Clinton's.

Gallup first measured Hillary Clinton's image in 1992 as her husband campaigned for the Democratic presidential nomination. Her image, like Bill Clinton's, was mixed in the spring of that year but then grew more positive. Her favorable ratings were above 60% at several points in 1993, and more than six in 10 Americans viewed her favorably at other points as well: when her husband was impeached by the House and tried by the Senate in 1998 and 1999, from 2009 through 2013 while she served as secretary of state, and in April 2013 after she returned to being a private citizen.

After launching her campaign last year and as her handling of emails while secretary of state became an increasingly public and controversial issue, Americans' views of Clinton began their downslide.

Americans' history of changing their views of Clinton from positive to negative and back to positive since 1992 suggests it's possible – although not highly likely, given recent trends – that her image could improve as the Democratic convention unfolds this week. Overall, 55% of Americans viewed her favorably and 39% unfavorably from 1992 through 2014. That long-term average is almost an exact flip of her current 38% favorable, 57% unfavorable rating. This shows how much more negatively the public views her now in the midst of her campaign and email controversy than they have historically.

Both Clinton's and Trump's unfavorable ratings are among the highest of any contemporary presidential candidates. The only comparable situation was in the 1992 presidential race. That year, Americans at times held similarly negative views of independent candidate Ross Perot (after he dropped out and then re-entered the campaign) and incumbent Republican President George H.W. Bush as he sought re-election.

Democrats' Favorable View of Clinton at 71%

Seventy-one percent of Democrats and Democratic-leaning independents view Clinton favorably, compared with fewer than one in 10 Republicans. Democrats were slightly more positive about Clinton last summer and through the winter, and were slightly less positive in April and May as she battled Bernie Sanders for the Democratic nomination. Republicans' favorable views have drifted down somewhat over the past 12 months from their already low starting point.

Hillary Clinton Favorability, by Party

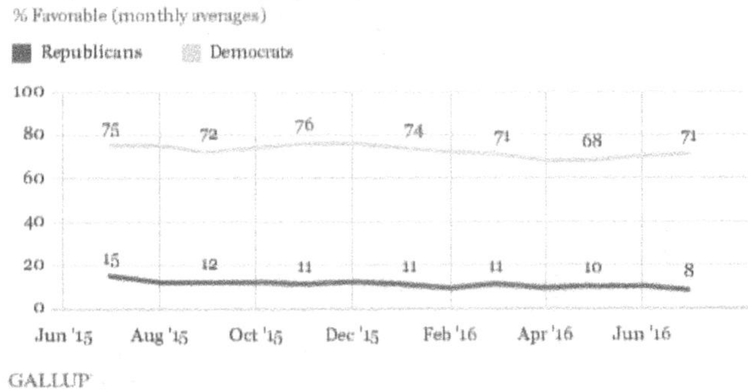

Over the past seven days, spanning the Republican convention at which he accepted his party's nomination, Trump's favorable rating among Republicans improved slightly, to 72%. He and Clinton now have nearly identical favorable ratings among their respective partisans.

Implications

Two highly unpopular candidates are waging the 2016 presidential campaign. Clinton enters her convention with almost six in 10 Americans holding a negative opinion of her, similar to Americans' negative views of her opponent, Trump.

Clinton is one of the best-known politicians in the U.S., with almost a quarter-century of national public exposure as a first lady, a U.S. senator, a secretary of state and now a candidate for president. While Americans' positive views of Clinton have moved up and down over the years, she now is on the verge of accepting the Democratic Party's presidential nomination with an image that is as negative as it has ever been.

A positive image is obviously not all it takes to win the presidency; two of the previous three Democratic nominees had majority-favorable images but ultimately lost. Plus, the parallel unpopularity of Clinton's opponent this year makes it a unique situation in which many voters will choose the least objectionable of two candidates they don't admire. Still, Clinton would clearly rather have a positive than negative image going into the last three months of the campaign, and now faces the significant challenge of attempting to rehabilitate her image to at least some degree during the convention week in Philadelphia.

Historical data are available in Gallup Analytics.

Survey Methods

Results for the latest seven-day averages are based on telephone interviews conducted July 16-23, 2016, on the Gallup U.S. Daily survey, with a random sample of 3,545 adults, aged 18 and older, living in all 50 U.S. states and the District of Columbia. For results based on the total sample of national adults, the margin of sampling error is ±3 percentage points at the 95% confidence level. All reported margins of sampling error include computed design effects for weighting.

July 25, 2016
TIM KAINE MATCHES MIKE PENCE IN LACKLUSTER INITIAL RATINGS

by Lydia Saad

Story Highlights

- *35% of voters call Kaine an excellent or pretty good choice*
- *Somewhat more, 49%, rate him only fair or poor*
- *Few know Kaine well enough to rate him personally*

PRINCETON, N.J. – U.S. voters' initial reaction to Hillary Clinton's selection of Virginia Sen. Tim Kaine as her running mate is similar to their muted response to Donald Trump's selection of Mike Pence a week ago. Thirty-five percent say Kaine is an "excellent" or "pretty good" choice, nearly matching the 37% who said the same of Pence just after Trump chose him.

U.S. Registered Voters' Reaction to Hillary Clinton's Choice of Tim Kaine for Vice President

How would you rate Hillary Clinton's choice of Tim Kaine for vice president? Would you rate this choice as – excellent, pretty good, only fair or poor?

	Excellent/Pretty good %	Only fair/ Poor %	No opinion %
2016: Tim Kaine	35	49	15
For comparison:			
2016: Mike Pence	37	45	18
2012: Paul Ryan	39	45	16
2008: Sarah Palin	46	37	17
2008: Joe Biden	47	33	20
2004: John Edwards	64	28	8
2000: Joe Lieberman	53	28	19
2000: Dick Cheney	55	34	11

Gallup, July 23-24, 2016

Forty-nine percent have a middling or negative reaction to Kaine in the July 23-24 poll, rating him "only fair" or "poor," again similar to voters' first reaction to Pence.

Democrats Mostly Fine With Kaine

Despite some discussion in the news that Kaine may not be liberal enough to satisfy Bernie Sanders supporters, just 3% of Democratic registered voters currently consider Kaine a poor choice. Instead, with more than six in 10 of these Democrats rating Kaine an excellent or pretty good choice, his party seems largely on board with him at the outset.

Still, fewer than three in 10 Democrats consider Kaine an *excellent* choice while slightly more consider him pretty good – a relatively restrained reaction to the Virginia senator from his own party, on par with Republicans' initial reaction to Pence.

U.S. Voters' Reaction to Tim Kaine as Clinton's VP Choice, by Party ID

	Excellent %	Pretty good %	Only fair %	Poor %	No opinion %
U.S. registered voters	13	22	30	19	15
Democrats	29	33	25	3	10
Independents	9	23	31	23	14
Republicans	2	13	32	31	23
(Reaction to Mike Pence, July 15-16, 2016)					
U.S. registered voters	13	24	23	22	18
Republicans	27	40	17	5	13
Independents	9	21	28	21	22
Democrats	4	10	26	42	18

Gallup, July 23-24, 2016

Six in 10 Voters Not Familiar With Kaine

More than six in 10 Americans (61%) have either never heard of Kaine or don't know enough about him to have an opinion in the new survey, similar to the 62% for Pence last week.

The remaining voters are a bit more likely to have a favorable (24%) than unfavorable (15%) opinion of Kaine. This is just slightly more positive than Pence's initial favorability scores.

U.S. Registered Voters' Impressions of Tim Kaine

Do you have a favorable or unfavorable opinion of Tim Kaine, or have you never heard of him?

	Favorable %	Unfavorable %	Never heard of %	No opinion %
2016: Tim Kaine	24	15	41	20
For comparison:				
2016: Mike Pence	21	18	44	18
2012: Paul Ryan	27	21	32	21
2008: Sarah Palin	22	7	51	20
2008: Joe Biden	34	15	23	28
2004: John Edwards	54	16	12	18
2000: Joe Lieberman	37	10	24	29
2000: Dick Cheney	51	11	7	31
1996: Jack Kemp	56	14	10	20
1992: Al Gore	59	13	–	28

Gallup, July 23-24, 2016

Kaine Neither Attracts Nor Repels Many Voters

In line with his low public profile, Kaine's inclusion on the Democratic ticket is not causing voters to rethink their willingness to vote for Clinton – one of the most well-known public figures in the country. Slightly more say having Kaine as her running mate makes them more likely to vote for Clinton rather than less likely, 12% vs. 9%, but three-quarters say he won't affect their vote. These figures are almost identical to how voters said Pence would affect their chances of backing Trump.

Effect of Tim Kaine on Likelihood of Voting for Hillary Clinton in November

Does having Tim Kaine as her running mate make you more likely to vote for Hillary Clinton in November, less likely or will it not have much effect on your vote?

	More likely %	Less likely %	No effect %	Net "more likely" pct. pts.
2016: Tim Kaine	12	9	77	4
For comparison:				
2016: Mike Pence	14	10	74	4
2012: Paul Ryan	17	13	68	4
2008: Sarah Palin	18	11	67	7
2008: Joe Biden	14	7	72	7
2004: John Edwards	24	7	66	17
2000: Joe Lieberman	16	4	76	12
2000: Dick Cheney	14	10	72	4
1996: Jack Kemp	26	8	63	18
1992: Al Gore	33	8	57	25
1988: Lloyd Bentsen §	26	9	60	17
1988: Dan Quayle ^	10	10	73	0

§ Time magazine poll; ^ USA Today poll; NOTE: all vice presidential nominees shown are non-incumbents

Gallup, July 23-24, 2016

Also mirroring the immediate reaction to Pence, Kaine earns middling ratings in voter perceptions that he is qualified to serve as president should it ever become necessary – ratings that are generally worse than those of vice presidential choices in prior years. While 47% of registered voters say he is qualified, 32% believe he is not and about one-fifth are unsure.

U.S. Voters' Perceptions of Tim Kaine as Qualified to Serve as President

Based on what you know about Tim Kaine, do you think he is qualified to serve as president if it becomes necessary, or not?

	Yes, qualified %	No, not %	No opinion %
2016: Tim Kaine	47	32	21
For comparison:			
2016: Mike Pence	46	33	22
2012: Paul Ryan	50	31	19
2008: Sarah Palin	39	33	29
2008: Joe Biden	57	18	26
2004: John Edwards	57	29	14
2000: Joe Lieberman	52	13	35
2000: Dick Cheney	57	18	25
1996: Al Gore	60	34	6
1996: Jack Kemp	61	16	23
1992: Al Gore	64	19	17

Gallup, July 23-24, 2016

Bottom Line

Voters' initial reaction to Kaine as Clinton's running mate suggests she has successfully chosen someone who, at a bare minimum, will do her candidacy no harm. While about a third consider Kaine an excellent or good choice for vice president, few – including almost no Democrats – think he is a poor choice. However, Kaine is still largely unknown to the majority of voters, highlighting the important role this week's Democratic National Convention will have in establishing his public identity.

More broadly, Kaine is now the third consecutive newly named vice presidential pick – after Pence and the 2012 Republican vice presidential nominee, Paul Ryan – to garner mediocre initial ratings from voters. By contrast, the five such nominees preceding them between 2000 and 2008 were viewed much more positively. This could partly reflect the relatively low profiles that Kaine, Pence and Ryan all had before being hand-picked for the vice presidential slot on their party's ticket – although that didn't prevent Sarah Palin from making a good first impression in 2008. Nevertheless, voters may not have much more than their partisanship to draw on in evaluating Pence and Kaine. And in an era when voters appear unwilling to say anything positive about the opposing party, their first impressions are mediocre at best.

Historical data are available in Gallup Analytics.

Survey Methods

Results for this Gallup poll are based on telephone interviews conducted July 23-24, 2016, on the Gallup U.S. Daily survey, with a random sample of 937 registered voters, aged 18 and older, living in all 50 U.S. states and the District of Columbia. For results based on the total sample of registered voters, the margin of sampling error is ±4 percentage points at the 95% confidence level. All reported margins of sampling error include computed design effects for weighting.

July 27, 2016

ROBO-ADVICE STILL A NOVELTY FOR U.S. INVESTORS

by Lydia Saad

Story Highlights

- *Less than half of investors are familiar with robo-advice*
- *Only 5% are highly familiar with it or have already used it*
- *Sizeable segments consider robo-advisers economical, simpler*

PRINCETON, N.J. - "Robo-advice" is not yet a widely known service among U.S. investors. Just five percent of U.S. investors say they have heard a lot about robo-advisers and 40% have heard a fair amount or only a little, while the rest have heard nothing.

U.S. Investors' Familiarity With Robo-Advisers

Robo-advisers are digital advisory services that use computer algorithms to select stocks and other investments for people based on the information people provide about their risk tolerance and goals. How much have you heard or read about robo-advisers before now?

	May 13-22, 2016 %
A lot	5
A fair amount	12
Only a little	28
Nothing	55
No opinion	*

Wells Fargo/Gallup Investor and Retirement Optimism Index survey

Given this low awareness, adoption has been slow. Just 5% of investors say they have already used robo-advice. Another 5% indicate they are very or somewhat likely to try it in the next year, and another 10% are not too likely. However, a full 80% either say they are not likely at all to use a robo-advisor (25%) or are not familiar with the technology (55%).

These findings are from the latest Wells Fargo/Gallup Investor and Retirement Optimism Index survey, conducted May 13-22, 2016, among 1,019 U.S. investors. In the survey, robo-advice was defined as "digital advisory services that use computer algorithms to select stocks and other investments for people based on the information people provide about their risk tolerance and goals." Approximately 40% of U.S. adults meet the survey's criteria as investors, which are having $10,000 or more invested in stocks, bonds or mutual funds, either in an investment or retirement account.

Investors Rate Human Advisers Higher on Most Qualities

The survey asked those who have heard at least a little about robo-advisers to say whether each of 10 positive qualities in an investment advisor applies more to robo-advisers or human advisers.

Human advisers lead on almost all qualities measured in the survey. However, on the continuum of things investors think humans do better, robo-advice is perceived relatively well on a few process-oriented items. Investors choose robo- over human advisers for charging lower fees. And at least one in four investors associate robo-advice with simplifying the investing process (36%), being more reliable in turbulent markets (30%) and matching clients' investments to their risk tolerance (29%).

U.S. Investors' Perceptions of Human vs. Robo-Advice

Next, as I read some statements about financial advisers, please say if you think each applies more to human advisers or more to robo-advisers?

	Robo-Adviser %	Human adviser %
Charges lower fees	63	26
Simplifies the investing process for investors	36	57
Is more reliable in turbulent markets	30	61
Matches clients' investments to their risk tolerance	29	62
Is focused on investors' best interests	21	72
Makes good investment recommendations	18	70
Takes each client's entire financial picture into account	15	77
Advises clients on risks they are taking	10	83
Makes people feel confident about their investments	5	90
Helps people understand their investments	3	91

Based on investors who have heard about robo-advisers
Wells Fargo/Gallup Investor and Retirement Optimism Index survey

Additionally, about one in five informed investors think robo-advisers are more likely than human advisers to be focused on investors' best interests (21%) and make good investment recommendations (18%). Along the same lines, 15% think robo-advisers take their client's entire financial picture into account. All of these qualities relate to the competence or integrity of financial advice.

At the same time, human advisers almost completely overshadow robo-advice on three communication-centric skills: helping people understand their investments, making people feel confident about their investments and advising clients on the risks they are taking.

Investors Most Value Integrity and Communication in Investment Advice

Gallup and Wells Fargo also asked all investors to say how important each of the 10 qualities is to them in deciding what type of advice to use to help manage their investments. The top-rated qualities all relate to integrity or communication, which investors see as weaker areas for robo-advice compared with human advice.

For the most part, human advisers are strongly preferred when it comes to the aspects of advice that are most important to investors, such as being focused on the investor's best interests and taking the investor's entire financial picture into account. By contrast, robo-advisers fare better, at least on a relative basis, on some of the least important factors – particularly simplifying the investing process and having the lowest fees.

Two somewhat important areas to investors on which they rate robo-advice relatively well are matching investors' investments to their risk tolerance and being more reliable in turbulent markets – both dealing with the competence of investment advice.

U.S. Investors' Ratings of Importance of Investment Advice Qualities

How important are each of the following in deciding what type of advice to use to help manage your investments – extremely important, very important, somewhat important or not too important?

	Extremely/ Very important %
Is focused on your best interests	70
Takes your entire financial picture into account	81
Makes good investment recommendations	79
Helps you understand your investments	75
Matches your investments to your risk tolerance	75
Makes you feel confident about your investments	72
Is more reliable in turbulent markets	69
Provides advice about how much risk you should take	66
Simplifies the investing process for you	64
Has the lowest fees	42

Based on investors who have heard about robo-advisers
Wells Fargo/Gallup Investor and Retirement Optimism Index survey

Bottom Line

"Robo-advice" provides consumers with a convenient way to customize and manage their investments online, relying on computer algorithms to design and manage portfolios. Because the technology is still in its infancy, few investors have fully embraced it or think it outperforms human advisers. However, enough investors already recognize its advantages for streamlining the investing process that investor demand for blending it with human advice is likely to grow.

Future installments in Gallup's analysis of this poll will review who already uses robo-advice and who is most interested in using it in conjunction with a personal adviser.

Survey Methods

Results for the Wells Fargo/Gallup Investor and Retirement Optimism Index survey are based on questions asked May 13-22, 2016, on the Gallup Daily tracking survey, of a random sample of 1,019 U.S. adults having investable assets of $10,000 or more.

For results based on the total sample of investors, the margin of sampling error is ±4 percentage points at the 95% confidence level. All reported margins of sampling error include computed design effects for weighting.

July 28, 2016
AMERICANS OFFER SOLUTIONS FOR PROBLEM OF DEADLY SHOOTINGS

by Frank Newport

Story Highlights

- *Americans suggest a number of ways to reduce deadly shootings*
- *Included are better relations, changes in black community and police changes*
- *Clear majority still optimistic that black-white problems can be solved*

PRINCETON, N.J. – When asked to name what can be done to reduce the number of deadly encounters between black men and police in the U.S. today, Americans – taken as a whole – offer suggestions that fall under three main headings: changes in society, changes in the black community and changes in the police.

Just your opinion, what do you think is the single most important thing that could be done to reduce the number of deadly encounters between black men and police in the U.S.?

	National adults %
General, structural changes	**36**
Better relations/Communication/Understanding	19
Gun control/Get rid of guns/Disband NRA	5
Less focus on race/Less racism	5
Better/More accurate reporting/Media, politicians not blow issue out of proportion	4
Eliminate stereotyping of blacks	1
Better leadership/President Barack Obama	1
Better drug enforcement	1
Changes among blacks	**27**
Change blacks' attitudes toward police/More respect/ Cooperation	8
Accountability/Responsibility for own actions/Obey the law	6
Education (non-specific)	5
More/Better jobs for blacks	2
Find religion/Jesus/Ethics	2
Educate on issues/Raise awareness/What to do if pulled over	1
Better education of underprivileged/Blacks	1
More responsibility/Better parenting among blacks/ Teach respect	1
Eliminate Black Lives Matter movement	1
Changes in police and police operations	**21**
Better/Additional police training	9
Police should be more patient/Slower to act/Use common sense/Less brutality	5
Better hiring practices/Hire more qualified police/ More diverse police	2
Improve police policies and procedures	1
Reform law enforcement/Criminal justice system	1
More technology/Cameras	1
Police need to be more strict/Do their job	1
Need more police	1
Other	2
Nothing	4
No opinion	11

Gallup Poll July 13-17, 2016

Americans name race relations and racism as the single most important problem facing the U.S. today, reflecting the aftermath of shootings of black men by police in Minnesota and Louisiana, and the shootings of police officers by black men in Texas and Louisiana. Americans' opinions about what to do to reduce these types of deadly encounters, from a July 13-17 Gallup survey, help inject the perspective of everyday Americans into the discussion. The public's views augment those voiced by politicians, pundits, community leaders, police officials, journalists and others who have easy media access.

Overall, no one solution dominates the American people's thinking, but instead Americans offer a spectrum of suggestions and ways of addressing the problem. The three most frequently occurring specific responses are better communications and relations (suggested by 19% of the public), better and additional police training (9%) and changes in blacks' attitudes toward the police (8%) – each exemplifying a broader category of similar-minded responses.

An approach to solving the problem of deadly shootings that emphasizes just one of these approaches would ignore the multifaceted set of solutions from the public that touch on a number of different aspects of the situation.

Democrats, Liberals Most Likely to Suggest Changes in Police

Recommendations vary among different subgroups of Americans, and particularly along political and ideological lines. Democrats and liberals' suggestions tend to focus more on changes in the way police operate, while Republicans and conservatives are more likely to suggest that changes are needed in the black community. The differences among any of these groups are not extremely large, however, with a good deal of overlap in the types of suggestions made by members in each.

Whites are somewhat more likely to suggest changes in black communities than changes involving the police, while nonwhites are more likely to suggest changes in the police.

Just your opinion, what do you think is the single most important thing that could be done to reduce the number of deadly encounters between black men and police in the U.S.?

	General/ Structural changes %	Changes among blacks %	Changes in police and police operations %
Republicans/leaners	31	37	14
Democrats/leaners	41	18	27
Conservative	33	35	14
Moderate	41	24	16
Liberal	34	19	35
Whites	36	28	17
Nonwhites	34	22	27

Gallup Poll July 13-17, 2016

Little Change in Americans' Optimism That a Solution Can Be Worked Out

About six in 10 Americans indicate in the mid-July survey that a solution to the problem of the relations between blacks and whites in the U.S. will eventually be worked out. This update is little changed from responses to the same question in June, despite the intervening occurrence of highly publicized deaths in early July of two black men at the hands of the police, and the killings of five police officers by a black man.

Do you think that relations between blacks and whites will always be a problem for the U.S., or that a solution will eventually be worked out?

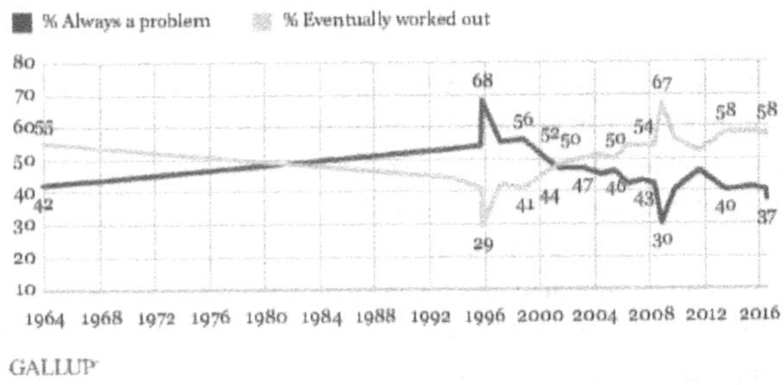

In fact, there has been little change over the past five years in Americans' attitudes about eventually finding a solution to problems that linger in black-white relations, even though this time period has included a long string of high-profile killings of black men by police officers. At the same time, however, Americans' ratings of black-white relations have also suffered.

Implications

The American public does not coalesce around one specific solution to the problem of deadly encounters between black men and police. Rather, Americans make a number of suggestions, including calling for broad changes in society and culture, changes in black communities and changes in the way the police are trained and operate. These results underscore the difficulty in coming up a quick answer to the problem, and emphasize how – at least from the American public's perspective taken as a whole – the issue needs to be addressed on many different fronts.

A majority of Americans continue to hold out hope that a solution to the broader issue of relations between whites and blacks will eventually be worked out. This optimism indicates the public is apparently open to suggestions and proposed actions that address this complex and highly important issue.

Historical data are available in Gallup Analytics.

Survey Methods

Results are based on telephone interviews conducted July 13-17, 2016, with a random sample of 1,023 adults, aged 18 and older, living in all 50 U.S. states and the District of Columbia. For results based on the total sample of national adults, the margin of sampling error is ±4 percentage points at the 95% confidence level. All reported margins of sampling error include computed design effects for weighting.

July 28, 2016

FEWER IN U.S. SAY MEN AND WOMEN HAVE EQUAL JOB OPPORTUNITIES

by Stephanie Marken

Story Highlights

- *About half believe men and women have equal job opportunities*
- *Percentage who feel opportunities are equal down from 2008*
- *Majority favor affirmative action programs for women*

WASHINGTON, D.C. – Approximately half of U.S. adults believe women have equal job opportunities as men, although women themselves (43%) are significantly less likely than men (61%) to agree. The 52% of U.S. adults saying men and women have equal job opportunities is down slightly from 57% in 2008, mostly related to a decline in the percentage of men who hold this view.

Do you feel that women in this country have equal job opportunities as men, or not?

% Yes

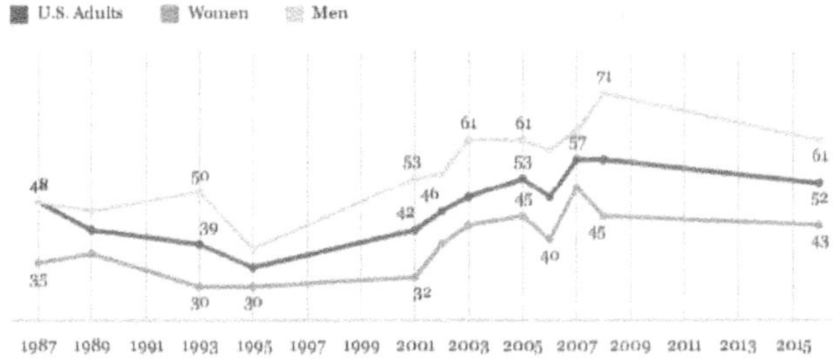

Gallup Poll Social Series

GALLUP

When Gallup first asked this question in 1987, 48% of U.S. adults believed women and men had equal job opportunities. The public grew more skeptical about gender equality in job opportunities, and by 1995, only 34% said they believed women and men had equal opportunities. That figure has increased steadily to a high of 57% in 2007 and 2008.

These results are based on Gallup's 2016 Minority Rights and Relations poll, conducted June 7-July 1 with more than 3,200 U.S. adults, including approximately 1,500 women and 1,700 men.

Majority Favor Affirmative Action for Women

A separate question from the poll shows six in 10 U.S. adults favor affirmative action programs for women, on par with the 59% who supported these programs in 2005, when Gallup last asked this question. Women (64%) are more likely than men (55%) to favor these programs, but the percentages of men *and* women favoring these programs are essentially unchanged from 2005.

Members of underrepresented minority groups are more likely than whites to report favoring affirmative action for women. Eighty-one percent of blacks and 69% of Hispanics say they support these programs, compared with 55% of whites. The percentages of these minority groups reporting they favor these programs for women remain similar to those found in 2005.

Do you generally favor or oppose affirmative action programs for women?

% Favor

	2001 %	2003 %	2005 %	2016 %
National adults	53	59	59	60
Women	57	62	65	64
Men	49	56	53	55
Whites	50	55	52	55
Blacks	77	77	80	81
Hispanics	72	69	76	69

Gallup

Implications

With 52% of Americans reporting that women in the U.S. have equal job opportunities as men, it is clear that concerns about gender equality in the workplace still exist, despite progress on many fronts over the past three decades. Perceptions of gender equality increased slightly in 2007, but Gallup data suggest this progress lacked staying power. Similarly, previous Gallup research found that women were more likely than men to report that they were denied a raise because of their gender, suggesting a gender gap still exists both in the opportunities available to members of each gender and in the experiences they have upon employment, including pay and promotion.

The outcome of the 2016 presidential election could affect Americans' perceptions of whether men and women have equal job opportunities. Hillary Clinton is now the first woman to be a major party's presidential nominee and could potentially be the first female president. This could signal to the public that women have equal job opportunities as men.

Survey Methods

Results for this Gallup poll are based on telephone interviews conducted June 7-July 1, 2016, with a random sample of 3,270 adults, aged 18 and older, living in all 50 U.S. states and the District of Columbia. For results based on the total sample of national adults, the margin of sampling error is ±3 percentage points at the 95% confidence level.

For results based on the total sample of 1,513 women, the margin of sampling error is ±5 percentage points. For results based on the total sample of 1,755 men, the margin of sampling error is ±4 percentage points. For results based on the total sample of 1,320 whites, the margin of sampling error is ±4 percentage points. For results based on the total sample of 912 blacks, the margin of sampling error is ±5 percentage points. For results based on the total sample of 906 Hispanics, the margin of sampling error is ±6 percentage points.

All reported margins of sampling error include computed design effects for weighting.

July 28, 2016

LESS THAN HALF IN U.S. OK WITH TREATMENT OF IMMIGRANTS, ARABS

by Art Swift

Story Highlights

- *45% in U.S. satisfied with how Arabs treated; 43% for immigrants*
- *Whites more satisfied than blacks with blacks' treatment*
- *Hispanics least likely to be satisfied with how immigrants are treated*

WASHINGTON, D.C. – Among six key groups in society, Americans are least satisfied with the way Arabs and immigrants are treated in the U.S. Less than half of Americans are satisfied with the treatment of either group. In contrast, Americans are most satisfied with the way Asians are treated (75% very or somewhat satisfied). A slim majority, 51%, are satisfied with the treatment of blacks.

Satisfaction With the Way Key Groups in U.S. Society Are Treated, 2015 vs. 2016

We'd like to know how you feel about the way various groups in society are treated. For each of the following groups please say whether you are very satisfied, somewhat satisfied, somewhat dissatisfied or very dissatisfied with the way they are treated. How about ... ?

	Very/Somewhat satisfied, 2015 %	Very/Somewhat satisfied, 2016 %
Asians	77	75
Women	64	63
Hispanics	58	54
Blacks	49	51
Arabs	49	45
Immigrants	44	43

Gallup

The results are based on Gallup's 2016 Minority Rights and Relations poll, conducted June 7-July 1 with more than 3,200 adults, including 1,300 non-Hispanic whites, 900 non-Hispanic blacks and 900 Hispanics.

The overall 2016 figures for this question remained relatively stable from last year, with the largest drop – four percentage points each – in Americans' perceptions about the treatment of Hispanics and Arabs. Perceptions of how blacks are treated are within two points of where they were last year. Treatment of Asians has remained consistently at the top of these satisfaction ratings since 2001.

The current stability stands in contrast to more substantial shifts earlier this decade. The most recent significant shift occurred between 2013 and 2015, when Americans' overall satisfaction with how blacks are treated dropped from 62% to 49% after high-profile killings of black men by white police officers. This year, satisfaction with how blacks are treated remains on the low side, but it has stabilized at 51%. The 2016 survey was conducted before the police-related shootings in Louisiana and Minnesota, along with the shootings of police officers in Dallas and Baton Rouge in July.

Blacks Least Satisfied With Society's Treatment of Them

Thirty-two percent of black Americans say they are satisfied with how society treats blacks, within two percentage points of the lowest reading over the past 15 years. Americans of other racial and ethnic identities are more positive about the treatment of blacks, however. Forty-seven percent of Hispanics and 56% of whites are satisfied with society's treatment of blacks.

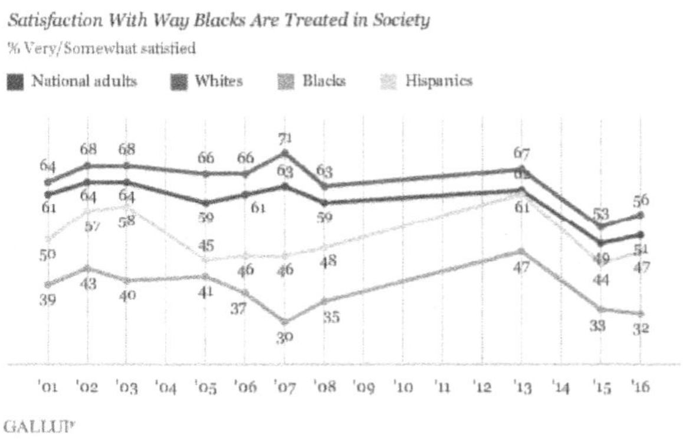

Since 2001, never have a majority of blacks been satisfied with the way society treats blacks. The highest satisfaction was in 2013, at 47%, but blacks' assessments plunged to 33% by 2015.

In 2007, the contrast between national adults and blacks was stark – a trend high of 71% of whites said they were satisfied with the way blacks are treated, yet only 30% of blacks themselves agreed with the same sentiment. Blacks currently are also less satisfied than whites with the way immigrants and Arabs are treated. But Hispanics are even less satisfied with immigrants' treatment. Blacks are also less satisfied with Hispanics' treatment than whites are.

Satisfaction With Treatment of Key U.S. Groups, by Race and Ethnicity

Very/Somewhat satisfied

	Whites %	Blacks %	Hispanics %
Asians	81	62	60
Women	68	49	56
Hispanics	59	43	46
Blacks	56	32	47
Arabs	47	35	44
Immigrants	46	38	32

Gallup, June 7-July 1, 2016

Gallup does not have a sufficient sample of Arabs to report on how they feel Arabs are treated in the U.S.

Bottom Line

In this election year, the issues of race and ethnicity have been at the forefront of the presidential campaign, and in "down-ballot" contests as well. Republican nominee Donald Trump has made blocking certain groups of immigrants from entering the U.S., including Muslims and Mexicans, a centerpiece of his campaign.

Gallup has not found much change in how Americans believe immigrants are treated in the past year since Trump became a candidate, however. While a sizable number of Arabs in the U.S. are Muslims, many are Christians, and there has only been modest change in the satisfaction with the treatment of Arabs in the past year. Still, immigrants and Arabs are viewed as getting worse treatment than other key minority groups.

The recent incidents of deadly encounters between blacks and police have forced race further to the front of the 2016 campaign. Blacks still have diminished satisfaction with how they believe blacks are treated in the U.S., while satisfaction with the treatment of blacks among other races and ethnicities, and among national adults overall, has modestly increased.

Historical data are available in Gallup Analytics.

Survey Methods

Results for this Gallup poll are based on telephone interviews conducted June 7-July 1, 2016, with a random sample of 3,270 adults, aged 18 and older, living in all 50 U.S. states and the District of Columbia. For results based on the total sample of national adults, the margin of sampling error is ±3 percentage points at the 95% confidence level. For results based on the total sample of 1,320 non-Hispanic whites, the margin of sampling error is ±4 percentage points at the 95% confidence level. For results based on sample of 912 non-Hispanic blacks and 906 Hispanics, the margin of sampling error is ±5 percentage points at the 95% confidence level. All reported margins of sampling error include computed design effects for weighting.

July 29, 2016
IN U.S., OPIOIDS VIEWED AS MOST SERIOUS LOCAL DRUG PROBLEM

by Alyssa Davis

Story Highlights

- *44% say prescription painkillers a crisis/very serious problem in their area*
- *42% say the same for heroin*
- *Both seen as more serious than tobacco, cocaine, alcohol and marijuana*

WASHINGTON, D.C. – More than four in 10 Americans see prescription painkillers and heroin as a "crisis" or "very serious problem" in their local areas. Smaller percentages of Americans – one in three or fewer – view cigarettes, alcohol, cocaine and marijuana as a crisis or very serious problem where they live.

Americans' Perceptions of Drugs as a Problem in Their Area

For each of the following drugs, please say how much of a problem you think it is in your area – is it a crisis, a very serious problem but not a crisis, a somewhat serious problem or not much of a problem?

	Crisis %	Very serious problem %	Somewhat of a problem %	Not much of a problem %	Total: Crisis/Very serious %
Prescription painkillers	14	30	28	24	44
Heroin	17	25	22	29	42
Cigarettes	10	23	33	33	33
Alcohol	8	24	35	32	32
Cocaine	8	20	29	37	28
Marijuana	6	17	25	50	23

Gallup, June 14-23, 2016

These data are based on a Gallup poll conducted June 14-23, before national and state leaders took steps this month to address the growing issue of prescription painkiller and heroin abuse. In a rare display of bipartisanship, Congress passed and President Barack Obama signed the Comprehensive Addiction and Recovery Act (CARA), which contains numerous prevention and treatment measures intended to reduce prescription opioid and heroin abuse.

Additionally, 46 state and U.S. territorial governors signed a pact through the National Governors Association committing themselves to reduce inappropriate prescribing of prescription painkillers, educate the public about opioid abuse and improve access to treatment.

Across key U.S. subgroups, there are notable differences in perceptions of opioids as a crisis or very serious problem:

- Women are slightly more likely than men to say prescription painkillers are a crisis or very serious problem in their area, 48% vs. 38%, respectively. The two groups are about equally likely to say heroin is a crisis or very serious problem.
- Those living in the East (59%) are much more likely than those in other regions to say heroin is a very serious problem or crisis, with those in the South having the least concern (33%). The regional differences are much smaller on views of prescription painkillers.
- Whites are more likely than nonwhites to see heroin as a problem in their area, 46% vs. 34%, respectively, but these groups' views of prescription painkillers are similar.
- Lower-income Americans are much less likely than those living in middle- and upper-income households to see prescription painkillers as a crisis or very serious problem where they live.
- Republicans are a bit more likely than Democrats to see prescription painkillers and heroin as a crisis or very serious, but these party differences are minor in comparison to those seen on many issues Gallup measures.

Americans' Perceptions of Drugs as a Problem in Their Area

% Crisis/Very serious problem

	Prescription painkillers %	Heroin %
Men	38	41
Women	48	43
East	48	59
Midwest	41	43
South	40	33
West	45	41
Whites	45	46
Nonwhites	40	34
Less than $36,000	30	41
$36,000 to $89,999	47	44
$90,000+	47	41
Democrats	43	38
Independents	39	43
Republicans	48	46

Gallup, June 14-23, 2016

Americans See Multiple Causes of Prescription Painkiller Problem

Presidential candidates from both parties have focused on opioid addiction on the campaign trail, particularly ahead of the Republican presidential debate in New Hampshire, a state ravaged by opioid overdose deaths. Eight in 10 Americans say they have heard or read about problems with prescription opioids, including 46% who have heard or read a lot, 19% some, and 15% only a little.

Americans who have heard or read about the prescription opioid problem do not rate any of four possible causes of prescription opioid addiction higher than any others, suggesting the public believes the problem needs to be attacked on multiple fronts. Slightly more than half place "a lot" of blame on "the pharmaceutical industry encouraging doctors to use opioids" and on "doctors overprescribing painkillers to their patients." Meanwhile, slightly less than half attribute a lot of the blame to a "lack of public knowledge about the dangers of opioids" and to "patients demanding that they be given a prescription to ease their pain."

Americans' Views on Causes of Opioid Problem

How much do you blame each of the following for the opioid problem – a lot, some, only a little or not at all?

	A lot %	Some %	Only a little %	Not at all %
The pharmaceutical industry encouraging doctors to use opioids	55	22	13	7
Doctors overprescribing painkillers to their patients	53	27	14	5
Lack of public knowledge about the dangers of opioids	49	28	14	8
Patients demanding that they be given a prescription to ease their pain	47	29	16	5

Among those who have heard at least a little about opioid problem
Gallup, June 14-23, 2016

Among those who have heard or read about the prescription opioid problem, Republicans are less likely than Democrats to blame pharmaceutical companies and lack of public knowledge about opioids for addiction problems. Republicans are more likely than Democrats to blame patients demanding that they be given prescription painkillers. Both are just as likely to blame doctors for overprescribing painkillers.

"A Lot" of Blame for Opioid Problem, by Party Identification

Among those who have heard about opioid problem

	Democrats %	Republicans %	Independents %
The pharmaceutical industry encouraging doctors to use opioids	57	47	60
Doctors overprescribing painkillers to their patients	47	49	60
Lack of public knowledge about the dangers of opioids	53	41	52
Patients demanding that they be given a prescription to ease their pain	40	52	49

Gallup, June 14-23, 2016

Bottom Line

More Americans see prescription painkillers and heroin as a crisis or very serious problem in their area than do so for any of the other four items Gallup asked about. Americans are also significantly more worried about drugs as a problem facing the country more broadly now than in recent years. In March, Gallup found 44% of Americans worry about drug use "a great deal," up 10 percentage points from two years ago.

The new federal opioid law and the pact that nearly all state governors signed address some of the factors Americans say are to blame for the opioid problem. The federal law encourages states to establish programs to monitor drug prescriptions, and the pact includes measures to reduce inappropriate prescribing of painkillers. Both feature public education components to increase awareness of the dangers of opioids. The federal law also establishes a task force for studying how to better address pain and offers incentives for pharmaceutical companies to develop non-opioid painkillers. However, Obama and congressional Democrats argue that the law does not provide enough funding to prevent and treat opioid abuse and addiction.

The outcome of the presidential election also could shape how opioid addiction will be addressed in the coming years. Hillary Clinton released a $10 billion plan last year that expands access to treatment programs. Donald Trump has said building a wall on the border between the U.S. and Mexico will keep drugs out of the country but hasn't offered other specifics on how to prevent or treat abuse and addiction.

Historical data are available in Gallup Analytics.

Survey Methods

Results for this Gallup poll are based on telephone interviews conducted June 14-23, 2016, with a random sample of 1,025 adults, aged 18 and older, living in all 50 U.S. states and the District of Columbia. For results based on the total sample of national adults, the margin of sampling error is ±4 percentage points at the 95% confidence level.

July 29, 2016

U.S. SUPREME COURT JOB APPROVAL RATING TIES RECORD LOW

by Jeffrey M. Jones

Story Highlights

- *42% job approval ties low from June 2005*
- *Approval has been below majority level since 2010*
- *Record party gap in approval from last summer has narrowed*

PRINCETON, N.J. – The U.S. Supreme Court's 42% job approval rating is down slightly from September and matches the low point in Gallup's 16-year trend, recorded in June 2005. The Supreme Court's approval ratings have not been above 50% since September 2010.

Do you approve or disapprove of the way the Supreme Court is handling its job?

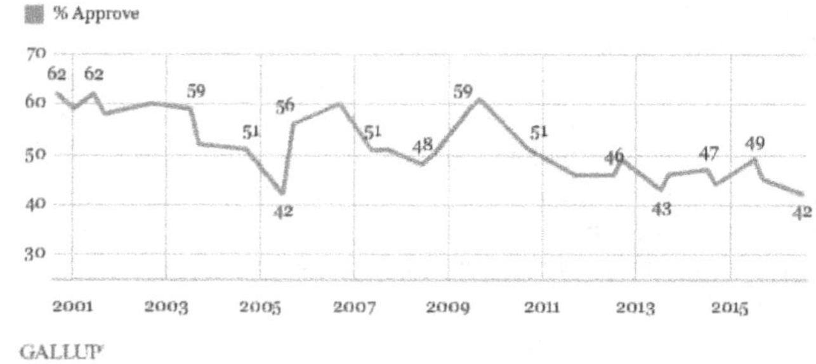

The latest results are from a July 13-17 Gallup poll. Although the current approval rating ties the historical low, it is not a major departure from updates over the last five years, when approval has ranged between 43% and 49% – including 45% when Gallup last measured it, in September 2015.

The Supreme Court recently concluded its 2015-2016 term, with eight justices serving since the death of Antonin Scalia in February and no progress made toward confirming Barack Obama's choice of Merrick Garland to fill the vacancy. As a result, the shorthanded court deadlocked on several potentially important decisions, upholding previous lower court rulings. One of the more significant decisions of the term was the court's ruling allowing colleges to continue to consider an applicant's racial or ethnic background as a factor in admissions decisions. Americans widely disapproved of that decision.

The prior low Supreme Court job approval rating came in June 2005, just after a court decision to permit governments to use the power of eminent domain to seize private property for economic development purposes. Approval of the Supreme Court fell to 42% immediately after that decision was announced, from 51% in the prior measurement. That proved to be a short-term decline, however, with approval back to 56% in Gallup's next update in September 2005.

Although the current approval rating ties the previous low, the 52% of Americans now disapproving of the Supreme Court is the highest in the trend. The prior high disapproval rating was 50% last September.

Democrats Still More Likely Than Republicans to Approve; Party Gap Narrows

Just after the Supreme Court legalized same-sex marriage nationwide and rejected a second major legal challenge to the 2010 Affordable Care Act last summer, Democrats' (76%) and Republicans' (18%) approval ratings of the court were the most polarized Gallup had ever measured. Today, Democrats remain significantly more likely to approve, 60% to 32%, but the party gap in approval ratings has narrowed, from 58 percentage points to 28 points.

Supreme Court Job Approval, by Political Party

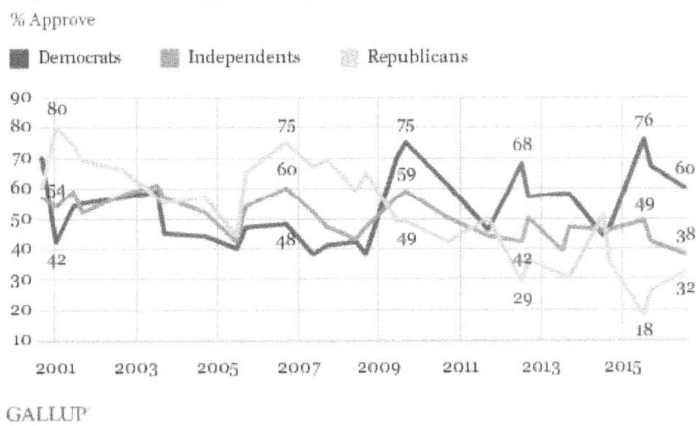

The record party polarization last summer was clearly a response to those two politically charged rulings, both of which were aligned with Democratic rather than Republican policy preferences on same-sex marriage and the Affordable Care Act. However, over time, the impact of those decisions on partisans' views of the Supreme Court has likely diminished. Republicans' approval has returned to its fall 2014 level, while Democrats' approval remains above where it was at that time.

Independents' approval of the court today is 38%, still down significantly from 46% in the fall of 2014, and the lowest approval rating among this group in Gallup's trend. This helps account for the all-time low Supreme Court approval rating among all Americans.

Implications

During the decade of the 2000s, a majority of Americans typically approved of the job the Supreme Court was doing, with the most notable exception occurring in 2005. That dip was short-lived, and Americans' positivity toward the Supreme Court was quickly restored.

However, in the past six years, Supreme Court job approval has yet to return to the majority level and is now tied for the low point in Gallup's trend. While Americans' views of the Supreme Court are often influenced by the decisions it issues, the current depressed ratings are likely also caused by Americans' long-standing dissatisfaction with the way things are going in the country, their frustrations with the government and diminished confidence in U.S. institutions more generally.

Gallup has documented that Americans' more basic trust in government institutions has eroded in recent years, and the Supreme Court, often the most popular and trusted of the three branches of the federal government, has not been immune.

Historical data are available in Gallup Analytics.

Survey Methods

Results for this Gallup poll are based on telephone interviews conducted July 13-17, 2016, with a random sample of 1,023 adults, aged 18 and older, living in all 50 U.S. states and the District of Columbia. For results based on the total sample of national adults, the margin of sampling error is ±4 percentage points at the 95% confidence level. All reported margins of sampling error include computed design effects for weighting.

Each sample of national adults includes a minimum quota of 60% cellphone respondents and

August 01, 2016

AMERICANS MORE POSITIVE ABOUT DEMOCRATIC THAN GOP CONVENTION

by Jeffrey M. Jones

Story Highlights

- *44% view Democratic Party more favorably after convention*
- *35% were more positive about GOP after its convention*
- *Clinton's acceptance speech rated better than Trump's*

PRINCETON, N.J. – Americans are evenly divided on whether they view the Democratic Party more favorably (44%) or less favorably (42%) after the party's national convention last week. However, their ratings of the Republican Party after the GOP convention two weeks ago were significantly worse, with 35% saying they viewed the party more favorably and 52% less favorably.

Effect of Conventions on Images of the Democratic and Republican Parties

From what you have seen or heard about this week's [Democratic/Republican] convention, do you have a more favorable or a less favorable opinion of the [Democratic/Republican] Party?

	More favorable %	Less favorable %
2016 Democratic convention	44	42
2016 Republican convention	35	52

Gallup, July 23-24 and July 29-30, 2016

The results are based on Gallup polls conducted in the days immediately after each party's convention – the Republican convention in Cleveland from July 18-21 and the Democratic convention in Philadelphia from July 25-28.

Americans' assessments of the effect of the conventions on their image of each party largely mirror their assessments of how the convention will affect their vote in the 2016 election. By 45% to 41%, Americans say they are more rather than less likely to vote for Hillary Clinton based on what they saw or read about the Democratic convention. In contrast, many more Americans said they were less likely (51%) rather than more likely (36%) to vote for Donald Trump as a result of what they saw or read about the Republican convention.

Gallup has asked this question about Democratic and Republican national conventions since 1984, with the exceptions of the 1984 and 1992 Republican conventions. The 2016 Republican convention is the first after which a greater percentage of Americans have said they are "less likely" rather than "more likely" to vote for the party's presidential nominee.

Likelihood to Vote for Party's Presidential Candidate Based on What You Saw/Read About Party's Convention

Based on national adults

	More likely %	Less likely %	No difference/ No opinion %	Net (more likely minus less likely) pct. pts.
Democratic conventions				
2016	45	41	14	+4
2012	43	38	20	+5
2008	43	29	27	+14
2004	44	30	26	+14
2000	43	28	29	+15
1996	44	29	27	+15
1992	60	15	25	+45
1988	56	21	23	+35
1984	45	29	26	+16
Republican conventions				
2016	36	51	14	-15
2012	40	38	21	+2
2008	43	38	19	+5
2004	41	38	21	+3
2000	44	27	29	+17
1996	45	34	21	+11
1992	n/a	n/a	n/a	n/a
1988	43	27	30	+16
1984	n/a	n/a	n/a	n/a

Gallup

Since 1984, an average of 45% of Americans have said they are more likely to vote for a party's presidential candidate after the party's convention; thus, the Democratic Party's 2016 convention is right at the historical norm. At the same time, the 41% of Americans who say they are less likely to vote for Clinton after the party's convention is among the highest Gallup has measured, while the 14% who said the convention made no difference in their vote or who had no opinion is historically low.

Americans' ratings of recent conventions have tended to be less positive than those of 2000 and before, likely because of the greater party polarization in Americans' attitudes. That is borne out in looking at the results by political party identification of the 2016, 2008 and 2000 conventions – all years in which an incumbent was not running in either party. In recent election years, supporters of each party have been more inclined to react positively to their own party's convention, but also much more likely to react negatively to the other party's convention. Fewer in each party now say the other party's convention made no difference to their vote or offer no opinion at all.

Likelihood to Vote for Party's Presidential Candidate Based on What You Saw/Read About Party Convention, by Political Party

Based on national adults

	More likely %	Less likely %	No difference/ No opinion %	Net (more likely minus less likely) pct. pts.
2016 Democratic convention				
Democrats/Democratic leaners	81	9	10	+72
Republicans/Republican leaners	8	82	10	-74
2016 Republican convention				
Democrats/Democratic leaners	2	88	10	-86
Republicans/Republican leaners	73	13	14	+60
2008 Democratic convention				
Democrats/Democratic leaners	74	8	18	+66
Republicans/Republican leaners	8	59	33	-51
2008 Republican convention				
Democrats/Democratic leaners	11	70	19	-59
Republicans/Republican leaners	78	7	15	+71
2000 Democratic convention				
Democrats/Democratic leaners	67	9	24	+58
Republicans/Republican leaners	15	53	32	-38
2000 Republican convention				
Democrats/Democratic leaners	22	49	29	-27
Republicans/Republican leaners	67	8	25	+59

Gallup

Clinton's Speech Rated More Positively Than Trump's

The most anticipated event at modern political conventions is the presidential nominee's acceptance speech. Overall, 44% of Americans gave Clinton's speech a positive rating, saying it was either "excellent" or "good." That is significantly higher than the 35% who rated Trump's speech positively. In fact, as many Americans rated Trump's speech negatively, saying it was "poor" or "terrible."

Trump's speech was rated less positively than any Gallup has asked about since 1996. The positive rating of Clinton's speech is slightly below the historical average of 47%, but similar to Barack Obama's 2012 acceptance speech. Obama's 2008 speech got the highest percentage of positive ratings at 58%.

Ratings of Presidential Nominee Acceptance Speeches

From what you have heard or read, how would you rate [nominee's] acceptance speech at the [Democratic/Republican] convention on Thursday night, as – excellent, good, just OK, poor or terrible?

	Excellent/ Good %	Just OK %	Poor/Terrible %	Didn't see/ No opinion %
2016, Clinton	44	17	20	19
2016, Trump	35	18	36	11
2012, Obama	43	17	16	23
2012, Romney	38	21	16	26
2008, McCain	47	22	12	19
2008, Obama	58	15	7	20
2004, Bush	49	19	8	24
2004, Kerry	52	19	9	20
2000, Gore	51	18	6	24
2000, Bush	51	17	4	28
1996, Clinton	n/a	n/a	n/a	n/a
1996, Dole	52	21	7	20

Gallup

Implications

The Democratic Party's convention left a considerably more positive impression on the American public than the Republican Party's convention. That is likely to aid the Democratic Party in its quest to win a third consecutive presidential election. However, the Democratic convention's historically average ratings are beneficial only in contrast to the Republicans' historically negative ratings, meaning both parties could have done a better job of appealing to Americans this year.

In the short term, it appears the Democratic Party will leave the convention phase better off than before it began. Gallup tracking finds Clinton's post-convention favorable rating at 44%, up six percentage points from mid-July. That is much higher than Trump's 32% favorable rating in the days after the Democratic convention. Also, Obama's job approval rating is now up to 54%, tied for the highest it has been since early 2013.

In the weeks ahead, both Clinton's favorable rating and Obama's approval rating could fall back somewhat as the campaign moves further away from the Democratic convention. But as of now, these key election indicators suggest the Democrats are in a stronger electoral position than the Republicans, and Trump and the GOP have a little more than three months left to try to change that.

Historical data are available in Gallup Analytics.

Survey Methods

Results for this Gallup poll are based on telephone interviews conducted July 23-24 (Republican convention) and July 29-30 (Democratic convention), 2016, on the Gallup U.S. Daily survey, with random samples of approximately 1,000 adults each, aged 18 and older, living in all 50 U.S. states and the District of Columbia. For results based on the total samples of national adults, the margin of sampling error is ±4 percentage points at the 95% confidence level. All reported margins of sampling error include computed design effects for weighting.

August 01, 2016
U.S. CONSUMERS REPORT A SURGE IN SPENDING IN JULY

by Justin McCarthy

Story Highlights

- *Daily spending reports averaged $100 in July*
- *July's average $12 higher than the prior month*
- *Highest average for any month since July 2008*

WASHINGTON, D.C. – Americans' daily self-reports of spending averaged $100 in July, a $12 increase from June. Gallup's measure of consumer spending has not been at this level since July 2008, though it reached $99 in December.

Amount of Money Americans Report Spending "Yesterday," Monthly Averages

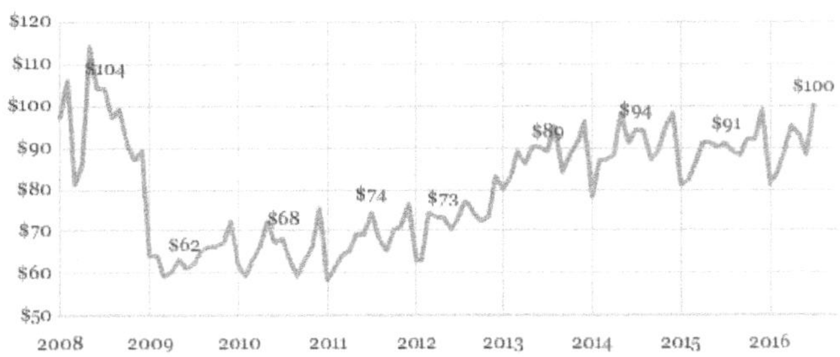

Note: Figures shown are for July of each year.
Gallup U.S. Daily tracking

GALLUP

These results are based on Gallup Daily tracking interviews conducted throughout July. Gallup asks Americans each night to report how much they spent "yesterday," excluding normal household bills and major purchases such as a home or car. The measure gives an indication of discretionary spending.

After dropping dramatically in 2008 and early 2009 amid the global financial crisis, Americans' reported spending levels gradually held at low levels – mostly in the $60 to $70 range – through late 2012. At that point, they began to increase and have typically been in the $80 to $90 range since. Spending estimates have reached the $100 average only a few times in Gallup's trend prior to July, all before the financial crisis took hold in 2008.

July typically ranks among the highest spending months in Gallup's nearly nine-year trend. However, large increases between June and July, such as those this year, are not common. The average June-to-July increase had been $2 before this year.

Spending Up Among All Income Groups

Spending among Americans with annual household incomes of less than $90,000 increased by $5 from June's average, erasing the decline observed among this group from May to June. The current monthly figure for lower- and middle-income Americans is one of the highest in the past year.

Americans whose households earn $90,000 or more annually saw a much more significant increase – $18 – from June to July. The latest monthly spending average for this income group, $161, essentially matches the $162 from December, when the spending average among all Americans was $99.

Consumer Spending by Annual Household Income, July 2015 to July 2016

Gallup U.S. Daily tracking

GALLUP

Bottom Line

The latest spending average is a notable marker in the post-recession spending trend, as monthly averages have not reached or exceeded $100 since 2008.

While spending was slightly depressed in June, this could have been because Americans anticipated spending more in July. Gallup observed a notable pullback in spending in the second half of June compared with the first. In addition to robust spending during the July Fourth holiday, the month had five weekends as opposed to four. Since Americans spend proportionately more on weekends than weekdays, according to Gallup data, this helped keep the spending at a higher level for the month of July.

These data are available in Gallup Analytics.

Survey Methods

Results for this Gallup poll are based on telephone interviews conducted July 1-31, 2016, on the Gallup U.S. Daily survey, with a random sample of 14,181 adults, aged 18 and older, living in all 50 U.S. states and the District of Columbia. For results based on the total sample of national adults, the margin of error for the spending mean is ±$5 at the 95% confidence level. All reported margins of sampling error include computed design effects for weighting.

August 02, 2016
AMERICANS' INTEREST IN WATCHING OLYMPICS TUMBLES TO NEW LOW

by Art Swift

Story Highlights

- *48% in U.S. say they plan to watch a "great deal" or "fair amount"*
- *wSharp decline among women fuels drop in interest*
- *Fewer know where games will take place compared with previous years*

WASHINGTON, D.C. – Forty-eight percent of Americans say they plan to watch a "great deal" or "fair amount" of the 2016 Summer Olympics. This is a sharp drop from 59% in 2012 and easily the lowest percentage planning to watch compared with the past four Summer Games.

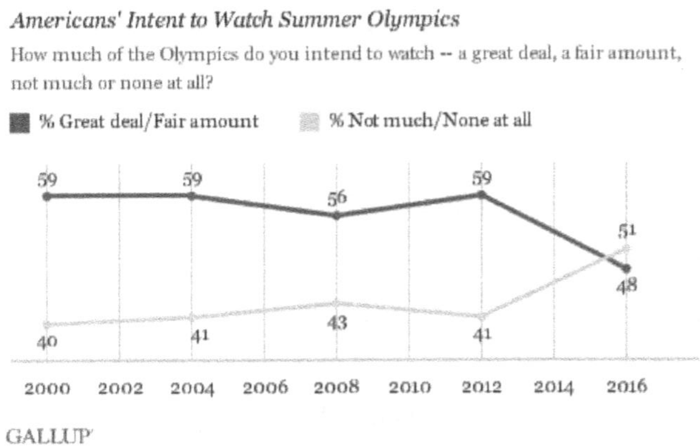

Thirty percent say they plan to watch "not much" of the Olympics, and 21% say "none at all" – the highest percentage saying so since Gallup began asking this question in 2000.

These results come from a July 13-17 Gallup poll asking Americans about their plans to watch the Olympics, which begin this week in Rio de Janeiro. Many athletes' decisions to opt out of the games because of concerns about the Zika virus have already blemished the Rio Olympics. Other controversies have marred the games, including the banishment of the Russian track and field and weightlifting teams due to their widespread drug use. Reports of rooms in the Olympic Village smelling like gas, along with blocked toilets and exposed wires – as well as accounts of sewage in the waters that athletes will swim and row in – have dominated headlines. All of these issues may explain why Americans find the idea of watching the Rio Olympics less appealing than previous Summer Games.

Sharp Decline Among Women Fuels Drop in Viewing

Men (49%) and women (47%) have roughly the same interest in watching the Rio Olympics. Yet the decline in interest among women is stark: For the 2012 London Olympics, 63% of women said they planned to watch the Olympics a great deal or fair amount.

Americans' Intent to Watch Summer Olympics, by Gender

% Great deal/Fair amount

	Men %	Women %
2016	49	47
2012	53	63
2008	56	56
2004	57	60
2000	57	61

Gallup

In previous Olympic Games, men and women were roughly even in their intentions to watch – although in three of the last four Summer Olympics, women outpaced men at least slightly in their interest in watching. This year, men have a slight edge in interest level for the first time since 2000.

Knowledge of Olympics' Host City Declines

Despite controversies in the news about the Rio Olympics, fewer Americans are able to identify where the Olympics are taking place than in years past. Less than half (46%) know the Olympics will be held in Rio, with an additional 17% correctly identifying Brazil as the host nation. This is down from 65% who correctly named London as the location for the 2012 Games, in addition to 8% who were partially correct in naming England as the site of the games.

Americans' Knowledge of Olympics' Location

Do you, by chance, know where the Summer Olympics are being held this month?

	Correct response %	Partially correct %	Incorrect %	No opinion %
2016	46 (Rio de Janeiro)	17 (Brazil)	4	34
2012	65 (London)	8 (England)	2	24
2008	43 (Beijing)	36 (China)	2	19
2004	45 (Athens)	26 (Greece)	8	21
2000	44 (Sydney)	30 (Australia)	3	23
1952	28 (Helsinki)	4 (Europe)	27	41
1948	20 (London)	17 (England)	12	51

Gallup

While still a solid combined majority at 63% for 2016, in Olympics past Americans' awareness of the location has been much higher. In 2008, 79% knew that the Olympics would take place in Beijing or China, along with 71% in 2004 and 74% in 2000.

In 1948 and 1952, a time with far less television and no social media, less than half of Americans could name London and Helsinki as the locations for those respective years' games.

Bottom Line

For the first time since Gallup began asking this question in 2000, Americans are almost evenly split as to whether they will watch the Olympics. The Olympic Games have been a rallying cry for nations since ancient times, and certainly since the modern Olympics resumed in 1896. Yet with concerns about the Zika virus keeping many American athletes at home, on top of allegations of drug use among participants and recent reports of unsafe conditions in the Olympic Village, Americans seem to have lost interest.

Though U.S. adults are less likely to watch the Olympics than in years past, they may tune in in greater numbers if there are captivating storylines to drive interest early in the games – such as "underdog" athletes winning unexpectedly, the U.S. outperforming other nations or even further controversies. Whether or not Americans watch the Summer Games, they are likely to remain a highly observed global event this month.

Historical data are available in Gallup Analytics.

Survey Methods

Results for this Gallup poll are based on telephone interviews conducted July 13-17, 2016, with a random sample of 1,023 adults, aged 18 and older, living in all 50 U.S. states and the District of Columbia. For results based on the total sample of national adults, the margin of sampling error is ±4 percentage points at the 95% confidence level. All reported margins of sampling error include computed design effects for weighting.

August 03, 2016
BEER REIGNS AS AMERICANS' PREFERRED ALCOHOLIC BEVERAGE

by Zac Auter

Story Highlights

- *Beer continues to edge out wine, liquor as preferred alcoholic drink*
- *65% of Americans say they drink alcoholic beverages*
- *A quarter of drinkers say they occasionally drink too much*

WASHINGTON, D.C. – Beer remains the alcoholic beverage of choice among Americans who imbibe alcohol. While 43% of Americans who drink alcohol say they prefer beer, 32% say wine and 20% say liquor.

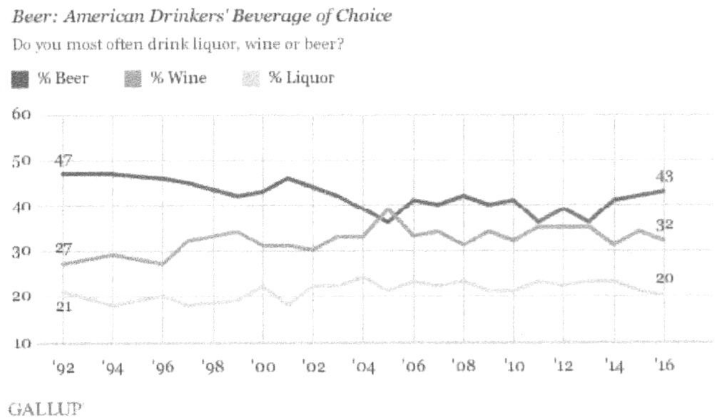

These results come from Gallup's 2016 Consumption Habits survey, conducted July 13-17. The 43% of U.S. adult drinkers who say they drink beer most often is the highest since 2002, when 44% said the same. At several points since 2005, wine and beer essentially tied as the preferred alcoholic beverage, but in the last three years beer has held firmly as the top choice.

Americans' drink of choice differs by gender, as it has since the 1990s. Half of female drinkers prefer wine, based on combined data from 2010 through 2016, while beer and liquor tie as their next-favored beverage (23%). Meanwhile, 54% of male drinkers name beer as their preferred drink, followed by liquor (22%) and wine (18%). These gender differences largely echo men's and women's alcoholic beverage preferences from the previous decade (2001-2009).

American Drinkers' Alcoholic Beverage Choice, by Gender

Do you most often drink liquor, wine or beer?

	Men, 2001-2009 %	Men, 2010-2016 %	Women, 2001-2009 %	Women, 2010-2016 %
Liquor	19	22	25	23
Wine	20	18	47	50
Beer	57	54	24	23

Gallup, July 13-17, 2016

Most Americans Drink, but Higher-Income More Likely

Since 1939, Gallup has consistently found that a solid majority of Americans consume alcohol; however, the precise percentage has varied between 55% and 71%. The low point came in 1958, while the high occurred in the late 1970s. This year, 65% of Americans say they imbibe and 35% say they wholly abstain.

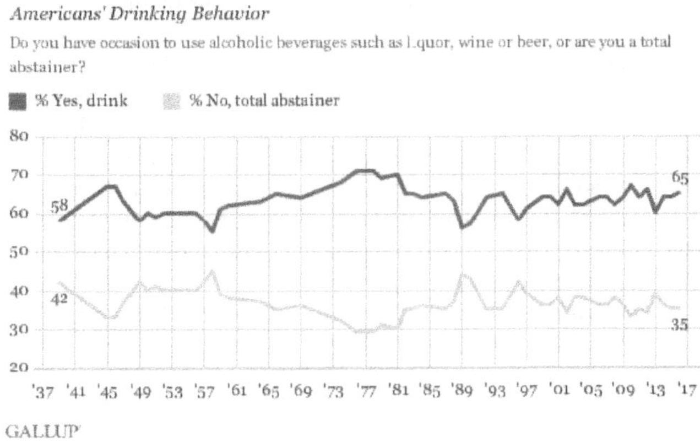

The choice to drink alcohol varies markedly among income groups. Between 2010 and 2016, 79% of higher-income Americans said they have occasion to imbibe, compared with 63% of middle-income Americans and 49% of lower-income Americans. These differences may stem from higher-income Americans having more disposable income to spend on alcoholic beverages.

Americans' Reports of Drinking Behavior, by Annual Household Income

2010-2016

	Have occasion to drink %
Less than $30,000	49
$30,000 to less than $75,000	63
$75,000 or more	79

Gallup, July 13-17, 2016

Drinking Not an Issue for Most Americans; More Problematic for Men

In the most recent poll, 25% of those who drink alcohol say they sometimes drink more than they should. Between 2010 and 2016, men (26%) were more likely than women (16%) to say they occasionally drink excessively – a gender discrepancy largely unchanged from the previous decade.

Reports of Occasionally Drinking Too Much, by Gender

	Occasionally drink too much %
Men, 2010-2016	26
Men, 2001-2009	28
Women, 2010-2016	16
Women, 2001-2009	16

Gallup, July 13-17, 2016

Bottom Line

Drinking remains a popular pastime for most Americans. For the nearly two in three Americans who imbibe, beer is consistently the preferred beverage of choice. However, more women continue to favor wine over beer and liquor. Gender differences in drinking behavior do not stop at favored alcoholic beverage, however. Men are more likely than women to say they occasionally drink more than they should.

A study by the University of Texas at Austin last year revealed that alcohol advertisement sales have increased 400% in the past four decades. This increase in advertisement sales could, in part, reflect a lack of growth in the percentage of Americans who drink alcohol and the stability of their preferred beverage of choice. Alcohol producers must compete with an ever-increasing number of producers and a population of drinkers that, rather than expanding, has remained relatively constant for decades.

Historical data are available in Gallup Analytics.

Survey Methods

Results for this Gallup poll are based on telephone interviews conducted July 13-17, 2016, with a random sample of 1,023 adults, aged 18 and older, living in all 50 U.S. states and the District of Columbia. For results based on the total sample of national adults, the margin of sampling error is ±4 percentage points at the 95% confidence level. For results based on the total sample of 682 adults who drink alcoholic beverages, the margin of sampling error is ±5 percentage points at the 95% confidence level. All reported margins of sampling error include computed design effects for weighting.

August 03, 2016
U.S. JOB CREATION REMAINS AT POST-RECESSION HIGH IN JULY

by Justin McCarthy

Story Highlights

- *U.S. Job Creation Index at +33 for third month in a row*
- *Gap narrowing between government and nongovernment hiring*

WASHINGTON, D.C. – U.S. workers' reports of hiring activity at their place of employment in July remained at a record high for the third month in a row. Gallup's U.S. Job Creation Index first reached the high score of +33 in its eight-year trend in May.

Gallup Job Creation Index -- Monthly Averages, Full Trend

The index is computed as the percentage of workers who say their employer is hiring workers/expanding the size of its workforce minus the percentage who say their employer is letting workers go/reducing the size of its workforce.

Note: Numbers shown are July readings for each year

Gallup U.S. Daily tracking

GALLUP

The latest holding pattern follows a period of relative stability in workers' perceptions of their employers' hiring activity. The index has ranged from +29 to +33 since February 2015.

Worker perceptions of hiring plummeted in 2008 amid that year's global financial crisis, resulting in more workers reporting layoffs rather than hiring at their places of employment between December 2008 and August 2009. Since then, perceptions of hiring have steadily improved, with the Job Creation Index climbing higher in each subsequent year before stabilizing in 2015. Index scores for 2016 so far have been slightly higher than those recorded by this point in 2015.

Gallup's Job Creation Index is based on employed U.S. adults' perceptions of their companies' hiring and firing practices. Gallup asks a random sample of employed adults each day whether their employers are hiring new people and expanding the size of their workforces, not changing the size of their workforces, or letting people go and reducing the size of their workforces. The resulting index – computed by subtracting the percentage of employers letting workers go from the percentage hiring – is nearly a real-time indicator of the nation's employment picture across all industry and business sectors.

In July, 44% of workers reported their companies were hiring, while 11% reported their companies were laying people off, resulting in the July Job Creation Index score of +33. These figures are unchanged from May and June. The latest results are based on interviews conducted July 1-31 with 16,753 full- and part-time U.S. workers.

Hiring and Firing Nationwide, Monthly Averages, January 2008-July 2016

Note: Numbers shown are July readings for each year

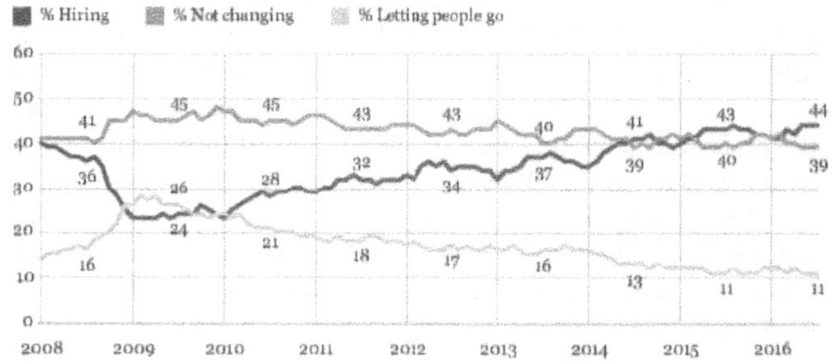

Gallup Daily tracking

GALLUP

Gap Narrowing Between Government and Nongovernment Hiring

Government hiring increased for the third month in a row in July, to +31 – the highest score for this sector in Gallup's trend. That increase had little effect on the overall Job Creation Index because the vast majority of U.S. workers are employed by nongovernment employers, among whom the July hiring index was +33, compared with +34 in June.

Net hiring scores among nongovernment workers have bested those of government workers for nearly all of Gallup's trend since late 2008, but that gap has narrowed recently. Net hiring plunged among both groups in late 2008, but nongovernment hiring recovered more quickly, returning to positive scores by late 2009 and steadily mounting thereafter. By contrast, net hiring among government workers remained in the red for three more years, turning positive only in late 2012.

Since then, government net hiring has been increasing at a faster pace than nongovernment net hiring, and the latest scores for each sector mark the closest the two have been since April 2009.

U.S. Job Creation Index for Government and Nongovernment Workers, August 2008–July 2016

Percentage who say their employers are expanding the workforce minus percentage who say their employers are reducing the workforce

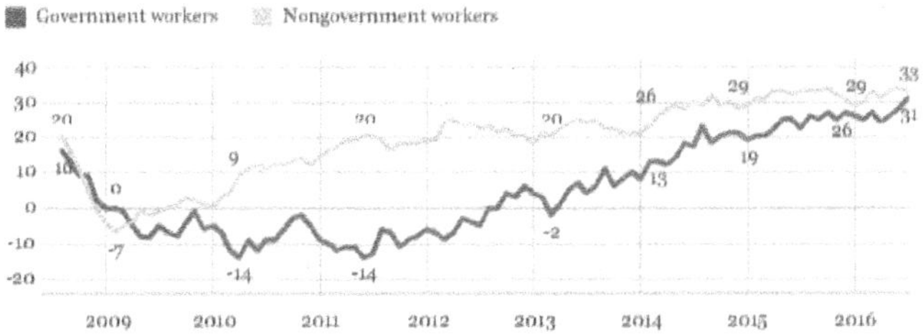

GALLUP

Bottom Line

Hiring activity in the U.S. remains at its best in eight years, according to U.S. workers themselves. This syncs with the Bureau of Labor Statistics' unemployment figures, which have been below 5% for most of 2016 so far. Gallup's Good Jobs measure is also healthy. The July update of the Good Jobs measure will be released on Thursday.

The private sector continues to provide the large majority of Americans' jobs, and hiring reports among private-sector workers remain strong. But government workers' reports are catching up and now barely trail those of nongovernment workers.

These data are available in Gallup Analytics.

Survey Methods

Results for this Gallup poll are based on telephone interviews conducted July 1-31, 2016, on the Gallup U.S. Daily survey, with a random sample of 16,753 workers, aged 18 and older, living in all 50 U.S. states and the District of Columbia. For results based on the total sample of workers, the margin of sampling error is ±1 percentage point at the 95% confidence level. All reported margins of sampling error include computed design effects for weighting.

August 04, 2016

U.S. SMALL-BUSINESS OWNERS' OPTIMISM INCHES UP

by Coleen McMurray and Frank Newport

Story Highlights

- *Index is at +68; up from +64 in the second quarter*
- *Small-business owners are somewhat more positive about cash flow*
- *Most owners say presidential candidates not talking about their issues*

PRINCETON, N.J. – U.S. small-business owners' optimism increased modestly this quarter. The Wells Fargo/Gallup Small Business Index is at +68, up from +64 in the second quarter of 2016 and nearly matching the eight-year high of +71, recorded in the first quarter of 2015.

Wells Fargo/Gallup Small Business Index

The Small Business Index consists of owners' ratings of their business' current situation and their expectations for the next 12 months, measured in terms of their overall financial situation, revenue, cash flow, capital spending, number of jobs and ease of obtaining credit.

Index conducted since August 2003 and quarterly from December 2003 to July 2016

GALLUP

These most recent data, collected July 6-12, are from the Wells Fargo/Gallup Small Business Index survey. The Wells Fargo/Gallup Small Business Index jumped in the first quarter of this year after posting declines for three consecutive quarters in 2015. The last three quarters' index scores have been within a few points of each other. The current score is close to the post-recession high of +71, recorded in the first quarter of 2015.

The Wells Fargo/Gallup Small Business Index consists of owners' ratings of their business' current situation and their expectations for the next 12 months, measured in terms of their overall financial situation, revenue, cash flow, capital spending, number of jobs and ease of obtaining credit. Small-business owners' assessments of these individual aspects of their current situation and future expectations are largely similar to the previous quarter. One exception is owners' reports about the status of their cash flow over the past year have increased modestly, helping lift the overall index. Now, 60% of owners say their cash flow over the past 12 months has been "somewhat good" or "very good," compared with 55% in quarter two.

Small-Business Owners' Top Challenge: Attracting Customers

When small-business owners were asked to identify the most important challenge facing their business, 14% cite attracting customers and finding new business, making this the top category of mentions. Other top concerns include government regulations (12%), the economy (10%) and hiring and retaining quality staff (11%). These challenges have been consistently reported as the top concerns of small-business owners since early 2013, although the order of these concerns shifts from quarter to quarter.

Few Owners Say Presidential Candidates Are Addressing Their Issues

Small-business owners continue to say they are following news about the presidential election. The 87% of owners who are following the election either "very closely" (57%) or "somewhat closely" (30%) is identical to the 87% found last quarter.

Small-business owners are more tuned into the presidential campaigns than the general public. In a national survey of adults in mid-June, Gallup found that 77% of national adults were following the election very closely (40%) or somewhat closely (37%).

While nearly half of small-business owners (48%) say the outcome of the November presidential election will have a major effect on their small businesses, few say that the presidential candidates are addressing their concerns. One-third of small-business owners surveyed (33%) said the presidential candidates are discussing the issues most important to them as small-business owners. This is up slightly from the 28% recorded in April. In comparison, 62% of national adults in a June Gallup poll said, in response to a more general question, that the candidates are addressing the issues about which they really care.

As far as you are concerned, are the presidential candidates discussing the issues most important to you as a small-business owner, or not?

	Yes %	No %	Don't know/Refused %
July 2016	33	62	5
April 2016	28	69	3

Wells Fargo/Gallup Small Business Index

More than half (54%) of small-business owners surveyed said they understand the candidates' positions on the issues that would affect their business "extremely well" or "very well," similar to the 47% who said so in April.

Bottom Line

Small-business owners are a bit more optimistic now than they were last quarter, but from a big picture perspective, optimism has yet to show signs of returning to the higher levels recorded before 2008. Small-business owners are not, apparently, holding out much hope that the next president will make specific changes that directly affect them; a clear majority say the candidates are not addressing the issues of importance to them.

Survey Methods

Results are based on telephone interviews with 603 U.S. small-business owners in all 50 states, conducted July 6-12, 2016. The margin of sampling error is ±4 percentage points at the 95% confidence level.

August 05, 2016

THIRD-PARTY CANDIDATES JOHNSON, STEIN LARGELY UNKNOWN

by Jeffrey M. Jones

Story Highlights

- *63% unfamiliar with Gary Johnson, 68% with Jill Stein*
- *Opinions of Johnson divided; views of Stein tilt negative*
- *Better known than most prior Green and Libertarian candidates*

PRINCETON, N.J. – Roughly two-thirds of U.S. adults are unfamiliar with third-party presidential candidates Gary Johnson of the Libertarian Party and Jill Stein of the Green Party. Those with an opinion are about evenly split in holding a positive or a negative view of Johnson, while they are slightly negative about Stein.

Opinions of Libertarian Party presidential candidate Gary Johnson and Green Party presidential candidate Jill Stein

	Favorable %	Unfavorable %	No opinion %
Gary Johnson	19	18	63
Jill Stein	13	18	68

Gallup, July 13-17, 2016

The results are based on a July 13-17 Gallup poll, conducted before the Republican and Democratic national conventions. It is unclear what impact, if any, those conventions have had on views of the Libertarian and Green Party candidates, who receive far less media attention than Republican candidate Donald Trump and Democratic candidate Hillary Clinton.

But given the unpopularity of Trump and Clinton, it is possible Americans will be searching for an alternative candidate to vote for this fall. Typically, the Libertarian and Green Party candidates receive 1% or less of the vote. Current presidential preference polls that include the third-party candidates show Johnson averaging about 7% of the vote and Stein 3%, a stronger showing than each had in summer preference polls as their party's presidential candidate in 2012. However, support for third-party candidates in early campaign preference polls often greatly overstates the support they receive on Election Day.

Johnson, Stein Better Known Than Many Past Nominees

Gallup has asked Americans for their views of some third-party candidates in past elections, including Libertarian and Green Party candidates, but not Johnson and Stein in 2012. In general, Johnson and Stein this year are better known than many former minor-party candidates, perhaps because it is the second presidential campaign for each.

However, they are not nearly as well-known as other third-party candidates who had already had a national profile before running for president on a third-party ticket, including Ross Perot, Ralph Nader and Pat Buchanan.

Favorable Ratings of Prior Third-Party Candidates Measured in Gallup Polls

	Date	Have an opinion %	Favorable %	Unfavorable %
Ross Perot (R)	1996 ^	87	35	52
Ross Perot (I)	1992 ^	83	42	41
Ralph Nader (I)	2004 Sep	81	33	48
Pat Buchanan (R)	2000 Jul	77	28	49
Ralph Nader (I)	2008 Aug	73	29	44
Ralph Nader (G)	2000 Jul	64	42	22
Gary Johnson (L)	2016 Jul	37	19	18
Jill Stein (G)	2016 Jul	31	13	18
Bob Barr (L)	2008 Aug	27	10	17
David Cobb (G)	2004 Sep	27	6	21
Michael Badnarik (L)	2004 Sep	23	7	16
Michael Peroutka (C)	2004 Sep	18	5	13
Harry Browne (L)	2000 Jun	8	3	5

^ Perot's favorable rating was measured numerous times in 1992 and 1996; figures are average for the year; (R) = Reform Party, (I) = Independent, (G) = Green Party, (L) = Libertarian Party, (C) = Constitution Party
Gallup

For the most part, third-party candidates have not been especially popular, even among Americans who are familiar with them. Only Ralph Nader in 2000 had significantly higher favorable (42%) than unfavorable (22%) ratings, in a year when he won nearly 3% of the national popular vote. Nader was better known in his 2004 and 2008 campaigns for president, but much less liked, perhaps because of the belief he cost Al Gore the 2000 election. Perot, too, was better known but less liked in his second campaign for president in 1996 and received 8% of the vote, compared with 19% in 1992.

Johnson Less Appealing to the Political Right

Johnson is a former two-term Republican governor of New Mexico. As such, some experts view him as a greater electoral threat to Trump than to Clinton. And while that may still be the case in terms of how people cast their ballots, more conservatives and Republicans currently view Johnson negatively than positively. In contrast, moderates, liberals, independents and Democrats view him somewhat more positively than negatively. He is about equally unknown among all political groups.

Opinions of Libertarian Party Presidential Candidate Gary Johnson, by Ideology and Party Identification

	Favorable %	Unfavorable %	No opinion %
Liberal	22	15	63
Moderate	24	16	59
Conservative	14	20	66
Democratic	20	17	64
Independent	24	15	62
Republican	13	22	64

Gallup, July 13-17, 2016

The potential threat Johnson poses to Trump may be a reason for the negative tilt among Republicans and conservatives who know him. In other words, they may view Johnson as more of a spoiler candidate than as one who shares their political views on many issues, most notably a preference for limited government.

Political liberals have the most positive views of Stein, suggesting they view her as more of an ideological ally than as a potential spoiler. This may be partly because she is getting lower support in national preference polls than Johnson is. Also, the 45% of liberals who have an opinion of Stein is far greater than the roughly one-third or less of other political and ideological groups that do.

None of the other political and ideological groups view Stein positively. This includes Democrats – who might be more inclined to like her for her ideological views – and independents, who may be more positive toward a third-party candidate.

Opinions of Green Party Presidential Candidate Jill Stein, by Ideology and Party Identification

	Favorable %	Unfavorable %	No opinion %
Liberal	29	16	56
Moderate	10	19	72
Conservative	8	20	72
Democratic	16	16	68
Independent	16	18	66
Republican	7	22	71

Gallup, July 13-17, 2016

Implications

Johnson and Stein are similar to many prior third-party candidates in that they are unknown to most Americans. They are, however, better known than many past third-party candidates, including some who ran on the Libertarian and Green Party tickets. But they are not nearly as well-known as Perot and Nader, the third-party candidates who won the greatest share of the vote in recent elections.

As long as they remain lesser-known, the record indicates Johnson and Stein will not be significant factors in the 2016 election. At most, they have the potential to peel enough support from one of the major-party candidates to swing a close election or possibly alter the outcome in a few states.

And while both Johnson and Stein are registering perceptible support in national presidential preference polls today, the strong historical pattern has been for third-party candidate support levels to shrink as the election draws near. However, the 2016 campaign has already deviated from the historical playbook with a political outsider claiming the Republican nomination and both parties nominating candidates whom the American public views more negatively than positively, even after their nominating conventions. Thus, if more voters dissatisfied with Trump and Clinton choose to register their displeasure by voting for a third-party candidate rather than voting for the "lesser of two evils," this year's third-party candidates could surpass their parties' vote totals in prior elections.

Historical data are available in Gallup Analytics.

Survey Methods

Results for this Gallup poll are based on telephone interviews conducted July 13-17, 2016, with a random sample of 1,023 adults, aged 18 and older, living in all 50 U.S. states and the District of Columbia. For results based on the total sample of national adults, the margin of sampling error is ±4 percentage points at the 95% confidence level. All reported margins of sampling error include computed design effects for weighting.

August 05, 2016

U.S. INVESTORS SPLIT BETWEEN DIGITAL AND TRADITIONAL BANKING

by Lydia Saad

Story Highlights

- *Half of investors rely on financial firms' websites or mobile apps*
- *Majorities check their statements online*
- *Most investors aged 50+ still rely mainly on phone and branch office*

PRINCETON, N.J. – U.S. investors split into two camps when it comes to the method they prefer for interacting with the financial services firm that handles their investments. Fifty percent of investors say they rely mainly on the firm's website (40%) or mobile app (10%), while a combined 47% still turn to traditional methods including the branch office (25%) or telephone (22%).

U.S. Investors' Preferences for Interacting With Financial Services Firm

Next, thinking about the primary financial services firm you use for your investments, which of the following methods of interacting with that firm is most important to you?

	U.S. investors %
Website	40
Branch office	25
Telephone	22
Mobile app	10
(All equally)	1
No opinion	2

Wells Fargo/Gallup Investor and Retirement Optimism Index, May 13-22, 2016

More broadly, investors divide roughly into thirds when it comes to reliance on mobile apps and other online tools and services. About a third (31%) say they do everything they possibly can online, while 38% say they only do some things online and 31% do very little.

Naturally, there is a strong generational aspect to these preferences. Most strikingly, a combined 69% of investors aged 18 to 49 say that a website or mobile app is the most important means for them to interact with their primary financial firm, whereas 59% of older investors cite the telephone or branch office. Similarly, while 43% of younger investors say they do everything they possibly can online, an equal proportion of older investors, 45%, say they do very little online.

Summary of U.S. Investors' Preferences for Use of Online Tools – by Age

	18 to 49 %	50+ %
Most important channel for interacting with financial firm		
Website	53	31
Branch office	18	29
Telephone	12	30
Mobile app	16	6
TOTAL WEBSITE/MOBILE APP	69	37
TOTAL TELEPHONE/BRANCH OFFICE	30	59
Orientation to online tools and mobile apps		
Do everything you possibly can online	43	20
Do only some things online	41	35
Do very little online	16	45

Wells Fargo/Gallup Investor and Retirement Optimism Index, May 13-22, 2016

These findings are from the second quarter Wells Fargo/Gallup Investor and Retirement Optimism Index survey, conducted in May. The survey reflects the views of U.S. investors with $10,000 or more invested in stocks, bonds or mutual funds.

Investors Use Web for Routine Financial Tasks, but Not Advice

Despite these general orientations toward technology, about six in 10 investors indicate they do a variety of routine financial tasks online. This includes reviewing their investment statements, reviewing account fees and transferring money between funds. Fewer than half, however, say they use an online method to rebalance (45%) or make changes to their investments (46%) or to calculate their retirement needs (46%). And fewer still, just 24%, say they go online for investment advice.

How U.S. Investors Handle Various Investing Tasks

Now we'd like you to think about your investments, including your retirement accounts, stocks and any other investments you may have. Do you usually handle each of the following tasks related to your investments using an online method or some other method?

	Online method %	Some other method %
Reviewing account fees	62	35
Transferring money between funds	61	33
Reviewing your investment statements	60	37
Making changes to your investments	46	49
Calculating your retirement needs	46	48
Rebalancing your investments	45	49
Getting investment advice	24	70

Note: "Never do task" responses not included
Wells Fargo/Gallup Investor and Retirement Optimism Index, May 13-22, 2016

In line with the low percentage of investors who seek investment advice online, the survey found that just 5% of investors are highly familiar with or have already used robo-advice – that is, online advisory services that rely on computer algorithms to select and manage customers' investments.

Some of the variation in the percentage of investors using an online vs. "some other" method to do things like rebalance or calculate their retirement needs could reflect lower proportions of investors engaging in these activities at all; however, no more than 5% volunteered in the survey that they never engage in these tasks.

In line with their general preferences for interacting with their primary investing firm, majorities of investors younger than 50 say they use the web for almost all of the investing activities tested, whereas less than half of those 50 and older do so.

How U.S. Investors Handle Various Investing Tasks – by Age

Shown is percentage who handle each task online rather than via some other method

	18 to 49 %	50+ %
Reviewing account fees	79	49
Transferring money between funds	80	47
Reviewing your investment statements	80	47
Making changes to your investments	64	34
Calculating your retirement needs	63	34
Rebalancing your investments	60	33
Getting investment advice	30	20

Wells Fargo/Gallup Investor and Retirement Optimism Index, May 13-22, 2016

Investors who have a dedicated financial adviser tend to be less likely to handle various investing tasks for themselves online, but this does not explain the large age differences described above. First, younger investors are only slightly less likely than those 50 and older to have such an adviser. Moreover, the age gaps persist among investors who have and who do not have their own adviser.

Bottom Line

While the internet is ubiquitous in people's lives and offers numerous ways for investors to stay on top of their investments, nearly half of investors still rely mainly on in-person interactions, or at least the familiarity of the telephone, to conduct their investment transactions. However, a sea change is on the horizon, because investors younger than 50 show tremendous willingness not only to monitor their investments online but also to use digital tools to move money around and calculate their retirement needs.

Close to half of younger investors describe themselves as the kind of people who do everything they can online. The one digital offering they still resist is getting their investment advice through a computer or mobile app, meaning human advisers – whether working as personal financial advisers or in call centers – will continue to play an important role in investors' lives.

Survey Methods

Results for the Wells Fargo/Gallup Investor and Retirement Optimism Index survey are based on questions asked May 13-22, 2016, on the Gallup Daily tracking survey, of a random sample of 1,019 U.S. adults having investable assets of $10,000 or more.

For results based on the total sample of investors, the margin of sampling error is ±4 percentage points at the 95% confidence level. All reported margins of sampling error include computed design effects for weighting.

August 08, 2016

PERCENTAGE OF PACK-A-DAY SMOKERS HITS RECORD LOW IN U.S.

by Justin McCarthy

Story Highlights

- *New low of 26% of smokers report smoking a pack or more a day*
- *More than three in four smokers have tried to quit*
- *64% of former smokers quit after one or two attempts*

WASHINGTON, D.C. – The percentage of smokers in the U.S. who light up a pack or more of cigarettes a day has fallen sharply over the past decade and is now at an all-time low of 26% in Gallup's seven-decade trend. The figure topped 30% as recently as 2012 and routinely exceeded 50% until the late 1990s.

U.S. Smokers' Reported Quantity of Cigarette Consumption, 1944-2016

About how many cigarettes do you smoke each day?

(Asked of U.S. smokers)

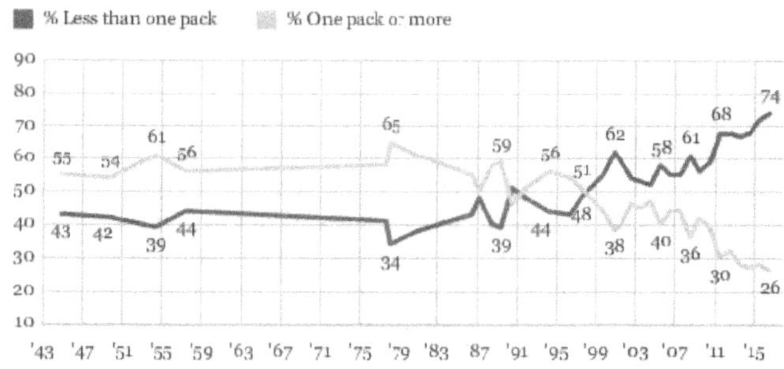

GALLUP

The latest findings are from Gallup's annual Consumption Habits poll, conducted July 13-17. The trend shows a continuous decline in the percentage of heavy smokers over the years – with a particularly sharp drop since the late 1990s, when public smoking bans were implemented in many states and municipalities.

The decline in the percentage of heavy smokers somewhat mirrors a long-term decline in the overall percentage of Americans who smoke. Gallup's data show that 19% of Americans report having smoked cigarettes in the past week, similar to recent years and well below the levels of 40% or higher in the 1940s to early 1970s.

Most Cigarette Smokers Have Tried to Quit

The percentage of current smokers would be even lower if smokers had their wish, as most (74%) say they would like to give up smoking, and the vast majority have made some attempt at kicking the habit. Smokers surveyed in 2013 and 2016 who have tried to quit are split between those who have tried once or twice (39%) and those who have made even more attempts (43%).

Number of Times Smokers Say They've Tried to Quit

How many different times in your life, if any, have you made serious attempts to quit smoking? [Open-ended]

	Never %	Once or twice %	Three to 10 times %	More than 10 times %
2013, 2016	17	39	38	5

Averages of polling from July 10-14, 2013, and July 13-17, 2016; Gallup

Six in 10 Former Smokers Kicked the Habit in One or Two Tries

Twenty-five percent of those interviewed in Gallup's 2013 and 2016 surveys say they are former smokers. The majority of this group, 60%, report that they were able to do away with their smoking habit in one or two attempts, with the rest saying it took more tries.

Number of Attempts It Took Former Smokers to Quit

How many different times in your life did you make serious attempts to quit smoking? [Open-ended]

	Once or twice %	Three to 10 times %	More than 10 times %
2013, 2016	60	31	5

Averages of polling from July 10-14, 2013, and July 13-17, 2016; Gallup

The fact that so many former smokers were able to quit in only one or two attempts, while current smokers have tried and failed multiple times, underscores the dilemma public health officials face when trying to further reduce the smoking rate. Those who continue to smoke apparently have an addiction to nicotine that is particularly acute.

Bottom Line

The laws and attitudes surrounding smoking in the U.S. have changed over the past several decades, and so have smoking habits. Public health officials have reason to be encouraged by record lows in both the percentage of Americans who smoke and the percentage of heavy smokers.

Though a strong majority of Americans who used to smoke were successful at quitting in their first or second attempt, four in 10 current smokers have tried to quit more than twice and still have not been able to. While tobacco may be a substance that is easy for many Americans to stop using, it's a heavier lift for the majority who still use it.

Historical data are available in Gallup Analytics.

Survey Methods

Results for this Gallup poll are based on telephone interviews conducted July 13-17, 2016, on the Gallup U.S. Daily survey, with a random sample of 1,023 adults, aged 18 and older, living in all 50 U.S. states and the District of Columbia. For results based on the total sample of national adults, the margin of sampling error is ±4 percentage points at the 95% confidence level. All reported margins of sampling error include computed design effects for weighting.

August 08, 2016

ONE IN EIGHT U.S. ADULTS SAY THEY SMOKE MARIJUANA

by Justin McCarthy

Story Highlights

- *13% report being current marijuana users, up from 7% in 2013*
- *43% of U.S. adults say they have tried it*
- *Use and experimentation differ by religiosity, age*

WASHINGTON, D.C. – Thirteen percent of U.S. adults tell Gallup they currently smoke marijuana, nearly double the percentage who reported smoking marijuana only three years ago.

Americans Who Say They Currently Smoke Marijuana

Keeping in mind that all of your answers in this survey are confidential, do you, yourself, smoke marijuana?

	Yes, do %	No, do not %
July 13-17, 2016^	13	87
July 8-12, 2015^	11	88
July 10-14, 2013^	7	93

^ Based on a half sample
Gallup

Although use of the drug is still prohibited by federal law, the number of states that have legalized recreational marijuana use has grown from two in 2013, Colorado and Washington, to four today – with the addition of Alaska and Oregon – plus the District of Columbia. Five states will vote on whether to legalize marijuana this November.

Half of U.S. states (including the four above) have some variation of a medicinal marijuana law on the books, and four more will be voting this fall on whether to legalize marijuana for medicinal use. Both major-party presidential candidates, Hillary Clinton and Donald Trump, have voiced support for medicinal marijuana but say they defer to the states in terms of policymaking on both recreational and medicinal marijuana use.

States' willingness to legalize marijuana could be a reason for the uptick in the percentage of Americans who say they smoke marijuana, regardless of whether it is legal in their particular state. Gallup finds residents in the West – home of all four states that have legalized recreational marijuana use – are significantly more likely to say they smoke marijuana than those in other parts of the country.

Gallup has found that majorities of Americans have supported legalizing marijuana since 2013.

More Than Four in 10 Say They Have Tried Marijuana

More broadly, 43% of Americans say they have ever tried marijuana, similar to the 44% recorded last year and up slightly from 38% in 2013. The percentage of Americans who say they have tried the drug has slowly increased from 4% in 1969.

Americans Who Say They Have Tried Marijuana

Keeping in mind that all of your answers in this survey are confidential, have you, yourself, ever happened to try marijuana?

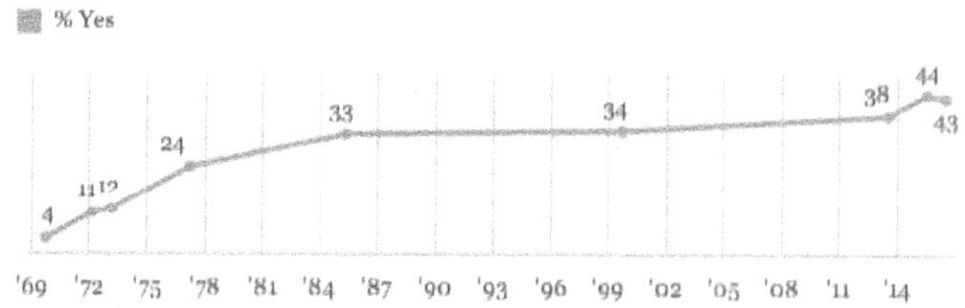

Latest data asked of half sample of 507 national adults

Question wording for 1969-1985 trend: Have you, yourself, ever happened to try marijuana?

GALLUP

Between 1969 and 1977, young adults were the group most likely to experiment with marijuana. But as those adults have aged and successive generations have joined their ranks, the overall percentage having ever tried it has sharply increased.

The latest data come from Gallup's July 13-17 Consumption Habits poll.

Age and Religiosity Key Predictors of Current Marijuana Use

To compare marijuana use among various subgroups, Gallup aggregated data from 2013, 2015 and 2016.

The results show that age and religiosity are key determinants of marijuana use. Almost one in five adults (19%) under the age of 30 report currently using it – at least double the rate seen among each older age group. Only 2% of weekly churchgoers and 7% of less frequent attenders say they use marijuana, but this rises to 14% of those who seldom or never attend a religious service.

The pattern by age in ever having used marijuana does not show the same skew toward the young; instead, it peaks among the middle-aged. About half of adults between the ages of 30 and 49 (50%) and between 50 and 64 (48%) report having *tried* it. Despite being less likely to currently smoke marijuana, these older Americans could be more likely than their younger peers to report having tried it because they've had more years to do so. But this difference in their rates of experimentation could also reflect generational cultures and attitudes toward marijuana that have shifted over time.

Marijuana Usage and Experimentation in the U.S., by Subgroup

	Smoke marijuana % Yes	Have tried marijuana % Yes
Men	12	48
Women	7	34
18 to 29 years old	19	38
30 to 49 years old	9	50
50 to 64 years old	7	48
65+ years old	3	21
Annual income less than $30,000	14	41
Annual income $30,000 to <$75,000	9	41
Annual income $75,000+	9	43
High school education or less	9	40
Some college	11	43
College graduate	11	42
Postgraduate	6	38
Attend church seldom/never	14	52
Attend church nearly weekly/monthly	7	36
Attend church weekly	2	26
East	9	38
Midwest	9	41
South	6	38
West	14	47

Based on aggregated data from July 10-14, 2013; July 8-12, 2015; and July 13-17, 2016

Income and education levels don't seem strongly related to an individual's likelihood of having tried marijuana. Americans who live in households that make less than $30,000 are a bit more likely to report currently using it, however, at 14%.

In the East, Midwest and South, both the percentages who use marijuana and the percentages who have experimented with it are generally slightly below the national averages. Meanwhile, Americans who live in the West are a bit more likely to report currently using (14%) or having tried (47%) pot. This could be because of marijuana's legal status in Colorado, Oregon, Alaska and Washington, but could also reflect a regional difference in attitudes, even as more Western states – including Arizona, California and Nevada – prepare to vote on recreational marijuana use in November.

Bottom Line

As nine states vote on various levels of marijuana legalization this fall, 2016 could mark a significant legal shift on the issue. Recreational use could become legal in as many as nine states (up from only four today), and medicinal use could become legal in an additional four states.

As for medical marijuana, pros and cons for the drug – including recreational use of it – are well-documented. The negative effects could keep many Americans from regularly using or even trying marijuana. Still, because a clear majority of Americans support legalizing marijuana and more states are considering it, it's likely that use of and experimentation with marijuana will increase.

Historical data are available in Gallup Analytics.

Survey Methods

Results for this Gallup poll are based on telephone interviews conducted July 13-17, 2016, with a random sample of 1,023 adults, aged 18 and older, living in all 50 U.S. states and the District of Columbia. The questions reported here are based on half samples of approximately 500 adults each. For results based on these samples of national adults, the margin of sampling error is ±5 percentage points at the 95% confidence level. All reported margins of sampling error include computed design effects for weighting.

August 10, 2016
VIEWS OF U.S. POLITICAL PARTIES UNCHANGED AFTER CONVENTIONS

by Zac Auter

Story Highlights

- *Americans are more favorable toward the Democratic than Republican Party*
- *Opinions of the two parties largely unchanged after the conventions*
- *Among Republicans, Trump elicits more favorability than Republican Party*

WASHINGTON, D.C. – Americans' perceptions of the Republican and Democratic parties at the conclusion of this summer's presidential nominating season are little changed from what they were before the conventions began. Overall, 44% of Americans hold a favorable view of the Democratic Party – similar to the 43% in mid-July. Meanwhile, just over a third (36%) of Americans have a favorable view of the Republican Party, compared with 37% before the conventions.

Percentage of Americans Viewing Each Major Political Party Favorably

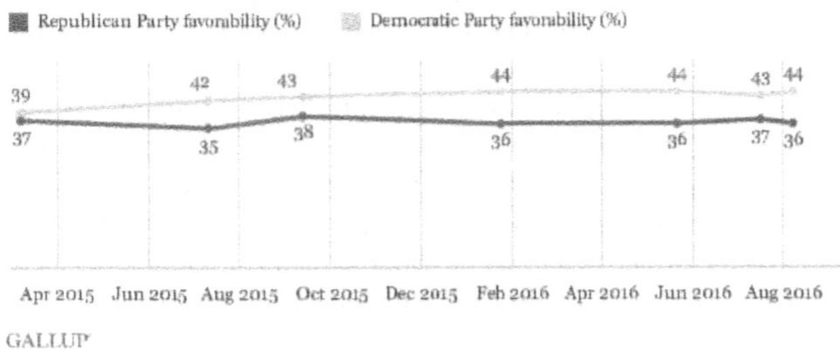

The latest results come from a Gallup poll conducted Aug. 3-7. The party favorable ratings remain relatively stable, with Americans consistently giving the Democratic Party a more positive image as they have all year – despite the heavy news coverage given to the Republican (July 18-21) and Democratic (July 25-28) conventions, as well as the 20 to 30 million viewers who tuned in each night to watch them live on television.

Democrats More Positive Toward Their Own Party

Eighty percent of Democrats and independents who lean Democratic have a favorable opinion of the Democratic Party. GOP supporters grade the Republican Party less positively, with 63% of Republicans and independents who lean Republican rating their party favorably. Neither Democratic nor Republican partisans' views of their own party changed significantly after the conventions.

Americans' Favorability Ratings of the Two Major Political Parties

	Pre-convention favorability among own partisans %	Post-convention favorability among own partisans %
Democratic Party	79	80
Republican Party	65	63

Gallup, Aug. 3-7, 2016

Democrats More Favorable Toward Clinton Than Republicans, Trump

Americans' views of the Democratic and Republican parties are, in general, quite similar to their views of each party's candidates, with 41% in the Aug. 3-7 survey viewing Hillary Clinton favorably (compared with 44% who view the Democratic Party favorably) and 34% who view Donald Trump favorably (compared with 36% who view the Republican Party favorably).

The same general pattern holds among the two partisan groups, with Democrats viewing their party and Clinton in broadly similar ways, and Republicans holding similar images of their own party and Trump. Nearly three-quarters of Democrats and independents who lean Democratic (74%) have a favorable opinion of Clinton, and 80% rate the Democratic Party favorably overall. Republicans' favorable opinions of both Trump and the GOP are also similar, albeit lower – with 69% holding a favorable opinion of Trump and 63% for the Republican Party overall.

Democrats' views of Clinton are thus six percentage points lower than their favorable views of the party, while Republicans' views of Trump are six points more positive than views of their party.

Americans' Post-Convention Views of Party and Nominee Image

	Post-convention favorability among own partisans %
Among Democrats and independents who lean Democratic	
Democratic Party	80
Hillary Clinton	74
Among Republicans and independents who lean Republican	
Republican Party	63
Donald Trump	69

Gallup, Aug. 3-7, 2016

Implications

All of the resources expended on the Republican and Democratic conventions failed to move the needle on either party's national image. Neither party gained nor lost ground in the eyes of the American public. Whether this is because Americans are resistant to changing their views of the parties or because the effect of the two conventions canceled each other out is unclear. Given the Democratic Party's edge on this measure entering the convention season, Americans' unchanged views of the two parties in the wake of the conventions may represent a win for Democrats.

Trump is running as the nominee of a party that is held in less favor in the eyes of the public than his opponent's, presenting his campaign with a politically challenging environment. At the same time, Republicans are slightly more positive about him than they are their own party, while Democrats are less positive about Clinton than they are the Democratic Party. One possible implication of this could be Trump's ability to generate higher turnout among his base than Clinton will be able to do among hers.

These data are available in Gallup Analytics.

Survey Methods

Results for this Gallup poll are based on telephone interviews conducted Aug. 3-7, 2016, on the Gallup U.S. Daily survey, with a random sample of 1,032 adults, aged 18 and older, living in all 50 U.S. states and the District of Columbia. For results based on the total sample of national adults, the margin of sampling error is ±4 percentage points at the 95% confidence level. All reported margins of sampling error include computed design effects for weighting.

August 10, 2016

MIKE PENCE SHOWS GREATER GAINS IN FAVORABILITY THAN TIM KAINE

by Art Swift

Story Highlights

- *36% of Americans have favorable impression of Mike Pence*
- *33% have favorable opinion of Tim Kaine*
- *Republicans' views of Pence more positive than Democrats' views of Kaine*

WASHINGTON, D.C. – Since their respective selections as vice presidential candidates, both Mike Pence and Tim Kaine have become much better known nationwide, but Pence's image has grown significantly more positive over this time than has been the case for Kaine. As of now, Republicans are embracing Pence more than Democrats are embracing Kaine.

Americans' Impressions of Vice Presidential Candidates Mike Pence and Tim Kaine

% Favorable

	Pre-convention %	Post-convention %
Mike Pence	18	36
Tim Kaine	24	33

Gallup, July 15-16 (Pence), July 23-24 (Kaine) and August 3-7 (both), 2016

At this stage in the previous campaigns, most non-incumbent vice presidential candidates had substantially higher favorable ratings than Kaine and Pence do. Al Gore was at 62% favorable at this point in 1992; Jack Kemp was at 56% in 1996; Dick Cheney was at 51% and Joe Lieberman was at 55% in 2000; and John Edwards was at 59% in 2004. Gallup did not have polling for Joe Biden and Sarah Palin at this point in August in 2008 or for Paul Ryan in 2012.

Both Pence's favorable and unfavorable ratings have risen, while the percentage of those who have never heard of him or have no opinion has dropped from 65% before the Republican convention to 39%. His favorable rating has gone up more than his unfavorable rating. The Indiana governor received some nationwide media attention last year for signing a "religious freedom" law that LGBT Indianans sharply criticized, and was facing a difficult gubernatorial re-election campaign before GOP presidential nominee Donald Trump chose him to be his running mate.

Americans' Impressions of Mike Pence

Do you have a favorable or unfavorable opinion of Mike Pence, or have you never heard of him?

	Favorable %	Unfavorable %	Never heard of/No opinion %	Net favorable pct. pts.
Aug 3-7, 2016	36	25	39	+11
Jul 15-16, 2016	18	16	65	+2

Gallup

Trump has garnered many headlines since the conventions, including his pronouncements about the Muslim family whose Army captain son was killed in Iraq, the tensions between him and House Speaker Paul Ryan, and whether nuclear weapons can or should be used. The conciliatory statements Pence made may be seen as an attempt to assuage the situation by endorsing Ryan days before Trump did and by sympathizing with the soldier's family. Yet while Trump's statements have not helped his own favorable ratings, Pence has gained substantially in net favorability – the percentage with a positive opinion of him minus the percentage with a negative opinion.

Americans Quickly Forming Impressions of Pence; Republicans Embracing Him

Pence is better known and liked across key subgroups than he was before the Republican convention, especially among members of his own Republican Party.

Sixty-four percent of Republicans have a favorable impression of Pence, up from 40% in mid-July. He has risen to 33% favorability among independents and even has a 17% score among Democrats, up from a paltry 5% in July.

Impressions of Mike Pence, by Subgroup

% Favorable

	Jul 15-16, 2016 %	Aug 3-7, 2016 %
Republicans	40	64
Independents	14	33
Democrats	5	17

Gallup

Kaine's Favorable Ratings See Slower Rise

Americans' overall image of Kaine has become somewhat more negative since the beginning of the Democratic convention, contrasting with Pence's more positive movement. The U.S. senator from Virginia and former Virginia governor has a favorable rating of 33%, up from 24% before the convention. But his unfavorable rating has increased from 14% to 30%. Kaine's running mate, Hillary Clinton, has been much more low-key in her public appearances and statements than Trump has been in the last several weeks, with less controversy surrounding the Democratic campaign.

Americans' Impressions of Tim Kaine

Do you have a favorable or unfavorable opinion of Tim Kaine, or have you never heard of him?

	Favorable %	Unfavorable %	Never heard of/ No opinion %	Net favorable pct. pts.
Aug 3-7, 2016	33	30	37	+3
Jul 23-24, 2016	24	14	63	+10

Gallup

As was true of Pence, a large share of Americans, 63%, had not heard of or had no opinion of Kaine at the time of his selection as a vice presidential candidate. In Gallup's early August poll, the percentage unfamiliar with Kaine has dropped to 37%. But while Pence has been able to convert proportionately more of those unfamiliar with him to a positive opinion, Kaine has had a proportionately greater gain in those having a negative opinion of him. As a result, Pence's net favorable is currently +11, compared with +3 for Kaine.

Among subgroups, Kaine has made gains, but these have been modest. Only among Democrats does Kaine have a majority favorable rating, at 54%, but this is worse than Pence's 64% favorable rating among Republicans. It is possible that Bernie Sanders voters may have wished that Clinton picked a more liberal running mate, and they are still holding that against Kaine.

Impressions of Tim Kaine, by Subgroup

% Favorable

	Jul 23-24, 2016 %	Aug 3-7, 2016 %
Republicans	7	19
Independents	22	28
Democrats	42	54

Gallup

Bottom Line

The American public is getting to know Pence and Kaine. The vice presidential nominees' favorable ratings are rising, but Pence's gains have been more substantial than Kaine's since their respective nominating conventions. In the next three months, the American people will continue to form opinions of Kaine and Pence, and their images may be affected by the forthcoming vice presidential debate on Oct. 4 at Longwood University in Virginia.

Historical data are available in Gallup Analytics.

Survey Methods

Results for this Gallup poll are based on telephone interviews conducted Aug. 3-7, 2016, on the Gallup U.S. Daily survey, with a random sample of 1,032 adults, aged 18 and older, living in all 50 U.S. states and the District of Columbia. For results based on the total sample of national adults, the margin of sampling error is ±4 percentage points at the 95% confidence level. All reported margins of sampling error include computed design effects for weighting.

August 11, 2016

TRUMP, CLINTON FAVORABILITY BACK TO PRE-CONVENTION LEVELS

by Frank Newport

Story Highlights

- *Clinton's 39% and Trump's 32% favorable ratings very similar to early July*
- *Both saw their images improve during the conventions, but that didn't last*
- *73% of Democrats see Clinton favorably; 68% of Republicans like Trump*

PRINCETON, N.J. – Americans' views of Donald Trump and Hillary Clinton are almost exactly the same now as they were in early July before their party's convention. Both of their favorable ratings improved after their party's convention, but those higher ratings did not persist.

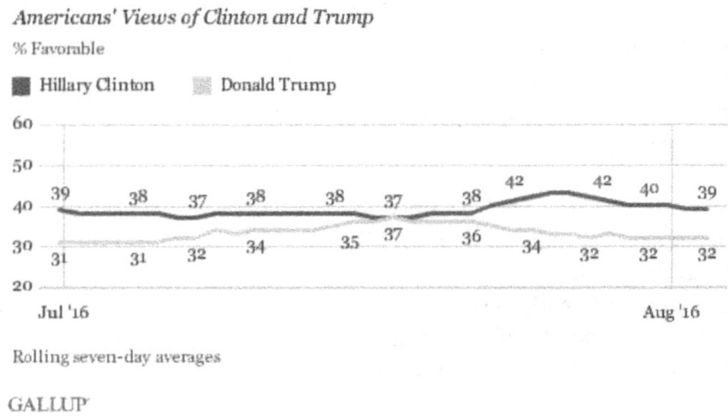

Trump's favorable rating became slightly more positive in the Republican convention environment, rising to 37% and matching Clinton's for the first and only time in Gallup's tracking. Then, as the Democratic convention was wrapping up, Clinton's favorable rating rose to 42%, and the gap between the two candidates' ratings expanded to 10 percentage points.

These shifts in the public's views of the two candidates were short-lived, however, and their images have now returned to where they were. Clinton is once again enjoying a modestly more positive image than Trump. Any hopes that either campaign had of using the conventions to create a major, lasting shift in Americans' images of the candidates did not materialize.

Partisans' Views of Their Candidates Also Little Changed

One of the traditional purposes of the summer political conventions is to rally each party's base around their candidate. But, as was the case for national adults, Democratic and Republican views of their party's nominee barely budged.

Seventy-three percent of Democrats (including Democrat-leaning independents) are positive about Clinton, similar to the 70% who rated her favorably prior to the conventions. Similarly, Trump's favorable rating among Republicans (including Republican-leaning independents) is 68%, up only three points since before the conventions.

Clinton and Trump Among Their Partisans

% Favorable

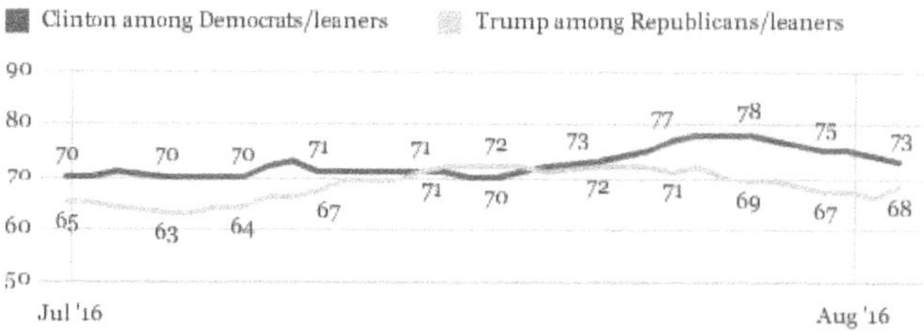

Rolling seven-day averages

GALLUP

This lack of improvement in partisan favorability was not what either campaign would have liked. Democratic Party unity had been roiled prior to the convention by many Democrats' loyalty to Bernie Sanders. The Vermont senator endorsed Clinton and said he was "proud to stand with her" in his convention speech, and while that may have helped boost her image among Democrats in the short term, it didn't create a major, lasting shift.

Trump too would have certainly liked to see improvement in his image among Republicans as a result of his convention. Trump's campaign had its own unity challenges, with establishment Republicans' reluctance to embrace his candidacy and an ugly primary campaign between Trump and his numerous GOP opponents. However, Trump's image among Republicans has ended up just marginally better than where it was in early July.

While Clinton's 73% approval rating among Democrats is slightly higher than Trump's 68% rating among Republicans, the historical record shows these are low compared with how partisans have evaluated their party's nominee in previous years. As one example, 94% of Republicans viewed John McCain favorably and 91% of Democrats viewed Barack Obama favorably in a Gallup poll conducted in September 2008 after both of that year's conventions. This underscores one of the unique features of this election – the negative aura which surrounds both major party candidates.

Implications

The conventions produced no major reset in Americans' or party loyalists' opinions of Clinton and Trump. Americans' views of the two candidates are basically back where they started in July.

With both candidates having historically high unfavorable ratings this year, many Americans may have to carefully assess their priorities in a "lesser of two evils" calculation when it comes to their vote – if they vote at all. But the candidate with the most favorable image almost always wins in presidential elections, and both Trump and Clinton would presumably like to craft more positive images as the campaign progresses.

Separate Gallup research shows that over seven in 10 Americans continue to report having read, seen or heard something about the candidates each day, giving Trump and Clinton at least a theoretical chance of altering people's perceptions of them. Beginning on Sept. 26, the three scheduled presidential debates will also provide a chance for the candidates to boost their images. The results of tracking through the conventions, however, suggest it may be hard to change opinions of the candidates in this election.

These data are available in Gallup Analytics.

Survey Methods

Results for the most recent candidate favorable ratings are based on telephone interviews conducted Aug. 3-9, 2016, on the Gallup U.S. Daily survey, with a random sample of 3,566 adults, aged 18 and older, living in all 50 U.S. states and the District of Columbia. For results based on the total sample of national adults, the margin of sampling error is ±3 percentage points at the 95% confidence level. All reported margins of sampling error include computed design effects for weighting.

August 11, 2016

IN U.S., OBAMA EFFECT ON RACIAL MATTERS FALLS SHORT OF HOPES

by Jeffrey M. Jones

Story Highlights

- *32% say Obama's presidency one of most important advances for blacks*
- *Down from 71% after his election, 58% in first year in office*
- *More say race relations have gotten worse than better*

PRINCETON, N.J. – Americans are far less positive today about what Barack Obama's presidency means for the advancement of blacks in the U.S. than they were shortly after his historic election. Currently, 32% say Obama's presidency is one of the most important advances for blacks in the past 100 years, down from 71% immediately after he was elected and 58% nine months into his first term. Today, nearly as many describe it as "not that important" as say it is one of the most important advances for blacks.

Views of Barack Obama's Presidency in Terms of Progress for Blacks in the U.S.

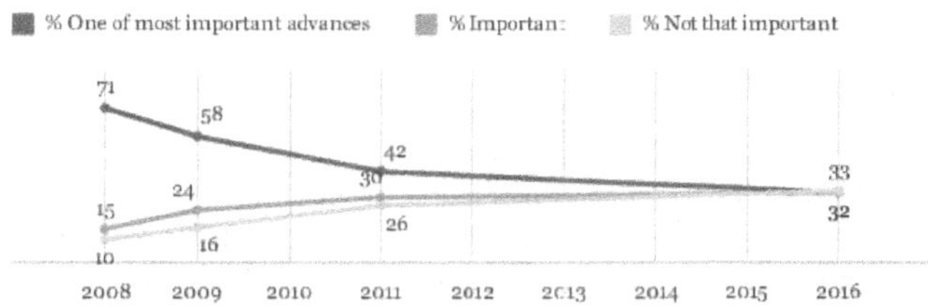

Note: The 2008-2011 surveys asked about Obama's election. The 2016 survey asked about his presidency.

GALLUP

The decline in perceived significance of Obama's election and presidency is evident among both blacks and whites, though blacks remain more positive overall. In October 2009, 71% of blacks considered Obama's election as one of the most important advances for blacks; today, 51% do. Among whites, the percentage has declined from 56% to 27%.

Views of Barack Obama's Election and Presidency as One of the Most Important Advances for Blacks in the U.S., by Race

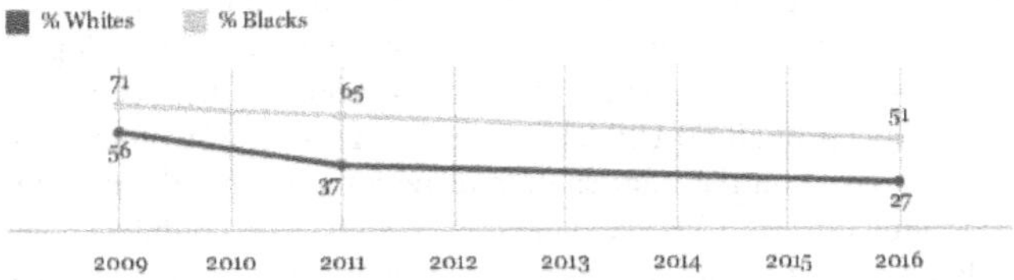

Note: The 2008-2011 surveys asked about Obama's election. The 2016 survey asked about his presidency.
The November 2008 poll did not include a large enough sample of blacks to report an estimate for that group. In that poll, 71% of whites said Obama's election was one of the most important advances for blacks.

GALLUP'

These results are based on Gallup's 2016 Minority Rights and Relations poll, conducted June 7-July 1, just before a renewed round of deadly racial incidents between police and black men in early July. Gallup interviewed 3,270 U.S. adults, including 1,320 non-Hispanic whites and 912 non-Hispanic blacks.

Americans' optimism about the effects that Obama's election and presidency would have on race relations has also declined significantly since he was elected in November 2008. At that time, 70% of Americans expected race relations in the U.S. to get better, while only 10% believed relations would get worse. Now, more say that race relations have gotten worse as a result of his presidency (46%) than say they have gotten better (29%).

Views of the Effect of Barack Obama's Election and Presidency on Race Relations in the U.S.

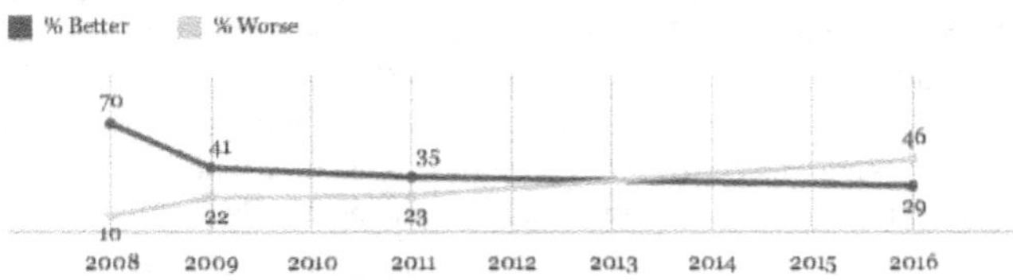

Note: The 2008-2011 surveys asked about Obama's election. The 2016 survey asked about his presidency.
Percent "no change" omitted from graph.

GALLUP'

Whites, by more than a 2-to-1 margin, now say race relations are worse rather than better. Blacks are more charitable in their evaluation of the effect of Obama's presidency on U.S. race relations, but they are divided on whether things are better or worse. Both blacks' and whites' opinions are more pessimistic than they were in October 2009, nine months into Obama's presidency.

Views of the Effect of Barack Obama's Election and Presidency on Race Relations in the U.S., by Race

	2009 %	2011 %	2016 %
Whites			
Better	39	31	23
No change	36	45	25
Worse	23	22	51
NET (Better-Worse)	+16	+9	-28
Blacks			
Better	53	48	37
No change	27	27	24
Worse	20	24	39
NET (Better-Worse)	+33	+24	-2

2009-2011 surveys asked about Obama's election; 2016 survey asked about his presidency. Not enough blacks in 2008 poll to report an estimate.

Gallup

These less-positive ratings may mostly acknowledge the state of race relations in the U.S., rather than serve as a criticism of Obama's work on the issue. Americans' positive assessments of black-white relations tumbled between 2013 and 2015 and remain lower in 2016, most likely in response to the string of deadly incidents between black men and police in recent years.

Gallup has found Obama's approval rating for handling racial issues ranging narrowly from 46% to 52% the four times it has been asked during his presidency, all since 2010. This includes 51% approval and 47% disapproval in a recent Aug. 3-7 poll.

The decline in positivity about what Obama's election has meant for black progress and for U.S. race relations to some degree reflects his overall job approval ratings, which have averaged a relatively weak 47%. The decline may also indicate that Americans' initial expectations for what he could do on these issues were unrealistic. The continuing racial incidents may underscore that it takes more than a change in who is president to improve the situation. Also, the early positive ratings may have been influenced by the historic nature of having a black president, an effect that could have worn off over time.

Majority of Blacks Say Obama Has Not Gone Far Enough to Help Them

During Obama's presidential campaign in 2008, there were questions about how his racial background might affect the policies he pursued as president. One such question was how a black president could balance a desire to aid the black community with the need to pursue policies designed to help Americans of all races and ethnicities.

From the time Obama was campaigning in 2008 until now, only between 21% and 26% of Americans have been concerned that his policies would go, or have gone, too far to help blacks. Initially, far fewer were concerned that his policies would not go far enough, but that has changed. Now, 33% say his policies haven't gone far enough, up from 8% immediately after his election and 18% during his first year in office.

Views of Barack Obama's Policies to Aid Blacks

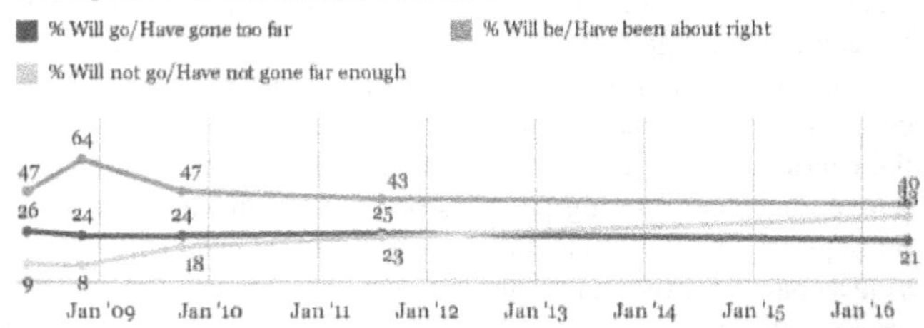

Note: The 2008-2011 surveys asked whether Obama's policies will go too far/will not go far enough. The 2016 survey asked whether Obama's polices have gone too far/have not gone far enough.

GALLUP'

Blacks have never expressed much concern that Obama's policies would go too far in aiding the black community. However, blacks' opinions have shifted from viewing Obama's policies to help blacks as "about right" to "not going far enough." Currently, 52% of blacks say his policies have not gone far enough, up from 20% during the 2008 campaign and 32% his first year in office. The plurality of whites, 39%, still believe his policies have been about right, while 30% say they have not gone far enough. The latter figure is up from 7% during the campaign and 16% his first year in office.

Views of Whether Barack Obama's Policies Designed to Aid the Black Community Go Too Far, by Race

	May 2008 %	Oct 2009 %	Aug 2011 %	Jun 2016 %
Whites				
Too far	27	28	29	25
About right	46	45	42	39
Not far enough	7	16	18	30
Blacks				
Too far	5	5	5	6
About right	64	55	47	39
Not far enough	20	32	43	52

2008-2011 surveys asked if Obama's policies will go too far/not go far enough; 2016 survey asked if his policies have gone too far/have not gone far enough
Gallup

Implications

Americans had high hopes for what the first black president could accomplish, particularly on matters of race. Obama's early-term job approval ratings were among the highest for a new president, consistent with these expectations. But governing is a challenging task for any president, particularly during a sluggish economy. Since his first year, his job approval rating has struggled to reach or stay above the majority level. Americans' assessments of the effect of Obama's presidency on blacks' lives and on race relations are likely heavily influenced by his general approval ratings.

Americans' expectations for what Obama could accomplish may also have been overly optimistic and perhaps could not have been predicted to persist for eight years after he was elected.

Regardless of how Americans feel about Obama and his policies, they believe black-white relations are much worse now than earlier in his presidency. The public may not necessarily fault Obama for those problems, as roughly half have consistently approved of how he has handled race relations throughout his time in office. But it is clear that the optimism Americans initially had for a black president's ability to improve race relations and the situation for blacks has long since faded.

Historical data are available in Gallup Analytics.

Survey Methods

Results for this Gallup poll are based on telephone interviews conducted June 7-July 1, 2016, with a sample of 3,270 adults, aged 18 and older, living in all 50 U.S. states and the District of Columbia, who had previously been interviewed in the Gallup Daily tracking poll and agreed to be re-interviewed for a later study. The sample is weighted to be representative of U.S. adults.

For results based on the total sample of national adults, the margin of sampling error is ±3 percentage points at the 95% confidence level. For results based on the sample of 1,320 non-Hispanic whites, the margin of sampling error is ±4 percentage points at the 95% confidence level. For results based on the sample of 912 non-Hispanic blacks, the margin of sampling error is ±5 percentage points at the 95% confidence level.

All reported margins of sampling error include computed design effects for weighting.

August 12, 2016

MICHELLE OBAMA MORE POPULAR THAN BILL CLINTON, MELANIA TRUMP

by Justin McCarthy

Story Highlights

- *64% view Michelle Obama favorably*
- *Images of Bill Clinton, Melania Trump about as favorable as unfavorable*
- *About half have favorable views of Chelsea Clinton, Ivanka Trump*

WASHINGTON, D.C. – While first lady Michelle Obama is not as popular as some of her predecessors, the American public views her far more favorably than either of the potential first spouses in the 2016 election. In contrast to Michelle Obama's 64% favorable and 32% unfavorable scores, Americans are about as likely to view Bill Clinton and Melania Trump positively as they are to view them negatively.

Favorable Ratings of Politicians' Spouses, Among National Adults

Next, we'd like to get your overall opinion of some people in the news. As I read each name, please say if you have a favorable or unfavorable opinion of that person – or if you have never heard of them.

	Favorable	Unfavorable	Never heard of/ No opinion
	%	%	%
Michelle Obama	64	32	3
Bill Clinton	49	46	4
Melania Trump	38	42	20

Gallup, Aug. 3-7, 2016

These latest data, collected in an Aug. 3-7 Gallup poll, come a little more than a week after the parties' national conventions ended.

Michelle Obama's current favorable rating is up from 58% before the Democratic convention, suggesting her prime-time speech may have caused some Americans to see her in a more positive light.

Although Gallup does not measure first lady favorability ratings frequently, Michelle Obama's favorable ratings have, on average, exceeded those of presidential candidate and former first lady Hillary Clinton when she served in the ceremonial role. Obama's average is 65% compared with Clinton's 56%. However, Obama's ratings are not quite as high as those of Laura Bush, who averaged a 73% favorable rating as first lady. Gallup measured opinions of Barbara Bush only near the end of her husband's term as president, but no less than 69%, and typically more than 80%, viewed her positively in 1992 and early 1993.

Both Bill Clinton and Melania Trump gave prime-time addresses at their spouses' respective party conventions, but neither speech did much to change how Americans view them in terms of their net favorability. While Clinton's favorable rating didn't budge, Trump's climbed 10 points after her speech – but so too did her unfavorable ratings amid the controversy her speech generated over accusations that she plagiarized parts of Michelle Obama's 2008 speech. While Trump is much better known after having given the speech, she is no better liked proportionally to the percentage who view her unfavorably.

Americans are about as likely to view Bill Clinton favorably (49%) as unfavorably (46%) – nearly identical to his ratings before the convention. This is unusual for a former president, as most presidents enjoy majority favorable ratings after their presidency. George W. Bush has generally been an exception to the rule, but even he had a higher favorable rating than Bill Clinton last month. Clinton's ratings were much higher than his current figure during periods when his wife was not running for office, suggesting that the recently subdued favorables could reflect the political ramifications of his involvement in his wife's current campaign.

Partisanship Influences Americans' Views of Candidates' Spouses

Perhaps unsurprisingly, Bill Clinton and Melania Trump are viewed most favorably by Americans who align with the party of their spouses. About seven in 10 Republicans view Trump favorably (69%), while an even higher 84% of Democrats have a favorable view of Clinton.

Clinton is more popular among women than men (54% vs. 45%), while Trump is slightly more popular among men than women (41% vs. 35%).

Trump is most popular among adults aged 50 to 64 (49%) and 65 and older (52%), while Clinton's popularity is greatest among adults younger than 50, a majority of whom view him favorably.

Favorable Ratings of Candidates' Spouses, by Group

Next, we'd like to get your overall opinion of some people in the news. As I read each name, please say if you have a favorable or unfavorable opinion of that person – or if you have never heard of them.

	Bill Clinton % Favorable	Melania Trump % Favorable
National adults	49	38
Men	45	41
Women	54	35
18 to 29	56	22
30 to 49	56	27
50 to 64	43	49
65+	45	52
Republicans	11	69
Independents	50	33
Democrats	84	19

Gallup, Aug. 3-7, 2016

Similar Favorable Ratings for Chelsea Clinton, Ivanka Trump

Both major parties' presidential candidates have put their children front and center at many points throughout their respective campaigns, with Chelsea Clinton and Ivanka Trump having introduced their parents before their convention speeches last month.

The candidates' daughters enjoy nearly identical favorable ratings, with about half of Americans viewing them favorably, and three in 10 expressing an unfavorable view. Sizable percentages of Americans have no opinion of either woman – 19% for Chelsea Clinton and 21% for Ivanka Trump.

Favorable Ratings of Candidates' Children, Among National Adults

Next, we'd like to get your overall opinion of some people in the news. As I read each name, please say if you have a favorable or unfavorable opinion of that person – or if you have never heard of them.

	Favorable	Unfavorable	Never heard of/ No opinion
	%	%	%
Chelsea Clinton	51	30	19
Ivanka Trump	49	30	21

Gallup, Aug. 3-7, 2016

Both women are viewed most favorably among the parties of their parents' respective affiliations.

While men and women are about equally as likely to view Ivanka Trump favorably, women (60%) are more likely than men (42%) to view Chelsea Clinton favorably – perhaps partly because her mother is the first female nominee of a major U.S. party.

Favorable Ratings of Candidates' Children, by Group

Next, we'd like to get your overall opinion of some people in the news. As I read each name, please say if you have a favorable or unfavorable opinion of that person – or if you have never heard of them.

	Chelsea Clinton % Favorable	Ivanka Trump % Favorable
National adults	51	49
Men	42	49
Women	60	48
Republicans	24	75
Independents	51	45
Democrats	80	32

Gallup, Aug. 3-7, 2016

Bottom Line

Campaigns typically employ family members to stand in for them at campaign events and even showcase them nationally to help soften or otherwise improve their image. But Hillary Clinton may receive the biggest boost from the convention speech of Michelle Obama, whose positive standing among nearly two in three Americans makes her one of the Democratic Party's most cherished figures.

Both candidates' daughters are arguably their biggest family assets, as Chelsea Clinton and Ivanka Trump enjoy favorable ratings that significantly outweigh their unfavorable ones.

Although Bill Clinton's status as a former president can be seen as an asset to his wife's campaign, the negative views he receives from Americans nearly cancel out the positive ones. The same can be said for Melania Trump: Any benefits she may provide to her husband's campaign are outweighed by her unfavorable ratings. It's possible that her ratings will improve if she becomes better known to Americans.

Historical data are available in Gallup Analytics.

Survey Methods

Results for this Gallup poll are based on telephone interviews conducted Aug. 3-7, 2016, with a random sample of 1,032 adults, aged 18 and older, living in all 50 U.S. states and the District of Columbia. For results based on the total sample of national adults, the margin of sampling error is ±4 percentage points at the 95% confidence level. All reported margins of sampling error include computed design effects for weighting.

August 12, 2016
AMERICANS' SATISFACTION RECOVERS IN AUGUST, THOUGH STILL LOW

by Art Swift

Story Highlights

- *Satisfaction now at 27%, up from 17% in July*
- *Democrats, independents fuel rebound in satisfaction*
- *Economy now most important problem in U.S.; racism drops from top spot*

WASHINGTON, D.C. – Americans' satisfaction with the way things are going in the U.S. rebounded this month, as national news coverage shifted away from several race-related controversies that occurred in early July. Twenty-seven percent of Americans are now satisfied with the state of affairs in the U.S., up sharply from 17% in July but similar to the level from February through June.

Satisfaction With U.S., Trend Since 2013

In general, are you satisfied or dissatisfied with the way things are going in the United States at this time?

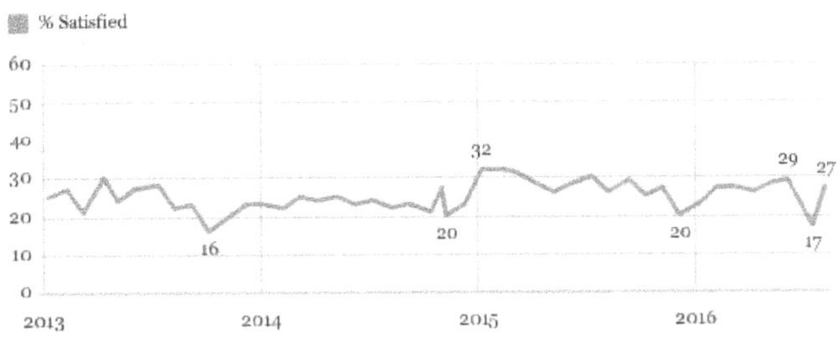

GALLUP

The 17% satisfied in July was the lowest satisfaction had been since October 2013, which came during a federal government shutdown. There have been two more recent low points of 20% satisfaction, in November 2014 and December 2015.

The latest data are from Gallup's monthly update of Americans' satisfaction, collected Aug. 3-7. The rebound in U.S. satisfaction comes at the same time that public concern about the issue that seemed responsible for low satisfaction in July – race relations – has subsided. Since the prior reading in mid-July, the U.S. has not experienced the level of disturbing incidents that made news in early July, namely, race-related shootings by police in Louisiana and Minnesota or against police officers in Dallas.

Last month, these incidents seemed to directly affect Americans' perceptions of the most important U.S. problem, with a sharp increase in the percentage naming race relations or racism. In August, race relations dropped from its No. 1 spot as most important, with mentions of it falling from 18% in July to 7% now. At the same time, mentions of the economy rose five percentage points to 17%.

These changes likely reflect a shift in the media's focus from race-related news events in early July to the national party conventions in mid- to late July.

Recent Trend, Most Important U.S. Problem

What do you think is the most important problem facing this country today?

	August 2016 %	July 2016 %	June 2016 %	May 2016 %
Economy in general	17	12	18	18
Dissatisfaction with government	13	16	13	13
Terrorism	9	5	4	4
Unemployment/Jobs	8	7	8	9
Immigration/Illegal aliens	8	6	7	7
National security	7	6	5	4
Elections/Election reform	7	5	6	5
Race relations/ Racism	7	18	5	5
Federal budget deficit/Federal debt	5	4	5	5
Crime/Violence	5	6	3	2
Poor healthcare/ hospitals	5	3	4	4

Gallup

Meanwhile, two issues that have typically topped the most important problem list this year – the economy and dissatisfaction with government – have returned to their places. Terrorism has risen slightly from 5% to 9%, despite a lack of high-profile terrorist incidents in the past several weeks in the U.S. The rise in mentions of the economy may be related to the Republican National Convention in Cleveland in mid-July. During the four-day event, speakers including GOP presidential nominee Donald Trump hammered on the economy as a major problem facing voters. In August, Republican mentions of the economy in general as the most important problem have jumped from 14% to 25%, fueling the rise in mentions among all Americans.

Democrats' Satisfaction Rebounds

Democrats' satisfaction with the way things are going in the U.S. plunged from 51% in June to 29% in July, largely explaining the drop in satisfaction last month. Now, that percentage has rebounded to 45%, while Republicans' satisfaction is unchanged at 6%. Independents' satisfaction rose to 27%, up from 16%.

Satisfaction With U.S. by Party ID, 2016

In general, are you satisfied or dissatisfied with the way things are going in the United States at this time?

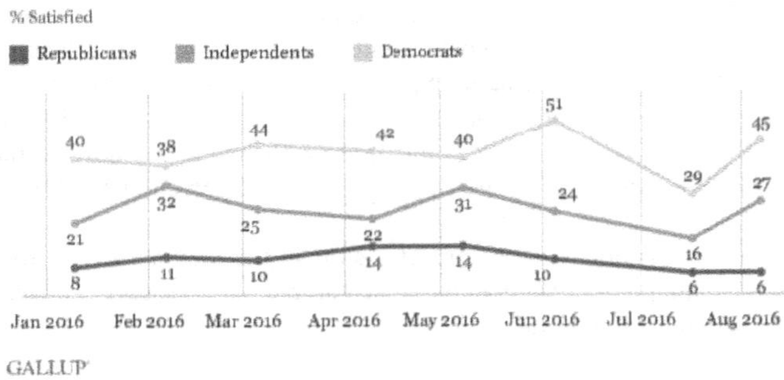

Apart from swings in overall U.S. satisfaction, the measure consistently reflects Americans' feelings about the party of the president. For example, in early 2007, during the presidency of George W. Bush, Republicans' satisfaction with the country's direction was in the low 60s, while Democrats' satisfaction ranged from 16% to 20%. By contrast, in August 2009, with Barack Obama in the White House, Democrats' satisfaction had risen to a high of 59% while Republicans' registered 15%. This dynamic has generally held throughout the Obama presidency.

Bottom Line

With fewer negative headlines regarding race relations and racism dominating news coverage in the past few weeks, Americans are currently less likely to cite race issues as the nation's most important problem, and their overall satisfaction with the state of the country has rebounded to the level of prior months. Mainstay problems such as the economy and government have returned to the forefront, though with neither topic reaching 20% of concern, no single problem dominates as the most important. Americans are generally more likely to be satisfied than they were last month, though only about one in four feel that satisfaction.

Historical data are available in Gallup Analytics.

Survey Methods

Results for this Gallup poll are based on telephone interviews conducted Aug. 3-7, 2016, on the Gallup U.S. Daily survey, with a random sample of 1,032 adults, aged 18 and older, living in all 50 U.S. states and the District of Columbia. For results based on the total sample of national adults, the margin of sampling error is ±4 percentage points at the 95% confidence level All reported margins of sampling error include computed design effects for weighting.

August 15, 2016

AMERICANS' APPROVAL OF OBAMA ON FOREIGN AFFAIRS RISES

by Justin McCarthy

Story Highlights

- *48% of Americans approve of Obama's handling of foreign affairs*
- *Approval of his performance on the economy is steady, at 48%*
- *Americans most approving of work in education, race relations*

WASHINGTON, D.C. – Nearly half of Americans (48%) approve of President Barack Obama's handling of foreign affairs in August, up markedly from 39% in February. The latest rating is the highest since November 2012 (49%), just days before Obama was re-elected.

Approval of President Obama's Handling of Foreign Affairs

Do you approve or disapprove of the way Barack Obama is handling foreign affairs?

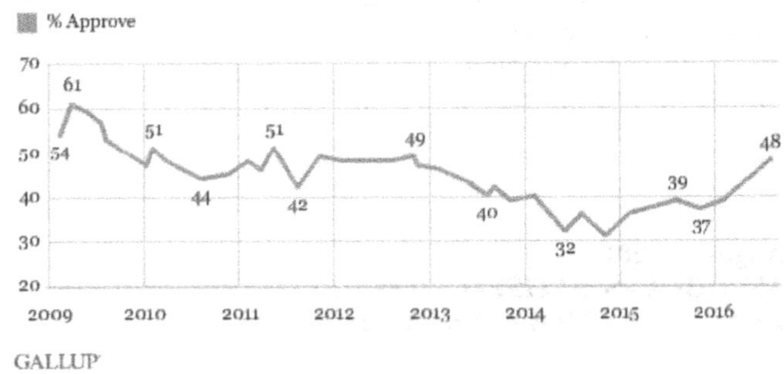

With just five months left in Obama's presidency, Americans are as likely to approve (48%) as to disapprove (48%) of his performance on foreign affairs. Obama's second-term approval ratings on the issue have been fairly weak, averaging 39% as the administration has struggled to deal with a number of international challenges such as the rise of the Islamic State group, tense relations with Russia and the conflict in Syria. Obama averaged a higher 50% approval rating on foreign affairs during his first term. His second-term average on foreign affairs is among the lowest Gallup has measured for presidents since Ronald Reagan. Only George W. Bush had a lower rating on foreign affairs in a presidential term, at 38%.

Obama's latest foreign affairs rating was recorded in an Aug. 3-7 Gallup poll, after he rebuffed allegations that his administration paid Iran $400 million in cash in exchange for hostages. More recently, the Republican nominee for president alleged that Obama is the founder of the Islamic State.

Obama's Approval Rating on the Economy at Seven-Year High

Americans' approval of Obama's handling of foreign affairs now matches his 48% approval on the economy, which has been steadily climbing over the past year. The recent low of 33% came just before the 2014 midterm elections that saw Obama's own party lose control of the Senate. But this figure has since steadily improved so that his rating is now at a seven-year high.

Approval of President Obama's Handling of the Economy

Do you approve or disapprove of the way Barack Obama is handling the economy?

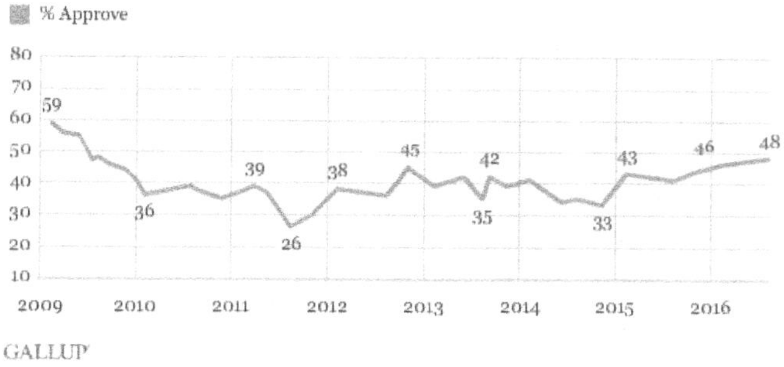

Obama's second-term average approval rating on the economy (40%) is about the same as his first-term average of 41% – as well as the second-term average for President George W. Bush (41%).

These are historically low ratings, with George H.W. Bush (35%) being the only president to have scored a lower average on this issue over the past nine presidential terms.

Approval Up on President's Handling of Most Issues

Americans have been more approving of Obama's overall job performance than his handling of specific issues, as has been the case for most presidents since Reagan. Obama's overall approval rating of 52% in this August's poll is at least one percentage point higher than his rating for any of the seven issues Gallup asked about.

Of the seven issues included in the current poll, Obama rates best on education and race relations, both at 51%. However, Gallup has found withering hopefulness among Americans on the latter issue. His 48% ratings on the economy and foreign affairs are not far behind, while his approval on terrorism (45%) and immigration (44%) lag a bit further. He fares worst on gun policy, with 37% approval.

Since August 2015, Obama's approval ratings on most issues have improved, nearly matching the five-point increase in his overall job approval between the two polls.

Though Obama's approval rating on gun policy was not measured last year, his rating has not improved from two polls conducted in 2013, when he received 40% and 42% approval.

Ratings of Obama's Handling of Issues, August 2015 vs. August 2016

% Approve

	August 2015 %	August 2016 %
Overall job approval	47	52
Education	44	51
Race relations	46	51
Foreign affairs	39	48
The economy	41	48
Terrorism	41	45
Immigration	36	44
Gun policy	–	37

Gallup

Bottom Line

As Obama's presidency nears its end and his overall job approval rating remains above the majority level, Americans' views of his handling of a variety of issues are improving as well. Americans' higher ratings of his performance on key issues reflect neither personal nor historical highs, but they do compare favorably with his ratings on these issues over the past seven-and-a-half years. His approval ratings on the economy and foreign affairs currently rank above the best since his first term.

His presidency is not yet over, however, and Obama's performance on these issues is a constant talking point for both presidential nominees – one who seeks to tie her record to his, and another who ridicules Obama's performance on most issues. Regardless of who succeeds him, Obama's ratings as he departs from the White House will serve as a benchmark for the next president.

Historical data are available in Gallup Analytics.

Survey Methods

Results for this Gallup poll are based on telephone interviews conducted Aug. 3-7, 2016, with a random sample of 1,032 adults, aged 18 and older, living in all 50 U.S. states and the District of Columbia. For results based on the total sample of national adults, the margin of sampling error is ±4 percentage points at the 95% confidence level. All reported margins of sampling error include computed design effects for weighting.

August 15, 2016

RESTAURANTS AGAIN VOTED MOST POPULAR U.S. INDUSTRY

by Lydia Saad

Story Highlights

- *Restaurants lead industries with 66% positive, 7% negative ratings*
- *Computer industry a close second at 66% positive, 13% negative*
- *Federal government again ranked last*

PRINCETON, N.J. – The restaurant and computer industries, long among the best-rated U.S. industries in Gallup's annual measure of U.S. business sectors, again lead the poll, with 66% of Americans rating each positively. However, with only 7% of Americans viewing the restaurant industry negatively vs. 13% for the computer industry, the restaurant industry enjoys the more positive overall image this year.

Top-Rated U.S. Business Sectors – Better Than 2-to-1 Positive

For each of the following business sectors in the United States, please say whether your overall view of it is very positive, somewhat positive, neutral, somewhat negative or very negative.

	Total positive %	Neutral %	Total negative %	Net positive pct. pts.
Restaurant industry	66	27	7	+59
Computer industry	66	19	13	+53
Grocery industry	54	28	18	+36
Farming and agriculture	55	23	20	+35
Accounting	45	40	12	+33
Travel industry	48	33	16	+32
Internet industry	53	21	24	+29
Automobile industry	50	26	23	+27
Retail industry	49	26	23	+26
Real estate industry	44	31	21	+23

Gallup, Aug. 3-7, 2016

The restaurant and computer sectors have vied for the most well-reviewed U.S. industry in each of Gallup's annual measures of this question since 2001. This year's +59 net-positive score for the restaurant industry is well above its average +51 since 2001, whereas the computer industry's +53 net-positive score is about average for that industry.

Two other industries connected with food – grocery and farming/agriculture – rank near the top in the Aug. 3-7 poll. The remaining six industries in the top 10 represent a hodgepodge of sectors including the accounting, travel, internet, automobile, retail and real estate industries. All of these enjoy better than 2-to-1 positive over negative ratings.

Americans view another 10 industries no worse than neutrally, but in most cases net-positively. The telephone and airline industries lead this group, and it includes several entertainment and communication-related arenas: sports, movies, television and radio, publishing and advertising. Electric and gas utilities, education and banking also make this list.

Second-Tier U.S. Business Sectors – Neutral to Somewhat Net-Positive Ratings

For each of the following business sectors in the United States, please say whether your overall view of it is very positive, somewhat positive, neutral, somewhat negative or very negative.

	Total positive %	Neutral %	Total negative %	Net positive pct. pts.
Telephone industry	42	31	27	+15
Airline industry	41	30	26	+15
Sports industry	41	31	27	+14
Publishing industry	39	32	27	+12
Movie industry	42	24	32	+10
Electric and gas utilities	42	23	33	+9
Education	44	17	38	+6
Television and radio	40	23	38	+2
Banking	38	23	36	+2
Advertising and public relations	35	27	35	0

Gallup, Aug. 3-7, 2016

Federal Government Edges Out Pharmaceuticals and Healthcare at Bottom

The bottom five industries are all reviewed more negatively than positively, with three – the federal government, pharmaceuticals and healthcare – receiving negative ratings from more than half of the public. The legal field plus oil and gas have just slightly higher negative than positive ratings. While fairly typical for the legal field, this represents a significantly improved positioning for the oil and gas industry, which had skewed strongly negative from 2004 through 2014.

Worst-Rated U.S. Business Sectors – Net-Negative Ratings

For each of the following business sectors in the United States, please say whether your overall view of it is very positive, somewhat positive, neutral, somewhat negative or very negative.

	Total positive %	Neutral %	Total negative %	Net positive pct. pts.
Oil and gas industry	37	17	44	-7
The legal field	31	28	39	-8
Healthcare industry	34	12	54	-20
Pharmaceutical industry	28	19	51	-23
The federal government	28	16	55	-27

Gallup, Aug. 3-7, 2016

Airline Industry Improves; Healthcare and Pharma Sink

The biggest improvement in industry ratings this year is for the airline industry, with its +15 net-positive rating up from +3 in 2015, and by far its best rating in more than a decade.

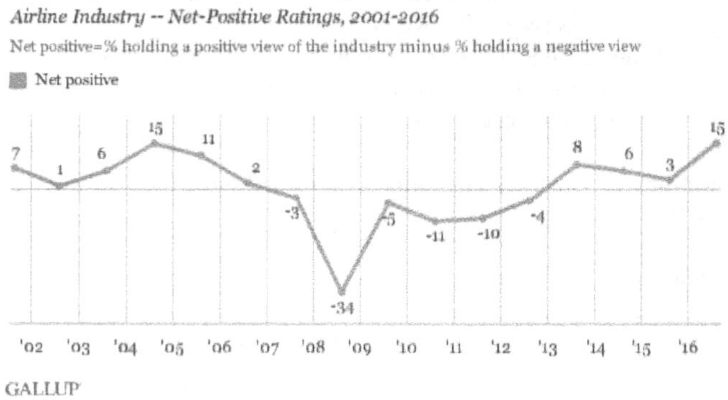

Two other industries – healthcare and pharmaceuticals – have gone down in public esteem. Although Democrats continue to be more positive than Republicans about the healthcare industry, as they have since 2013 when major components of the Affordable Care Act began to take effect, the healthcare industry is now at a five-year low. Its -20 net-positive score is down from -6 in 2015 and the lowest since 2011 because of declines in the past year among all party groups.

Relatedly, the pharmaceutical industry's -23 net-positive score is the worst in Gallup's 16-year trend, down from -8 in 2015.

Healthcare and Pharmaceutical Industries -- Net-Positive Ratings, 2001-2016

Net positive=% holding a positive view of the industry minus % holding a negative view

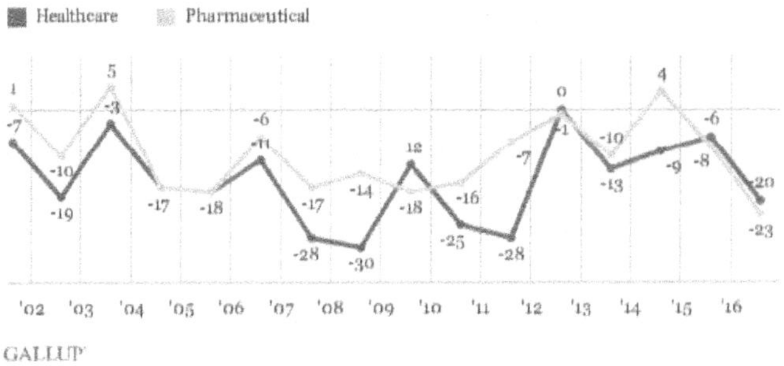

Positive ratings of the internet industry are also down sharply compared with 2015 but are similar to 2014. More generally, its ratings have tended to bounce around in recent years.

Internet Industry -- Net-Positive Ratings, 2001-2016

Net positive=% holding a positive view of the industry minus % holding a negative view

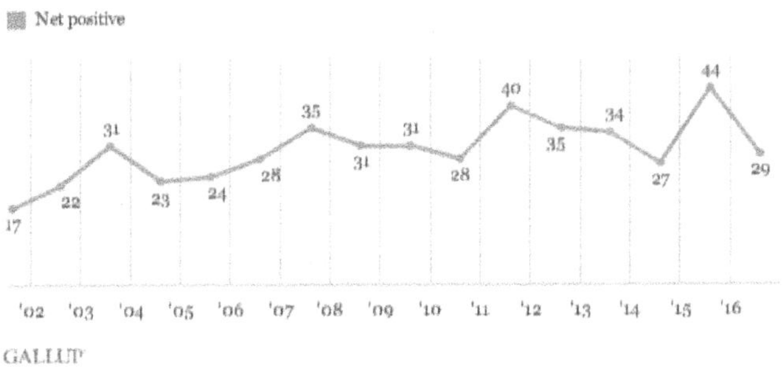

Bottom Line

At a time of persistently low public trust in the federal government, and with many more Americans rating the federal government negatively than positively, it is reassuring that Americans tend to view the bulk of 25 major U.S. business and industry sectors positively. Further, 10 of these – ranging from some of the nation's oldest to some of its newest industries – enjoy solidly positive ratings.

The top-scoring industries over the past 16 years – restaurants and computers – are both competitive ones that offer Americans enjoyment and efficiency while not stirring up major political controversies. The internet can also be a time saver in people's lives, but is known for significant privacy, security and crime risks that may keep it somewhat below computers in the overall ranking.

Historical data are available in Gallup Analytics.

Survey Methods

Results for this Gallup poll are based on telephone interviews conducted Aug. 3-7, 2016, with a random sample of 1,032 adults, aged 18 and older, living in all 50 U.S. states and the District of Columbia. Each industry was rated by a randomly chosen half sample of respondents. Results for each industry have a margin of sampling error of ±6 percentage points at the 95% confidence level. All reported margins of sampling error include computed design effects for weighting.

August 16, 2016

MOVIE INDUSTRY'S IMAGE IN U.S. MATCHES 16-YEAR HIGH

by Art Swift

Story Highlights

- *42% of Americans have positive views of the movie industry*
- *Those aged 18 to 34 have consistently given the industry higher ratings*
- *In recent years, Dems have had increasingly positive views compared with GOP*

WASHINGTON, D.C. – The movie industry's image in the U.S. ties for the most positive in Gallup's 16-year trend, with 42% of Americans saying they have positive views of it. The current rating matches previous highs found in 2003 and 2014.

Americans' Ratings of the Movie Industry

For each of the following business sectors in the United States, please say whether your overall view of it is very positive, somewhat positive, neutral, somewhat negative or very negative. How about the movie industry?

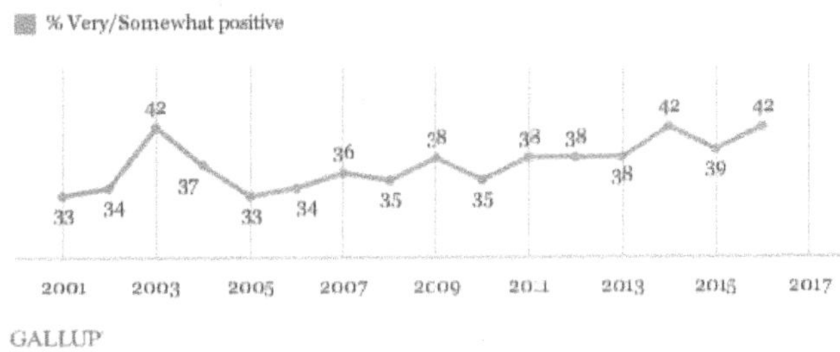

These results are from a Gallup poll conducted Aug. 3-7 asking Americans about their views of 25 U.S. industries, including the airline, healthcare, pharmaceutical, and oil and gas industries. The movie industry's image falls toward the middle of the pack, but it has risen steadily overall since Gallup began asking this question in 2001. In that year and in 2005, a low of 33% rated the movie industry positively.

Americans have more options than ever before when it comes to watching movies – at the theater, at home on TV, or streamed via computer or smartphone. Although movie ticket prices continue to climb, it has not dampened Americans' enthusiasm for the industry itself. Three of the movie industry's four best annual ratings have occurred in the past three years: 2014, 2015 and 2016. The fourth was in 2003, when "Finding Nemo" hit theaters and smashed previous box office records for animated films.

Democrats' Opinions of Movie Industry Steadily Rise

The gap between Democrats' and Republicans' positive views of the movie industry has widened since Gallup began asking this question in 2001. The two partisan groups had similar views until 2006, when Democrats began to extend more positive ratings. In 2016, 53% of Democrats and independents who lean Democratic view the movie industry positively, up from 36% in 2001. Meanwhile, the industry's positive image among Republicans and independents who lean Republican (30%) is essentially unchanged from 29% in 2001.

Americans' Ratings of the Movie Industry, by Party ID

% Very/Somewhat positive

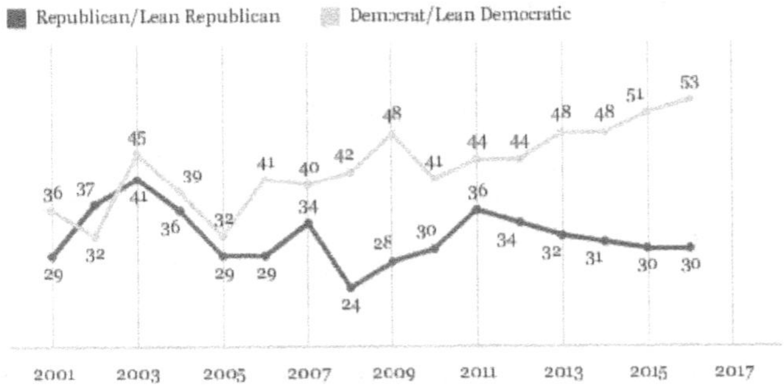

GALLUP

Younger Americans Most Positive About Movie Industry

Americans aged 18 to 34 typically rate the movie industry more positively than older age groups. This year, 56% hold positive views of it, on par with an average of 53% among this age group viewing it positively since 2010.

Americans' Ratings of the Movie Industry, by Age

% Very/Somewhat positive

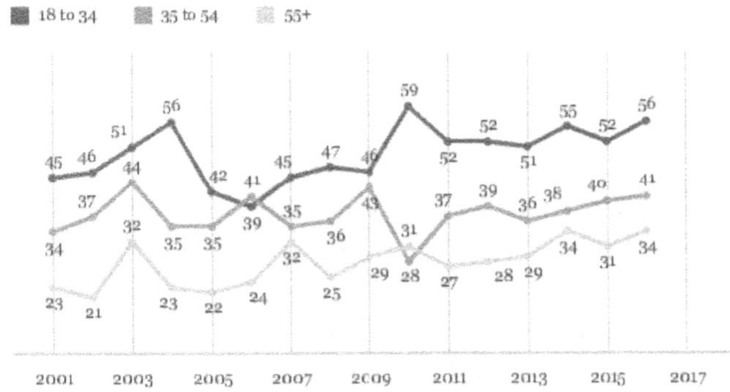

GALLUP

Older adults typically are the least positive about the movie industry – but the percentage of those aged 55 and older who view the industry positively has increased from 23% in 2001 to 34% today. Sentiments among those aged 35 to 54 have also improved from 34% to 41%. The higher levels seen among younger Americans since 2010 could potentially be attributed to the introduction of streaming services; Netflix pioneered this delivery method in 2007.

Bottom Line

Many factors could be contributing to the general increase in Americans' positive views of the movie industry. In an uncertain age marked by global terrorism and a seemingly divided domestic population, Americans may find solace in going to the movies. This also occurred during the Great Depression of the 1930s, often referred to as the "Golden Age of Hollywood." In a decade that has seen strained race relations and economic collapse, it is possible that Americans are turning to the movies – whether in a theater or, as is increasingly the case, at home – to escape reality. Movies have remained relatively inexpensive entertainment compared with going to major sporting events or music concerts.

It is also possible that Americans believe the movie industry is simply performing well. There are more ways to watch films than ever before, and movie production has expanded beyond the traditional Hollywood studio. Thus, Americans may have more options to see the movies they want to see, when they want to see them. Technology has allowed the industry more opportunities to showcase special effects and production values such as IMAX and 3D. And even as ticket prices continue to rise in theaters, streaming options and cable TV offer affordable ways to watch movies at home.

Historical data are available in Gallup Analytics.

Survey Methods

Results for this Gallup poll are based on telephone interviews conducted Aug. 3-7, 2016, with a random sample of 1,032 adults, aged 18 and older, living in all 50 U.S. states and the District of Columbia. For results based on the total sample of national adults, the margin of sampling error is ±4 percentage points at the 95% confidence level. All reported margins of sampling error include computed design effects for weighting.

August 17, 2016

SIX IN 10 AMERICANS SAY RACISM AGAINST BLACKS IS WIDESPREAD

by Jeffrey M. Jones

Story Highlights

- *Perceptions of racism against blacks remain elevated at 61%*
- *41% say racism against whites is widespread, up from 2015*

PRINCETON, N.J. – Six in 10 Americans say racism against blacks is widespread in the U.S., similar to the percentage measured last year but higher than what Gallup found in 2008-2009, the most recent prior measures. At the same time, 41% say racism against whites is widespread, a return to previous levels after the measure dipped to 33% last year.

Perceptions That Racism Against Blacks and Whites Is Widespread in U.S.

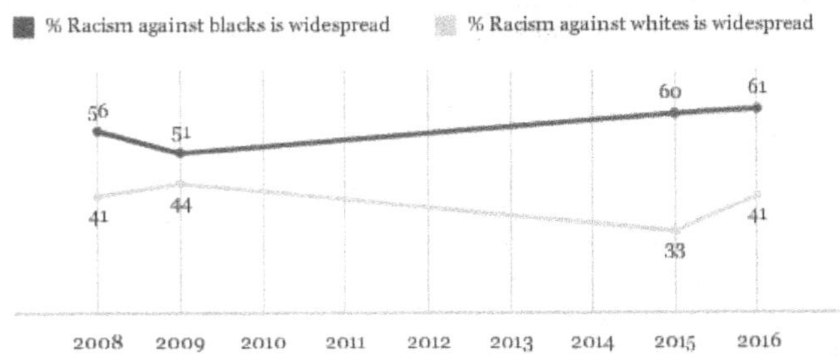

GALLUP

The latest results are based on Gallup's Minority Rights and Relations survey, conducted June 7-July 1 with 3,270 U.S. adults, including 1,320 non-Hispanic whites and 912 non-Hispanic blacks.

Americans' perceptions of widespread racism against blacks remain elevated this year after an uptick last year, likely in response to the highly publicized incidents in which black men were killed in confrontations with white police officers in 2014 and early 2015. The increase in perceptions of racism against blacks in 2015 was not as dramatic as the changes in Americans' assessments of black-white relations in last year's survey, for example, perhaps because the majority of Americans already thought racism was widespread.

There have been more recent deadly encounters between police and citizens this summer, including incidents in Dallas and Louisiana in which black men shot and killed white police officers, but those occurred after interviewing for the poll finished July 1.

Both blacks and whites are more likely to say racism against blacks is widespread today than they were in October 2009, during the first year of Barack Obama's presidency. Now, 82% of blacks and 56% of whites say racism against blacks is widespread, reflecting increases of 10 and seven percentage points, respectively.

Perceptions That Racism Against Blacks Is Widespread in U.S., by Race

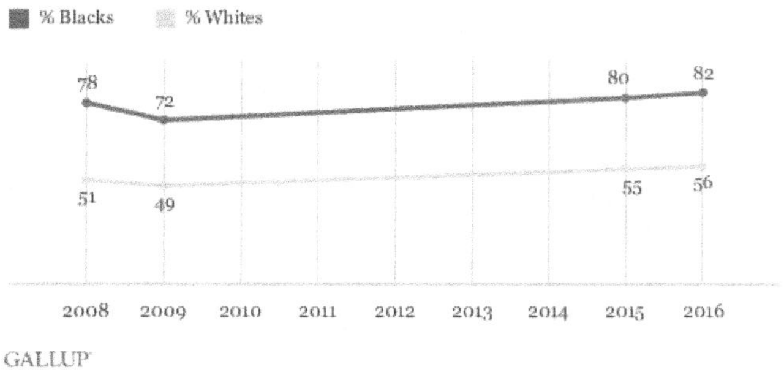

At 66%, Hispanics are more likely than whites but less likely than blacks to perceive racism against blacks as widespread. That figure is up from 59% in 2008. Gallup did not report an estimate among Hispanics in its 2009 survey.

Whites More Likely Than Last Year to Perceive Racism Against Whites

Currently, 43% of whites and 33% of blacks believe racism against whites is widespread. For whites, that essentially marks a return to 2008-2009 levels after a sharp drop to 32% last year. The percentage of blacks who perceive widespread racism against whites also fell last year, from 39% to 32%, but has not increased this year. As a result, whites are once again more likely than blacks to believe racism against whites is common.

Perceptions That Racism Against Whites Is Widespread in U.S., by Race

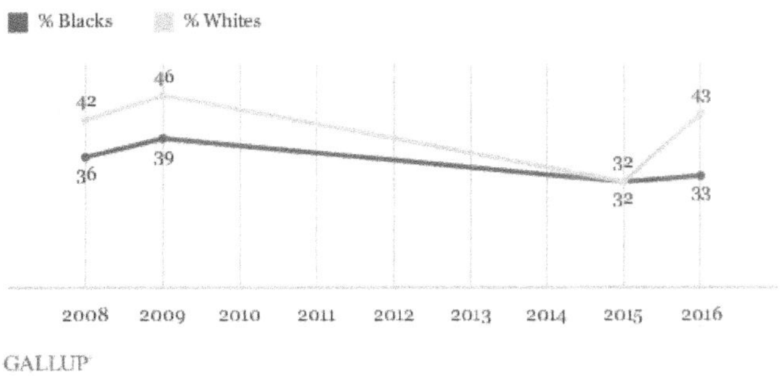

The trend on whites' opinions about racism against whites indicates 2015 was the unusual year. Perhaps the extensive news coverage of racial incidents, particularly those resulting in the deaths of black men, may have left the impression that racism in the U.S. was largely directed against blacks. Some whites may not have been as comfortable acknowledging racism toward whites against that backdrop. In the second half of 2015 and first half of 2016, relatively few deadly incidents between white police and blacks occurred, which could have made those incidents less of a factor this year in how white Americans assess racism against whites.

Hispanics' views are similar to those of whites – 42% of Hispanics believe racism against whites is widespread in the country.

Implications

Perceptions of racism against U.S. blacks were already high before several deadly confrontations between police and black citizens in 2014 and 2015 led to increased concerns about race relations in the U.S., but they have increased modestly since then. At the same time, Americans' belief in equality of opportunity for blacks in being able to find good jobs, a quality education, and any housing they can afford are the lowest they have been since at least the 1990s. These trends underscore that Americans perceive the situation for blacks as worse than it has been in the recent past.

Those heightened perceptions of racism could reflect the reality that racism is greater in the U.S. It is also possible that the actual prevalence of racism is unchanged but is perceived to be greater because of the increased news media attention devoted to matters of race. After the 2014-2015 police incidents, there was little change in blacks' self-reports of being treated unfairly in a variety of situations, including in dealings with police. This year's update continues to show between 12% and 25% of blacks reporting they have been treated unfairly in their dealings with police, while they are at work, while shopping or in other situations. Thus, while the problem of racism may be receiving greater or at least renewed attention, and deservedly so, it is unclear if the problem is actually worse than it was a few years ago.

Historical data are available in Gallup Analytics.

Survey Methods

Results for this Gallup poll are based on telephone interviews conducted June 7-July 1, 2016, with a sample of 3,270 adults, aged 18 and older, living in all 50 U.S. states and the District of Columbia, who had previously been interviewed in the Gallup Daily tracking poll and agreed to be re-interviewed for a later study. The sample is weighted to be representative of U.S. adults.

For results based on the total sample of national adults, the margin of sampling error is ±3 percentage points at the 95% confidence level. For results based on the sample of 1,320 non-Hispanic whites, the margin of sampling error is ±4 percentage points at the 95% confidence level. For results based on the sample of 912 non-Hispanic blacks, the margin of sampling error is ±5 percentage points at the 95% confidence level. For results based on the sample of 906 Hispanics, the margin of sampling error is ±6 percentage points at the 95% confidence level.

All reported margins of sampling error include computed design effects for weighting.

August 17, 2016

U.S. EDUCATION RATINGS SHOW RECORD POLITICAL POLARIZATION

by Lydia Saad

Story Highlights

- 53% of Democrats, 32% of Republicans satisfied with U.S. education
- Majority of Americans dissatisfied with education U.S. children receive
- Most parents satisfied with own child's education

PRINCETON, N.J. – Republicans' satisfaction with the education that U.S. students receive in grades K-12 has plummeted in the past two years to 32%, while Democrats' has edged a bit higher to 53%. The result is stark political polarization in Americans' views of U.S. education – something that has been uncommon in Gallup's 18-year trend. Only two years ago, Republican and Democratic satisfaction were tied at 48%.

Americans' Satisfaction With U.S. Education, by Party ID

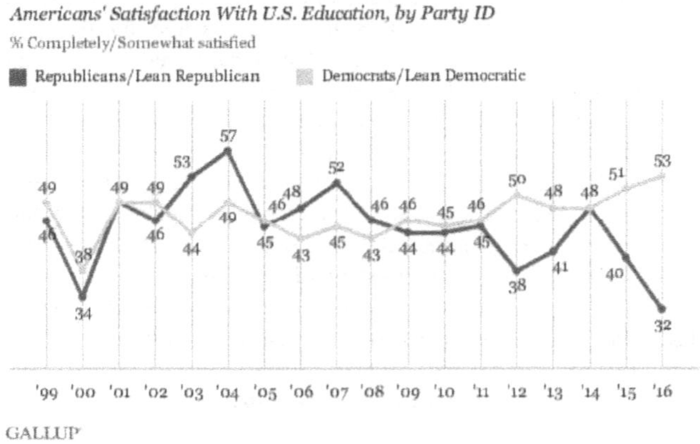

The reason for the increase in Republicans' satisfaction with students' education in 2014 is not clear. However, since then, criticism of the Common Core educational standards being implemented across the country – standards most Republicans view negatively – may help explain the decline in Republican satisfaction with education in 2015 and 2016. Various Republican leaders have taken issue with the Common Core for a number of years. However, strong opposition recently voiced by several Republican presidential contenders, including Donald Trump, may have heightened rank-and-file Republicans' concerns about the effect the standards are having on education.

Ratings of U.S. Education the Most Negative Since 2000

The recent decline in Republicans' satisfaction with education is partly neutralized by the rise in Democrats' satisfaction. Nevertheless, the 43% of all Americans now satisfied ties the lowest figure Gallup has recorded since dipping to 36% in 2000 – that low point likely reflecting a strong focus on education reform in the 2000 presidential campaign.

The 55% now dissatisfied with U.S. education is, by one percentage point, the highest Gallup has recorded since 2000.

Americans' Satisfaction With U.S. Education

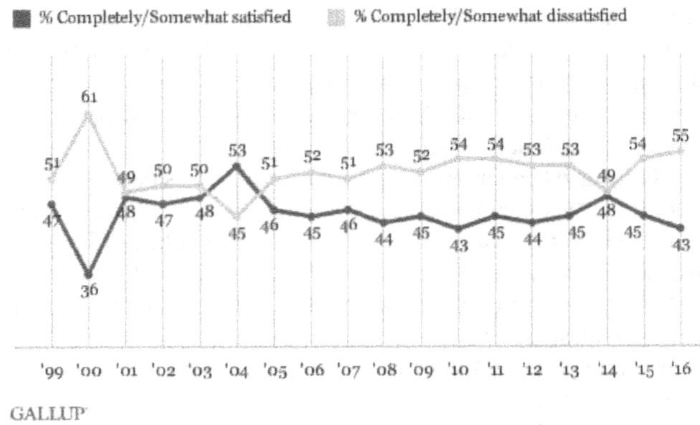

Parents' Experience With Education More Positive, Less Partisan

Although Americans overall hold a net-negative view of education, three-quarters of parents of K-12 students say they are satisfied with the education their oldest child receives, including 36% who say they are "completely satisfied" and another 40% who are "somewhat satisfied."

The combined 76% satisfied matches the trend average since 1999. Since then, only twice – in 2002 and 2013 – did parents' satisfaction drop much below the average.

Parents' Satisfaction With Oldest Child's Education

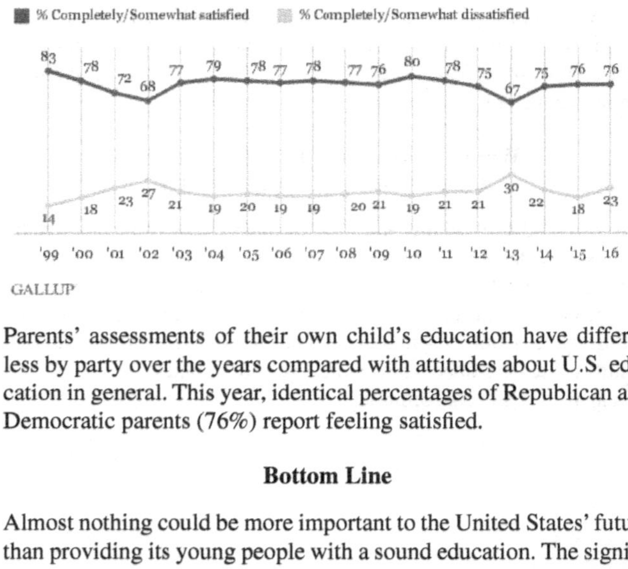

Parents' assessments of their own child's education have differed less by party over the years compared with attitudes about U.S. education in general. This year, identical percentages of Republican and Democratic parents (76%) report feeling satisfied.

Bottom Line

Almost nothing could be more important to the United States' future than providing its young people with a sound education. The significance of this goal may explain why the past two federal education laws – No Child Left Behind (NCLB) and now the Every Student Succeeds Act (ESSA), which replaces NCLB – both got through Congress with unusually broad bipartisan support.

One heartening finding is that those on the front lines of public education – parents of children enrolled in kindergarten through grade 12 – are largely satisfied with the education their oldest child receives. But only 36% are "completely satisfied," suggesting there is room for improvement.

Meanwhile, the partisanship that characterizes Americans' outlook on numerous U.S. policy issues – from the Affordable Care

Act to abortion to global warming – now appears to be affecting the public's views of K-12 education. If this is merely the result of presidential campaign rhetoric about problems with the U.S. educational system, the gap is likely to close in the next year or two. Alternatively, if ESSA succeeds in returning more control of educational standards back to school districts and teachers, that may allay Republicans' concerns about the Common Core. Otherwise, if partisanship on education continues, congressional gridlock on education – as seen with many other high-priority national issues – may follow.

Historical data are available in Gallup Analytics.

Survey Methods

Results for this Gallup poll are based on telephone interviews conducted Aug. 3-7, 2016, with a random sample of 1,032 adults, aged 18 and older, living in all 50 U.S. states and the District of Columbia. For results based on the total sample of national adults, the margin of sampling error is ±4 percentage points at the 95% confidence level. For results based on the total sample of 254 parents of children in kindergarten through grade 12, the margin of sampling error is ±8 percentage points at the 95% confidence level. All reported margins of sampling error include computed design effects for weighting.

August 18, 2016

CRUZ'S IMAGE AMONG REPUBLICANS TANKS AFTER GOP CONVENTION

by Jeffrey M. Jones

Story Highlights

- *Cruz's favorable rating among Republicans at 43%, down from 59%*
- *Fifty percent of Republicans view Cruz unfavorably*
- *Among U.S. adults, 29% see him favorably, 58% unfavorably*

PRINCETON, N.J. – Republicans' views of Texas Sen. Ted Cruz have gotten significantly worse since he refused to endorse Donald Trump at the Republican National Convention, with his favorable rating falling from 59% to 43%. Now more Republicans have an unfavorable opinion of Cruz than a favorable one, reverting to the pattern seen when he suspended his presidential campaign in early May. His image had recovered in the months leading up to the convention.

Opinions of Ted Cruz, Among Republicans and Republican-Leaning Independents

Recent Trend

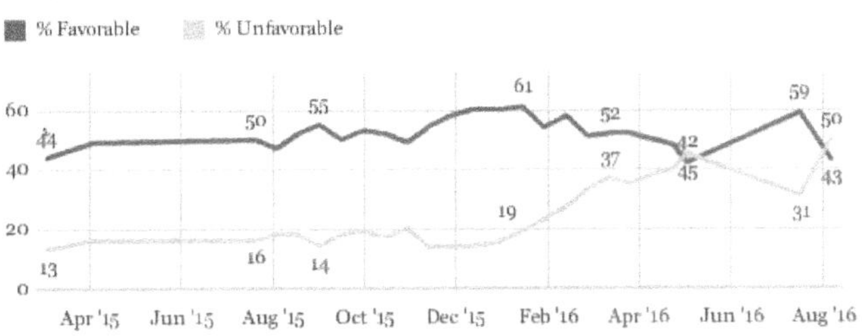

GALLUP

In late April and early May, slightly more Republicans had a negative view of him (45%) than a positive one (42%). With Trump's nomination looking more assured at the time, Cruz and Trump exchanged a flurry of personal insults. Cruz also attempted to jump-start his faltering campaign before the critical May 3 Indiana primary by making the unusual move of announcing Carly Fiorina as his vice presidential running mate.

Once Cruz ended his campaign after losing in Indiana, Republicans' feelings toward him quickly improved. He entered the convention with nearly twice as many Republicans rating him positively as negatively. His pre-convention 59% favorable rating among Republicans nearly tied his personal high of 61% from early January.

Cruz secured a prime-time speaking slot at the GOP convention, but he was roundly booed when he did not formally endorse Trump. That move rankled many Republican Party officials and, it appears based on the Aug. 3-7 Gallup poll, also many Republican Party supporters nationwide. His favorable ratings have dropped by similar amounts among both conservative Republicans and liberal/moderate Republicans.

Notably, Cruz's highly negative image among Democrats and Democratic leaners has changed little. Prior to the GOP convention, Democrats' opinions of Cruz were 19% favorable and 67% unfavorable; after, they were 21% favorable and 67% unfavorable.

Republicans' more negative opinions of Cruz have driven his favorable rating among all Americans down to 29% from 36% in mid-July. His unfavorable rating is up to 58% from 49%.

Opinions of Ted Cruz, Among All Americans

Recent Trend

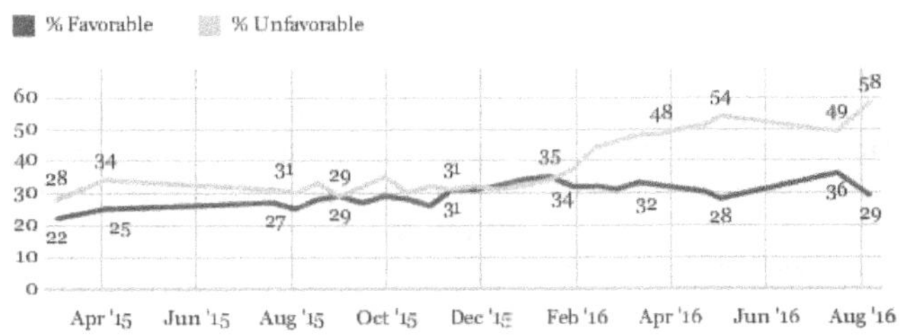

GALLUP

For most of 2015, Americans viewed Cruz slightly more negatively than positively. In late December and January, after several televised Republican debates but before voting in primaries and caucuses began, Americans' views were nearly evenly split. But as the campaign wore on and he became better known, negative opinions greatly outnumbered positive ones. Now, his unfavorable rating among all Americans is twice as high as his favorable rating.

Sanders, Ryan, Other Convention Speakers' Favorable Ratings Little Changed

Gallup tested Americans' views of several notable speakers before and after the Democratic and Republican conventions, including Republicans Cruz and Paul Ryan and Democrats Barack Obama, Bill Clinton, Bernie Sanders and Michelle Obama. None of these speakers saw much improvement in their images apart from Michelle Obama. This includes Sanders, Cruz's Democratic counterpart as the nomination runner-up. Unlike Cruz, Sanders formally endorsed his party's presidential nominee during the convention, and his already majority favorable rating edged up to 56%, a new high for him.

Only Cruz saw a significant drop in his favorable rating after the two political conventions.

Opinions of Convention Speakers Before and After 2016 Political Conventions

% Favorable

	Before %	After %	Change pct. pts.
Republicans			
Ted Cruz	36	29	-7
Paul Ryan	44	44	0
Democrats			
Barack Obama	51	54	+3
Bill Clinton	49	49	0
Bernie Sanders	53	56	+3
Michelle Obama	58	64	+6

July 13-17, 2016 and Aug. 3-7, 2016 Gallup polls

Presidential nominees Hillary Clinton and Trump both saw slight increases in their favorable ratings after their respective conventions, but both of these upticks have faded, and opinions of the nominees are essentially the same as they were in mid-July.

Implications

Should Cruz decide to mount another run for president in 2020, he has a lot of work to do to repair his image. Twice as many Americans view him negatively as positively, and his own party's supporters view him unfavorably on balance. Notably, Americans' opinions of Cruz right now are very similar to those of his formal rival, Trump. However, despite tepid support for Trump's nomination, at no point have Republicans viewed Trump more negatively than positively.

In fact, in Gallup's available polling on presidential nomination candidates, it has been extremely rare for a major nomination contender to be viewed more negatively than positively by his or her own party. Cruz's image among his party's supporters was net-negative near the end of his campaign, and is again now as a former candidate.

Cruz's future in presidential politics may depend on Americans, especially Republicans, having short memories or being able to forgive him for anything he has done to cause them to view him negatively. That appeared to be the case for Republicans in the two months after Cruz ended his 2016 presidential bid, but any goodwill he recovered has been lost.

Historical data are available in Gallup Analytics.

Survey Methods

Results for this Gallup poll are based on telephone interviews conducted Aug. 3-7, 2016, with a random sample of 1,032 adults, aged 18 and older, living in all 50 U.S. states and the District of Columbia. For results based on the total sample of national adults, the margin of sampling error is ±4 percentage points at the 95% confidence level.

For results based on the total sample of 469 Republicans and Republican-leaning independents, the margin of sampling error is ±6 percentage points at the 95% confidence level. All reported margins of sampling error include computed design effects for weighting.

August 18, 2016
U.S. APPROVAL OF CONGRESS IMPROVES, BUT STILL LOW AT 18%

by Justin McCarthy

Story Highlights

- *Approval of Congress up five percentage points since July*
- *Congress approval mostly aligns with satisfaction with U.S.*
- *Republicans remain least approving of Congress among party groups*

WASHINGTON, D.C. – Americans' approval of the U.S. Congress remains low at 18%, though the rating has recovered after dropping to 13% in July. The rating in August ties with the highest measured in 2016 so far. Approval of the institution has been below 20% in most of Gallup's monthly measures since February 2010.

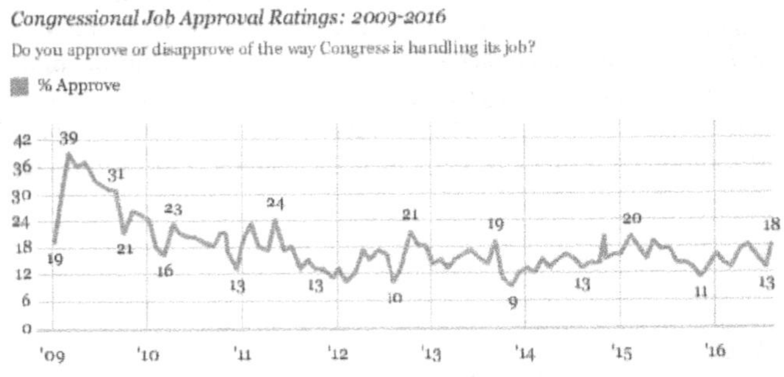

Approval ratings of Congress were in the 30% range in 2009 during the honeymoon period for President Barack Obama and a newly installed Democratic majority. However, by early 2010, approval faltered and has since averaged 16%.

This month's improvement in Americans' approval of Congress, recorded in an Aug. 3-7 Gallup poll, coincides with a 10-percentage-point increase in the percentage of adults who say they are satisfied with the direction of the U.S. Both measures had taken a hit in July before they rebounded this month.

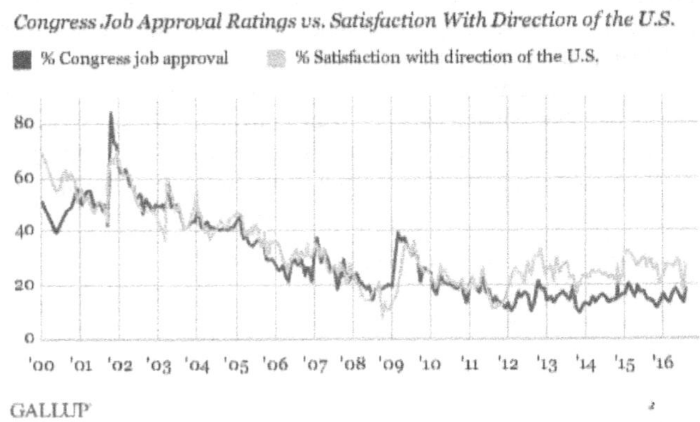

Over more than 15 years, Americans' approval of Congress has largely paralleled their satisfaction with the way things are going in the U.S. at large. In most polls between 2001 and 2012, the two measures have come within 10 points of each other. On only a few occasions – after the attacks on 9/11, prior to the March 2003 invasion of Iraq and in the first couple of months of Obama's presidency – did Congress' approval rating surpass that of satisfaction with the U.S. by more than 10 points.

Early in 2012, Americans' satisfaction with the direction of the U.S. improved while their approval of Congress did not. Since then, the two metrics have continued to run in parallel, but satisfaction has consistently outpaced Congress' job approval by as much as 17 percentage points. This more negative attitude toward Congress mirrors other indicators showing that Americans are at or near record lows in their confidence in the executive and judicial branches, and the federal government in general.

Despite controlling both chambers of Congress, Republicans remain least approving of the institution, at 13%, while about one in five independents (20%) and Democrats (19%) approve of the job Congress is doing.

Congress Job Approval, by Party Group

Do you approve or disapprove of the way Congress is handling its job?

	Approve %
Republicans	13
Independents	20
Democrats	19

Aug. 3-7, 2016

Bottom Line

The increase in Congress' job approval this month is a modestly positive sign for the institution, but 18% is still historically low. In addition to being the least trusted branch of government, the legislative branch's approval rating has not seen any lasting improvements in recent years.

The improvement is likely related to the cheerier views Americans hold about the direction of the country more generally, although neither measure is doing well by historical standards.

Historical data are available in Gallup Analytics.

Survey Methods

Results for this Gallup poll are based on telephone interviews conducted Aug. 3-7, 2016, with a random sample of 1,032 adults, aged 18 and older, living in all 50 U.S. states and the District of Columbia. For results based on the total sample of national adults, the margin of sampling error is ±4 percentage points at the 95% confidence level. All reported margins of sampling error include computed design effects for weighting.

August 19, 2016

LESS THAN HALF OF REPUBLICANS PLEASED WITH TRUMP AS NOMINEE

by Frank Newport

Story Highlights

- *46% of Republicans satisfied with Trump as GOP nominee*
- *56% of Democrats are satisfied with Clinton as party's nominee*
- *Young Democrats most likely to wish nominee were someone else*

PRINCETON, N.J. – Less than half of Republicans, 46%, are pleased that Donald Trump is their party's presidential nominee, while a slight majority, 52%, wish their party had nominated someone else. Democrats are more satisfied with Hillary Clinton, with 56% saying they are pleased while 42% wish someone else were the Democratic Party's nominee.

Now thinking about the candidates for president this year, are you pleased that Donald Trump is the Republican nominee, or do you wish someone else were the nominee?

	Republicans/Leaners %
Pleased Trump is the nominee	46
Wish someone else were the nominee	52
Don't know/Refused	3

Gallup, Aug. 15-16, 2016

Now thinking about the candidates for president this year, are you pleased that Hillary Clinton is the Democratic nominee, or do you wish someone else were the nominee?

	Democrats/Leaners %
Pleased Clinton is the nominee	56
Wish someone else were the nominee	42
Don't know/Refused	2

Gallup, Aug. 15-16, 2016

Neither of these assessments is a ringing endorsement; both represent pretty much the status quo compared with results from other Gallup questions, asked before the July conventions, which measured satisfaction with the party's nominee or likely nominee. For example, two Gallup surveys in May showed 48% and 51% of Republicans were pleased with the prospect of Trump as the GOP nominee, slightly higher than his current post-convention 46%. In mid-May, 56% of Democrats said they would rather see Clinton than Bernie Sanders as their party's nominee, identical to the current percentage saying they are pleased with Clinton in the role.

In previous elections, similar questions asked before the conventions showed that satisfaction with the prospect of various nominees ranged widely among Republicans and Democrats. Some partisan satisfaction levels (for example, for George H.W. Bush in June 1992 and Barack Obama in May 2012) were as high as 80%.

Young Democrats in Particular Wish Someone Else Was Their Party's Nominee

Both age and race are significant predictors of satisfaction with Clinton as the Democratic Party nominee. Only 38% of Democrats and Democratic leaners between the ages of 18 and 39 are satisfied with Clinton, compared with 67% of those 40 and older.

Pleased With Hillary Clinton as Democratic Presidential Nominee, by Age

Among Democrats/leaners

	Pleased Clinton is the nominee %	Wish someone else were the nominee %
18 to 39	38	60
40+	67	32

Gallup, Aug. 15-16, 2016

This age pattern most likely reflects the residue of support for erstwhile Democratic contender Sanders, who consistently during the primary campaign demonstrated a strong appeal to young Democrats. Sanders endorsed Clinton and praised her at the Democratic convention, but apparently some of his youthful supporters continue to wish he was their party's nominee.

Additionally, less than half (47%) of non-Hispanic white Democrats are satisfied with Clinton as their party's nominee, compared with 67% of nonwhite Democrats. This reinforces the idea that Clinton will depend heavily on support from black, Hispanic and other nonwhite Democrats in her effort to get a winning coalition to the polls in November.

Young Republicans are somewhat less likely to be satisfied with Trump than those 40 and older (36% vs. 50%), and those who have lower levels of education are somewhat more likely than Republicans with more education to be pleased with Trump.

Bottom Line

There is not a great deal of enthusiasm among Republicans or Democrats for their party's nominees this year. Both candidates had to fight off challengers to procure their nominations during the primary process, and the residual effect of those battles is most likely still affecting partisan views of Trump and Clinton. Both nominees also have significantly negative top-of-mind images, helping explain why both are less popular with their party's base than the typical nominee whose post-convention partisan favorables are in the 80% to 90% range.

It's not clear what effect these relatively low levels of satisfaction will have on Election Day. More than half of Republicans wish someone other than Trump were their party's nominee, but less than a third hold an unfavorable opinion of Trump. This suggests that the dissatisfaction levels may overstate the degree to which Trump might be hurt by a lack of support or voting turnout among Republicans. Similarly, while more than four in 10 Democrats say they wish someone other than Clinton were their party's nominee, about two in 10 view her unfavorably.

Regardless of whether one looks at the satisfaction measure or basic favorability, however, Trump clearly faces the challenge of a less positive party base. Both measures show about a 10-percentage-point gap between Republicans and Democrats in positive assessments of their respective nominees.

Trump has recently shaken up his staff in an effort to regain his campaign's momentum, but his choice of the chairman of the highly conservative Breitbart website to be his campaign chief doesn't signal that Trump is focused on reaching out to expand his appeal to more centrist or moderate voters.

Clinton faces the continuing challenge of particularly low satisfaction among younger Democrats, who may still be pining for Sanders. Younger voters are generally less likely to vote, meaning they are potentially not as valuable as voters from other age groups. But the Clinton campaign would certainly like to generate as much support from millennials as possible, including preventing them from defecting to a third-party candidate such as Gary Johnson or Jill Stein. Clinton also faces the challenge of generating more enthusiasm for her candidacy among white Democrats, the majority of whom still wish that someone else were their party's nominee, and whose votes she will need to win in November.

Historical data are available in Gallup Analytics.

Survey Methods

Results for this Gallup poll are based on telephone interviews conducted Aug. 15-16, 2016, on the Gallup U.S. Daily survey, with a random sample of 1,013 adults, aged 18 and older, living in all 50 U.S. states and the District of Columbia. For results based on the total sample of 466 Republicans and Republican-leaning independents, the margin of sampling error is ±6 percentage points at the 95% confidence level. For results based on the total sample of 451 Democrats and Democratic-leaning independents, the margin of sampling error is ±6 percentage points at the 95% confidence level. All reported margins of sampling error include computed design effects for weighting.

August 19, 2016
U.S. PARENTS' FEARS FOR CHILD'S SAFETY AT SCHOOL UNCHANGED

by Zac Auter

Story Highlights

- *28% of U.S. parents are concerned for their children's safety at school*
- *Mothers, minority and lower-income parents most likely to express concern*
- *13% of parents say their children have expressed fear about school safety*

WASHINGTON, D.C. – U.S. parents' concern for their children's physical safety at school has held steady this year at 28%. Parents' fears most recently edged up to 33% in 2012 and 2013 after the mass shooting in Newtown, Connecticut, in December 2012. Since then, the percentage of parents who fear for their children's safety has returned to the levels seen from 2009 to mid-2012.

U.S. Parents' Concerns for Their Children's Safety at School

Thinking about your oldest child, when he or she is at school, do you fear for his or her physical safety?

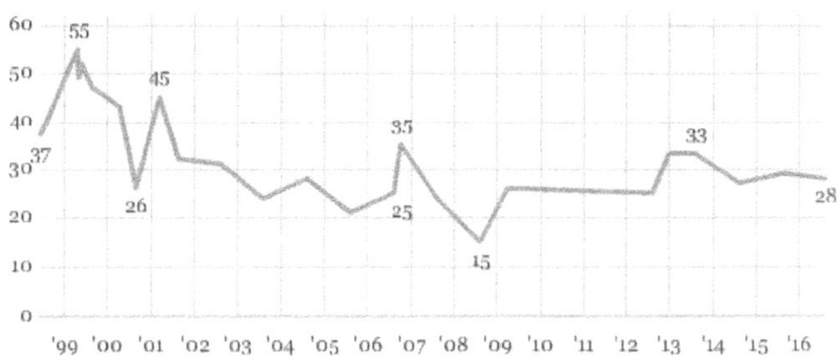

GALLUP

Gallup's 18-year trend documents spikes in parents' concern about school safety after major incidents of gun violence at schools, including the April 1999 Columbine massacre (55%) and the March 2001 shooting at Santana High (45%), and an uptick after the December 2012 Newtown shooting (33%).

The combined data since 2012 demonstrate that parents' worry varies among key subgroups. Mothers (33%) are more likely than fathers (25%), nonwhite parents (40%) are more likely than white parents (23%), and lower-income parents (41%) are nearly twice as likely as high-income parents (21%) to be concerned.

Parents' Concern for Their Children's Safety at School

	Fear for child's safety at school %	Child has expressed worry about safety at school %
U.S. parents overall	28	13
Men	25	8
Women	33	13
Whites	23	9
Nonwhites	40	14
Income less than $30,000	41	19
Income $30,000 to $74,999	30	7
Income $75,000 or more	21	8
Parent of child in public school	30	11
Parent of child in private school	28	6
Parent of elementary school student (K-5th grade)	30	8
Parent of middle school student (6th-8th grade)	34	13
Parent of high school student (9th-12th grade)	26	11

Combined data from 2012-2016
Gallup, Aug. 3-7, 2016

Despite the racial and income differences, concern among parents whose children attend public versus private schools does not differ significantly. However, parents of elementary and middle school students are slightly more likely than parents of high school students to be concerned about their children's safety at school.

Roughly One in Eight Students Express Fear for Their Own Safety

Currently, 13% of parents say their children have expressed fear about their safety at school. This is the highest level of fear recorded since 2001, when 22% of parents said their child indicated concern shortly after the Santana High School shooting. However, the current figure is largely consistent with the 8% to 12% range seen since 2012.

U.S. Parents Who Say Child Expressed Concerns About Safety at School

Have any of your school-aged children expressed any worry or concern about feeling unsafe at their school when they go back to school this fall?

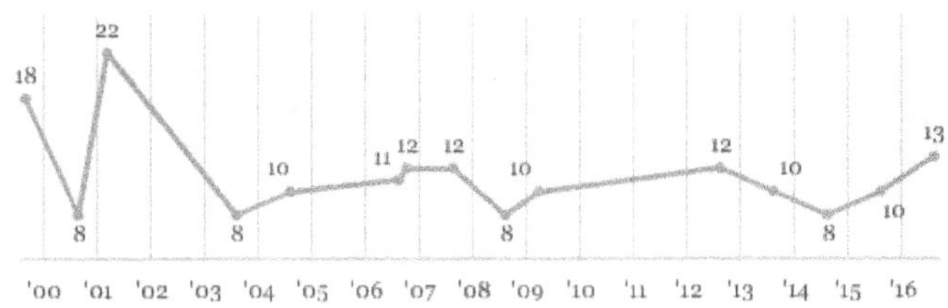

GALLUP

Parents' reports since 2012 that their children have expressed fear are higher among mothers than fathers, nonwhites than whites, and low-income than middle- and high-income parents. These patterns match those seen among parents' own concerns for their children's safety. Additionally, 11% of parents with children in public schools say their children have expressed fear about their safety in school, nearly double the rate among parents of children in private schools (6%).

Implications

The spikes in parents' fear for their children's safety in the wake of high-profile school shootings have receded in recent years. After the 1999 Columbine shooting that left 12 students dead, a majority of U.S. parents admitted concern for their children's safety at school. However, after 20 children were killed at Sandy Hook Elementary in Connecticut in 2012, one-third of U.S. parents expressed fear for their children's physical safety at school.

According to the FBI, there have been as many as 50 mass murders or attempted mass murders in U.S. schools since the Columbine shooting. Parents' muted response to high-visibility school shootings in recent years could reflect an increasing desensitization to school violence.

Historical data are available in Gallup Analytics.

Survey Methods

Results for this Gallup poll are based on telephone interviews conducted Aug. 3-7, 2016, with a random sample of 254 parents of children in grades kindergarten through 12, aged 18 and older, living in all 50 U.S. states and the District of Columbia. For results based on the total sample of national adults, the margin of sampling error is ±8 percentage points at the 95% confidence level. All reported margins of sampling error include computed design effects for weighting.

August 22, 2016

NEARLY HALF OF BLACKS TREATED UNFAIRLY 'IN LAST 30 DAYS'

by Jim Norman

Story Highlights

- *Percentage treated unfairly similar to 2015, down from 2004*
- *Whites now more likely to think their community discriminates*
- *Blacks' views of discrimination in community mostly unchanged*

WASHINGTON, D.C. – Just before two fatal police shootings of black men in July sparked nationwide protests and an attack on police officers in Dallas, close to half (46%) of U.S. blacks reported being treated unfairly in at least one of five different situations within the past 30 days. These results, from a June Gallup poll, are similar to the 43% seen in 2013 and 2015. However, the figure is lower than the 59% recorded in 2004, the first time Gallup measured all five situations.

Perceptions of Unfair Treatment in Past 30 Days, Among U.S. Blacks

Can you think of any occasion in the last 30 days when you felt you were treated unfairly in the following places because you were black? (% Yes)

	2004 %	2013 %	2015 %	2016 %
In a store where you were shopping	28	24	24	25
In a restaurant, bar, theater or other entertainment place	26	16	20	19
At your place of work	22	15	18	19
In dealings with the police, such as traffic incidents	25	17	18	16
While getting healthcare for yourself or a family member	20	9	12	12
Treated unfairly in any of the five situations	59	43	43	46

Gallup

Gallup has asked about unfairness in four of the five situations in 10 different years but included the question about healthcare only in 2004, 2013, 2015 and this year. In all 10 polls, blacks have been most likely to report unfair treatment while shopping. The first year Gallup asked these questions, 1997, was also the year that the highest percentage said they had been treated unfairly while shopping (30%).

Among the 46% of blacks who in 2016 reported receiving unfair treatment in at least one situation, slightly less than half (45%) listed only one of the situations. Twenty-five percent listed two, 20% listed three, 7% mentioned four, and 3% named all five.

Perceptions of Discrimination Growing Among Whites, Unchanged Among Blacks

In addition to asking U.S. blacks to report on their own treatment, Gallup has often asked Americans more broadly how they perceive blacks being treated in their community and in specific situations such as shopping and while at work. Combining the data from the 2004 and 2007 polls and the data from the 2015 and 2016 polls provides large enough samples to show changes over time. While blacks have become less likely to report being personally treated unfairly in recent years, their assessments of how blacks are treated in their community show little change from the 2004/2007 results to those from 2015/2016. Meanwhile, whites have become more likely in the past two years than previously to perceive that blacks are being treated less fairly than whites in their community.

Perceptions of Unfair Treatment and Discrimination, by Race

Can you think of any occasion in the last 30 days when you were treated unfairly (shopping, at work, in entertainment places, in dealings with police) because you were black? Just your impression, are blacks in your community treated less fairly than whites (in dealings with police, in stores downtown and shopping malls, in neighborhood shops, at work, in entertainment places)?

	2004/2007 %	2015/2016 %
Blacks reporting being treated unfairly in past 30 days in any of the situations	53	42
Blacks believing blacks in their community are treated less fairly in any of the situations	84	83
Whites believing blacks in their community are treated less fairly in any of the situations	37	46

Gallup polls in 2004, 2007, 2015 and 2016

In this year's poll, both blacks (67%) and whites (40%) are more likely to perceive that blacks are treated unfairly in "dealings with the police" than in any of the other four situations asked about. Among blacks, more than half also say blacks are treated less fairly "on the job or at work" and "in stores downtown or in the shopping mall." In every situation included in the poll, blacks are significantly more likely than whites to say that discrimination exists in their community.

- Fifty-two percent of blacks and 17% of whites say that blacks are treated less fairly on the job or at work.
- Fifty-two percent of blacks and 17% of whites perceive discrimination in stores downtown or in the shopping mall.
- Forty-one percent of blacks and 16% of whites think there is discrimination in neighborhood shops.
- Thirty-seven percent of blacks and 15% of whites think there is discrimination in restaurants, bars, theaters or other entertainment places.

Bottom Line

Blacks have been less likely to report unfair treatment in the past few years than they were in the 2004 and 2007 polls. Over the same period, the percentage of blacks saying their community discriminates against blacks has remained largely unchanged, while whites have become more likely to think blacks are treated less fairly.

With the widespread coverage of fatal police shootings of black men and subsequent protests across the nation in the past two years, it is not surprising that more whites have come to conclude that their community discriminates against blacks. Meanwhile, attitudes among blacks, who do not have to rely on news reports to become aware of such discrimination, have changed little.

That fewer blacks are saying they have experienced unfair treatment because of their race than were doing so several years ago is encouraging. Optimism about this trend, however, needs to be judged within the context that almost half of blacks in this year's poll reported at least one incident within a span of a month or less.

Survey Methods

Results for this Gallup poll are based on telephone interviews conducted June 7-July 1, 2016, with a sample of 3,270 adults, aged 18 and older, living in all 50 U.S. states and the District of Columbia, who had previously been interviewed in the Gallup Daily tracking poll and agreed to be re-interviewed for a later study. The sample is weighted to be representative of U.S. adults.

For results based on the total sample of national adults, the margin of sampling error is ±3 percentage points at the 95% confidence level. For results based on the sample of 1,320 non-Hispanic whites, the margin of sampling error is ±4 percentage points at the 95% confidence level. For results based on the sample of 912 non-Hispanic blacks, the margin of sampling error is ±5 percentage points at the 95% confidence level.

All reported margins of sampling error include computed design effects for weighting.

August 22, 2016

FOUR IN FIVE AMERICANS SUPPORT VOTER ID LAWS, EARLY VOTING

by Justin McCarthy

Story Highlights

- *63% of Americans support automatic voter registration*
- *Democrats (85%) most likely to favor early voting*
- *Republicans overwhelmingly support voter ID laws (95%)*

WASHINGTON, D.C. – As partisan-fueled court battles over state voting laws are poised to shape the political landscape in 2016 and beyond, new Gallup research shows four in five Americans support both early voting and voter ID laws. A smaller majority of 63% support automatic voter registration.

Americans' Support for Election Law Policies

In general, do you favor or oppose each of the following election law policies?

	Favor	Oppose
Early voting, which gives all voters the chance to cast their ballot prior to Election Day	80%	18%
Requiring all voters to provide photo identification at their voting place in order to vote	80%	19%
Automatic voter registration, whereby citizens are automatically registered to vote	63%	34%

Gallup, Aug. 15-16, 2016

These data come from an Aug. 15-16 Gallup poll.

While providing early voting opportunities and requiring voters to show photo identification at polling stations are popular among a majority of Americans, both are contentiously debated by party leaders and are being contested in state courts. Most recently, a federal judge in Ohio ruled against limiting early voting, saying the move would discriminate against black voters. There are electorally strategic reasons as to why each major political party has a stake in the two contested policies.

Majorities of Democrats and Republicans support early voting, but the option finds more favor among Democrats (85%) than Republicans (74%). Early voting typically benefits Democratic candidates, who have performed well electorally among early voters in many states that allow the option. Blacks and lower-income Americans – key Democratic support blocs – disproportionately opt to vote early.

Americans' Support for Election Law Policies, by Party

Do you favor or oppose each of the following election law policies? (% Favor)

	Early voting %	Photo ID requirement %	Automatic voter registration %
Republicans	74	95	51
Independents	80	83	58
Democrats	85	63	80

Gallup, Aug. 15-16, 2016

Studies have shown that voter ID laws reduce voting among blacks and young adults, who tend to vote Democratic. Many Republican leaders and Republican state legislatures have worked to put them into law. While majorities of Republicans and Democrats favor voter ID laws, Republicans (95%) overwhelmingly support them. Democratic support is more tepid, at 63%. GOP-led states have been the most active proponents of voter ID laws. Republicans who have championed these laws claim they prevent voter fraud, while opponents argue that there are too few cases to justify the legislation.

Meanwhile, a majority of U.S. adults (63%) also favor automatic voter registration, whereby citizens are automatically registered to vote when they do business with the Department of Motor Vehicles or certain other state agencies. This policy, which Democratic presidential nominee Hillary Clinton advocated about a year before her party included it in its official 2016 platform, has been implemented in five states. Although Democrats (80%) are more likely than Republicans (51%) to favor the idea, in April, the Republican-controlled legislature of West Virginia made the state the third to enact automatic voter registration.

Majorities Among Racial Groups, Regions Support Election Laws

Though many of the arguments for early voting and against voter ID laws frequently cite minorities' voting access, nonwhites' views of the two policies don't differ markedly from those of whites. Seventy-seven percent of nonwhites favor both policies, while whites favor each at 81%. Nonwhites are, however, more likely to support automatic voter registration (71%) than are whites (59%).

More than four in five residents of the Midwest, South and West, regions where at least half of states have early voting, support the policy. The East, where the policy is favored least (71%), is unique in that only the District of Columbia and two states – Maryland and West Virginia – have a formal process of early voting.

But some states in the region offer alternatives to formal early voting. Three other Eastern states – Maine, New Jersey and Vermont – have what the National Conference of State Legislatures (NCSL) refers to as "in-person absentee" voting. This is a less formal process of early voting in which a voter can apply in person for an absentee ballot and immediately cast that ballot before an election. In Massachusetts, early voting is allowed in even-year elections. The region's most populous states, New York and Pennsylvania, have no form of early voting.

Voter ID laws are most popular among residents living in the South (84%) and Midwest (84%), the regions in which eight of the strictest state voter ID laws are enforced, according to the NCSL. Nationally, election laws requiring voter identification exist – with some variation of the requirement – in 34 states, 33 of which are in effect for the 2016 election. West Virginia's law goes into effect in 2018.

Americans' Support for Election Law Policies, by Race and Region

Do you favor or oppose each of the following election law policies? (% Favor)

	Early voting %	Photo ID requirement %	Automatic voter registration %
Whites	81	81	59
Nonwhites	77	77	71
East	71	73	69
Midwest	83	84	56
South	82	84	60
West	81	78	66

Gallup, Aug. 15-16, 2016

Automatic voter registration is most popular in the East (69%) and West (66%), the only regions in which states have enacted it – including Oregon and California in the West, and Connecticut, Vermont and West Virginia in the East.

The number of states offering automatic voter registration could increase nearly seven-fold, however. In 2016, 29 states and the District of Columbia have considered measures that would put in place some form of the policy.

Majority of Republicans View Voter Fraud as a 'Major' Problem

The survey also asked Americans about their general concern that ineligible voters would cast votes, and that eligible voters would be kept from casting theirs. Americans are fairly split on their degree of concern about votes being cast by people who, by law, are not eligible to vote. More than a third view it as a major problem (36%), while nearly as many view it as either a minor problem (32%) or not a problem at all (29%).

A majority of Republicans (52%) perceive voter fraud as a major problem, which is reflected in the policy stances of many GOP state governors. By contrast, just 26% of Democrats expect ineligible persons voting to be a major problem this year. Southerners (42%) are more likely than those in other regions to view it as a major problem. The South is the most Republican region in the country, and the only region where some variation of a voter ID law is in effect in every state.

Concerns About Voter Fraud and Eligible Voters Not Being Allowed to Vote

In this year's election, do you think each of the following will be a major problem, a minor problem or not a problem at all across the country? (% Major problem)

	Votes being cast by people not eligible to vote %	Eligible voters not being allowed to cast a vote %
U.S. adults	36	32
Republicans	52	22
Independents	33	31
Democrats	26	40
Whites	37	25
Nonwhites	35	46
East	34	35
Midwest	34	26
South	42	32
West	33	32

Gallup, Aug. 15-16, 2016

The poll finds a bit narrower partisan gap over the issue of eligible voters not being allowed to cast a vote. Four in 10 Democrats, versus two in 10 Republicans, say keeping eligible voters from voting is a major problem. Mirroring these partisan attitudes, nonwhites are more likely than whites to say it is a problem.

Bottom Line

Despite widespread public support for early voting and voter ID laws – including majority support among partisans on both sides – the two parties' leaders often have strong preferences for one and not the other. The political squabbling over efforts to pass or restrict these laws in many states is therefore not representative of public opinion.

A smaller majority of Americans favor automatic voter registration, which could become more popular in the future as more states become acquainted with it. This is likely, as dozens of states have considered the policy in 2016.

In sum, Americans want easier processes for registering to vote and casting their ballots, as well as stronger checks against fraud.

Historical data are available in Gallup Analytics.

Survey Methods

Results for this Gallup poll are based on telephone interviews conducted Aug. 15-16, 2016, with a random sample of 1,013 adults, aged 18 and older, living in all 50 U.S. states and the District of Columbia. For results based on the total sample of national adults, the margin of sampling error is ±4 percentage points at the 95% confidence level. All reported margins of sampling error include computed design effects for weighting.

August 24, 2016
IN U.S., SUPPORT FOR DECREASING IMMIGRATION HOLDS STEADY

by Frank Newport

Story Highlights

- *38% want to see immigration levels decreased, similar to recent years*
- *21% want immigration levels increased*
- *Three times as many Republicans as Democrats want it decreased*

PRINCETON, N.J. – Despite Donald Trump's continued emphasis on the harmful effects of various types of immigrants coming to the U.S., there is no evidence of a surge in the percentage of Americans wanting to see immigration levels decreased. Thirty-eight percent of U.S. adults say the level of immigration should be decreased, similar to recent years, while an equal percentage say immigration should be kept at its present level. The relatively small percentage of Americans who want immigration increased, however, has edged down this year to 21%.

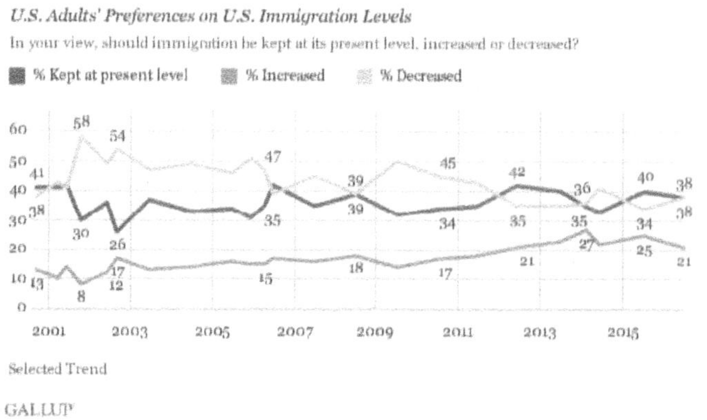

Since 2012, Americans generally have remained split between maintaining the current level of immigration and decreasing immigration, with less interest in increasing immigration. By contrast, before 2012 – and particularly in the years immediately after 9/11 – Americans tended to be more in favor of decreased immigration.

Gallup's question about changes in the volume of "immigration" does not specify whether it is legal or illegal, meaning respondents could, in theory, be taking both into account.

Immigration has been a major focus of Trump's presidential campaign since it began, including proposals to restrict the number of low-wage workers coming into the U.S. legally. He has also proposed restricting legal immigration among those who come from certain regions of the world with a history of exporting terrorism, who don't pass an ideology test or who identify with the Muslim faith. Trump has also proposed building a wall between the U.S. and Mexico to prevent illegal immigration and to deport the millions of immigrants living illegally in the U.S. – although news reports now indicate that he may alter his position on that issue.

Partisanship Creates the Biggest Divide on Immigration Attitudes

Americans' views on changes in the volume of immigration vary across key subgroups, particularly along party and ideological lines. Republicans and conservatives are most likely to want immigration decreased, while Democrats and liberals are least likely to want it decreased. The range across the political and ideological subgroups goes from 60% of Republicans and Republican leaners who want immigration decreased down to 20% among Democrats and Democratic leaners.

In your view, should immigration be kept at its present level, increased or decreased?

In rank order by percent "Decreased"

	Decreased %	Kept at present level %	Increased %
Republicans/Republican leaners	60	27	11
Conservatives	58	27	12
Non-Hispanic whites	42	36	20
Born in U.S. and parent born in U.S.	40	36	21
National adults	38	38	21
Hispanics	35	43	18
Born in U.S., but parent not born in U.S.	35	42	21
Hispanics born in Mexico	35	44	15
Moderates	32	44	23
Not born in U.S.	26	45	24
Non-Hispanic blacks	25	43	30
Liberals	21	45	31
Democrats/Democratic leaners	20	46	31

June 7-July 1, 2016
Gallup

There is less variation among racial and ethnic groups in views on immigration levels. Whites are somewhat more likely than Hispanics to want immigration decreased, while blacks are the least likely. The small group of those interviewed who identify as immigrants (12% of survey respondents in this poll) are somewhat less likely to want immigration decreased than are those who have been in the U.S. for at least two generations (26% vs. 40%, respectively). Twenty-four percent of immigrants want immigration increased, not far from the overall sample average.

Most Americans Define Immigration in General as "Good"

A separate question confirms that most Americans (72%) believe that immigration is a "good thing for this country today." Americans' positive views about immigration dipped to a low point after 9/11 and have fluctuated since then, but the 72% and 73% "good thing" percentages measured in 2013, 2015 and this year are the highest in Gallup's trend dating back to 2001.

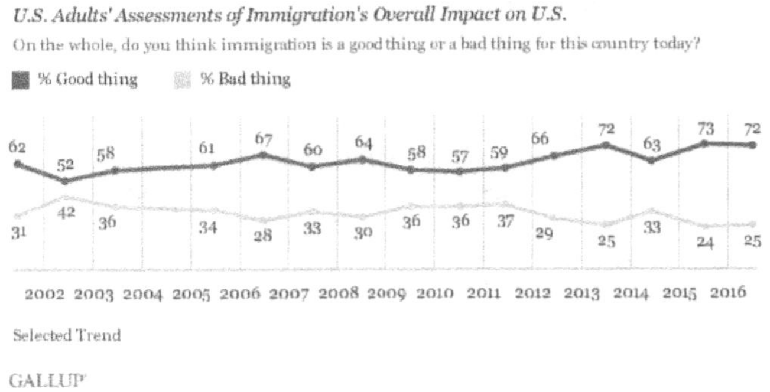

Bottom Line

While most Americans believe immigration is good for the country, a relatively small percentage would like to see the nation's level of immigration increased, while the rest want it either to remain the same or to decrease. Despite the strong rhetoric on immigration emanating from the Trump presidential campaign, there has been no uptick in the past year of those wanting to see immigration decreased, suggesting that Trump is not so much changing public opinion as he is taking advantage of existing attitudes. Trump generally finds support for the idea of decreasing immigration among his conservative, Republican base. But the significantly lower level of support for decreasing immigration among non-Republicans underscores the challenge Trump faces in the general election – given how closely tied he is to the issue – and helps explain why he may be shifting his tone on some immigration-related policies.

Historical data are available in Gallup Analytics.

Survey Methods

Results for this Gallup poll are based on telephone interviews conducted June 7-July 1, 2016, with a sample of 3,270 adults, aged 18 and older, living in all 50 U.S. states and the District of Columbia, who had previously been interviewed in the Gallup Daily tracking poll and agreed to be re-interviewed for a later study. The sample is weighted to be representative of U.S. adults.

For results based on the total sample of national adults, the margin of sampling error is ±3 percentage points at the 95% confidence level. For results based on the sample of 1,320 non-Hispanic whites, the margin of sampling error is ±4 percentage points at the 95% confidence level. For results based on the sample of 912 non-Hispanic blacks, the margin of sampling error is ±5 percentage points at the 95% confidence level. For results based on the sample of 906 Hispanics, the margin of sampling error is ±6 percentage points at the 95% confidence level.

All reported margins of sampling error include computed design effects for weighting.

August 25, 2016

HALF OF AMERICANS NOW VIEW AUTO INDUSTRY POSITIVELY

by Art Swift

Story Highlights

- *50% view auto industry positively, consistent with recent years*
- *Young Americans' views similar to national average*
- *Democrats more likely than GOP to view industry positively*

WASHINGTON, D.C. – Half of Americans view the auto industry positively, the highest since 2003. Ratings of the industry have been fairly stable in recent years after recovering from a sharp downturn after the 2007-2009 recession and subsequent government bailout and recovery.

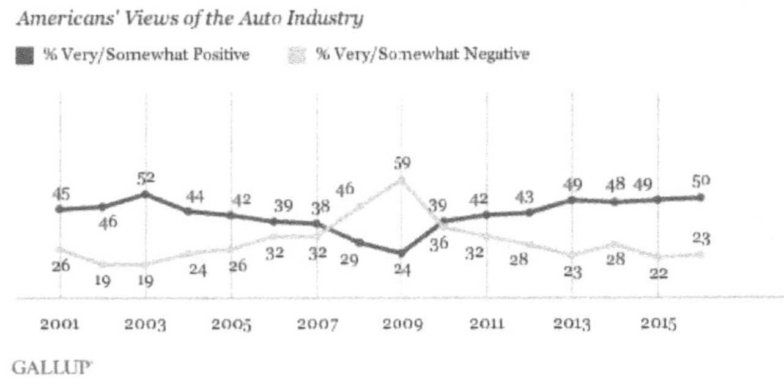

The auto industry's sales have risen since the Obama administration cemented a deal to bail out GM and Chrysler in 2009. Since then, U.S. auto sales have climbed from 10.4 million automobiles in 2009 to an estimated 17.5 million automobiles in 2015, the best year on record. The sales in the last two years have been buoyed by lower gas prices in the U.S. and the subsequent increase in the sales of higher-priced SUVs and trucks. Amid these developments, 23% of Americans rate the industry negatively, down significantly from 59% in 2009. This places the auto industry's image eighth among 25 industries Gallup measures.

Younger Americans' Views of Auto Industry Match National Average

Much has been written about younger Americans, millennials namely, being uninterested in buying cars. There may not be much truth to that recently since in 2015, millennials were second to baby boomers as the largest segment buying an automobile, according to industry estimates. Earlier in the decade, the industry said millennials were buying far fewer cars as a result of the economy and members of the age group getting their licenses later.

Regardless of their purchasing behavior, millennials' views of the auto industry over the past 15 years have been as positive or more positive than those who were older. Young adults were more positive than their elders from 2001-2005 and from 2008-2009, while their attitudes about the auto industry over the past four years are now about on par with others.

Americans' Views of the Auto Industry, By Age

% Very/Somewhat positive

	2001-2005 %	2008-2009 %	2013-2016 %
18-34	52	34	51
35-54	42	22	46
55 and older	45	25	51

Gallup

Democrats, Republicans Differ on Positive Views of Auto Industry

Democrats (53%) have had a more positive view of the auto industry over the past four years than have Republicans (46%). Both political groups had a comparatively negative view of the industry during the Great Recession in 2008 and 2009. From 2001-2005, when George W. Bush was president, Republicans (50%) were slightly more likely than Democrats (42%) to have a positive view of the auto industry.

Americans' Views of the Auto Industry, By Party ID

% Very/Somewhat positive

	2001-2005 %	2008-2009 %	2013-2016 %
Republican/Lean Republican	50	27	46
Democrat/Lean Democratic	42	27	53

Gallup

Bottom Line

Americans' views of the auto industry crashed during the Great Recession, but recovered fairly quickly. Americans' image of the industry today roughly matches what it was 15 years ago. Americans are buying cars at a record rate, many of these are more expensive large sport utility vehicles. Even though Americans' views of the industry have recovered, they are still not overwhelmingly positive.

The roots of why only half the nation views the auto industry positively may have to do with the politicized nature of the industry this decade. The auto bailout garnered great media attention when leaders were initially debating and implementing it and when President Barack Obama and Mitt Romney used it as a campaign issue in the 2012 presidential election. That may explain why a majority of Democrats have a positive view of the auto industry this decade, while a minority of Republicans see the industry the same way.

Historical data are available in Gallup Analytics.

Survey Methods

Results for this Gallup poll are based on telephone interviews conducted Aug. 3-7, 2016, with a random sample of 518 adults aged 18 and older, living in all 50 U.S. states and the District of Columbia. For results based on the total sample of national adults, the margin of sampling error is ±6 percentage points at the 95% confidence level. All reported margins of sampling error include computed design effects for weighting.

August 26, 2016

CLINTON HISPANIC ADVANTAGE SMALLER AMONG U.S.-BORN HISPANICS

by Justin McCarthy

Story Highlights

- *Her favorability is twice as high among foreign-born Hispanics*
- *72% of foreign-born Hispanics say they are not registered to vote*
- *Hispanics less likely to be registered than blacks, whites*

WASHINGTON, D.C. – Though U.S. Hispanics overall view Hillary Clinton three times more favorably than they do Donald Trump (65% to 21%), her edge is significantly smaller among U.S.-born Hispanics (43% to 29%). Meanwhile, foreign-born Hispanics are almost seven times more likely to view Clinton (87%) than Trump (13%) favorably.

Very Favorable/Favorable Ratings of Presidential Candidates Among Hispanics: Native-Born and Foreign-Born

Next, please tell me whether you have a very favorable, favorable, unfavorable or very unfavorable opinion of – [RANDOM ORDER]?

	Hillary Clinton %	Donald Trump %
All U.S. Hispanics	65	21
U.S.-born Hispanics	43	29
Hispanics born in another country	87	13

Gallup, June 7-July 1, 2016

These data come from Gallup's annual Minority Rights and Relations poll, conducted June 7-July 1.

Notably, U.S.-born Hispanics' views of the candidates are similar to those of the larger population of national adults. Forty-three percent of U.S.-born Hispanics and 44% of national adults view Clinton favorably. Twenty-nine percent of U.S.-born Hispanics view Trump favorably, while his favorability is 34% among national adults.

Therefore, Clinton owes a lot of her overall image advantage among Hispanics to those born outside the U.S.

Clinton is working to transform her higher favorability among Hispanics into solid electoral support. And while Hispanics' Democratic voting history makes it more likely they will vote for Clinton than for Trump, more uncertain is how many Hispanics will turn out to support her.

Fifty-eight percent of Hispanics say they are registered to vote, far less than the 95% of non-Hispanic whites and 87% of non-Hispanic blacks who say the same. But the lower rate of reported Hispanic voter registration is almost entirely attributable to low registration among foreign-born Hispanics. Just 28% of Hispanics born outside the U.S. – the group that views Clinton so positively – say they are registered to vote, compared with 87% of those born in the U.S.

This lower voter registration rate could be related partly to citizenship issues, as some foreign-born Hispanics may not be legal U.S. citizens, and therefore are ineligible to vote.

Percentage of U.S. Hispanics Who Are Registered to Vote, Native-Born and Foreign-Born

Are you now registered to vote in your precinct or election district, or not?

	Registered to vote	Not registered to vote
	%	%
All U.S. Hispanics	58	42
U.S.-born Hispanics	87	13
Hispanics born in another country	28	72

Gallup, June 7-July 1, 2016

Less Than Half of Nonregistered Hispanics Plan to Register

Trump's rhetoric on immigration has hardly won him supporters among U.S. Hispanics, particularly those who were born outside the U.S. Some have speculated that Hispanics may become much more involved in the political process this year in an effort to defeat Trump. To some degree, the Gallup data already reflect an increase in Hispanic registration, with self-reported registration now up to 58%, compared with 51% in 2013.

Gallup also asked nonregistered voters whether they intend to register. Among Hispanics, about four in 10 of those not registered – equivalent to 17% of all U.S. Hispanics – say they are very or somewhat likely to register to vote before the presidential election this year. Theoretically, that could boost voter registration among Hispanics to 75%, but it's unclear how many Hispanics will actually follow through on their intention to register to vote.

An additional 8% of U.S.-born Hispanics say they are very or somewhat likely to register to vote, which could result in a total of 95% of registered voters among this group – on par with the rate of U.S.-born whites.

Meanwhile, nearly half of foreign-born U.S. Hispanics (45%) have resigned themselves to not being likely to register to vote. However, the foreign-born group overall – 27% of whom are registered to vote – could theoretically double its voting size to a slim majority, as an additional 27% of foreign-born Hispanics report being very or somewhat likely to register before Election Day.

Registered Voter Status, Among Hispanics

Are you now registered to vote in your precinct or election district, or not? (Asked of those not registered to vote) How likely are you to register to vote before the presidential election this November – very likely, somewhat likely, not too likely or not likely at all?

	Registered	Very/Somewhat likely to register	Not too/Not at all likely to register
	%	%	%
All U.S. Hispanics	58	17	25
U.S.-born Hispanics	87	8	5
Hispanics born in another country	28	27	45

Gallup, June 7-July 1, 2016

Bottom Line

With a population of 55 million, about one in six Americans are Hispanic, according to the U.S. Census Bureau. Though the minimum percentage of Hispanic support a candidate must garner in a national election is debatable, it is not a constituency a candidate can afford to ignore.

Trump's comments and campaign positions have offended many Hispanics, but his image has suffered less among those who were born in the U.S. While he is certainly not popular among U.S.-born Hispanics, the group hardly holds warm feelings about Clinton either. U.S.-born Hispanics do view Clinton significantly more favorably than Trump, which should help her fare better at the polls among this group, the vast majority of whom are registered to vote.

Clinton, however, is highly popular among foreign-born Hispanics, and her support among this group is the primary reason she has such a large advantage in favorability over Trump among all U.S. Hispanics. But low reported voter registration among foreign-born Hispanics limits her ability to leverage them as a voting bloc. This makes it clear why Clinton's campaign could most likely benefit by prioritizing the registration of the roughly one in six nonregistered Hispanics who want to register but have still not done so.

Historical data are available in Gallup Analytics.

Survey Methods

Results for this Gallup poll are based on telephone interviews conducted June 7-July 1, 2016, with a random sample of 3,270 adults, aged 18 and older, living in all 50 U.S. states and the District of Columbia. For results based on the total sample of national adults, the margin of sampling error is ±3 percentage points at the 95% confidence level. For results based on the total sample of 1,320 non-Hispanic whites, the margin of sampling error is ±4 percentage points at the 95% confidence level. For results based on the total sample of 912 non-Hispanic blacks, the margin of sampling error is ±5 percentage points at the 95% confidence level. For results based on the total sample of 906 Hispanics, the margin of sampling error is ±6 percentage points at the 95% confidence level. All reported margins of sampling error include computed design effects for weighting.

August 26, 2016
IMAGE OF REAL ESTATE INDUSTRY CONTINUES TO IMPROVE

by Jim Norman

Story Highlights

- *44% view real estate industry positively, 21% negatively*
- *Net positive of +23 points is above 25-industry average*
- *Overall positive image a huge swing from -40 in 2008*

WASHINGTON, D.C. – The image of the U.S. real estate industry improved for the fifth year in a row in 2016, with 44% of Americans now viewing it positively and 21% viewing it negatively. The public's 23-percentage-point net positive rating gives real estate, for the first time since 2006, a higher rating than the overall average for the 25 industries Gallup measures annually.

Real Estate Image Climbs Above Industry Average

Net positive ratings (percentage with a positive view minus percentage with a negative view) for the real estate industry compared with the average for industries included in Gallup poll

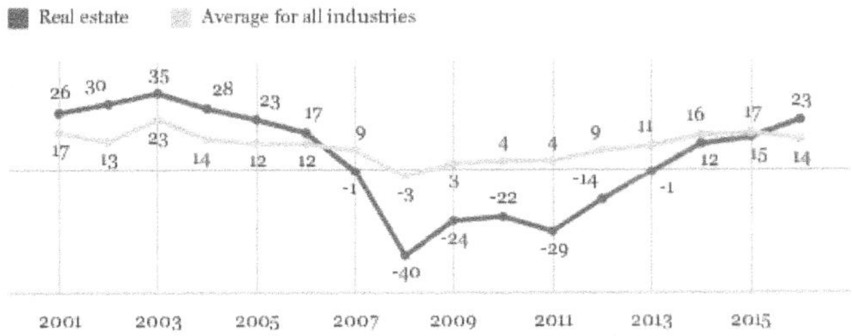

Industry average includes 24 industries in 2001 and 2002, and 25 industries in 2003-2016; question is asked annually

GALLUP

The industry's climb back into public favor began in 2009 following a spectacular five-year fall after the housing bubble burst in the middle of the last decade. During that five-year span, the public's net positive rating of real estate tumbled from +35 in 2003 to -40 in 2008. The 75-point ratings loss was the largest any industry has suffered since Gallup began asking the question in 2001. Three other industries sustained smaller, but still sizable, losses in their ratings from their high points in the early to mid-2000s. All three have since regained at least some of the ground they lost.

- The auto industry fell 68 points, from a +33 net positive rating in 2003 to -35 in 2009, then rose to +27 this year.
- The banking industry dropped 67 points, from +39 in 2006 to -28 in 2009, and now stands at +2.
- Soaring gas prices in 2004, 2005 and 2006 sent the oil and gas industry's rating tumbling 54 points, from -8 in 2003 down to -62 in 2006, the lowest net positive rating Gallup has recorded. The industry now stands at -7.

Image Gains Put Real Estate Near Middle of Pack for Industry Ratings

Even with its highest rating of +35 in 2003, the real estate industry's image has never approached the net positive ratings of such American favorites as the restaurant and computer industries. On the other hand, the public's -40 net positive real estate rating – coming during the 2008 mortgage crisis that resulted in millions of defaulted home loans – pushed real estate near the bottom of the 25 rated industries. Only the federal government (-42) and the oil and gas industry (-61) were viewed more negatively at the time.

This year, real estate's +23 net positive puts it near the middle of the ratings, closest to the retail (+26) and automobile (+27) industries.

Bottom Line

No industry's reputation suffered more than the real estate sector's during the financial calamities that began with the collapse of the housing bubble in 2006 and 2007. Year by year, however, this industry has managed to turn around the negative views of many Americans as housing prices have climbed past pre-crash levels. The public now holds an overall view of the sector that is the most positive since 2005. The industry's image improved in 2016 even as the overall ratings for the 25 industries tracked by Gallup slipped slightly. Combined with the public's renewed belief that real estate is the best long-term investment, the higher ratings give cause for optimism in an industry that has seen more than its share of ups and downs since the turn of the new century.

Survey Methods

Results for this Gallup poll are based on telephone interviews conducted Aug. 3-7, 2016, with a random sample of 1,032 adults, aged 18 and older, living in all 50 U.S. states and the District of Columbia. Each industry was rated by a randomly chosen half sample of respondents. Results for each industry have a margin of sampling error of ±6 percentage points at the 95% confidence level. All reported margins of sampling error include computed design effects for weighting.

August 29, 2016
UNINSURED DOWN SINCE OBAMACARE; COST, QUALITY STILL CONCERNS

by Nader Nekvasil

Story Highlights

- *Uninsured rate down significantly since the healthcare law took effect*
- *Percentage who have trouble affording necessary care/medicines at record low*
- *U.S. adults don't see improvement in healthcare costs and quality*

This is the first article in a five-part series examining changes in Americans' health and well-being during Barack Obama's presidency.

WASHINGTON, D.C. – During his presidential campaign and first term in office, President Barack Obama made healthcare reform the foundation of his domestic agenda. Now, six years after the Affordable Care Act was signed into law and a few months before Obama leaves office, Gallup and Healthways are reviewing how his signature legislative achievement has affected the public's perceptions of the law's primary goals. These goals include: increasing healthcare accessibility, reducing healthcare costs and improving healthcare quality.

To make healthcare more accessible, the Affordable Care Act requires Americans to carry health insurance or risk paying a fine – a provision often referred to as the "individual mandate." The percentage of U.S. adults without health insurance has dropped significantly since the individual mandate took effect in early 2014, according to data from the Gallup-Healthways Well-Being Index. The uninsured rate declined from 17.3% in 2013 to 10.8% so far in 2016, the lowest percentage of uninsured adults Gallup and Healthways have recorded in more than eight years of tracking. This translates to roughly 16.1 million previously uninsured adults gaining health insurance since 2013.

Percentage of U.S. Adults Without Health Insurance

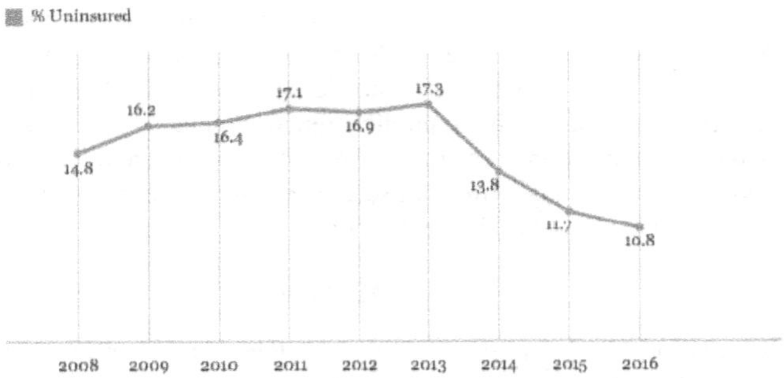

2016 data reflect Jan. 2–July 31, 2016
Gallup-Healthways Well-Being Index

GALLUP

When Obama took office, the uninsured rate was increasing amid the worst economic recession since the Great Depression. Many Americans lost their jobs and, consequently, their healthcare coverage. The uninsured rate climbed to a six-year high of 17.3% in 2013 but dropped significantly after the individual mandate took effect in early 2014. While the drop in the uninsured rate appears to be tied to the individual mandate, declining unemployment also might have played a role.

Minorities, young adults and lower-income Americans have seen the sharpest drops in their uninsured rates. Regardless, these groups still have the highest uninsured rates across key demographic groups. Further, Gallup-Healthways research shows that collectively, states that have expanded Medicaid to provide coverage to more individuals and have established a state-run marketplace exchange have seen a greater decline in their uninsured rate than have states that took neither or just one of these actions.

Percentage With Trouble Affording Necessary Care or Medicine at Record Low

The percentage of U.S. adults who say they were unable to afford healthcare or medicines for themselves or their families at some point in the past 12 months is also at a record low after nearly eight years of Obama's presidency. Since Gallup and Healthways began tracking this metric in 2008, it has dropped more than four percentage points, with a majority of that decline occurring after the individual mandate took effect in early 2014. The increase in the percentage of U.S. adults with health insurance appears to be a key reason why fewer U.S. adults report having difficulty affording healthcare or medicines.

Have there been times in the past 12 months when you did not have enough money to pay for healthcare and/or medicines that you or your family needed?

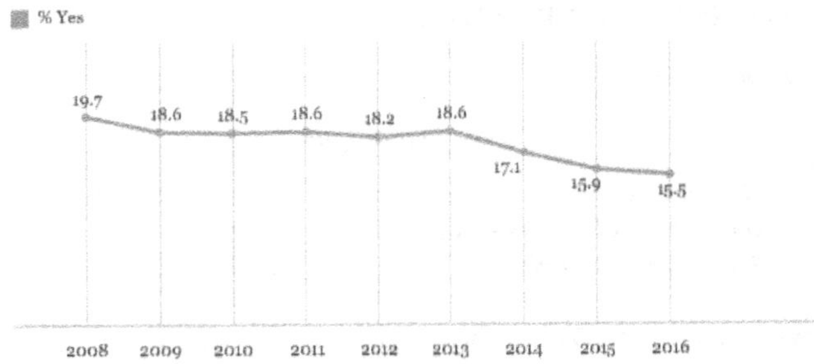

2016 data reflect Jan. 2–July 31, 2016
Gallup-Healthways Well-Being Index

GALLUP

Even though fewer Americans are struggling to afford healthcare, other Gallup trends suggest that the Affordable Care Act may not be meeting its goal of reducing healthcare costs. U.S. adult satisfaction with the total cost they pay for their healthcare has remained relatively steady over the past 14 years, including after the healthcare law was passed. Gallup also previously reported that since the individual mandate took effect, there has been a rise in the percentage of U.S. adults paying for all or some of their health insurance premiums who say that their premiums have gone up "a lot" over the past year.

Healthcare Quality Remains a Concern

To improve healthcare quality and lower long-term costs, the Affordable Care Act includes various provisions to encourage preventive and primary care. The percentage of U.S. adults with a personal doctor has remained relatively unchanged since early 2014, according to data from the Gallup-Healthways Well-Being Index.

Do you have a personal doctor?

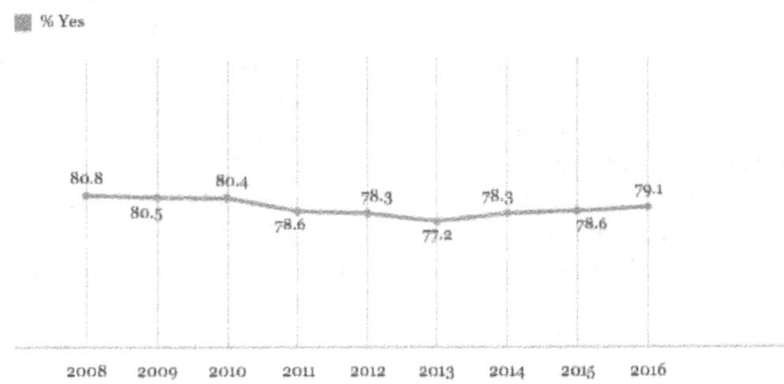

2016 data reflect Jan. 2–July 31, 2016
Gallup-Healthways Well-Being Index

GALLUP

Other Gallup trends suggest healthcare quality remains a concern. Gallup reported in late 2015 that the percentage of U.S. adults rating the quality of their healthcare and their healthcare coverage as "excellent" has dropped over the previous two years.

Bottom Line

Barack Obama's legacy is focused, to some degree, around the passage of the landmark Affordable Care Act and how it has affected healthcare in the U.S. The uninsured rate was rising during Obama's first term amid high unemployment during the economic recession. The uninsured rate has fallen since the Affordable Care Act took effect and is now back to the levels recorded before the 2007-2009 recession. The uninsured rate has dropped most among groups who previously struggled with access to healthcare, such as young adults, minorities and lower-income Americans.

However, despite the increase in healthcare accessibility, the two other original goals of the Act – increasing the quality and decreasing the cost of healthcare in the U.S. – remain in question. Fewer Americans say the quality of their healthcare is "excellent," and they are no more likely than they were before the law was passed to be satisfied with the total cost of their healthcare.

The sustainability of the Affordable Care Act in its current state has come under scrutiny. Aetna recently joined other health insurance groups in withdrawing from the healthcare marketplace, leading some experts to question the viability of the Affordable Care Act in its current form. Further, the next presidential administration could try to repeal or significantly reshape the Affordable Care Act.

Still, even with the cost, quality and future of healthcare in question, it is clear that millions of U.S. adults have gained access to healthcare through the Affordable Care Act.

These data are available in Gallup Analytics.

Survey Methods

Results are based on telephone interviews conducted January 2008-July 2016 as part of the Gallup-Healthways Well-Being Index survey, with a random sample of 2,415,499 adults, aged 18 and older, living in all 50 U.S. states and the District of Columbia. For results based on the total sample of national adults, the margin of sampling error is ±.08 percentage points at the 95% confidence level. All reported margins of sampling error include computed design effects for weighting.

August 29, 2016
U.S. WORKERS' SATISFACTION WITH JOB DIMENSIONS INCREASES

by Frank Newport and Jim Harter

Story Highlights

- *Workers' satisfaction with various job dimensions has improved in 2016*
- *Highest satisfaction is with safety and relations with coworkers*
- *Workers generally least satisfied with stress, benefits and pay*

PRINCETON, N.J. – U.S. workers continue to be most positive about their physical safety on the job, their relations with coworkers, their flexibility of hours and their job security. Workers are least satisfied with other aspects of their jobs, including their health benefits, the money they earn, their chances for promotion, retirement plans and on-the-job stress – the last of which is at the bottom of the list. From last year to this year, workers have become more satisfied with most aspects of their jobs.

U.S. Employees' Satisfaction With 13 Job Aspects – Recent Trend

% Completely satisfied, ranked by 2016

	2015 %	2016 %	Change over past year (pct. pts.)
The physical safety conditions of your workplace	70	76	+6
Your relations with coworkers	72	71	-1
The flexibility of your hours	58	67	+9
Your job security	57	65	+8
Your boss or immediate supervisor	54	61	+7
The amount of work that is required of you	53	58	+5
The amount of vacation time you receive	57	56	-1
The recognition you receive at work for your work accomplishments	45	55	+10
The retirement plan your employer offers	35	44	+9
Your chances for promotion	35	43	+8
The amount of money you earn	33	41	+8
The health insurance benefits your employer offers	40	37	-3
The amount of on-the-job stress in your job	28	34	+6

Based on adults employed full or part time
Gallup

These results are from Gallup's annual Work and Education survey, conducted Aug 3-7. In that survey, U.S. workers convey increased levels of contentment with their work or workplace: Satisfaction with 10 of the 13 job-related aspects measured has edged up from 2015. This trend coincides with a recent uptick in "good jobs" – the percentage of Americans who work full time for an employer.

Workers' Satisfaction With Tangible Benefits Up Over Time

Workers' increased satisfaction this year with tangible benefits, such as the amount of money they earn and retirement benefits, is part of a long-term trend. Based on three-year rolling averages beginning in 2003, 26% of workers were completely satisfied with the amount of money they earned between 2001 and 2003, while 35% have been satisfied over the past three years, including 41% in 2016. Satisfaction with retirement plans has followed the same pattern.

U.S. Workers' Satisfaction With Money Earned and Retirement Plan

% Completely satisfied, three-year rolling averages

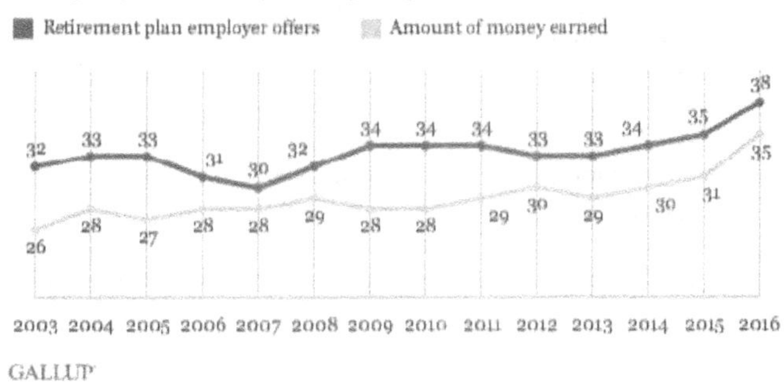

This rise in worker satisfaction with tangible benefits in the workplace coincides with government economic data showing that wages have risen by 2.6% over the past 12 months, Gallup data showing that the majority of workers say their pay has gotten better in recent years, and the increase in Gallup's "good jobs" measure.

Workers' satisfaction with vacation time has also edged up in recent years.

More Satisfaction With the Recognition Received at Work

Workers' satisfaction with the recognition they receive at work – one of the less tangible aspects of work included in Gallup's trends – improved more than any other dimension year over year and has shown a broad uptick over time since the early 2000s. The majority of workers (51%) interviewed over the past three years feel completely satisfied with the recognition they receive for their work, up from 42% in 2001 through 2003.

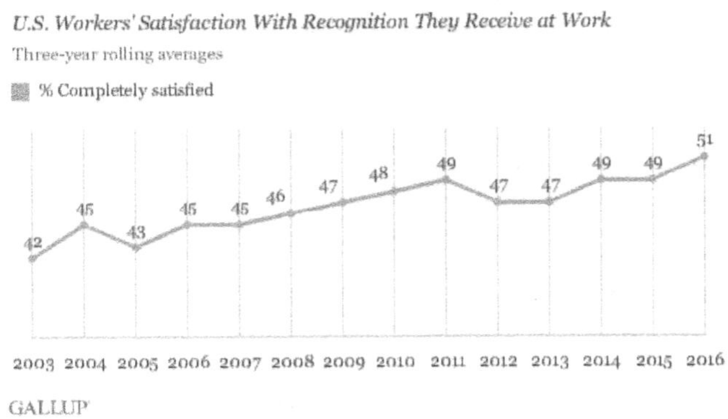

Worker Satisfaction and Worker Engagement

While satisfaction with work seems to be improving in the U.S., this trend needs to be viewed in the context of a different aspect of the workplace: engagement. Engaged employees – a smaller subset of those who may be satisfied with their job – are involved in and enthusiastic about their work and workplace. They are more likely to show up to work, are less likely to leave the organization, treat customers better and are more productive. Gallup finds that business units with an above-average number of highly engaged employees average 21% higher profitability than business units with few engaged employees.

As is the case for worker satisfaction, the percentage of engaged employees has grown slightly in recent years. But that leaves approximately two-thirds of U.S. employees whom Gallup classifies as either "not engaged" or "actively disengaged," which is significantly higher than the percentage who report being dissatisfied with aspects of their jobs. The result? Many workers are satisfied but are not engaged at work.

For example, while more U.S. workers in 2016 are reporting that they are completely satisfied with their retirement plans, flexible hours and pay, Gallup research shows that workers who are happy with these tangible benefits, but who are not engaged, produce little in return to their employers for these benefits. And past Gallup research has found that workers who are engaged have lower stress and higher well-being, regardless of hours worked, vacation time or flextime policies.

From an employer's perspective, this research shows that increasing workers' satisfaction with their workplace alone is not the formula to improve productivity, retention and output. Employers should also strive to have engaged employees – those who are not just content with their job, but who are highly involved in and enthusiastic about it.

In an ideal world, American business and industry would have employees who are highly satisfied with all aspects of their job and, at the same time, highly engaged.

Employers can increase workers' *satisfaction* with their compensation by paying them fairly, can increase satisfaction with retirement plans by putting more money into 401(k) matches, and can boost satisfaction with vacation time by offering appropriate amounts so that employees are thriving in their overall lives.

Increasing *engagement*, on the surface, may seem like a less straightforward process. Gallup finds that boosting engagement involves focused efforts on complex elements that drive day-to-day performance – including role clarity, opportunities to develop, and feedback and progress discussions. This type of focus on engagement, however, can have a powerful effect on the factors that matter most to an organization's performance management and human capital strategies. And, while about one-third of U.S. employees are engaged at work, many organizations have bucked this trend and have achieved more than double this rate – particularly by identifying and developing managers with the skills to increase engagement effectively.

Survey Methods

Results for this Gallup poll are based on telephone interviews conducted Aug. 3-7, 2016, with a random sample of 521 adults employed full or part time, aged 18 and older, living in all 50 U.S. states and the District of Columbia. For results based on this sample, the margin of sampling error is ±6 percentage points at the 95% confidence level. All reported margins of sampling error include computed design effects for weighting.

August 30, 2016
AMERICANS' LIFE EVALUATIONS IMPROVE DURING OBAMA ERA

by Dan Witters

Story Highlights

- *Life evaluations across all racial/ethnic groups have improved since 2008*
- *Blacks' life evaluations have dropped during Barack Obama's second term*
- *Life evaluations among whites now at highest point in nine-year period*

This is the second article in a five-part series examining changes in Americans' health and well-being during Barack Obama's presidency.

WASHINGTON, D.C. – In the nearly eight years since President Barack Obama took office in January 2009, the percentage of U.S. adults who evaluate their lives well enough to be considered "thriving" has improved by nearly four percentage points. The 55.4% who are thriving so far in 2016 is on pace to be the highest recorded in the nine years Gallup and Healthways have tracked it.

Life Evaluations (% Thriving) Among U.S. Adults

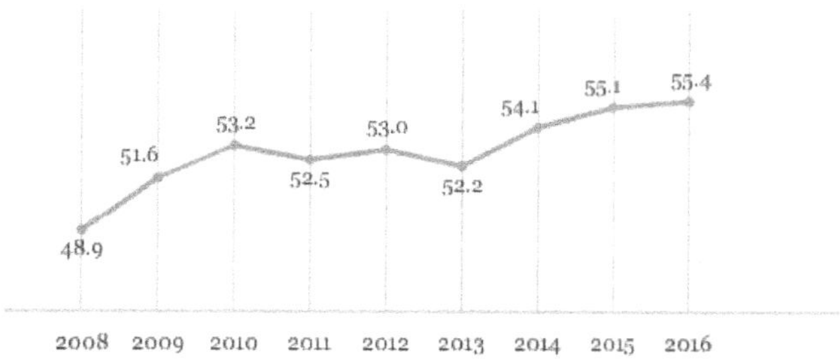

Gallup-Healthways Well-Being Index
Note: 2016 results are from Jan. 2-July 31, 2016

GALLUP

Gallup and Healthways classify Americans as "thriving," "struggling" or "suffering" according to how they rate their current and future lives using a ladder scale with steps numbered from 0 to 10, based on the Cantril Self-Anchoring Striving Scale. Those who rate their present life a 7 or higher and their life in five years an 8 or higher are classified as thriving.

In 2008, George W. Bush's final year in office, 48.9% of U.S. adults were classified as thriving. By 2010, the second year of Obama's presidency, this figure had bumped up to 53.2%, where it generally remained through 2013. In 2014, the percentage of adults classified as thriving crossed the 54% mark for the first time, only to be topped again at 55.1% in 2015. Life evaluations are currently on pace to reach another record high in 2016.

Under Obama, Life Evaluations Improve for All Major Racial and Ethnic Groups

The percentages of U.S. whites, blacks, Hispanics and Asians who are thriving have all increased during the Obama era, although not uniformly. Blacks' life evaluations improved by nearly 13 points between 2008 and 2010, more than any other group. By 2010, blacks' life evaluations were second only to those of Asians. Some of the increase among blacks – particularly the seven-point increase that occurred between 2008 and 2009 – could be explained by Obama coming into office, which may have made blacks feel more optimistic about their current and future lives even if his being in office hadn't yet had any tangible effect on their lives.

However, blacks' life evaluations have waned in Obama's second term, averaging below 54% each year since 2013 and now registering below that of whites and Hispanics. These results dovetail with blacks' collective sentiment that Obama has not done enough to improve black Americans' standard of living.

Life Evaluations (% Thriving) Among U.S. Adults, by Race/Ethnicity

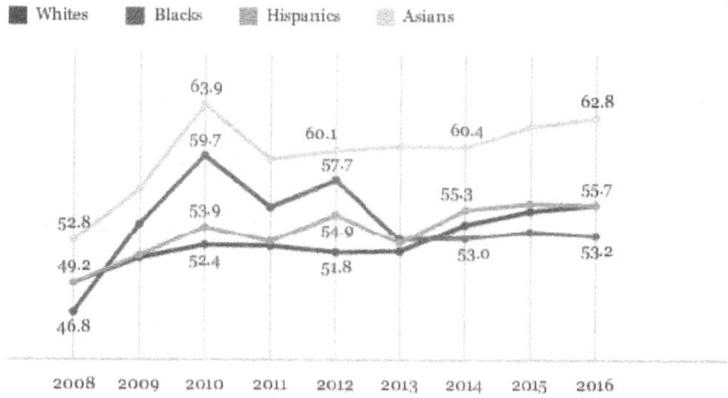

Gallup-Healthways Well-Being Index
Note: 2016 results are from Jan. 2-July 31, 2016

GALLUP

Whites' and Hispanics' life evaluations improved much more modestly in the first two years of Obama's presidency. The percentage thriving among whites rose from 49.2% in 2008 to 52.4% in 2010 and stayed near that level through 2013. Similarly, the percentage of Hispanics thriving rose from 49.2% in 2008 to 53.9% in 2010 and remained in the 52% to 55% range for the next three years. Since then, both groups have improved to an identical 55.7% thus far in 2016.

Asians, who experienced marked improvement between 2008 and 2010, have historically maintained the highest life evaluations of all four groups. The percentage of Asians thriving is currently on pace to be above 60% for the fifth straight year.

Implications

U.S. adults' life evaluations are better today than when President Obama took office in January 2009. During the Great Recession, the rapid decline in the labor market played an instrumental role in suppressing life evaluations nationally, setting the scene for improvement to come. Many factors could help explain the subsequent uptick in life evaluations, including the election of the president himself. Obama's first term showed a major improvement in blacks' life evaluations, especially among black Democrats. White Democrats' life evaluations improved as well, but this was partially offset by a modest decline in life evaluations among white Republicans.

Obama's second term, however, shows an improvement in whites' life evaluations – particularly those of white Republicans – and corresponding declines among blacks and black Democrats during a period when the presidency did not change. This finding suggests that some improvements in the economy after the Great Recession have likely played a more significant role in the overall gains that have been measured. For example, the percentage of U.S. adults who can't afford food and the percentage who have experienced healthcare insecurity within the past 12 months are both at their lowest levels since Gallup and Healthways began tracking them in 2008, and the uninsured rate has dropped over six percentage points since late 2013. The percentage of U.S. adults who have a good job – those who work full time for an employer – is now at its highest point since measurement began in 2010. Additionally,

Gallup's Job Creation Index – U.S. workers' reports of employer hiring activity – is at its highest point since measurement began in 2008.

Social turmoil also may be affecting some Americans' life evaluations. For example, recent high-profile incidents of police shooting black men have resulted in unrest in many black communities, which may be contributing to the decline seen in blacks' life evaluations in Obama's second term.

Finally, Gallup research shows that Asians do well in many of the areas that drive positive life evaluations, including having enough money to buy what one needs, using strengths daily and making time for trips or vacations with family or friends. Each of these aspects of well-being strongly influences life evaluations – and in all cases, Asians substantially outpace their counterparts.

Survey Methods

Results are based on telephone interviews conducted Jan. 2-Dec. 30, 2008-2015, and Jan. 2-July 31, 2016, as part of the Gallup-Healthways Well-Being Index, with a random sample of adults aged 18 and older, living in all 50 U.S. states and the District of Columbia. The national sample size averaged 350,000 in 2008-2012, approximately 175,000 in 2013-2015 and about 105,000 for the first seven months of 2016. In each year since 2013, Gallup has interviewed about 130,000 whites, 16,000 blacks, 16,000 Hispanics and 4,000 Asians. The margin of sampling error for each reported racial/ethnic group is no more than ±1 percentage point in most cases, but climbs to ±1.6 points for Asians in 2016. All reported margins of sampling error include computed design effects for weighting.

August 31, 2016
IN U.S., SMOKING DIPS, BUT FEWER EATING HEALTHY SINCE '09

by Nader Nekvasil

Story Highlights

- *Fewer Americans, 64.2%, report eating healthy on any given day*
- *Percentage exercising regularly edges up slightly to 53.8%*
- *Smoking rate among U.S. adults drops to 18.0%*

This is the third article in a five-part series examining changes in Americans' health and well-being during Barack Obama's presidency.

WASHINGTON, D.C. – Americans' exercise and smoking habits have improved while their eating habits have worsened slightly over the nearly eight years of Barack Obama's presidency. These findings are based on interviews conducted daily from January 2008 through July 2016 as part of the Gallup-Healthways Well-Being Index.

So far in 2016, 64.2% of U.S. adults report that they ate healthy all day yesterday, which is on the lower end of what Gallup and Healthways have recorded since beginning to track this metric in 2008. The percentage of Americans who said they ate healthy peaked at 67.7% in 2010, but generally declined through 2013 and has remained steady since.

Did you eat healthy all day yesterday?

% Yes

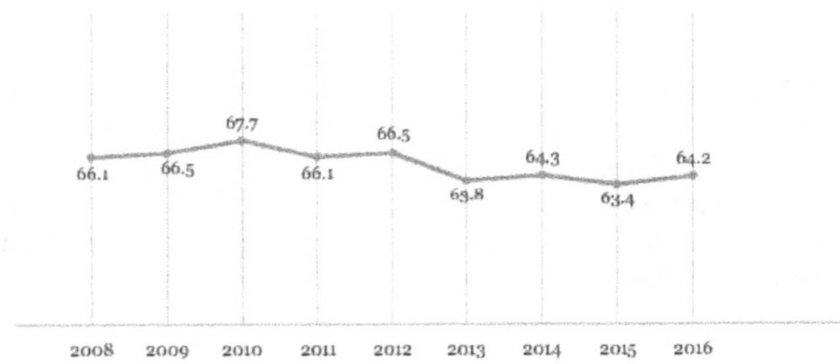

2016 data reflect Jan. 2-July 31, 2016
Gallup-Healthways Well-Being Index

GALLUP

While Americans' reports of healthy eating have declined slightly over the past eight years, the percentage who consume produce frequently has generally held steady. To measure produce consumption, Gallup and Healthways ask Americans to report on how many days they consumed five or more servings of fruits and vegetables in the past seven days.

Percentage of Americans Who Consume Produce Frequently

% who had five or more servings of fruits and vegetables at least four days last week

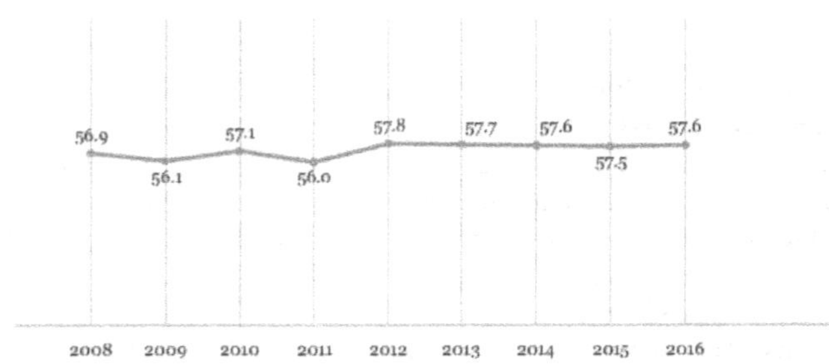

2016 data reflect Jan. 2-July 31, 2016
Gallup-Healthways Well-Being Index

GALLUP

One possible explanation for the slight decline in healthy eating while frequent produce consumption has remained steady is that more U.S. adults may be aware of the nutritional content of their food and drink. During his tenure, President Obama has made some strides in shedding light on proper nutrition. Some restaurants and vending machine owners have voluntarily posted nutrition information ahead of an FDA regulation requiring large restaurant chains and vending machine operators to list calorie information. And in May, the U.S. Food and Drug Administration approved new nutrition labels for the first time in more than 20 years. The updated labels include a new design, up-to-date nutritional science and different standards for serving size. The updated labeling is significant as Gallup previously found that 68% of Americans pay attention to nutrition labels either a great deal or a fair amount on food packages, more than the percentage who say the same about restaurant menus (43%).

Percentage Who Exercise Regularly Edged Up Slightly

The percentage of Americans who report exercising regularly has edged up in 2016 to 53.8%, and from a longer-term perspective, has increased 2.4 percentage points since 2008. To assess exercise habits, U.S. adults are asked to report on how many days in the past week they exercised for at least 30 minutes.

Percentage of Americans Who Exercise Regularly

% who exercised for 30 minutes or more at least three days last week

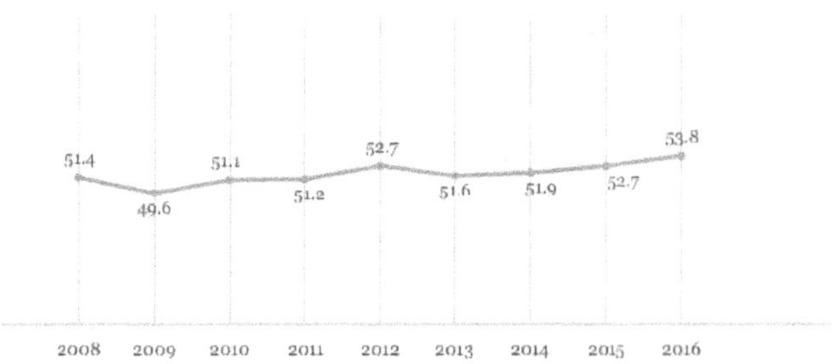

2016 data reflect Jan. 2–July 31, 2016
Gallup-Healthways Well-Being Index

GALLUP

But the quality of Americans' exercise may still be falling short of what is needed to achieve the maximum health benefits. According to the CDC, just 21% of U.S. adults are meeting the physical activity guidelines for both muscle-strengthening and aerobic activity.

U.S. Smoking Rate Continued to Decline

While Americans' exercise habits have improved slightly, their smoking habits have improved significantly, with the smoking rate dropping three points since 2009. The percentage of U.S. adults who smoke has declined nearly every year during Obama's two terms, a continuing trend that began long before Obama took office. The smoking rate among U.S. adults is now 18.0%, down from 21.0% in 2009.

Do you smoke?

% Yes

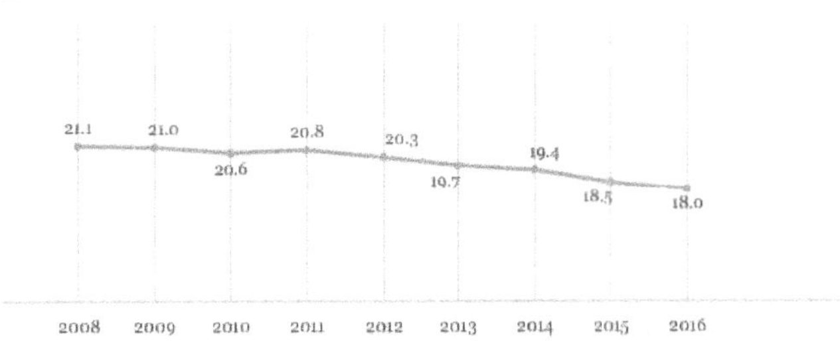

2016 data reflect Jan. 2–July 31, 2016
Gallup-Healthways Well-Being Index

GALLUP

Across age groups, the smoking rate has declined the most among young adults – those aged 18-29 – during Obama's years in office. Young adults had the highest smoking rate in the early 2000s, but their smoking rate is now closer to the national average. The percentage of U.S. adults who smoke varies widely by state, with residents of southern and Midwestern states more likely to smoke.

As the smoking rate has declined, Americans' negative views on smoking have persisted. More than half of U.S. adults say smoking should be illegal in all public places while an increasing percentage say that smoking should be totally illegal.

Bottom Line

A president can encourage citizens to live a healthy lifestyle and advocate for legislation and regulatory actions that promote healthy choices. President Obama and the first lady have taken some concrete steps in doing so by implementing initiatives such as Let's Move! to encourage regular exercise and leading the movement to update nutrition labels on food and drink. Obama also signed the Family Smoking Prevention and Tobacco Control Act in 2009, which gave the FDA the power to regulate tobacco products. Even so, it is unclear whether most Americans are aware of these actions and to what extent they might influence their behavior.

As Barack Obama completes his final term as president, U.S. adults' health habits have changed only marginally, with the exception of smoking. Although fewer U.S adults say they eat healthy, this decline could be a result of adults having a better understanding of what foods are nutritious, as opposed to making a deliberate choice to eat less healthy. Americans are slightly more likely to exercise frequently, but that alone is unlikely to be enough to reduce the record-high obesity rate. Regardless, the new low in smoking among U.S. adults is an encouraging sign that long-term improvement in health habits remains possible.

These data are available in Gallup Analytics.

Survey Methods

Results are based on telephone interviews conducted from 2008-2016 as part of the Gallup-Healthways Well-Being Index survey, with a random sample of 2,415,499 adults, aged 18 and older, living in all 50 U.S. states and the District of Columbia. For results based on the total sample of national adults, the margin of sampling error is ±.08 percentage points at the 95% confidence level. All reported margins of sampling error include computed design effects for weighting.

August 31, 2016

IN U.S., SLIM MAJORITY AGAIN SEES UNIONS AS HELPING ECONOMY

by Jeffrey M. Jones

Story Highlights

- *52% say unions help the U.S. economy, 41% say they hurt it*
- *In 2009, 39% said unions help the economy; 51% said they hurt it*
- *56% approval of unions still below the historical norm*

PRINCETON, N.J. – A slim majority of Americans, 52%, say labor unions mostly help the U.S. economy, while 41% believe unions mostly hurt it. After a sharp 14-point decline between 2006 and 2009 in the percentage of Americans who believe unions mostly help the economy, public opinion is essentially back to what it was before the recession.

Overall, do you think labor unions mostly help or mostly hurt ... the U.S. economy in general?

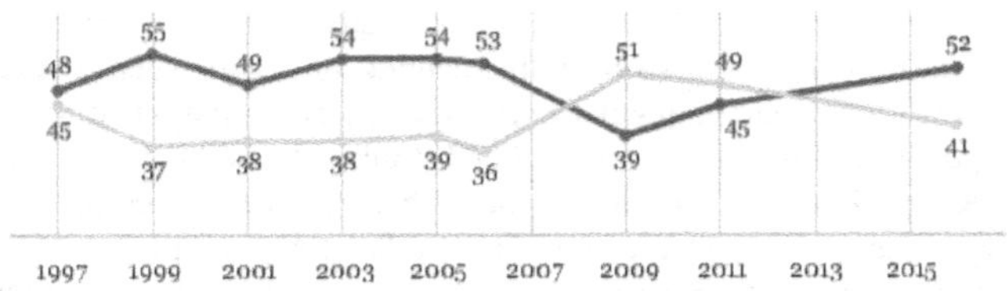

Democrats, Republicans and independents became less optimistic about unions' effect on the economy during and after the Great Recession, but all three groups have grown more positive. Republicans, the group showing the least amount of faith in unions' ability to help the economy, have not quite recovered to their pre-recession levels, but independents and Democrats have. Currently, 71% of Democrats, 53% of independents and 28% of Republicans believe unions mostly help the economy.

Perceptions That Labor Unions "Mostly Help" the U.S. Economy, by Political Party

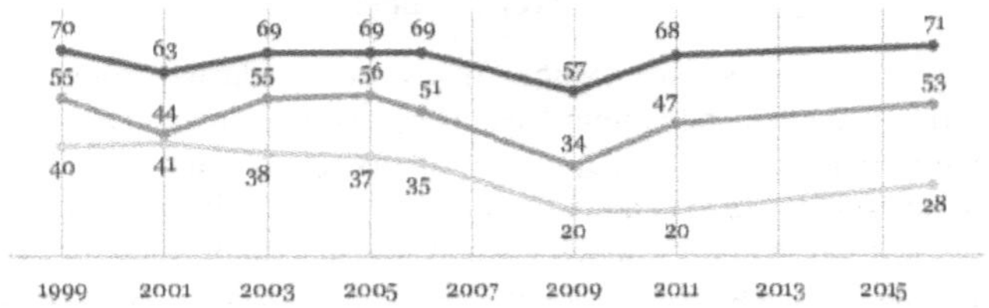

The results are based on Gallup's annual Work and Education poll. In this year's poll, conducted Aug. 3-7, Gallup asked Americans for the first time since 2011 to assess unions' effect on the U.S. economy, on unionized companies, and on union and nonunion workers.

Americans are most likely to say unions mostly help union workers themselves – 70% hold this view. That is nearly twice the percentage who say unions benefit workers who are not members of unions (38%). Fifty-five percent say unions mostly help companies where workers are unionized, similar to the 52% who say unions benefit the U.S. economy.

Americans' Views of Effect of Labor Unions

Overall, do you think labor unions mostly help or mostly hurt ...?

	Mostly help %	Mostly hurt %
Workers who are members of unions	70	24
The companies where workers are unionized	55	39
The U.S. economy in general	52	41
Workers who are not members of unions	38	54

Gallup

Americans' opinions of whether unions help unionized companies, union workers and nonunion workers all declined slightly in 2009 during the recession by four or five percentage points each. Those are much smaller declines than the 14-point drop in assessments of whether unions mostly helped the U.S. economy during the same year. The public's views of labor unions' effect on workers and companies are similar now to what they were before the recession.

Labor Union Approval at 56%

Americans have long approved of labor unions, including the 56% majority in the latest poll. Gallup first asked Americans whether they approved or disapproved of labor unions in 1936; since then, approval has averaged 62%, indicating Americans' current approval rating is below the historical norm.

Union approval fell to an all-time low of 48% in 2009 and has recovered modestly since then, though it has yet to reach the 59% it held in the last pre-recession reading. Americans were also less approving of unions when the economy declined in the late 1970s and early 1980s. Union approval reached its high points of 75% in 1953 and 1957 Gallup polls.

Do you approve or disapprove of labor unions?

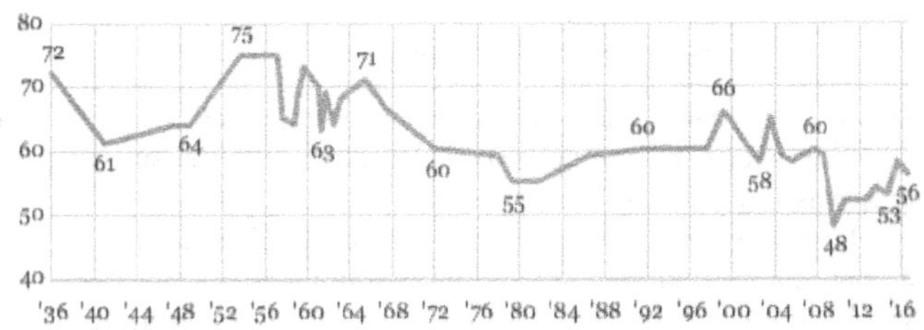

One reason recent opinions on unions have remained less positive than in the past is that Republicans have become increasingly negative toward them. Currently, 32% of Republicans approve of unions, compared with an average 43% approval from 2001 to 2007. Democrats' and independents' current approval ratings of unions – 78% and 57%, respectively – are essentially unchanged from 2001 to 2007 averages (76% of Democrats and 59% of independents).

Implications

Americans have historically evaluated unions more positively than negatively, a trend that continued even as union membership in the U.S. declined significantly in recent decades. It wasn't until the Great Recession that union approval dropped below the majority level and Americans' assessments of unions' effect on the economy, workers and companies also grew more negative at that time.

Now, Americans' opinions of unions have mostly recovered to what they were before the recession began. But their approval of labor unions remains slightly below pre-recession levels, largely because Republicans have become increasingly negative toward them. This is consistent with other trends toward greater partisan divides on political opinions such as presidential job approval and attitudes on policy issues such as global warming. That may make it difficult for labor union approval to return to the same level of support it enjoyed from the 1930s through the early 2000s, when approval ratings were mostly in the 60% range.

Historical data are available in Gallup Analytics.

Survey Methods

Results for this Gallup poll are based on telephone interviews conducted Aug. 3-7, 2016, with a random sample of 1,032 adults, aged 18 and older, living in all 50 U.S. states and the District of Columbia. For results based on the total sample of national adults, the margin of sampling error is ±4 percentage points at the 95% confidence level. All reported margins of sampling error include computed design effects for weighting.

September 01, 2016

AMERICANS' HEALTH ASSESSMENTS WORSEN DURING OBAMA YEARS

by Dan Witters and Diana Liu

Story Highlights

- *Americans are less likely to report "excellent" health now than in 2008*
- *Obesity and diabetes rates are steadily climbing*
- *High cholesterol has declined across all major racial/ethnic groups*

This is the fourth of a five-part series examining changes in Americans' health and well-being during Barack Obama's presidency.

WASHINGTON, D.C. — Americans' self-assessments of overall health have slipped since 2008. Currently, 19.0% of U.S. adults report that their health is "excellent," compared with 22.6% in 2008, before President Barack Obama took office. The percentage of U.S. adults who report "poor" or "fair" health has remained stable during this period at around 20%.

Overall Self-Assessments of Health in U.S., 2008-2016

"Would you say your own health, in general, is excellent, very good, good, fair or poor?"

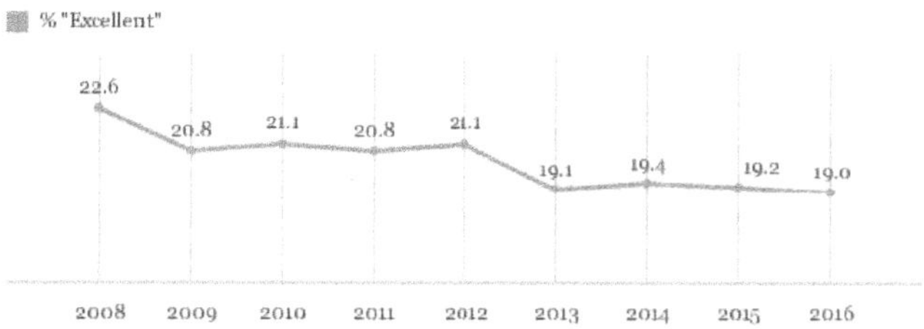

Gallup-Healthways Well-Being Index, 2008-2016 YTD
2016 results are from Jan. 2-July 31

GALLUP

This drop in reports of excellent health since 2008 is largest among those younger than 45, with no change measured among seniors aged 65 and older. Personal health assessments worsened across all four major racial and ethnic groups – whites, blacks, Hispanics and Asians – with the greatest drops coming from Asians (down 5.5 percentage points) and whites (down 3.8 points). Blacks' and Hispanics' assessments each dropped by less than two points.

Overall Health Assessments in U.S., by Age, 2008-2009, 2015-2016 YTD

Would you say your own health, in general, is excellent, very good, good, fair or poor? (% Excellent)

	2008 %	2009 %	2015 %	2016 YTD %	Change since 2008 (pct. pts.)
18 to 29	29.2	26.9	23.6	22.5	-6.7
30 to 44	26.8	24.2	20.5	20.5	-6.3
45 to 64	20.7	19.4	17.9	18.0	-2.7
65+	14.1	13.4	14.9	14.9	+0.8

2016 results are from Jan. 2-July 31
Gallup-Healthways Well-Being Index

While the percentage of adults who consider their health to be excellent has declined, the percentage who report ever having been diagnosed with various major chronic diseases presents a more mixed picture. Since 2008, obesity has increased by nearly three points to 28.3%, and lifetime diagnoses of diabetes have increased about one point to 11.5%, a statistically significant climb. Self-reports of clinical diagnoses of depression have also edged up since 2008.

On the other hand, the percentage of Americans who report having been diagnosed with high cholesterol in their lifetimes has declined by 3.5 points since 2008, while reports of high blood pressure and cancer are essentially unchanged.

Incidence of Key Health Indicators in U.S., 2008-2009, 2015-2016 YTD

	2008 %	2009 %	2015 %	2016 YTD %	Change since 2008 (pct. pts.)
Obesity	25.5	26.5	28.0	28.3	+2.8
High blood pressure (lifetime)	29.4	30.5	28.9	28.8	-0.6
High cholesterol (lifetime)	26.5	27.5	23.7	23.0	-3.5
Diabetes (lifetime)	10.6	11.0	11.4	11.5	+0.9
Cancer (lifetime)	6.9	7.2	7.2	7.0	+0.1
Depression (lifetime)	16.1	16.5	17.4	17.7	+1.6

2016 results are from Jan. 2-July 31
Gallup-Healthways Well-Being Index

Historically, blacks have disproportionately suffered from chronic conditions, including obesity and high blood pressure.

These results are based on more than 100,000 interviews thus far in 2016, 175,000 interviews conducted in 2015 and more than 350,000 interviews conducted in 2008 and 2009 as part of the Gallup-Healthways Well-Being Index. Unlike some government estimates of obesity, the Well-Being Index uses respondents' self-reported height and weight to calculate body mass index (BMI). It does not involve in-home clinical measurements, which typically result in higher obesity rates at a population level. All other chronic conditions are measured based on responses to the question: "Has a doctor or nurse ever told you that you have ___?"

Obesity's Overall Increase Driven Primarily by Whites

Whites' obesity rates have risen more since 2008 than those of blacks, Asians and Hispanics. Overall, the obesity rate among whites has climbed three points to 27.2% thus far in 2016. The remaining three groups, in turn, have all seen their obesity rates increase by less than two points during that time.

Obesity Trended, by Race/Ethnicity, 2008-2009, 2015-2016 YTD

Based on a BMI >30 via self-reported height and weight

	2008 %	2009 %	2015 %	2016 YTD %	Change since 2008 (pct. pts.)
Whites	24.2	25.2	27.0	27.2	+3.0
Blacks	35.1	36.2	35.6	36.9	+1.8
Asians	8.6	9.6	9.8	9.9	+1.3
Hispanics	27.4	28.3	28.6	28.6	+1.2

2016 results are from Jan. 2-July 31
Gallup-Healthways Well-Being Index

High cholesterol is the one major chronic condition that has diminished in the U.S. adult population over the course of the Obama era, even as the rate of obesity, often associated with high cholesterol, has continued to climb. The percentage of adults who have been diagnosed with high cholesterol has decreased across all four major racial and ethnic groups in the U.S.

Those with health insurance are more likely to have been diagnosed with most of the aforementioned chronic diseases than are those without insurance. Declining uninsured rates since 2013 could theoretically be playing a role in the increasing percentage of adults who have been diagnosed with any given condition in 2016 compared with the pre-Affordable Care Act era in 2008 or 2009. A Gallup analysis demonstrates that this potential influence has at best only a minor effect on change in diagnosis rates, at least thus far.

High Cholesterol Trended, by Health Insurance Status, 2008-2009, 2015-2016 YTD

Has a doctor or nurse ever told you that you have high cholesterol?

	2008 %	2009 %	2015 %	2016 YTD %	Change since 2008 (pct. pts.)
Insured	28.2	29.5	25.1	24.1	-4.1
Not insured	16.5	17.2	13.3	13.0	-3.5
Difference	11.7	12.3	11.8	11.1	-0.6

2016 results are from Jan. 2-July 31
Gallup-Healthways Well-Being Index

Implications

Obama's signature legislative achievement, the Patient Protection and Affordable Care Act (ACA), will ultimately be judged based largely on three major criteria: the reduction in the percentage of Americans without health insurance, the rate of increase in healthcare costs over time, and trends in the overall health of the American public. While the uninsured rate has declined since the ACA was fully implemented, the changes in various health conditions measured as a part of the Well-Being Index reveal a mixed picture.

The ongoing climb in both obesity and diabetes is likely tied to the decline in Americans' overall self-assessments of their general health. The percentages of adults who have been diagnosed with high blood pressure and cancer, however, are essentially unchanged, while the proportion who report having been diagnosed with high cholesterol has noticeably declined. Smoking is linked to high cholesterol, so it is possible that the decline in the high cholesterol rate is related partly to the ongoing decline in smoking that began decades ago and has continued throughout the Obama era. Despite this positive trend, the rising obesity rate remains a significant problem, as its incidence in the population is closely linked to the other chronic conditions.

Obesity is most effectively addressed through both a holistic approach to well-being and a realistic and personalized plan. "A fundamental shift to lifestyle management is what we see on the horizon to help slow and reverse the rising rates of obesity in our country," says Stacey Jensen, Senior Vice President at Healthways. "It is not a one-size-fits-most approach, but rather one that provides precision planning around meals and exercise that is tailored to meet an individual's needs. An effective plan should take into account topics such as what food individuals like, the amount of exercise they can commit to, and the availability of safe environments for exercise."

While conventionally understood influences on obesity such as poor exercise, smoking and eating habits are all strongly linked to obesity, so too are less obvious factors such as not having a safe place to exercise, struggling to afford food, being from a low-income household and suffering poor social well-being. Therefore, taking a holistic approach that focuses on Americans' purpose, social, financial and community well-being is an effective strategy to help reduce obesity and other chronic diseases, thus improving overall health in the U.S.

Survey Methods

Results are based on telephone interviews conducted Jan. 2-Dec. 30, 2008-2015, and Jan. 2-Jul. 31, 2016, as part of the Gallup-Healthways Well-Being Index, with a random sample of adults aged 18 and older, living in all 50 U.S. states and the District of Columbia. The national sample size was about 350,000 in 2008-2012, about 175,000 surveys in 2013-2015 and about 105,000 cases through the end of July 2016. In a typical year since 2013, about 130,000 whites, 16,000 blacks, 16,000 Hispanics and 4,000 Asians are interviewed. The margin of sampling error for each reported race or ethnic group is no more than ±1 percentage point in most cases, but climbs to ±1.6 percentage points for Asians in 2016. All reported margins of sampling error include computed design effects for weighting.

September 02, 2016

STANDARD OF LIVING RATINGS RISE DURING OBAMA PRESIDENCY

by Art Swift

Story Highlights

- *Standard of Living Index has risen overall since 2009*
- *Views of current standard of living have improved*
- *Views of standard of living as "getting better" have risen more sharply*

This is the fifth article in a five-part series examining changes in Americans' health and well-being during Barack Obama's presidency.

WASHINGTON, D.C. — Americans' ratings of their standard of living have increased since President Barack Obama took office in 2009, with the Gallup Standard of Living Index rising steadily for the past 7 ½ years.

Gallup U.S. Standard of Living Index, Yearly Averages

Are you satisfied with your standard of living, all the things you can buy and do? Right now, do you feel your standard of living is getting better or getting worse?

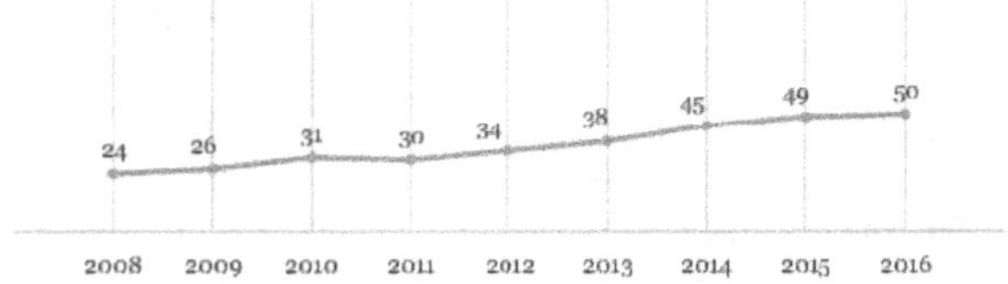

2016 data reflect Jan. 2-July 31, 2016, polling

GALLUP

When Obama entered the White House, the United States was in the midst of the Great Recession, which damaged the housing market, left many Americans out of work and caused the U.S. gross domestic product to plummet. For 2009, the Gallup Standard of Living Index averaged +26, little better than the +24 found in 2008. It has edged up in most years since then, and for the first seven months of 2016, it averaged +50.

Gallup's Standard of Living Index is a composite of Americans' responses to two questions: one asking U.S. adults whether they are satisfied or dissatisfied with their standard of living, and the other asking whether their standard of living is getting better or worse. The index has a theoretical maximum of 100 (if all respondents say they are satisfied with their standard of living and say it is getting better) and a theoretical minimum of -100 (if all respondents are dissatisfied with their standard of living and say it is getting worse).

Satisfaction With Current Standard of Living Has Increased Steadily

Americans have been largely satisfied with their current standard of living over the past eight years, even during the depths of the recession. At the beginning of the Obama presidency, 73% of Americans said they were satisfied with their current standard of living. By 2015, that figure had risen to 79%, and it is 80% so far in 2016.

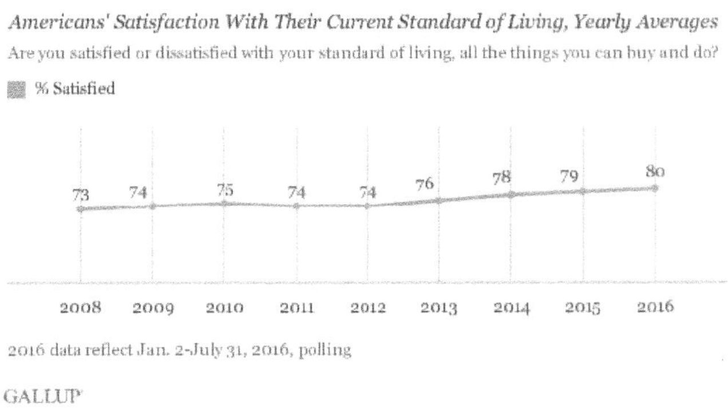

Future Expectations Have Risen More Sharply During Obama Years

Americans' expectations for their standard of living going forward have changed more significantly over the past eight years than their assessments of their current standard of living. In 2009, 42% of Americans said their standard of living was getting better, while nearly the same percentage, 40%, said it was getting worse. The percentage saying their standard of living is getting better has climbed steadily for the past 7 ½ years, amid battles over the federal budget and sequestration. In 2012, the percentage rose to 50%, and more recently, it moved into the 60% range. This range has held constant thus far in 2016.

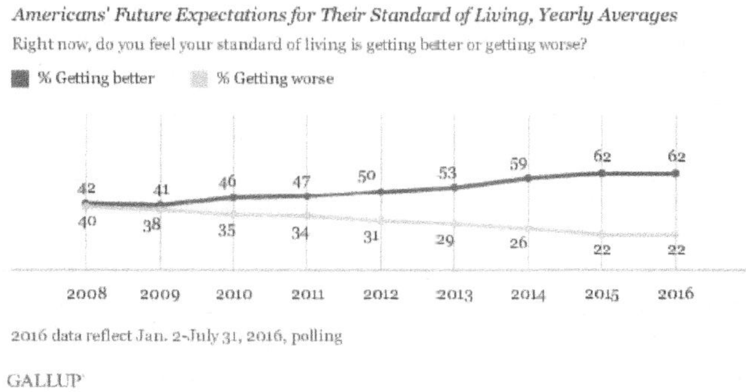

Standard of Living Ratings Rise Across Income Groups

Americans' evaluations of their standard of living have improved significantly across all income groups during the Obama era. The improvement is similar across all groups, even though those with lower incomes have lower Standard of Living Index scores than those with higher incomes.

Standard of Living Index, by Annual Household Income

	2008	2016 YTD	Change
Less than $24,000	3	25	+22
$24,000 to $59,999	19	45	+26
$60,000 to $89,999	35	54	+19
$90,000+	44	69	+25

Gallup, 2008 and 2016

Non-Hispanic black Americans have reported the highest gains in the Standard of Living Index during the Obama years, with a 34-point jump between 2008 and 2016 to date. Hispanics are next with a jump of 31 points, and registered the highest index score among ethnic groups and races, at 62 in 2016. Non-Hispanic white Americans have an index of 47 in 2016 so far, a jump of 22 points from their 25 index in 2008.

Standard of Living Index, by Racial/Ethnic Group

	2008	2016 YTD	Change
Non-Hispanic whites	25	47	+22
Non-Hispanic blacks	16	50	+34
Hispanics	31	62	+31

Gallup, 2008 and 2016

Bottom Line

Standard of living is a chief component of a person's financial well-being. Though Americans' views of the U.S. economy are now more negative than positive after having been slightly positive for part of 2014 and 2015, their assessments of their personal standard of living have always been positive and have improved during Obama's presidency.

The increase in perceived standard of living over the past seven-plus years reflects in large part the low starting point when Obama took office during the aftermath of a crippling recession. Since 2009, Americans' belief that their standard of living is getting better has increased steadily, as has been the case with other economic indicators such as job creation, and this is true across all income groups.

Financial well-being is about more than just income. It also reflects Americans' ability to manage their money to reduce financial stress. Those with lower incomes who manage their finances effectively could weather storms caused by a global recession. Yet even if there is another recession, it is possible that Gallup's Standard of Living Index will not dip considerably, especially the percentage who are satisfied with their current standard of living.

These data are available in Gallup Analytics.

Survey Methods

Results are based on telephone interviews conducted Jan. 2-Dec. 30, 2008-2015, and Jan. 2-July 31, 2016, as part of the Gallup U.S. Daily survey, with a random sample of adults aged 18 and older, living in all 50 U.S. states and the District of Columbia. The national sample size averaged 350,000 in 2008-2012, approximately 175,000 in 2013-2015 and about 105,000 for the first seven months of 2016. In each year since 2013, Gallup has interviewed about 130,000 whites, 16,000 blacks, 16,000 Hispanics and 4,000 Asians. The margin of sampling error for each reported racial/ethnic group is no more than ±1 percentage point in most cases, but climbs to 1.6 percentage points for Asians in 2016. All reported margins of sampling error include computed design effects for weighting.

September 06, 2016
U.S. ECONOMIC CONFIDENCE UP IN AUGUST AS DNC RALLY PERSISTS

by Andrew Dugan

Story Highlights

- *Economic Confidence Index averages -11 in August, up from -15 in July*
- *Democrats' confidence rose in late July and remained higher in August*
- *Current conditions index at -2; Economic outlook index at -19*

WASHINGTON, D.C. — The Gallup U.S. Economic Confidence Index rose to a five-month high of -11 in August, up from -15 in July. This month's four-point gain notwithstanding, the index remains well below its post-recession high of +3 in January 2015 and is one point below this March's -10, the monthly high for 2016.

Gallup's U.S. Economic Confidence Index – Monthly Averages

January 2008-August 2016

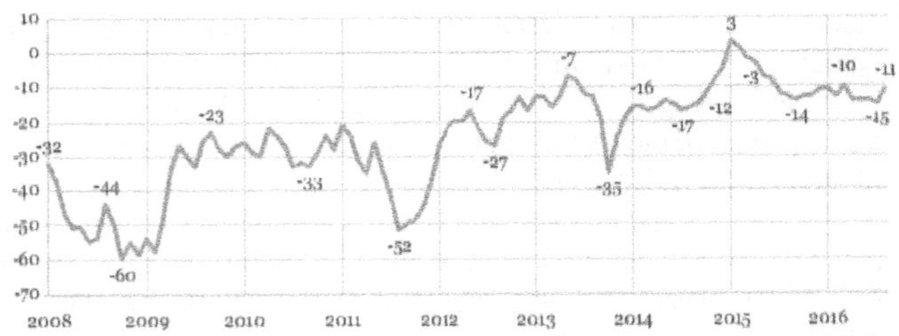

Gallup Daily tracking

GALLUP'

The recent uptick in Americans' confidence in the economy began in the final week of July when the index's weekly average rose six points to -10. Democrats' brighter assessments of the economy after the Democratic National Convention largely drove this increase, with their economic confidence growing 13 points to +28 in the last week of July. Democrats' higher level of confidence persisted throughout August. Meanwhile, Republicans saw no comparable gains in economic confidence over this time period.

Democrats' confidence in the economy held at that higher level in August, averaging +26 on Gallup's index, up from +13 for July. In contrast, Republicans' already low confidence slipped to -46 in August from -41 in July. Independents' confidence improved by four points in August but remained net negative at -14.

Economic Confidence by Self-Identified Party Affiliation

January 2015-August 2016

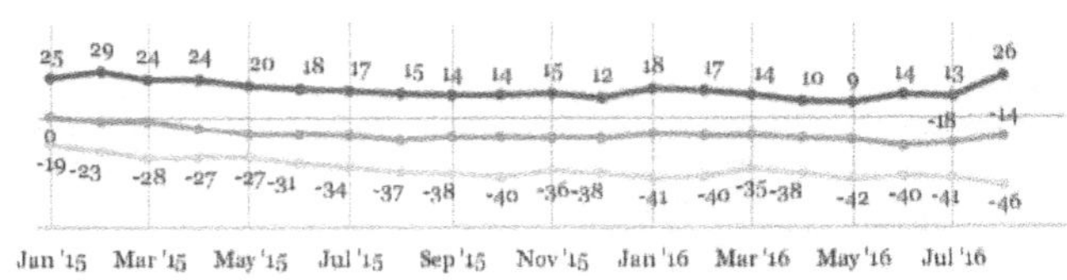

Gallup Daily tracking

GALLUP'

Americans More Positive About Economy's Current State Than Its Future Direction

Gallup's U.S. Economic Confidence Index is the average of two components: how Americans rate current economic conditions and whether they feel the economy is improving or getting worse. The index has a theoretical maximum of +100 if all Americans say the economy is doing well and improving, and a theoretical minimum of -100 if all Americans say the economy is doing poorly and getting worse.

In August, 27% of U.S. adults described the current conditions of the economy as "excellent," or "good," while 29% said conditions were "poor," yielding a current conditions index score of -2. This is up slightly from a current conditions score of -5 in July.

Gallup's U.S. Economic Confidence Index Components -- Monthly Averages

January 2015-August 2016

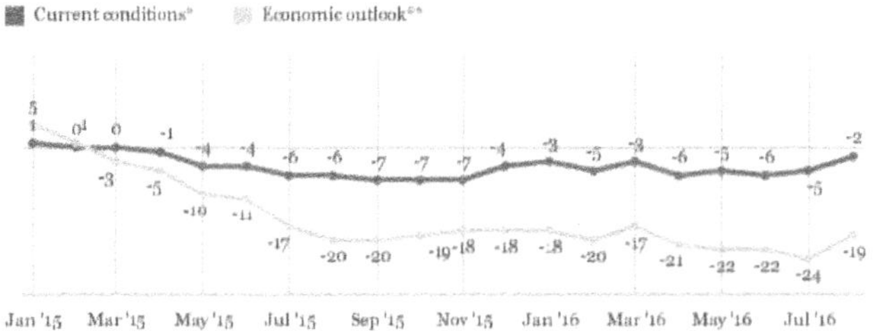

* % (Excellent + Good) minus % Poor

** % Getting better minus % Getting worse

Gallup Daily tracking

GALLUP

The economic outlook index rose in August to -19 from July's -24. The August outlook score reflects the 38% of Americans who said the economy was "getting better" and the 57% who said it was "getting worse."

Though the outlook score improved slightly in August, Americans' views of the direction of the economy remain low compared with the recent past: The outlook index has fallen from its apex of +5 in January 2015 to as low as -24 in July of this year and now stands at -19. By contrast, Americans' assessments of current economic conditions have remained relatively stable over this same time frame: The -2 score observed last month is only a few points below the January 2015 high of +1, and the index fell no lower than -7 in the intervening months.

There are many possible explanations for this drop in Americans' economic outlook, including the rebound in gas prices that began around the spring of 2015. Another possible reason is the uncertainty surrounding the 2016 presidential election – both Democrats' and Republicans' economic outlook scores have fallen sharply since January 2015. Thanks to the post-DNC rally, however, Democrats' economic outlook is recovering.

These data are available in Gallup Analytics.

Survey Methods

Results for this Gallup poll are based on telephone interviews conducted Aug. 1-31, 2016, on Gallup Daily tracking, with a random sample of 15,175 adults, aged 18 and older, living in all 50 U.S. states and the District of Columbia. For results based on the total sample of national adults, the margin of sampling error is ±1 percentage point at the 95% confidence level. All reported margins of sampling error include computed design effects for weighting.

September 06, 2016

U.S. SPENDING RETURNS TO MORE TYPICAL LEVELS IN AUGUST

by Justin McCarthy

Story Highlights

- *Daily spending reports averaged $91 last month*
- *August spending down $9 from unusually high July spending*
- *Higher-earning Americans' spending average down sharply*

WASHINGTON, D.C. — Americans' daily self-reports of spending averaged $91 in August, down from $100 in July, which was the highest average for any month since July 2008. Last month's average is in line with the $89 reported in August 2015, but slightly below the averages for the same month in 2013 ($95) and 2014 ($94).

Amount of Money Americans Report Spending "Yesterday," Monthly Averages

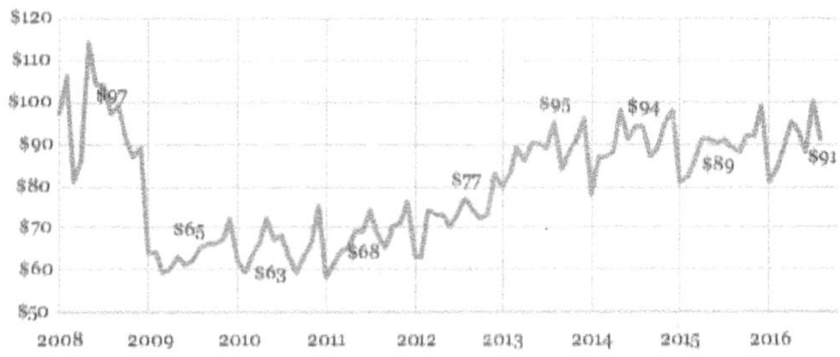

Note: Figures shown are for August of each year.

Gallup U.S. Daily tracking

GALLUP

These results are based on Gallup Daily tracking interviews conducted throughout August. Gallup asks Americans each night to report how much they spent "yesterday," excluding normal household bills and major purchases such as a home or car. The measure gives an indication of discretionary spending.

Since December 2012, Americans' daily spending estimates have consistently averaged $80 or higher in all but one month. By contrast, in the four years prior, which included part of the Great Recession and periods of high unemployment that ensued, monthly spending averages were as low as $58 and never above $77.

The spending average for August is on par with the average of $90 for 2016 so far. In Gallup's nearly nine-year trend, August has generally not been a standout month for spending, ranking neither among the highest nor the lowest spending months in most years.

Looking forward, Americans typically report less spending on average in September than in August, including each year since 2010. On this basis, it's not likely spending will rise in the coming month.

Higher-Earning Americans' Spending Average Slid Last Month

Both higher- and lower-earning Americans reported lower spending on average in August than in July. The drop was more pronounced among Americans whose annual household incomes are $90,000 or higher, whose self-reported daily spending average fell $21, to $140. This earning group consistently reports spending a lot more on average than lower-income Americans, and its spending estimates tend to vary more over time.

Spending dropped less in August among Americans whose annual household incomes are lower than $90,000. Spending among this group dropped only $3 to an average of $72. Monthly averages for lower-earning Americans have been much steadier over time compared with those who earn $90,000 or more annually.

Consumer Spending by Annual Household Income, August 2015 to August 2016

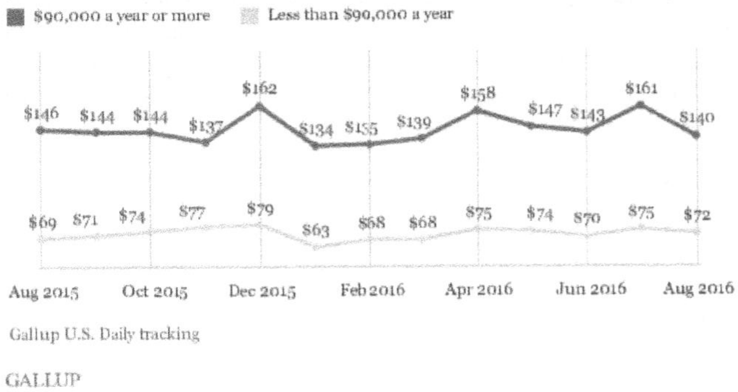

Bottom Line

After reporting higher-than-usual discretionary spending in July, Americans pulled back slightly to more typical levels in August. The average for spending in August is still on par with the 2016 average so far, and remains healthy compared with sub-$80 figures from 2009 to 2012.

The dip in spending does, however, come amid a slowing of spending in manufacturing and construction industries. But given Americans' improved confidence in the U.S. economy last month, it doesn't appear that their return to normal spending is a reaction to larger economic forces.

These data are available in Gallup Analytics.

Survey Methods

Results for this Gallup poll are based on telephone interviews conducted Aug. 1-31, 2016, on the Gallup U.S. Daily survey, with a random sample of 15,249 adults, aged 18 and older, living in all 50 U.S. states and the District of Columbia. For results based on the total sample of national adults, the margin of error for the spending mean is ±$4 at the 95% confidence level. All reported margins of sampling error include computed design effects for weighting.

September 07, 2016

CLINTON, TRUMP FAVORABLE RATINGS REMAIN DEFLATED

by Lydia Saad

Story Highlights

- *At 38%, Clinton's favorable rating is one point from her record low*
- *Trump's favorable rating is worse, at 34%, but still above his low*
- *Blacks' views of Clinton have slipped since pre-convention period*

PRINCETON, N.J. — After sinking in August from their convention highs, the favorable ratings for Donald Trump and Hillary Clinton show little to no positive momentum as the campaign passes the symbolic Labor Day milestone. Clinton's current 38% favorable rating essentially ties her personal low of 37%, first reached during the GOP convention. Trump's latest rating, at 34%, is just a bit better than where he stood at the close of the Democratic convention (33%).

Candidate Favorable Ratings Among U.S. Adults

Seven-day rolling averages from July 1-7, 2016, through Aug. 31-Sept. 6, 2016

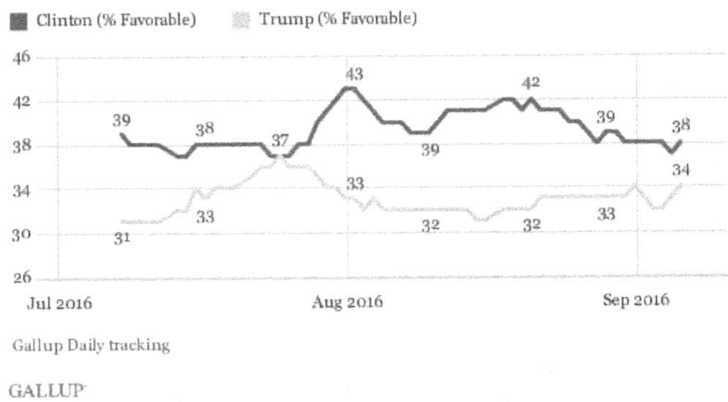

Today's low favorable ratings for the major party candidates mean that their unfavorable ratings are correspondingly high: 58% for Clinton and 62% for Trump. Clinton's unfavorable rating matches her campaign high, recorded during the Republican convention. Trump's is slightly below his record high, 66%, last reached in April during the competitive phase of the Republican primaries.

These trends are based on seven-day rolling averages of Gallup Daily tracking interviews with U.S. adults. The latest figures are based on interviews conducted Aug. 31-Sept. 6, 2016.

Both candidates' images changed slightly during the convention period in the second half of July, showing improvements during their own party's convention and declines during the other. But those changes proved fleeting, and neither candidate is much better off today than before the party conventions.

The following charts detail each candidate's key subgroup ratings in the first half of July, prior to the back-to-back conventions, and in the most recent seven-day tracking period of Aug. 31-Sept. 6.

Clinton's overall favorable rating is the same, at 38%. Her current ratings among men and women, all age groups, and all party groups are within a few percentage points of their pre-convention levels.

The notable exception to her subgroup stability is her favorable rating among blacks, which, at 63%, is seven points below where it stood in the first half of July. It is also her lowest weekly favorable rating among blacks this year, after occasionally dipping to as low as 65%.

Hillary Clinton Favorable Ratings

Pre-convention period compared with most recent weekly averages

	July 1-17 %	Aug. 31-Sept. 6 %	Change (pct. pts.)
U.S. adults	38	38	0
Men	34	32	-2
Women	43	43	0
18 to 29	34	33	1
30 to 49	39	40	+1
50 to 64	41	38	-3
65+	39	39	0
Non-Hispanic whites	28	29	+1

	July 1-17 %	Aug. 31-Sept. 6 %	Change (pct. pts.)
Non-Hispanic blacks	70	63	-7
Hispanics	59	56	-3
Republicans	7	6	-1
Independents	30	30	0
Democrats	77	79	+2

Gallup Daily tracking

Trump Still at Square One With Key Demographic Groups

Trump's current 34% rating among national adults is just slightly better than his average 32% rating in the first half of July – the same as his average since January. At the same time, like Clinton's, most of Trump's subgroup ratings are remarkably similar to where they were before the start of the conventions – most within two points of his July 1-17 scores. The one notable change is a five-point increase in his rating among Republicans, which helps account for his two-point overall increase in favorability between the two periods.

Donald Trump Favorable Ratings

Pre-convention period compared with most recent weekly averages

	July 1-17 %	Aug. 31-Sept. 6 %	Change (pct. pts.)
U.S. adults	32	34	+2
Men	37	39	+2
Women	27	28	+1
18 to 29	18	18	0
30 to 49	29	31	+2
50 to 64	39	43	+4
65+	42	44	+2
Non-Hispanic whites	41	44	+3
Non-Hispanic blacks	7	8	+1
Hispanics	14	12	-2
Republicans	69	74	+5
Independents	28	27	-1
Democrats	7	6	-1

Gallup Daily tracking

Bottom Line

As noted previously on Gallup.com, the slight boost the conventions provided to the candidates' national images – pushing Clinton's favorable rating to 43% and Trump's to 38% – were short-lived, and neither has since picked up as the calendar moves past Labor Day. Clinton remains near her record-low favorability, with the added concern that her favorability is slumping among blacks. Trump's 34% favorable rating is better than his 2016 low of 27%, recorded in April, but remains near the 32% to 34% range seen throughout August and still lags Clinton's current rating.

Rather than offering a sign that voters are finally warming up to one candidate or the other, the latest ratings underscore the historic nature of this year's election as one featuring the two most unpopular nominees since the advent of scientific polls.

Historical data are available in Gallup Analytics.

Survey Methods

The results for this Gallup poll are based on telephone interviews conducted Aug. 31-Sept. 6, 2016, on the Gallup Daily tracking survey, with a random sample of 3,561 adults, aged 18 and older, living in all 50 U.S. states and the District of Columbia. For results based on the total sample of national adults, the margin of sampling error is ±2 percentage points at the 95% confidence level. Results based on subgroups are associated with higher margins of error. All reported margins of sampling error include computed design effects for weighting.

September 07, 2016

U.S. JOB CREATION INDEX HOLDS STEADY AT POST-RECESSION HIGH

by Jim Norman

Story Highlights

- Job Creation Index at +33 for fourth straight month
- Government job creation at highest level in eight years

WASHINGTON, D.C. — U.S. workers' reports of hiring activity at their places of employment in August held steady at a post-recession high for the fourth month in a row. Gallup's Job Creation Index, a measure that began in January 2008, now stands at +33, the same as in May, June and July.

Job Creation Index -- Monthly Averages, January 2008-August 2016

Percentage of U.S. workers who say their employers are hiring new workers minus the percentage who say their employers are letting workers go

Numbers shown are August readings for each year

GALLUP

The latest results, based on interviews conducted Aug. 1-31 with 17,894 full- and part-time U.S. workers, continue a pattern seen over the past 19 months, during which the index never dipped below +29.

Gallup asks a random sample of employed adults each day whether their employer is hiring new people and expanding the workforce, not changing the workforce, or letting people go and reducing the size of the workforce. In August, 44% of workers reported an increase and 11% a decrease, resulting in the Job Creation Index score of +33.

Since the index bottomed out at -5 in early 2009 in the midst of the nation's economic crash, it has taken a slow, bumpy path upward, with numerous minor downticks from month to month. However, every August reading since 2010 has shown improvement over the previous August. The near-negligible one-point improvement this

August from last August's +32 is the smallest since the index began its climb.

Government, Non-Government Hiring Show No Major Change

The Job Creation Index for both government and non-government workers showed no material change in August. The index for government workers (local, state and federal) rose a single point to +32 – the highest level since Gallup began identifying government workers in August 2008. This score is based on 45% of government workers reporting their employers are hiring new workers and 13% reporting their workplace is letting people go. The government index is up from +26 a year ago when 42% reported their government employers were adding workers and 16% reported workers were being let go.

Meanwhile, the index for non-government workers in August stood at +34. Forty-four percent report their employers are hiring new workers, 10% say they are cutting back.

Government Hiring Workers and Letting Workers Go, August 2008-August 2016

Percent of workers who say their company or employer is hiring new people and expanding the size of its workforce, or letting people go and reducing the size of its workforce

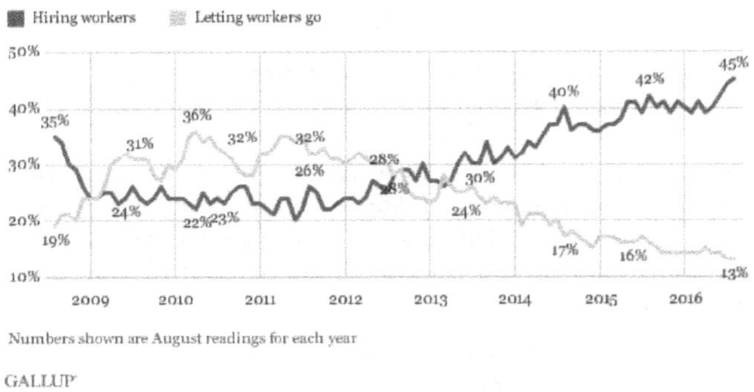

After the economic crash of 2008, net government hiring moved into the red in early 2009 and stayed there for more than three years, not moving into positive territory until late 2012. A major gap opened between non-government and government workers, driven in large part by the high percentage of government workers reporting that their employers were letting people go. In April 2010, 36% in government jobs said their employers were letting people go, while 19% in non-government jobs reported cutbacks at their workplace. The percentage of non-government workers reporting cutbacks has stayed in the teens since then, but the percentage of government workers reporting cutbacks did not dip below 20% until 2014.

Bottom Line

U.S. workers in August were far more likely to report a growing workforce than a shrinking one at their workplaces, sustaining the solid hiring reports that are now well into the second year. The 19-month period that the index has stayed within a four-point range (+29 to +33) is the longest period of time since the index began in which it has been so stable.

The move toward hiring and away from cutting back continues to hold steady in the government sector this year, where reports from government workers give evidence of solid gains over the last 12 months.

Survey Methods

Results for this Gallup poll are based on telephone interviews conducted Aug. 1-31, 2016, on Gallup Daily tracking, with a random sample of 17,894 workers, aged 18 and older, living in all 50 U.S. states and the District of Columbia. For results based on the total sample of workers, the margin of sampling error is ±1 percentage point at the 95% confidence level. All reported margins of sampling error include computed design effects for weighting.

September 08, 2016
MORE AMERICANS NEGATIVE THAN POSITIVE ABOUT ACA

by Art Swift

Story Highlights

- *51% disapprove of ACA; 44% approve*
- *18% say the law has helped their families; 29% say it has hurt them*
- *Long term, most Americans say law will hurt or not make much difference*

WASHINGTON, D.C. — In a summer that saw many insurers drop out of the Affordable Care Act's health insurance exchanges, Americans' support for the healthcare law continues to be slightly more negative than positive. Now, 44% of Americans support the law, also known as Obamacare, and 51% disapprove of it – similar to what Gallup measured last November.

Do you generally approve or disapprove of the 2010 Affordable Care Act, signed into law by President Obama that restructured the U.S. healthcare system?

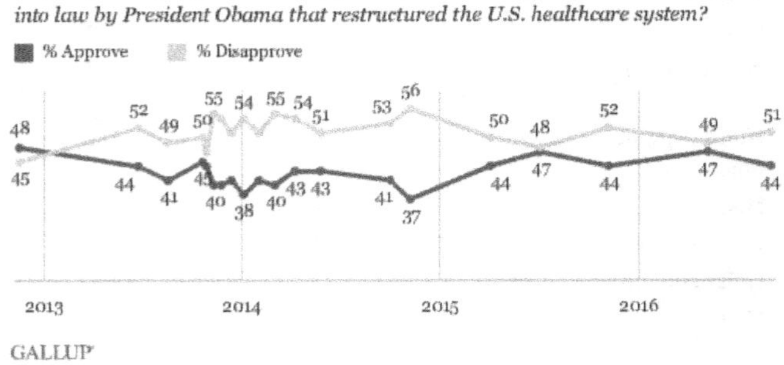

Insurance giant Aetna decided in August to pull out of most of the healthcare exchanges it had entered in 2014 and announced it would not expand into any more states. This news followed similar announcements from other major insurers such as United Healthcare and Humana. There have also been reports that the cost of individual plans offered through health insurance exchanges in many states is likely to jump significantly in the coming years as federal subsidies disappear. Since the spring, the percentage who approve of the law has declined slightly from 47% to 44%, while disapproval has risen two percentage points to 51%.

Percentage of Americans Saying ACA Hurt Their Family Rises to New High

Currently, 29% of Americans say Obamacare has hurt them and their family, up from 26% in May, and the highest Gallup has measured to date. Meanwhile, the percentage who say the ACA has helped their family dropped from 22% to 18%. The bulk of Americans, 51%, continue to say the law has "had no effect." As more provisions of the law have taken effect over the years, the "no effect" percentage has dropped from the first reading of 70%, in early 2012.

The Affordable Care Act's Effect on Families

As you may know, a number^ of the provisions of the healthcare law have already gone into effect. So far, has the law -- [ROTATED: helped you and your family, not had an effect (or has it) hurt you and your family]?

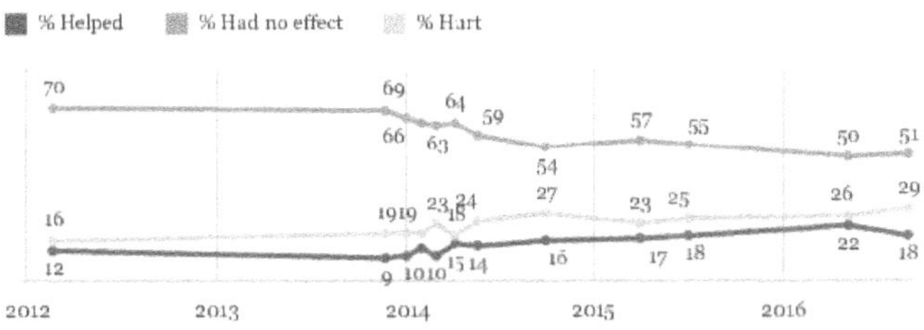

^ Wording from 2012 to April 2014: "a few"

GALLUP

Because Republicans are much more likely (46%) than Democrats (9%) to say the new law has hurt their family, it is possible that some of those who say "hurt" are giving a political response rather than an actual report on the law's effect on their lives.

The number of uninsured Americans has declined under Obamacare, a positive outcome of the law. But the actions of Aetna and other insurers raise doubts about whether the law is sustainable financially, not only for private insurance companies but also for the federal and state governments that help shoulder the costs, and whether insurance will be affordable for Americans themselves.

Americans Divided on Long-Term Effects

More Americans expect the ACA to make their family's healthcare situation worse in the long run (36%) than say it will make it better (24%). Thirty-seven percent say they expect the law not to make much difference. The current percentage who believe the law will make things better reflects no change since Gallup began asking this question in 2012.

Americans' Views of the ACA's Ability to Improve Their Family's Healthcare Situation

In the long run, how do you think the healthcare law will affect your family's healthcare situation? Will it -- [ROTATED: make things better, not make much difference (or will it) make things worse]?

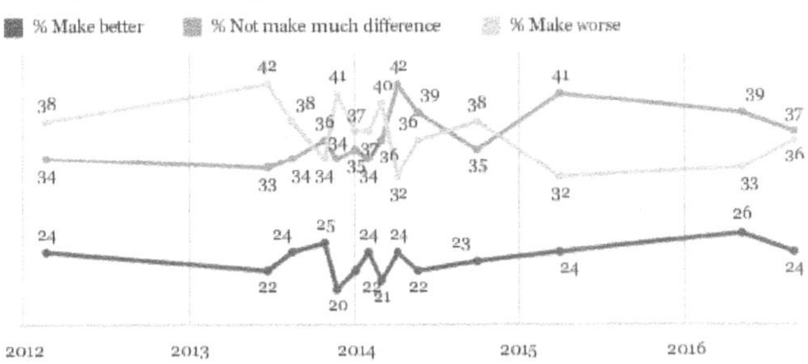

GALLUP

Gallup also asked Americans about the law's effect on the U.S. so far. Thirty-seven percent say the law has helped the healthcare situation in the U.S., while 45% say it has hurt it. A much smaller percentage (12%) say it has had no effect.

Bottom Line

Six years after passage of the ACA, it appears that much of the American public hasn't embraced the healthcare law and still holds serious reservations about it. Although opinion has fluctuated somewhat over time, Americans have remained at least slightly more negative than positive about the law for three years. This partly reflects the highly politicized views of the controversial law – with Republicans overwhelmingly opposed to it and unlikely to change their views, while Democrats have shown consistently high support.

At the same time, more Americans than at any previous point are reporting that the law has hurt their healthcare situation. The percentage who believe their family will be hurt in the long run by Obamacare is up slightly since May. It is possible that these feelings are related to negative media attention to the law this summer; that the lack of positive news has returned sentiments to previous levels; or that they simply reflect underlying political predispositions to the law. In any case, President Barack Obama's signature legislative achievement still has miles to go before a majority of the public considers it a positive. With Hillary Clinton vowing to strengthen Obamacare, and Donald Trump pledging to undo it, the healthcare law's future hangs in the balance this election season.

Historical data are available in Gallup Analytics.

Survey Methods

Results for this Gallup poll are based on telephone interviews conducted Aug. 30-31, 2016, on the Gallup U.S. Daily survey, with a random sample of 1,015 adults, aged 18 and older, living in all 50 U.S. states and the District of Columbia. For results based on the total sample of national adults, the margin of sampling error is ±4 percentage points at the 95% confidence level. All reported margins of sampling error include computed design effects for weighting.

September 09, 2016

ABOUT SIX IN 10 CONFIDENT IN ACCURACY OF U.S. VOTE COUNT

by Justin McCarthy

Story Highlights

- *Confidence in accurate vote counting was higher from 2004-2007*
- *About three in four Democrats confident, compared with just half of GOP*
- *Americans more confident in accuracy of count at their voting facility*

WASHINGTON, D.C. — About six in 10 Americans are confident that votes will be accurately cast and counted in the coming election. This is similar to their confidence level in 2008, but down from levels from 2004 to 2007 when confidence ranged between 71% and 75%.

Confidence in the Accuracy of U.S. Vote Counting, 2004-2016

How confident are you that, across the country, the votes will be accurately cast and counted in this year's election -- very confident, somewhat confident, not too confident or not at all confident?

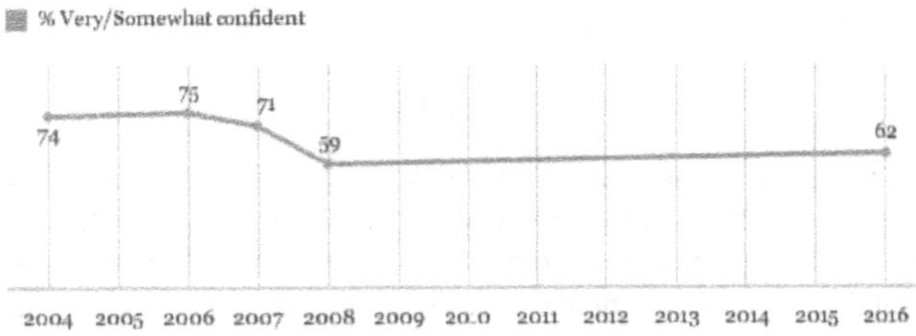

Note: 2004 wording: "... the votes for president will be accurately cast and counted in this year's election"; 2007 wording: "... the votes will be accurately cast and counted in next year's election"

GALLUP'

Despite the controversy over ballot accuracy in the 2000 election, Gallup's trend shows that the highest level of voting confidence was in 2004 – the first time Gallup polled on this question – four months before that year's presidential election. Confidence remained similarly high in the 2006 midterm and in December 2007, shortly before the 2008 presidential primaries and caucuses started. Before the 2008 election, confidence in the accuracy of vote counting had dropped sharply, perhaps as an indirectly related response to the global financial crisis that sent Americans' satisfaction with the way things were going in the U.S. into the single digits. Eight years later, the confidence level in voting accuracy is not much higher.

Prominent political figures and former federal security officials raised concerns about a compromised vote count leading up to Gallup's latest measurement, taken in an Aug. 15-16 poll.

In April, supporters of Democratic primary candidate Bernie Sanders raised questions after more than 100,000 voters were purged from the New York City Board of Elections. More recently, Republican presidential nominee Donald Trump suggested that the election is going to be rigged, saying courts that have thrown out state voter ID laws have left voting systems vulnerable to fraud.

Though these examples of doubts about the election's accuracy could be politically motivated, there are real threats. Due to the patchwork of state voting systems, some of which have electronic vulnerabilities, many security officials warn of the prospect of foreign hacking, especially in the wake of Russia's suspected involvement in the successful infiltration of the Democratic National Committee's email system. Just after Gallup's August poll, the FBI alerted that one state's Board of Election site was compromised and that another state's election system had an attempted intrusion.

Dems Much More Confident Than Republicans in Vote Count Accuracy

Perhaps related to their party nominee's view, only half of Republicans say they are "very confident" or "somewhat confident" that votes will be accurately cast and counted in this year's election. This is the lowest Gallup has recorded for the GOP in five measures, and much lower than current confidence among independents (59%) and Democrats (77%).

Americans have expressed more confidence when a president of their same party occupies the White House, helping to explain why Republicans were much more confident in the vote count during George W. Bush's presidency and why Democrats are much more confident under President Barack Obama. However, both parties expressed equally slim confidence in the accuracy of vote counting in 2008, at 57%.

Confidence in the Accuracy of U.S. Vote Counting, 2004-2016, by Party I.D.

How confident are you that, across the country, the votes will be accurately cast and counted in this year's election -- very confident, somewhat confident, not too confident or not at all confident?

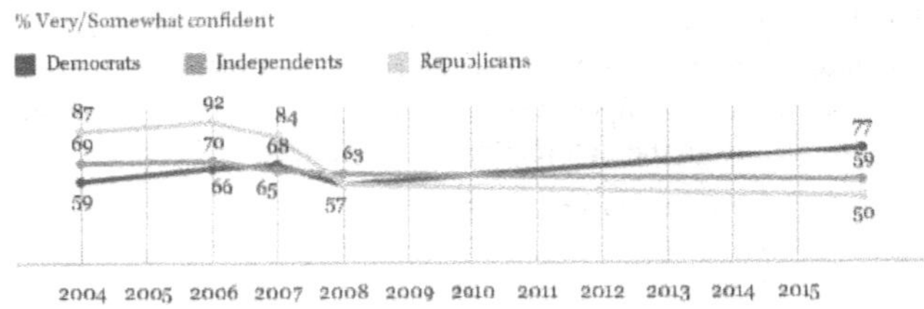

Note: 2004 wording: "... the votes for president will be accurately cast and counted in this year's election"; 2007 wording: "... the votes will be accurately cast and counted in next year's election"

GALLUP'

Americans More Confident in Their Own Voting Facilities

While many Americans have doubts about the integrity of the vote count in the nation at large, they are much more likely to express confidence in the facilities where they vote.

About four in five Americans (81%) say they are very or somewhat confident in the accuracy of vote casting and counting at their local polling station, though this is down from 91% in 2006 and 88% in 2007.

Confidence in Accurate Vote Counting at Americans' Own Voting Facilities

How confident are you that, at the voting facility where you vote, the votes will be accurately cast and counted in this year's election – very confident, somewhat confident, not too confident or not at all confident?

	% Very/Somewhat confident	% Not at all/Not very confident
2016	81	16
2007*	88	12
2006	91	8

* 2007 wording: "... in next year's election"
Gallup

The current measures are consistent with Americans' tendency to rate local conditions and their own personal situation better than the situation in the country as a whole, including on crime, healthcare and economic matters.

Bottom Line

Though a majority of Americans still say they have faith in the accuracy of U.S. elections, the level of confidence isn't what it once was. And with legitimate threats to state voting systems, Americans have reason to have some doubt about their accuracy, while some may subscribe to a more politically motivated idea of it being rigged.

There is a political element to views of the integrity of the vote count, however. Americans have been more likely to feel confident when a member of their party occupies the White House. And these political bents are reflected in Republicans' and Democrats' respective level of support for voter ID laws and early voting.

A strong majority of U.S. adults have faith in their local polling facility's accuracy, suggesting that they are less concerned about their own vote not being cast and counted properly as they are about fraud elsewhere in the country. Their lower confidence about voting accuracy nationally could have ramifications for a new president whose constituents have doubts about the legitimacy of the win.

Historical data are available in Gallup Analytics.

Survey Methods

Results for this Gallup poll are based on telephone interviews conducted Aug. 15-16, 2016, on the Gallup U.S. Daily survey, with a random sample of 1,013 adults, aged 18 and older, living in all 50 U.S. states and the District of Columbia. Each question was asked of a randomly selected half-sample of approximately 500 adults. For results based on each half-sample of national adults, the margin of sampling error is ±6 percentage points at the 95% confidence level. All reported margins of sampling error include computed design effects for weighting.

September 09, 2016
MORE FAVOR MAJOR GOVERNMENT ROLE IN ASSISTING MINORITIES

by Jeffrey M. Jones

Story Highlights

- *38% favor major government role to help minorities*
- *Up from 32% in 2013 and 27% in 2011*
- *64% of blacks, 28% of whites favor major government role*

PRINCETON, N.J. — As both major party presidential candidates tout ways their policies will benefit blacks and other minority groups, Americans are now, more so than in recent years, open to a prominent government role to help racial minorities. Currently, 38% say the government should have "a major role" in trying to improve the social and economic position of minorities, up from 32% in 2013 and 27% in 2011, but similar to what Gallup measured in 2004 and 2005.

How much of a role, if any, do you think the government should have in trying to improve the social and economic position of blacks and other minority groups in this country -- a major role, a minor role or no role at all?

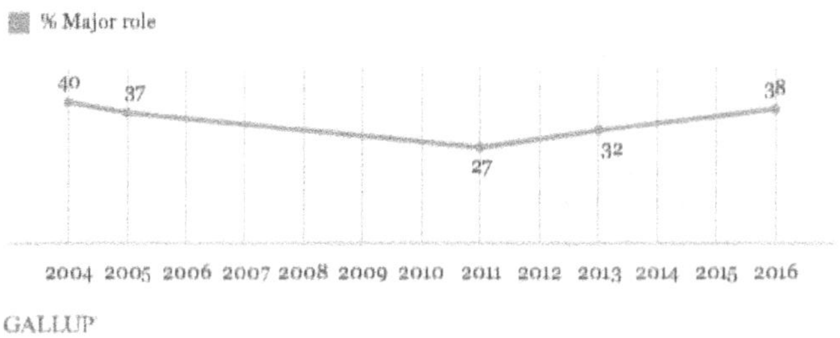

The June 7-July 1 Gallup Minority Rights and Relations survey also finds that 40% of Americans want the government to play "a minor role" in helping minorities, while 22% do not want the government to have any role in this area. The latter figure is down slightly from 26% in 2011 but remains up significantly from 14% in 2004.

Gallup's 2011 and 2013 polls were conducted at a time of historically low trust in government and subdued concern about matters relating to race. While Americans' trust in government remains low, they have grown increasingly concerned about race relations since 2013 following a series of highly publicized incidents in which black men were killed in confrontations with white police officers.

Blacks have consistently been much more likely than whites to prefer a major role for the government in improving the position of minorities in the U.S. In the latest poll, 64% of blacks and 28% of whites hold this view.

Both blacks' and whites' opinions have shown similar changes over the last 12 years. Support for a major government role was relatively high in 2004 and 2005, fell sharply in 2011 and stayed relatively low in 2013 before increasing significantly this year.

Preference for a Major Government Role to Improve the Social and Economic Positions of Minority Groups, by Race

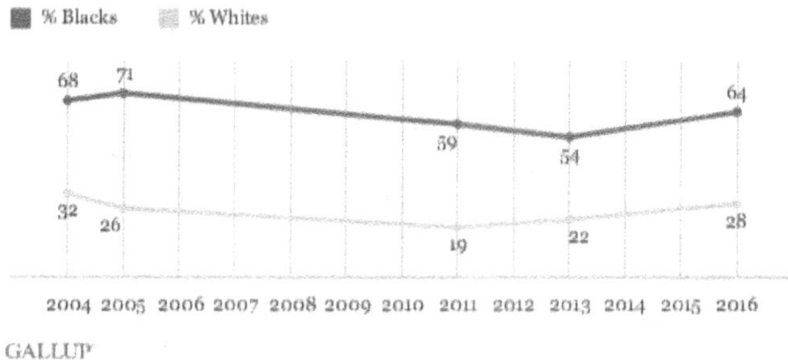

At 63%, Hispanics are just as likely as blacks to favor a major government role to help minority groups. Hispanics' preferences have varied less than blacks' and whites' over time, ranging from a low of 60% favoring a major role in 2013 to a high of 67% in 2004.

Democrats Favor Larger Government Role Than Republicans Do

Beyond race, there is a major political divide on this question that reflects the political parties' long-standing views of the appropriate role of government. Sixty-three percent of Democrats, but only 15% of Republicans, say the government should have a major role in assisting minority groups. More than twice as many Republicans, 33%, favor no government role as favor a major one. Independents' views are closer to those of Republicans than Democrats, as 33% of independents believe the federal government should have a major role.

Support for a major government role was lower among all party groups in 2011 and 2013 than in the mid-2000s, and all have shown an increase since 2013. But Democrats are more likely today than in 2004 and 2005 to favor a major government role, while Republicans are less likely to do so. That shift could be an example of increasing party polarization on key issues, but it may also reflect the way partisans' attitudes are influenced by the party of the president, with a Republican president in 2004 and 2005 and a Democratic president today.

Preference for a Major Government Role to Improve the Social and Economic Positions of Minority Groups, by Political Party

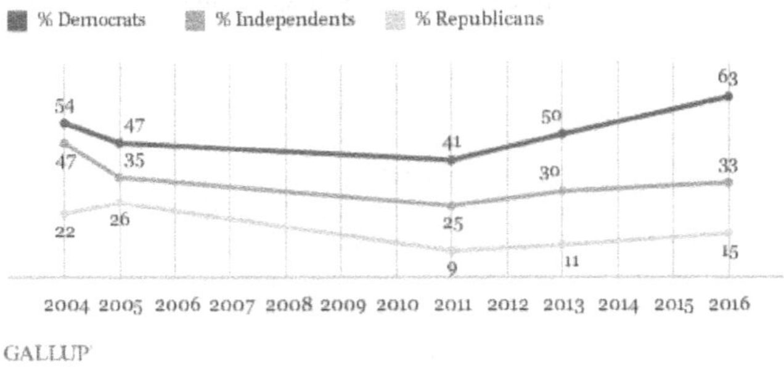

Women are significantly more likely than men to say the government should have a major role in improving the position of minorities. Notably, this gender difference holds across racial and political groups. Women may have more empathy than men, and that may influence the degree to which they support government action to assist disadvantaged groups.

Gender Differences in Preference for a Major Government Role to Improve the Social/Economic Position of Racial Minorities

	Women %	Men %	Difference pct. pts.
National adults	44	32	12
Whites	33	24	9
Blacks	72	54	18
Hispanics	73	53	20
Democrats	68	57	11
Independents	37	30	7
Republicans	18	12	6

June 7-July 1, 2016

Implications

Race has been a major factor in the presidential campaign. Hillary Clinton won the Democratic nomination over Bernie Sanders in large part because of her greater support among blacks and other minority voters. Republican presidential candidate Donald Trump has recently made overt appeals to black voters, undaunted by their historically overwhelming support for Democratic presidential candidates.

Clinton and Trump have both argued that their policies – in particular, their economic plans – would benefit blacks and other minority voters. Beyond that, the Clinton campaign has outlined a number of specific policy proposals to directly address racial inequality and injustice. Trump's argument has mainly focused on the failures of Democratic policies to improve the situation for many blacks, but he recently called for a new civil rights agenda in a highly publicized visit to a Detroit church.

Americans' greater openness to a major government role to improve the position of minorities means such policy proposals could make more of a difference for voters in this year's presidential election than in the last presidential election.

Historical data are available in Gallup Analytics.

Survey Methods

Results for this Gallup poll are based on telephone interviews conducted June 7-July 1, 2016, with a sample of 3,270 adults, aged 18 and older, living in all 50 U.S. states and the District of Columbia, who had previously been interviewed in the Gallup Daily tracking poll and agreed to be re-interviewed for a later study. The sample is weighted to be representative of U.S. adults.

For results based on the total sample of national adults, the margin of sampling error is ±3 percentage points at the 95% confidence level. For results based on the sample of 1,320 non-Hispanic whites, the margin of sampling error is ±4 percentage points at the 95% confidence level. For results based on the sample of 912 non-Hispanic blacks, the margin of sampling error is ±5 percentage points at the 95% confidence level. For results based on the sample of 906 Hispanics, the margin of sampling error is ±6 percentage points at the 95% confidence level.

All reported margins of sampling error include computed design effects for weighting.

September 12, 2016
POPULAR PRESIDENTS FACTOR LITTLE IN NON-INCUMBENT ELECTIONS

by Lydia Saad

Story Highlights

- *Two of three popular incumbents saw party's nominee lose*
- *Current U.S. satisfaction in a gray zone as election indicator*
- *Economic confidence similar to 2012, when Obama won*

PRINCETON, N.J. — The Ronald Reagan presidency offers the most recent historical clues as to whether President Barack Obama's popularity could affect voters' choices for president in November. Like Obama, Reagan was earning job approval ratings in the low to mid-50s in the second half of his eighth year. And the Republican nominee for president that year, George H.W. Bush, won the election. In contrast, two second-term presidents with even higher job approval ratings – Bill Clinton in 2000 and Dwight D. Eisenhower in 1960 – each saw their party's candidate lose the election.

Presidential Approval of Outgoing Presidents

% Approve in August-October of final year in office

	Aug %	Sep %	Oct %
2016: Barack Obama (D)	52	50	–
Outgoing presidents whose party won			
1988: Ronald Reagan (R)	53	54	51
Outgoing presidents whose party lost			
2008: George W. Bush (R)	33	31	25
2000: Bill Clinton (D)	62	60	58
1968: Lyndon Johnson (D)	35	42	–
1960: Dwight Eisenhower (R)	63	58	58

	Aug %	Sep %	Oct %

Based on U.S. adults
Gallup

Al Gore is one of two candidates – the other being Republican Richard Nixon who narrowly lost the popular vote in 1960 – who failed to inherit the high popularity of their party's sitting president and enjoy an easy win. The 2000 election, however, requires a footnote because Gore won the popular vote by 0.5% but ended up losing the Electoral College.

The 1968 election was another example of a close race in the popular vote; however, the outcome – Nixon's victory – conformed with the outgoing Democratic incumbent Lyndon B. Johnson's relatively low job approval rating amid extensive public concern about the Vietnam War. Similarly, the 2008 election was another logical case of the opposing party candidate – Obama – winning an open race when the two-term incumbent, George W. Bush, was highly unpopular.

This hodgepodge of outcomes relative to presidential approval in non-incumbent election years sharply contrasts with incumbent re-election years when the president's job approval rating has been a strong indicator of a second term.

High U.S. Satisfaction Also Not a Guarantee for President's Party

Gallup has found useful relationships between incumbent re-election and other measures of the nation's mood, namely Americans' satisfaction with the direction of the country and their degree of concern with the national economy. However, both metrics have less predictive value in non-incumbent years.

Data on the "country's direction" question are not available for 1960 and 1968. However, the readings in 1988, 2000 and 2008 indicate that, as is the case with a president's job approval rating, U.S. satisfaction is not destiny for the president's party. While extremely low public satisfaction with the country's direction in October 2008 (9%) may have doomed the Republican presidential nominee, extraordinarily high satisfaction in 2000 (63%) did not ensure a Democratic win. Only in 1988 did high satisfaction correspond with the sitting president's party retaining the White House. Today's 27% U.S. satisfaction rating is on the low side, but not nearly as low as in 2008.

Americans' Satisfaction With Direction of the U.S. Under Outgoing Presidents

% Satisfied in August-October of final year in office

	Aug %	Sep %	Oct %
2016: Barack Obama	27	–	–
2008: George W. Bush	17	21	9
2000: Bill Clinton	63	–	–
1988: Ronald Reagan	–	56	–

Based on U.S. adults
Gallup

U.S. satisfaction is a bit easier to interpret in the context of incumbent re-election years, as every president running when satisfaction was 30% or higher won, while the only president running when it was lower – George H.W. Bush in 1992 – lost.

Weak Economic Ratings Matter More Than Strong Ones

Gallup's economic indicators offer better news for the Democrats, as the economy is not nearly as dominant a national concern in Americans' minds as it was in 2008, even though it isn't as remote of a concern as it was in 2000. Thirty-five percent of Americans name a major economic problem as one of the nation's top problems, which is higher than the 17% found in October 2000 but well below the 69% in October 2008.

Also, according to the Gallup Economic Confidence Index, Americans' overall view of the economy today tilts slightly more negative than positive, with a -12 index score. While that is nowhere near the highly positive reading in October 2000 (+44), it is not nearly as negative as the -65 recorded at the same point in 2008. Perhaps most notably, the Economic Confidence Index today is nearly identical to where it stood when Obama was re-elected in 2012, and thus it may not be a great liability for Hillary Clinton.

Americans' Economic Views Under Outgoing Presidents

Data shown are for August-October in final year in office

	Aug %	Sep %	Oct %
Mentions of key economic issues as Most Important Problem			
2016: Barack Obama	61	–	–
2008: George W. Bush	59	60	69
2000: Bill Clinton	–	–	21
Gallup Economic Confidence Index	Index	Index	Index
2016: Barack Obama	-12	–	–
2008: George W. Bush	-46	-39	-65
2000: Bill Clinton	+52	–	+44

Based on U.S. adults
Gallup

Bottom Line

Ultimately, all three dimensions – approval of the incumbent president, satisfaction with the direction of the country and perceptions of the U.S. economy – point to a similar conclusion. The mood of the country is not a good indicator of the outcome of open-seat presidential elections, at least not when the mood is good, such as it was in 2000 and to a lesser extent in 1960. A sour public mood – as in 2008 and 1968 – may have more influence in open elections, making it difficult for the president's party to hold the White House.

Additionally, the reality that the president's party has lost in four of the last five open presidential elections suggests voters may simply be ready for a change after a president has served two terms.

The bottom line for the 2016 election is that, while Obama's relatively high job approval ratings may make it easier for Clinton to make her case to the voters, attaching herself to the incumbent is not as simple as in 2000 when all of the major indicators of public mood were positive. Further, even if all of the indicators were positive, the historical patterns show Clinton's election would be far from guaranteed.

The deciding factor could be something entirely different, namely Americans' reaction to the candidates as people. Gallup trends since 1992 show that the candidate with the higher favorable rating always wins. Thus far, Clinton has the upper hand in favorability, but it is within the context of both major party candidates maintaining unprecedentedly low favorable ratings, so it is not assured that the historical pattern of "the better-liked candidate always wins" will apply.

Historical data are available in Gallup Analytics.

Survey Methods

Results for President Obama's job approval rating and U.S economic confidence are based on telephone interviews conducted Sept. 6-8, 2016, on the Gallup U.S. Daily survey, with a random sample of 1,520 adults, aged 18 and older, living in all 50 U.S. states and the District of Columbia. For results based on the total sample of national adults, the margin of sampling error is ±3 percentage points at the 95% confidence level. All reported margins of sampling error include computed design effects for weighting.

Results for U.S. satisfaction and the Most Important Problem are based on Gallup's August Work and Education Survey, conducted by telephone Aug. 3-7, 2016, with a random sample of, 1,032 adults, aged 18 and older, living in all 50 U.S. states and the District of Columbia. For results based on the total sample of national adults, the margin of sampling error is ±4 percentage points at the 95% confidence level. All reported margins of sampling error include computed design effects for weighting.

September 13, 2016
U.S. WORKERS STILL WORRY MOST ABOUT BENEFITS CUTS

by Jeffrey M. Jones

Story Highlights

- *30% worry about having benefits reduced*
- *20% worry about pay cut, 19% about being laid off*
- *Worker worries have eased since 2014 after spiking in 2009*

PRINCETON, N.J. — More U.S. workers say they worry about having their benefits reduced (30%) than worry about having their wages cut (20%), being laid off (19%), having their hours cut back (17%), or their company moving their jobs overseas (8%). Benefits cuts consistently have been the top worry since Gallup first asked the question in 1997. U.S. workers' worries about these possibilities generally have eased since 2014 after rising sharply following the financial crisis and staying elevated during the ensuing period of high unemployment.

U.S. Workers' Worries About Possible Job Setbacks

Next, please indicate whether you are worried or not worried about each of the following happening to you, personally, in the near future.

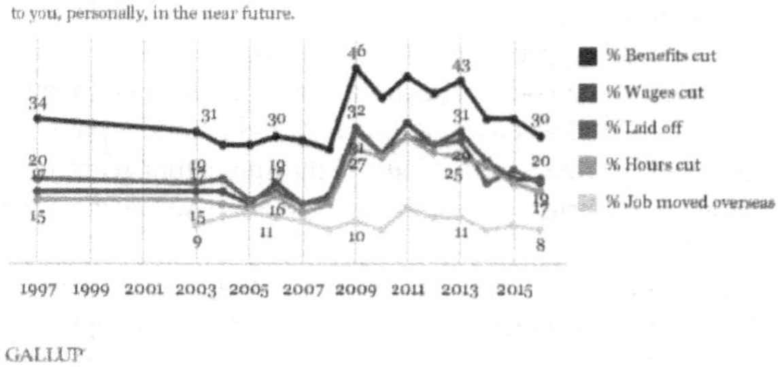

The data are based on Gallup's annual Work and Education poll, conducted each August. U.S. workers' concern about having their benefits cut spiked to 46% in 2009 and did not show sustained recovery until falling to 34% in 2014. The 30% who worry about benefits reductions today is essentially back to where it was before the September 2008 financial crisis.

Workers' concerns about having their wages cut or their hours reduced remain at least slightly higher than they were at any point before the 2007-2009 recession. While the 19% worried about being laid off is also higher than just before the financial crisis (15%), it is similar to what Gallup measured in the late 1990s and early 2000s.

Relatively few American workers worry about their company moving jobs overseas – the one concern that did not dramatically increase after the financial crisis.

Nearly Half of Government, Union Workers Fear Benefits Cuts

Government workers and unionized workers are significantly more likely than nongovernment and nonunion workers to worry about having their benefits reduced. According to combined data from the 2014-2016 Work and Education surveys, 46% of government workers and 45% of union workers say they worry their benefits will be reduced. That compares with 32% of those employed by a private company and 31% of nonunion workers.

Government workers, many of whom are also unionized, often have more generous benefits packages than private sector workers, and thus more to lose if their employers cut benefits. Previous Gallup research showed government workers and, to a lesser extent, union workers are more satisfied with their retirement, health insurance and vacation benefits than nongovernment and nonunion workers, respectively.

Gallup consistently has found a gap between union and nonunion workers' concerns about having their benefits cut, perhaps because each new round of collective bargaining brings the possibility of reduced benefits.

By contrast, government and private sector workers had similar levels of worry about benefits reductions before the financial crisis. Both groups grew more concerned from 2009 to 2013 about losing their benefits, but the increase was sharper among government workers. Government workers may have grown more concerned because government spending drew greater scrutiny as many state governments struggled to balance their budgets and the federal debt became a more salient political issue in those years. Now, private sector employee worries about benefits cuts are essentially back to where they were before the financial crisis, while government workers' worries remain significantly higher than before.

Percentage of Government vs. Private Sector Workers Worried About Having Their Benefits Reduced

	2005-2008 %	2009-2013 %	2014-2016 %
Government workers	33	56	46
Private sector workers	30	41	32

Aggregated data from Gallup annual Work and Education polls

The combined 2014-2016 data also reveal that concerns about job setbacks vary for different types of workers.

- Part-time workers (36%) are twice as likely as full-time workers (17%) to say they worry their hours will be cut back. In fact, a reduction in hours is part-time workers' top worry, surpassing benefits cuts (30%), being laid off (27%), and having their pay cut (23%).

- Professionals or executives (12%) are far less likely than blue-collar workers (26%) and white-collar workers who are not professionals or executives (22%) to worry about having their hours cut. Most professional and executive workers report they are paid a salary while most blue-collar (and nonprofessional/executive white-collar) workers say they are paid by the hour.
- Blue-collar workers are also most likely among employee groups to worry about their company moving jobs overseas, although the 14% who worry is still small on an absolute basis. In comparison, 5% of professional workers and 7% of nonprofessional white-collar workers worry that their company will move jobs overseas.

Aside from these differences, the various employee groups express generally similar worry about the other job setbacks tested in the survey.

Implications

It is clear the financial crisis and periods of high unemployment caused an increasing number of U.S. workers to feel insecure in their jobs, including worrying about their pay, benefits and whether they would keep their jobs at all. Those fears remained elevated for several years after the recession before finally showing some signs of receding in the last three years. Americans' various job worries are not all back to prerecession levels, but those that haven't already recovered are getting closer to that mark.

A lasting effect of the recession appears to be heightened worry about benefits cuts among public sector employees. Some state and local governments have struggled to balance their budgets and have been forced to re-examine whether they can pay promised levels of retirement and health benefits for current and past employees. As a result, some governments have proposed benefits cuts as a way to close budget shortfalls, which persist in some states and localities even as the economy has improved in recent years.

Historical data are available in Gallup Analytics.

Survey Methods

Results for this Gallup poll are based on telephone interviews conducted Aug. 3-7, 2016, with a random sample of 521 adults, aged 18 and older, living in all 50 U.S. states and the District of Columbia, who are employed full or part time. For results based on the total sample of workers, the margin of sampling error is ±6 percentage points at the 95% confidence level. All reported margins of sampling error include computed design effects for weighting.

September 14, 2016
AMERICANS' TRUST IN MASS MEDIA SINKS TO NEW LOW

by Art Swift

Story Highlights

- *32% say they have "a great deal" or "a fair amount" of trust*
- *14% of Republicans express trust, down from 32% last year*
- *Confidence drops among younger and older Americans*

WASHINGTON, D.C. — Americans' trust and confidence in the mass media "to report the news fully, accurately and fairly" has dropped to its lowest level in Gallup polling history, with 32% saying they have a great deal or fair amount of trust in the media. This is down eight percentage points from last year.

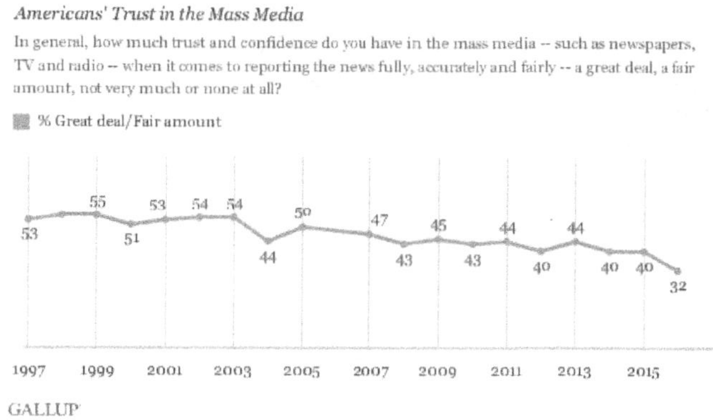

Gallup began asking this question in 1972, and on a yearly basis since 1997. Over the history of the entire trend, Americans' trust and confidence hit its highest point in 1976, at 72%, in the wake of widely lauded examples of investigative journalism regarding Vietnam and the Watergate scandal. After staying in the low to mid-50s through the late 1990s and into the early years of the new century, Americans' trust in the media has fallen slowly and steadily. It has consistently been below a majority level since 2007.

Republicans Fuel Drop in Media Trust

While it is clear Americans' trust in the media has been eroding over time, the election campaign may be the reason that it has fallen so sharply this year. With many Republican leaders and conservative pundits saying Hillary Clinton has received overly positive media attention, while Donald Trump has been receiving unfair or negative attention, this may be the prime reason their relatively low trust in the media has evaporated even more. It is also possible that Republicans think less of the media as a result of Trump's sharp criticisms of the press. Republicans who say they have trust in the media has plummeted to 14% from 32% a year ago. This is easily the lowest confidence among Republicans in 20 years.

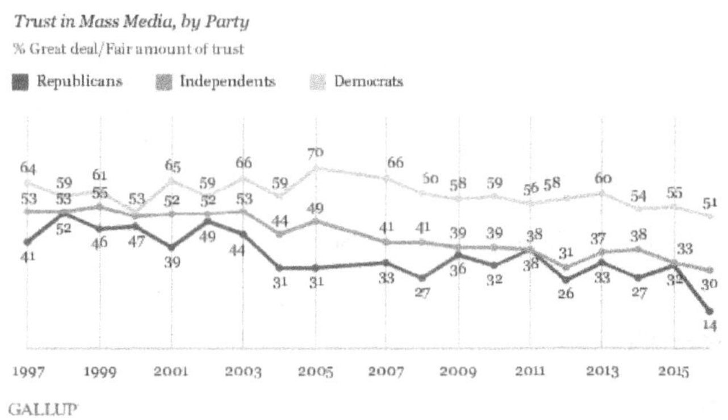

Democrats' and independents' trust in the media has declined only marginally, with 51% of Democrats (compared with 55% last year) and 30% of independents (versus 33% last year) expressing trust. Over the past 20 years, Democrats have generally expressed more trust than Republicans in the media, although in 2000, the two parties were most closely aligned, with 53% of Democrats and 47% of Republicans professing trust.

Trust in Mass Media Falls Across Age Groups

Older Americans are more likely than younger Americans to say they trust the media, but trust has declined among both age groups this year. Currently, 26% of those aged 18 to 49 (down from 36% last year) and 38% of those aged 50 and older (down from 45%) say they have a great deal or fair amount of trust in the media.

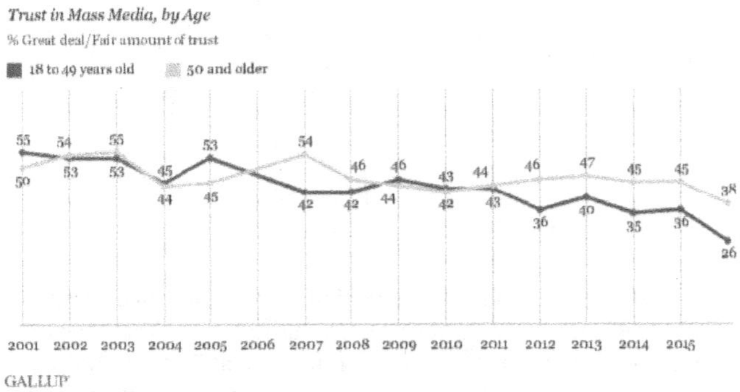

In 2001, younger Americans (55%) were more likely than older Americans (50%) to express trust and confidence in mass media. This gap emerged again in 2005 when 53% of 18- to 49-year-olds had trust and 45% of those 50 and older expressed the same sentiment. Yet in the past decade, older Americans have mostly had more confidence than younger Americans, and this year, the gap between these age groups is 12 points. And 2016 marks the first time that confidence among older Americans has dropped below 40% in polling since 2001.

Bottom Line

The divisive presidential election this year may be corroding Americans' trust and confidence in the media, particularly among Republicans who may believe the "mainstream media" are too hyperfocused on every controversial statement or policy proposal from Trump while devoting far less attention to controversies surrounding the Clinton campaign. However, the slide in media trust has been happening for the past decade. Before 2004, it was common for a majority of Americans to profess at least some trust in the mass media, but since then, less than half of Americans feel that way. Now, only about a third of the U.S. has any trust in the Fourth Estate, a stunning development for an institution designed to inform the public.

With the explosion of the mass media in recent years, especially the prevalence of blogs, vlogs and social media, perhaps Americans decry lower standards for journalism. When opinion-driven writing becomes something like the norm, Americans may be wary of placing trust on the work of media institutions that have less rigorous reporting criteria than in the past. On the other hand, as blogs and social media "mature," they may improve in the American public's eyes. This could, in turn, elevate Americans' trust and confidence in the mass media as a whole.

Historical data are available in Gallup Analytics.

Survey Methods

Results for this Gallup poll are based on telephone interviews conducted Sept. 7-11, 2016, with a random sample of 1,020 adults, aged 18 and older, living in all 50 U.S. states and the District of Columbia. For results based on the total sample of national adults, the margin of sampling error is ±4 percentage points at the 95% confidence level. All reported margins of sampling error include computed design effects for weighting.

September 15, 2016
AMERICANS' SATISFACTION WITH HEALTHCARE SYSTEM EDGES DOWN

by Zac Auter

Story Highlights

- *65% of Americans satisfied with healthcare system, down from 67% in 2014*
- *Americans with government health plans most satisfied*
- *Republicans much less satisfied than Democrats*

WASHINGTON, D.C. — Sixty-five percent of Americans are satisfied with the way the healthcare system works for them, down slightly from 67% in 2014. Americans with Medicare, Medicaid and military or veterans' insurance continue to express the most satisfaction, at or near 75%, while uninsured Americans report the lowest (40%).

Satisfaction With the U.S. Healthcare System, by Insurance Type

	2014 %	2015 %	2016 YTD* %	Difference between 2014 and 2016 pct. pts.
Overall satisfaction	67	66	65	-2
Medicare	77	76	75	-2
Military or veterans'	78	77	75	-3
Medicaid	75	74	73	-2
Union	74	71	71	-3
Current or former employer	69	68	66	-3
Plan fully paid for by you or family member	66	64	62	-4
Uninsured	39	40	40	+1

Gallup, *2016 data are from Jan. 2-Aug. 31, 2016

Since 2014, personal satisfaction with the way the healthcare system works is down among all insured groups, including a four-percentage-point drop, from 66% to 62%, among adults who pay for their own insurance, and three-point drops among those covered by an employer, union, or military or veterans' insurance. Even though satisfaction has declined, Americans whose healthcare is subsidized by the government have consistently expressed the highest satisfaction.

Republicans Least Likely to Be Satisfied With Healthcare System

Republicans (58%) and independents (62%) are less satisfied than Democrats (75%) with the way the healthcare system works for them. While Democrats' satisfaction has been stable between 2014 and 2016, Republicans' satisfaction has declined four points. These differences could be, at least in part, a result of Republicans' more negative views of the Affordable Care Act (ACA). Only 9% of Republicans approve of the ACA, compared with 78% of Democrats.

Satisfaction With the U.S. Healthcare System, by Party I.D.

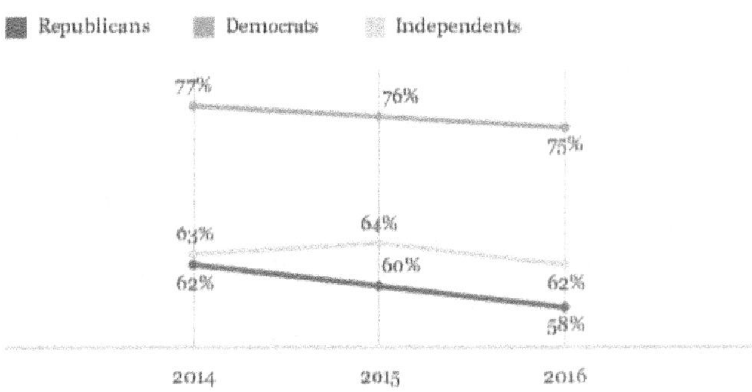

2016 data are from Jan. 2-Aug. 31

GALLUP

Among other key demographic groups, satisfaction with the healthcare system displays little variation. Low-, middle- and high-income Americans show similar satisfaction. About seven in 10 blacks, Hispanics and Asians say they are satisfied with the way the healthcare system works for them, while whites express the least satisfaction (63%). Americans aged 65 and older are more satisfied than their younger counterparts, which comports with Americans' high level of satisfaction with Medicare – the government's health insurance program for older Americans.

Satisfaction With the U.S. Healthcare System, by Key Demographic Groups

	% Satisfied
Annual income	
Less than $36,000	64
$36,000-$89,999	63
$90,000 or more	67
Age	
18-29	67
30-49	59
50-64	61
65+	77
Race	
White	63
Black	72
Hispanic	69
Asian	70

Gallup, 2016 data are from Jan 2.-Aug. 31

Bottom Line

Americans' satisfaction with the healthcare system has declined slightly since 2014, even as the percentage of Americans without health insurance has reached its lowest point in the more than eight years that Gallup and Healthways have tracked it. Americans' concern about the quality of healthcare could be contributing to somewhat-decreased satisfaction, as the number of Americans who described their healthcare coverage as "excellent" has fallen in recent years. Additionally, since the ACA was implemented in 2014, Americans have cited cost and access to healthcare as urgent problems facing the country.

Americans' slightly reduced satisfaction with how the U.S. healthcare system is working for them comes during a presidential election campaign in which the ACA has been hotly debated. While Hillary Clinton supports the ACA signed into law by President Barack Obama, Donald Trump advocates repealing it. The politicization of the ACA has, in part, colored Americans' satisfaction with the U.S. healthcare system more broadly, as both parties continue to debate the fundamental nature of the country's healthcare system and the government's role in it.

Survey Methods

Results for this Gallup poll are based on telephone interviews conducted Jan. 2-Aug. 31, 2016, as part of Gallup Daily tracking, with a random sample of 119,931 adults, aged 18 and older, living in all 50 U.S. states and the District of Columbia. For results based on the total sample of national adults, the margin of sampling error is ±1 percentage point at the 95% confidence level. All reported margins of sampling error include computed design effects for weighting.

September 15, 2016

GOP LOSING GROUND AS BETTER PARTY TO HANDLE FOREIGN THREATS

by Jim Norman

Story Highlights

- *47% favor GOP, 40% Democrats on protecting nation*
- *GOP has slight edge on keeping country prosperous*

WASHINGTON, D.C. — More Americans say the Republican Party will do a better job than the Democratic Party of protecting the country from foreign threats, but the gap between the parties has narrowed in the last year. The Republicans now lead by seven percentage points, 47% to 40%, down from their 16-point lead a year ago (52% to 36%).

Americans Typically Lean to GOP to Protect U.S. From Outside Threats

Looking ahead for the next few years, which party do you think will do a better job of protecting the country from international terrorism and military threats?

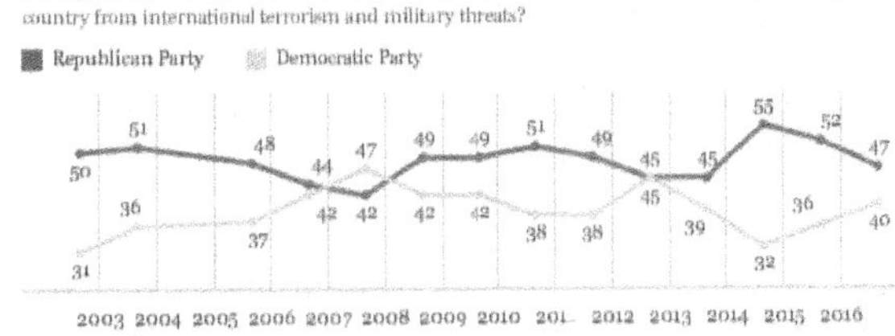

GALLUP

Americans have favored the Republican Party in all but two years since the question was first asked in 2002, though often by less than a majority.

The only time the Democrats were favored was in September 2007, when 47% said the Democrats could do a better job, compared with 42% for the GOP. At that time, most Americans had become pessimistic about the chances of the U.S. winning the Iraq War and were unhappy with Republican President George W. Bush's handling of foreign policy. A year later, however, Republicans once again edged out Democrats on this issue, 49% to 42%, in a poll conducted shortly after the Republican National Convention. The Republican candidate that year was war hero and veteran Sen. John McCain, running against freshman Sen. Barack Obama.

In September 2012, in a poll conducted immediately after Obama was nominated for re-election at the Democratic National Convention, Americans were evenly split (45% for each party) on which party would better defend the nation against foreign threats.

The slide in support for the GOP this year could be tied to the upcoming presidential election. Democratic nominee Hillary Clinton has experience as both a U.S. senator and as secretary of state, while GOP nominee Donald Trump has no direct experience in conducting foreign policy.

GOP Has Slight Lead on Keeping Country Prosperous

Americans, by a narrow 46% to 43% margin, say the Republican Party would do a better job than the Democratic Party of keeping the country prosperous. These views are almost exactly the same as they were a year ago, but are a significant shift from views in the final months of the past two presidential elections, when the Democrats led. In September 2012, 51% said the Democrats would do a better job of keeping the country prosperous, compared with 42% who favored the Republican Party. In September 2008, 52% preferred the Democratic Party, with 39% saying the GOP could do a better job.

Looking ahead to the next few years, which political party do you think will do a better job of keeping the country prosperous?

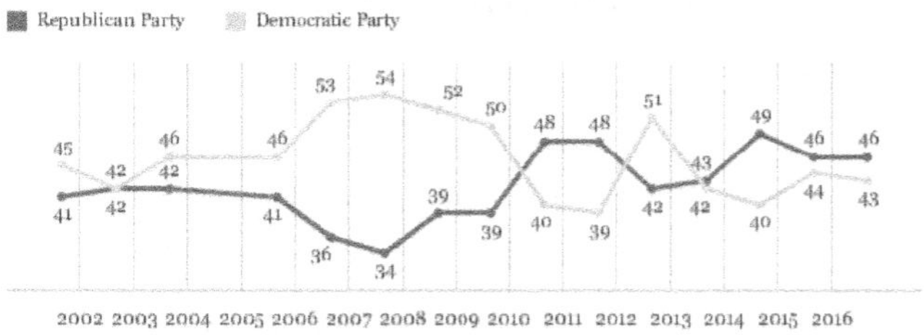

GALLUP

From 2001, when Gallup began routinely asking the question each September, through the eight years of George W. Bush's two terms as president, Americans either were more likely to think Democrats would do a better job of keeping the nation prosperous, or were almost evenly divided on the subject. Since Obama took office in 2009, public opinion has shifted back and forth between the two parties.

Key voting groups have become much less likely to think the Democratic Party will do a better job of keeping the country prosperous since the last presidential election.

- In 2012, a clear majority of women (58%) said the Democrats would do a better job, with only 38% naming the GOP. Now, women are almost evenly split – 44% favor the Democratic Party and 43% the Republican Party.
- Among moderates, the percentage favoring the Democratic Party has dropped from 61% in 2012 to 47% now.
- Fifty-seven percent of middle-income Americans – those with annual household incomes between $30,000 and $75,000 – favored the Democratic Party in 2012. The number has shrunk to 42%.
- Forty-eight percent of independents in 2012 thought the Democratic Party would do a better job. This year, only 35% feel that way.

GOP Holds Edge When Looking at Both Prosperity and Foreign Threats

Forty-one percent now say the Republican Party would do a better job both of protecting the nation from foreign threats and keeping the country prosperous, compared with 35% saying Democrats would do a better job on both. Few Americans have split opinions, favoring one party on one issue and the other party on the other. Only 4% say the GOP is better on defending the country, but the Democrats on prosperity; only 3% go in the other direction – choosing Democrats on defense and Republicans on prosperity. The remaining 17% have no opinion on at least one of the questions.

Bottom Line

Public opinion about which of the nation's two major parties does a better job on the economy and national security becomes more complicated in a presidential election year, as Americans' opinions of the parties comingle with their views about the party nominees. The process is even more complex this year when assessing a Republican Party's nominee who challenged much of the GOP establishment in winning the nomination.

Attitudes have clearly changed since Trump first began his race for the presidency in 2015. On the one hand, the percentage of Americans who believe the Republican Party could do a better job of protecting the nation from foreign threats dropped from 55% in 2014, before Trump announced he would run, to 47% now. On the other hand, more Americans still side with the GOP than the Democrats, reflecting the traditional GOP advantage on this issue.

Americans give only a slight edge to the Republicans on "keeping the country prosperous," but that is a considerable improvement for the GOP when compared with attitudes leading up to the last two presidential elections.

These views about the parties could wind up being overwhelmed in the presidential election by voters' views of the candidates themselves. Even if that happens, the more positive views of the Republican Party in this election than in 2012 could pay dividends in the battles for control of Congress.

Survey Methods

Results for this Gallup poll are based on telephone interviews conducted Sept. 7-11, 2016, with a random sample of 1,020 adults, aged 18 and older, living in all 50 U.S. states and the District of Columbia. For results based on the total sample of national adults, the margin of sampling error is ±4 percentage points at the 95% confidence level. All reported margins of sampling error include computed design effects for weighting.

September 16, 2016
APPROVAL OF CONGRESS INCHES UP TO 20% IN SEPTEMBER

by Art Swift

Story Highlights

- *20% approval is up slightly from 18% in August*
- *Democrats' approval up to 30% from 2016 low of 13% in June*
- *Republicans and independents lower on scale of approval*

WASHINGTON, D.C. — Americans' job approval rating of Congress continues to edge upward to 20% in September, an increase of two percentage points from last month and seven points from July. The 20% mark is notable given that congressional approval has reached this level only three times since 2012.

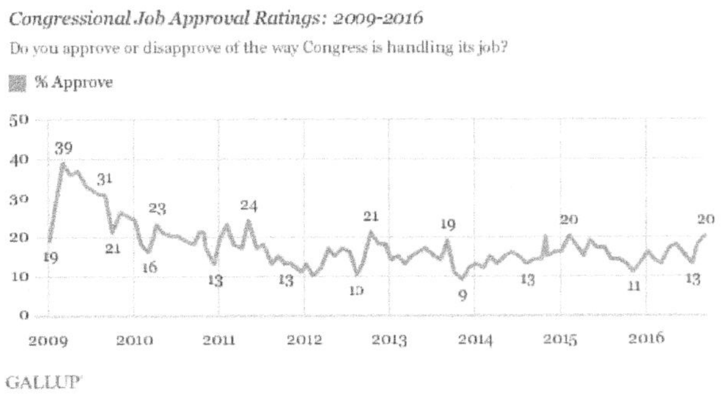

Congressional approval was in the 30% range for the first several months of President Barack Obama's first term in office, before sliding into the 20s later in 2009. Throughout most of his presidency, congressional approval has teetered from the 10s to the 20s, even falling to 9% in November 2013 after the government partially shut down in September. The current 20% reading comes from a Sept. 7-11 Gallup poll.

Democrats Rise Rapidly Since June

At 30%, Democrats' approval of Congress is the highest it has been in the past year and is a marked increase from their 2016 low of 13% recorded in June. Democrats have bounced between the 10s and 20s all year.

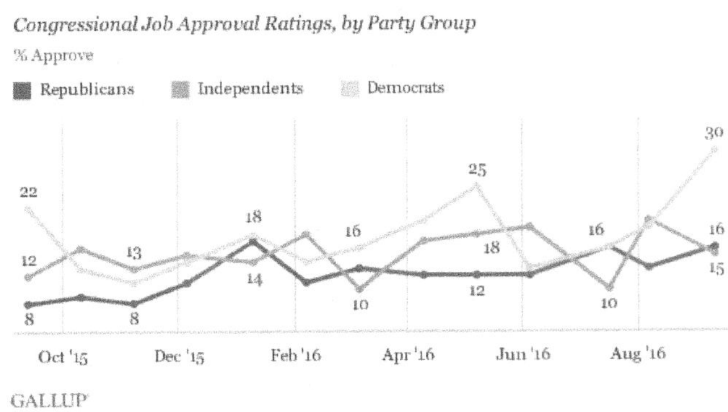

Republicans' approval of Congress, on the other hand, has been mired in the single digits and teens in the past year. At 16%, Republicans' current approval is double what it was one year ago but abysmally low for the party in control of Congress. Historically, Gallup has found that supporters of the majority party in Congress rate the institution much more positively than do nonsupporters of that party. Since taking control of Congress in early 2015, Republicans have expressed frustration with their congressional leaders. Though they view House Speaker Paul Ryan more positively than negatively, the change in speakership last fall has done little to brighten Republicans' outlook.

Independents' approval of Congress is at 15%, down slightly from 20% in August. Approval among those who identify as independents has stayed in a tight 10% to 20% range for the past year.

Bottom Line

Congressional approval is modestly improving, but only one in five Americans say they approve of the legislative branch – still historically low. With few legislative accomplishments this year, Congress may still fail to inspire Americans to rate the institution highly, even though it has avoided political brinkmanship involving government shutdowns and other budgetary impasses seen in the recent past.

Democrats' improved rating of Congress is more peculiar. It is possible that Democrats may believe the Senate – and possibly the House – is in play for a Democratic takeover this fall, fueling a rise in approval of the branch. Since 2009, Democrats have generally been more favorable than Republicans toward Congress, likely because a Democrat is in the White House. The election season has also brought about a decline in congressional activity, including GOP-led attempts to block Obama's agenda.

Republicans' low approval of Congress could reflect frustration with Congress not fulfilling the GOP agenda since Republicans assumed control of the House after the 2010 midterm election.

If there is one party controlling both the executive and legislative branches come January, it is possible that ratings of Congress will improve, as they did at the beginning of Obama's first term, when Democrats also had the majority in both houses of Congress. Many political experts expect Republicans to keep control of the House, so unified control of government is more likely if Republicans maintain their Senate majority and Donald Trump defeats Hillary Clinton.

Historical data are available in Gallup Analytics.

Survey Methods

Results for this Gallup poll are based on telephone interviews conducted Sept. 7-11, 2016, with a random sample of 1,020 adults, aged 18 and older, living in all 50 U.S. states and the District of Columbia. For results based on the total sample of national adults, the margin of sampling error is ±4 percentage points at the 95% confidence level. All reported margins of sampling error include computed design effects for weighting.

September 19, 2016
AMERICANS STILL MORE TRUSTING IN LOCAL OVER STATE GOVERNMENT

by Justin McCarthy

Story Highlights

- *71% trust local government, compared with 62% for state*
- *Republicans have greatest trust in both levels of government*

WASHINGTON, D.C. — For the past 15 years, Americans have expressed more confidence in their local government than their state government to handle problems. Similar to polls since 2013, about seven in 10 (71%) say they have a "great deal" or a "fair amount" of trust in local government to handle problems, compared with about six in 10 (62%) who say the same for their state government.

How much trust and confidence do you have in ...

% Great deal/Fair amount of trust

■ The local governments in the area where you live when it comes to handling local problems?

■ The government of the state where you live when it comes to handling state problems?

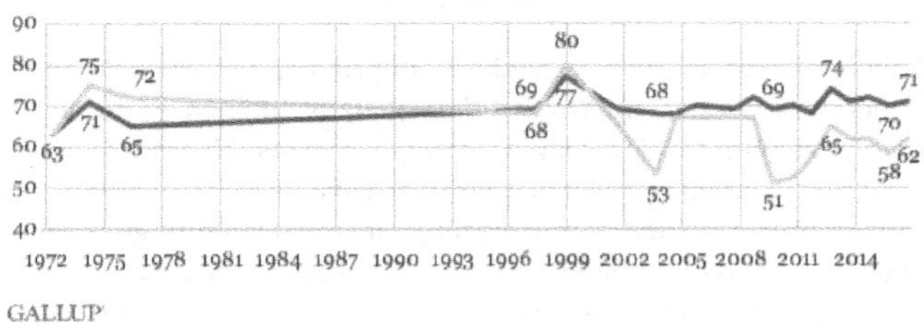

These data were collected as part of Gallup's Sept. 7-11 Governance poll, just two months before a dozen state gubernatorial elections and thousands of state legislative races take place alongside the presidential election.

Americans express much greater confidence in their local and state governments than they do in the executive and legislative branches of federal government. Confidence in state government roughly ties confidence in the judicial branch (61%), including the Supreme Court.

Trust in local government has been fairly steady since Gallup first polled Americans on the topic in 1972, ranging between 63% in that year to as high as 77% in 1998 amid good economic conditions for the country at large. Confidence in state government, however, has varied more, from as high as 80% during the relative good economic times of 1998 to as low as 51% in 2009 as the economy soured after the 2008 Wall Street financial crisis and many states faced revenue shortfalls.

GOP Confidence in State Government Has Waned, but Remains Strongest

From 1997 to 2011, differences in political partisans' views of state government have not varied tremendously – though Republicans generally displayed slightly greater confidence than Democrats in state government, usually ranging from three to eight percentage points higher. But after losing a large number of governorships in 2008, Republicans have since made a significant rebound, earning a dozen additional state governors' offices, bringing their total to 31.

With so many gubernatorial victories, Republicans' confidence in state government soared past Democrats' in 2012, rising to a 15-point advantage in 2013. Their trust in state government has been tempered in the past three years, however, ebbing from 73% in 2014 to the current 66% – still slightly higher than for independents (62%) and Democrats (58%). Republicans could give their representation at the state level particular significance because their party is not in control of the presidency, therefore leaving state governors to promote the party's platform as executives of individual states.

Trust in State Government, by Party

Figures are percentages with a great deal/fair amount of trust in the level of government

■ Republicans ■ Independents ■ Democrats

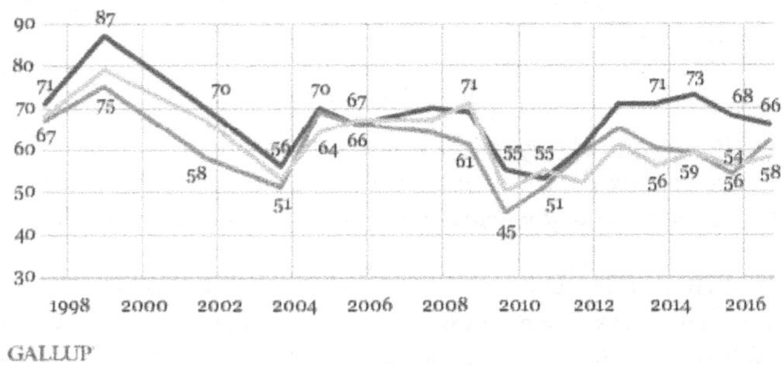

Two-Thirds or More of Each Party Group Expresses Trust in Local Government

Similar to their confidence in state government, Republicans have generally expressed more trust than Democrats in local government – this was the case in all but three polls Gallup has taken since 1997. Overall, however, solid majorities of all three party groups have expressed confidence in their local governments.

Currently, three in four Republicans say they have a great deal or a fair amount of confidence in local governments, compared with 71% of independents and 66% of Democrats.

Trust in Local Government, by Party

Figures are percentages with a great deal/fair amount of trust in the level of government

■ Republicans ■ Independents ■ Democrats

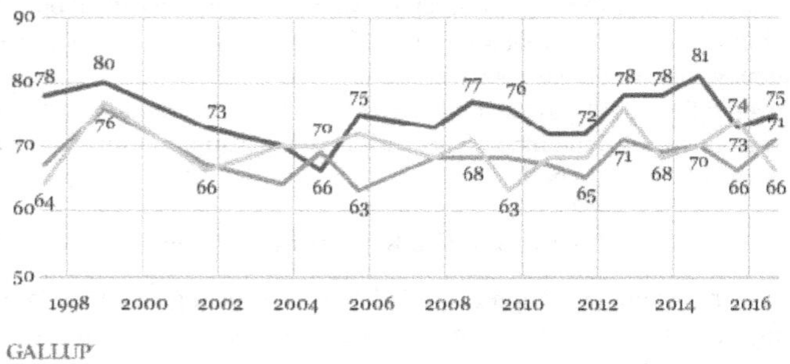

Bottom Line

Despite Republicans' high trust in state and local governments, even independents and Democrats have had fairly high confidence in these lower levels of government – especially compared with their confidence in the federal government's executive and legislative branches. Majorities of each party group have had confidence in both the state and local levels of government in Gallup's trend in nearly every poll since 1997.

This is likely related to the increased value of state residents' votes in local and state elections, paired with the more direct interaction they have with these governments in their everyday lives. This greater familiarity may make lower levels of governments seem more trustworthy.

Historical data are available in Gallup Analytics.

Survey Methods

Results for this Gallup poll are based on telephone interviews conducted Sept. 7-11, 2016, with a random sample of 1,020 adults, aged 18 and older, living in all 50 U.S. states and the District of Columbia. For results based on the total sample of national adults, the margin of sampling error is ±4 percentage points at the 95% confidence level. All reported margins of sampling error include computed design effects for weighting.

September 19, 2016
"EMAIL" DOMINATES WHAT AMERICANS HAVE HEARD ABOUT CLINTON

by Frank Newport, Lisa Singh, Stuart Soroka, Michael Traugott and Andrew Dugan

Story Highlights

- *Data based on daily interviewing July 11-Sept. 18*
- *Americans report hearing more varied information about Trump*
- *Significant majority getting information about candidates each day*

PRINCETON, N.J. — Americans' reports of what they have read, seen or heard about Hillary Clinton over the past two months are dominated by references to her handling of emails while she was secretary of state.

What Americans Have Heard or Read About Hillary Clinton

What specifically do you recall reading, hearing or seeing about Hillary Clinton in the last day or two?

GALLUP DAILY TRACKING
JULY 17-SEPT 18, 2016

By contrast, Americans' reports of what they have read, seen or heard about Donald Trump over this same period have been more varied and related to his campaign activities and statements.

What Americans Have Heard or Read About Donald Trump

What specifically do you recall reading, hearing or seeing about Donald Trump in the last day or two?

GALLUP DAILY TRACKING
JULY 17-SEPT 18, 2016

These findings are based on an ongoing research project conducted by Gallup together with the University of Michigan and Georgetown University. Gallup conducted more than 30,000 interviews with U.S. adults from July 11-Sept. 18 to measure Americans' daily recall of what they read, saw or heard about the two major party candidates.

The word maps use font size to indicate the relative frequency of which specific words appeared for each candidate over the past 10 weeks.

Americans' frequent mention of "email" in response to the question about Hillary Clinton are followed by "lie," "health," "speech," "scandal" and "foundation," the latter referencing recent concerns about conflicts of interest with the Clinton Foundation.

The top substantive words Americans use when reporting on Trump include "speech," "president," "immigration," "Mexico," "convention," "campaign" and "Obama." Though Clinton has attacked Trump on several issues related to his character, no specific words representing negative traits have "stuck" to Trump the way the word "email" has to Clinton. Instead, Americans' recollection of information about Trump shifts in response to his campaign schedule, speeches, comments and the resulting controversies that sometimes arise from those comments.

This conclusion is reinforced by an analysis of changes in what Americans recall about the candidates over time. Americans have most frequently used the word "email" to describe Clinton in eight of the 10 weeks of this project so far. The only two times when this was not the case were the week of the Democratic National Convention, when "convention" became the most frequently cited word, and this past week, when mentions of Clinton's "health" and "pneumonia" rose to the top of the list.

The most frequently mentioned words for Trump have changed during the campaign, and these words often reflect his actions and travels as well as what he says about his opponent or President

Barack Obama. In early August, Americans' most recalled words were associated with his comments about the Muslim parents of a fallen U.S. soldier, and then in the second week of August words associated with his claims that Obama started ISIS. Later, Americans used words associated with Trump's travel to Louisiana to view flood damage, and more recently his trip to Mexico. This past week, "health" was the second most frequently used word associated with Trump.

What Have You Read, Seen or Heard About Hillary Clinton and Donald Trump in the Past Several Days?

Most Frequently Used Words

	Top Words Used in Response to: "What Read, Seen or Heard About Hillary Clinton?"	Top Words Used in Response to: "What Read, Seen or Heard About Donald Trump?"
Sep 12-18	Health Pneumonia Sick Issue	Obama Health Bear President
Sep 5-11	Email Lie Scandal Interview	Mexico Immigration President Speech
Aug 29-Sep 4	Email FBI Release Lie	Mexico Immigration Speech President
Aug 22-28	Email Foundation Scandal Lie	Immigration Change Campaign Policy
Aug 15-21	Email Foundation Lie Health	Campaign Speech Louisiana Change
Aug 8-14	Email Lie Foundation Tax	Obama ISIS Amendment Second
Aug 1-7	Email Lie Convention Campaign	Family Muslim Ryan Son
Jul 25-31	Convention Email Democratic Speech	Russia Email Convention Speech
Jul 18-24	Email President Convention Pick	Convention Speech Republican Wife
Jul 11-17	Email Sanders FBI Scandal	President Pick Pence Mate

Gallup

Most Americans Hearing News About the Presidential Candidates

On most days over the past 10 weeks, at least 60% and often 70% or 80% or more of Americans said they were aware of having read, seen or heard information about the candidates in the past few days. Over this period, an average of 76% recalled information about Trump, compared with an average 73% for Clinton.

In early July, Americans were more likely to report getting information about Clinton than Trump. Trump then became more prominent in Americans' minds during the GOP convention in July, rising to the point where 81% recalled hearing about him. Clinton gained more attention than Trump again during the Democratic convention, peaking at 82% recall. Soon after the conventions, however, Trump regained the lead on this recall measure and remained on top throughout the entire month of August and early September.

Americans' reports of hearing news about Clinton jumped during the week of Sept. 12 after she fell ill at a 9/11 memorial service, announced that she had pneumonia and took a brief break from the campaign trail to recuperate. Clinton's 84% recall average for Sept. 12-18 – reflecting the intense focus on her health and brief withdrawal from the campaign trail – is the highest so far, slightly besting the percentages recorded for her and Trump during their conventions.

Candidates' Influence Among National Adults

Did you read, hear or see anything about Hillary Clinton/Donald Trump in the last day or two?

% Yes

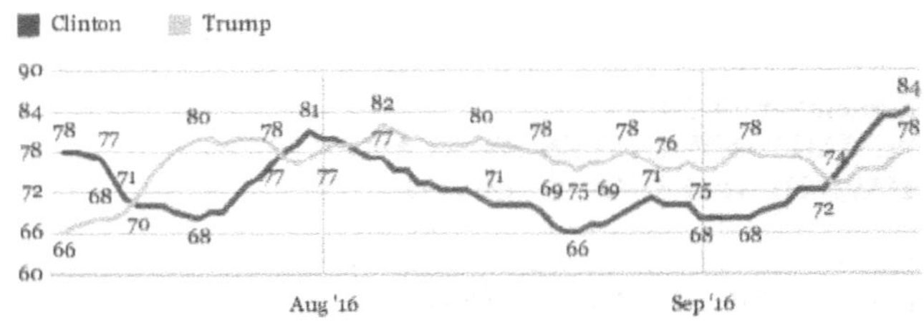

Based on a seven-day rolling average

GALLUP

Implications

This project's objective is to understand the dynamics of the presidential campaign from the U.S. public's perspective, expanding the typical journalists' and pundits' assessments of the race and the two major party candidates.

While research often tracks Americans' opinions of the candidates or their changing vote intentions, few studies have assessed what information the public is absorbing from the campaign on a daily basis. With the enormous expansion of news sources and information available in today's environment, it is no longer possible to assume that what traditional news outlets cover is what is getting through to the public. Many Americans now get information about the candidates from social media, bloggers, partisan news sources, television, radio, the internet and social networks. The "read, seen or heard" data reported here encompass all of this election-related information.

This project will continue through to the election. Upcoming reports will look at differences in what subgroups of the population report about the candidates as well as the relationship between these reports and views of the candidates.

Lisa Singh is an associate professor of computer science at Georgetown University; Stuart Soroka is a professor of communication sciences and political science at the University of Michigan; and Michael W. Traugott of the University of Michigan is a Gallup Senior Scientist.

Survey Methods

Results for this Gallup poll are based on telephone interviews conducted beginning on July 11, 2016, on the Gallup U.S. Daily survey, with a random sample of 500 adults, aged 18 and older, living in all 50 U.S. states and the District of Columbia. For results based on each weekly samples of approximately 3,500 national adults, the margin of sampling error is ±2 percentage points at the 95% confidence level. All reported margins of sampling error include computed design effects for weighting.

September 19, 2016

AMERICANS' CONFIDENCE IN GOVERNMENT TAKES POSITIVE TURN

by Lydia Saad

Story Highlights

- *Confidence in judicial branch highest, at 61%; up eight points*
- *Democrats fuel six-point increase in executive branch rating*
- *Confidence in legislative branch still low, but improved*

PRINCETON, N.J. — Americans express as much or slightly more confidence in each of the three branches of the federal government than they did in 2014 and 2015, when their confidence fell to record or near-record lows. Public confidence in the judicial branch has recovered to 61% after slipping to 53% in 2015. Meanwhile, since 2014, confidence in the executive branch has climbed eight percentage points to 51%, and confidence in the legislative branch has improved seven points to 35%.

Americans' Trust and Confidence in Three Branches of Federal Government

% Great deal/Fair amount

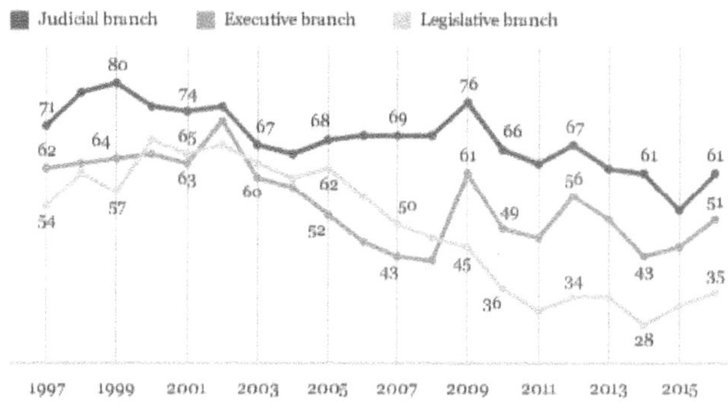

GALLUP

Confidence in each government branch is now similar to where it stood in 2013, but is still well below the averages in Gallup's annual trend since 1997 (68% for the judicial branch, 55% for the executive branch and 49% for the legislative branch).

The latest results are based on Gallup's 2016 Governance poll, conducted Sept. 7-11, and represent the percentage of Americans saying they have a "great deal" or "fair amount" of confidence in each branch of government.

At the other end of the scale, 24% of Americans currently say they have no confidence in the executive branch. Another 20% have no confidence in the legislative branch, while just 9% have no confidence in the judiciary. The remainder have "not very much" confidence in each branch or express no opinion.

Democrats More Confident Than GOP in the Presidency, Judiciary

The recent increase in public trust in the executive branch largely comes from Democrats' rising confidence, which jumped from 77% in 2015 to 84% this year, consistent with President Barack Obama's improved job approval ratings. By contrast, increased confidence in the legislative branch has occurred about equally among Republicans and Democrats, although confidence remains in the 30% range among both groups.

After plummeting in 2015 to 43% – likely in reaction to Supreme Court decisions essentially upholding the Affordable Care Act and legalizing gay marriage – Republicans' confidence in the judicial branch has increased to 51%. However, it remains below pre-2015 levels. Democrats' confidence in the judiciary is now at 71%, up from 64% in 2015.

Americans' Confidence in Three Branches of Government, by Party ID

How much trust and confidence do you have at this time in [the executive branch headed by the president/the judicial branch headed by the U.S. Supreme Court/the legislative branch, consisting of the U.S. Senate and House of Representatives] – a great deal, a fair amount, not very much or none at all?

	2014 %	2015 %	2016 %
Executive branch			
Republicans/Lean Republican	16	16	18
Democrats/Lean Democratic	77	77	84
Legislative branch			
Republicans/Lean Republican	28	32	37
Democrats/Lean Democratic	28	28	34
Judicial branch			
Republicans/Lean Republican	60	43	51
Democrats/Lean Democratic	67	64	71
Recent trend			

Gallup

Government Seen as More Capable of Handling Problems

In the same poll, Gallup asked Americans about their confidence in the federal government to handle domestic and, separately, international problems. Here too, declining confidence since 2011 and 2012 appears to have arrested, and confidence has started to trend upward.

Currently, 49% of Americans are confident in the government to handle international problems, up slightly from 45% a year ago and 43% in 2014. Confidence in the government to handle domestic problems is now at 44%, up from 38% in 2015.

Americans' Trust in Federal Government to Handle Problems, 1997-2016

% Great deal/Fair amount

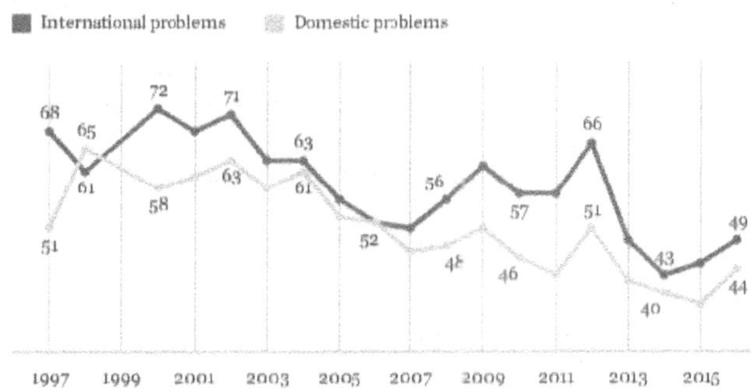

GALLUP

As with partisan confidence in the executive branch, increases in public trust in the government to handle domestic and international problems are mainly a function of higher trust among Democrats. This likely reflects their support for Obama in his final year in office after Republican presidential nominee Donald Trump and other Republican candidates for office have attacked his leadership.

Democrats' confidence in the government to handle domestic problems has risen by 11 points over the past year, to 64%, and has increased by 10 points to 72% for international problems. Republicans' confidence in the government to handle each dimension is unchanged.

Americans' Trust in Federal Government to Handle Problems, by Party ID

How much trust and confidence do you have in our federal government in Washington when it comes to handling [international problems/domestic problems] – a great deal, a fair amount, not very much or none at all?

	2014 %	2015 %	2016 %
Domestic problems			
Republicans/Lean Republican	26	24	26
Democrats/Lean Democratic	58	53	64
International problems			
Republicans/Lean Republican	26	29	27
Democrats/Lean Democratic	64	62	72
Recent trend			

Gallup

Bottom Line

After several years of Americans' confidence in the federal government – particularly in the White House and Congress – wasting away, confidence has rebounded some. This is mainly because Democrats are feeling more positive. Republicans' views of the executive and legislative branches have not changed much; their confidence in each remains low. But their confidence in the judiciary has rebounded some after dropping sharply a year ago.

These trust ratings are highly political, with Democrats and Republicans' views especially dependent on the party occupying the White House. The current pattern of high Democratic confidence and low Republican confidence will likely continue if Democrat Hillary Clinton wins the presidential election. Conversely, partisan confidence levels could reverse if Trump prevails. Meanwhile, confidence in the Supreme Court is mainly dependent on the nature of its big decisions. Any more cases that deeply disappoint the political right could send its confidence rating back down. Otherwise, it seems on course to recover.

Historical data are available in Gallup Analytics.

Survey Methods

Results for this Gallup poll are based on telephone interviews conducted Sept. 7-11, 2016, with a random sample of 1,020 adults, aged 18 and older, living in all 50 U.S. states and the District of Columbia. For results based on the total sample of national adults, the margin of sampling error is ±4 percentage points at the 95% confidence level. All reported margins of sampling error include computed design effects for weighting.

September 21, 2016
AMERICANS CONTINUE TO WANT POLITICAL LEADERS TO COMPROMISE

by Frank Newport

Story Highlights

- *53% want leaders to compromise; 21% want them to stick to principles*
- *Democrats and Republicans both favor compromise over strict principles*
- *Democrats remain more likely than Republicans to favor compromise*

PRINCETON, N.J. — A majority of Americans continue to believe that political leaders in Washington should compromise in order to get things done, while less than half as many say leaders should stick to their beliefs even if little gets done. These attitudes are particularly relevant to the current situation in Washington, where Senate and House members face a Sept. 30 deadline to pass a stopgap budget resolution to avoid a government shutdown.

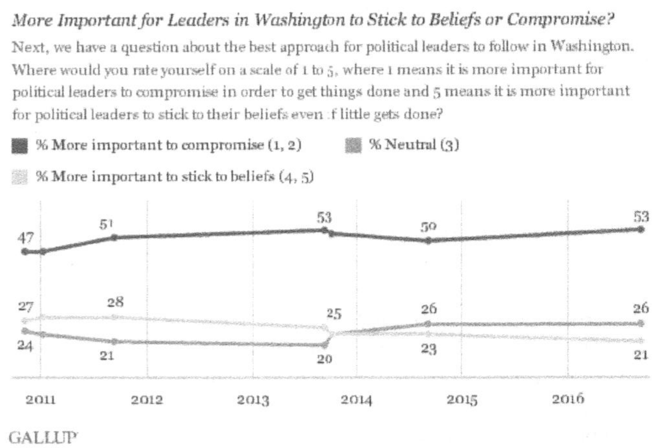

Although Congress' job approval ratings have edged up to 20%, they are still historically low and reflect Americans' general antipathy toward their elected representatives. Previous Gallup research shows that gridlock is the top reason Americans give for disapproving of Congress, and leaders seem to agree. President Barack Obama said in his latest weekly radio address, "This is America – we can do anything. We just need a Congress that works as hard as you do. At the very least, we should expect that they do their jobs."

Gallup has asked Americans seven times since 2010 to indicate where they stand on this issue using a 1-to-5 scale, where "1" represents the belief that it is important to compromise in order to get things done and "5" represents the belief that it is important for leaders to stick to their principles even if little gets done. Americans have favored "compromise" over "sticking to principles" in each of these surveys, ranging from 53% this year and in 2013 to 47% when the question was first asked in late 2010 and early 2011. The current 21% of Americans who prefer that their leaders stick to their principles is the lowest Gallup has recorded; 28% in 2011 was the highest.

Democrats and Republicans continue to look at this philosophic question through somewhat different lenses, although some evidence suggests that both partisan groups are shifting their positions. The current 56% of Democrats and Democratic-leaning independents who favor the compromise position is down from 67% in 2014 when Gallup last asked this question. Republicans and Republican-leaning independents, by contrast, have become somewhat *more* likely to favor compromise than in 2014 and less likely to believe leaders should stick to their principles. This means the gap between Republicans' and Democrats' preferences for compromise is smaller than it was in either 2013 or 2014.

More Important for Leaders in Washington to Stick to Beliefs or Compromise?

	2013 %	2014 %	2016 %
Republicans/Republican leaners			
More important to stick to beliefs	33	32	22
Neutral	25	31	29
More important to compromise	42	37	48
Democrats/Democratic leaners			
More important to stick to beliefs	19	13	20
Neutral	17	18	24
More important to compromise	63	67	56

Gallup

The reason for Democrats' and Republicans' shifts are not clear. Republicans' increased interest in compromise could reflect House Speaker Paul Ryan's apparent interest in passing legislation rather than holding out for specific provisions at all costs. It's also possible that in September 2014, when Gallup last asked this question, Republicans were focused on winning the Senate and attempting to limit Obama's influence and thus less interested in compromise.

Rank-and-file Democrats could be less interested in compromise because of the possibility that it would be GOP presidential candidate Donald Trump with whom they would be compromising – or perhaps because of the lingering influence of Bernie Sanders and his strongly held, uncompromising beliefs. Whatever their reasons, both Republicans and Democrats, by a ratio of more than 2-to-1, say they want their leaders to compromise rather than stick to their principles.

Bottom Line

Americans continue to want their leaders in Washington to find a way to compromise and get things done rather than hold out for what they believe at the cost of inaction. Both presidential candidates appear to agree. Trump has said that when dealing with Congress, he would get everyone together in one room and get them to act for the good of the people. Hillary Clinton has pointed out that "the tendency to put ideology ahead of political progress [has] led to gridlock in Congress." The data show that more Democrats and Republicans would agree with these sentiments than would disagree. Of course, when either Trump or Clinton wins the presidency, how much Americans who identify with the opposite party will actually want their representatives to compromise and go along with the new president remains to be seen.

Survey Methods

Results for this Gallup poll are based on telephone interviews conducted Sept. 7-11, 2016, with a random sample of 1,020 adults, aged 18 and older, living in all 50 U.S. states and the District of Columbia. For results based on the total sample of national adults, the margin of sampling error is ±4 percentage points at the 95% confidence level. All reported margins of sampling error include computed design effects for weighting

September 21, 2016

AMERICANS' TRUST IN POLITICAL LEADERS, PUBLIC AT NEW LOWS

by Jeffrey M. Jones

Story Highlights

- *42% have a "great deal" or "fair amount" of trust in political leaders*
- *56% trust American people to make decisions under democratic system*
- *Trust in both groups down about 20 percentage points since 2004*

PRINCETON, N.J. — Americans' trust in their political leaders and in the American people themselves to make political decisions continues to decline. The percentages trusting the American people (56%) and political leaders (42%) are down roughly 20 percentage points since 2004 and are currently at new lows in Gallup's trends.

Trust in Political Leaders and in the American People

% Great deal/Fair amount of trust

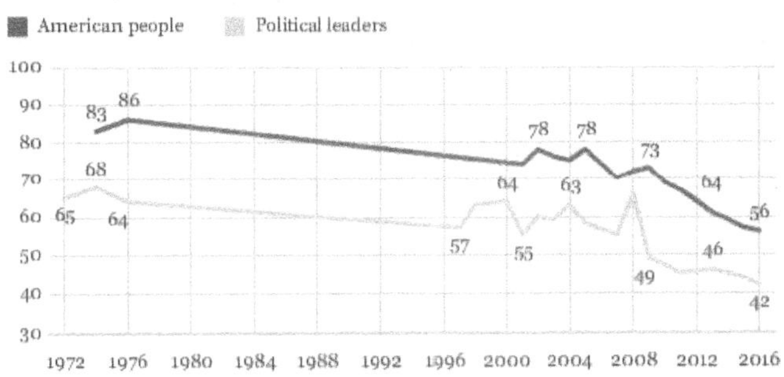

GALLUP

More specifically, the survey asks U.S. adults how much they trust "the men and women in political life in this country who either hold or are running for political office" and how much trust they have in the American people to make "judgments under our democratic system about the issues facing our country."

These items are included in Gallup's annual Governance poll, conducted each September, alongside questions measuring Americans' trust in the three branches of the federal government, state and local governments, and the mass media.

Trust in most of these institutions is lower now than a decade ago. This is possibly a symptom of Americans' low levels of satisfaction with the way things are going in the country. In the past decade, Americans' top concerns have been the economy, the Iraq War and the way the government is working in general.

However, while levels of trust in political leaders, the American people and the mass media all continue to erode this year, trust in the three branches of the federal government and in state and local governments has improved.

Current Gap in Trust Between People, Leaders Is Typical

Not surprisingly, more Americans have always said they trust the American people than have said they trust political leaders. The current 14-point gap in trust between these groups matches the average in Gallup's trend, first measured during the Watergate era and updated more regularly since the early 2000s.

The high point in trust in the American people was 86% in 1976. The high point in trust in political leaders, ironically, was 68% in April 1974, just months before President Richard Nixon resigned the presidency because of the Watergate scandal. At that time, Americans' loss of faith appeared to be limited to Nixon and the executive branch of government (40% trust) and not to Congress (68% trust) or other political institutions.

Americans' trust in political leaders also spiked to 66% in September 2008, in the midst of the presidential election campaign between Barack Obama and John McCain. That increase represented the only major interruption in the steady decline in trust in political leaders over the past decade-plus.

Democrats Have More Trust in Political Leaders

Democrats (61%) are more likely than Republicans (37%) to say they trust political leaders, with independents being the least trusting (30%) among the major political groups. Democrats' and Republicans' trust levels were generally similar until 2009, when Republicans' trust fell, likely in response to Democratic President Obama taking office. Since then, Democrats have typically expressed more trust than Republicans, apart from a few isolated years, including 2015.

Trust in Political Leaders, by Political Party (Recent Trend)

% Great deal/Fair amount of trust

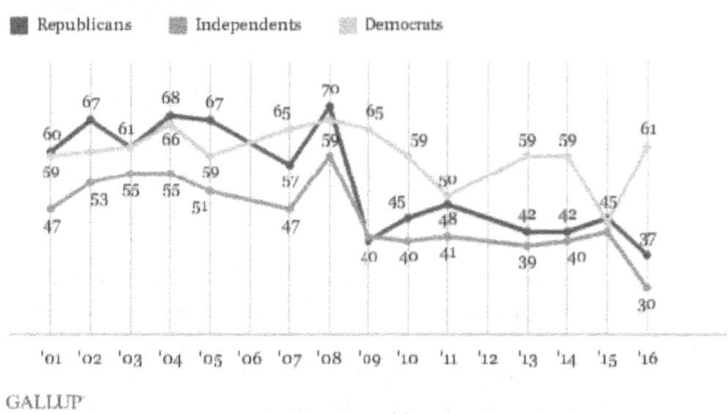

Trust in political leaders has declined at least somewhat among all party groups since the mid-2000s, with more change seen among independents and Republicans than among Democrats.

Historically, there have been only modest party differences in trust in the American people, something that is less plainly connected to the current party power structure in Washington than is trust in political leaders. Currently, 58% of Democrats, 55% of independents and 53% of Republicans say they have a "great deal" or "fair amount" of trust in the American people to make judgments about the issues facing the country. All party groups have significantly less trust in the American people today than in the mid-2000s.

Trust in American People, by Political Party (Recent Trend)

% Great deal/Fair amount of trust

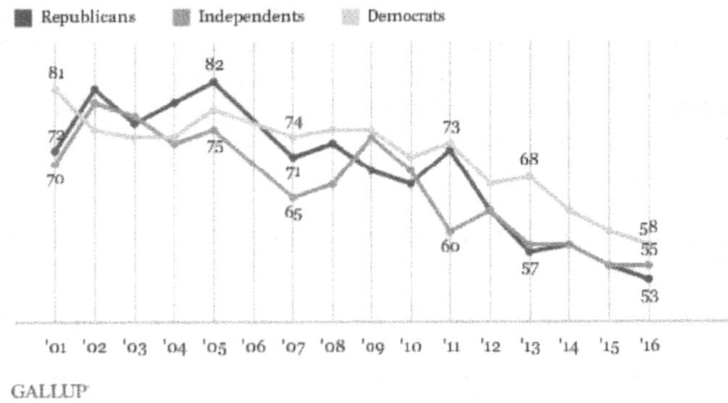

Implications

At no point in the last four decades have Americans expressed less trust than they do today in U.S. political leaders or in the American people who voted those leaders into office. Both trends were already in place long before this year's presidential campaign saw primary voters choose, and their political parties nominate, the worst-rated presidential candidates in recent memory.

Americans' dour view of the state of the nation appears to be affecting the way they view many U.S. institutions, both political and nonpolitical. Americans' trust in political leaders and in the American people as a whole began declining during George W. Bush's second term, the same time their confidence in nonpolitical institutions started heading downward. These trends have yet to recover even after the U.S. ended major military operations in Iraq and after the economy emerged, albeit sluggishly, from the worst economic recession in several generations.

Voter frustration was arguably a major factor behind Donald Trump's victory in the GOP primaries and Bernie Sanders' unexpectedly strong challenge to Hillary Clinton in the Democratic primaries. Whether Trump or Clinton is elected in November, the winner will be governing at a time when Americans' trust in nearly all major U.S. institutions – including the American people themselves – is at or near historical lows.

Historical data are available in Gallup Analytics.

Survey Methods

Results for this Gallup poll are based on telephone interviews conducted Sept. 7-11, 2016, with a random sample of 1,020 adults, aged 18 and older, living in all 50 U.S. states and the District of Columbia. For results based on the total sample of national adults, the margin of sampling error is ±4 percentage points at the 95% confidence level. All reported margins of sampling error include computed design effects for weighting.

September 22, 2016

NUMBER OF AMERICANS CLOSELY FOLLOWING POLITICS SPIKES

by Zac Auter

Story Highlights

- *39% say they follow national politics "very closely," up from 31% in 2015*
- *Republicans more likely than Democrats to follow national politics very closely*
- *Younger Americans' attention to national politics has waned since 2008*

WASHINGTON, D.C. — In this presidential election year, nearly four in 10 Americans say they are following news about national politics "very closely." Americans' attention to national politics traditionally peaks in presidential election years compared with intervening years, and that is the case in 2016. The 39% who say they are following national politics very closely is up from 31% in 2015 and is similar to the percentages who paid close attention in 2012, 2008 and 2004.

Percentage of Americans Who Follow News About National Politics "Very Closely"

Overall, how closely do you follow news about national politics -- very closely, somewhat closely, not too closely or not at all?

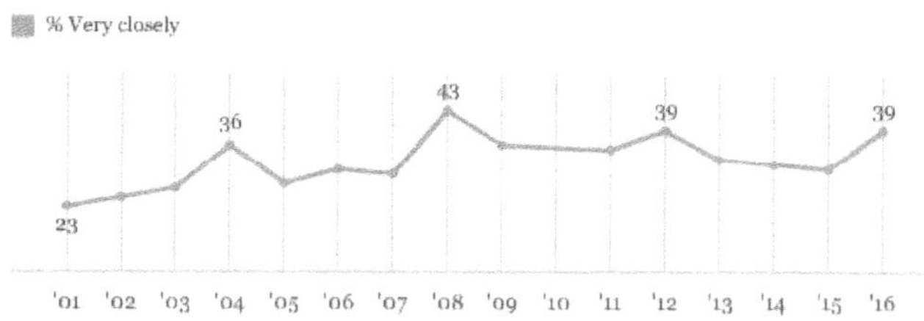

Data are from September of each year.

GALLUP

As more Americans report following politics "very closely" this year compared with 2015, fewer report following it "somewhat closely" – down seven percentage points to 39%. This suggests those who followed political news on a slightly more casual basis last year have intensified their interest this year. Meanwhile, since 2013, a fairly consistent 23% of adults, on average, have said they follow news about politics "not too closely" or "not at all."

The latest results come from Gallup's annual Governance survey, conducted Sept. 7-11. Because Gallup has asked Americans about their attention to national politics in September of each year since 2001, the measures are drawn from similar points in each presidential election cycle.

Republicans Pay Slightly More Attention to Politics Than Democrats Do

Since 2001, Republicans have been slightly more likely than Democrats to say they follow national politics very closely. During President Barack Obama's first term, however, the gap widened. Between 2009 and 2012, Republicans' attention to national politics outpaced Democrats' by an average of nine points, compared with a four-point gap in the years before his first term and six points afterward.

Democrats' and Republicans' close attention to national politics has peaked in presidential election years since at least 2004. However, independents' attention to national politics has not spiked in recent presidential years after doing so in 2004 and 2008.

In 2016, the percentage of Republicans and Democrats paying very close attention to national politics jumped nine and 14 points, respectively, from 2015. These increases are exceeded only by those seen from 2007 to 2008 among Republicans (18 points) and Democrats (15 points). Those spikes may have taken place because that presidential election was the first to feature a black major-party nominee and was one in which the winner would confront two major wars and a bad economy.

The 2016 presidential election does not appear to be drawing independents' attention, which is essentially unchanged from last year. This marks a change from the presidential election eight years ago, when the percentage of independents following national politics very closely increased by seven points from 2007 to 2008.

Percentage of Americans Who Follow News About National Politics "Very Closely," by Partisan Identification

Overall, how closely do you follow news about national politics -- very closely, somewhat closely, not too closely or not at all?

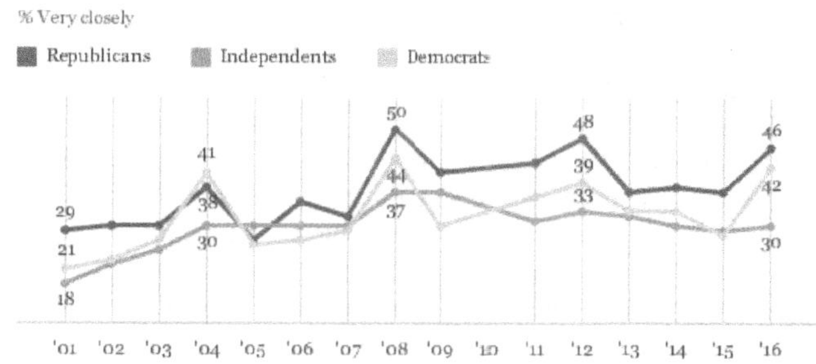

GALLUP

Older Americans More Attentive Than Younger Americans to National Politics

Older Americans consistently follow news about national politics more closely than middle-aged and younger Americans, but age groups' attention typically increases in presidential election years. Four in 10 middle-aged Americans in 2016 are paying very close attention to national politics, up from 27% last year, which represents the largest increase among all age groups. Younger Americans (20% "very closely") are paying the least attention to national politics this year, while older Americans, as is typically the case, are paying the most attention (49%).

Percentage of Americans Who Follow News About National Politics "Very Closely," by Age Group

Overall, how closely do you follow news about national politics -- very closely, somewhat closely, not too closely or not at all?

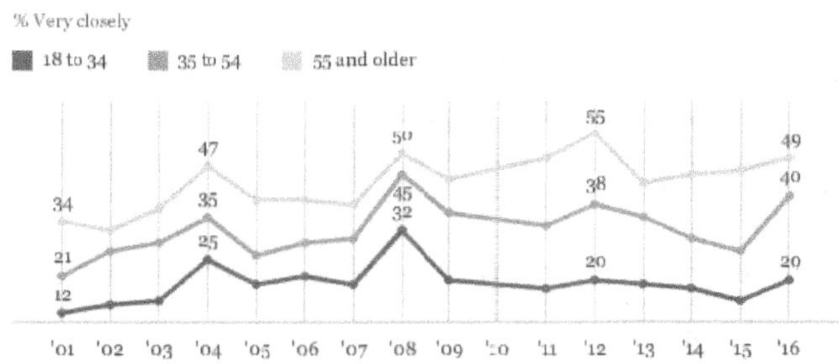

GALLUP

Middle-aged and younger Americans' attention peaked in 2008, when 45% and 32%, respectively, said they followed national politics "very closely." Among younger Americans, this could have reflected interest in Obama's presidential campaign which was, in part, driven by a coalition that prominently featured younger voters.

Since 2008, the share of attentive younger Americans has faded substantially, with only a fifth paying very close attention in 2012 and 2016 – similar to non-presidential-election years. Older Americans' attention peaked in 2012, when 55% said they followed national politics "very closely."

Bottom Line

While political independents and younger adults generally pay less attention to national politics than Democrats, Republicans and older Americans do, these groups' attention has waned since the 2008 presidential election year. In 2016, this could reflect the presidential candidates' failure to resonate with young adults and independents, who represent critical voting blocs. Hillary Clinton and Donald Trump are posting historically bad image ratings for presidential candidates overall, and both candidates have been particularly unpopular with young adults and independents.

Gallup recently reported that 33% of 18- to 29-year-old adults had a favorable image of Clinton, while 18% had a favorable image of Trump – the lowest favorability among all age groups for both candidates. Similarly, less than a third of independents hold favorable images of Clinton and Trump. To the extent that close attention to politics translates into voter turnout, this could be an indication of low turnout among younger Americans and independents on Election Day.

Historical data are available in Gallup Analytics.

Survey Methods

Results for this Gallup poll are based on telephone interviews conducted Sept. 7-11, 2016, with a random sample of 1,020 adults, aged 18 and older, living in all 50 U.S. states and the District of Columbia. For results based on the total sample of national adults, the margin of sampling error is ±4 percentage points at the 95% confidence level. All reported margins of sampling error include computed design effects for weighting.

September 22, 2016

MORE AMERICANS SAY PRESIDENTS SHOULD RELEASE MEDICAL INFO

by Art Swift

Story Highlights

- *51% say a president should release all medical information*
- *More Republicans than Democrats believe it should be released*
- *75% say Trump healthy enough to serve; 62% for Clinton*

WASHINGTON, D.C. — Amid recent concerns about the health of Hillary Clinton and Donald Trump, 51% of Americans say a president should release all medical information that might affect his or her ability to serve. Nearly half (46%) say a president should have the same right as every other citizen to keep medical records private. This is a change from 2004, the last time Gallup asked this question, when 38% said presidents should release all information and 61% said they should be able to keep records private.

Releasing Health Records vs. Keeping Them Private

Which comes closer to your view – [ROTATED: a president should publicly release all medical information that might affect his or her ability to serve as president, (or) a president should have the same right as every other citizen to keep his or her medical records private]?

	2004 %	2016 %
Should release all information	38	51
Should have right to keep records private	61	46

Gallup

The candidates' health has erupted into a central campaign issue as both Clinton and Trump have fielded calls to release their full medical records. Instead, the Clinton and Trump campaigns have released records in a gradual fashion, leading some critics to suggest they are both being less than forthcoming. Clinton's apparent fainting spell at a 9/11 memorial event in New York City has forced this issue to the forefront. Trump too has been questioned; he released a vague, one-page health summary from his doctor last week. He then appeared on the "Doctor Oz Show" to ostensibly clarify his medical situation.

Republicans More Likely to Say Presidents Should Release Records

Sixty-six percent of Republicans say presidents should release all medical information, while 34% say they should have the right to keep their records private. Democrats are more evenly split, with 47% calling for presidents to release their medical information and 50% saying presidents should be able to keep it private. Independents align more closely with Democrats than with Republicans on this issue; 45% say presidents should release the information, and 52% believe they have the right to keep it private.

Releasing Health Records vs. Keeping Them Private, by Party ID

Which comes closer to your view – [ROTATED: a president should publicly release all medical information that might affect his or her ability to serve as president, (or) a president should have the same right as every other citizen to keep his or her medical records private]?

	Republicans %	Independents %	Democrats %
Should release all information	66	45	47
Should have right to keep records private	34	52	50

Gallup

Republicans may have picked up on Trump's focus on health this election cycle in forming their responses. In 2004, when Republican President George W. Bush ran for re-election, 34% said a president should release all medical information, and 65% said he or she should have the right to keep it private. Democrats, at 42%, said all information should be released, while 57% said a president should have the right to privacy.

Most Americans Say Health of President "Very Important"

A majority of Americans (61%) say the health of a president is "very important" to his or her ability to be a good president. Another 31% say it is "somewhat important." These percentages are similar to 2004, when 70% said health is "very important." Overall, more than 90% of Americans in both 2004 and 2016 said a president's health is very or somewhat important.

Importance of Health in Ability to Be a Good President

How important would you say the health of a president is to his or her ability to be a good president – very important, somewhat important, not too important or not at all important?

	2004 %	2016 %
Very important	70	61
Somewhat important	26	31
Not too important	3	5
Not at all important	1	2

Gallup

More Say Trump "Healthy Enough to Be President" Than Clinton

Gallup also asked Americans about a series of characteristics and qualities that may or may not apply to each candidate. Included in this list was "is healthy enough to be president." Seventy-five percent of Americans say this quality applies to Trump, while 62% say it applies to Clinton.

Health of Presidential Candidates

Thinking about the following characteristics and qualities, please say whether you think each applies or doesn't apply to [Hillary Clinton/Donald Trump]. How about "is healthy enough to be president"? (% Applies)

	U.S. adults %
Hillary Clinton	62
Donald Trump	75

Gallup

These ratings vary by political affiliation, suggesting that Americans' assessments may be influenced as much by their basic feelings toward the candidates as by any health-related information they have heard or read. A majority of Republicans (96%), independents (78%) and Democrats (54%) say Trump is healthy enough to be president. For Clinton, the percentages are lower across the board – 27% of Republicans say this statement applies to her, compared with 63% of independents and 89% of Democrats.

Health of Presidential Candidates, by Party ID

Thinking about the following characteristics and qualities, please say whether you think each applies or doesn't apply to [Hillary Clinton/Donald Trump]. How about "is healthy enough to be president"? (% Applies)

	Republicans %	Independents %	Democrats %
Hillary Clinton	27	63	89
Donald Trump	96	78	54

Gallup

Bottom Line

Americans believe that a president's health is important to his or her ability to be a good leader. While that may seem like an obvious statement, Americans have long had presidents who were not in the best of health, and some concealed their health problems. Dwight Eisenhower was hospitalized for a heart attack, John F. Kennedy privately struggled with Addison's disease, Franklin Roosevelt experienced paralysis, and Ronald Reagan may have suffered from Alzheimer's disease while in office. In this social media age, however, it is exceedingly difficult to hide much from the public; the health problems of presidents past would likely be impossible to conceal today. Along with scrutiny over tax returns, legal records and other personal effects, a candidate's medical background has moved to the forefront of the presidential vetting process this year.

More Republicans now than in 2004 say a president should release all medical information. This increase may be related to recent media coverage of Clinton's alleged health problems, or perhaps the GOP believes Trump to be a vigorous, healthy candidate. Overall, more Americans say Trump is healthy enough to be president than say the same about Clinton, although a majority believe the former first lady is healthy enough. With both candidates being tentative (to varying degrees) about releasing their full health records, this issue is likely to remain prevalent through Election Day.

Historical data are available in Gallup Analytics.

Survey Methods

Results for these Gallup polls are based on telephone interviews conducted Sept. 16-17, 2016, and Sept. 14-18, 2016, with a random sample of 1,033 adults, aged 18 and older, living in all 50 U.S. states and the District of Columbia. For results based on the total sample of national adults, the margin of sampling error is ±4 percentage points at the 95% confidence level. All reported margins of sampling error include computed design effects for weighting.

September 23, 2016

AS DEBATE LOOMS, VOTERS STILL DISTRUST CLINTON AND TRUMP

by Frank Newport

Story Highlights

- *33% say "honest and trustworthy" applies to Clinton, 35% to Trump*
- *Clinton does best relative to Trump on having experience it takes to be president*

- *Trump bests Clinton on being healthy, standing up to special interests*

PRINCETON, N.J. — Both Hillary Clinton and Donald Trump continue to struggle to overcome Americans' perceptions of their lack of honesty. About a third of U.S. voters are willing to say that the terms "honest and trustworthy" apply to either Clinton or to Trump, putting honesty at or near the bottom of a list of 11 attributes tested.

U.S. Voters' Views of the Qualities and Characteristics of Hillary Clinton and Donald Trump

Thinking about the following characteristics and qualities, please say whether you think each applies or doesn't apply to Hillary Clinton/Donald Trump. How about – [RANDOM ORDER]? (Rank ordered by % saying applies to Clinton)

	Applies to Clinton %	Applies to Trump %
Has the experience it takes to be president	69	29
Can get things done	60	56
Is healthy enough to be president	60	77
Is a strong and decisive leader	56	57
Would display good judgment in a crisis	54	39
Can manage the government effectively	54	41
Is likable	50	38
Cares about the needs of people like you	48	40
Stands up to special interest groups	46	52
Can bring about the changes this country needs	41	41
Is honest and trustworthy	33	35

Gallup, Sep 14-18, 2016

These results are from Gallup's Sept. 14-18 update of Americans' assessments of how well each of 11 qualities and characteristics fits the two major-party presidential candidates. The data provide an understanding of how the public views the candidates heading into the first presidential debate on Monday.

"Honesty and trustworthy" was last among the 11 attributes for Clinton and was second-worst for Trump, only above his rating on "has the experience it takes to be president." Trump's low rating on experience contrasts with Clinton's high rating – it is her top dimension – creating the biggest gap in U.S. voters' views of the two candidates across all qualities tested.

Overall, Clinton does statistically better than Trump on five of the dimensions tested. In addition to experience, Clinton's perceived advantages include displaying good judgment in a crisis, managing the government effectively, being likable and caring about people like you.

Trump does better than Clinton on two dimensions: being healthy enough to be president and standing up to special interest groups.

The two candidates are essentially tied on the other four dimensions tested, including being honest and trustworthy, being a strong and decisive leader, being able to get things done and being able to bring about change the country needs.

U.S. Voters' Views of the Qualities and Characteristics of Hillary Clinton and Donald Trump

Thinking about the following characteristics and qualities, please say whether you think each applies or doesn't apply to Hillary Clinton/Donald Trump. How about – [RANDOM ORDER]?

	Applies to Clinton %	Applies to Trump %	Difference (Clinton minus Trump) pct. pts.
Has the experience it takes to be president	69	29	+40
Would display good judgment in a crisis	54	39	+15
Can manage the government effectively	54	41	+13
Is likable	50	38	+12
Cares about the needs of people like you	48	40	+8
Can get things done	60	56	+4
Can bring about the changes this country needs	41	41	0
Is a strong and decisive leader	56	57	-1
Is honest and trustworthy	33	35	-2
Stands up to special interest groups	46	52	-6
Is healthy enough to be president	60	77	-17

Gallup, Sep 14-18, 2016

Health has been in the news often over the past two weeks and provides the second-biggest gap (17 percentage points) in views of the two candidates. The latest research was in the field just after Clinton fell ill at a 9/11 ceremony in New York, leading her to announce that she had pneumonia and would take a break from the campaign trail for several days. Last week, Trump also released some of his medical information on the "Dr. Oz" television program. Other Gallup research shows that Americans feel the health of a president is important to his or her ability to be a good leader.

Americans, on average, rate the two candidates lowest on honesty and being able to bring about the changes the country needs. This provides some understanding of possible reasons why both candidates get such high unfavorable ratings overall, and it provides an indication of the challenges both candidates will need to address in the coming debate.

On the other hand, Americans give the two candidates the highest combined average scores for being healthy, being strong and decisive leaders, and getting things done.

Americans' ratings of Clinton on all dimensions (excluding health, which Gallup included for the first time in September) are modestly higher now than they were when Gallup last tested them in May – an increase that could reflect the timing of the May survey, when Clinton was still competing against Bernie Sanders. But the relative rank order of the dimensions for each candidate has not changed at all. In other words, even with the enormous amount of campaign-related activity that has taken place over the past four months, including the two conventions in July, the public's views of the *relative* strengths and weaknesses of both candidates have remained remarkably stable.

This lack of change in the rank order of the dimensions for each candidate reflects that both candidates are very well-known and established figures, and it shows their images are pretty fixed in the public's mind.

Bottom Line

The first presidential debate on Sept. 26 at Hofstra University in Long Island will put the two candidates simultaneously on the same stage for the first time in this long campaign. It will provide Americans with a renewed opportunity to assess where the candidates stand on important issues as well as their personal characteristics. Clinton and Trump will enter the debate with high unfavorable ratings and a populace that tends to doubt their honesty and trustworthiness.

Clinton clearly has the edge over Trump in terms of the perception that she has the experience needed to be president, but the Republican challenger will most likely continue to attempt to turn that into a liability rather than an asset. At the same time, the data show that just 41% of voters say that either candidate can bring about the changes the country needs, suggesting that Trump has not yet been able to turn his political newcomer status into a major differentiator against his opponent.

Still, Americans appear to be relatively fixed in the way they rate each candidate on these dimensions, which could suggest that despite the probable record-high viewership of the debate, Americans' post-debate views of the candidates may not change much.

Historical data are available in Gallup Analytics.

Survey Methods

Results for this Gallup poll are based on telephone interviews conducted Sept. 14-18, 2016, with a random sample of 1,033 adults, aged 18 and older, living in all 50 U.S. states and the District of Columbia. For results based on the total sample of national adults, the margin of sampling error is ±4 percentage points at the 95% confidence level. All reported margins of sampling error include computed design effects for weighting.

September 26, 2016

AMERICANS LESS SURE THEY'LL VOTE FOR PRESIDENT

by Lydia Saad

Story Highlights

- *69% of U.S. adults are sure they will vote, down from 76% in 2012*
- *72% have given a lot of thought to the election; lowest figure since 2000*
- *Intent to vote is down sharply among U.S. adults aged 18 to 34*

PRINCETON, N.J. — Amid the news frenzy leading up to the first general election debate of 2016, fewer U.S. adults rate themselves highly likely to vote for president than did so in September of each of the past four presidential election years. Sixty-nine percent of Americans currently rate their chances of voting a "10" on a 1-to-10 likelihood of voting scale. That is down from 76% in 2012 and 80% in 2008, the year with the highest turnout since 2000.

U.S. Adults' Self-Ratings of Likelihood of Voting for President

I'd like you to rate your chances of voting in November's election for president on a scale of 1 to 10. If "1" represents someone who definitely will not vote and "10" represents someone who definitely will vote, where on this scale of 1 to 10 would you place yourself?

	2000 %	2004 %	2008 %	2012 %	2016 %
10	74	78	80	76	69
8 or 9	14	11	9	9	11
1 to 7	10	10	9	14	18
Not sure	3	1	2	1	3
Voter turnout^	51.2	56.7	58.2	54.9	n/a

^ Based on voting age population (VAP); source: http://www.presidency.ucsb.edu/data/turnout.php; polls conducted in September of each year

Gallup

Gallup has historically asked this question as part of a set of questions gauging likelihood to vote. Another likely voter question asks Americans how much thought they have given to the election – quite a lot or only a little. The 72% currently giving "a lot" of thought to the race is similar to what Gallup recorded in September 2012, but is down from 2004 and 2008.

U.S. Adults' Self-Reported Reflections on Presidential Elections

How much thought have you given to the upcoming election for president – quite a lot, or only a little?

	2000 %	2004 %	2008 %	2012 %	2016 %
Quite a lot	59	77	80	74	72
Some (volunteered)	8	3	4	4	2
Only a little	30	16	15	20	22
None (volunteered)	2	3	1	2	4
No opinion	1	0	0	0	0

Polls conducted in September of each year

Gallup

These figures could change between now and Election Day. However, while the percentage giving quite a lot of thought to the election usually increases by several percentage points between September and November, the percentage rating their likelihood of voting a "10" typically does not.

Final Pre-Election Attitudes

Based on U.S. adults

	2000 %	2004 %	2008 %	2012 %
Have given "quite a lot" of thought to election				
September	59	77	80	74
Final pre-election	70	84	81	78
Will definitely vote ("10")				
September	74	78	80	76
Final pre-election	67	82	77	75

Gallup

Intent to Vote Sagging Among Both Major Party Groups

Democrats and independents who lean Democratic currently report giving the same level of thought to the election as they did in September 2012 (70%), whereas thought given is down slightly among Republicans and independents who lean Republican, from 81% to 75%. At the same time, intent to vote is down by a similar proportion among both party groups.

Still, by 76% to 65%, Republicans remain more likely than Democrats to say they will definitely vote – a gap that is similar to 2012, but higher than in previous elections. Further, the 65% of Democrats saying they will definitely vote is well below their average for the prior four presidential elections (77%), whereas the 76% of Republicans saying they will definitely vote is only a bit lower than their prior average (81%).

Summary of U.S. Adults' Attitudes About Voting, by Party ID

Polls conducted in September of each year

	2000 %	2004 %	2008 %	2012 %	2016 %
Have given "quite a lot" of thought to election					
Republicans/Republican leaners	65	81	81	81	75
Democrats/Democratic leaners	57	76	80	70	70
Will definitely vote ("10")					
Republicans/Republican leaners	79	81	82	83	76
Democrats/Democratic leaners	74	78	80	74	65

Gallup

One reason for the decline in Democrats' intent to vote could be the depressed percentage of young voters this year saying they will definitely vote – now at 47%, down from 58% in 2012 and from a peak of 74% in 2008.

In contrast to the 11-point drop since 2012 in young adults' voting intention, there has been a seven-point decline among 35- to 54-year-olds and virtually no decline among those aged 55 and older.

Percentage Saying They Will Definitely Vote ("10"), by Age

Polls conducted in September of each year

	2000 %	2004 %	2008 %	2012 %	2016 %
U.S. adults	74	78	80	75	69
18 to 34	60	67	74	58	47
35 to 54	77	81	81	79	72
55+	81	84	82	83	82

Gallup

Given Hispanics' lower propensity to vote due to citizenship and other issues, this recent decline in intent to vote among 18- to 34-year-olds may partly reflect the influence of the growing and disproportionately youthful Hispanic population. But even when looking only at non-Hispanic adults, intent to vote among those aged 18 to 34 has dropped substantially more than among older Americans.

Percentage of Non-Hispanic U.S. Adults Saying They Will Definitely Vote ("10"), by Age

Polls conducted in September of each year

	2000 %	2004 %	2008 %	2012 %	2016 %
Non-Hispanic U.S. adults	75	79	81	79	73
18 to 34	61	66	76	62	51
35 to 54	78	81	81	81	78
55+	82	84	83	86	83

Gallup

Bottom Line

While Americans are giving a similar level of thought to the presidential election compared with previous years, the percentage saying they are certain they will vote is lagging, particularly among young adults. This likely reflects the persistently poor images of both major party nominees, as well as Hillary Clinton's difficulty in winning over the young adults who were much more favorable toward Bernie Sanders than toward her when Sanders was running for the Democratic nomination. Thus, while the debates could attract record audiences and the election is sure to dominate news coverage for the next several weeks, as long as Clinton and her Republican rival, Donald Trump, remain unpopular, voter turnout – particularly among younger Americans – may suffer.

Historical data are available in Gallup Analytics.

Survey Methods

Results for this Gallup poll are based on telephone interviews conducted Sept. 14-18, 2016, with a random sample of 1,033 adults, aged 18 and older, living in all 50 U.S. states and the District of Columbia. For results based on the total sample of national adults, the margin of sampling error is ±4 percentage points at the 95% confidence level. All reported margins of sampling error include computed design effects for weighting.

September 26, 2016

VOTERS PREFER TRUMP ON ECONOMY, CLINTON ON MOST OTHER ISSUES

by Zac Auter

Story Highlights

- *Registered voters prefer Trump to Clinton on economic issues*
- *Registered voters prefer Clinton to Trump on education, foreign affairs*
- *Young adults choose Clinton over Trump on nearly all issues*

WASHINGTON, D.C. — With the presidential election less than two months away, U.S. registered voters say Donald Trump is better able to handle economic issues – such as employment and taxes – than Hillary Clinton. However, these voters see Clinton as better suited than Trump on issues such as the treatment of minority groups, social issues, foreign affairs, education and immigration. Overall, of the 17 issues that Gallup asked registered voters about, Clinton leads Trump on 10.

Registered Voters' Perceptions of Which Candidate Is Best Able to Handle Key Issues

Regardless of which presidential candidate you support, please tell me if you think Hillary Clinton or Donald Trump would better handle each of the following issues.

	Prefer Hillary Clinton %	Prefer Donald Trump %	Advantage pct. pts.
The treatment of minority groups in this country	65	30	Clinton +35
Climate change	62	29	Clinton +33
Social issues such as gay marriage and abortion	63	33	Clinton +30
Foreign affairs	61	35	Clinton +26
Education	61	36	Clinton +25
Healthcare and the Affordable Care Act	56	41	Clinton +15
Immigration	55	42	Clinton +13
The distribution of income and wealth in the U.S.	50	44	Clinton +6
Trade with other nations	51	47	Clinton +4
Terrorism and national security	48	47	Clinton +1
The federal budget deficit	44	53	Trump +9
Government regulation of Wall Street and banks	43	52	Trump +9
The size and efficiency of the federal government	44	52	Trump +8
Gun policy	45	52	Trump +7
Taxes	45	51	Trump +6
Employment and jobs	47	51	Trump +4
The economy	47	50	Trump +3

Gallup, Sept. 14-18, 2016

While Clinton leads Trump on only three more issues total (10 for Clinton, seven for Trump), her average advantage far outpaces his. Clinton leads by an average of 19 percentage points, while Trump's average advantage is seven points.

The disparity in leads between Clinton and Trump in these policy spheres exceeds the gap between the major-party candidates in the two most recent presidential elections. In September 2008, John McCain led Barack Obama on six issues by an average of 12 points, while Obama led McCain on four issues by an average of nine points. In September 2012, Obama led Mitt Romney on seven issues by an average of 11 points – driven largely by a 26-point advantage on social issues – whereas Romney's lead on two issues averaged nine points.

Trump Weaker Among Republicans Than Clinton Is Among Democrats

Trump receives less support on these policy issues among registered Republicans than Clinton receives among registered Democrats. Republicans choose Trump over Clinton by an average of 71 points. Meanwhile, Clinton's advantage over Trump among Democrats across all policy spheres averages 81 points.

Among registered Republicans, Trump receives especially weak support on social issues, the treatment of minorities and climate change – issues on which about three in 10 Republicans say Clinton is better suited. On economic issues – such as taxes, the economy and the federal budget deficit – Trump scores especially strongly among his political compatriots, with almost nine in 10 Republicans preferring him to Clinton.

Clinton's weakest point among registered Democrats is on the issue of government regulation of Wall Street and banks, on which slightly less than one-fifth of Democrats prefer Trump. However, in all other policy spheres, no fewer than eight in 10 Democrats say Clinton would be better able than Trump to handle the issue.

Perceptions of Which Candidate Is Best Able to Handle Key Issues Among Registered Voters, by Partisan Identification

Regardless of which presidential candidate you support, please tell me if you think Hillary Clinton or Donald Trump would better handle each of the following issues.

	Trump's advantage among Republicans pct. pts.	Clinton's advantage among Democrats pct. pts.	Advantage among independents pct. pts.
The distribution of income and wealth in the U.S.	72	82	Clinton +1
Immigration	74	87	Clinton +10
Healthcare and the Affordable Care Act	73	93	Clinton +10
Education	60	94	Clinton +28
Trade with other nations	74	72	Clinton +3
Foreign affairs	53	85	Clinton +33
Social issues such as gay marriage and abortion	46	88	Clinton +37
Climate change	35	87	Clinton +38
The treatment of minority groups in this country	43	96	Clinton +41
The economy	88	77	Trump +10
Employment and jobs	87	79	Trump +16
The size and efficiency of the federal government	87	72	Trump +16
Government regulation of Wall Street and banks	76	61	Trump +20
The federal budget deficit	88	72	Trump +21
Gun policy	85	78	Trump +21
Terrorism and national security	77	77	Trump +7
Taxes	88	70	Trump +8

Gallup, Sept. 14-18, 2016

Independents strongly prefer Clinton to Trump on the treatment of minority groups in the U.S. (+41), climate change (+38), social issues (+37) and foreign affairs (+33). On immigration – an issue central to Trump's campaign – independents choose Clinton over Trump.

Trump's advantages over Clinton among independents reflect some of his strongest issues among Republicans. He leads Clinton on the budget deficit (+21), gun policy (+21) and government regulation of Wall Street (+20). However, on issues where Trump leads Clinton among independents, he averages a 15-point advantage, compared with Clinton's 22-point average advantage on issues where she leads.

Clinton Leads Trump on Nearly All Issues Among Young Americans

Both campaigns have struggled to resonate with young Americans, as both candidates' favorable ratings are lowest among young voters. When 18- to 34-year-olds are asked which candidate they believe to be best suited to handle particular policy issues, younger voters largely prefer Clinton over Trump. For issues on which Clinton leads, her advantage averages 31 points. In fact, young adults choose Clinton over Trump on nearly all issues that Gallup asks about. The only issue where young voters choose Trump over Clinton is on the regulation of Wall Street and banks (+7).

Young U.S. Registered Voters' Perceptions of Which Candidate Is Best Able to Handle Key Issues

Regardless of which presidential candidate you support, please tell me if you think Hillary Clinton or Donald Trump would better handle each of the following issues.

	Prefer Hillary Clinton %	Prefer Donald Trump %	Advantage pct. pts.
Terrorism and national security	57	38	Clinton +19
Gun policy	50	47	Clinton +3
Immigration	67	30	Clinton +37
Healthcare and the Affordable Care Act	68	28	Clinton +40
Foreign affairs	72	25	Clinton +47
The federal budget deficit	51	47	Clinton +4
Education	75	22	Clinton +53
Social issues such as gay marriage and abortion	76	19	Clinton +57
Climate change	79	15	Clinton +64
Employment and jobs	52	45	Clinton +7
The economy	53	45	Clinton +8
The size and efficiency of the federal government	57	40	Clinton +17
Trade with other nations	60	38	Clinton +22
The distribution of income and wealth in the U.S.	60	36	Clinton +24
The treatment of minority groups in this country	81	16	Clinton +65
Government regulation of Wall Street and banks	44	51	Trump +7
Taxes	49	49	Tie

Based on 18- to 34-year-olds who are registered to vote

Gallup, Sept. 14-18, 2016

Bottom Line

Americans cite the economy and unemployment as some of the most important problems facing the country. While Trump leads Clinton among registered voters in terms of which candidate can best handle these issues, his advantage is relatively small. And among young adults, Clinton leads Trump by seven or eight points on these issues.

Trump, meanwhile, continues to emphasize his stance on immigration. "Immigration" is still one of the most frequently used words Americans use to describe what they've recently heard about Trump. However, registered voters overall and independents prefer Clinton to Trump on the immigration issue by margins of 13 and 10 points, respectively.

Historical data are available in Gallup Analytics.

Survey Methods

Results for this Gallup poll are based on telephone interviews conducted Sept. 14-18, 2016, on the Gallup U.S. Daily survey, with a random sample of 1,033 adults, aged 18 and older, living in all 50 U.S. states and the District of Columbia. For results based on the total sample of national adults, the margin of sampling error is ±4 percentage points at the 95% confidence level. For results based on the total sample of 931 registered voters, the margin of sampling error is ±4 percentage points at the 95% confidence level. All reported margins of sampling error include computed design effects for weighting.

September 26, 2016

FEW HAVE HIGH HOPES FOR CLINTON OR TRUMP PRESIDENCY

by Justin McCarthy

Story Highlights

- *One in three say Clinton would be a good or great president*
- *One in four say a Trump presidency would be good or great*
- *Dems more optimistic about Clinton than GOP is about Trump*

WASHINGTON, D.C. — The campaigning over the past four months has done little to improve Americans' confidence in the potential presidencies of either major-party candidate. Americans are about as likely to say Hillary Clinton (33%) and Donald Trump (25%) would be a "great" or "good" president as they were in May. More Americans still think each candidate would make a "poor" or "terrible" president than a "good" or "great" one.

Americans' Views of Potential Clinton and Trump Presidencies

In your view, what kind of president would each of the following be if he or she were elected in November 2016 – great, good, average, poor, terrible or don't you know enough to say?

	Great/Good %	Average %	Poor/ Terrible %	No opinion/ Don't know %
HILLARY CLINTON				
Sept. 14-18, 2016	33	20	39	8

	Great/Good %	Average %	Poor/ Terrible %	No opinion/ Don't know %
May 18-22, 2016	32	19	47	3
DONALD TRUMP				
Sept. 14-18, 2016	25	15	51	9
May 18-22, 2016	29	14	52	4

Gallup

While more than half of Americans remain pessimistic about the performance of a Trump presidency, fewer are pessimistic about a Clinton presidency now (39%) than in May (47%). This is due to Democrats who initially showed resistance to her nomination (either by supporting Bernie Sanders or saying they wish someone else were the nominee) giving her slightly less negative ratings now than in May. Republicans also rate Clinton a bit less negatively. Among both of these groups, the percentage who rated Clinton's potential presidency as "poor" or "terrible" decreased by five percentage points or more since May. So, while they are not more likely to describe her presidency as "good" or "great," her negative ratings have fallen slightly.

These latest data, collected Sept. 14-18, mirror the lack of movement in each candidate's favorable ratings. Despite the events of the past four months, which included both Clinton and Trump accepting their respective parties' nominations, Americans are no more optimistic about the two potential presidencies than they were a few months ago.

Democrats, Nonwhites Most Optimistic About a Clinton Presidency

Across major subgroups, Democrats (69%) are most likely to say Clinton would be a "great" or "good" president, followed by nonwhites (50%). Clinton doesn't come close to the 50% mark with any other group – the closest being adults over the age of 55, at 38%.

Meanwhile, four in five Republicans say she would be a "poor" or "terrible" president" (79%), while half of whites rate her just as negatively.

Views of Potential Clinton Presidency by Group

In your view, what kind of president would each of the following be if he or she were elected in November 2016 – great, good, average, poor, terrible or don't you know enough to say?

	Great/Good %	Average %	Poor/Terrible %
Men	29	23	42
Women	36	18	37
White	24	18	50
Nonwhite	50	23	15
18-34	27	29	33
35-54	31	21	37
55+	38	14	44
Republicans	3	11	79
Independents	22	27	38
Democrats	69	19	6

Gallup, Sept. 14-18, 2016

Republicans' Ratings for Trump Lower Than Democrats' for Clinton

Trump's ratings from his own party are somewhat more subdued than Clinton's among her own party – 59% of Republicans say he would be a "great" or "good" president compared with 69% of Democrats who say the same for Clinton. In no other group does the percentage saying Trump would be a good or great president reach a majority, though about one in three whites (32%) and adults over the age of 55 (32%) have a positive view of Trump as president.

Democrats overwhelmingly view a Trump presidency as "poor" or "terrible" (84%), slightly higher than the percentage of Republicans who view a potential Clinton presidency as poor or terrible. More than six in 10 nonwhites (66%) and 18- to 34-year-olds (61%) share this sentiment. Smaller majorities of women (54%) and independents (51%) are just as negative about a potential Trump presidency.

Views of Potential Trump Presidency by Group

In your view, what kind of president would each of the following be if he or she were elected in November 2016 – great, good, average, poor, terrible or don't you know enough to say?

	Great/Good %	Average %	Poor/Terrible %
Men	28	17	49
Women	22	13	54
White	32	14	45
Nonwhite	8	15	66
18-34	12	16	61
35-54	26	13	50
55+	32	15	46
Republicans	59	19	14
Independents	18	17	51
Democrats	3	8	84

Gallup, Sept. 14-18, 2016

Bottom Line

The past four months have been eventful for the presidential race, but clearly not consequential in terms of Americans' outlooks for either a Clinton or Trump presidency.

The public is no more likely to view a Clinton presidency positively than in May, but fewer now have negative expectations if she were to win. But views of a Trump White House have hardly budged, and a majority continues to think he would be a poor or terrible president.

Beyond the two candidates' respective political parties, no demographic group has high expectations for either of their possible performances as president – though Clinton does receive positive ratings from half of nonwhites. This underscores the incredibly negative tone of the race and how difficult it will be for either candidate to overcome such dismal assessments from Americans with less than two months left before Election Day.

Enthusiasm for either Clinton or Trump in the White House remains fairly subdued, which raises the stakes for their performance in the debates and in the final weeks of the campaign.

Historical data are available in Gallup Analytics.

Survey Methods

Results for this Gallup poll are based on telephone interviews conducted Sept. 14-18, 2016, with a random sample of 1,033 adults, aged 18 and older, living in all 50 U.S. states and the District of Columbia. For results based on the total sample of national adults, the margin of sampling error is ±4 percentage points at the 95% confidence level. All reported margins of sampling error include computed design effects for weighting.

September 28, 2016
PARTISAN DIVIDE ON GOVERNMENT REGULATIONS REMAINS WIDE

by Justin McCarthy

Story Highlights

- *About three in four Republicans say business regulations are too much*
- *One in five Democrats see too much regulation*
- *Attitudes shifted after Obama's election*

WASHINGTON, D.C. — Donald Trump's assertion at Monday night's presidential debate that he would cut regulations while Hillary Clinton would "increase regulations all over the place" is consistent with the sensitivity to government regulation of business among members of his party. Republicans (76%) are more than three times as likely as Democrats (21%) to say there is "too much" government regulation of business and industry. Since President Barack Obama took office in 2009, Republicans' and Democrats' views on the matter have been widely at odds.

Americans' Views on Government Regulation of Business, by Party ID

In general, do you think there is too much, too little or about the right amount of government regulation of business and industry?

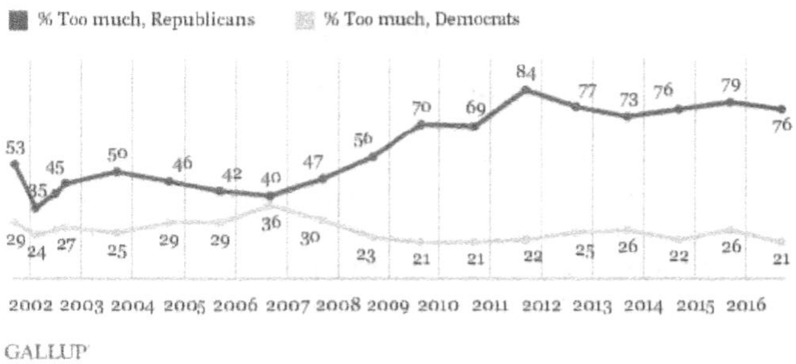

For her part, Clinton claimed that her proposals would "cut regulations and streamline them for small businesses," but this may have been directed more at those outside of her party, as relatively few Democrats (21%) say there is too much government regulation. In fact, too much business regulation was not a major concern of Democrats even before Obama's presidency. Since 2002, the percentage saying there was too much regulation of business has been between 21% and 29% in all but two polls.

Democrats are currently more likely to say the government regulates business too little (35%) or about the right amount (39%).

Republicans have typically been more likely than Democrats to be concerned with too much business regulation, even during the administration of Republican President George W. Bush. The percentage of Republicans citing too much regulation ranged from 35% to 56% throughout Bush's presidency. This jumped to 70% at the start of Obama's first term in 2009 and reached an apex of 84% in 2011.

The latest results come from Gallup's Sept. 7-11 annual Governance poll. Overall, about half of U.S. adults (47%) believe that the government regulates business and industry too much. Meanwhile, 27% say there is about the right amount of government regulation, while the smallest segment, 22%, believe there is too little.

Americans' Perceptions on Government Regulation of Business

In general, do you think there is too much, too little or about the right amount of government regulation of business and industry?

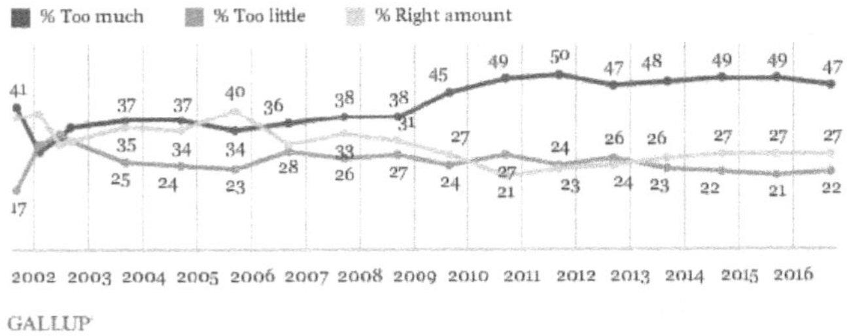

In line with the changes observed among Republicans and Democrats, Americans' views on business regulation shifted between the Bush and Obama administrations. Throughout the better part of Bush's two terms, the public was closely divided between saying there was too much versus about the right amount of government regulation of business and industry. Since Obama took office, close to half of the public has said there is too much regulation – driven by the dramatic rise in this view among Republicans – and the other half has split between saying there is about the right amount or too little.

Bottom Line

Americans' attitudes about government regulation of business and industry shifted when Obama became president, mainly because Republicans increasingly adopted the view that there was too much regulation. Those views would likely persist if Clinton is elected but could recalibrate if Trump wins.

Since 2009, Americans have been most likely to feel there is too much regulation, which could be related to the hundreds of regulations that went into effect on Obama's watch. Analysis by George Washington University's Regulatory Studies Center finds that Obama's regulations have outpaced those of the prior two presidents.

As Election Day nears, both major parties' candidates have made regulation-related pledges. But Republicans and Democrats do not share the same level of concern that government regulation is a problem.

Historical data are available in Gallup Analytics.

Survey Methods

Results for this Gallup poll are based on telephone interviews conducted Sept. 7-11, 2016, with a random sample of 1,020 adults, aged 18 and older, living in all 50 U.S. states and the District of

Columbia. For results based on the total sample of national adults, the margin of sampling error is ±4 percentage points at the 95% confidence level. All reported margins of sampling error include computed design effects for weighting.

September 28, 2016
IN U.S., PREFERENCE FOR DIVIDED GOVERNMENT LOWEST IN 15 YEARS

by Art Swift

Story Highlights

- *20% of Americans say they want divided government*
- *Fewer Republicans want divided government now than four years ago*
- *Fewer Democrats want the same party to control Congress than four years ago*

WASHINGTON, D.C. — One in five Americans believe it is best for the president to be from one political party and for Congress to be controlled by another, the lowest level of public support for divided government in Gallup's 15-year trend. The remainder are evenly divided between those who favor one party controlling both the presidency and Congress (36%) and those saying it makes no difference how political power is allocated (36%).

Americans' Views on Divided Government

Do you think it is better for the country to have a president who comes from the same political party that controls Congress, does it make no difference either way or do you think it is better to have a president from one political party and Congress controlled by another?

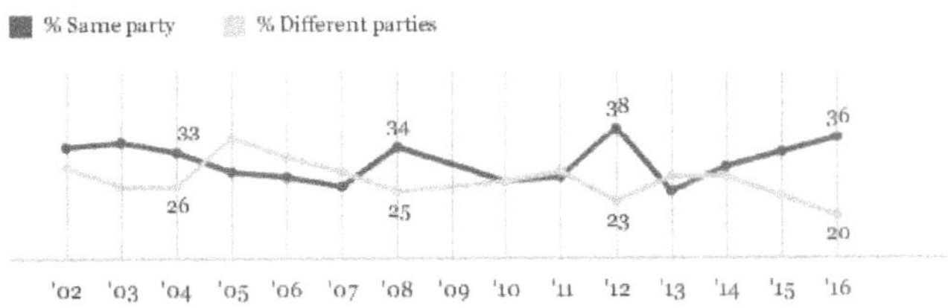

"No difference" not shown

GALLUP

Americans' current preference for one party controlling both the presidency and Congress is near the record high of 38% from four years ago. That fits with a pattern of heightened support for single-party control seen in the past two presidential election years. In 2004, the preferences were more evenly divided. These results are based on Gallup's annual Governance poll, conducted Sept. 7-11.

Divided government has been a regular occurrence in Washington, D.C., since 1969, with one party controlling the presidency and Congress for a little more than 12 of those years – 1977-1981, 1993-1995, 2003-2007, 2009-2011 and part of 2001. Looking back on the last five decades, Americans may be uncomfortable giving one party full control of the federal government. This may have compelled voters to restore divided government in three recent midterm elections (1994, 2006 and 2010) after two or four years when one party had controlled both the White House and Capitol Hill.

Fewer Republicans Prefer Divided Government

Party groups' preference for single-party control of the presidency and Congress during the past few presidential election years depends on the party in control of the presidency. In 2004, when Republican George W. Bush was in the White House, 44% of GOP voters said they wanted the same party to control Congress and the presidency, compared with 26% of Democrats who expressed a similar sentiment. Eight years later, when Democrat Barack Obama was seeking re-election, party views were flipped – 49% of Democrats said they wanted the same party to control Congress and the presidency, versus 36% of Republicans. This year, however, there is little difference in these views among the two groups.

Preferences for Control of Government

By party ID

	2004 %	2008 %	2012 %	2016 %
Republicans				
Same party	44	46	36	42
Different parties	17	21	27	19
Makes no difference	36	29	31	29
Independents				
Same party	26	23	27	28
Different parties	30	29	30	27
Makes no difference	38	35	35	38
Democrats				
Same party	26	35	49	40
Different parties	32	22	13	14
Makes no difference	38	39	32	37

Gallup

The percentage of Democrats who want the same party to control government is now 40%, down from 49% in 2012. However, Democrats' preference for divided government is essentially unchanged; it is now 14%, versus 13% in 2012. In the four most recent presidential election years, the percentage of Democrats who have said the division of power in Washington "makes no difference" has stayed relatively consistent, between 32% and 39%.

Independents tend to be indifferent on retaining divided government, at 38% "makes no difference." Unlike views of Democrats or Republicans, independents' views on this issue have not fluctuated much in the four most recent presidential election years. Independents notably are much less likely than both major parties in 2016 to say they want the same party to control the political branches of government.

Bottom Line

Since President Richard Nixon was paired with a Democratic Congress in 1969, party control of the political branches of the U.S. government has usually been divided. For nearly the past six years, the federal government has operated under this arrangement, with Obama having to work with at least one Republican-controlled branch of Congress. In recent presidential election years dating back to 2008, Americans' preference for the "same party" controlling the government has been more pronounced than in non-presidential years. This is likely because many Americans have witnessed the government increasingly in gridlock, believing that legislation will get passed only if there is one party in control and that party pushes it through.

In a presidential election year, Americans may hope that their party will gain control of the legislative and executive branches of government and pass legislation with which they agree. During the Obama presidency, one notable example was the Affordable Care Act, which Democrats passed without Republican support in the House of Representatives or the Senate.

In recent past election years, those who supported the party of the president in office tended to want the same party to control both political branches of the U.S. government. For example, in 2004, more Republicans than Democrats wanted same-party rule, and the opposite occurred when a Democrat was in the White House in 2012.

This year, relatively few Democrats or Republicans wish for divided government. In addition to each group possibly feeling optimistic about their party's chances in the election, another reason so few support divided government could be a desire to overcome political gridlock and pass legislation. In any case, Americans have no clear preference for whether the same party should control both political branches or whether it makes no difference.

Historical data are available in Gallup Analytics.

Survey Methods

Results for this Gallup poll are based on telephone interviews conducted Sept. 7-11, 2016, with a random sample of 1,020 adults, aged 18 and older, living in all 50 U.S. states and the District of Columbia. For results based on the total sample of national adults, the margin of sampling error is ±4 percentage points at the 95% confidence level. All reported margins of sampling error include computed design effects for weighting.

September 29, 2016

CLINTON'S VICTORY ON THE LARGER SIDE FOR MODERN DEBATES

by Lydia Saad

Story Highlights

- *By 61% to 27%, more say Clinton than Trump did the better job*
- *Long line of first-debate winners have failed to win the presidency*
- *Clinton dominated in perceptions of understanding the issues*

PRINCETON, N.J. — By 61% to 27%, Americans who tuned in to Monday night's presidential debate believe Hillary Clinton, rather than Donald Trump, did the better job. Her 34-percentage-point lead is among the more robust victories presidential candidates have earned in Gallup's post-debate polls stretching back to 1960, on par with Bill Clinton's debate wins over Bob Dole in 1996. However, as the record shows, the winner of the first debate does not necessarily win the next debate, or the election.

Presidential Candidate Perceived as Performing Best in Debate

Among U.S. adults who watched or listened to each debate; shown is percentage-point lead over next-highest-rated opposing candidate

	First debate	Second debate	Third debate
2016	H. Clinton (+34)	–	–
2012	Romney (+52)	Obama (+13)	Obama (+23)
2008	Obama (+12)	Obama (+33)	Obama (+26)
2004	Kerry (+32)	Kerry (+15)	Kerry (+14)
2000	Gore^ (+7)	G.W. Bush^ (+13)	Gore^ (+2)
1996	B. Clinton (+35)	B. Clinton^ (+30)	–
1992	Perot^ (+17)	B. Clinton (+42)	Perot^ (+9)
1988	Dukakis (+9)	–	–
1984	Mondale^ (+19)	Reagan^ (+3)	–
1976	Ford (+7)	–	–
1960	Kennedy (+21)	–	–

^ Based on debate reaction poll conducted the same night with respondents interviewed in advance who planned to watch the debate and agreed to be called back

Gallup

Most notably, Mitt Romney was the runaway leader in public perceptions of who performed better in the opening debate of 2012, with 72% of debate watchers choosing him versus just 20% naming Barack Obama – the widest debate lead Gallup has ever recorded. Yet Obama eclipsed Romney in the next two debates and won the election. Equally striking is that John Kerry was the perceived winner of all three debates against George W. Bush in 2004, including by 32 points in the first debate, but lost the election.

In terms of other first debates, viewers thought Al Gore outperformed George W. Bush in 2000, and they believed Ross Perot bested both Bill Clinton and George H.W. Bush in 1992. Viewers also gave Michael Dukakis better marks than Bush in 1988. They thought Walter Mondale outperformed Ronald Reagan in 1984 and determined that Gerald Ford beat Jimmy Carter in 1976. But the credential carried none of these debate winners to presidential victory.

On the other hand, decisive first-debate showings by John F. Kennedy in 1960, Bill Clinton in 1996 and Obama in 2008 all foreshadowed positive outcomes for these candidates in the elections that followed.

Democrats Much Happier Than GOP With Candidate's Performance

Hillary Clinton's strong lead in public perceptions of who won Monday night's debate is explained by her much higher support from fellow Democrats (92% of whom said she did the better job) than Trump received from Republicans (53% thought he did the better job). Additionally, 59% of political independents thought Clinton prevailed, adding to her overall strong showing. Gallup conducted this poll Sept. 27-28 with 1,020 national adults, including 791 who said they watched or heard the debate.

Regardless of which candidate you happen to support, who do you think did the better job in [last/Monday] night's debate – [Hillary Clinton (or) Donald Trump]?

Among U.S. adults who watched or listened to the debate

	Clinton %	Trump %	Neither (vol.) %	Both equally (vol.) %	No opinion %
All debate viewers	61	27	5	6	2
Democrats	92	3	2	2	2
Independents	59	30	5	4	2
Republicans	28	53	6	12	1

"vol." = volunteered response

Gallup, Sept. 27-28, 2016

Viewers of the first debate between Clinton and Trump, held Sept. 26 at Hofstra University in New York, also thought Clinton outshone Trump on each of four personal qualities that could be important to voters when casting their ballots in November, although by varying margins.

She did best against Trump, 62% to 26%, in perceptions of which candidate better demonstrated a good understanding of the issues – but led by nearly as much, 59% to 27%, for appearing presidential.

Trump edged closer to Clinton in viewers' opinions of which candidate came across as more likable and inspiring, but he still trailed her by double digits on both qualities.

Viewers' Perceptions of Qualities Exhibited at First Debate

Thinking about the following characteristics and qualities, please say whether you think each one better described Hillary Clinton or Donald Trump during [last/Monday] night's debate.

	Clinton %	Trump %	Clinton advantage (pct. pts.)
Had a good understanding of the issues	62	26	+36
Appeared presidential	59	27	+32
Was more likable	55	36	+19
Was inspiring	46	34	+12

Gallup, Sept. 27-28, 2016

Bottom Line

Clinton's success over Trump in debate viewers' perceptions of who prevailed Monday night may support the maxim that "he who fails to prepare, prepares to fail." Her confidence in detailing one policy plan after another likely contributed to viewer perceptions that she had a good command of the issues and was more "presidential." And her 36- and 32-point leads, respectively, over Trump on these qualities mirror her 34-point lead in overall perceptions of who did the better job in the debate. The telltale sign that Trump came up short is that barely half of Republicans believe he won, compared with almost all Democrats believing Clinton won.

Debate performances do not always line up with election outcomes, and a poor showing in the initial debate doesn't mean a candidate can't come back and win the next one. Obama's recovery after losing badly in the first 2012 debate best illustrates this. George W. Bush even won the presidency in 2004 without winning any of that year's debates, although he at least improved his showing in the final two. Hillary Clinton's reportedly meticulous preparation won her the first round, and the stakes are now raised for Trump in rounds two and three.

Historical data are available in Gallup Analytics.

Survey Methods

Results for this Gallup poll are based on telephone interviews conducted Sept. 27-28, 2016, on the Gallup Daily tracking survey, with a random sample of 1,020 adults, aged 18 and older, living in all 50 U.S. states and the District of Columbia. For results based on the total sample of national adults, the margin of sampling error is ±4 percentage points at the 95% confidence level. For results based on the total sample of 791 adults who watched or listened to the debate, the margin of sampling error is ±4 percentage points at the 95% confidence level. All reported margins of sampling error include computed design effects for weighting.

September 29, 2016
MOST REPUBLICANS CONTINUE TO DISAPPROVE OF SUPREME COURT

by Michael Smith and Frank Newport

Story Highlights

- *67% of Republicans say the court is too liberal*
- *67% of Democrats approve of the court*
- *39% of Americans say court's ideology is "about right"*

WASHINGTON, D.C. — As the eight-person Supreme Court prepares to reconvene next Monday for its fall term, Americans' views of the court remain highly partisan. Slightly more than one in four Republicans (26%) approve of the how the court is handling its job, compared with 42% of independents and 67% of Democrats.

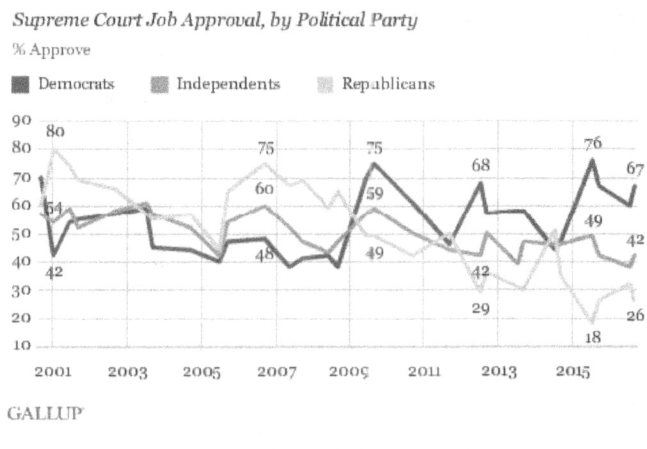

These results are from Gallup's Sept. 7-11 Governance poll. If Hillary Clinton wins the presidential election, it could result in a left-leaning justice filling the vacant seat left by the late conservative

Justice Antonin Scalia in February 2016, giving the liberal wing majority control of the court.

The current 41-percentage-point gap between Democrats and Republicans is not as large as the gap Gallup found in July 2015 – after the Supreme Court legalized same-sex marriage and rejected a challenge to the Affordable Care Act – when 76% of Democrats and 18% of Republicans approved. A year before that, in a July 2014 survey, there was no party difference in approval of the court. From 2000 to 2014, partisans' views varied, influenced partly by the party of the president, but also by the direction of some of the court's decisions.

Supreme Court Job Approval Remains Below 50%

Overall, 45% of Americans now approve of the way the Supreme Court is handling its job, up slightly from 42% in mid-July, but generally in line with the range of approval ratings since 2011.

Do you approve or disapprove of the way the Supreme Court is handling its job?

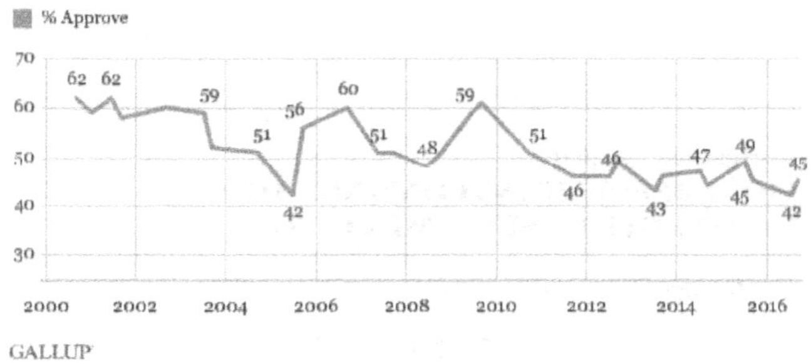

With a few exceptions, Americans' approval of the Supreme Court was significantly higher in the years before 2011, including the all-time highs of 62% in 2000 and 2001. Approval was at its lowest (42%) this past summer and in 2005. This summer, the court ruled that colleges and universities can continue to use race as a factor in their admissions decisions, a ruling that just over one-quarter of Americans supported. Meanwhile, the court deadlocked 4-4 on President Barack Obama's immigration plan. This decision essentially left in place a lower court's decision that blocked the president's immigration plan, which would have prevented up to 5 million undocumented immigrants from being deported.

"Too Liberal" Perceptions of Court Constant at 37%

Americans continue to have mixed feelings about the court's ideological bent. Currently, 37% of Americans think the court is "too liberal," while about as many (39%) say the court's ideology is "about right" and 20% say it is too conservative. These views are essentially the same as they were last year, which marked a seven-point increase from 2014 in the percentage believing the court was too liberal. That shift likely came in response to the court's 2015 landmark rulings that legalized same-sex marriage and upheld the Affordable Care Act. In the two decades prior to that, the percentage of Americans who thought the court was too liberal was consistently less than one-third. Thirty-two percent gave the "too liberal" response in 2010, soon after two new liberal justices, Sonia Sotomayor and Elena Kagan, replaced fellow liberals David Souter and John Paul Stevens, respectively.

In general, do you think the current Supreme Court is too liberal, too conservative or just about right?

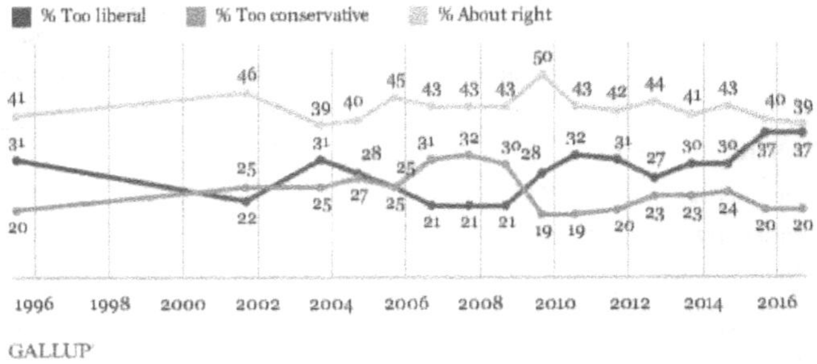

Almost the same percentage of Republicans say the court is too liberal (67%) as disapprove of the court's handling of its job (66%). That is in sharp contrast to Democrats, of whom 17% say it's too liberal.

Bottom Line

Since the conservative Scalia died, the empty ninth seat has been part of the backdrop of this year's presidential election. The winner of the election will affect the court's balance of power. This reality and liberal victories in several major decisions handed down by the court in recent years, such as legalized same-sex marriage and the upholding of constitutional protection for abortion rights, help explain Americans' politically polarized views when asked to rate the court. This polarization could become even more pronounced if a liberal justice replaces Scalia, swinging the court's balance of power to the left on the political spectrum. On the other hand, as long as Justice Anthony Kennedy remains on the court as a swing vote, a conservative or moderate appointment might keep the status quo.

Historical data are available in Gallup Analytics.

Survey Methods

Results for this Gallup poll are based on telephone interviews conducted Sept. 7-11, 2016, with a random sample of 1,020 adults, aged 18 and older, living in all 50 U.S. states and the District of Columbia. For results based on the total sample of national adults, the margin of sampling error is ±4 percentage points at the 95% confidence level. All reported margins of sampling error include computed design effects for weighting.

September 30, 2016

AMERICANS' DESIRE FOR THIRD PARTY PERSISTS THIS ELECTION YEAR

by Jeffrey M. Jones

Story Highlights

- *57% say a third major party is needed*
- *In 2008 and 2012, less than half favored a third party*
- *Just over half of Republicans favor a third party*

PRINCETON, N.J. — A majority of Americans, 57%, continue to say that a third major U.S. political party is needed, while 37% disagree, saying the two parties are doing an adequate job of representing the American people. These views are similar to what Gallup has measured in each of the last three years. However, they represent a departure from public opinion in 2008 and 2012 – the last two presidential election years – when Americans were evenly divided on the need for a third party.

Americans' Views on Need for Third Party

In your view, do the Republican and Democratic parties do an adequate job of representing the American people, or do they do such a poor job that a third major party is needed?

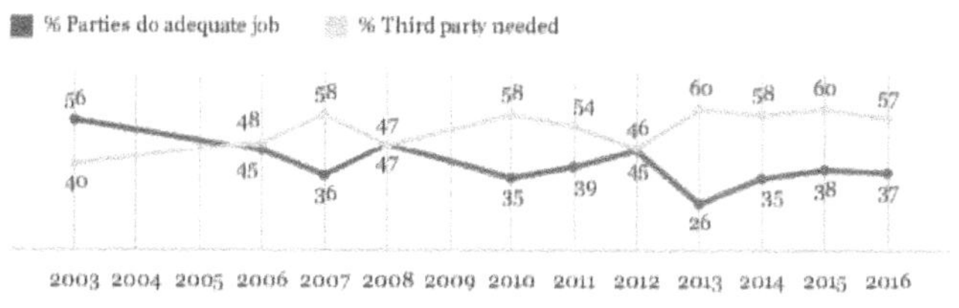

Note: 2007 and 2011 represent average of two polls conducted those years.

GALLUP

These results are based on Gallup's annual Governance poll. The poll was conducted Sept. 7-11, at a time when Americans' views of the Republican and Democratic parties are near historical lows, and when Americans hold highly negative opinions of both major-party presidential nominees. In 2008 and 2012, Americans' favorable ratings of the parties were slightly more positive than today, but their favorable ratings of the presidential candidates were far better.

In those years, third-party presidential candidates received less than 2% of the popular vote for president. This year, third-party candidates are getting about 10% of the vote combined in presidential preference polls. Should that level of support hold between now and Election Day, it would be the strongest performance for third-party candidates since the 1992 and 1996 campaigns, when Ross Perot ran for president.

When Gallup first asked Americans about the need for a third party in 2003, a majority said the parties were doing an adequate job, leaving 40% advocating for a third party. By 2006, Americans were evenly divided, but they have shown a clearer preference for a third party since then, apart from 2008 and 2012.

Half of Republicans Say Third Party Needed

As might be expected, independents have consistently been most likely among the major political groups to believe a third party is needed. Currently, 73% of independents, 51% of Republicans and 43% of Democrats favor the formation of a third party. Republicans' preference for a third party today ranks among the highest Gallup has found for a partisan group, along with a 52% reading among Republicans in 2013 and 50% for Democrats in 2006.

Support for a Third Major U.S. Political Party, by Political Party Affiliation

Figures are percentages saying a third party is needed

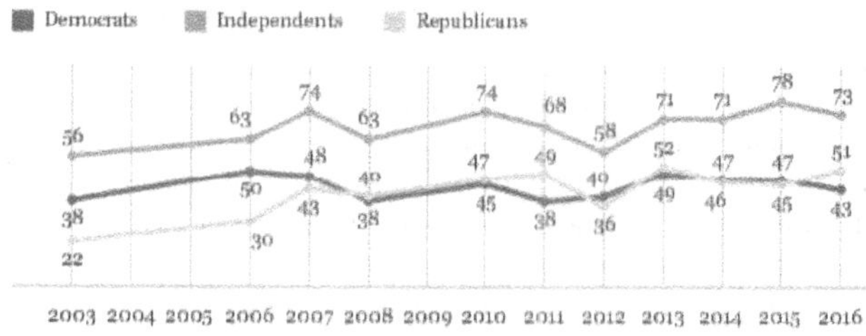

Note: 2007 and 2011 data represent average of two polls

GALLUP

In the 2008 and 2012 presidential election years, the decline in support for a third party was the result of a sharp drop from the prior year among independents, coupled with a similar, double-digit drop among the major-party group looking to win control of the White House – Democrats in 2008 and Republicans in 2012.

This year, independents' desire for a third party declined only modestly, from 78% in 2015 to 73%, while Democrats' desire also declined slightly and that of Republicans increased. The increase could reflect some Republicans' frustration with the party's internal divisions, both between conservatives and party leaders in government, and between party establishment figures and Donald Trump.

Implications

Americans' usual preference for a third major political party had subsided in the last two presidential election years, but that pattern did not repeat itself this year. In 2008 and 2012, Americans' general contentment with the major-party nominees may have led them to believe the parties were doing an adequate job of representing their views, and thus there was little appetite for a third party. This was the case in 2012, even as the well-funded "Americans Elect" movement aimed at providing the infrastructure for a credible third-party candidate could not field a viable candidate.

The political environment is different this year, with Hillary Clinton's favorable ratings struggling to break 40%, while Trump's have been stuck even lower at around 33%. Four years ago, Gary Johnson and Jill Stein combined for just over 1% of the national popular vote as the Libertarian and Green Party presidential nominees, respectively. This year, with those two third-party candidates nominated again, their support in pre-election polls among likely voters is nearly 10%.

Those polls portend a significant increase in the third-party vote this year, but well short of what it would take any third-party candidate to win the election. Their main impact on the outcome would likely be to play "spoiler" by taking away enough votes from one major-party candidate to allow the other to prevail.

With 57% of Americans favoring a third major political party, but only about one in 10 voters currently saying they will vote for a third-party candidate, Americans' appetite for a third party may not be as great as they say it is. The gap between preference for a third party and support for third-party candidates in this year's election may also reflect the structural challenges third parties face, Americans' unfamiliarity with the third-party candidates and possibly Americans' reluctance to cast their vote for a candidate with little chance of winning.

Historical data are available in Gallup Analytics.

Survey Methods

Results for this Gallup poll are based on telephone interviews conducted Sept. 7-11, 2016, with a random sample of 1,020 adults, aged 18 and older, living in all 50 U.S. states and the District of Columbia. For results based on the total sample of national adults, the margin of sampling error is ±4 percentage points at the 95% confidence level. All reported margins of sampling error include computed design effects for weighting.

October 03, 2016
U.S. CONSUMER SPENDING HIGHEST FOR ANY SEPTEMBER SINCE 2008

by Jim Norman

Story Highlights

- *September spending averages $91 a day, identical to August*
- *Spending had dropped from August to September in last six years*
- *Spending typically rises from September to October*

WASHINGTON, D.C. – Americans' daily self-reports of spending averaged $91 in September, unchanged from August, but the highest average for the month since 2008. The stability in September comes after wide swings during the summer months – when spending rose from June's $88 average to an eight-year high of $100 in July, then fell to $91 in August.

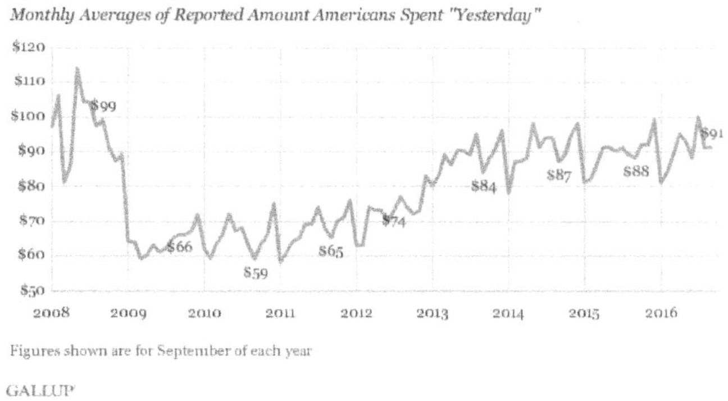

Results are based on Gallup Daily tracking interviews conducted throughout September. Gallup asks Americans each night to report how much they spent "yesterday," excluding normal household bills and major purchases such as a home or car. The measure gives an indication of discretionary spending.

Since December 2012, Americans' daily spending estimates have consistently averaged $80 or higher in all but one month. By contrast, in the four years prior, which included part of the Great Recession and periods of high unemployment that ensued, monthly spending averages were as low as $58 and never above $77.

Spending Avoids Usual September Slump

Although spending in the U.S. had been lower in September than in August in each of the past six years, it held steady this year. In all but one of those years it subsequently rose in October. The exception was 2012, when the average dropped in both September and October. Last year, September's average of $88 was only a dollar lower than August's $89.

Monthly Consumer Spending Averages, 2008-2016

	August $	September $	October $
2008	97	99	91
2009	65	66	66
2010	63	59	63
2011	68	65	70
2012	77	74	72
2013	95	84	88
2014	94	87	89
2015	89	88	92
2016	91	91	

Gallup Daily Tracking

Bottom Line

American consumers this year avoided the September slump in spending typically seen in recent years. That has helped keep average spending for the first nine months of 2016 the highest for any year since 2008. Spending patterns of the past decade for the months of October, November and December suggest that spending will increase even further.

However, there are some reasons to believe spending might not follow the normal pattern this year. While the relatively high level of September spending could indicate that Americans stayed in a buying mood even after the end of summer vacations and back-to-school shopping, it could also mean that the customary September-to-October rise in spending has already taken place. And although presidential elections generally do not affect consumer spending, Americans' negative views about the two major-party candidates could affect consumer confidence and spending in ways not seen in 2008 or 2012.

Survey Methods

Results for this Gallup poll are based on telephone interviews conducted Sept. 1-30, 2016, on the Gallup U.S. Daily survey, with a random sample of 14,743 adults, aged 18 and older, living in all 50 U.S. states and the District of Columbia. The margin of error for the spending mean is ±$5 at the 95% confidence level. All reported margins of sampling error include computed design effects for weighting.

October 04, 2016
TRUMP SEEN AS LESS CONSERVATIVE THAN PRIOR GOP CANDIDATES

by Justin McCarthy

Story Highlights

- *47% say Trump is conservative – less than Romney, McCain and Bush*
- *Voters split on Trump being more conservative, liberal than they are*
- *Nearly one in five registered voters describe Trump as liberal*

WASHINGTON, D.C. – Donald Trump's political views, in the eyes of U.S. registered voters, are the least conservative of GOP presidential candidates in recent history. About six in 10 registered voters have viewed recent Republican nominees as conservative or very conservative, with George W. Bush's 68% in 2004 the highest. Trump stands out from the rest of the group with less than half of voters (47%) describing him as conservative or very conservative.

Voters' Views of Republican Presidential Candidates, 1992-2016

How would you describe the political views of [candidate]: very liberal, liberal, moderate, conservative or very conservative?

	Total liberal %	Moderate %	Total Conservative %
2016 **Views of Donald Trump**	19	22	47
2012 **Views of Mitt Romney**	11	21	60
2008 **Views of John McCain**	9	26	62
2004 **Views of George W. Bush**	8	18	68
1992 **Views of George H.W. Bush**	9	20	59

Gallup

These results come from a Sept. 14-18 Gallup poll, conducted prior to last week's presidential debate. Respondents were asked to describe the presidential candidates' views as "very liberal," "liberal," "moderate," "conservative" or "very conservative." Gallup has asked voters to rate the presidential candidates and themselves using the same five-point ideology scale in most presidential elections since 1992.

The 58% of voters describing Hillary Clinton's views as liberal or very liberal is similar to Barack Obama's 60% in 2012 and 62% in 2008. Voters were somewhat less likely to perceive John Kerry in 2004 (48%) and Bill Clinton in 1992 (42%) as liberal.

Voters' Views of Democratic Presidential Candidates, 1992-2016

How would you describe the political views of [candidate]: very liberal, liberal, moderate, conservative or very conservative?

	Total liberal %	Moderate %	Total Conservative %
2016 **Views of Hillary Clinton**	58	25	12
2012 **Views of Barack Obama**	60	22	12
2008 **Views of Barack Obama**	62	24	11
2004 **Views of John Kerry**	48	32	15
1992 **Views of Bill Clinton**	42	32	15

Gallup

Nearly One in Five Voters Describe Trump as Liberal

While about half of registered voters describe Trump as conservative or very conservative, 22% describe him as moderate and 19% as liberal or very liberal.

Roughly equal proportions of Democrats and Democratic-leaning independents (51%) and Republicans and Republican-leaning independents (47%) perceive the GOP candidate's views as conservative or very conservative. At the same time, Republicans and Republican leaners (33%) are three times as likely as Democrats and Democratic leaners (11%) to describe Trump as a moderate.

About one in five registered voters say Trump is liberal or very liberal, including 16% of Republicans and 21% of Democrats.

Voters' Perceptions of Donald Trump's Political Views, by Party ID

How would you describe the political views of Donald Trump: very liberal, liberal, moderate, conservative or very conservative?

	All Voters %	Republican/ Leaners %	Democrats/ Leaners %
Very liberal	8	3	12
Liberal	11	13	9
Moderate	22	33	11
Conservative	31	38	26
Very conservative	16	9	25

Gallup, Sept. 14-18, 2016

Perceptions that Trump is liberal could be related to his former left-leaning stances on issues such as abortion, gun rights and healthcare. His current views on trade often align with liberal economists. It's worth noting that while only 5% of registered voters don't have an opinion on the ideology of Clinton's political views, 12% have no opinion on Trump's views.

About Six in 10 Voters Say Clinton Is Liberal

U.S. voters are most likely to describe Clinton as liberal (31%) or very liberal (27%). One in four consider her a political moderate (25%), while much smaller percentages describe her as conservative (9%) or very conservative (3%).

Perceptions of Clinton's ideology differ sharply by voters' partisan identification or leanings. More than three-quarters of registered voters who identify as Republicans or as Republican-leaning independents (77%) describe Clinton as liberal or very liberal, compared with 41% of Democrats and Democratic-leaning independents.

And while few Republicans and Republican leaners describe Clinton as either conservative or very conservative (6%), a sizable minority of Democrats and Democratic leaners (17%) describe Clinton's political views this way.

Voters' Perceptions of Hillary Clinton's Political Views, by Party ID

How would you describe the political views of Hillary Clinton: very liberal, liberal, moderate, conservative or very conservative?

	All Voters %	Republican/ Leaners %	Democrats/ Leaners %
Very liberal	27	49	6
Liberal	31	28	35
Moderate	25	10	40
Conservative	9	4	13
Very conservative	3	2	4

Gallup, Sept. 14-18, 2016

Half of Voters Say Clinton Is More Liberal Than They Are

While about half of registered voters describe Clinton's political views as "a lot more liberal" or "somewhat more liberal" than their own, they are divided as to whether Trump is more conservative (35%) or more liberal (31%) than they are.

One in four Americans describe themselves as very liberal (8%) or liberal (17%), while more than one in three say their political views are moderate (37%). Thirty-six percent describe their political views as conservative, including 9% who say they are very conservative.

Gallup combined voters' self-reported ideology and their ratings of the candidates to compute political difference scores indicating how each candidate compares with the respondent's own political views.

Voters' Political Views vs. Those of Presidential Candidates

Figures are computed by combining registered voters' self-reported ideology with their ratings of the ideology of each candidate.

	Hillary Clinton %	Donald Trump %
A lot more liberal than self	34	13
Somewhat more liberal	15	18
Same views	24	22
Somewhat more conservative	15	14
A lot more conservative than self	6	21
No opinion/Undesignated	5	12

Gallup, Sept. 14-18, 2016

Bottom Line

Clinton is slightly more likely than Trump to represent the ideology often associated with each candidate's respective party, as 58% consider her a liberal versus 47% calling Trump a conservative. At the same time, slightly more voters consider Trump a liberal than call Clinton a conservative. As a result, the two receive about equal ratings as "moderates."

When comparing these perceptions with voters' own political views, similar proportions of voters – between 22% and 24% – place themselves and the candidate at the same point on the left-right ideological continuum. Nearly half of voters place Clinton to the left of themselves, while smaller, similar proportions put Trump to the left and to the right of their own views.

Trump stands out more from a historical perspective, however, as he is less likely to be considered a conservative than any other recent Republican presidential candidate.

Meanwhile, Clinton – who has been accused by some on the left of not being liberal enough – will have to work to win over those who may feel her views are too far to the left of their own. However, perceptions of Clinton as being liberal are about the same as the man she hopes to succeed as president.

Historical data are available in Gallup Analytics.

Survey Methods

Results for this Gallup poll are based on telephone interviews conducted Sept. 14-18, 2016, with a random sample of 931 registered voters, aged 18 and older, living in all 50 U.S. states and the District of Columbia. For results based on the total sample of registered voters, the margin of sampling error is ±4 percentage points at the 95% confidence level. All reported margins of sampling error include computed design effects for weighting.

October 05, 2016

OBAMA JOB APPROVAL UP MOST AMONG CONSERVATIVE DEMOCRATS

by Jeffrey M. Jones

Story Highlights

- *Overall approval has increased from 46% to 52% since last October*
- *All Democratic groups more approving, especially conservative Democrats*
- *Little to no change in Republican job approval*

PRINCETON, N.J. – President Barack Obama's job approval has increased from 46% in October 2015 to 52% last month. His ratings have risen among most party and ideological groups, but his largest gain – 13 percentage points – has come among conservative Democrats. Regardless of their ideology, Republicans' opinions of Obama are virtually unchanged.

President Barack Obama Job Approval Ratings, October 2015 vs. September 2016

	October 2015 %	September 2016 %	pct. pts.
National adults	46	52	+6
Liberal Democrats	87	93	+6
Moderate Democrats	80	88	+8
Conservative Democrats	67	80	+13
Non-leaning independents	38	46	+8
Moderate/Liberal Republicans	23	25	+2
Conservative Republicans	6	7	+1

Party groups include independents who lean to the party.
Gallup Daily Tracking

Over the past year, moderate Democrats and liberal Democrats have shown eight- and six-point increases, respectively. Those changes are smaller than the change among conservative Democrats, in part because liberal and moderate Democrats already had high approval ratings of Obama.

Approval among non-leaning independents – those who initially identify as political independents and say they do not lean toward either the Democratic or Republican Party – also increased significantly over the past year, from 38% to 46%.

Liberal Democrats currently give Obama his highest approval rating at 93%. His ratings decrease moving rightward on the political spectrum to a low of 7% approval among conservative Republicans. Although the precise level of support for Obama among the various political and ideological groups has varied over the course of his presidency, the rank order of the groups has been consistent.

In this analysis, partisanship is based on a respondent's self-identification as a Republican, independent or Democrat. Independents are subsequently asked if they lean more to the Republican Party or the Democratic Party. Party leaners are grouped with those who initially identify with the relevant party, since partisan leaners often share similar opinions with party identifiers. Ideological orientation is also based on self-identification as a liberal, moderate or conservative.

The latest results are based on Gallup Daily tracking interviews conducted throughout September. Obama's 52% average job approval rating last month ties January 2013 and June 2016 ratings as the best monthly averages during his second term in office. The highest monthly average approval rating he has had in his presidency was 65% in May 2009, during the "honeymoon" phase of his presidency. He also averaged 66% job approval between his inauguration on Jan. 20, 2009, and the end of that month.

The six-point improvement in Obama's job approval rating over the past year is similar to what occurred leading up to his re-election in 2012. His approval rating increased seven points from November 2011 (43%) to October 2012 (50%).

Back then, Obama's approval rating increased a substantial 18 points among conservative Democrats – more than any other political group. He also enjoyed double-digit increases among liberal Democrats, moderate Democrats and non-leaning independents. His job approval rating declined over the course of that year among Republicans, who mostly supported GOP nominee Mitt Romney in his attempt to deny Obama a second term as president in the 2012 election.

President Barack Obama Job Approval Ratings, November 2011 vs. October 2012

	November 2011 %	October 2012 %	pct. pts.
National adults	43	50	+7
Liberal Democrats	83	93	+10
Moderate Democrats	74	87	+13
Conservative Democrats	66	84	+18
Non-leaning independents	31	43	+12
Moderate/Liberal Republicans	22	19	-3
Conservative Republicans	7	5	-2

Party groups include independents who lean to the party.
Gallup Daily Tracking

These trends indicate that opinions of the president become more politicized during a presidential election year, a time when Americans' partisanship is continually reinforced by news coverage and discussion of the campaign. Conservative Democrats likely agree less with a liberal Democratic president's policies and actions than moderate or liberal Democrats do. As a result, they may be less inclined to approve of the job he is doing in nonelection years when political news coverage may be focused more on what the president is doing in office and less on party politics. When the discussion turns to re-electing the president, or choosing his successor, as is the case this year, a person's attachment to the political party becomes more influential than other considerations in how they evaluate the president's performance.

Bottom Line

For most of Barack Obama's White House career, less than half of Americans have approved of the job he is doing. Now, in his last year in office, as attention turns to finding his successor and evaluating his historical legacy, Americans are seeing him in a more positive light.

Obama's recent approval ratings have consistently been above 50% and among the best of his second term. That rise has mostly been fueled by increased support from Democrats of all ideological orientations, especially conservative Democrats. As a result, the gap between Democrats who are conservative and those who are moderate and liberal has narrowed.

The increase among Democratic groups has likely been aided by the presidential campaign, which serves to activate Americans' partisanship and thus cause them to view politicians of their preferred party more positively.

The most obvious historical parallel to Obama's eighth-year increase from below 50% approval to above it is that of Ronald Reagan. Reagan's job approval ratings pushed above 50% in 1988, creating a favorable political environment for George H.W. Bush to win the political equivalent of a third Reagan term. Democrats surely hope that they can capitalize on a similar trend and see the party win a rare third consecutive presidential election.

These data are available in Gallup Analytics.

Survey Methods

Results for this Gallup poll are based on telephone interviews conducted Sept. 1-30, 2016, on the Gallup U.S. Daily survey, with a random sample of 14,743 adults, aged 18 and older, living in all 50 U.S. states and the District of Columbia. For results based on the total sample of national adults, the margin of sampling error is ±1 percentage point at the 95% confidence level.

For results based on the total samples of 2,735 liberal Democrats and 2,505 moderate Democrats, the margin of sampling error is ±2 percentage points at the 95% confidence level.

For results based on the sample of 845 conservative Democrats, the margin of sampling error is ±4 percentage points at the 95% confidence level.

For results based on the samples of 1,610 non-leaning independents and 2,141 liberal or moderate Republicans, the margin of sampling error is ±3 percentage points at the 95% confidence level.

For results based on the sample of 4,267 conservative Republicans, the margin of sampling error is ±2 percentage points at the 95% confidence level.

All reported margins of sampling error include computed design effects for weighting.

October 06, 2016

AVERSION TO OTHER CANDIDATE KEY FACTOR IN 2016 VOTE CHOICE

by Lydia Saad

Story Highlights

- *Top rationale for vote choice is opposition to other candidate*
- *Many Clinton voters also cite her experience and qualifications*
- *Trump voters are disproportionately issue-driven, want change*

PRINCETON, N.J. – The lead reason U.S. registered voters give for their choice of president in the 2016 election involves not liking something about the opposing candidate. All told, 28% of voters – including equal proportions of Hillary Clinton and Donald Trump supporters – cite reasons such as believing the other candidate is dishonest, unqualified or of poor temperament. The remaining voters offer more positive reasons for their choice of president, including their own candidate's qualifications (24%), policy stances (17%), personal qualities (14%) or party affiliation (9%).

Summary of Reasons Voters Support Hillary Clinton or Donald Trump

In your own words, why are you most likely to vote for [Hillary Clinton/Donald Trump]?

	All voters %	Clinton voters %	Trump voters %
Negative assessment of opponent	28	28	28
Qualifications/Experience	24	31	16
Issues/Policies	17	11	23
Personal qualities	14	13	15
Partisanship	9	12	6
Want change	4	<1	9
Other	2	2	2
No opinion	2	3	2

Based on U.S. registered voters who plan to vote for either Clinton or Trump
Gallup, Sept. 14-18, 2016

Thes55e results are from a Sept. 14-18 Gallup survey in which self-identified U.S. registered voters were first asked whether they are voting for Democrat Hillary Clinton or Republican Donald Trump, and then asked to explain why in their own words.

In contrast to today, in 2008 – the last presidential election without an incumbent seeking a second term – hardly any respondents said the main reason they were supporting either Barack Obama or John McCain was that they objected to the opposing candidate. Many Obama supporters explained their vote in terms of wanting change from the current Republican administration, but not explicitly because they rejected McCain.

Similarly, in the 2000 election, another open-seat race, Gallup found relatively few voters basing their preference for George W. Bush or Al Gore on their objection to the opposing candidate.

The Anti-Vote for Clinton vs. Trump Is a Wash

As noted, 28% of both Clinton and Trump voters say they are backing that person because of something they don't like about the other candidate. Among the specific responses that make up this category, Trump voters are most likely to cite their lack of trust in Clinton. This is followed by their dislike of her, their determination to vote against her and their decision to vote *for* Trump as the "lesser of two evils."

Clinton voters are a bit more likely to give the "lesser of two evils" response, followed by saying that they dislike Trump and that he doesn't have the temperament to be president.

"Anti-Vote" Reasons Voters Support Hillary Clinton or Donald Trump

	All voters %	Clinton voters %	Trump voters %
Negative assessment of opponent (Total)	6	2	10
Don't trust other candidate/Dishonest/Lack of integrity	6	7	4
Lesser of two evils	4	5	4
Do not like other candidate	4	3	4
Voting against other candidate	3	5	1
Other does not have temperament to be president	2	3	1
Do not favor other's agenda, ideas, platform	2	3	1
Other is not qualified to be president/Not a good candidate	1	0	1
Other has not done his/her job/Done a poor job	6	2	10
Other is too liberal	<1	0	1

Based on U.S. registered voters who plan to vote for either Clinton or Trump
Gallup, Sept. 14-18, 2016

Clinton Voters Drawn to Experience, Trump Voters to Issues

The perception that she has experience or is otherwise qualified to be president is the key reason 31% of Clinton voters give for backing her, nearly twice the percentage citing experience for Trump (16%). Clinton voters are also twice as likely as Trump voters, 12% vs. 6%, to say their candidate's party affiliation is the major factor in their decision. (See the full list of detailed responses in the "View complete question responses" document linked in the Survey Methods section.)

Meanwhile, Trump's voters (23%) are about twice as likely as Clinton's (11%) to cite agreement with their preferred candidate on issues or policy matters. (It should be noted that Gallup conducted this poll before the first presidential debate, for which viewers gave Clinton far more credit than Trump for having a good grasp of the issues.) For both candidates, most mentions in this category are general, rather than specific to individual policies.

Issue-Related Reasons Voters Support Hillary Clinton or Donald Trump

	All voters %	Clinton voters %	Trump voters %
Issues/Policies (Total)	**17**	**11**	**23**
Favor his/her agenda, ideas, platform	10	9	12
Cares about poor, old, middle class, average person	1	2	1
Conservative policies	1	<1	2
Economic issues	1	0	2
Immigration issues	1	0	2
Defense/Military issues	1	0	1
Foreign policy issues	1	1	0
Reduce spending	<1	0	1
Create jobs/Lower unemployment	<1	0	1
Want less government/Reduce government	<1	0	1
Healthcare issues	<1	0	1

Based on U.S. registered voters who plan to vote for either Clinton or Trump
Gallup, Sept. 14-18, 2016

Trump voters are also unique in naming "change" as a key reason for their vote choice, mentioned by 9% of his supporters compared with less than 1% of hers – not surprising given that the current president is a Democrat.

Similar proportions of Clinton (13%) and Trump (15%) voters identify positive personal qualities about their own candidate as their primary motivation for backing that person. Among the specific responses falling into this category, 5% of Clinton voters say they "like her" and 3% say she has good morals or ethics. For Trump, 4% of his supporters cite his credibility or ability to keep promises, while 3% cite his leadership qualities and 2% simply say they like him.

Quality-Related Reasons Voters Support Hillary Clinton or Donald Trump

	All voters %	Clinton voters %	Trump voters %
Personal qualities (Total)	**14**	**13**	**15**
Like him/her	3	5	2
Good morals, ethics, values	2	3	2
Credible/Reliable/Keeps promises	2	<1	4
Trustworthy/Honest/Integrity	2	1	3
Leadership qualities	2	1	3
Represents women/Favor woman for president	1	2	0

Based on U.S. registered voters who plan to vote for either Clinton or Trump
Gallup, Sept. 14-18, 2016

Bottom Line

When voters are asked why they support Clinton or Trump in this election, the first reason nearly three in 10 give involves what they think is wrong with the opposing candidate. This is extraordinary when compared with recent open-seat elections, when few voters mentioned anything unflattering about the opponent as a reason for their vote. The current pattern does fit, however, with both candidates' lackluster favorable ratings thus far in 2016. Unusually high proportions of their own party members view both negatively – 21% for Clinton and 31% for Trump in the latest Gallup Daily tracking figures. These disgruntled partisans may account for many of those who say they are voting for their preferred candidate as the "lesser of two evils."

Still, the majority of each candidate's voters do offer a positive reason for backing that person. Clinton's voters are about twice as likely as Trump's to cite their candidate's experience and qualifications to be president, while Trump's are twice as likely to cite policy positions. Additionally, Clinton has more people voting for her out of party loyalty, while Trump voters are more likely to say they expect him to be a change agent.

The upcoming presidential debates offer these candidates a final opportunity to boost their favorable ratings, display presidential gravitas and present ideas that appeal to swing voters. If after the third debate these improvements haven't materialized, even more voters may decide that the best reason to vote for one of the two is that he or she isn't the other.

Survey Methods

Results for this Gallup poll are based on telephone interviews conducted Sept. 14-18, 2016, with a random sample of 1,033 adults, aged 18 and older, living in all 50 U.S. states and the District of Columbia, including 931 registered voters. For results based on the total sample of registered voters, the margin of sampling error is ±4 percentage points at the 95% confidence level. For results based on the 444 registered voters who support either Hillary Clinton or the 407 registered voters who support Donald Trump, the margin of sampling error is ±6 percentage points at the 95% confidence level. All reported margins of sampling error include computed design effects for weighting.

October 07, 2016
U.S. UNINSURED RATE AT NEW LOW OF 10.9% IN THIRD QUARTER

by Stephanie Marken

Story Highlights

- *Uninsured rate reaches nine-year low*
- *Rate down 6.2 points since individual mandate took effect*
- *Uninsured rate has dropped most among low-income households, Hispanics*

WASHINGTON, D.C. – In the third quarter of 2016, 10.9% of U.S. adults were without health insurance, representing a new low in Gallup's and Healthways' nearly nine years of trending the rate of uninsured. This is down from 11.9% in the fourth quarter of 2015, before the 2016 open enrollment period that allowed U.S. adults to obtain insurance through the government health insurance exchanges.

The uninsured rate has declined 6.2 percentage points from 17.1% in the fourth quarter of 2013, right before the Affordable Care Act's requirement that Americans carry health insurance took effect in early 2014.

Results for the third quarter are based on approximately 44,000 interviews with U.S. adults aged 18 and older from July 1- Sept. 30, 2016, conducted as part of the Gallup-Healthways Well-Being Index. Gallup asks 500 U.S. adults each day whether they have health insurance, which, on an aggregated basis, allows for precise and ongoing measurement of the percentage of Americans with and without health insurance.

Largest Change Among Low-Income Households and Hispanics

Among key groups, the largest declines in the uninsured rate between the last quarter of 2013 and the third quarter of 2016 took place among low-income households and Hispanics. However, these groups remain the ones with the highest uninsured rates. In the fourth quarter of 2013, 30.7% of low-income Americans were uninsured, compared with 20.1% in the third quarter of 2016. In the last quarter of 2013, 38.7% of Hispanics were uninsured, compared with 27.0% in the third quarter of 2016.

Percentage of Uninsured U.S. Adults, by Subgroup

	Q4 2013 %	Q3 2016 %	Net change (pct. pts.)
National adults	17.1	10.9	-6.2
18 to 25	23.5	14.2	-9.3
26 to 34	28.2	19.1	-9.1
35 to 64	18.0	11.4	-6.6
65+	2.0	1.7	-0.3
Whites	11.9	7.1	-4.8
Blacks	20.9	11.6	-9.3
Hispanics	38.7	27.0	-11.7
Less than $36,000	30.7	20.1	-10.6
$36,000 to $89,999	11.7	9.2	-2.5
$90,000+	5.8	2.9	-2.9

Gallup-Healthways Well-Being Index

Largest Change Among Self-Paid Plans

To assess changes among Americans with different types of insurance coverage, Gallup and Healthways focus on adults aged 18 to 64, because nearly all of those aged 65 and older have Medicare. Since the fourth quarter of 2013, the largest change has occurred among those with an insurance plan fully paid for by themselves or their families, most likely reflecting insurance purchased on the government's health insurance exchanges or individual plans purchased directly from an insurer. In the final quarter of 2013, 17.6% of U.S. adults aged 18 to 64 were insured through these individually purchased health insurance plans, compared with 21.5% in the third quarter of 2016. The percentage of Americans with Medicaid coverage has also risen as the percentage who are uninsured has declined.

Type of Health Insurance Coverage in the U.S., Among 18- to 64-Year-Olds

Is your health insurance coverage through a current or former employer, a union, Medicare, Medicaid, military or veteran's coverage, or a plan fully paid for by you or a family member? Primary and secondary insurance combined

	Q4 2013 %	Q3 2016 %	Change (pct. pts.)
Current or former employer	44.2	43.4	-0.8
Plan fully paid for by self or family member	17.6	21.5	3.9
Medicaid	6.9	9.4	2.5
Medicare	6.1	7.9	1.8
Military/Veteran's	4.6	4.9	0.3
A union	2.5	2.8	0.3
Something else	3.5	4.2	0.7
No insurance	20.8	13.3	-7.5

Gallup-Healthways Well-Being Index

Gallup and Healthways began asking Americans about the source of their health insurance using the current question wording in August 2013, in anticipation of shifts in how people would receive their health insurance through the Affordable Care Act. Respondents are asked, "Is your primary health insurance coverage through a current or former employer, a union, Medicare, Medicaid, military or veteran's coverage, or a plan fully paid for by you or a family member?" Respondents are also asked if they have secondary health insurance coverage and, if so, what type of coverage it is. The results reported here are a combined estimate of primary and secondary insurance types.

Implications

The sharp declines in the uninsured rates in the first year of the individual mandate and insurance exchanges have leveled off. The declines remained mostly steady in the third year after the introduction of the individual mandate, from 11.9% in the fourth quarter of 2015 to 10.9% in the third quarter of 2016. These changes in the second and third years after the individual mandate went into effect are not surprising since the remaining uninsured are likely among the hard-to-reach populations or those most resistant to complying with the law. Additionally, a majority of the states that have expanded Medicaid coverage did so early in 2014; since that time, Medicaid expansion has occurred gradually, one state at a time.

The fourth open enrollment period, set to begin on Nov. 1, will be a critical one for the law. In some states and counties, consumers who have or are seeking insurance through government exchanges or direct purchase with insurers will see higher premiums and fewer insurers offering individual policies. Results from the first quarter of 2017 will illustrate how these rate increases may affect the percentage of U.S. adults who remain without health insurance.

Survey Methods

Results are based on telephone interviews conducted July 1-Sept. 30, 2016, as part of the Gallup-Healthways Well-Being Index survey, with a random sample of 44,028 adults, aged 18 and older, living in all 50 U.S. states and the District of Columbia. For results based on the total sample of national adults, the margin of sampling error is ±1 percentage point at the 95% confidence level. Each quarter dating to Quarter 1, 2014, has approximately 44,000 respondents. Each quarter from 2008 through 2013 has approximately 88,000 respondents.

October 10, 2016
AMERICANS TILT TOWARD VIEW THAT GOVERNMENT IS DOING TOO MUCH

by Frank Newport

Story Highlights

- *54% of Americans say the government is trying to do too many things*
- *About four in 10 say the government should do more to solve problems*
- *Republicans and Democrats continue to have widely divergent views*

PRINCETON, N.J. – One of the fundamental questions that have divided the U.S. this election year – and, in fact, since its founding 240 years ago – concerns the appropriate role of the federal government. A new update of a longstanding Gallup trend shows that Americans continue to favor a smaller role for government, with 54% saying the government is attempting to do too many things that should be left to individuals and businesses, and 41% saying it should do more to solve the country's problems.

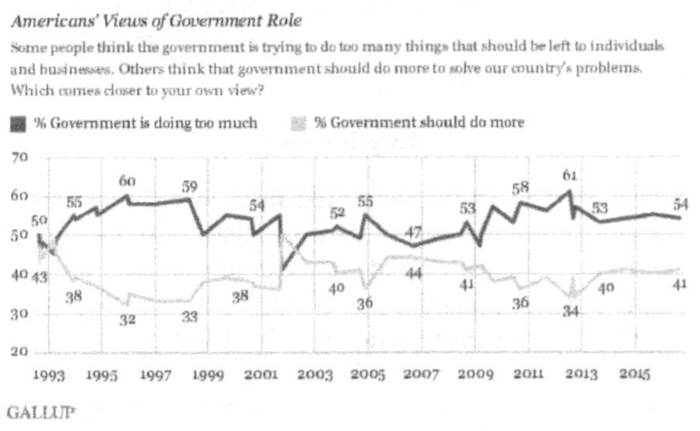

With a few exceptions, the current results are typical of Americans' responses since 1992. One exception was in late 1992 and early 1993 as Bill Clinton campaigned for and took over the presidency. At that time, Americans were highly concerned about the economy. The second exception occurred in October 2001, just after the Sept. 11 terrorist attacks, when Americans were focused on the government's response to the most significant domestic terrorist attack in the country's history. Otherwise, across more than 40 surveys over 25 years, including the most recent Sept. 7-11 update, the public has tilted by at least a small margin toward believing that the government is trying to do too much.

The margin between "doing too much" and "should do more" was somewhat larger during the last seven years of the Clinton administration and the entire Barack Obama presidency than in the George W. Bush years. This most likely reflects a counteraction to perceptions that the two Democratic presidents were oriented toward increasing the government's role.

These broad general population trends mask the fact that Republicans and Democrats have widely divergent views on the issue, consistent with each party's philosophy on the role of government. Republicans overwhelmingly favor the "doing too much" option, and Democrats are almost as likely to favor "should do more."

The accompanying graph shows the trends in the views of Republicans and Democrats compiled from 16 annual Gallup Governance surveys conducted each September since 2001. The graph shows the percentage of each party choosing the "doing too much" option (a display of partisan differences on the alternative option would show, in essence, a mirror image).

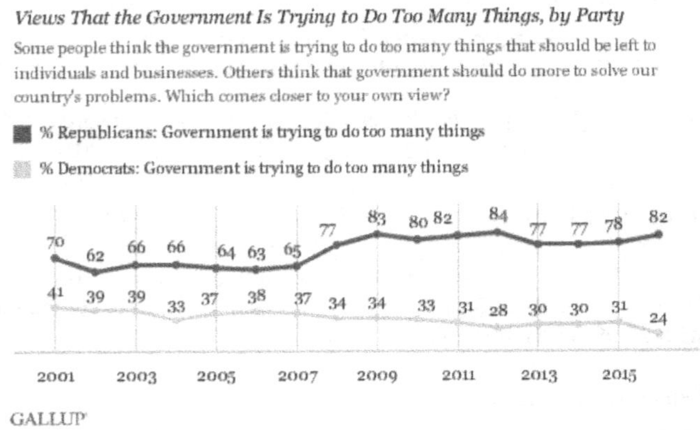

It's clear that Republicans' choice of the conservative viewpoint edged up in 2008 as the financial crisis took hold and the Bush administration struggled to right the economy, while Democrats' choice of that option began to edge down. The overall gap between the views of the two partisan groups on this measure went from the 30-percentage-point range to a high of 58 points in the latest survey.

Differences in these views across other segments of the U.S. population are generally related to the political orientation of each segment. Women, minorities and young adults are more likely to be Democrats and are least likely to say the government is doing too many things that should be left to individuals and businesses.

The details of the differences in these attitudes across racial and ethnic population segments are worth highlighting. Blacks' and Hispanics' views of what government's role should be are almost exactly the opposite of those of non-Hispanic whites, helping clarify at least one reason why race and ethnicity are such powerful determinants of support for Hillary Clinton and Donald Trump in the presidential election.

Americans' Views of Role of Government, by Race and Ethnicity

Some people think the government is trying to do too many things that should be left to individuals and businesses. Others think that government should do more to solve our country's problems. Which comes closer to your own view?

	Government is doing too much %	Government should do more %
Non-Hispanic white	62	32
Black	29	65
Hispanic	33	63

Aggregated Gallup Polls conducted 2013-2016
Gallup

Bottom Line

Republican candidate Trump has not made smaller government a major part of his campaign rhetoric – certainly not in the way it became a centerpiece of the campaign of his chief competitor for the nomination, Ted Cruz, who called for shutting down whole departments and federal agencies. Still, if Trump is elected, it would be expected that the number of Republicans saying the government is trying to do too much would drop, at least marginally.

Democratic candidate Clinton's governing philosophy as president is likely to be similar in many ways to Obama's, with an underlying faith in the idea of using and expanding the government to right wrongs and ameliorate society's problems. If she is elected, the type of gap found now between the two partisan groups' views on the government's role would most likely stay large.

Survey Methods

Results for this Gallup poll are based on telephone interviews conducted Sept. 7-11, 2016, with a random sample of 1,020 adults, aged 18 and older, living in all 50 U.S. states and the District of Columbia. For results based on the total sample of national adults, the margin of sampling error is ±4 percentage points at the 95% confidence level. All reported margins of sampling error include computed design effects for weighting.

October 10, 2016
FINANCIAL INSECURITY HIGHER FOR THOSE WHO FAVOR TRUMP

by Jonathan Rothwell

WASHINGTON, D.C. – Many political analysts have tried to pinpoint the reasons why Donald Trump, a political outsider, has won the Republican party's presidential nomination. A new Gallup analysis offers one clue: Americans who view Trump favorably are significantly more likely than other Americans to report feeling financially insecure. The large gap in financial insecurity persists even after controlling for income, education, occupation, party affiliation and various other measures of objective economic circumstances.

This analysis is based on interviews conducted July 2015 through August 2016 as part of Gallup Daily tracking. Over this period, Gallup asked a random sample of U.S. adults two of the eight questions measuring financial worry, shown below.

Gallup U.S. Financial Anxiety Index

Questions Measuring Financial Worry

1	You are watching your spending very closely.
2	Would you be able right now to make a major purchase, such as a car, appliance or furniture, or pay for a significant home repair if you needed to?
3	At this time, are you cutting back on how much money you spend each week, or not?
4	Are you feeling pretty good these days about the amount of money you have to spend, or not?
5	Did you worry yesterday that you spent too much money, or not?
6	You have more than enough money to do what you want to do.
7	Do you have enough money to buy the things you need, or not?
8	Are you feeling better about your financial situation these days, or not?

Items 1, 3 and 5 are coded as affirmative if respondent agrees, whereas the others are coded as affirmative if respondent disagrees.
Gallup Daily tracking, July 2015-August 2016

Americans with a favorable opinion of Trump report relatively high levels of financial anxiety across seven of eight survey questions when compared with those holding an unfavorable view of Trump. For example, those with a favorable opinion of Trump are 23 percentage points more likely to say they are not feeling better about their financial situation these days, 17 points more likely to say they do not feel good about the amount of money they have to spend and 13 points more likely to say they are cutting back on spending.

Republicans and conservatives have reported higher levels of financial insecurity than Democrats and liberals since at least 2013, but these party and ideological differences do not account for the gap in financial insecurity between those who do and do not favor Trump. Republicans who view Trump favorably are still more likely to express economic insecurity on each item than Republicans who view him unfavorably.

For example, 59% of Republicans who have a favorable view of Trump report that they do not feel good about the amount of money they have to spend, compared with 45% of Republicans who have an unfavorable view of Trump. Republicans who have a favorable view of Trump are also 15 points more likely than fellow Republicans who do not favor Trump to say they are not feeling better about their financial situation these days.

Percentage Reporting Financial Anxiety, by View of Trump and Republican Party Affiliation

	U.S. Adults - Favorable View of Trump %	U.S. Adults - Unfavorable View of Trump %	Republicans - Favorable View of Trump %	Republicans - Unfavorable View of Trump %
Watching spending	91	86	92	89
Can't make major purchase	45	44	41	38
Cutting back	67	54	66	59
Don't feel good about amount of spending money	59	42	59	45
Worry-ing about spending too much	31	27	31	27
Don't have enough money for wants	70	62	67	62
Don't have enough money for needs	29	26	25	21
Not feeling better about financial situation	62	39	64	49

Differences between columns 1 and 2 are statistically significant at 95% confidence intervals except row 2. Differences between columns 3 and 4 are significant.
Gallup Daily tracking, July 2015-August 2016

Financial Insecurity Particularly High Among Affluent Trump Supporters

Financial anxiety is generally lower among those with higher household incomes, but across income groups, those who view Trump favorably are more likely to be worried about their personal finances.

The largest gaps in worries about personal finances tend to be found in households earning $200,000 or more in annual income. Among these affluent households, 51% of those who favor Trump say they don't have enough money to buy what they want, compared with just 31% of those who do not favor Trump. Those who favor Trump are also twice as likely as those who do not favor Trump to report that they are not feeling better about their financial situation (52% vs. 25%). Similar differences occur on the other financial questions tested.

Percentage Expressing Financial Insecurity, by View of Trump and Household Income

	Income $100K-$200K - Favorable View of Trump %	Income $100K-$200K - Unfavorable View of Trump %	Income > $200K - Favorable View of Trump %	Income > $200K - Unfavorable View of Trump %
Watching spending	89	81	82	68
Can't make major purchase	25	20	20	12
Cutting back	61	39	50	31
Don't feel good about amount of spending money	52	27	47	20
Worry-ing about spending too much	30	23	26	17
Don't have enough money for wants	64	48	51	31
Don't have enough money for needs	16	8	11	6
Not feeling better about financial situation	57	27	52	25

Differences between columns comparing >$200K income are statistically significant at 95% confidence. The same is true for $100K-$200K.
Gallup Daily tracking, July 2015-August 2016

The differences in financial worry between those who do and do not favor Trump are smaller among households with annual income below $100,000, although even within this group, statistically significant gaps remain for seven of the eight questions.

Percentage Expressing Financial Insecurity, by View of Trump and Household Income

	Income <$100K – Favorable View of Trump %	Income <$100K - Unfavorable View of Trump %
Watching spending	93	90
Can't make major purchase	55	55
Cutting back	71	61
Don't feel good about amount of spending money	64	49
Worrying about spending too much	35	31
Don't have enough money for wants	76	71
Don't have enough money for needs	36	33
Not feeling better about financial situation	64	44

Differences between columns comparing <$100K income are statistically significant at 95% confidence, except for row 2.

Gallup Daily tracking, July 2015-August 2016

Heightened Insecurity Not Readily Explained by Objective Circumstances

Donald Trump has a more positive image among people who worry about their finances, no matter how grounded those concerns are in the apparent reality of their circumstances.

The financial insecurity gap between those who do and do not view Trump favorably cannot be explained by income or other objective economic and social circumstances. The relationship between viewing Trump favorably and feeling financially insecure holds even after statistically controlling for individual factors such as age, veteran status, gender, race, ethnicity, employment status, education, occupational category, religion, party affiliation and ideology.

Likewise, the gap remains even after taking into account the local cost of living, the average income of people living in the respondents' ZIP codes and income growth in those ZIP codes. For additional details on other variables included in this analysis, see the survey methods section.

It is unclear what is behind the significant relationship between the high levels of financial insecurity and having a favorable opinion of Trump. It may be that there are unmeasured economic factors or experiences not considered here that explain the correlation, or the financial insecurity gap may be attributable to other differences – such as knowledge, media consumption, cultural practices or some other factor – between those who favor Trump and those who do not.

Survey Methods

Results for this Gallup poll are based on telephone interviews conducted July 8, 2015, through August 31, 2016, on the Gallup U.S. Daily tracking survey, with a random sample of 112,995 adults, aged 18 and older, living in all 50 U.S. states and the District of Columbia. All reported means and statistical significance include computed design effects for weighting.

Each sample of national adults includes a minimum quota of 60% cellphone respondents and 40% landline respondents, with additional minimum quotas by time zone within region. Landline and cellular telephone numbers are selected using random-digit-dial methods.

October 12, 2016
AHEAD OF ELECTIONS, U.S. CONGRESS APPROVAL AT 18%

by Justin McCarthy

Story Highlights

- *In final measure before Election Day, Congress approval at 18%*
- *Republicans remain least approving of Congress*

WASHINGTON, D.C. – With less than a month to go before the U.S. congressional elections, 18% of Americans approve of the job Congress is doing. This rating has been low for some time, and has not cracked 25% since 2009.

Congressional Job Approval Ratings: 2009-2016

Do you approve or disapprove of the way Congress is handling its job?

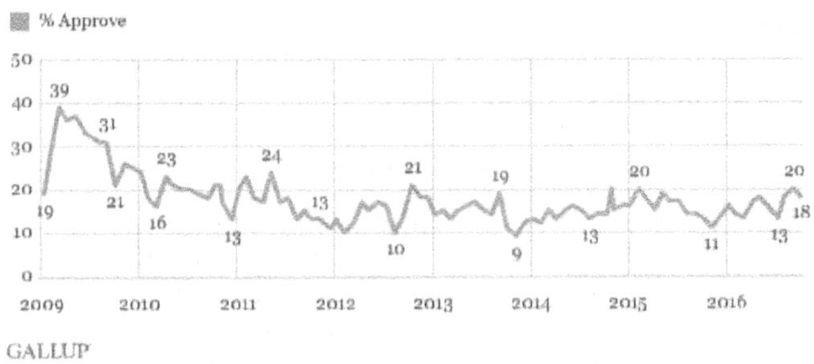

The latest figure, from an Oct. 5-9 Gallup poll, represents Americans' final job approval rating of Congress before the November elections, and is similar to the ratings found in final pre-election polls in 2008, 2010, 2012 and 2014, when Congress approval ranged between 18% and 21%.

Republicans Remain Least Approving of Congress

Supporters of the majority party in Congress tend to rate the institution more favorably than do supporters of the minority party, but the GOP bucked the trend when its supporters' approval did not improve after the party took the second chamber of Congress in 2014. Despite controlling both the House and Senate, Republicans (14%) are currently less likely than Democrats (22%) to approve of the job Congress is doing.

Congressional Job Approval Ratings, by Party Group

% Approve

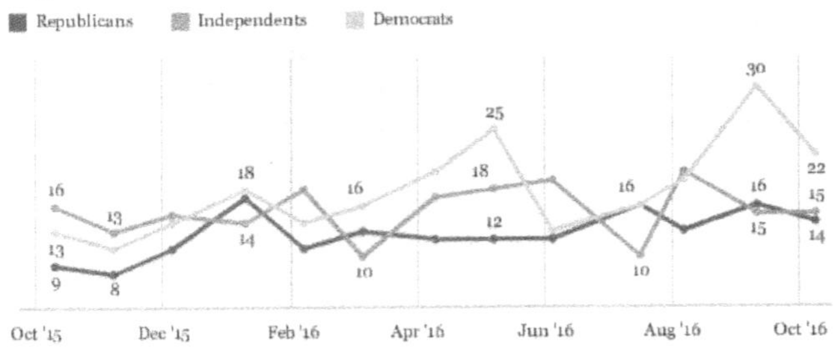

GALLUP

This could reflect the split between conservative and moderate Republicans in Washington that has been palpable throughout Barack Obama's presidency. Regardless of the side on which national Republicans fall, their frustration with this breach could be affecting their approval of Congress as a whole.

Bottom Line

Many political observers believe Democrats have a reasonable chance of regaining party control of the Senate. Republicans, who won many Senate seats in a significant wave in 2010, are defending those same seats in 2016 – arguably in a less favorable political climate for the party than was the case six years ago. The GOP seems to have a better chance of holding its House majority, though even that could be in jeopardy if a Democratic wave emerges.

Since World War II, Congress' party composition has generally changed most significantly in non-presidential election years, so while individual seats and control of each chamber may be in play, it's likely that the overall party layout of Congress will not change drastically.

Survey Methods

Results for this Gallup poll are based on telephone interviews conducted Oct. 5-9, 2016, on the Gallup U.S. Daily survey, with a random sample of 1,017 adults, aged 18 and older, living in all 50 U.S. states and the District of Columbia. For results based on the total sample of national adults, the margin of sampling error is ±4 percentage points at the 95% confidence level. All reported margins of sampling error include computed design effects for weighting.

October 13, 2016
TRUMP'S IMAGE SLIDES AMONG REPUBLICANS

by Frank Newport and Andrew Dugan

Story Highlights

- *Trump's unfavorables rose from 30% to 33% among Republicans*
- *Both candidates receive high unfavorables from the opposite party*
- *Independents are slightly more positive about Clinton*

PRINCETON, N.J. – Donald Trump's favorable rating among Republicans dropped from 69% to 64% in the fallout after *The Washington Post* released a 2005 video in which he made lewd comments about women, and after the second presidential debate on Sunday night. Trump's unfavorable rating ticked up slightly from 30% to 33%. There was virtually no change in Trump's already poor image among independents or Democrats.

Donald Trump Favorables, by Party, October 2016

	Favorable %	Unfavorable %
Republicans		
Oct 1-6	69	30
Oct 7-11	64	33
Independents/Other/Don't know		
Oct 1-6	26	67
Oct 7-11	26	68
Democrats		
Oct 1-6	5	93
Oct 7-11	5	92

Gallup

Hillary Clinton over the past five days has seen her favorable rating rise from 81% to 84% among Democrats, but take a slightly negative turn among independents, from 35% to 32%. Clinton herself has been the focus of news events, including WikiLeaks-released transcripts of emails involving Clinton, her campaign strategy and Wall Street speeches. Gallup polling finds that debate watchers saw Clinton as the winner of Sunday night's debate.

Hillary Clinton Favorables, by Party, October 2016

	Favorable %	Unfavorable %
Republicans		
Oct 1-6	7	92
Oct 7-11	7	92
Independents/Other/Don't know		
Oct 1-6	35	58
Oct 7-11	32	60
Democrats		
Oct 1-6	81	16
Oct 7-11	84	13

Gallup

The gulf between the partisan ratings of the two candidates at this point is substantial. Trump now has a 64% favorable rating among Republicans (for Oct. 7-11), while Clinton enjoys an 84% favorable rating among Democrats. Both candidates have high unfavorables among those in the opposing party, while Clinton has a slight edge among independents.

Though the 2005 video of Trump came out before Gallup interviewing began on Friday, his image did not begin to deteriorate among Republicans until the weekend, perhaps reflecting a delayed reaction to Republican leaders' public drop in support. Across the four days, Oct. 8-11, Trump's favorable among Republicans is 61% with a 36% unfavorable rating.

Given the lack of change in ratings among independents and Democrats, the effect of these events on Trump's image among Americans as a whole is slight. For the six days through Oct. 6, Trump averaged a 32% favorable, 64% unfavorable rating. Over the past five days, Oct. 7-11, Trump's favorable rating was 31%, with a similar one-percentage-point rise in his unfavorables, to 65%. Clinton's favorable among all Americans also remained stable, with her favorable dropping by one point (to 41%) while her unfavorable went up by one point (to 55%).

Americans Continue to Report More Recall of News About Trump Than Clinton

By Monday night, 92% of Americans recalled having read, seen or heard something about Trump in the last day or two. That compares with 84% for Clinton – even though the two presidential candidates had nearly equal speaking time on stage at Sunday's debate in St. Louis. The 92% recall figure for Trump is the highest for either candidate since Gallup tracking of this measure began in July. Recall of hearing about Trump dropped somewhat by Tuesday night, but remained higher than for Clinton. This pattern contrasts with the days after the first debate (Sept. 26), when Americans' recall of having heard about the two candidates was essentially equal.

The release of the video on Friday did not appear to increase Americans' recall of having heard about the candidates, perhaps because attention to news is lower over the weekend in general. It wasn't until the day after the debate that recall jumped for both candidates.

Did you read, see or hear anything about Donald Trump/Hillary Clinton in the last day or two?

% Yes

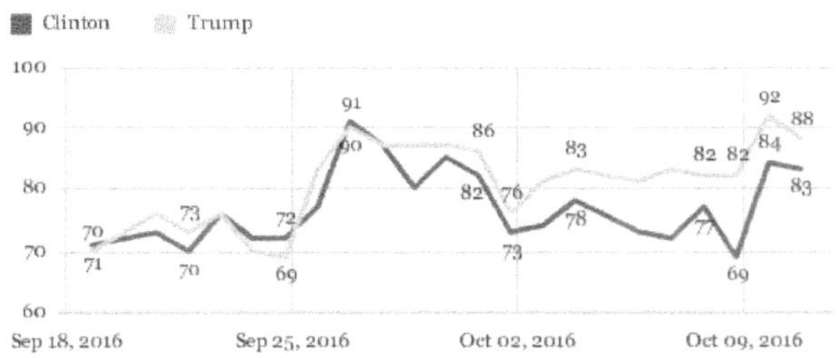

GALLUP

What Americans Are Reading, Hearing or Seeing About the Candidates

In conjunction with Georgetown University and the University of Michigan, Gallup is tracking exactly what Americans say they have read, seen or heard about the candidates on a daily basis. The following summarizes the findings for each of the past five days.

- **Oct. 7.** The story of Trump's 2005 comments broke Friday afternoon, and by Friday evening, it was apparent that many U.S. adults had heard about it. The most common word Americans used in reporting what they had heard about Trump on Friday night was "woman," more frequently mentioned than words such as "debate" and "tax." The most common word Republicans used in their recall of Trump was "debate," while "woman" was the most common for Democrats and independents.

  Meanwhile, Clinton was less prominent in Americans' minds, as noted previously. The most frequent words used to describe what people had heard about Clinton were "email," "debate" and "campaign."
- **Oct. 8.** References to the Trump video dominated Americans' descriptions of what they recently heard about Trump on Saturday. "Women" or "woman" was about three times more common in people's answers than the next-most-frequent word.

  For Clinton, "email" was the most common word used in people's descriptions of what they heard, twice as likely as the next-most-common word, "speech."
- **Oct. 9.** Interviewing on Sunday was conducted before the beginning of the second presidential debate. For Trump, the most common word used in respondents' answers was "woman" or "women." The word "email" remained the most common one used in the description of what respondents recently heard about Clinton.
- **Oct. 10.** In a rare convergence, the most common word Americans used when recalling what they had read, seen or heard about both candidates was the same: "debate." However, "woman" was the second-most-mentioned word for Trump and "email" was in second place for Clinton.
- **Oct. 11**. "Debate" continued to be the most common word for both candidates Tuesday night, but the respective controversies surrounding each candidate did not fade from the public eye. After "debate," the next two most common substantive words for Trump were "woman"/"women" and "tape." Trump's claim, repeated several times in Sunday's debate, that the video represented "locker room talk" also percolated into the results. The words "locker" and "room" were among the 10 most common words Americans used to describe what they recently heard about Trump.

  For Clinton, Americans frequently used the words "email," "leak," "lie" and "WikiLeak" in their responses. Still, "debate" was by far the most common word.

Bottom Line

Gallup typically reports Americans' attitudes about the candidates on the basis of seven-day rolling averages in order to provide reliably stable estimates. It will thus be this coming weekend before the effect of the recent events on the two candidates' images can be fully assessed. At this point, the data suggest that Americans are paying close attention to campaign events – particularly the debate – and that, at least in the short term, Trump's image among his own partisans has taken a hit, while Clinton has modestly shored up her image among Democrats.

Survey Methods

Results for this Gallup poll are based on telephone interviews conducted Oct. 1-11, 2016, on the Gallup U.S. Daily survey, with random samples of approximately 500 adults per night, aged 18 and older, living in all 50 U.S. states and the District of Columbia. For results based on one night's sample of national adults, the margin of sampling error is ±5 percentage points at the 95% confidence level. For results based on the aggregated samples over Oct. 1-6, and 7-11, the margin of sampling error is ±3 percentage points at the 95% confidence level. All reported margins of sampling error include computed design effects for weighting.

October 13, 2016
VIEWERS SAY CLINTON WINS SECOND DEBATE

by Lydia Saad

Story Highlights

- *Clinton perceived winner of second debate, 53% to 35%, over Trump*
- *Republicans much more positive about Trump in second debate*
- *Majority of Americans would not be proud with either as president*

PRINCETON, N.J. – Following her solid victory in the first presidential debate two weeks ago, Democrat Hillary Clinton performed well in the second debate Sunday night, with 53% of those tuning in saying she did the better job, compared with 35% naming Republican Donald Trump. Winning the first two debates hasn't guaranteed presidential candidates success in their election. Still, two of the past three candidates who managed this feat – Barack Obama in 2008 and Bill Clinton in 1996 – went on to win.

Presidential Candidate Perceived as Performing Best in Debate

Among U.S. adults who watched or listened to each debate; shown is percentage-point lead over next-highest-rated opposing candidate

	First debate	Second debate	Third debate
2016	H. Clinton (+34)	H. Clinton (+18)	n/a
2012	Romney (+52)	Obama (+13)	Obama (+23)
2008	Obama (+12)	Obama (+33)	Obama (+26)
2004	Kerry (+32)	Kerry (+15)	Kerry (+14)
2000	Gore^ (+7)	G.W. Bush^ (+13)	Gore^ (+2)
1996	B. Clinton (+35)	B. Clinton^ (+30)	n/a
1992	Perot^ (+17)	B. Clinton (+42)	Perot^ (+9)
1988	Dukakis (+9)	n/a	n/a
1984	Mondale^ (+19)	Reagan^ (+3)	n/a
1976	Ford (+7)	n/a	n/a
1960	Kennedy (+21)	n/a	n/a

^Based on debate reaction poll conducted the same night with respondents interviewed in advance who planned to watch the debate and agreed to be called back
Gallup

Clinton earned an 18-percentage-point lead over Trump in television viewer perceptions of who did a better job in Sunday night's town hall-style debate at Washington University in St. Louis. While impressive, the lead is down from her 34-point advantage in the first debate. Sixty-one percent of those watching or listening to the Sept. 26 debate at Hofstra University in Hempstead, New York, considered her the winner, versus 27% naming Trump.

The latest results are from Gallup polling conducted in the first two days after the second debate, Oct. 10-11, and before an article was published in *The New York Times* stating that two women claim to have been touched inappropriately by Trump.

The narrowing of Clinton's debate victory is reminiscent of 2004 when John Kerry followed a 32-point winning margin among watchers of the first debate against President George W. Bush with a 15-point victory in the second. By contrast, in 2008, Obama gained momentum between the first and second debates – with his margin over John McCain swelling from 12 points to 33. Also, viewers gave President Bill Clinton a 30-point or better margin over Bob Dole for both debates in 1996.

Republicans Happier With Trump's Performance

Clinton's diminished debate advantage is mainly the result of Republicans giving Trump more credit in the second debate than they did in the first: 71% say he did a better job than Clinton in the second debate, compared with 53% who say the same about the first debate. Meanwhile, Democratic debate watchers were nearly unanimous in their choice of Clinton as the winner of both events.

Independents also thought Clinton did best in both debates, although the percentage naming her the winner fell from 59% to 51%, while the percentage of independents saying neither did a better job rose from 5% to 13%.

Regardless of which candidate you happen to support, who do you think did the better job in [last/Sunday or Monday] night's debate – [Hillary Clinton (or) Donald Trump]?

Among U.S. adults who watched or listened to each debate

	Clinton %	Trump %	Neither (vol.) %
All debate watchers			
Second debate	53	35	8
First debate	61	27	5
Republicans			
Second debate	15	71	8
First debate	28	53	6
Independents			
Second debate	51	32	13
First debate	59	30	5
Democrats			
Second debate	93	3	2
First debate	92	3	2

First debate based on poll conducted Sept. 27-28, 2016. Second debate based on poll conducted Oct. 10-11, 2016.
Gallup

Women Rate Trump Better in Second Debate

The first segment of the St. Louis debate focused on criticism of Trump over his treatment of women, specifically referencing a recently released videotape from 2005 in which he bragged about making aggressive sexual advances toward women.

Despite this, women were more likely to say Trump did a better job in the second debate than the first debate, a significantly higher increase than among men. Almost a third of women (32%) who saw or listened to the St. Louis debate thought Trump did the better job, up from 21% after the first debate. That 11-point increase exceeds the five-point increase among men, from 33% choosing Trump for the New York debate to 38% choosing him for St. Louis.

Regardless of which candidate you happen to support, who do you think did the better job in [last/Sunday or Monday] night's debate – [Hillary Clinton (or) Donald Trump]?

Among U.S. adults who watched or listened to each debate

	Clinton %	Trump %	Net Clinton %
Women			
Second debate	58	32	+26
First debate	69	21	+48
Men			
Second debate	49	38	+11
First debate	53	33	+20

First debate based on poll conducted Sept. 27-28, 2016. Second debate based on poll conducted Oct. 10-11, 2016.
Gallup

Trump may have lost a little ground between the two debates in perceptions that he came across as a likable person. The percentage of watchers naming him as the more likable of the two candidates in the debates fell from 36% to 31%, while the percentage of those who name Clinton as most likable rose from 55% to 59%.

There was virtually no change, however, in how debate viewers compared the candidates on three other dimensions. Clinton maintains a large advantage over Trump for having a good understanding of the issues and appearing presidential, while she holds a slimmer lead for being inspiring.

Viewers' Perceptions of Qualities Exhibited at Each Debate

Thinking about the following characteristics and qualities, please say whether you think each one better described Hillary Clinton or Donald Trump during [last/Sunday or Monday] night's debate. Among U.S. adults who watched or listened to each debate.

	Clinton %	Trump %	Clinton advantage pct. pts.
Second debate			
Had a good understanding of the issues	59	28	+31
Appeared presidential	56	27	+29
Was more likable	59	31	+28
Was inspiring	44	34	+10
First debate			
Had a good understanding of the issues	62	26	+36
Appeared presidential	59	27	+32
Was more likable	55	36	+19
Was inspiring	46	34	+12

First debate based on poll conducted Sept. 27-28, 2016. Second debate based on poll conducted Oct. 10-11, 2016.
Gallup

Clinton Seen as Qualified, But Neither Inspires Much Pride

Not only do debate watchers associate positive personal qualities more with Clinton than with Trump, but she is almost twice as likely as Trump to be seen as qualified to be president. Fifty-eight percent of debate watchers say this applies to her versus 36% to Trump. Clinton leads by an even larger margin – 62% versus 32% – in perceptions of having the character and temperament to occupy the Oval Office.

Trump comes a bit closer to Clinton in debate watchers' perceptions that each would be an effective president (50% for Clinton versus 39% for Trump). Neither is well-rated for being someone debate watchers would be proud to call president (46% for Clinton versus 32% for Trump).

Finally, Clinton also won Sunday night's debate on the positions she articulated. Debate watchers preferred her over Trump by an 18-point margin, 56% to 38%, as the candidate who shared better ideas during the debate for addressing the issues facing the country.

Bottom Line

Clinton didn't quite repeat her strong first debate performance when sharing the stage with Trump in St. Louis Sunday night, but she was still perceived as the winner by a majority of Americans who tuned in. Trump earned a higher share of Republican votes than he did the first time, helping him cut into Clinton's overall lead on this post-debate measure. Still, almost all Democrats and about half of independents considered Clinton the winner.

Should the third debate not go his way, the Republican candidate may hope his campaign follows the 2004 example in which Bush prevailed in the election in spite of losing all three debates, but there is a major difference between 2004's and this year's presidential campaigns. While Bush and Kerry both had respectable favorable ratings from the American people – registering in the low 50s in October 2004 – Trump and Clinton continue to garner historically low favorability ratings, with Trump's now markedly lower than Clinton's, 32% versus 40%, respectively. This liability for Trump is reflected in debate watchers' response to whether they would feel proud to have each candidate as president. The figure is relatively low for both, but the 32% for Trump is a major hurdle for him to overcome between now and Nov. 8.

Survey Methods

Results for this Gallup poll are based on telephone interviews conducted Oct. 10-11, 2016, on the Gallup U.S. Daily survey, with a random sample of 1,017 adults, aged 18 and older, living in all 50 U.S. states and the District of Columbia. For results based on the total sample of 693 national adults who watched or heard the debate, the margin of sampling error is ±5 percentage points at the 95% confidence level. All reported margins of sampling error include computed design effects for weighting.

October 13, 2016
U.S. SATISFACTION REMAINS LOW LEADING UP TO ELECTION

by Michael Smith and Jeffrey M. Jones

Story Highlights

- *28% are satisfied with the direction of the U.S.*
- *8% of Republicans and 49% of Democrats are satisfied*
- *Satisfaction similar to level seen before 2012 election*

WASHINGTON, D.C. – With the presidential election less than a month away, 28% of Americans are satisfied with the way things are going in the U.S. This continues the low satisfaction levels that started near the end of the George W. Bush administration and have persisted under President Barack Obama. Satisfaction remains significantly below the historical average of 37% since Gallup began measuring it in 1979.

Satisfaction With U.S., Trend Since 1979

In general, are you satisfied or dissatisfied with the way things are going in the United States at this time?

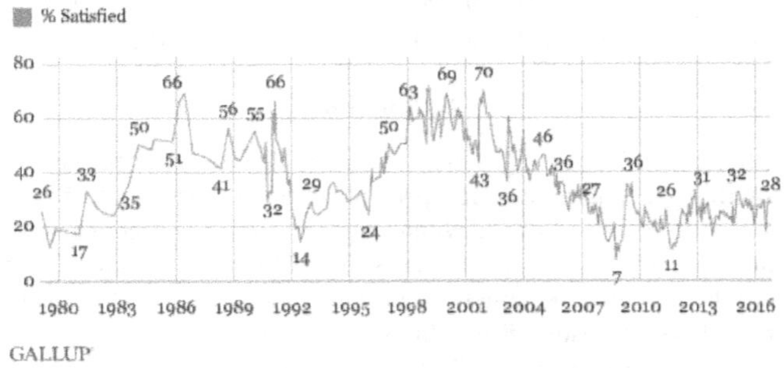

Americans' current level of satisfaction is similar to where it has been for most of 2016, with the notable exception of July. That month, 17% of Americans were satisfied according to the July 13-17 poll, conducted shortly after incidents in which police officers killed black men in Louisiana and Minnesota, and after five police officers in Dallas were fatally shot. July's satisfaction rating was the lowest since October 2013. By August, with news coverage focused more on other events such as the political conventions, satisfaction rebounded to the levels seen before July.

Satisfaction With U.S., 2016

In general, are you satisfied or dissatisfied with the way things are going in the United States at this time?

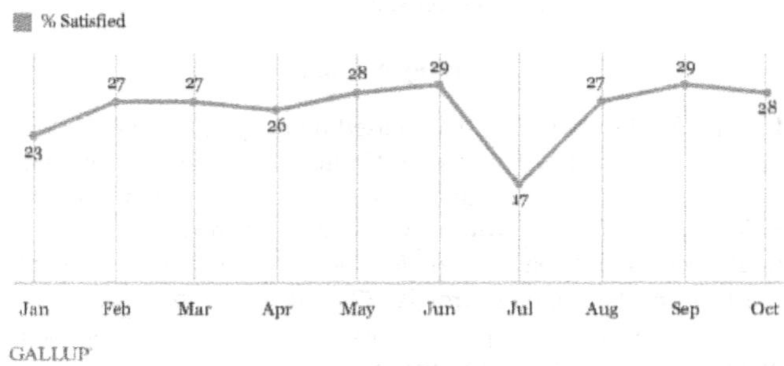

Americans' Satisfaction Similar to a Month Before 2012 Election

Hillary Clinton has said she is the only candidate who will continue Obama's policies, so her supporters might be worried that less than a third of Americans are satisfied with the country's direction near the end of Obama's second term. But a month before the 2012 election, in which Obama handily defeated Mitt Romney, the U.S. satisfaction level was 30%, similar to today's figure. Satisfaction did rise slightly to 33% immediately before the election, possibly because Americans approved of the way Obama handled the effects of Superstorm Sandy.

Heading into the Nov. 8 general election this year, 49% of Democrats, 24% of independents and 8% of Republicans are satisfied with the country's direction. Republican numbers are almost identical to four years ago – when 7% were satisfied. Democrats (53%) and independents (29%) were slightly more likely to be satisfied in October 2012 than they are now.

Bottom Line

The finding that fewer than one in three Americans are satisfied with the way things are going in the U.S. could appear ominous for the Democratic Party's chances of holding on to the White House in 2016. But satisfaction today is similar to what it was four years ago, when Obama won a second term. So while Clinton may pin her hopes for winning on convincing Americans of the need to continue with the course Obama has set, she would also benefit from convincing voters she can improve on what Obama has accomplished.

On the other hand, Republican Donald Trump has been able to focus heavily on his claims about what has gone wrong with the direction of the U.S. under Obama. With seven in 10 Americans expressing dissatisfaction with the nation's course, Trump has a large audience who agrees with his contention that the country is on the wrong track, even if many may not agree with his explanations for why that is the case. Trump's challenge is to convince Americans that he would be able to make things better in the future if elected.

In addition to influencing the outcome of the election, Americans' low satisfaction level could affect voter turnout on Nov. 8. When citizens are frustrated with the way things are going in the nation, they may be motivated to vote for change. Alternatively, their frustration could discourage them from voting. Gallup research from September found Americans were *less* sure they will vote in this year's election than they were in each of the past four presidential elections. One reason voters may be less inclined to vote despite high dissatisfaction levels is their dislike of the two candidates. Both Clinton and Trump have historically low favorability ratings.

Survey Methods

Results for this Gallup poll are based on telephone interviews conducted Oct. 5-9, 2016, with a random sample of 1,017 adults, aged 18 and older, living in all 50 U.S. states and the District of Columbia. For results based on the total sample of national adults, the margin of sampling error is ±4 percentage points at the 95% confidence level. All reported margins of sampling error include computed design effects for weighting.

October 14, 2016

AMERICANS DIVIDED ON PRIORITIES FOR CRIMINAL JUSTICE SYSTEM

by Justin McCarthy

Story Highlights

- *49% favor strengthening law and order*
- *43% prioritize reducing bias against minorities*
- *Stark political party differences exist in justice system priorities*

WASHINGTON, D.C. – Americans are almost evenly divided on whether strengthening law and order through more police and greater enforcement of the laws (49%) or reducing bias against minorities in the criminal justice system by reforming court and police practices (43%) should be the higher priority for the U.S. criminal justice system. Republicans prioritize law and order, while Democrats are more likely to say reducing bias is more important.

Americans' Views of Priorities for the U.S. Justice System, by Political Party

Which do you think should be the bigger priority for the U.S. criminal justice system today – [ROTATED: strengthening law and order through more police and greater enforcement of the laws (or) reducing bias against minorities in the criminal justice system by reforming court and police practices]?

	Strengthening law and order %	Reducing bias against minorities %	No opinion %
National adults	49	43	8
Republicans	77	17	6
Independents	41	52	8
Democrats	32	60	8

Gallup, Oct 5-9, 2016

The latest data, collected Oct. 5-9, reflect stark party differences in approaches to the U.S. justice system – ones that have been on display throughout the 2016 presidential race.

Trump has declared himself the "law and order candidate," while his vice presidential running mate, Mike Pence, has said that he and Trump "believe there's been far too much of this talk of institutional bias or racism within law enforcement." Meanwhile, Democratic candidate Hillary Clinton has advocated for reform in the criminal justice system to reduce racial and ethnic bias.

More than three in four Republicans (77%) say the bigger priority should be to strengthen law and order through more police and greater enforcement of the laws, while 17% say the priority should be to reduce bias against minorities. Majorities of both Democrats (60%) and independents (52%) prioritize reducing bias against minorities in the criminal justice system by reforming court and police practices. However, Republicans tilt more toward strengthening law and order than both of these groups do toward reducing bias.

Whites, Nonwhites Take Opposing Stances on Criminal Justice Priorities

Largely reflecting their likelihood to lean Republican, a majority of whites (56%) favor strengthening law and order, while 57% of nonwhites – a group that leans Democratic – prioritize reducing minority bias. But substantial minorities of both whites and nonwhites take the opposing views.

Americans who live in towns and rural areas are nearly twice as likely to prioritize strengthening law and order over reducing racial and ethnic bias. Among suburban residents, 55% prioritize reducing minority bias, and 40% prioritize strengthening law and order. Residents of large and small cities, however, are evenly divided on the question.

Americans' Views of Priorities for the U.S. Justice System, by Race and Area of Living

Which do you think should be the bigger priority for the U.S. criminal justice system today – [ROTATED: strengthening law and order through more police and greater enforcement of the laws (or) reducing bias against minorities in the criminal justice system by reforming court and police practices]?

	Strengthening law and order %	Reducing bias against minorities %	No opinion %
National adults	49	43	8
Whites	56	38	6
Nonwhites	33	57	10
Large/Small city	45	48	8
Suburb	40	55	5
Town/Rural area	59	31	11

Gallup, Oct 5-9, 2016

Bottom Line

Criminal justice statistics show that blacks and Hispanics are much more likely than whites to be searched, arrested, detained and imprisoned, and many Americans feel this is an issue that needs addressing. Views on priorities for criminal justice reform, however, are largely divided along political lines. But while law and order is a popular rallying cry within the GOP, some Republicans are attempting to address institutional race disparities in the criminal justice system, such as House Speaker Paul Ryan's efforts at sentencing reform, which have bipartisan support.

The future of criminal justice reform largely hinges on who assumes the presidency in January, as each major party candidate has taken a starkly different approach toward the issue.

Survey Methods

Results for this Gallup poll are based on telephone interviews conducted Oct. 5-9, 2016, on the Gallup U.S. Daily survey, with a random sample of 1,017 adults, aged 18 and older, living in all 50 U.S. states and the District of Columbia. For results based on the total sample of national adults, the margin of sampling error is ±4 percentage points at the 95% confidence level. All reported margins of sampling error include computed design effects for weighting.

October 14, 2016

AMERICANS CONTINUE TO CITE THE ECONOMY AS TOP PROBLEM

by Zac Auter

Story Highlights

- *17% cite the economy, 12% problems with government as top issue*
- *7% name the election as top problem facing the country*
- *Overall, 31% name at least one economic issue as top concern*

WASHINGTON, D.C. – With the presidential election looming, more Americans cite the economy (17%) than any other issue as the most important U.S. problem in October, followed by dissatisfaction with the government (12%). Americans' concerns about the major problems facing the country are largely consistent with what they have been throughout 2016.

Americans' Views of the Most Important U.S. Problem, October 2016

What do you think is the most important problem facing this country today?

	Oct 5-9, 2016 %
Economy in general	17
Dissatisfaction with government	12
Race relations/Racism	10
Immigration/Illegal aliens	7
Elections/Election reform	7
National security	7
Unemployment/Jobs	6
Terrorism	5
Federal budget deficit/Federal debt	4
Poor healthcare/High cost of healthcare	4
Ethics/Moral/Religious decline	3
Crime/Violence	3
Environment/Pollution	3

Gallup

Racism and race relations is the only other issue that at least 10% of Americans mentioned as a top problem in the Oct. 5-9 survey. This is down slightly from its 2016 peak of 18% in July when racial tensions flared after police killed black men in Louisiana and Minnesota and a black man killed five police officers in Dallas.

In the midst of the ongoing presidential campaign, 7% of Americans cite the election as the top U.S. problem in October – higher than Gallup has found at this stage in recent presidential election years. In October of each presidential election year from 2000 to 2012, no more than 1% of Americans mentioned the election as one of the country's top concerns.

Concerns About Economic Issues Down From Recent Election Years

While 17% of Americans currently name the economy in general as the top problem, a combined 31% name at least one of several different economic issues, including the economy, unemployment, the wealth gap and taxes, among others. This marks the lowest level of concern about economic issues at this point in presidential election years since 2000, when 21% of Americans mentioned an economic issue as the top problem.

In October 2012 and 2008, 72% and 69% of Americans, respectively, named some economic issue as the top problem. In the 2004 presidential election, when overall mentions of the economy took a back seat to noneconomic issues such as the situation in Iraq and terrorism, 40% of Americans named an economic issue as the top concern in October.

Percentage of Americans Who Cite Economic Issues as Most Important Problem, Month Before Presidential Elections, 2000-2016

What do you think is the most important problem facing this country today?

	Economic issues as most important problem %
October 2016	31
October 2012	72
October 2008	69
October 2004	40
October 2000	21

Gallup

Implications

Americans have typically named the economy in general as the top issue facing the country in 2016. As recently as September, registered voters chose Donald Trump over Hillary Clinton as the candidate better able to handle the economy, employment and taxes.

Though Trump holds a slight edge over Clinton among registered voters on economic issues, the 2016 presidential campaign has not centered on economic issues recently. In the days after Sunday's presidential debate, for example, a different set of issues has been foremost in Americans' thoughts about the campaign. According to Gallup's daily measurement of what Americans are hearing in the news, those issues include revelations that Trump has made lewd comments about women and Clinton's email scandal.

While Americans may cite the economy as the most important problem facing the country, the campaign in the past week has instead focused on the candidates' personal scandals. Thus, it is unclear to what extent Americans' current top concern will factor into this year's election outcome.

Survey Methods

Results for this Gallup poll are based on telephone interviews conducted Oct. 5-9, 2016, on the Gallup U.S. Daily survey, with a random sample of 1,017 adults, aged 18 and older, living in all 50 U.S. states and the District of Columbia. For results based on the total sample of national adults, the margin of sampling error is ±4 percentage points at the 95% confidence level. All reported margins of sampling error include computed design effects for weighting.

October 17, 2016

CONSUMERS' HOLIDAY SPENDING ESTIMATE MATCHES RECENT YEARS

by Lydia Saad

Story Highlights

- *U.S. adults expect to spend $785 on Christmas gifts*
- *Figure consistent with range since 2013*
- *Nearly nine in 10 intend to spend something*

PRINCETON, N.J. – Americans, on average, anticipate spending $785 on Christmas gifts this year. This is consistent with the range in October spending estimates since 2013 and represents a meaningful improvement over the post-recession lows near $700 recorded in

2010 and 2011. However, it is still not as high as the $900 averages recorded just prior to the recession.

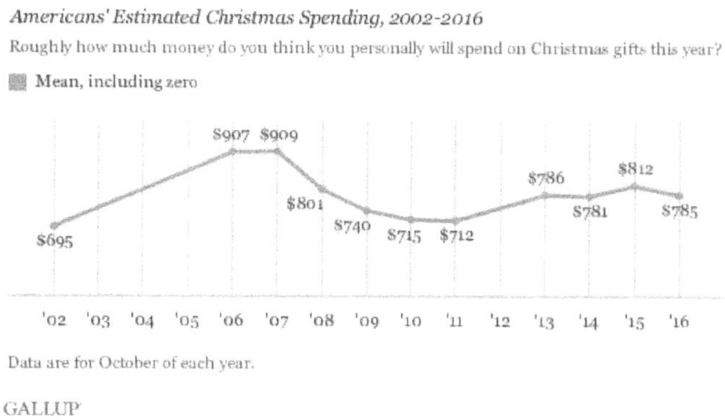

This is Gallup's preliminary look at 2016 holiday spending, based on an Oct. 5-9 poll. Gallup repeats the measure each November, and those results, which often show a shift from October in spending intentions, tend to be more indicative of how holiday spending plays out.

The slight decline since 2015 in Americans' October spending estimate is within the margin of error for these results and does not presage an actual decline in holiday retail spending compared with 2015. In fact, with the exception of 2008 when the Wall Street economic crisis sent a shock wave through the economy, holiday retail spending almost always increases year over year; what changes is the magnitude of that increase. According to National Retail Federation (NRF) estimates since 2002, that increase has been as low as 0.3% to as high as 6.8%, with the recent average near 3.5%.

Regardless of the amount spent, Christmas gift giving remains an important cultural and economic tradition in the U.S. Nearly nine in 10 U.S. adults intend to spend something on gifts, including 3% who think they will spend less than $100, 53% who plan to spend $100 to $999 and 31% who will lay out $1,000 or more. All of these figures nearly match the 2015 levels for each spending range.

Another 6% are unsure how much they'll spend this year, leaving just 7% who say they won't spend anything or that they don't celebrate the holiday.

Americans' October Christmas Spending Estimates for 2015-2016

Roughly how much money do you think you personally will spend on Christmas gifts this year?

	Oct 7-11, 2015 %	Oct 5-9, 2016 %
$1,000 or more	32	31
$500 to $999	23	23
$250 to $499	13	14
$100 to $249	17	16
Less than $100	3	3
None/Don't celebrate	8	7
Not sure	4	6
Average (including zero)	$812	$785
Average (excluding zero)	$887	$849

Gallup

Relatively Few Intend to Spend "Less"

The latest survey includes a separate question asking Americans, regardless of what dollar amount they say they plan to spend, whether that amount is higher, lower or the same compared with the previous year. The results offer news that is slightly more positive for holiday retailers, as a relatively low proportion – 21% – expressly say they will spend less on gifts this year. That is similar to the percentage a year ago saying they would spend less, but down from 35% at the height of the Wall Street financial crisis in 2008 and from elevated levels for several years thereafter.

As is typical, the majority of adults (63%) say they will spend about the same amount on gifts as the year prior, while the smallest percentage, now 14%, plan to spend more.

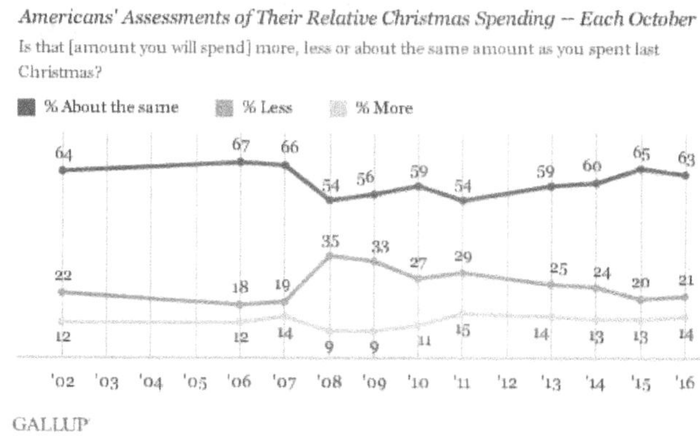

Bottom Line

Americans' enthusiasm for gift buying this holiday season is broadly in line with their October spending predictions in each of the past three years, suggesting that holiday spending will be similar to last year when, according to the NRF, holiday spending grew by 3.2%. However, because Americans' holiday spending estimate often changes as the season progresses, it will be important to see where this stands in Gallup's November update. That figure could be especially relevant this year if the presidential election has any effect – positive or negative – on consumers' comfort with spending.

Historical data are available in Gallup Analytics.

Survey Methods

Results for this Gallup poll are based on telephone interviews conducted Oct. 5-9, 2016, with a random sample of 1,017 adults, aged 18 and older, living in all 50 U.S. states and the District of Columbia. The margin of sampling error for the spending mean is ±$69 at the 95% confidence level. This sampling error includes the computed design effect for weighting.

October 17, 2016

ONE IN THREE U.S. WOMEN WORRY ABOUT BEING SEXUALLY ASSAULTED

by Jeffrey M. Jones

Story Highlights

- *34% of women worried, up from an average 30% in 2013-2015*
- *Younger women worry more than older women*
- *Increase was apparent before Trump tapes were released*

PRINCETON, N.J. – Thirty-four percent of U.S. women say they worry "frequently" or "occasionally" about being sexually assaulted. That percentage essentially matches the 33% average in Gallup's 17-year trend but is up slightly from an average 30% who worried from 2013 through 2015. Relatively few men (5%) worry about being sexually assaulted.

Concern About Being a Victim of Sexual Assault, by Gender

How often do you, yourself, worry about the following things -- frequently, occasionally, rarely or never? How about -- being sexually assaulted?

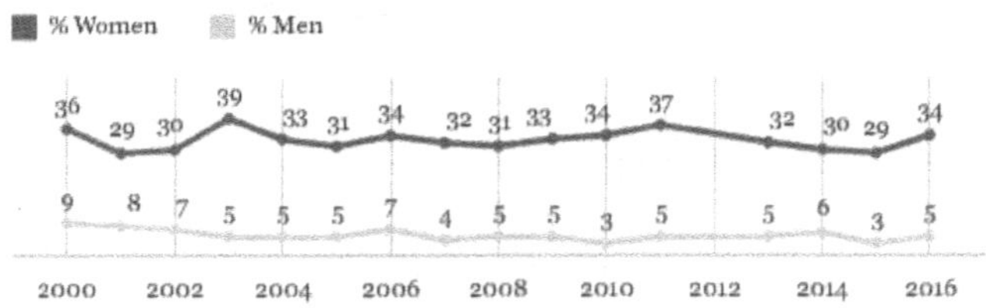

Figures are percentage who worry frequently or occasionally about being sexually assaulted

GALLUP

Gallup's annual Crime Poll was conducted Oct. 5-9, which included two days before and three days after the Oct. 7 release of audiotapes of Republican presidential candidate Donald Trump making references in 2005 to kissing and touching women without their consent. The release of the tapes had no apparent immediate effect on women's worry about being sexually assaulted – the percentage worried was already up from 2013-2015 levels in Oct. 5-6 polling and was no higher in Oct. 7-9 polling.

The audio recording of Trump has made sexual assault and the treatment of women more generally a major issue in the presidential campaign. Trump attempted to dismiss the conversation as nothing more than "locker room talk." Last week, however, several women came forward accusing Trump of making sexual advances on them without their consent. Trump has denied those accusations.

Younger women report a greater level of concern than older women about being sexually assaulted – 42% of women under the age of 50 say they worry at least occasionally about it, compared with 25% of women aged 50 and older. That age gap has been the norm in Gallup's polling on the matter, with an average 38% of younger women and 26% of older women concerned since 2000.

Overall, 20% of all U.S. adults say they worry frequently or occasionally about being sexually assaulted. The current percentage is back up from a low of 16% last fall, and matches the historical average in Gallup's trend dating to 2000, mostly because of an increase in women's concern.

Concern About Being a Victim of Sexual Assault

How often do you, yourself, worry about the following things -- frequently, occasionally, rarely or never? How about -- being sexually assaulted?

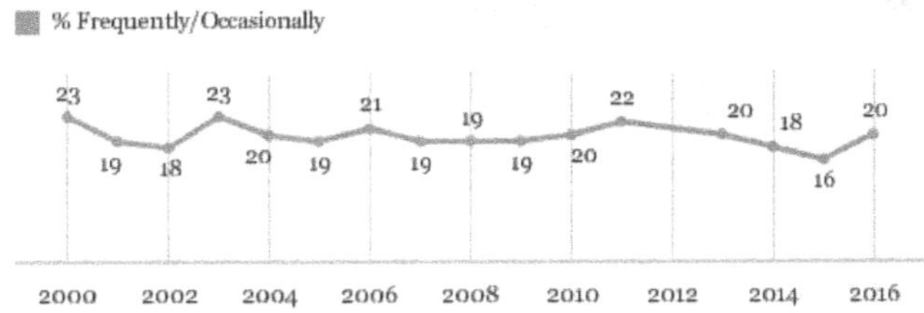

GALLUP

One Percent in U.S. Report Being Victims of Sexual Assault

As part of its annual Crime survey, Gallup also asks Americans whether they have been the victims of specific types of crimes, including sexual assault. Typically about 1% of Americans say they or a member of their household has been a victim of sexual assault within the past 12 months, and slightly less than 1% say they, personally, were the victim. That is a lower household victimization rate than for other violent crimes tested, including physical assault (3%) and armed robbery (2%).

Gallup data from 2000 to the present, encompassing more than 15,000 interviews, indicate that women – particularly younger women – are more likely to say they themselves or a member of their household has been sexually assaulted. Slightly more than 2% of women younger than 50 say a member of their household has been the victim of sexual assault, including just over 1% who say they were personally the victim.

Last 12 Months: Been Victim of Sexual Assault

Based on aggregated data from 15 polls conducted between 2000 and 2016

	Respondent personally %	Respondent or other household member %	N size
All U.S. adults	0.6	1.2	15,197
Women	0.9	1.6	7,621
Men	0.3	0.7	7,576
Women 18 to 49	1.2	2.2	2,970
Women 50+	0.5	0.9	4,504
Men 18 to 49	0.5	0.9	3,504
Men 50+	0.2	0.5	3,985

Gallup

These data indicate that greater worry among women – particularly younger women – is consistent with their greater likelihood of being sexually assaulted.

Implications

Although the sexual assault issue has been prominent in the campaign this past week, the release of the Trump tapes does not appear to have affected women's concerns about their own risk of being a sexual assault victim, at least as of Oct. 9. More Americans, and more women, are concerned about sexual assault than in recent years, but that may just reflect a return to more normal levels of concern after those levels dipped between 2013 and 2015.

Typically, sexual assault has not ranked among Americans' top crime concerns – with theft of credit card information, identity theft, burglary and car theft usually ranking higher. The lesser concern about sexual assault may have more to do with the frequency of the crime than the seriousness of it. Along these lines, Americans also worry less about being murdered than about crimes involving theft or damage of property, for example.

But Americans as a whole also worry less about sexual assault because it is primarily a concern held by women, with few men worrying about it, whereas for most other crimes the gender gap in worry is smaller or nonexistent.

Survey Methods

Results for this Gallup poll are based on telephone interviews conducted Oct 5-9, 2016, with a random sample of 1,017 adults, aged 18 and older, living in all 50 U.S. states and the District of Columbia. For results based on the total sample of national adults, the margin of sampling error is ±4 percentage points at the 95% confidence level. All reported margins of sampling error include computed design effects for weighting.

October 18, 2016
U.S. MINORITY STUDENTS LESS EXPOSED TO COMPUTER SCIENCE

by Dawn Royal and Art Swift

Story Highlights

- *Black students are less likely than white students to have access to classes*
- *Fewer blacks and Hispanics than whites frequently use a computer at home*
- *Black students more likely to see computer science in TV shows, movies*

WASHINGTON, D.C. – Black students are less likely than white and Hispanic students in grades seven through 12 in the U.S. to be exposed to computer science learning at school, according to a new study conducted by Gallup and Google. Specifically, black students are less likely than white and Hispanic students to say their school offers classes dedicated to computer science. Black students are also less likely to say computer science is taught as part of other classes at their school.

Students' Access to Computer Science Classes

Are there classes where only computer science is taught in your school? Is computer science taught as part of other classes at your school? (% Yes)

	Whites %	Blacks %	Hispanics %
Classes where only computer science is taught	58	47	59
Computer science taught as part of other classes	53	44	56

Google-Gallup study conducted Dec. 7, 2015-Jan. 17, 2016

Black students may have less access to computer science classes at school, but they are more likely than their white classmates to be aware of specific websites where they can learn computer science (73% vs. 62%, respectively). Blacks are about as likely as Hispanics (71%) to be aware of these websites.

Black students who have learned computer science are more likely than white students to have done so in a group or club at school (34% vs. 18%, respectively). They are also more likely to have learned computer science in a formal group or program outside of school, such as a camp or a summer program (38% of blacks vs. 17% of whites). These findings also show that when black students say computer science is taught at their school, or that their school offers computer science clubs, they have a greater interest in learning about it.

While Hispanic students have similar exposure to computer science at school as their white counterparts, they are less likely, at 49%, than whites (68%) and blacks (65%) to say they have an adult in their life who works with computers or other types of technology. This lack of role models or a personal lack of confidence in learning computer science may be a barrier for Hispanic students – only 51% are "very confident" they could learn computer science, compared with 68% of black students and 56% of white students.

These findings are from the second year of Google and Gallup's multiyear study on computer science education among seventh- to 12th-grade students and their parents. Google and Gallup also interviewed elementary and high school teachers, principals and superintendents. Only white, black and Hispanic student and parent data were analyzed in this article due to insufficient sample sizes for other racial and ethnic groups.

Blacks, Hispanics Less Likely Than Whites to Use a Computer at Home

Sixty-three percent of seventh- to 12th-grade students overall in the U.S. use a computer at home every day or most days per week. White students (68%) are more likely than black (58%) and Hispanic (50%) students to use a computer at home at least most days per week. Just 5% of students overall say they never use a computer at home. These disparities in exposure to technology at home and in school may influence whether underrepresented minorities learn and practice computer science in the future.

Computer Access at Home

In a typical week, how often do you use a computer at home?

	Every day/Most days %
Whites	68
Blacks	58
Hispanics	50

Google-Gallup study conducted Dec. 7, 2015-Jan. 17, 2016

Blacks More Likely to See Computer Science in TV Shows, Movies

Exposure to seeing others perform computer science activities can influence perceptions of the industry and potentially the desire to be part of the industry. About one in four students report often seeing people "doing computer science" in TV shows or movies. Among whites, these figures are 20% for TV shows and 24% for movies; among Hispanics, it is 23% for both TV shows and movies. Among blacks, 34% of students say they see people "doing computer science" in TV shows, while 36% say the same about movies. The greater media exposure for black students could potentially boost their future involvement in computer science.

Students' Observations of Computer Science in Media

How often do you see or read about people doing computer science in each of the following places? (% Often)

	Whites %	Blacks %	Hispanics %
In TV shows	20	34	23
In movies	24	36	23
Online through social media, articles or videos	34	32	36

Google-Gallup study conducted Dec. 7, 2015-Jan. 17, 2016

The percentage of students seeing someone "doing computer science" online through social media, articles or videos is higher for whites (34%) and Hispanics (36%) but lower for blacks (32%).

The amount of exposure children have to computer science may affect their interest in doing this type of work later in life. If students do not see people "doing computer science" very often, especially people they can relate to, they may struggle to imagine themselves ever doing the same work. Just one in six students (16%) who say they see computer science in the media say it is often people like them they see doing this type of work. This is true of even fewer Hispanic students (13%).

"People Like You" Doing Computer Science

Thinking about all of the people you see or read about doing computer science in TV shows, in movies or online, how often do you see people like you doing computer science?

	Overall %	Whites %	Blacks %	Hispanics %
Often	16	16	26	13
Sometimes	59	59	54	65
Never	24	25	20	22

Among those who see people "doing computer science" on TV, movies or online
Google-Gallup study conducted Dec. 7, 2015-Jan. 17, 2016

Bottom Line

Many students from underrepresented groups in the computer science field, including black, Hispanic and female students, do not have the same computer science learning opportunities as their peers. This may reflect a lack of awareness of or access to computer science learning opportunities, less frequent use of computers at home and in school, and less exposure to computer science in various forms of media.

Blacks and Hispanics are more interested than whites in learning computer science, but both black and Hispanic students are also less likely to use a computer at home at least most days per week. Limited computer use could lessen exposure to computer science in general – and stifle the possibilities of pursuing it as a career.

It is important that all students have the opportunity to learn computer science skills during their K-12 education, as these skills become increasingly important in many areas of life. Schools should make an extra effort to attract female, black and Hispanic students to computer science learning opportunities, as these groups are traditionally underrepresented in computing fields.

Survey Methods

Results for this Google-Gallup computer science education poll are based on telephone interviews conducted Dec. 7, 2015-Jan. 17, 2016, among a random sample of 1,672 students in grades seven through 12 currently living in all 50 states and the District of Columbia, based on samples drawn using the nationally representative Gallup Daily tracking re-contact sample.

For results based on the total sample of students, the margin of sampling error is ±3.4 percentage points at the 95% confidence level. The design effect is ±2.1 percentage points. All reported margins of sampling error include computed design effects for weighting.

October 19, 2016

SUPPORT FOR LEGAL MARIJUANA USE UP TO 60% IN U.S.

by Art Swift

Story Highlights

- *Highest percentage of support recorded in 47-year trend*
- *Favoring legalization is up among all age groups in the past decade*
- *Large majorities of Democrats, independents favor legalization*

WASHINGTON, D.C. – With voters in several states deciding this fall whether to legalize the use of marijuana, public support for making it legal has reached 60% – its highest level in Gallup's 47-year trend.

Americans' Views on Legalizing Marijuana

Do you think the use of marijuana should be made legal, or not?

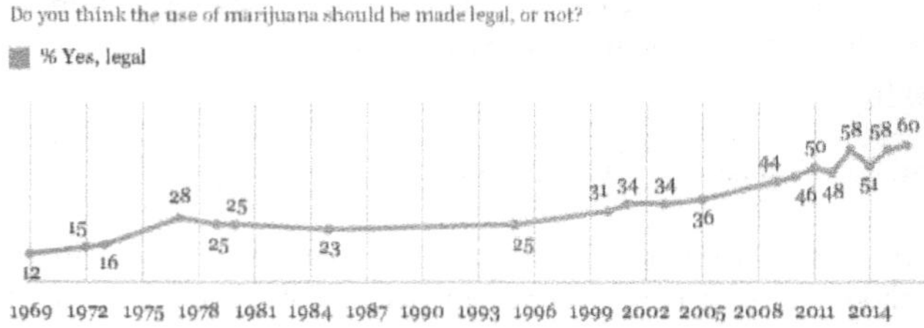

GALLUP

Marijuana use is currently legal in four states and the District of Columbia, and legalization measures are on the ballot in five more – California, Arizona, Massachusetts, Maine and Nevada – this

November. As a result, the percentage of Americans living in states where pot use is legal could rise from the current 5% to as much as 25% if all of these ballot measures pass.

When Gallup first asked this question in 1969, 12% of Americans supported the legalization of marijuana use. In the late 1970s, support rose to 28% but began to retreat in the 1980s during the era of the "Just Say No" to drugs campaign. Support stayed in the 25% range through 1995, but increased to 31% in 2000 and has continued climbing since then.

In 2013, support for legalization reached a majority for the first time after Washington and Colorado became the first states to legalize the recreational use of marijuana. Since then, a majority of Americans have continued to say they think the use of marijuana should be made legal.

Today's 60% is statistically similar to the previous high of 58% reached in 2013 and 2015, so it is unclear whether support has stabilized or is continuing to inch higher.

Support Up From a Decade Ago Among All Age Groups

Support for legalizing marijuana use has increased among most subgroups in the past decade, but more so among certain groups than others. For example, support is up 33 percentage points to 77% among adults aged 18 to 34, while it is up 16 points among adults aged 55 and older to 45%.

Support for the Legalization of Marijuana, by Age Group

	2003 and 2005 %	2016 %
National adults	35	60
18-34	44	77
35-54	35	61
55+	29	45

Note: Analysis combines data from 2003 and 2005 because each survey asked the question of a half-sample of respondents
Gallup

Democrats and Independents Soar to Majorities Favoring Legalization

Additionally, support is up more among independents and Democrats than it is among Republicans, partly because of the older age skew of the last group. Seventy percent of independents and 67% of Democrats support legal pot use, a major increase since the combined survey of 2003 and 2005 when 46% of independents and 38% of Democrats supported the idea. While less than a majority of members in any political party backed legalizing marijuana in 2003 and 2005, Democrats and independents have fueled the recent nationwide surge in support.

Support for the Legalization of Marijuana, by Political Party

	2003 and 2005 %	2016 %
National adults	35	60
Republicans	20	42
Independents	46	70
Democrats	38	67

Note: Analysis combines data from 2003 and 2005 because each survey asked the question of a half-sample of respondents
Gallup

Republicans' support has doubled from more than a decade ago, yet only 42% of GOP members now support legal marijuana use.

Bottom Line

If recreational marijuana use becomes legal in California this year, many other states will likely follow, because the "Golden State" often sets political trends for the rest of the U.S. As more states legalize marijuana, the question of *whether* the drug should be legal may become *when* it will be legal. The transformation in public attitudes about marijuana over the past half-century has mirrored the liberalization of public attitudes about gay rights and the same-sex-marriage movement, the latter of which the U.S. Supreme Court deemed legal last year. It is possible that it might take a Supreme Court case to settle this matter, too.

Survey Methods

Results for this Gallup poll are based on telephone interviews conducted Oct. 5-9, 2016, with a random sample of 1,017 adults, aged 18 and older, living in all 50 U.S. states and the District of Columbia. For results based on the total sample of national adults, the margin of sampling error is ±4 percentage points at the 95% confidence level. All reported margins of sampling error include computed design effects for weighting.

October 19, 2016
CANDIDATES' IMAGES WHERE THEY WERE IN EARLY JULY

by Frank Newport and Andrew Dugan

Story Highlights

- *Trump's image slightly less positive now than before debates*
- *53% have strongly unfavorable views of Trump; 43% of Clinton*
- *Partisans have relatively lukewarm feelings about their candidate*

PRINCETON, N.J. – Although Americans' views of Hillary Clinton and Donald Trump fluctuated during the July political conventions and in recent weeks, the public's current views of the two candidates are about where they were before the conventions. Trump's 31% favorable rating for the period spanning Oct. 11-17 is essentially where it was in the first week of July, while Clinton's current 41% favorable rating is about the same as her 40% rating in early July.

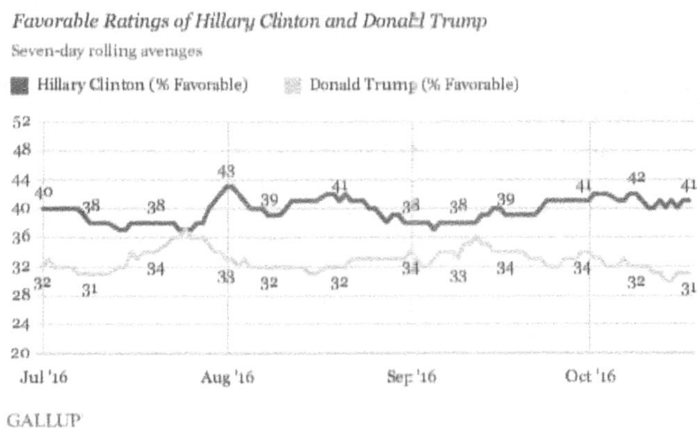

Since the conventions, the American public has witnessed two presidential debates, as well as swirling controversy over a 2005 video of Trump making lewd and controversial comments about women and more WikiLeaks releases of emails sent by Clinton and her campaign.

All of this has minimally affected the images of the two candidates. Trump's favorable score edged down a few percentage points between early September and mid-October, while Clinton's favorable rating moved up a few points. However, these changes do not represent a major shift from earlier times and underscore the stable nature of the public's views of these two high-profile candidates at this late point in the campaign.

Americans More Likely to Have Strongly Negative Than Strongly Positive Views

To the extent that Clinton and Trump evoke passion in the U.S. public, it is significantly more likely to be negative than positive. Most of those who view Clinton or Trump unfavorably say they feel strongly about those negative sentiments. In comparison, only about half of those with positive views of each candidate feel strongly favorable.

This measure is based on a follow-up question Gallup began including on Oct. 13 that asks Americans if they feel strongly or not strongly about their opinions of the candidates. Overall, 43% of Americans interviewed Oct. 13-17 say they have a strongly unfavorable opinion of Clinton, while 21% have a strongly favorable opinion. For Trump, an even higher 53% say they have strongly unfavorable views, with 16% holding a strongly favorable opinion.

Hillary Clinton and Donald Trump Images

	Hillary Clinton %	Donald Trump %
Strongly favorable	21	16
Somewhat favorable	23	15
Somewhat unfavorable	13	15
Strongly unfavorable	43	53

Gallup, Oct. 13-17, 2016

Republicans, Democrats Not Likely to Feel Strongly About Party Nominee

Eight in 10 Democrats and Democratic-leaning independents have favorable views of Clinton. Among this group, about half say that it is a strongly favorable view, suggesting a less-than-passionate attachment to their nominee. A similar pattern exists among those Republicans and Republican leaners who have a favorable opinion of Trump (63% overall), with a little more than half saying they strongly hold this view.

Clinton does better than Trump in terms of partisans' unfavorable views. The 36% of Republicans who have unfavorable views of Trump split evenly between those whose views are strongly unfavorable and somewhat unfavorable. Democrats with unfavorable views of Clinton (20%) are less intense, and by about a 2-to-1 margin are more likely to say they hold somewhat unfavorable rather than strongly unfavorable views.

Hillary Clinton and Donald Trump Images, by Party ID

	Clinton (among Democrats) %	Trump (among Republicans) %
Strongly favorable	40	34
Somewhat favorable	39	29
Somewhat unfavorable	13	18
Strongly unfavorable	7	18

Gallup, Oct. 13-17, 2016

The mixed feelings partisans have toward their candidate are in stark contrast to how they feel about the opposite party's candidate – 83% of Republicans strongly dislike Clinton, and 84% of Democrats strongly dislike Trump.

Bottom Line

Americans have become slightly more positive about Clinton and slightly less positive about Trump in recent weeks, but from a long-range perspective, the two are positioned in the minds of Americans about where they were in early July. Clinton's image is currently 10 points more favorable than Trump's.

At the same time, neither Clinton nor Trump is particularly well-liked. Only about half of those who view either candidate favorably say they have strongly favorable views. By contrast, most of those who have unfavorable views of Clinton or Trump say they are strongly unfavorable. This reinforces the idea that for many voters, the 2016 election is a choice between "the lesser of two evils."

The presidential candidate with the most favorable image is almost always the one who wins the election, clearly giving Clinton the overall edge at this point. Additionally, fewer Democrats hold negative views of Clinton than Republicans hold negative views of Trump – and among these groups, Republicans are more likely to say their negative views are strong. The impact of these attitudes on voter turnout, however, is still unclear.

Survey Methods

Results for this Gallup poll are based on telephone interviews conducted Oct. 11-17, 2016, on the Gallup U.S. Daily survey, with a random sample of 3,582 adults, aged 18 and older, living in all 50 U.S. states and the District of Columbia. For results based on the total sample of national adults, the margin of sampling error is ±2 percentage points at the 95% confidence level. All reported margins of sampling error include computed design effects for weighting.

October 20, 2016
AMERICANS' VIEWS SHIFT ON TOUGHNESS OF JUSTICE SYSTEM

by Justin McCarthy

Story Highlights

- *Percentage who say justice system "not tough enough" shrinks to 45%*
- *38% say drug crime sentencing guidelines are "too tough"*

WASHINGTON, D.C. – Americans' views of how the criminal justice system is handling crime have shifted considerably over the past decade. Currently, 45% say the justice system is "not tough enough" – down from 65% in 2003 and even higher majorities before then. Americans are now more likely than they have been in three prior polls to describe the justice system's approach as "about right" (35%) or "too tough" (14%).

Americans' Views of the U.S. Justice System's Handling of Crime, 1992-2016

In general, do you think the criminal justice system in this country is too tough, not tough enough or about right in its handling of crime?

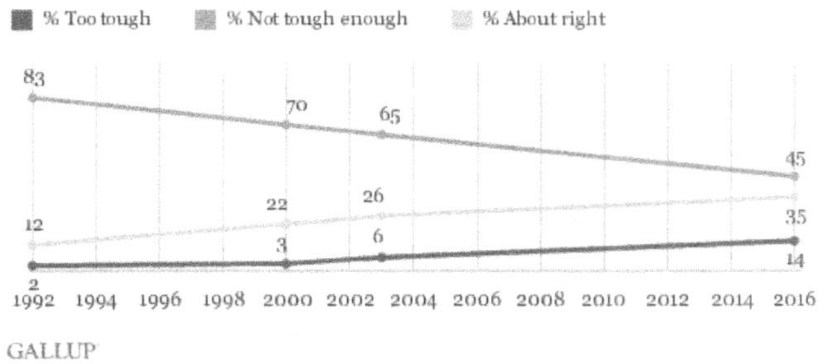

Incarceration rates in the U.S. have soared over the past few decades, and political leaders, justice officials and reform advocates have sought criminal justice reform as a result. With this, Americans' views of the criminal justice system have shifted with the national conversation, with less than a majority now saying the system is "not tough enough." Although considerably higher than in the past, relatively few believe the system is "too tough."

Views of the justice system's toughness vary across racial and political party lines. The majority of Republicans and Republican-leaning independents say it is "not tough enough" (65%), with most of the rest describing it as "about right" (30%). Democrats and Democratic-leaning independents, on the other hand, are most likely to say the system is "about right" (42%), with the rest dividing about evenly between saying it is "too tough" (22%) or "not tough enough" (29%).

A majority of whites (53%) say the system's handling of crime is "not tough enough," while a third (32%) say it is "about right." One in 10 whites say the system is "too tough." Nonwhites – who as a group make up a disproportionate percentage of the U.S. incarcerated population – are more than twice as likely as whites to say the system is "too tough" (23%). They are also more likely than whites to say it is "about right" (40%). Meanwhile, 30% of nonwhites say the system's handling of crime is "not tough enough."

Americans' Views of the U.S. Justice System's Handling of Crime, by Group

In general, do you think the criminal justice system in this country is too tough, not tough enough or about right in its handling of crime?

	Too tough %	Not tough enough %	About right %
Republicans/Republican leaners			
Oct. 5-9, 2016	2	65	30
Oct. 6-8, 2003	2	72	25
Aug. 29-Sept. 5, 2000	1	79	16
Democrats/Democratic leaners			
Oct. 5-9, 2016	22	29	42
Oct. 6-8, 2003	9	58	29
Aug. 29-Sept. 5, 2000	6	62	27
Whites			
Oct. 5-9, 2016	10	53	32
Oct. 6-8, 2003	6	67	25
Aug. 29-Sept. 5, 2000	3	72	21
Nonwhites			
Oct. 5-9, 2016	23	30	40
Oct. 6-8, 2003	8	57	28
Aug. 29-Sept. 5, 2000	7	57	28

2000-2016
Gallup

Americans More Likely to Describe Drug Crime Sentencing as "Too Tough"

Against a backdrop of bipartisan efforts in Congress to reform drug sentencing in 2016, 38% of U.S. adults describe guidelines for sentencing of people convicted of routine drug crimes as "too tough." A slightly smaller percentage say they are "not tough enough" (34%), while a quarter say they are "about right" (25%).

Fifty percent of Democrats say drug crime sentencing guidelines are "too tough" – twice as high as the percentage of Republicans (26%) who say the same. Republicans are more likely than Democrats to describe drug crime sentencing as "not tough enough" (47%).

Differences in views between whites and nonwhites are less pronounced on drug crime sentencing guidelines compared with their views of the criminal justice system's handling of crime more generally. Both whites and nonwhites have sizable percentages, ranging from 21% to 39%, of those who describe drug crime sentencing guidelines as "too tough," "not tough enough" or "about right."

Americans' Views of Drug Crime Sentencing Guidelines, by Race and Party Leanings

In general, do you think the current sentencing guidelines for people convicted of routine drug crimes are too tough, not tough enough or about right?

	Too tough %	Not tough enough %	About right %	No opinion %
National adults	38	34	25	4
Whites	39	35	21	4
Nonwhites	36	28	33	3
Republicans/ Republican leaners	26	47	22	6
Democrats/Democratic leaners	50	22	26	3

Oct. 5-9, 2016
Gallup

Bottom Line

Americans' views about the toughness of the criminal justice system have clearly shifted in recent decades, with less than a majority now saying the system is "not tough enough" and more Americans describing it as "about right" or "too tough." Although more than in the past believe the system is overly tough, this view is still held by a relatively small minority. U.S. adults are much more likely, however, to describe drug crime sentencing guidelines as "too tough" compared with their opinions of the system's handling of overall crime, and this is the case among both racial and political party groups.

Reform of drug-related sentencing may be a more agreeable point for larger discussions of criminal justice reform, and this topic seems to have gained some degree of bipartisan traction in the House of Representatives recently.

These data are available in Gallup Analytics.

Survey Methods

Results for this Gallup poll are based on telephone interviews conducted Oct. 5-9, 2016, on the Gallup U.S. Daily tracking survey, with a random sample of 520 adults, aged 18 and older, living in all 50 U.S. states and the District of Columbia. For results based on the total sample of national adults, the margin of sampling error is ±5 percentage points at the 95% confidence level. All reported margins of sampling error include computed design effects for weighting.

NOTE: ABOVE ARTICLE WAS CUT OFF...

October 21, 2016

OBAMA AVERAGES 52.0% JOB APPROVAL IN 31ST QUARTER

by Jeffrey M. Jones

Story Highlights

- *Best quarterly average in Obama's second term*
- *Ties as fourth-best quarter in his presidency*
- *One of four presidents above 50% approval in 31st quarter*

PRINCETON, N.J. – During his 31st quarter in office, President Barack Obama averaged 52.0% job approval, up one percentage point from the 30th quarter and the highest in his second term as president. His most recent quarterly average essentially ties a 51.9% average in his 16th quarter as the fourth-best of his entire presidency.

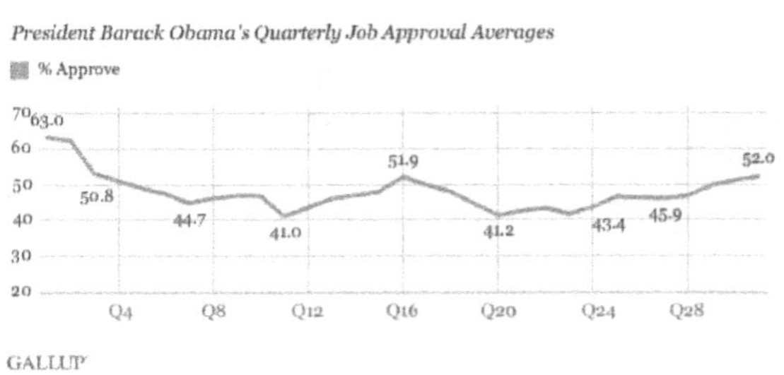

Since his first year in office, Obama's job approval ratings have mostly been below the majority level. The notable exception was slightly higher ratings in his 16th quarter in office, when he was re-elected and enjoyed a rally in support in subsequent weeks. It was not until his 30th quarter, from April 20 through July 19, that he again averaged above 50% job approval, reaching 50.9%, and improving further in the most recent quarter.

The upward momentum in Obama's approval ratings is continuing, as he has averaged 54% job approval so far in October.

Americans' evaluations of Obama have grown more positive as voters prepare to elect his successor next month. Neither of the major contenders – Hillary Clinton nor Donald Trump – is viewed favorably, and Americans may rate Obama more positively given the contrast.

The presidential election also helps focus Americans' attention on how the country is doing and on Obama's performance in office as they prepare to cast their votes.

Obama's job approval has improved about equally among Democrats and independents. In his 31st quarter in office, Obama's approval rating reached 90% among Democrats and 50% among independents – both figures up two points from the previous quarter and up roughly seven points each over the past year.

Republicans' 12% approval of Obama is unchanged from the previous quarter and is up two points from one year ago.

Obama's Rating in 31st Quarter Most Similar to Reagan's

Of the six presidents who served 31 quarters in office, Obama is the fourth to have majority approval at that point in his presidency. Dwight Eisenhower and Bill Clinton were considerably more popular, with approval ratings near 60%. Harry Truman and George W. Bush were much less popular, with approval ratings near 30%. Ronald Reagan's 53.5% job approval during his 31st quarter in office is the closest to Obama's.

Average Presidential Job Approval Ratings During 31st Quarter in Office, Gallup Polls

	Dates of 31st quarter %	Average approval rating %	Number of polls %
Truman	Oct 20, 1952-Jan 19, 1953	32.0	1
Eisenhower	Jul 20-Oct 19, 1960	61.3	6
Reagan	Jul 20-Oct 19, 1988	53.5	2
Clinton	Jul 20-Oct 19, 2000	59.1	7
G.W. Bush	Jul 20-Oct 19, 2008	29.4	8
Obama	Jul 20-Oct 19, 2016	52.0	88

Gallup

Gallup has found a weak relationship between a two-term president's job approval rating and the outcome of the ensuing presidential election. However, like Reagan's, Obama's approval ratings have been on an upward trajectory in his final year. That may aid Hillary Clinton as she seeks to lead the Democrats to a third consecutive presidential election victory, as Reagan's improving ratings may have done for his Republican successor George H.W. Bush in 1988.

Implications

Obama has averaged 47.6% job approval throughout his presidency. Even if his approval ratings in his final quarter in office stay above 50%, his eight-year approval average will rank among the lowest of post-World War II presidents. This is largely because Republicans' extremely low ratings of him have suppressed his overall ratings. This reflects the highly polarized nature of the modern political environment. The gap in Republicans' and Democrats' ratings of Obama rank among the highest for any president in Gallup's polling history.

But like Eisenhower, Clinton and Reagan, Obama is on pace to leave office with relatively solid approval ratings. That may serve his legacy as Americans evaluate his presidency from a historical perspective. Generally speaking, Americans' historical assessments of presidents are more strongly related to presidents' final year approval ratings than to their overall term averages.

Survey Methods

Results for this Gallup poll are based on telephone interviews conducted July 20-Oct. 19, 2016, on the Gallup U.S. Daily survey, with a random sample of 44,728 adults, aged 18 and older, living in all 50 U.S. states and the District of Columbia. For results based on the total sample of national adults, the margin of sampling error is ±1 percentage point at the 95% confidence level. All reported margins of sampling error include computed design effects for weighting.

October 21, 2016

SHARP DROP IN VIEWS THAT CANDIDATES TALK ABOUT KEY ISSUES

by Frank Newport

Story Highlights

- *48% say candidates talking about issues, down from 56% in September*
- *Drop evident among both Republicans and Democrats*
- *Lowest response since 1992*

PRINCETON, N.J. – The proportion of Americans who say the presidential candidates are talking about the issues that they – the people – really care about has dropped to its lowest point yet in the current election cycle. Less than half of Americans (48%) say the candidates are talking about the issues that really matter, down sharply from the nine previous months, and the lowest in Gallup's history.

Next, please try to answer each of the following questions based on what you may have heard or read so far about the presidential campaign and candidates from the Democratic and Republican parties.

Are the presidential candidates talking about issues you really care about, or not?

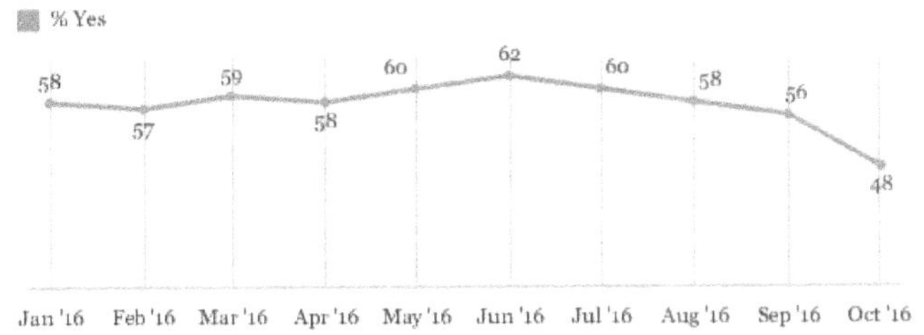

GALLUP

These results are from Gallup's Oct. 17-18 update on key election indicators, measured after the first two presidential debates but just before Wednesday night's final debate. The current percentage of Americans who say the candidates are "talking about issues you really care about" marks an eight-percentage-point drop in agreement since September and is 11 points below the January through September average of 59%.

Before this year, Gallup asked this question periodically between 1992 and 2011. During that time, the lowest percentage of Americans saying the candidates were addressing the issues they care about was 53% in February/March and April 1992, when the political coverage was focused in part on Bill Clinton's past, including extramarital affairs.

But in that election year, in which Democrat Clinton and independent Ross Perot challenged the incumbent George H.W. Bush, Americans became *more* likely to say candidates were addressing important issues as the campaign progressed. By late October 1992, 76% said the candidates were talking about important issues.

Gallup observed a similar increase during 2000, with 77% of registered voters in October of that year saying the candidates were addressing the issues – compared with 54% in January.

So not only is the current measure the lowest in Gallup's trend, it stands in contrast to these two prior election years in which Americans became more likely to believe the candidates were talking about important issues as the campaigns progressed.

Are the presidential candidates talking about issues you really care about, or not?

	Yes %
Dec 15-18, 2011	57
Jan 10-13, 2008	72
Oct 13-15, 2000^	77
Mar 10-12, 2000	60
Jan 7-10, 2000	54
May 9-12, 1996	57
Oct 23-25, 1992	76
Sep 11-15, 1992	66
Apr 20-22, 1992	53
Feb 28-Mar 1, 1992	53
Jan 6-9, 1992	60

^ Based on registered voters
Gallup

Americans' lower level of agreement that the candidates are talking about important issues occurred as the news focused on the release of a 2005 videotape showing Donald Trump making lewd and controversial comments about women. Trump also has attempted to draw attention to women who have accused former President Clinton of sexual improprieties, bringing up this topic in the second debate on Oct. 9.

Two other measures included in the October election update were unchanged from September, suggesting that the public has not so much been souring on the presidential campaign over the past month as specifically noting the shift in campaign focus. About three in 10 Americans say the campaign is being conducted in a way that "makes you feel as though the election process is working as it should." Almost six in 10 say there is at least one candidate running who would make a good president.

Downturn Evident Among Both Republicans and Democrats

Perceptions that the candidates are talking about the right issues have nosedived among both Republicans and Democrats. The 51% of Republicans and Republican-leaning independents and 49% of Democrats and leaners who answer "yes" are the lowest of the year for both groups. (Thirty percent of the small group of independents and those who don't have a party identification answer yes.)

With few exceptions this year, Republicans have been more likely than Democrats to say the candidates are talking about issues they care about. Republicans were particularly positive on this measure in the early months of the year and again in June and July.

Are the presidential candidates talking about issues you really care about, or not?

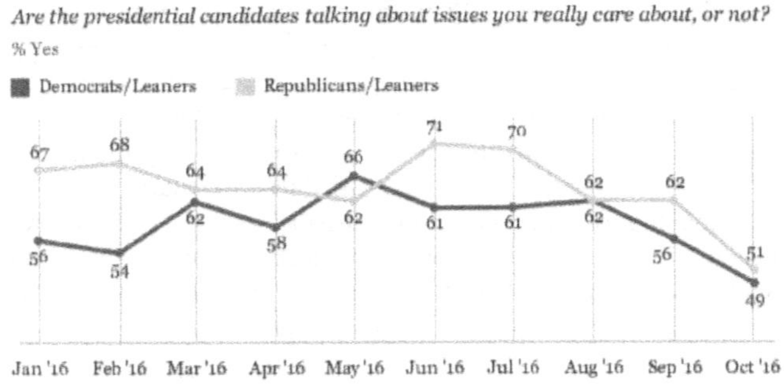

Implications

The drop in the percentage of Americans who say the candidates are talking about the issues they care about almost certainly reflects the increased focus on the character and temperament of Trump and Hillary Clinton. Separate Gallup research shows that Americans on a daily basis have mentioned the word "women" more than any other when asked in recent weeks what they have read, seen or heard about Trump, while "emails" is the most commonly mentioned word for Clinton, as it has been throughout the campaign.

The question doesn't ask if Americans think this shift away from issues is a good or a bad thing. Given that perceptions that the campaign is working the way it should didn't change this month, Americans may not be that concerned that issues have taken a back seat. Plus, the third presidential debate occurred just after these interviews were conducted. Although the headlines coming out of the event focused on Trump's comment about not accepting the results of the election, most of the 90 minutes focused on the candidates' positions on issues. If the candidates spend more time talking about their plans and issues and less time attempting to denigrate each other, public perceptions about the campaign's focus could change in the remaining weeks before Election Day.

Survey Methods

Results for this Gallup poll are based on telephone interviews conducted Oct. 17-18, 2016, on the Gallup U.S. Daily survey, with a random sample of 1,013 adults, aged 18 and older, living in all 50 U.S. states and the District of Columbia. For results based on the total sample of national adults, the margin of sampling error is ±4 percentage points at the 95% confidence level. All reported margins of sampling error include computed design effects for weighting.

October 24, 2016
AMERICANS' RESPECT FOR POLICE SURGES

by Justin McCarthy

Story Highlights

- *76% say they have "a great deal" of respect for the police in their area*
- *Respect for law enforcement up since 2015 among whites and nonwhites*
- *Majorities in major party, age groups report having respect for police*

WASHINGTON, D.C. – Three in four Americans (76%) say they have "a great deal" of respect for the police in their area, up 12 percentage points from last year.

Americans' Respect for Police in Their Areas, 1965-2016

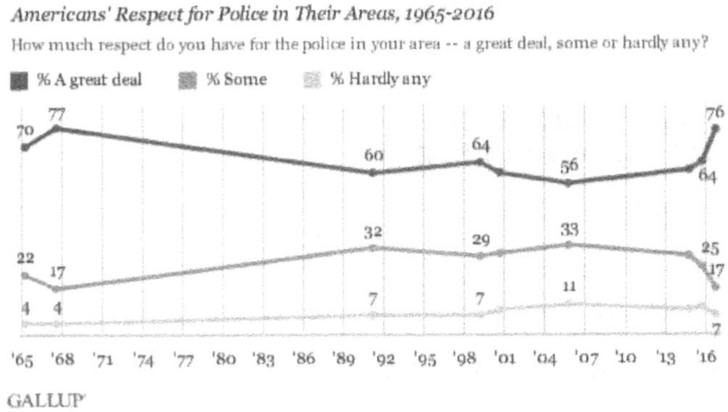

In addition to the large majority of Americans expressing "a great deal" of respect for their local police, 17% say they have "some" respect while 7% say they have "hardly any."

Gallup has asked this question nine times since 1965. The percentage who say they respect the police is significantly higher now than in any measurement taken since the 1990s and is just one point below the high of 77% recorded in 1967. Solid majorities of Americans have said they respect their local law enforcement in all polls conducted since 1965.

The latest figures, from Gallup's Oct. 5-9 annual poll on crime, show Americans' respect for police increased as the number of on-duty police officers who were shot and killed was on the rise.

Americans' confidence in police has also increased after falling to a 22-year low in 2015 and recovering in this year's poll. The latter was conducted in early June, before police officers were shot and killed in separate incidents in Texas and Louisiana.

Respect for Police Up Sharply Among Both Whites and Nonwhites

The increase in shootings of police coincided with high-profile incidents of law enforcement officials shooting and killing unarmed black men. Despite the flaring of racial tensions after these incidents, respect for local police has increased among both whites and nonwhites.

Four in five whites (80%) say they have a great deal of respect for police in their area, up 11 points from last year. Meanwhile, two in three nonwhites (67%) report having the same level of respect, an increase of 14 points from last year.

Since 2000, whites have been more likely than nonwhites to say they respect local law enforcement.

Americans' Respect for Police in Their Areas, by Race -- 2000-2016

How much respect do you have for the police in your area -- a great deal, some or hardly any?

% A great deal

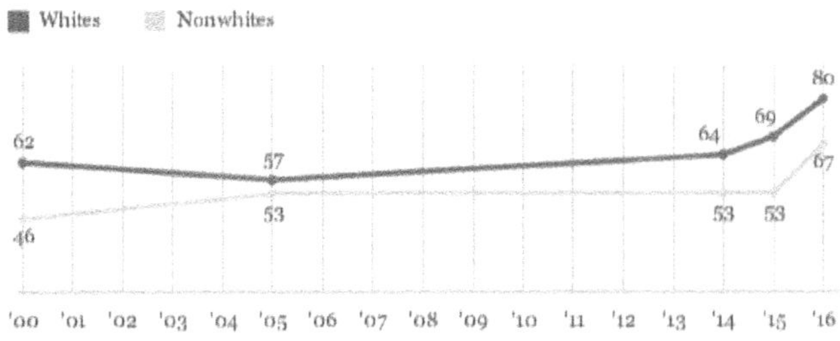

GALLUP

Respect for Police Up Among Age and Party Groups in 2016

In addition to the increases across racial groups, respect for local law enforcement has increased among most political party, ideological and age groups. It has also improved among city, suburban and rural area residents. Liberals, rural residents and young adults saw the sharpest increases – of 19 to 21 points – from 2015 to 2016.

Americans' Respect for Police in Their Areas, by Group – 2015 vs. 2016

How much respect do you have for the police in your area – a great deal, some or hardly any?

	Oct 7-11, 2015 % "A great deal"	Oct 5-9, 2016 % "A great deal"	Change (pct. pts.)
Whites	69	80	+11
Nonwhites	53	67	+14
Conservatives	69	85	+16
Moderates	67	72	+5
Liberals	50	71	+21
Republicans	82	86	+4
Independents	60	75	+15
Democrats	54	68	+14
Large/Small city	61	68	+7
Suburb	71	82	+11
Town/Rural area	61	80	+19
18 to 34	50	69	+19
35 to 54	61	77	+16
55+	77	81	+4

Gallup

Respect for police remains highest among Republicans (86%) and conservatives (85%), but solid majorities of Democrats (68%) and liberals (71%) report the same level of respect.

Adults aged 55 and older (81%) are more likely than those aged 18 to 34 (69%) to have a great deal of respect for police.

About four in five Americans who say they live in a suburb (82%) or a town or rural area (80%) report having a great deal of respect for local police officers, higher than the percentage of those who live in small or large cities (68%) who say the same.

Bottom Line

The sharp increase over the past year in professed respect for local law enforcement comes as many police say they feel they are on the defensive – both politically and for their lives while they are on duty – amid heated national discussions on police brutality and shootings. After an officer was killed by a gunman in Harlem last year, then-New York City Police Commissioner Bill Bratton warned that the U.S. has fostered "an anti-police attitude that has grown" and that the national dialogue on police-community relations needs to discourage individuals who "exhibit anti-police behavior or attitudes."

Louisiana became the first state to pass a bill that treats acts targeted against police officers as a hate crime. Other states are discussing passing similar laws. It's unclear whether the spike in respect for police will have staying power or if it reflects mostly a reaction to the retaliatory killings against police officers last summer.

Although confidence in police varies among subgroups, majorities of all groups say they have a great deal of respect for their local police. And the percentage of national adults who say they have "hardly any" respect for local law enforcement remains small.

Survey Methods

Results for this Gallup poll are based on telephone interviews conducted Oct. 5-9, 2016, with a random sample of 1,017 adults, aged 18 and older, living in all 50 U.S. states and the District of Columbia. For results based on the total sample of national adults, the margin of sampling error is ±4 percentage points at the 95% confidence level. All reported margins of sampling error include computed design effects for weighting.

October 24, 2016

CLINTON WINS THIRD DEBATE, GAINS GROUND AS 'PRESIDENTIAL'

by Lydia Saad

Story Highlights

- *Clinton beat Trump 60% to 31% in perceptions of who won debate*
- *Clinton gained ground for appearing presidential*
- *Trump competitive on economic issues*

PRINCETON, N.J. – Hillary Clinton won round three of the 2016 presidential debates, according to Americans who watched or listened to the event on Wednesday evening. Six in 10 of those who tuned in thought Clinton did the better job, while 31% chose Donald Trump.

Perceptions of Who Won Each Debate – by Party ID

Regardless of which candidate you happen to support, who do you think did the better job in [last/Wednesday] night's debate – [Hillary Clinton (or) Donald Trump]?

	Hillary Clinton %	Donald Trump %	Candidate advantage (pct. pts.)
All debate viewers			
Third debate	60	31	Clinton +29
Second debate	53	35	Clinton +18
First debate	61	27	Clinton +34
Democrats			
Third debate	96	2	Clinton +94
Second debate	93	3	Clinton +90
First debate	92	3	Clinton +89
Independents			
Third debate	58	35	Clinton +23
Second debate	51	32	Clinton +19
First debate	59	30	Clinton +29
Republicans			
Third debate	19	64	Trump +45
Second debate	15	71	Trump +56
First debate	28	53	Trump +25

Among U.S. adults who watched or listened to each debate
Gallup; post-debate polls based on interviewing conducted Sept. 27-28, 2016, Oct. 10-11, 2016, and Oct. 20-21, 2016

Clinton's sweep of all three debates puts her in the company of Barack Obama in 2008, John Kerry in 2004 and Bill Clinton in 1996. Each won all of the presidential debates that took place in those election years, although Kerry still failed to win the 2004 election.

In addition to nearly unanimously being perceived as the winner by rank-and-file Democrats (96%) for her performance in the debate at the University of Nevada, Las Vegas, Clinton was the solid pick among political independents (58%). Nearly one in five Republicans (19%) also chose her as the winner.

The 29-percentage-point overall advantage for Clinton in perceptions of who won the third debate is almost as big as her 34-point lead over Trump in the first debate. A bare majority of Republicans thought Trump won the first debate – his worst performance of the three. And Clinton's third-debate advantage is a clear improvement over her 18-point lead in overall perceptions of who won the second debate.

Two-Thirds of Female Viewers Pick Clinton as the Winner

Part of the reason for Clinton's strong advantage over Trump in all three post-debate polls is the high proportion of women naming her as the winner in each. Most recently, 67% of women watching the third debate said Clinton performed best, whereas 26% chose Trump – better than 2-to-1. Men also chose Clinton over Trump, but by a slimmer 19-point margin (54% vs. 35%).

Perceptions of Who Won Each Debate – by Gender

Regardless of which candidate you happen to support, who do you think did the better job in [last/Wednesday] night's debate – [Hillary Clinton (or) Donald Trump]?

	Hillary Clinton %	Donald Trump %	Clinton advantage (pct. pts.)
Women			
Third debate	67	26	+41
Second debate	58	32	+26
First debate	69	21	+48
Men			
Third debate	54	35	+19
Second debate	49	38	+11
First debate	53	33	+20

Among U.S. adults who watched or listened to each debate
Gallup; post-debate polls based on interviewing conducted Sept. 27-28, 2016, Oct. 10-11, 2016, and Oct. 20-21, 2016

Clinton Stretches Her Advantage as "Presidential"

After each debate, Gallup has asked viewers to compare the candidates' performance on four specific personal dimensions, including their command of the issues, appearance as presidential, likability and ability to be inspiring.

Clinton excelled on perceptions of competency in the first debate, with 62% saying she had the better understanding of issues versus 26% naming Trump on this dimension. In the second debate, her ratings for being likable inched higher while the others held steady or sagged slightly. In the third debate, she made some headway on the final two qualities:

- Sixty-four percent of viewers chose Clinton as the more presidential of the two candidates on the Nevada stage, up from 56% in the second debate and 59% in the first.
- The percentage choosing Clinton as the more inspiring increased slightly – to 50% from 44% in the second debate and 46% in the first.

Perceptions of Candidates' Personal Qualities

Thinking about the following characteristics and qualities, please say whether you think each one better described Hillary Clinton or Donald Trump during [last/Wednesday] night's debate.

	Hillary Clinton %	Donald Trump %	Clinton advantage (pct. pts.)
Appeared presidential			
Third debate	64	26	+38
Second debate	56	27	+29
First debate	59	27	+32
Had a good understanding of the issues			

Third debate	63	26	+37
Second debate	59	28	+31
First debate	62	26	+36
Was more likable			
Third debate	59	31	+28
Second debate	59	31	+28
First debate	55	36	+19
Was inspiring			
Third debate	50	31	+19
Second debate	44	34	+10
First debate	46	34	+12

Among U.S. adults who watched or listened to each debate
Gallup; post-debate polls based on interviewing conducted Sept. 27-28, 2016, Oct. 10-11, 2016, and Oct. 20-21, 2016

The moderator of the third debate, Fox News anchor Chris Wallace, stuck to the handful of policy-based issues he pre-announced he would focus on.

Clinton came out significantly ahead of Trump in viewers' ratings of their performance on most of these, holding a particularly strong edge in perceptions of who would best deal with international crises as president. Sixty percent chose her, compared with 35% naming Trump.

Clinton also led by roughly 15 points as the better candidate to deal with immigration, the Supreme Court, Social Security and Russia.

At the same time, Trump came within four points of Clinton in ratings of which would be better for the economy and the federal debt, indicating a potential vulnerability for Clinton in the closing days of the campaign.

Perceptions of Who Was Better on Issues at Third Debate

Now, based on what you heard or saw in the debate, which candidate – [Hillary Clinton (or) Donald Trump] – do you think would better handle each of the following issues if elected president?

	Hillary Clinton %	Donald Trump %	Clinton advantage (pct. pts.)
Dealing with international crises	60	35	+25
Immigration	56	41	+15
The Supreme Court	56	40	+16
Social Security	55	39	+16
Dealing with Russia	54	39	+15
The economy	50	46	+4
The federal debt	49	45	+4

Among U.S. adults who watched or listened to the third debate
Gallup; Oct. 20-21, 2016

Debate Viewers Ready to Accept Election Outcome

Reiterating his concerns about voter fraud and other ways the presidential election might be corrupted, Trump refused to guarantee that he would "absolutely accept the result of this election" when Wallace asked the Republican nominee if he agreed with his running mate's pledge.

However, 83% of Americans who watched or heard the third debate responded affirmatively to the same question, including 94% of Democrats, 80% of independents and 77% of Republicans. While 12% of Republicans said they would not accept the results, nearly as many (9%) said "it depends," possibly reflecting the Trump campaign's post-debate spin that a recount would be warranted if Trump were to lose by a narrow margin.

Willingness to Accept Election Outcome

No matter who wins in November, will you absolutely accept the result of this election, or not?

	Yes, will %	No, will not %	Depends (vol.) %	No opinion %
All debate viewers	83	12	4	1
Democrats	94	6	0	<1
Independents	80	16	3	2
Republicans	77	12	9	2

Among U.S. adults who watched or listened to the third debate; "vol." = volunteered response
Gallup; Oct. 20-21, 2016

Bottom Line

Whatever the outcome of the presidential election, Clinton accomplished a trifecta in the debates, leading Trump by substantial margins in viewer perceptions of who won each contest. And, as evident in her gains on the personal qualities Gallup tracked across the debates, Clinton maintained or strengthened her image as an informed leader with the temperament to be president.

On the issues, Clinton earned a commanding lead in the third debate for being better prepared to handle international crises and led Trump on two of his signature themes – dealing with Russia and immigration. The one area where she may be vulnerable is the economy, for which debate viewers were nearly as likely to say Trump would be the more effective of the two if elected president.

Survey Methods

Results for this Gallup poll are based on telephone interviews conducted Oct. 20-21, 2016, on the Gallup U.S. Daily survey, with a random sample of 682 adults, aged 18 and older, living in all 50 U.S. states and the District of Columbia who watched or listened to the Oct. 19 debate. For results based on the total sample of U.S. debate viewers, the margin of sampling error is ±5 percentage points at the 95% confidence level. All reported margins of sampling error include computed design effects for weighting.

October 25, 2016
U.S. DEATH PENALTY SUPPORT AT 60%

by Jeffrey M. Jones

Story Highlights

- *Gallup has not found a lower level of support since 57% in 1972*
- *Support peaked at 80% in 1994*
- *Less than half of Democrats now favor the death penalty*

PRINCETON, N.J. – As voters in several states prepare to vote on death penalty initiatives, 60% of Americans say they are in favor of the death penalty for persons convicted of murder. This figure is similar to the 61% average since 2011 but down from 66% support between 2000 and 2010 and the all-time high of 80% in 1994. Support for the death penalty has not been lower since it was 57% in November 1972.

Are you in favor of the death penalty for a person convicted of murder?

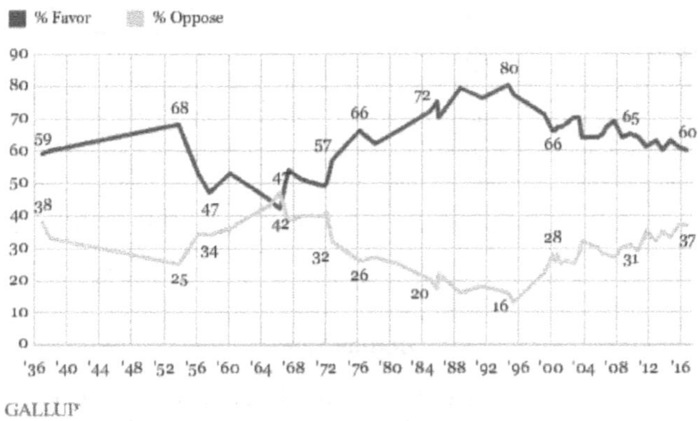

California, Nebraska and Oklahoma are the latest in a series of states to reconsider their death penalty laws. Voters will decide on the legality of the death penalty in those states in Election Day referenda.

The latest results on Gallup's basic death penalty question are based on Gallup's annual Crime poll, conducted Oct. 5-9. Gallup first asked this question in 1936 and has measured it 47 times in total, including at least annually since 1999.

Americans' current level of support for capital punishment is similar to what Gallup measured in 1936, when 59% favored the death penalty and 38% opposed it. These attitudes have fluctuated a great deal over the 80 years since.

Support for the death penalty increased to 68% in a 1953 survey conducted shortly after Julius and Ethel Rosenberg were convicted of spying for the Soviet Union and executed for their crimes. Americans' support for the death penalty then declined for the remainder of the 1950s and throughout much of the 1960s. During this time, legal experts debated whether the death penalty constituted "cruel and unusual punishment." Several successful legal challenges to various aspects of state death penalty laws led to a decade-long moratorium on U.S. executions from the mid-1960s to the mid-1970s.

In 1966, more Americans were opposed (47%) than in favor (42%) of the death penalty, the only time that has occurred in Gallup's trend. In 1972, the U.S. Supreme Court struck down all state death penalty statutes because of concerns of arbitrary sentencing.

Support for the death penalty recovered in the 1970s as states rewrote their statutes to address the Supreme Court's concerns and the new laws generally passed court muster. By 1976, less than a year before executions resumed in the U.S., two-thirds of Americans expressed support for the death penalty.

The percentage of Americans favoring the death penalty increased to 72% in January 1985 and stayed above 70% through 1999. This included the peak of 80% in 1994, a time when Americans overwhelmingly mentioned "crime" as the most important problem facing the U.S.

The year 2000 brought about renewed questions regarding the manner in which certain states applied the death penalty. Illinois adopted a moratorium after several death row inmates were exonerated of their crimes. In February 2000, 66% of Americans were in favor of the death penalty, with support holding at about that level through 2010. Eight states, including Illinois, have abolished the death penalty since 2007, and four others have moratoria in place.

The recent decline in U.S. support for the death penalty is mostly attributable to a decline in the percentage of Democrats favoring the practice. Democratic support has now dropped below the majority level, to an average 47% over the last five years from 55% in the prior decade. Independents have shown a smaller decrease over this time, with virtually no change among Republicans. Eight in 10 Republicans, and 61% of independents, favor the death penalty.

Recent Changes in Support for the Death Penalty, by Political Party

	2000-2010 %	2011-2016 %	Change (pct. pts.)
Democrats			
Favor	55	47	-8
Oppose	39	49	+10
Independents			
Favor	64	61	-3
Oppose	30	35	+5
Republicans			
Favor	80	79	-1
Oppose	16	17	+1

Gallup

In stark contrast to now, in 1994 there were small party differences in death penalty support. Back then, 75% of Democrats, 80% of independents and 85% of Republicans said they favored capital punishment.

Half in U.S. Say Death Penalty Applied Fairly

Critics of the death penalty often argue it is applied unfairly in the U.S. For example, crime statistics show blacks are much more likely than whites to receive death sentences. Americans as a whole are more inclined to say the death penalty is applied fairly (50%) than to say it is not (44%). However, the percentage saying the death penalty is applied fairly is the lowest in Gallup's 17-year trend, although there have been several other readings near 50%.

Generally speaking, do you believe the death penalty is applied fairly or unfairly in this country today?

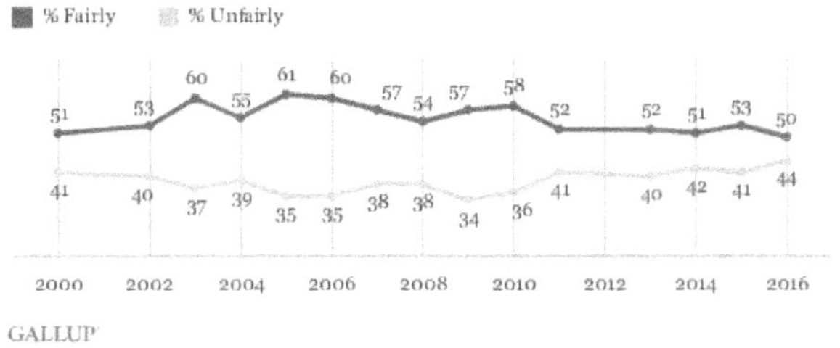

Since 2011, an average 52% of Americans have said the death penalty is applied fairly. From 2000 to 2010, the average was 57%. That matches the five-percentage-point decline in the percentage of Americans who favor the death penalty.

When asked about the frequency with which the death penalty is used, the largest proportion of Americans say it is not used often enough rather than used too often or used about the right amount. But the percentage of Americans who believe the death penalty is not imposed often enough has decreased in recent years. From 2001 to 2010, an average 48% of Americans said the death penalty was not used enough; over the past five years, the average is 41%. At the same time, 25% in this decade – compared with 21% in the prior decade – say the death penalty is imposed too often.

In your opinion, is the death penalty imposed -- [ROTATED: too often, about the right amount (or) not often enough]?

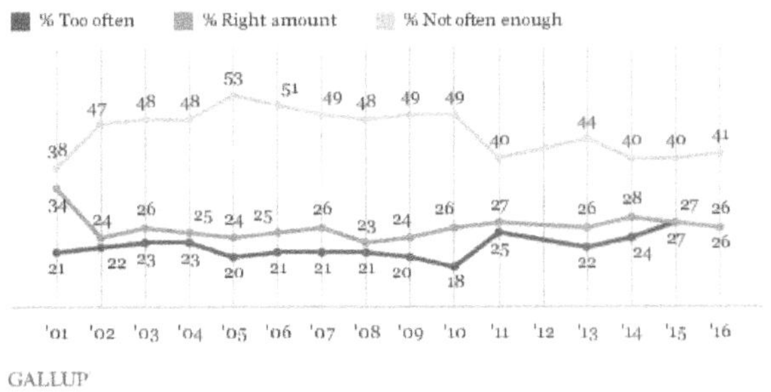

Implications

Americans historically have been more likely to favor than oppose the death penalty, and a solid majority of 60% still endorse it. But support has slipped in recent years and is the lowest Gallup has measured since 1972, when the Supreme Court invalidated capital punishment laws.

This is reflected in, or perhaps the force behind, changes in death penalty laws in recent years, with a total of 12 states abolishing the death penalty or imposing a moratorium in the last decade alone. Although there are exceptions, most Democratic-leaning states have abolished the death penalty, whereas most Republican-leaning states, particularly those in the South and West, continue to allow it.

In several states, including Nebraska, California and Oklahoma, voters this fall will attempt to decide the future of the death penalty in their state. Nebraska legislators abolished the death penalty in 2015, and this year voters will decide whether that action will stand or be turned back. California voters will determine whether the death penalty remains legal in their state. And Oklahoma voters are deciding on a measure that would formally add language to the state's constitution to recognize the death penalty as a legal form of punishment.

Survey Methods

Results for this Gallup poll are based on telephone interviews conducted Oct. 5-9, 2016, with a random sample of 1,017 adults, aged 18 and older, living in all 50 U.S. states and the District of Columbia. For results based on the total sample of national adults, the margin of sampling error is ±4 percentage points at the 95% confidence level. All reported margins of sampling error include computed design effects for weighting.

October 26, 2016
LGBT COMMUNITY STILL VIEWS CLINTON MORE FAVORABLY THAN TRUMP

by Gary J. Gates

Story Highlights

- *Clinton's favorability among LGBT adults is 55%; Trump's is 12%*
- *LGBT adults favor Clinton more, Trump less than non-LGBT adults*
- *Race and ethnicity are not a factor in LGBT views of candidates*

WASHINGTON, D.C. – Democratic candidates have historically garnered widespread support among the lesbian, gay, bisexual and transgender (LGBT) community, and this year is no exception. So far in October, 55% of LGBT adults view Democrat Hillary Clinton favorably, similar to the majority viewing her favorably since the primaries wrapped in June. By contrast, barely one in eight LGBT adults (12%) view Republican Donald Trump favorably, also consistent with ranges since June.

Favorability of Hillary Clinton and Donald Trump per Month, by LGBT Identification

We'd like to get your overall opinion of some people in the news. As I read each name, please say if you have a favorable or unfavorable opinion of that person -- or if you have never heard of them.

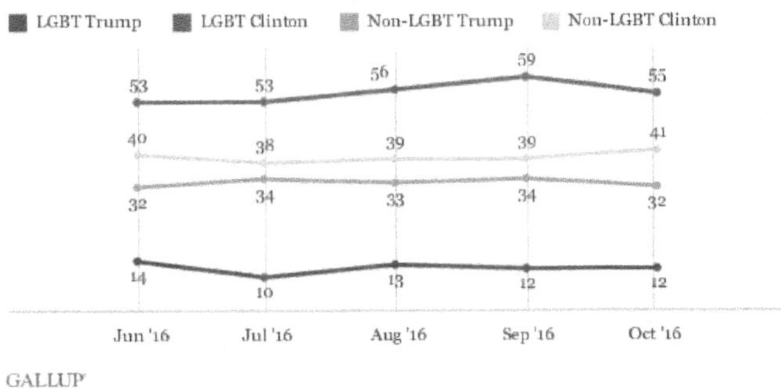

LGBT Americans view Clinton more positively than non-LGBT Americans do, with 55% and 41%, respectively, rating her favorably. At the same time, LGBT Americans, at 12%, view Trump much *less* favorably than non-LGBT Americans do, at 32%. The favorability of both candidates has not varied much since June.

These results are based on Gallup Daily tracking and include more than 450 individuals each month who self-identify as lesbian, gay, bisexual or transgender from June through September, and 282 from Oct. 1-20. Before June, LGBT adults were slightly more favorable toward Trump, giving him an average 17% favorable rating from January through May, compared with 32% of the non-LGBT population. Opinions of Clinton from January through May were similar to where they have been in recent months among both groups.

Although vote preferences cannot be directly inferred from favorable ratings, the favorability data suggest Clinton should fare much better among LGBT voters than Trump, consistent with the LGBT community's previous support for Democratic presidential candidates. For example, 76% of LGBT adults supported Democratic nominee Barack Obama in the 2012 election, compared with 22% who voted for Republican candidate Mitt Romney.

Candidate Favorability by Demographic Characteristics

Previous Gallup research shows that images of Clinton and Trump differ across a number of demographics. For example, women have less favorable views of Trump than men do, those with a college degree are more likely to view Clinton favorably, and blacks and Hispanics hold Clinton in much higher regard than they do Trump.

These patterns are not entirely the same within the LGBT population, according to combined data from June through Oct. 20, 2016. For example, among non-LGBT Americans, non-Hispanic white individuals report a substantially higher level of favorability toward Trump than their nonwhite counterparts (43% vs. 13%, respectively). But among LGBT adults, the differences by race or ethnicity are minor, with Trump being viewed favorably by just 13% of non-Hispanic whites and 11% of nonwhite adults.

LGBT support for Clinton also varies little by race or ethnicity, contrasting with the significantly stronger favorability she receives among the nonwhite, non-LGBT population. The lack of big differences in favorability by race or ethnicity among LGBT individuals can, in part, be explained by the fact that party identification doesn't differ as much between non-Hispanic white and nonwhite LGBT adults as it does for their non-LGBT counterparts. Among both white and nonwhite LGBT adults, more than 70% say they are Democrats or lean Democratic. Among non-LGBT individuals, 61% of nonwhite adults identify as Democrat, compared with only 35% of their non-Hispanic white counterparts.

Favorability of Hillary Clinton and Donald Trump, by LGBT Identification, Gender and Race/Ethnicity

	LGBT: Favorable view of Trump %	LGBT: Favorable view of Clinton %	Non-LGBT: Favorable view of Trump %	Non-LGBT: Favorable view of Clinton %
Male	16	56	39	33
Female	9	55	28	45
White	13	54	43	29
Nonwhite	11	57	13	62

Gallup, Oct 1-20

While Trump has better favorability among men than women overall, the gender gap in favorability is particularly striking in the LGBT population, as LGBT men are nearly twice as likely as LGBT women to have a favorable view of Trump (16% vs. 9%, respectively). Among non-LGBT adults, 39% of men and 28% of women view Trump favorably.

Clinton's image is least positive among young adults (those aged 18 to 34) for both LGBT and non-LGBT adults. Forty-six percent of LGBT young adults view her favorably, compared with 36% of non-LGBT Americans in this age group. Trump's favorability is highest among those aged 55 and older, regardless of LGBT identity. Slightly more than one in five LGBT adults aged 55 and older (21%) have a favorable view of Trump, compared with 41% of non-LGBT adults in this age range.

Favorability of Hillary Clinton and Donald Trump, by LGBT Identification, Age and Party Affiliation

	LGBT: Favorable view of Trump %	LGBT: Favorable view of Clinton %	Non-LGBT: Favorable view of Trump %	Non-LGBT: Favorable view of Clinton %
18-34	10	46	23	36
35-54	12	65	34	40
55+	21	68	41	41
Republican/ Lean	51	19	67	8
Independent	14	20	17	26
Democrat/ Lean	4	69	6	73

Gallup, Oct 1-20

While 15% of LGBT adults in the Gallup data identify as Republican or lean Republican, LGBT Republicans report less favorable views of Trump and more favorable views of Clinton compared with non-LGBT Republicans. Barely more than half of LGBT Republicans (51%) have a favorable view of Trump, compared with 67% of non-LGBT Republicans. Among Republicans, 19% of LGBT adults have a favorable view of Clinton, compared with just 8% of their non-LGBT counterparts. Among independents and Democrats, patterns of candidate favorability do not differ much by LGBT identity.

Bottom Line

While Trump has attempted to position himself as more receptive to LGBT issues than previous Republican nominees, the Republican Party's platform still opposes marriage equality, bathroom choice for transgender individuals and parenting rights for same-sex couples. In contrast, Clinton supports marriage equality and wants to pass a federal law that would prohibit discrimination based on sexual orientation and gender identity.

To the extent that favorable views of presidential candidates translate to votes, it appears the LGBT community leans strongly toward Clinton. However, the patterns of support among various constituencies are not entirely consistent among LGBT and non-LGBT adults. Notably, race and ethnicity do not appear to be a factor in gauging support for either candidate among LGBT individuals.

Analyses of 2012 voting patterns suggest that without the support of the 5% of voters in four key swing states who identified as LGBT, President Barack Obama may have lost those states, jeopardizing his re-election. Current polling shows Clinton faring much better against Trump at this point in the election cycle compared with Obama's position relative to Romney. The closer the popular vote, the more likely it is for the LGBT community and other small voting blocs in swing states to have a clear effect on the election results. Assuming that favorability translates into votes, Gallup polling on the images of the two candidates suggests that Clinton, similar to Obama, will garner the lion's share of LGBT support. But unless the race tightens, it's unlikely that LGBT support will play a decisive role in determining the next president.

Survey Methods

Results for the most recent candidate favorable ratings are based on telephone interviews conducted June 1-Oct. 20, 2016, on the Gallup U.S. Daily survey, with a random sample of 69,075 adults, aged 18 and older, living in all 50 U.S. states and the District of Columbia. Of this group, 2,220 respondents identified as lesbian, gay, bisexual or transgender. For results based on the non-LGBT sample of national adults, the margin of sampling error is ±0.5 percentage points at the 95% confidence level. For LGBT adults, the comparable margin of error is ±2 percentage points at the 95% confidence level. Margins of error within subpopulations of both groups are higher and vary depending on sample size. All reported margins of sampling error include computed design effects for weighting.

October 26, 2016
IN U.S., SUPPORT FOR ASSAULT WEAPONS BAN AT RECORD LOW

by Art Swift

Story Highlights

- *36% favor a ban on assault rifles, down from 44% four years ago*
- *Half of Democrats and a quarter of Republicans favor this ban*
- *A majority of those in households without guns oppose such a ban*

WASHINGTON, D.C. – The fewest Americans in 20 years favor making it illegal to manufacture, sell or possess semi-automatic guns known as assault rifles. Thirty-six percent now want an assault weapons ban, down from 44% in 2012 and 57% when Gallup first asked the question in 1996.

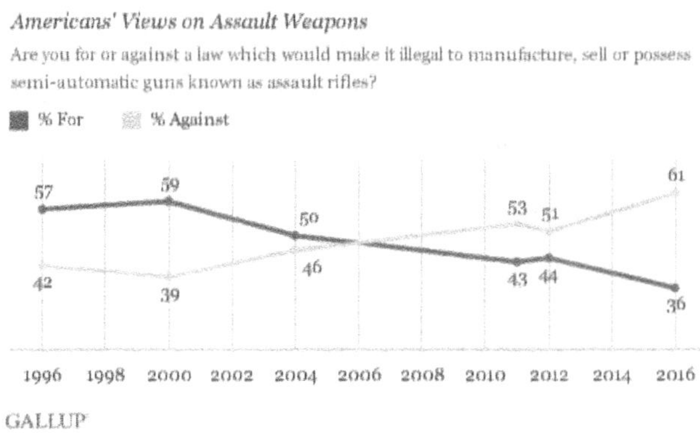

Assault rifles have been a contentious issue in American life for decades. Two years after President Bill Clinton signed a federal assault weapons ban in 1994, Gallup found that a solid majority of Americans favored such a ban. By the time the 10-year ban expired in 2004, Americans were evenly divided. And by 2011, public opinion had tilted against the assault weapons ban, with 53% opposed and 43% in favor. In Gallup's 2016 Crime poll, conducted Oct. 5-9, opposition now exceeds support by 25 percentage points, 61% to 36%.

Perhaps paradoxically, opposition toward a ban has increased against a backdrop of multiple mass shootings and terrorist attacks in which the perpetrators used assault rifles. These guns were used in high-profile incidents, including the terrorist attacks in San Bernardino, California, and Orlando, and the mass shootings in Aurora, Colorado, and Newtown, Connecticut.

Support for Ban Wanes Among Democrats, Republicans

In the past 20 years, support for an assault weapons ban has fallen among all partisan groups, but more so among Republicans than Democrats. Currently, 50% of Democrats and 25% of Republicans favor a ban; in 1996, 63% of Democrats and 50% of Republicans did so. The partisan gap in support has doubled, from 13 points in 1996 to 25 points today.

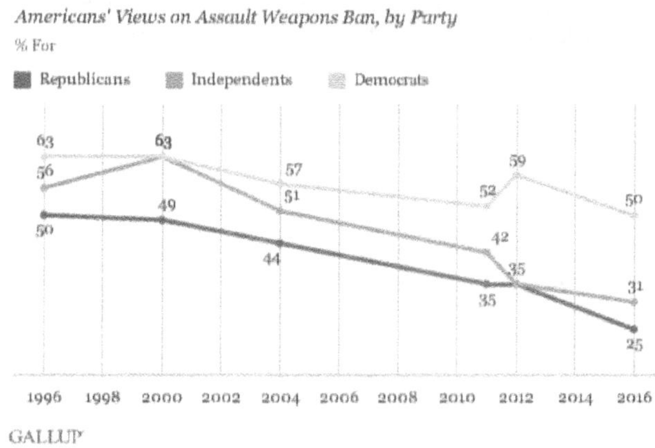

Independents also have grown less inclined to back an assault weapons ban, dropping from a peak of 63% in favor of a ban in 2000 to 31% in the latest poll. From 2004 to 2011, support among independents plunged from 51% to 42%, echoing the nine-point drop among Republicans during that period.

Both Gun and Non-Gun Households Retreat in Ban Support

Support for a ban has declined among both those with and those without a gun in the home. In 2004, 55% of those in non-gun households supported a ban; this year, 45% do. Likewise, while those with a gun in the home have never favored a ban on assault weapons, support is now at an all-time low of 26%.

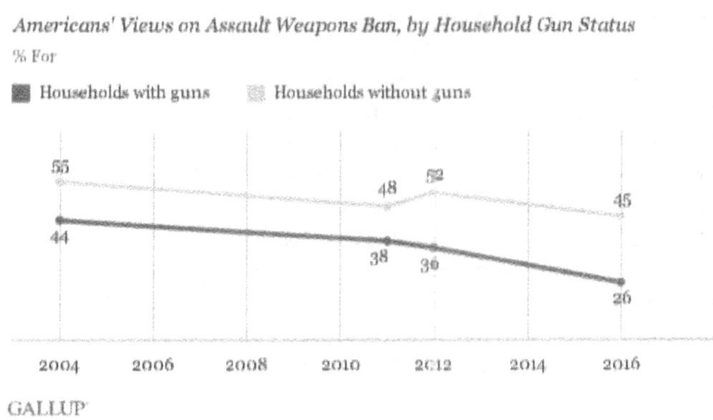

Americans living in households with guns have consistently been less likely than those in non-gun households to favor a ban. The percentage of those with a gun in the home who favor an assault weapons ban has declined steadily since 2004.

Americans Less Likely to Favor Tougher Gun Laws in General

The decline in support for an assault weapons ban mirrors the trend for those saying there should be a law banning the possession of handguns, except by the police or other authorized people. Currently, 23% of Americans favor such a ban, down from 26% in 2011 and 36% in 2004.

At the same time, 55% of Americans say laws covering the sale of firearms should be made more strict, with 10% saying the laws should be less strict and 34% saying they should be kept as they are now. The percentage favoring stricter gun laws has fluctuated between 43% and 60% since 2004, with no clear increase or decrease in support. But it is down from levels consistently at or above 60% in the 1990s, including a high of 78% in 1990.

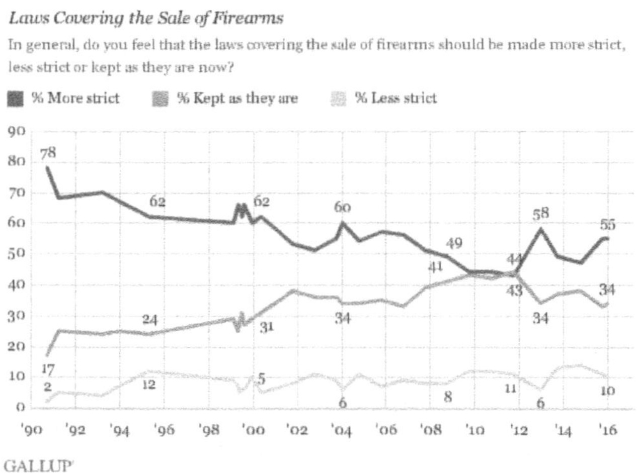

Bottom Line

In an era of ongoing terrorist attacks and mass shootings in the U.S., Americans are now more likely to oppose an assault weapons ban than they have been in two decades. One reason may be the large increase in opposition to such a ban among Republicans. Whereas 20 years ago half of Republicans were open to such legislation, now only one in four are. But politics alone do not explain the declining support, since it has dropped among independents and Democrats as well, although on a smaller scale.

It is possible this represents a backlash against calls by some in the national media and the federal government to ban certain weapons after mass shootings occur. This backlash may reflect growing apprehension that the government may infringe upon particular civil and personal liberties. Gallup finds even lower levels of support for other potential bans, such as those on handguns and cigarettes.

It is striking – and unusual – that fewer Democrats than ever support an assault weapons ban, since the Democratic Party has been instrumental in pushing for stricter gun laws.

However, it is worth noting that a majority of Americans still believe there should be stricter laws governing the sale of firearms, even as they are reluctant to endorse a ban on handguns and assault weapons. In general, a majority of Americans say they are dissatisfied with the nation's gun laws, furthering the complexity of this issue.

Survey Methods

Results for this Gallup poll are based on telephone interviews conducted Oct. 5-9, 2016, with a random sample of 1,017 adults, aged 18 and older, living in all 50 U.S. states and the District of Columbia. For results based on the total sample of national adults, the margin of sampling error is ±4 percentage points at the 95% confidence level. All reported margins of sampling error include computed design effects for weighting.

October 27, 2016

AMERICANS: CREDIT CARD INFORMATION STILL GETTING HACKED

by Jim Norman

Story Highlights

- *27% say information hacked from cards used in stores*
- *Thefts come despite increased use of chip-enabled cards*
- *Thefts affect affluent much more than low-income households*

WASHINGTON, D.C. – Americans are more likely than they were a year ago to say their households were the victims of credit card information theft, despite recent efforts to make the use of credit cards in stores safer. More than one in four (27%) now say they or someone in their household had information stolen from a credit card used in a store, up from a dip to 22% in 2015.

Credit Card Theft Tops List of Crimes

Crimes more than 10% of respondents said occurred to someone in their household in last 12 months

	2014 %	2015 %	2016 %
Credit card information used at a store stolen	27	22	27
Money, property stolen	15	15	17
Identity theft	N/A	16	17
Home, car, property vandalized	14	15	14

N/A = Not asked

Gallup Crime Survey, Oct 5-9, list of nine crimes

Americans are significantly more likely to say their households have been victimized by credit card information theft than to say they were victims of any of the other eight crimes Gallup measured in its 2016 Crime survey. Theft of credit card information has topped the list all three years since Gallup first included it in 2014.

The increase in reports of credit card information theft come at a time when both Visa and MasterCard are aggressively replacing magnetic-stripe credit cards as a way to protect information from hackers. The replacement cards use a chip that generates a unique code for every transaction. Both credit card companies have more than doubled the number of chip-enabled cards in the last year, with MasterCard reporting in July that 88% of their consumer credit cards have the chip.

Things are not moving as swiftly among U.S. businesses. About a third of U.S. stores were able to process chip transactions in August, according to Visa. The National Retail Federation, which has complained the cards are "cumbersome" and do not provide enough security, contends that card companies' slowness in signing off on chip-reading terminals has been a major factor in the delays.

Credit Card Information Victims Vary Greatly by Income, Age

Theft of credit card information is the crime most Americans have in common, but it is much more of a problem for high earners and those aged 35 to 54. At least part of the reason for the discrepancy between high and low earners is that those in higher income brackets are much more likely to have credit cards. In a 2014 Gallup poll, 88% of those with annual household incomes of $75,000 or more said they had at least one card, compared with 41% of those with incomes of less than $30,000. Nearly three in four of those in the $30,000-$74,999 income bracket said they had a card. Among age groups, about half of those under 35 had a credit card, and about three-fourths of those 35 and older had one.

Credit Card Information Theft Higher Among Affluent, 35- to 54-Year-Olds

Percent saying someone in household had credit card information used at a store stolen by hackers in last 12 months

	Yes %	No %
Age		
18-34	19	80
35-54	39	61
55 and older	23	77
Household income		
Less than $30,000	14	86
$30,000-$74,999	25	75
$75,000 and above	41	58

Gallup Crime Survey, Oct 5-9

Americans in higher-earning households, though most likely to report credit card information theft and most likely to have cards, are slightly less likely to worry frequently about it happening to them (40%) than are middle-income Americans (46%). Lower-income Americans are least likely (30%) to say it worries them frequently.

Overall, 38% of Americans say they worry frequently about having their credit card information stolen, the highest percentage for any of the 14 crimes Gallup asked about. The only other crimes which at least a third of Americans say they worry about frequently involve computer hacking:

- 35% worry frequently about having their email, passwords or electronic records hacked into.
- 33% worry frequently about being a victim of identity theft.
- 18% worry frequently about having their car broken into or stolen – the crime most often mentioned by respondents that did not involve computer hacking.

Bottom Line

Concerns about hacking have produced a worldwide transition to machines that accept chip-enabled cards. The pressure on businesses in the U.S. ratcheted up last year on Oct. 1 when merchants without chip-reading terminals became liable for fraudulent transactions from counterfeit cards.

At this point the changes taking place in the U.S. have neither allayed the fears of consumers that their credit card information will be stolen nor reduced the percentage of Americans saying their households have been victimized.

As differences between merchants and credit card companies are resolved, a broader rollout of chip-reading terminals in U.S. businesses could bring a drop in credit card information theft and a subsequent lessening of worries about the crime.

Survey Methods

Results for this Gallup poll are based on telephone interviews conducted Oct. 5-9, 2016, with a random sample of 1,017 adults, aged 18 and older, living in all 50 U.S. states and the District of Columbia. For results based on the total sample of national adults, the margin of sampling error is ±4 percentage points at the 95% confidence level. All reported margins of sampling error include computed design effects for weighting.

October 28, 2016
IN U.S., 65% SAY DRUG PROBLEM 'EXTREMELY' OR 'VERY SERIOUS'

by Jeffrey M. Jones

Story Highlights

- *Down from 83% in 2000 and 73% in 2007*
- *Less than half of young adults say problem is "very serious"*
- *One-third say drugs are a serious problem in their local area*

PRINCETON, N.J. – Sixty-five percent of Americans describe the problem of illegal drugs in the U.S. as "extremely" or "very serious." Although still well above the majority level, the percentage is down significantly from 83% in 2000 and 73% in 2007.

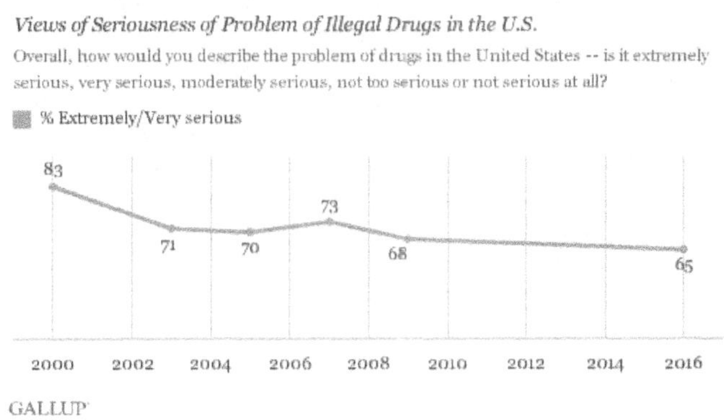

The results are based on Gallup's annual Crime poll, conducted Oct. 5-9. The U.S. has long struggled with problems coming from the sale and use of illegal drugs, such as drug-related crime and drug addiction.

Americans have frequently mentioned drugs as the most important problem facing the country in the past. It ranked as the No. 1 problem on the list from May 1989 through April 1990, including September 1989 when a high of 63% mentioned it. That poll was conducted shortly after President George H.W. Bush gave a nationally televised address to outline his anti-drug strategy in an attempt to fight the crack cocaine epidemic and the international threat posed by Colombian drug lords.

Mentions of Drugs as the Most Important Problem Facing the U.S., 1969-2016

From 1970 through 2000, an average of 8% of Americans named drugs as the most important problem facing the country. Since 2007, the average has been 1%.

The fall in concern about drugs may also reflect less-prominent federal anti-drug efforts in recent years than in the 1970s, 1980s and 1990s. In fact, more recently, much of the news about drug policy has focused on state-level efforts to decriminalize marijuana. Those efforts are consistent with shifts in public opinion, as Americans' support for legalizing marijuana has nearly doubled, from 31% in 2000 to 60% today.

Americans' perceptions of the drug problem in the U.S. may also have become more politicized over time. In 2000, Republicans (84%), Democrats (84%) and independents (79%) were about equally likely to describe the drug problem as "extremely" or "very serious." Today, there is a wide partisan gap, as 81% of Republicans and 57% of Democrats hold that view.

Republicans may view the U.S. drug situation more negatively because a Democratic president is in office. When George W. Bush was president in 2007, Republicans (69%) were less likely than Democrats (75%) to describe the U.S. drug problem as being serious. Republicans this year may also be responding to Donald Trump's making drug traffic from Mexico a campaign issue.

Aside from Republicans, every major subgroup in the U.S. is much less likely today than in 2000 to believe illegal drugs are an extremely or very serious problem in the country. Declines have been largest among Democrats, young adults and nonwhites, who now rank among the groups least likely to view the U.S. drug situation as this serious.

In fact, less than a majority of 18- to 29-year-olds, 45%, now hold this view – compared with 71% in 2000. This drop could reflect a generational change, as today's young adults were between the ages of 2 and 13 in 2000, and are therefore likely unfamiliar with strong government anti-drug efforts of the past.

Views of Drugs in U.S. as an Extremely/Very Serious Problem, by Subgroup

	2000 %	2007 %	2016 %
Gender			
Men	77	66	59
Women	86	80	70
Age			
18 to 29 years	71	71	45
30 to 49 years	80	63	63
50 to 64 years	88	77	72
65+ years	91	89	77
Race			
White	80	71	69
Nonwhite	90	80	57
Party identification			
Republican	84	69	81
Independent	79	74	58
Democrat	84	75	57
Church attendance			
Weekly	91	82	76
Monthly	82	73	68
Seldom/Never	76	68	59
Education			
College graduate	74	65	59
College nongraduate	85	77	67
Household income			
Less than $30,000	86	83	68
$30,000 to $74,999	82	76	66
$75,000+	73	59	60
Place of residence			
Big/Small city	82	n/a	62
Suburb	78	n/a	59
Town/Rural area	72	n/a	73

n/a = not available
Gallup Crime Polls

One in Three Say Drugs Are Serious Problem in Local Area

Americans express far less concern about drugs being a problem in their local area. The poll finds 32% of Americans describing drugs as an extremely or very serious problem in the area where they live. That is consistent with what Gallup has measured on six other occasions since 2000, with the percentage typically near 30%.

Views of Seriousness of Problem of Illegal Drugs "in the Area Where You Live"

Overall, how would you describe the problem of drugs in the area where you live -- is it extremely serious, very serious, moderately serious, not too serious or not serious at all?

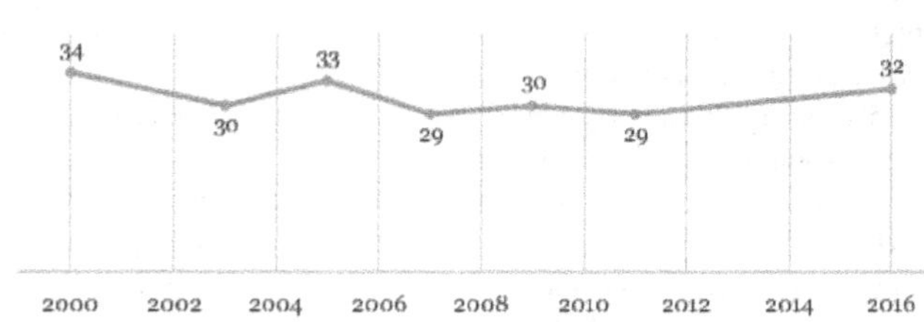

In addition to the 32% who currently describe drugs as an extremely or very serious problem in their local area, 35% say it is a "moderately serious problem," and 31% say it is "not too serious" or "not serious at all."

Americans' more positive assessments of the drug situation in their local area than nationally are consistent with their tendency to rate their own situation much better than the situation in the rest of the country. This includes assessments of crime, education, healthcare, and their overall satisfaction.

Americans who describe their local area as suburban (22%) are much less likely than those who say they live in a city (33%) or a town or rural area (39%) to rate drugs as an extremely or very serious problem in their area.

Implications

A majority of Americans continue to believe drugs are a serious problem in the U.S., but the percentage has fallen significantly since 2000. The continuing high concern about drugs probably reflects Americans' recognition that drugs can harm people, but the decline in the level of concern might reflect reduced news media and government focus on drugs as a problem. Both presidential candidates have raised the drug issue during the campaign, although it has not received nearly as much attention as other issues such as immigration and trade, or character concerns about the candidates.

Younger adults, who have never known a time when drugs were among the most prominent issues on the national landscape, show far less concern about drugs than older adults do. They have also come of age at a time when Americans, particularly those in their age cohort, support legalizing marijuana. Given the differences by age in concern about the drug problem, the trend toward lesser concern about drugs could continue in the decades to come.

Survey Methods

Results for this Gallup poll are based on telephone interviews conducted Oct. 5-9, 2016, with a random sample of 1,017 adults, aged 18 and older, living in all 50 U.S. states and the District of Columbia. For results based on the total sample of national adults, the margin of sampling error is ±4 percentage points at the 95% confidence level. All reported margins of sampling error include computed design effects for weighting.

October 31, 2016

AS USUAL, VOTERS SAY THIS ELECTION MORE IMPORTANT THAN MOST

by Lydia Saad

Story Highlights

- *Seven in 10 U.S. voters say 2016 election matters more than prior ones*
- *Republicans lead Democrats in this belief, 80% to 69%*
- *Party out of the White House typically thinks election matters more*

PRINCETON, N.J. – Seven in 10 U.S. voters say the outcome of the presidential election matters more to them this year than it did in prior election years – in line with what Gallup recorded at this stage of the past three presidential campaigns. However, before 2004, voters were far less likely to believe presidential elections meant that much.

Does the outcome of this year's presidential election matter to you more than in previous years, less than in previous years or about the same?

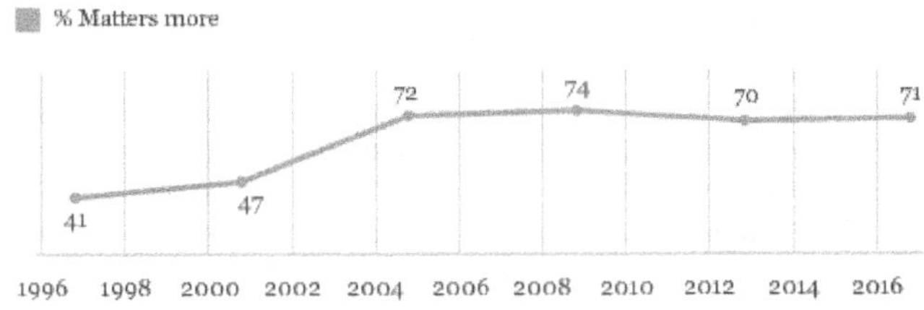

Based on registered voters

GALLUP

Across the 20 years Gallup has asked this question, including in the latest update – from an Oct. 25-26, 2016, poll – few voters say the election matters *less* than in the past, including just 3% this year. Instead, most of those who don't think it matters more (29% this year) say it matters about the same.

Belief Election Matters Relates to Turnout

Since 1996, the percentage of Americans who show up at the polls on Election Day has followed the same trajectory as voter attitudes about the importance of each election. In 1996 and 2000, when less than half of voters believed the election was especially important, voter turnout failed to reach 55%. But from 2004 to 2012, when 70% or more of voters have consistently said the election matters more than usual, turnout among the U.S. voting-age population has been at or near 60%.

U.S. Voters' Investment in the Presidential Election

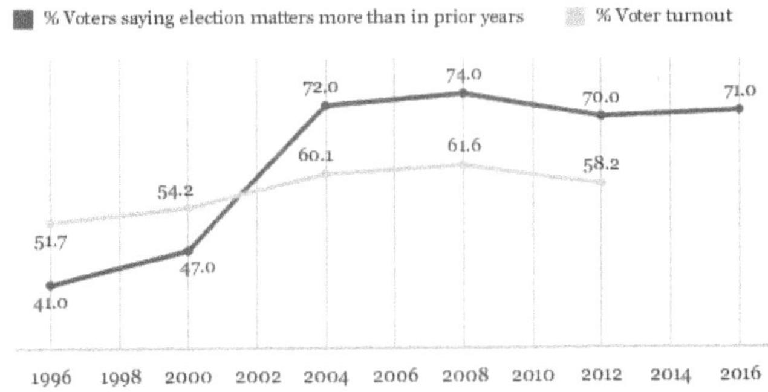

^ Source for voter turnout: http://www.electproject.org/national-1789-present

GALLUP

Party Out of Power Cares More

Given the historical pattern, turnout in the 2016 election could be on the high side, similar to 2012. However, the effect on the election's outcome depends on whether one party turns out at a higher rate than the other. That is not readily forecast from the trend in

Republicans' and Democrats' answers to whether the election matters more than in the past.

Voters aligned with the party in opposition to the sitting president's party typically think the election is more important than those affiliated with the president's party. So Republicans were more likely to think the outcome was highly significant in 2000 and 2012, when the sitting president was a Democrat, and Democrats were more likely to feel this way in 2004 and 2008, when a Republican was in office. However, in only half of those years – 2000 and 2008 – did the party with the higher percentage saying the election mattered more win the election.

Currently, 80% of Republicans and 69% of Democrats say the election's outcome matters more to them than it did in prior elections. While that 11-percentage-point margin may seem advantageous for Republican nominee Donald Trump, Republicans' even greater 19-point advantage on this measure in 2012 did not correspond with the GOP winning the White House. Likewise, Democrats had the edge in 2004 and 2008, but lost in 2004 while winning in 2008. In 2000, Republicans had the advantage and won in the Electoral College but lost the popular vote.

Voters' Belief That Outcome of Presidential Election Matters More Than in Prior Years

Based on registered voters

	Democrats %	Independents %	Republicans %	Democratic advantage (pct. pts.)
2016	69	66	80	-11
2012	66	62	85	-19
2008	80	68	74	6
2004	77	73	69	8
2000	45	43	52	-7
1996	45	34	47	-2

Gallup

Bottom Line

Believing that each presidential election is more consequential than the last has been the new normal for voters since 2004 and may be one reason for higher voter turnout in recent elections. This year is no exception, and it would not be surprising to find that overall turnout is high.

As Gallup has noted previously, voters' greater psychological investment in the presidential election since 2004 may reflect intensifying problems facing the country, including terrorism, the Iraq War and a struggling economy. It may also be a reaction to the 2000 election, whose outcome was decided by a handful of votes in Florida after an extensive recount. The rise of social media could be another factor affecting voters, possibly contributing to heightened political awareness and polarization. Whatever the cause, the stakes feel high for about eight in 10 Republicans and seven in 10 Democrats, enough to keep the country on edge for the remaining week of the campaign, but not necessarily dictating who will win.

Survey Methods

Results for this Gallup poll are based on telephone interviews conducted Oct. 25-26, 2016, on the Gallup U.S. Daily survey, with a random sample of 926 registered voters, aged 18 and older, living in all 50 U.S. states and the District of Columbia. For results based on the total sample of national adults, the margin of sampling error is ±4 percentage points at the 95% confidence level. All reported margins of sampling error include computed design effects for weighting.

November 01, 2016

AHEAD OF ELECTION, AMERICANS' CONFIDENCE IN ECONOMY STEADY

by Andrew Dugan

Story Highlights

- *Index averaged -11 in October, similar to -10 in September*
- *Economic perceptions relatively stable for past year and a half*
- *Current conditions score at -2; economic outlook at -20*

WASHINGTON, D.C. – Americans' confidence in the U.S. economy has been stable for three months since the Democratic National Convention held in late July helped boost assessments of the economy. The index averaged -11 in October, similar to the -11 and -10 recorded in August and September, respectively.

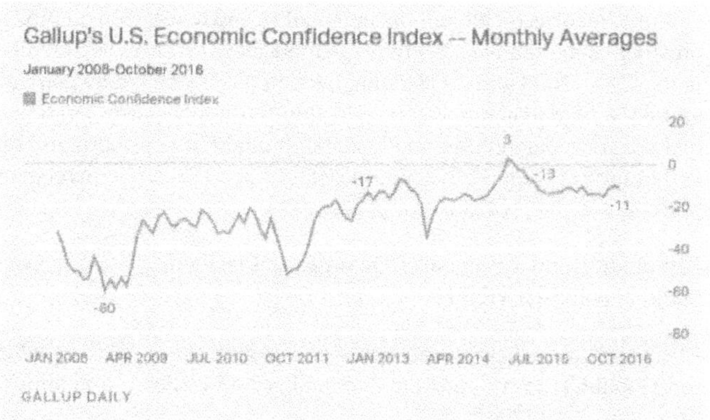

From a long-term perspective, Americans' views of the economy have been relatively stable since August 2015. That month marked the end of the index's 16-point decline from +3 in January 2015. Since then, the index's monthly averages have remained within a narrow range of -10 to -15.

Gallup has tracked economic confidence daily for the past three presidential election years. In previous presidential election years:

- Gallup's U.S. Economic Confidence Index fell to a record low of -60 in October 2008 as the U.S. experienced its worst financial crisis in decades. The plunge in economic confidence likely contributed to Americans' decision to eject Republicans from the White House and elect Democrat Barack Obama in early November.
- The index stood at -17 in October 2012 – which was, at the time, tied for the highest monthly score since Gallup began tracking economic confidence daily in 2008. Although Americans were more negative than positive about the economy, their views were much less negative than when Obama took office. Obama won re-election the next month.

The current -11 for October is better than the scores for either of the two previous election-year Octobers. But unlike the past two elections, economic confidence has not been trending in a positive or negative direction in the months preceding Election Day, but rather has remained flat.

While Gallup did not track economic confidence on a daily basis before 2008, it did conduct regular surveys measuring Americans' economic confidence in presidential election years from 1992 to 2004. The methodologies used in the pre-2008 and 2008-2016 polls differ enough that precise comparisons cannot be made. Generally speaking, however, Gallup's data from the pre-2008 polls show:

- Americans' ratings of the economy were quite negative in 1992 just before George H.W. Bush lost his re-election bid.
- Ratings were very positive in 2000 when Republican George W. Bush won a contested election to succeed Democrat Bill Clinton.
- They were slightly more positive than negative when Bush won re-election in 2004. That October, more Americans named the Iraq War as the nation's most important problem than named the economy.

Americans More Negative About Economy's Outlook Than Current Conditions

Gallup's U.S. Economic Confidence Index is the average of two components: how Americans rate current economic conditions and whether they feel the economy is improving or getting worse. The index has a theoretical maximum of +100 if all Americans were to say the economy is doing well and improving, and a theoretical minimum of -100 if all Americans were to say the economy is doing poorly and getting worse.

In October, about as many Americans said the economy is "excellent" or "good" (27%) as said the economy is "poor" (29%), resulting in a current conditions score of -2. Americans' assessments of the current state of the economy are about as positive as they have been in the past eight years; the best score for this index component is +1, recorded in January 2015.

Americans remain much more negative about the direction the economy is headed. Thirty-eight percent believe the economy is "getting better" and 58% say it is "getting worse," resulting in an economic outlook score of -20. This index component has fallen sharply since reaching its post-recession high of +5 in January 2015, though it has held steady over the past several months.

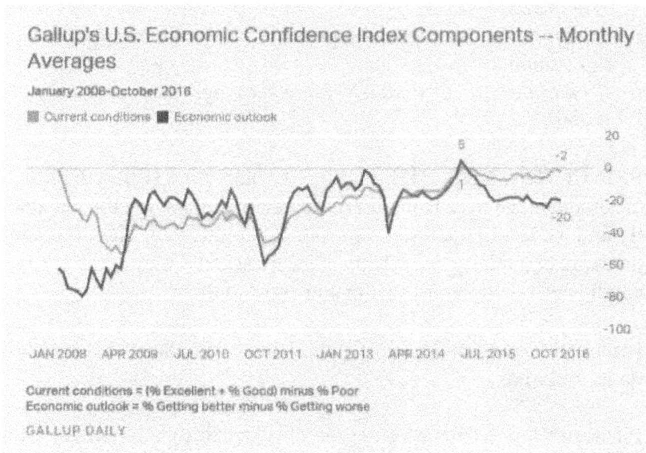

Bottom Line

Gallup's U.S. Economic Confidence Index has been largely stable, though in negative territory, for the past 17 months. Americans' economic perceptions could indicate how willing consumers are to spend their discretionary income or could signal real shifts occurring in the economy. But how Americans feel the economy is doing, particularly when many think the economy is in bad shape, can be the reason why some voters decide to vote the way they do. In 2008, for instance, Americans' confidence in the economy fell steeply in the months preceding Election Day, just as Obama jumped to his largest lead of the campaign season.

In 2012, by contrast, economic confidence remained negative but demonstrated clear improvement, particularly toward the end of Obama's first term. The index in October 2012 matched the highest score recorded since 2008, suggesting that many Americans, particularly Democrats, felt conditions were improving.

This year, however, confidence is neither strengthening nor faltering. This could indicate that Americans voting primarily on economic issues may be more divided on which candidate to support than was the case in 2008 and 2012.

Survey Methods

Results for this Gallup poll are based on telephone interviews conducted Oct. 1-31, 2016, on the Gallup U.S. Daily survey, with a random sample of 15,193 adults, aged 18 and older, living in all 50 U.S. states and the District of Columbia. For results based on the total sample of national adults, the margin of sampling error is ±1 percentage point at the 95% confidence level. All reported margins of sampling error include computed design effects for weighting.

November 01, 2016

CLINTON HOLDS CLEAR EDGE ON HAVING PRESIDENTIAL QUALITIES

by Frank Newport

Story Highlights

- *Just over half say Clinton has presidential character; 32% say Trump does*
- *Trump is the worst-rated candidate on this dimension in Gallup's trend*
- *Candidates rated similarly on voters agreeing with them on issues*

PRINCETON, N.J. – U.S. registered voters give Hillary Clinton a clear advantage over Donald Trump in terms of having the personality and leadership qualities a president should have. The two candidates are essentially tied when voters are asked if they agree with the candidates on the issues that matter most to them.

Personality and Leadership Qualities and Agreement With Candidates on Issues

Please tell me whether you agree or disagree that – [Hillary Clinton/Donald Trump] – has the personality and leadership qualities a president should have. Please tell me whether you agree or disagree with – [ROTATED: Hillary Clinton/Donald Trump] – on the issues that matter most to you.

	%
Has personality and leadership qualities a president should have	
Clinton	51
Trump	32
Agree with candidate on issues that matter most to you	
Clinton	45
Trump	46

Among registered voters
Gallup, Oct. 27-28, 2016

The results are from Gallup interviewing conducted Oct. 27-28. News broke Friday that the FBI would review whether a new set of emails belonging to Clinton's top aide Huma Abedin are related to the FBI's investigation of Clinton's private server while Clinton was secretary of state. Americans' responses to these questions on Friday did not differ significantly from Thursday. Moreover, there were no immediate signs that the news was affecting the two candidates' images over the weekend.

Voters rate Trump worse than any other presidential candidate in Gallup's records on having the personality and leadership qualities a president should have. Previous readings were taken in late October in the 2000, 2004 and 2008 campaigns. In those years, between 52% and 61% of registered voters said the two major-party candidates had the right personality and leadership qualities – a sharp contrast to Trump's current 32%. Clinton's rating of 51% is one percentage point below the previous low score.

Personality and Leadership Qualities a President Should Have – Gallup Historical Trend

Please tell me whether you agree or disagree that – [Hillary Clinton/Donald Trump] – has the personality and leadership qualities a president should have.

	Agree %	Disagree %	No opinion %
2016 Oct 27-28			
Registered voters			
Hillary Clinton	51	47	1
Donald Trump	32	67	1
For comparison: Final pre-election measurement, based on registered voters			
2008 Oct 23-26			
Barack Obama	61	37	2
John McCain	60	38	2
2004 Oct 22-24			
John Kerry	52	44	4
George W. Bush	57	41	2
2000 Oct 20-22			
Al Gore	59	37	4
George W. Bush	57	39	4

Gallup

In contrast, U.S. voters' agreement with candidates on issues today is similar to what Gallup measured in late October 2004 and 2008. Historically, voters have been about evenly divided on whether the two major-party candidates' issue positions align with their own, as they are in this election.

Trump and Clinton on Issues, Plus Historical Trend

Please tell me whether you agree or disagree with – [ROTATED: Hillary Clinton/Donald Trump] – on the issues that matter most to you.

	Agree %	Disagree %	No opinion %
2016 Oct 27-28			
Registered voters			
Hillary Clinton	45	54	1
Donald Trump	46	53	*
For comparison: Final pre-election measurement, based on registered voters			
2008 Oct 23-26			
Barack Obama	51	46	3
John McCain	48	50	3
2004 Oct 22-24			
John Kerry	49	49	2
George W. Bush	50	48	2

* Less than 0.5%; Note: Question not asked in 2000
Gallup

Gallup did not ask these two questions in October 2012, but did in the summer of that year. The results were generally similar to those measured in 2000, 2004 and 2008. Fifty-four percent of voters said in July 2012 that Barack Obama had the personality and leadership qualities needed in a president; 57% said Mitt Romney held these qualities.

Trump's deficit on perceived personality and leadership is also evident in the views among party groups. Sixty percent of Republican voters and independent voters who lean Republican say Trump has presidential personality and leadership qualities, substantially lower than the 87% of Democratic voters and leaners who say that about Clinton. This corresponds to the less positive image Republicans have of Trump and Democrats' more positive views of Clinton. For the two days of interviewing, Oct. 27-28, for example, 80% of Democratic registered voters on average had a favorable view of Clinton, compared with 65% of Republican voters who had a favorable view of Trump.

Republicans are just as likely as Democrats to say they agree with their respective nominee on the issues that matter most to them.

Personality and Leadership Qualities and Agreement With on Issues: Clinton and Trump

	Democrats/Leaners % Agree	Republicans/ Leaners % Agree
Has personality and leadership qualities to be president		
Clinton	87	16
Trump	6	60
Agree with candidate on issues that matter most to you		
Clinton	82	11
Trump	12	83

Among registered voters
Gallup, Oct. 27-28, 2016

Implications

Trump and Clinton are about equal in voters' agreement with them on the issues, in line with what Gallup has measured previously and reflecting the general division of the U.S. electorate on political matters. From this standpoint, Trump is no different from prior GOP or Democratic nominees.

However, Trump stands out for his low ratings on having the personality and leadership qualities a president should have, relative to Clinton and to any other presidential candidate Gallup has measured.

Trump's approach to campaigning may be what made it possible for a businessman with no government credentials to become the Republican nominee for president. But his unique style and personality could also be holding him back in his quest to defeat Clinton in the general election.

Survey Methods

Results for this Gallup poll are based on telephone interviews conducted Oct. 27-28, 2016, on the Gallup U.S. Daily survey, with a random sample of 945 registered voters, aged 18 and older, living in all 50 U.S. states and the District of Columbia. For results based on the total sample of registered voters, the margin of sampling error is ±4 percentage points at the 95% confidence level. All reported margins of sampling error include computed design effects for weighting.

November 01, 2016

UPDATE: AMERICANS' CONFIDENCE IN VOTING, ELECTION

by Justin McCarthy and Jon Clifton

Story Highlights

- *As election nears, 66% very or somewhat confident in vote*
- *Percentage who report being "very" confident grows to 35%*
- *Democrats remain much more confident than Republicans*

WASHINGTON, D.C. – As claims that next Tuesday's presidential election is "rigged" continue to swirl, two in three Americans (66%) say they are "very" or "somewhat confident" that votes will be cast and counted accurately across the country. This is similar to the 62% Gallup recorded in August, after GOP presidential nominee Donald Trump first suggested that the only way he could lose "is if cheating goes on."

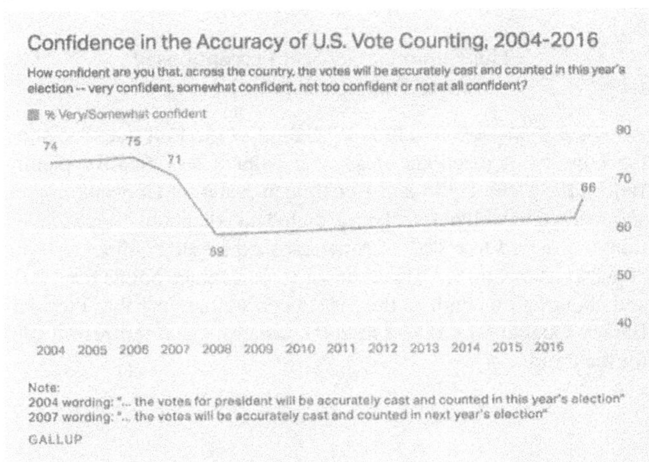

Americans' current level of confidence in the accuracy of the vote is also similar to the 59% recorded in 2008 but remains lower than what they expressed from 2004 to 2007, when more than seven in 10 were "very" or "somewhat confident."

Trump has repeatedly asserted in recent months that weak voter identification laws could imperil the integrity of the election's results and has encouraged his supporters to monitor polling stations for fraudulent activity. The Democratic National Committee has responded with a lawsuit against the Republican National Committee, saying the GOP is coordinating to intimidate voters at the polls.

Americans Now More Likely to Say They Are "Very Confident" in Vote Count

Democrats' overall confidence in votes being accurately counted this year is stable; however, the percentage who say they are *very* confident increased to 54% from 37%. Republicans' overall confidence was already low in August and remains that way today. As a result of Democrats' rising confidence, the percentage of all Americans feeling very confident that votes will be accurately counted in this year's election rose from 24% to 35%.

Confidence in the Accuracy of U.S. Vote Counting, by Party – August vs. October 2016

How confident are you that, across the country, the votes will be accurately cast and counted in this year's election – very confident, somewhat confident, not too confident or not at all confident?

	Very confident %	Somewhat confident %	Very/ Somewhat confident %
National adults			
Oct 25-26, 2016	35	31	66
Aug 15-16, 2016	24	38	62
Democrats/Democratic leaners			
Oct 25-26, 2016	54	29	83
Aug 15-16, 2016	37	39	76
Republicans/Republican leaners			
Oct 25-26, 2016	19	37	56
Aug 15-16, 2016	15	37	52

Gallup

This Summer, General Perceptions of "Honesty" of Elections at New Low

Americans' answers to a broader Gallup World Poll question about the honesty of elections *in general* paint a less positive picture. Before the Democratic and Republican National Conventions this summer – and well before Trump dialed up talk about "rigged" elections – a record-low 30% of Americans expressed confidence in the "honesty of elections." This is down 10 percentage points from 2015 and about half as high as the 59% recorded the year that President Barack Obama took office in 2009, which is also the record high for the trend.

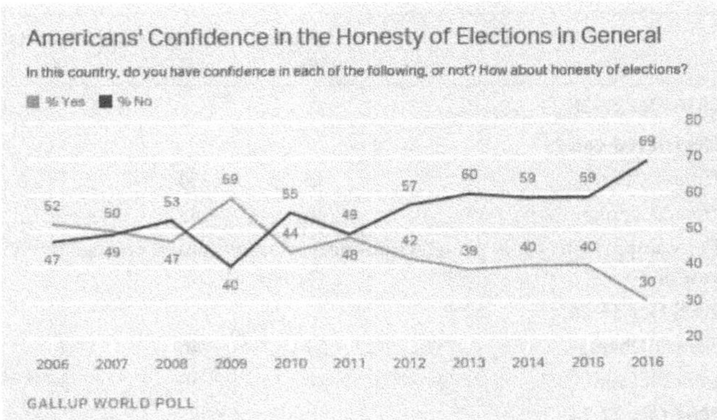

Globally, the U.S. ranks 90th out of 112 countries that Gallup has asked this question in so far this year. While the percentage in the U.S. is undoubtedly low, the ranking may be slightly misleading because a number of countries with higher scores than the U.S. are not considered electoral democracies. But even among those that are, including the wealthy OECD member states, only Mexico (19%) ranks lower than the U.S.

The decline between 2015 and 2016 may reflect Americans' overall dissatisfaction with the primaries and the nominees who emerged from them rather than the voting process itself. According to a recent Pew study, only 35% of voters said that they thought the primaries were a good way of determining the best-qualified nominees for president. And, according to recent Gallup polls, Trump and Hillary Clinton are two of the least liked candidates in the history of Gallup's tracking, and both get low ratings as being honest and trustworthy.

Bottom Line

Trump's warnings about voter fraud in recent months haven't weakened Americans' faith in the accuracy of the U.S. vote count. But the fact remains that one in three national adults have low confidence that votes across the country will be properly cast and counted. Perhaps even more negatively, 30% said that they have confidence in the honesty of elections earlier this year. The latter finding suggests that the public thinks about more than the voting process itself when thinking about elections, perhaps considering things such as the honesty of the candidates themselves or the sources of money behind the campaigns.

Americans have shown strong support for various changes in how and when people can vote, such as facilitating early voting and strengthening voter identification laws, but these aren't uniformly implemented across states. Relatedly, sizable minorities of Americans have expressed concerns about voter fraud and eligible voters being turned away. Regardless of their levels of concern, voter fraud has been found to be fairly rare in U.S. elections.

However, perceived accuracy may be just as important as actual accuracy in vote counting. The legitimacy of a candidate's electoral victory, whether accurate or not, can be undermined by popular beliefs about fraud. And with a major party nominee making voter fraud a central focus of his speeches in the final days of the election season, the issue could carry into the elected president's first term.

Survey Methods

Results for this Gallup poll are based on telephone interviews conducted Oct. 25-26, 2016, on the Gallup U.S. Daily survey, with a random sample of 1,011 adults, aged 18 and older, living in all 50 U.S. states and the District of Columbia. For results based on the total sample of national adults, the margin of sampling error is ±6 percentage points at the 95% confidence level. All reported margins of sampling error include computed design effects for weighting.

November 02, 2016

U.S. JOB CREATION INDEX HOVERS NEAR POST-RECESSION HIGH

by Justin McCarthy

Story Highlights

- *Gallup's U.S. Job Creation Index at +32 for October*
- *Latest score matches that of the prior October*
- *Hiring gap between government, nongovernment sectors narrows*

WASHINGTON, D.C. – American workers' reports of hiring activity at their place of employment remained relatively strong in October, with many more saying their employer was adding rather than subtracting jobs. Gallup's U.S. Job Creation Index (JCI), a measure of net hiring, was +32 for the month. This score is identical to the one in October 2015 and nearly matches the post-recession high of +33 in each of the past five months.

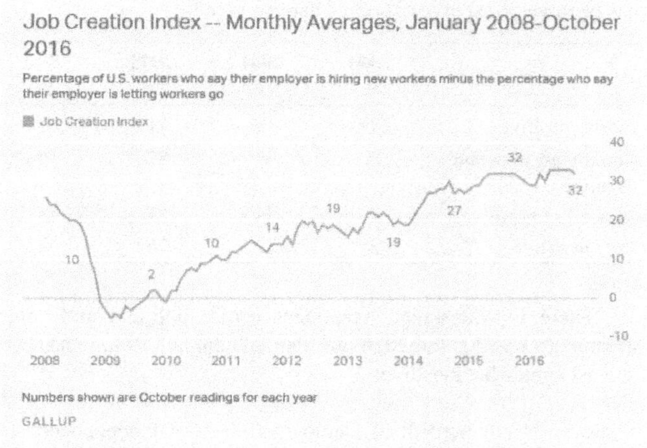

Gallup's JCI is a broad measure of the U.S. labor market based on full- and part-time workers' perceptions of hiring activity where they work. The index gradually recovered and improved to new heights after bottoming out at -5 in February and April of 2009 amid the Great Recession, and has been fairly steady recently. Over the past two years, it has ranged between +27 and +33.

Gallup asks a random sample of employed U.S. adults each day whether their employer is hiring new people and expanding the size of its workforce, not changing the size of its workforce, or letting people go and reducing the size of its workforce. Gallup computes the JCI by subtracting the percentage of employers letting workers go (11%) from the percentage bringing on new workers (43%), providing an indication of net hiring across all industry and business sectors. Additionally, 41% of workers in October said their employer is not changing the size of its workforce.

Net Hiring Gap Narrows Between Government, Nongovernment Sectors

For nearly all of Gallup's JCI trend since August 2008, net hiring in the private sector has far outpaced government net hiring. But the latest poll shows the narrowest gap between net hiring in the two sectors since April 2009, with nongovernment hiring (+32) essentially tied with government hiring (+31). The private sector represents the majority of U.S. jobs.

While both sectors have shown great gains in net hiring, the gains reported by government workers have climbed more steeply, which has gradually narrowed the gap between government and nongovernment net hiring.

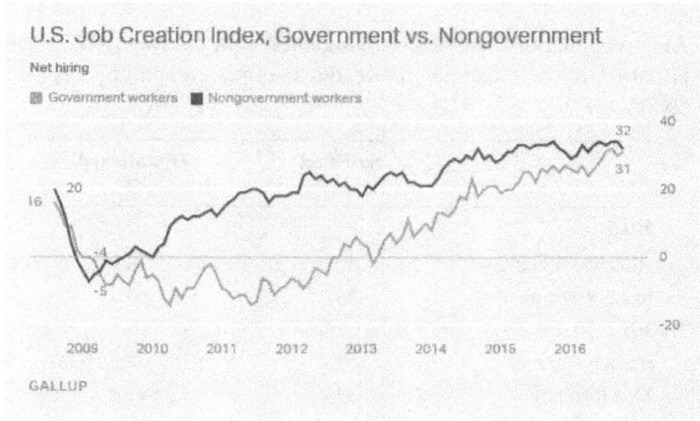

Bottom Line

As in most presidential elections, the candidates this year have laid out their economic plans and proposals for job creation. Although Democrats and Republicans may differ in their perceptions of how strong the job market is, Gallup's Job Creation Index suggests perceived hiring activity is about the best it has been since the Great Recession. It is also greatly improved over the last presidential election in 2012.

Both Donald Trump and Hillary Clinton claim their economic plans will create millions of new jobs. But unlike his or her predecessor, the next president will take office at a time when the job market is relatively strong, and improving it may be a difficult task.

Survey Methods

Results for this Gallup poll are based on telephone interviews conducted Oct. 1-31, 2016, on the Gallup U.S. Daily survey, with a random sample of 18,466 workers, aged 18 and older, living in all 50 U.S. states and the District of Columbia. For results based on the total sample of national adults, the margin of sampling error is ±1 percentage point at the 95% confidence level. All reported margins of sampling error include computed design effects for weighting.

November 02, 2016

RATINGS OF TRUMP CAMPAIGN WORST IN RECENT ELECTION YEARS

by Jim Norman

Story Highlights

- *Sixty-nine percent dissatisfied with Trump campaign*
- *Public split on satisfaction with Clinton campaign*
- *Fifty-nine percent find campaign tone "very negative"*

WASHINGTON, D.C. – As Republican nominee Donald Trump enters the home stretch of his campaign for the U.S. presidency, more than two-thirds of Americans say they are dissatisfied with the way his campaign has been conducted. This level of dissatisfaction is 21 percentage points higher than for Democratic nominee Hillary Clinton's campaign and 10 points higher than for any nominee's since Gallup first asked the question in 2000.

Satisfaction With Campaigns Takes a Dive in 2016

Are you generally satisfied or dissatisfied with the way [ROTATED: Hillary Clinton's campaign/Donald Trump's campaign] has been conducted?

	Satisfied %	Dissatisfied %
2016		
Hillary Clinton	50	48
Donald Trump	29	69
2012		
Barack Obama	58	37
Mitt Romney	54	41
2008		
Barack Obama	66	31
John McCain	40	59
2004		
John Kerry	51	46
George W. Bush	55	42
2000		
Al Gore	61	30
George W. Bush	58	31

Gallup

The campaign that garnered the highest dissatisfaction other than Trump's was Republican nominee John McCain's in 2008, at 59%. Clinton's is the next highest at 48%.

On the flip side, the largest percentage to be *satisfied* came in 2008, when 66% expressed satisfaction with Barack Obama's campaign. The 29% who say they are satisfied with Trump's campaign is the lowest, followed by McCain's 40%.

Barely half of Republicans (51%) say they are satisfied with Trump's campaign, compared with 81% of Democrats satisfied with the Clinton campaign. Trump's tempestuous campaign this year has put him at odds with both Clinton supporters and leaders of his party. The two highest ranking Republicans in Congress, Senate Majority Leader Mitch McConnell and House Speaker Paul Ryan, denounced Trump's call last December to ban all Muslims from the U.S. Ryan has criticized Trump's comments on several occasions and has avoided public appearances with the presidential nominee. Numerous Republicans have said they would not vote for Trump, including 2012 presidential nominee Mitt Romney.

Taken together, 27% of Americans say they are dissatisfied with both campaigns, and 8% are satisfied with both. These numbers represent a stark contrast to four years ago when 9% were dissatisfied and 24% were satisfied with both campaigns.

Two major groups driving the overall dissatisfaction with the campaigns are Republicans and whites.

More Republicans (47%) are dissatisfied with Trump's campaign than with any of the last four GOP candidates, and more are dissatisfied with Clinton's campaign (82%) than with Democratic candidates in the last four elections. Among whites, majorities are dissatisfied with both Clinton's (60%) and Trump's (63%) campaigns. Democrats are no more likely to be dissatisfied with Clinton than they were with the Democratic candidates in 2004 or 2000.

Public Overwhelmingly Sees Campaign's Tone as Negative

Given high levels of dissatisfaction with the campaign, it is not surprising that 77% of the public believes this year's presidential campaign has been at least somewhat negative in tone. This percentage is 27 points higher than in any of the previous three elections (2000, 2004 and 2008) when Gallup asked the question. Fifty-nine percent say the tone has been "very negative," more than double the same responses in the three other elections.

Campaign Tone Turns More Negative

How would you describe the tone of the presidential campaign so far? Would you say it has been mostly positive, about equally positive and negative, or mostly negative in tone? Would you say that it has been very negative or somewhat negative?

	2000 %	2004 %	2008 %	2016 %
Mostly positive	26	13	11	7
Equally positive and negative	55	37	37	15
Somewhat negative	12	25	24	18
Very negative	3	23	26	59

Gallup

There is widespread agreement across political and demographic groups that the 2016 presidential campaign's tone has been at least somewhat negative:

- Seventy-four percent of Democrats, 78% of independents and 79% of Republicans say this.
- Seventy-nine percent of women and 75% of men say this.
- Seventy-nine percent of those ages 18-34, 76% of those 35-54 and 77% of those 55 and older say this.

Bottom Line

As the presidential campaign approaches the finish line, Americans are looking back with displeasure on the way the candidates ran their campaigns and on the overall tenor of the race. While almost half of Americans are dissatisfied with Clinton's campaign, that is far better than the 69% who are dissatisfied with Trump's campaign.

That wide disparity in Clinton's favor may not guarantee her an election win because the public is still split on which candidate is better on the important issues. But there is little doubt about how Americans will view the campaign's conduct once it is over. The question now is whether the long slide from the campaign of 2000, which only 15% saw as negative, to 2016, when 77% feel this way, will result in a move to improve the tone of future elections or whether it marks the new reality of presidential politics in the U.S.

Survey Methods

Results for this Gallup poll are based on telephone interviews conducted Oct. 27-28, 2016, on the Gallup U.S. Daily survey, with a random sample of 945 registered voters, aged 18 and older, living in all 50 U.S. states and the District of Columbia. For results based on the total sample of registered voters, the margin of sampling error is ±4 percentage points at the 95% confidence level. All reported margins of sampling error include computed design effects for weighting.

November 30, 2016
U.S. CONSUMERS REPORT SOLID BLACK FRIDAY WEEKEND SPENDING

by Lydia Saad

Story Highlights

- Consumer daily spending averaged $128 over Black Friday weekend
- While similar to 2014-2015 spending, the figure is up from 2008-2013 spending
- Consumers' spending estimate rose even before Thanksgiving week

PRINCETON, N.J. – U.S. consumers' self-reported daily spending over Black Friday weekend was statistically similar to the average for each of the past two Black Friday weekends but remains well above the levels recorded in the immediate post-recession period.

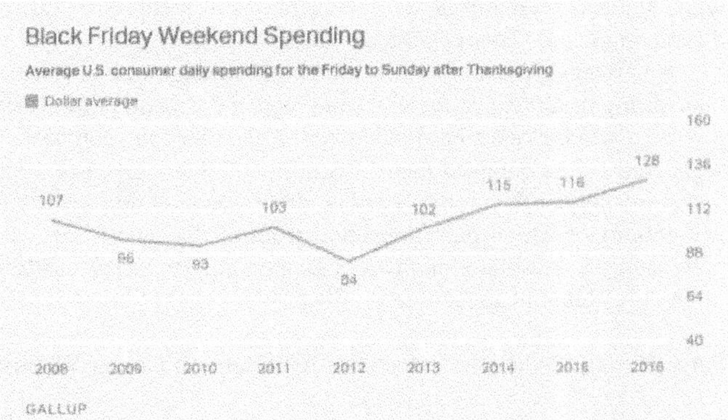

Consumers' self-reported $128 in average daily spending from Friday, Nov. 25, through Sunday, Nov. 27, is within the margin of error of the $115 and $116 averages over the same three days in 2014 and 2015. However, it is higher than the $102 recorded in 2013 and several sub-$100 readings in earlier years. These averages do not include spending on Cyber Monday – the Monday following Thanksgiving, which, because of deep online discounts that day, has become the biggest digital shopping day of the year.

Gallup's spending measure asks consumers to estimate how much they spent on retail goods or services "yesterday," either in person or online, not counting home or vehicle purchases. While this kind of spending would include gift purchases, it also covers money spent at restaurants, grocery stores, gas stations, hair salons and other places not associated with gift-buying, but easily influenced by consumers' holiday activities.

The seven-day average of consumers' daily spending over the entire Thanksgiving week – from Sunday, Nov. 20, through Saturday, Nov. 26 – averaged $106. That falls within the $100 to $110 range for Thanksgiving week reached from 2013 to 2015, supporting Gallup's finding that holiday retail sales appear on track to be about average.

But Will Spending Stay Higher Longer?

Although Gallup's late November consumer spending figures are on par with recent years, week-by-week spending in November shows that spending kicked up a bit earlier than usual. Average daily spending jumped to $103 in the third week of the month from an average of $87 in the second week. That $16 increase contrasts with an average $1 increase between the second and third weeks of November over the eight years from 2008 through 2015.

Thus, it appears that holiday spending may have gotten off to an early start, perhaps aided by the recent boost in Americans' outlook on the economy.

Americans' Daily Spending Estimates – Weekly November Averages

	Nov week 1	Nov week 2	Nov week 3	Nov week 4
2016	$95	$87	$103	$106
2015	$86	$92	$92	$101
2014	$88	$89	$98	$110
2013	$91	$90	$83	$100
2012	$66	$68	$74	$67
2011	$74	$70	$64	$83
2010	$64	$60	$66	$79
2009	$65	$62	$69	$69
2008	$99	$81	$74	$92

Based on U.S. consumers' estimate of daily spending in stores and online
Gallup

The key question for retailers is whether this momentum will continue in December. Last year, consumers' self-reported spending dipped to about $90 in the first half of December after reaching an average $101 in late November, but then surged in the third and fourth weeks of December.

These 2015 shifts – which were statistically significant, given the weekly sample sizes – conform with analysis by the National Retail Federation that warm December weather, combined with consumers' increasing reliance on online shopping and determination to wait for pre-Christmas sales, may have pushed the 2015 holiday shopping peak to later in the season.

Americans' Daily Spending Estimates – Weekly December Averages

	Dec week 1	Dec week 2	Dec week 3	Dec week 4
2016	n/a	n/a	n/a	n/a
2015	$90	$91	$119	$113
2014	$98	$104	$101	$97
2013	$103	$82	$106	$91
2012	$90	$75	$104	$63
2011	$70	$78	$78	$83
2010	$66	$66	$77	$85
2009	$75	$73	$74	$70
2008	$95	$94	$93	$68

Based on U.S. consumers' estimate of daily spending in stores and online
Gallup

Gallup's weekly spending estimates this December will help clarify whether the 2015 pattern was the start of a new model of consumer behavior driven by internet shopping or if it was unique to that year – perhaps more weather-driven.

Bottom Line

Consumers' holiday shopping spree started a bit early this year and, even without factoring in Cyber Monday sales, spending over Black Friday weekend was brisk. More broadly, the extent to which consumer spending results in average or above-average holiday sales for retailers is still largely dependent on what happens next month, and that is far from predictable.

Although factors such as the weather are beyond retailers' control, reaching consumers online, connecting with their attachment to Christmas (around nine in 10 Americans indicate they celebrate the holiday) and offering them value in a highly competitive marketplace are not. While much of this spending may occur online in the final week before Christmas, the fact that the holiday falls on a Sunday this year means many procrastinators may take advantage of Christmas Eve being a Saturday to finish their holiday shopping the old-fashioned way – pounding the pavement at malls.

Historical data are available in Gallup Analytics.

Survey Methods

Results for 2016 Black Friday weekend spending are based on telephone interviews conducted Nov. 26-28, 2016, on the Gallup U.S. Daily survey, with a random sample of 1,512 adults, aged 18 and older, living in all 50 U.S. states and the District of Columbia. For results based on the total sample of national adults, the margin of sampling error is ±$22 at the 95% confidence level. Gallup's weekly spending estimates are generally based on 3,500 interviews with a nationwide sample of U.S. adults on the Gallup U.S. Daily survey, and have a margin of sampling error of approximately ±$12 at the 95% confidence level. All reported margins of sampling error include computed design effects for weighting.

November 03, 2016

MAJORITY OF U.S. VOTERS THINK MEDIA FAVORS CLINTON

by Gary J. Gates

Story Highlights

- *52% of registered voters say election media bias favors Clinton*
- *Opinions about candidates are a strong predictor of perceived bias*
- *Perceptions of bias are more partisan today than in 2004*

WASHINGTON, D.C. – Republican presidential nominee Donald Trump frequently accuses the media of biasing its coverage of the 2016 election campaign in favor of his Democratic opponent Hillary Clinton. A majority of registered voters (52%) agree with the Republican nominee. Meanwhile, 8% think the media favors Trump and 38% perceive no media bias.

Perception of Media Bias in Favor of Hillary Clinton or Donald Trump

Thinking about the media coverage of the election so far this year, do you think it has been biased in favor of Hillary Clinton, not biased in favor of either candidate, or biased in favor of Donald Trump?

	Biased in favor of Clinton %	No bias toward either candidate %	Biased in favor of Trump %	No opinion %
Registered voters	52	38	8	2

Gallup, Oct 27-28, 2016

Therefore, not only do the slight majority of U.S. registered voters believe the media is biased in favor of Clinton, but 87% of voters who perceive any media bias believe that bias favors Clinton.

The findings are based on Gallup Daily tracking data collected Oct. 27-28, 2016. About half of respondents were interviewed prior to the Friday release of a letter from FBI Director James Comey to Congress about the discovery of additional emails that might pertain to the FBI's investigation into Clinton's use of a private email server while she was secretary of state. Perceptions of media bias did not differ significantly between the two days.

Americans' perception of media bias is stronger in this election than during the 2004 presidential campaign, the only other time Gallup has asked the question. In October of that election year, 45% of registered voters believed there was no media bias, seven percentage points higher than today. Further, there was a bit more parity in perceptions of which party benefited from media favoritism, with 35% saying it was biased in favor of Democrat John Kerry and 16% in favor of Republican George W. Bush.

Perception of Media Bias in Favor of John Kerry or George W. Bush

Thinking about the media coverage of the election so far this year, do you think it has been biased in favor of John Kerry, not biased in favor of either candidate, or biased in favor of George W. Bush?

	Biased in favor of Kerry %	No bias toward either candidate %	Biased in favor of Bush %	No opinion %
Registered voters	35	45	16	4

Gallup, Oct 22-24, 2004

Among registered voters who perceived media bias, 69% thought that the bias favored Kerry in 2004, 18 points lower than the perceived bias favoring Clinton in 2016.

Opinions About Candidates Strongly Linked to Perceptions of Media Bias

Voters' perceptions of media bias in 2016 are closely related to their underlying opinions of Clinton and Trump. Among voters who have a favorable opinion of Trump, 90% say that the media is biased in favor of Clinton. By contrast, nearly two-thirds (63%) of those who view Clinton favorably say the media is not biased toward either candidate. Notably, more of these Clinton supporters believe the media is biased toward her over Trump, 23% vs. 13%, respectively.

Perception of Media Bias in Favor of Hillary Clinton or Donald Trump Among Registered Voters by Candidate Favorability

	Biased in favor of Clinton %	No bias toward either candidate %	Biased in favor of Trump %	No opinion %
Favorable view of Clinton	23	63	13	2
Favorable view of Trump	90	7	3	1

Gallup, Oct 27-28, 2016

Party Affiliation Also Linked to Perceptions of Media Bias

Voters' perceptions of media bias in 2016 are also related to political party affiliation. Majorities of Democrats (63%) and independents (52%) do not believe that the media is biased toward either candidate. By contrast, the vast majority of Republicans (86%) perceive media bias, and nearly all of them (80%) believe the bias favors Clinton. Among independents and Democrats who perceive bias, large majorities also believe the bias favors Clinton.

Perception of Media Bias in Favor of Hillary Clinton or Donald Trump Among Registered Voters by Party Affiliation

	Biased in favor of Clinton %	No bias toward either candidate %	Biased in favor of Trump %	No opinion %
Republican/ Lean	80	12	6	2
Independent	41	52	2	5
Democrat/ Lean	25	63	10	2

Gallup, Oct 27-28, 2016

Similar to today, a majority of Democrats (51%) and independents (72%) did not perceive media bias in 2004. But the perception of bias has grown substantially among Republicans, increasing by 26 points from 60% in 2004 to 86% today.

Bottom Line

In the U.S., perceptions of a liberal media bias have been prevalent throughout this century. However, the perceived tilt in bias toward the Democratic candidate among registered voters was less pronounced in the 2004 election than it is today.

The overall percentage believing the media is biased toward either candidate is nine points higher today than in 2004, 60% vs. 51%, respectively. But among those who perceive bias, almost all in 2016 (87%) see Clinton as the beneficiary versus 69% saying Kerry benefited in 2004. The increased perception of media bias among voters is largely driven by Republicans. While they were more likely than independents and Democrats to perceive bias in 2004 and are again more likely to do so in 2016, that gap has widened substantially.

This shift could be related to how often Trump publicly laments media bias in favor of Clinton and has perhaps elevated the issue to a higher profile in this campaign than in past elections.

Despite evidence of the partisanship in patterns of media-bias perception, Americans who perceive bias – regardless of their favorability of Clinton or Trump or their party affiliation – generally agree that media coverage favors Clinton.

Survey Methods

Results regarding media bias in the 2016 campaign are based on telephone interviews conducted Oct. 27-28, 2016, on the Gallup U.S. Daily survey, with a random sample of 1,017 adults, aged 18 and older, living in all 50 U.S. states and the District of Columbia. Of this group, 940 respondents identified as registered voters. For results based on registered voters, the margin of sampling error is ±4 percentage points at the 95% confidence level. Margins of error within subpopulations of both groups are higher and vary depending on sample size. All reported margins of sampling error include computed design effects for weighting.

November 04, 2016

PERCEPTIONS OF CLINTON'S HONESTY UNCHANGED AFTER FBI LETTER

by Frank Newport and Michael Smith

Story Highlights

- *Despite new email investigations, Clinton's honesty ratings stable*
- *Clinton scores higher on judgment and getting things done*
- *Trump scores low on having good judgment*

WASHINGTON, D.C. – About a third of Americans (32%) say "honest and trustworthy" applies to Hillary Clinton, essentially unchanged from 35% in mid-September and in May. Americans' views of Donald Trump's honesty and trustworthiness have also been stable – 36% say the term applies to him now versus 33% in September. The latest figures are from the Gallup poll conducted after an FBI letter revealed the agency would look into emails on a private computer at the home of Clinton aide Huma Abedin.

Do the Following Characteristics and Qualities Apply to Clinton/Trump?

	Nov. 2-3 % Applies	Sept. 14-18 % Applies	May 18-22 % Applies
Hillary Clinton			
Can get things done	57	61	56
Would display good judgment in a crisis	50	55	48
Is honest and trustworthy	32	35	32
Donald Trump			
Can get things done	53	56	58
Would display good judgment in a crisis	36	38	39
Is honest and trustworthy	36	33	33

Gallup

The Nov. 2-3 poll also measured the public's views of whether two other terms applied to the candidates: "can get things done" and "would display good judgment in a crisis" – qualities both candidates claim make them uniquely qualified for the presidency.

More than half of U.S. adults say both Clinton and Trump can get things done – 57% for the former, and 53% for the latter. Both figures are similar to those found in September and in May. At the same time, Trump receives substantially lower ratings than Clinton for displaying good judgment in a crisis, 36% vs. 50%, also broadly similar to previous measures.

Implications

The lack of substantive change in these measures since September is an indication of the relative stability of Americans' views of the two candidates. Both were well-known figures before they entered the race, and each candidate's favorable ratings have been relatively consistent – Clinton at roughly 41% and Trump at roughly 33% – amid the long campaign for president.

Both candidates have historically high unfavorable ratings for presidential candidates. Their low ratings on honesty and trustworthiness are also the lowest Gallup has recorded for presidential candidates in election campaigns, providing one key indicator of why their overall images are so low.

Survey Methods

Results for this Gallup poll are based on telephone interviews conducted Nov. 2-3, 2016, on the Gallup U.S. Daily tracking survey, with a random sample of 1,019 adults, aged 18 and older, living in all 50 U.S. states and the District of Columbia. For results based on the total sample of national adults, the margin of sampling error is ±4 percentage points at the 95% confidence level. All reported margins of sampling error include computed design effects for weighting.

November 07, 2016

TRUMP AND CLINTON FINISH WITH HISTORICALLY POOR IMAGES

by Lydia Saad

Story Highlights

- *Trump's 61% unfavorable score is worst in presidential polling history*
- *Clinton's 52% unfavorable score is second-worst*
- *Candidates roughly matched in highly unfavorable images*

PRINCETON, N.J. – Donald Trump and Hillary Clinton head into the final hours of the 2016 presidential campaign with the worst election-eve images of any major-party presidential candidates Gallup has measured back to 1956. Majorities of Americans now view each of them unfavorably on a 10-point favorability scale, a first for any presidential standard-bearer on this long-term Gallup trend. Trump's image is worse than Clinton's, however, with 61% viewing him negatively on the 10-point scale compared with 52% for her.

Final Pre-Election "Scalometer" Favorable Ratings of Major-Party Presidential Nominees, 1956-2016

Based on U.S. adults; ranked by % total unfavorable

	Nominee	Total favorable % (+1 to +5)	Total unfavorable % (-1 to -5)
2016 Nov 2-5	D. Trump	36	61
2016 Nov 2-5	H. Clinton	47	52
1964 Oct 8-13	B. Goldwater	43	47
2012 Oct 27-28	M. Romney	55	43
1972 Oct 13-16	G. McGovern	55	41
2004 Oct 22-24	J. Kerry	57	40
1992 Oct 23-25	G.H.W. Bush	59	40
2004 Oct 22-24	G.W. Bush	61	39
2012 Oct 27-28	B. Obama	62	37
1980 Oct 10-13	R. Reagan	64	37
2008 Oct 23-26	B. Obama	62	35
2008 Oct 23-26	J. McCain	63	35
1984 Sep 21-24	W. Mondale	66	34
1992 Oct 23-25	B. Clinton	64	33
1980 Oct 10-13	J. Carter	68	32
1956 Oct 18-23	A. Stevenson	61	31
1984 Sep 21-24	R. Reagan	71	30
1968 Oct 17-22	H. Humphrey	72	28
1968 Oct 17-22	R. Nixon	79	22
1972 Oct 13-16	R. Nixon	76	21
1976 Sep 24-27	G. Ford	78	20
1960 Oct 18-23	R. Nixon	79	16

	Nominee	Total favorable % (+1 to +5)	Total unfavorable % (-1 to -5)
1976 Sep 24-27	J. Carter	81	16
1960 Oct 18-23	J. Kennedy	80	14
1964 Oct 8-13	L. Johnson	81	13
1956 Oct 18-23	D. Eisenhower	84	12

No data for 1988, 1996 and 2000
Gallup

These findings are based on Gallup's historical "scalometer" favorability measure, which asks respondents for their general opinion of each candidate using a 10-point positive-to-negative scale. Respondents can use any number from +1 to +5 to indicate that they have a favorable view of a candidate, with +5 being highly favorable. They can use any number from -1 to -5 for an unfavorable view, with -5 being highly unfavorable. The latest survey was conducted by telephone Nov. 2-5 with a nationwide sample of U.S. adults.

The scalometer measure tends to produce higher positive ratings than the binary favorable/unfavorable choice that has been the mainstay of Gallup's favorability measurement since 1992, although that is currently more true for Clinton than for Trump. Clinton's straight-up "favorable" rating is 40% in Gallup Daily tracking for the week ending Nov. 6, while Trump's is 35%.

2016 Campaign Sets Record-High Unfavorability Scores

The extent of Americans' distaste for the two major-party candidates is further evident in the extraordinarily high percentages viewing each highly unfavorably – rating them a -5 or -4 on the scale. Forty-two percent of Americans view Trump highly unfavorably, unchanged from Gallup's prior measure in June. Clinton's highly unfavorable rating is nearly as high, at 39%, but up from 33% in June.

Both candidates' highly unfavorable ratings far outpace any Gallup has recorded before for a major-party presidential nominee, with the next-highest being Republican Barry Goldwater's 26% score in 1964. Even the former Alabama governor and proponent of racial segregation, George Wallace, who ran for president as a third-party candidate in 1968, earned a lower high unfavorability score that year (32%) than the 2016 candidates do today.

Highly Favorable and Highly Unfavorable Ratings of Major-Party Presidential Nominees, 1956-2016

Based on U.S. adults; ranked by % highly unfavorable

	Nominee	Highly favorable % (+4 to +5)	Highly unfavorable % (-4 to -5)
2016 Nov 2-5	D. Trump	14	42
2016 Nov 2-5	H. Clinton	21	39
1964 Oct 8-13	B. Goldwater	17	26
2012 Oct 27-28	B. Obama	36	24
2004 Oct 22-24	G.W. Bush	34	23
2004 Oct 22-24	J. Kerry	22	22
2012 Oct 27-28	M. Romney	30	22
2008 Oct 23-26	B. Obama	37	22
1972 Oct 13-16	G. McGovern	21	20
2008 Oct 23-26	J. McCain	28	20
1984 Sep 21-24	R. Reagan	43	18
1980 Oct 10-13	J. Carter	31	17
1992 Oct 23-25	G.H.W. Bush	20	16
1980 Oct 10-13	R. Reagan	26	16
1956 Oct 18-23	A. Stevenson	34	16
1992 Oct 23-25	B. Clinton	27	15
1984 Sep 21-24	W. Mondale	28	15
1968 Oct 17-22	H. Humphrey	29	11
1972 Oct 13-16	R. Nixon	41	11
1976 Sep 24-27	G. Ford	29	9
1968 Oct 17-22	R. Nixon	39	8
1960 Oct 18-23	R. Nixon	37	5
1976 Sep 24-27	J. Carter	42	5
1960 Oct 18-23	J. Kennedy	43	5
1964 Oct 8-13	L. Johnson	49	5
1956 Oct 18-23	D. Eisenhower	57	4

No data for 1988, 1996 and 2000
Gallup

Bottom Line

Americans' fundamental reactions to their 2016 presidential candidates are at least as negative today as when Clinton and Trump emerged as their respective parties' presumptive nominees in June. The subsequent ups and downs of the campaign have resulted in no meaningful change to Trump's image, and have had a modest negative effect on Clinton's, with her highly unfavorable rating inching up to match Trump's.

The 2016 election is the only one in Gallup's polling history to feature two broadly unpopular candidates. Further, when factoring in the high percentages viewing each very negatively, Trump and Clinton are the two most negatively reviewed U.S. presidential candidates of the modern era, and probably ever.

There has been a trend toward harsher ratings of candidates in recent elections. Indeed, as Gallup noted in June, no presidential candidate since Ronald Reagan in 1984 has ended a campaign with a total favorable scalometer score above 70%. But even in the last two elections, all candidates enjoyed total favorable scores of 55% or higher, far better than either candidate today.

In sum, this contest of historically unpopular candidates concludes with Clinton the apparent "lesser of two evils," and that could be what decides the election.

Survey Methods

Results for this Gallup poll are based on telephone interviews conducted Nov. 2-5, 2016, on the Gallup U.S. Daily survey, with a random sample of 1,033 adults, aged 18 and older, living in all 50 U.S. states and the District of Columbia. For results based on the total sample of national adults, the margin of sampling error is ±4 percentage points at the 95% confidence level. For results based on the total sample of 947 registered voters, the margin of sampling error is ±4 percentage points at the 95% confidence level. All reported margins of sampling error include computed design effects for weighting.

November 08, 2016

U.S. SATISFACTION RISES TO MATCH HISTORICAL NORM

by Jeffrey M. Jones

Story Highlights

- *37% of Americans satisfied with way things are going in U.S.*
- *Up from 28% in October*
- *Low satisfaction usually associated with incumbent party losing*

PRINCETON, N.J. – On this Election Day, 37% of Americans say they are satisfied with the way things are going in the country. That is up significantly from 28% in October and now matches the historical average since Gallup first asked the question in 1979. It also ties the average figure in Gallup's final pre-election polls in prior presidential election years.

Satisfaction With Way Things Are Going in the U.S., Final Pre-Election Measure in Presidential Election Years

	Satisfied %	Incumbent party	Winning party
2016 Nov 1-6	37	Democrat	
2012 Nov 1-4	33	Democrat	Democrat
2008 Oct 31-Nov 2	13	Republican	Democrat
2004 Oct 29-31	44	Republican	Republican
2000 Oct 6-9	62	Democrat	Republican
1996 Oct 26-29	39	Democrat	Democrat
1992 Aug 28-Sep 2	22	Republican	Democrat
1988 Sep 25-Oct 1	56	Republican	Republican
1984 Sep 28-Oct 1	48	Republican	Republican
1979 Nov 2-5	19	Democrat	Republican

Note: No satisfaction measures were taken in 1980, but satisfaction was 19% in November 1979 and 17% in January 1981, indicating it was likely similar in 1980.
Gallup

The current results are based on a Nov. 1-6 Gallup poll. Low satisfaction can be an indicator that Americans are ready to change the government as a means of trying to improve the situation in the country. Consistent with that pattern, the incumbent party lost the 1980, 1992 and 2008 campaigns, all election cycles in which U.S. satisfaction was no greater than 22%.

However, the incumbent party has won elections when satisfaction was well below the majority level. In the 2012 election, Barack Obama won re-election when 33% of Americans were satisfied. In 1996, Bill Clinton won re-election when 39% were satisfied. Both presidents may have benefited from satisfaction being significantly higher than it was four years earlier when each was elected. George W. Bush won re-election when 44% of Americans were satisfied in 2004, even though satisfaction was lower at that time than it was when Bush was first elected in 2000.

Therefore, by no means is majority satisfaction necessary for the incumbent party to win a presidential election. Rather, satisfaction near the historical average of 37% may be enough, as it was in 1996 and 2012.

However, above-average satisfaction does not guarantee a favorable outcome for the incumbent party. The major exception occurred in 2000 when 62% of Americans were satisfied – the highest it has been at the time of a presidential election in Gallup's trend. That year, Democrat Al Gore won the popular vote, but Republican George W. Bush won the presidency in the Electoral College after the Supreme Court sided with Bush in a legal dispute over the Florida results.

In contrast, George H.W. Bush was elected president in 1988 to succeed Ronald Reagan at a time when 56% of Americans were satisfied with the state of the nation.

Satisfaction Up Among All Major Political Groups Since October

The current 37% satisfaction figure is the highest in President Obama's time in office by one percentage point over a reading in August 2009, during his first year in office. The last time satisfaction was higher was in September 2005, when it was 39%.

Americans from all three major political party groups are more satisfied now than they were one month ago. Democrats' satisfaction has increased the most – 13 percentage points – to 62%. Independents (34%) and Republicans (14%) are much less satisfied than Democrats, which is to be expected with a Democratic president in office, but both have shown meaningful gains in satisfaction in the past month.

Change in Satisfaction With Way Things Are Going in the U.S., by Political Party

	Oct 5-9, 2016 %	Nov 1-6, 2016 %	Change (pct. pts.)
National adults	28	37	+9
Democrats	49	62	+13
Independents	24	34	+10
Republicans	8	14	+6

Gallup

In each of the past four presidential election years, Gallup has measured increases in satisfaction from early October to right before the election. This included three-percentage-point gains in 2004 and 2012, a six-point gain in 2008 and a nine-point gain this year. Thus, something about the approaching election – either satisfaction with the democratic process or optimism about the prospect of their preferred candidate winning – may make Americans feel modestly better about the way things are going in the country.

Implications

The surge in satisfaction right before the election is a promising sign for Democratic presidential candidate Hillary Clinton as she attempts to succeed a Democratic president in office. Another positive sign for the Clinton campaign is that satisfaction is well above the levels associated with the levels when incumbent parties were defeated in 1980, 1992 and 2008. At least two incumbent presidents, Obama in 2012 and Bill Clinton in 1996, have been re-elected when satisfaction was similar to what it is now.

There have been only three prior presidential elections that did not involve an incumbent president in the years in which Gallup has asked the satisfaction question. The link between satisfaction and the election outcome is not clear-cut in those cases, with the incumbent party winning in 1988 when satisfaction was above average, losing in 2000 when satisfaction was above average, and losing in 2008 when satisfaction was well below average.

In non-incumbent presidential elections, voters' evaluations of the candidates' characteristics, assessments of the candidates' ideology and policy positions, and party leanings may matter more than assessments of how the nation is doing when they decide which candidate to vote for.

Survey Methods

Results for this Gallup poll are based on telephone interviews conducted Nov. 1-6, 2016, with a random sample of 1,532 adults, aged 18 and older, living in all 50 U.S. states and the District of Columbia. For results based on the total sample of national adults, the margin of sampling error is ±3 percentage points at the 95% confidence level. All reported margins of sampling error include computed design effects for weighting.

November 09, 2016

AMERICANS' PERCEPTIONS OF U.S. CRIME PROBLEM ARE STEADY

by Art Swift

Story Highlights

- *Perceptions of nationwide crime unchanged from 2015*
- *Perceptions of local crime also steady*
- *60% of Americans believe crime problem in U.S. extremely or very serious*

WASHINGTON, D.C. – Seven in 10 Americans say there is more crime in the U.S. than a year ago, unchanged from 2015. Two in 10 believe there is less crime. The percentage who believe crime is up from a year ago is near the recent high of 74% in 2009, but still significantly below the record high of 89% in 1992.

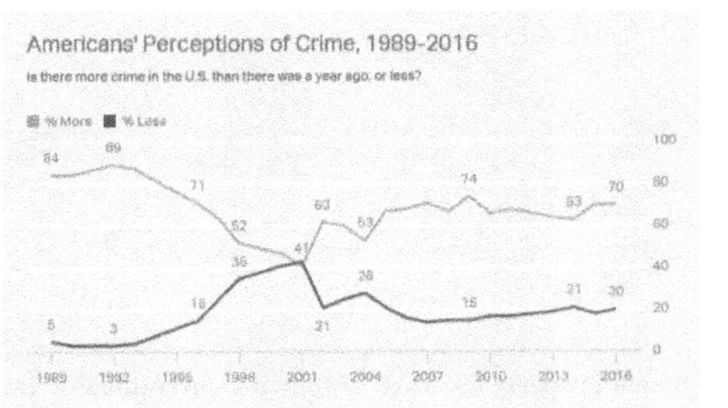

Since Gallup began asking this question in 1989, a majority of Americans have usually said there is more crime than there was the year before. A notable exception was in October 2001, soon after the Sept. 11 attacks, when 41% expressed this sentiment. By the next year, perceptions of there being more crime in the U.S. than in the prior year returned to the majority level, possibly because of the 2002 D.C. sniper shootings, and have since remained there.

The FBI announced in September of this year that homicides were up by 11% in 2015 from the previous year. The violent crime rate also increased, by about 4%, in 2015 and was the highest in three years. Gallup measured a seven-percentage-point increase from 2014 to 2015 in perceptions that there was more crime in the U.S. than the prior year, but found no change this year. Government data on crime rates for 2016 won't be released until next year, so it is unclear whether Americans' perceptions about crime in the U.S. are consistent with the actual crime trend.

Perceptions of Local Crime Steady From Last Year

In line with this year's stability in Americans' beliefs about U.S. crime, Americans' perceptions of crime in the area where they live were unchanged from 2015. Forty-five percent now say there is more crime locally than last year, essentially unchanged from 46% a year ago. Thirty-three percent now say there is less local crime and 20% say there is the same amount.

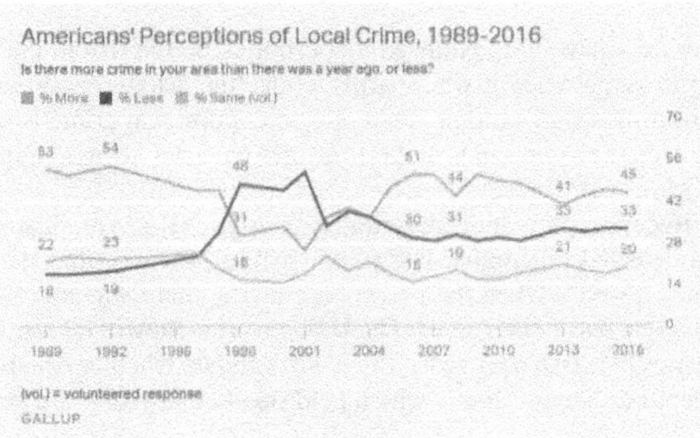

As noted, Americans' perceptions of crime locally and nationally are unchanged this year, even as violent crime is reportedly up from the previous year in certain major cities such as Chicago and Los Angeles. Donald Trump made the perception that violent crime is rising in the U.S. a hallmark of his campaign, especially in his acceptance speech at the Republican National Convention in July. In reply, President Barack Obama said murder and violent crime rates are much lower today than when Ronald Reagan was president. Gallup's trend underscores this long-term decline. A majority of Americans from 1989 to 1992 thought local crime was increasing, almost 10 percentage points higher than today.

Perceived Seriousness of U.S. Crime Problem Remains High

Along with the stability in Americans' perceptions of the national and local crime rate, Americans' views of the seriousness of the national crime problem are unchanged. Amid the noise of the presidential election year, with Trump frequently citing crime as a chief concern in the U.S., 60% of Americans say the problem of crime in the nation is "extremely" or "very" serious. This is essentially unchanged from October 2015 but tied for the high point over the past 16 years.

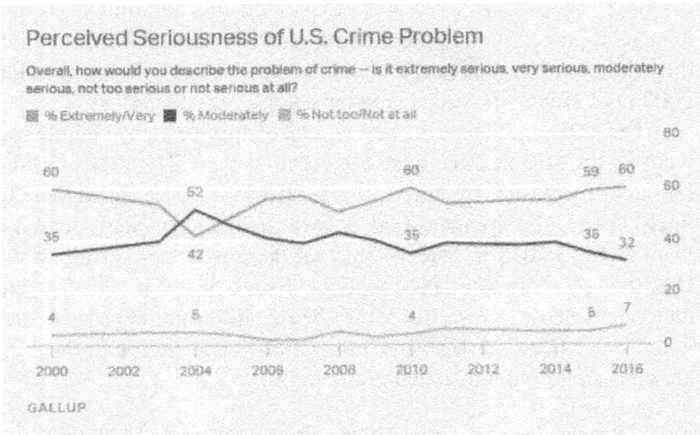

While in most years, the majority of Americans have said the crime problem was "extremely" or "very serious," that has not been the case in all years. In 2004, perceptions of the seriousness of crime dropped, with 42% saying the crime problem was extremely or very serious – and more saying it was moderately serious or not serious.

Bottom Line

Americans have long believed that crime is on the rise in the U.S., even in years when it was sharply in decline. Media reports about high-profile crimes might create the perception that crime is on the rise, even if changes in actual crime rates have not always supported that idea.

Recent reports indicate crime was up in 2015. Americans may have detected this uptick last year – before official crime statistics were released – when the percentage saying there was more crime than a year earlier increased. The U.S. government will release crime statistics for 2016 next year, which will validate whether Americans' perceptions about crime – which held steady this year – are correct.

Survey Methods

Results for this Gallup poll are based on telephone interviews conducted Oct. 5-9, 2016, with a random sample of 1,017 adults, aged 18 and older, living in all 50 U.S. states and the District of Columbia. For results based on the total sample of national adults, the margin of sampling error is ±4 percentage points at the 95% confidence level. All reported margins of sampling error include computed design effects for weighting.

November 10, 2016
AMERICANS' REPORTS OF CRIME VICTIMIZATION AT HIGH EBB

by Lydia Saad

Story Highlights

- *29% of U.S. adults indicate household was victimized in past year*
- *Household victimization up from average 24% in prior decade*
- *17% of Americans say they were personally victimized, holding steady*

PRINCETON, N.J. – Twenty-nine percent of U.S. adults report that they or someone in their household was the victim of at least one form of conventional – meaning nondigital – crime in the past year. This is in line with the average 27% over the past four years, but up from an average of 24% in the early 2000s.

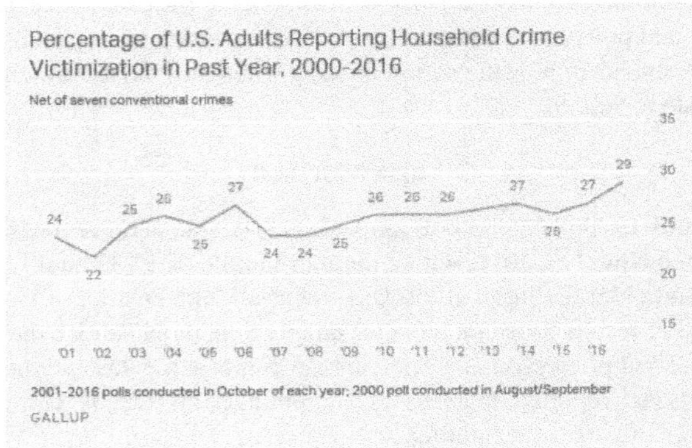

More generally, Americans' self-reported experience with crime has been trending up since about 2001 and is now at a numerical high. Although not significantly higher than the 27% recorded in 2015, it could suggest the continuation of the upward trend and bears watching in the coming years.

The latest results are from Gallup's annual Crime poll, conducted Oct. 5-9.

The household victimization index reflects U.S. adults' responses to whether they or anyone in their household was the victim of each of seven different crimes spanning theft, vandalism and violent crimes. Those who say their household experienced a listed crime are then asked whether it happened to them personally or to another family member.

Overall, 16% of U.S. adults say that they were personally the victim of at least one crime in the past year, similar to the 17% found in 2015 and about the middle of the 14% to 19% range seen since 2001.

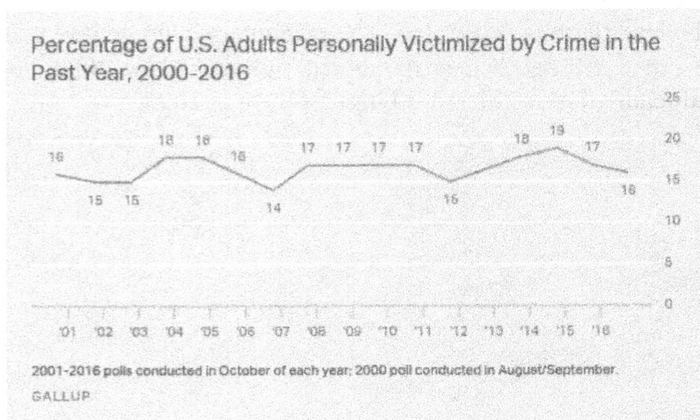

Stolen Property the Most Common Conventional Crime

The conventional crimes that comprise Gallup's crime victimization metrics include four different property crimes and three violent crimes that Gallup has asked about each year since 2000. In terms of the household numbers:

- 17% of Americans say that property or money was stolen from someone in their household in the past year
- 14% report having a home, car or other property vandalized

- 5% say their home was broken into
- 4% say a household member's car was stolen

Smaller proportions of Americans say that a member of their household was a victim of any sort of violent crime in the past year. Of the three types asked about, the most common is a mugging or physical assault (3%), followed by armed robbery (2%) and sexual assault (1%).

The index does not include two types of digital crimes that Gallup began measuring more recently – experiencing identity theft and having credit card information stolen. More Americans tend to report being victimized by these than by most conventional crimes.

As Gallup reported last month, 27% of Americans say that they or someone in their household had information from a credit card stolen by computer hackers. That is similar to the level in 2014, but up from 22% in 2015. At the same time, 17% say that a household member was the victim of identity theft, similar to 2015 (16%), but significantly higher than the 8% to 12% range seen from 2009 to 2013.

Bottom Line

Americans' direct experience with crime is at a 16-year high, consistent with a gradual increase – from 22% in 2001 to 29% today – in the percentage saying that they or a household member was the victim of a robbery, vandalism or violent crime in the past year.

In the same poll, Americans' perceptions of the seriousness of crime nationally and in their local area was unchanged from 2015. But longer term, it has worsened slightly since 2001. As a result, while crime was not at the top of the candidates' or voters' agenda in the 2016 presidential campaign, the issue may be ripe for policymakers at all levels of government to address.

Survey Methods

Results for this Gallup poll are based on telephone interviews conducted Oct. 5-9, 2016, with a random sample of 1,017 adults, aged 18 and older, living in all 50 U.S. states and the District of Columbia. For results based on the total sample of national adults, the margin of sampling error is ±4 percentage points at the 95% confidence level. All reported margins of sampling error include computed design effects for weighting.

November 11, 2016
TRUMP VICTORY SURPRISES AMERICANS; FOUR IN 10 AFRAID

by Jim Norman

Story Highlights

- *Trump's win surprises both Republicans and Democrats*
- *42% describe one of their reactions as "afraid"*
- *Reactions are far different from those eight years ago*

WASHINGTON, D.C. – Americans on both sides of the 2016 presidential race are reacting strongly to Donald Trump's victory Tuesday: 80% of Trump voters say they are "excited," while 76% of Hillary Clinton voters say they are "afraid." A large majority (75%) share one reaction: surprise.

Americans' Reactions to Trump Victory Vary Widely

Percent who said each of the following describes their reaction to Donald Trump being elected president

	National adults	Trump voters	Clinton voters
	%	%	%
Surprised	75	62	88
Afraid	42	5	76
Relieved	40	91	9
Excited	35	80	5
Devastated	34	3	66
Proud	32	75	2
Angry	29	3	58

Gallup

Trump's tumultuous campaign often put him at odds with leaders of his own Republican Party and resulted in the highest unfavorable ratings for any presidential candidate in Gallup polling history. A majority of Americans also viewed Democratic nominee Clinton unfavorably, making this the first time since Gallup began measuring favorability that both major-party candidates had negative ratings.

Nevertheless, when asked whether each of six adjectives describes how they are reacting to the election results, Americans do not overwhelmingly identify with the most negative terms. Almost as many say they are "relieved" (40%) as say they are "afraid" (42%). About the same percentages describe their reaction as "excited" (35%) and "devastated" (34%).

Huge differences exist between Trump voters and Clinton voters, with somewhat smaller differences between Republicans and Democrats as well as between younger and older Americans.

- Sixty-six percent of Democrats and independents who lean Democratic say they are "afraid," compared with 11% of Republicans and leaners.
- Sixty-three percent of Republicans and leaners are "excited," compared with 13% of Democrats and leaners.
- More than half of Americans aged 40 and younger (54%) say they are "afraid," compared with only a fourth of those 60 and older (25%).
- The situation reverses for those who say they are "relieved": More than half of those aged 60 or older (57%) say they are "relieved," while less than a fourth of those 40 or younger (22%) feel the same way.

Reactions Differ Greatly From Historic Obama Win in 2008

Americans reacted far differently in 2008 when Barack Obama won election as the first black president.

- Thirty-two percent of Americans say they are "proud" after Trump's election. The night after Obama's historic election, 67% described themselves as "proud."

- Thirty-five percent are "excited" about Trump's election. In 2008, 59% said they felt this way.
- Forty-two percent are "afraid" now, compared with 27% in 2008.

Obama's re-election four years ago did not evoke the same level of excitement as his historic win in 2008 did. Significantly fewer said they were "proud" or "excited," and more said they were "afraid."

Americans' Reactions to 2008, 2012 and 2016 Elections

Percent who say each of the words describes their reaction to the elections in 2008, 2012 and 2016

	2008 %	2012 %	2016 %
Proud	67	48	32
Excited	59	40	35
Afraid	27	36	42

Gallup

Bottom Line

Eight years ago, the vast majority of Americans felt "proud" that their country had elected a black president, seeing it as a monumental milestone. More than two-thirds had a favorable view of Obama, who won the race by more than 9 million votes.

Two presidential elections later, reactions are far different to Trump, who has the lowest favorable rating of any major presidential candidate in more than 50 years and who trails Clinton in the popular vote.

However, a comparison of reactions this year with those in 2012 shows the percentages of Americans "excited" about and "afraid" of each outcome do not greatly differ. Further, 66% of Republicans in 2012 said they were "afraid" when reacting to Obama's re-election, the same as the percentage of Democrats who now say they are "afraid." (In 2008, 53% of Republicans said the election outcome made them "afraid.")

Obama's re-election in 2012 and his subsequent inauguration occurred without widespread unrest or challenges to his legitimacy. The question moving forward after numerous anti-Trump protests Wednesday night and the threat of more to come on Inauguration Day is whether the anger and fear of those who oppose Trump will produce a different result.

Survey Methods

Results for this Gallup poll are based on telephone interviews conducted Nov. 9, 2016, on the Gallup U.S. Daily survey, with a random sample of 511 U.S. adults, aged 18 and older, living in all 50 U.S. states and the District of Columbia. For results based on the total sample of national adults, the margin of sampling error is ±5 percentage points at the 95% confidence level. All reported margins of sampling error include computed design effects for weighting.

Polls conducted entirely in one day, such as this one, are subject to additional error or bias not found in polls conducted over several days.

November 11, 2016

IN U.S., 84% ACCEPT TRUMP AS LEGITIMATE PRESIDENT

by Jeffrey M. Jones

Story Highlights

- *76% of Clinton voters say Trump is legitimate president*
- *60% of Clinton voters say election has caused permanent harm to U.S.*
- *Views of this election similar to 2000 election*

PRINCETON, N.J. – After Donald Trump's surprise defeat of Hillary Clinton in the highly contentious 2016 presidential campaign, 84% of Americans say they accept Trump as the legitimate president, but 15% do not. Among Clinton voters, 76% accept Trump and 23% do not.

Now that Donald Trump has been declared the winner and will be inaugurated in January, will you accept him as the legitimate president, or not?

	National adults %	Trump voters %	Clinton voters %
Yes, accept	84	100	76
No, do not	15	0	23

Nov. 9, 2016
Gallup

The results are from a one-night Gallup poll conducted Nov. 9, the day after the presidential election. Trump's victory spurred protests around the nation, with protesters commonly chanting "not my president." Those protesters' sentiments are shared by about one in six Americans, and one in four Clinton voters.

Gallup asked the same question about George W. Bush in December 2000, and found 83% of Americans accepting Bush as the legitimate president, essentially the same as the percentage who now accept Trump. That poll was conducted just after the Supreme Court voted 5-4 to end a contentious recount in Florida, which allowed Bush's original slim Florida vote margin to stand and effectively made him president.

Perhaps understandably, Al Gore supporters were somewhat less likely (68%) than Clinton voters today (76%) to accept the president-elect as legitimate. The overall numbers are similar, though, because Americans with no candidate preference in 2000 were more likely to accept Bush as legitimate than the comparable group this year is to accept Trump.

Like Gore, Clinton won the popular vote but lost the Electoral College. However, Trump's Electoral College tally is more decisive than Bush's and not dependent on favorable legal rulings. Still, just as many Americans say they cannot accept Trump as president as said the same about Bush. Trump's controversial statements, actions and policy proposals may cause some Americans to view him as unworthy of the office, even though his victory was beyond dispute.

Substantial Minority Say Election Process Has Done Permanent Harm

The 2016 election campaign was characterized by its negative tone. Much of the campaign and discussion in the presidential debates centered on personal attacks. Americans rated the campaign more negatively than any in recent memory. Even so, the majority, 58%, say the 2016 election process has not caused permanent harm to the U.S., although 38% say it has. Clinton voters are much more likely than Trump voters to say the campaign has caused permanent harm to the country, 60% to 17%.

Which comes closer to your view – [ROTATED: there has been permanent harm done to the United States as a result of the election process this year, (or) there has been no permanent harm done to the United States as a result of the election process this year]?

	National adults %	Trump voters %	Clinton voters %
Permanent harm	38	17	60
No permanent harm	58	82	38

Nov. 9, 2016
Gallup

Gallup asked the same question in the aftermath of the 2000 election, and found similar results, with 59% of Americans saying the election process did not cause permanent harm but 39% disagreeing and saying it did.

Although there were differences between Gore (50%) and Bush (28%) supporters in their perceptions that the process caused permanent harm, the 22-percentage-point gap was not nearly as large as the 43-point gap between Trump and Clinton voters today. The widening gap between candidate support groups since 2000 may reflect the more polarized political environment of recent years.

Implications

Trump frequently claimed the election process was rigged against him and famously would not commit to accepting the outcome of the election in the third presidential debate. Now, the often mean-spirited presidential campaign has ended – with Trump winning, Clinton conceding and both candidates calling on Americans to put aside their differences and come together as a nation.

The vast majority of Americans, 84%, say they accept Trump as president, and 58% do not believe the election process has permanently harmed the nation. Whether those figures are typical for most elections is unclear, although they are almost identical to what Gallup measured in 2000, when the outcome was in doubt until the Supreme Court sided with Bush.

While most of Clinton's supporters have followed her lead in acknowledging Trump as the legitimate president, about one in four still have not. Many Clinton voters in the same Nov. 9 poll expressed a wide array of negative emotional reactions to the outcome, including being afraid, angry and devastated. Some of those emotions have been on display in the anti-Trump protests.

Those negative emotions may take time to heal, given the unexpected nature of Trump's victory. Most pre-election polls and forecasting models pointed toward a Clinton win. Trump was the most unpopular presidential candidate in modern polling history, and a majority of Americans had a strongly unfavorable view of him during the campaign. Consequently, he faces a steep climb to win over the public. And while new presidents typically enjoy a honeymoon phase in the early months of their presidencies, Trump may begin his term with less public support than any prior president.

Survey Methods

Results for this Gallup poll are based on telephone interviews conducted Nov. 9, 2016, on the Gallup U.S. Daily survey, with a random sample of 511 adults, aged 18 and older, living in all 50 U.S. states and the District of Columbia. For results based on the total sample of national adults, the margin of sampling error is ±5 percentage points at the 95% confidence level. All reported margins of sampling error include computed design effects for weighting. Polls conducted entirely in one day, such as this one, are subject to additional error or bias not found in polls conducted over several days.

November 14, 2016

AMERICANS' WORRIES ABOUT MOST CRIMES SIMILAR TO 2015

by Justin McCarthy

Story Highlights

- *Identity theft and credit card hacking remain greatest worries*
- *Worries about terrorism up 8 points from 2015*

WASHINGTON, D.C. – Americans are about as worried as they were last year about being victims of a host of different crimes. Their fears have increased on three of the 13 crimes that Gallup asked them about in both years: being a victim of terrorism, being attacked while driving and getting mugged.

Americans' Worries About Various Crimes, 2015 vs. 2016

How often do you, yourself, worry about the following things – frequently, occasionally, rarely or never? How about?

	2015 % Frequently or occasionally worry	2016 % Frequently or occasionally worry	Change (pct. pts.)
Being a victim of terrorism	27	35	8
Being attacked while driving your car	17	23	6
Getting mugged	25	30	5
Your home being burglarized when you are not there	39	43	4
Being sexually assaulted	16	20	4
Having your car stolen or broken into	40	43	3
Being the victim of a hate crime	19	22	3
Being a victim of identity theft	69	70	1
Having a school-aged child of yours physically harmed while attending school	33	34	1
Your home being burglarized when you are there	25	26	1
Getting murdered	17	18	1

	2015 % Frequently or occasionally worry	2016 % Frequently or occasionally worry	Change (pct. pts.)
Being assaulted/killed by a coworker/employee where you work	7	8	1
Having the credit card information you have used at stores stolen by computer hackers	69	69	0
Having your email, passwords or electronic records hacked into	–	64	–

Oct. 5-9, 2016
Gallup

Worries about nearly all of these crimes have varied since Gallup first asked about them in 2000, but almost all are within three percentage points of their historical averages. One issue – fear of being the victim of a hate crime – is on the high end of its 13% to 22% range since 2000 and is up three points from last year, but this is within the margin of error.

Crimes that Gallup introduced to the list in more recent years – identity theft (70%) and credit card hacking (69%) – have not varied much, and remain atop the list of Americans' crime worries. Concerns about email and password hacking (64%), new to the list this year, also rank near the top of the list.

Worries About Being Victim of Terrorism at Highest Since 2009

More than a third of Americans (35%) say they frequently or occasionally worry about being a victim of terrorism, the highest since 2009, when the same percentage reported this level of worry. This is not as high, however, as concerns about terrorism in the first five years after 9/11, which ranged from 38% to 47% – the latter being the high reached immediately after the terrorist attacks.

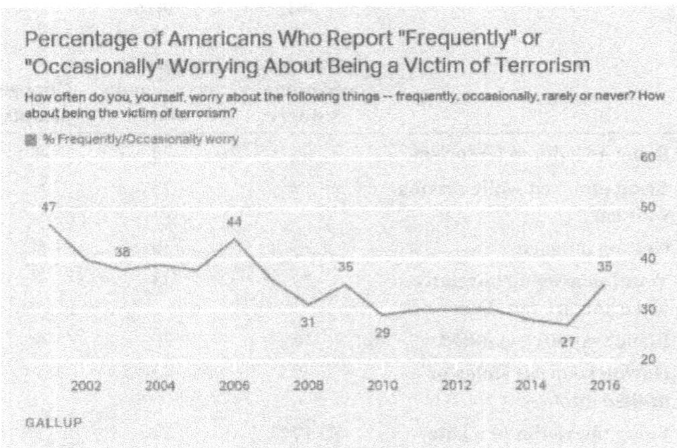

Increased concern about terrorism this year comes after a shooter in San Bernardino, California, took 14 lives last December and a shooter in Orlando, Florida, killed 49 people in June – the latter being the deadliest mass shooting in U.S. history.

Bottom Line

For the most part, Americans' worries about being the victim of a variety of crimes are at about their respective averages, and none of them have decreased since last year. Gallup reports that household crime victimization is at a new high and Americans' perceptions of crime in the U.S. remain elevated.

Americans slightly favor law and order when it comes to the priorities of the criminal justice system, and President-elect Donald Trump's emphasis on this in the 2016 campaign may have been a factor in his success at the ballot box. If, as president, he is successful in bringing a greater sense of general security for Americans, their concerns about various crimes may decrease.

Survey Methods

Results for this Gallup poll are based on telephone interviews conducted Oct. 5-9, 2016, on the Gallup U.S. Daily survey, with a random sample of 1,017 adults, aged 18 and older, living in all 50 U.S. states and the District of Columbia. For results based on the total sample of national adults, the margin of sampling error is ±4 percentage points at the 95% confidence level. All reported margins of sampling error include computed design effects for weighting.

November 14, 2016

EXPECTATIONS OF TRUMP HIGH ON ECONOMY, LOW ON RACE RELATIONS

by Gary J. Gates

Story Highlights

- *60% of Americans think Trump administration will improve the economy*
- *Just over a third think Trump will improve race relations*
- *Portion who think president-elect can avoid war is lower than in the past*

WASHINGTON, D.C. – Six in 10 Americans say President-elect Donald Trump's administration will be able to reduce unemployment and create new jobs (62%) and improve the economy (60%). On the other hand, about one in three believe he will improve race relations (35%) and improve the environment (35%), and 38% think he will keep the nation out of war.

Expectations of Donald Trump After the Election

Regardless of which presidential candidate you preferred, do you think the Trump administration will or will not be able to do each of the following?

	Yes, will %	No, will not %	No opinion %
Reduce unemployment and create new jobs	62	35	3
Improve the economy	60	37	2
Control illegal immigration	59	38	3
Keep the U.S. safe from terrorism	57	40	3
Improve education	53	45	2
Improve the healthcare system	52	46	3

	Yes, will %	No, will not %	No opinion %
Appoint good justices to the U.S. Supreme Court	52	46	3
Cut your taxes	51	46	3
Improve the way the federal government works	49	48	3
Increase respect for the United States abroad	47	51	2
Substantially reduce the federal budget deficit	46	52	2
Improve conditions for minorities and the poor	44	53	2
Reduce the crime rate	43	54	3
Heal political divisions in this country	39	57	4
Keep the nation out of war	38	57	5
Improve the quality of the environment	35	61	4
Improve race relations	35	62	3

Gallup, Nov. 10-11, 2016

In addition to Trump's stronger scores on economic issues, Gallup's Nov. 10-11 poll finds Americans generally positive about the Trump administration's ability to control illegal immigration (59%) and keep the U.S. safe from terrorism (57%).

While Americans are optimistic about Trump's prospects of improving the economy overall, they are more divided on whether he will be able to improve education (53%), cut taxes (51%) and substantially reduce the federal deficit (46%). Americans are also divided on whether the Trump administration will improve healthcare (52%), appoint good U.S. Supreme Court justices (52%) and improve the way the federal government works (49%).

In addition to Americans' skepticism about Trump's ability to improve race relations, improve the environment and avoid war, Americans seem pessimistic that he will be able to heal political divisions (39%). Slightly more Americans believe he will improve conditions for minorities and the poor (44%) and reduce the crime rate (43%).

Economic Prospects Similar to Past; Immigration Expectations Higher

After presidential elections, Americans are typically positive about the prospect of an improved economy – and this year is no different, with large majorities expressing optimism about the economy and job growth. In elections dating back to 1988, Gallup has asked Americans about their economic expectations in several different ways, sometimes right after the election and other times after an inauguration. Americans' views about the prospect of a better economy range from a low of 54% in 2012 after Barack Obama's second election to a high of 74% in 1989 after the inauguration of George H.W. Bush.

Historic Expectations for the Economy After Elections or Inaugurations

Regardless of which presidential candidate you preferred, do you think the administration will or will not be able to do each of the following?

	Yes, will %	No, will not %	No opinion %
Create a strong economic recovery	54	45	2
Barack Obama (2012)			
Create a strong economic recovery	64	34	2
Barack Obama (2008)			
Keep America prosperous	62	35	3
George W. Bush (2005)			
Keep America prosperous	63	33	4
George W. Bush (2001)			
Improve the economy	59	35	6
Bill Clinton (1992)			
Keep America prosperous	74	15	10
George H.W. Bush (1989)			

Gallup

The 59% of Americans who believe Trump will curb illegal immigration marks an issue where he gets high marks compared with Obama. In 2008, a third of Americans (35%) thought the Obama administration would do so.

The 39% who expect Trump to be able to heal political divisions is similar to the 41% recorded in 2001 after George W. Bush's election, but lower than the 54% who believed this of Obama in 2008, before his first term.

Compared With Predecessors, Expectations Low on Many Issues

Americans are more pessimistic about Trump's potential on several issues than they were in surveys conducted after the election of his predecessors. These include:

- **Improving the environment:** Americans express the least optimism about Trump's potential to improve the quality of the environment since Gallup first asked this question in 1988 after the election of George H.W. Bush.
- **Improving education:** While 53% think the Trump administration will improve education, that figure is the lowest of all of his predecessors dating back to George H.W. Bush in 1988.
- **Keeping the U.S. safe from terrorism:** Expectations for Trump's ability to keep the U.S. safe from terrorism (57%) are lower than those for his two most recent predecessors. In 2008, 62% thought Obama would keep the country safe from terrorists. And in 2005, after George W. Bush's election to a second term, the comparable figure was 68% (the terrorism question was not asked following the 2000 election).
- **Increasing respect for the U.S.:** The 47% of Americans who think that Trump will increase respect for the U.S. is low compared with expectations for Obama and George H.W. Bush. In 2008, 76% expected Obama to enhance the international reputation of the country. In 1988, 64% thought Bush would increase respect for the U.S. abroad.
- **Keeping the nation out of war:** The 38% of Americans who think the Trump administration can avoid war is sharply lower than the 70% and 60%, respectively, who thought George H.W. Bush and Bill Clinton would keep the nation out of war.

A complete summary of public expectations from past elections can be found here.

Bottom Line

U.S. elections over the past several decades have come with generally buoyant expectations for an improved economy, regardless of the party taking office. This year is no different, as a solid majority of Americans think the economy will improve under President-elect Trump as he lowers unemployment and creates new jobs.

Expectations for a Trump presidency regarding race relations, the environment and foreign policy, however, are much lower than after past elections. These are all issues for which the Hillary Clinton campaign and Trump critics raised substantial doubt regarding his competence. Perhaps as a result, Americans show historically low levels of optimism that he can improve racial tensions and have a positive impact on the environment. Of note, public opinions of Trump's prospects are even more negative than those of his Republican predecessors.

In particular, the often-repeated refrain about the danger of Trump having access to the nuclear codes represented a main argument of Clinton's campaign against her opponent. Former officials of the two Bush administrations also publicly challenged Trump's foreign policy credentials.

Few Americans think Trump can avoid war. This suggests that despite Trump's election victory, the skepticism his critics created during the campaign remains.

Survey Methods

These results are based on telephone interviews with a random sample of 1,000 U.S. adults, aged 18 and older, living in all 50 states and the District of Columbia, conducted Nov. 10-11, 2016. Each respondent rated 12 of 17 items, and each item was asked of approximately 700 adults. The margin of error for each item is ±4 percentage points at the 95% confidence level. All reported margins of sampling error include computed design effects for weighting.

November 15, 2016
OBAMA JOB APPROVAL JUMPS TO FOUR-YEAR HIGH

by Frank Newport

Story Highlights

- *President Obama's job approval rating for week ending Nov. 13 is 57%*
- *Since 2009, only other average that high was 57% in December 2012*
- *Obama's favorable rating, 62%, also higher than at any time since 2009*

PRINCETON, N.J. – President Barack Obama's job approval rating rose to 57% last week, his highest weekly average since late December 2012. Prior to 2012, Obama's weekly approval rating had not reached 57% since July 2009.

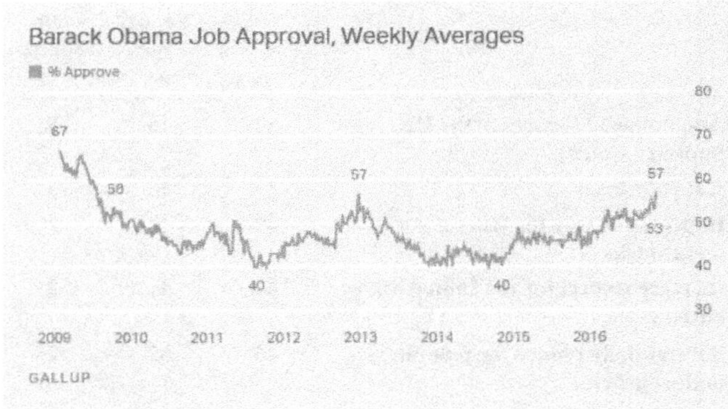

Last week's uptick in Obama's approval rating continues a broader trend in Americans' more positive evaluations of his job performance this year. Job approval for his 31st quarter in office, which ended Oct. 19, was the best quarterly average in his second term and ties as the fourth best of his presidency.

The improvement in Obama's approval rating also reflects the "post-election bounce" that lame duck presidents typically have enjoyed in November of their last year in office.

George H.W. Bush, who lost his bid for re-election in 1992, saw his approval rating rise nine percentage points after the election, the biggest such increase of the five most recent presidents. The other four presidents served two full terms and were not up for re-election, and saw post-election increases ranging from three to six points. Obama's four-point uptick this past week is within the range of what would be expected based on these previous trends.

Outgoing Presidents' Job Approval Ratings, Pre- and Post-Election

	Year	Dates of interviewing	Approval rating
Barack Obama	2016	Nov 7-13	57%
	2016	Oct 31-Nov 6	53%
	Change		+4
George W. Bush	2008	Nov 7-9	28%
	2008	Oct 31-Nov 2	25%
	Change		+3
Bill Clinton	2000	Nov 13-15	63%
	2000	Oct 25-28	57%
	Change		+6
George H.W. Bush	1992	Nov 20-22	43%
	1992	Oct 13-15	34%
	Change		+9
Ronald Reagan	1988	Nov 11-14	57%
	1988	Oct 21-24	51%
	Change		+6

Gallup

Obama's Favorable Rating, Approval on the Economy Also Up

In a Gallup Nov. 9-13 survey, 62% of Americans say they have a favorable opinion of Obama, while 37% hold an unfavorable opinion. This compares with a 54% favorable and 43% unfavorable reading when Gallup last updated this measure in August.

Gallup has measured Obama's favorable rating 47 times since he first took office, and his current 62% is his highest since July 2009. His lowest favorable rating was 42% in November 2014.

Gallup also measured the public's approval of Obama's handling of key issues in the most recent survey. Half of Americans say they approve of the way he is handling the economy, slightly higher than in August and reaching the 50% level for the first time since May 2009. Obama's job approval ratings on handling foreign affairs and healthcare policy are 47% and 41%, respectively, and are essentially unchanged from previous measurements.

Bottom Line

The increase in Obama's job approval rating this past week continues a gradual improvement seen most of the year, and reflects the typical post-election bump that most lame duck presidents enjoy toward the end of their time in the White House. It is possible that Obama's approval rating could rise further. George H.W. Bush's approval reached 56% in January 1993 just before he left office, up 23 points from October of the previous year. Ronald Reagan's rose to 63% in his last measure, recorded in December 1988, from 51% that October.

Survey Methods

Results for this Gallup poll are based on telephone interviews conducted Nov. 7-13, 2016, on the Gallup U.S. Daily survey, with a random sample of 3,561 adults, aged 18 and older, living in all 50 U.S. states and the District of Columbia. For results based on this total sample of national adults, the margin of sampling error is ±2 percentage points at the 95% confidence level. Results are also based on telephone interviews conducted Nov. 9-13, 2016, with a random sample of 1,019 adults. For this sample, the margin of sampling error is ±4 percentage points at the 95% confidence level. All reported margins of sampling error include computed design effects for weighting.

November 16, 2016
AMERICANS' SATISFACTION WITH U.S. MAKES A U-TURN

by Jim Norman

Story Highlights

- *Satisfaction dropped from 37% to 27% just after election*
- *Rate dropped back below historical average of 37%*
- *Among Democrats, rate fell almost 30 percentage points after election*

WASHINGTON, D.C. – Americans' satisfaction with the way things are going in the U.S. plunged 10 percentage points in the aftermath of the presidential election – retreating from a decade high of 37% in the run-up to last Tuesday's vote. The 27% of Americans who are satisfied matches the 2016 average so far but is 10 points below the historical average for the more than 300 times Gallup has asked the question since 1979.

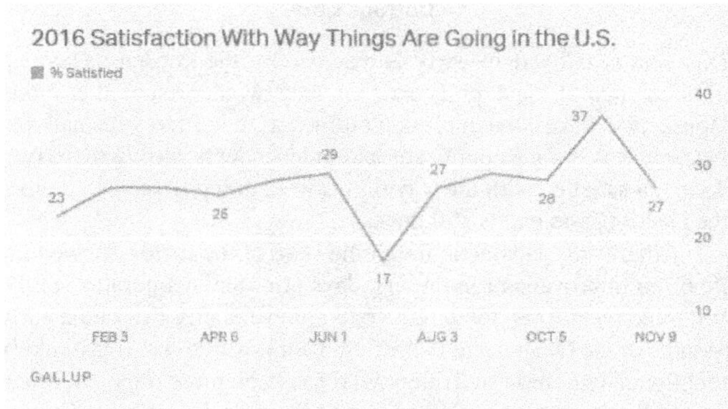

A sharp decline in satisfaction among Democrats explains most of the drop. Before the election, 62% of Democrats were satisfied; now, 34% are. Widespread forecasts that Democratic nominee Hillary Clinton would win gave Democrats' outlook a boost in the week before the election. The increase among Democrats from 49% in October to 62% in the days leading up to the election was more than erased after Clinton lost.

Republicans' attitudes were much less volatile over the past two months. The satisfaction rate rose slightly from 8% in October to 14% just before the election, and then climbed a few more points to 17% after Republican Donald Trump's victory.

Satisfaction Rates Before and After 2016 Presidential Election

	All adults %	Republicans %	Independents %	Democrats %
Oct 5-9	8	24	49	8
Nov 1-6	14	34	62	14
Nov 9-13	17	27	34	17

Gallup

Though the percentage of Republicans saying they are satisfied with the way things are going rose only three points after the election, the 17% is still the highest satisfaction rate among Republicans since President Barack Obama first took office in January 2009. Democrats' current satisfaction level is slightly below their 39% average for Obama's time in office and 10 points below their 44% average for 2016.

Satisfaction levels followed a similar pattern after the White House changed parties in 2008. In the days following that election, satisfaction dropped more among Republicans (26% to 19%) than it rose among Democrats (4% to 7%). The real increase among Democrats came right after Obama's inauguration in January (rising to 22%) and in the first months of his presidency, reaching 50% in May.

Obama Years Marked by Low Satisfaction Rates

Obama, who was elected as the U.S. reeled from a series of economic shocks, has seen an increase in the average satisfaction rate, from 15% in the year before he took office to 27% this year. Over the nearly eight years of his presidency, the satisfaction rate has averaged 24%, the lowest average for any president's term of office since Ronald Reagan was inaugurated in 1980.

Bottom Line

Democrats, buoyed in early November by the consensus among political pundits and pollsters that they would retain the White House, now have a much bleaker outlook as they survey the national landscape. Among Republicans and independents, strong majorities were not satisfied with the way things were going in the U.S. before the election, and that is still the case.

Americans' satisfaction with the state of the nation showed little or no improvement in the first days after the inauguration of the last three presidents, though the rate did eventually rise in the early months of the Obama and Bill Clinton administrations. It is unlikely that the inauguration of Trump, who has been more unpopular than any of the past three presidents when they ran for office, will produce an immediate major increase in the number of Americans who are satisfied with the way things are going. However, if the majority of Americans are right in their belief that Trump will cut unemployment and improve the economy, his presidency could be marked by a major change in the satisfaction rate.

Survey Methodology

Results for this Gallup poll are based on telephone interviews conducted Nov. 9-13, 2016, with a random sample of 1,019 adults, aged 18 and older, living in all 50 U.S. states and the District of Columbia. For results based on the total sample of national adults, the margin of sampling error is ±4 percentage points at the 95% confidence level. All reported margins of sampling error include computed design effects for weighting.

November 17, 2016

TRUMP FAVORABILITY UP, BUT TRAILS OTHER PRESIDENTS-ELECT

by Jeffrey M. Jones

Story Highlights

- *42% now view Trump favorably, up from 34% before election*
- *Highest rating for Trump since 2011*
- *Other recent president-elect favorable ratings were 58% or higher*

PRINCETON, N.J. – Donald Trump's favorable rating has improved from 34% to 42% after his election as president. While a majority in the U.S. still have an unfavorable view of him, his image is the best it has been since March 2011 when 43% viewed him positively.

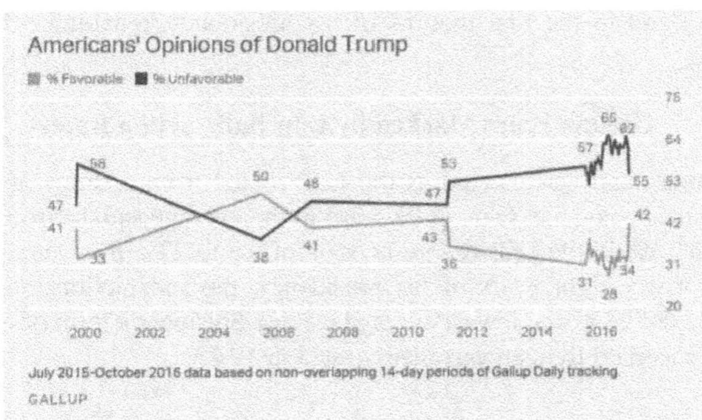

Gallup measured opinions of Trump infrequently from 1999 through 2015, and then on a continuous basis from June 2015 through the election. Americans have consistently viewed Trump more negatively than positively. The sole exception in Gallup's trend came in 2005, when Trump's reality show *The Apprentice* was among the most popular TV programs. At that time, 50% of Americans had a favorable opinion of Trump and 38% an unfavorable one.

Trump's favorability ratings have increased among all political party groups since the election. Republicans have shown the greatest increase – 11 percentage points – to 82%. Thirty-nine percent of independents, up from 32%, and 10% of Democrats, up from 5%, view Trump positively.

Changes in Favorable Ratings of Donald Trump, Before and After the 2016 Presidential Election

	Nov 1-6, 2016 %	Nov 9-13, 2016 %	Change (pct. pts.)
National adults	34	42	+8
Republicans	71	82	+11
Independents	32	39	+7
Democrats	5	10	+5

Gallup

Other Presidents-Elect Viewed Much More Positively

Gallup has asked Americans to rate political figures using the current favorable/unfavorable format since 1992. The last three presidents-elect had much higher favorable ratings at comparable time periods than Trump currently does. Then President-elect Barack Obama had the highest favorable rating, 68%, in November 2008. Fifty-nine percent of Americans viewed George W. Bush positively just after the Supreme Court effectively decided the 2000 election in his favor in December of that year. Bill Clinton's favorable ratings were also just shy of 60% after he won the 1992 election.

Favorable Ratings of Recent Presidents-Elect

	Date	Favorable %	Unfavorable %
Donald Trump	2016 Nov 9-13	42	55
Barack Obama	2008 Nov 7-9	68	27
George W. Bush	2000 Dec 15-17	59	36
Bill Clinton	1992 Nov 10-11	58	35

Gallup

Trump's ratings lag behind those of other presidents-elect in large part because Democrats' views of him are much worse than the opposition party's supporters' ratings have been in the past. Whereas 10% of Democrats view Trump favorably, 25% of Republicans had a positive opinion of Clinton, 31% of Democrats had a positive opinion of Bush and 35% of Republicans viewed Obama favorably.

Trump's favorable rating among independents, 39%, is also significantly worse than those of his predecessors. It is 15 points lower than Clinton's rating among independents and 31 points worse than Obama's.

And Trump's 82% favorability among his party's supporters also is lower than that for prior presidents-elect, which range from 88% for Clinton to 95% for Obama.

Favorable Ratings of Presidents-Elect, by Political Party

	Date	Republicans %	Independents %	Democrats %
Donald Trump	2006 Nov 9-13	82	39	10
Barack Obama	2008 Nov 7-9	35	70	95
George W. Bush	2000 Dec 15-17	93	59	31
Bill Clinton	1992 Nov 10-11	25	54	88

Gallup

Implications

Trump, like his predecessors, will have to govern a nation that is divided politically. But Trump's challenge may be even greater, because the nation is arguably more divided than when his predecessors took office, perhaps as evidenced by several days of protests nationwide after his election. Trump also has far less public goodwill than Obama, Bush and Clinton did after they were elected. He won the election despite a historically low favorability rating and is the first candidate to win with a lower favorable rating than his opponent.

However, Trump's favorability is improving. His inauguration may provide an additional boost in popularity, and all prior presidents have enjoyed a "honeymoon period" in the initial months of their presidency. But with so much ground to make up in public support, and a difficult presidential transition for a political newcomer to navigate, Trump may very well start his term with the lowest job approval ratings for any president.

Survey Methods

Results for this Gallup poll are based on telephone interviews conducted Nov. 9-13, 2016, with a random sample of 1,019 adults, aged 18 and older, living in all 50 U.S. states and the District of Columbia. For results based on the total sample of national adults, the margin of sampling error is ±4 percentage points at the 95% confidence level. All reported margins of sampling error include computed design effects for weighting.

November 17, 2016

ECONOMY, ELECTIONS TOP PROBLEMS FACING U.S.

by Gary J. Gates

Story Highlights

- *Race relations, healthcare, unemployment also mentioned*
- *Concerns about elections highest Gallup has recorded*
- *Unifying country, lack of respect for others also at new highs*

WASHINGTON, D.C. – The economy and elections top the list of the nation's most important problems in Gallup's first post-election update of this question. Fourteen percent of Americans identify the economy as the most important problem, and 11% name elections or election reform. Prior to this year, "elections" has never been this high on the list. Nearly as many mention race relations or racism (10%), healthcare (10%) and unemployment or jobs (9%).

Most Important Problems Facing the Nation

What do you think is the most important problem facing this country today?

	Oct 5-9 %	Nov 9-13 %
Economy in general	17	14
Elections/Election reform	7	11
Race relations/Racism	10	10
Healthcare	4	10
Unemployment/Jobs	6	9
Dissatisfaction with government/Poor leadership	12	8
Unifying the country	2	6
Immigration/Illegal aliens	7	5
Lack of respect for each other	2	5
Federal budget deficit/Federal debt	4	3
Ethics/Moral/Religious/Family decline	3	3
Environment/Pollution	3	3
National security	7	3
Gap between rich and poor	2	2
Foreign policy/Foreign aid/Focus overseas	2	2
Poverty/Hunger/Homelessness	2	2
Terrorism	5	2
Judicial system/Courts/Laws	1	2
	Oct 5-9 %	**Nov 9-13** %
Education	2	2
Lack of money	1	1
Taxes	1	1
High cost of living/Inflation	*	1
Wage issues	*	1
Crime/Violence	3	1
Welfare	1	1
Abortion	*	1
Drugs	*	1
Energy/Lack of energy sources	*	1
Lack of military defense	1	1
Situation in Iraq/ISIS	1	1

* = Less than 0.5%
Gallup

Overall, 31% of the public mention issues related to the economy as the nation's most important problem. Besides the economy in general and unemployment, these economic problems include the federal debt (3%) and the gap between the rich and the poor (2%). The percentage of total economic mentions is unchanged from October's reading, despite sharp increases in economic confidence since the election.

While the economy ranking at the top of the list is not new, the 11% of Americans mentioning elections as the country's top problem is the largest percentage to say so since Gallup started tracking this question monthly in 2001. The plurality of Americans voted for a candidate (Hillary Clinton) who will not become president. Dissatisfaction with the election results largely explains the increase – from 7% in October to 11% in November – in the percentage mentioning elections and election reform as the top problem in the U.S. The vast majority of the mentions in this category refer to Donald Trump's election, in particular, as the nation's top problem.

Also likely reflecting the election results and the ensuing nationwide protests, new highs say "unifying the country" (6%) and "a lack of respect for each other" (5%) are the most important problems facing the nation. The percentage of Americans concerned about race relations (10%) is unchanged from October and remains on the higher end of what Gallup has measured since 2001. It was lower, ranging from 5% to 7%, in the first half of 2016.

Americans' mentions of healthcare as the nation's most important problem have more than doubled since the election, rising to 10% from 4% in October. Since April, no more than 5% of Americans had cited this as the country's most important problem. The spike in November could reflect uncertainty associated with Trump's campaign promise to repeal and replace the Affordable Care Act, known as Obamacare.

Dissatisfaction with government has declined since October, from 12% to 8%. Of note, President Barack Obama's job approval rating is currently at a four-year high. Americans' frustrations with politics may center more on the election than the incumbent government.

Bottom Line

Domestic policy issues such as the economy, elections, race relations, healthcare and unemployment dominate the problems that Americans say are the most important facing the country. Recent Gallup polling shows Americans have relatively high expectations that the president-elect can effectively address some of these major concerns. Substantial majorities (upward of 60%) believe the Trump administration will improve the economy and create jobs. A slim majority (52%) say he'll improve the healthcare system.

But Americans are more skeptical of Trump's ability to improve race relations, perhaps reflecting some of the divisive comments he made during the campaign. Slightly more than one-third (35%) think he will be successful in dealing with that issue.

Foreign policy issues rank relatively low among the nation's most important problems. Just 3% cite national security and 2% cite foreign policy as big concerns, and another 2% mention terrorism. Expectations for the Trump administration on these issues are mixed – 57% say Trump will keep the U.S. safe from terrorism, while 38% say he will keep the nation out of war.

If the president-elect were to use these data as a guide, the results suggest that his top priorities should be the economy and jobs, unifying the country after a close election, race relations, healthcare, and providing strong leadership.

Survey Methods

These results are based on telephone interviews with a random sample of 1,019 adults aged 18 and older, living in all 50 states and the District of Columbia, conducted Nov. 9-13, 2016. The margin of error for each item is ±4 percentage points at the 95% confidence level. All reported margins of sampling error include computed design effects for weighting.

November 18, 2016

PAUL RYAN'S FAVORABLE RATING EDGES UP TO NEW HIGH

by Justin McCarthy

Story Highlights

- *Nearly half of Americans (48%) have favorable view of Ryan*
- *About one in five (18%) still unfamiliar with the House speaker*
- *Ryan edges out Mike Pence, Donald Trump and Melania Trump in favorability*

WASHINGTON, D.C. – After navigating a shaky political tightrope throughout 2016, House Speaker Paul Ryan has reached his highest favorable rating to date. Nearly half of Americans (48%) hold a positive view of Ryan, up slightly from 44% in July and August before the election.

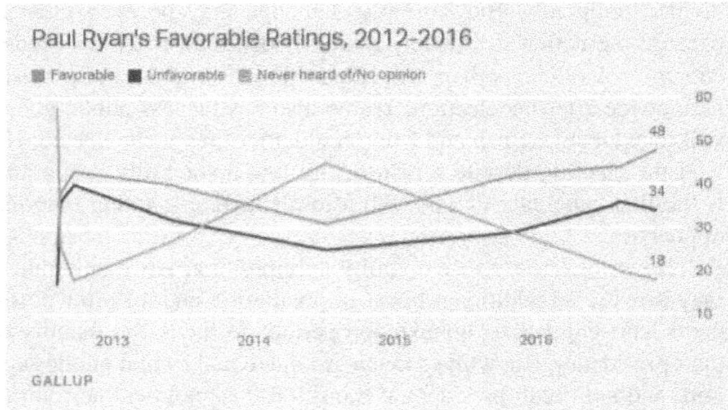

The latest favorable rating for the speaker is from a Nov. 9-13 Gallup poll. Thirty-four percent of U.S. adults view him unfavorably, essentially unchanged from 36% in August. About one in five have never heard of Ryan or have no opinion of him.

Ryan was recently re-elected as speaker of the House after a politically challenging year. He was first elected to the leadership position late last year, with many seeing him as a leader who could unite the divided Republican conference. But Ryan's election came amid a contentious GOP presidential primary season that put pressure on him to endorse Donald Trump, the controversial eventual nominee. Ryan denounced many of Trump's inflammatory comments, leading Trump to threaten not to endorse the speaker during his primary race in his Wisconsin home district. Despite their complicated relationship, the two GOP leaders maintained their endorsements of one another and must now work together in a GOP-controlled government.

When he became Mitt Romney's running mate in August 2012, Ryan was an unfamiliar face to more than half of Americans (58%) and registered his lowest favorable rating of 25%. His rating improved to 43% before the unsuccessful campaign's end.

Americans became less familiar with Ryan as he returned to his role as a U.S. congressman after the election. As a result, his favorable ratings ebbed to 31% by 2014. But Ryan's election to speaker of the House in 2015 boosted both Americans' familiarity with and favorability of him. He became better known as the highest-ranking elected Republican during the contentious 2016 presidential campaign; his favorable ratings rose to 44%, while his unfavorable ratings held steady, ranging from 34% to 36% since July. The speaker now emerges from the 2016 election with his most positive image to date.

Ryan Stacks Up Well Against Other Republican Party Figures

The speaker's ratings narrowly edge out not only those of Trump (42%), but also those of Vice President-elect Mike Pence (46%) and incoming first lady Melania Trump (43%).

Favorable Ratings of Republican Political Figures

	Favorable %	Unfavorable %	Never heard of/ No opinion %
Paul Ryan	48	34	18
Mike Pence	46	33	21
Melania Trump	43	39	18
Donald Trump	42	55	4

GALLUP, Nov 9-13, 2016

Like Ryan, Pence and Melania Trump have much lower *unfavorable* ratings than the president-elect, largely because about one in five U.S. adults are unfamiliar with each of them. All three have seen their images improve since August.

Pence has seen the biggest improvement in both favorability and familiarity in that time. His favorable rating has increased by 10 percentage points, while the percentage unfamiliar with the vice president-elect dropped by nearly half, from 39% to 21%. Meanwhile, Melania Trump's favorable rating has improved modestly from 38% in August. Her image is now slightly more positive than negative, whereas before it tilted negative.

Bottom Line

Considering all that could have gone wrong for Ryan in recent months, the speaker's image is stronger than at any point in Gallup's trend. He faced a primary challenge from his home district in Wisconsin; his House GOP majority was thought to be imperiled; and, more recently, his chances of re-election as speaker were in question. But Ryan endured it all.

His next challenge will be moving past a rocky relationship to work with Trump. Despite their recent history, the two appear to be supporting each other in key ways now that the election is over.

Trump could stand to buoy his poor favorable ratings by embracing Ryan, who has emerged from the election in perhaps the best standing among Trump's allies. This puts Ryan in a strong position as a key leader in a newly Republican-controlled government.

Survey Methods

Results for this Gallup poll are based on telephone interviews conducted Nov. 9-13, 2016, with a random sample of 1,019 adults, aged 18 and older, living in all 50 U.S. states and the District of Columbia. For results based on the total sample of national adults, the margin of sampling error is ±4 percentage points at the 95% confidence level.

November 18, 2016
IMAGE OF DEMOCRATIC PARTY REMAINS MORE POSITIVE THAN GOP

by Michael Smith

Story Highlights

- *Democratic Party viewed more favorably (45%) than Republican Party (40%)*
- *Current favorable rating is Democratic Party's highest since 2013*
- *First time since 2014 that GOP has cracked 40% favorability*

WASHINGTON, D.C. – Americans continue to view the Democratic Party more favorably than the Republican Party, with little evident change after the election that saw the GOP win the White House and keep control of both houses of Congress. In a Gallup survey conducted Nov. 9-13, 45% of Americans view the Democratic Party favorably, compared with 40% for the Republican Party.

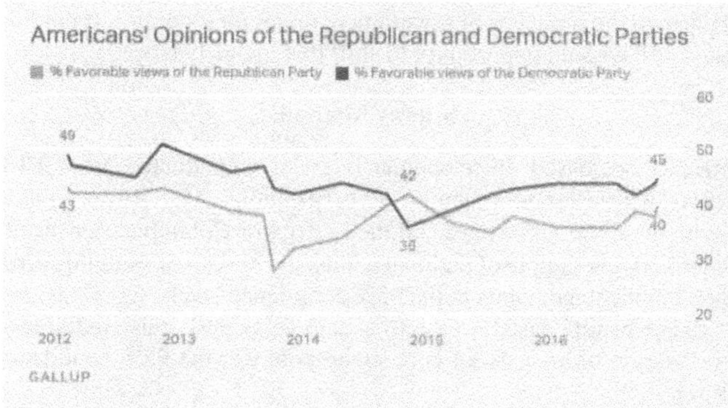

Americans have viewed the Democratic Party more favorably than the Republican Party for most of the past four years of the Barack Obama administration, except at one point immediately after the 2014 midterm elections.

This year's election did not drastically change how Americans view the country's two major political parties, which is normal after presidential elections, with a few exceptions. In 2012, favorable views of the Democratic Party edged up from 45% to 51% after the election. In 2008, the Republican Party's favorable image dropped from 40% before to 34% after the election. Party images were essentially stable after the 2004 election.

Approval Ratings Lower Than in Past

The Democratic Party's favorable rating has been lower in recent years than the average before 2010. The Republican Party's favorable rating has clearly been lower in recent years than it was during the beginning of the George W. Bush administration. Democrats enjoyed their highest favorability advantages over the Republican Party between 1996 and 1999, and again between 2005 and 2009. As noted, they have enjoyed a more positive image in most years since 2011. Republicans have never had a more positive image than Democrats for any consistent period over the past quarter century.

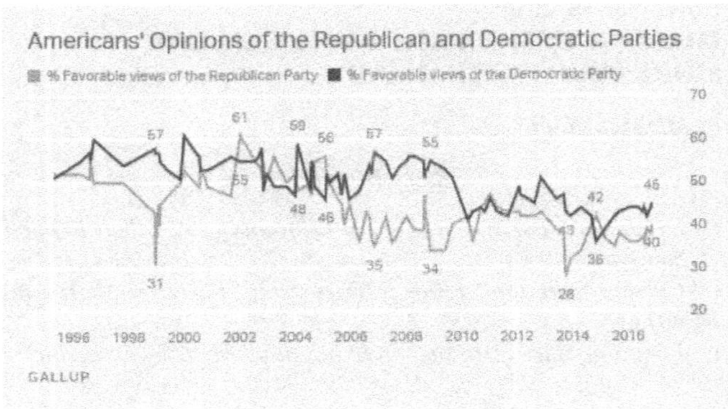

Bottom Line

The Nov. 8 election does not appear to have changed Americans' modestly more positive views of the Democratic Party, at least in the short term. Beginning in January, Republicans will add the White House to the branches of government under their control, providing the GOP with an opportunity to shift this image balance.

Survey Methods

Results are based on telephone interviews conducted Nov. 9-13, 2016, with a random sample of 1,019 adults, aged 18 and older, living in all 50 U.S. states and the District of Columbia. For results based on this sample of national adults, the margin of sampling error is ±4 percentage points at the 95% confidence level.

For results based on the total sample of 940 registered voters, the margin of error is ±4 percentage points at the 95% confidence level.

November 21, 2016

VIEWS OF QUALITY JOB MARKET SYNC WITH U.S. UNEMPLOYMENT RATE

by Frank Newport

Story Highlights

- *43% say now is a good time to find a quality job*
- *This is roughly the same as Gallup has measured since early 2015*
- *Views of the job market are highly related to U.S. unemployment rate*

PRINCETON, N.J. – Forty-three percent of Americans currently say now is a good time to find a quality job. This percentage, from a Gallup poll conducted right after the election, is essentially the same as the 42% recorded in October and about average for the measure since early 2015.

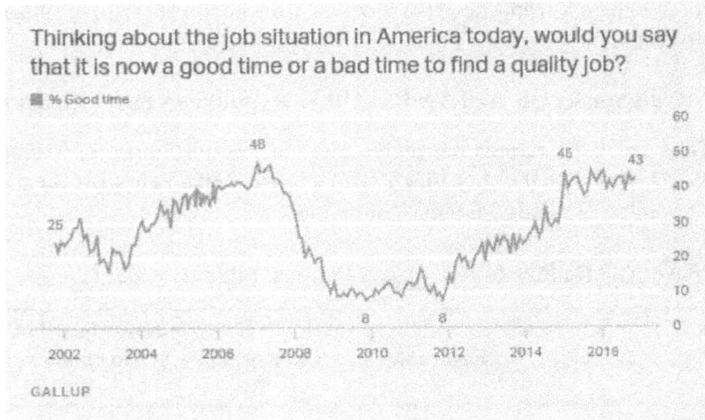

Americans' views of the job market have gone through several phases since Gallup began measuring them each month in October 2001, when roughly a quarter saw positive job market conditions. Attitudes about jobs improved from 2004 through early 2007, including the 15-year high of 48% in January 2007. Then, with the start of the 2007-2009 recession, perceptions of the job market fell dramatically, bottoming out at 8% in November 2009 and remaining low through much of 2011. Views improved from 2012 through the beginning of 2015 and have been fairly stable since, in the low- to mid-40% range.

Just as Americans' impressions of the job market are the same this month compared with October, there was no short-term change in views when Barack Obama was elected for the first time in November 2008.

Americans' Views of Job Market Closely Mirror BLS Unemployment Rate

Gallup's measure of Americans' subjective views about the job market is designed to augment the objective economic data from government and other sources. But the reality is that Americans' perceptions track closely with the unemployment rate that the U.S. government publishes each month. Views that it is a good time to find a quality job rise when the unemployment rate falls, are generally stable when the rate is stable and drop when the rate goes up.

The accompanying chart displays trends on both Gallup's quality job measure and the monthly Bureau of Labor Statistics (BLS) unemployment rate. Because the two measures are on different scales, each has been indexed to its average over the October 2001 to October 2016 period, with 1.0 representing the average for each.

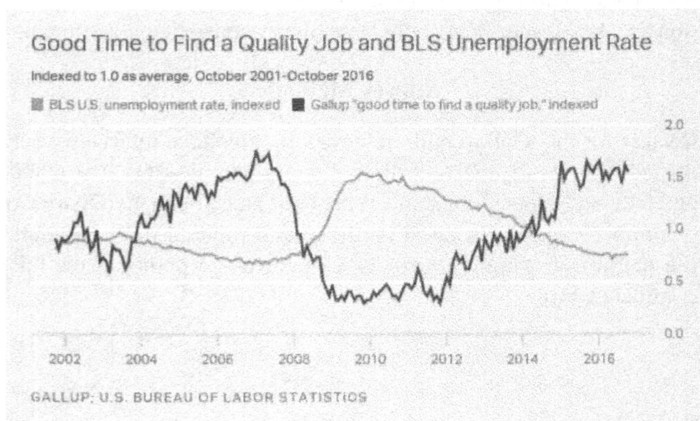

The overall correlation between the monthly BLS unemployment rate and Americans' belief that it is a good time to find a quality job is -.88.

The strong relationship between these measures suggests Americans may be aware of the official, widely reported employment rate when it comes out each month, and may consider that rate when asked to assess the job market. Broader reporting about the economy's health, such as GDP growth, may influence the public's views as well. Americans may also more directly assess the jobs-related reality they see around them daily, the same reality that is reflected when the government assesses employment trends each month.

Whatever the underlying reasons, the key takeaway is that Americans' collective views of the job market appear to be mostly grounded in employment reality – at least as measured by the government.

Bottom Line

President-elect Donald Trump maintained during his campaign that Americans were experiencing economic malaise, including increased worry about the availability of good jobs. The percentage of Americans who say it is a good time to find a quality job (43%) is not high on an absolute basis but is generally in sync with what one would expect based on the patterns over the past 15 years – given an unemployment rate hovering near 5%. Americans do not appear to be in an unusual funk, but rather reflect the objective reality in the same way they have since 2001.

If the unemployment rate drops in the months ahead, history shows that the percentage saying it is a good time to find a quality job could rise closer to 50%. The most positive view of the job market Gallup has measured was 48% in early 2007, when the unemployment rate was hovering in the mid-4% range.

Survey Methods

Results for this Gallup poll are based on telephone interviews conducted Nov. 9-13, 2016, with a random sample of 1,019 adults, aged 18 and older, living in all 50 U.S. states and the District of Columbia. For results based on the total sample of national adults, the margin of sampling error is ±4 percentage points at the 95% confidence level. All reported margins of sampling error include computed design effects for weighting.

November 21, 2016

RECORD-HIGH 77% OF AMERICANS PERCEIVE NATION AS DIVIDED

by Jeffrey M. Jones

Story Highlights

- *Previous high was 69% in 2012*
- *21% say nation is united and in agreement on values*
- *Public split on whether Trump will do more to unite or divide nation*

PRINCETON, N.J. – Seventy-seven percent of Americans, a new high, believe the nation is divided on the most important values, while 21% believe it is united and in agreement. Over the past 20+ years, the public has tended to perceive the nation as being more divided than united, apart from two surveys conducted shortly after the 9/11 terrorist attacks.

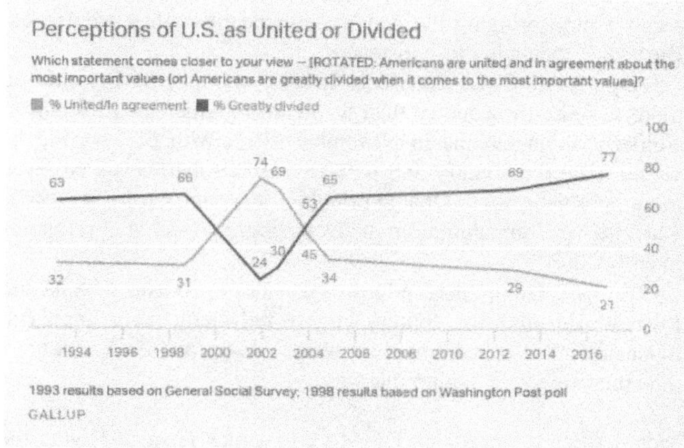

The latest poll was conducted Nov. 9-13 after a contentious presidential campaign involving the two of the least popular candidates in postwar U.S. history, and as protests erupted nationwide in response to Donald Trump's victory.

All major subgroups of Americans share the view that the nation is divided, though Republicans (68%) are less likely to believe this than independents (78%) and Democrats (83%). That is consistent with the findings in the past two polls, conducted after the 2004 and 2012 presidential elections, in which the winning party's supporters were less likely to perceive the nation as divided.

Perceptions That Americans Are Greatly Divided on the Most Important Values, by Political Party

	Republicans %	Independents %	Democrats %
2016 Nov 9-13	68	78	83
2012 Nov 9-12	80	67	63
2004 Nov 19-21	59	70	70

Gallup

Public Not Convinced Trump Will Unite the Country

Americans are split about evenly on whether Trump will do more to unite the country (45%) or do more to divide it (49%). These views largely follow party lines, with 88% of Republicans believing Trump will do more to unite the country and 81% of Democrats saying he will do more to divide it. Independents predict Trump will do more to divide (51%) than to unite the country (43%).

In the next four years, do you think Donald Trump will do more to – [ROTATED: unite the country (or more to) divide the country]?

	More to unite %	More to divide %
U.S. adults	45	49
Republicans	88	10
Independents	43	51
Democrats	12	81

Gallup

Gallup has asked this question on a few prior occasions, including in November 2004 after George W. Bush was re-elected, in February 2008 during the presidential primaries, and in November 2012 after Barack Obama was re-elected. Americans are less optimistic about Trump bringing the country together than they were about Bush and Obama in those instances.

By 57% to 39%, Americans in 2004 thought Bush would do more to unite the country than to divide it. Americans responded similarly about Obama in November 2012, with 55% saying he would unite the country and 42% divide it. Americans were even more optimistic about Obama bringing the country together (66%) when he was campaigning in the Democratic presidential primaries in early 2008.

As with Trump, perceptions of whether Presidents Obama and Bush would unite the country largely fell along party lines. But independents were more inclined to see Obama and Bush as uniters than they are to see Trump this way.

Would Elected Presidents Do More to Unite Than to Divide the Country, Previous Elections, by Political Party

	More to unite	More to divide
	%	%
Barack Obama (2012)		
U.S. adults	55	42
Republicans	12	86
Independents	52	42
Democrats	92	6
George W. Bush (2004)		
U.S. adults	57	39
Republicans	94	4
Independents	58	37
Democrats	21	76

Gallup

Implications

Trump prepares to take office as a record number of Americans perceive the nation as divided and less than half believe his actions will help unite the country. Those perceptions may reflect his blunt speaking manner and sometimes divisive campaign rhetoric, though he did call for Americans to come together in his victory speech.

Obama and Bush made unifying the country key goals of their campaigns and administrations, and Americans perceived each as likely to do more to bring the country together than drive it apart. But each wound up having job approval ratings among the most politically polarized in Gallup's history. That polarization may have resulted from the realities of partisan politics in Washington and the difficulty of bringing together a governing coalition that crosses party lines. It may also have resulted from the rise of new media as a forum for opinion leaders on the right and left to express their views and for Americans to seek out news coverage and commentary that fits their political predispositions.

Trump's ability to unite the country is also handicapped by the limited goodwill he has from the opposition party. About one in 10 Democrats have a positive opinion of Trump, far less than the three in 10 Democrats who viewed Bush positively in 2000 and the roughly one in three Republicans rating Obama positively in 2008.

Survey Methods

Results for this Gallup poll are based on telephone interviews conducted Nov. 9-13, 2016, with a random sample of 1,019 adults, aged 18 and older, living in all 50 U.S. states and the District of Columbia. For results based on the total sample of national adults, the margin of sampling error is ±4 percentage points at the 95% confidence level. All reported margins of sampling error include computed design effects for weighting.

November 22, 2016

U.S. ECONOMIC CONFIDENCE REMAINS POSITIVE AFTER ELECTION

by Justin McCarthy

Story Highlights

- *Americans maintain slightly positive views of economy after the election*
- *Index at +4, rivals the January 2015 post-recession high*
- *Both current conditions, economic outlook components are positive*

WASHINGTON, D.C. – Gallup's U.S. Economic Confidence Index was +4 for the week ending Nov. 20, the first full week of interviewing after the Nov. 8 presidential election. This is the first positive weekly reading in more than a year and a half.

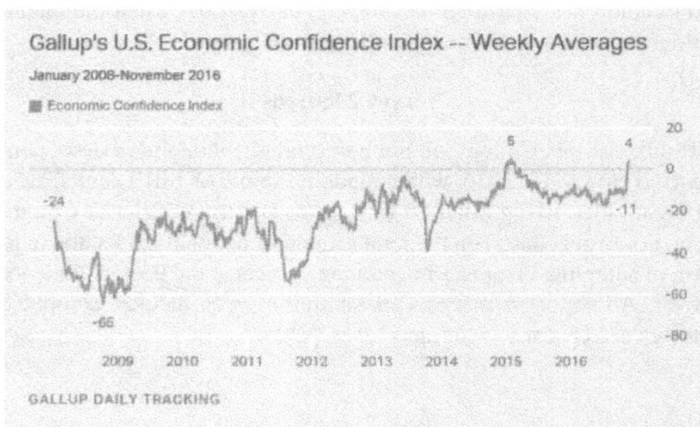

Last week, Gallup reported an improvement in Americans' views of the economy in the first few days after the presidential election. This moved the weekly average from -11 in the last full week before the election to 0 for the week of Nov. 7-13, which included both pre-election and post-election interviewing.

Gallup's U.S. Economic Confidence Index is the average of two components: how Americans rate current economic conditions and whether they feel the economy is improving or getting worse. The index has a theoretical maximum of +100 if all Americans were to say the economy is doing well and improving, and a theoretical minimum of -100 if all Americans were to say the economy is doing poorly and getting worse. If Americans are equally balanced in their positive and negative views on both measures, the score would be 0, as it was the week ending Nov. 13.

The index has registered a handful of positive weekly averages over Gallup's U.S. Daily tracking trend beginning in 2008. All of these occurred during a three-month stretch from late December 2014 to mid-March 2015 after a sustained period of declining gas prices. The latest figure rivals the record-high weekly average of +5 recorded in late January 2015.

In the year leading up to the election, Americans were consistently negative about the economy, with weekly index scores ranging from -7 to -17.

Since Donald Trump's victory in the presidential election, Republicans have become substantially more positive about the economy – particularly about its direction – while Democrats' former optimism has collapsed.

Both Current Conditions, Economic Outlook Components in Positive Territory

Twenty-nine percent of Americans rated the economy as "excellent" or "good" last week, while 23% said it was "poor," resulting in a current conditions index of +6. That is up from a score of 0 the week before the election and one point shy of the high of +7 recorded in January 2008.

The economic outlook component experienced an even greater improvement. For the week ending Nov. 20, this component edged into positive territory at +1, compared with -5 one week earlier and -21 the week before the election. The latest score is the result of 47% of Americans saying economic conditions in the country are "getting better" and 46% saying they are "getting worse."

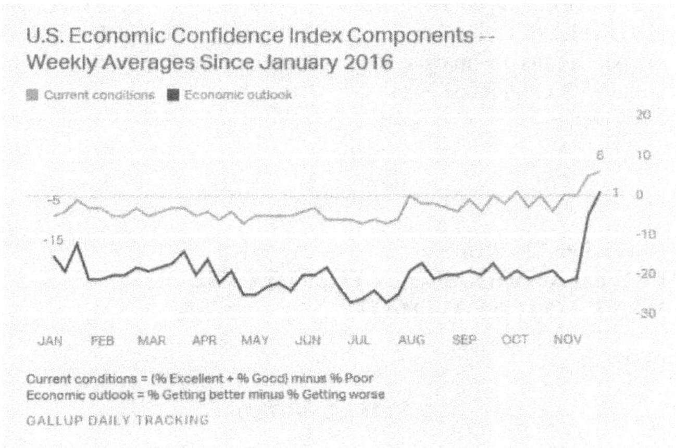

Bottom Line

Americans' confidence in the economy is now higher than it has been for most of Gallup's tracking trend over the past nine years.

The heightened confidence places Trump on much better footing than what his predecessor Barack Obama started his first term with, but it could also set a high bar for the incoming president's performance. If Trump rises to the challenge of further improving the U.S. economy, the index could reach heights it hasn't touched in nearly a decade. But the high hopes could also lead to disappointment if Americans feel Trump hasn't kept his promises of economic progress, which could cause the economic outlook component to retreat into negative territory.

Historical data are available in Gallup Analytics.

Survey Methods

Results for this Gallup poll are based on telephone interviews conducted Nov. 14-20, 2016, on the Gallup U.S. Daily survey, with a random sample of 3,546 adults, aged 18 and older, living in all 50 U.S. states and the District of Columbia. For results based on the total sample of national adults, the margin of sampling error is ±2 percentage points at the 95% confidence level. All reported margins of sampling error include computed design effects for weighting.

November 23, 2016

RECORD ONE IN FIVE IN BAD MOOD ON DAY AFTER ELECTION

by Alyssa Davis

Story Highlights

- *Election Day and day after were among most stressful days since 2008*
- *Bad mood percentage spiked more on 2016 Election Day than prior two*
- *Recovery in Americans' mood consistent with prior elections*

WASHINGTON, D.C. – Election Day 2016 and the day after were two of the most stressful days on record since Gallup and Healthways began tracking Americans' mood in January 2008. On Nov. 8, 19% of U.S. adults were classified as being in a bad mood – experiencing a lot of stress or worry without a lot of happiness and enjoyment. That metric rose to 20% on Nov. 9. Before Election Day 2016, the metric had reached 19% or higher only three times in nearly nine years. The 2016 Election Day and day after figures are much higher than the daily average of 11%.

Days With Highest Percentage of U.S. Adults in Bad Mood Since January 2008

Bad mood calculated as percentage who report a lot of stress or worry without a lot of happiness and enjoyment

	Bad mood %
Nov 9, 2016	20
Feb 11, 2014	20
Jun 3, 2013	20
Nov 8, 2016	19
Feb 20, 2013	19

Gallup-Healthways Well-Being Index

These results are based on interviews with approximately 500 U.S. adults each day since 2013 and 1,000 adults from 2008 to 2012 as part of the Gallup-Healthways Well-Being Index. Interviewers read respondents a series of emotions and ask them to say whether they experienced each one "during a lot of the day yesterday." The "bad mood" metric is defined as the percentage of U.S. adults who, reflecting on the day before they were interviewed, say they experienced a lot of stress or worry and did not experience a lot of happiness and enjoyment.

Previous Gallup research shows that increases in self-reported daily stress or worry and declines in happiness and enjoyment coincide with negative events such as the Sandy Hook school massacre, economic turmoil, natural disasters and tax day. Americans' mood is also more negative during the workweek than on the weekend.

Bad Mood Increases More on Election Day 2016 Than in Previous Election Years

Being a high-stakes, high-drama event, Election Day typically fosters a relatively high level of stress and worry in the population. The percentage of U.S. adults in a bad mood increased on the day of the election in 2008 and 2012 – as well as 2016 – compared to the average for the seven days prior.

However, the jump in bad mood on Election Day in 2016 is larger than the increase seen in the previous two elections. Americans' bad mood on Election Day 2016 was nine percentage points higher than the average of the seven previous days. Election Day 2012 and 2008 had a six-point and three-point difference, respectively, compared with the average of the seven previous days.

Percentage of U.S. Adults in Bad Mood: Elections 2016, 2012 and 2008

Bad mood defined as percentage of U.S. adults who experienced a lot of stress and worry without a lot of happiness and enjoyment

	Seven days before election (avg.) %	Election Day %	Day after election %	*Next seven days (avg.) %
Nov 8, 2016	10	19	20	12
Nov 6, 2012	10	16	15	12
Nov 4, 2008	10	13	15	13

*Average of seven days after the day following the election
Gallup-Healthways Well-Being Index

In all three election years, Americans' bad mood generally held steady the day after the election.

While Americans' mood deteriorated much more than usual on Election Day 2016, it appears to be bouncing back just as quickly as it did in 2008 and 2012.

Implications

Americans' mood soured on Election Day, something that typically has happened in election years. But the drop in mood was significantly worse this Election Day than in previous presidential election years.

There are several potential explanations for the increase in bad mood on Election Day and the day after. Beyond the public being anxious about the outcome of a particularly heated campaign, President-elect Donald Trump's victory largely was unexpected. Gallup found that three in four Americans were surprised that Trump won. Most media outlets and polls were predicting that Hillary Clinton would win, leaving many of her supporters without time to mentally prepare for stress and worry that might accompany a Trump victory.

Unlike the previous two elections, the candidate who won the Electoral College and thus the election did not win the popular vote. This could have contributed to more Americans, particularly Clinton supporters, experiencing a bad mood.

In addition, Trump and Clinton were the most unfavorably evaluated candidates in Gallup's polling history, which could have led to more anxiety at the prospect of either candidate winning.

Since the election, Americans' mood has improved but has not yet returned to levels seen before the election – as was the case in 2008 and 2012. Still, the improvement so far is notable given the bitterness of the campaign and the protests against Trump taking place in many cities. The ongoing recovery in mood since the election could be an encouraging sign that most Americans who felt stressed and worried by the outcome are no longer letting these concerns affect their day-to-day lives.

Trump's actions since the election may be driving the mood boost. Gallup recently reported that 51% of U.S. adults are more confident in Trump's ability to serve based on his actions and statements since the election.

Also, the rise in Americans' confidence in the economy and record highs in the stock market could be boosting the nation's mood.

If previous patterns hold true, Americans' mood should fully recover this week as many gather for Thanksgiving. Previous research shows that Americans' happiest days of the year fall on holidays.

Survey Methods

Results are based on telephone interviews conducted Jan. 2, 2008, through Nov. 16, 2016, as part of the Gallup-Healthways Well-Being Index survey, with a random sample of approximately 500 adults per day, aged 18 and older, living in all 50 U.S. states and the District of Columbia. For results based on the total sample of national adults, the margin of sampling error is ±5 percentage points at the 95% confidence level.

November 22, 2016

FEWER AMERICANS IN THIS DECADE WANT TO LOSE WEIGHT

by Art Swift

Story Highlights

- *Average wanting to lose weight drops from 59% in 2000s to 53% in 2010s*
- *Gap between men and women is slimmer in this decade than in 1950s*
- *Fewer Americans today than in 1990s describe themselves as overweight*

WASHINGTON, D.C. – Americans in this decade are less likely than in the prior decade to say they want to lose weight, with the average dropping from 59% in 2000-2009 to 53% in 2010-2016. The percentage of Americans wanting to lose weight is now back to where it was in the 1990s, but still well above the 35% average that Gallup measured in the 1950s.

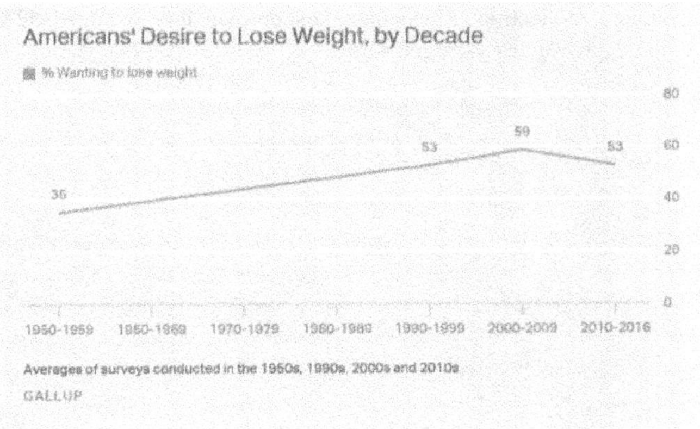

Losing weight was likely less important to Americans in the 1950s because obesity was far less prevalent – or perhaps because Americans were not as conscious of fitness 60 years ago and that social norms regarding size were different then. However, whether these attitudes changed quickly or slowly isn't clear because Gallup did not ask this question in the 1960s, 1970s or 1980s. When Gallup polls picked it up again in the 1990s, the average percentage wanting to lose weight had jumped nearly 20 percentage points.

Smaller Gap Between Men, Women Wanting to Lose Weight

In the current decade, on average, 60% of women and 46% of men say they are interested in losing weight. While both figures are lower than they were in the 1990s, they are also much higher than averages in the 1950s. However, the gap between men and women who say they want to lose weight has narrowed since the 1950s, when more than twice as many women as men professed wanting to lose weight. In the 2000s, the gap decreased to 13 points (65% for women and 52% for men).

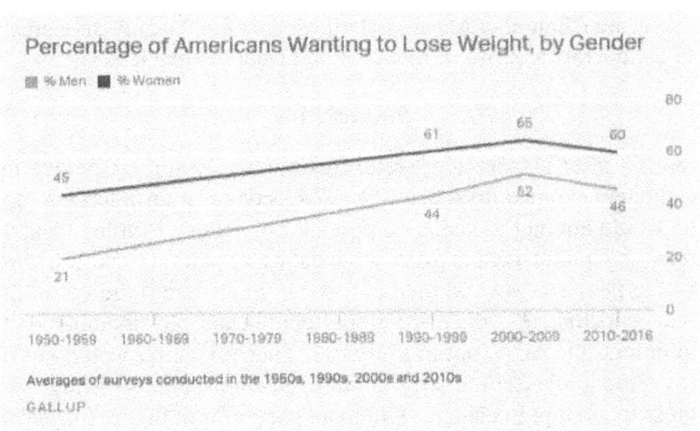

The gender gap is still narrower today than in the 1950s – suggesting that men, who may have been more indifferent toward weight loss in the 1950s, remain more concerned about it in recent years.

Fewer Americans in This Decade Say They Are Overweight

A smaller percentage of Americans now describe themselves as overweight than did so in the 1990s. The percentage saying they are overweight is down to 37% this decade from 41% in the 2000s and 44% in the 1990s.

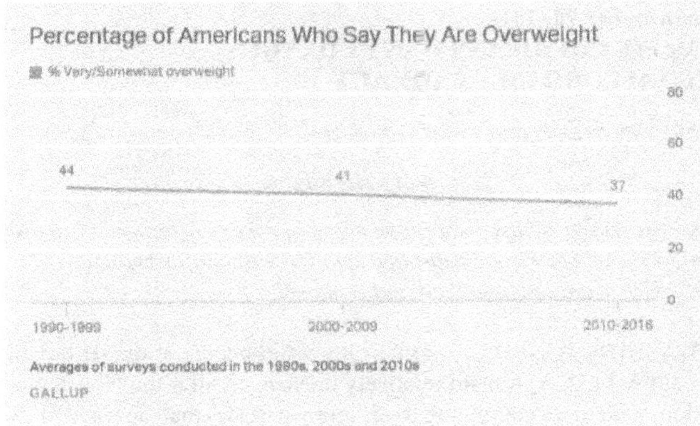

Americans' perceptions of their ideal weight and self-reports of their actual weight have been trending upward since the 1990s. During the 1990s, Americans' average ideal weight was 153 pounds. In the 2000s, it expanded to 158; in the 2010s, ideal weight has ticked up to 161. Americans' average self-reported weight has also increased, from 166 in the 1990s to 174 in the 2000s and 176 in the current decade.

Ideal Weight vs. Current Weight

	1990s	2000s	2010s
Ideal weight	153	158	161
Actual weight	166	174	176

Averages of surveys conducted in the 1990s, 2000s and 2010s
Gallup

Bottom Line

Body weight is a sensitive topic for many Americans. The U.S. obesity rate has actually risen to its highest point since Gallup began tracking this measure. In the 1950s, many more women than men said they wanted to lose weight – yet in recent decades, men have almost caught up with women in their desire for a trimmer body. On the other hand, fewer Americans now than in the past two decades believe they are overweight, and the benchmark for their ideal weight continues to be set higher. These concepts may make it easier for Americans to enjoy extra portions this Thanksgiving season, especially if they feel content being a little heavier than in decades past.

Survey Methods

Results for this Gallup poll are based on telephone interviews conducted Nov. 9-13, 2016, with a random sample of 1,019 adults, aged 18 and older, living in all 50 U.S. states and the District of Columbia. For results based on the total sample of national adults, the margin of sampling error is ±4 percentage points at the 95% confidence level.

For results based on the sample of 530 men, the margin of sampling error is ±5 percentage points. For results based on the sample of 489 women, the margin of sampling error is ±5 percentage points.

November 28, 2016

MOST AMERICANS WANT CHANGES TO AFFORDABLE CARE ACT

by Riley Brands and Frank Newport

Story Highlights

- *More Americans disapprove than approve of Affordable Care Act*
- *43% of Americans want law kept but with major changes*
- *37% want law repealed and replaced*

WASHINGTON, D.C. – Americans' assessments of the Affordable Care Act (ACA) remain relatively unchanged after the Nov. 8 election, with more continuing to disapprove (53%) than approve (42%) of the law. Going forward, the vast majority of Americans want to see the law changed. This includes the 37% who want it repealed and replaced, along with a total of 43% of Americans who want the law kept, but with major changes.

Americans' Approval of the Affordable Care Act and Preferred Corrective Actions

Based on national adults

	%
Approve	42
Keep in place as is	14
Keep but change significantly	28
Unspecified	1
Disapprove	53
Keep but change significantly	15
Repeal and replace	37
Unspecified	1
No opinion	5

GALLUP, Nov. 9-13, 2016

In its annual November Healthcare update, conducted Nov. 9-13, Gallup asked Americans who approve of the ACA if they would like it kept in place as is, or kept but with significant changes. Similarly, Americans who disapprove of the ACA were asked if they wanted to keep it but with significant changes, or repeal and replace it.

Putting the responses to these two questions together, an overall total of 43% of Americans – a group that includes some who approved of it initially (28%) and some who disapproved (15%) – want to change the ACA significantly without repealing it. That is a slightly larger percentage than the 37% who disapprove and wish to see it repealed and replaced. Fourteen percent of Americans approve of the ACA and wish to keep it as is.

Disapproval of the ACA Has Been the Norm

Since Gallup began regularly tracking Americans' overall evaluations of the ACA four years ago, approval has exceeded disapproval only once, in November 2012, shortly after President Barack Obama's re-election. Since then, disapproval has averaged 52%, while approval has averaged 42%.

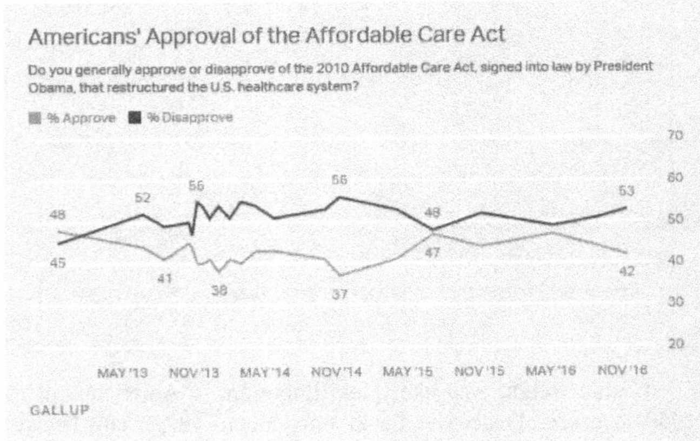

Attitudes toward the ACA continue to be highly partisan. The act's common name "Obamacare" highlights the degree to which it is attached to the Democratic president. The legislation, which was passed into law in 2010 despite "no" votes from all 178 Republican members of the House, became a point of contention between Donald Trump and Hillary Clinton during the election. Not surprisingly, rank-and-file Democrats have consistently been much more likely to approve of the ACA than Republicans. This month, 7% of Republicans say they approve of the ACA, compared with 76% of Democrats. This is fairly typical of the partisan spread in approval measured prior to the election.

Seventy-one percent of Republicans disapprove of the law and want to repeal it, essentially in line with Trump's campaign promise. Few Democrats want to see the ACA repealed and replaced. Instead, 59% of Democrats, including those who either approve or disapprove of the law in general, want to keep it with significant changes, mirroring Clinton's campaign platform position. Twenty-six percent of Democrats approve of the ACA and want to keep it as is.

Bottom Line

Shortly after his election earlier this month, Trump moderated his campaign promise to repeal the ACA, saying in an interview that he would attempt to keep two popular provisions: banning insurers from excluding people with pre-existing conditions and allowing young people to stay on their parents' insurance until the age of 26. It appears that, to avoid disruption, Republicans may attempt to vote to defund the ACA, but in a way that such an action would not be triggered until after the 2018 midterm elections, thus allowing Congress to attempt to change significant parts of it in the meantime.

Whatever the exact course of action that ensues once Trump and the new Congress take office, it is clear that about eight in 10 Americans favor changing the ACA significantly (43%) or replacing it altogether (37%).

Survey Methods

Results for this Gallup poll are based on telephone interviews conducted Nov. 9-13, 2016, on the Gallup Poll Social Series, with a random sample of 1,019 adults, aged 18 and older, living in all 50 U.S. states and the District of Columbia. For results based on the total sample of national adults, the margin of sampling error is ±4 percentage points at the 95% confidence level. For results based on the total sample of adults who approve of the Affordable Care Act, the margin of sampling error is ±6 percentage points at the 95% confidence level. For results based on the total sample of adults who disapprove of the Affordable Care Act, the margin of sampling error is ±5 percentage points at the 95% confidence level. All reported margins of sampling error include computed design effects for weighting.

November 28, 2016
MAJORITY IN U.S. SAY TRUMP WILL TRY TO WORK WITH DEMOCRATS

by Frank Newport

Story Highlights

- *58% say Donald Trump and Democrats in Congress will try to cooperate*
- *49% say Republicans in Congress will cooperate with Democrats*
- *Public was more optimistic about cooperation after Obama's 2008 election*

PRINCETON, N.J. – Although Republican President-elect Donald Trump will take office with his party in firm control of Congress, a majority of Americans (58%) are optimistic that he will make a sincere effort to work with Democrats to find solutions to the nation's problems. The same majority also believe that Democrats in Congress will sincerely try to work with Trump. Americans are less sure (49%) that Republicans in Congress will reach across the aisle.

Sincere Efforts of Donald Trump, Democrats and Republicans to Work With One Another

Among U.S. adults

	Yes %	No %
Trump will make sincere effort to work with Democrats in Congress	58	40
Democrats in Congress will make sincere effort to work with Trump and Republicans	58	39
Republicans in Congress will make sincere effort to work with Democrats	49	49

Gallup, Nov 9-13, 2016

These results, from Gallup's Nov. 9-13 post-election survey, are updates to similar questions Gallup asked after the 2008 and 2012 elections. Americans were significantly more hopeful in 2008 about the possibilities of newly elected President Barack Obama than they are now about Trump. Eight in 10 Americans at the time expected Obama would cooperate with the opposing party in Congress. Like Trump, Obama had campaigned in 2008 on the need to bring about change – but Obama was much better-liked after his election, with a 68% favorable rating, compared with Trump's post-election 42%.

After contending with a GOP-led House in 2011 and 2012, Obama in 2012 was less widely seen as able to work with the Republicans in Congress to find solutions. Even so, the 65% of Americans still saying this about Obama after his re-election was a bit more positive than Trump's current evaluation.

Although the political circumstances were different four years ago than they are now, just like today, Americans then gave more credit to the Democrats than to the Republicans in Congress for willingness to cooperate with the other party. Immediately after the 2008 election, however, the public was about equally optimistic about the potential cooperation of both parties' leaders.

Sincere Efforts of Barack Obama/Donald Trump, Democrats and Republicans to Work With One Another

Among U.S. adults

	Yes %	No %
President will make sincere effort to work with opposing party in Congress		
2016 (Trump)	58	40
2012 (Obama)	65	33
2008 (Obama)	80	19
Democrats in Congress will make sincere effort to work with opposing party		
2016	58	39
2012	57	40
2008	59	40
Republicans in Congress will make sincere effort to work with opposing party		
2016	49	49
2012	48	48
2008	62	37

Gallup

Implications

Although a record number of Americans believe the nation is divided after this election, Trump will enter office with fairly positive expectations that he will cooperate with Democrats in Congress and that Democrats will cooperate with him. Perhaps reflecting the political gridlock seen since the GOP took control of the House in 2011, Americans are less positive that GOP leaders will cooperate with Democrats.

Trump has the advantage of working with a Republican-controlled House and Senate, which should mean that he will be less at odds with Congress than has been the case for Obama over the past two years. Additionally, Trump can make a number of changes by implementing executive actions without congressional approval. But Democrats in Congress will still be needed for a number of actions on the Trump agenda to become law, meaning that cooperation between the two parties will continue to be important.

Previous Gallup research shows that Americans want their leaders in Washington to cooperate to get things done, including a significant percentage of rank-and-file Republicans who want compromise from their leaders. The likelihood of that occurring after the contentious 2016 election campaign is unknown, although Americans are somewhat optimistic that it will.

Survey Methods

Results for this Gallup poll are based on telephone interviews conducted Nov. 9-13, 2016, with a random sample of 1,019 adults, aged 18 and older, living in all 50 U.S. states and the District of

Columbia. For results based on the total sample of national adults, the margin of sampling error is ±4 percentage points at the 95% confidence level. All reported margins of sampling error include computed design effects for weighting.

November 29, 2016
U.S. ECONOMIC CONFIDENCE HIGHEST IN NINE YEARS

by Justin McCarthy

Story Highlights

- *Weekly U.S. Economic Confidence Index score at +6*
- *Three-day average also reaches new high, at +9*
- *Both current conditions and economic outlook scores are up*

WASHINGTON, D.C. – Americans expressed more positivity about the U.S. economy last week than they have at any other time during the nine years that Gallup has been tracking the U.S. Economic Confidence Index. The latest score of +6 for the week ending Nov. 27 inched past the previous high of +5 recorded in January 2015.

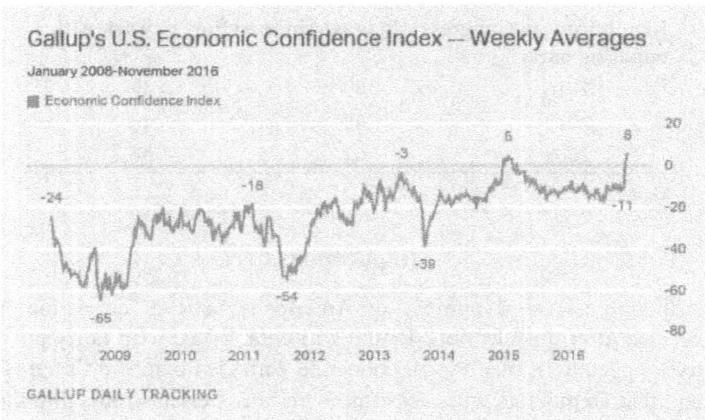

Americans' confidence in the economy recently shifted from negative to positive territory after Donald Trump was elected president three weeks ago. The index was -11 in the last full week before the Nov. 8 election, but then jumped to +4 the week after. Gallup noted that the change was largely attributable to Republicans becoming more optimistic about the economy's direction. Registering at +9 for Nov. 25-27, this three-day average bests the previous high of +7, which Gallup recorded after this November's election, as well as once before in January 2015.

Gallup's U.S. Economic Confidence Index is the average of two components: how Americans rate current economic conditions and whether they feel the economy is improving or getting worse. The index has a theoretical maximum of +100 if all Americans were to say the economy is doing well and improving, and a theoretical minimum of -100 if all Americans were to say the economy is doing poorly and getting worse.

Economic confidence has been below zero nearly continuously since 2008, hitting its lowest level of -65 in October 2008 at the onset of the financial crisis. Aside from the recent pair of positive index readings, Gallup's weekly scores were positive several times during a brief, three-month span from late 2014 to early 2015, when U.S. consumers enjoyed a sustained drop in gasoline prices.

Assessments of Current Economic Conditions Best in Nine Years

Thirty percent of Americans rated the economy as "excellent" or "good" last week, while 22% said it was "poor," resulting in a current conditions index of +8 – this is, by one point, the highest score recorded for this component over the past nine years. The latest current conditions score is up two points from the prior week.

The economic outlook component is at its highest since February of last year. For the week ending Nov. 27, this component moved further into positive territory at +4, compared with +1 the previous week. The latest score is the result of 49% of Americans saying economic conditions in the country are "getting better" and 45% saying they are "getting worse."

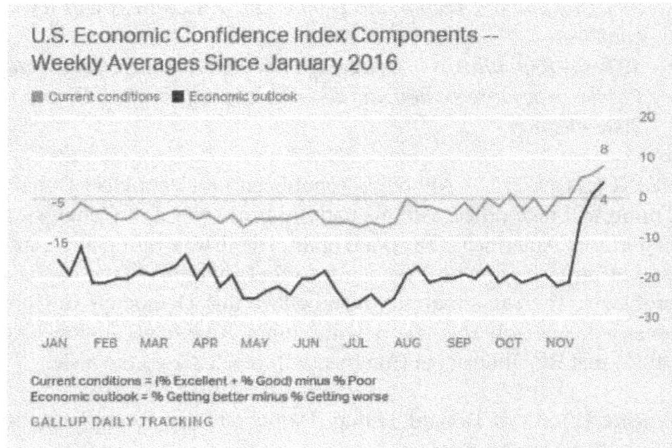

Bottom Line

It's not just Americans who have felt more economically exuberant since the election – U.S. markets have skyrocketed, with the Dow closing above 19,000 this week for the first time in its 120-year history.

So, while the election's results may have improved Americans' outlook on the economy, favorable market conditions may have driven their confidence further upward. This also comes as many economists expect that potential U.S. economic growth could have a significant effect worldwide.

It's too early to tell whether this uptick in Americans' positivity will last as Trump's term begins in January. But two weeks of positive index readings on the heels of his unexpected victory reveals a degree of economic confidence Americans have not expressed since the recession.

Survey Methods

Results for this Gallup poll are based on telephone interviews conducted Nov. 21-27, 2016, on the Gallup U.S. Daily survey, with a random sample of 3,049 adults, aged 18 and older, living in all 50 U.S. states and the District of Columbia. For results based on the total sample of national adults, the margin of sampling error is ±2 percentage points at the 95% confidence level. All reported margins of sampling error include computed design effects for weighting.

December 02, 2016
AMERICANS' SUPPORT FOR ELECTORAL COLLEGE RISES SHARPLY

by Art Swift

Story Highlights

- *47% want to keep Electoral College, up from 35% in 2011*
- *Republicans shift decisively in favor of Electoral College*
- *Most Americans correctly answer that Hillary Clinton won popular vote*

WASHINGTON, D.C. — Americans' support for keeping the Electoral College system for electing presidents has increased sharply. Weeks after the 2016 election, 47% of Americans say they want to keep the Electoral College, while 49% say they want to amend the Constitution to allow for a popular vote for president. In the past, a clear majority favored amending the U.S. Constitution to replace the Electoral College with a popular vote system.

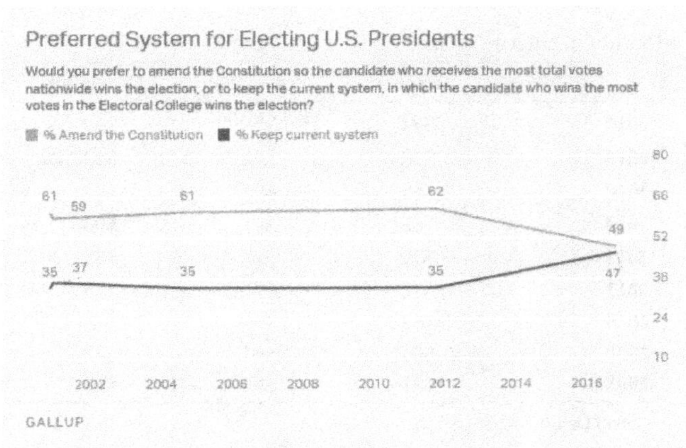

Donald Trump secured enough electors in the Electoral College to win the presidency, despite Hillary Clinton winning the popular vote. With Clinton's popular lead total continuing to expand, now at more than 2.5 million votes, there have been persistent calls since Election Day to abolish the Electoral College. Such sentiment has clearly prevailed when Gallup asked this question twice in 2000 – after George W. Bush won the Electoral College while Al Gore won the popular vote – in 2004 and in 2011. In each instance, support for a constitutional amendment hovered around 60%.

From 1967 through 1980, Gallup asked a slightly different question that also found majority support for an amendment to base the winner on the popular vote. Support for an amendment peaked at 80% in 1968, after Richard Nixon almost lost the popular vote while winning the Electoral College. Ultimately, he wound up winning both by a narrow margin, but this issue demonstrated the possibility of a candidate becoming president without winning the popular vote. In the 1976 election, Jimmy Carter faced a similar situation, though he also won the popular vote and Electoral College. In a poll taken weeks after the election, 73% were in favor of an amendment doing away with the Electoral College.

This year, for the first time in the 49 years Gallup has asked about it, less than half of Americans want to replace the Electoral College with a popular vote system.

The reason for this shift in opinion is clear: In the aftermath of this year's election, the percentage of Republicans wanting to replace the Electoral College with the popular vote has fallen significantly.

Currently, 19% of Republicans and Republican-leaning independents favor basing the winner on the popular vote, down from 49% in October 2004 and 54% in 2011. Democrats and Democratic-leaning independents already widely favored having the popular vote determine the winner and are slightly more likely to do so now than in the past.

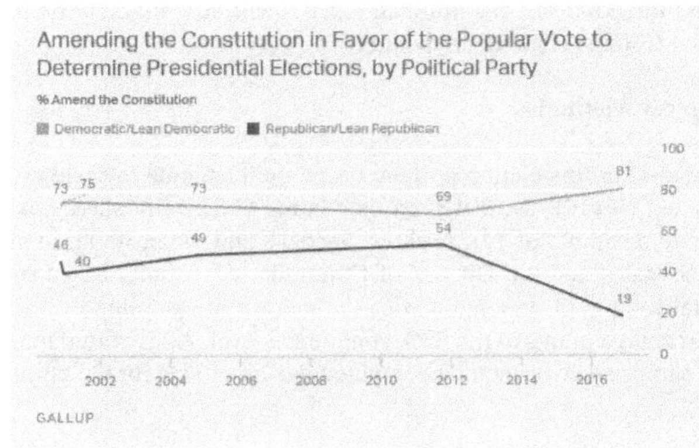

Most Americans Know Hillary Clinton Won the Popular Vote

Because of the divergence of the Electoral College and popular vote, the popular vote is garnering particular attention this year. Two-thirds of Americans correctly name Clinton as the winner of the popular vote, while 15% incorrectly name Trump and 18% say they are unsure. Eighty-five percent of Democrats correctly name Clinton as the winner of the popular vote compared with 56% of Republicans.

Winning the National Popular Vote

From what you have heard or read, who won the national popular vote this year – that is, the most votes in the country overall – Hillary Clinton (or) Donald Trump, or are you unsure?

	Clinton %	Trump %	Unsure %
National adults	66	15	18
Democrats	85	8	8
Republicans	56	23	20
Independents	59	16	25

Gallup, Nov 28-29, 2016

Americans' ability to correctly identify the winner is similar to what it was after the disputed 2000 election – 65% named Gore the popular vote winner, 16% said Bush was and 18% were unsure. The results by party in 2000 were also similar to what they are today.

Bottom Line

Despite some Democratic elected officials and media pundits calling for intensively studying, if not doing away with, the Electoral College, the country is now sharply divided on the issue.

In previous years, Americans preferred amending the U.S. Constitution to abolish the Electoral College, but not in 2016. One possible reason is that Republicans are aware that President-elect Trump would not have won the presidency without winning the Electoral College, and that Republicans possess a state-by-state advantage in this area, at least for now. Also, the popular vote is clearly advantageous to Democrats, who can accumulate big totals in heavily Democratic states such as California.

With two-thirds of Congress and two-thirds of states needed to pass this kind of constitutional amendment, it is unlikely the Electoral College is going anywhere.

Survey Methods

Results for this Gallup poll are based on telephone interviews conducted Nov. 28-29, 2016, on the Gallup U.S. Daily survey, with a random sample of 1,021 adults, aged 18 and older, living in all 50 U.S. states and the District of Columbia. For results based on the total sample of national adults, the margin of sampling error is ±4 percentage points at the 95% confidence level. All reported margins of sampling error include computed design effects for weighting.

December 05, 2016

U.S. CONSUMER SPENDING RISES IN NOVEMBER

by Justin McCarthy

Story Highlights

- *November spending averaged $98 per day, up from $93 in October*
- *Highest spending average for month of November in Gallup's trend*
- *Spending increased more among lower- and middle-income Americans*

WASHINGTON, D.C. — Americans' daily self-reports of spending averaged $98 in November, up from $93 in October. The latest figure exceeds the $92 average recorded in the same month a year ago and is the highest for any November since Gallup began tracking consumer spending in 2008.

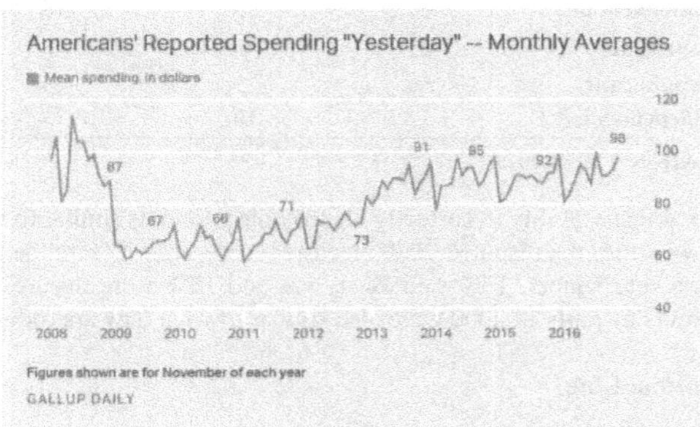

These results are based on Gallup Daily tracking interviews conducted Nov. 1-29. Gallup asks Americans each night to report how much they spent "yesterday," excluding normal household bills and major purchases such as a home or car. The measure gives an indication of discretionary spending.

The highest monthly averages on this self-reported spending measure came in the early months of 2008. Since the recession ended, self-reported spending has gradually increased. In several months recently, including November, the monthly average has been in the high $90 range, reaching $100 in July.

The November figure provides a strong springboard for the usual surge in holiday spending in December. Gallup has recorded an increase in December spending over November's figure in every year since 2008, with an average increase of $6.

The $5 increase in November spending compared with October is larger than usual. In some years, spending between these two months has stayed flat or even dipped. Generally, average daily spending rises $1 to $3. One exception was 2014 when spending increased $6 between October and November.

Average Reported U.S. Consumer Spending, October-December

Monthly averages

	October	November	December
2016	$93	$98	–
2015	$92	$92	$99
2014	$89	$95	$98
2013	$88	$91	$96
2012	$72	$73	$83
2011	$70	$71	$76
2010	$63	$66	$75
2009	$66	$67	$72
2008	$91	$87	$89

Gallup Daily

November Increase Driven by Middle- and Lower-Income Families

Spending among lower- and middle-income families is up relatively sharply on both a monthly (up $7) and year-over-year (up $5) basis. Americans with an annual household income of less than $90,000 spent an average of $82 per day in November, the highest for this group in nearly two years.

By contrast, spending among upper-income Americans – those with an annual household income of $90,000 or more – averaged $146 in November, similar to October's $143 but higher than the average for November of last year ($137).

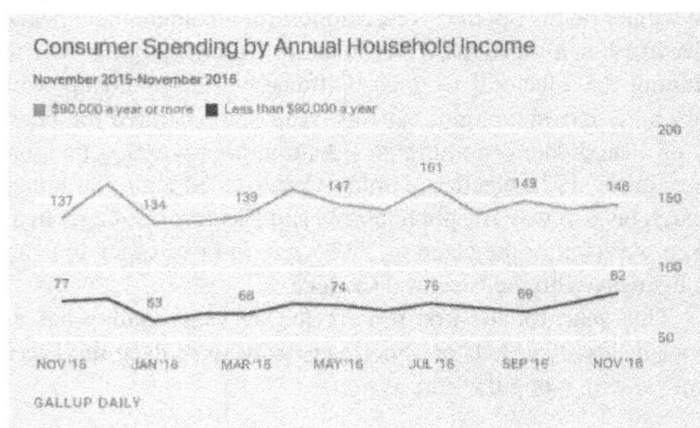

Bottom Line

U.S. Department of Commerce data show that consumer spending improved markedly in recent months, including a combined 4.3% increase in year-over-year sales in September and October. Now Gallup's data indicate that trend may have continued into November, offering a positive sign for holiday retailers.

Americans have matched or exceeded their previous monthly spending average not only this month but also five other months this year. If this trend continues, next year's monthly spending averages could rival the record highs seen in 2008.

Historical data are available in Gallup Analytics.

Survey Methods

Results for this Gallup poll are based on telephone interviews conducted Nov. 1-29, 2016, on the Gallup Daily tracking survey, with a random sample of 13,724 adults, aged 18 and older, living in all 50 U.S. states and the District of Columbia. For results based on the total sample of national adults, the margin of sampling error is ±$5 at the 95% confidence level. All reported margins of sampling error include computed design effects for weighting.

December 05, 2016

FOR OLDER ADULTS, HAWAII LEADS U.S. STATES IN WELL-BEING

by Dan Witters

Story Highlights

- *Hawaii again leads U.S. in well-being among older residents*
- *West Virginia's older residents have lowest well-being*
- *Hawaii, Arizona among top five states in three well-being elements*

WASHINGTON, D.C. — For the second consecutive year, Hawaii led all U.S. states in well-being among residents aged 55 and over, with a Well-Being Index score of 67.0. The other four states with a Well-Being Index score of 65 or higher are Arizona, New Hampshire, North Dakota and Colorado. West Virginia, Kentucky, Oklahoma, Ohio and Indiana are the states with the lowest well-being among older residents, unchanged from last year.

States With Highest and Lowest Well-Being Among Residents Aged 55+

State	Well-Being Index Score	State	Well-Being Index Score
Hawaii	67.0	West Virginia	59.9
Arizona	65.2	Kentucky	61.2
New Hampshire	65.2	Oklahoma	62.0
North Dakota	65.2	Ohio	62.5
Colorado	65.1	Indiana	62.7
Alaska	64.9	Vermont	62.7
Minnesota	64.9	Georgia	62.9
Wisconsin	64.9	Missouri	62.9
Iowa	64.7	Arkansas	62.9
South Dakota	64.7	New Jersey	62.9

Gallup-Healthways Well-Being Index, Q1 2015 through Q1 2016

These state-level data are based on more than 115,000 interviews with U.S. adults across all 50 states, conducted from Jan. 2, 2015, through March 31, 2016. The Well-Being Index is calculated on a scale of 0 to 100, where 0 represents the lowest possible well-being and 100 represents the highest possible well-being. The Gallup-Healthways Well-Being Index scores for the nation and for each state consist of metrics affecting overall well-being and each of the five essential elements of well-being:

- **Purpose:** liking what you do each day and being motivated to achieve your goals
- **Social:** having supportive relationships and love in your life
- **Financial:** managing your economic life to reduce stress and increase security
- **Community:** liking where you live, feeling safe and having pride in your community
- **Physical:** having good health and enough energy to get things done daily

In most cases, a difference of 1.0 point in the Well-Being Index score between any two states represents a statistically significant gap.

Hawaii Leads All States in Three Elements of Well-Being

Hawaii holds the highest well-being of older residents in three of the five elements: purpose, community and physical well-being. Older residents of Arizona, South Carolina and Florida report the highest social well-being, while those living in North Dakota, Iowa and Minnesota lead in financial well-being. Across the five elements, Hawaii and Arizona each rank among the top five states three times, while Iowa, New Hampshire and North Dakota each appear twice.

West Virginia's older residents report the lowest purpose, social and physical well-being, and rank among the five states with the lowest well-being in all five elements. Older residents of Mississippi, Georgia and Louisiana have the lowest financial well-being, while those living in New Jersey, West Virginia and Maryland report the lowest community well-being.

States With Highest Well-Being Across Each Element

Purpose	Social	Financial	Community	Physical
Hawaii	Arizona	North Dakota	Hawaii	Hawaii
Mississippi	South Carolina	Iowa	Montana	Colorado
Texas	Florida	Minnesota	North Dakota	New Hampshire
Arizona	New Hampshire	Alaska	South Dakota	Connecticut
Alabama	Maryland	Wisconsin	Iowa	Arizona

States With Lowest Well-Being Across Each Element

Purpose	Social	Financial	Community	Physical
West Virginia	West Virginia	Mississippi	New Jersey	West Virginia
Vermont	Wyoming	Georgia	West Virginia	Kentucky
Kentucky	Vermont	Louisiana	Maryland	Oklahoma
Massachusetts	Montana	South Carolina	Illinois	Arkansas
New Jersey	Kentucky	West Virginia	Connecticut	Tennessee

Gallup-Healthways Well-Being Index, Q1 2015 through Q1 2016

Older Residents of New Hampshire Have Largest Well-Being Advantage

New Hampshire's older residents have the largest well-being advantage compared with the general population of the state, with residents aged 55 or older having a Well-Being Index score of 65.2 compared with 62.1 for residents overall – a difference of 3.1 points. For comparison, older adults in the U.S. generally have higher well-being compared with the broader adult population, with an average gap of 1.7 points. The well-being edge for New Hampshire's older residents significantly boosts its state ranking from 21st for the overall population to the third-highest among residents aged 55 and older. Three other states with notably higher well-being among older residents compared with the general population are North Dakota, Mississippi and Oregon.

States in Which Well-Being of Older Residents Is Most Significantly Better Than That of All Residents

	Well-Being Index Score All adults	Well-Being Index Score 55 and older	Difference
New Hampshire	62.1	65.2	3.1
North Dakota	62.3	65.2	2.9
Mississippi	60.9	63.8	2.9
Oregon	61.7	64.3	2.6

Gallup-Healthways Well-Being Index, Q1 2015 through Q1 2016

The older residents in four states have a much smaller advantage or no advantage in well-being compared with the overall population: Wyoming, Montana, Utah and Alaska. In each of these states, the Well-Being Index score among older residents is the same as or only slightly higher than the score found among all adults in the state.

States in Which Well-Being of Older Residents Is Closest to That of All Residents

	Well-Being Index Score All adults	Well-Being Index Score 55 and older	Difference
Wyoming	63.5	63.5	0.0
Montana	63.8	64.2	0.4
Utah	63.1	63.8	0.7
Alaska	64.1	64.9	0.8

Gallup-Healthways Well-Being Index, Q1 2015 through Q1 2016

Each of these four states ranked in the top 10 for highest overall well-being in 2015. So while there is not a large jump in well-being among older residents, the high well-being found among the general adult population is preserved. These results suggest that one common characteristic of the nation's states with the highest well-being is high well-being across age groups rather than just among those who are older, underscoring a broader and deeper culture of well-being that might not be present elsewhere.

Implications

Americans aged 55 and over have higher well-being across all five elements than do their younger adult counterparts, including better eating habits, significantly reduced money worries and greater pride in their community compared with those between the ages of 18 and 54.

This elevated state of well-being upon reaching older age manifests itself in many other ways:

- Older Americans feel better about their physical appearance.
- Daily emotions such as happiness, worry and stress improve with age in the U.S., although this is less consistent internationally.
- Smoking rates drop substantially among older Americans.
- Financial well-being improves substantially after age 65, although retirement remains Americans' top financial worry.
- The rate of those aged 65 and older without health insurance plummets.

"People in the United States are now living significantly longer than prior generations, a trend that stands to continue," said Joe Coughlin, founder and director of the Massachusetts Institute of Technology AgeLab. "As a nation, we must improve upon advances in well-being while developing new strategies to help Americans age well and thrive in later life."

Prior research has demonstrated that high well-being among individuals is closely linked to lower healthcare costs and increased productivity. As the average retirement age continues to climb, boosting well-being for older Americans who remain in the workforce should be a critical goal for U.S. employers.

"Our research paints a powerful picture of how we age as a population, and the important link between the physical and social aspects of well-being, especially for older Americans," said Dr. Sheri Pruitt, Ph.D., vice president and chief behavioral scientist at Healthways. "When older adults thrive, they are more active, assert good physical and mental health, and achieve higher life satisfaction."

Survey Methods

Results are based on telephone interviews conducted Jan. 2, 2015, to March 31, 2016, as part of the Gallup-Healthways Well-Being Index survey, with a random sample of 115,572 adults, aged 55 and older, living in all 50 U.S. states and the District of Columbia. The margin of sampling error for most states is about ±1.5 points, although this increases to about ±2.1 points for the smallest-population states such as North Dakota, Wyoming, Hawaii and Delaware.

December 06, 2016

ECONOMIC CONFIDENCE KEEPS IMPROVING, REACHING NEW HIGHS

by Jeffrey M. Jones

Story Highlights

- *Gallup Economic Confidence Index averaged +8 for week ending Dec. 4*
- *Democrats, Republicans now equally confident in economy*
- *Democrats more positive about current economy, Republicans about future*

PRINCETON, N.J. — Americans' confidence in the economy continues its post-election improvement, with Gallup's U.S. Economic Confidence Index averaging +8 for the week ending Dec. 4. That is the highest weekly average in Gallup's tracking trend, which dates back to January 2008.

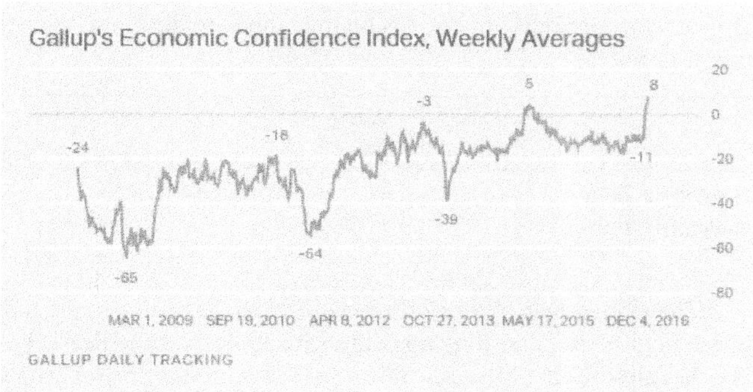

Last week's confidence average included a score of +12 for Dec. 2-4 interviewing, the highest three-day average in Gallup's tracking trend.

Gallup's U.S. Economic Confidence Index is based on Americans' evaluations of current conditions and their perceptions of whether the economy is getting better or worse. It has a theoretical range of -100 (if all Americans rated the economy as "poor" and said it was getting worse) to +100 (if all Americans rated the economy as "excellent" or "good" and said it was getting better).

Since 2008, the index has mostly been in negative territory. The major exception came during an eight-week period from late December 2014 through mid-February 2015 when U.S. consumers reacted to a sustained drop in gasoline prices and the weekly average for Gallup's index reached as high as +5.

Confidence has now been above the neutral mark for three consecutive weeks. In November, confidence averaged +1, up from -11 in October. This was the third time in Gallup's trend that the monthly average has been positive, along with January 2015 (+3) and February 2015 (+1).

Republicans See Economy in More Positive Light After Election

The recent increase in economic confidence appears mostly to be a reaction to the presidential election – chiefly among Republicans, who are much more likely to view the economy positively after Donald Trump's victory. Republicans have shifted dramatically from a decidedly negative evaluation of the economy before the election to a positive one after it.

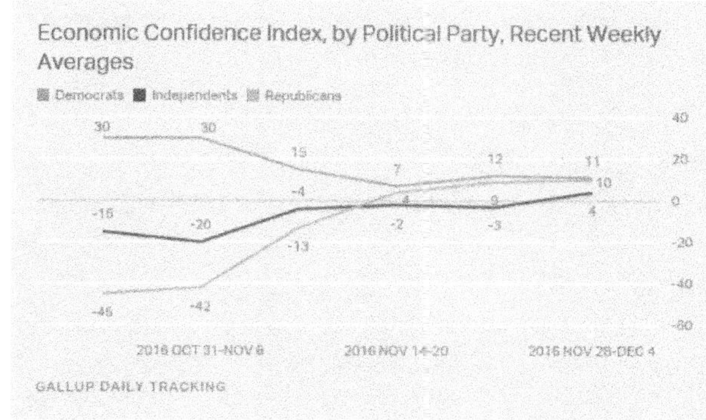

For the week before the election, the index among Republicans was -42. Now, it is +10. Democrats, who were quite positive about the economy before the election (+30), remain so, but to a far lesser degree (+11). The net result of these changes is that Republicans and Democrats are now about equally confident in the economy.

Independents are slightly less optimistic, with a +4 index score, but that is also a significantly improvement from their -20 score the week before the election.

Before the election, Democrats were much more optimistic than Republicans were about both current economic conditions and the outlook for the economy. Democrats still rate current economic conditions better than Republicans do, while Republicans are more positive than Democrats are about the economy's direction. These shifting perceptions likely result from the political reality: A Democratic president is in office and currently presiding over the nation, but a Republican president is set to take over early next year.

In the most recent weekly average, 58% of Republicans said the economy was "getting better," and 37% said it was "getting worse," for an economic outlook score of +21. That is sharply higher than the -66 average among Republicans (15% "getting better" and 81% "getting worse") just before the election.

Meanwhile, 49% of Democrats said the economy was "getting better," and 46% said "getting worse," for an economic outlook score of +3. That is down from +30 among Democrats before the election.

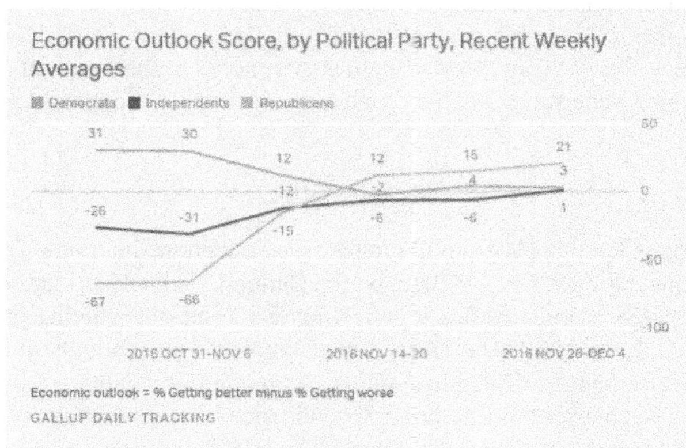

For the week ending Dec. 4, 37% of Democrats rated current economic conditions as "excellent" or "good," while 18% said they were "poor." That yielded a +19 current conditions score among Democrats, down 11 points from before the election. Republicans' score on that component was -2 for last week, up 17 points from the week before Trump was elected. Last week, 25% of Republicans rated current conditions as "excellent" or "good," and 27% said they were "poor."

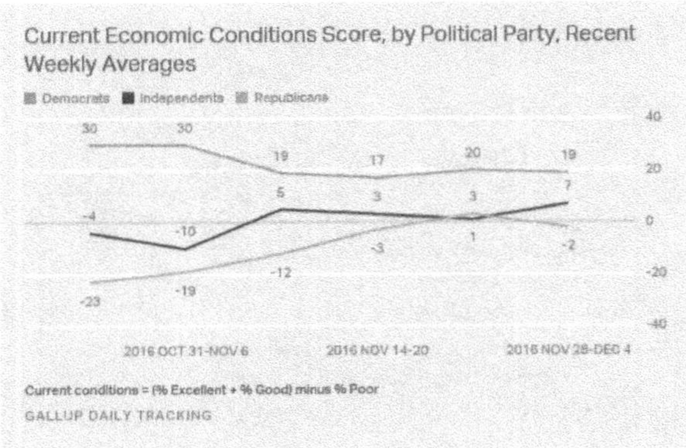

Implications

Americans' evaluations of the economy have changed considerably since Election Day. Republicans are much more likely to say the economy is "getting better" and even see current economic conditions in a more positive light. Democrats' confidence has declined, but they still rate the economy more positively than negatively – a situation that may persist as long as President Barack Obama is in office.

Republicans' increase in economic confidence since the election has been greater than Democrats' decrease. Independents have also gained confidence and now are more positive than negative about the economy. These factors have led to a net increase in Gallup's Economic Confidence Index among all Americans, from -11 the week before the election to last week's +8.

Confidence may stay higher as long as both Democrats and Republicans have reasons to be positive about the economy, given the current and future political situations. Outside the political sphere, the economy has also seen record-high stock prices in recent weeks, reports of greater economic growth in the third quarter than in past years and a positive unemployment report released late last week.

Given the strong influence of partisanship on how Americans view the state of the nation, including the economy, Democrats' confidence may sharply decline once Trump is in office. The degree to which Republicans' views improve beyond what their current levels may determine whether confidence nationally remains high or retreats.

Survey Methods

Results for this Gallup poll are based on telephone interviews conducted Nov. 28-Dec. 4, 2016, on the Gallup U.S. Daily survey, with a random sample of 3,029 adults, aged 18 and older, living in all 50 U.S. states and the District of Columbia. For results based on the total sample of national adults, the margin of sampling error is ±2 percentage points at the 95% confidence level. For results based on the total samples of 929 Democrats, 974 Republicans and 1,030 independents, the margin of sampling error is ±4 percentage points at the 95% confidence level. All reported margins of sampling error include computed design effects for weighting.

December 07, 2016

FEWER IN U.S. SEE JAPAN AS AN ECONOMIC THREAT

by Art Swift

Story Highlights

- *24% say Japan is an economic threat, down from 77% in 1991*
- *64% have friendly feelings toward Japanese people*
- *Most Americans still know what happened at Pearl Harbor*

WASHINGTON, D.C. — On the 75th anniversary of the Japanese bombing of Pearl Harbor, and decades after Japan's economy grew exponentially following World War II, most Americans no longer consider Japan an economic threat to the U.S. Twenty-four percent of Americans say Japan is an economic threat, down sharply from 77% in 1991.

Americans' Perceptions of Japan as an Economic Threat

Do you consider Japan to be an economic threat to the United States today, or not?

	Yes %	No %
November 2016	24	72
November 1991	77	20

Gallup

The United States' relationship with Japan has come to the fore of public discussion leading up to the 75th anniversary of Pearl Harbor. Japanese Prime Minister Shinzo Abe will honor this milestone by becoming the first Japanese leader to visit Pearl Harbor in Hawaii later this month.

After it surrendered to the Allied forces at the end of World War II, Japan rapidly became an economic powerhouse – and by 1968 had become the second-largest economy in the world, behind the U.S.

Gallup first asked Americans if they considered Japan an economic threat in 1991. At the time, Japan was nearing the end of a long period of remarkable economic growth and about to enter what economists have called the "lost decade" – an economic crash of sorts, occurring roughly from 1991 to 2000. Americans were still unaware of the effects of that crash 25 years ago and remained nervous about global competition from Japan. Today, however, China seems to have emerged as a bigger threat in Americans' minds.

More Americans Have Friendly Feelings Toward the Japanese

Along with a decline in their belief that Japan poses an economic threat, Americans have grown more likely to view the Japanese people positively. Currently, 64% of Americans say they have friendly feelings toward the Japanese people, with 33% saying they have neutral feelings and 2% professing unfriendly feelings. "Friendly feelings" are up by 12 percentage points since Gallup last asked this question in 1994, and up by 21 points since 1991.

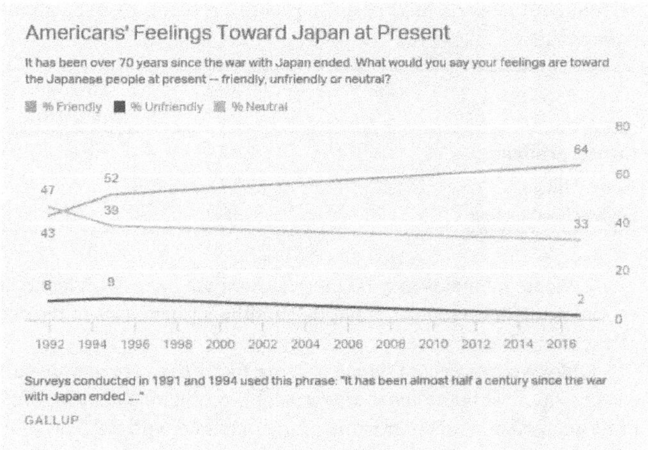

Gallup asked a similar question twice in the decades prior to 1991. In 1953, a period of less intense economic competition, 56% said they had friendly feelings toward the Japanese. In 1949, in the immediate aftermath of World War II, 34% said they felt friendly toward Japan, with 27% saying they had unfriendly feelings.

Most Americans Remember Historical Events of Dec. 7

Although most Americans today were not alive on Dec. 7, 1941, the public is still widely aware of what happened at Pearl Harbor. When asked in an open-ended fashion to say what happened on that date relating to Pearl Harbor, 73% of Americans correctly cite the Japanese attack on the U.S. An additional 5% mention the "beginning of U.S. involvement in World War II." These percentages are almost identical to the last time this question was asked, just before the 50th anniversary of Pearl Harbor in 1991.

Americans' Remembrance of Pearl Harbor

As you may know, this Dec. 7 marks the 75th anniversary of Pearl Harbor. Would you know specifically what happened 75 years ago, relating to Pearl Harbor? (Open-ended)

	November 2016 %	November 1991 %
Japanese attack on U.S./bombing of U.S. military base in Pearl Harbor	73	72
Beginning of U.S. involvement in World War II	5	5
Other	2	3
No opinion	20	20

Surveys conducted in 1991 used this phrase: "As you may know, this Dec. 7 marks the 50th anniversary of Pearl Harbor ...."
Gallup

Bottom Line

Japanese Prime Minister Abe is making a historic visit to the memorial at Pearl Harbor on the 75th anniversary of his country's attack there, which follows President Barack Obama's historic visit this past May to the site of America's bombing of Hiroshima, Japan. With decades of temporal distance from the horrors of the attack on Pearl Harbor, Americans' feelings about the Japanese people are the most positive Gallup has recorded in five measurements since 1949. The chief reason for this may be the rapid growth of the Chinese economy at a time when Japan's growth has tapered off.

Survey Methods

Results for this Gallup poll are based on telephone interviews conducted Nov. 28-29, 2016, on the Gallup U.S. Daily survey, with a random sample of 1,021 adults, aged 18 and older, living in all 50 U.S. states and the District of Columbia. For results based on the total sample of national adults, the margin of sampling error is ±4 percentage points at the 95% confidence level. All reported margins of sampling error include computed design effects for weighting.

December 07, 2016

COST EDGES ACCESS AS MOST URGENT U.S. HEALTH PROBLEM

by Jeffrey M. Jones

Story Highlights

- *27% of Americans name cost as top health problem; 20% name access*
- *Cost and access were tied as top health problem in 2014 and 2015*
- *College graduates most likely to cite cost as top health problem*

PRINCETON, N.J. — More Americans now mention healthcare costs (27%) than mention access (20%) when asked to name the most urgent health problem facing the U.S. These two issues typically rank at the top of the list in Gallup's annual poll but have tied for first the past two years.

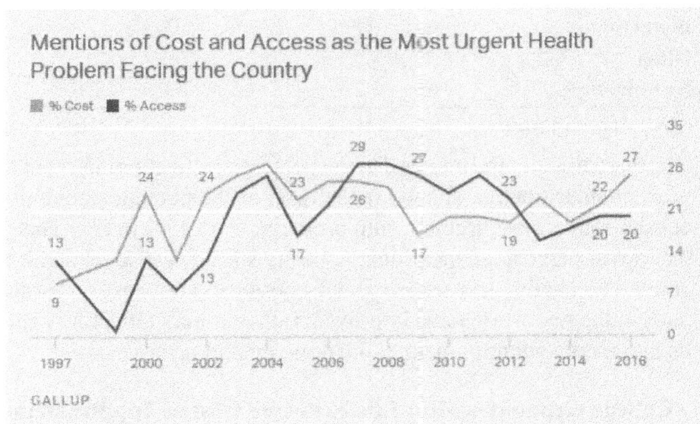

The Affordable Care Act was designed to address the problems of cost and access in the U.S. healthcare system. Since the law was implemented, the percentage of uninsured Americans has declined significantly. At the same time, many who have bought plans through federal and state health insurance exchanges are facing steep increases in what they will have to pay for those plans. Attention to those price increases from the news media and politicians this year may be one reason cost has edged ahead of access this year in Americans' identification of the most urgent health problem.

These results are from Gallup's Nov. 9-13 Health and Healthcare poll, conducted before the government released a report showing healthcare spending increased rapidly in 2015 and totaled $3.2 trillion in the U.S.

The last time that cost or access did not finish first as the most urgent health problem was in 2001. That year, bioterrorism edged cost and access amid a nationwide scare involving the mailing of letters containing anthrax spores to government and news media officials, resulting in five deaths.

Further back, AIDS was named the most urgent health problem in the 1980s and 1990s, including in 1987 when a record-high 68% mentioned it.

After cost and access, Americans today identify several other health conditions as the most urgent health problem, including cancer, obesity, diabetes, drug and alcohol abuse, and mental illness. Likely because of major advances in the treatment and prevention of the condition, AIDS now barely generates any mentions, with less than 1% naming it in 2016.

What would you say is the most urgent health problem facing this country at the present time? (Open-ended)

	% Mentioning
Cost	27
Access	20
Cancer	12
Obesity	8
Diabetes	3
Drug\Alcohol abuse	3
Mental illness	3
Flu/Viruses	2
Heart disease	2
Finding cures for diseases	1
Government interference	<1
AIDS	<1
Bioterrorism	0
Other	8
No opinion	11

Gallup, Nov 9-13, 2016

In addition to the increase in the percentage mentioning cost this year, another notable change is the drop in the percentage naming obesity as the most urgent health problem, from 15% to 8%. That is the lowest percentage mentioning obesity since 8% also named it in 2009. The decline in concern about obesity is not because obesity rates in the real world have improved; rather, it may reflect less public and media attention paid to the issue than in prior years.

College Graduates Most Likely to Cite Cost as Top Problem

The increased salience of cost as an urgent health problem this year is primarily driven by college graduates. Mentions of the issue are up 11 percentage points among college graduates, while other education groups' figures are similar to last year. Currently, 37% of college graduates name cost as the most urgent health problem. That compares with 27% of those with some college and 19% of those with a high school education or less.

Mentions of Cost as Most Urgent Health Problem, by Educational Attainment

	2015 %	2016 %	Change (pct. pts.)
College graduates	26	37	+11
Some college	27	27	0
High school or less	16	19	+3

Gallup

College graduates may be more aware than those with less education of the news reports about the significant increases in the cost of exchange-based plans.

Older Americans are typically more likely than younger Americans to say cost is the most urgent health problem. This year, 32% of those aged 50 and older name cost, compared with 24% of 30- to 49-year-olds and 18% of 18- to 29-year-olds.

Republicans, independents and Democrats do not differ meaningfully in their perceptions that cost is the most urgent health problem facing the country.

Implications

During his presidential campaign, Donald Trump promised to repeal the Affordable Care Act. With a Republican president and a Republican majority in Congress, the odds of a successful repeal are greater. The law has been controversial since its passage, and while it has helped to significantly reduce the percentage of Americans who lack health insurance, it is unclear whether it has helped to rein in healthcare costs. The recent government report on healthcare spending casts doubt on whether the law has achieved that objective.

Costs are now uppermost in Americans' minds when they are asked to name the most urgent health problem in the U.S., and that was the case even before the government report came out. Irrespective of whether Trump and the Republicans are ultimately successful in repealing the Affordable Care Act and possibly putting new legislation in place, it appears likely that healthcare costs will remain a major political issue throughout the next four years.

Survey Methods

Results for this Gallup poll are based on telephone interviews conducted Nov. 9-13, 2016, with a random sample of 1,019 adults, aged 18 and older, living in all 50 U.S. states and the District of Columbia. For results based on the total sample of national adults, the margin of sampling error is ±4 percentage points at the 95% confidence level. All reported margins of sampling error include computed design effects for weighting.

December 08, 2016

AMERICANS STILL SPLIT ON GOVERNMENT'S HEALTHCARE ROLE

by Justin McCarthy

Story Highlights

- *Slight majority says healthcare is a government responsibility*
- *Majority continues to favor system based on private insurance*
- *Party divisions reflected in views on both questions*

WASHINGTON, D.C. — Slightly more Americans agree (52%) than disagree (45%) that the federal government is responsible for making sure all Americans have healthcare coverage. This balance of views is similar to last year but represents a shift from 2012 to 2014, when majorities said ensuring healthcare coverage for all was not the government's job.

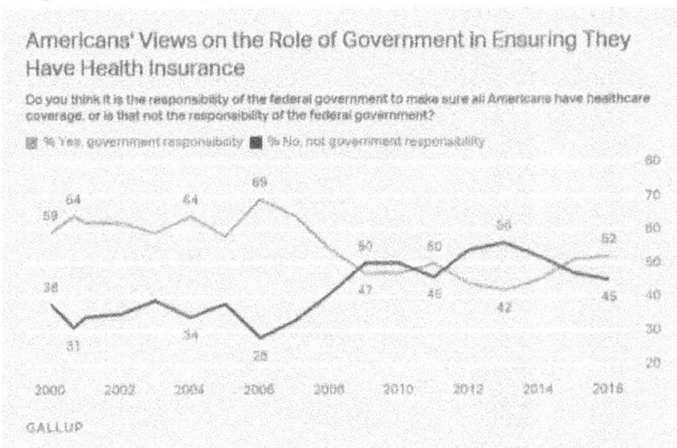

The latest findings are from Gallup's annual Health and Healthcare survey, conducted Nov. 9-13.

Compared with today, Americans were more widely inclined to say ensuring healthcare coverage is a federal responsibility between 2000 and 2008, with majorities of 54% to 69% saying this. But as President Barack Obama's Affordable Care Act was debated and implemented, the issue became politicized, leading to a nearly even division on the question from 2009 to 2011.

By 2012, sentiment against healthcare being a government responsibility swelled to 54%, and it remained the majority view through 2014. But last year's poll found Americans shifting more toward the view that the government should ensure all have healthcare, and this holds today.

Smaller Majority Prefers Private Healthcare System

When asked if they would prefer a government-run healthcare system or a system based on private insurance, majorities of Americans have consistently said they prefer a private system. However, this year's 10-percentage-point gap in favor of a private system (53%) compared with a government system (43%) is the narrowest in Gallup's trend.

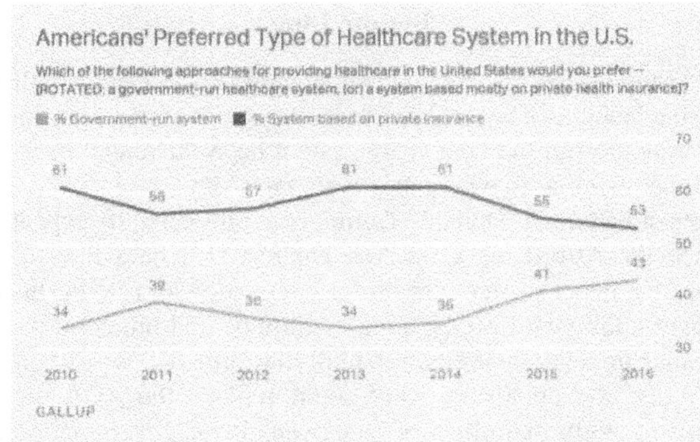

Parties Split in Views on Healthcare Responsibility, Approach

When Americans' views on both questions are assessed, they largely fall into two similarly sized camps. One group, capturing 39% of the public, consists of those who say ensuring healthcare for all is *not* the government's responsibility and would prefer a system based on private insurance. The other group, 35%, consists of Americans who say it is the government's responsibility to provide healthcare and would prefer a government-run healthcare system. A much smaller 14% believe it's the government's responsibility make sure everyone has healthcare, but want the system itself to be based on private insurance.

Nearly three-quarters of Republicans (72%) fall into the "free-enterprise group," saying it is *not* the government's responsibility and preferring a system based on private insurance. Meanwhile, a majority of Democrats (56%) fall into the "pro-government group," contending that it *is* the government's responsibility to provide healthcare and preferring a government-run system. Roughly equal percentages of Democrats believe it is the government's responsibility to ensure insurance coverage but prefer a private system (16%) or take the "free-enterprise" view (14%).

Independents are evenly split between the two major groups, with 36% falling into each.

Americans' Views of Government Responsibility to Ensure Healthcare Coverage vs. Healthcare System Preference, by Party

Aggregated data from 2015 and 2016

	National adults %	Republicans %	Independents %	Democrats %
Government should ensure/Prefer government system	35	8	36	56
Government should ensure/Prefer private system	14	12	15	16
Government should not ensure/Prefer government system	6	4	7	7
Government should not ensure/Prefer private system	39	72	36	14
Undesignated *	6	4	5	8

*Undesignated row represents the percentage who had no opinion on either or both questions.
Gallup

Bottom Line

Americans' views on the federal government's responsibility in ensuring healthcare coverage and whether government or the private sector should run the healthcare system have fluctuated over time, but remain similar to where they were last year.

President-elect Donald Trump has promised to repeal and replace the Affordable Care Act, but has said he'd like to keep certain elements of the current system – such as forcing insurers to cover adults with pre-existing conditions and allowing parents' insurance to cover their children until they are 26.

While the details of what could replace the ACA are still unknown, slight majorities of Americans favor government ensuring healthcare coverage and, separately, a system based on private insurance – both of which are major elements of the act as it currently stands. This could complicate the president-elect's efforts to undo the ACA while appealing to the interests of the Americans who recently elected him.

Survey Methods

Results for this Gallup poll are based on telephone interviews conducted Nov. 9-13, 2016, with a random sample of 1,019 adults, aged 18 and older, living in all 50 U.S. states and the District of Columbia. For results based on the total sample of national adults, the margin of sampling error is ±4 percentage points at the 95% confidence level. All reported margins of sampling error include computed design effects for weighting.

December 09, 2016

AMERICANS RATE HEALTHCARE QUALITY HIGH, COST LOW

by Art Swift

Story Highlights

- *56% say they are satisfied with total cost they pay for healthcare*
- *33% rate U.S. healthcare coverage as "excellent" or "good"*
- *Most Americans say the quality of healthcare nationwide is excellent or good*

WASHINGTON, D.C. — Americans are more likely to be positive about the cost, coverage and quality of their own healthcare than they are about the same aspects of healthcare nationwide. For both their own healthcare and healthcare nationally, they are most positive about quality and least positive about cost, with coverage falling in the middle.

Americans' Views of Healthcare Quality, Coverage and Cost, Personally and in the U.S.

	Own care %	Healthcare nationally %
Rate quality excellent/good	76	55
Rate coverage excellent/good	65	33
Satisfied with cost	56	19

Nov. 9-13, 2016
Gallup

These results are based on Gallup's annual Healthcare poll, conducted Nov. 9-13. The current patterns – that Americans are more positive about their own healthcare than about healthcare nationally, rate quality better than coverage and rate coverage better than cost – have been consistent in Gallup's polling since 2001. Currently, the personal versus national gaps in positive ratings are smallest in terms of quality (21 percentage points) and largest on cost (37 points).

Americans More Positive About Quality of Own Care Than Quality Nationally

Since 2001, Americans have been quite positive about the quality of the healthcare they personally receive. This year, 76% rate the quality of their healthcare as excellent or good, just a bit lower than the peak of 83% in 2007 and 2008. However, fewer Americans – although still a majority – are positive about healthcare quality in the U.S. In 2016, 55% say they are satisfied, down from a high of 62% in 2010 and 2012.

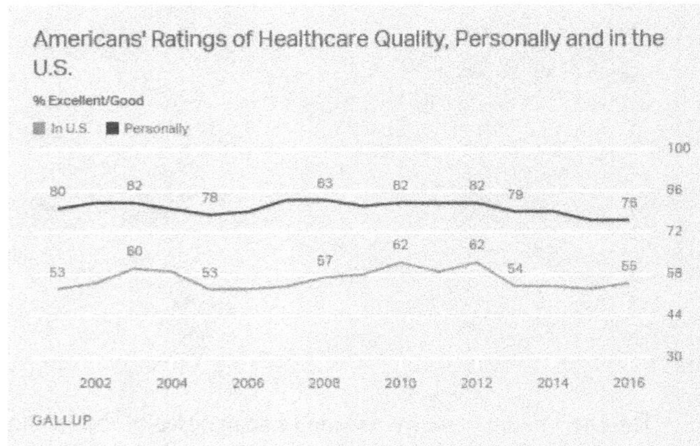

Americans Generally Satisfied With Their Own Healthcare Coverage

Sixty-five percent of Americans rate their own healthcare coverage as "excellent" or "good." This personal satisfaction has been roughly constant over the past 15 years, including after the Affordable Care Act was enacted in 2010 and the healthcare exchanges first opened in 2014.

While 65% of Americans rate their personal healthcare coverage positively, about half as many say healthcare coverage nationwide is excellent or good.

Americans' ratings of healthcare coverage nationally have improved modestly from the past decade. In 2005, 21% rated U.S. healthcare coverage excellent or good, and this rose to 26% in 2008. In 2009, before Obamacare became law but before it was fully implemented in 2014, ratings of healthcare coverage in the U.S. spiked, reaching 39% in 2010 and 41% in 2012 before dipping back down over the past several years.

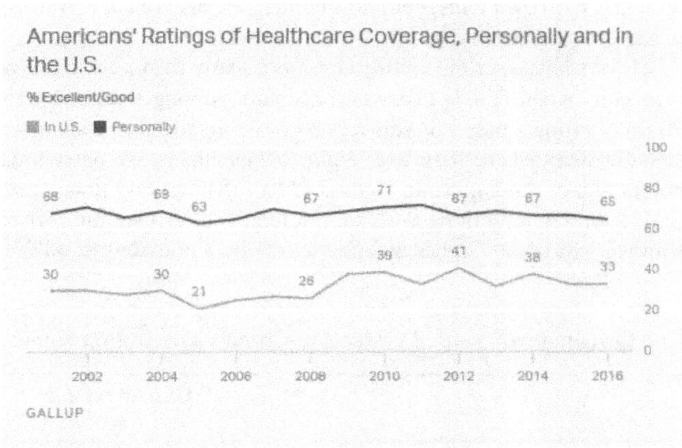

Americans Aren't as Satisfied With National Healthcare Costs

Americans are less satisfied with the cost of their healthcare than with their healthcare quality or coverage. This year, 56% say they are satisfied with the total cost they pay for healthcare, a figure that has been relatively stable over the past 15 years. It is down from a high point of 64% in 2001 and from 62% in 2009, the year before the ACA was signed into law. In 2006, 54% of Americans said they were satisfied with their healthcare costs, the low point in Gallup's trend.

While a majority of Americans say they are satisfied with their healthcare costs, few (19%) are satisfied with healthcare costs nationally. Satisfaction with nationwide costs rose to 26% in 2009, President Barack Obama's first year in office, but that uptick was not sustained. The 19% satisfied this year is within two points of the lowest Gallup has measured.

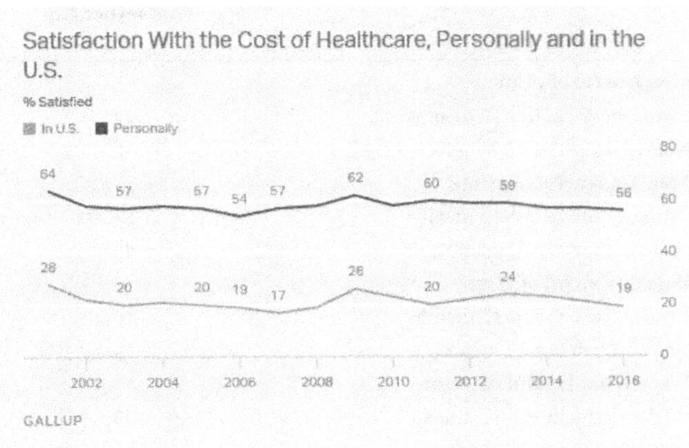

Bottom Line

Americans are more content with their own healthcare coverage, quality and costs than they are with those same aspects for Americans nationwide. This local versus national divergence is similar to how Americans rate education, crime and government.

Americans generally believe healthcare in the U.S. is high quality, though they widely believe such care is too costly. More money is spent in the U.S. on healthcare than in any other nation.

Obamacare will remain a central point of debate in the near term. Premium increases for the ACA next year may be affecting Americans' perceptions of healthcare costs nationwide, and there is fresh talk of repeal now that Donald Trump has been elected president and will have a GOP Congress to work with. Republicans in Congress have talked about "repealing and replacing" Obamacare since the law went into effect, and this discourse may still be influencing Americans' perceptions of the law. With this as a front-burner issue in Washington, it will be interesting to see if one year from now there is a significant shift in U.S. healthcare policy, and in Americans' perceptions on these questions.

Survey Methods

Results for this Gallup poll are based on telephone interviews conducted Nov. 9-13, 2016, with a random sample of 1,019 adults, aged 18 and older, living in all 50 U.S. states and the District of Columbia. For results based on the total sample of national adults, the margin of sampling error is ±4 percentage points at the 95% confidence level. All reported margins of sampling error include computed design effects for weighting.

December 12, 2016

CRIME VICTIMS MORE LIKELY TO OWN GUNS

by Riley Brands and Jeffrey M. Jones

Story Highlights

- *33% of victims vs. 28% of nonvictims own guns*
- *Pattern holds, taking into account gender, fear of crime*

WASHINGTON, D.C — Americans who have been recent crime victims report higher rates of gun ownership than those who have not been victims, according to an analysis of aggregated data from Gallup Crime surveys. Thirty-three percent of U.S. adults who have been recent victims of assault, theft or property crimes own a gun, compared with 28% of those who have not been victims – a statistically significant difference.

Gun Ownership Among Americans by Crime Victimization Status

	Gun ownership %
Crime victim in last 12 months	33
Nonvictim in last 12 months	28

Gallup Annual Crime Surveys, 2000, 2005, 2007-2011, 2013-2016

As part of its annual Crime survey, Gallup asks Americans whether in the past 12 months they personally have been the victim of a number of crimes, including burglary, property theft, assault and vandalism. In most years the survey has also asked Americans whether they personally own a gun, including in 2000, 2005, 2007-2011 and 2013-2016. The analysis is based on a combined 11,165 interviews from those surveys. Overall, an average of 17% of Americans reported being the victim of at least one of the crimes in those polls, and 29% said they personally owned a gun.

Although it is not possible to know from the survey questions whether the crime prompted the individual to buy a gun or if the person owned a gun before the crime occurred, the modest yet significant relationship between recent crime victimization and gun ownership is clear. Also, because the survey asks only about crime victimization in the last 12 months, it is possible many people victimized by crimes in the more distant past bought a gun in reaction to those crimes. Thus, the analysis may understate the relationship between crime victimization and gun ownership.

Past Gallup analysis has shown that men are far more likely than women to own a gun – in fact, gender is the strongest predictor of gun ownership. For both men and women, gun ownership is higher among crime victims than nonvictims. Specifically, 48% of men who have experienced a recent personal or property crime own a gun, compared with 43% of men who have not been victimized. Meanwhile, 19% of female crime victims own a gun, compared with 14% of all other women.

Gun Ownership by Gender and Crime Victimization Status

	Gun ownership %
Men	
Crime victim in last 12 months	48
Nonvictim in last 12 months	43
Women	
Crime victim in last 12 months	19
Nonvictim in last 12 months	14

Gallup Annual Crime Surveys, 2000, 2005, 2007-2011, 2013-2016

Gun ownership overall is also much higher among those living in towns or rural areas (39%) than those living in suburbs (28%) or cities (22%). Suburban and rural crime victims show higher gun ownership rates than their nonvictim counterparts, but this is not true among urban residents. To some degree, tougher restrictions on gun ownership in many cities may make it harder for crime victims to obtain guns.

Gun Ownership by Place of Residence and Crime Victimization Status

	Gun ownership %
Live in big/small city	
All	22
Crime victim in last 12 months	22
Nonvictim in last 12 months	23
Live in suburb of big/small city	
All	28
Crime victim in last 12 months	39
Nonvictim in last 12 months	26
Live in town/rural area	
All	39
Crime victim in last 12 months	47
Nonvictim in last 12 months	38

Gallup Annual Crime Surveys, 2000, 2005, 2007-2011, 2013-2016

Even Accounting for Fear, Crime Victims More Likely to Own Guns

Being a crime victim can understandably motivate someone to purchase a gun, but so can the fear of becoming a victim, even for those who have not been victims. The relationships between crime fears and gun ownership are complex, largely because subgroups who are more likely to own guns, particularly men, are also much *less* likely to say they are afraid of crime.

Nevertheless, crime victims are more likely than nonvictims to own guns when fear is taken into account. Among those who are afraid of crime – based on self-reports of being afraid to walk alone at night near where they live – gun ownership is six percentage points higher among crime victims (27%) than among nonvictims (21%). And among those who are not fearful of crime, gun ownership is eight points higher among victims than nonvictims, 40% to 32%.

Gun Ownership by Fear of Crime and Crime Victimization Status

	Gun ownership %
Fearful of crime	
Crime victim in last 12 months	27
Nonvictim in last 12 months	21
Not fearful of crime	
Crime victim in last 12 months	40
Nonvictim in last 12 months	32

Crime fear based on response to question: "Is there any area near where you live – that is, within a mile – where you would be afraid to walk alone at night?"
Gallup Annual Crime Surveys, 2000, 2005, 2007-2011, 2013-2016

The patterns hold by gender as well: Taking into account fear of crime and gender, gun ownership is at least marginally higher among crime victims than among nonvictims.

Gun Ownership by Fear of Crime and Crime Victimization Status, Among Men and Women

	Gun ownership %
Men fearful of crime	
Crime victim in last 12 months	44
Nonvictim in last 12 months	36
Men not fearful of crime	
Crime victim in last 12 months	51
Nonvictim in last 12 months	45
Women fearful of crime	
Crime victim in last 12 months	16
Nonvictim in last 12 months	14
Women not fearful of crime	
Crime victim in last 12 months	23
Nonvictim in last 12 months	15

Crime fear based on response to question: "Is there any area near where you live – that is, within a mile – where you would be afraid to walk alone at night?"
Gallup Annual Crime Surveys, 2000, 2005, 2007-2011, 2013-2016

A separate statistical analysis that takes into account the influence of several factors related to gun ownership – including gender, marital status and place of residence – shows that crime victimization has a unique effect on gun ownership. Although gender is the strongest single predictor of gun ownership, being a crime victim is one of the more important factors in likelihood to own a gun.

Bottom Line

Although the analysis demonstrates a statistically significant relationship between crime victimization and gun ownership, it cannot answer why the relationship exists. An obvious explanation is some of those who have been a crime victim purchase a gun as a reaction to that event. The Gallup data do not explore when the gun purchase was made in relation to when the crime occurred, so it is not possible to know to what extent this explains the relationship.

It does not appear that those who live in higher-crime areas, and who therefore may be more likely to become a victim, are also more likely to own guns. Gallup's Crime surveys show urban residents are much more likely than rural residents to report being crime victims, 20% to 15%, but rural residents are far more likely to own guns. The data do suggest, though, that crime victimization has a greater effect on gun ownership among suburban and rural residents than among urban residents.

Nor does fear of crime explain the relationship, because gun ownership is higher among victims than nonvictims when fear is held constant. It is possible some other unmeasurable psychological, cultural or situational characteristics could be related to both one's likelihood of buying a gun and one's vulnerability to being a crime victim.

In 2013, Gallup asked gun owners why they keep a weapon. The majority, 60%, cited personal safety or protection. More broadly, Americans tend to believe that having a gun in the home or carrying concealed weapons would do more to keep people safe than to put them at risk of harm.

U.S. gun policy has come under increased scrutiny in recent decades, driven partly by mass shootings but also by the high rate of gun-related homicides. For crime victims, the threat of victimization is no longer a possibility but a reality. Crime victims' desire to protect themselves may explain why many gun owners do not favor stricter gun laws, and why gun owners as well as nonowners are reluctant to back outright bans on guns.

Survey Methods

Results for this Gallup poll are based on aggregated telephone interviews from Gallup's annual Crime survey, conducted each October. The analysis is based on a random sample of 11,165 adults, aged 18 and older, living in all 50 U.S. states and the District of Columbia. For results based on the total sample of national adults, the margin of sampling error is ±1 percentage point at the 95% confidence level.

For results based on the sample of 1,667 adults who had personally been the victim of a crime in the past 12 months, the margin of sampling error is ±3 percentage points at the 95% confidence level. The crimes included in the survey are having their house or apartment broken into, having money or property stolen, having a car stolen, having property vandalized, having money or property taken by force, being mugged or physically assaulted, and being sexually assaulted.

For results based on the sample of 9,498 adults who had not personally been the victim of a crime in the past 12 months, the margin of sampling error is ±1 percentage point at the 95% confidence level.

December 12, 2016

FOUR IN 10 IN U.S. DISSATISFIED WITH THEIR HEALTHCARE COSTS

by Lydia Saad

Story Highlights

- *Dissatisfaction at 48% among those with private health insurance*
- *Rising premiums, lack of employer help spur dissatisfaction*
- *Many in dissatisfied group have put off treatment*

PRINCETON, N.J. — Even as the majority of Americans applaud the quality, cost and coverage of their healthcare, four in 10 adults – a conspicuous minority in the era of the Affordable Care Act – are dissatisfied with their healthcare costs. Americans who are covered by Medicare or Medicaid are the least dissatisfied (29%), while dissatisfaction is highest among the uninsured (62%) and averages 48% among those with private insurance.

Are you generally satisfied or dissatisfied with the total cost you pay for your healthcare?

	Satisfied %	Dissatisfied %	No opinion %
U.S. adults	56	42	3
Type of health insurance			
Medicaid/Medicare	69	29	2
Private insurance	52	48	<1
No insurance	31	62	7

Based on 2014-2016 Gallup Healthcare polls
Gallup

These figures are based on combined data from Gallup's 2014, 2015 and 2016 Health and Healthcare polls, conducted each November. Across this period, coinciding with the implementation of the individual mandate component of the Affordable Care Act (ACA), an average 42% of U.S. adults report being dissatisfied with their healthcare costs. That is up from 38% on average from 2011-2013, although similar to satisfaction levels a decade ago.

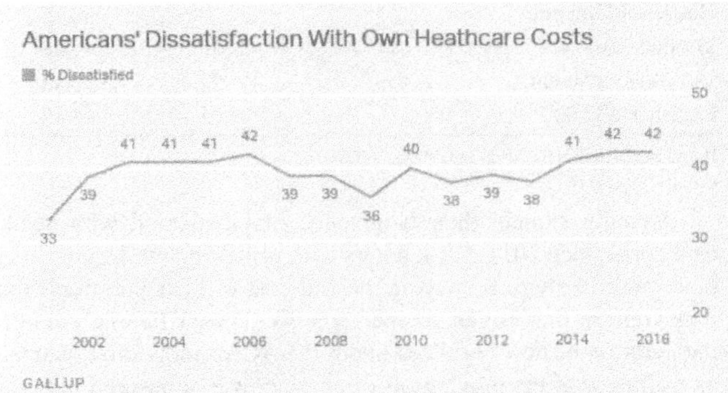

Just over a third of Americans in Gallup's 2014-2016 healthcare polling (37%) report being enrolled in a government healthcare plan such as Medicaid or Medicare; 52% get their healthcare through private insurance; and 11% have no insurance.

Among the three groups, dissatisfaction has increased the most in recent years for those with private insurance, rising to 49% in

2016 from an average 40% during 2011-2013, and more broadly from 31% in 2001.

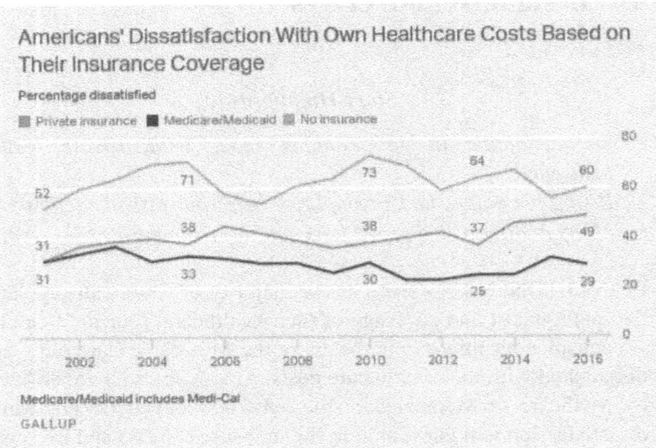

Which Privately Insured Americans Are Most Cost-Sensitive?

Satisfaction with healthcare costs among Americans with private health insurance does not appear to be related to their own income level, but is related to the degree to which they contribute to their own insurance premiums.

Among those whose employer pays the full amount, just 27% are dissatisfied. This rises to 46% among those who share premium costs with their employer and to 60% who pay the full costs themselves.

Satisfaction With Healthcare Costs Among U.S. Adults With Private Health Insurance

	Satisfied %	Dissatisfied %
Who pays healthcare premium		
Employer pays full amount	72	27
Costs are shared	53	46
Consumer pays full amount	40	60
Household income		
$75,000 or more	51	48
$30,000 to $74,999	52	48
Less than $30,000	55	45

Based on 2014-2016 Gallup Healthcare polls
Gallup

Helping explain their heightened dissatisfaction with healthcare costs since 2011-2013, adults with private health insurance are now more likely to be paying the full cost of their premiums than they were in that earlier period, 28% vs. 21%. This likely reflects the addition of new enrollees under the ACA's individual mandate, as well as workers moving off of an employer-sponsored plan – in some cases after being dropped – and into the ACA exchanges.

Cost increases also appear irksome to healthcare consumers because the percentage of Americans who are dissatisfied is directly related to the extent to which their healthcare premiums went up in the prior year.

- A third of adults with private health insurance say the amount they pay for health insurance went up a lot in the prior year. Of this group, 81% are dissatisfied with their healthcare costs.
- Another 38% of private health insurance holders say their premiums went up a little. Forty percent of this group is dissatisfied with their costs.
- Just over a quarter of private insurance holders say their premiums were steady or declined, and 28% of this group is dissatisfied with their healthcare costs.

Consumers' dissatisfaction with healthcare costs is more than a mindset – it is rooted in difficult decisions. Fifty percent of those who are dissatisfied with what they pay say that they or a family member put off medical treatment in the past year because of the cost. This includes 32% who say the delay was related to a serious medical condition. By contrast, among those who are satisfied with their costs, 18% put off a medical treatment of any kind, including 11% for whom it was a serious condition.

Bottom Line

While it may be hard for average consumers to be "satisfied" with the price of anything that can cost them thousands of dollars, dissatisfaction with healthcare costs depends a lot on the type of coverage a person has. Medicare recipients enjoy fairly broad coverage with relatively low health insurance premiums unless they opt for supplemental insurance. The uninsured pay no monthly premiums but have the burden of paying all of their medical bills. Privately insured adults are largely satisfied with their benefits, but also bear a lot of the costs. Their growing dissatisfaction with those costs likely reflects the squeeze from all sides: reduced employer health insurance benefits, rising health insurance premiums and rising deductibles at a time when medical costs are outpacing inflation.

The Affordable Care Act has made health insurance available to millions of Americans who previously had no insurance and provides subsidies for those least able to pay on their own. The program's provisions requiring insurance companies to cover preexisting conditions also likely contribute to Americans' continued high satisfaction with the level of coverage they receive. However, healthcare costs remain a vexing problem for the system as a whole, as well as for individual Americans.

Survey Methods

The 2014-2016 results reported here are based on combined results from Gallup's 2014, 2015 and 2016 Health and Healthcare surveys. The surveys were conducted by telephone each November with a random sample of at least 800 adults, aged 18 and older, living in all 50 U.S. states and the District of Columbia. For results based on the combined sample of 2,868 national adults, the margin of sampling error is ±2 percentage points at the 95% confidence level.

For results based on the combined sample of 1,409 adults with private health insurance, the margin of sampling error is ±3 percentage points at the 95% confidence level. For results based on the combined sample of 1,257 adults on Medicare or Medicaid, the margin of sampling error is ±3 percentage points at the 95% confidence level. For results based on the combined sample of 192 adults with no health insurance, the margin of sampling error is ±9 percentage points at the 95% confidence level.

December 14, 2016
TRUMP'S TRANSITION APPROVAL LOWER THAN PREDECESSORS'

by Jeffrey M. Jones

Story Highlights

- *48% approve, 48% disapprove of how Trump is handling transition*
- *Past three presidents-elect had approval at or above 65%*
- *Transition approval has usually exceeded initial job approval ratings*

PRINCETON, N.J. — Americans are evenly divided in their assessment of the way Donald Trump is handling his presidential transition, with 48% approving and 48% disapproving. By contrast, 65% or more approved of the way the past three presidents-elect were handling their transitions at similar points in time, including 75% for Barack Obama in December 2008.

Do you approve or disapprove of the way ... is handling his presidential transition?

	Dates	Approve %	Disapprove %
Donald Trump	2016 Dec 7-11	48	48
Barack Obama	2008 Dec 12-14	75	17
George W. Bush	2001 Jan 5-7	65	26
Bill Clinton	1992 Dec 18-20	67	15

Based on mid-December readings; Bush's reading was his first after being named winner in mid-December
Gallup

Trump's rating is based on a new Dec. 7-11 Gallup poll and gives an initial read on how Americans think the president-elect is handling the transition process. Trump has announced his choices for many of the cabinet-level positions in his administration, selecting many business and military leaders and relatively few with prior political experience. In addition, he has held public rallies in states crucial to his victory and weighed in on some issues on Twitter.

One major reason Trump's transition approval lags well behind his predecessors' is that members of the opposition party are far more critical of Trump than they were of prior presidents-elect. Whereas 17% of Democrats approve of Trump's presidential transition, the ratings for Obama and Bill Clinton among Republicans and for George W. Bush among Democrats were near 50%.

Presidential Transition Approval Ratings, by Political Party

	Dates	Democrats %	Independents %	Republicans %
Donald Trump	2016 Dec 7-11	17	46	86
Barack Obama	2008 Dec 12-14	93	75	53
George W. Bush	2001 Jan 5-7	46	59	93
Bill Clinton	1992 Dec 18-20	83	64	50

Based on mid-December readings; Bush's reading was his first after being named winner in mid-December
Gallup

Democrats' low level of approval of Trump may foreshadow a high degree of political polarization in his forthcoming job approval ratings as president, which has been the case for Obama during his time in office.

Trump also does significantly worse among independents than the past three presidents-elect did: 46% approve of the way Trump is handling his transition, compared with 64% for Clinton, 59% for Bush and 75% for Obama.

Trump receives a high 86% approval rating among Republicans, but that is still slightly lower than approval ratings for Bush (93%) and Obama (93%) among their parties' supporters. However, it is similar to Clinton's 83% transition approval among Democrats.

Transition Approval Ratings Usually Exceed Initial Job Approval Ratings

Transition approval ratings taken in December and January have tended to be higher than presidents' initial job approval rating after they were inaugurated. On average, recent presidents' transition approval ratings have been about eight points higher than their first presidential job approval ratings.

Transition Approval Ratings Versus Initial Job Approval Ratings, Recent Presidents

	Transition approval, mid-December/early January %	Transition approval, mid-January %	Initial job approval %
Obama	75	83	68
Bush	65	61	57
Clinton	67	68	58

Gallup

If the recent historical pattern holds, Trump's initial job approval rating after he takes office could be in the low 40% range. To date, the lowest initial job approval rating in Gallup's records is 51%, held by both Ronald Reagan in 1981 and George H.W. Bush in 1989.

The difference in transition approval versus initial job approval is mostly attributable to an increase in the percentage of Americans who do not have an opinion of the job the newly inaugurated president is doing. For the past three presidents, an average of 20% of Americans did not have an opinion of the job each was doing in Gallup's first measurement. That compares with an average 11% not having an opinion of the way the president was handling his transition in the final Gallup update on that measure for each.

Implications

In a little more than one month, Donald Trump will take office as the nation's 45th president. Presidents-elect generally enjoy broad public support during their transition phase, but that has not been the case for Trump – with as many Americans disapproving of the way he is handling his transition as approving of it.

Trump has a stiff challenge in winning over the public, given his low favorable ratings, which may have been a factor in him losing the popular vote. George W. Bush also took office having lost the popular vote, but he was a more well-liked figure and enjoyed solid public support during his transition phase and in the first weeks after he took office.

Trump still has time to turn the tide and avoid starting his presidency with the lowest public support in Gallup's polling history, but that would largely entail gaining the support of independents and, in particular, Democrats – most of whom appear reluctant to back him.

Survey Methods

Results for this Gallup poll are based on telephone interviews conducted Dec. 7-11, 2016, with a random sample of 1,028 adults, aged 18 and older, living in all 50 U.S. states and the District of Columbia. For results based on the total sample of national adults, the margin of sampling error is ±4 percentage points at the 95% confidence level. All reported margins of sampling error include computed design effects for weighting.

December 14, 2016

LIFE EVALUATIONS OF LGBT AMERICANS DECLINE AFTER ELECTION

by Gary J. Gates

Story Highlights

- *Percentage of LGBT adults "thriving" dropped 10 points after election*
- *Far fewer Democrats in general classified as thriving after election*
- *Republican life evaluations improved post-election*

WASHINGTON, D.C. — The election of Donald Trump as president had a significant negative effect on American adults who identify as lesbian, gay, bisexual or transgender (LGBT). The percentage of LGBT adults rating their lives positively enough to be classified as "thriving" declined 10 percentage points after the election, from 51% to 41%. There was little change in life evaluations among non-LGBT Americans.

U.S. Life Evaluation: Americans Classified as "Thriving," by LGBT Status

	% Thriving
LGBT	
Oct 1-Nov 8	51
Nov 9-Dec 6	41
Non-LGBT	
Oct 1-Nov 8	57
Nov 9-Dec 6	55

Gallup-Healthways Well-Being Index

Americans' life evaluations are tracked as part of the Gallup-Healthways Well-Being Index. Gallup and Healthways classify Americans as "thriving," "struggling" or "suffering" according to how they rate their current and future lives on a ladder scale with steps numbered from 0 to 10, based on the Cantril Self-Anchoring Striving Scale. Those who rate their present life a 7 or higher and their life in five years an 8 or higher are classified as thriving.

The LGBT community traditionally has been among the most reliable Democratic constituencies. Before the election, Gallup research showed that 12% of LGBT adults had a favorable opinion of Trump, contrasted with a 55% favorable opinion of Hillary Clinton. Additionally, exit polls showed that 77% of LGBT voters picked Clinton on Nov. 8, slightly higher than the 70% who voted for Barack Obama in 2008.

This drop in life evaluations among LGBT adults after the election is part of a more general pattern evident among all Democrats, whose outlook on life also dropped significantly. In the month before the election, Democrats were slightly more likely than Republicans to be classified as thriving (59% to 56%, respectively). That changed after the election, however – 50% of Democrats are now considered thriving (a nine-point drop), compared with 60% of Republicans (a four-point increase).

U.S. Life Evaluation: Americans Classified as "Thriving," by Party ID

	% Thriving
Democrats	
Oct 1-Nov 8	59
Nov 9-Dec 6	50
Independents	
Oct 1-Nov 8	50
Nov 9-Dec 6	49
Republicans	
Oct 1-Nov 8	56
Nov 9-Dec 6	60

Gallup-Healthways Well-Being Index

The large decline in life evaluations among LGBT adults does not appear to be simply a result of their Democratic leanings. Across a variety of demographic characteristics, including gender, race/ethnicity and education, Democrats tend to show large drops in "thriving" while most Republicans report modest increases. However, among LGBT individuals, the 10-point overall decline in "thriving" is seen in both Democrats and Republicans. This suggests that concerns about the prospects of a Trump administration cross party lines among LGBT people.

Bottom Line

Declining life evaluations among those in the losing party after a presidential election are not without precedent. After Obama's 2012 election, a win for Democrats, Gallup data showed that the percentage of Republicans classified as thriving had dropped from 47% in October to 40% in December. Democrats, on the other hand, increased from 54% to 57%. After Obama's first election in 2008, life evaluations among racial and ethnic minorities improved – particularly among black Americans – though this was not true after his 2012 win.

The LGBT community has had substantial political success during Obama's presidency. In his first term, Congress repealed the military's "don't ask, don't tell" policy that barred open service among lesbians, gay men and bisexuals. In 2015, the U.S. Supreme Court ruled that same-sex couples have a constitutional right to marriage. And this year, the Defense Department lifted the ban on transgender people serving openly in the military. The precipitous decline in life evaluations among LGBT Americans after Trump's election may indicate a particular vulnerability in a group concerned about holding on to these political gains.

Survey Methods

These results are based on telephone interviews with a random sample of 31,898 U.S. adults, aged 18 and older, living in all 50 states and the District of Columbia, conducted Oct. 1-Dec. 6, 2016, as part of the Gallup-Healthways Well-Being Index survey. Before the election on Nov. 8, 18,736 individuals were surveyed; 13,162 were surveyed after the election. The margin of error varies by subgroup sample size. For political party affiliation, it is ±2 to ±3 percentage points at the 95% confidence level. For LGBT status, it is ±5 percentage points. All reported margins of sampling error include computed design effects for weighting.

December 15, 2016

AMERICANS' IDENTIFICATION AS MIDDLE CLASS EDGES BACK UP

by Frank Newport

Story Highlights

- *58% identify as upper-middle or middle class in 2016*
- *This is up from 50% in 2012 and 51% in 2015*
- *The rise in middle-class identification has occurred across income groups*

PRINCETON, N.J. — The percentage of Americans who say they belong in the upper-middle and middle class has edged up to an average 58% this year, compared with 50% in 2012 and 51% in 2015.

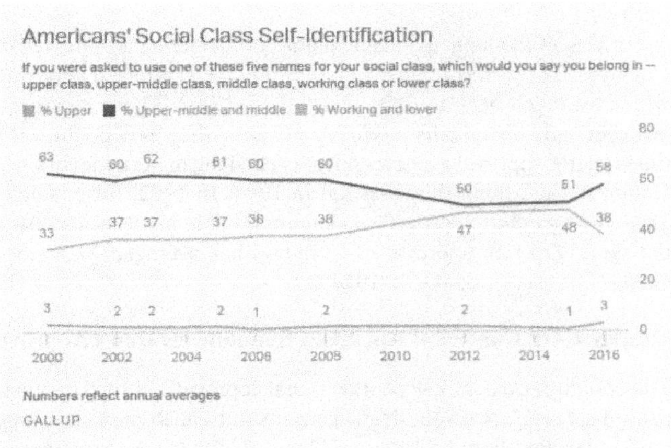

The 2016 figure is based on the average of three separate polls conducted in September, October and December. Despite this year's recovery in middle-class identification compared with 2015 and 2012, middle-class identification remains slightly below the 61% average measured between 2000 and 2008.

This year's uptick in middle-class identification was not directly related to the presidential election, even as economic confidence rose sharply after Nov. 8. Two of the three recent surveys showing higher middle-class identification were conducted before the election, and there was little change in the third, post-election survey conducted Dec. 7-11.

Gallup's class identification question gives Americans five categories from which to choose. Across nine surveys conducted since June 2008, only between 1% and 3% of Americans say they are upper class, with the rest spread out across upper-middle-, middle-, working- and lower-class categories. In 2012 and 2015, almost twice as many Americans put themselves in the "lower class" category as did in 2008 and 2016. This, combined with a slight increase in working-class identification in 2012 and 2015, resulted in the drop in middle-class identification during those years.

Americans' Social Class Self-Identification

	2008 %	2012-2015 %	2016 %
Upper class	2	2	3
Upper-middle class	18	12	15
Middle class	44	39	43
Working class	28	33	30
Lower class	8	15	8

Figures represent averages for June 2008 and two September 2008 surveys, one 2012 and one 2015 survey, and three 2016 surveys
Gallup

Americans' self-identified social class does not necessarily reflect their actual socioeconomic status because in responding to the question, Americans can choose to place themselves in any category they want. However, there is a strong relationship between respondents' self-reported income and their self-placement on the social class spectrum. Americans are two to three times more likely to identify as upper-middle or middle class if they report a household income of at least $75,000 than they are if their income is under $30,000, based on aggregated data across the three time periods.

Identification as Upper-Middle/Middle Class, by Income

	2008 %	2012-2015 %	2016 %
Income			
<$30,000	28	25	36
$30,000 to <$75,000	59	48	53
$75,000+	86	78	82
National average	62	51	58

Figures represent averages for June 2008 and two September 2008 surveys, one 2012 and one 2015 survey, and three 2016 surveys
Gallup

The shifts in class identification between 2008 and the present occurred across income categories. Although the patterns fluctuate, middle-class identification dipped in each income group in 2012-2015 and recovered in each group at least somewhat this year.

The shifting percentages over the past eight years in those identifying as middle class occurred mostly among those without a college degree. Middle-class identification among those with college degrees has been more stable – and high.

Identification as Upper-Middle/Middle Class, by Education

	2008 %	2012-2015 %	2016 %
Education			
Less than high school	36	29	36
High school graduate	50	38	49
Some college	60	45	53
College graduate	80	76	79
National average	62	51	58

Figures represent averages for June 2008 and two September 2008 surveys, one 2012 and one 2015 survey, and three 2016 surveys
Gallup

Even though the political circumstances have changed significantly since 2008, the dip in 2012 and 2015 (compared with 2008) and then the recovery this year was fairly similar among Republicans, independents and Democrats.

Implications

With the exceptions of 2012 and 2015, Americans' subjective class identification has been fairly consistent over the past 16 years. Relatively few see themselves as lower class, and even fewer identify as upper class. That leaves the bulk of the population viewing themselves as working or middle class, with the rest in the upper-middle-class category.

Gallup did not measure subjective class identification between 2008 and 2012, and it's possible that the drop in middle-class identification in the latter year, along with 2015, reflected the lingering aftermath of the Great Recession and mortgage crisis.

The uptick this fall, across three separate surveys, could reflect many factors. The rise was not confined to just one partisan group and was not a direct result of the election of Donald Trump. Perhaps most importantly, middle-class household incomes rose last year, and the shift from lower- and working-class to middle-class identification could reflect these real-world circumstances.

Researchers over the years have made many attempts to classify who is and who is not middle class, based on income and household composition. The Pew Research Center, for example, analyzed government data and reported that the percentage objectively in the middle class has declined significantly from 1971 to last year. It is, however, still too early for analysts to determine whether the percentage of Americans who can be grouped in the middle class based on their incomes and household compositions did in fact rise in the final months of this year.

Survey Methods

Results for the most recent Gallup polls reported in this article are based on telephone interviews conducted in surveys conducted Sept. 14-18, Oct. 5-9 and Dec. 7-11, 2016, with random samples of 1,033, 1,017 and 1,028 adults, respectively, aged 18 and older, living in all 50 U.S. states and the District of Columbia. For results based on each of these samples of national adults, the margin of sampling error is ±4 percentage points at the 95% confidence level. All reported margins of sampling error include computed design effects for weighting.

December 15, 2016

U.S. CONGRESSIONAL APPROVAL AVERAGES WEAK 17% FOR 2016

by Art Swift

Story Highlights

- *2016 average consistent with average approval ratings in the 2010s*
- *Seventh consecutive year approval has averaged below 20%*
- *Republicans, Democrats nearly even in approval of Congress*

WASHINGTON, D.C. — For the seventh year in a row, less than 20% of Americans approved of the job that Congress is doing. In 2016, approval averaged 17% for the year, only slightly better than the all-time low average of 14% in 2013.

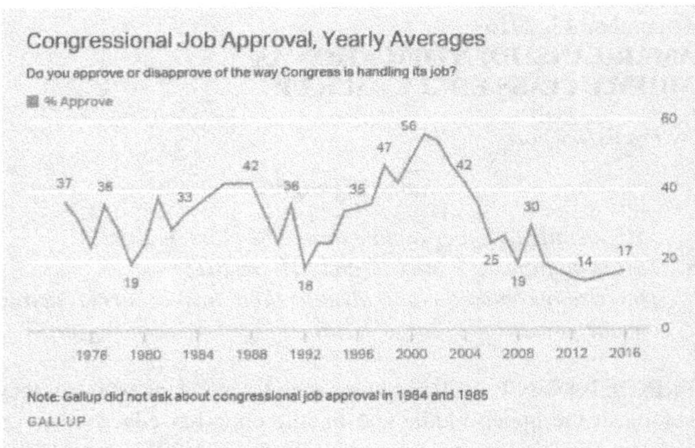

The last time the yearly average exceeded the teens was in 2009 (30%).

It wasn't too long ago that a majority of Americans approved of Congress. The terrorist attacks of Sept. 11, 2001, affected approval, which averaged 56% in 2001 and 54% in 2002. Those measures, however, are historically atypical, because they reflect the only times yearly approval averages have reached the majority level since Gallup began asking this question in 1974. In 1992, for example, 18% of Americans approved of Congress, while in 1979, 19% said the same. Overall, approval of Congress has averaged 31% since Gallup first measured this in 1974.

Despite GOP Control of Congress, Republicans Don't Approve

The ongoing streak of low congressional approval is rooted in bipartisan displeasure with the legislative institution. Republicans may have controlled both branches of Congress for the past two years, but they aren't any more likely to approve of Congress now than when Congress was divided or when Democrats controlled both houses from 2007 to 2010.

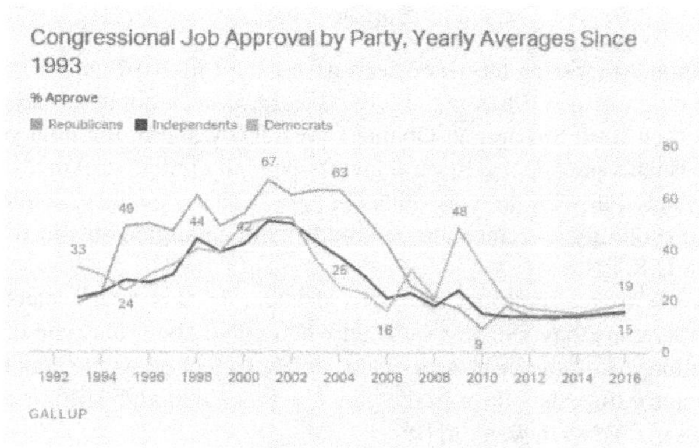

Since 1992, those who identified with the party in control of Congress have tended to be more approving than those identifying with the party out of power. From 1995 through 2006, more Republicans than Democrats approved of Congress, and in the mid-2000s, Republicans' approval of Congress far exceeded Democrats'. In 2004, for example, 63% of Republicans approved of Congress, compared with 25% of Democrats.

When Democrats retook both houses in 2007, GOP support plummeted while Democratic support rose modestly, but enough so that Democratic approval generally exceeded Republican approval during the period of Democratic control that lasted through 2010. In only two years – 2009 and 2010, when Democrats controlled Congress and Barack Obama was president – did Democratic approval tower over Republican approval.

From 2011 through 2014, with Democrats controlling the Senate and Republicans controlling the House, neither party's supporters held Congress in high esteem. When Republicans took control of both houses in 2015, there was a brief period when GOP supporters were more likely than Democratic supporters to approve. However, that didn't last, perhaps because loyalists were frustrated with the lack of progress on issues of importance to the party.

Even with a new president-elect in place to lead a unified Republican Congress next year, partisan views about Congress haven't changed. In December 2016, 18% of Americans, including 16% of Democrats and 16% of Republicans, approve of Congress.

Bottom Line

Congressional approval in the U.S., while never high, saw the bottom fall out in the 2010s. Americans have given Congress low approval ratings throughout the decade, possibly owing to the hyperpartisanship and gridlock resulting from divided party control of government, plus perceptions that Congress is controlled by major donors and lobbyists.

While disapproval of Congress by party differed, often markedly, in the Bill Clinton and George W. Bush administrations, disapproval has been particularly acute during the Obama years, as both parties have given Congress abysmal ratings. This could be related to Americans' frustration with the seeming inability of Congress to get important things done, and their frequent selection of the government as the nation's most important problem. In the previous two presidential administrations, supporters of the party in power generally were favorable toward Congress, but that has not been the case in recent years. It remains to be seen whether a President Donald Trump, joined by a Republican Congress, will bolster the overall ratings of Congress somewhat by the end of 2017, especially among Republicans.

Survey Methods

Results for this Gallup poll are based on telephone interviews conducted throughout 2016, with a random sample of 12,258 adults, aged 18 and older, living in all 50 U.S. states and the District of Columbia. For results based on the total sample of national adults, the margin of sampling error is ±1 percentage point at the 95% confidence level. All reported margins of sampling error include computed design effects for weighting.

December 16, 2016

SATISFACTION WITH U.S. DIRECTION STEADY BUT HISTORICALLY LOW

by Michael Smith

Story Highlights

- *27% of Americans satisfied in December with the way things are going in U.S.*
- *2016 average of 27% is similar to 2012-2015 combined average of 25%*
- *Republicans' satisfaction improving, Democrats' worsening since election*

WASHINGTON, D.C. — In 2016, an average of 27% of Americans have been satisfied with the way things are going in the U.S. This is comparable to averages since 2012 but is lower than the 37% yearly average over the 37 years Gallup has tracked this measure.

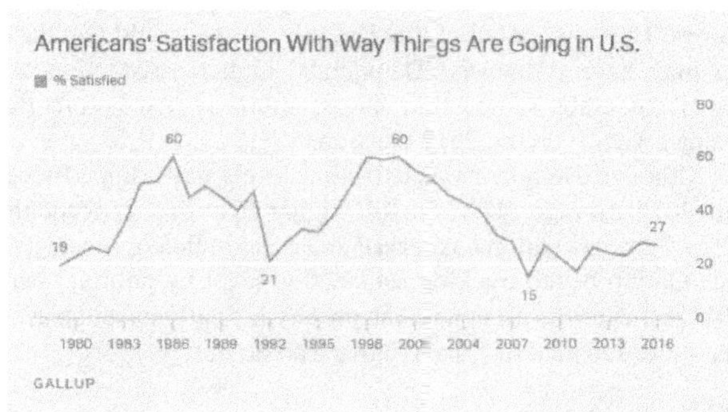

Satisfaction in 2016 Resembles Recent Years but Is Historically Low

In the past decade, the U.S. has faced a range of domestic and international challenges including the Iraq War, the global financial crisis, several high-profile mass shootings, increased racial tensions and partisan gridlock in the federal government – all of which could have negatively affected Americans' perceptions of the way things were going in the country.

This year's average satisfaction is similar to the combined average of 25% from 2012-2015 and is slightly higher than the 22% combined average from 2007-2011 The latter period included record-low yearly averages of 15% in 2008 and 17% in 2011.

In the recent trend, 2006 was a transitional year; satisfaction dropped nine percentage points from the previous year, coinciding with Americans' decreasing approval of then-President George W.

Bush and an increase in their belief that the Iraq War was a mistake. Lower satisfaction levels in 2006 likely contributed to the Democrats taking control of the House of Representatives for the first time in 12 years. Before 2006, the yearly average satisfaction level for the previous 26 years measured was 42%.

Overall Satisfaction in December Equals Immediate Post-Election Level

In December polling, 27% of Americans are satisfied with the way things are going in the U.S. This matches the November reading taken just after the election. Americans' satisfaction levels each month of this year mostly remained near the annual average. Two exceptions were in July (17%) when the killings of police officers in Dallas and the fatal shootings of black men in Minnesota and Louisiana dominated headlines, and in the first week of November when 37% of the country was satisfied heading into the election.

The lack of overall change in December masks some shifts among partisan groups. Twenty-four percent of Republicans in December are satisfied with the way things are going in the U.S., up from 17% last month. While still low overall, it is Republicans' highest satisfaction level since right before the 2008 presidential election, which ended eight years of Republican leadership in the White House. Republicans' anticipation of President-elect Donald Trump's transition has likely boosted their satisfaction with the nation's direction.

While Republicans' satisfaction has increased, Democrats' satisfaction continues to head in the opposite direction. Thirty percent of Democrats are satisfied in December, slightly below the 34% satisfied just after the election. Both figures are down dramatically from a poll conducted shortly before Election Day when 62% of Democrats were satisfied with the way things were going in the country. The popular belief that Hillary Clinton would win the election may have influenced Democrats' higher satisfaction at that time. Democrats' satisfaction surged similarly just before Barack Obama's victory in the 2012 election.

Although Democrats' satisfaction levels have dipped recently, their 2016 average (43%) is still higher than that of Republicans (12%). Party affiliation has served as a good indicator of satisfaction since Gallup began tracking satisfaction level by political party in 1992, as those who align with the president's party have, on average, been more satisfied than have those who do not.

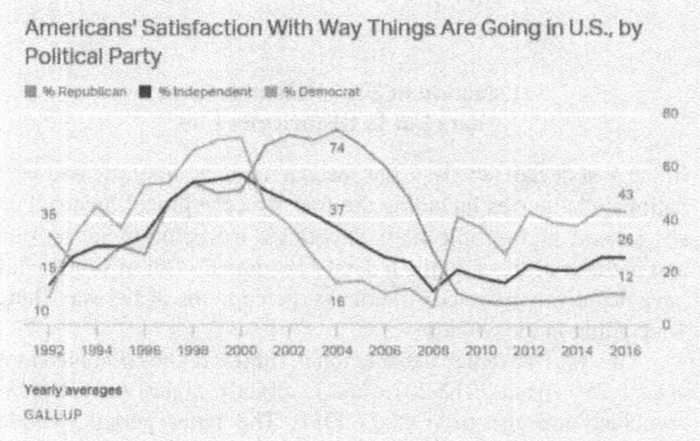

Bottom Line

While Americans have not been as satisfied in 2016 as they were in much of the 1980s and 1990s, they have been about as satisfied as they were throughout Obama's presidency and in the final years of Bush's presidency. Several factors typically influence Americans' satisfaction with the way things are going in the country, including the economy and the status of any foreign entanglements in which the U.S. is involved.

With the political divisions existent in this year's election, Americans may feel less satisfied when asked about the state of the country. But this year, Americans appear to feel no worse about the country than they have in the past few years – though still far from as satisfied as they could be.

Survey Methods

Results are based on telephone interviews conducted Dec. 7-11, 2016, with a random sample of 1,028 adults, aged 18+, living in all 50 U.S. states and the District of Columbia. For results based on this sample of national adults, the margin of sampling error is ±4 percentage points at the 95% confidence level. All reported margins of sampling error include computed design effects for weighting.

December 16, 2016

TRUMP MAINTAINS POST-ELECTION BOUNCE, BUT NO NEW GAINS

by Justin McCarthy

Story Highlights

- *At 42%, no movement in Trump's rating since post-election poll*
- *Barack Obama and Hillary Clinton's ratings also unchanged*

WASHINGTON, D.C. — After jumping from 34% in Gallup's final pre-election poll to 42% right after his election victory, President-elect Donald Trump's favorable rating from the American people remains at 42% today. The slight majority, 55%, still view him unfavorably.

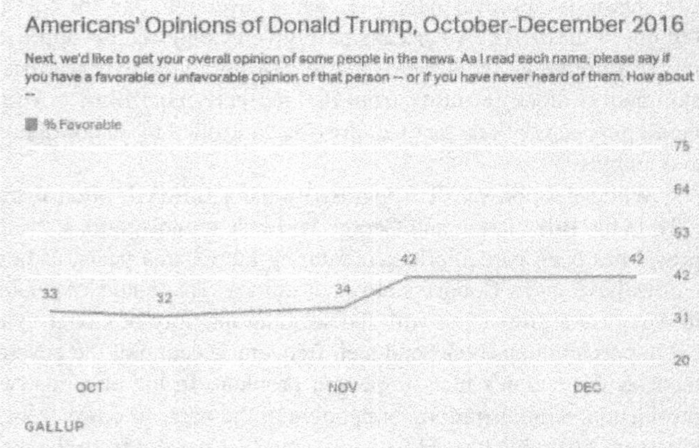

The latest results are from a Dec. 7-11 Gallup poll.

The eight-percentage-point post-election increase in Trump's favorability rating was slightly larger than the boosts experienced by Barack Obama in 2008 (+6), George W. Bush in 2000 (+4) and Bill Clinton in 1992 (+7). But Trump also had a much lower rating to start with, meaning that even with the bump in favorable views, he remains significantly less popular at this point than his predecessors. Obama, Bush and Clinton all had favorable ratings ranging from 58% to 68% after their initial election.

The three previous presidents also enjoyed additional boosts in their favorability between their elections and polls taken just before their inaugurations. Bush experienced the smallest bump of three points, while Obama enjoyed the largest bump of 10 points. Clinton saw his favorability climb eight points between his election and his inauguration.

The lack of change in Trump's favorable rating halfway through his transition period suggests that his favorable image may have stalled, making it likely that he will arrive on Inauguration Day with a significantly less positive image than Obama and Clinton, and perhaps Bush as well. Additionally, his 48% approval rating for his handling of the transition lags far behind those of previous presidents at a similar point in the process.

Obama's and Hillary Clinton's Ratings Steady Since Election

Like Trump's, the favorable ratings of his opponent, Democratic presidential nominee Hillary Clinton (41%), have held steady since the election. Clinton's image began to improve after her unsuccessful bid for the Democratic nomination in 2008, and as secretary of state in the years that followed, as many as two-thirds of Americans viewed her favorably. It is not out of the realm of possibility that her image could make a comeback as she retreats from the political limelight.

Barring any major problems for Obama over the next month, he is poised to exit the White House with higher favorable ratings than did Bill Clinton (57%) or George W. Bush (40%). Presidents have also generally become more favorably viewed after leaving office.

Favorable Ratings of Barack Obama and Hillary Clinton, November vs. December

Next, we'd like to get your overall opinion of some people in the news. As I read each name, please say if you have a favorable or unfavorable opinion of that person – or if you have never heard of them. How about –

	Nov 9-13 %	Dec 7-11 %
Barack Obama	62	61
Hillary Clinton	43	41

Gallup

Bottom Line

Though Trump experienced a typical post-election bump, it is too soon to say if he will experience the same boost in favorability that previous presidents have enjoyed from the time of their election to their Inauguration Days. At the moment, though, he struggles with historically low transition approval ratings, suggesting that his cabinet selections and preparations for the White House through early December have done nothing to change how many Americans view him.

But while Trump's presidency has yet to begin, Obama is ending his on a positive note, on par with several of his popular predecessors. And since the images of former presidents often take on a post-White House glow, it's possible that Obama's ratings could further increase in the coming years. Meanwhile, Hillary Clinton's current ratings are not among her best. But this could change, as Americans have changed their minds about her many times before.

Survey Methods

Results for this Gallup poll are based on telephone interviews conducted Dec. 7-11, 2016, on the Gallup U.S. Daily survey, with a random sample of 1,028 adults, aged 18 and older, living in all 50 U.S. states and the District of Columbia. For results based on the total sample of national adults, the margin of sampling error is ±4 percentage points at the 95% confidence level. All reported margins of sampling error include computed design effects for weighting.

December 19, 2016

AMERICANS RATE HEALTHCARE PROVIDERS HIGH ON HONESTY, ETHICS

by Jim Norman

Story Highlights

- *Nurses rated highest among professions for 15th straight year*
- *College teachers' ratings dropped*
- *41% say journalists' standards are "low" or "very low"*

WASHINGTON, D.C. — Most Americans trust their healthcare providers to be honest and ethical, but few other professions fare so well in Gallup's annual look at honesty and ethical standards among various fields. Nurses top the list with 84% of the public rating their standards as "high" or "very high," while members of Congress fall to the bottom – the only profession for which a majority of Americans (59%) rate honesty and ethical standards as "low" or "very low."

Americans' Ratings of Honesty and Ethical Standards in Professions

Please tell me how you would rate the honesty and ethical standards of people in these different fields – very high, high, average, low or very low?

	Very high/High %	Very low/Low %	Average %
Nurses	84	3	13
Pharmacists	67	8	26
Medical doctors	65	7	29
Engineers	65	5	29
Dentists	59	7	34
Police officers	58	13	29
College teachers	47	18	32
Clergy	44	13	39

Chiropractors	38	13	45
Psychiatrists	38	12	45
Bankers	24	30	46
Journalists	23	41	34
Lawyers	18	37	45
State governors	18	35	45
Business executives	17	32	50
HMO managers	12	31	48
Senators	12	50	37
Stockbrokers	12	39	46
Advertising practitioners	11	40	46
Insurance salespeople	11	38	51
Car salespeople	9	46	45
Members of Congress	8	59	31

Gallup, Dec 7-11, 2016

Nurses have topped the list every year but one since Gallup first asked about them in 1999. In 2001, Gallup included firefighters in the list based on their heroic efforts in the wake of the 9/11 terrorist attacks, and 90% of the public rated their honesty and ethical standards as "high" or "very high."

A majority of Americans viewed only six of the 22 professions Gallup measured in its Dec. 7-11 poll as having "high" or "very high" ethical standards. For 10 of those professions, fewer than one in five Americans rated the standards as "high" or "very high" – including key aspects of American society such as lawyers, lawmakers and business executives.

College Teachers' Rating Falls Below 50%

College teachers' honesty and ethical standards rating dropped to 47% this year from 53% in 2012. The first four ratings for college teachers, conducted between 1976 and 1983, were below 50%, bottoming out at 42% in 1977. The rating rose to 53% in 1985 and stayed above 50% in all but one of the next 18 polls through 2012.

The percentage of Americans saying college teachers' standards were either "low" or "very low" reached a new high of 18%, surpassing the 11% recorded in 2009.

Ratings of college teachers showed strong partisan differences, with 33% of Republicans giving them a "high" or "very high" rating, compared with 63% of Democrats.

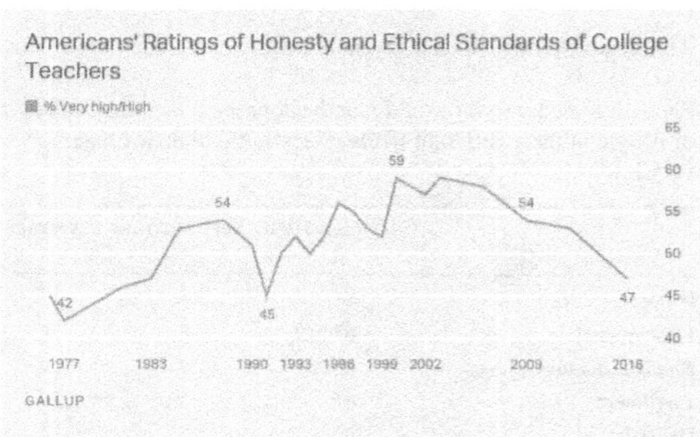

More Americans Rate Journalists' Standards as "Low" or "Very Low"

The 23% who rated journalists' honesty and ethical standards as "high" or "very high" this month is within a few points of the 20% who rated it "high" or "very high" in 1994. The percentage saying their honesty and ethical standards were "low" or "very low" climbed to 41%, 10 percentage points above the previous high of 31% measured in 2008 and 2009. In previous polls, more Americans rated journalists' standards as "average."

Twenty-one percent of Democrats rated journalists' honesty and ethical standards as "low" or "very low," compared with 63% of Republicans.

Ratings of Clergy's Honesty and Ethical Standards Continue Slow Descent

Americans' "high" or "very high" ratings of the clergy slipped to 44%, its lowest point since Gallup first asked the question in 1977. The clergy rating first dropped below 50% in 2013 to 47% and slipped one point to a new low in each of the past three years.

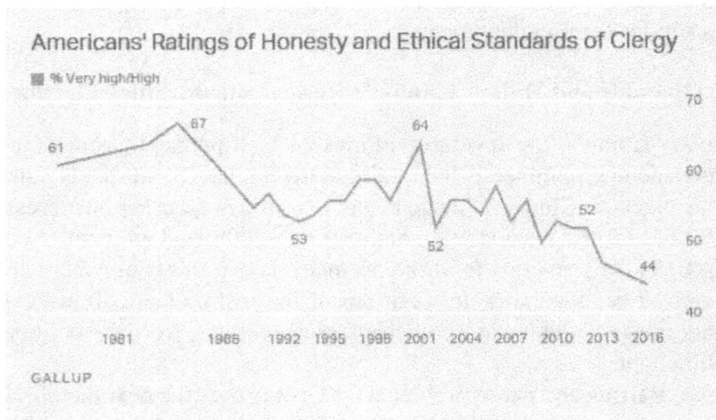

Clergy ranked at the top of the list in 1977 with a 61% rating when Gallup first included the profession in the list. In 2001, almost two-thirds of Americans rated the honesty and ethical standards of the clergy as "high" or "very high." But the sexual abuse scandal that engulfed the Roman Catholic Church in 2002 brought the rating down to 52% that year. By 2013, after a series of further revelations of abuse, less than half of the public gave the clergy a "high" or "very high" rating.

Among those most likely to give the clergy a "high" or "very high" rating this month were Protestants (59%), those aged 65 and older (58%), those who attend religious services at least weekly (57%), and Republicans (56%).

The groups least likely to rate the clergy's standards as "high" or "very high" were the nonreligious (22%), 18- to 29-year-olds (30%), those with annual household incomes under $30,000 (31%), those with a high school education or less (37%), and liberals (37%).

Bottom Line

Healthy majorities of the American public continue to show a willingness to trust the honesty and ethical standards of healthcare providers – nurses, doctors, pharmacists and dentists. However, Americans do not, by and large, rate the honesty and ethical standards of American professions highly.

Further, for the fourth year in a row – in a nation where religion is an important part of life for three-fourths of the population – less than half of Americans think religious leaders have high ethical standards. Meanwhile, two groups of professionals linked to the bitter political battles of 2016 – college teachers and journalists – are at or near their all-time lows, with views split along partisan lines.

As Americans consider how much to trust the honesty and ethical standards of many of the country's major professions in the next few years, politics may be a major factor. With the public expecting President-elect Donald Trump to make major changes to the federal government, the fierce political battles to come could produce a litany of charges of dishonesty and corruption. Trump is already embroiled in controversy concerning what should happen to his business holdings, and that may turn out to be a precursor to the ethics charges and countercharges that lie ahead.

Survey Methods

Results for this Gallup poll are based on telephone interviews conducted Dec. 7-11, 2016, with a random sample of 1,028 adults, aged 18 and older, living in all 50 U.S. states and the District of Columbia. For results based on the total sample of national adults, the margin of sampling error is ±4 percentage points at the 95% confidence level. All reported margins of sampling error include computed design effects for weighting.

December 19, 2016

ECONOMY TOP PROBLEM IN A CROWDED FIELD

by Michael Smith and Lydia Saad

Story Highlights

- *Economy averaged 16% mentions in 2016, lowest since 2007*
- *Unemployment, government dissatisfaction also prominent*
- *Record-high 8% said race relations is most important problem*

PRINCETON, N.J. — No single problem dominated Gallup's list of the most important problems facing the U.S. in 2016, but, at 16%, the economy averaged the most mentions. Dissatisfaction with the government followed closely at 13%. Unemployment or jobs has ranked in the top four every year since 2009, and ranked third this year with 9%. Race relations ranked fourth with 8%, the highest annual average for this issue in recent years.

Top Four Issues Americans Named as Most Important Problem Facing the U.S.

	Issue 1	Issue 2	Issue 3	Issue 3 (tie)/4
2016	Economy, 16%	Gov't, 13%	Jobs, 9%	Race relations, 8%
2015	Gov't, 16%	Economy, 13%	Jobs, 8%	Immigration, 8%
2014	Gov't, 18%	Economy, 17%	Jobs, 15%	Healthcare, 10%
2013	Economy, 22%	Gov't, 20%	Jobs, 16%	Healthcare, 10%
2012	Economy, 31%	Jobs, 25%	Gov't, 13%	Fed. deficit, 10%
2011	Economy, 30%	Jobs, 29%	Gov't, 12%	Fed. deficit, 12%
2010	Economy, 29%	Jobs, 27%	Healthcare, 13%	Gov't, 12%
2009	Economy, 40%	Jobs, 16%	Healthcare, 15%	Gov't, 7%
2008	Economy, 39%	Iraq, 18%	Gas prices, 10%	Healthcare, 8%
2007	Iraq, 33%	Healthcare, 10%	Immigration, 9%	Gov't, 8%
2006	Iraq, 26%	Immigration, 10%	Gov't, 9%	Economy, 9%
2005	Iraq, 22%	Economy, 11%	Gov't, 8%	Terrorism, 8%
2004	Iraq, 22%	Economy, 19%	Jobs, 14%	Terrorism, 14%
2003	Economy, 27%	Iraq, 17%	Jobs, 12%	Terrorism, 10%
2002	Terrorism, 24%	Economy, 22%	Iraq, 9%	Jobs, 7%
2001	Economy, 14%	Terrorism, 10%	Ethics/Morals, 9%	Education, 9%

Annual averages of monthly results
Gallup

Each month, Gallup asks Americans to name, in their own words, the most important problem facing the U.S. The 2016 results are based on the average responses for each issue across the 12 national surveys.

At 7%, immigration was the fifth-most-important issue in 2016, just below the 8% recorded in 2015, when it tied for the third-highest-mentioned issue.

Economy Still Concerning, but Less So Than in Recent Years

The economy has historically been among the top few issues Americans identify as the nation's most important problem. However, reflecting the better economic conditions of recent years, the percentage naming it has dwindled from 40% in 2009 to less than 20% in each of the past three years. The average 16% naming the economy in 2016 is the second-lowest since the financial crisis hit in 2008, after last year's 13%. The relatively low mentions of the economy as the top problem coincide with a rise in overall economic confidence to nine-year highs.

Signaling that Americans' concerns are more spread out than in years past, 2016 was the second straight year that only two issues averaged double-digit mentions as the nation's top problem, after seven years when three or more issues routinely averaged at least 10%.

The 13% mentioning government encompasses a variety of complaints about the leadership of the federal government, including the Republican-controlled Congress and President Barack Obama. The government first appeared among the top four problems in 2005 and has remained there every year except 2008, when gas prices zoomed up in public concern.

Race Relations and Elections Surge

The 8% of Americans naming race relations over the course of 2016 is up from 5% last year and 3% in 2014, and it is the highest in Gallup polling since 1970. The 2016 average included a spike to 18% in July after well-publicized incidents involving police officers killing black men, as well as fatal shootings by black men of police officers in Dallas and Louisiana. From 2001 through 2015, only 1% of Americans, on average, thought race relations was the most important U.S. problem.

Elections or the need for election reform also garnered unusually high public concern in 2016. The 6% naming it the nation's most important problem was by far the highest for this category in Gallup polling history. Mentions were generally higher in the second half of the year – after the presidential nominees were selected – than in the first half, peaking at 11% in November. By contrast, before this year's highly contentious presidential race between Donald Trump and Hillary Clinton, the percentage citing the election process as the top problem averaged less than 1%. Even in the past presidential election years of 2008 and 2004, just 1% named the election or the need for election reform, and in 2012 the category didn't register a single percent.

Most Important Problems Facing the U.S. in 2016

	2016 yearly total^ %	Highest monthly result %	Lowest monthly result %
Economy	16	18	12
Government	13	16	8
Unemployment/Jobs	9	11	5
Race relations	8	18	5
Immigration	7	12	5
Terrorism	6	9	2
Elections/Election reform	6	11	2
National security	5	7	3
Fed. deficit/debt	5	6	3
Healthcare	5	10	3
Ethics/Morals	4	6	1
No opinion	4	7	2
Other noneconomic	3	4	2
Unifying the country	3	6	1
Lack of respect for each other	3	6	1
Crime/Violence	3	4	1
Poverty/Homelessness	3	4	1
Education	3	5	1
Environment/Pollution	2	3	1
Judicial system	2	3	1
Lack of money	2	3	1
Gap between rich and poor	2	4	1
Foreign aid	2	3	1
Situation in Iraq	2	3	1
Guns	2	7	1

Issues averaging 2% or higher; ^Based on average of 12 monthly surveys
Gallup

Bottom Line

With unemployment much lower today than at its peak in 2009 and with economic confidence at new nine-year highs, far fewer Americans in 2016 than in recent years named the economy as the nation's top problem. Yet, at 16%, it still averaged more mentions in 2016 than any other issue, perhaps reflecting the presidential campaign's economic themes. The government remains the object of many Americans' ire (13%). But each of the other top 10 issues – including unemployment/jobs, race relations, immigration, terrorism, election reform, national security, the federal deficit and healthcare – garnered less than 10%.

As a result, Trump will assume the presidency at a time when a variety of serious issues are important to small segments of people. That is different from the situation Obama faced when he was first elected in 2008, when Americans largely agreed that the economy was the foremost problem. In that year, an average 39% of Americans said the economy was the nation's most important problem, and it remained No. 1 as Obama was sworn in for his second term in 2013.

The current issue landscape is more reminiscent of 2000, when George W. Bush was first elected, but only in the sense that Americans' concern was highly dispersed across multiple issues. However, at that time the economy ranked sixth, mentioned by 7%, and terrorism had not yet emerged as a serious national security concern. The leading issues were more standard domestic fare such as education, ethical/moral decline, crime and healthcare. Of course, any intention Bush may have had to focus his administration on those items was upended by the 9/11 terrorist attacks in his first year, completely resetting the national agenda.

.Survey Methods

Results for the monthly Gallup Poll Social Series surveys included in this analysis are based on telephone interviews conducted with a random sample of approximately 1,000 adults, aged 18 and older, living in all 50 U.S. states and the District of Columbia. The yearly averages from the combined results are based on the total sample of approximately 12,000 national adults, with a margin of sampling error of ±1 percentage point at the 95% confidence level.

December 20, 2016
AMERICANS' QUALITY JOBS OUTLOOK HOLDS STEADY IN 2016

by RJ Reinhart

Story Highlights

- *Optimism about the job market averaged 42% in 2016*
- *Job market optimism has leveled off after four years of increases*
- *Americans' optimism about the job market colored by political views*

WASHINGTON, D.C. — In 2016, an average of 42% of Americans said it was a good time to find a quality job. This matches the average for 2015, signifying that optimism about the job market has leveled off after rising steadily since 2012.

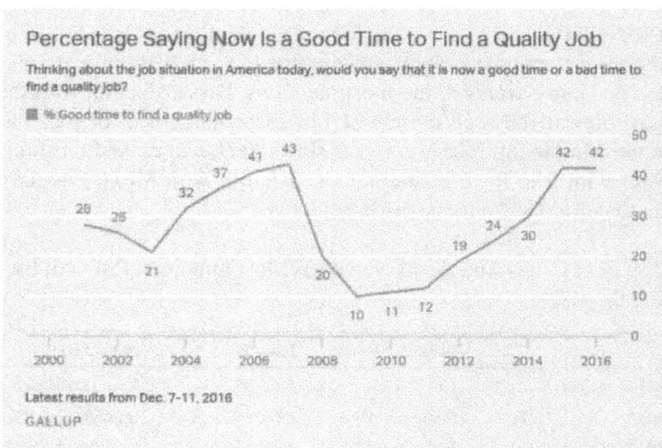

Gallup began measuring Americans' assessments of the job market in 2001. In 2007, a record-high 43% of Americans, on average, said it was a good time to find a quality job. Beginning in 2008, as the Great Recession took hold, Americans' perceptions of the health of the job market began a steep decline.

Americans' optimism toward the job market bottomed out in 2009, when 10% indicated it was a good time to find a quality job. Optimism about the job market increased slightly to 12% by 2011 and then steadily improved each year through 2015. Americans' optimism about finding a quality job did not return to prerecession levels until January 2015.

Partisanship Continues to Color Views of Job Market

The latest monthly reading from a Dec. 7-11 Gallup poll shows 43% of Americans are optimistic about the job market, similar to the 42% average for the entire year. Optimism about the job market among Republicans and Democrats has shifted since the presidential election.

In October 2016, before the election, 26% of Republicans and Republican-leaning independents said it was a good time to find a job. That figure increased to 34% in November and held steady in December at 35%, a 2016 high for this group.

On the other hand, optimism about the job market has dwindled among Democrats and Democratic-leaning independents. In October, before the election, 56% of Democrats said it was a good time to find a quality job. This figure fell to 51% in November and 49% in December, down significantly from its 2016 peak of 58% in January. Although Democrats' optimism currently sits below levels recorded just before the election, it remains higher than April's low of 47%.

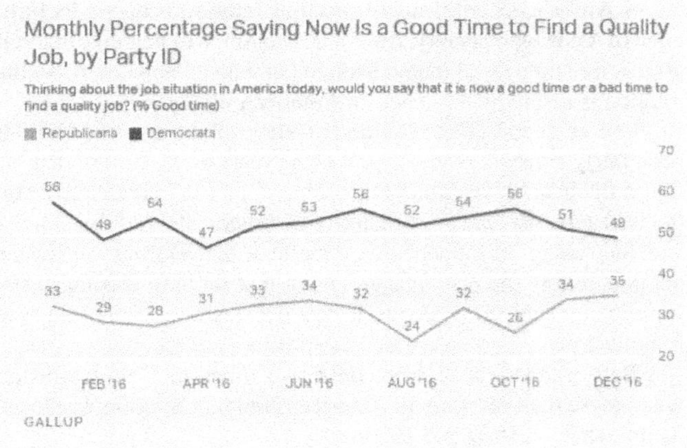

Bottom Line

Despite the unemployment rate being at or below 5% throughout 2016, Americans' overall optimism about the U.S. job market leveled off this year. This occurred even as economic confidence improved in late 2016 and the percentage of Americans mentioning the economy as the most important problem facing the country fell to its second-lowest level since 2008.

President-elect Donald Trump has promised to create millions of new jobs once he takes office, and Gallup's quality jobs metric will be a good indicator of whether Americans believe he is succeeding in keeping that promise.

Survey Methods

Results for this Gallup poll are based on telephone interviews conducted Dec. 7-11, 2016, with a random sample of 1,028 adults, aged 18 and older, living in all 50 U.S. states and the District of Columbia. For results based on the total sample of national adults, the margin of sampling error is ±4 percentage points at the 95% confidence level. All reported margins of sampling error include computed design effects for weighting.

December 23, 2016
FIVE KEY FINDINGS ON RELIGION IN THE U.S.

by Frank Newport

Story Highlights

- *Almost eight in 10 identify with a religion, mostly Christian*
- *21% have no religious identity, up from 15% in 2008*
- *Over seven in 10 say religion is losing its influence in U.S. society*

PRINCETON, N.J. — Religion remains an integral part of most Americans' lives, but Gallup's ongoing research shows how this has changed over time. The following are five important findings about religion in the U.S.:

1. America remains a largely Christian nation, although less so than in the past. Seventy-four percent of Americans identify with a Christian religion, and 5% identify with a non-Christian religion. The rest of the U.S. adult population, about 21%, either say they don't have a formal religious identity or don't give a response.

Religious Identification in the U.S.: 2016

	%
Protestant/Other Christian	48.9
Catholic	23.0
Mormon	1.8
Jewish	2.1
Muslim	0.8
Other non-Christian religion	2.5
None/Atheist/Agnostic	18.2
No response given	2.6

Based on 173,229 interviews conducted Jan. 2-Dec. 9, 2016
Gallup

The dominance of Christianity in the U.S. is not new, but it has changed over time. The U.S. has seen an increase in those with no formal religious identity (sometimes called "nones") and a related decrease in those identifying with a Christian religion. Since 2008, when Gallup began tracking religion on its daily survey, the "nones" have increased by six percentage points, while those identifying as Christian have decreased by six points. The 5% who identify with a non-Christian religion has stayed constant.

In the late 1940s and 1950s, when Gallup began regularly measuring religious identity, over nine in 10 American adults identified as Christian – either Protestant or Catholic – with most of the rest saying they were Jewish.

2. The trend away from formal religion continues. The most significant trend in Americans' religiosity in recent decades has been the growing shift away from formal or official religion. About one in five U.S. adults (21%) don't have a formal religious identity. This represents a major change from the late 1940s and 1950s when only 2% to 3% of Americans did not report a formal religious identity when asked about it in Gallup surveys. The increase in those claiming no religious identity began in the 1970s, with the percentage crossing the 10% threshold in 1990 and climbing into the teens in the 2000s.

Americans are also significantly less likely now than they were in the past to claim membership in a church, synagogue or mosque. In 1937, when Gallup first asked about church membership, 73% said they were a member of a church. This figure dropped into the upper 60% range in the 1980s and continued to decrease from that point on. It fell to its lowest point of 54% in 2015 but increased slightly to 56% this year.

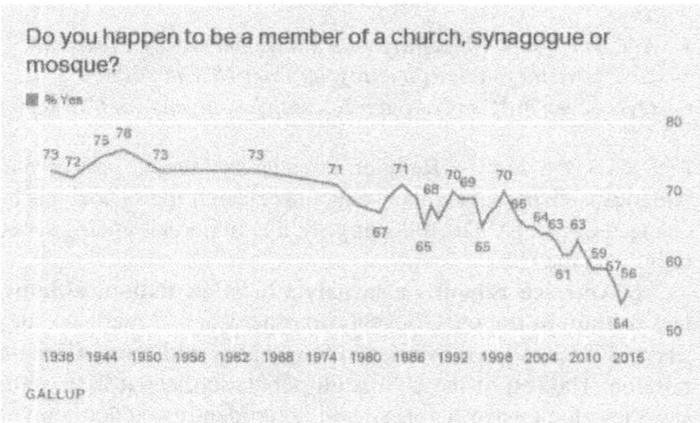

Self-reported church attendance is also lower than it has been in past decades – although perhaps not as low as might be expected, given the drop in church membership and the increase in the percentage of those with no religious identity.

Gallup's longest-running religious service attendance question asks, "Did you, yourself, happen to attend church, synagogue or mosque in the last seven days, or not?" In 1939, when Gallup first asked this question, 41% said "yes." That percentage dropped to 37% in 1940 and rose to 39% in 1950. It continued to climb, reaching as high as 49% at multiple points in the 1950s. Attendance then settled down to figures around 40% for decades, before dropping to 36% for the past three years.

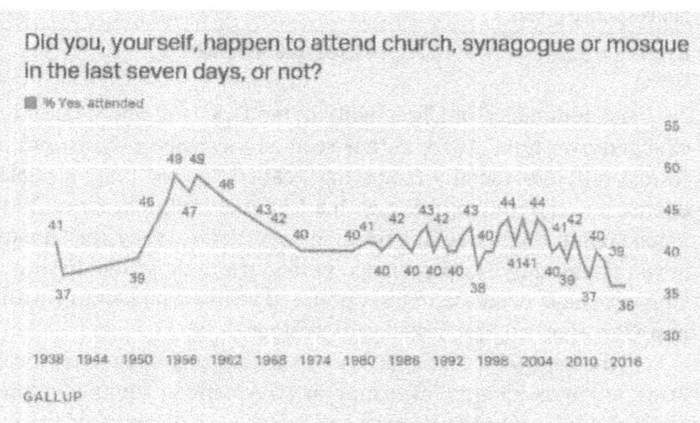

3. A majority still say religion is important in their lives. A majority of Americans (53%) say that religion is "very important" in their lives. This is down marginally from recent years, but the trend over time has shown less of a decline than have other religious indicators such as religious identification or church membership. In 1965, 70% said that religion was "very important" in their lives, but figures have since ranged from 52% to 61%. The percentage reporting that religion is "very important" hit the low end of this range in the 1980s and has done so again in more recent years. The 53% who say religion is "very important" this year is low on a relative basis but is similar to what Gallup measured in 1978 and 1987.

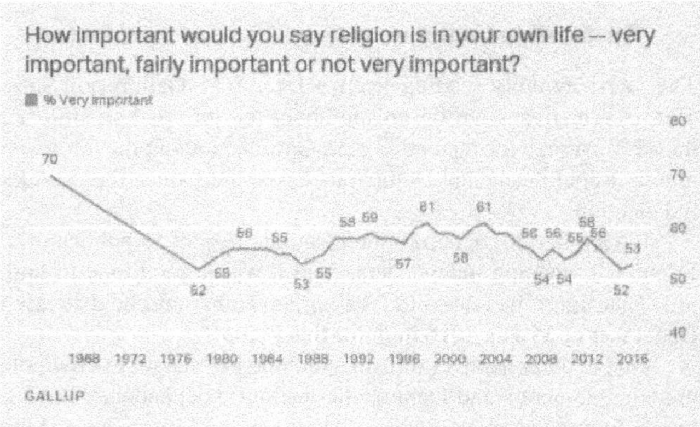

A different question included on Gallup Daily tracking since 2008 offers two choices, asking if religion is "important in your daily life" or not. Sixty-four percent of those interviewed in 2016 say that religion is important, down two points since 2008.

4. Americans continue to say that religion is losing its influence in American society. Americans continue to perceive that religion is less influential than it used to be, with 72% in 2016 say that religion is losing its influence on American life.

The perception that religion is losing influence in the U.S. has been fairly constant over the past eight years or so. Before that, the figure fluctuated over time. For example, in 1957 and shortly after the 9/11 terrorist attacks, a majority of Americans said that religion was increasing its influence on American life. During the Reagan administration, the percentages saying that religion was increasing in influence and those saying it was decreasing in influence were roughly equal.

Before 2009, there were only two times in Gallup's history when more than seven in 10 Americans thought religion was losing its influence: in 1969 and 1970.

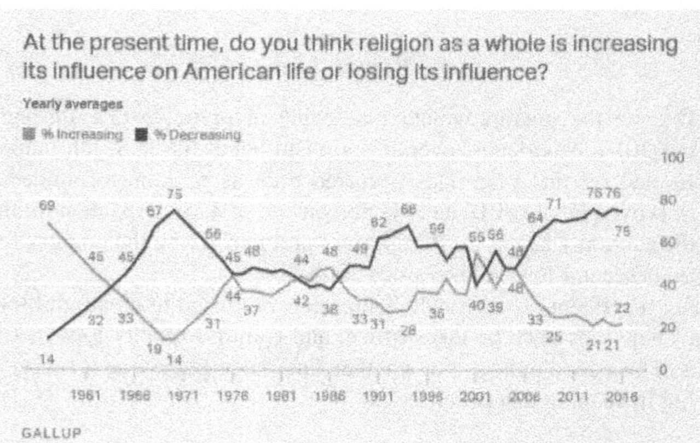

5. Religion remains intertwined with political self-identification. Religiosity continued in 2016 to significantly correlate with partisan identification. Slightly more than half of Republicans this year are "highly religious," based on a combination of their self-reported religious service attendance and the importance of religion in their daily life. That compares with a third of independents and Democrats who say the same. By contrast, 20% of Republicans are not religious, compared with 37% of the two other political groups.

Political Party Identification Within Partisan Groups in the U.S.: 2016

	Republicans %	Independents %	Democrats %
Highly religious	51	33	33
Moderately religious	29	30	30
Not religious	20	37	37

Based on 173,229 interviews conducted Jan. 2-Dec. 19, 2016
Gallup

Gallup began tracking religiosity on a continual basis in 2008, and although overall religiosity is down across all political groups since then, it remains much higher among Republicans than among the other two political groups.

The connection between religion and politics manifested itself in the presidential election this fall. Exit poll data showed that among those who reported attending religious services weekly, 55% voted for Donald Trump and 41% voted for Hillary Clinton. Among those who never attend religious services, 62% voted for Clinton and 30% voted for Trump.

Bottom Line

Gallup data in 2016 show a leveling off in downward trends in church attendance, the importance of religion and the perception that religion is losing influence in society. This may be a short-term phenomenon or an indication of a more lasting pattern. Demographics in a broad sense could predict an uptick in religiosity if the same historical patterns continue to hold. Large numbers of baby boomers and millennials are entering the age ranges in which religiosity has traditionally been higher. But these patterns may change, and it will take years of data collection to determine if formal religiosity will continue to decrease or level off.

December 28, 2016
U.S. INVESTOR OPTIMISM ENDS 2016 AT NINE-YEAR HIGH

by Lydia Saad

Story Highlights

- *Investor index remains at nine-year high in fourth quarter*
- *Investors most upbeat about maintaining or increasing their income*
- *Republican and Democratic investors swap outlooks after election*

PRINCETON, N.J. — After reaching a nine-year high in the third quarter, the Wells Fargo/Gallup Investor and Retirement Optimism Index rose further in the fourth quarter to its highest point since January 2007. The index now stands at +96, up from +79 last quarter and from +40 in the first quarter after stock market volatility rattled investor confidence.

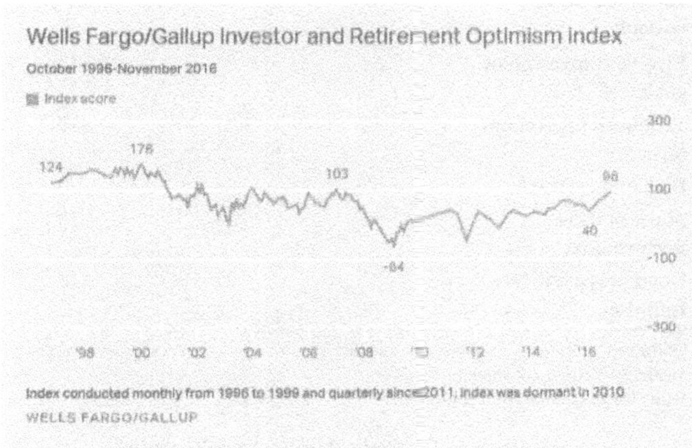

The fourth-quarter reading is based on telephone interviews conducted Nov. 16-20 with a nationally representative sample of 1,012 U.S. investors who report having $10,000 or more in stocks, bonds, mutual funds, or a self-directed IRA or 401(k).

Reflecting the results of the 2016 presidential election, investor confidence zoomed 155 points in the post-election poll among investors who identify as Republican, from an index score of 0 in the third quarter to +155 in the fourth. Conversely, Democrats' confidence fell by nearly as much, from +174 to +25. At the same time, the index rose only slightly among those with $100,000 or more in investments, from +99 to +105, while it jumped from +55 to +87 among lower-asset investors.

The Wells Fargo/Gallup Investor and Retirement Optimism Index has been conducted quarterly since 2011. The Gallup Index of Investor Optimism, which provides the historical trend, was conducted monthly from October 1996 through October 2009. The index has a theoretical range of +400 to -400, but in practice has ranged from +178 at its highest point in January 2000 to -64 at its lowest in February 2009.

Investors More Confident About Personal Than Economic Factors

Of the seven elements that form the index, investors are the most confident this quarter about maintaining or increasing their income over the next 12 months – 69% are optimistic about this while 15% are pessimistic, for a +54 net optimism score.

Investors are nearly as hopeful about reaching their five-year investment goals, with 68% optimistic. Slightly fewer are optimistic about achieving their 12-month investment targets (58%) and in their 12-month outlook for U.S. economic growth (57%) and stock market performance (54%).

Net optimism about the unemployment rate is just a notch below investors' outlook for the economy and stock market, while investors are split in their outlook for inflation.

Components of U.S. Investor Optimism – Q4, 2016

Wells Fargo/Gallup Investor and Retirement Optimism Index

	Optimistic %	Pessimistic %	Net optimism (pct. pts.)
12-month income outlook	69	15	+54
Five-year investment goals	68	20	+48
12-month investment targets	58	21	+37
Economic growth	57	27	+30
Stock market performance	54	24	+30
Unemployment rate	52	27	+25
Inflation	37	36	+1

Optimistic = % Very/Somewhat optimistic; Pessimistic = % Very/Somewhat pessimistic; % Neither not shown

Wells Fargo/Gallup, Nov. 16-20, 2016

Optimism Typically Highest on Income, Five-Year Investing Outlook

The rank order of investors' confidence in the three personal financial components of the index has been fairly constant in recent years. Investors tend to be the most optimistic about the 12-month outlook for their income, as well as the outlook for reaching their five-year investment goals. They tend to be a bit less optimistic about achieving their 12-month investment targets. However, solid majorities are now optimistic on all three dimensions.

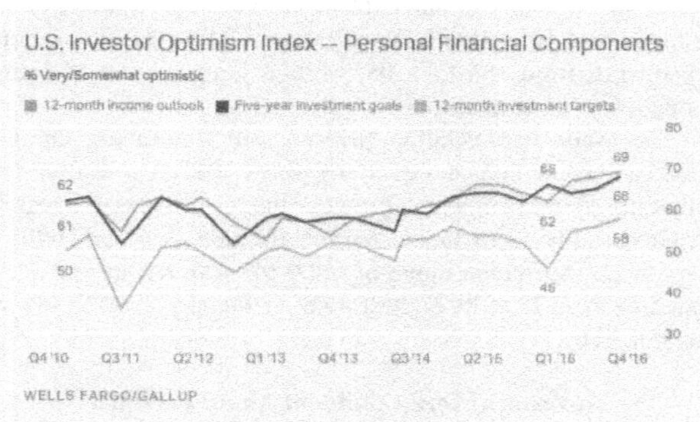

Investor optimism about the four economic factors included in the index have been more variable since 2011 but also stand at recent high points. This reflects a sharp increase in investor optimism about economic growth since last quarter – from 45% to 57% – as well as steady long-term gains in investor optimism about the U.S. unemployment rate.

Since early 2011, the percentage of investors expressing optimism about unemployment has risen 18 percentage points, compared with a 13-point increase in optimism about economic growth, a seven-point rise on inflation and a five-point rise on stock market performance.

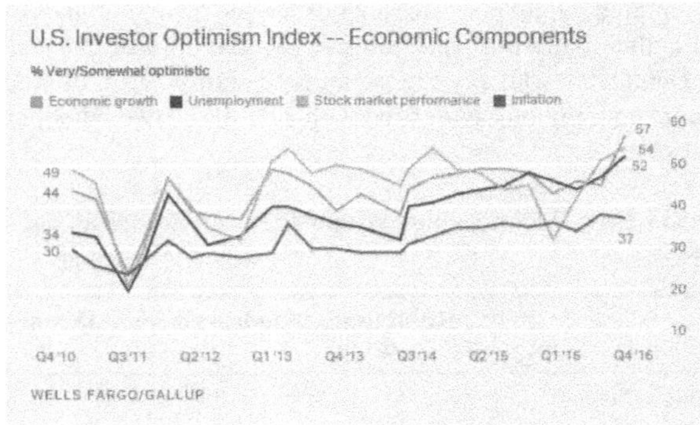

Bottom Line

Investors' willingness to purchase equities in 2017, thus helping to maintain the bull market, will depend on many factors, not the least of which is their broad outlook on the investment climate as measured by the Wells Fargo/Gallup Investor and Retirement Optimism Index. The index presents a fairly positive picture at the close of 2016 and is considerably improved over a year ago after three consecutive quarters of gains. While Republican exuberance about Donald Trump's victory may explain some of this, the fourth-quarter jump only added to long-term gains in confidence – particularly in optimism about unemployment – that should provide a good foundation to build on in 2017.

Survey Methods

Results for the Wells Fargo/Gallup Investor and Retirement Optimism Index survey are based on questions asked Nov. 16-20, 2016, on the Gallup Daily tracking survey, of a random sample of 1,012 U.S. adults having investable assets of $10,000 or more.

December 28, 2016

OBAMA BESTS TRUMP AS MOST ADMIRED MAN IN 2016

by Jeffrey M. Jones

Story Highlights

- *22% name Barack Obama as most admired man; 15% name Donald Trump*
- *Hillary Clinton is the most admired woman*
- *9th time Obama has won; 21st time for Clinton*

PRINCETON, N.J. — Americans are most likely to name President Barack Obama as the man they admire most in 2016. Twenty-two percent mentioned Obama in response to the open-ended question. President-elect Donald Trump was second at 15%. It is Obama's ninth consecutive win, but the seven-percentage-point margin this year is his narrowest victory yet.

Most Admired Man, Recent Trend

What man that you have heard or read about, living today in any part of the world, do you admire most? And who is your second choice?

	2016 %	2015 %	2014 %	2013 %	2012 %	2011 %	2010 %	2009 %
1. Barack Obama	22	17	19	16	30	17	22	30
2. Donald Trump	15	5	*	–	*	1	*	–
3. Pope Francis	4	5	6	4	–	–	–	–
4. Bernie Sanders	2	3	–	–	–	*	–	–
5. Rev. Billy Graham	1	1	2	2	2	2	2	2
6t. Benjamin Netanyahu	1	*	1	*	*	*	*	*
6t. The Dalai Lama	1	1	*	*	1	1	1	*
6t. Bill Clinton	1	1	3	2	1	2	4	1
6t. Bill Gates	1	2	1	1	*	1	2	2
10. Mike Pence	1	–	–	–	–	–	*	–
Ben Carson	1	1	1	–	*	*	–	–
Stephen Hawking	1	*	1	–	*	*	*	*
Warren Buffett	1	*	*	*	*	2	*	*
Joe Biden	1	*	–	–	1	*	–	*
Elon Musk	*	1	*	–	–	–	–	–
George W. Bush	*	1	2	4	2	3	5	4
Jimmy Carter	*	1	*	1	*	*	2	1
George H.W. Bush	*	*	1	*	1	1	*	1
Prince William	*	–	1	*	*	*	*	–
Mark Zuckerberg	*	1	–	–	–	*	–	–
Michael Jordan	*	1	–	–	*	*	–	1
Mitt Romney	*	*	1	1	2	1	*	*
Thomas Monson	*	*	*	*	–	1	1	*
Friend/Relative	8	9	9	9	8	9	7	7
Other	24	30	34	40	25	35	37	35
None/No opinion	23	25	23	27	29	32	25	25

Combined responses; Ranked according to number of responses; * Less than 0.5%
Gallup

The results are based on a Dec. 7-11 poll. Since 1946, Gallup has asked Americans to name the man, living anywhere in the world, whom they admire most.

Incumbent presidents typically win the distinction – in the 70 times Gallup has asked the question, the president has won 58 times. The 12 exceptions were mostly times when the sitting president was unpopular, including 2008, when Americans named President-elect Obama over President George W. Bush. Obama and Dwight Eisenhower in 1952 are the only presidents-elect to win the distinction. Eisenhower finished first 12 times, more than any other man in history. Obama is now second all-time with nine first-place finishes.

Obama's win over Trump this year is largely a result of the president earning more mentions among Democrats than Trump receives from Republicans. Fifty percent of Democrats named Obama as most admired, compared with 34% of Republicans choosing Trump.

The remainder of this year's top 10 most admired man list includes Pope Francis, Vermont Sen. Bernie Sanders, the Rev. Billy Graham, Israeli Prime Minister Benjamin Netanyahu, The Dalai Lama, former President Bill Clinton, businessman and philanthropist Bill Gates, and Vice President-elect Mike Pence.

This year marks the 60th time Graham has finished in the top 10 – a Gallup record. That includes making it into the top 10 every year since 1955, with the exception of the 1962 survey and in 1976, when the question was not asked.

Pence is the only newcomer among the top 10 men this year. Trump has finished in the top 10 five prior times – in 1988, 1989, 1990, 2011 and 2015. Clinton made the top 10 for a 25th time and Gates for a 17th. Former President George W. Bush finished outside the top 10 for the first time since he was elected in 2000.

Hillary Clinton Most Admired Woman a Record 21st Time

Americans named Hillary Clinton the Most Admired Woman for the 15th consecutive year and 21st time overall. Since her initial win in 1993 as first lady, Clinton has topped the list every year but 1995 and 1996 (when she finished behind Mother Teresa) and 2001 (behind Laura Bush). Eleanor Roosevelt has the second-most No. 1 finishes among women, at 13.

First lady Michelle Obama finished second on the Most Admired Woman list this year, tied with 2012 as her best finish. The remainder of the top 10 most admired women include German Chancellor Angela Merkel, former and current talk-show hosts Oprah Winfrey and Ellen DeGeneres, Queen Elizabeth of England, human rights activist Malala Yousafzai, former Secretary of State Condoleezza Rice, Massachusetts Sen. Elizabeth Warren, and former Alaska Gov. Sarah Palin.

Most Admired Woman, Recent Trend

What woman that you have heard or read about, living today in any part of the world, do you admire most? And who is your second choice?

	2016 %	2015 %	2014 %	2013 %	2012 %	2011 %	2010 %	2009 %
1. Hillary Clinton	12	13	12	15	21	17	17	16
2. Michelle Obama	8	4	3	5	5	5	5	7
3. Angela Merkel	3	2	1	1	1	1	*	1
4. Oprah Winfrey	3	4	8	6	4	7	11	8
5. Ellen DeGeneres	2	1	1	*	1	2	*	*
6. Queen Elizabeth	2	2	1	1	2	2	2	2
7. Malala Yousafzai	2	5	5	2	2	–	–	–
8. Condoleezza Rice	2	1	4	2	3	3	2	2
9. Elizabeth Warren	1	1	1	*	1	–	–	–
10. Sarah Palin	1	1	2	5	2	4	12	15
Dolly Parton	1	–	–	*	*	–	–	*
Princess Kate	1	*	2	1	1	1	*	–
Carly Fiorina	*	2	–	–	–	–	–	*
Barbara Bush	*	*	1	1	1	1	1	*
Madeleine Albright	*	*	*	–	*	–	*	1

	2016 %	2015 %	2014 %	2013 %	2012 %	2011 %	2010 %	2009 %
Sonia Sotomayor	*	–	–	–	–	–	–	1
Aung San Suu Kyi	*	1	*	–	1	1	1	*
Laura Bush	*	*	1	1	*	2	1	1
Angelina Jolie	*	*	2	1	1	1	1	1
Friend/Relative	12	11	9	13	13	12	11	8
Other	22	23	24	27	18	22	23	22
None/No opinion	31	31	26	28	29	29	22	23

Combined responses; Ranked according to number of responses; * Less than 0.5%
Gallup

All of this year's leading women have finished in the top 10 multiple times before, led by Queen Elizabeth's record 48. Winfrey's 29th top 10 finish this year moved her ahead of Jacqueline Kennedy for the third-most-frequent appearances behind Queen Elizabeth and Margaret Thatcher (34). Clinton's 25 top 10 finishes rank fifth-best all-time. Rice has finished in the top 10 a total of 16 times, while Obama and Palin each made their ninth appearances in the top 10 this year.

Clinton was the top choice among Democrats, with 26% naming her, followed by Michelle Obama at 18%. Republicans did not have a consensus choice – 5% named Queen Elizabeth, 4% each named Clinton and DeGeneres, and 3% each named Rice and Palin.

Implications

Barack Obama and Hillary Clinton have been the most admired man and woman every year since 2008. Now, as both move into the post-political phase of their careers, their future status as most admired is uncertain.

Given the prominence of incumbent presidents as the most admired man, Trump may be the favorite to win the distinction next year, provided he does not have low job approval ratings in December 2017. Even if Obama does not win the honor next year, his relative youth and high favorable ratings could make him a fixture in the top 10 for years. Many ex-presidents have enjoyed long runs on the most admired man list after leaving office.

Clinton may have a better chance of staying most admired woman based on history. Former first ladies have won the title more than any other role – 35 times in the 67 years the question has been asked. Most of those wins are for Roosevelt and Clinton, but Mamie Eisenhower, Kennedy and Betty Ford also won after their husband's term ended. Clinton may also be advantaged in the future because she will be in a less overt political role. Her highest favorable ratings to date came when she was first lady and secretary of state, while they fell significantly during her two presidential campaigns.

Survey Methods

Results for this Gallup poll are based on telephone interviews conducted Dec. 7-11, 2016, with a random sample of 1,028 adults, aged 18 and older, living in all 50 U.S. states and the District of Columbia. For results based on the total sample of national adults, the margin of sampling error is ±4 percentage points at the 95% confidence level. All reported margins of sampling error include computed design effects for weighting.

Index